LEGISLATIVE LAW AND STATUTORY INTERPRETATION: CASES AND MATERIALS

Fourth Edition

LEGISLATIVE LAW AND STATUTORY INTERPRETATION: CASES AND MATERIALS

Fourth Edition

OTTO J. HETZEL
Professor of Law Emeritus
Wayne State University

MICHAEL E. LIBONATI
Laura H. Carnell Professor and Professor of Law
Temple University

ROBERT F. WILLIAMS
Distinguished Professor of Law
Rutgers University, Camden

ISBN: 978-1-4224-0745-5

Hetzel, Otto J.
Legislative law and statutory interpretation : cases and materials / Otto J. Hetzel, Michael E. Libonati,
Robert F. Williams. -- 4th ed.
  p. cm.
Includes and index.
ISBN 978-1-4224-0745-5 (hard cover)
1. Legislation--United States. 2. Legislative power--United States. 3. Separation of powers--United States. I.
Libonati, Michael E., 1944- II. Williams, Robert F. (Robert Forrest), 1945- III. Title.
KF4930.H47 2008
328.73'077--dc22   2008021815

Editorial Offices
744 Broad Street, Newark, NJ 07102 (973) 820-2000
201 Mission St., San Francisco, CA 94105-1831 (415) 908-3200
www.lexisnexis.com

MATTHEW ◊ BENDER

Preface

Preface to the Fourth Edition

During the first decade of the twenty-first century the interest among judges, lawyers, and legal academics in statutory interpretation and legislative process issues continued unabated from the 1980's and 1990's. This Fourth Edition continues the basic structure of the first three editions, but has been improved in a number of important ways.

Chapter 1 has been expanded slightly to introduce students to the wide variety of lawmaking mechanisms in addition to common law development. New material on judicial rulemaking, executive orders, and the use of statutory change to affect pending litigation have been added.

Chapter 2 continues its central focus on the interaction of legislation and statutory changes in the common law system, particularly the use of statutes as precedents, or in reasoning by analogy. New materials indicate other indirect effects of statutes, such as in the area of preemption.

Chapter 3 has been completely revised and shortened, with a specific focus on aspects of the legislative process that have specific consequences for statutory interpretation.

Chapter 4 has also been completely revised, with a single, lengthy state case illustrating a wide variety of the state constitutional restrictions on the legislative process. Materials from the prior edition, reflecting the federal legislative process, have been retained.

A new Chapter 5 has been created, utilizing the materials from the earlier edition concerning the executive branch roles in the legislative process.

The materials on statutory interpretation are retained as Chapters 6 through 9 of this Fourth Edition. Chapter 6, on textual approaches to statutory interpretation remains much the same, having been updated to reflect the recent literature. Section F has been expanded to include material from the former Chapter 10 on the federal appropriations process, as an introduction to the materials on substantive legislation in appropriations acts.

Chapter 7, on legislative intent and purpose also remains much the same, with some additional material on the *Weber* case and the debate over the use of legislative history in statutory interpretation.

Chapter 8, concerning canons of interpretation, has been expanded to include important new literature on the canons.

Chapter 9, on institutional competence, has been expanded to include an updated section on *Chevron* deference, and an expanded section on severability. Finally, there is a new section on interpretation of state statutes in federal courts and *vice versa*.

Chapters 10, on the appropriation process, and 11, on lobbying, have both been eliminated from this edition.

DEDICATIONS

This Edition is again dedicated to the memory of my parents who stimulated me in my passion for teaching, to those students over the years who have shared their experiences in legislative matters with me on many occasions contributing to my own knowledge as well, and especially to the steadfast support for my creative efforts by my wife, Bonnie, who has endured the tolls of the production of these editions and has contributed her excellent editing skills to my prose, when requested.

OJH

To the memory of my father Roland V. Libonati who served thirty-two years as a member of both chambers of the Illinois state legislature and the U.S. House of Representatives:

Sunt hic etiam praemia laudi

Sunt lacrimae rerum et mentem mortalia tangunt.

Solve metus: feret haec aliquam tibi fama salutem.

MEL

For Alaine, Sarah and Tyler.

RFW

ACKNOWLEDGMENTS

I want to express my appreciation for the greater understanding of legislative law, process, and interpretation that a number of my colleagues, elected officials, professional, and academic, have provided me over the years, especially from those who have served in state and federal legislative bodies, that has enabled me to share their experiences to others interested in these subjects through these materials.

OJH

Many thanks to the library staff, in particular Paul Carino, John Necci, and the ever forbearant and resourceful Larry Reilly.

Shirley Hall continues to be the First Lady of word-processing, remarkable for her patience and fortitude.

MEL

I would like to acknowledge the ongoing learning experience of working with Michael Libonati and Otto Hetzel, and the tireless assistance of Denise Johnson-Steinert and David Batista, without whose help and competence this project could not have been completed. I have also had an ongoing, reciprocal learning experience with the Rutgers law students.

RFW

TABLE OF CONTENTS

TABLE OF CONTENTS

TABLE OF CONTENTS

TABLE OF CONTENTS

TABLE OF CONTENTS

TABLE OF CONTENTS

TABLE OF CONTENTS

TABLE OF CONTENTS

TABLE OF CONTENTS

TABLE OF CONTENTS

Chapter 8   **JUDICIALLY CREATED CANONS, ASSUMPTIONS, AND PRESUMPTIONS OF STATUTORY INTERPRETATION**

TABLE OF CONTENTS

TABLE OF CONTENTS

TABLE OF CONTENTS

Part I

INTRODUCTION

Chapter 1

LAWYERS AND LEGAL CHANGE

A. THE IMPACT OF LEGISLATION ON SOCIAL AND ECONOMIC CHANGE

INTRODUCTORY NOTE

There is a popular conception that society's problems can be resolved by creating new legal rights or new machinery to protect existing rights. The legislative branch is now the first place to turn to accomplish these objectives, although in areas subject to common-law treatment, the judiciary has been a source of change through its power to develop the common law in response to changed circumstances. Thus, in these instances, the legislature and the judiciary exercise concurrent power to accomplish legal change. Lawmaking may also take place through judicial rulemaking and executive orders. Advocates of change therefore have a choice of forum, albeit with great differences, in seeking their objectives. Sometimes several avenues of change may be pursued at the same time. Opponents of such change will often, in addition to resisting the proposals on their merits, argue that it is inappropriate for the courts, the legislature or the executive, as the case may be, to exercise their or its power to change the law. Of course, even in areas where the legislature has already acted to regulate by statute, many matters are left for judicial decision through interpretation of the statute in actual controversies. In both the common-law and statutory interpretation realms, however, the legislature is supreme — it has the final say as to what shall be the law.

The lawyer's skills as an advocate in these other lawmaking contexts differ somewhat from those of the more familiar litigation advocate. Still, the ability to make persuasive arguments, gather and present facts, find and follow procedural rules, and educate decisionmakers are central to the lawyer's professional role.

The legislature has fact-finding mechanisms available to gather the data necessary to determine whether a new right is needed and how it might best be fashioned. Further, the legislature, in contrast to the courts, is not limited to the facts of an individual controversy, or by the rules of evidence applicable to the courts. The legislature need not wait for a problem to be brought to it, as the courts must do. A legislative investigative committee has the flexibility to examine all information necessary to develop an appropriate solution to the entire problem. That the legislative branch does not always make effective use of the tools available to it reflects more upon its operation than on its potential.

Although some look first to the legislature for responses to changing situations, the courts also have the ability to react, often with greater dispatch and effectiveness, to society's demands for solutions to pressing problems. During the period of the Warren Supreme Court, lower federal courts and, to a greater degree recently, some "activist" state courts fashioned judicial remedies where the legislature had failed to respond to social issues. Typical of such developments were reapportionment, access to birth control devices, school desegregation, unequal school funding, elimination of inter-spousal and sovereign immunity, freedom of expression on private property, abortions, same-sex marriage and limitations on the use of the death penalty. Interestingly, although many of these decisions can be viewed as natural evolution of constitutional law, they are often within the realm of legislative policymaking, and most came only after the legislature failed to act.

Some scholars in the past generation have begun to question whether constitutional law-reform litigation in the courts has really been very effective. For example, Prof. Gerald Rosenberg has contended that courts are rarely able to produce "significant social reform" through litigated cases because there are three structural constraints on the American judiciary:

   a)   Constitutional rights are of a limited nature;
   b)   Lack of judicial independence;
   c)   The judiciary lacks the power to implement its decisions.

Despite these constraints, under some conditions the results of litigation may result in significant social change:

   a)   There is already existing legal precedent for the change that is sought through litigation; and
   b)   The executive and a substantial number of legislators support the change; and
   c)   Some of the citizens support the change, or at least not very many citizens oppose the change; and, either
   1)   There are positive incentives for compliance with the court's decree; or
   2)   Failure to comply will result in costs being imposed; or
   3)   Market implementation can support compliance with the judicial decision; or
   4)   Officials or those whose support is crucial for implementing the judicial decision are willing to engage in such implementation and they see judicial decisions as enabling them to leverage additional resources or as something they can "hide behind" as they implement the judicial decision.

Needless to say, Professor Rosenberg finds that there are very few circumstances where these constraints can be overcome and the required conditions met. *See* GERALD N. ROSENBERG, THE HOLLOW HOPE: CAN COURTS BRING ABOUT SOCIAL CHANGE? 35–36 (1991). For a similar pessimistic assessment, see STUART A. SCHEINGOLD, THE POLITICS OF RIGHTS: LAWYERS, PUBLIC POLICY, AND POLITICAL CHANGE (1989). For a similar assessment based on a study of courts in other countries, see RAN HIRSCHL, TOWARDS JURISTOCRACY: THE ORIGINS AND CONSEQUENCES OF THE NEW CONSTITUTIONALISM (2004). *But see* Robert F. Williams, *Juristocracy in the American States?* 65 MD. L. REV. 68 (2006) (a slightly more optimistic view of *state* court decisions). For an argument that the Civil Rights Act of 1964 has had much more positive influence than the Supreme Court's civil rights rulings, see Rebecca E. Zietlow, *To Secure These Rights: Congress, Courts and the 1964 Civil Rights Act*, 57 RUTGERS L. REV. 945 (2005).

    The choice of where to pursue change is based on a determination of which arena will be most receptive to the proposal. Sometimes the courts are preferred over a politically unresponsive legislature; at other times the legislature is perceived as a more fertile territory for achieving the desired goal. Sometimes both are pursued at the same time. The forum selection process is also affected by other issues. Once a right is created, who will enforce it, and how? How susceptible will a decisive court decision or statute be to subsequent pressures for change? Can the resultant action be easily undercut by those charged with its administration? And, of foremost importance, which forum will respond more quickly?

    The judicial system is not generally noted for its speed. Significant change, particularly in legal doctrine, is effectuated only through courts of last resort, after expensive and time-consuming appeals. Doctrinal change is slow because concepts of *stare decisis* usually require adherence to the status quo. Nevertheless, although significant delay is often occasioned in reaching the highest court, fewer persons are required for consensus once there. The compromises required among a handful of justices are minimal compared to the tradeoffs necessary to assure passage before a large legislative body.

    In the past, lawyers have often exhibited a strong bias toward the *judicial* resolution of social problems. The judiciary is the branch with which lawyers are most familiar, and in which they have felt most comfortable. So, despite the benefits of legislative solutions, many lawyers in the past have turned to the judiciary. This is now changing, and, of course, there are many legal changes which simply can not be accomplished by the judiciary.

The courts' approach to interpretation of legislation also has influenced their role in social change. When dealing with a statute, a court can address the problem either as one of reasoning from a new, legislatively-derived principle or of preserving existing legal doctrines until specifically instructed to the contrary by the legislature. The issue of which judicial philosophy should generally prevail has generated much commentary over more than half a century, with little observable change in judicial attitudes. By expanding upon legislative policy, courts can play a positive role in social change. The nature of the change, however, will depend upon the underlying political philosophy to be implemented.

Depending upon the degree of controversy generated by the particular measure, resort to the legislature for change can also involve long delays. The process of enactment is sufficiently strewn with obstacles to permit a small but well-informed and organized opposition the opportunity to delay or defeat any proposal. The leadership in both houses, as well as chairpersons on key committees, often have power to virtually dictate what proposals will be heard and when. Their personal predilections can have inordinate weight within the body. Further, the sheer number of participants in the legislative process means that extensive and time-consuming compromise is often required.

The executive also must be recognized as having a major role in fashioning social change. Recent administrations at both the federal and state levels have graphically demonstrated the power of the executive. Some have exercised immense power in initiating legislation and forcing its enactment; others have shown how easily legislation can either be forestalled or given direction and content more to the executive's liking. The power to influence votes flows from such things as the chief executive's discretionary appointment authority, power to assist with a legislator's reelection, or to bestow economic benefits upon a legislator's constituency; it is especially effective because of the leverage available from exercise of the veto power.

The executive also can respond most rapidly to newly perceived needs through flexible administration of the laws, a discretion often accorded by the legislature. The executive may also utilize executive orders. Policy can be changed simply by directive or regulation requiring few, if any, compromises. The executive is likely to be constrained in rapidly implementing a new policy only when it fails to follow prescribed procedures. For instance, courts have overridden the administrative judgment inherent in environmental impact statements approving government funded projects where a procedural requirement has not been followed, such as the failure to collect sufficient data to demonstrate adequate support for the position taken.

In its role as implementer and principal interpreter of statutes, however, the executive can resist as well as create change. A recalcitrant executive can foil implementation despite direction, and even redirection, by both the legislature and the courts. For example, continued legislative efforts failed to make the executive more sensitive to the relocation needs of persons displaced by urban renewal and highway programs. Finding the administrators intractable, Congress finally mandated financial benefits to those displaced, sufficient to offset many of the hardships caused by the restrictive administration of these programs.

Each branch of the government alone can have a direct role in social change. Similarly, each can affect the ability of the other branches to act, by utilizing its negative "check" on the other branches' activities.

An example of the interplay between the three branches of government in effecting social change was the battle over the provision of legal services to the poor. As Office of Economic Opportunity (OEO) legal services (now Legal Services Corporation) attorneys began to play a significant role in law reform in the late 1960s, they naturally turned to the arena in which they were most comfortable and knowledgeable — the courts. To some extent, the attorneys also participated in legislative law reform, but when a subsequent administration took office, Congressional and Legal Services Corporation directives substantially restricted the attorneys in their legislative representation. Their access to the courts was circumscribed, in addition, first by their client's interest, and then by judicial restrictions affecting the utility of class actions. Decisions requiring each class plaintiff to meet minimal jurisdictional amounts and placing the burden for notice upon plaintiffs further limited the effectiveness of resort to the judicial forum for "law reform." Certain of these restrictions were declared unconstitutional in *Legal Services Corp. v. Velasquez*, 531 U.S. 533 (2001).

The three branches of our governmental structure have separate strengths and weaknesses, can override and be overridden, and can directly initiate or indirectly circumscribe social change. The role of each and the relationship of each to the others form the basis for organization of subsequent materials in this coursebook. It is important, however, to remember that policy change is one thing, while its direction is an entirely different matter. The determination of what is acceptable social change may well be rooted in the eye of the perceiver.

ROSCOE POUND,
COMMON LAW AND LEGISLATION
21 HARVARD LAW REVIEW 383 (1908)*

Not the least notable characteristics of American law today are the excessive output of legislation in all our jurisdictions and the indifference, if not contempt, with which that output is regarded by courts and lawyers. Text-writers who scrupulously gather up from every remote corner the most obsolete decisions and cite all of them, seldom cite any statutes except those landmarks which have become a part of our American common law, or, if they do refer to legislation, do so through the judicial decisions which apply it. The courts, likewise, incline to ignore important legislation; not merely deciding it to be declaratory, but sometimes assuming silently that it is declaratory without adducing any reasons, citing prior judicial decisions and making no mention of the statute. In the same way, lawyers in the legislature often conceive it more expedient to make of a statute the barest outline, leaving details of the most vital importance to be filled in by judicial lawmaking. It is fashionable to point out the deficiencies of legislation and to declare that there are things that legislators cannot do try how they will. It is fashionable to preach the superiority of judge-made law. It may be well, however, for judges and lawyers to remember that there is coming to be a science of legislation and that modern statutes are not to be disposed of lightly as off-hand products of a crude desire to do something, but represent long and patient study by experts, careful consideration by conferences or congresses or associations, press discussions in which public opinion is focused upon all important details, and hearings before legislative committees. It may be well to remember also that while bench and bar are never weary of pointing out the deficiencies of legislation, to others the deficiencies of judge-made law are no less apparent. To economists and sociologists, judicial attempts to force Benthamite conceptions of freedom of contract and common-law conceptions of individualism upon the public of today are no less amusing — or even irritating — than legislative attempts to do away with or get away from these conceptions are to bench and bar. The nullifying of these legislative attempts is not regarded by lay scholars with the complacent satisfaction with which lawyers are wont to speak of it. They do not hesitate to say that "the judicial mind has not kept pace with the strides of industrial development." They express the opinion that "belated and anti-social" decisions have been a fruitful cause of strikes, industrial discord, and consequent lawlessness. They charge that "the attitude of the courts has been responsible for much of our political immorality."

There are two ways in which the courts impede or thwart social legislation demanded by the industrial conditions of today. The first is narrow and illiberal construction of constitutional provisions, state and federal. "Petty judicial interpretations," says Professor Thayer, "have always been, are now, and will always be, a very serious danger to the country." The second is a narrow and illiberal attitude toward legislation conceded to be constitutional, regarding it as out of place in the legal system, as an alien element to be held down to the strictest limits and not be applied beyond the requirements of its express language. The second is by no means so conspicuous as the first, but is not on that account the less unfortunate or the less dangerous.

. . . .

Formerly it was argued that common law was superior to legislation because it was customary and rested upon the consent of the governed. Today we recognize that the so-called custom is a custom of judicial decision, not a custom of popular action. We recognize that legislation is the more truly democratic form of lawmaking. We see in legislation the more direct and accurate expression of the general will. We are told that lawmaking of the future will consist in putting the sanction of society on what has been worked out in the sociological laboratory. That courts cannot conduct such laboratories is self evident. Courts are fond of saying that they apply old principles to new situations. But at times they must apply new principles to situations both old and new. The new principles are in legislation. The old principles are in common law. The former are as much to be respected and made effective as the latter — probably more so as our legislation improves. The public cannot be relied upon permanently to tolerate judicial obstruction or nullification of the social policies to which more and more it is compelled to be committed.

NOTES AND QUESTIONS

1. Pound, in 1908, seems to have felt that: (1) the legal profession tends to carefully scout up every available judicial decision yet ignore all but the most obvious statutes when arguing by analogy from the law of other jurisdictions; (2) that legislators seem to leave all but the barest framework of a statute for courts and administrators to fill in; (3) that there is a prejudice among lawyers which leads them to extoll the value of judicial decisions over legislative enactments; and (4) that part of the conflict between the judicial system and the legislative branch is one of basic policies, the former favoring the status quo as well as concepts of individualism and the latter more collectivist in its attempt through "social legislation" to spread wealth and the burdens of responsibility over a larger part of society. Which of these perceptions are still valid or widely held today?

2. Considering the kinds of pressures that can be exerted on legislative bodies by special interest groups, is legislation really "the more democratic form of lawmaking"? Are the courts more or less free from this kind of influence? If less, does this independence make them any more or less democratic? Why would lawyers be more comfortable with judicial opinions than statutes as sources of law?

3. Do the procedures used to select judges or the interests they represented when they practiced as attorneys, have any influence on which value systems judges apply to the facts in reaching their decisions? How do the procedures for selecting legislators compare?

4. Is it usually true that legislation creates "new" legal principles, while the common law perpetuates old values? How often has legislation simply incorporated common-law principles? Are statutes often used to effectively create "privileges," or to prevent certain persons from protecting their interests? For instance, have trends toward limiting the doctrine of *caveat emptor* given "consumers" rights equal to merchants? When consumers are granted such rights, how important are the means provided for enforcing them?

5. What are the differences in the forms of legislative and judicial policymaking? Once the policy is made, which branch has responsibility for further fine tuning of the policy?

FRANK P. GRAD,
THE ASCENDANCY OF LEGISLATION:
LEGAL PROBLEM SOLVING IN OUR TIME
9 Dalhousie Law Journal 228, 233–34, 251–53 (1985)*

I. *Introduction*

Law making in our time depends on legislation, and our primary reliance on statutory law is being increasingly recognized, even though, as James Williard Hurst recently put it, "Judge-made law is still the darling of legal philosophers." It has also remained at the misplaced center of much of our legal education . . . . The New Deal Legislation of the 1930's not only applied legislation to the solution of the economic, social, and ultimately legal problems of its times, but it also changed the very nature of the legislative product. The ascendancy of legislation resulted not only in a far greater legislative output, but also in the development of massive programmatic legislation, unique in its character and different in kind from the narrow, limited statutes that had preceded it. So significant is this new form that some of the older rules of statutory construction seem hardly relevant in their application. But the new legislative approach, here referred to as programmatic legislation, imposes a responsibility for legal training which develops to the fullest the ability to use legislation as the way to solve today's legal problems.

. . . .

The sentiment against statutory law of the 1890's recognized a unique characteristic of legislation — its capacity for making major changes in the existing social order. Common law is private law. Legislation opens the field of public law. No judicial decision on a work-place injury can have as far-reaching effects as the legislative establishment of a workers' compensation system. As noted, case law is limited by the nature of the case that gave rise to the decision, and even landmark cases will not have an impact beyond a fairly limited legal field. The decision of a case may have significant and direct impact on the law, but it is not likely to have any such direct impact on the social order. The legislation to establish workers' compensation had an impact on employer-employee relations which was not only different in degree, but different in kind from the impact of even the most significant decisions in individual cases on employer liability for work-place accidents. A case establishing a pharmacists' liability for improperly labeling a medication, however influential in the law of product liability, is quite different in its impact from a comprehensive food and drug act, which sets labeling requirements prospectively.

. . . .

V. *The Development and Prevalence of Programmatic Legislation*

The significant change in the twentieth century is in the character of the laws. The dominant form of legislation today, starting with the New Deal legislation of the thirties, is what I shall call *programmatic legislation*. It is a new form which responds to new needs. During much of the nineteenth century, legislation had limited targets, and much state legislation was of a limited remedial nature — to remedy problems of private law which common law decisions had created, or which common law decisional approaches were unable or unwilling to resolve. A great deal of that legislation, it appears, dealt with matters that could have been resolved by decisional law *if* an appropriate case for such a decision had emerged, or *if*, having emerged, the courts had been willing to create new case law for the future. There was also a great deal of private, local, and special legislation, and there was very little public law, and even less legislation that created any public programs.

Programmatic legislation is precisely the kind of legislation the eighteen nineties would have been afraid of. It consists of public law that cannot be formulated or promulgated by the courts. In essence, programmatic legislation creates a governmental program — its usual pattern is the establishment or designation of an agency, and the assignment of a task. Frequently, the task is broadly defined, leaving the agency with the obligation to articulate the details of its own mandate. The breadth of the delegation grows out of the complexity of the assigned task. If the statute is to provide substantial schemes of social insurance, or sound regulation of hazardous or toxic pollutants, or decent controls on the distribution of sophisticated medical technology, it must delegate the details of eligibility requirements, technical details of health and safety requirements, or details of economic controls over scarce medical resources to agencies that have been provided with the means and expertise to carry out their legislatively defined task. It should be added that programmatic legislation uses the tools of administrative law because it must. Administrative law, which has many other applications, does not, however, define the field of programmatic legislation.

Other recurring aspects of programmatic legislation may be noted. Generally, in establishing a new program, the legislature seeks to occupy the entire field it regulates, leaving no room for other lawmaking in the area. This feature of programmatic legislation has resulted in formidable, lengthy, detailed and complex statutes, because it usually takes a lot of law to cover a field. The development of good programmatic legislation requires a thorough knowledge of the area to be regulated, and the interplay between factual background — be it technical, scientific or economic — and the necessary legal analysis is always part of the process of shaping statutes to resolve complex contemporary problems.

. . . .

NOTES AND QUESTIONS

1. How effective and thorough are the legislative mechanisms for fact-finding? Are they used impartially? Are there adequate protections to assure objectivity? To what extent are rational or factually based legislative decisions overridden by political trade-offs? Are these decisions better made by courts armed with the relevant facts as presented by adversaries? For a critique of the congressional fact finding process in the context of the enactment of a specific statute, see David A. Hyman, *Lies, Damned Lies, and Narrative*, 73 IND. L. REV. 797 (1998).

2. How true is it that the common law is a slow and cumbersome mechanism for change, bringing only incremental revisions at best, while legislation is rapid and brings radical change? What role do the United States Supreme Court and state supreme courts play in bringing about such social change?

3. The legislature has endowed administrative agencies with the power to supervise many segments of society and the economy. Does this reflect a legislative "solution," or simply the creation of new institutions to deal with the same problem? What types of problems for the legislative branch are created when power is delegated?

4. Professor Edward Rubin makes a distinction between a "transitive statute," that "speaks directly to private persons" and an "intransitive statute" that "speaks exclusively to the implementation mechanism and instructs that mechanism to make the rules." Edward L. Rubin, *Modern Statutes, Loose Canons, and the Limits of Practical Reason: A Response to Farber and Ross*, 45 VAND. L. REV. 579, 581–82 (1992). He then draws distinctions as to judicial interpretation of the different kinds of statutes:

Even if we restrict ourselves to the judicial interpretation of statutes, the relative degrees of transitivity that characterize contemporary statutes will make an enormous difference. It is one thing for the court to interpret a statute that states transitive rules, applicable in terms to private persons. It is quite another thing for the court to interpret a statute that instructs an administrative agency to formulate the applicable rules. Two differences are particularly notable. First, the type of language that is appropriate for imposing obligations on private persons is quite distinct from the language appropriate for issuing instructions to a government agency. Second, the role of the court is different; in one case, it is the primary implementation mechanism, responsible for imposing the statutory obligations on private persons; in the other case, the court is evaluating the implementation strategy of a separate governmental unit and deciding whether that unit has exceeded the bounds of its instructions.

Id. at 582–83.

5. Professor Grad describes a different type of legislation since the New Deal — "programmatic legislation." What different challenges does such legislation present for the courts?

6. For a treatment of the problems of dealing with "programmatic legislation," see CASS R. SUNSTEIN, AFTER THE RIGHTS REVOLUTION: RECONCEIVING THE REGULATORY STATE (1990), and Rand E. Rosenblatt, *Statutory Interpretation and Distributive Justice: Medicaid Hospital Reimbursement and the Debate Over Public Choice*, 35 ST. LOUIS U. L. REV. 793 (1991).

7. If statutes are now the dominant source of law, what role remains for common law? *See* Daniel A. Farber & Philip P. Frickey, *In the Shadow of the Legislature: The Common Law in the Age of the New Public Law*, 89 MICH. L. REV. 875 (1991).

8. In *Wisconsin Knife Works v. National Metal Crafters*, 781 F.2d 1280, 1285–86 (7th Cir. 1986), Judge Richard Posner described the differing approaches to contract modification under the common law and the Uniform Commercial Code:

Because the performance of the parties to a contract is typically not simultaneous, one party may find himself at the mercy of the other unless the law of contracts protects him. Indeed, the most important thing which that law does is to facilitate exchanges that are not simultaneous by preventing either party from taking advantage of the vulnerabilities to which sequential performance may give rise. If A contracts to build a highly idiosyncratic gazebo for B, payment due on completion, and when A completes the gazebo B refuses to pay, A may be in a bind — since the resale value of the gazebo may be much less than A's cost — except for his right to sue B for the price. Even then, a right to sue for breach of contract, being costly to enforce, is not a completely adequate remedy. B might therefore go to A and say, "If you don't reduce your price I'll refuse to pay and put you to the expense of suit"; and A might knuckle under. If such modifications are allowed, people in B's position will find it harder to make such contracts in the future, and everyone will be worse off.

The common law dealt with this problem by refusing to enforce modifications unsupported by fresh consideration . . . . Thus in the hypothetical case just put B could not have enforced A's promise to accept a lower price. But this solution is at once overinclusive and underinclusive — the former because most modifications are not coercive and should be enforceable whether or not there is fresh consideration, the latter because, since common law courts inquire only into the existence and not the adequacy of consideration, a requirement of fresh consideration has little bite. B might give A a peppercorn, a kitten, or a robe in exchange for A's agreeing to reduce the contract price, and then the modification would be enforceable and A could no longer sue for the original price . . . .

The draftsmen of the Uniform Commercial Code took a fresh approach, by making modifications enforceable even if not supported by consideration (see section 2-209(1)) and looking to the doctrines of duress and bad faith for the main protection against exploitive or opportunistic attempts at modification, as in our hypothetical case. See UCC § 2-209, official comment 2. But they did another thing as well. In section 2-209(2) they allowed the parties to exclude oral modifications . . . .

The common law did not enforce agreements such as section 2-209(2) authorizes. The "reasoning" was that the parties were always free to agree orally to cancel their contract and the clause forbidding modifications not in writing would disappear with the rest of the contract when it was canceled. "The most ironclad written contract can always be cut into by the acetylene torch of parol modification supported by adequate proof." *Wagner v. Graziano Constr. Co.*, 390 Pa. 445, 448, 136 A.2d 82, 83–84 (1957). This is not reasoning; it is a conclusion disguised as a metaphor. It may have reflected a fear that such clauses, buried in the fine print of form contracts, were traps for the unwary; a sense that they were unnecessary because only modifications supported by consideration were enforceable; and a disinclination to allow parties in effect to extend the reach of the Statute of Frauds, which requires only some types of contract to be in writing. But the framers of the Uniform Commercial Code, as part and parcel of rejecting the requirement of consideration for modifications, must have rejected the traditional view; must have believed that the protection which the doctrines of duress and bad faith give against extortionate modifications might need reinforcement — if not from a requirement of consideration, which had proved ineffective, then from a grant of power to include a clause requiring modifications to be in writing and signed. An equally important point is that with consideration no longer required for modification, it was natural to give the parties some means of providing a substitute for the cautionary and evidentiary function that the requirement of consideration provides; and the means chosen was to allow them to exclude oral modifications.

9. The Uniform Electronic Signature Act, proposed by the National Conference of Commissioners on Uniform State Laws to give legal effect to electronic signatures and electronic records, has now been adopted by a number of states. Could such a change have been accomplished by the common law? As a statute "in derogation" of the common law, should it be strictly construed in the way Roscoe Pound described?

10. Some statutes encourage, or delegate, a form of common law decisionmaking to courts. Various sections of the Uniform Commercial Code are examples of this. Another well-known example is the California Civil Code provision on negligence and contributory negligence, which the California Supreme Court relied on to abolish the doctrine of contributory negligence and substitute in its place the doctrine of comparative negligence. *See Li v. Yellow Cab Co.*, 532 P.2d 1226 (Cal. 1975).

11. For an interesting argument that "expansive" judicial interpretation of complex, programmatic statutes actually inhibits further legislative development of such statutes, see Daniel B. Rodriguez & Barry Weingast, *The Paradox of Expansionist Statutory Interpretations*, 101 Nw. U. L. Rev. 1207 (2007).

NOTE ON JUDICIAL LEGISLATION

Pound, in 1908, and Grad, more recently, suggest that legislation has become the primary vehicle for change in the law. Similarly, in *Some Reflections on the Reading of Statutes*, 47 Colum. L. Rev. 527 (1947), Felix Frankfurter noted a dramatic increase in the role of statutory law in the cases that come before the Supreme Court.

. . . Broadly speaking, the number of cases disposed of by opinions has not changed from term to term. But even as late as 1875 more than 40% of the controversies before the Court were common-law litigation, fifty years later only 5%, while today cases not resting on statutes are reduced almost to zero.

It is therefore accurate to say that courts have ceased to be the primary makers of law in the sense in which they "legislated" the common law. It is certainly true of the Supreme Court that almost every case has a statute at its heart or close to it.*

What, then, should be the role of the judiciary, whose traditions are rooted in the court-fashioned common law, in a legal world increasingly populated by legislative rather than judicial law? To some, statutory enactments provide additional opportunities for judicial activism. Judges analyzing statutory language simply adopt all the same methods of lawmaking which they use in dealing with judicial authority — interpretation, clarification, expansion, distinction and limitation. Through these processes courts continue to make law even in those cases "resting on statutes."

Lawmaking through interpretation of legislation is not limited to consideration of the words of the statute. Courts also look to the policy behind the act in the same way they consider the rationale used in judicial precedents. In *Johnson v. United States*, 163 F. 30, 32 (1908), Justice Holmes wrote for the majority:

> We recognize that courts have been disinclined to extend statutes modifying the common law beyond the direct operation of the words used, and that at times this disinclination has been carried very far. But it seems to us that there may be statutes that need a different treatment. A statute may indicate or require as its justification a change in the policy of the law, although it expresses that change only in the specific cases most likely to occur to the mind. The Legislature has the power to decide what the policy of the law shall be, and if it has intimated its will, however indirectly, that will should be recognized and obeyed. The major premise of the conclusion expressed in a statute, the change of policy that induces the enactment, may not be set out in terms, but it is not an adequate discharge of duty for courts to say: We see what you are driving at, but you have not said it, and therefore we shall go on as before.

On first reading, this statement appears to be a call for judicial restraint and deference to legislative enactments. It is critical of judges who resist statutory encroachment into areas previously controlled by the judicially-determined common law. Professor F. Reed Dickerson in *Statutory Interpretation: A Peek into the Mind and Will of a Legislature*, 50 IND. L.J. 206, 230 (1975), suggests that Justice Holmes, by deferring to what he determined to be the purpose of the statute, may in reality have been asserting judicial lawmaking power rather than shunning it:

> Because the specific formulation of purpose was Holmes's, how could he be reasonably sure that he was stating a purpose that Congress would recognize as its own? Or was he merely creating a sensible policy, well served by the clear elements of the statute, that he could thereafter use to interpret more broadly what was otherwise narrow language? Although the result was probably sensible and fair, can it be supported as something cognitively discoverable from the statute and its proper context? Or was it in significant aspects a judicial purpose that Holmes himself assigned to the statute? So far as it may have been the latter, the result must be sustained, not as the ascertainment of statutory meaning, but as an act of judicial lawmaking.

To the extent that courts are involved in interpretation of statutes, they can either extend or contract the scope of the legislation. The occasion for this assessment arises simply because a legislature seldom will have the ability to accurately forecast the variety of factual circumstances to which the enactment may be applied. Courts have performed this function in two ways. One has been to view its role as preserving the status quo unless there are specific instructions to the contrary. Alternatively, the court has chosen as Holmes did, to reason from a legislative precedent.

---

* Reprinted with permission from Columbia Law Review.

For instance, faced with the necessity to decide whether the use of coaxial cable to transmit television signals (known as CATV) is within the definition of "wire" as used in the act empowering the Federal Communications Commission (FCC) to regulate "all interstate and foreign communications by wire or radio," the Court decided to expand the scope of the federal language. Whether or not it is useful to denigrate this decision as "judicial lawmaking" as defined by Professor Dickerson, the case illustrates the critical role the courts can play in fashioning social change. It may be that the Court felt that cable television represented an area that required federal regulation and that the FCC was an appropriate place to locate this responsibility — Congress could reassign this role if it so wished. Or, the Court may have felt that Congress intended that such evolving technology be encompassed within the general purpose of the Communications Act as reflected in its terms.

A court does not evade the label of judicial legislation, however, by imposing a limiting interpretation of the Act. To have decided that CATV was *not* within the grant of authority to the FCC would have involved the same degree of interpretation, and therefore lawmaking, as a determination that such activity came within the provisions of the Act. Barring an explicit statement of congressional intent on the specific point, it is difficult to imagine how one cognitively discovers a legislative meaning from the statute and its context without incorporating some of the perceptions of the interpreter in that process. As long as there is a bona fide attempt to determine what the legislature means by an enactment, rather than an assertion of the personal policy predilections of the court (however disguised by the incantation of Latin maxims or other euphemisms), this judicial role seems proper and necessary.

Is not Holmes, in the last sentence of the excerpt from *Johnson*, really expressing a distaste for the judicial habit of ignoring the relatively clear expression of the legislature ("we see what you are driving at") because the judges prefer the existing state of the law or a version more consistent with their own values? And does Holmes not appear to be saying that it is the judge who refuses to give legal effect to a determinable but not explicitly stated legislative policy who is improperly engaging in judicial lawmaking? Professor Julius Cohen has coined a term to describe a judge's attempt to make an earnest search for legislative purpose — "legisputation." The court engaged in legisputation, he feels, is acting within its legitimate authority and not illicitly "making law."

What is significant is that the court can effectuate change through its interpretative role. Whether or not one agrees with judges' decisions or labels what they have done as judicial legislation, it must realistically be understood that the court exercises more than a mechanical, value-free, interpretive function when considering the scope and application of statutes. In their present role, courts are called upon to fashion the law and will do so in one manner or another. So long as courts must decide cases involving statutes, they will perform a legislative role. Referring to this process as judicial legislation or activism is simply applying a label and does little to advance the discussion of how this responsibility should be exercised.

Judicial interpretation of statutes should be distinguished from the court's role in evaluating the constitutional validity of legislation. These judicial functions become intertwined to the extent that the court interprets legislation to determine whether its intended scope exceeds constitutional boundaries. Courts often have decided that a narrow interpretation of a statute is appropriate to avoid constitutional complications, inferring that the legislature did not intend to enact an unconstitutional provision. Such judicial interpretations, however, are quite different from the court's establishing constitutional doctrine that may invalidate existing legislation or circumscribe the scope of future legislation.

ROBERT F. WILLIAMS,
STATUTORY LAW IN LEGAL EDUCATION:
STILL SECOND CLASS AFTER ALL THESE YEARS
35 MERCER LAW REVIEW 803, 828–29, 833–35 (1984)*

. . . .

A practicing lawyer in modern times needs legislative skills, if not for the development and drafting of statutes, at least for their application.

The lawyer's predictive function on behalf of clients can be as important in legislative development of the law as in judicial development. Because traditional legal education and legal materials have not prepared most lawyers adequately for this function, legislative developments often take lawyers and clients by surprise. Frank Horack said that "[t]he development of legislative policy follows as predictable a system as does the judicial opinion." This predictive skill can be developed only by better understanding of the process by which statutes are created and adopted.

A lawyer trained by the case method (even in statutory interpretation) with either real or hypothetical facts always given, may have difficulty predicting the effect of proposed or newly-enacted legislation. He must conjure up hypothetical facts, and the reasoning process is basically deductive instead of inductive. This type of "issue recognition" is the opposite of regular law practice (or law school) in which the client gives the lawyer facts and the lawyer picks out the legal issues. Here, by contrast, the lawyer is given the legal rule, and he must create fact situations in which the rule might apply to the client. These are two very different mental operations.

Lawyers may be called upon to represent clients directly before the legislature and its committees. More and more professional, community, public interest, and small trade association groups are seeking legislative representation. Even legal services lawyers now are representing clients in the legislative process. In addition, lawyers have an obligation to advise clients of relevant statutory developments as they are taking place. Finally, on the other side, there are some unique problems in representing policy-making persons or bodies.

. . . .

Statutes, on their faces, do not explain the reasoning processes that led to the conclusions they contain, as judicial decisions purport to do. An understanding of the reasoning behind a statute usually must come from outside the text. The reasoning for adoption of the statute has been "merged" into the text. All of the words are of equal value (there being no "dictum"), unlike judicial decisions, which tell a story and have a rhythm and an ebb and flow. Thus, legislation presents itself in a one-dimensional "monotone." Cases, by contrast, are "easy reading." Judicial decisions persuade; statutes command. Statutes, with their "big bang" origins, are just not aesthetically pleasing to lawyers trained in the case method. Furthermore, common-law doctrine, formed in actual controversies, is always instrumental. Statutes, by contrast, may be passed or remain on the books for purely symbolic reasons. The legal profession, with its focus on the adversary system and judicial enforcement, obviously will have little interest in these statutes.

Because statutes usually are not applied by analogy beyond their express terms, they do not appear to contain the same *potential* as cases. In other words, a judicial decision will at once provide rules of law to decide the instant case and the raw materials for extrapolation in future analogous cases. Cases, therefore, hold a dual interest for the lawyer in a way not readily apparent in statutes. Not only are cases more interesting to read, but they also have these two levels of interest — the resolution of the instant case through the formulation of a rule and the foundation for common-law reasoning in the future. Future common-law decisions are put off for

---

another day, while the statutes seem to prejudge future cases.

Dean Landis illustrated this distinction by opining that *Rylands v. Fletcher* probably would have had no effect beyond its express terms if it had been a statutory rule instead of a common-law decision. It would have lacked *potential*. Instead, it became the basis for major developments in the law of torts over many decades.

Another ramification of thinking like a common-law lawyer is distrust of law created in a *political*, group struggle process instead of a process of "legal reasoning." A common assumption is that legislative bodies do not respond to rational argument but only to the influence of power and, therefore, that rational argument need not be developed nor attempted. This view does not leave much room for thinking like a lawyer.

Although most law professors and lawyers currently acknowledge the political content of judicial decisions, at least the legal profession maintains a virtual monopoly over the judiciary. Lawyers speak the same language. Certainly the same cannot be said for the legislature. Legal training is not a required qualification for legislative service. Entrance into the legal profession brings with it a heightened social class not necessarily obtained by nonlawyer legislators. When was the last time a bar association went on record for increased *legislative* salaries?

NOTES AND QUESTIONS

1. In 1989, the Legislation Section of the Association of American Law Schools, in its "Statement on Teaching Legislation in Law School," strongly recommended that all law schools offer courses in legislation and statutory interpretation.

2. Jeremy Waldron analyzed the differences between common law and statutory lawmaking in *The Dignity of Legislation*, 54 Md. L. Rev. 633 (1995). He noted:

> My point then is not that legislatures are suffering from overall academic neglect, but that, in jurisprudence at any rate, we have not bothered to develop any idealistic or normative picture of legislation. Our silence here is deafening compared to our philosophical loquacity on the subject of courts. There is nothing about legislatures or legislation in modern philosophical jurisprudence remotely comparable to the discussion of decision-making by judges. No one seems to have seen the need for an ideal type or theoretical model that would do for our understanding of legislation what, for example, Ronald Dworkin's "Hercules" purports to do for adjudicative reasoning.

> It may be thought that the reason is obvious: Judicial reasoning poses a special problem for jurisprudence in the way that the reasoning of legislators does not. Argument in a legislature is explicitly and unashamedly political. It is either the interplay of interests, or the direct clash of policy proposals and ideologies. Legislators do not need jurists to tell them how to argue. The processes by which courts reach their decisions, by contrast, are supposed to be special and distinctive, not directly political, but interpretative of already established political conclusions or expressive of some underlying spirit of legality.

Id. at 644

3. Even Benjamin Cardozo, toward the end of his celebration of the common law, made this concession concerning statutes:

> I do not mean to deprecate unduly the value of the statute as an instrument of reform. Legislation can eradicate a cancer, right some hoary wrong, correct some definitely established evil, which defies the feebler remedies, the distinctions and the fictions, familiar to the judicial process. Legislation, too, can sum up at times and simplify the conclusions reached by courts, and give them new vitality.

BENJAMIN N. CARDOZO, THE GROWTH OF THE LAW 134 (1924).

4. Although the nineteenth-century movement to codify all of the common law did not succeed, many areas of the law of contracts, commercial law, and torts, among others, were codified in the twentieth century. Mark Rosen argues that this move from common law to statutes affected the judicial development of the law. Mark D. Rosen, *What Has Happened to the Common Law? — Recent American Codifications, and Their Impact on Judicial Practice and the Law's Subsequent Development*, 1994 WIS. L. REV. 1119 (1994).

B. THE LAWYER'S ROLE IN THE LEGISLATIVE PROCESS

INTRODUCTORY NOTE

The ability to function as a lawyer in a court setting is not inherited but learned. Similarly, the role of a lawyer in the legislative process involves a set of acquired skills. Unfortunately, all too often these legislative skills are not taught in law schools. They can be developed through actual experience, although apprenticeship is neither an optimal nor an efficient educational technique. Instead, practical exposure to judicial and legislative proceedings can be provided along with applicable conceptual issues through a classroom component. Just as clinical programs involving court representation of clients seek to fill the gap between classroom learning and on-the-job training, legislative research clinics and drafting exercises in legislation courses have attempted to provide some of the practical training regarding the drafting and handling of legislative matters. Similarly, simulated legislative drafting and research projects have been used as training devices.

Lawyers must be prepared to perform a broad range of tasks in legislative work. Different skills are required to participate in legislative hearings, to draft bills, to effectively use procedural requirements, and to develop legislative history as well as to subsequently interpret and, if necessary, revise legislation.

Whether representing a public body or private client, lawyers will encounter legislation in a number of contexts, but primarily as a source of legal doctrine to be interpreted and analyzed for its impact upon clients. To establish legislative meaning requires a capacity for research, an understanding of the process of enactment, and a knowledge of the interpretative techniques of the courts.

Clients also must be represented at legislative hearings. Clients may appear as advocates with respect to a measure under consideration or they may be subpoenaed as subjects of inquiry. Here the lawyer will be needed to prepare or at least preview the client's statement, to provide the client with a fact book or briefing materials prior to the appearance, to draft questions for friendly legislators to present the client's position clearly and to advise the client at the hearing.

At times, a proposed bill or amendment will be needed to properly present a client's concerns. Then, lawyers must learn enough about the subject, related legislation and judicial decisions to draft a document that can effectively express the client's position.

As the bill comes up for legislative scrutiny the attorney must be sufficiently versed in legislative procedures as well as the political dynamics of the body to assure that the client's concerns will be fully considered. Thus, lawyers must know what steps the particular bill will undergo for passage and the predispositions of key legislators (particularly those on committees that will consider it), as well as the parliamentary rules and how they may affect consideration of the measure, *e.g.*, how a bill can be discharged from a committee "sitting" on it or how cloture works to prevent a filibuster.

Lawyers must also understand the role of those who assist legislators — their personal staff aides and committee staff. These positions, moreover, are often filled by lawyers and therefore constitute a significant field of legal practice. Such persons perform a number and variety of functions, depending upon their positions. Personal aides to legislators, if lawyers, often perform an analytical role and brief the legislator before the vote. Committee staff have prime allegiance to the legislator who hired them (just as with personal staff aides), but must also properly service other committee members. Services will include: obtaining witnesses and assembling documents, preparation of questions and briefing papers for the committee, editing transcripts and writing hearing reports, drafting bills and amendments, and dealing with the various lobbyists representing both private interests and public agencies concerned with the legislation.

Committee staff are expected to have a thorough working knowledge of subjects under the committee's jurisdiction. A legislator's aide, however, is a generalist. Only where the particular legislator has a continuing area of interest will the aide develop detailed knowledge of a subject. Additionally, a working knowledge of the legislature's procedures, its internal power structure and the ability to accurately forecast the political policy positions of the legislator(s) for whom they work is required of both staffs.

It is equally important for attorneys to know what functions are performed by legislative drafting bureaus, law revision commissions and legislative reference or research services. All of these offices play an increasingly important role in the initiation and revision of legislation. Such offices usually employ lawyers who have an expertise in the legislative process, solid drafting skills and well developed legislative research techniques. Their abilities give credence to any policy change they recommend and the specific language they suggest to accomplish it. Where statutory revisions are requested, such persons will proceed after gaining detailed knowledge of the subject area and will generally present the available alternatives. As professionals, they are more likely to be receptive to logical arguments and language clarifications, and their drafting expertise can be of great assistance.

An attorney's role as lobbyist on particular legislation can raise difficult questions. There are significant ethical concerns which must be addressed. The lawyer operates with a different set of restrictions than others involved in influencing the course and language of legislation. Disclosure of the interest an attorney represents while participating in the legislative process is critical, whether such interest is personal, as a member of an organized bar committee, agency advisory committee, or as a representative of a private client or public agency. Similar concerns apply to the manner in which the lawyer can influence the outcome of the legislative action. Some rather fine lines may distinguish what seems appropriate behavior for an attorney from what does not. Unfortunately, there is little in the way of specific directives for the lawyer's conduct. Clearly, there is nothing improper in performing traditional lawyer tasks of marshaling facts and focusing attention on the critical issues involved. Whether this activity properly should encompass drafting of floor speeches or questions for hearings, arranging dialogues for floor discussion, preparing drafts of committee reports and other types of work which clearly a legislator or his staff should perform is a more difficult question.

Finally, whether the lawyer is actually a legislator, plays a support role as staff for committee, legislator or service bureau, operates as a lobbyist for private interests or as legislative liaison for a government agency, an obligation exists to partake in reform of the legislative process itself. Lawyers are the major participants in the judicial system, whether as advocates or judges. There they participate in helping make that system operate more effectively. In the legislative arena, the legal profession also predominates numerically over any other occupational group. Their training and abilities are equally critical in undertaking the self-study and reform of legislative procedures that are clearly needed. Federal and state judicial systems have been revolutionized by open discovery and other procedural devices designed to arrive at a more just result. The game theory has been made less critical than protecting the rights involved. These same objectives must be further enhanced in the legislative forum; to make the legislature more responsive and responsible requires the assistance of those lawyers involved.

No occupational group stands in more regular and intimate relations to American politics than the legal profession. Lawyers make up a large proportion of American politicians at all levels and in all branches of government, in the political parties, and in other political organizations. The affinity of law and politics as vocations is a matter of record. In the United States, probably more than in any other nation, lawyers are the "high priests of politics." The legal profession provides the most substantial reservoir of political personnel.

H. Eulau & J.D. Sprague, Lawyers in Politics: A Study in Professional Convergence 11 (1964). *See also* Mark C. Miller, The High Priests of American Politics: The Role of Lawyers in American Political Institutions (1995).

Why is a lawyer particularly well qualified for lobbying? The answer is that he is trained to interpret laws and provide legal analysis for his clients. One who can interpret and analyze existing laws can also analyze the need for remedial legislation and the specifics for achieving it. In addition, the lawyer is trained as a skillful gatherer and interpreter of facts. And facts, properly presented and carefully analyzed, provide the rationale for most legislation, the cynics notwithstanding.

Charles D. Abalard, *The Washington Lawyer-Lobbyist*, 38 Geo. Wash. L. Rev. 641, 643 (1970).

For a very interesting description of "legislative people," those who run for and are elected as state legislators, see Alan Rosenthal, *Legislators and Legislatures, in* The State of the States 29, 29–38 (Carl Van Horn, ed., 2006).

Several circumstances are associated with the emergence and development of the lawyer as policymaker.[10] First, this profession, like that of the physician, outstrips most others in prestige — evidently an important factor both to party organizations in search of candidates and to voters in quest of representatives. Second, like all successful politicians, the lawyer is an adroit broker of ideas as well as of interests. Legal training, if deficient and illiberal on some counts, is extraordinarily successful in assisting its recipients to master the intricacies of human relations, to excel in verbal exchange, to understand complex and technical information, and to employ varying tactics to seize advantage. These qualities of mind and makeup serve the legislator no less than the campaigner. Third, the lawyer, unlike the usual farmer, teacher, or mechanic, ordinarily finds it convenient to link professional work to steady participation in politics; and political involvement may well bring an unearned increment by attracting, through publicity and social visibility, new clients and higher fees. Finally, whereas people in the workaday activities of other occupations stand on the outskirts of power, the lawyer, with professional knowledge and skills, is automatically the representative of power:

The attorney is the accepted agent of all politically effective groups of the American people. As the lawyer is habitually the representative of the grasping and abused in litigation, as he is increasingly the negotiator between businessmen with conflicting interests, as he is more and more the spokesman of individual and corporation in public relations — so is the lawyer today depended upon to represent citizens in the lawmaking body.[11]

---

[10] Many citizens disapprove of Congress because it does not conform to their expectations. As the public sees it, Congress is too partisan and too driven by the career orientations of its members; in addition, as the public sees it, it has too many lawyers. David Kimball and Samuel C. Patterson, "*Living Up to Expectations: Public Attitudes Toward Congress*," Journal of Politics, LIX (August 1997), 701–28.

[11] Hyneman, "Who Makes Our Laws?" 569.

William J. Keefe & Morris S. Ogul, The American Legislative Process: Congress and the States 158 (2000).

RICHARD B. STEWART,
FOREWORD: LAWYERS AND THE LEGISLATIVE PROCESS
10 Harvard Journal on Legislation 151 (1973)*

Writing over 40 years ago, James Landis complained of law schools — as he might have of the legal literature and much of the legal profession — that in the main they disregarded "both the content of the statute book and the manner of its making." Because the law has become increasingly statutory in its foundations, the profession today has escaped from the dominating spell of the common law to the extent that most practitioners and law students have a tolerable working knowledge of at least some portions of the statute books. Moreover, the legal literature now abounds with analyses of the content of statutes and their interpretation and application. But the second half of Landis' complaint — disregard of the process of statute making — is still apt.

A statute does not spring full blown from the legislature, but the lawyer often acts as if it had. In contrast to judge-made law, where the origins and development of a rule elicit close attention, statutory law is typically taken as a "given," with scant professional concern for the social, economic, and political soil out of which the statute grew or the parliamentary procedures and strategic compromises which shaped its content. The lawyer's concern is generally fixed on the statute's implementation by administrators and courts, and any quarrying he may undertake in the legislative history is usually limited to a search for quotations that can be used as ammunition in the battle of statutory interpretation.

. . . .

This lack of expressed interest on the part of lawyers in the legislative process is surprising when we consider not only the importance of statutory law today, but also the fact that lawyers have long been major participants in that process. In recent years well over half of all United States Senators and Representatives have been lawyers, and while the percentage in state legislatures is lower, it is still considerable. Moreover, lawyers are prominent in a variety of legislative roles other than that of legislator. In Congress lawyers man technical facilities, such as the legislative drafting service, and serve as professional staff for committees, the leadership, or individual congressmen. In addition, they play important roles in the legislative process as lobbyists or counsel for both governmental and private clients.

. . . .

There is also little published on the extent of the bar's professional responsibilities in the legislative arena. At one level, there are important unresolved issues concerning the ethical limits of legislative advocacy. Is it proper for a lawyer to engage in the "manufacture" of legislative history, and, if so, what are the proper limits of the practice? May a lawyer-lobbyist devote himself to advancing his clients' interests with the same wholehearted zeal he may assume in the context of adversary litigation, or must he also take account of larger and potentially conflicting obligations to the public interest, however defined? Charles Horsky attempted to raise some of these issues, but elsewhere in the legal literature such questions are normally passed over, if they are recognized at all. The Canons of Ethics and the new Code of Professional Responsibility provide little illumination on such questions.

In addition there are larger issues of the profession's responsibilities as a body. First, there is the question of expanding the provision of legal representation to various interests affected by the legislative process. Are interest groups which can afford to hire lawyer-lobbyists significantly advantaged in the legislative struggle compared to

---

*   Reprinted with permission of Harvard Journal on Legislation.

those that cannot? If so, is the bar under an obligation, similar to that it has accepted in criminal proceedings and has begun to recognize in civil proceedings in courts and before administrative agencies, to provide such representation to all? How should any such obligation be discharged? Second, does the bar have an obligation to improve the quality of statutory law from the perspective of society as a whole? The efforts of the American Law Institute, the American Bar Association, and other law-reform agencies in drafting and advocating legislation appear to presuppose such an obligation, although such efforts have sometimes been attacked as covert promotions of clients' interests. Third, there is the related matter of the bar's responsibility in improving the legislature as an institution. While the bar investigates and proposes reforms of almost every conceivable aspect of the workings of courts and agencies, there is scarcely any organized professional study of or concern with the functioning and possible improvement of the legislature.

The bar's responsibilities in these areas are rooted in the ongoing and substantial involvement in the legislative process of lawyers acting in various professional capacities. This involvement implies a correlative duty to ensure that the process is equitable and yields sound results from the viewpoint of society as a whole. Moreover, lawyers have a responsibility to the sound working of the legal order as a whole, and it is myopic to suppose this goal can be achieved by focusing on the functioning of courts or agencies alone and in isolation, when all parts of the legal order, including the legislature, act in dynamic interdependence.

. . . .

However, lawyers may often neglect valuable opportunities to advance clients' interests through the legislative process, in large part because they have not been trained to be effective participants in it. If so, the law schools must bear a considerable measure of responsibility, for they have largely neglected the training of lawyers in legislative roles.

This neglect may account in part for the attitude that lobbying is a somewhat disreputable activity for a lawyer, or that the legislative process does not call upon the distinctive intellectual skills of the profession. This latter attitude is illustrated by an exchange occurring some years ago between two senators, both lawyers. Senator Reed, who had but recently joined the Senate from law practice, had engaged the veteran Senator Norris over a question of law:

> Senator Reed: "How long has the gentleman been in Congress?"
>
> Senator Norris: "Twenty-nine years."
>
> Senator Reed: "It is too much to expect a senator to remain a lawyer after all that time."

Such attitudes may explain in part why the legal literature contains so little about the legislative process and lawyers' involvement in it, but the difficulties of the subject are also a factor. Contrast, for example, the analysis of a statute with that of a court decision. A judicial opinion will contain within itself the controlling facts, the pertinent background, the surrounding state of the law, and the reasoning behind the result. A statute, on the other hand, contains little or nothing about the problem it was designed to solve or the pertinent facts. The complex process by which the particular provisions in question came to be law remain hidden behind the general words of the enacting clause. These facts can be ascertained, if at all, only by protracted labor in the legislative history. Many of the most important aspects of a statute's history, including the private initiatives for its enactment, the reactions of antagonistic interest groups, and the compromise negotiations which occurred, rarely appear in any printed record. These difficulties are obviously multiplied when we pass from the enactment of a particular statute to a consideration of the legislative process as a whole.

NOTES AND QUESTIONS

1. In considering whether a lawyer needs to understand the legislative process, is the manner in which a statute comes into being relevant to the way in which the statute should be applied? Is it important to know what prompted the legislature to pass a particular law? Should a law's meaning differ because it was a result of an exchange of favors between legislators? What if a law resulted from intensive and well-financed lobbying? Should the fact that it was a rider attached to a bill about a totally different subject at the last minute have any significance?

2. Records of legislative activity are not extensively available. Is there a due process problem if such materials are to be used in a law's interpretation? Should citizens be presumed to know not only the law as it is written in the statute books, but also an act's legislative history? Is this any different from presuming awareness and comprehension of all relevant court decisions?

3. Is there any reason a lawyer should need to know about the gestation of a law once it is passed other than to deal with the courts and administrative agencies? How do bodies such as law reform commissions, agency advisory committees, and bar associations' legislative committees decide upon needed legislative changes? Is it sufficient for them to make their decisions simply by reference to appellate court interpretations? Are there aspects of the process of changing a law they also should need to know? What effect might an act's legislative history and its enactment process have on revision efforts?

4. What is meant by the term "manufacture" of legislative history? Assuming that this is used in a pejorative sense, how would you distinguish it from the legitimate creation of a legislative record? If the principal difference is that manufactured legislative history is intentionally or artificially produced while the legitimate variety derives naturally or accidentally, why should the second variety be accorded more respect than the first? What is there about the creation of legislative history that makes it ethically suspect for a lawyer to engage in it?

5. What ethical constraints should be put on the legislative activity of lawyers? In what ways, if any, should these differ from limitations on the judicial activity of lawyers? How compatible are these restrictions with the lawyer's role as an advocate? How does the quality of the public interest and the need to protect it differ between legislative and judicial advocacy? Is the adversary process an appropriate way to deal with the kinds of issues handled by legislatures? What is the impact on the public interest of the application of the adversary process to legislatures?

6. What should be the obligation of the lawyer in assisting those who are not presently having their interests considered by the legislature? What is the obligation of the organized bar in this regard? What specific recommendations could be made to implement these responsibilities? What practical obstacles would be confronted, and how could these be surmounted?

7. Most of the judicial process is extremely public. Virtually all of its sessions are open, most of its proceedings are recorded and its decisions are not only reprinted at length in the public record but are widely available and extensively cross-referenced, annotated, and analyzed. Conversely, as Stewart points out, most of the similar information about the legislative process is not as readily accessible, and much of it does not exist in any form. In fact, one reason courts are reluctant to give much weight to legislative history is the lack of authoritative sources. The consequences of this inadequacy are not limited to post-enactment concerns. One of the most effective means of client representation is to influence the development of a bill before it is enacted. However, the vast number of pending measures and the almost total lack of timely information about them exclude all but a few lawyers and well-financed special interest

groups from active participation in the ongoing legislative process. What is the ability and obligation of lawyers and bar associations to reform closed procedures, inadequate legislative history and the virtually nonexistent compilations, cross-referencing, and analysis which characterizes the legislative lawmaking?

EDWIN G. KRASNOW & STEPHEN KURZMAN, LAWYERS FOR THE LAWMAKERS
51 AMERICAN BAR ASSOCIATION JOURNAL 1191 (1965)*

Generally speaking, Representatives and Senators can call upon four kinds of lawyers for aid in carrying out their legislative duties — personal aides in their own Congressional offices, the staff members of the various committees and subcommittees, the draftsmen in the Legislative Counsel's office, and the attorneys in the Legislative Reference Service of the Library of Congress. Each of these four categories of legislative lawyers differs in regard to the breadth and variety of the subject matter it is expected to cover.

The Personal Staff Aide

The personal assistants of members of Congress generally have the widest range of subject matter responsibility, although this varies with the scope of the member's interests and the size of his personal staff. Senators, because of their larger constituencies, have bigger salary allowances and office space for staff than Representatives. While virtually every Senator has at least one lawyer on his staff and some as many as four, the number is not nearly as great in the House and some Representatives have no lawyers on their staffs.

A member expects his staff man to draft answers to reams of constituent mail, shepherd constituents through the maze of the executive branch on individual problems and literally shepherd constituents through the Capitol's corridors. A staff man who is a lawyer often, but not always, is designated "legislative assistant." In addition to all the functions he shares with other personal staff members, he is usually responsible for analyzing legislation going through the member's committees and being considered on the floor, briefing and counseling the member on what is involved, both as a matter of law and as a matter of policy, and recommending a position for the member to take. He is also expected to prepare bills and amendments for the member himself to introduce, help buttonhole cosponsors for the proposals and lobby for action on them.

In all these functions he cannot, of course, be expected to be an expert on the subject matter. In fact, he often is really no more than an informed "brain-picker," calling upon the expertise of the Library of Congress, the committee staffs, the Legislative Counsel of the Senate or House, the executive departments and agencies, bar and trade associations, colleges and universities, and lobbyists.

A personal staff assistant is so closely identified with the member for whom he works that he is often expected to act as his employer's alter ego. Occasionally he is called on to stand in for the member at speaking engagements or to testify on his behalf before committees. In executive, or closed "mark-up," sessions of his member's own committees, if proxy votes are authorized, a staff assistant may be expected to advise the chairman or ranking minority member as to how his principal would wish to be recorded as voting. Sometimes, when an important vote is close an assistant who is without specific instructions may suddenly find himself the object of considerable attention from members of the committee!

The price exacted for this close association and identification with his employer-member is usually a fairly high degree of anonymity for the assistant outside the confines of the Congressional staff milieu. His role is basically that of house counsel: to

---

* Reprinted with permission from American Bar Association Journal.

give sound advice in his employer's best interest and, once his employer's position has been taken, to defend it to the best of his ability, whatever his own views may be.

Committee Counsel

Somewhat more specialized subjects are assigned to lawyers on committee and subcommittee staffs. They are generally held to a higher standard of personal expertise than are personal staff assistants, at least as to the subjects within the jurisdiction of their committees or subcommittees. However, this is only relatively true as contrasted, say, with the greater degree of specialization common today among lawyers in the executive branch and in private practice.

. . . .

The Library of Congress analyzed the make-up of Senate committee staffs in some detail in a 1963 report, "Senate Committee Staffing," Senate Document No. 16, 88th Congress, First Session. The library found that there were some 256 professional staff employees of Senate committees and subcommittees. It concluded that while the Legislative Reorganization Act of 1946 requires professional and clerical employees of the committees to be appointed on a vote of the majority of the committee, in practice staff appointments are generally made instead by committee chairmen and, in the case of minority staff, by the chairmen after consultation with or on the recommendations of the ranking minority members. It also found that there are three types of committee staffs: (1) nonpartisan, without distinction as to political affiliation in hiring or in service; (2) partisan-sponsored staffs who work together as a team, serving members of both parties in varying degrees; and (3) staffs divided between majority and minority not only as to sponsorship but as to working relationships as well. Four of the Senate's sixteen standing committees were found to fall into the first category; the bulk of the remaining ones were considered to be in the second grouping. Much the same pattern could be found in House committee staffing.

. . . .

Legislative Counsel

The most traditionally craftsman-like work on the Hill is performed by the attorneys in the Office of Legislative Counsel. Each of the two houses has its own office offering bill-drafting services to its members and committees. These services are available at any stage of the legislative process, from preparing a bill for a member to drop in the hopper and drafting an amendment to be offered on the floor, to ironing out technical difficulties arising in a House-Senate conference committee. Often they simply check over drafting done first by members themselves or by lawyers on personal or committee staffs.

Attorneys in the Office of Legislative Counsel emphasize that their role is limited to the technical one of shaping legislative language to achieve the policy goals given to them, not defining those goals. However, as every lawyer knows, the choice of words and the choice of policy are inextricably intertwined. Thus, it is often legislative counsel's function to point out to the member whose bill he is drafting the choices of policy involved in various alternative wordings. Like a private practitioner drafting a will, legislative counsel must elicit from his "client," who is often a member's personal staff aide or committee counsel, as many facts as possible about the policy goals sought. In jest it is sometimes said that all a member has to do is call up the legislative counsel's office and say, "I've got a lot of farmers in my district. Draw me up a farm bill." A member would never make such a request and, even if one did so, legislative counsel could not honor it.

Drafting language that will conform to the style and content of the huge mass of existing legislation is a complex and specialized skill. One cannot successfully draft an amendment to the parity provisions of the agricultural laws, for example, without a considerable familiarity with the entire scheme of our farm legislation and how that legislation has been interpreted, both administratively and in the courts. Accordingly, the Office of Legislative Counsel tends to break down its organization along subject-matter lines, so that its attorneys generally work in the same few fields and with the same committees. But, since there are fewer than two dozen attorneys in each office, the scope of each attorney is formidably broad.

Legislative Reference Service

The Legislative Reference Service is the arm of the Library of Congress devoted to furnishing factual information to members and committees of Congress. The American Law Division of the Legislative Reference Service in turn supplies information about the state of existing law and is composed largely of lawyers. Its staff performs research and prepares memoranda in all fields of federal and state statutory and decisional law. The service employs on a nonpartisan basis some 120 lawyers, whose specialization depends in part upon seniority.

. . . .

Like the service performed by the legislative counsel, the demands on the Legislative Reference Service appear staggering to a newcomer on Capitol Hill. Literally, any question of fact submitted to the service by a member or committee of Congress or their staffs will be given an answer.

. . . .

As these brief descriptions indicate, lawyers in a variety of roles are highly important to the effective functioning of today's Congress. They provide the analytical skills and common law perspective developed by legal education and increasingly in demand in fields of endeavor previously thought to be independent of the practice of law. In an age of rapidly accelerating specialization in the legal as well as other professions, lawyers on Capitol Hill are among the last of the generalists. Perhaps more often than their brothers practicing privately, they have the gratification of grappling with issues of national and international importance and of influencing their resolution.

NOTES AND QUESTIONS

1. How comparable are the jobs of a legislative aide and a judicial clerk? For which job would you expect the selection process to be more political? Should a more objective and nonpartisan method of hiring legislative aides be developed or is some sort of political intimacy important in those positions? Conversely, should a judge choose clerks on the basis of their judicial philosophy? To the extent that personal and committee staff members have a fealty to their legislative sponsor, how does this influence their obligation to exercise independent professional judgment?

2. Is it appropriate for legislative aides to have lobbyists work on questions, committee reports, or other matters which are normally the aides' responsibility? Is there any difference between a staff member asking a lobbyist for assistance and a legislator personally making the same request? What difference does it make whether this work is done by the legislators, an aide, or a lobbyist? Is it appropriate for legislative staff aides to request or accept drafting assistance from an administrative agency over which their legislator or committee has oversight responsibilities? Working relationships between committee staff members and their counterparts in administrative agencies often are quite close. Are such close relationships proper? What problems can be foreseen?

3. What is the drafter's responsibility to unswervingly embody directives of the legislator requesting assistance? Can drafting ever really be value free? Is this a desirable goal? What are the limitations and advantages of having a legislature's drafting done by a single bureau? What incentives are there for members of such bureaus to provide legislators with creative alternatives?

4. How effective can personal staff aides be in advising a legislator since they cannot specialize in all or even a significant portion of the subject areas in which their sponsor is involved? What other sources of advice are available to the legislator? What problems does use of those sources involve?

5. Virtually all of the lawyers' roles described in the foregoing excerpt about Congress also exist in the state legislatures.

**ROBERT L. NELSON, JOHN P. HEINZ,
EDWARD O. LAUMANN & ROBERT H. SALISBURY,
PRIVATE REPRESENTATION IN WASHINGTON:
SURVEYING THE STRUCTURE OF INFLUENCE**

1987 AMERICAN BAR FOUNDATION RESEARCH JOURNAL 141, 142–44, 146–47, 191–93 (1987)[*]

Judging from the number of participants in the process, private representation has become an increasingly significant aspect of our governmental system. Since 1970 the vast and complex establishment of lobbyists and lawyers in the nation's capital has grown at a rate that far outstrips the growth of the federal government. Even a presidential administration dedicated to curbing the size of the government has had little impact on the expansion of this community . . . .

Studies of Washington lobbyists and lawyers treat the individual as the primary unit of action, thus presenting an overly individualized conception of representation. Although the interest group literature often recognizes the potential significance of representatives to the political behavior of organizations, in the absence of empirical data it largely proceeds as though the units of action are the organizations themselves and treats the actual lobbying and related activity as if it were undertaken directly by the organization, with the individual representatives having no separate existence or autonomy of action. This produces an undersocialized view of interest representation that tends to ignore the fact that both individual representatives and organizations are embedded in a broader social structure. For strategic reasons, we would expect interest organizations to retain or employ representatives who have the knowledge and connections needed to advance the organizations' interests. But beyond strategic considerations, the recruitment of representatives may well reflect an organization's attachment to particular geographic regions; ethnic, ideological, or occupational groups; or political parties. The social, political, and professional characteristics of representatives may in turn affect how an organization defines its goals, the sorts of strategies it employs, and the kinds of resources it can use to affect policy. Thus, the structure of relationships between client organizations and representatives will have important implications for the nature of interest group politics and the functioning of national policy-making systems.

. . . .

The most pervasive professional group among representatives — and the profession that has received the most theoretical attention with respect to the issue of its autonomy and influence in processes of representation — is the legal profession. Thus, theoretical discussions of the role of lawyers in representation are of considerable interest. Charles Horsky, the distinguished Washington attorney, credited Washington lawyers with being "an essential part of our present scheme of government" in that they serve as "principal interpreter between government and private person, explaining to each the needs, desires and demands of the other." Horsky's characterization of Washington lawyers was a grounded version of the functionalist conception of the role of the professions in modern society, which was given its most influential expression in the work of Talcott Parsons . . . . Because professionals were disposed to conform to a set of common ethical beliefs that reflected widely shared value commitments, Parsons suggested that "the lawyer stands as a kind of buffer between the illegitimate desires of his clients and the social interest. Here in a sense he 'represents' the law rather than the client."

Even with respect to lawyers, however, the Horsky/Parsons model of the representative as an autonomous mediating influence has been questioned . . . . Mark Green suggests a far different perspective on the power of Washington lawyers from that offered by Horsky, contending that Washington lawyers are only too willing to exploit their knowledge of the process of government and their influence with officials at the expense of the public interest.[29]

. . . .

Our findings strongly suggest that the Horsky/Parsons model of autonomous professional representation does not accurately describe Washington representation. The model implies that lawyers are at the center of the system and that representation, like government itself, is becoming increasingly professionalized. But our preliminary mapping of the terrain of representation indicates that lawyers and professionals in general are much less significant to national policy making than is another feature of the system — the organizational apparatus developed by interest groups to monitor and participate in the policy-making process. The dominant direction of the change in the character of representation is not professionalization, but organizational rationalization — the progressive internalization and control of representation by client organizations. As a result, representatives display little structural autonomy from clients.

. . . .

. . . The strong implication is that lawyers are not as influential in private representation as has been thought. Their function as interpreter between government and private interests now is limited largely to specialized questions of legal technique. Organization executives and government affairs personnel have taken over the day-to-day oversight of the client's portfolio of policy concerns. Perhaps in previous eras client organizations were dependent on outside legal counsel for the interpretation of events and the evaluation of potential strategies, but the evidence suggests that organization insiders are now in a position to call the shots on questions of law and policy. In their role as technical experts, lawyers may be more autonomous from clients than are other representatives. But the price of autonomy may be the loss of influence over the objectives clients pursue in the policy-making process.

JILL E. FISCH,
HOW DO CORPORATIONS PLAY POLITICS?:
THE FEDEX STORY
58 VAND. L REV. 1495 (2005)[*]

The Article uses a case study methodology to examine the political activity of a single firm, Federal Express ("FedEx"), over a forty-year period. Focusing primarily on the federal legislative process, the Article considers the business context surrounding FedEx's political activity, the details of the legislative process, and the significant interest group participants, as well as traditional campaign finance materials. An analysis of FedEx's involvement in legislative policymaking reveals that corporate participation in politics extends beyond the purchase of political favors in a spot market. The Article also demonstrates the relationship between FedEx's political activity and its business operations. In particular, it explores the manner in which FedEx has used its political influence to shape legislation and, in turn, the extent to which FedEx's political successes have shaped its business strategy.[18]

---

[29] GREEN, THE OTHER GOVERNMENT (New York: Grossman, 1975) . . . .

[*] Reprinted with permission. Copyright 2005 by Vanderbilt Law Review.

[18] The selection of FedEx represents a conscious choice — FedEx is relatively more active and arguably

. . . .

FedEx's investment in political capital extends beyond monetary donations. FedEx has carefully developed its reputation in Washington. Founder and CEO Fred Smith has maintained an active presence in Washington politics since founding the company; he travels to Washington once a month to meet with political officials and testifies regularly before Congress. As early as 1976, Smith testified before Congress on at least five separate occasions within a six month period in connection with legislative proposals to deregulate the air cargo industry. Washington insiders identify Smith's reputation and interest in politics as a substantial factor in FedEx's political success.

FedEx has also cultivated relationships with Washington insiders.

. . . .

The company maintains a six person office in Washington, D.C., expressly dedicated to government affairs. Specifically, FedEx staffs this office with Washington insiders who have experience in key areas of lawmaking interest to the company, thus extending the scope of the company's relationships. A. Doyle Cloud, FedEx's Vice President for Government Affairs, headed the Washington, D.C. office for a considerable period of time. The office also includes David H. Pryor Jr., the son of former Senator and FedEx consultant David H. Pryor, D-Ark. In 2002, FedEx hired Gina Adams, formerly a nine-year Transportation Department counsel-advisor, to be vice president of the office.

In addition, FedEx values political expertise outside its Washington office.

. . .

FedEx has a reputation for going beyond mere advocacy in its political efforts. FedEx regularly drafts legislation and provides research and other supporting information for government officials.[82] Additionally, FedEx is known for its ability to build coalitions within the industry. FedEx has built "rent chains," enlisting constituencies such as customers and employees to demonstrate broader support for its initiatives.[84] FedEx is politically active, both as an individual firm and as a member of industry groups.

. . . .

FedEx further enhances its reputation through a broad program of high profile charitable activities. In 1986, FedEx donated the use of its jets to airlift hay to drought stricken South Carolina, earning the long term loyalty of South Carolina Democratic Senator Ernest F. ("Fritz") Hollings.

. . . .

II. FedEx and Regulatory Change: The Nature and Role of Political Activity

This Part analyzes FedEx's political participation in a series of major regulatory reforms. Obviously, large public corporations are affected by many legal issues; this Article focuses on how FedEx participated in the creation of several pieces of federal

---

more successful than many of its peers. *See* Neil A. Lewis, *A Lobby Effort That Delivers the Big Votes; Federal Express Knows its Way Around Capital*, N.Y. TIMES, Oct. 12, 1996, at 37 (describing FedEx as "one of the most formidable and successful corporate lobbies in the capital").

[82] A corporation may be most effective in influencing legislative policy by presenting issue papers that inform a legislator on nonsalient political issues. Gerald D. Keim & Carl P. Zeithaml, *Corporate Political Strategy and Legislative Decision Making: A Review and Contingency Approach*, 11 ACAD. MGMT. REV. 828, 840 (1986).

[84] *See* DAVID P. BARON, BUSINESS AND ITS ENVIRONMENT 223 (3d ed. 2000) (explaining the concept of "rent chains" and applying it to FedEx); *see also* Thomas P. Lyon & John W. Maxwell, *Astroturf: Interest Group Lobbying and Corporate Strategy*, 13 J. ECON. & MGMT. STRAT. 561, 563–65 (2004) (describing other nonmarket strategies through which corporations can influence the lobbying behavior of other interest groups, thereby increasing the effectiveness of their own lobbying).

legislation that were of key importance to its business activities. FedEx has been involved in lawmaking efforts beyond the scope of this case study, including its participation in state regulatory change (in addition to trucking deregulation which is discussed in Section II.B *infra*) and activities directed at the Executive Department. With respect to the latter, FedEx's efforts to obtain greater access to foreign routes have been of particular importance. A corporation's litigation strategy also relates to its role in legislative lawmaking. This Part highlights several such connections but does not evaluate FedEx's litigation activities independently.

For each issue examined in this case study, the Article considers the nature of the regulatory changes sought by FedEx, the relationship between the applicable legal rules and FedEx's business operations, the methods employed by FedEx to obtain the change, the result of these efforts, and the significance of the issue for the company. In particular, the Article considers the role of money in the process, the participation of significant interest groups, and the importance of the other types of political participation described in Part I above.

A. Air Cargo Deregulation

Any analysis of FedEx's political activity must start with air cargo deregulation because this development was critical for FedEx to operate as a viable business. When Smith founded FedEx in 1971, the airline industry was extensively regulated. Most commercial airlines were subject to the restrictive regulations of the Civil Aeronautics Board ("CAB") which made rates and routes subject to CAB approval. New entrants had to undergo burdensome certification procedures, after which they were subject to CAB regulation. Critics charged that the CAB generally kept rates unreasonably low and routinely refused requests by carriers to expand into new markets. Initially, FedEx was able to avoid these regulations by carrying cargo in small Falcon jets under an exemption designed to permit air taxi operations. Using small aircraft to deliver cargo was inefficient, however, and FedEx hovered near bankruptcy for its first few years of operation. Indeed, Smith reported that he flew to Las Vegas in 1973 to play blackjack in an effort to generate the cash to keep the company solvent.

When the CAB denied FedEx's request to extend the exemption to bigger planes, Smith went to Washington. He lobbied extensively and testified before Congress, seeking modification of the law so as to enable FedEx to operate larger aircraft and to expand into new markets. Some reports describe air cargo deregulation as an easy political battle. Smith found several strong allies for his cause, including CAB Chair Alfred Kahn, who viewed the Cargo Act as the first step in his effort to deregulate the airline industry, and the National Industrial Traffic League — the most prestigious association of shippers. Many academics also supported airline deregulation.

Nonetheless, air cargo deregulation was not without opponents.

. . . .

Despite these obstacles, FedEx's efforts to obtain legal change were successful. In 1977, Congress enacted and President Carter signed the Air Cargo Deregulation Act ("ACDA"). The statute created substantial new opportunities for the development of the air cargo industry through deregulation by broadly facilitating competition within the industry. In particular, the statute granted certified carriers — those recognized by the CAB as "fit, willing and able" — complete freedom to enter domestic markets and to charge any nonpredatory rates.

The legislation also provided specific benefits tailored to FedEx. As an existing air cargo company, FedEx immediately received nationwide cargo operating authority, including freedom from CAB regulation. Moreover, the statute gave existing air cargo companies advantages over new entrants, including a one-year window during which they could enter new markets without competition.

. . . .

How did FedEx accomplish this regulatory change? FedEx's sustained lobbying efforts were clearly a factor. Smith personally testified before congressional committees on more than a dozen occasions, and a variety of FedEx officials participated in the deregulation efforts. FedEx also recognized the importance of professional lobbyists and enlisted their efforts in its campaign. Congressional staff members observed that FedEx did "an outstanding job" presenting its case to Congress. These efforts were supported by the relationships that FedEx already had begun to build with members of the congressional subcommittees on Aviation, whom FedEx recognized would continue to play an important role in evaluating regulatory changes that would affect its future.

. . . .

B. Trucking Deregulation

In latter stages of air cargo deregulation, FedEx and Flying Tiger raised the issue of trucking deregulation. As with air transportation, trucking was extensively regulated in the 1970s. This regulation affected FedEx's ability to transport packages to and from its aircraft. Consequently, after air cargo deregulation, FedEx turned its attention to trucking deregulation. Trucking deregulation occurred in two separate steps. Initial deregulation of interstate trucking, step one, followed closely upon the heels of airline deregulation. Two years after the Federal Express Act was signed into law, Congress passed, and President Carter signed, the Motor Carrier Act of 1980 ("MCA"). The MCA did not eliminate state authority to regulate intrastate trucking. Full deregulation of intrastate trucking, step two, did not occur until 1995.

. . . .

2. Intrastate Trucking Deregulation

After the adoption of the MCA, federal regulation of trucking was reduced, increasing rate competition and entry. The Motor Carrier Act, however, explicitly preserved state authority to regulate intrastate trucking. As a result, state regulation of intrastate trucking remained extensive. As of 1986, approximately forty states continued to regulate intrastate trucking. The regulations varied, but most included entry controls, tariff filing and rate regulation, restrictions on operations, and grants of antitrust immunity for carriers to set rates collectively.

. . . .

III. Implications of the Case Study

A. Political Activity and Corporate Operations

The FedEx case study demonstrates that the characterization of corporate political activity as a diversion of operating funds is, at best, naive. U.S. corporations operate within a complex legal infrastructure, and the regulatory environment is an integral part of market decisions for corporations as well as a key factor in their growth and strategic planning. FedEx, and indeed the entire air cargo industry, could not have gotten off the ground without air cargo deregulation. FedEx's ability to develop and serve its customer base was critically enhanced by the urgent letter exemption, which enabled it to deliver letters as well as freight. Noise standards, labor rules, and trucking regulation directly affected FedEx's operating costs, influencing the manner in which FedEx developed its business plan, affecting its pricing structure, and defining its key industry competitors.

Campaign finance scholars and the Supreme Court have isolated corporate political activity without considering the relationship of politics to the firm's business strategy. Corporate scholars may emphasize marketplace competition at the cost of overlooking nonmarket strategies. Yet, as the FedEx story shows, firm competition takes place both in the marketplace and in the political arena; the dynamics of one environment affect the other.

. . . .

There are several key implications of the FedEx story. First, the case study predicts that existing regulatory efforts to limit corporate political participation are unlikely to succeed, both because they use an artificially narrow conception of political participation and because of the relationship between a corporation's market and nonmarket activities. Second, it suggests that such efforts may be misguided in that advocates of such restrictions overstate the social costs of corporate political participation and overlook the ways in which such participation may enhance the legislative process. Finally, the study reveals several factors that policymakers should consider in their efforts to regulate corporate political activity, including transparency, provision of information, and firm specialization with respect to political capital.

Regulation has become an important factor for U.S. businesses. As a result, corporate political activity must be integrated within a corporation's overall business strategy, and corporations need to develop and manage their political capital in the same way that they manage other business assets. The FedEx story demonstrates the importance of politics to business and explains the growing investment by corporations in political capital. It further explains how the business world has responded, and will continue to respond, to regulatory restrictions by developing alternative mechanisms for exerting political influence. By understanding how and why corporations participate in politics, policymakers can better address concerns about the effect of corporate political influence.

NOTES AND QUESTIONS

1. These excerpts reflect the efforts of advocates who constructed arguments to modify the kind of "programmatic legislation" described by Professor Frank Grad earlier in this Chapter. These modifications were sought to facilitate the client's execution of its business model or plan. Further, those who advocated for Federal Express, including their lawyers, made use of forums in all three branches of the federal government, as well as state lawmaking mechanisms.

2. Those who seek to participate in these varied lawmaking activities must take account of the role of politics and the influence of organized interest groups. The role of lawyers and interest groups in developing "programmatic legislation" regulating the airline industry, to the advantage of the early participants in that industry, is documented in JOSEPH GOULDEN, THE SUPERLAWYERS 6-37 (1971).

ROBERT J. MARTIN,
ELIMINATION OF LITIGATION BY LEGISLATION:
THE STATUTORY SALVATION OF ST. VIRGIL SCHOOL
31 SETON HALL LEGIS. J. 353 (2007)*

I. *Introduction*

This article highlights an often-overlooked strategy in coping with pending litigation: enactment of a statute as a means for defendants to prevail without having to endure the expense and uncertainty of a full-blown trial or settlement. The article seeks to increase litigators' awareness of the possibility of changing the basic rules in mid-game by securing passage of legislative remedies directly targeted at influencing the outcome of pending litigation.

Of course, diligent litigators are probably familiar with at least some instances of legislative intervention to alter the course of judicial proceedings; but, typically, such legislation has been enacted to assist prospective plaintiffs — not previously named defendants. And, even when legislation has been enacted on behalf of defendants, it has usually occurred only *after* their case has resulted in an unfavorable decision.

In this article I have sought to demonstrate how a defendant may secure legislative relief to gain removal from a *pending* lawsuit. The case in question, *United States v. Cadillac Plastics Group* and *N.J. Dep't of Envtl. Prot. v. Beckman Coulter* (two separate actions which were subsequently consolidated),[4] is still awaiting final disposition despite a decade of ongoing discovery and settlement conferences. The case has evolved into one of the most extensive environmental lawsuits in the country, emanating from the pollution created at a notorious Superfund site, Combe Fill South Landfill. The governmental plaintiffs have sought damages pursuant to the Comprehensive Environmental Response Compensation and Liability Act of 1980 ("CERCLA") and New Jersey's Spill Compensation and Control Act of 1977. By 2001 there were thirty named defendants, of which thirteen had also assumed the role of third-party plaintiffs by subsequently impleading 276 additional parties as third-party defendants.

Most of the third-party defendants were added to the lawsuit because they had allegedly placed hazardous waste materials in refuse that had been transported to the landfill. Although many of them were large corporations, including both private entities (such as A&P, Acme, and Pathway supermarkets) and public entities (such as the United States Army and the municipalities of Darien and Greenwich, Connecticut), some of the third-party defendants were quite small.

One of the smallest third-party defendants was St. Virgil School, a parochial grammar school in Morris Plains, New Jersey. It presumably disposed of routine school refuse that technically fell within the definition of "hazardous waste" for purposes of CERCLA. Lacking insurance coverage to handle the cost to defend and pay potential damages, St. Virgil faced a serious financial hardship because of the joint and several liability exposure imposed by statute. In assessing St. Virgil's dilemma, the school's pro bono attorney, Michael Carlucci, concluded that the imposition of heavy penalties against this insignificant defendant, which had certainly never intended to pollute the environment, was fundamentally unfair. Thus, Mr. Carlucci looked for a way to get his client out of the lawsuit. Having been active in politics, Mr. Carlucci recognized that enactment of a statutory exception might provided the best solution.

How the "statutory salvation" of St. Virgil School was pursued and ultimately achieved forms the central theme of this article. As it turned out, the enactment of a bill into law proved an arduous process, taking almost three years to achieve passage. That bill, eventually named S. 682, underwent numerous amendments and encountered opposition from both liberal environmental and conservative business lobbyists, both of which sought to derail or revamp the legislation.

As the New Jersey state senator who served as prime sponsor of S. 682, I not only witnessed first-hand the manner in which the "dance of legislation" was performed, I took the lead in waltzing the bill through the legislative process. I believe that it is an intriguing story, one that pits a modern David against multiple Goliaths. Most significantly, its telling may serve several purposes.

This article may prove instructive to law school students and lawyers not well acquainted with the legislative process in that it is deliberately designed to expose the nitty-gritty of how a bill becomes law at the state level. It should also prove useful to policymakers as a reminder that their decision-making, when not fully thought out, can cause a great deal of anguish and damage to unintended parties. Just as importantly, the article illustrates how legislators can undertake remedial action to correct problems brought about by their previous lawmaking.

. . . .

---

[4] *See* Second Am. Complaint, *N.J. Dep't of Envtl. Protection v. Beckman Coulter, Inc.*, No. 98-CV-4781 (D.N.J. filed 2001) [hereinafter Second Amended Complaint]. The two cases were consolidated by order of the United States District Court of New Jersey, which has retained jurisdiction. *Id.*

V. The Dance of Legislation, Part 1: The Rise and Fall of S. 1866

Once begin the dance of legislation, you must struggle through its mazes as best you can to the breathless end — if any end there be . . . .
     — *Woodrow Wilson*[112]

Commentators have compared a legislature metaphorically to a circus, a marketplace, a zoo, and, quite frequently, a sausage factory.[113] It was Germany's "Iron Chancellor," Otto von Bismarck, who is credited with originating the phrase, "There are two things you don't want to see being made — sausage and legislation."[114]

The imagery engendered by a sausage factory and its product seems particularly appropriate in describing the lawmaking that takes place inside America's fifty state capitols. Indeed, when seen up close, the state legislative process may appear distasteful and its resulting product difficult to swallow, much less digest. It also can be quite mystifying. Alan Rosenthal, one of the foremost authorities on state legislatures, has acknowledged: "I have been a student of the legislative process for more than 30 years, but I still can't figure it out. The legislature is too human, too democratic and too messy to be totally comprehensible."

. . . .

Unfortunately, the express language of the statute did not directly state whether it was meant to apply retroactively or only prospectively. The bill's proponents had obviously intended the legislation to apply to pending litigation; in fact, this was the very reason they had sought its enactment. They thought that its purpose was so apparent they did not even bother to ensure that such language was included in their bill. In retrospect, this proved to be a serious omission, since Mr. Carlucci was now confronted with having to gather indirect evidence that S. 682 was intended to apply retroactively, and specifically to St. Virgil School.[235] Although he was reasonably certain he could do so, he recognized that a contested court issue is never clear-cut.

Presumably, Mr. Carlucci's biggest challenge would be to overcome the legal presumption that statutes should generally be applied prospectively, not retroactively. Fortunately for Mr. Carlucci, this presumption in not strongly adhered to in most jurisdictions, since it is widely acknowledged that "[s]tatutes, except for those establishing crimes, may be applied retroactively, and whether they are or are not depends on the language of the statute and its interpretation." Moreover, New Jersey case law has consistently followed this reasoning.

---

[112] Woodrow Wilson, Congressional Government (quoted in Eric Redman, The Dance of Legislation (1973)). This analogy of legislation to dancing is also discussed in Shirley S. Abrahamson & Robert L. Hughes, *Shall We Dance? Steps for Legislators and Judges in Statutory Interpretation*, 75 Minn. L. Rev. (1991).

[113] National Conference of State Legislatures, *In Search of the Perfect Metaphor*, http://ncsl.org/programs/pubs/901sausge.htm (last visited June 21, 2005). In this article two more recent metaphors, cited from John A. Straayer's book, *The Colorado General Assembly* (1990) are mentioned. The first compares the legislature to an arena in which "a score of basketball games are progressing, all at one time, on the same floor, with games at different stages, with participants playing on several teams at once, switching at will, opposing each other in some instances and acting as teammates in others." *Id.* The second compares the legislature to a casino, "where there are lots of tables, lots of games, the stakes are high, there are winners and losers, but the outcome is never final, for there is always a new game ahead." *Id.*

[114] Alan Rosenthal, *The Legislature as Sausage Factory: It's About Time We Examine This Metaphor*, *available at* http://ncsl.org/programs/pubs/901sausge.htm (last visited June 21, 2005) . . . .

[235] This was primarily a failure on my part, as prime-sponsor of S. 682. When the bill was first being drafted, I had contemplated putting in express language indicating that the exemption would apply to pending litigation but had decided against it. I thought such language might raise a "red flag" about the bill's potential impact, thus giving more ammunition to those who might oppose it. Although I believed such language was unnecessary, in hindsight I have recognized that such language should definitely have been included, even if it might have made the bill harder to enact.

. . . .

VIII: Conclusion

Trial lawyers may sometimes find it beneficial to fight their legal battles on two fronts: the courthouse *and* the statehouse. Yet many trial lawyers often fail to consider the advantages of opening a secondary front that might enable them to eliminate litigation through legislation. For despite its confusion and uncertainty, the legislative process may, given the proper circumstances, provide a means of relief that cannot be achieved, or as easily achieved, through litigation alone.

Indeed, if pursued early and skillfully enough, legislation may give trial lawyers the added ammunition necessary to defeat their legal adversaries. Employment of this strategy is often best applied when one merely needs to enact "minor legislation" to gain a decisive legal advantage. Although it may be of little consequence to the public in general and a majority of the legislature, minor legislation always has major significance to those directly affected; otherwise a bill's advocates would never go through the trouble of seeking its enactment. One must bear in mind, however, that even "little" laws can run into big procedural problems as they become entwined in the "dance of legislation," and these problems can occur at almost any step of the legislative process.

Accordingly, trial lawyers seeking a statutory solution must be aware of the requirements and potential roadblocks at every stage of lawmaking. In doing so, it is imperative to remember that the "hallmark of the American legislative process is the difficulty of legislative enactment, not its ease." Some of the greatest obstacles involve:

- Finding a sympathetic legislator, one who has the willingness and political clout to pursue the proposed legislation to a satisfactory conclusion.
- Having the proposed bill drawn correctly at its inception to ensure that the sponsor's purpose is accomplished and to circumvent the difficulty and potential delay in trying to procure clarifying amendments.
- Enlisting the support of key legislators, especially those in leadership positions in both political parties, to assist in moving the bill along.
- Getting the bill on the legislative calendar of the appropriate committee of the house of introduction.
- Shepherding the bill through each voting checkpoint inherent in the legislative process (i.e. the floor of both houses and those committees to which the bill is assigned).
- Keeping a close watch on potential opponents, especially powerful lobbying groups and organizations, and taking corrective action to ward off, defeat, or minimize hostile amendments.
- Ensuring that the governor and heads of the various departments and agencies of government do not seek to derail or detrimentally revise the legislation.
- Overcoming the frustration that frequently occurs because of the uncertainty, tension, and vagaries of the legislative process.

As one can glean, lawmaking can be messy and quirky and therefore not always susceptible to a predictable outcome. Just because a majority of legislators support a bill does not mean that it will ever be enacted. The reality is that the legislative process is highly nuanced and frequently filled with unpleasant surprises, including complications caused by last-minute amendments and inexplicable political intrigue.

Beyond recognition of the unpredictability of this line of attack, one daring enough to contemplate legislation to eliminate litigation must realize that timing *alone* can become a serious and perhaps fatal impediment, since, if pending litigation proceeds faster than anticipated legislation, the opportunity for success may expire before statutory relief comes to the rescue. Thus, this approach is usually available only for cases involving complex litigation that are not scheduled to be arbitrated or tried relatively quickly. Moreover, one must realize that the employment of legislation to eliminate litigation "ain't over till it's [*finally*] over," and that occurs only when the court, not the legislature, deems it is. Because of these shortcomings, one simply cannot rely with confidence on legislation to secure favorable results in ongoing litigation.

But surely the same can be said of any litigation strategy; for no matter how zealous and clever their trial advocacy, lawyers can never be guaranteed a satisfactory conclusion to pending court cases. What has been emphasized here, however, is that it is sometimes better to pursue litigation in combination with legislation in order to double one's chances for success.

NOTES AND QUESTIONS

1. For a similar example of "opening a secondary front," of advocacy, including a proposed state constitutional amendment, and judicial rulemaking, see Robert F. Williams, *The Anatomy of Law Reform: Dissecting a Decade of Change in Florida* in Forma Pauperis *Law*, 12 STETSON L. REV. 363, 370–75, 380–81, 385–86 (1983).

2. We will see a similar legislative intervention into pending litigation in *Robertson v. Seattle Audubon Society*, in Chapter 6F.

3. The issue of interpreting statutes to be retroactive is considered in Chapter 9D.

C. OTHER FORMS OF LAWMAKING

1. Judicial Rulemaking

BUSIK v. LEVINE
63 N.J. 351, 307 A.2d 571 (1973)

WEINTRAUB, C.J.

The principal charge is that prejudgment interest is a matter of "substantive" law and as such beyond the constitutional grant to the Supreme Court of the power to "make rules governing . . . the practice and procedure" in all courts, Art. VI, sec. 2, para. 3. Hence, it is argued, we trespassed upon the legislative domain in adopting the rule, in breach of the principle of separation of powers embodied in Art. III, sec. 1, of the Constitution. The argument is supplemented with the proposition that defendants were thereby deprived of the opportunity to be heard required by due process of law.

. . . .

We repeat there is no conflict with any statute; there is no statute on the subject. Nor can it be doubted that the Court has the power and the continuing responsibility to change these judge-made rules of law as justice may require. In short, had the proposition in paragraph (b) been announced in case of A against B, there could be no claim that the Court lacked the power or in any way transgressed upon the area constitutionally allotted to the Legislature. Thus it is not our power to act that is questioned; it is the method we chose to exercise that power.

But if we erred in adopting that method (we will demonstrate in Point II below that we did not), this litigation would not end. For plaintiffs here are entitled to ask for the same result which the challenged rule provides. They cannot be denied their due merely because we mistakenly expressed our view in a rule of court. The underlying issue is thus before us. The merits have been argued fully, and the litigants thus afforded a hearing. Nothing new, however, emerged. This is not surprising, for the subject is not new, and was fully explored at a public hearing before we adopted the rule.

. . . .

II

A

Defendants point out that the rule-making power granted the Supreme Court in Art. VI, sec. 2 para. 3, relates to "practice and procedure," and from this grant defendants would infer that this constitutional provision inferentially dictates the mode whereby the Supreme Court may make "substantive" law. But the constitutional provision is what it purports to be — a grant of power with respect to "practice and procedure." It does not purport to deal with substantive law or to prescribe a format for the discharge of the Court's responsibility as to that topic. Limitations of course do exist, but they arise, not from the cited section of the Constitution, but from the nature of the judicial process and of the Court's responsibility.

Nor, for that matter, is the constitutional grant of power with respect to "practice and procedure" a mandate that that subject may be dealt with only in a rule-making process. Many matters of practice and procedure repose in case law. Sometimes the procedures established in a judicial opinion will later be embodied in a formal rule of practice and procedure.[5] Commonly they are not.[6] Or a formal rule may expressly call for a case-by-case exposition, as for example, R. 4:4-4(i) relating to service of process which expressly leaves the outer reaches of substituted service to "due process of law." Indeed the most valued rights upon which life, liberty, and property depend are "procedural" and are embedded in the Constitutions of the United States and of this State. Although those rights are procedural, the courts have not chosen to particularize those rights by way of a rule-making process. Cases are legion which expound their meaning and the consequences of infringement. And, finally, a matter of practice may be prescribed in an administrative directive.

The constitutional grant of rule-making power as to practice and procedure is simply a grant of power; it would be a mistake to find in that grant restrictions upon judicial techniques for the exercise of that power, and a still larger mistake to suppose that the grant of that power impliedly deprives the judiciary of flexibility in the area called "substantive" law.

B

"Substantive" law of course is regularly established in cases brought before the Court. But there is no constitutional mandate that a court may not go beyond what is necessary to decide a case at hand. Whether an issue will be dealt with narrowly or expansively calls for a judge's evaluation of many things, including the need for guidance for the bar or agencies of government or the general public. To that end, the Court may express doubts upon existing doctrines, thereby inviting litigation, or may itself raise an issue it thinks should be resolved in the public interest, or may deliberately decide issues which need not be decided when it believes that course is warranted. So a court may decide an issue even though the litigation has become moot, again in the public interest . . . .

Defendants refer to the statement in *Winberry v. Salisbury*, 5 N.J. 240, 248, 74 A.2d 406, 410 (1950), *cert. denied*, 340 U.S. 877, 71 S. Ct. 123, 95 L. Ed. 638 (1950), that "While the courts necessarily make new substantive law through the decision of specific

---

[5] For example, the procedure outlined in *New Jersey Dept. of Health v. Roselle*, 34 N.J. 331, 169 A.2d 153 (1961), for the handling of contempt matters was thereafter incorporated in the formal rule, R. 1:10. In *State v. Abbott*, 36 N.J. 63, 77–78, 174 A.2d 881 (1961), we dealt with the problem of offers of proof in criminal matters and thereafter incorporated the suggested practice in R. 1:7-3.

[6] For example, in *State v. Guido*, 40 N.J. 191, 199–200, 191 A.2d 45 (1963), we suggested a procedure to deal with the problem of the recalcitrant witness.

cases coming before them, they are not to make substantive law *wholesale* through the exercise of the rule-making power" (emphasis ours). There can be no quarrel with that proposition, but one might note in passing that *Winberry* is a classic example of a deliberate decision upon a far-reaching issue, involving the respective powers of the Supreme Court and the Legislature, which no doubt could have been avoided but which the majority believed should be decided then in the public interest.

C

And finally it is simplistic to assume that all law is divided neatly between "substance" and "procedure." A rule of procedure may have an impact upon the substantive result and be no less a rule of procedure on that account. Speaking of the proposition that a court may not promulgate rules governing substantive law in the exercise of their rule-making power, Professors Levin and Amsterdam agreed that "rational separation is well-nigh impossible." *Legislative Control Over Judicial Rule-making: A Problem in Constitutional Revision*, 107 U. Pa. L. Rev. 1, 14–15 (1958). *See also State v. Otis Elevator Co.*, 12 N.J. 1, 24, 95 A.2d 715 (1953) (Jacobs, J., dissenting). As said in *Hanna v. Plumer*, 380 U.S. 460, 471, 85 S. Ct. 1136, 1144, 14 L. Ed. 2d 8, 16–17 (1965), "The line between 'substance' and 'procedure' shifts as the legal context changes. 'Each implies different variables depending upon the particular problem for which it is used.' " One context is conflict of laws; another is retrospective application of statutes: and a third is law-making, the subject at hand.

. . . .

And, finally, in the context of rule-making, other factors may come into play. The Court may be spurred by the needs of the judicial system measured, not only by the private interests of all litigants, but also by the interest of public. Or the Court, mindful of the problem of exclusivity and its impact upon the delicate relations among the co-equal branches of government, may be reluctant to move or to go as far as it would if the Legislature retained the power to disagree.

To illustrate, what is the statute of limitations? For conflict of laws purposes, it is usually said to be "procedural," meaning that the law of the forum will be applied, *Marshall v. Geo. M. Brewster & Son, Inc.*, 37 N.J. 176, 179–182, 180 A.2d 129 (1962); *see* RESTATEMENT (2D) OF CONFLICT OF LAWS (1971) sec. 142, although even there the just course may be to apply the law of another State if the parties were there throughout its period of limitations and the suit was brought after that period had run. In the context of retrospective application of a statute, there may be no substantial reason to refuse to apply a change in a period of limitations retrospectively so long as a barred cause of action is not thereby revived or an existing cause of action is not thereby barred without a fair opportunity to sue. But when we turn to the third context, whether the statute of limitations is within the Court's rule-making power, the considerations may well be different. We need but say that thus far it has not been suggested that this subject matter is "procedural" within the meaning of our constitutional provision. On the other hand, time for appeal, which must resemble a statute of limitation, may confidently be said to come within the Court's rule-making power. R. 2:4.

What is "evidence"? It arguably is "procedural," "substantive" or a hybrid. It smacks of "procedure" insofar as it controls what may enter the mix, but it is quite "substantive" as an ingredient of the end product, the judgment. Some rules of evidence, particularly those relating to privileges, may themselves be thought to generate rights or values of a "substantive" cast. In the context of conflict of laws, evidence generally would be for the forum. RESTATEMENT (2D) OF CONFLICT LAWS (1971) sec. 138 adopts that view, with, however, certain exceptions. In the context of retrospective application of a statute, it would likely again be "procedural" in most respects. But the third context, the respective powers of the legislative and judicial branches, brings other values into view.

We participated in a process whereby a code of evidence was adopted "wholesale," to use a word in the quotation above from *Winberry*. The rules of evidence were adopted cooperatively by the three branches of government under the Evidence Act, 1960 (L. 1960, c. 52; N.J.S.A. 2A:84A-1, et seq.) after the Supreme Court and the Legislature conducted their separate studies. Under the statutory arrangement, some of the rules, notably those embodying privileges, were fixed in the statute itself while other rules, prepared by the Court after consideration at a Judicial Conference, were filed with the legislature to become effective unless disapproved by a joint resolution signed by the Governor. Thus we did not pursue to a deadlock the question whether "evidence" was "procedural" and therefore, according to the *Winberry* dictum, the sole province of the Supreme Court. Nor were we deterred by the specter of the criticism that, if "evidence" is "substantive," it was unseemly or worse for the Court to participate in the "wholesale" promulgation of substantive law. The single question was whether it made sense thus to provide for the administration of justice, and the answer being clear, we went ahead. We add that the United States Supreme Court, which does not have a constitutional grant of rulemaking power as to practice and procedure, is pursuing a similar project in cooperation with the Congress. 18 U.S.C.A. sections 3402, 3771, 3772 (1964); 28 U.S.C.A. sections 2072, 2075 (1958).

D

What then is "interest"? As we have said, it is compensatory as to the parties and represents "damages" for delay in payment. "Damages" constitute a "remedy." And "remedy" promptly connotes "procedure." 1 Am. Jur. 2d, Actions, sec. 6, p. 546. But in the context of conflict of laws, the majority view is that "damages" go to the substance, i.e., that it would disserve the values involved to apply the law of the forum rather than the law of the place of the wrong . . . .

In the light of the foregoing it surely cannot be said to have been palpably inappropriate to think of prejudgment interest as a matter of procedure in the context of law-making. The question was of general concern, affecting many thousands of pending tort actions. The issue could have been raised in any of those cases, at the instance of the litigant or on the court's own motion. Had the issue been raised that way, all litigants would have been bound by the result notwithstanding that they were not heard upon the merits. One of the consequences of the stubborn myth that courts do not make law is the continuing failure to develop a technique whereby all may be heard who are interested in a legal proposition and might contribute to an informed decision. In this respect the rule-making approach is clearly superior. Here all interests were heard at a public meeting. Surely the litigants themselves lost nothing in that process. And when there is added the signal fact that the rule, while serving the cause of justice as between litigants, has the equally important objective of expediting the disposition of cases, thereby to advance the welfare of all litigants and the welfare of the taxpayers who must support the system, we have no doubt of the propriety of the course we followed. The rule concerns the practice and procedure in the courts in any view of that subject notwithstanding that the rule has also a "substantive" impact upon the dollar result. It made sense to invoke the rule-making process in such circumstances. It was a responsible exercise of our responsibility.

. . . .

It is insisted we cannot uphold the rule for prejudgment interest without also deciding whether the rule comes within the *Winberry* dictum that the Court's authority as to practice and procedure is exclusive. We see no need to meet that issue. The sole question is whether the Court may treat the subject by a rule rather than by a judicial decision despite the substantive aspect of the subject. The issue of exclusivity involves a touchy matter, the relations among the three branches of government. It will be time enough to talk about exclusivity when there is an impasse and no way around it.[10] A coordinate branch should not invite a test of strength by proclamation. Our form of government works best when all branches avoid staking out the boundaries which separate their powers.

NOTES AND QUESTIONS

1. What are the implications of a ruling that a subject is procedural rather than substantive? Does it really not matter, as the Court in *Busik* seems to say, whether the court relies on its power to make "substantive" rather than "procedural" law?

2. Once a state supreme court has determined that something is properly treated by a procedural rule is it likely to change its mind? The Pennsylvania Supreme Court did on a rule very similar to New Jersey's in *Craig v. Magee Memorial Rehabilitation Center*, 515 A.2d 1350 (Pa. 1986). For similar self-corrections, see *Consolidated Construction Services, Inc. v. Simpson*, 813 A.2d 260 (Md. 2002), and *Boyd v. Becker*, 627 So. 2d 481, 484 (Fla. 1993).

3. Should prior judicial interpretations of judicial rules be entitled to more or less precedential value than other precedents? Chief Justice Feldman of the Arizona Supreme Court wrote:

> The issue in this case requires us to reevaluate our holding in *Lambright*, and we believe a preliminary explanation of why we have chosen to revisit *Lambright* is warranted. In matters relating to the interpretation and application of court rules and procedures, this court must pay constant attention to developments in court procedures and changing circumstances in order to fulfill our constitutional role. *See* Ariz. Const. art. 6, § 5. In furtherance of this responsibility, we will reevaluate prior decisions regarding court procedures, where principles of *stare decisis* might counsel otherwise in substantive matters involving common law decisionmaking or statutory or constitutional interpretation. *See, e.g., State v. Mendoza*, 170 Ariz. 184, 823 P.2d 51 (1992) (overruling the interpretation of Rule 8.2(a), Ariz. R. Crim. P., 17 A.R.S., established for DUI cases in *Hinson v. Coulter*, 150 Ariz. 306, 723 P.2d 655 (1986)).

Hedlund v. Sheldon, 840 P.2d 1008, 1009 (Ariz. 1992).

2.   Executive Orders

BOURQUIN v. CUOMO
652 N.E.2d 171 (N.Y. 1995)

KAYE, CHIEF JUDGE.

This case requires us to decide whether an Executive Order issued by the Governor violates the principle of separation of powers under the New York State Constitution. We conclude that the Governor acted within his authority, and therefore reverse the order of the Appellate Division declaring the Executive Order unconstitutional.

On January 3, 1991, then-Governor Mario Cuomo issued Executive Order No. 141 (9 NYCRR 4.141) authorizing the creation of a private, not-for-profit corporation known as the Citizens' Utility Board (CUB) intended, among other things, to represent the interests of residential utility customers in ratemaking and other proceedings before the Public Service Commission. In issuing the order creating the CUB, the Governor

---

[10] In some instances our rules expressly accept statutory provisions relating to the same subject matters. *See* R. 4:27-2; R. 4:42-8(a); R. 4:52-7; R. 4:59-1; R. 4:83-1. After the adoption of the prejudgment interest rule here involved, the Legislature enacted the New Jersey Tort Claims Act, N.J.S.A. 59:1-1, et seq., which provides in N.J.S.A. 59:9-2a that "No interest shall accrue prior to the entry of judgment against a public entity or public employee." We have approved an amendment to our rule of Court which will except that situation.

cited "the policy of this State to foster and encourage citizen participation in utility matters and to facilitate effective representation and advocacy of the interests of residential utility customers in the regulatory process." He noted as well that "individual participation by residential utility customers . . . is impracticable because of the expertise required and the disproportionate expense of taking such action."

In addition to establishing the CUB, Executive Order No. 141 provided that the Board would have access to as many as four State agency mailings per year for the purpose of disseminating information to New York citizens about the CUB's purpose and activities and soliciting memberships and contributions. The Board was required to reimburse the agencies for any increase in postage attributable to its enclosures.

Five months after the issuance of the Executive Order, plaintiff-respondent Pierre Bourquin, a New York "citizen, resident and taxpayer," as well as various other nonprofit corporations "primarily engaged in educating the public about government expenditures . . . [and] representing . . . individuals, organizations and corporations in constitutional and public policy-oriented litigation," challenged Executive Order No. 141 as violative of the separation of powers doctrine. Plaintiffs also sought a preliminary injunction enjoining implementation of the Executive Order.

. . . .

The constitutional principle of separation of powers, "implied by the separate grants of power to each of the coordinate branches of government" . . . requires that the Legislature make the critical policy decisions, while the executive branch's responsibility is to implement those policies . . . .

Despite this functional separation, this Court has always understood that the duties and powers of the legislative and executive branches cannot be neatly divided into isolated pockets . . . . We have thus acknowledged that there need not be a specific and detailed legislative expression authorizing a particular executive act as long as "the basic policy decisions underlying the regulations have been made and articulated by the Legislature." . . . In other words, "[i]t is only when the Executive acts inconsistently with the Legislature, or usurps its prerogatives, that the doctrine of separation is violated." . . .

Recognizing the necessity of "some overlap between the three separate branches" of government as well as the "great flexibility" to be accorded the Governor in determining the methods of enforcing legislative policy, this Court in *Clark v. Cuomo*, 66 N.Y.2d 185, 189, 495 N.Y.S.2d 936, 486 N.E.2d 794, *supra* upheld against a separation of powers challenge then-Governor Cuomo's issuance of an Executive Order establishing a Voter Registration Task Force with access to State agencies in distributing its materials. The decision in *Clark*, like others that followed (e.g., *Matter of New York State Health Facilities Assn. v. Axelrod*, 77 N.Y.2d 340, 568 N.Y.S.2d 1, 569 N.E.2d 860, *supra*), resulted from this Court's long-standing and steadfast refusal to construe the separation of powers doctrine in a vacuum, instead viewing the doctrine from a common sense perspective. As Chief Judge Cardozo explained more than a half-century ago: "[t]he exigencies of government have made it necessary to relax a merely doctrinaire adherence to a principle so flexible and practical, so largely a matter of sensible approximation, as that of the separation of powers" (*Matter of Richardson*, 247 N.Y. 401, 410, 160 N.E. 655 [1928]).

As legislative authorization for the creation of the Task Force at issue in *Clark*, the Governor relied on Election Law § 3-102(13) which provided that "the state board of elections shall have the power and duty . . . to encourage the broadest possible voter participation in elections." In support of Executive Order No. 141, the Governor relied on article 20 of the Executive Law — containing nearly identical language — empowering the Consumer Protection Board to "promote and encourage the protection of the legitimate interests of consumers within the state" . . . . A simple comparison of the above-quoted Election Law provision at issue in *Clark* with the Executive Law provision at issue here compels the conclusion that the statutes are analogous. Each vests a particular entity (Boards of Elections or the Consumer Protection Board) with the power to promote a broad, even "general" legislative purpose (promoting voter registration or protecting the interests of utility consumers).

The analogy between the two cases is strengthened by the fact that in each case, the Governor — by Executive Order — created an entity other than that contemplated by the Legislature (the Voter Registration Task Force and the CUB) to implement those statutory goals. In *Clark*, we explicitly rejected the argument that the Legislature's decision to repose certain powers in local Boards of Elections prevented the Governor from establishing another governmental body intended to promote those same policies (*Clark*, 66 N.Y.2d at 190, 495 N.Y.S.2d 936, 486 N.E.2d 794).

Indeed, that the creation of the CUB was fully consistent with existing legislative policy is evidenced by the fact that three other entities already had overlapping authority to protect utility customers — the Consumer Protection Board, the Attorney-General and the Public Service Commission. In creating the CUB, the Governor recognized that in part because of the enormous demands on them from other duties, none of these agencies were adequately representing the interests of residential utility customers who lack the incentive to hire lawyers and lobbying groups to advance their interests.

Executive Order No. 141, like the order at issue in *Clark*, does not formulate a specific policy with respect to utility companies or their residential customers. It does not, for example, instruct the CUB to press for lower utility rates or to seek greater disclosure of the financial status of utility companies. Unlike the detailed and comprehensive Executive Orders and administrative regulations that this Court has struck down in the past . . . *Rapp v. Carey* . . . Executive Order No. 141 has no substantive content beyond that of creating the CUB itself and giving it access to State mailings for a three-year period. What the CUB, a private not-for-profit corporation, ultimately chooses to do with the funds it solicits is a decision entrusted solely to its membership. Executive Order No. 141 is thus well within the boundaries of this Court's recognition in *Clark* that the executive branch's mere creation of a new procedural, administrative mechanism, such as a task force or consumer board, to better implement a legislative policy does not offend the Constitution.

Indeed, there is yet another important parallel between the instant case and *Clark*. In each case, the Legislature considered but failed to enact a bill substantially similar to the provisions of the Executive Orders ultimately issued by the Governor. In each case, the plaintiffs argued that such failure should be taken as proof of hostile legislative intent. As we said in *Clark*, however, "that proposed legislation similar to [the] Executive Order . . . was not passed does not indicate legislative disapproval of the programs contemplated by the order. Legislative inaction, because of its inherent ambiguity, 'affords the most dubious foundation for drawing positive inferences.' " . . .

SMITH, JUDGE (dissenting).

The primary issue here is whether Executive Order No. 141, which directs the Department of Public Service (Department) to certify the establishment of a Citizens' Utility Board (CUB), violates the principle of separation of powers under the New York State Constitution. Because I conclude that it does, I dissent and vote to affirm the order of the Appellate Division.

    . . . .

We have previously held that the doctrine of separation of powers was not violated where the executive action was a clear implementation of State legislative policy . . . . On the other hand, we have concluded that the doctrine was violated by executive action which went beyond the legislative policy or enforcement directives . . . *Rapp v. Carey*, 44 N.Y.2d 157, 404 N.Y.S.2d 565, 375 N.E.2d 745 [Governor could not promulgate an Executive Order requiring executive branch employees to file financial disclosure forms and to refrain from certain political and business activities where the Legislature had not adopted such a policy] . . . .

The Legislature's policy favoring the protection of residential consumers does not translate into legislation authorizing the creation of a private not for-profit corporation with authority to speak on behalf of all residential utility customers. By this Executive Order, the Governor has effectively fashioned public policy in an area where the Legislature has not yet acted, clearly exceeding his authority and violating the principle of separation of powers.

As defendant concedes, the Legislature has expressed its desire that the interests of residential consumers be protected in the area of utilities. To this end, the Legislature has established the Consumer Protection Board which functions primarily to protect consumer interests. Further, the office of the Attorney-General and the Public Service Commission, the rate setting body within the Department of Public Service, are similarly charged to protect consumer interests in Public Service Commission proceedings. Nevertheless, such express legislative policy is insufficient authority for the certification of a single, State-wide CUB with access to State mailings.

. . . .

The specific ways in which the Executive Order establishes State policy are (1) by authorizing a new remedy for consumer involvement in utility rate setting through the establishment of a private corporation, whose interim board is created pursuant to procedures of the Department of Public Service, with access to State agency mailings to solicit members and financial contributions and (2) by involving State agencies in the approval of the content of communications (through a determination of whether it is false or misleading) sent to State residents by a private entity. Since such actions have not been adopted by the State Legislature, they violate the doctrine of separation of powers . . . .

NOTES AND QUESTIONS

1. How broad should the governor's power be to utilize executive orders? Should the situation be different when the legislature has *delegated* this power to the governor?

2. See *McCulloch v. Glendening*, 701 A.2d 99 (Md. 1997), upholding an executive order granting unionization and collective bargaining rights to executive branch employees.

3. On executive orders generally, see Note, *Gubernatorial Executive Orders as Devices for Administrative Discretion and Control*, 50 Iowa L. Rev. 78 (1964). For an in-depth study and analysis of executive orders in New Jersey, see Michael S. Herman, *Gubernatorial Executive Orders*, 30 Rutgers L.J. 987 (1999). Mr. Herman concludes that the New Jersey courts have not been attentive to policing the overuse of executive orders.

4. Similar issues may arise, of course, concerning Presidential executive orders. See, *e.g.*, *Chamber of Commerce of U.S. v. Reich*, 74 F.3d 1322 (D.C. Cir. 1996), *reh. den.*, 83 F.3d 442 (D.C. Cir. 1996), striking down President Clinton's executive order (after proposed legislation failed) barring the federal government from contracting with employers who hired permanent replacement workers during a lawful strike. The court held that the executive order conflicted with the National Labor Relations Act and therefore did not reach the question of Presidential power in the absence of such conflict. In *Building and Construction Trades Dept., AFL-CIO v. Allbaugh*, 295 F.3d 28 (D.C. Cir. 2002), *cert. den.* 537 U.S. 1171 (2003), the same court upheld President George W. Bush's executive order barring federal agencies from either requiring or prohibiting "project labor agreements" in federally-funded construction contracts.

3. Administrative Rulemaking

Another important source of law is the rules promulgated by state and federal administrative agencies, pursuant to statutory authority. Generally speaking the interpretative approaches covered in this book apply to administrative rules. In Chapter 9[B] we cover the specific statutory interpretation question of whether an agency's rules fit within the legislature's statutory delegation to the agency.

Part II

THE LEGISLATURE AND
THE JUDICIARY

Chapter 2

THE INTERACTION OF LEGISLATION AND OUR COMMON-LAW TRADITIONS

INTRODUCTION

The common law, and other forms of judge-made law, have enjoyed a long history of respect from the legal profession. At one time this translated into a superiority of common law over statutory enactments as reflected in such doctrines as strict construction for statutes in derogation of the common law. This preference for the common law has been eroding as statutory laws, particularly the Uniform Commercial Code but also many others, have gained wide acceptance. Nevertheless, case law is still the predominant vehicle by which lawyers are taught legal reasoning and the framing of legal issues, a process which continually reinforces common-law traditions.

The reverence of lawyers for the common law also derives from a strongly held belief that judges trained as lawyers are better able to develop legal principles than are legislators, whose work products are often the synthesis of hard-fought political compromises. The lawyers' resistance to the use of legislation is further reinforced by the lack of any official formulation of legislative history; coherent and accepted compilations of the underlying concepts and processes involved in the enactment of specific legislation are generally unavailable. Under such circumstances lawyers are naturally more comfortable with the common law.

The increasing extent to which our law has been derived from legislation has affected the interaction between common-law concepts and legislative doctrine. Respect is now accorded to a statute's intended scope without restricting its effects to the narrowest extent possible. Residual effects of common-law tradition, however, are reflected in the fact that courts, when faced with ambiguities, have been loath to expand the legislation beyond its easily discernible limits. If the legislative policy were to be extended, courts have felt more comfortable with having the legislature do so specifically.

Some courts have exercised greater comity with the legislative branch by beginning to use legislation as a basis for reasoning by analogy. A gradual transition to the use of legislative principles in arriving at new legal doctrines has occurred. One form of using legislation as precedent is that of reasoning from a statute which is not directly applicable in order to develop judge-made standards of conduct to be applied to the situation before the court. For instance, Justice Traynor suggests the use of penal statutes to establish standards for negligence for civil liability. The following materials provide an example of the process of such reasoning from statutes.

Our common-law experiences are deeply entrenched and we need to consider more carefully how legislative policies interact with these traditions. Lawyers and judges must become aware of other sources of policy that can be opened up by new techniques of analysis to supplement concepts of *stare decisis* and "rules" of statutory construction. Legislation constitutes an additional resource from which to derive policies to deal with contemporary problems. As a contrast to common-law approaches, the use of legislation as a source of law in civil law jurisdictions shows how the judiciary in such a system is expected to ascertain legal doctrine from statutes.

A. LEGISLATION AS PRECEDENT

The use of legislation as a source of legal doctrine from which to reason by analogy is not of recent origin.

Roscoe Pound, in his article *Common Law and Legislation*, enumerated four ways in which courts might deal with legislative innovations:

> (1) They might receive it fully into the body of the law as affording not only

a rule to be applied but a principle from which to reason, and hold it, as a later and more direct expression of the general will, of superior authority to judge-made rules on the same general subject; and so reason from it by analogy in preference to them. (2) They might receive it fully into the body of the law to be reasoned from by analogy the same as any other rule of law, regarding it, however, as of equal or co-ordinate authority in this respect with judge-made rules upon the same general subject. (3) They might refuse to receive it fully into the body of the law and give effect to it directly only; refusing to reason from it by analogy but giving it, nevertheless, a liberal interpretation to cover the whole field it was intended to cover. (4) They might not only refuse to reason from it by analogy and apply it directly only, but also give to it a strict and narrow interpretation, holding it down rigidly to those cases which it covers expressly.

Roscoe Pound, *Common Law and Legislation*, 21 Harv. L. Rev. 383, 385–86 (1908).

HARLAN FISKE STONE,
THE COMMON LAW IN THE UNITED STATES
50 Harvard Law Review 4, 12–14 (1936)

The reception which the courts have accorded to statutes presents a curiously illogical chapter in the history of the common law. Notwithstanding their genius for the generation of new law from that already established, the common-law courts have given little recognition to statutes as starting points for judicial lawmaking comparable to judicial decisions. They have long recognized the supremacy of statutes over judge-made law, but it has been the supremacy of a command to be obeyed according to its letter, to be treated as otherwise of little consequence. The fact that the command involves recognition of a policy by the supreme lawmaking body has seldom been regarded by courts as significant, either as a social datum or as a point of departure for the process of judicial reasoning by which the common law has been expanded.

. . . .

. . . I can find in the history and principles of the common law no adequate reason for our failure to treat a statute much more as we treat a judicial precedent, as both a declaration and a source of law, and as a premise for legal reasoning. We have done practically that with our ancient statutes, such as the statutes of limitations, frauds and wills, readily molding them to fit new conditions within their spirit, though not their letter, possibly because their antiquity tends to make us forget or minimize their legislative origin. Professor Landis of this Law School has recently pointed out in a valuable discussion of "Statutes and the Sources of Law," numerous examples in the Year Books of the application of the doctrine of the "equity of the statute" by which statutes were treated, in effect, as sources of law which by judicial decision could be extended to apply to situations analogous to those embraced within their terms. Apart from its command, the social policy and judgment, expressed in legislation by the lawmaking agency which is supreme, would seem to merit the judicial recognition which is freely accorded to the like expression in judicial precedent. But only to a limited extent do modern courts feel free, by resort to standards of conduct set up by legislation, to impose liability or attach consequences for the failure to maintain those or similar standards in similar but not identical situations, or to make the statutory recognition of a new type of right the basis for the judicial creation of rights in circumstances not dissimilar. Professor Landis and others have developed the subject with a detail unnecessary to consider now. It is enough for my purpose that they show that the legislative function has been reduced to mere rule making by the process of narrow judicial interpretation of statutes, and in consequence of the renunciation by the courts, where statutes are concerned, of some of their own lawmaking powers.

NOTES AND QUESTIONS

1. Compare Stone's view of the potential contribution of statutes to common-law reasoning with that of Pound.

2. How useful in practice is the following example of the purpose and policies of a statute? Which is more useful, the "Purposes" or "Official Comment"? What are the existing legislative analogies to Official Comments?

UNIFORM COMMERCIAL CODE

1-102. Purposes; Rules of Construction; Variation by Agreement

  (1)   This Act shall be liberally construed and applied to promote its underlying purposes and policies.

  (2)   Underlying purposes and policies of this Act are

  (a)   to simplify, clarify and modernize the law governing commercial transactions;

  (b)   to permit the continued expansion of commercial practices through custom, usage and agreement of the parties;

  (c)   to make uniform the law among the various jurisdictions.

Official Comment

Purposes of Changes:

1. Subsections (1) and (2) are intended to make it clear that:

This Act is drawn to provide flexibility so that, since it is intended to be a semi-permanent piece of legislation, it will provide its own machinery for expansion of commercial practices. It is intended to make it possible for the law embodied in this Act to be developed by the courts in the light of unforeseen and new circumstances and practices. However, the proper construction of the Act requires that its interpretation and application be limited to its reason.

Courts have been careful to keep broad acts from being hampered in their effects by later acts of limited scope. *Pacific Wool Growers v. Draper & Co.*, 158 Or. 1, 73 P.2d 1391 (1937), and compare Section 1-104. They have recognized the policies embodied in an act as applicable in reason to subject-matter which was not expressly included in the language of the act, *Commercial Nat. Bank of New Orleans v. Canal-Louisiana Bank & Trust Co.*, 239 U.S. 520, 36 S. Ct. 194, 60 L. Ed. 417 (1916) (bona fide purchase policy of Uniform Warehouse Receipts Act extended to case not covered but of equivalent nature). They have done the same where reason and policy so required, even where the subject-matter had been intentionally excluded from the act in general. *Agar v. Orda*, 264 N.Y. 248, 190 N.E. 479 (1934) (Uniform Sales Act change in seller's remedies applied to contract for sale of choses in action even though the general coverage of that Act was intentionally limited to goods "other than things in action"). They have implemented a statutory policy with liberal and useful remedies not provided in the statutory text. They have disregarded a statutory limitation of remedy where the reason of the limitation did not apply. *Fiterman v. J.N. Johnson & Co.*, 156 Minn. 201, 194 N.W. 399 (1923) (requirement of return of the goods as a condition of rescission for breach of warranty; also, partial rescission allowed). Nothing in this Act stands in the way of the continuance of such action by the courts.

The Act should be construed in accordance with its underlying purposes and policies. The text of each section should be read in the light of the purpose and policy of the rule or principle in question, as also of the Act as a whole, and the application of the language should be construed narrowly or broadly, as the case may be, in conformity with the purposes and policies involved.

3. In *United States v. Hext*, 444 F.2d 804 (5th Cir. 1971), the court, although deciding federal law was to apply to a suit arising from a Federal Housing Administration (FHA) loan transaction, declined to fashion "a specialized, esoteric body of federal law, confined in terms to suits by the United States seeking to impose conversion liability on persons who deal with property mortgaged under the FHA loan program." Rather, the court decided that:

> . . . [I]t is evident that the principal fount of general commercial law governing secured transactions is now Article 9 of the Uniform Commercial Code. We perceive no reason why the rights of the United States arising out of secured transactions pursuant to the FHA loan program should be any different than those of other financiers of farming operations under the Uniform Commercial Code. We have therefore determined that in fashioning the federal law that is applicable to suits arising from the FHA loan program we shall be guided by the principles set forth in Article 9 and other relevant portions of the Uniform Commercial Code.[17]

Such a course meets the principal reason advanced for requiring a federal rule of decision in these cases, that of uniformity, while at the same time assuring that an individual state's modifications of the Code's scheme cannot be employed to defeat federal rights. Taking this step is not inconsistent with the prior decisions applying federal law to suits arising from the FHA program since, in our judgment, in every case in which federal law has been so applied . . . the same result would have been reached under the Code. The Code has now been adopted in every state save Louisiana. By evaluating the issues involved in suits concerning FHA secured transactions in light of Article 9, the federal courts will have a coherent, unified body of law with which to deal and can benefit from the general body of precedent developed by the state courts under the Code. This is not to say, of course, that the interpretation of the Code made by any particular state court will be controlling nor that any modification of the Code enacted by a particular state legislature need be followed. Such interpretations and modifications may be followed only if the federal courts deem them reflective of the weight of authority, consistent with the operation to the FHA program, or desirable as precedent.

On this basis it is our judgment that the Code itself and the general body of precedent developed by the Code states provide the most logical source material supplying the content of federal common law to govern suits arising from FHA secured transactions. In this fashion the federal law governing FHA loans and the state law of secured transactions will coalesce to reinforce each other.

ROGER J. TRAYNOR,
STATUTES REVOLVING IN COMMON LAW ORBITS
17 Catholic University Law Review 401 (1968)*

Suppose, for example, a statute bearing a phrase like *X number of years*, specifying that it shall apply to A and B and clearly unconcerned with anyone else. Why not an equivalent rule for C?, the judge might ask himself, when there is a perplexing C before the court who appears to be a little cousin, if not the sibling, of A and B. Before the

---

[17] In so doing we are merely exercising the traditional judicial technique of making "use of a statutory rule as a model for the creation of an analogous judicial rule" which has been so ably discussed by Justice Roger J. Traynor of the Supreme Court of California. *See* Traynor, "Statutes Revolving in Common-Law Orbits," 17 Cath. U.L. Rev. 401, 420 (1968) . . . .

* Reprinted with permission from Catholic University Law Review.

fortuitous appearance of the statute, the judge might have deemed it prudent to abandon C to his legislative fate. Now he might deem it proper to compose a judgment as to C that would be in keeping with the newly declared legislative policy, even though the legislative authors had ended their text with B. He would thus make law to govern C by virtue of the analogy he would draw from the statute governing A and B. Whatever he chose to call his method, he would be creating law with a capital C. There was nothing in the statute that bade him thus to carry on. True, he was acting under the influence of a statute but the rule he created was his own.

    . . . .

    . . . Given their built-in controls, judges have little difficulty in keeping them on course in cases involving direct violations of a statute. The problem of judicial guidance is not with the statutes themselves, but with all the unidentified flying objects that do not come strictly within their orbit. Judges have still to make optimum use of penal or regulatory statutes in civil cases on negligence, involving the very conduct forbidden by the statutes.

In these cases judges have long been invoking such statutory standards as a test for civil liability, though in varying ways. Within a single case in California one finds large differences of judicial opinion. One opinion was that a violation of the statute was merely evidence of negligence. Another opinion was that such a violation engendered a rebuttable presumption of negligence. This opinion prevailed and still does. My own opinion was, and still is, that the statutory standard for penal liability was the appropriate one for civil liability and hence that a violation of the statute was negligence *per se.*

It is fair to ask why the statutory standard should govern civil liability when the statute prescribes criminal sanctions only. My answer is that it establishes a minimum standard of reasonableness, for a legislature responds to community experience in determining when conduct is likely to cause harm of such magnitude as to call for its prohibition in a penal statute. The rational course for a court is hence to adopt such a standard instead of delegating the formulation of one to a jury. It bears noting that "The decision as to what should be the controlling standard is made by the court, whether it instructs the jury to determine what would have been due care of a man of ordinary prudence under the circumstances or to follow the standard formulated by a statute." If a judge gives the latter instruction, he thereby guides the flying objects of civil litigation on a course that can be rationally synchronized with that of the pilot penal statute.

    . . . .

It would be wasteful for courts not to utilize such statutory materials when they are so readily available for analogy as well as for adoption. The statutes that protect specified classes of people from specified risks in specified areas are rich sources of analogy. "Suppose, for example, a penal statute regulates conduct only on the public highways, in a jurisdiction where all crimes are statutory. The court could not properly extend the area of crime by applying the statute to conduct on private roads. If the statute sets forth an appropriate standard of reasonable conduct for all roads, however, the court should be free to invoke it in a civil case involving negligence on a private road even though there has been no criminal violation.

"The court should also be free to make broad use of the standards in penal statutes preoccupied with the protection of a particular class. It is literal in the extreme to regard that preoccupation as indicative of indifference to the protection of any others. Yet the rule persists that a plaintiff cannot base a cause of action for negligence on the violation of a penal statute unless he is a member of the class the statute was designed to protect. Thus one who is not an employee is precluded from invoking a statute designed solely to protect employees even though he is injured by the very conduct proscribed. It is logic run riot that a state requiring the barricading of an open well or elevator shaft for the protection of employees cannot, by virtue of its particularity, be invoked for the protection of any others."

. . . .

The Uniform Commercial Code, far from diminishing the interaction of statutes and judicial decisions, has greatly accelerated it. The Code itself suggests in several comments that it should serve as a basis for analogous judicial rules to govern situations it has not expressly covered. Law journals have discussed extensively the possibilities of using various sections of the Code, particularly Article Two, Sales, as a basis for judicial analogy. Comments on decisions have also noted the implications of the Code even when it has not been directly controlling. When so formidable a code begins to revolve in common-law orbits, it dramatically compels even those who may hitherto have been unheeding, to note that in the vanguard as well as in the wake of such a skymark there are many less spectacular planets.

There are usually visible portents that a skymark is on the way. It would be unrealistic to say that it has no bearing on the scene until the day it bears down in full view. Hence courts have recognized the Uniform Commercial Code as influential when they have formulated kindred common-law rules to govern transactions that occurred before the effective date of the Code. Judge Wright, speaking for the United States Court of Appeals for the District of Columbia, found the code section on unconscionableness to be "persuasive authority for following the rationale of the cases from which the section is explicitly derived." Other courts have referred to the code as an appropriate source of law even though it has not yet been enacted in their jurisdictions. It has been viewed as "entitled to as much respect and weight as courts have been inclined to give to the various Restatements. It, like the Restatements, has the stamp of approval of a large body of American scholarship."

The Uniform Commercial Code has become a major influence in the development of common law in the federal courts to govern cases involving government contracts and other commercial transactions. Judge Friendly, speaking for the Court of Appeals for the Second Circuit, has reinforced with appellate approval the established practice of lower courts and federal agencies to make use of the Code as a source of federal law. He notes that its widespread enactment put it "well on its way to becoming a truly national law of commerce" and that this promise of uniformity would be disserved if transactions with the government were not subject to kindred rules.

. . . .

Only when a case is not governed by a statute is the court free to work out its own solution. Only then is it free to copy an appropriate model in a statute. A judicial rule that thus emerges signifies a discriminating choice of policy, in sharp contrast to the routine compliance with a legislative policy when the statute encompassing it governs.

The process of discriminating choice involves more than the usual deliberation characteristic of the judicial process. A judge may have to evaluate more than one policy and more than one model for a rule from whatever source, if they appear relevant, and in doing so he may decide to reject rather than accept one model or another. He is free to reject a statutory rule as a model, arriving instead at another or at a rule without benefit of any model that becomes itself a prototype, because the rule he rejects does not in any event govern the instant case. Its very rejection signifies a considered judgment that it is not appropriate to govern the case, just as its acceptance would signify a considered judgment that it is.

Once a court formulates a rule by analogy from a statutory rule, it creates a precedent of the same force as any other. Its continuing force, like that of any other precedent, depends on its continuing fitness to survive as it ages. It may endure for generations or succumb to rapid obsolescence.

It should not surprise us that such judicial rules analogized from statutes are at one with other judicial lawmaking. They always have been, despite the protestations of those who would have us believe that judicial rules and statutory rules are like set pieces of an automaton clock, springing from separate covertures to make wooden appearances at separate times.

. . . .

There is no orderly research of statutes comparable to the orderly research of cases. The problem at the outset is that they are not systematically catalogued as cases are. There are no comparable cross-references to make their interrelations clear or to identify their antecedents. How can a judge be sure that between counsel's efforts and his own all pertinent materials have been rounded up? Suppose there lies undiscovered some pertinent statute still at large? Cases may arise in which no statute is even in issue, and yet a statute may exist that would be of the greatest relevance as a basis for judicial analogy, and that a judge should study as closely as any judicial precedent if he is to make a rational decision.

. . . .

We are still far from betterment measured by the goal of rational processes of lawmaking in all the lanes of law. We might well concentrate on a preliminary goal, better use in the judicial process of the good laws that often emerge amid the variegated products of the legislative process. There must be teamwork to that end. If the librarians and researchers will systematize the study of statutes, if the watchbirds will sharpen their watch on legislatures in action, if commentators will set forth salient qualities or defects of legislative products, the judges will surely make better use than they have of the statutes revolving in common-law orbits. Then benefits will flow in every direction, *pro bono Hugo, pro bono Roberto*, but above all *pro lege et grege*.

NOTES AND QUESTIONS

1. Traynor states that judicial rules analogized from statutes are a form of judicial lawmaking, and create precedent of the same weight as any other form of judicial ruling. Can this form of judicial creativity be viewed as part of the evolving process of the common law? If not, what is it?

2. The use of statutes as a source of law beyond their specific provisions is viewed by Traynor as an improved use of legislation. Consider his example of applying the criminal standard of negligence to civil cases. What objections can be raised to this argument? The problem is compounded when a question of first impression arises. To what sources of law, other than legislation, should a judge look when faced with an unresolved issue? How does legislation compare with these alternatives as a legitimate source of law?

3. Which of Pound's four hypotheses most closely resembles Traynor's view on the use of legislation? For an excellent discussion of the use of legislation as a source of law, see Michael J. Bean, Note, *The Legitimacy of Civil Law Reasoning in the Common Law: Justice Harlan's Contribution*, 82 YALE L.J. 258 (1972).

4. Traynor emphasizes that the current legislative materials are inadequate, and stresses the need for systematic cataloguing, research, and criticism of legislation. Given that little of state legislative materials exists, what sorts of legislative histories, rationales for enactment and descriptions of the policies inherent in the provisions should be provided if the statutes are to constitute a "source of law"?

5. The Supreme Court of Illinois ruled unconstitutional a statute which voided exculpatory clauses in leases because the statute provided exceptions for certain business leases. Holding that the statute made discriminatory classifications without any reasonable basis, the court turned to common-law doctrine which recognized the validity of exculpatory clauses, and thus upheld the clause in question. The court noted that the legislature might not have enacted the statute without the unconstitutional exceptions, and stated its preference to leave the matter to the legislature. In dissent, Justice Schaefer noted:

I agree that the statute as written violates the constitution, for the reasons stated in the opinion of the majority. But I regard the enactment of the statute as an expression of the public policy of the State which this court should respect, even though it cannot be given complete effect according to its terms. That statute declares "void as against public policy and wholly unenforceable" every exculpatory clause in any lease, business or residential, with the narrow and irrational exception in favor of particular lessors and lessees of business property which totally defeats its major purpose. I would hold that the statute, despite its invalidity, is an expression of public policy which fully justifies this court in now holding, as a matter of common law, that exculpatory clauses in leaseholds are void.

Sweney Gasoline & Oil Co. v. Toledo, Peoria & W. R.R., 42 Ill. 2d 265, 247 N.E.2d 603, 606 (1969).

The majority failed to ask if there was a residual principle in the legislation, thereby forcing the legislature two years later to declare *all* exculpatory lease clauses void. Rather than rejecting such "underinclusive" legislation or looking for a rationale to uphold it sufficient to withstand equal protection challenge, the courts could expand the principle to encompass all parties analogously situated. What reasoning might have caused the court to reject this option?

In general, where application of an "underinclusion" provision is held unconstitutional, the unconstitutionality is removed by expanding its scope where benefits are extended and by striking down any application of the provision where a regulatory purpose is involved. Would simply extending the application in all circumstances be justified on the basis of Justice Schaefer's rationale? Have the courts made this distinction between the conferring of benefits or regulatory purposes on the basis of their conception of an implicit legislative intent in each circumstance? What is the basis for inferring these differing legislative intentions?

ROBERT F. WILLIAMS,
STATUTES AS SOURCES OF LAW BEYOND THEIR TERMS
IN COMMON-LAW CASES
50 George Washington Law Review 554, 563–64, 566, 567 (1982)[*]

II.

Legislative "Negative Preemption"

. . . Attempts to rely on statutes as persuasive precedent raise questions as to what conclusion, if any, should be drawn from the fact that the legislature did not "cover" the circumstances before a court. Courts often conclude, explicitly or implicitly, that if a pertinent statute does not expressly or impliedly mandate the result proposed by counsel (that is, if the statute is "silent"), then the legislature has forbidden courts to reach that result as a matter of common law. This is sometimes referred to by the civil-law term *argumentum a contrario* or "negative-opposite construction." Negative-opposite construction postulates that legislative enactment of a rule for one situation implies the opposite rule for any other situation. In other words, legislative silence is mistaken for legislative approval, ratification, or freezing of the common law not directly changed by the statute. This obviously creates a critical impediment to judicial use of statutes as sources of law beyond their terms in common-law cases.

Courts do not have a similar problem with "negative opposite construction" when they evaluate judicial precedents urged as persuasive. That a precedent does not directly hold the proposition being advocated is not taken to imply that the prior court

---

decided against the proposition. Extension of precedents is part of the accepted judicial function. Because the precedents are of judicial origin, persuasive extension in this context should not raise difficult questions about the role of the courts vis-a-vis the other lawmaking branch of government. Once a statute is introduced into a legal discussion, however, lawyers and judges often seem to become mesmerized by its express terms and to lose their peripheral vision as to issues the statute does not directly cover. They become so preoccupied with what the legislature did not do in the statute that they forget what judges can do.[51]

Analysis of a source of analogy for negative intent is an integral part of any proper reasoning by analogy . . . .

. . . [C]ourts should not limit their inquiry to whether a statute's terms reach a given situation; judges should also examine whether a statute forbids or negatives a contemplated common-law decision. The relevant question then becomes whether the legislature was "excluding by implication, or simply omitting without prejudice." Legislative silence, without more, should push a court in neither direction. Analysis should focus on whether any discernible legislative intent underlies legislative inaction. Courts that fully appreciate their own powers and obligations with respect to decisional law will not be deterred from a desirable result by inference from legislative silence, but only by some indication of legislative intent to preclude the proposed result.[65] This is not to say that in the absence of such negative intent, courts should automatically accept the proposed result, for *argumentum a pari* is as unjustified as *argumentum a contrario*. Rather, courts should exercise their freedom to evaluate the persuasiveness of statutes and then accept or reject arguments based on them. Incomplete statutory treatment does not put "off limits" the issues a legislature has failed to resolve.

NOTES AND QUESTIONS

1. In *Moragne v. States Marine Lines*, 398 U.S. 375, 390–93 (1970), Justice Harlan considered a wrongful death case on the high seas for which there was no directly applicable wrongful death statute. In rejecting the argument that the common law did not recognize a cause of action for wrongful death, and in the absence of a directly applicable statute no such claim would lie, he observed:

The legislature does not, of course, merely enact general policies. By the terms of a statute, it also indicates its conception of the sphere within which the policy is to have effect. In many cases the scope of a statute may reflect nothing more than the dimensions of the particular problem that came to the attention of the legislature, inviting the conclusion that the legislative policy is equally

---

[51] Judge Breitel observed:

An overly simple and insufficiently informed approach to legislative inaction readily becomes a barefaced question-begging process. Just as often as not the same judicial result can be sustained variously — for instance, on the argument that, since the legislature has not acted, the courts should move to relieve the legal condition, or that, since the legislature has not acted, it is quite clear that it is satisfied with the existing condition.

Breitel, *The Courts and Lawmaking, in* Legal Institutions, Today and Tomorrow 1, 25 (M. Paulsen ed., 1959).

[65] One scholar has taken the position that judicial use of statutes beyond their terms subverts legislative supremacy only if the statute has preempted the area by negative implication. R. Dickerson, Statutory Interpretation, *supra* note 12, at 205 (1975). This concept of "negative preemption" formulates but does not answer the question. Its importance, however, is that it targets the inquiry on whether the legislature has indicated some intent to prevent a judge-made decision based on statutes beyond their terms. "The first issue in such a case is whether the legislature has excluded judicial creativity by preempting the area through negative implication. If the statute carries no such implication, the court has inherent power to apply the principles announced by the statute to situations falling outside the statute . . . ." *Id.* at 201; *see Markle v. Mulhollands, Inc.*, 265 Or. 259, 272–73, 509 P.2d 529, 535 (1973); *Vincent v. Pabst Brewing Co.*, 47 Wis. 2d 120, 140–41, 177 N.W.2d 513, 522–23 (1970) (Hallows, C.J., dissenting); *see also* Dickerson, *Prosser's Folly, supra* note 52, at 469 (legislative supremacy requires courts to respect a statute's negative implications).

applicable to other situations in which the mischief is identical. This conclusion is reinforced where there exists not one enactment but a course of legislation dealing with a series of situations, and where the generality of the underlying principle is attested by the legislation of other jurisdictions. *Id.*, at 215–216, 220–222. On the other hand, the legislature may, in order to promote other, conflicting interests, prescribe with particularity the compass of the legislative aim, erecting a strong inference that territories beyond the boundaries so drawn are not to feel the impact of the new legislative dispensation. We must, therefore, analyze with care the congressional enactments that have abrogated the common-law rule in the maritime field, to determine the impact of the fact that none applies in terms to the situation of this case . . . .

. . . We find that Congress has given no affirmative indication of an intent to preclude the judicial allowance of a remedy for wrongful death to persons in the situation of this petitioner.

Does he also reject "negative preemption"?

2. Justice Harlan's reasoning is analyzed in Michael J. Bean, Note, *The Legitimacy of Civil Law Reasoning in the Common Law: Justice Harlan's Contribution*, 82 YALE L.J. 258, 274–76 (1972). *See also* Robert E. Keeton, *Statutory Analogy, Purpose, and Policy in Legal Reasoning: Live Lobsters and a Tiger Cub in the Park*, 52 MD. L. REV. 1192 (1993).

3. According to the traditional common-law view, as acknowledged by Justice Harlan, there was no cause of action for wrongful death. When wrongful death statutes were enacted, and included a time period within which such claims had to be filed, these were often viewed as *substantive elements* of the wrongful death claim and therefore not subject to relaxation under the "discovery rule" or the doctrine of equitable tolling. Could Justice Harlan's conclusion that wrongful death had, in fact, become part of the common law lead to a change in this view? *See LaFage v. Jani*, 766 A.2d 1066, 1076–80 (N.J. 2001).

CINTRONE v. HERTZ TRUCK LEASING
45 N.J. 434, 212 A.2d 769 (1965)

FRANCIS, J.

Plaintiff Francisco Cintrone was injured while a passenger in a truck leased by his employer from the defendant . . . .

Plaintiff presents two grounds of appeal: the trial court erred (1) in dismissing the warranty count of the complaint and in refusing to submit that issue to the jury . . . . Study of the record has led us to the conclusion the judgment should be reversed because, on the facts proved, the contract for the leasing and use of the truck gave rise to an implied warranty that it was fit for the use contemplated by plaintiff's employer.

. . . .

Schipper v. Levitt & Sons, Inc., 44 N.J. 70 (1965), *Santor v. A & M Karagheusian, Inc.*, 44 N.J. 52 (1965), and *Henningsen v. Bloomfield Motors, Inc.*, 32 N.J. 358 (1960), have made it plain that if the relationship in the present case between Contract Packers and Hertz were manufacturer or dealer and purchaser, an implied warranty of fitness for operation on the public highway would have come into existence at the time of the sale. Moreover, under those cases, breach of the warranty which caused personal injury to an employee of the purchaser would be actionable by the employee. It must be recognized, however, that the occasions have been relatively few when the courts have been asked to imply warranties in personal injury cases as an incident of transactions other than sales of chattels. Certainly in New Jersey there is no case precisely like this one involving the contention that a bailment for hire of a motor vehicle by a bailor or lessor engaged in such rental business carries with it an implied warranty that the rented vehicle is fit and will continue to be fit for the rental period for the ordinary and expected purposes of the rental.

There is no good reason for restricting such warranties to sales. Warranties of fitness are regarded by law as an incident of a transaction because one party to the relationship is in a better position than the other to know and control the condition of the chattel transferred and to distribute the losses which may occur because of a dangerous condition the chattel possesses. These factors make it likely that the party acquiring possession of the article will assume it is in a safe condition for use and therefore refrain from taking precautionary measures himself. 2 Harper and James, Torts, § 28.19 (1956). Harper and James point out that the presence of such factors in sales set in motion the development of the doctrine of implied warranties. They decry the notion, however, that because the doctrine had its origin in sales, the warranty protection should be withheld in other situations when the same considerations obtain. And they argue persuasively that in the face of present-day forms of business enterprise, development of the warranty doctrine in sales should point the way by suggestive analogy to similar results in cases where a commodity is leased. *Id.*, at p. 1577.

In this connection it may be observed also that the comment to the warranty section of the Uniform Commercial Code speaks out against confining warranties to sales transactions. The comment says:

> "Although this section is limited in its scope and direct purpose to warranties made by the seller to the buyer as part of a contract of sale, the warranty sections of this Article are not designed in any way to disturb those lines of case law growth which have recognized that warranties need not be confined either to sales contracts or to the direct parties to such a contract. They may arise in other appropriate circumstances such as in the case of bailments for hire, whether such bailment is itself the main contract or is merely a supplying of containers under a contract for the sale of their contents . . . ." *See* Comment, N.J.S. 12A:2-313, p. 190, n.2.

See also, Prosser, Torts, § 95, pp. 655–656 (3d ed. 1964); 1 Frumer and Friedman, Products Liability, § 19.02 (1964); Vold, Sales, § 94, p. 454, fn. 42a (2d ed. 1959); Annotation, 68 A.L.R.2d 850 (1959); *and see* Farnsworth, "Implied Warranties of Quality in Non-Sales Cases," 57 Colum. L. Rev. 653, 673–674 (1957):

> "The expansion of enterprises engaged solely in bailment for hire seems to justify increasing imposition of absolute warranties, at least to the extent that they would be imposed upon a seller of similarly used goods. In addition, reliance is greater than in the typical sale, for it is generally true that the bailee for hire spends less time shopping for the article than he would in selecting like goods to be purchased, and since the item is not one he expects to own, he will usually be less competent in judging its quality."

     . . . .

A bailor for hire, such as a person in the U-drive-it business, puts motor vehicles in the stream of commerce in a fashion not unlike a manufacturer or retailer . . . . We held in *Santor* the liability of the manufacturer might be expressed in terms of strict liability in tort. *Santor v. A & M Karagheusian, Inc., supra* (44 N.J., at pp. 66–67); *see also*, Restatement (Second), Torts, § 402A, comment m, pp. 9–10 (Tent. Draft No. 10, 1964). By analogy the same rule should be made applicable to the U-drive-it bailor-bailee relationship. Such a rental must be regarded as accompanied by a representation that the vehicle is fit for operation on the public highways.

NOTES AND QUESTIONS

1. Was the court in *Cintrone* interpreting the statute? Could it have interpreted the statute to cover leases?

2. Is the court's use of the statute by analogy, rather than expanding it through interpretation, a better technique?

3. The legislature provided for warranties in the buyer-seller relationship. Should a court, therefore, wait for the legislature to expand these warranties to the lessor-lessee relationship?

4. What can the legislature do if it disagrees with *Cintrone*? What can lawyers for the leasing industry do?

E. ALLEN FARNSWORTH,
IMPLIED WARRANTIES OF QUALITY IN NON-SALES CASES
57 COLUMBIA LAW REVIEW 653, 667–69 (1957)[*]

IV.

Advantage of Reasoning by Analogy

The preceding discussion indicates that there is respectable authority for the extension of implied warranties to non-sales cases, in spite of a tendency to overlook the possibility. In borderline cases reasoning by analogy to sales law should not be merely a technique of last resort to be used only where the facts will not support the finding of a sale. It is preferable to categorization of the contract as one of sale and direct application of the sales statute. It has five advantages.

The first is greater ease of adjusting legal rules to altered social conditions. If a new duty is to be imposed, it is awkward and misleading for a court to explain that what yesterday was not a sale, is today a sale. The restaurant cases afforded a good example, for this is the basic approach of most cases which hold restauranteurs in implied warranty. Certainly there have been some changes in the nature of the service of food from the time of the inn to the day of the automat, but the cardinal change is not in the nature of the transaction but in the obligations which are attached to it. There can be considerable sympathy for courts which maintain that the serving of food is no more a sale today than it was one hundred years ago. This, however, should not preclude a change in the duties of the restaurateur.

The second is that it avoids the application of sales rules that have no place in a transaction which is comparable to a sale only in respect to the supplier's obligation as to the quality of his goods. The Massachusetts court which in *Friend v. Childs Dining Hall Co.* imposed a warranty upon the restaurateur without regard to whether there was a sale, now takes the position that there is a sale and that the Uniform Sales Act applies in toto. One consequence is that the buyer must notify the seller of the breach within a reasonable time after he knows or ought to know of it. This rule of sales law has been criticized in its application to consumer-buyers who sustain personal injuries, yet the denomination of the transactions as a sale leaves the court little choice but to apply the sale rule in situations of this character. Under the Uniform Commercial Code the service of food is only classified as a sale for the purpose of raising an implied warranty. Nevertheless, a state enacting the Code would appear free to retain or adopt a rule that the service of food is a sale for all purposes under the Code. Sales law is even more clearly inapplicable to exchanges of goods for services and to bailments, and the implication of quality warranties would be severely limited if a necessary concomitant were subjection of the transaction to rules designed for the sale of goods.

A third advantage to reasoning by analogy is that it can be used to extend implied warranties to many transactions which could not be defined as sales but which are so like other cases where warranties are implied that they should be treated similarly. If a jurisdiction implies a warranty in the serving of food by a restaurant, it will be apt to reach the same result in the serving of food by a hospital, a children's camp, or a hotel on the American plan. Where the warranty is imposed upon the restaurant by the mechanical process of finding a sale, it would be more likely that the other situations would be distinguished as not being sales, and warranty would be implied.

The fourth advantage is, in a sense, the reverse of the third. Not only is it easier to extend warranties to appropriate cases, but it is also easier to avoid extending them to similar cases which are merely homologous rather then analogous.[117]

. . . .

The fifth advantage is that reasoning by analogy lays bare the real reasons for implying a warranty, reasons which are only too easily obscured if the ultimate decision is to rest upon the denomination of the transaction.

ROBERT F. WILLIAMS,
STATUTES AS SOURCES OF LAW BEYOND THEIR TERMS
IN COMMON LAW CASES
50 George Washington Law Review 554, 594–96 (1982)*

IV.

Advantages of Statutory Analogy

In close cases, courts must choose between extensively interpreting a statute so as to make it apply and acknowledging the statute's inapplicability and using it instead as a source of law for reasoning by analogy to create a judge-made solution. There may be reasons for preferring the use of statutes beyond their terms over extensive interpretations.

Professor Farnsworth, writing about the use of the Sales Act warranty provisions in non-sales situations, strongly favored the technique of analogy.

. . . .

Professor Dickerson identified an additional advantage.[245]

In some jurisdictions, courts consider decisions interpreting statutes to be binding "one-shot" matters, in effect merging with the statute. They view legislative silence as to an interpretation as tantamount to amending the statute in accordance with the decision (and thereby withdrawing the judicial power to modify its interpretation).[246]

The use of statutes by analogy, however, cannot legislatively bind courts, for it does not present legislatures with statutory interpretations they may be deemed to ratify tacitly.

Thus, statutory analogy can provide a useful alternative to extensive interpretation by providing courts with a degree of flexibility in choosing the premises from which to

---

[117] The terms are employed here in the sense in which they are used in the biology.

* Copyright © 1982 by *George Washington Law Review*. Reprinted with permission.

[245] R. Dickerson, Statutory Interpretation, *supra* note 12, at 204–05.

[246] *Id.* at 252–55; *see e.g., Zimmerman v. Wisconsin Elec. Power Co.*, 38 Wis. 2d 626, 633–34, 157 N.W.2d 648, 651 (1968). *But see Boys Markets, Inc. v. Retail Clerks Union*, 398 U.S. 235, 240–42 (1970).

reason. Once a statute has been held to apply, this judicial choice disappears. A holding in an extreme case that a statute applies will tend to prejudge the statute's direct applicability to less extreme cases that may arise in the future. A decision based on the persuasive qualities of the statute, by contrast, can leave future issues for case-by-case determination. While the legislature retains the power to overturn or modify decisions with which it disagrees, the judiciary can enjoy the flexibility that is the hallmark of common law.[247]

In addition to affording courts needed flexibility, statutory analogy provides an important basis for common-law decisionmaking. When courts are called upon to create new law, they need a complete understanding of the legal backdrop against which the current issue appears. Statutes make up part of the body of law into which courts must integrate their decisions, thus, a rule founded on existing legal concepts, derived from both common law and analogous statutory law, is more likely to satisfy the need for consistency than one based on common law alone.

NOTES AND QUESTIONS

1. For critical consideration of the "one-shot" theory of statutory interpretation precedents, see Chapter 8, Section A.

2. *Norcon Power Partners, L.P. v. Niagara Mohawk Power Corp.*, 705 N.E.2d 656 (N.Y. 1998), confronted a situation where one party to a complex contract had substantial reason to doubt the other party's ability to perform in the future. Because the Uniform Commercial Code provision, § 2-609 (demand for adequate assurance of due performance) did not apply to this contract because it was not for the sale of "goods," the court had to consider creating such a common-law mechanism. It reasoned:

> The Uniform Commercial Code settled on a mechanism for relieving some of this uncertainty. It allows a party to a contract for the sale of goods to demand assurance of future performances from the other party when reasonable grounds for insecurity exist (see, UCC 2-609; II Farnsworth, Contracts § 8.23). When adequate assurance is not forthcoming, repudiation is deemed confirmed, and the nonbreaching party is allowed to take reasonable actions as though a repudiation had occurred (see, 4 Anderson, Uniform Commercial Code § 2-609:3 [3d ed. 1997 rev.]).

> . . . .

> Indeed, UCC 2-609 has been considered so effective in bridging the doctrinal, exceptional and operational gap related to the doctrine of anticipatory breach that some States have imported the complementary regimen of demand for adequate assurance to common-law categories of contract law, using UCC 2-609 as the synapse (see, e.g., *Lo Re v. Tel-Air Communications*, 200 N.J. Super. 59, 490 A.2d 344 (1985) [finding support in UCC 2-609 and Restatement (Second) of Contracts § 251 for applying doctrine of adequate assurance to contract to purchase radio station]; *Conference Ctr. v. TRC-The Research Corp. of New England*, 189 Conn. 212, 455 A.2d 857 [analogizing to UCC 2-609, as supported by Restatement (Second) of Contracts § 251, in context of constructive eviction]).

Commentators have helped nudge this development along. They have noted that the problems redressed by UCC 2-609 are not unique to contracts for sale of goods, regulated under a purely statutory regime. Thus, they have cogently

---

[247] Whether judicial use of statutory analogy is justifiable depends to a large extent on one's perception of the proper role of the judiciary in making law. One could argue that criticism of undemocratic "judicial legislation" could be somewhat muted if courts made routine use of cognate statutory materials in reaching decisions. The counterargument often advanced is that the mere fact that the legislature created a rule for a given situation should preclude courts from making their own rules in similar situations.

identified the need for the doctrine to be available in exceptional and qualifying common-law contractual settings and disputes because of similar practical, theoretical and salutary objectives (e.g., predictability, definiteness, and stability in commercial dealings and expectations) . . . .

The American Law Institute through its Restatement (Second) of Contracts has also recognized and collected the authorities supporting this modern development . . . .

. . . .

Niagara Mohawk, before our Court through the certified question from the Federal court, urges a comprehensive adaptation of the exceptional demand tool. This wholesale approach has also been advocated by the commentators (see generally, Dowling, op. cit.; Campbell, op. cit.). Indeed, it is even reflected in the breadth of the wording of the certified question.

This Court's jurisprudence, however, usually evolves by deciding cases and settling the law more modestly (*Rooney v. Tyson*, 91 N.Y.2d 685, 694, 674 N.Y.2d 616, 697 N.E.2d 571, citing Cardozo, at 115, 134 [Margaret E. Hall ed. 1947] [observing that Judges proceed interstitially]). The twin purposes and functions of this Court's work require significant professional discipline and judicious circumspection.

We conclude, therefore, that it is unnecessary, while fulfilling the important and useful certification role, to promulgate so sweeping a change and proposition in contract law, as has been sought, in one dramatic promulgation. That approach might clash with our customary incremental common-law developmental process, rooted in particular fact patterns and keener wisdom acquired through observations of empirical application of a proportioned, less than absolute, rule in future cases.

It is well to note the axiom that deciding a specific case, even with the precedential comet's tail its rationale illuminates, is very different from enacting a statute of general and universal application (see, Breitel, The Lawmakers, 2 Benjamin N. Cardozo Memorial Lectures 761, 788 [1965] ["(P)rocedurally, courts are limited to viewing the problem as presented in a litigated case within the four corners of its record. A multiplication of cases will broaden the view because of the multiplication of records, but the limitation still persists because the records are confined by the rules of procedure, legal relevance, and evidence."]).

Experience and patience thus offer a more secure and realistic path to a better and fairer rule, in theory and in practical application. Therefore, this Court chooses to take the traditionally subtler approach, consistent with the proven benefits of the maturation process of the common law, including in the very area of anticipatory repudiation which spawns this relatively newer demand for assurance corollary (see, Garvin, op. cit., at 77–80; Robertson, op. cit., at 307–310; Dowling, op. cit., at 1359–1362; see also, Breitel, op. cit., at 781–782 [1965] ["The commonplace, for which the Holmeses and the Cardozos had to blaze a trail in the judicial realm, assumes the rightness of courts in making interstitial law, filling gaps in the statutory and decisional rules, and at a snail-like pace giving some forward movement to the developing law. Any law creation more drastic than this is often said and thought to be an invalid encroachment on the legislative branch."]).

This Court is now persuaded that the policies underlying the UCC 2-609 counterpart should apply with similar cogency for the resolution of this kind of controversy. A useful analogy can be drawn between the contact at issue and a contract for the sale of goods. If the contract here was in all respects the same, except that it was for the sale of oil or some other tangible commodity instead of the sale of electricity, the parties would unquestionably be governed by the demand for adequate assurance of performance factors in UCC 2-609. We are convinced to take this prudent step because it puts commercial parties in these kinds of disputes at relatively arm's length equilibrium in terms of reliability and uniformity of governing legal rubrics. The availability of the doctrine may even provide an incentive and tool for parties to resolve their own differences, perhaps without the necessity of judicial intervention. Open, serious renegotiation of dramatic developments and changes in unusual contractual expectations and qualifying circumstances would occur because of and with an eye to the doctrine's application.

The various authorities, factors and concerns, in sum, prompt the prudence and awareness of the usefulness of recognizing the extension of the doctrine of demand for adequate assurance, as a common-law analogue.

Id. at 660–62.

3. The New York Court of Appeals mentioned the role of the American Law Institute Restatements urging the use of statutes in common-law reasoning. In its April 5, 1999, discussion Draft of The Third Restatement of the Law of Torts: General Principles, the American Law Institute suggested the following:

§ 12. Statutory Violations as Negligence Per Se

An actor is negligent if, without excuse, the actor violates a statute that is designed to protect against the type of accident the actor's conduct causes, and if the accident victim is within the class of persons the statute is designed to protect.

Comment:

. . . .

c. *Rationale.* The rule in this section presupposes a statute that declares conduct unlawful but which is silent as to civil liability, and which cannot be readily interpreted as impliedly creating civil liability. The section hence acknowledges that the statute may not itself create civil liability. The section nevertheless concludes that courts, exercising their common-law authority to develop tort doctrine, not only should regard the actor's statutory violation as evidence admissible against the actor, but should treat that violation as actually determining the actor's negligence. An unexcused violation of the statute is thus negligence per se.

. . . .

REPORTER'S NOTE

. . . .

Many of the recent statutes that require motorists and passengers to wear seat belts include specific provisions stating that the violation of the statute is not admissible in tort claims for damages. See, e.g., Utah Code Ann. § 41-6-186 (1993), given effect in *Ryan v. Gold Cross Services, Inc.*, 903 P.2d 423 (Utah 1995); *see also* Tenn. Code Ann. § 55-9-604 (Supp. 1996). For another example of a statute that declares its violation inadmissible in a tort case, *see Reed v. Phillips*, 452 S.E.2d 708 (W. Va. 1994). The *Reed* opinion, dealing with the defendant's violation of two different statutes, in fact engages in a rather complex process of reasoning.

Do statutes such as these constitute explicit "negative preemption" by the legislature?

4. A Pennsylvania statute requires eye doctors to report patients with poor vision to the Department of Transportation, which issues drivers licenses. An ophthalmologist examined a patient with very poor eyesight but failed to report. Later the patient struck

and killed a bicyclist in an accident attributable to her poor eyesight. What are the arguments for and against a negligence per se claim against the doctor? *See Estate of Witthoeft v. Kiskaddon,* 733 A.2d 623 (Pa. 1999).

So far, we have been looking at plaintiffs' use of statutes beyond their terms. Now consider the following from the Restatement of Torts, Third:

§ 14 Statutory Compliance

(a) An actor's compliance with a pertinent statute, while evidence of non-negligence, does not preclude a finding that the actor is negligent under § 4 for failing to adopt precautions in addition to those mandated by the statute.

(b) If the actor's adoption of a precaution would require the actor to violate a statute, the actor cannot be found negligent for failing to adopt that precaution.

Read the next case with this perspective in mind.

RAMIREZ v. PLOUGH
863 P.2d 167 (Cal. 1993)

KENNARD, JUSTICE.

We granted review in this case to determine whether a manufacturer of nonprescription drugs may incur tort liability for distributing its products with warnings in English only. Recognizing the importance of uniformity and predictability in this sensitive area of the law, we conclude that the rule for tort liability should conform to state and federal statutory and administrative law. Because both state and federal law now require warnings in English but not in any other language, we further conclude that a manufacturer may not be held liable in tort for failing to label a nonprescription drug with warnings in a language other than English.

I

Plaintiff Jorge Ramirez, a minor, sued defendant Plough, Inc., alleging that he contracted Reye's syndrome as a result of ingesting a nonprescription drug, St. Joseph Aspirin for Children (SJAC), that was manufactured and distributed by defendant. Plaintiff sought compensatory and punitive damages on theories of negligence, products liability, and fraud. The trial court granted summary judgment for defendant. On plaintiff's appeal, the Court of Appeal reversed, 15 Cal. App. 4th 1110, 12 Cal. Rptr. 2d 423.

. . . .

In March 1986, when he was less than four months old, plaintiff exhibited symptoms of a cold or similar upper respiratory infection. To relieve these symptoms, plaintiff's mother gave him SJAC. Although the product label stated that the dosage for a child under two years old was "as directed by doctor," plaintiff's mother did not consult a doctor before using SJAC to treat plaintiff's condition. Over a two-day period, plaintiff's mother gave him three SJAC tablets. Then, on March 15, plaintiff's mother took him to a hospital. There, the doctor advised her to administer Dimetapp or Pedialyte (nonprescription medications that do not contain aspirin), but she disregarded the advice and continued to treat plaintiff with SJAC.

Plaintiff thereafter developed Reye's syndrome, resulting in severe neurological damage, including cortical blindness, spastic quadriplegia, and mental retardation.

. . . .

The cause of Reye's syndrome was unknown in 1986 (and apparently remains unknown), but by the early 1980s several studies had shown an association between ingestion of aspirin during a viral illness, such as chicken pox or influenza, and the subsequent development of Reye's syndrome. These studies prompted the United

States Food and Drug Administration (FDA) to propose a labeling requirement for aspirin products warning of the dangers of Reye's syndrome. (*See* 50 Fed. Reg. 51,400 (Dec. 17, 1985).) The FDA published a regulation to this effect on March 7, 1986. (51 Fed. Reg. 8,180.) Unless extended, the regulation was to expire two years after its effective date. (*Id.* at p. 8182.) In 1988, the FDA revised the required warning to state explicitly that Reye's syndrome is reported to be associated with aspirin use, and it made the regulation permanent. (53 Fed. Reg. 21,633 (June 9, 1988).)

Even before the federal regulation became mandatory, packages of SJAC displayed this warning: "Warning: Reye Syndrome is a rare but serious disease which can follow flu or chicken pox in children and teenagers. While the cause of Reye Syndrome is unknown, some reports claim aspirin may increase the risk of developing this disease. Consult doctor before use in children or teenagers with flu or chicken pox." The package insert contained the same warning, together with this statement: "The symptoms of Reye syndrome can include persistent vomiting, sleepiness and lethargy, violent headaches, unusual behavior, including disorientation, combativeness, and delirium. If any of these symptoms occur, especially following chicken pox or flu, call your doctor immediately, even if your child has not taken any medication. REYE SYNDROME IS SERIOUS, SO EARLY DETECTION AND TREATMENT ARE VITAL."

These warnings were printed in English on the label of the SJAC that plaintiff's mother purchased in March 1986. At that time, plaintiff's mother, who was born in Mexico, was literate only in Spanish. Because she could not read English, she was unable to read the warnings on the SJAC label and package insert. Yet she did not ask anyone to translate the label or package insert into Spanish, even though other members of her household could have done so. Plaintiff's mother had never heard, seen, or relied upon any advertising for SJAC in either English or Spanish. In Mexico, she had taken aspirin for headaches, both as a child and as an adult, and a friend had recommended SJAC.

Plaintiff, by and through his mother as guardian ad litem, filed suit against defendant in August 1989, alleging causes of action for fraud, negligence, and product liability, all premised on the theory of failure to warn about the dangers of Reye's syndrome.

. . . .

II

A

Defendant concedes, as it must, that a manufacturer of nonprescription drugs has a duty to warn purchasers about dangers in its products. For purposes of the summary judgment motion, it also concedes, at least for argument's sake, that it had a duty to warn purchasers of SJAC about the reported association between aspirin use and Reye's syndrome. The issue presented, then, is not the existence of a duty to warn as such, or the class of persons to whom the duty extends, but the nature and scope of the acknowledged duty. Specifically, the issue is whether defendant's duty to warn required it to provide label or package warnings in Spanish. Issues such as this, which concern the scope of an established duty, are resolved by reference to the governing standard of care: "Once the existence of a legal duty is found, it is the further function of the court to determine and formulate the standard of conduct to which the duty requires the defendant to conform." (Rest. 2d Torts, § 328B, com. f, p. 153.)

. . . .

In most cases, courts have fixed no standard of care for tort liability more precise than that of a reasonably prudent person under like circumstances. (*Greenwood v. Summers* (1944) 64 Cal. App. 2d 516, 520, 149 P.2d 35; see also *Warner v. Santa*

Catalina Island Co. (1955) 44 Cal.2d 310, 317, 282 P.2d 12; Rest. 2d Torts, § 328C, com. (b); Prosser and Keaton on Torts (5th ed. 1984) § 35, pp. 217–219.) "But the proper conduct of a reasonable person under particular situations may become settled by judicial decision or be prescribed by statute or ordinance." (*Satterlee v. Orange Glenn School Dist.* (1947) 29 Cal. 2d 581, 587, 177 P.2d 279, overruled on other grounds in *Alarid v. Vanier* (1958) 50 Cal. 2d 617, 624, 327 P.2d 897; accord, *Barker v. Wah Low* (1971) 19 Cal. App. 3d 710, 722, 97 Cal. Rptr. 85; *Beauchamp v. Los Gatos Golf Course, supra*, 273 Cal. App. 2d 20, 26–27, 77 Cal. Rptr. 914; Rest. 2d Torts, § 285.)

Justice Traynor explained the rationale for using a statute to define the standard of care in the following way: "The significance of a statute in a civil suit for negligence lies in its formulation of a standard of conduct that the court adopts in the determination of such liability. (See Holmes, The Common Law, 120–129; Morris, *The Relation of Criminal Statutes to Tort Liability*, 46 HARV. L. REV. 453.) The decision as to what the civil standard should be still rests with the court, and the standard formulated by a legislative body in a police regulation or criminal statute becomes the standard to determine civil liability only because the court accepts it. In the absence of such a standard the case goes to the jury, which must determine whether the defendant has acted as a reasonably prudent man would act in similar circumstances. The jury then has the burden of deciding not only what the facts are but what the unformulated standard is of reasonable conduct. When a legislative body has generalized a standard from the experience of the community and prohibits conduct that is likely to cause harm, the court accepts the formulated standards and applies them [citations], except where they would serve to impose liability without fault. [Citations.]" (*Clinkscales v. Carver* (1943) 22 Cal. 2d 72, 75, 136 P.2d 777; accord, *Casey v. Russell* (1982) 138 Cal. App. 3d 379, 383, 188 Cal. Rptr. 18.)

Statutory standards of conduct are commonly invoked by plaintiffs in negligence actions to establish a breach of duty by the defendant. In this setting, proof of the defendant's violation of a statutory standard of conduct raises a presumption of negligence that may be rebutted only by evidence establishing a justification or excuse for the statutory violation. (Evid. Code, § 669; see *Gruss v. Coast Transport, Inc.* (1957) 154 Cal. App. 2d 85, 88, 315 P.2d 339; *Lotta v. City of Oakland* (1944) 67 Cal. App. 2d 411, 413, 154 P.2d 25.)

Less common is the use of a statutory standard of conduct by a defendant to establish that no breach of duty occurred. Courts have generally not looked with favor upon the use of statutory compliance as a defense to tort liability. The Restatement Second of Torts summarizes the prevailing view in these terms: "Where a statute, ordinance or regulation is found to define a standard of conduct for the purposes of negligence actions, . . . the standard defined is normally a minimum standard, applicable to the ordinary situations contemplated by the legislation. This legislative or administrative minimum does not prevent a finding that a reasonable [person] would have taken additional precautions where the situation is such as to call for them." (Rest. 2d Torts, § 288C, com. a, p. 40; *see also Elsworth v. Beech Aircraft Corp.* (1984) 37 Cal. 3d 540, 547, 208 Cal. Rptr. 874, 691 P.2d 630 [manufacturer's compliance with federal aircraft safety regulations does not preclude liability for defective design]; *Buccery v. General Motors Corp.* (1976) 60 Cal. App. 3d 533, 540–541, 132 Cal. Rptr. 605 [compliance with federal motor vehicle safety standards does not preclude liability for defective design].)

But there is some room in tort law for a defense of statutory compliance. Where the evidence shows no unusual circumstances, but only the ordinary situation contemplated by the statute or administrative rule, then "the minimum standard prescribed by the legislation or regulation may be accepted by the triers of fact, or by the court as a matter of law, as sufficient for the occasion . . . ." (Rest. 2d Torts, § 288C, com. a, p. 40; see also *Arata v. Tonegato* (1957) 152 Cal. App. 2d 837, 842–843, 314 P.2d 130 [jury entitled to consider compliance with federal labeling requirements for hair dye as factor in determining negligence]; Model U. Product Liability Act, § 108, subd. (A) [compliance with legislative or administrative safety standards relating to product warnings deemed proof that warnings were adequate "unless the claimant proves by a preponderance of the evidence that a reasonably prudent product seller could and would have taken additional precautions"]; see generally, 1 American Law of Products Liability 3d (1987) § 12-8.)

Here, defendant manufacturer argues, in substance, that the standard of care for packaging and labeling nonprescription drugs, and in particular the necessity or propriety of foreign-language label and package warnings, has been appropriately fixed by the dense layer of state and federal statutes and regulations that control virtually all aspects of the marketing of its products. To evaluate this argument, we proceed to review the applicable statutes and regulations.

. . . .

The FDA has stated that it "encourages the preparation of labeling to meet the needs of non-English speaking or special user populations so long as such labeling fully complies with agency regulations." (53 Fed. Reg. 21,633, 21,636 (June 9, 1988).) But the controlling regulation requires only that manufacturers provide full English labeling for all nonprescription drugs except those "distributed solely in the Commonwealth of Puerto Rico or in a Territory where the predominant language is one other than English. . . ." (21 C.F.R. § 201.15(c)(1) (1993).) The regulation further states that if the label or packaging of any drug distributed in the 50 states contains "any representation in a foreign language," then all required "words, statements, and other information" must appear in the foreign language as well as in English. (*Id.*, § 201.15(c)(2)–(3).) Finally, the regulation states that "use of label space for any representation in a foreign language" is not a basis to exempt a manufacturer from the general obligation to make required language prominent and conspicuous. (21 C.F.R. § 201.15(b)(3) (1993).)

California law parallels and reinforces federal law on the points discussed here. The Health and Safety Code mandates conspicuous English language warnings in section 25900, which provides: "Cautionary statements which are required by law, or regulations adopted pursuant to law, to be printed upon the labels of containers in which dangerous drugs, poisons, and other harmful substances are packaged shall be printed in the English language in a conspicuous place in type of conspicuous size in contrast to the typography, layout, or color of the other printed matter on the label." (See also *id.*, §§ 26633, 26637.5.) Although warnings in English are expressly required, no California statute requires label or package warnings in any other language.

C

Defining the circumstances under which warnings or other information should be provided in a language other than English is a task for which legislative and administrative bodies are particularly well suited. Indeed, the California Legislature has already performed this task in a variety of different contexts, enacting laws to ensure that California residents are not denied important services or exploited because they lack proficiency in English.

. . . .

These statutes demonstrate that the Legislature is able and willing to define the circumstances in which foreign-language communications should be mandated. Given the existence of a statute expressly requiring that package warnings on nonprescription drugs be in English, we think it reasonable to infer that the Legislature has deliberately chosen not to require that manufacturers also include warnings in foreign languages. The same inference is warranted on the federal level. The FDA's regulations abundantly demonstrate its sensitivity to the issue of foreign-language labeling, and yet the FDA regulations do not require it. Presumably, the FDA has concluded that despite the obvious advantages of multilingual package warnings, the associated problems and costs are such that at present warnings should be mandated only in English.

. . . .

Were we to reject the applicable statutes and regulations as the proper standard of care, there would be two courses of action open to us. The first would be to leave the issue for resolution on a case-by-case basis by different triers of fact under the usual "reasonable person" standard of care. This was the approach that the Court of Appeal adopted in this case. As a practical matter, such an open-ended rule would likely compel manufacturers to package all their nonprescription drugs with inserts containing warnings in multiple foreign languages because, simply as a matter of foreseeability, it is foreseeable that eventually each nonprescription drug will be purchased by a non-English-speaking resident or foreign tourist proficient only in one of these languages. The burden of including warnings in so many different languages would be onerous, would add to the costs and environmental burdens of the packaging, and at some point might prove ineffective or even counterproductive if the warning inserts became so large and cumbersome that a user could not easily find the warning in his or her own language.

The other alternative would be to use our seldom-exercised power to judicially declare a particularized standard of care, giving precise guidance on this issue. But this determination would involve matters that are peculiarly susceptible to legislative and administrative investigation and determination, based upon empirical data and consideration of the viewpoints of all interested parties. A legislative body considering the utility of foreign-language label warnings for nonprescription medications would no doubt gather pertinent data on a variety of subjects, including the space limitations on nonprescription drug labels and packages, the volume of information that must be conveyed, the relative risks posed by the misuse of particular medications, the cost to the manufacturer of translating and printing warnings in languages other than English, the cost to the consumer of multilingual package warnings in terms of higher prices for, or reduced availability of, products, the feasibility of targeted distribution of products with bilingual or multilingual packaging, the number of persons likely to benefit from warnings in a particular language, and the extent to which nonprescription drug manufacturers as a group have used foreign-language advertisements to promote sales of their products. Legislation and regulations would no doubt reflect findings on these and other pertinent questions.

Lacking the procedure and the resources to conduct the relevant inquiries, we conclude that the prudent course is to adopt for tort purposes the existing legislative and administrative standard of care on this issue. The feasibility and advisability of foreign-language labeling for nonprescription drugs will, no doubt, be reviewed periodically by the FDA and other concerned agencies. Indeed, we are conscious that our decision here may prompt review of this issue by the California Legislature. That is as it should be, for further study might persuade the Legislature, the FDA, or any other concerned agency to revise the controlling statutes or regulations for nonprescription drugs.

NOTES AND QUESTIONS

1. Notice that this is a "programmatic statute," where it is actually compliance with *administrative regulations* that provides the evidence of non-negligence.

2. What if the FDA issued regulations specifying that compliance with its regulations constituted evidence of non-negligence or even non-negligence *per se*?

3. Could the FDA issue regulations specifying that they *preempt* state tort actions?

B. IMPLIED PREEMPTION

GEIER v. AMERICAN HONDA MOTOR COMPANY, INC.
529 U.S. 861 (2000)

JUSTICE BREYER delivered the opinion of the Court.

This case focuses on the 1984 version of a Federal Motor Vehicle Safety Standard promulgated by the Department of Transportation under the authority of the National Traffic and Motor Vehicle Safety Act of 1966, 80 Stat. 718, 15 U.S.C. § 1381 *et seq.* (1988 ed.). The standard, FMVSS 208, required auto manufacturers to equip some but not all of their 1987 vehicles with passive restraints. We ask whether the Act pre-empts a state common-law tort action in which the plaintiff claims that the defendant auto manufacturer, who was in compliance with the standard, should nonetheless have equipped a 1987 automobile with airbags. We conclude that the Act, taken together with FMVSS 208, pre-empts the lawsuit.

I

In 1992, petitioner Alexis Geier, driving a 1987 Honda Accord, collided with a tree and was seriously injured. The car was equipped with manual shoulder and lap belts which Geier had buckled up at the time. The car was not equipped with airbags or other passive restraint devices.

Geier and her parents, also petitioners, sued the car's manufacturer, American Honda Motor Company, Inc., and its affiliates (hereinafter American Honda), under District of Columbia tort law. They claimed, among other things, that American Honda had designed its car negligently and defectively because it lacked a driver's side airbag. App. 3. The District Court dismissed the lawsuit. The court noted that FMVSS 208 gave car manufacturers a choice as to whether to install airbags. And the court concluded that petitioners' lawsuit, because it sought to establish a different safety standard — *i.e.*, an airbag requirement — was expressly pre-empted by a provision of the Act which pre-empts "any safety standard" that is not identical to a federal safety standard applicable to the same aspect of performance, 15 U.S.C. § 1392(d) (1988 ed.); Civ. No. 95-CV-0064 (D.D.C., Dec. 9, 1997), App. 17. (We, like the courts below and the parties, refer to the pre-1994 version of the statute throughout the opinion; it has been recodified at 49 U.S.C. § 30101 *et seq.*)

The Court of Appeals agreed with the District Court's conclusion but on somewhat different reasoning. It had doubts, given the existence of the Act's "saving" clause, 15 U.S.C. § 1397(k) (1988 ed.), that petitioners' lawsuit involved the potential creation of the kind of "safety standard" to which the Safety Act's express pre-emption provision refers. But it declined to resolve that question because it found that petitioners' state-law tort claims posed an obstacle to the accomplishment of FMVSS 208's objectives. For that reason, it found that those claims conflicted with FMVSS 208, and that, under ordinary pre-emption principles, the Act consequently pre-empted the lawsuit. The Court of Appeals thus affirmed the District Court's dismissal. 166 F.3d 1236, 1238–1243 (C.A.D.C. 1999).

Several state courts have held to the contrary, namely, that neither the Act's express pre-emption nor FMVSS 208 pre-empts a "no airbag" tort suit. . . . All of the Federal Circuit Courts that have considered the question, however, have found pre-emption. One rested its conclusion on the Act's express pre-emption provision. *See, e.g., Harris v. Ford Motor Co.*, 110 F.3d 1410, 1413–1415 (9th Cir. 1997). Others, such as the Court of Appeals below, have instead found pre-emption under ordinary pre-emption principles by virtue of the conflict such suits pose to FMVSS 208's objectives, and thus to the Act itself. . . . We granted certiorari to resolve these differences. We now hold that this kind of "no airbag" lawsuit conflicts with the objectives of FMVSS 208, a standard authorized by the Act, and is therefore pre-empted by the Act.

In reaching our conclusion, we consider three subsidiary questions. First, does the Act's express pre-emption provision pre-empt this lawsuit? We think not. Second, do ordinary pre-emption principles nonetheless apply? We hold that they do. Third, does this lawsuit actually conflict with FMVSS 208, hence with the Act itself? We hold that it does.

II

We first ask whether the Safety Act's express pre-emption provision pre-empts this tort action. The provision reads as follows:

"Whenever a Federal motor vehicle safety standard established under this subchapter is in effect, no State or political subdivision of a State shall have any authority either to establish, or to continue in effect, with respect to any motor vehicle or item of motor vehicle equipment[,] any safety standard applicable to the same aspect of performance of such vehicle or item of equipment which is not identical to the Federal standard." 15 U.S.C. § 1392(d) (1988 ed.).

American Honda points out that a majority of this Court has said that a somewhat similar statutory provision in a different federal statute — a provision that uses the word "requirements" — may well expressly pre-empt similar tort actions. *See, e.g.*, *Medtronic, Inc. v. Lohr*, 518 U.S. 470, 502–504, 116 S. Ct. 2240, 135 L. Ed. 2d 700 (1996) (plurality opinion); *id.*, at 503–505, 116 S. Ct. 2240 (Breyer, J., concurring in part and concurring in judgment); *id.*, at 509–512, 116 S. Ct. 2240 (O'Connor, J., concurring in part and dissenting in part). Petitioners reply that this statute speaks of pre-empting a state-law "safety *standard*," not a "requirement," and that a tort action does not involve a safety *standard*. Hence, they conclude, the express pre-emption provision does not apply.

We need not determine the precise significance of the use of the word "standard," rather than "requirement," however, for the Act contains another provision, which resolves the disagreement. That provision, a "saving" clause, says that "[c]ompliance with" a federal safety standard "does not exempt any person from any liability under common law." 15 U.S.C. § 1397(k) (1988 ed.). The saving clause assumes that there are some significant number of common-law liability cases to save. And a reading of the express pre-emption provision that excludes common-law tort actions gives actual meaning to the saving clause's literal language, while leaving adequate room for state tort law to operate — for example, where federal law creates only a floor, *i.e.*, a minimum safety standard. *See, e.g.*, Brief for United States as *Amicus Curiae* 21 (explaining that common-law claim that a vehicle is defectively designed because it lacks antilock brakes would not be pre-empted by 49 C.F.R. § 571.105 (1999), a safety standard establishing minimum requirements for brake performance). Without the saving clause, a broad reading of the express pre-emption provision arguably might pre-empt those actions, for, as we have just mentioned, it is possible to read the pre-emption provision, standing alone, as applying to standards imposed in common-law tort actions, as well as standards contained in state legislation or regulations. And if so, it would pre-empt all nonidentical state standards established in tort actions covering the same aspect of performance as an applicable federal standard, even if the federal standard merely established a minimum standard. On that broad reading of the pre-emption clause little, if any, potential "liability at common law" would remain. And few, if any, state tort actions would remain for the saving clause to save. We have found no convincing indication that Congress wanted to pre-empt, not only state statutes and regulations, but also common-law tort actions, in such circumstances. Hence the broad reading cannot be correct. The language of the pre-emption provision permits a narrow reading that excludes common-law actions. Given the presence of the saving clause, we conclude that the pre-emption clause must be so read.

III

We have just said that the saving clause *at least* removes tort actions from the scope of the express pre-emption clause. Does it do more? In particular, does it foreclose or limit the operation of ordinary pre-emption principles insofar as those principles instruct us to read statutes as pre-empting state laws (including common-law rules) that "actually conflict" with the statute or federal standards promulgated thereunder? *Fidelity Fed. Sav. & Loan Assn. v. de la Cuesta*, 458 U.S. 141, 153, 102 S. Ct. 3014, 73 L. Ed. 2d 664 (1982). Petitioners concede, as they must in light of *Freightliner Corp. v. Myrick*, 514 U.S. 280, 115 S. Ct. 1483, 131 L. Ed. 2d 385 (1995), that the pre-emption provision, by itself, does not foreclose (through negative implication) "any possibility of implied [conflict] pre-emption," *id.*, at 288, 115 S. Ct. 1483 (discussing *Cipollone v. Liggett Group, Inc.*, 505 U.S. 504, 517–518, 112 S. Ct. 2608, 120 L. Ed. 2d 407 (1992)). But they argue that the saving clause has that very effect.

We recognize that, when this Court previously considered the pre-emptive effect of the statute's language, it appeared to leave open the question of how, or the extent to which, the saving clause saves state-law tort actions that conflict with federal regulations promulgated under the Act. *See Freightliner, supra*, at 287, n.3, 115 S. Ct. 1483 (declining to address whether the saving clause prevents a manufacturer from "us[ing] a federal safety standard to immunize itself from state common-law liability"). We now conclude that the saving clause (like the express pre-emption provision) does *not* bar the ordinary working of conflict pre-emption principles.

Nothing in the language of the saving clause suggests an intent to save state-law tort actions that conflict with federal regulations. The words "[c]ompliance" and "does not exempt," 15 U.S.C. § 1397(k) (1988 ed.), sound as if they simply bar a special kind of defense, namely, a defense that compliance with a federal standard automatically exempts a defendant from state law, whether the Federal Government meant that standard to be an absolute requirement or only a minimum one. *See* Restatement (Third) of Torts: Products Liability § 4(b), Comment *e* (1997) (distinguishing between state-law compliance defense and a federal claim of pre-emption). It is difficult to understand why Congress would have insisted on a compliance-with-federal-regulation precondition to the provision's applicability had it wished the Act to "save" all state-law tort actions, regardless of their potential threat to the objectives of federal safety standards promulgated under that Act. Nor does our interpretation conflict with the purpose of the saving provision, say, by rendering it ineffectual. As we have previously explained, the saving provision still makes clear that the express pre-emption provision does not of its own force pre-empt common-law tort actions. And it thereby preserves those actions that seek to establish greater safety than the minimum safety achieved by a federal regulation intended to provide a floor. *See supra*, at 1917–1918.

Moreover, this Court has repeatedly "decline[d] to give broad effect to saving clauses where doing so would upset the careful regulatory scheme established by federal law." *United States v. Locke, ante*, at 106–107, 120 S. Ct. 1135; *see American Telephone & Telegraph Co. v. Central Office Telephone, Inc.*, 524 U.S. 214, 227–228, 118 S. Ct. 1956, 141 L. Ed. 2d 222 (1998) *(AT&T)*; *Texas & Pacific R. Co. v. Abilene Cotton Oil Co.*, 204 U.S. 426, 446, 27 S. Ct. 350, 51 L. Ed. 553 (1907). We find this concern applicable in the present case. And we conclude that the saving clause foresees — it does not foreclose — the possibility that a federal safety standard will pre-empt a state common-law tort action with which it conflicts. We do not understand the dissent to disagree, for it acknowledges that ordinary pre-emption principles apply, at least sometimes. *Post*, at 1934–1936 (opinion of Stevens, J.).

Neither do we believe that the pre-emption provision, the saving provision, or both together, create some kind of "special burden" beyond that inherent in ordinary pre-emption principles — which "special burden" would specially disfavor pre-emption here. *Cf. post*, at 1934–1935. The two provisions, read together, reflect a neutral policy, not a specially favorable or unfavorable policy, toward the application of ordinary conflict pre-emption principles. On the one hand, the pre-emption provision itself reflects a desire to subject the industry to a single, uniform set of federal safety standards. Its pre-emption of *all* state standards, even those that might stand in harmony with federal law, suggests an intent to avoid the conflict, uncertainty, cost, and occasional risk to safety itself that too many different safety-standard cooks might otherwise create. *See* H.R.Rep. No. 1776, 89th Cong., 2d Sess., 17 (1966) ("Basically, this preemption subsection is intended to result in uniformity of standards so that the public as well as industry will be guided by one set of criteria rather than by a multiplicity of diverse standards"); S.Rep. No. 1301, 89th Cong., 2d Sess., 12 (1966). This policy by itself favors pre-emption of state tort suits, for the rules of law that judges and juries create or apply in such suits may themselves similarly create uncertainty and even conflict, say, when different juries in different States reach different decisions on similar facts.

On the other hand, the saving clause reflects a congressional determination that occasional nonuniformity is a small price to pay for a system in which juries not only create, but also enforce, safety standards, while simultaneously providing necessary compensation to victims. That policy by itself disfavors pre-emption, at least some of the time. But we can find nothing in any natural reading of the two provisions that would favor one set of policies over the other where a jury-imposed safety standard actually conflicts with a federal safety standard.

Why, in any event, would Congress not have wanted ordinary pre-emption principles to apply where an actual conflict with a federal objective is at stake? Some such principle is needed. In its absence, state law could impose legal duties that would conflict directly with federal regulatory mandates, say, by premising liability upon the presence of the very windshield retention requirements that federal law requires. *See, e.g.*, 49 C.F.R. § 571.212 (1999). Insofar as petitioners' argument would permit common-law actions that "actually conflict" with federal regulations, it would take from those who would enforce a federal law the very ability to achieve the law's congressionally mandated objectives that the Constitution, through the operation of ordinary pre-emption principles, seeks to protect. To the extent that such an interpretation of the saving provision reads into a particular federal law toleration of a conflict that those principles would otherwise forbid, it permits that law to defeat its own objectives, or potentially, as the Court has put it before, to " 'destroy itself.' " *AT&T, supra*, at 228, 118 S. Ct. 1956 (quoting *Abilene Cotton, supra*, at 446, 27 S. Ct. 350). We do not claim that Congress lacks the constitutional power to write a statute that mandates such a complex type of state/federal relationship. *Cf. post*, at 1935, n. 16. But there is no reason to believe Congress has done so here.

The dissent, as we have said, contends nonetheless that the express pre-emption and saving provisions here, taken together, create a "special burden," which a court must impose "on a party" who claims conflict pre-emption under those principles. *Post*, at 1934–1935. But nothing in the Safety Act's language refers to any "special burden." Nor can one find the basis for a "special burden" in this Court's precedents. It is true that, in *Freightliner Corp. v. Myrick*, 514 U.S. 280, 115 S. Ct. 1483, 131 L. Ed. 2d 385 (1995), the Court said, in the context of interpreting the Safety Act, that "[a]t best" there is an "inference that an express pre-emption clause forecloses implied pre-emption." *Id.*, at 289, 115 S. Ct. 1483 (emphasis added). But the Court made this statement in the course of *rejecting* the more absolute argument that the presence of the express pre-emption provision entirely foreclosed the possibility of conflict pre-emption. *Id.*, at 288, 115 S. Ct. 1483. The statement, headed with the qualifier "[a]t best," and made in a case where, without any need for inferences or "special burdens," state law obviously would survive, *see id.* at 289–290, 115 S. Ct. 1483, simply preserves a legal possibility. This Court did not hold that the Safety Act *does* create a "special burden," or still less that such a burden necessarily arises from the limits of an express pre-emption provision. And considerations of language, purpose, and administrative workability, together with the principles underlying this Court's pre-emption doctrine discussed above, make clear that the express pre-emption provision imposes no unusual, "special burden" against pre-emption. For similar reasons, we do not see the basis for interpreting the saving clause to impose any such burden.

. . . .

IV

The basic question, then, is whether a common-law "no airbag" action like the one before us actually conflicts with FMVSS 208. We hold that it does.

In petitioners' and the dissent's view, FMVSS 208 sets a minimum airbag standard. As far as FMVSS 208 is concerned, the more airbags, and the sooner, the better. But that was not the Secretary's view. The Department of Transportation's (DOT's) comments, which accompanied the promulgation of FMVSS 208, make clear that the standard deliberately provided the manufacturer with a range of choices among different passive restraint devices. Those choices would bring about a mix of different devices introduced gradually over time; and FMVSS 208 would thereby lower costs, overcome technical safety problems, encourage technological development, and win widespread consumer acceptance — all of which would promote FMVSS 208's safety objectives. *See generally* 49 Fed. Reg. 28962 (1984).

A

The history of FMVSS 208 helps explain why and how DOT sought these objectives. . . .

. . . .

B

Read in light of this history, DOT's own contemporaneous explanation of FMVSS 208 makes clear that the 1984 version of FMVSS 208 reflected the following significant considerations. First, buckled up seatbelts are a vital ingredient of automobile safety. *Id.*, at 29003; *State Farm, supra*, at 52, 103 S. Ct. 2856 ("We start with the accepted ground that if used, seatbelts unquestionably would save many thousands of lives and would prevent tens of thousands of crippling injuries"). Second, despite the enormous and unnecessary risks that a passenger runs by not buckling up manual lap and shoulder belts, more than 80% of front seat passengers would leave their manual seatbelts unbuckled. 49 Fed. Reg. 28983 (1984) (estimating that only 12.5% of front seat passengers buckled up manual belts). Third, airbags could make up for the dangers caused by unbuckled manual belts, but they could not make up for them entirely. *Id.*, at 28986 (concluding that, although an airbag plus a lap and shoulder belt was the most "effective" system, airbags alone were *less* effective than buckled up manual lap and shoulder belts).

Fourth, passive restraint systems had their own disadvantages, for example, the dangers associated with, intrusiveness of, and corresponding public dislike for, nondetachable automatic belts. *Id.*, at 28992–28993. Fifth, airbags brought with them their own special risks to safety, such as the risk of danger to out-of-position occupants (usually children) in small cars. *Id.*, at 28992, 29001; *see also* 65 Fed. Reg. 30680, 30681–30682 (2000) (finding 158 confirmed airbag-induced fatalities as of April 2000, and amending rule to add new requirements, test procedures, and injury criteria to ensure that "future air bags be designed to create less risk of serious airbag-induced injuries than current air bags, particularly for small women and young children"); U.S. Dept. of Transportation, National Highway Traffic Safety Administration, National Accident Sampling System Crashworthiness Data System 1991–1993, p. viii (Aug.1995) (finding that airbags caused approximately 54,000 injuries between 1991 and 1993).

Sixth, airbags were expected to be significantly more expensive than other passive restraint devices, raising the average cost of a vehicle price $320 for full frontal airbags over the cost of a car with manual lap and shoulder seatbelts (and potentially much more if production volumes were low). 49 Fed. Reg. 28990 (1984). And the agency worried that the high replacement cost — estimated to be $800 — could lead car owners to refuse to replace them after deployment. *Id.*, at 28990, 29000–29001; *see also id.*, at 28990 (estimating total investment costs for mandatory airbag requirement at $1.3 billion compared to $500 million for automatic seatbelts). Seventh, the public, for reasons of cost, fear, or physical intrusiveness, might resist installation or use of any of the then-available passive restraint devices, *id.*, at 28987–28989 — a particular concern with respect to airbags, *id.*, at 29001 (noting that "[a]irbags engendered the largest quantity of, and most vociferously worded, comments").

FMVSS 208 reflected these considerations in several ways. Most importantly, that standard deliberately sought variety — a mix of several different passive restraint systems. It did so by setting a performance requirement for passive restraint devices and allowing manufacturers to choose among different passive restraint mechanisms, such as airbags, automatic belts, or other passive restraint technologies to satisfy that requirement. *Id.*, at 28996. And DOT explained why FMVSS 208 sought the mix of devices that it expected its performance standard to produce. *Id.*, at 28997. DOT wrote that it had *rejected* a proposed FMVSS 208 "all airbag" standard because of safety concerns (perceived or real) associated with airbags, which concerns threatened a "backlash" more easily overcome "if airbags" were "not the only way of complying." *Id.*, at 29001. It added that a mix of devices would help develop data on comparative effectiveness, would allow the industry time to overcome the safety problems and the high production costs associated with airbags, and would facilitate the development of alternative, cheaper, and safer passive restraint systems. *Id.*, at 29001–29002. And it would thereby build public confidence, *id.*, at 29001–29002, necessary to avoid another interlock-type fiasco.

The 1984 FMVSS 208 standard also deliberately sought a *gradual* phase-in of passive restraints. *Id.*, at 28999–29000. It required the manufacturers to equip only 10% of their car fleet manufactured after September 1, 1986, with passive restraints. *Id.*, at 28999. It then increased the percentage in three annual stages, up to 100% of the new car fleet for cars manufactured after September 1, 1989. *Ibid.* And it explained that the phased-in requirement would allow more time for manufacturers to develop airbags or other, better, safer passive restraint systems. It would help develop information about the comparative effectiveness of different systems, would lead to a mix in which airbags and other nonseatbelt passive restraint systems played a more prominent role than would otherwise result, and would promote public acceptance. *Id.*, at 29000–29001.

. . . .

In sum, as DOT now tells us through the Solicitor General, the 1984 version of FMVSS 208 "embodies the Secretary's policy judgment that safety would best be promoted if manufacturers installed *alternative* protection systems in their fleets rather than one particular system in every car." Brief for United States as *Amicus Curiae* 25; see 49 Fed. Reg. 28997 (1984). Petitioners' tort suit claims that the manufacturers of the 1987 Honda Accord "had a duty to design, manufacture, distribute and sell a motor vehicle with an effective and safe passive restraint system, including, but not limited to, airbags." App. 3 (Complaint, ¶ 11).

In effect, petitioners' tort action depends upon its claim that manufacturers had a duty to install an airbag when they manufactured the 1987 Honda Accord. Such a state law — *i.e.*, a rule of state tort law imposing such a duty — by its terms would have required manufacturers of all similar cars to install airbags rather than other passive restraint systems, such as automatic belts or passive interiors. It thereby would have presented an obstacle to the variety and mix of devices that the federal regulation sought. It would have required all manufacturers to have installed airbags in respect to the entire District-of-Columbia-related portion of their 1987 new car fleet, even though FMVSS 208 at that time required only that 10% of a manufacturer's nationwide fleet be equipped with any passive restraint device at all. It thereby also would have stood as an obstacle to the gradual passive restraint phase-in that the federal regulation deliberately imposed. In addition, it could have made less likely the adoption of a state mandatory buckle-up law. Because the rule of law for which petitioners contend would have stood "as an obstacle to the accomplishment and execution of" the important means-related federal objectives that we have just discussed, it is pre-empted.

. . . .

One final point: We place some weight upon DOT's interpretation of FMVSS 208's objectives and its conclusion, as set forth in the Government's brief, that a tort suit such as this one would " 'stan[d] as an obstacle to the accomplishment and execution' " of those objectives. Brief for United States as *Amicus Curiae* 25–26 (quoting *Hines, supra*, at 67, 61 S. Ct. 399). Congress has delegated to DOT authority to implement the statute; the subject matter is technical; and the relevant history and background are complex and extensive. The agency is likely to have a thorough understanding of its own regulation and its objectives and is "uniquely qualified" to comprehend the likely impact of state requirements. *Medtronic*, 518 U.S., at 496, 116 S. Ct. 2240; *see id.*, at 506, 116 S. Ct. 2240 (Breyer, J,. concurring in part and concurring in judgment). And DOT has explained FMVSS 208's objectives, and the interference that "no airbag" suits pose thereto, consistently over time. Brief for United States as *Amicus Curiae* in *Freightliner Corp. v. Myrick*, O.T.1994, No. 94-286, pp. 28–29; Brief for United States as *Amicus Curiae* in *Wood v. General Motors Corp.*, O.T.1989, No. 89-46, pp. 7, 11–16. In these circumstances, the agency's own views should make a difference.

. . . .

The judgment of the Court of Appeals is affirmed.

It is so ordered.

JUSTICE STEVENS, with whom JUSTICE SOUTER, JUSTICE THOMAS, and JUSTICE GINSBURG join, dissenting.

Airbag technology has been available to automobile manufacturers for over 30 years. There is now general agreement on the proposition "that, to be safe, a car must have an airbag." *Ante* this page. Indeed, current federal law imposes that requirement on all automobile manufacturers. *See* 49 U.S.C. § 30127; 49 C.F.R. § 571.208, S4.1.5.3 (1998). The question raised by petitioners' common-law tort action is whether that proposition was sufficiently obvious when Honda's 1987 Accord was manufactured to make the failure to install such a safety feature actionable under theories of negligence or defective design. The Court holds that an interim regulation motivated by the Secretary of Transportation's desire to foster gradual development of a variety of passive restraint devices deprives state courts of jurisdiction to answer that question. I respectfully dissent from that holding, and especially from the Court's unprecedented extension of the doctrine of pre-emption. As a preface to an explanation of my understanding of the statute and the regulation, these preliminary observations seem appropriate.

"This is a case about federalism," *Coleman v. Thompson*, 501 U.S. 722, 726, 111 S. Ct. 2546, 115 L. Ed. 2d 640 (1991), that is, about respect for "the constitutional role of the States as sovereign entities." *Alden v. Maine*, 527 U.S. 706, 713, 119 S. Ct. 2240, 144 L. Ed. 2d 636 (1999). It raises important questions concerning the way in which the Federal Government may exercise its undoubted power to oust state courts of their traditional jurisdiction over common-law tort actions. The rule the Court enforces today was not enacted by Congress and is not to be found in the text of any Executive Order or regulation. It has a unique origin: It is the product of the Court's interpretation of the final commentary accompanying an interim administrative regulation and the history of airbag regulation generally. Like many other judge-made rules, its contours are not precisely defined. . . .

. . . .

III

When a state statute, administrative rule, or common-law cause of action conflicts with a federal statute, it is axiomatic that the state law is without effect. U.S. Const., Art. VI, cl. 2; *Cipollone v. Liggett Group, Inc.*, 505 U.S. 504, 516, 112 S. Ct. 2608, 120 L. Ed. 2d 407 (1992). On the other hand, it is equally clear that the Supremacy Clause does not give unelected federal judges *carte blanche* to use federal law as a means of imposing their own ideas of tort reform on the States. Because of the role of States as separate sovereigns in our federal system, we have long presumed that state laws — particularly those, such as the provision of tort remedies to compensate for personal injuries, that are within the scope of the States' historic police powers — are not to be pre-empted by a federal statute unless it is the clear and manifest purpose of Congress to do so. *Medtronic, Inc. v. Lohr*, 518 U.S. 470, 485, 116 S. Ct. 2240, 135 L. Ed. 2d 700 (1996); *Gade v. National Solid Wastes Management Assn.*, 505 U.S. 88, 116–117, 112 S. Ct. 2374, 120 L. Ed. 2d 73 (1992) (Souter, J., dissenting) ("If the [federal] statute's terms can be read sensibly not to have a pre-emptive effect, the presumption controls and no pre-emption may be inferred").

. . . .

Our presumption against pre-emption is rooted in the concept of federalism. It recognizes that when Congress legislates "in a field which the States have traditionally occupied . . . [,] we start with the assumption that the historic police powers of the States were not to be superseded by the Federal Act unless that was the clear and manifest purpose of Congress." *Rice v. Santa Fe Elevator Corp.*, 331 U.S., at 230, 67 S. Ct. 1146; see *Jones v. Rath Packing Co.*, 430 U.S. 519, 525, 97 S. Ct. 1305, 51 L. Ed. 2d 604 (1977). The signal virtues of this presumption are its placement of the power of pre-emption squarely in the hands of Congress, which is far more suited than the Judiciary to strike the appropriate state/federal balance (particularly in areas of traditional state regulation), and its requirement that Congress speak clearly when exercising that power. In this way, the structural safeguards inherent in the normal operation of the legislative process operate to defend state interests from undue infringement. . . . In addition, the presumption serves as a limiting principle that prevents federal judges from running amok with our potentially boundless (and perhaps inadequately considered) doctrine of implied conflict pre-emption based on frustration of purposes — *i.e.*, that state law is pre-empted if it "stands as an obstacle to the accomplishment and execution of the full purposes and objectives of Congress." *Hines v. Davidowitz*, 312 U.S. 52, 67, 61 S. Ct. 399, 85 L. Ed. 581 (1941).

While the presumption is important in assessing the pre-emptive reach of federal statutes, it becomes crucial when the pre-emptive effect of an administrative regulation is at issue. Unlike Congress, administrative agencies are clearly not designed to represent the interests of States, yet with relative ease they can promulgate comprehensive and detailed regulations that have broad pre-emption ramifications for state law. We have addressed the heightened federalism and nondelegation concerns that agency pre-emption raises by using the presumption to build a procedural bridge across the political accountability gap between States and administrative agencies. Thus, even in cases where implied regulatory pre-emption is at issue, we generally "expect an administrative regulation to declare any intention to pre-empt state law with some specificity." . . . This expectation, which is shared by the Executive Branch, serves to ensure that States will be able to have a dialog with agencies regarding pre-emption decisions *ex ante* through the normal notice-and-comment procedures of the Administrative Procedure Act (APA), 5 U.S.C. § 553.

. . . .

Because neither the text of the statute nor the text of the regulation contains any indication of an intent to pre-empt petitioners' cause of action, and because I cannot agree with the Court's unprecedented use of inferences from regulatory history and commentary as a basis for implied pre-emption, I am convinced that Honda has not overcome the presumption against pre-emption in this case. I therefore respectfully dissent.

NOTES AND QUESTIONS

1. This may be the only place in law school where students study federal preemption. It is a set of doctrines that is of great importance in our legal system. *See, e.g.*, Mary J. Davis, *Unmasking the Presumption in Favor of Preemption*, 53 S. CAR. L. REV. 967 (2002); Richard C. Ausness, *Preemption of State Tort Law by Federal Safety Statutes: Supreme Court Preemption Jurisprudence Since* Cipollone, 92 KY. L.J. 913 (2003–04); Michael S. Greve & Jonathan Klick, *Preemption in the Rehnquist Court: A Preliminary Empirical Analysis*, 2006 SUP. CT. ECON. REV. 43 (2006) (identifying and describing outcomes in 105 preemption cases decided between 1986 and 2003). *See generally* ERWIN CHEMERINSKY, CONSTITUTIONAL LAW 374–401 (2d ed. 2002).

2. Even where there is *express* congressional preemption, sometimes questions of statutory interpretation remain. *Implied* preemption cases, however, always involve statutory interpretation. This case reflects a number of statutory interpretation approaches we will study later in Part IV, such as the interaction of different sections of the same statute (the express preemption and "savings" clause), legislative history (committee reports), legislative intent, deference to administrative interpretation of statutes, judge-made doctrines of statutory interpretation ("special burden," presumption against preemption or clear statement requirement, and federalism deference to states), consideration of legislative and judicial roles, and the operation of complex, "programmatic statutes" discussed by Professor Frank P. Grad in Chapter 1. How many of these have you already encountered in your law studies?

3. In what way does this case illustrate application of a statute beyond its terms?

4. In *Riegel v. Medtronic, Inc.*, ___ U.S. ___, 2008 U.S. LEXIS 2013, No. 06-179 (2008), the Court held, 8-1, that the Medical Device Amendments of 1976 provision preempting state "requirements" that were "different from, or in addition to" the Act's standards for FDA pre-market approval of medical devices preempted state common law claims based on negligent design of such medical devices.

C. A DEBATE: SHOULD THE COMMON LAW BECOME A REFORM MECHANISM FOR OBSOLETE STATUTES?

GUIDO CALABRESI, A COMMON LAW FOR THE AGE OF STATUTES
1–2, 82–83, 101–02, 118 (1982)[*]

The last fifty to eighty years have seen a fundamental change in American law. In this time we have gone from a legal system dominated by the common law, defined by courts, to one in which statutes, enacted by legislatures, have become the primary source of law. The consequences of the "orgy of statute making," in Grant Gilmore's felicitous phrase, are just beginning to be recognized. The change itself and its effect on our whole legal-political system have not been systematically treated.

In this book I will argue that many disparate current legal-political phenomena are reactions to this fundamental change and to the problems it has created. These phenomena include events as diverse as: the increasing tendency of courts to find that constitutions, and especially notions of equal protection, require the invalidation of statutes; the development of "passive-virtue" theories, associated especially with

[*] Reprinted by permission of the publishers from *A Common Law for the Age of Statutes* by Guido Calabresi. Cambridge, Mass.: Harvard University Press. Copyright © 1983 by the President and Fellows of Harvard College.

Alexander Bickel, which would enable courts to force legislatures to take a second look at constitutionally doubtful statutes; the development of theories and practices of judicial interpretation of statutes which would make even the proverbial Jesuit blush if they were viewed as attempts to discern any kind of legislative intent; the delegation of substantial authority in lawmaking to administrative agencies; the pressure for sunset laws, which would automatically repeal statutes or regulations after a fixed number of years; and the insistent suggestions for radical reform of our legislatures or even of our whole system of checks and balances.

The "statutorification" of American law is not the only reason for these varied proposals and events. Each one has independent reasons that might explain it. Nevertheless, I believe that as a group they cannot be adequately explained except as a series of *ad hoc* reactions to deeper change in American law. More specifically, they are reactions to the feeling that, because a statute is hard to revise once it is passed, laws are governing us that would not and could not be enacted today, and that *some* of these laws not only could not be reenacted but also do not fit, are in some sense inconsistent with, our whole legal landscape.

. . . .

There is an alternate way of dealing with the problem of legal obsolescence: granting to courts the authority to determine whether a statute is obsolete, whether in one way or another it should be consciously reviewed. At times this doctrine would approach granting to courts the authority to treat statutes as if they were no more and no less than part of the common law. At other times it would be used to enable courts to encourage, or even to induce, legislative reconsideration of the statute. Employing a variety of techniques, the courts might begin a "common law" process of renovation in the obsolete law, update the statute directly by replacing it with new rules (derived either from the common law or from statutory sources), or do no more than create a situation in which conscious legislative reconsideration of law was made likely. The object in all cases would be to permit courts to keep anachronistic laws from governing us without thereby requiring them to do tasks for which they are not suited, or denying to the legislatures the decisive word in the making of constitutionally valid laws.

. . . .

To state the approach in summary form is easy; to outline, let alone fill out, its workings is far more difficult. So I will state the approach as a hypothesis. Let us suppose that common law courts have the power to treat statutes in precisely the same way that they treat the common law. They can (without resort to constitutions or passive virtues or strained interpretations) alter a written law or some part of it in the same way (and with the same reluctance) in which they can modify or abandon a common law doctrine or even a whole complex set of interrelated doctrines. They can use this power either to make changes themselves or, by threatening to use the power, to induce legislatures to act. Let us not, for the moment, concern ourselves with the question of whether this authority has been given explicitly to the courts by the legislatures or has been asserted independently by the courts themselves, in a common law way. ("We have, in fact, been doing this indirectly[;] it is time we said what we were doing and, so to speak, gave a name and a legitimacy to what has simply grown to be the law.")

How should such a power be used? Should all or only some kinds of statutes be subject to it? Should many courts or only the highest courts of a jurisdiction be permitted to exercise it? When should courts using this power act on their own, and when should they instead use the power to press legislatures or administrative agencies into acting? Are there differences in the proper employment of this power and in the proper employment of the traditional judicial authority to update common law rules?

. . . .

Can Common Law Power Apply to Statutes?

Should an old legislative decision determine the starting point, the allocation of the burden of inertia, or should that be decided on the basis of conformity to the legal landscape? I don't think one can give an all-or-nothing answer to the question. Too much depends on the type of statute, the type of majority and legislature that enacted it, and the statute's relation to fundamental or constitutional principles, not to mention the obvious question of how old the statute is. All these factors will be important in any attempt to develop limits appropriate to the kind of doctrine we are now analyzing. For now, however, I am more concerned with the question of whether there does exist a significant category of cases in which the burden of inertia is, in a democratic society, better assigned by courts acting in a principled, common law fashion than by leaving the burden where a long past legislative majority placed it. . . . So long as the legislature can alter judge-made law, a judge-made law immediately commands the identical majoritarian basis as an old statute, if the statue's claim of legitimacy is grounded on no more than the negative fact of nonrepeal. It would follow that judge-made common law rules should also be outside the scope of judicial revision. And that has never been our law.

. . . .

Legitimacy — Conclusion

In the end the question of legitimacy, like all legal questions, is a profoundly practical one. We cannot avoid a decision on who should bear the burden of inertia in lawmaking, but we can choose among several possible approaches. The first would let the burden automatically fall on those who would change the will of a past majority or majoritarian body. This is the system that makes old rules untouchable (except by legislatures). The second would, just as automatically, put the burden of inertia on those who would keep in force any law that was enacted more than a fixed number of years before. This is the radical sunsetter's approach. If the first position presumes a *continuation of majoritarian support in all cases*, until proven otherwise by an overcoming of inertia, the second approach presumes *the absence of such support after a set period*, unless proven otherwise. The third approach would let a semirepresentative body decide where the burden would lie. It would allow an administrative agency or a legislative or executive committee to decide which laws must be reconsidered and tested for current support in the legislature. Such an approach is the hardest to justify in majoritarian terms, for it relies on the essentially unfettered desires of members of an only partly majoritarian body to determine the burden of inertia. The last approach would make the allocation of the burden a judicial junction. It would ask courts to look at statutes, as they did common law rules, and decide which are ripe for reconsideration.

NOTES AND QUESTIONS

1. Dean Calabresi's book did, in fact, generate a wide range of comment. Much of this commentary examined the problems with identifying statutes that were "obsolete," and no longer fitting within the "legal landscape," as well as defining the legal landscape; the obvious blurring of legislative and judicial power; practical workability problems; the apparent over-reliance on judicial wisdom; and alternatives to the Calabresi proposal, such as a renewed legislative concern with statutory obsolescence. *See, e.g.,* Abner J. Mikva, *The Shifting Sands of Legal Topography*, 96 HARV. L. REV. 534 (1982); Archibald Cox, *Book Review*, 70 CAL. L. REV. 1463 (1982); Frank M. Coffin, *The Problem of Obsolete Statutes: A New Role for Courts?*, 91 YALE L.J. 827 (1982); Allan C. Hutchinson & Derek Morgan, *Calabresian Sunset: Statutes in the Shade*, 82 COLUM. L. REV. 1752 (1982); Robert Weisberg, *The Calabresian Judicial Artist: Statutes and the New Legal Process*, 35 STAN. L. REV. 213 (1983).

2. In 1979, Jack Davies, a state senator in Minnesota introduced a "Nonprimacy of Statutes Act." *See* Jack Davies, *A Response to Statutory Obsolescence: The Nonprimacy of Statutes Act*, 4 VT. L. REV. 203 (1979). For Dean Calabresi's reactions to Senator Davies' proposed Nonprimacy of Statutes Act, see GUIDO CALABRESI, A COMMON LAW FOR THE AGE OF STATUTES 82 n.3, 90, 131–32 (1982); Guido Calabresi, *The Nonprimacy of Statutes Act: A Comment*, 4 VT. L. REV. 247 (1979).

OTTO J. HETZEL,
INSTILLING LEGISLATIVE INTERPRETATION SKILLS IN THE CLASSROOM AND THE COURTROOM
48 UNIVERSITY OF PITTSBURGH LAW REVIEW 663, 667–71 (1987)*

. . . .

The heart of Dean Calabresi's argument is that "enlightened" judges should "update" obsolete legislation. While this proposition is helpful because it will spur dialogue concerning the need to upgrade skills and to provide a place in the curriculum for legislative interpretation, his thesis appears to be an unworkable and inherently invalid assertion. Dean Calabresi's basic premise, that obsolete legislation can and should be updated by judges who should be empowered to carry out that task, raises a number of questions. These include semantic problems concerning what statutes are "obsolete" and the need to reorder or at least redefine our constitutional system of the separation of powers to implement his proposal. Despite these difficulties, his revolutionary proposal apparently has an emotional attraction for a constituency that yearns to return to the simpler times and legal systems of the past.

Clearly, Dean Calabresi wants to return to the age of the philosopher kings, whose enlightened rulings provided order in a much less complicated time. The attractiveness of his thesis has been nurtured by the current state of legal education, which instills in lawyers and judges a belief that the common law is a more flexible and valuable source of support for decisions than statutes and that judges are far better shepherds of society than a democratic majority. As will be illustrated in the next Section, this reverence for the common law is but one problem with Dean Calabresi's proposal.

III.

An Unjustified Infatuation with the Common Law

. . . .

At its core, Dean Calabresi's theory exhibits a fascination with judicial activism. He would have us literally return to the age when judges exercised the kind of power they possessed in the heyday of the common law without considering the objectives of much legislation that was necessitated by obsolete or unacceptable common law concepts. In his system, judges would identify and discard "obsolete" statutes, substituting their own analysis with more appropriate doctrine. Presumably, this analysis would often be derived from previously discarded common law doctrines that may, in hindsight, appear more appropriate in the current circumstances.

Significant semantic and definitional problems intrude upon Dean Calabresi's proposal. A key issue is what grounds we will use to determine that statutes are "obsolete," and the mechanical problems attendant to making this determination. Several obvious questions arise. First, who will decide what statutes are obsolete and in need of updating? Will the concept for obsolescence become a grounds on which to challenge any legislation, so long as the party can pass the "red-faced test" in mounting an argument alleging some perceived deficiency in its current applications, or will the

---

* Reprinted with permission.

obsolescence issue be restricted to use by the court? Regardless of who can raise the issue, at what level court, trial or appellate, can the argument be presented and a decision rendered? What would be the impact of permitting such challenges to legislation on concepts of *stare decisis* and on objectives such as obtaining consistency and certainty of treatment under the law? What criteria should be used to determine obsolescence? Furthermore, if a statute is found to be obsolete, what does the judge substitute and on what value theory does he act in making those revisions?

Although some may believe that the judiciary effectively interprets legislation, few observers would suggest that judges at any level demonstrate a notable capacity to handle the legislative interpretation tasks we now assign them. Thus, the inappropriateness of having judges carry out the responsibilities Dean Calabresi would re-invest in them makes his proposal simply unacceptable.

. . . .

Unfortunately, the implications of such a change are largely ignored or misunderstood by those who postulate the propriety of judicial action to spur legislative responses. Regardless of its nature, intervention will change an existing balance of political power and the separation of powers between the three branches of government. One interest group or the other will be adversely affected by the court's intervention. Different values are likely to undergird the decisions of particular judges on a variety of economic and moral issues. Empowering judges to "update" "obsolete" statutes would change the balance of power and tilt in one direction or another a statute's meaning, causing a profound change in the role of the judiciary as it is currently constitutionally mandated.

. . . .

Beyond the constitutional issue, and more pertinent to this Article, Dean Calabresi's proposal would have far-reaching implications for statutory interpretation. That seems clear even though his proposal is fetchingly disguised as the need to revise "worn-out" solutions for newly redefined problems, the "allocation of the burden of inertia" in his shorthand terminology. In essence, Dean Calabresi makes a call to usurp those interpretation techniques and doctrines that courts have generally felt impelled to respect in our system of government. This radical proposal will undoubtedly generate a spirited dialogue and revisiting of underlying questions concerning the judiciary's role in statutory interpretation.

Part III

THE LEGISLATURE AND LEGISLATIVE PROCESS

Chapter 3

THE LEGISLATURE AS AN INSTITUTION

This chapter aims at providing law students with a straightforward overview of the structure and function of the legislative process. The presentation is keyed to the U.S. Congress both because that body is the most studied legislature in the world, *see, e.g.,* DONALD C. BACON, ROGER H. DAVIDSON & MORTON KELLER, THE ENCYCLOPEDIA OF THE UNITED STATES CONGRESS (4 vols., 1995), and because the case law and materials in subsequent chapters presupposes a familiarity with the standard operating procedures of the U.S. Congress.

As you read through the materials in this chapter, remember the various roles that lawyers play in the legislative process sketched in Chapter 1B. The lawyer engaged in legislative advocacy needs to be familiar with the phases of legislative decision-making that offer possibilities of well-timed strategic and tactical intervention on behalf of a client's interest. The lawyer engaged in research relevant to statutory interpretation will find evidence of potential probative value deposited in the interstices of the procedural phases outlined in this chapter. Moreover, the legal researcher familiar with the ebb and flow of the legislative policy-making process will be in a better position to evaluate the probative force of that evidence in bolstering the client's case or in contravening the claims of the adversary.

A. REPRESENTATION

1. The Function of Representation

DAVID J. VOGLER
THE POLITICS OF CONGRESS
6, 51, 52–53, 61–62, 69–71, 71–73 (6th ed., 1993)·

The republican principle of the Constitution rests on two central ideas: representation and deliberation. The first, that of having government decisions made by elected representatives held accountable through free elections, distinguishes the United States political system from a direct democracy, in which the people themselves make the decisions of government (in assemblies such as town meetings or by voting directly on a policy in a referendum). The Framers of the Constitution made Congress the principal representative institution of government. This is most evident in the population-based membership and two-year terms of the House of Representatives; after the 17th Amendment established the direct election of senators in 1921, the Senate, too, has claimed its place as a representative institution in the national government.

The second idea is so central to American government that the term *deliberative democracy* has been used to describe the system of government created by the Constitution. That system is based on a belief that representatives of the people can, in Madison's words, "refine and enlarge the public views," through deliberation, an extensive debate and careful consideration of alternative courses of action, and in that way make laws that better serve majority interests than would policies chosen by the people themselves.

Representation and deliberation are the primary responsibilities of Congress in our constitutional system. Almost everything that Congress does, or is expected to do, is connected in some way to representation or deliberative policymaking. We also expect

Congress and its members to oversee the administration of programs by the executive branch, to engage the public in democratic discussions about policies through hearings and other public forums, and to help constituents with problems ranging from individuals not getting their social security checks to businesses losing government contracts. In the discussion that follows, those three functions are identified as congressional oversight of administration, democratic education, and constituent service. They also contribute to the broader functions of representation and deliberative policymaking.

. . . .

Everyone agrees that representation is a cardinal principle of American democracy. But the concept of representation raises a number of questions. How are constituencies defined and representatives selected? Do representatives need to be like the people they are supposed to represent? Does a belief that their interests are represented in government policymaking affect how willing constituents are to pay their taxes and obey unpopular laws? How closely would a representative follow constituency opinion in voting on issues? What happens when what the representative believes to be in the best interest of constituents is not the same as what constituents themselves say they want from government? Such questions direct our attention to four dimensions of representation: formal, descriptive, symbolic, and substantive representation.

FORMAL REPRESENTATION:
REAPPORTIONMENT AND REDISTRICTING

. . . .

Formal representation is the authority to act in another's behalf, gained through an institutional arrangement such as elections. The essence of representation is that the representatives are authorized in advance to act in behalf of their constituents, who agree to be bound by the representatives' collective decisions. This idea of representation as a process requiring formal transfer of authority from many people to one delegate was a central part of Thomas Hobbes's conception of the state. In *Leviathan* (1651), Hobbes observed: "A multitude of men are made one person, when they are by one man, or one person, represented; so that it be done with the consent of every one of that multitude in particular." The covenant between the people and the person selected to act in their behalf was also central to a definition of representation articulated by Joseph Tussman in the twentieth century.

The essence of representation is the delegation or granting of authority. To authorize a representative is to grant another the right to act for oneself. Within the limits of the grant of authority one is, in fact, submitting himself in advance to the decision or will of another . . . .

The fact that our rulers are elected does not make them any less our rulers . . . . To say that we send our representatives to Congress is not to say that we have sent our servants to market. We have simply designated the person or persons to whose judgment or will we have subordinated ourselves. Nor does the fact that at a later date we must redesignate a representative alter the fact that an act of subordination has occurred.

Formal representation in the U.S. Congress is achieved through the apportionment of seats in the House of Representatives (each state is guaranteed one seat and additional seats are determined by population) and the Senate (each state gets two seats regardless of population) and the boundaries of House districts within each state. The Constitution directs that a national census be taken every ten years and that representatives in the House be apportioned among the states according to their respective populations. *Reapportionment* is the process of reallocating House seats on the basis of state populations after each census. *Redistricting* is the process of redrawing electoral district lines in those states that gained or lost seats in the reapportionment following the decennial census.

DESCRIPTIVE REPRESENTATION:
CONGRESS AS A MIRROR OF SOCIETY

. . . .

Descriptive representation is the extent to which representatives reflect the characteristics of the people they formally represent. It is measured by looking at qualities such as ethnic background, social class, education, sex, age, place of residence, religion, occupation, and similar characteristics. That is the meaning of representation implicit in John Adams's statement during the American Revolution that a representative legislature "should be an exact portrait, in miniature, of the people at large." Descriptive representation is also evident in Congressman (and later House Speaker) Jim Wright's description of Congress in 1964 as a "mirror of the people" — one which includes "just about the same percentage of saints and sinners, fools and geniuses, rogues and heroes as does the general populace."

Descriptive representation rests on a belief that how legislators behave is to some degree a product of who they are. As one legislator put it:

> Basically you represent the thinking of the people who have gone through what you have gone through and who are what you are. You vote according to that. In other words, if you come from a suburb you reflect the thinking of people in the suburbs, if you are of depressed people, you reflect that. You represent the sum total of your background.

. . . .

SYMBOLIC REPRESENTATION:
CONSTITUENTS' TRUST

A republican government rests on the confidence of the people. Federalists and Anti-Federalists disagreed on whether the structure of congressional representation would inspire this trust, but they agreed that the future of American government would depend on its ability to sustain the confidence of the governed. Trust is also central to the concept of symbolic representation; for the essence of symbolic representation is not what representatives are but what they are perceived to be by their constituents. Here is the way Hannah Pitkin describes symbolic representation:

> The crucial test of political representation (according to this definition) will be the existential one: Is the representative believed in? And the basis of such belief will seem irrational and affective because no rational justification of it is possible. Hence, political representation will not be an activity but a state of affairs, not an acting for others, but a "standing for"; so long as people accept or believe, the political leader represents them, by definition.

In Washington, senators and representatives can propose what David Mayhew calls a "purely symbolic congressional act" by introducing or voting for a bill or resolution "expressing an attitude by prescribing no policy effects. An example would be a resolution deploring communism or poverty." And "in a large class of legislative undertakings," Mayhew says, "the electoral payment is for positions rather than for effects." A common form of symbolic representation is for members to sponsor or cosponsor a bill, and thus gain credit for taking a position, even when they do not want or expect the bill to be passed. In fact, most bills introduced in Congress every term have so little support that even their sponsors do not expect them to become law. Why bother? Walter Oleszek points to a number of reasons why members sponsor legislation they know is doomed from the start — some of which illustrate symbolic representation:

> To go on record in support of a given proposal, to satisfy individual constituents or interest groups from the member's district or state, to convey a

message to executive agencies, to publicize an issue, to attract media attention, or to fend off criticism during political campaigns.

Once a member has introduced a bill, he or she can claim "action" on the issue and can blame the committee to which the bill has been referred for its failure to win enactment . . . .

In the district, symbolic representation is most likely to focus not on policy issues but rather on the qualities of the person chosen to represent the people in that district. "Most people get a gut feeling about the kind of human being they want to represent them," one House member observes. Another comments: "My constituents don't know how I vote, but they know me and they trust me . . . . They say to themselves, 'everything we know about him tells us he's up there doing a good job for us.' It's a blind faith type of thing." Richard Fenno found that constituents trusted a representative only when they were convinced that the representative was qualified for the job, identified with them, and understood and cared about their situation.

What is it about this type of representation in Washington and in the district that makes it symbolic representation? Pitkin says that symbols represent something by making it "present by their presence although it is not present in fact." This is the sense in which the flag is said to represent the entire nation or the president to represent the government. What, then, is "not present in fact" in the types of symbolic representation we have discussed? In the case of symbolic representation in Washington, the answer is policy. In the case of symbolic representation in the district, the answer seems to be the government, or more specifically, Congress. The discussion of Washington-style symbolic representation emphasized the separation between individual position-taking and the passing of legislation and the separation between policy enactment and policy implementation. By simply taking position on issues or by introducing or cosponsoring measures that will never pass, legislators are able to present the appearance of a policy that is in fact not there. The focus of home style is the individual not the institution. There is, in fact, an anti-Congress or antigovernment theme to much of that representation. Members are perceived as representatives to the government rather than representatives of the government. What is lacking in both types of symbolic representation, some would say, is a policy accountability that many consider the essence of representative democracy.

SUBSTANTIVE REPRESENTATION: DELEGATE OR TRUSTEE

. . . .

Hannah Pitkin's definition of substantive representation illustrates both how important and how complex this meaning of representation really is:

> Representing here means acting in the interest of the represented, in a manner responsive to them. The representative must act independently; his action must involve discretion and judgment, he must be the one who acts.
>
> The represented must also be (conceived as) capable of independent action and judgment, not merely being taken care of.
>
> And, despite the resulting potential for conflict between representative and represented about what is to be done, that conflict must not normally take place. The representative must act in such a way that there is no conflict or if it occurs an explanation is called for. He must not be found persistently at odds with the wishes of the represented without good reason in terms of their interest, without a good explanation of why their wishes are not in accord with their interest.

Notice how Pitkin distinguishes between constituents' wishes and interests in this definition, and how substantive representation calls for a reconciliation of any conflicts between these wishes and interests. That is just the beginning. The concept of substantive representation raises all sorts of conflicting views and competing principles about how constituencies are defined, the role of representatives in a national legislature, and the competing values of representation and deliberative policymaking . . . . Consider, for example, the distinction between constituents' interests and wishes. Members of Congress who attend to constituents' interests are said to be acting as *trustees*; those who respond to constituents' wishes are identified as *delegates*.

Acting as a trustee means that the representative votes for what he or she considers to be in the best interests of constituents, regardless of those constituents' own expressed preferences. Eighteenth-century British statesman Edmund Burke captures the essence of the trustee role when he said: "Your representative owes you, not his industry only, but his judgment; and he betrays, instead of serving you, if he sacrifices it to your opinion." Senators and representatives often echo Burke in explaining why they adopted a trustee perspective. West Virginia Senator Robert Byrd, for example, used some of Burke's words as well as his ideas two hundred years later in explaining his vote for the Panama Canal treaties during the Carter administration:

> There's no political mileage in voting for the treaties. I know what my constituents are saying. But I have a responsibility not only to follow them, but to inform them and lead them. I'm not going to betray my responsibility to my constituents. I owe them not only my industry but my judgment. That's why they send me here.

. . . .

Not everyone believes that a good representative must be a trustee. "What snarls up the system," a congressman once complained, "is these so-called statesmen-congressmen who vote for what they think is the country's best interest." He had a decidedly different view of the representative's job: "I'm here to represent my district. This is part of my actual belief as to the function of a congressman. What is good for the majority of districts is good for the country." The delegate role stands in sharp contrast to that of trustee. Instead of looking to one's own judgment and conscience, a delegate is expected to vote in accordance with majority opinion in his or her constituency. "Damn it, home comes first," is the way one representative put it. A nineteenth-century political essayist provided a clear picture of the delegate role. "A representative is but the mouthpiece and organ of his constituents. What we want in legislation as in other trusts, are honest fiduciaries, men who will perform their duties according to our wishes."

These conflicting ideas about whether representatives should be trustees or delegates also raise questions about formal representation as well, particularly whether constituencies are defined as cities and towns, states, a corporate "people," or individual citizens. The extent to which representatives see themselves as delegates or trustees is also important in judgments about the ability of Congress to identify and work toward a national interest or a common good. Indeed, the whole idea of Congress as a deliberative policymaker requires legislators to be open to the arguments of their colleagues rather than simply recording the views of their constituency.

In what sense might there be less here than meets the eye in this distinction between the representative roles of trustee and delegate? Most members of Congress are not one or the other; they are not always a delegate or always a trustee, they are both. They will follow what they see as the wishes of a majority of constituents on some issues but rely on their own judgment about long-term constituency and national interests on other issues. Sometimes they know how a majority of constituents wants them to vote, but most of the time they do not. And there would be no point in members putting in the long hours of Washington work . . . unless it provided them with information and insights beyond those of most constituents.

NOTES AND QUESTIONS

1. Wouldn't legislators be best described as agents of their political parties? *See* HANNAH FENICHEL PITKIN, THE CONCEPT OF REPRESENTATION 83, 291–92 (1967).

2. The Equal Protection Clause of the U.S. Constitution speaks to the issue of how constituencies are defined:

a. Apportionment of the U. S. House of Representatives is subject to a strict equipopulation principle in drawing districts. Even a minor deviation in population between the largest and smallest districts shifts the burden of proof to the state to justify a disparity by a particularized state interest such as compactness, respecting municipal or county boundaries, preserving the core of prior districts, or avoiding conflict between incumbents. *Karcher v. Daggett*, 462 U.S. 725 (1983) (invalidating a 0.1384% population disparity); *Vieth v. Pennsylvania*, 195 F. Supp. 2d 672 (M.D. Pa. 2002) (invalidating 19 person deviation where it was possible to draw a district map with zero deviation).

b. Should a different standard be applied to the apportionment of state legislatures based on a policy of respecting the boundaries of political subdivisions? *Mahan v. Howell*, 410 U.S. 315 (1973) (sustaining 16.4% deviation from the ideal district population).

c. The Board of Estimate of New York City exercised authority to modify and approve the city's capital expense budget, over zoning and planning, city property, city contracts, and salaries of city officers and personnel. Each of the city's five boroughs was entitled to a seat on the board. The population disparity between the largest and smallest boroughs was 78%. What result in the face of a challenge based on the equipopulation principle? *Board of Estimate v. Morris*, 489 U.S. 688 (1989).

3. Which concepts of representation are at play in these cases? In the provision of the U.S. Constitution assigning two senators to each state?

4. Should the equipopulation principle apply to elective judicial districts? In the leading case, a three judge panel observed that "the rationale behind the one-man, one-vote principle, which evolved out of efforts to preserve a truly representative form of government, is simply not relevant to the makeup of the judiciary" since "judges . . . are not representatives in the same sense as are legislators on the executive. Their function is to administer the law, not to espouse the cause of a particular constituency." *Wells v. Edwards*, 347 F. Supp. 453, 455–56 (1972), *aff'd*, 409 U.S. 1095 (1973).

5. During a primary contest for City Council in New York City, a black challenger accused a black incumbent of favoring Jewish organizations in the district. In another district, a black candidate complained that she was being judged by whether she is light or dark skinned and by whether she is American-born or of West Indian heritage. A black challenger in a district currently represented by an incumbent white Jewish female asserted that "The laws of nature require that if a people are a dominant group, that the political representation reflect that." Steven Roberts, *In Some Council Races, It's Still Us Against Them*, N.Y. TIMES, Sept. 2, 1991, at 21, 24. What views of representation are reflected in these various assertions?

6. Would you feel comfortable arguing in court that a certain legislator's views ought to be either given weight or disregarded because of that legislator's ethnicity, color, creed, gender, or sexual orientation? Would your answer differ if you were engaged in debate in a legislative body? Testifying before a legislative committee?

7. One commentator asserted that "in every apportionment rule there lurked an implicit theory of representation . . . ." ABIGAIL J. THERNSTROM, WHOSE VOTES COUNT? 64 (1987).

Under the Voting Rights Act, as amended in 1982, certain states are required to obtain federal approval for redistricting plans for state legislative and congressional district boundaries. Section 2 of the Voting Rights Act provides as follows:

> Sec. 2 (a) No voting qualification or prerequisite to voting or standard, practice, or procedure shall be imposed or applied by any State or political subdivision in a manner which results in a denial or abridgement of the right of any citizen of the United States to vote on account of race or color, or in contravention of the guarantees set forth in section 4(f)(2), as provided in subsection (b).
>
> (b) A violation of subsection (a) is established if, based on the totality of circumstances, it is shown that the political processes leading to nomination or election in the State or political subdivision are not equally open to participation by members of a class of citizens protected by subsection (a) in that its members have less opportunity than other members of the electorate to participate in the political process and to elect representatives of their choice. The extent to which members of a protected class have been elected to office in the State or political subdivision is one circumstance which may be considered: Provided, That nothing in this section establishes a right to have members of a protected class elected in numbers equal to their proportion in the population.

42 U.S.C. § 1973.

What implicit theory of representation lurks within this section of the Voting Rights Act?

8. In *Chisom v. Roemer*, 501 U.S. 380 (1991), the Supreme Court interpreted the term "representatives" in § 1973(b) of the Voting Rights Act to include judicial elections. In so doing, the Court made the following observations:

> Respondents argue . . . that the term "representatives" was used to extend § 2 coverage to executive officials, but not to judges. We think, however, that the better reading of the word "representatives" describes the winners of representative, popular elections. If executive officers, such as prosecutors, sheriffs, state attorney generals, and state treasurers, can be considered "representatives" simply because they are chosen by popular election, then the same reasoning should apply to elected judges . . . .
>
> . . . Moreover, this Court has recently recognized that judges do engage in policymaking at some level. *See Gregory v. Ashcroft*, 501 U.S. 452, 466–467 (1991) ("It may be sufficient that the appointee is in a position requiring the exercise of discretion concerning issues of public importance. This certainly describes the bench, regardless of whether judges might be considered policymakers in the same sense as the executive or legislature."). A judge brings to his or her job of interpreting texts "a well-considered judgment of what is best for the community." *Id.*, at 466. As the concurrence notes, Justice Holmes and Justice Cardozo each wrote eloquently about the "policymaking nature of the judicial function." *Id.*, at 482 (WHITE, J., concurring in part, dissenting in part, and concurring in judgment).

Is *Wells v. Edwards*, *supra* Note 4 wrongly decided?

9. A candidate for elective judicial office in Minnesota challenged a provision of the state code of judicial conduct that barred him from "announcing" his views on disputed legal or political issues. In striking down the ban on First Amendment grounds, Justice Scalia made the following counterargument:

> But in any case, Justice Ginsburg greatly exaggerates the difference between judicial and legislative elections. She asserts that "the rationale underlying unconstrained speech in elections for political office — that representative

government depends on the public's ability to choose agents who will act at its behest — does not carry over to campaigns for the bench." This complete separation of the judiciary from the enterprise of "representative government" might have some truth in those countries where judges neither make law themselves nor set aside the laws enacted by the legislature. It is not a true picture of the American system. Not only do state-court judges possess the power to "make" common laws, but they have the immense power to shape the States' constitutions as well. *See, e.g., Baker v. State*, 170 Vt. 194, 744 A.2d 864 (1999). Which is precisely why the election of state judges became popular.

Republican Party of Minnesota v. White, 536 U.S. 765, 784 (2002).

2. Limitations on Representation

The Legislative branch of the Federal Government has evolved, unconstrained by any limitations imposed by the Constitution, into a complex, well paid full-time institution with ample staff and support resources. Most legislative bodies in the United States, however, embody a different ideal, that of the "citizen legislator" particularly at the level of local government. *See generally* Jon C. Teaford, *Local Legislative Institutions*, 1 ENCYCLOPEDIA OF THE AMERICAN LEGISLATIVE SYSTEM 233–47 (Joel H. Sibley, ed., 1994). In many states, the state constitution contains provisions designed to implement the citizen legislator concept by constraining the length of sessions, fixing low levels of pay, and imposing term limits.

The question of eligibility for office was much debated during the period from 1776 to 1787. The "radical" Pennsylvania Constitution of 1776, for example, mandated both annual elections and that "no person shall be capable of being elected a member to serve in the house of representatives of the freemen of this commonwealth more than four years in seven." Pa. Const. § 8 (1776). The principle of rotation in office was, however, not adopted by the Framers of the Federal Constitution — a decision which was attacked by Antifederalists. GORDON S. WOOD, THE CREATION OF THE AMERICAN REPUBLIC 521–22 (1972).

A constitutional initiative, approved by California voters in 1990, returned these issues to the forefront of the political agenda.

CALIFORNIA CONSTITUTION

Article IV Legislative

1.5 Incumbency powers: restrictions

Sec. 1.5. The people find and declare that the Founding Fathers established a system of representative government based upon free, fair, and competitive elections. The increased concentration of political power in the hands of incumbent representatives has made our electoral system less free, less competitive, and less representative.

The ability of legislators to serve unlimited number of terms, to establish their own retirement system, and to pay for staff and support services at state expense contribute heavily to the extremely high number of incumbents who are reelected. These unfair incumbent advantages discourage qualified candidates from seeking public office and create a class of career politicians, instead of the citizen representatives envisioned by the Founding Fathers. These career politicians become representatives of the bureaucracy, rather than of the people whom they are elected to represent.

To restore a free and democratic system of fair elections, and to encourage qualified candidates to seek public office, the people find and declare that the powers of incumbency must be limited. Retirement benefits must be restricted, state-financed incumbent staff and support services limited, and limitations placed upon the number of terms which may be served.

2. Senate and Assembly; membership; terms

Sec. 2. (a) The Senate has a membership of 40 Senators elected for 4-year terms, 20 to begin every 2 years. *No Senator may serve more than 2 terms.*

The Assembly has a membership of 80 members elected for 2-year terms. *No member of the Assembly may serve more than 3 terms.*

Their terms shall commence on the first Monday in December next following their election.

(b) Election of members of the Assembly shall be on the first Tuesday after the first Monday in November of even-numbered years unless otherwise prescribed by the Legislature. Senators shall be elected at the same time and places as members of the Assembly.

(c) A person is ineligible to be a member of the Legislature unless the person is an elector and has been a resident of the legislative district for one year, and a citizen of the United States and a resident of California for 3 years, immediately preceding the election.

(d) When a vacancy occurs in the Legislature the Governor immediately shall call an election to fill the vacancy.

7. 5. Compensation. Operating expenses and equipment; spending limits

Sec. 7.5. In the fiscal year immediately following the adoption of this Act, the total aggregate expenditures of the Legislature for the compensation of members and employees of, and the operating expenses and equipment for, the Legislature may not exceed an amount equal to nine hundred fifty thousand dollars ($950,000) per member for that fiscal year or 80 percent of the amount of money expended for those purposes in the preceding fiscal year, whichever is less. For each fiscal year thereafter, the total aggregate expenditures may not exceed an amount equal to that expended for those purposes in the preceding fiscal year, adjusted and compounded by an amount equal to the percentage increase in the appropriations limit for the state established pursuant to Article XIII B.

Article V. Executive

2. Governor; term; qualifications; other offices

Sec. 2. The Governor shall be elected every fourth year at the same time and places as members of the Assembly and hold office from the Monday after January 1 following the election until a successor qualifies. The Governor shall be an elector who has been a citizen of the United States and a resident of this State for 5 years immediately preceding the Governor's election. The Governor may not hold other public office. *No Governor may serve more than 2 terms.*

11. Election of lieutenant governor and other constitutional officers; term limits

Sec. 11. The Lieutenant Governor, Attorney General, Controller, Secretary of State, and Treasurer shall be elected at the same time and places and for the same term as the Governor. *No Lieutenant Governor, Attorney General, Controller, Secretary of State, or Treasurer may serve in the same office for more than 2 terms.*

LEGISLATURE OF THE STATE OF CALIFORNIA v. EU
816 P.2d 1309 (Cal. 1991)

LUCAS, CHIEF JUSTICE.

In this proceeding, we consider constitutional challenges to an initiative measure adopted at the November 6, 1990, General Election. This measure, entitled by its framers "The Political Reform Act of 1990," was designated on the ballot as Proposition 140. Its stated purpose is to "restore a free and democratic system of fair elections, and to encourage qualified candidates to seek public office" by limiting "the powers of incumbency." (Cal. Const., art. IV, § 1.5, added by Prop. 140.) The measure seeks to accomplish these goals by these three separate reforms: "Retirement benefits [of legislators] must be restricted, state-financed incumbent staff and support services limited, and limitations placed upon the number of terms which may be served." (*Ibid.*) . . . .

II

Discussion

A. Lifetime Ban or Limit on Consecutive Terms

As a preliminary matter, we must address the interpretive question whether Proposition 140 imposes a "lifetime ban" on officers who have served the specified number of terms, or merely limits the number of *consecutive* terms they may serve. With respect to state legislators, petitioners and intervener assume that once a legislator has served the prescribed maximum number of terms, the measure would forever bar him or her from running for a seat in the legislative house previously served. Respondent Secretary of State contends, however, that the term limitation "is directed only at the *incumbent office holder.*" (Italics in original.) In her view, the measure simply limits the number of consecutive terms served, and she suggests that a former legislator might run for a new term of office if he or she is not currently holding that office.

. . . .

We conclude that Proposition 140's term limitations extend over the lifetime of each affected office holder.

B. Lifetime Ban or Limit on Consecutive Terms

1. Character and Extent of Injury to Protected Rights

Two important rights are affected by Proposition 140, namely, the incumbent's right to run for public office, and the voter's right to reelect the incumbent to that office. Consequently, the "injury" to those rights resulting from the application of Proposition 140 is also twofold, namely, lifetime exclusion of the incumbent from the office previously held, and a corresponding permanent inability of the voters to return the incumbent to that office.

a. Effect on Candidates

As previously explained, Proposition 140 imposes a lifetime ban on legislators once they have completed the maximum number of terms. Petitioners argue, "In the long run, the term limitations permanently ban those who are arguably the most qualified candidates — incumbents with the experience and expertise in the legislative process necessary to the most effective representation of their constituencies." According to petitioners, qualified incumbents will be "purged" solely to seat "massive numbers" of inexperienced "newcomers." Petitioners predict that only a few qualified persons will be attracted to short term public office.

Respondents, of course, dispute petitioners' premise that long-term legislators are inevitably better qualified than other candidates, and they believe that term limitations will encourage, rather than inhibit, new qualified candidates seeking short term public service. They characterize the term limitations of Proposition 140 as additional candidacy requirements, akin to age, integrity, training or residency, which have generally been upheld . . . .

Respondents also stress three features of Proposition 140 that assertedly serve to mitigate the severity of its lifetime ban: First, the effected incumbent is not barred from seeking any other public office, including a seat in another legislative house or a statewide constitutional office. A former Senator may seek a seat in the Assembly, and vice versa. Second, the term limitations arise only after the incumbent already has had the opportunity to serve a significant period in office (i.e., eight years for a Senator, and six years for a member of the Assembly). Finally, the term limitations are generally applicable to persons elected or appointed on or after November 6, 1990. Except for some incumbent Senators, past terms served do not count in calculating the limitation. Thus, by the time the term limitations of Proposition 140 come into play, the incumbent will have already served, and indeed may continue to serve, several terms in public office.

b. Effect on Voters

Petitioners also stress the impact on the voters who are prevented from casting their ballots for the particular candidate of their choice. Just as incumbent legislators are permanently barred from running for another term once they have served the prescribed numbers of terms, the voters are permanently barred from voting for such persons, at least for the legislative office they once held. According to petitioners, the voters thus will be denied the right to vote for those persons who arguably possess the best qualifications.

Additionally, petitioners note that because Proposition 140 was adopted on a statewide basis, "the disability [on candidates and voters] is imposed not by those who have the right to vote for the candidate, but rather by those outside the district." Petitioners thus suggest the resulting impact on or injury to the voters is aggravated or enhanced by reason of the ability of voters residing outside a particular voting district to essentially "veto" particular candidates within that district.

Respondents reply by citing federal court cases (e.g., *Burdick v. Takushi, supra*, 927 F.2d 469, 473–474) stating that voters have no constitutional right to vote for particular candidates. Additionally, respondents observe that the challenged measure does not fall into any of the categories of prior cases in which the right to vote was found impermissibly infringed. No identifiable groups of voters are excluded from voting or otherwise unduly burdened in the exercise of their franchise. Characterizing the term limitations of Proposition 140 as additional candidacy qualifications akin to age or residency, respondents submit that Proposition 140 does not truly impair the franchise, for the voters retain the basic fundamental right to cast their ballots for the *qualified* candidate of their choice.

Moreover, respondents observe that neither voter choice nor candidate eligibility is restricted based on the content of protected expression, political affiliation, or inherently arbitrary factors such as race, religion or sex. The only criterion used is incumbency. Voters retain the ability to vote for any qualified candidate holding the beliefs or possessing the attributes they may desire in a public officeholder. Under these circumstances, First Amendment protection of political expression and promotion of the marketplace for ideas continue unabated.

Respondents further note that petitioners have cited no case supporting their theory that a voting restriction on "local" offices would be invalid if imposed by voters on a statewide basis. Indeed, such a rule would seemingly call in question any statewide legislation affecting the qualification of candidates for local elections, such as age or residency requirements.

Finally, respondents suggest that because Proposition 140 was an initiative measure adopted by the people at a statewide election, any resulting injury to the exercise of the franchise should be deemed self-inflicted, and thus not constitutionally protected.

c. Summary of Impact on Candidates and Voters

In sum, although Proposition 140 does affect the rights of voters and candidates to a degree, there are several mitigating aspects, including the voters' continued right to vote for any qualified candidates, as well as the candidates' ability to run for other public offices, their entitlement to a significant period of service in office before the term limitations apply, and the "prospective" application of the limitation provision. Additionally, we should bear in mind that it is presently unclear under federal law whether and to what extent voters retain a constitutional right to vote for particular candidates such as the incumbent legislators affected by the challenged measure. Thus, the legal impact of Proposition 140 on the voters remains uncertain.

Having discussed the extent of the "asserted injury to the rights protected" (*Anderson v. Celebrezze, supra*, 460 U.S. at p. 789), we next analyze the "precise interests put forward by the State as justifications for the burden imposed by its rule" (*ibid.*).

2. The Interests of the State

Balanced against the foregoing negative impact on candidates and voters flowing from the challenged measure are the considerable state interests assertedly promoted thereby. In the words of new article IV, section 1.5, of the state Constitution, term limitations are deemed necessary to restore "free, fair, and competitive elections," to "encourage qualified candidates to seek public office," and to eliminate "unfair incumbent advantages" that have resulted in an "extremely high number of incumbents" and created "a class of career politicians" instead of the "citizen representatives envisioned by the Founding Fathers."

According to respondents, the state's interest in limiting incumbency should support measures considerably stronger than a mere temporary disability from holding office. As respondents argue, the state's strong interests in protecting against an entrenched, dynastic legislative bureaucracy, and in thereby encouraging new candidates to seek public office, are both legitimate and compelling ones that support a lifetime ban from the office and outweigh any interest in incumbent legislators, or the voting public, may have in perpetuating the incumbents' positions of control.

The legitimacy of the foregoing asserted state interests in limiting incumbency are well recognized in analogous contexts. As stated by the West Virginia Supreme Court of Appeals in rejecting a similar challenge to a state constitutional amendment limiting the right of the Governor to seek a third consecutive term, "Constitutional restrictions circumscribing the ability of incumbents to succeed themselves appear in over twenty state constitutions, and exist in the Twenty-second Amendment to the Constitution of the United States with regard to the Presidency. The universal authority is that restriction upon the succession of incumbents serves a rational public policy and that, while restrictions may deny qualified men an opportunity to serve, as a general rule the over-all health of the body politic is enhanced by limitations on continuous tenure. [Citations and fn. Omitted]." (*State ex rel. Maloney v. McCartney* (1976) 159 W. Va. 513, 223 S.E.2d 607, 611 [hereafter *Maloney*], *app. dism. sub nom. Moore v. McCartney* (1976) 425 U.S. 946, . . . ; Chemerinsky, *Protecting the Democratic Process: Voter Standing to Challenge Abuses of Incumbency* (1988) 49 Ohio St. L.J. 773 et seq.; Tribe, American Constitutional Law (2d ed. 1988) §§ 13–18, at p. 1097 ["Democracy envisions rule by successive temporary majorities. The capacity to displace incumbents in favor of the representatives of a recently coalesced majority is, therefore, an essential attribute of the election system in a democratic republic."]; cf. Annot. (1958) 59 A.L.R.2d 716 [construction and effect of incumbency limitation laws].)

The *Maloney* decision continues by describing at length the substantial reasons for limiting the right of incumbents to succeed themselves. These include "The power of incumbent officeholders to develop networks of patronage and attendant capacities to deliver favorably disposed voters to the polls," "fears of an entrenched political machine which could effectively foreclose access to the political process," and the belief that regularly disrupting those "machines" "would stimulate criticism within political parties" and "insure a meaningful, adversary, and competitive election." (223 S.E.2d at p. 611.)

In addition, *Maloney* explains that "it has long been felt that a limitation upon succession of incumbents removes the temptation to prostitute the government to the perpetuation of a particular administration. [Citation.] . . . Meretricious policies which sacrifice the well-being of economic, social, racial, or geographic minorities are most likely where a political figure, political party, or political interest group can rely upon electorate inertia fostered by the hopelessness of encountering a seemingly invincible political machine." (223 S.E.2d at pp. 611–612.)

Petitioners observe that *Maloney* involved a limitation on *consecutive* terms of a *Governor*, rather than a lifetime ban on incumbent legislators. They suggest that term limitations on the executive branch are justified by the need to check the substantial concentration of power that the chief executive possesses, a consideration assertedly not applicable to the legislative branch. But we think that many, if not all, of the considerations mentioned in *Maloney* (e.g., eliminating unfair incumbent advantages, dislodging entrenched political machines, restoring open access to the political process, and stimulating electorate participation) would apply with equal force to the legislative branch.

. . . .

3. Necessity of Imposing Restrictions

We turn next to the "necessity" of imposing the restrictions of Proposition 140 on the dual rights at issue here (see *Anderson v. Celebrezze, supra*, 460 U.S. at 789–790). Petitioners contend that a lifetime ban on candidacy was unnecessary and that other less "drastic" alternatives, such as a limitation on consecutive terms, together with additional restrictions on campaign contributions to legislators, decreased fringe and pension benefits, and additional incentives for early retirement, would have been sufficient to promote and accomplish the state interests previously discussed.

As will appear, we conclude that the less drastic alternatives suggested by petitioners would have been inadequate to accomplish the declared purpose of Proposition 140 to eliminate the "class of career politicians" that assertedly had been created by virtue of the "unfair incumbent advantages" referred to in that measure. (Cal. Const., art. IV, § 1.5.)

Respondents stress the substantial advantages incumbent legislators enjoy in this state, advantages that permitted 92 percent of all incumbents to win reelection at this state's November 1990 General Election. Indeed, respondents note that nine of these incumbents ran unopposed.

Respondents seem correct in this regard. Whether by reason of superior fund raising ability, greater media coverage, larger and more experienced staffs, greater name recognition among the voters, favorably drawn voting districts, or other factors, incumbents do indeed appear to enjoy considerable advantages over other candidates. (See *Service Employees v. Fair Political Practices* (E.D. Cal. 1990) 747 F. Supp. 580, 588; *Watson v. Fair Political Practices Com.* (1990) 217 Cal. App. 3d 1059, 1074, & fn. 13, 266 Cal. Rptr. 408.) As Proposition 140's introductory statement indicates, the framers of the measure believed these substantial advantages of incumbency were unfair to other candidates and tended to create "a class of career politicians, instead of the citizen representatives envisioned by the Founding Fathers." (Cal. Const., art. IV, § 1.5.)

Petitioners suggest that a more reasonable alternative existed to the measure's lifetime ban: disqualification of the incumbent for the forthcoming term, thus "forcing the legislator to take one term off, before being eligible to run for the body." Yet, as respondents observe, the framers reasonably concluded that a lifetime ban was necessary to assure that a former office holder could not reinvoke at least some of the advantages of incumbency to gain reelection after leaving office for a term or more.

Additionally, we believe the framers might well have reasonably concluded that a mere ban on consecutive terms could encourage popular "career politicians" to trade terms with each other, or to attempt to arrange for a "caretaker" candidate, such as a spouse or relative, to hold office for them during the interrupted term. For example, when in 1966 George Wallace became legally ineligible to run for reelection as Governor of Alabama because of state term limitations applicable to that office, his wife Lurleen successfully ran in his place, and served as Governor until her death in 1968. George Wallace was reelected as Governor in 1970 and again in 1974. (See 12 THE NEW ENCYCLOPEDIA BRITANNICA, MICROPAEDIA (15th ed. 1990) Wallace, George C. at p. 467.)

Realistically, only a lifetime ban could protect against various kinds of continued exploitation of the "advantages of incumbency" captured through past terms in office. The remainder of petitioners' suggested "alternatives" essentially involve narrow changes in the system of providing contributions or compensation for legislators, changes that would afford "career politicians" with independent resources little incentive to voluntarily terminate public service.

4. Conclusion

On balance, we conclude the interests of the state in incumbency reform outweigh any injury to incumbent office holders and those who would vote for them . . . .

NOTES AND QUESTIONS

1. A study of turnover in state legislatures finds that "27% of all the state legislators initially elected to the lower chambers for the 1979–1980 term were still serving in that chamber 12 years later." The retention rate in the upper chamber at the end of twelve years is 33.6%. Gary F. Moncrief, Joel A. Thompson, Michael Haddon & Norman R. Hoyer, *For Whom the Bell Tolls: Term Limits and State Legislatures*, 17 LEGIS. STUD. Q. 37, 39–42 (1992). A substantial number of state legislators (one-half in the lower chamber and one-third in the upper chamber) leave by the fifth and sixth years in office. Professor Luttbeg's data indicates that state legislative careers are typically brief, that incumbency in office "[l]ittle influences the ease of reelection," and that voluntary retirement is common. Norman R. Luttbeg, *Legislative Careers in Six States: Some Legislatures More Likely to be Responsive?*, 17 LEGIS. STUD. Q. 49, 63 (1992). Do these studies suggest that the problem identified by the proponents of Proposition 140 is overblown?

The article by Moncrief et al. indicates that term limitations may impact primarily on legislative leaders, thus reducing the expertise and experience of the legislature as an institution. *Id.* at 44. Is Proposition 140 better viewed as an attack on the seniority system?

2. The California legislature has been viewed as a model professional legislature. One study concludes that "the California legislature must be placed in the front rank among the world's lawmaking assemblies for its ability to recognize problems and to mobilize support around their solution." WILLIAM K. MUIR, JR., LEGISLATURE: CALIFORNIA'S SCHOOL FOR POLITICS 202 (1982).

The hallmarks of the California model for legislative reform are a nonpartisan staff, a specialized committee system, and an internal set of procedures designed to make legislators accountable for the long-run consequences of legislative action. Why did the California electorate seek to dismantle an institution regarded as a paradigm of rational, deliberative decisionmaking?

One explanation is that divided government, negative campaigning, and recurring scandal have undermined whatever positives legislative reform may have generated in the public mind. Alan Ehrenhalt, *An Embattled Institution*, GOVERNING, Jan. 1992, at 28, 31.

3. Is it possible that strengthening the state legislature as an institution might make officeholding too desirable and too satisfying for incumbents? That it might induce legislators to orient their activities toward raising money to secure reelection rather than toward making good public policy? That legislators seeking leadership positions would complete for support based on their skill in raising funds for their supporters? *See* Alan Rosenthal, *The Legislative Institution; Transformed and at Risk, in* THE STATE OF THE STATES 69 (Carl E. Van Horn ed. 1989).

4. Knowledge and experience are important power bases. Would term limits shift power from elected legislators to legislative staff? From the legislative branch to the executive branch?

5. Budget reductions impair the legislature's ability to gather policy-relevant information from internal sources. Do the budget limits contained in Article IV, § 7.5 shift power from staff to lobbyists? Will the legislature become more dependent on information screened and vetted by the executive branch?

6. Isn't the correct inference from a 95% reelection rate that "the political process is working and that officeholders are conforming to the wishes of their constituents"? Robert S. Barro, *A Free Marketeer's Case Against Term Limits*, WALL ST. J. Dec. 24, 1991, p. 8, cols. 3–6. The author, an economist, is puzzled that those who espouse free markets in economics advocate term limits. Do term limits cast doubt upon the capability of voters to act in their own best interest when making political choices — "an argument which, if true, would mean that democracy is seriously flawed . . . ." *Id.* How would Professor Barro meet the counterargument that Proposition 140 itself is a product of the free market in ideas spawned by the initiative process?

7. Some states' constitutions seek to implement the citizen legislature concept by providing for low, per diem legislative salaries and by limiting the length of legislative sessions. Are these more desirable solutions than term limits? Would you recommend that these policies be included in the California Constitution? *See Eberle v. Nielson*, 78 Idaho 572, 306 P.2d 1083 (1957).

8. Is Justice Mosk correct when he asserts in his omitted dissenting opinion that an initiative proposition which would affect the judiciary in the same way as Proposition 140 impacted the legislature would have been struck down as an unconstitutional revision of the California Constitution?

9. Rule 14, paragraph 6 of the U.S. House Republican Conference limits a Member to three consecutive two year terms (6 years):

> as Chairman or Ranking Member of a standing, select, joint, or ad hoc Committee or Subcommittee beginning with the 104th Congress.

Is this approach preferable to a constitutional amendment like the one enacted in California?

10. As of 2002, 17 states have placed term limits on their state legislatures. California and five other states (Arkansas, Michigan, Missouri, Nevada, and Oklahoma) impose lifetime bans. Arizona, Colorado, Florida, Louisiana, Maine, Montana, Nebraska, Ohio, South Dakota, Utah, and Wyoming assure rotation in office by banning consecutive terms. ALAN ROSENTHAL, BURDETT A. LOOMIS, JOHN R. HIBBING & KARL T. KURTZ, REPUBLIC ON TRIAL 168–69 (2003).

For further information on this and other issues concerning state legislatures, consult the website of the National Conference of State Legislatures, www.ncsl.org.

11. For further discussion, see, generally, JOHN M. CAREY, RICHARD G. NIEMI & LYNDA W. POWELL, TERM LIMITS IN STATE LEGISLATURES (2000); GERALD BENJAMIN & MICHAEL J. MALBIN, EDS., LIMITING LEGISLATIVE TERMS (1992).

3. Direct Democracy: The Initiative, Referendum, and Recall

The initiative allows voters to propose a legislative measure (statutory initiative) or a constitutional amendment (constitutional initiative) by filing a petition bearing a required number of citizen signatures.

The referendum refers a proposed or existing law or statute to voters for their approval or rejection . . . . Measures referred by legislatures (statutes, constitutional amendments, bonds, or advisory questions) are the most common ballot proposition. A popular or petition referendum . . . refers an already enacted measure to the voters before it can go into effect . . . .

Recall is a procedural device that allows voters to discharge and replace a public official.

THOMAS E. CRONIN, DIRECT DEMOCRACY 2, 125 (1989).

All three devices are traceable to the political agenda of the Populist and Progressive movements of the late nineteenth and early twentieth century. *See* People's Party Platform of 1892, *reprinted in* DANIEL J. BOORSTIN, ED., AN AMERICAN PRIMER 539–40 (1966). *See generally* RICHARD N. HOFSTADTER, THE AGE OF REFORM (1955); WILLIAM B. MUNRO, ED., THE INITIATIVE, REFERENDUM, AND RECALL (1912). These procedures reflect the same public distrust of representative democracy which inform the citizen legislature concept treated in the previous section. Each procedure is unknown to the national government, although each is afforded to citizens at the state or local government level in a majority of states. CRONIN, *supra* 51, 126–27.

The proponents of direct democracy claim the following benefits flow from their adoption:

Citizen initiatives will promote government responsiveness and accountability. If officials ignore the voice of the people, the people will have an available means to make needed law.

Initiatives are freer from special interest domination than the legislative branches of most states, and so provide a desirable safeguard that can be called into use when legislators are corrupt, irresponsible, or dominated by privileged special interests.

The initiative and referendum will produce open, educational debate on critical issues that otherwise might be inadequately discussed.

Referendum, initiative, and recall are nonviolent means of political participation that fulfill a citizen's right to petition the government for redress of grievances.

Direct democracy increases voters' interest and election-day turnout. Perhaps, too, giving the citizen more of a role in governmental processes might lessen alienation and apathy.

Finally (although this hardly exhausts the claims), citizen initiatives are needed because legislators often evade the tough issues. Fearing to be ahead of their time, they frequently adopt a zero-risk mentality. Concern with staying in office often makes them timid and perhaps too wedded to the status quo. One result is that controversial social issues frequently have to be resolved in the judicial branch. But who elected the judges?

CRONIN, *supra*, at 10–11. Based on your understanding of the legislature as an institution and the concepts of representation, what are the counterarguments against the initiative? the referendum? recall?

LUKER v. CURTIS
136 P.2d 978 (Idaho 1943)

AILSHIE, JUSTICE

This is an original proceeding for a writ of prohibition, restraining defendant, as Secretary of State, from publishing in the session laws of the twenty-seventh legislative session, H.B. No. 74, passed by the twenty-seventh legislative session, which act purports to repeal the "Senior Citizens' Grant Act," initiated by the people and approved and passed by vote of the people at the general election of November, 1942 . . . .

Now, passing to the question as to the power of the legislature to repeal an initiative act adopted by popular vote, we must examine the provisions of the constitution, see. 1, art. III, which provides as follows:

Sec. 1. *Legislative power — Enacting clause — Referendum — Initiative. —* The legislative power of the state shall be vested in a senate and a house of representatives. The enacting clause of every bill shall be as follows: "Be it enacted by the Legislature of the State of Idaho."

The people reserve to themselves the power to approve or reject at the polls any act or measure passed by the legislature. This power is known as the referendum, and legal voters may, under such conditions and in such manner as may be provided by acts of the legislature, demand a referendum vote on any act or measure passed by the legislature and cause the same to be submitted to a vote of the people for their approval or rejection.

The people reserve to themselves the power to propose laws, and enact the same at the polls independent of the legislature. This power is known as the initiative, and legal voters may, under conditions and in such manner as may be provided by acts of the legislature, initiate any desired legislation and cause the same to be submitted to the vote of the people at a general election for their approval or rejection provided that legislation thus submitted shall require the approval of a number of voters equal to a majority of the aggregate vote cast for the office of governor at such general election to be adopted.

The italicized portion of the foregoing, being the initiative clause, was adopted in 1912 (1913 Sess. Laws, Amendment No. 16, p. 675). Acting under procedures prescribed by the legislature (1933 Session Laws, chap. 210 p. 431), the requisite number of electors initiated an act designated and known as the "Senior Citizens' Grants Act," which was submitted to and adopted by the voters at the November, 1942, election. The act was certified as passed and, by the Governor, declared in force November 23, 1942. The legislature, which convened in January, 1943, by H.B. No. 74, repealed the "Senior Citizens' Grants Act."

In the first place, let it be noted, the initiative provision of the constitution places no limitation whatever on the power of amendment or repeal of an initiative act.

This power of legislation, reclaimed by the people through the medium of the amendment to the constitution, did not give any more force or effect to initiative legislation than to legislative acts but placed them on an equal footing. The power to thus legislate is derived from the same source and, when exercised through one method of legislation, it is asserted, is just as binding and efficient as if accomplished by the other method; that the legislative will and result is as validly consummated the one way as the other.

It is contended, however, that the legislature has no power or authority to amend or repeal an *initiative act,* for the alleged reason that an initiative act comes directly from the people. That may very well be answered by the fact that the legislators, who convene on the first Monday of January, following adoption of initiative measure, also come direct from the people, having been elected at the same time and by the same electors who adopted the initiative measure. If the legislature repeals or amends an initiative act, the people have at least two remedies, both of which they may exercise at the same time, to redress their grievance, if indeed they have a grievance, over the act of the legislature: First, they may reenact the measure by another initiative and, second, at the same time ad at the same election, may elect other members of the legislature who will, or may, better heed their wishes.

The enactment of law by the legislature takes a very different course from enactment by initiative. In the legislature, a Bill must be introduced, printed, read on three several days; and the members thereby have an opportunity of debating the act and offering and making amendments so that the law, if on a controversial subject, is ordinarily much discussed and analyzed. On the other hand, an initiative measure is drafted by a single person, or group of persons (*Wallace v. Zinman*, 200 Cal. 585, 254 P. 946, 62 A.L.R. 1341, 1345), and after it is circulated and filed, there is no opportunity for amendment or change until after it is voted upon. Indeed, the public, except the signers of the initiative petition, have no ready opportunity of seeing or reading an initiative measure until the Secretary of State mails copies out to the auditors of the several counties for distribution, preceding the general election . . . .

It may have been, and is, altogether probable, that the framers of the initiative amendment to the constitution had these considerations in mind, when they drafted the amendment, and therefore refrained from inserting any prohibition against the legislature amending an initiative act; but rather preferred to leave that entire legislative field of deliberation to the people and their chosen legislators. It is not unreasonable to infer, that the people themselves realized that emergencies might arise requiring amendment, alternation or repeal of initiative laws, as well as legislative acts, that could not, with safety to the public welfare, be deferred for two years or until the next general elections. That, however, is a political question involving governmental authority and policy, over which the courts have no jurisdiction to consider or pass upon.

    . . . .

About half a century ago (in the '90's), a number of new theories of legislation and political policies came into vogue and resulted in the formation of various political and civic organizations, advancing new theories of popular government. It is generally considered, however, that the first *initiative and referendum amendment* to an American constitution (12 Encyc. Brit., p. 358) was adopted by the people of South Dakota in 1898. Const. sec. 1, art. 3; *State ex rel. Richards v. Whisman*, 36 S.D. 260, 154 N.W. 707, 709, L.R.A. 1917B, 1. That amendment, while differently phrased, was in substance and effect the same as the Idaho initiative and referendum amendment *supra*. The scope and effect of the amendment came under review of the supreme court of South Dakota in *State v. Whismen, supra*; and the court, among other things, said:

> As we view this constitutional amendment, there is nothing therein contained which, either expressly or impliedly, in any degree, conflicts with, inhibits, limits, abridges, or prohibits any part of the legislative power originally granted to it to enact, amend, or repeal any law which it might have enacted before the adoption of this amendment. The fact that the people themselves may propose or enact laws in connection with the Legislature in no manner conflicts with or prohibits the Legislature from itself also enacting the same law that might be desired by the people. If the Legislature of its own volition should enact the same law desired by the people, the initiative would then become unnecessary and useless as to such law. The evident purpose of this constitutional amendment was not to curtail or limit the powers of the Legislature to enact laws, but the purpose was to compel enactment by the Legislature of measures desired by the people, and, if the Legislature neglected to act as so desired by the people, that then the people, by means of the initiative might enact such measures into laws themselves. And, recognizing the right of the Legislature to enact laws as it pleased, within all its constitutional powers, the referendum was designed as a check upon all legislative enactments not favored by the people. The only

prohibition or inhibition or limitation in relation to legislative power appearing in the initiative portion of the amendment is that which relates to the veto power, and which reads:

"The veto power of the executive shall not be exercised as to measures referred to a vote of the people."

If the framers of this constitutional amendment had placed therein language something like the following: "No Legislature shall have power to repeal any initiative measure referred to vote of the people," then the Constitution would have expressly prohibited the Legislature from amending or repealing initiated laws; or, if they had placed something like this in the constitutional amendment: "Initiated laws can be amended or repealed only by a vote of the people" — then this constitutional amendment would, by necessary implication, have prohibited the Legislature from repealing initiated laws. But no such limitation of the legislative power appears in such amendment or elsewhere in the Constitution. Appellants are, in effect, now asking this court to read into the Constitution something that is not, either expressly or by implication therein.

. . . .

The initiative principle of legislating has been attacked in the courts from time to time, on the theory that it was contrary to and destructive of a *representative* form of government and therefore in violation of the Federal constitution. That contention was finally set at rest by the Supreme Court of the United States in *Pacific States Tel. & Tel. Co. v. Oregon*, 223 U.S. 118, wherein the court, speaking through Chief Justice White, held that the manner, method and instrumentalities, through which the people of a state determine to *legislate*, are *political* (23 Am. Jur., 153) and not judicial questions; and that the courts can not consider the wisdom or unwisdom of the methods or instrumentalities by which the people of a state determine to accomplish legislation . . . .

We conclude and hold that the legislature had the constitutional power to enact the repealing statute. We express no opinion as to the wisdom or unwisdom of the act.

HOLDEN, CHIEF JUSTICE (dissenting).

Whether the "Senior Citizens' Grants Act" was, or is, wise or unwise and whether, for instance, a pension of $20.00 per month is too little or a pension of $100.00 per month too much, are social questions, and not *judicial* questions; also whether the initiative principle of legislation as provided by Section 1, Article III of our State Constitution, was, or is, wise or unwise, is a *political* and not a *judicial* question. With the determination of such questions this court has nothing whatsoever to do. So that the sole question presented to this court for determination is: Has the legislature power to repeal an initiative act adopted by popular vote under and pursuant to Section I, Article III of the Constitution of the State of Idaho?

It is therein provided that: "The people reserve to themselves the power to propose laws, and enact the same at the polls *independent of the legislature*." (Emphasis mine.) In other words, it is expressly provided, without any qualification or exception whatever, that all legislation initiated and enacted by the people, shall be "Independent of the legislature." To hold, as the majority does, the legislature had power to repeal legislation enacted by the people under and pursuant to this provision of the Constitution, at once makes such legislation absolutely dependent upon the will of the legislature, not "independent of the legislature," as our Constitution so clearly provides. Not only can no hint be found giving the legislature power to repeal initiative legislation, but, on the contrary, the above quoted language of the Constitution, expressly negatives any such power. Furthermore, if the legislature has the power to repeal, as the majority holds, then, it could repeal, any and all legislation enacted by the people, as often as enacted, thus not only annulling this provision of the Constitution, but at the same time rendering it useless, absurd and ridiculous.

. . . .

. . . The effect of the holding of the majority of this court is, of course, to render Section1, of Article III, *supra*, a mere worthless "scrap of paper."

NOTES AND QUESTIONS

1. For a critical discussion of the early experience with the Oregon provisions, see Robert Treat Platt, *Some Experiments in Direct Legislation*, 18 YALE L.J. 40, 47–48 (1908):

> Against the theoretical view of direct legislation little can be said. If communities were small and intelligent, and newspapers fair and intelligent, direct legislation ought to be a success. As to whether the great mass of voters in a big commonwealth will advise themselves sufficiently, and will so act, is one of the great questions connected with this form of legislation.

2. *See generally* Note, *The Power of the Legislature to Amend or Repeal Direct Legislation*, 27 WASH. U. L.Q. 437 (1942).

Article II, section 10(c) of the California Constitution provides:

> The legislature may . . . amend or repeal an initiative statute by another statute that becomes effective only when approved by the electors unless the initiative statute permits amendment or repeal without their approval.

3. For a survey of current provisions on direct lawmaking, see Note, *Initiative and Referendum — Do They Encourage or Impair Better State Government?*, 5 FLA. U. L. REV. 925 (1977); Note, *The California Initiative Process: A Suggestion for Reform*, 48 S. CAL. L. REV. 92 (1975).

4. Derrick A. Bell provides an important view of minorities with respect to the majority rule initiative process in *The Referendum; Democracy's Barrier to Racial Equality*, 54 WASH. L. REV. 1 (1978). *See also* Hans A. Linde, *When Initiative Lawmaking Is Not Republican Government: The Campaign Against Homosexuality*, 72 OR. L. REV. 19 (1993).

5. In *Romer v. Evans*, 517 U.S. 620 (1996), the Supreme Court ruled that an initiative amendment to the Colorado Constitution barring state or local legislation protecting gays and lesbians to be an unconstitutional violation of the Equal Protection Clause of the Fourteenth Amendment. Would the Court's rationale apply to an identically worded statutory initiative in Idaho even though the legislature is free to repeal the measure?

6. *See generally* DAVID B. MAGLEBY, DIRECT LEGISLATION: VOTING ON BALLOT PROPOSITIONS IN THE UNITED STATES; Richard Briffault, *Distrust of Democracy*, 63 TEX. L. REV. 1347 (1985) (reviewing MAGLEBY, DIRECT LEGISLATION).

7. An excellent source of information on state, local, and international aspects of direct democracy is maintained by the University of Southern California Law School's Initiative and Referendum Institute. The Website may be accessed at: www.iandrinstitute.org.

8. Recall provisions may be differentiated according to the required contents of recall petitions:

1) Some are purely political in that no grounds for removal need be stated in the petition;

2) some require that grounds be stated in the recall petition or that the stated grounds relate to competency or official conduct in office, but, in either case, the truth or sufficiency for the grounds are for the voters alone to decide;

3) in some jurisdictions, the stated grounds must constitute malfeasances, misfeasance or other legal cause relating to official misconduct, which grounds are subject to judicial review.

C. DALLAS SANDS, MICHAEL E. LIBONATI & JOHN MARTINEZ, LOCAL GOVERNMENT LAW § 10.54 (1982).

Can a recall petition be based on words uttered by a legislator in speech or debate? *See In re Call*, 109 Wash. 2d 954, 749 P.2d 674 (1988).

B. THE CONGRESS

CHARLES W. JOHNSON, HOW OUR LAWS ARE MADE
1–4 (rev. ed., 2003)

Article I, Section 1, of the United States Constitution, provides that:

All legislative Powers herein granted shall be vested in a Congress of the United States, which shall consist of a Senate and House of Representatives.

The Senate is composed of 100 Members — two from each state, regardless of population or area — elected by the people in accordance with the 17th Amendment to the Constitution. The 17th Amendment changed the former constitutional method under which Senators were chosen by the respective state legislatures. A Senator must be at least 30 years of age, have been a citizen of the United States for nine years, and, when elected, be a resident of the state for which the Senator is chosen. The term of office is six years and one-third of the total membership of the Senate is elected every second year. The terms of both Senators from a particular state are arranged so that they do not terminate at the same time. Of the two Senators from a state serving at the same time the one who was elected first — or if both were elected at the same time, the one elected for a full term — is referred to as the "senior" Senator from that state. The other is referred to as the "junior" Senator. If a Senator dies or resigns during the term, the governor of the state must call a special election unless the state legislature has authorized the governor to appoint a successor until the next election, at which time a successor is elected for the balance of the term. Most of the state legislatures have granted their governors the power of appointment.

Each Senator has one vote.

As constituted in the 108th Congress, the House of Representatives is composed of 435 Members elected every two years from among the 50 states, apportioned to their total populations. The permanent number of 435 was established by federal law following the Thirteenth Decennial Census in 1910, in accordance with Article I, Section 2, of the Constitution . . . .

Under a former apportionment in one state, a particular Representative represented more than 900,000 constituents, while another in the same state was elected from a district having a population of only 175,000. The Supreme Court has since held unconstitutional a Missouri statute permitting a maximum population variance of 3.1 percent from mathematical equality. The Court ruled in *Kirkpatrick v. Preisler*, 394 U.S. 526 (1969), that the variances among the districts were not unavoidable and, therefore, were invalid. That decision was an interpretation of the Court's earlier ruling in *Wesberry v. Sanders*, 376 U.S. 1 (1964), that the Constitution requires that "as nearly as is practicable one man's vote in a congressional election is to be worth as much as another's."

A law enacted in 1967 abolished all "at-large" elections except in those less populous states entitled to only one Representative. An "at-large" election is one in which a Representative is elected by the voters of the entire state rather than by the voters in a congressional district within the state.

A Representative must be at least 25 years of age, have been a citizen of the United States for seven years, and, when elected, be a resident of the state in which the Representative is chosen. Unlike the Senate where a successor may be appointed by a governor when a vacancy occurs during a term, if a Representative dies or resigns during the term, the executive authority of the state must call a special election pursuant to state law for the choosing of a successor to serve for the unexpired portion of the term.

Each Representative has one vote.

In addition to the Representatives from each of the States, a Resident Commissioner from the Commonwealth of Puerto Rico and Delegates from the District of Columbia, American Samoa, Guam, and the Virgin Islands are elected pursuant to federal law. The Resident Commissioner, elected for a four-year term, and the Delegates, elected for two-year terms, have most of the prerogatives of Representatives including the right to vote in committees to which they are elected. However, the Resident Commissioner and the Delegates do not have the right to vote on matters before the House.

Under the provisions of Section 2 of the 20th Amendment to the Constitution, Congress must assemble at least once every year, at noon on the third day of January, unless by law they appoint a different day.

A Congress lasts for two years, commencing in January of the year following the biennial election of Members. A Congress is divided into two sessions.

The Constitution authorizes each House to determine the rules of its proceedings. Pursuant to that authority, the House of Representatives adopts its rules on the opening day of each Congress. The Senate considers itself a continuing body and operates under continuous standing rules that it amends from time to time.

Unlike some other parliamentary bodies, both the Senate and the House of Representatives have equal legislative functions and powers with certain exceptions. For example, the Constitution provides that only the House of Representatives originates revenue bills. By tradition, the House also originates appropriation bills. As both bodies have equal legislative powers, the designation of one as the "upper" House and the other as the "lower" House is not appropriate.

The chief function of Congress is the making of laws. In addition, the Senate has the function of advising and consenting to treaties and to certain nominations by the President. However under the 25th Amendment to the Constitution, both Houses confirm the President's nomination for Vice-President when there is a vacancy in that office. In the matter of impeachments, the House of Representatives presents the charges — a function similar to that of a grand jury — and the Senate sits as a court to try the impeachment. No impeached person may be removed without a two-thirds vote of the Senate. The Congress under the Constitution and by statute also plays a role in presidential elections. Both Houses meet in joint session on the sixth day of January, following a presidential election, unless by law they appoint a different day, to count the electoral votes. If no candidate receives a majority of the total electoral votes, the House of Representatives, each state delegation having one vote, chooses the President from among the three candidates having the largest number of electoral votes. The Senate, each Senator having one vote, chooses the Vice President from the two candidates having the largest number of votes for that office.

Article 1 of the U. S. Constitution sets forth a framework for the internal exercise of powers within each branch of the legislature. Pay careful attention to these excerpted texts when reading *Powell v. McCormack*.

ARTICLE 1

Section 1.

All legislative Powers herein granted shall be vested in a Congress of the United States which shall consist of a Senate and House of Representatives.

Section 2.

[1] The House of Representatives shall be composed of Members chosen

every second Year by the People of the several States . . . .

[2] No Person shall be a Representative who shall not have attained to the Age of twenty five Years, and been seven Years a Citizen of the United States, and who shall not, when elected, be an Inhabitant of that State in which he shall be chosen.

Section 3.

[3] No Person shall be a Senator who shall not have attained to the Age of thirty Years, and been nine Years a Citizen of the United States, and who shall not, when elected, be an Inhabitant of that State for which he shall be chosen.

Section 5.

[1] Each House shall be the Judge of the Elections, Returns and Qualifications of its own Members, and a Majority of each shall constitute a Quorum to do Business; but a smaller Number may adjourn from day to day, and may be authorized to compel the Attendance of absent Members, in such Manner, and under such Penalties as each House may provide.

[2] Each House may determine the Rules of its Proceedings, punish its Members for disorderly Behavior, and, with the Concurrence of two thirds, expel a Member . . . .

Section 6.

[1] The Senators and Representatives . . . shall in all Cases, except Treason, Felony and Breach of the Peace, be privileged from Arrest during their Attendance at the Session of their respective Houses, and in going to and returning from the same; and for any Speech or Debate in either House, they shall not be questioned in any other Place.

POWELL v. McCORMACK
395 U.S. 486 (1969)

Mr. Chief Justice Warren delivered the opinion of the Court.

In November 1966, petitioner Adam Clayton Powell, Jr., was duly elected from the 18th Congressional District of New York to serve in the United States House of Representatives for the 90th Congress. However, pursuant to a House resolution, he was not permitted to take his seat. Powell (and some of the voters of his district) then filed suit in Federal District Court, claiming that the House could exclude him only if it found he failed to meet the standing requirements of age, citizenship, and residence contained in Art. I, § 2, of the Constitution — requirements the House specifically found Powell met — and thus had excluded him unconstitutionally. The District Court dismissed petitioners' complaint "for want of jurisdiction of the subject matter." A panel of the Court of Appeals affirmed the dismissal, although on somewhat different grounds, each judge filing a separate opinion. We have determined that it was error to dismiss the complaint and that petitioner Powell is entitled to a declaratory judgment that he was unlawfully excluded from the 90th Congress.

I

Facts

During the 89th Congress, a Special Subcommittee on Contracts of the Committee on House Administration conducted an investigation into the expenditures of the Committee on Education and Labor, of which petitioner Adam Clayton Powell, Jr., was chairman. The Special Subcommittee issued a report concluding that Powell and certain staff employees had deceived the House authorities as to travel expenses. The report also indicated there was strong evidence that certain illegal salary payments had been made to Powell's wife at his direction. *See* H.R. Rep. No. 2349, 89th Cong., 2d Sess., 6–7

(1966). No formal action was taken during the 89th Congress. However, prior to the organization of the 90th Congress, the Democratic members-elect met in caucus and voted to remove Powell as chairman of the Committee on Education and Labor. *See* H.R. Rep. No. 27, 90th Cong., 1st Sess., 1–2 (1967).

When the 90th Congress met to organize in January 1967, Powell was asked to step aside while the oath was administered to the other members-elect. Following the administration of the oath to the remaining members, the House discussed the procedure to be followed in determining whether Powell was eligible to take his seat. After some debate, by a vote of 363 to 65 the House adopted House Resolution No. 1, which provided that the Speaker appoint a Select Committee to determine Powell's eligibility. 113 Cong. Rec. 26–27. Although the resolution prohibited Powell from taking his seat until the House acted on the Select Committee's report, it did provide that he should receive all the pay and allowances due a member during the period.

The Select Committee, composed of nine lawyer-members, issued an invitation to Powell to testify before the Committee. The invitation letter stated that the scope of the testimony and investigation would include Powell's qualifications as to age, citizenship, and residency; his involvement in a civil suit (in which he had been held in contempt); and "[m]atters of . . . alleged official misconduct since January 3, 1961." *See* Hearings on HR. Res. No. 1 before Select Committee Pursuant to HR. Res. No. 1, 90th Cong., 1st Sess., 5 (1967) (hereinafter Hearings). Powell appeared at the Committee hearing held on February 8, 1967. After the Committee denied in part Powell's request that certain adversary-type procedures be followed[1] Powell testified. He would, however, give information relating only to his age, citizenship, and residency; upon the advice of counsel, he refused to answer other questions.

On February 10, 1967, the Select Committee issued another invitation to Powell. In the letter, the Select Committee informed Powell that its responsibility under the House Resolution extended to determining not only whether he met the standing qualifications of Art. I, § 2, but also to "inquir[ing] into the question of whether you should be punished or expelled pursuant to the powers granted . . . the House under Article I, Section 5, . . . of the Constitution. In other words, the Select Committee is of the opinion that at the conclusion of the present inquiry, it has authority to report back to the House recommendations with respect to . . . seating, expulsion or other punishment." *See* Hearings 110. Powell did not appear at the next hearing, held February 14, 1967. However, his attorneys were present, and they informed the Committee that Powell would not testify about matters other than his eligibility under the standing qualifications of Art. II, § 2. Powell's attorneys reasserted Powell's contention that the standing qualifications were the exclusive requirements for membership, and they further urged that punishment or expulsion was not possible until a member had been seated. *See* Hearings 111–113.

The Committee held one further hearing at which neither Powell nor his attorneys were present. Then, on February 23, 1967, the Committee issued its report, finding that Powell met the standing qualifications of Art. I, § 2. HR. Rep. No. 27, 90th Cong., 1st Sess., 31 (1967). However, the Committee further reported that Powell had asserted an unwarranted privilege and immunity from the processes of the courts of New York;

---

[1] Powell requested that he be given (1) notice of the charges pending against him, including a bill of particulars as to any accuser; (2) the opportunity to confront any accuser, to attend all committee sessions where evidence was given, and the right to cross-examine all witnesses; (3) public hearings; (4) the right to have the Select Committee issue its process to summon witnesses for his defense; (5) and a transcript of every hearing. Hearings on HR. Res. No. 1 before Select Committee Pursuant to H.R. Res. No. 1, 90th Cong., 1st Sess., 54 (1967).

The Select Committee noted that it had given Powell notice of the matters it would inquire into, that Powell had the right to attend all hearings (which would be public) with his counsel, and that the Committee would call witnesses upon Powell's written request and supply a transcript of the hearings. *Id.*, at 59.

that he had wrongfully diverted House funds for the use of others and himself; and that he had made false reports on expenditures of foreign currency to the Committee on House Administration. *Id.*, at 31–32. The Committee recommended that Powell be sworn and seated as a member of the 90th Congress but that he be censured by the House, fined $40,000 and be deprived of his seniority. *Id.*, at 33.

The report was presented to the House on March 1, 1967, and the House debated the Select Committee's proposed resolution. At the conclusion of the debate, by a vote of 222 to 202 the House rejected a motion to bring the resolution to a vote. An amendment to the resolution was then offered; it called for the exclusion of Powell and a declaration that his seat was vacant. The Speaker ruled that a majority vote of the House would be sufficient to pass the resolution if it were so amended. 113 Cong. Rec. 5020. After further debate, the amendment was adopted by a vote of 248 to 176. Then the House adopted by a vote of 307 to 116 House Resolution No. 278 in its amended form, thereby excluding Powell and directing that the Speaker notify the Governor of New York that the seat was vacant.

. . . .

[In a footnote the Court indicated: " . . . On April 11, 1967, Powell was reelected to the House of Representatives in a special election called to fill his seat. The formal certification of election was received by the House on May 1, 1967, but Powell did not again present himself to the House or ask to be given the oath of office." — Eds.]

. . . In November 1968, Powell was again elected as the representative of the 18th Congressional District of New York, and he was seated by the 91st Congress. The resolution seating Powell also fined him $25,000 . . . .

III

Speech or Debate Clause

Respondents assert that the Speech or Debate Clause of the Constitution, Art. I, § 6, is an absolute bar to petitioners' action. This Court has on four prior occasions — *Dombrowski v. Eastland*, 387 U.S. 82 (1967); *United States v. Johnson*, 383 U.S. 169 (1966); *Tenney v. Brandhove*, 341 U.S. 367 (1951); and *Kilbourn v. Thompson*, 103 U.S. 168 (1881) — been called upon to determine if allegedly unconstitutional action taken by legislators or legislative employees is insulated from judicial review by the Speech or Debate Clause. Both parties insist that their respective positions find support in these cases and tender for decision three distinct issues: (1) whether respondents in participating in the exclusion of petitioner Powell were "acting in the sphere of legitimate legislative activity," *Tenney v. Brandhove, supra*, at 376; (2) assuming that respondents were so acting, whether the fact that petitioners seek neither damages from any of the respondents nor a criminal prosecution lifts the bar of the clause; and (3) even if this action may not be maintained against a Congressman, whether those respondents who are merely employees of the House may plead the bar of the clause. We find it necessary to treat only the last of these issues.

The Speech or Debate Clause, adopted by the Constitutional Convention without debate or opposition, finds its roots in the conflict between Parliament and the Crown culminating in the Glorious Revolution of 1688 and the English Bill of Rights of 1689. Drawing upon this history, we concluded in *United States v. Johnson, supra*, at 181, that the purpose of this clause was "to prevent intimidation [of legislators] by the executive and accountability before a possibly hostile judiciary." Although the clause sprang from a fear of seditious libel actions instituted by the Crown to punish unfavorable speeches made in Parliament, we have held that it would be a "narrow view" to confine the protection of the Speech or Debate Clause to words spoken in debate. Committee reports, resolutions, and the act of voting are equally covered, as are "things generally done in a session of the House by one of its members in relation to the business before it." *Kilbourn v. Thompson, supra*, at 204. Furthermore, the clause not only provides a defense on the merits but also protects a legislator from the burden of defending himself. *Dombrowski v. Eastland, supra*, at 85, *see Tenney v. Brandhove, supra*, at 377.

Our cases make it clear that the legislative immunity created by the Speech or Debate Clause performs an important function in representative government. It insures that legislators are free to represent the interests of their constituents without fear that they will be later called to task in the courts for that representation. Thus, in *Tenney v. Brandhove, supra*, at 373, the Court quoted the writings of James Wilson as illuminating the reason for legislative immunity: "In order to enable and encourage a representative of the publick to discharge his publick trust with firmness and success, it is indispensably necessary, that he should enjoy the fullest liberty of speech, and that he should be protected from the resentment of every one, however powerful, to whom the exercise of that liberty may occasion offence."

Legislative immunity does not, of course, bar all judicial review of legislative acts. That issue was settled by implication as early as 1803, *see Marbury v. Madison*, 1 Cranch 137 and expressly in *Kilbourn v. Thompson*, the first of this Court's cases interpreting the reach of the Speech or Debate Clause. Challenged in *Kilbourn* was the constitutionality of a House Resolution ordering the arrest and imprisonment of a recalcitrant witness who had refused to respond to a subpoena issued by a House investigating committee. While holding that the Speech or Debate Clause barred Kilbourn's action for false imprisonment brought against several members of the House, the Court nevertheless reached the merits of Kilbourn's attack and decided that, since the House had no power to punish for contempt, Kilbourn's imprisonment pursuant to the resolution was unconstitutional. It therefore allowed Kilbourn to bring his false imprisonment action against Thompson, the House's Sergeant at Arms, who had executed the warrant for Kilbourn's arrest.

The Court first articulated in *Kilbourn* and followed in *Dombrowski v. Eastland* the doctrine that, although an action against a Congressman may be barred by the Speech or Debate Clause, legislative employees who participated in the unconstitutional activity are responsible for their acts. Despite the fact that petitioners brought this suit against several House employees — the Sergeant at Arms, the Doorkeeper and the Clerk — as well as several Congressmen, respondents argue that *Kilbourn* and *Dombrowski* are distinguishable. Conceding that in *Kilbourn* the presence of the Sergeant at Arms and in *Dombrowski* the presence of a congressional subcommittee counsel as defendants in the litigation allowed judicial review of the challenged congressional action, respondents urge that both cases concerned an affirmative act performed by the employee outside the House having a direct effect upon a private citizen. Here, they continue, the relief sought relates to actions taken by House agents solely within the House. Alternatively, respondents insist that Kilbourn and Dombrowski prayed for damages while petitioner Powell asks that the Sergeant at Arms disburse funds, an assertedly greater interference with the legislative process. We reject the proffered distinctions.

That House employees are acting pursuant to express orders of the House does not bar judicial review of the constitutionality of the underlying legislative decision.

Kilbourn decisively settles this question, since the Sergeant at Arms was held liable for false imprisonment even though he did nothing more than execute the House Resolution that Kilbourn be arrested and imprisoned. Respondents' suggestions thus ask us to distinguish between affirmative acts of House employees and situations in which the House orders its employees not to act or between actions for damages and claims for salary. We can find no basis in either the history of the Speech or Debate Clause or our cases for either distinction. The purpose of the protection afforded legislators is not to forestall judicial review of legislative action but to insure that legislators are not distracted from or hindered in the performance of their legislative tasks by being called into court to defend their actions. A legislator is no more or no less hindered or distracted by litigation against a legislative employee calling into question the employee's affirmative action than he would be by a lawsuit questioning the employee's failure to act. Nor is the distraction or hindrance increased because the claim is for salary rather than damages, or because the litigation questions action taken by the employee within rather than without the House. Freedom of legislative activity and the purposes of the Speech or Debate Clause are fully protected if legislators are relieved of the burden of defending themselves. In *Kilbourn* and *Dombrowski* we thus dismissed the action against members of Congress but did not regard the Speech or Debate Clause as a bar to reviewing the merits of the challenged congressional action since congressional employees were also sued. Similarly, though this action may be dismissed against the Congressmen petitioners are entitled to maintain their action against House employees and to judicial review of the propriety of the decision to exclude petitioner Powell. As was said in *Kilbourn*, in language which time has not dimmed:

> "Especially is it competent and proper for this court to consider whether its [the legislature's] proceedings are in conformity with the Constitution and laws, because, living under a written constitution, no branch or department of the government is supreme; and it is the province and duty of the judicial department to determine in cases regularly brought before them, whether the powers of any branch of the government, and even those of the legislature in the enactment of laws, have been exercised in conformity to the Constitution; and if they have not, to treat their acts as null and void." 103 U.S., at 199.

IV

Exclusion or Expulsion

The resolution excluding petitioner Powell was adopted by a vote in excess of two-thirds of the 434 Members of Congress — 307 to 116. 113 Cong. Rec. 5037–5038. Article I, § 5, grants the House authority to expel a member "with the Concurrence of two thirds." Respondents assert that the House may expel a member for any reason whatsoever and that, since a two-thirds vote was obtained, the procedure by which Powell was denied his seat in the 90th Congress should be regarded as an expulsion not an exclusion. Cautioning us not to exalt form over substance, respondents quote from the concurring opinion of Judge McGowan in the court below:

> "Appellant Powell's cause of action for a judicially compelled seating thus boils down, in my view, to the narrow issue of whether a member found by his colleagues . . . to have engaged in official misconduct must, because of the accidents of timing, be formally admitted before he can be either investigated or expelled. The sponsor of the motion to exclude stated on the floor that he was proceeding on the theory that the power to expel included the power to exclude, provided a 2/3 vote was forthcoming. It was. Therefore, success for Mr. Powell on the merits would mean that the District Court must admonish the House that it is form, not substance, that should govern in great affairs, and accordingly command the House members to act out a charade." 129 U.S. App. D.C., at 383–384, 395 F.2d, at 606–607.

Although respondents repeatedly urge this Court not to speculate as to the reasons for Powell's exclusion, their attempt to equate exclusion with expulsion would require a similar speculation that the House would have voted to expel Powell had it been faced with that question. Powell had not been seated at the time House Resolution No. 278 was debated and passed. After a motion to bring the Select Committee's proposed resolution to an immediate vote had been defeated, an amendment was offered which mandated

Powell's exclusion.[28] Mr. Celler, chairman of the Select Committee, then posed a parliamentary inquiry to determine whether a two-thirds vote was necessary to pass the resolution if so amended "in the sense that it might amount to an expulsion." 113 Cong. Rec. 5020. The Speaker replied that "action by a majority vote would be in accordance with the rules." *Ibid.* Had the amendment been regarded as an attempt to expel Powell, a two-thirds vote would have been constitutionally required. The Speaker ruled that the House was voting to exclude Powell, and we will not speculate what the result might have been if Powell had been seated and expulsion proceedings subsequently instituted.

Nor is the distinction between exclusion and expulsion merely one of form. The misconduct for which Powell was charged occurred prior to the convening of the 90th Congress. On several occasions the House has debated whether a member can be expelled for actions taken during a prior Congress and the House's own manual of procedure applicable in the 90th Congress states that "both Houses have distrusted their power to punish in such cases." Rules of the House of Representatives, H.R. Doc. No. 529, 89th Cong., 2d Sess., 25 (1967); *see* G. Galloway, History of the House of Representatives 32 (1961). The House rules manual reflects positions taken by prior Congresses. For example, the report of the Select Committee appointed to consider the expulsion of John W. Langley states unequivocally that the House will not expel a member for misconduct committed during an earlier Congress:

> "[I]t must be said that with practical uniformity the precedents in such cases are to the effect that the House will not expel a Member for reprehensible action prior to his election as a Member, not even for conviction for an offense. On May 23, 1884, Speaker Carlisle decided that the House had no right to punish a Member for any offense alleged to have been committed previous to the time when he was elected a Member, and added, 'That has been so frequently decided in the House that it is no longer a matter of dispute.'" H.R. Rep. No. 30, 69th Cong., 1st Sess., 1–2 (1925).[29]

Members of the House having expressed a belief that such strictures apply to its own power to expel, we will not assume that two-thirds of its members would have expelled Powell for his prior conduct had the Speaker announced that House Resolution No. 278 was for expulsion rather than exclusion.[30]

---

[28] House Resolution No. 278, as amended and adopted, provided: "That said Adam Clayton Powell . . . be and the same hereby *is excluded* from membership in the 90th Congress . . . ." 113 Cong. Rec. 5020. (Emphasis added.)

[29] Other Congresses have expressed an identical view. The Report of the Judiciary Committee concerning the proposed expulsion of William S. King and John G. Schumaker informed the House:

> "Your committee are of opinion that the House of Representatives has no authority to take jurisdiction of violations of law or offenses committed against a previous Congress. This is purely a legislative body, and entirely unsuited for the trial of crimes. The fifth section of the first article of the Constitution authorizes 'each house to determine the rules of its proceedings, punish its members for disorderly behavior, and, with the concurrence of two thirds, expel a member.' This power is evidently given to enable each house to exercise its constitutional function of legislation unobstructed. It cannot vest in Congress a jurisdiction to try a member for an offense committed before his election; for such offense a member, like any other citizen, is amenable to the courts alone." H.R. Rep. No. 815, 44th Cong, 1st Sess, 2 (1876).

See also 15 Cong. Rec. 4434 (1884) (ruling of the Speaker); HR. Rep. No. 81, 42d Cong., 3d Sess., 8 (1873) (expulsion of James Brooks and Oakes Ames); H.R. Rep. No. 179, 35th Cong., 1st Sess., 4–5 (1858) (expulsion of Orsamus B. Matteson).

[30] We express no view as to whether such a ruling would have been proper. A further distinction between expulsion and exclusion inheres in the fact that a member whose expulsion is contemplated may as a matter or right address the House and participate fully in debate while a member-elect apparently does not have a similar right. In prior cases the member whose expulsion was under debate has been allowed to make a long and often impassioned defense. *See* Cong. Globe, 42d Cong., 3d Sess., 1723 (1873) (expulsion of Oakes Ames); Cong. Globe, 41st Cong., 2d Sess., 1524–1525, 1544 (1870) (expulsion of B.F. Whittemore); Cong. Globe, 34th Cong., 3d Sess., 925–926 (1857) (expulsion of William A. Gilbert); Cong. Globe, 34th Cong., 3d Sess., 947–951

Finally, the proceedings which culminated in Powell's exclusion cast considerable doubt upon respondents' assumption that the two-thirds vote necessary to expel would have been mustered.

. . . .

VI

Justiciability

. . . .

Political Question Doctrine

1. Textually Demonstrable Constitutional Commitment.

. . . .

Respondents' first contention is that this case presents a political question because under Art. I, § 5, there has been a "textually demonstrable constitutional commitment" to the House of the "adjudicatory power" to determine Powell's qualifications. Thus it is argued that the House alone, has power to determine who is qualified to be a member.

In order to determine whether there has been a textual commitment to a co-ordinate department of the Government, we must interpret the Constitution. In other words, we must first determine what power the Constitution confers upon the House through Art. I, § 5, before we can determine to what extent, if any, the exercise of that power is subject to judicial review. Respondents maintain that the House has broad power under § 5, and, they argue, the House may determine which are the qualifications necessary for membership. On the other hand, petitioners allege that the Constitution provides that an elected representative may be denied his seat only if the House finds he does not meet one of the standing qualifications expressly prescribed by the Constitution.

If examination of § 5 disclosed that the Constitution gives the House judicially unreviewable power to set qualifications for membership and to judge whether prospective members meet those qualifications, further review of the House determination might well be barred by the political question doctrine. On the other hand, if the Constitution gives the House power to judge only whether elected members possess the three standing qualifications set forth in the Constitution,[41] further consideration would be necessary to determine whether any of the other formulations of the political question doctrine are "inextricable from the case at bar." *Baker v. Carr*, [369 U.S. 186, 217 (1962)].

In other words, whether there is a "textually demonstrable constitutional commitment of the issue to a coordinate political department" of government and what is the scope of such commitment are questions we must resolve for the first time in this case.

(1857) (expulsion of William W. Welch); 9 Annals of Cong. 2966 (1799) (expulsion of Matthew Lyon). On at least one occasion the member has been allowed to cross-examine other members during the expulsion debate. 2 A. Hinds, Precedents of the House of Representatives § 1643 (1907).

[41] In addition to the three qualifications set forth in Art. I, § 2, Art. I, § 3, cl. 7, authorizes the disqualification of any person convicted in an impeachment proceeding from "any Office of honor, Trust or Profit under the United States"; Art. I, § 6, cl. 2, provides that "no Person holding any Office under the United States, shall be a Member of either House during his Continuance in Office"; and § 3 of the 14th Amendment disqualifies any person "who, having previously taken an oath . . . to support the Constitution of the United States, shall have engaged in insurrection or rebellion against the same, or given aid or comfort to the enemies thereof." It has been argued that each of these provisions, as well as the Guarantee Clause of Article IV and the Oath requirement of Art. VI, cl. 3, is no less a "qualification" within the meaning of Art. I, § 5, than those set forth in Art. I, § 2. Dionisopoulos, *A Commentary on the Constitutional Issues in the Powell and Related Cases*, 17 J. Pub. L. 103, 111–15 (1968).

For, as we pointed out in *Baker v. Carr, supra,* "[d]eciding whether a matter has in any measure been committed by the Constitution to another branch of government, or whether the action of that branch exceeds whatever authority has been committed, is itself a delicate exercise in constitutional interpretation, and is a responsibility of this Court as ultimate interpreter of the Constitution." *Id.,* at 211, 7 L. Ed. 2d at 682.

In order to determine the scope of any "textual commitment" under Art. I, § 5, we necessarily must determine the meaning of the phrase to "be the Judge of the Qualifications of its own Members." Petitioners argue that the records of the debates during the Constitutional Convention; available commentary from the post-Convention, pre-ratification period; and early congressional applications of Art. I, § 5, support their construction of the section. Respondents insist, however, that a careful examination of the pre-Convention practices of the English Parliament and American colonial assemblies demonstrates that by 1787, a legislature's power to judge the qualifications of its members was generally understood to encompass exclusion or expulsion on the ground that an individual's character or past conduct rendered him unfit to serve. When the Constitution and the debates over its adoption are thus viewed in historical perspective, argue respondents, it becomes clear that the "qualifications" expressly set forth in the Constitution were not meant to limit the long-recognized legislative power to exclude or expel at will, but merely to establish "standing incapacities," which could be altered only by a constitutional amendment. Our examination of the relevant historical materials leads us to the conclusion that petitioners are correct and that the Constitution leaves the House without authority to *exclude* any person, duly elected by his constituents, who meets all the requirements for membership expressly prescribed in the Constitution.

. . . .

Conclusion

To summarize, we have determined the following: (1) This case has not been mooted by Powell's seating in the 91st Congress. (2) Although this action should be dismissed against respondent Congressmen, it may be sustained against their agents. (3) The 90th Congress' denial of membership to Powell cannot be treated as an expulsion. (4) We have jurisdiction over the subject matter of this controversy. (5) The case is justiciable.

Further, analysis of the "textual commitment" under Art. I, § 5 (*see* Part VI, B(1)), has demonstrated that in judging the qualifications of its members Congress is limited to the standing qualifications prescribed in the Constitution. Respondents concede that Powell met these. Thus, there is no need to remand this case to determine whether he was entitled to be seated in the 90th Congress. Therefore, we hold that, since Adam Clayton Powell, Jr., was duly elected by the voters of the 18th Congressional District of New York and was not ineligible to serve under any provision of the Constitution, the House was without power to exclude him from its membership.

. . . .

Mr. Justice Douglas.

While I join the opinion of the Court, I add a few words. As the Court says, the important constitutional question is whether the Congress has the power to deviate from or alter the qualifications for membership as a Representative contained in Art. I, § 2, cl. 2, of the Constitution. Up to now the understanding has been quite clear to the effect that such authority does not exist. To be sure, Art. I, § 5, provides that: "Each House shall be the Judge of the Elections, Returns and Qualifications of its own Members . . . ." Contests may arise over whether an elected official meets the "qualifications" of the Constitution, in which event the House is the sole judge. But the House is not the sole judge when "qualifications" are added which are not specified in the Constitution.

A man is not seated because he is a Socialist or a Communist.

Another is not seated because in his district members of a minority are systematically excluded from voting.

Another is not seated because he has spoken out in opposition to the war in Vietnam.

The possible list is long. Some cases will have the racist overtones of the present one. Others may reflect religious or ideological clashes.

At the root of all these cases, however, is the basic integrity of the electoral process. Today we proclaim the constitutional principle of "one man, one vote." When that principle is followed and the electors choose a person who is repulsive to the Establishment in Congress, by what constitutional authority can that group of electors be disenfranchised?

By Art. I, § 5, the House may "expel a Member" by a vote of two-thirds. And if this were an expulsion case I would think that no justiciable controversy would be presented, the vote of the House being two-thirds or more. But it is not an expulsion case. Whether it could have been won as an expulsion case, no one knows. Expulsion for "misconduct" may well raise different questions, different considerations. Policing the conduct of members, a recurring problem in the Senate and House as well, is quite different from the initial decision whether an elected official should be seated. It well might be easier to bar admission than to expel one already seated.

The House excluded Representative-elect Powell from the 90th Congress allegedly for misappropriating public funds and for incurring the contempt of New York courts. Twenty-six years earlier, members of the upper chamber attempted to exclude Senator-elect William Langer of North Dakota for like reasons. Langer first became State's Attorney for Morton County, North Dakota, from 1914 to 1916, and then served as State Attorney General from 1916 to 1920. He became Governor of the State in 1932 and took office in January 1933. In 1934 he was indicted for conspiring to interfere with the enforcement of federal law by illegally soliciting political contributions from federal employees, and suit was filed in the State Supreme Court to remove him from office. While that suit was pending, he called the State Legislature into special session. When it became clear that the court would order his ouster, he signed a Declaration of Independence, invoked martial law, and called out the National Guard. Nonetheless, when his own officers refused to recognize him as the legal head of state, he left office in July 1934. As with Adam Clayton Powell, however, the people of the State still wanted him. In 1937 they re-elected him Governor and, in 1940, they sent him to the United States Senate.

During the swearing-in ceremonies, Senator Barkley drew attention to certain complaints filed against Langer by citizens of North Dakota, yet asked that he be allowed to take the oath of office "without prejudice, which is a two-sided proposition — without prejudice to the Senator and without prejudice to the Senate in the exercise of its right [to exclude him]."

The matter of Langer's qualifications to serve in the Senate was referred to committee which held confidential hearings on January 9 and 16, 1941, and open hearings on November 3 and 18, 1941. By a vote of 14 to 2, the committee reported that a majority of the Senate had jurisdiction under Art. I, § 5, cl. 1, of the Constitution to exclude Langer; and, by a vote of 13 to 3, it reported its recommendation that Langer not be seated.

The charges against Langer were various. As with Powell, they included claims that he had misappropriated public funds[16] and that he had interfered with the judicial

---

[16] It was alleged that he had conspired as Governor to have municipal and county bonds sold to a friend of his who made a profit of $300,000 on the purchase, and purportedly rebated as much as $56,000 to Langer himself. Hearings 822–823.

process in a way that beclouded the dignity of Congress.[17] Reference was also made to his professional ethics as a lawyer.[18]

Langer enjoyed the powerful advocacy of Senator Murdock from Utah. The Senate debate itself raged for over a year. Much of it related to purely factual allegations of "moral turpitude." Some of it, however, was addressed to the power of the Senate under Art. I, § 5, cl. 1, to exclude a member-elect for lacking qualifications not enumerated in Art. I, § 3.

. . . .

The Senate was . . . troubled by the suggestion that the Constitution compelled it to accept anyone whom the people might elect, no matter how egregious and even criminal his behavior. No need to worry, said Murdock. It is true that the Senate cannot invoke its majority power to "judge" under Art. I, § 5, cl. 1, as a device for excluding men elected by the people who possess the qualifications enumerated by the Constitution. But it does have the power under Art. I, § 5, cl. 2, to expel anyone it designates by a two-thirds vote. Nonetheless, he urged the Senate not to bypass the two-thirds requirement for expulsion by wrongfully invoking its power to exclude.

. . . .

Mr. Murdock [quoting senator Philander Knox]. "I know of no defect in the plain rule of the Constitution for which I am contending . . . . I cannot see that any danger to the Senate lies in the fact that an improper character cannot be excluded without a two-thirds vote. It requires the unanimous vote of a jury to convict a man accused of crime; it should require, and I believe that it does require, a two-thirds vote to eject a Senator from his position of honor and power, to which he has been elected by a sovereign State."

Thus, after a year of debate, on March 27, 1942, the Senate overruled the recommendation of its committee and voted 52 to 30 to seat Langer.

I believe that Senator Murdock stated the correct constitutional principle governing the present case.

NOTES AND QUESTIONS

1. Elected members of the House and Senate are not just plain folks. They possess, by virtue of the Speech or Debate Clause, Art I, § 6, cl. 1, immunities from civil and criminal liability not shared by ordinary citizens.

Many state legislators enjoy an analogous privilege conferred by the state constitution. *See* Steven F. Huefner, *The Neglected Value of the Legislative Privilege in State Legislatures*, 45 WM. & MARY L. REV. 221 (2003).

Some more recent cases indicate the scope of "legitimate legislative activity" protected by the Speech or Debate Clause. In *United States v. Brewster*, 408 U.S. 501 (1972), the Supreme Court held that the government could not offer evidence, in a bribery prosecution, that a member actually performed a legislative act such as voting for a bill or making a speech on the floor supporting a bill. And in *Gravel v. United States*, 408 U.S. 606 (1972), neither a Senator nor his aide could be required to testify before a grand jury with respect to events occurring at a subcommittee hearing at

---

[17] At the retrial of his conviction for conspiring to interfere with the enforcement of federal law, he was said to have paid money to have a friend of his, Judge Wyman, be given control of the litigation, and to have "meddled" with the jury. Hearings 20–42, 120–130.

[18] He was charged as a lawyer with having accepted $2,000 from the mother of a boy in prison on the promise that he would obtain his pardon, when he knew, in fact, that a pardon was out of the question. He was also said to have counseled a defendant-client of his to marry the prosecution's chief witness in order to prevent her from testifying against him. And finally, it was suggested that he once bought an insurance policy during trial from one of the jurors sitting in judgment of his client. Hearings 820–30.

which a classified document, the Pentagon Papers, was introduced into the public record. In *Eastland v. United States Servicemen's Fund*, 421 U.S. 491 (1975), a civil injunction against a senate subcommittee and its chief counsel seeking to subpoena bank records pursuant to an investigation of subversive activities was quashed. However, *Hutchinson v. Proxmire*, 443 U.S. 111 (1979), a civil suit for defamation, held that statements made by a Senator in press releases and newsletters were unprotected. And in *Doe v. McMillan*, 412 U.S. 306 (1973), parents of school children sued House members, committee staff, the public printer and superintendent of documents and others for defaming their children by name in a committee report on the District of Columbia school system. The members and committee staff were held to be immune from civil liability but the printer and superintendent of documents who distributed the materials were held to be outside the protections of the Clause to the extent they had printed excess copies of the report for use other than internally by Congress.

2. Soon after the Republicans regained control over both the House and the Senate for the first time in forty years, the Congressional Accountability Act of 1995, 2 U.S.C. § 1301 et seq. was enacted. That law applied, for the first time, the provisions of a variety of labor and civil rights protective statutes to the legislative branch of government including the Fair Labor Standards Act, Title VII of the 1964 Civil Rights Act, the Americans with Disabilities Act, the Age Discrimination in Employment Act and the Occupational Safety and Health Act. That statute contains the following provisions:

§ 1413. Privileges and immunities

The authorization to bring judicial proceedings under . . . this title shall not constitute a waiver of sovereign immunity for any other purpose, or of the privileges of any Senator or Member of the House of Representatives under article I, section 6, clause 1, of the Constitution, or a waiver of any power of either the Senate or the House of Representatives under the Constitution . . . or under the rules of either House relating to records and information within its jurisdiction.

Would this statute have any effect on the cases discussed in note 1 *supra?* Would a statute purporting to waive Speech or Debate Clause immunity be constitutional?

3. *In re Chapman*, 166 U.S. 661, 669–60 (1897), stands for the proposition that each branch of the legislature has a broad and expansive power to expel. But in *Powell*, the Court tied the power to exclude to the qualifications spelled out in the Constitution. What is the basis for the Court's broad construction of the power to expel and its narrow construction of the power to exclude? Is it because the power to expel is expressly stated whereas the power to exclude is not?

4. The Court in *Powell* relies on statements in the House Rules that rejected any power to punish conduct occurring during a prior Congress. In concurrence, Douglas cites the experience with Senator Langer as precedent for a lack of congressional authority.

If the House expelled a member whose misconduct was known to his constituents at the time of his reelection, would such action unconstitutionally substitute the House's own standards for the standards of those who voted to reelect him?

5. The Select Committee recommended that Mr. Powell be censured, fined, and stripped of seniority. The chair of the Select Committee, Rep. Celler (D.N.Y.), asserted that if the House followed the Select Committee's recommendation Mr. Powell would have no "right to appeal except to the Lord Almighty." Does *Powell v. McCormack* undermine the force of Rep. Celler's remarks?

If not, given your understanding of legislative representation, how effective a representative is one who has been censured and fined by his colleagues and who possesses no committee seniority?

If, upon Mr. Powell's readmission to the House, his colleagues in the House

Democratic Caucus had refused to give him a committee assignment, would he have a constitutional claim?

Suppose a conservative Democrat on the House Ways and Means Committee has consistently voted with his Republican colleagues on issues crucial to his party. Can the House Democratic caucus strip him of seniority or transfer him to a less significant committee without violating the member's rights of free expression under the First Amendment?

See *Skaggs v. Carle*, 110 F.3d 831 (D.C. Cir. 1997) (rejecting a First Amendment challenge to House Rule XXI(5)(d): "It shall not be in order to consider any bill, joint resolution or conference report carrying a retroactive Federal income tax increase.").

6. What procedure should a legislature use to determine the relevant facts before acting to exclude or expel a member convicted of a crime? Should the conviction be conclusive, should it be *prima facie* evidence, or must all the evidence be resubmitted for an independent determination by the legislature itself? Who should hear the facts and what role should be given to a committee? Videotapes used in his criminal prosecution were made available to members before they voted in 1980 to expel Congressman Myers.

In the United States House of Representatives, the Ethics Committee prosecutes, determines facts, and imposes sanctions, subject to the vote of the full house. Few members are anxious to undertake these roles and sit in judgment of their colleagues. In 1979, a proposal was made to separate these functions. The committee would act as a "grand jury." Upon finding grounds to proceed, *e.g.*, "credible evidence," four members of each party were to be chosen by lot to act as judges. The proposal was strongly supported by committee members who saw a way to avoid passing judgment on their fellow members.

Are there interim sanctions which would avoid a redetermination of the facts, *e.g.*, loss of leadership roles or suspension of voting privileges? Would voters from the member's district have standing to challenge suspension of the member's voting privileges?

7. The following hypothetical situations may be useful in exploring the dimensions of a legislature's power over its members:

(a) A federal statute requires that a federal legislator convicted of bribery be removed from office.

Is the statute constitutional? *Cf. Burton v. United States*, 202 U.S. 344 at 369 (1905).

(b) A member of the United States House is convicted of embezzling funds through an elaborate scheme. He increased his aides' salaries, who in turn loyally returned the funds to him through a tacit agreement that the monies be deposited in his special account.

Is there a sufficient basis for expulsion by a two-thirds vote of the House? Would these acts constitute grounds for exclusion from the next Congress if the member is reelected subsequently? Is exclusion by a simple majority vote a legal alternative?

(c) Should there be a different result if the convicted legislator was a lawyer who had embezzled funds from a client?

See generally JACK MASSEY, EXPULSION, CENSURE, REPRIMAND & FINE: LEGISLATIVE DISCIPLINE IN THE HOUSE OF REPRESENTATIVES (CRS Report, April 16, 2002).

8. What redress does the member have who is excluded or expelled on the basis of a conviction that is later reversed?

9. What conduct is deemed covered by the language of Article 1, § 5, "disorderly behavior," so as to justify imposition of sanctions? Several members of Congress were expelled during the Civil War when they joined the Confederacy in open revolt against the Union. Does their action come within § 5? What other constitutional provisions discussed in *Powell* would justify such congressional action? What is the rationale for giving the body power to discipline its members? Should a distinction be drawn between disciplining a member for conduct outside Congress prior to election to the Congress and for conduct committed while in Congress but in a prior session?

10. In some states, conviction of a felony involving moral turpitude may disqualify the person from holding office. This would justify the legislature's excluding or expelling that person from membership. Assuming, however, that the conviction is appealed, must the legislature delay action until all appeals are final? In such states, should conviction of felonies not involving moral turpitude be considered a sufficient basis to deny member?

11. How sound is the following comment on the majority's reasoning on the justiciability issue:

> The Court's failure to note the lack of any historical support for judicial review of cases of exclusion from Congress is related to a more fundamental defect in its analysis of the justiciability of Powell's claim. Having begun by asking the right question, whether there was a "constitutional commitment of the issue" to the House, the Court proceeded to answer a quite different one, whether the "qualifications" which Article I, Section 5 authorized the House to "judge" were only those specified in Article I, Section 2 (and perhaps elsewhere in the Constitution). The opinion reflects, in short, a classic instance of confusion between "jurisdiction" — the power to decide — and "the merits" — the correctness of decisions.
>
> The source of this confusion, it seems fairly clear is the Court's assumption that it bears "responsibility . . . to act as the ultimate interpreter of the Constitution." On that premise, it is but a short step to the conclusion that the Court is obligated to intervene when another branch of government acts in a manner prohibited by the Constitution. If the Constitution permits the House to judge only the "standing" qualifications of those who have been elected to membership, *e.e.*, those specified in the Constitution, the Court, as the body ultimately responsible for the Constitution, must have the authority to review the decisions of the House to assure that constitutional limitations have been observed.

Terrance Sandalow, *Comments on Powell v. McCormack*, 17 UCLA L. Rev. 164, 172–73 (1969).

Has the author adequately weighed the framer's concerns lest the legislature "usurp 'the indisputable right [of the people] to return who they thought proper' to the legislature"? *Powell v. McCormack, supra* at 535.

12. In *Nixon v. United States*, 506 U.S. 224, 237 (1993), the Supreme Court observed:

> Our conclusion in *Powell* was based on the fixed meaning of "qualifications" set forth in Article I § 2. The claim by the House that its power to "be the judges of the Elections, Returns and Qualifications of its own members" was a textual commitment of unreviewable authority was defeated by the existence of this separate provision specifying the only qualifications which may be imposed for House membership. The decision as to whether a member satisfied these qualifications was placed within the House, but the decision as to what those qualifications consisted of was not.

Do you agree with the *Nixon* Court's reading of *Powell?*

13. Suppose that the voters of California extended term limit restrictions to members of California's congressional delegation. Would that measure survive the analysis in *Powell v. McCormack, supra? See U.S. Term Limits, Inc. v. Thornton*, 514 U.S. 779, 787–819 (1995) (extensive discussion of *Powell v. McCormack*).

C. SOURCES OF LEGISLATION

These materials deal both with the generation of ideas for legislation and with the hard task of translating ideas into legislative language.

CHARLES W. JOHNSON,
HOW OUR LAWS ARE MADE
4–5 (2003)

Sources of ideas for legislation are unlimited and proposed drafts of bills originate in many diverse quarters. Primary among these is the idea and draft conceived by a Member. This may emanate from the election campaign during which the Member had promised, if elected, to introduce legislation on a particular subject. The Member may have also become aware after taking office of the need for amendment to or repeal of an existing law or the enactment of a statute in an entirely new field.

In addition, the Member's constituents, either as individuals or through citizen groups, may avail themselves of the right to petition and transmit their proposals to the Member. The right to petition is guaranteed by the First Amendment to the Constitution. Many excellent laws have originated in this way, as some organizations, because of their vital concern with various areas of legislation, have considerable knowledge regarding the laws affecting their interests and have the services of legislative draftspersons for this purpose. Similarly, state legislatures may "memorialize" Congress to enact specified federal laws by passing resolutions to be transmitted to the House and Senate as memorials. If favorably impressed by the idea, a Member may introduce the proposal in the form in which it has been submitted or may redraft it. In any event, a Member may consult with the Legislative Counsel of the House or the Senate to frame the ideas in suitable legislative language and form.

In modern times, the "executive communication" has become a prolific source of legislative proposals. The communication is usually in the form of a message or letter from a member of the President's Cabinet, the head of an independent agency, or the President himself, transmitting a draft of a proposed bill to the Speaker of the House of Representatives and the President of the Senate. Despite the structure of separation of powers, Article II, Section 3, of the Constitution imposes an obligation on the President to report to Congress from time to time on the "State of the Union" and to recommend for consideration such measures as the President considers necessary and expedient. Many of these executive communications follow on the President's message to Congress on the state of the Union. The communication is then referred to the standing committee or committees having jurisdiction of the subject matter of the proposal. The chairman or the ranking minority member of the relevant committee usually introduces the bill promptly either in the form in which it was received or with desired changes. This practice is usually followed even when the majority of the House and the President are not of the same political party, although there is no constitutional or statutory requirement that a bill be introduced to effectuate the recommendations. The committee or one of its subcommittees may also decide to examine the communication to determine whether a bill should be introduced. The most important of the regular executive communications is the annual message from the President transmitting the proposed budget to Congress. The President's budget proposal, together with testimony by officials of the various branches of the government before the Appropriations Committees of the House and Senate, is the basis of the several appropriation bills that are drafted by the Committee on Appropriations of the House.

Many of the executive departments and independent agencies employ legislative counsels who are charged with the drafting of bills. These legislative proposals are forwarded to Congress with a request for their enactment.

The drafting of statutes is an art that requires great skill, knowledge, and experience. In some instances, a draft is the result of a study covering a period of a year or more by a commission or committee designated by the President or a member of the Cabinet. The Administrative Procedure Act and the Uniform Code of Military Justice are two examples of enactments resulting from such studies. In addition, congressional committees sometimes draft bills after studies and hearings covering periods of a year or more.

The following observations by an assistant counsel in the Office of Legislative Counsel of the U.S. House of Representatives illustrate the constraints and complexities involved in legislative drafting.

SANDRA STROKOFF,
HOW OUR LAWS ARE MADE: A GHOST WRITER'S VIEW
(Updated April 19, 2002)

Frequently, on the floor of the House of Representatives, one will hear a Member refer to another as the "author" of a bill who has "carefully crafted" the language of the proposed legislation. Statements like these make me smile, because if the Members are the authors, then I and my colleagues in the Office of the Legislative Counsel of the House of Representatives are the ghost writers.

The Office of the Legislative Counsel, created by statute originally in 1918, currently composed of 30-plus attorneys who generally toil in anonymity, at least as far as those outside the legislative process are concerned. Attorneys are charged with taking the idea of any Member or committee of the House of Representatives requesting the services of the Office and transforming it into legislative language or, as one of my clients used to say, "the magic words." We participate in all stages of the legislative process, be it preparing a bill for introduction, drafting amendments, participating in any conference of the two Houses of Congress to resolve differences between the two versions of the bill, or incorporating changes in the bill at each stage for publication and ultimately for presentation to the President. Frequently, we draft while debate is going on — both during committee consideration and on the House Floor, and may be asked to explain the meaning or effect of legislative language.

Although the Office has drafting manuals and guidelines, drafting legislation is without question a matter of on-the-job training. For up to two years, a new attorney in the Office, while communicating directly with clients (congressional staff members, but occasionally the Members themselves) on legislative requests, works under the tutelage of a senior attorney in preparing for introduction a wide variety of bills to gain as much experience as possible in developing drafting skills. Typically, only legislation that is unlikely to pass is given to a new attorney, Ironically a new attorney's work will almost always include drafting a few amendments to the U.S. Constitution.

Members of the Office of the Legislative Counsel are bound by statute not to express views on or make policy with respect to legislation. Our responsibility is to reflect the ideas of Members of Congress accurately in legislative language. That isn't to say that we can't affect policy by pointing out the consequences or meanings of the printed word. Trying to close loopholes before they open is a constant challenge. It is easy to overlook the consequences of the simplest word. Some years ego, a House bill authorizing the President to impose controls on exports to any foreign country for foreign policy reasons was amended to prohibit placing these controls on "food." When the House was in conference with the Senate on the bill, the Senate staff referred to the provision as the "Twinkies amendment" because "food" meant any kind of food, exported for any reason. The conference agreement modified the provision to prohibit controls on exports of food, but only food used to combat malnutrition. Most would not put Twinkies in that category.

Attorneys in our office "specialize" in particular areas of law with which we become reasonably conversant over a period of time; however, because of the relatively small number of attorneys handling anything that comes in the door, we use the term "specialist" loosely. I, for example, am responsible for legislation involving trade with other countries, exports from the United States, controlling the proliferation of arms and weapons of mass destruction, all forms of intellectual property, and matters affecting the Federal courts and civil actions, and I share responsibility with other attorneys on all other matters affecting international relations. We work best when we can rely on the expertise of congressional staff, the executive branch, the Library of Congress, and even outside groups, who are able to answer our questions regarding the practical effect of a particular policy.

We draft legislation for all sides on the issues at the same time, both Republicans and Democrats, and factions within each party. We may be drafting the same legislation for different individuals. At times, it would be much more efficient to be able to hook up several different clients who want to do roughly the same thing at the same time, instead of having to produce multiple documents with enough modifications to make them look different. But we are strictly bound by the rules of attorney-client confidentiality. We are therefore frequently in the position of knowing what all sides are up to before anyone else does.

While drafting legislation primarily involves knowing what existing law is and how to change it to do only what is asked and no more, we of course have to be mindful of the constraints of the Constitution. Bill of Rights issues do occasionally arise, but far more likely are issues regarding Federal versus State powers. I have become aware of parts of the Constitution I didn't know existed in law school, such as Article 1, section 9, clause 5, which prohibits the imposition of a tax on exports from any State, and Article I, section 10, clauses 2 and 3, which require the consent of Congress to any State-imposed duty on imports or exports and to any interstate compact (e.g. the agreement between Pennsylvania and New Jersey establishing the Delaware River Port Authority, which is supposed to keep the bridges connecting the two States from falling down). Sometimes we are asked to draft a constitutional fix for a provision that the courts have struck down as unconstitutional. Far more common, however, are proposals to amend existing law to change an interpretation of it by the courts that was unintended when the law was first enacted.

Of more pervasive impact than the Constitution are procedural issues. The rules of the House of Representatives and the Senate have tremendous significance at all stages of the legislative process once a bill has been introduced. An amendment to be offered to a bill in committee or on the House floor has to be *germane* to the bill (a term meaning, roughly, to be within the jurisdictional scope of the bill), and has to be offered at the appropriate time and in the appropriate form (e.g. as an amendment, an amendment to an amendment, a substitute to an amendment, an amendment to a substitute, etc.). But more significantly, before each bill is considered on the House floor, a rule is adopted (as reported by the Committee on Rules of the House) that stipulates how it is to be considered. Whereas in the past most bills had an "open rule," that is, a rule under which anyone could offer an amendment to the bill, more recently the norm is either a rule making in order a short list of amendments submitted in advance to the Rules Committee, or a rule prescribing a limited time within which consideration of the bill, and all amendments thereto, must be completed. Both of these so-called "modified open rules" have the effect of cutting off debate. The result is that many ideas are never debated at all.

In recent years the volume of work, coupled with extraordinary time constraints within which to do it, have made the job as legislative counsel increasingly demanding. There has also been the advent of the "megabill", that is, instead of a bill dealing with a specific subject within the jurisdiction of one committee that more than likely began as the idea of one Member of the House, a bill on a general subject for which many committees contribute provisions within their respective jurisdictions. The major megabills created by the budget process mandated by law are the budget reconciliation bills, encompassing changes in law required for each committee to meet prescribed budget targets for the coming fiscal year for matters within their respective jurisdictions. Our office is assigned the task of assembling these massive bills, which by their nature require coordinating the efforts of many attorneys in the Office who handle the different jurisdictions.

If, as we are all aware, legislation is not perfect, the circumstances under which it is put together prevent its being so: being asked to draft major proposals or multiple requests (as in preparation for committee or floor consideration) in short periods of time; being told to leave language ambiguous so as to avoid a particular interpretation or to gain the support of a particular constituency; generally not having enough time to read and reread proposed legislation for consistency and technical correctness. And, in some cases, the services of legislative counsel are not even used. The extraordinary agenda of the House of Representatives in the 104th Congress of *completing* consideration of major pieces of legislation in the now famous first "100 days," coupled with the major downsizing of congressional staff (and with it, a significant loss of expertise and institutional memory) have made the job of legislative counsel all the more challenging.

Complaints aside, what keeps the job interesting and intellectually stimulating is the steady stream of new issues to tackle. To be presented with a problem that seeks a legislative solution, and then to put the pieces together in the matrix of existing law, much like solving a puzzle, can be very gratifying.

. . . .

Being a participant . . . in the legislative process has been at times exhilarating, at other times frustrating, and many times nerve-wracking. Most legislation that is enacted is a comprise of divergent points of view, and that, perhaps, is the essence of the democratic process. There are times, purely for the sake of that compromise, when I am asked to draft provisions that may not make much logical, let alone policy, sense. At such times I am happy to remain a ghost writer as I mutter the title of a pamphlet given to me on my first day in the Office 20 years ago: "How our laws are made."

NOTES AND QUESTIONS

James Madison, in Federalist 37, made the following reflections on the task of drafting that are still pertinent:

> When we pass from the works of nature, in which all the delineations are perfectly accurate, and appear to be otherwise only from the imperfection of the eye which surveys them, to the institutions of man, in which the obscurity arises as well from the object itself as from the organ by which it is contemplated, we must perceive the necessity of moderating still further our expectations and hopes from the efforts of human sagacity. Experience has instructed us that no skill in the science of government has yet been able to discriminate and define, with sufficient certainty, its three great provinces — the legislative, executive, and judiciary; or even the privileges and powers of the different legislative branches. Questions daily occur in the course of practice, which prove the obscurity which reigns in these subjects, and which puzzle the greatest adepts in political science.

> The experience of ages, with the continued and combined labors of the most enlightened legislators and jurists, has been equally unsuccessful in delineating the several objects and limits of different codes of laws and different tribunals of justice. The precise extent of the common law and the statute law, the maritime law, the ecclesiastical law, the law of corporations, and other local laws and customs, remains still to be clearly and finally established in Great Britain,

where accuracy in such subjects has been more industriously pursued than in any other part of the world. The jurisdiction of her several courts, general and local, of law, of equity, of admiralty, etc., is not less a source of frequent and intricate discussions, sufficiently denoting the indeterminate limits by which they are respectively circumscribed. All new laws, though penned with the greatest technical skill, and passed on the fullest and most mature deliberation, are considered as more or less obscure and equivocal, until their meaning be liquidated and ascertained by a series of particular discussions and adjudications. Besides the obscurity arising from the complexity of objects, and the imperfection of the human faculties, the medium through which the conceptions of men are conveyed to each other adds a fresh embarrassment. The use of words is to express ideas. Perspicuity, therefore, requires not only that the ideas should be distinctly formed, but that they should be expressed by words distinctly and exclusively appropriate to them. But no language is so copious as to supply words and phrases for every complex idea, or so correct as not to include many equivocally denoting different ideas. Hence it must happen that however accurately objects may be discriminated in themselves, and however accurately the discrimination may be conceived, the definition of them may be rendered inaccurate by the inaccuracy of the terms in which it is delivered. And this unavoidable inaccuracy must be greater or less, according to the complexity and novelty of the objects defined. When the Almighty himself condescends to address mankind in their own language, his meaning, luminous as it must be, is rendered dim and doubtful by the cloudy medium through which it is communicated.

Here, then, are three sources of vague and incorrect definitions: indistinctness of the object, imperfection of the organ of perception, inadequateness of the vehicle of ideas . . . .

THE FEDERALIST 225–27 (Robert Scigliano, ed., 2000).

A well-known maxim about the legislative process is that "the President proposes and Congress disposes." PAUL DICKSON & PAUL CLANCY, THE CONGRESS DICTIONARY 273 (1993). The following materials reveal how the executive branch seeks to influence the legislative process.

OFFICE OF MANAGEMENT AND BUDGET, CIRCULAR NO. A-19
(revised September 20, 1979)

TO THE HEADS OF EXECUTIVE DEPARTMENTS AND ESTABLISHMENTS

SUBJECT: Legislative coordination and clearance

1. **Purpose.** The Circular outlines procedures for the coordination and clearance by the Office of Management and Budget (OMB) of agency recommendations on proposed, pending, and enrolled legislation. It also includes instructions on the timing and preparation of agency legislative programs . . . .

3. **Background.** OMB performs legislative coordination and clearance functions to (a) assist the President in developing a position on legislation, (b) make known the Administration's position on legislation for the guidance of the agencies and information of Congress, (c) assure appropriate consideration of the views of all affected agencies, and (d) assist the President with respect to action on enrolled bills.

4. **Coverage.** All executive branch agencies (as defined in section 5b) are subject to

the provisions of this Circular, except those agencies that are specifically required by law to transmit their legislative proposals, reports, or testimony to the Congress without prior clearance. OMB will, however, honor requests from such agencies for advice on the relationship of particular legislation, reports, or testimony to the program of the President. The municipal government of the District of Columbia is covered to the extent that legislation involves the relationship between it and the Federal Government. Agencies of the legislative and judicial branches are not covered by this Circular

5. **Definitions.** For the purpose of this Circular, the following definition apply.

a. **Advice.** Information transmitted to an agency by OMB stating the relationship of particular legislation and reports thereon to the program of the President or stating the views of OMB as a staff agency for the President with respect to such legislation and reports.

b. **Agency.** Any executive department or independent commission, board, bureau, office, agency, Government-owned or controlled corporation, or other establishment of the Government, including any regulatory commission or board and also the municipal government of the District of Columbia.

c. **Proposed legislation.*** A draft bill or any supporting document (e.g., Speaker letter, section-by-section analysis, statement of purpose and justification, etc.) that an agency wishes to present to Congress for its consideration. Also, any proposal for or endorsement of Federal legislation included in an agency's annual or special report or in other written form which an agency proposes to transmit to Congress, or to any Member or committee, officer or employee of Congress, or staff of any committee, or the public.

d. **Pending bill.** Any bill or resolution that has been introduced in Congress or any amendment to a bill or resolution while in committee or when proposed for House or Senate floor consideration during debate. Also, any proposal placed before the conferees on a bill that has passed both Houses.

e. **Report** (including testimony). Any written expression of official views prepared by an agency on a pending bill for (1) transmittal to any committee, Member, officer or employee or Congress, or staff of any committee or Member, or (2) presentation as testimony before a congressional committee. Also, any comment or recommendation on pending legislation included in an agency's annual or special report that an agency proposes to transmit to Congress, or any Member or committee, or to make available to any study group, commission, or the public.

f. **Enrolled bill.** A bill or resolution passed by both Houses of Congress and presented to the President for action.

g. **Views letter.** An agency's written comments provided at the request of OMB on a pending bill or on another agency's proposed legislation, report, or testimony.

6. **Agency legislative programs.**

a. **Submission to OMB.** Each agency shall prepare and submit to OMB annually its proposed legislative program for the next session of Congress. If an agency has no legislative program, it should submit a statement to this effect.

b. **Purposes of legislative program submission.** The essential purposes for requiring agencies to submit annual legislative programs are: (1) to assist agency planning for legislative objectives; (2) to help agencies coordinate their legislative program with the preparation of their annual budget submissions to

---

* The terms "proposed legislation" and "report" do not include materials submitted in justification of appropriation requests or proposals for reorganization plans.

OMB; (3) to give agencies an opportunity to recommend specific proposals for Presidential endorsement; and (4) to aid OMB and other staff of the Executive Office of the President in developing the President's legislative program, budget, and annual and special messages.

c. Timing of submission to OMB. (1) Each agency shall submit its proposed legislative program to OMB at the same time as it initially submits its annual budget request . . . . Timely submission is essential if the programs are to serve the purposes set forth in section 6b.

(2) Items that are not included in an agency's legislative program and have significant upward budget impact will not be considered after the budget is prepared unless they result from circumstances not foreseeable at the time of final budget decisions . . . .

e. Program content. Each agency shall prepare its legislative program in accordance with the instructions in Attachment A. Agency submission shall include:

(1) All items of legislation that an agency contemplates proposing to Congress (or actively supporting, if already pending legislation) during the coming session, including proposals to extend expiring laws or repeal provisions of existing laws. These items should be based on policy-level decisions within the agency and should take into account the President's known legislative, budgetary, and other relevant policies. Agencies' proposed legislative programs should identify those items of sufficient importance to be included in the President's legislative program.

(2) A separate list of legislative proposals under active consideration in the agency that are not yet ready for inclusion in its proposed legislative program. For each item in this list, the agency should indicate when it expects to reach a policy-level decision and, specifically, whether it expects to propose the item in time for its consideration for inclusion in the annual budget under preparation.

(3) A separate list of all laws or provisions of law affecting an agency that will expire between the date the program is submitted to OMB and the end of the two following calendar years, whether or not the agencies plans to propose their extension.

(4) All items in the submissions that are proposed, or expected to be proposed, for inclusion in the annual budget shall be accompanied by a tabulation showing amounts of budget authority and outlays or other measure of budgetary impact for the budget year and for each of the four succeeding fiscal year . . . .

(5) All items covered by section 6e(4) above shall also be accompanied by estimates of work-years of employment and of personnel required to carry out the proposal in the budget year and four succeeding fiscal years.

f. Relationship to advice. Submission of a legislative program to OMB does not constitute a request for advice on individual legislative proposals. Such request should be made in the manner prescribed in section 7 of this Circular.

7. Submission of agency proposed legislation and reports.

a. Submission to OMB. Before an agency transmits proposed legislation or a report (including testimony) outside the Executive branch, it shall submit the proposed legislation or report or testimony to OMB for coordination and clearance.

b. Agency scheduling of submission. Agencies should not commit themselves to testify on pending bills or to submit reports or proposed legislation to Congress on a time schedule that does not allow orderly coordination and clearance. To facilitate congressional action on Administration proposals and to forestall hasty, last-minute clearance requests, agencies should plan their submissions to OMB on a time schedule that will permit orderly coordination and clearance. Particular care should be given to ensuring that draft legislation to carry out Presidential legislative recommendations is submitted promptly to OMB to allow sufficient time for analysis and review.

c. Timing of agency submissions.

(1) Agencies should submit proposed legislation, reports, and testimony to OMB well in advance of the desired date of transmittal to Congress.

(2) Agencies should include in their submissions to OMB of proposed reports and testimony a copy of any committee request for such reports and testimony, if the request calls for special information or includes specific questions to be covered in the reports or testimony.

(3) Depending on the complexity and significance of the subject matter, the policy issues involved, and the number of agencies affected, an adequate period for clearance by OMB may range from several days to a number of months. Agencies shall consult with OMB staff as to necessary periods for clearance, particularly in cases of major or complex legislation.

(4) On occasion, very short periods for clearances may be unavoidable because of congressional time schedules or other factors. Nevertheless, agencies should make every effort to give OMB a minimum of five full working days for clearance of proposed reports or testimony.

(5) Agencies shall state in their transmittal letters to OMB any information on congressional schedules or other special circumstances that may require expedited clearance . . . .

e. Submission of legislation authorizing the enactment of new budget authority.

f. Items to be included in agency submission.

(1) Agencies should identify proposed legislation submitted to OMB by using the number assigned to the proposal in the agency's legislative program submission e.g., Agriculture, 96-12 (see Attachment A). Each legislative proposal shall include a draft transmittal letter to the Speaker of the House and the President of the Senate as well as background information and justification, including where applicable.

(a) a section-by-section analysis of the provisions of the proposed legislation;

(b) Comparison with existing law presented to "Ramseyer" or "Cordon" rule form by underscoring proposed addition to existing law and bracketing the text of proposed deletions (This need be done only when it would facilitate understanding of the proposed legislation);

(c) budgetary and personnel impacts as described in sections 6e(4) and (5), including statement of the relationship of these estimates to those previously incorporated in the President's budgetary program. (Public Law 89-554, 5 U.S.C. 2953, requires in certain cases that agencies, in proposing legislation and in submitting reports favoring legislation, provided estimates of expenditures and personnel that would be needed. Public Law 91-510, sections 252(a) (2U.S.C. 190j) and 252(b) imposes similar requirements on congressional committees.);

(d) comparison with previous agency proposals or related bills introduced in the Congress;

(e) an identification of other agencies that have an interest in the proposal;

(f) an indication of any consultation with other agencies in the development of the proposal; and

(g) information required by statute or by Administration policies, as, for example, that noted in section 7h below.

(2) Similarly, in their letters to OMB requesting advice on reports or testimony, agencies should identify related bills and set forth any relevant comments not included in the report or testimony itself. As indicated in section 7f(1)(c), certain reports or testimony favoring legislation are required by law to include budget and personnel estimates. Where such estimates are not included in other reports or in testimony favoring or opposing legislation, agencies should provide in their letters to OMB a statement of budgetary and personnel impacts as described in sections 6e(4) and (5), including a statement of the relationship of these estimates to those previously incorporated in the President's budgetary program.

(3) In cases where legislation carries out a Presidential recommendation, agencies should include in the proposed report or the letter transmitting proposed legislation a statement identifying the recommendation and indicating the degree to which the legislation concerned will carry it out.

g. Views letters. In views letters to OMB, an agency should indicate whether it supports, opposes, or has no objection to all or part of a pending bill or of another agency's proposed legislation, report, or testimony and should state the reasons for its position. If an agency proposes changes to a pending bill or to another agency's submission, its views letter should recommend, insofar as practicable, specific substitute language.

h. Certain statutory and other requirements and Administration policies. Agencies shall carefully consider and take into account certain requirements of existing statutes and Executive orders and Administration policies and directives that are of general applicability. Agency reports and proposed legislation shall, to the maximum extent possible, contain or be accompanied by appropriate recommendations, statements, or provisions to give effect to such requirements, including but not limited to:

(1) Civil rights

(2) Environmental impact

(3) Economic impact

(4) Federal budgetary impact and personnel requirements

(5) Federal and non-federal paperwork requirements

(6) State and local government impact

(7) Urban and community impact.

i. Drafting service. Agencies need not submit for clearance bills that they prepare as a drafting service for a congressional committee or a Member of Congress, provided that they state in their transmittal letter that the drafting service does not constitute a commitment with respect to the position of the Administration or the agency. Agencies shall advise OMB of these drafting service requests while the requests are being complied with, and supply a copy of the request, if in writing. A copy of each such draft bill and the accompanying letter should be furnished to OMB at the time of transmittal, together with an explanatory statement of what the bill would accomplish if that is not contained in the transmittal letter.

j. Use of "no comment" reports. Agencies should submit no comment reports only when they have no interest in the pending legislation or nothing to contribute by way of informed comment. Agencies should submit such reports for clearance, unless a different procedure is informally arranged with OMB. In either event, they should furnish OMB with one copy of each such report at the time it is transmitted for Congress.

8. Clearance of agency proposed legislation and reports.

a. OMB action on agency submissions.

(1) OMB will undertake the necessary coordination with other interested agencies of an agency's proposed legislation or report. If congressional committees have not requested reports from all of the interested agencies, OMB will request other agency views within specified time limits. OMB will consult with the President, when appropriate, and undertake such staff work for him as may be necessary in cooperation with other Presidential staff. OMB may request the originating agency to provide additional information or may call interagency meetings to exchange views, resolve differences of opinion, or clarify the facts.

(2) When coordination is completed, OMB will transmit advice to the appropriate agencies, either in writing or by telephone. In transmitting advice, OMB may indicate considerations that agencies should or may wish to take into account before submitting proposed legislation or reports to Congress.

b. Forms of OMB advice. The exact forms of OMB advice will vary to suit the particular case. The basic forms of advice that are commonly used are set forth and explained in Attachment C.

c. Agency action on receipt of advice from OMB.

(1) Agencies shall incorporate the advice received from OMB in their reports and in their letters transmitting proposed legislation to Congress. Advice on testimony is usually not included in the testimony as delivered unless it would be likely to have a significant effect on a committee's consideration of particular legislation or would not otherwise be available to a committee through a written report.

(2) In the case of reports, receipt of advice contrary to views expressed does not require any agency to change its views. In such cases, however, the agency will review its position. If it decides to modify its views, the agency shall consult with OMB to determine what change, if any, in advice previously received is appropriate. If, after the review, the views of the agency are not modified, it shall incorporate in its report the full advice it received.

(3) In the case of proposed legislation, the originating agency shall not submit to Congress any proposal that OMB has advised is in conflict with the program of the President or has asked the agency to reconsider as a result of the coordination process. In such cases, OMB will inform the agency of the reasons for its action.

(4) Agencies are expected to transmit reports and proposed legislation to Congress promptly after receiving OMB clearance. Should circumstances arise that make prompt transmittal inadvisable, the agency shall immediately notify OMB. Similarly, in the case of cleared testimony, the agency shall immediately notify OMB if its testimony has been cancelled or rescheduled.

(5) Agencies should observe the instructions in House and Senate rules to forward proposed legislation or various reports required by law to the Speaker of the House and the President of the Senate. Reports that have been requested by committee chairmen on bills and resolutions pending before their committees should be transmitted directly to the requesting committees . . . .

d. Agency action where prior clearance has not been effected.

(1) Agencies shall not submit to Congress proposed legislation that has not

been coordinated and cleared within the Executive branch in accordance with this Circular.

(2) If congressional time schedules do not allow an agency to send its proposed report to OMB in time for the normal clearance and advice, the agency shall consult informally with OMB as to the advice to be included in the proposed report. OMB may advise the agency to state in its report that time has not permitted securing advice from OMB as to the relationship of the proposed legislation to the program of the President. Agencies shall send to OMB six copies of such reports at the same time that they are transmitted to Congress. Where appropriate, OMB will subsequently furnish advice on the report, which the agency shall transmit promptly to Congress.

(3) In cases where an agency has not submitted a report for clearance and its views on pending legislation are to be expressed in the form of oral, unwritten testimony, OMB will undertake such coordination and give such advice as the circumstances permit. In presenting oral testimony, the agency should indicate what advice, if any, has been received from OMB. If no advice has been obtained, the agency should so indicate.

e. Reclearance requirements. The advice received from OMB generally applies to all sessions of each Congress, but it does not carry over from one Congress to the next. Generally, agencies do not need to seek reclearance of reports on which they have already received advice before making the same reports on identical bills introduced in the same Congress, unless considerable time has elapsed or changed conditions indicate that the need for reclearance is appropriate or should be rechecked. Prior to transmitting such reports, however, agencies shall consult informally with appropriate OMB staff to determine whether reclearance is necessary. In cases where reclearance does not take place, agencies shall include in the subsequent report appropriate reference to the advice received on the original report. They shall also send one copy of any subsequent report to OMB at the same time that it is transmitted to Congress. The transmittal letter to OMB should identify the related report that was previously cleared.

9. Interagency Consultation. In carrying out their legislative functions, agencies are encouraged to consult with each other in order that all relevant interests and points of view be considered and accommodated, where appropriate, in the formulation of their positions. Such consultation is particularly important in cases of overlapping interest, and intensive efforts should be made to reach interagency agreement before proposed legislation or reports are sent to OMB. In order that the President may have the individual views of the responsible heads of the agencies, however, proposed legislation or reports so coordinated shall be sent to OMB by the individual agencies involved, with appropriate reference to the interagency consultation that has taken place.

. . . .

11. Agency legislative liaison officers. To assist in effecting interagency coordination, each agency shall furnish OMB with the name of a liaison officer who has been designated by the agency to handle the coordination of legislative matters under this Circular. From time to time, OMB will send agencies lists of the liaison officers so designated. Agencies should promptly notify OMB of any change in their liaison officers.

ATTACHMENT A

INSTRUCTIONS RELATING TO THE PREPARATION OF AGENCY LEGISLATIVE PROGRAMS

1. Agencies' proposed legislative programs should be divided into two parts:

PART I — PRESIDENT'S PROGRAM PROPOSALS

Those items that the agency believes are of sufficient importance to be included in the President's legislative program and given specific endorsement by him in one of the regular annual messages, such as the budget message, or in a special message.

PART II — ALL OTHER PROPOSALS

2. Within each Part, agencies should list the items in order of relative priority. Each item of proposed legislation should be given a separate number for purposes of ready identification, using a numbering system which identifies the Congress; e.g., Agriculture, 96-12.

3. With respect to each item, agencies should provide the following information:

    a.   A brief description of the proposal, its objectives, and its relationship to existing programs. Agencies should include greater detail on the specific provisions of proposals included in Part I or where the subject matter of the proposal contains new policies or programs or raises complex issues;

    b.   Pertinent comments as to timing and readiness of draft legislation;

    c.   Pertinent references to bills and reports concerning the subject of the proposal in current or recent sessions of Congress;

    d.   An estimate for each of the first five fiscal years of (1) any budget authority and outlays that would be required, (2) any savings in budget authority and outlays, (3) any changes in budget receipts, and (4) work years of employment and numbers of personnel . . . .

4. The lists of (a) legislative proposals still under consideration in an agency and (b) expiring laws (see section 6 of the Circular) should be presented separately from Parts I and II. The following special instructions apply to them:

    a.   Items still under consideration should be listed in approximate order of priority and each briefly described in terms of subject matter and status.

    b.   Each expiring law should be described in terms of (1) the subject, (2) the citation, (3) the date of expiration, (4) the agency's views as to whether the law should be extended or permitted to expire, and (5) other pertinent information. If an agency recommends extension, the proposal should also be included in Part I or Part II, as appropriate . . . .

EXHIBIT FOR ATTACHMENT A

DEPARTMENT OF GOVERNMENT

PROPOSED LEGISLATIVE PROGRAM FOR THE SESSION

OF THE CONGRESS

(Items in each Part are listed in order of priority)

PART I — PRESIDENT'S PROGRAM PROPOSALS

96-3 Amend the provisions of the 1902 Reclamation Act regarding acreage limitation, residency, leasing, excess land sales, the use of Class I Equivalency, contracts and contracting procedures, and certain administrative procedures. This proposal would modify and update the acreage limitation provisions of Federal Reclamation law to reflect and accommodate modern agricultural practices, but at the same time retain the basic concept of the Reclamation program — providing opportunities for family farms.

The Department has recommended that legislation amending the law reflect the following: Eligibility to receive project water would be limited to adults — 18 years of age or older. Residency as provided in the Reclamation Act of 1902, and defined as a maximum distance of 50 miles from the land, would be reimposed on both lessors and lessees of project lands, with specific guidelines for phasing in the requirement; the acreage entitlement for which project water would be available would be increased 60 320 acres owned per adult individual, with an additional allowance of 160 acres leased, or the entire 480 acres could be leased (family corporations and multiple ownerships could hold up to 960 acres without regard to the number of people in the arrangement); Class I equivalency would be authorized for general use for projects with a frost-free growing season of 180-days or less and would be applied on a project-by-project basis; contracts with districts containing provisions for exemption from acreage limitation provision upon payout of construction charges would be approved; Sale of excess land by the owner to immediate family members, long-time tenants, employees, or adjoining neighbors would be permitted; Charitable and religious organizations holding project lands on January 1, 1978, would be exempt from acreage limitations.

Cost: The estimated cost to the government of administering this proposal would he comparable to the estimated cost of implementing the compliance program under regulations which are being promulgated at this rime, The estimated cost of the compliance program for the 5-year period after the final rules are published . . .

	FY 1980	FY 1981	FY 1982	FY 1983	FY 1984
(millions)	2.4	2.4	2.0	2.0	2.0

Personnel requirements: Estimated personnel requirements are:

	FY 1980	FY 1981	FY 1982	FY 1983	FY 1984
(work-years)	76	76	64	64	64
(personnel)	85	85	70	70	70

PART II — ALL OTHER PROPOSALS

96-14 Amend Federal Power Commission Act of 1920. This proposal would amend the Federal Power Commission Act of 1920 to provide that a license will he issued only after the Secretary administering affected public lands makes a determination that the license will not interfere or he inconsistent with the purposes for which such lands are reserved. The Federal Power Commission has interpreted Section 4(e) to require only consideration of the affected Secretary's recommendations.

The proposal would also amend the act to provide for extinguishment of withdrawals created by the Federal Energy Regulatory Commission (FERC) applications if the FERC has not responded to the applicant within 6 months or as of date of denial or expiration, surrender, revocation or termination of the license. Most applications do not result in FEC licenses; yet the land is withdrawn. The administrative process of removing the withdrawals is cumbersome and time consuming and constrains the land managing agency from fully managing these lands for their resource values or from using these lands in exchanges. Revocation of the FERC withdrawal within a specified time period would he consistent with the provisions of Title II of the Federal Lands Policy and Management Act relating to withdrawals.

No additional appropriations or outlays would be required.

ATTACHMENT C
Circular No. A-19
Revised

BASIC FORMS OF OMB ADVICE

The basic forms of advice and their implications are set forth below:

1. **"In accord (not in accord) with the program of the President."** When an agency or a committee of Congress is advised that enactment of a bill would be in accord with the program of the President, the advice means that the bill is of sufficient importance for the President to give it his personal and public support. That identification of the legislative proposal with the President is made in a variety of ways; e.g., by inclusion in one of his regular messages (State of the Union, Economic, Budget), a special message, speech, press conference, letter, or leadership meeting.

"Not in accord" advice indicates that a bill is so contrary to the President's legislative proposals or other policies or is otherwise so objectionable that should it be enacted in its current form, a veto would be considered. It is not, however, necessarily a commitment to veto.

2. **"Consistent with"** advice is used where the relationship of a legislative proposal to the Administration's objectives is direct and the Administration's expressed support is desirable, but the item does not warrant personal identification with, or support by, the President. "Not consistent with" advice signals to Congress that there are major objections to a bill, but does not indicate as clearly as "not in accord" advice that a veto would be considered if it were enacted.

3. **"No objection from the standpoint of the Administration's program."** Advice that there is no objection to a bill from the standpoint of the Administration's program is given on the large number of agency draft bills that deal with matters primarily of agency concern and do not bear a direct or immediate relationship to the President's program or the Administration's objectives, In effect, such advice indicates to Congress that OMB knows of no reason why the President would not approve the bill if Congress should enact it.

Advice to an agency that there is no objection from the standpoint of the Administration's program to its submission of a report (or testimony) on a bill to a committee of Congress does not indicate any commitment as to ultimate Presidential approval or disapproval of the bill if it is enacted. Nevertheless, such "no objection" clearance does set up certain presumptions. If all agencies' views are favorable, the presumption is that no major objection to the bill is known and that the agencies affected will recommend Presidential approval if it becomes enrolled. If all agencies' views are adverse, the presumption is that the agencies may wish to recommend a veto if the bill becomes enrolled.

Infrequently, "no objection" clearance is given to agency reports expressing divergent views on the same bill. When this is done, it normally means that there is no objection to the bill if Congress acts favorably after considering the adverse views. Occasionally, it means that the Administration's position is being reserved pending resolution of the agencies' differences, and this reservation may be explicitly stated. The interested agencies are advised of each other's differing views in these cases.

4. **Qualified advice.** In some cases the advice given is qualified. For example, the advice

may be that there would be no objection to enactment of the bill from the standpoint of the Administration's program, or that the bill would be consistent with the Administration's objectives, if it were revised in specified respects.

NOTES AND QUESTIONS

To what extent should a lawyer giving advice to a client on the meaning of newly enacted legislation pay attention to differences between administration proposals and the text of enacted laws? Should the lawyer find out whether the proposal was a Presidential program proposal or a Part II proposal?

As Circular A-19 makes clear, the Executive branch is constantly engaged in drafting legislation. In doing so, the following executive order spells out some guidelines and considerations that highlight recurring issues in performing the task of legislative drafting.

EXECUTIVE ORDER 12988,
61 Fed Reg. 4729, 4731–4732
(February 5, 1996)

Civil Justice Reform

By the authority vested in me as President by the Constitution and the laws of the United States of America, including section 301 of title 3, United States Code, and in order to . . . who wish to improve legislative and regulatory drafting to reduce needless litigation . . . .

. . . .

Sec. 3. Principles to Enact Legislation and Promulgate Regulations Which Do Not Unduly Burden the Federal Court System

(a) General Duty to Review Legislation and Regulations. Within current budgetary constraints and existing executive branch coordination mechanisms and procedures established in OMB Circular A-19 and Executive Order No. 12866, each agency promulgating new regulations, reviewing existing regulations, developing legislative proposals concerning regulations, and developing new legislation shall adhere to the following requirements:

(1) The agency's proposed legislation and regulations shall be reviewed by the agency to eliminate drafting errors and ambiguity;

(2) The agency's proposed legislation and regulations shall be written to minimize litigation; and

(3) The agency's proposed legislation and regulations shall provide a clear legal standard for affected conduct rather than a general standard, and shall promote simplification and burden reduction.

(b) Specific Issues for Review. In conducting the reviews required by subsection (a), each agency formulating proposed legislation and regulations make every reasonable effort to ensure:

(1) that the legislation, as appropriate —

(A) specifies whether all causes of action arising under the law are subject to statutes of limitations;

(B) specifies in clear language the preemptive effect, if any, to be given to the law;

(C) specifies in clear language the effect on existing Federal law, if any, including all provisions repealed, circumscribed, displaced, impaired, or modified;

(D) provides a clear legal standard for affected conduct;

(E)   specifies whether private arbitration and other forms of private dispute resolution are appropriate under enforcement and relief provisions; subject to constitutional requirements;

(F)   specifies whether the provisions of the law are severable — if one or more of them is found to be unconstitutional;

(G)   specifies in clear language the retroactive effect, if any, to be given to the law;

(H)   specifies in clear language the applicable burdens of proof;

(I)   specifies in clear language whether it grants private parties a right to sue and, if so, the relief available and the conditions and terms for authorized awards of attorney's fees, if any;

(J)   specifies whether State courts have jurisdiction under the law and, if so, whether and under what conditions an action would be removable to Federal court;

(K)   specifies whether administrative proceedings are to be required before parties may file suit in court and, if so, describes those proceedings and requires the exhaustion of administrative remedies;

(L)   sets forth the standards governing the assertion of personal jurisdiction, if any;

(M)   defines key statutory tens, either explicitly or by reference to other statutes that explicitly define those terms;

(N)   specifies whether the legislation applies to the Federal Government or its agencies;

(O)   specifies whether the legislation applies to States, territories, the District of Columbia, and the Commonwealths of Puerto Rico and of the Northern Mariana Islands;

(P)   specifies what remedies are available such as money damages, civil penalties, injunctive relief, and attorney's fees; and

(Q)   addresses other important issues affecting clarity and general draftsmanship of legislation set forth by the Attorney General, with the concurrence of the Director of the Office of Management and Budget ("OMB") and after consultation with affected agencies, that are determined to be in accordance with the purposes of this order.

(2)   that the regulation, as appropriate —

(A)   specifies in clear language the preemptive effect, if any, to be given the regulation;

(B)   specifies in clear language the effect on existing Federal law or regulation, if any, including all provisions repealed, circumscribed, displaced, impaired, or modified;

(C)   provides a clear legal standard for affected conduct rather than a general standard, while promoting simplification and burden reduction;

(D)   specifies in clear language the retroactive effect, if any, to be given to the regulation;

(E)   specifies whether administrative proceedings are to be required before parties may file suit in court and, if so, describes those proceedings and requires the exhaustion of administrative remedies;

(F)   defines key terms, either explicitly or by reference to other regulations or statutes that explicitly define those items; and

(G)   addresses other important issues affecting clarity and general draftsmanship of regulations set forth by the Attorney General, with the concurrence of the Director of OMB and after consultation with affected agencies, that are determined to be in accordance with the purposes of this order.

(c) Agency Review. The agencies shall review such draft legislation or regulation to determine that either the draft legislation or regulation meets the applicable standards provided in subsections (a) and (b) of this section, or it is unreasonable to require the particular piece of draft legislation or regulation to meet one or more of those standards.

NOTES AND QUESTIONS

Keep these caveats in mind when working through the materials on statutory interpretation.

D.   FORMS OF LEGISLATIVE ACTION

1.   The U.S. Congress

CHARLES W. JOHNSON,
HOW OUR LAWS ARE MADE
5–8 (2003)

The work of Congress is initiated by the introduction of a proposal in one of four forms: the bill, the joint resolution, the concurrent resolution, and the simple resolution. The most customary form used in both Houses is the bill. During the 107th Congress (2001–2002), 8,948 bills and 178 joint resolutions were introduced in both Houses. Of the total number introduced, 5,767 bills and 125 joint resolutions originated in the House of Representatives.

For the purpose of simplicity, this discussion will be confined generally to the procedure on a House of Representatives bill, with brief comment on each of the forms.

BILLS

A bill is the form used for most legislation, whether permanent or temporary, general or special, public or private.

The form of a House bill is as follows:

A BILL

For the establishment, etc. [as the title may be].

Be it enacted by the Senate and House of Representatives of the United States of America in Congress assembled, That, etc.

The enacting clause was prescribed by law in 1871 and is identical in all bills, whether they originate in the House of Representatives or the Senate.

Bills may originate in either the House of Representatives or the Senate with one notable exception provided for in the Constitution. Article I, Section 7, of the Constitution provides that all bills for raising revenue shall originate in the House of Representatives but that the Senate may propose or concur with amendments. By tradition, general appropriation bills also originate in the House of Representatives.

There are two types of bills — public and private. A public bill is one that affects the public generally. A bill that affects a specified individual or a private entity rather than the population at large is called a private bill. A typical private bill is used for relief in matters such as immigration and naturalization and claims against the United States.

A bill originating in the House of Representatives is designated by the letters "H.R." followed by a number that it retains throughout all its parliamentary stages. The letters signify "House of Representatives" and not, as is sometimes incorrectly assumed,

"House resolution". A Senate bill is designated by the letter "S." followed by its number. The term "companion bill" is used to describe a bill introduced in one House of Congress that is similar or identical to a bill introduced in the other House of Congress.

A bill that has been agreed to in identical form by both bodies becomes the law of the land only after —

(1) Presidential approval; or

(2) failure by the President to return it with objections to the House in which it originated within 10 days (Sundays excepted) while Congress is in session; or

(3) the overriding of a presidential veto by a two-thirds vote in each House.

It does not become law without the President's signature if Congress by their final adjournment prevent its return with objections. This is known as a "pocket veto".

JOINT RESOLUTIONS

Joint resolutions may originate either in the House of Representatives or in the Senate — not, as is sometimes incorrectly assumed, jointly in both Houses. There is little practical difference between a bill and a joint resolution and the two forms are often used interchangeably. One difference in form is that a joint resolution may include a preamble preceding the resolving clause. Statutes that have been initiated as bills have later been amended by a joint resolution and vice versa. Both are subject to the same procedure except for a joint resolution proposing an amendment to the Constitution. When a joint resolution amending the Constitution is approved by two-thirds of both Houses, it is not presented to the President for approval. Following congressional approval, a joint resolution to amend the Constitution is sent directly to the Archivist of the United States for submission to the several states where ratification by the legislatures of three-fourths of the states within the period of time prescribed in the joint resolution is necessary for the amendment to become part of the Constitution.

The form of a House joint resolution is as follows:

Authorizing, etc. [as the title may be].

Resolved by the Senate and House of Representatives of the United States of America in Congress assembled, That all, etc.

The resolving clause is identical in both House and Senate joint resolutions as prescribed by statute in 1871. It is frequently preceded by a preamble consisting of one or more "whereas" clauses indicating the necessity for or the desirability of the joint resolution.

A joint resolution originating in the House of Representatives is designated "H.J. Res." followed by its individual number which it retains throughout all its parliamentary stages. One originating in the Senate is designated "S.J. Res." followed by its number.

Joint resolutions, with the exception of proposed amendments to the Constitution, become law in the same manner as bills.

CONCURRENT RESOLUTIONS

A matter affecting the operations of both Houses is usually initiated by a concurrent resolution. In modern practice, and as determined by the Supreme Court in *INS v. Chadha*, 462 U.S. 919 (1983), concurrent and simple resolutions normally are not legislative in character since not "presented" to the President for approval, but are used merely for expressing facts, principles, opinions, and purposes of the two Houses. A concurrent resolution is not equivalent to a bill and its use is narrowly limited within these bounds. The term "concurrent", like "joint", does not signify simultaneous introduction and consideration in both Houses.

A concurrent resolution originating in the House of Representatives is designated "H.

Con. Res." followed by its individual number, while a Senate concurrent resolution is designated "S. Con. Res." together with its number. On approval by both Houses, they are signed by the Clerk of the House and the Secretary of the Senate and transmitted to the Archivist of the United States for publication in a special part of the Statutes at Large volume covering that session of Congress.

SIMPLE RESOLUTIONS

A matter concerning the rules, the operation, or the opinion of either House alone is initiated by a simple resolution. A resolution affecting the House of Representatives is designated "H. Res." followed by its number, while a Senate resolution is designated "S. Res." together with its number. Simple resolutions are considered only by the body in which they were introduced. Upon adoption, simple resolutions are attested to by the Clerk of the House of Representatives or the Secretary of the Senate and are published in the Congressional Record.

2. State Legislatures

State constitutions typically contain a variety of provisions that impose constraints on the form and procedures of state law-making that are not found in the Federal Constitution. These are covered in Chapter 4. *See generally* G. ALAN TARR, UNDERSTANDING STATE CONSTITUTIONS 118–21 (1998).

E. INTRODUCTION AND REFERRAL TO COMMITTEE

CHARLES W. JOHNSON,
HOW OUR LAWS ARE MADE
8–9 (2003)

Any Member, Delegate or the Resident Commissioner from Puerto Rico in the House of Representatives may introduce a bill at any time while the House is in session by simply placing it in the "hopper", a wooden box provided for that purpose located on the side of the rostrum in the House Chamber. Permission is not required to introduce the measure. The Member introducing the bill is known as the primary sponsor. An unlimited number of Members may cosponsor a bill. To prevent the possibility that a bill might be introduced in the House on behalf of a Member without that Member's prior approval, the primary sponsor's signature must appear on the bill before it is accepted for introduction. Members who cosponsor a bill upon its date of introduction are original cosponsors. Members who cosponsor a bill after its introduction are additional cosponsors. Cosponsors are not required to sign the bill. A Member may not be added or deleted as a cosponsor after the bill has been reported by the last committee authorized to consider it, but the Speaker may not entertain a request to delete the name of the primary sponsor at any time. Cosponsors names may be deleted by their own unanimous consent request or that of the primary sponsor. In the Senate, unlimited multiple sponsorship of a bill is permitted. Occasionally, a Member may insert the words "by request" after the Member's name to indicate that the introductions of the measure is at the suggestion of some other person or group — usually the President or a member of his Cabinet.

In the Senate, a Senator usually introduces a bill or resolution by presenting it to one of the clerks at the Presiding Officer's desk, without commenting on it from the floor of the Senate. However, a Senator may use a more formal procedure by rising and introducing the bill or resolution from the floor. A Senator usually makes a statement about the measure when introducing it on the floor. Frequently, Senators obtain consent to have the bill or resolution printed in the Congressional Record following their formal statement.

If any Senator objects to the introduction of a bill or resolution, the introduction of the bill or resolution is postponed until the next day. If there is no objection, the bill is read by title and referred to the appropriate committee. If there is an objection, the bill is placed on the Calendar.

In the House of Representatives, it is no longer the custom to read bills — even by title — at the time of introduction. The title is entered in the Journal and printed in the Congressional Report, thus preserving the purpose of the custom. The bill is assigned its legislative number by the Clerk. The bill is then referred as required by the rules of the House to the appropriate committee or committees by the Speaker, the Member elected by the Members to be the Presiding Officer of the House, with the assistance of the Parliamentarian. The bill number and committee referral appear in the next issue of the Congressional Report. It is then sent to the Government Printing Office where it is printed in its introduced form and printed copies are made available in the document rooms of both Houses. Printed and electronic versions of the bill are also made available to the public.

Copies of the bill are sent to the office of the chairman of the committee to which it has been referred. The clerk of the committee enters it on the committee's Legislative Calendar.

JUDY SCHNEIDER,
HOUSE AND SENATE RULES OF PROCEDURE:
A COMPARISON
1–2 (updated May 12, 2003)

Referral of Legislation

In both the House and Senate, the presiding officer . . . refers newly-introduced legislation and measures passed by the other chamber to the appropriate standing committee. Upon advice from the Parliamentarian, the presiding officer bases referral decisions on the chamber's rules and precedents for subject matter jurisdiction. Legislation passed by the other body usually receives floor consideration without reference to a committee if there already is a companion bill on a calendar . . . .

The House changed its referral rule (Rule XII, clause 2) at the beginning of the 104th Congress. This change was aimed at reducing the number of measures referred to more than one committee commonly called "multiple referrals." The rules change eliminated joint referrals, a type of multiple referral where a measure is simultaneously referred to two or more committees. Under the new rule, the Speaker designates "a committee of primary jurisdiction" (based on the committee jurisdictions itemized in Rule X) when referring measures to more than one committee. In practice, two types of multiple referrals can take place if the Speaker first selects a primary committee: a *sequential referral* (the measure is referred to one committee, then to another, and so on; the Speaker can establish time limits for each committee's consideration); and a *split referral* (specifically designated portions of a measure are referred to one or more committees). In the 108th Congress, House rules were changed to allow the Speaker to not designate a primary committee "under exceptional circumstances."

House committees often develop "memorandums of understanding" (sometimes referred to as "letters of agreement") which explain an agreement between committees about how to divide jurisdiction over specific policy issues. These memorandums are sent to the Speaker in the form of letters from the involved committee chairmen, and are sometimes printed in the *Congressional Record*. The memorandums seek to advise the Speaker on referral decisions where committee jurisdictions are unclear or overlapping.

Under the Senate's referral rule (Rule XVII, paragraph 1), legislation is referred to "the committee which has jurisdiction over subject matter which predominates" in the measure (sometimes referred to as "predominant jurisdiction"). Senate Rule XXV lists the subjects for which the standing committees are responsible. Senate Rule XIV requires that measures be read twice on different legislative days (see "Adjournment and Legislative Days" section) before being referred to a committee. Most bills and joint resolutions, however, are considered as having been read twice and are referred to committee upon introduction. Under Rule XIV, when a Senator demands two readings and there is objection to the measure's second reading, the measure is placed directly on the Calendar of Business without reference to committee.

Three types of multiple referrals — *joint, sequential and split* — are allowed in the Senate. In practice, measures are referred to multiple committees by unanimous consent. Under the Senate's standing rules (Rule XVII, paragraph 3), the Senate Majority and Minority Leaders can make a joint leadership motion to jointly or sequentially refer legislation to multiple committees. However, this rule has never been used since its adoption by the Senate in 1977. In general multiple referrals are more common in the House than in the Senate.

NOTES AND QUESTIONS

1. Should the views of a sponsor or cosponsor of a bill be afforded a greater weight in determining the meaning of a statute? Should that depend on whether the views are those of a member of the House rather than a Senator?

2. A measure may be drafted with an eye to committee jurisdiction. DAVID C. KING, TURF WARS: HOW CONGRESSIONAL COMMITTEES CLAIM JURISDICTION 106–07 (1997) (discussing how the House Agriculture Committee gained jurisdiction over pesticide regulation by persuading the White House to change its proposal from one amending the Toxic Substances and Control Act, which was within the jurisdiction of the Commerce Committee, to one amending the Federal Insecticide, Fungicide and Rodenticide Act).

Dr. King also points out that the House and Senate Parliamentarians create significant "common-law" precedents when resolving ambiguities in published House and Senate referral rules. *Id.* at 78–104.

3. In state legislatures, a bill that appropriates money may also be referred to the Appropriations committees. OTTO J. HETZEL, LEGISLATIVE LAW AND PROCESS 477 (1980).

F. COMMITTEE CONSIDERATION

Stephen Breyer, who served as counsel to the Senate Judiciary Committee before serving on the bench, described Congress as a "bureaucratic organization." Stephen Breyer, *Uses of Legislative History in Interpreting Statutes*, 65 S. CAL. L. REV. 845, 858 (1992). Standard operating legislative procedures involve committee hearings, committee markups and committee reports in each chamber. Although not every piece of even major legislation receives the considered deliberation that attends orthodox lawmaking[*] neither users of the Legislative's work product nor legislative advocates can afford to be uninformed about this part of the dance of legislation.

JUDY SCHNEIDER,
THE COMMITTEE SYSTEM IN THE U.S. CONGRESS
1–4 (updated May 2, 2003)

Introduction

Decentralization is the most distinctive characteristic of the congressional committee system. Due to the high volume and complexity of its work, Congress divides its legislative, oversight, and internal administrative tasks among committees and

---

[*] *See generally* BARBARA SINCLAIR, UNORTHODOX LAW MAKING (2d. ed., 2000).

subcommittees. Within assigned subject areas, committees and subcommittees gather information; compare and evaluate legislative alternatives; identify policy problems and propose solutions to them; select, determine the text of, and report out measures for the full chambers to consider; monitor executive branch performance of duties (oversight); and look into allegations of wrongdoing (investigation).

Although Congress has used committees since its first meetings in 1789, the 1946 Legislative Reorganization Act (60 Stat. 812) set the foundation of today's committee system. The House and Senate each have their own committees and related rules of procedure, which are similar but not identical. Within the guidelines of chamber rules, each committee adopts its own rules addressing organizational, structural, and procedural issues; thus, even within a chamber, there is considerable variation among panels.

Within their respective areas of responsibility, committees generally operate rather independently of each other and of their parent chambers. The difficult tasks of aggregating committees' activities, and of integrating policy in areas where jurisdiction is shared, fall largely to the chambers' party leaderships.

Structure and Organization

Type of Committees.

There are three types of committees — standing; select; and joint.

Standing committees are permanent panels identified in chamber rules. The rules also list the jurisdiction of each committee. Because they have legislative jurisdiction, standing committees consider bills and issues and recommend measures for consideration by the respective chambers. They also have oversight responsibility to monitor agencies, programs, and activities within their jurisdictions, and in some cases in areas that cut across committee jurisdictions. Most standing committees recommend authorized levels of funds for government operations and for new and existing programs within their jurisdiction. Standing committees also have jurisdiction over appropriations (in the case of the Appropriations Committee), taxation (in the case of the House Ways and Means and Senate Finance Committees), various other revenues such as user fees, and direct spending such as Social Security, veterans' pensions, and some farm support programs.

Select committees usually are established by a separate resolution of the parent chamber, sometimes to conduct investigations and studies, sometimes to consider measures. A select committee is established because the existing standing committee system does not address an issue comprehensively, or because a particular event sparks interest in an investigation. A select committee may be permanent or temporary. *Special committees* tend to be similar in constitution and function and that distinction from select committees is generally thought to be only semantic.

Joint committees are made up of Members of both chambers. Today, they usually are permanent panels that conduct studies or perform housekeeping tasks rather than consider measures. A *conference committee* is a temporary joint committee formed to resolve differences in Senate- and House-passed versions of a particular measure.

Subcommittees.

Most committees form subcommittees with legislative jurisdiction to consider and report bills on particular issues with the purview of the full committee. Committees may assign their subcommittees such specific tasks as the initial hearings held on measures and oversight of laws and programs in their areas. Subcommittees are responsible to and work within guidelines established by their parent committees. Consequently, subcommittees' number, independence and autonomy vary between committees.

Composition.

Party leaders generally determine the size of committees and the ratio of majority to minority members on each of them. Each party is primarily responsible for choosing its committee leaders and assigning its Members to committees, and, once assigned to a particular committee, a Member often makes a career there. Each committee distributes its members among its subcommittees, on which only members of the committee may serve. There are limits on the number and type of committees and subcommittees on which each Member may serve. Members, especially in the House, tend to specialize in the issues of their assigned committees.

Leadership.

A committee's authority is centered in its chair. In practice, a chair's prerogatives usually include determining the committee's agenda, deciding when to take or delay action, presiding during meetings, and controlling most funds allocated by the matter in the legislation. Singly referred measures have been more likely than multiply referred ones to pass their chamber and to be enacted into law, in part because of the difficulty in coordinating the work of multiple panels.

To distribute committee power, chamber and party caucus rules limit the number of full and subcommittee chair or ranking minority positions a single Member may hold. Only the Republicans have committee leadership term limits. No House Republican may serve as chair (or ranking minority member) of a committee or subcommittee for more than three consecutive terms, effective with the 104th Congress, and no Senate Republican may serve more than six years as chair and six years as ranking member of any standing committee, effective with the 105th Congress. Waivers can be granted.

Staff.

Approximately 2,000 aides provide professional, administrative and clerical support to committees. Their main job is to assist with writing, analyzing, amending, and recommending measures to the full chamber, as well as overseeing the executive branch's implementation of laws and the operation of programs. Pursuant to funding resolutions and other mechanisms, committees receive varying levels of operating funds for their expenses, including the hiring of staff. From these funds, each hires its own staff, and committees employ varying numbers of aides ranging from a few to dozens. (Committees may also fire staff.) Most staff and resources are controlled by the chair of a committee, although in general a portion must be shared with minority-party members. Further, some committees assign staff directly to their subcommittees, and give subcommittee leaders considerable authority in hiring and supervising subcommittee staff. Each committee sets staff pay levels within limits contained in chamber salary policies.

Oversight.

Committees conduct oversight to assure that the policy intentions of legislators are carried out by those administering programs, and to assess the adequacy of programs for changing conditions. Some committees, especially in the House, establish separate oversight subcommittees to oversee the implementation of all program within their jurisdiction. Also, each chamber has assigned to specific committees oversight responsibility for certain issues and programs that cut across committee jurisdictions and each has a committee responsible for overseeing comprehensively the efficiency and economy of government activities.

Operations and Procedures

Referral.

Each committee has nearly exclusive right to consider measures within its jurisdiction. In general, committees are not required to act on any measure, and a measure can not come to the floor for consideration unless through the action or at least concurrence of a committee. A procedure to discharge a committee from consideration is rarely successful.

Any introduced measure generally gets referred immediately to a committee. Especially in the House, some measures are referred to two or more panels, usually because policy subjects are split among committees. When more than one House committee receives a referral, a primary committee is designated. Other panels receive a sequential referral. In the Senate, referral is determined by the predominant subject matter in the legislation. Singly referred measures have been more likely than multiply referred ones to pass their chamber and to be enacted into law, in part because of the difficulty in coordinating the work of multiple panels.

Committees receive varying numbers of measures. Committees dispose of these measures as they please, selecting only a small percentage for action, for a number of reasons. For instance, a committee usually receives many proposals in each major policy area. While those measures not chosen usually receive no further congressional action, the idea, specific provisions, or entire text of some of these measures may be incorporated through the amendment process into others that the committees and chambers consider and that become law. Determining the fate of measures and, in effect, helping to set a chamber's agency make committees very powerful.

Committee often send their measures to subcommittees for initial consideration, but only a full committee can report a measure to the floor for consideration . . . .

Executive Agency Comment.

As a matter of practice and cooperation between the legislative and executive branches, a committee asks relevant executive agencies for written comments on measures it is studying.

NOTES AND QUESTIONS

1. When reelected to Congress, would Congressman Powell have legal recourse against his party caucus if it refused to assign him to a committee?

2. Suppose that the partisan composition of the House as a whole consists of 218 elected representatives of the majority party and 217 elected representatives of the minority party. Further suppose that the majority party fixes the committee ratios on powerhouse committees like Appropriations at 2:1. Would the minority have legal recourse against the majority? *Cf. Vander Jagt v. O'Neill*, 699 F.2d 1166 (D.C. Cir. 1983).

CHRISTOPHER M. DAVIS,
LEGISLATIVE PROCEDURES AND THE LEGISLATIVE AGENDA
IN THE HOUSE OF REPRESENTATIVES
7, 12 (Updated August 7, 2003)

The Committee System and Agenda Control

During the 107th Congress (2001–2002), 5,892 bills and joint resolutions were introduced in the House of Representatives; another 226 such measures were passed by the Senate and sent to the House for consideration. Of this total of 6,118 bills and joint resolutions — which represented the possible legislative agenda for that two-year Congress — only 383, or about 6.2%, became law . . . .

Thus, the legislative process in the House of Representatives (and the Senate) is in part a process of agenda control — a process of selecting from among the thousands of measures introduced the relatively few that will reach enactment . . . .

The committees constitute a system of division of labor by which the House designates certain of its Members to become experts in certain arenas of policy and to make recommendations to the full membership. But the committees are equally important for what they do not do. During the 107th Congress, the standing committees of the House reported (or recommended for passage) a total of 487 bills and joint resolutions from among the total of 6,118 that Representatives introduced or the Senate passed. What makes this figure so significant is that a measure that is not reported stands little chance of becoming law. Committee approval is not necessarily conclusive; committee disapproval or inaction usually is.

. . . .

In light of the powerful veto that committees can and do exercise, proponents of legislation attempt to influence committee and subcommittee agendas. The President as well as private individuals and groups may lobby for committee action, both by arguing the merits of their case and by demonstrating the breadth and intensity of support for the bill they endorse. The bill's supporters in Congress may attempt to persuade their colleagues on the committee and demonstrate support for the bill within the House by such methods as seeking co-sponsors for the bill from a broad cross-section of the House and especially from influential Representatives — including, if possible, members of the committee itself. In some cases, the goal of such efforts is not to transform opponents into proponents, but instead to increase the visibility of a bill that otherwise might simply be lost in the press of other business. On the other hand, opponents can be equally successful in stressing the political and policy disadvantages of the bill, and in encouraging their allies on the committee to prolong the process of committee consideration, in the hope that the bill will be removed eventually from the committee's agenda in favor of more pressing and less controversial matters. By and large, the advantage normally rests with the opponents of legislative action.

1.   Committee Hearings

The following excerpts from publicly available documents written by inhouse experts on legislative process, primarily by the staff of the Congressional Research Service, are edited to highlight those aspects of the process most salient to law students. That is, the excerpts focus on items, such as committee reports, that are commonly resorted to in the search for the legislative history of a statute.

RICHARD C. SACHS,
TYPES OF COMMITTEE HEARINGS
1–2 (June 24, 2004)

Congressional committee hearings may be broadly classified into four types: *legislative, oversight, investigative, and confirmation.* Hearings may be held on Capitol Hill or elsewhere, perhaps a committee member's district or state or a site related to the subject of the hearing. (These latter ones are often referred to as *field hearings.*) . . .

All hearings have a similar formal purpose, to gather information for use by the committee in its activities. Often, this information is used to shape legislation, even when the hearing is not specifically a legislative hearing. For this reason, all four types of hearings share common characteristics, and the differences among them may appear indistinct. For example, investigative hearings are sometimes seen as a type of oversight hearings. Hearings on a bill might also provide oversight opportunities.

One reason for these common characteristics is that a single set of rules in each chamber governs the different kinds of hearings (Senate Rule XXVI and House Rule X, particularly clauses 2 and 3, and Rule XI, particularly clauses 2, 4, and 5). Some of these rules, however, are more pertinent to certain kinds of hearings than to others. And, within the rules, a chair has broad latitude in the organization and conduct of hearings.

Legislative Hearings.

The most familiar type of congressional hearing gathers information about the subject matter of one or more measures in anticipation that the committee will eventually mark up and report legislation. By deciding to hold a hearing, a committee takes a bill (or often several that bear on the same issue) from the many that are referred to the committee and indicates that the bill involves a subject that the panel must act on (for example, a reauthorization, without which a program will expire) or is otherwise worthy of attention.

A bill does not have to be introduced and referred to a committee for the panel to hold a legislative hearing. Sometimes, a hearing will be held prior to the introduction of a bill for the purpose of gathering information the committee can use in shaping legislation.

There is no requirement that legislation be drafted based in whole or in part on hearing testimony, or that, if hearings are held, the committee must mark up and report a measure. In only a few procedural circumstances, for example, consideration of the annual budget resolution, are there any requirements that a committee hold a hearing on a bill in order to take action on it. If a bill is referred to more than one committee, each committee has the discretion to decide whether to hold a hearing.

Oversight Hearings.

Congress has historically engaged in oversight of the executive, specifically the review, monitoring, and supervision of the implementation of public policy. Oversight hearings are one technique a committee can use in this evaluation. Hearings may be held because a committee has a commitment to review ongoing programs and agencies, or it believes that a program is being poorly administered or that an agency is unresponsive to the committee. A committee may also hold an oversight hearing when a program under its jurisdiction is set to expire and needs to be reauthorized in order to continue.

Investigative Hearings.

An investigative hearing differs from a legislative or oversight hearing in that investigations usually involve allegations of wrongdoing by public officials acting in their official capacity, or private citizens whose activities may suggest the need for a legislative remedy.

By their nature, investigative hearings may be more likely than other kinds to be confrontational and adversarial. For this reason, witnesses in these hearings are more likely to appear under subpoena and to be sworn. As a consequence, certain of the rules that govern hearings are often most pertinent to this type of hearing. For example, there are rules that specify procedures for the treatment of witnesses and govern the issuance of subpoenas. Authorizing a major investigation sometimes requires the passage of a House or Senate resolution. This authorizing resolution commonly establishes special procedures for the hearings stage of a committee's investigation.

Confirmation Hearings.

Each Senate committee has the authority to hold confirmation hearings on presidential nominations to executive and judicial positions within its jurisdiction. Article II of the Constitution authorizes the President to nominate certain government officials with the "advise and consent" of the Senate. Senate Rule XXXI, setting procedures on presidential nominees, is silent on hearings. Committees are not required to hold a hearing, and most nominations, for example military promotions, are forwarded directly to the Senate floor.

Hearings are commonly held only for the very highest positions, such as nominees to become members of the President's Cabinet or the Supreme Court. Some committee rules require that nominees provide biographical, financial, and other information to the committee. A committee may also request reports of FBI background checks on the nominee done for the White House. This information may be used in questioning a nominee or other witnesses.

Confirmation hearings may also offer Senators an opportunity for oversight. For example, questions about how a nominee might manage an agency or administer a program may help Senators evaluate an agency's effectiveness.

NOTES AND QUESTIONS

On investigative hearings, see, generally, MORTON ROSENBERG, INVESTIGATIVE OVERSIGHT: AN INTRODUCTION TO THE LAW, PRACTICE, AND PROCEDURE OF CONGRESSIONAL INQUIRY (April 7, 1995).

RICHARD C. SACHS,
HEARINGS IN THE HOUSE OF REPRESENTATIVES:
A GUIDE FOR PREPARATION AND PROCEDURE
2–4, 5–7, 10–11, 14, 24–26 (Updated July 28, 2004)

Hearings in the Committee Process

Hearings are the broad information-gathering technique committees use — and have always used — in policy making and oversight. Hearings may be held on issues in the absence of specific legislation, but many are held on particular legislative proposals. In either case, Congress benefits from hearings in a variety of ways. Hearings inform Members, staff, and the public about measures and issues, and help assess the intensity of support for proposals. Hearings serve to monitor government programs and activities, and expose problems that Congress can later correct.

Hearings give citizens an opportunity to participate in the policy process, and help build the public record for a measure or issue.

House committees act on a minority of the measures introduced and referred to them, for a number of reasons. For instance, a committee usually receives many proposals in each major policy area within its jurisdiction, but ultimately chooses one measure as its vehicle in each such area. Also, a committee usually does not act on measures that it opposes. When a committee does act, it usually sends a bill to subcommittee for initial consideration, although committees do not uniformly require such referral. A committee may decide to send a bill to subcommittee for initial scrutiny because of the technical nature of the issue, the history of prior handling of the matter, and political factors, among other reasons. When a committee or a subcommittee considers a measure, it generally takes four actions. Where a subcommittee initiates some of the four actions, the extent to which the full committee repeats some of these steps varies among committees and from issue to issue. The sequence of actions assumes the committee favors a measure, but at any time the committee may discontinue action.

First, a committee may seek agency comment by sending a copy of the measure to the executive departments or agencies having relevant policy expertise and soliciting their written evaluation of the proposal. The executive agency typically sends a copy of the measure to the Office of Management and Budget (OMB) for a determination as to consistency with the President's program.

Second, a committee may decide to hold one or more hearings. Further committee action without hearings is the exception, although hearings have been bypassed to move measures expeditiously through committee or because of action on a related bill in the previous Congress. The importance of this action is well stated by congressional scholar Walter J. Oleszek:

> The decision to hold a hearing is often a critical point in the life of a bill. Measures brought to the floor without first undergoing the scrutiny of hearings will likely receive sharp criticism . . . . The importance of the committee stage is based on the assumption that the experts — the committee members —

carefully scrutinize a proposal, and hearings provide a demonstrable record of that scrutiny.[3]

Third, a committee will meet to "mark up," or recommend amendments to the legislation, in part based on information received at hearings. Markup is the critical stage where the committee decides how the language of the bill should appear when it is presented to the House for consideration. While a bill can be subsequently amended on the House floor, committees have the important prerogative of shaping legislation before consideration by the full chamber.

Fourth, the full committee will report the legislation to the floor; subcommittees must report to their parent committees. When a committee reports a measure, it is also required to issue a written report that typically describes and explains the measure's purposes and provisions and tells Members why the measure should be passed. The report also may summarize any relevant hearings that were held. This reporting requirement may be waived.

. . . .

Preparation for Hearings

Preliminary Issues

A committee considers a variety of issues in deciding whether to hold a hearing. A committee must define the information it needs, evaluate the policy matters or the political message it wishes to communicate, and then determine whether a hearing is the best method of achieving its goals. A hearing agenda is influenced by several factors, including the salience of issues to the nation, the importance of policies to interest groups, and matters of significance to the President, House leaders, and other Representatives. Programs under a committee's jurisdiction that need to be reauthorized generally receive committee scrutiny, as do instances of reported waste, fraud, or abuse.

Each committee receives dozens or even hundreds of proposals for possible examination and studies matters not embodied in specific legislation. In the context of this overall workload, a committee must decide whether holding a particular hearing is the best use of staff and funds. A committee also considers whether and how a hearing would fit into its overall schedule. It may be particularly difficult for committees with broad jurisdictions to allocate limited resources and to fit matters into the schedule.

To obtain approval for a hearing, committee staff often prepare a preliminary hearing memorandum for the chair that includes information such as the scope and purpose of the hearing, the expected outcome, possible witnesses, how many hearing days are planned, and perhaps the views of the minority party. Informal discussion with committee members and staff may suffice.

Sources of Outside Assistance

Numerous governmental and non-governmental resources are available to committees to assist with hearings. Because most hearings focus on government programs, or potential programs, executive agencies often are major providers of information. Committees may request information directly from specific offices, or may place requests through an agency's congressional liaison, an office established to respond to congressional requests for information.

Each of the three congressional support agencies can assist with hearings. The Congressional Research Service (CRS) can assist in

- framing the agenda for hearings;
- preparing background and policy studies; preparing bibliographies and conducting database searches;
- providing information on positions of interest groups and other key players;
- suggesting witnesses and drafting questions for Members to ask them;
- making its experts available on a nonpartisan basis as witnesses;
- analyzing testimony;
- preparing studies or documentation for inclusion in the hearing record;
- supplying information on program accomplishments; and
- evaluating legislative proposals and discussing alternative approaches.

The Government Accountability Office (GAO) provides assistance to committees principally by reviewing executive branch programs through independent audits, investigations, and evaluations. Its reviews measure the effectiveness of government programs. GAO's reports contribute to the background study and examination necessary for hearings. For instance, reports on investigations of waste, fraud, and abuse in federal entities may be used at oversight and investigative hearings probing government programs, or at hearings to craft legislation to correct problems exposed. In addition to its routine, periodic reviews, GAO may be asked for studies specific to a committee hearing. Also, GAO experts frequently appear as witnesses.

The Congressional Budget Office (CBO) furnishes Congress with key information relating to the U.S. economy, the federal budget, and federal programs. It assists committees by preparing cost estimates of legislation. Its assistance to Congress in carrying out the Congressional Budget Act provides a framework and useful background and analysis for committee hearings. Its responsibilities include

- estimating the five-year budgetary costs of legislation;
- tracking congressional budget actions against targets established in budget resolutions (scorekeeping); estimating costs to state, local, and tribal governments of carrying out mandates to be imposed by legislation;
- making periodic forecasts of economic trends and baseline projections of spending and revenue levels against which proposed changes in taxing and spending policies can be measured; conducting studies of programmatic or policy issues that affect the federal budget; and
- preparing an annual report on spending and revenue options for reducing the federal deficit.

Nongovernmental organizations provide a wealth of resources for committees. Knowledgeable individuals in universities, policy research institutes, law and consulting firms, and trade and other non-profit associations often are willing to assist committees with data, analysis, and testimony. Interest groups with public policy concerns become involved at the hearing stage in an attempt to frame the issues early in the legislative process. Studies indicate that lobbyists believe testifying at congressional hearings is an important and effective technique for influencing legislation. In addition to consulting policy experts and special interest groups, committees seek information and assistance from ordinary citizens who have direct experience with a proposed policy or whose lives will bear the impact of Congress's eventual decision.

Choosing and Inviting Witnesses

Choosing witnesses is often one of the most important issues in planning a hearing. Committees pay careful attention to which viewpoints will be represented, who should testify, and the order and format for presenting witnesses.

In some cases a committee will strive to make sure that all reasonable points of view are represented, while in other cases witnesses expressing only particular points of view will be invited. House rules allow the minority party members of a committee to call witnesses of their choice on at least one day of a hearing, if a majority of them makes this request to the committee chair before completion of the hearing (House Rule XI, clause 2(j)(1)). In lieu of this formal option, the minority sometimes works informally with the majority to invite witnesses representing its views.

In order to testify, a witness must be invited by the committee. Before officially inviting a witness, committee staff identify and often interview prospective candidates. When suitable witnesses are found, the committee chair sends a formal letter of invitation. This letter generally gives the witness some basic information, including the purpose, subject, date, time, and place of the hearing. In addition to specifying the portion of a measure or issue the witness should address, the letter may contain a limitation on the length of the witness's oral testimony.

The committee may send the witness additional information. This information may include a list of committee members, the committee's rules, the measure under consideration, and material from the media relating to the issue. Often a staff contact is indicated. Staff will sometimes meet with witnesses before a hewing to answer questions and to review procedure.

Briefing Books

Committees often ask staff to prepare summary and background material for use by their members before and during a hearing. This information is sometimes assembled into briefing books or folders to present issues in a systematic, uniform way. Briefing books might include a variety of items, including a description of the subject, scope, and purpose of the hearing. For legislative hearings, a copy and an explanation of each measure under consideration, and a comparison of all measures to be discussed, are useful. Background material might include pertinent statutes and regulations, court decisions, press articles, agency reports, academic studies, and a chronology of major events. To assist members with witnesses, the books might contain a list of witnesses in their order of appearance, a copy or summary of written testimony, and biographical information. Briefing material might also include questions or talking points for committee members to use in opening statements and in examining witnesses.

Before a hearing, committee staff sometimes brief members and other staff may conduct oral briefings in addition to, or in lieu of, preparing briefing books. These sessions provide an opportunity to discuss matters of particular interest to individual committee members . . . .

Post-Hearing Activities

After examining the last witness, the committee chair closes the hearing. The chair may summarize what has been learned about the issue, and comment on the future committee schedule or expected action.

After a day of hearings, staff may be asked to prepare a summary of testimony. The summary may be distributed to committee members and the press and become part of any published hearing. Follow-up questions can be prepared and submitted to witnesses for written replies to clear up points not resolved during the hearing. If the hearing is investigative, the committee can prepare and issue its report, If the hearing is legislative, the committee may proceed to mark up and report a measure to the House . . . .

Printing Hearings

Committees are required to keep transcripts of their hearings. Most committees regularly ask the Office of Official Reporters, Clerk of the House, to provide a reporter to transcribe a hearing. Transcripts must be substantially verbatim (House Rules XI, clause 2(e)(1)(A)). Only technical, grammatical, and typographical corrections authorized by the person making the remarks are allowed.

Further, committees usually publish their transcripts, although publication is not required. House rules encourage committees to publish their hearings on reported measures. In general, if hearings have been held on any measure or matter reported by committee, the rules require the committee to make every reasonable effort to have the hearings printed and available to Members before floor consideration (House Rule XIII, clause 4(b)). General appropriations bills may not be considered in the House until printed hearings and a committee report have been available for at least three calendar days, excluding Saturdays, Sundays, and legal holidays, except when the House is in session on such a day (House Rule XIII, clause 4(c)). In addition, testimony taken in executive session may not be released or used in public sessions without the consent of a majority of the committee present (House Rule XI, clause 2(k)(7)) . . . .

The rules of some committees address the authority to print hearings. Transcripts of Budget Committee hearings may be printed if the chair so decides or if a majority of the members so requests. The Appropriations Committee requires that a transcript of all hearings on the federal budget as a whole be printed and distributed to Members.

Each committee may establish procedures for correcting its transcripts, and some committees have rules to expedite this process. The Committee on Ways and Means, for example, requires each witness to correct and return the transcript, and members must correct their testimony and return the corrected transcripts as soon as possible. Further, the committee chair can order a transcript printed without the corrections of a member or witness if the chair determines that a reasonable time has elapsed and that further delay would impede the legislative process.

Each committee also has discretion to print supplemental materials as part of the printed hearing. For example, in its printed hearing a committee might include written statements of witnesses, charts, and research materials prepared by committee staff; and letters and testimony from individuals who did not appear as witnesses. A printed hearing also might include witness responses to questions posed during the hearing that the witness could not answer on the spot, or witness responses to follow-up questions. The rules of some committees address the printing of supplemental material or information. For instance, the Committee on Agriculture's hearings must include the attendance of members during the hearings.

House rules require that, to the maximum extent feasible, committees are to make their publications available to the public in electronic form (House Rule XI, clause 2(e)(4)). This rules change in the 105th Congress was intended to encourage committees to make printed, public materials available on the Internet. While a number of committee rules restate this House rule, those of the Committee on Small Business expressly state that the proposed testimony of witnesses must be provided to the public in electronic form. Since the 106th Congress, most committees have made written testimony and/or hearing transcripts available online. (See [http://www.house.gov/house/CommitteeWWW.html].)

House rules require that a committee's hearings, records, and other documents be kept separate from the personal office records of the chair, and generally allow all Members of the House access to a committee's records (House Rule XI, clause 2(e)(2)). The Legislative Reorganization Act of 1946 requires that at the end of each session of Congress, each committee's printed hearings must be bound by the Library of Congress. In addition, at the end of each Congress, the chair of each committee is to transfer to the Clerk of the House the noncurrent records of the committee (House Rule VII, clause I). Noncurrent committee records are preserved and made available by the

National Archives and Records Administration, in accordance with House and committee rules.

1. What materials generated by congressional hearings are most useful to the lawyer seeking to advise a client on the meaning of a newly enacted statute? What materials are less useful?

2. From the point of view of a lawyer engaged in legislative advocacy, what aspects of the hearing process offer the best opportunity to influence legislative outcomes?

2.   Committee Markups

JUDY SCHNEIDER,
HOUSE COMMITTEE MARKUP: PREPARATION
1–2 (May 5, 2003)

Markups provide Members on a committee an opportunity to change parts of a bill prior to its consideration by the full House. A number of administrative, procedural, and substantive steps must be undertaken in preparation for a markup, and other steps could or should be undertaken. Generally, the markup should be strategically planned to minimize controversy, provide Members with political dividends, and position the committee for future action.

. . . .

The following checklist, one of a series on legislative process, is generally applicable in full committee markup, although much of it also applies to a subcommittee markup.

Informational Preparation

- Compile background material for Members on the committee, including a summary of the measure to be marked up and summaries of hearing testimony. Packets also usually include information provided by the subcommittee, including details of subcommittee action.
- Hold briefings for legislative assistants prior to the committee meeting to review the bill, discuss possible amendments, and provide opportunities for questions. These briefings can be held for one party only or both parties together.
- Prepare advocacy material and talking points on possible amendments and the measure to be marked up.

Political Preparation

- Work with "key constituents" and advocacy groups
- Discuss with the administration, if desirable, and Senate sponsors
- Develop plan to work with the press

Chairman's Preparation

- Meet with chairman to review markup vehicle and potential amendments
- Draft opening statement
- Draft procedural script and have available scripts for members that my be used
- Meet with members of party to discuss procedural and political strategy prior to markup

Procedural Preparation

- Comply with committee rules' notification requirements
- Compile amendment roster
- Prepare script for possible procedural motions
- Determine Member schedules to ensure attendance at markup and determine where they can be reached if their presence is needed in the committee. (Each party does this for its own Members. Quorum requirements differ among committees, although a majority must be physically present to report a measure from committee.)

JUDY SCHNEIDER,
THE COMMITTEE MARKUP PROCESS IN THE
HOUSE OF REPRESENTATIVES
3, 7, 8, 10, 19, 20–22 (Dec. 1, 2004)

Selecting the Text

A key initial decision that can shape the course and outcome of a markup is the selection of the text that the committee considers. Essentially, there are two choices. First, the committee may mark up the text of one of the bills that Members had introduced and that the House parliamentarian, acting for the Speaker, had referred to the committee.

Second, the committee may mark up the draft of a bill that has not yet been formally introduced and referred to the committee. The chair can direct the committee's staff to prepare the draft of a bill, usually written with the assistance of attorneys in the House's Office of Legislative Counsel, that reflects the chair's policy preferences. The committee then may mark up this draft bill which, in its printed form, may be called a "discussion draft" or a "staff draft." Such a draft is now often known informally as a "chair's mark." This phrase originated in committee consideration of budget resolutions, but now is commonly used to denote any draft that constitutes the legislative starting point from which a committee chair thinks a markup should begin.

In either case, the text that a committee marks up already may have been marked up by one or more of the committee's subcommittees If there has been a subcommittee markup, the subcommittee then makes its legislative recommendations to its parent committee. In turn, the committee most often uses the product of the subcommittee's markup as the starting point for its own markup.

The selection of the text — or the "base text" or the "vehicle," as Members sometimes call it — that the committee will mark up is important because it sets the framework within which the markup, and the policy debates it inspires, will take place. Each provision of the selected text will survive the markup and be recommended to the House for passage unless a committee member takes the initiative to propose an amendment to it that the committee adopts. The burden is on those who would change the provisions of the base text; it is up to them to devise alternatives to that text and convince a majority of their committee colleagues to vote — for those alternatives. Clearly, then, it is advantageous to be able to select the vehicle from among the bills that were referred to the committee, or to devise the vehicle by drafting anew text that very well may draw on selected provisions of the introduced bills on which the committee held hearings.

Beginning the Markup

A committee markup meeting usually begins by the chair calling the committee to order and announcing the matters that the committee is expected to consider at that meeting. The chair also may announce that the requisite quorum of members is present. The chair begins the markup itself by announcing that the committee will proceed to the consideration of the bill, resolution, or draft that is scheduled for consideration. The chair also may note that whatever requirements for prior notification the committee's rules impose have been satisfied.

First Reading

The committee clerk then is to read the entire text of the bill (or whatever text is being considered). However, this reading usually is waived by unanimous consent when all committee members already have had an opportunity to become familiar with the text. If unanimous consent cannot be obtained, a committee member may move to waive the first reading of a bill or resolution. Clause l(a)(1)(B) of House Rule XI provides for a privileged and nondebatable motion to waive this first reading in committee or subcommittee if printed copies of the measure are available.

Opening Statements

Either before or after the chair formally presents the bill to the committee for consideration, he or she may entertain opening statements on the bill and the issues it raises. The chair typically makes the first statement and next recognizes the ranking minority party member. The chair then recognizes other members to speak, alternating between the parties. Members usually are recognized in the order of their seniority on the committee (to the extent that the party ratio permits). However, chairs sometimes recognize members in the order in which they arrived at the committee meeting, just as chairs sometimes follow this practice in recognizing members to question witnesses at committee hearings.

Members normally are recognized for no more than five minutes each to make their opening statements, though chairs may allot more time to themselves and to their ranking minority members. In principle, members who have been recognized may yield to colleagues or request unanimous consent for additional time, but they are much less likely to do so while making opening statements than when debating amendments . . . .

Offering and Debating Amendments

After opening statements and after the first reading of the bill has been completed or dispensed with, the committee begins the markup process per se by entertaining, debating, and voting on amendments . . . .

Offering Amendments

If a full committee is marking up a bill that one of its subcommittees already has marked up, the chair is most likely to give priority consideration to any subcommittee-approved amendments to each section (or to whatever part of the text is open to amendment) To offer additional amendments to each section, the chair usually first recognizes a senior member of his or her party. After the committee disposes of that amendment (and any amendment to it), the chair normally recognizes a senior member of the minority party to offer another amendment to that section. Thereafter the chair typically recognizes other members to offer amendments to the section in order of their seniority, alternating between members of the two parties. However, there is nothing in House rules that requires chairs to follow these recognition practices. Committee chairs sometimes offer amendments themselves (unlike Members who preside over the House's floor sessions).

. . . .

Debating Amendments

Each amendment is debated under the five-minute rule, much as members debate amendments on the floor in Committee of the Whole. The chair first recognizes the amendment's sponsor for five minutes to explain and justify the amendment. Then the chair recognizes a member who opposes the amendment to speak for five minutes. Thereafter, each committee member may be recognized to speak for five minutes unless the committee votes to stop the debate . . . .

Motions to Conclude Markups

It bears repeating that no House committee has the authority to actually change the text of a measure that has been introduced and referred to it, nor do committees vote directly on the merits of bills and resolutions. The committee votes instead on the amendments that it will recommend to the House. The House then considers and votes on these committee amendments when it acts on the bill itself.

Markups may begin with an amendment in the nature of a substitute being offered by or on behalf of the chair, sometimes for the tactical reasons . . . . Members then offer their amendments to that complete substitute, rather than to the text of the underlying bill. In such a case, the final vote the committee takes on amendments is on agreeing to the amendment in the nature of a substitute, as it may have been amended. When the committee reports the bill back to the House, the bill will be accompanied by only that one amendment in the nature of a substitute, even though the committee may have adopted several or even many amendments to it during the course of the markup.

Ordering the Bill Reported

The committee does not conclude its markup by voting on the bill itself. After voting on the last amendment to be offered, the chair recognizes a majority party member to move that the committee order the bill reported to the House with whatever amendments the committee has adopted during the markup, and with the recommendation that the House agree to those amendments and then pass the bill as amended. The bill is actually reported (as opposed to the committee *ordering* it reported) when the committee chair takes the bill and the accompanying committee report to the floor when the House is in session, files the report, and returns the bill to the House. The committee report then is printed, the bill is reprinted to show the committee's action and its recommended amendments, and the bill is listed on the Union Calendar if it authorizes or appropriates funds or affects revenues, or otherwise on the House Calendar.

The Committee's Reporting Options

A House committee has several options in deciding how it will report to the House after it has completed a markup.

Committee Amendments. If the committee has marked up a bill that was introduced and referred to it — HR. 1, for example, the committee may vote to order H.R. 1 reported with one or more amendments.

If, at its last vote on amendments, the committee agreed to an amendment in the nature of a substitute (perhaps as amended), the committee may vote to order H.R. 1 reported with that one amendment, even though the amendment constitutes an entirely new text of the bill that may not resemble the text of H.R. 1 as it was introduced and referred to the committee.

If the committee has marked up H.R. 1 and agreed to several different amendments to it, each amendment affecting a different provision of the bill, the committee may vote to order H.R. 1 reported with those separate amendments. Instead, though, the committee may authorize the chair to incorporate those amendments into a single amendment in the nature of a substitute. The reason for doing so is that it is more convenient for the House, when considering a bill on the floor, to act on a single committee substitute than to act on a series of discrete committee amendments. The committee may agree to a unanimous consent request that the committee report an amendment in the nature of a substitute instead of the several amendments. Alternatively, a member may offer the amendment in the nature of a substitute as the last amendment to be considered during the markup. (In the latter case, however, any committee member has the right to insist that the substitute actually be drafted and available in writing at the time it is offered.)

Clean Bills. Alternately, the committee may vote to report what is known as a *clean bill* instead of reporting H. R. 1 with one or more amendments. A clean bill is a new bill that has a new number instead of H.R. 1 and that typically lists as its sponsor the committee chair, not the Member who had introduced H.R. 1. This new bill is known as a clean bill because it incorporates all the amendments that the committee adopted during its markup of H.R. 1. For this reason, the committee reports the new bill without amendment; in this sense, it is "clean."

The effect of reporting a clean bill is much the same as reporting the marked-up bill with an amendment in the nature of a substitute. In either case, all the committee's proposed changes in the marked up text are incorporated into a single new text. Then why would a committee report a clean bill?

There are at least two reasons. First, if the committee has marked up a staff draft (discussion draft, chair's mark) instead of HR. 1, that marked-up text must be introduced and reported as a bill before the House can consider it. Second, there are instances in which the committee (or its chair) decides to assume complete responsibility (and credit) for the bill it orders reported. Imagine, for example, that the committee has marked up H.R. 1 in ways that the original sponsor of the bill finds unacceptable. In that case, the sponsor may wish to disavow further responsibility for H.R. 1, and so welcomes the committee's decision to report a clean bill instead of reporting HR. 1 with a committee substitute. In other cases, the chair may prefer a clean bill in order to have his or her name most closely associated with it.

Technically, the committee must have the clean bill in its possession before it can vote to order it reported. This means that, at the conclusion of the markup, the marked-up text must be prepared as a bill, it must be introduced while the House is in session, and the newly introduced clean bill must be numbered and referred back to the committee before the committee may act on it. In practice, committees sometimes short-circuit this process if no one objects. Immediately after the committee completes its markup, it may authorize the chair to report the clean bill. So long as the clean bill is introduced on that same calendar day, the official records of the House's proceedings do not indicate whether the clean bill actually was introduced and referred to committee before or after the committee's markup ended.

Other Views

Immediately after the committee votes to order the bill reported, the ranking minority member or another minority party member usually claims the right for all committee members to submit their own supplemental, minority, or dissenting views for printing as part of the committee's report on the bill. Clause 2(l) of Rule XI provides that:

> If at the time of approval of a measure or matter by a committee (other than the Committee on Rules) a member of the committee gives notice of intention to file supplemental, minority, or additional views for inclusion in the report to the House thereon, that member shall be entitled to not less than two additional calendar days after the day of such notice (excluding Saturdays, Sundays, and

legal holidays except when the House is in session on such a day) to file such views, in writing and signed by that member, with the clerk of the committee.

NOTES AND QUESTIONS

1. Although Committees seldom publish transcripts of markup sessions, markups usually take place in open public sessions. ROGER H. DAVIDSON & WALTER J. OLESZEK, CONGRESS AND ITS MEMBERS 218 (9th ed., 2004). If you are retained as a lobbyist concerning a measure scheduled for markup would you attend? Why?

2. If markup transcripts are available, how useful do you think they would be in determining the meaning of the measure?

G. REPORTED BILLS

CHARLES W. JOHNSON,
HOW OUR LAWS ARE MADE
16–18 (2003)

If the committee votes to report the bill to the House, the committee staff writes a committee report. The report describes the purpose and scope of the bill and the reasons for its recommended approval. Generally, a section-by-section analysis is set forth explaining precisely what each section is intended to accomplish. All changes in existing law must be indicated in the report and the text of laws being repealed must be set out. This requirement is known as the "Ramseyer" rule. A similar rule in the Senate is known as the "Cordon" rule. Committee amendments also must be set out at the beginning of the report and explanations of them are included. Executive communications regarding the bill may be referenced in the report.

If at the time of approval of a bill by a committee, except for the Committee on Rules, a member of the committee gives notice of an intention to file supplemental, minority, or additional views, that member is entitled to not less than two additional calendar days after the day of such notice (excluding Saturdays, Sundays, and legal holidays unless the House is in session on those days) in which to file those views with the clerk of the committee. Those views that are timely filed must be included in the report on the bill. Committee reports must be filed while the House is in session unless unanimous consent is obtained from the House to file at a later time or the committee is awaiting additional views.

The report is assigned a report number upon its filing and is sent to the Government Printing Office for printing. House reports are given a prefix-designator that indicates the number of the Congress. For example, the first House report is the 108th Congress was numbered 108-1.

In the printed report, committee amendments are indicated by showing new matter in italics and deleted matter in line-through type. The report number is printed on the bill and the calendar number is shown on both the first and back pages of the bill. However, in the case of a bill that was referred to two or more committee for consideration is sequence, the calendar number is printed only on the bill as reported by the last committee to consider it. . . .

Committee reports are perhaps the most valuable single element of the legislative history of a law. They are used by the courts, executive departments, and the public as a source of information regarding the purpose and meaning of the law.

CONTENTS OF REPORTS

The report of a committee on a measure that has been approved by the committee must include: (1) the committee's oversight findings and recommendations; (2) a statement required by the Congressional Budget Act of 1974, if the measure is a bill or joint resolution providing new budget authority (other than continuing appropriations) or an increase or decrease in revenues or tax expenditures; (3) a cost estimate and comparison prepared by the Director of the Congressional Budget Office whenever the Director has submitted that estimate and comparison to the committee prior to the filing of the report; and (4) a statement of general performance goals and objectives, including outcome-related goals and objectives, for which the measure authorizes funding. Each report accompanying a bill or joint resolution relating to employment or access to public services or accommodations must describe the manner in which the provisions apply to the legislative branch. Each of these items are set out separately and clearly identified in the report.

With respect to each record vote by a committee, the total number of votes cast for, and the total number of votes cast against any public measure or matter or amendment thereto and the names of those voting for and against, must be included in the committee report.

In addition, each report of a committee on a public bill or public joint resolution must contain a statement citing the specific powers granted to Congress in the Constitution to enact the law proposed by the bill or joint resolution. Committee reports that accompany bills or resolutions that contain federal unfunded mandates are also required to include an estimate prepared by the Congressional Budget Office on the cost of the mandates on state, local, and tribal governments. If an estimate is not available at the time a report is filed, committees are required to publish the estimate in the Congressional Record. Each report also must contain an estimate, made by the committee, of the costs which would be incurred in carrying out that bill or joint resolution in the fiscal year reported and in each of the five fiscal years thereafter or for the duration of the program authorized if less than five years. The report must include a comparison of the estimates of those costs with any estimate made by any Government agency and submitted to that committee. The Committees on Appropriations, House Administration, Rules, and Standards of Official Conduct are not required to include cost estimates in their reports. In addition, the committee's own cost estimates are not required to be included in reports when a cost estimate and comparison prepared by the Director of the Congressional Budget Office has been submitted prior to the filing of the report and included in the report.

FILING OF REPORTS

Measures approved by a committee must be reported by the Chairman promptly after approval. If not, a majority of the members of the committee may file a written request with the clerk of the committee for the reporting of the measure. When the request is filed, the clerk must immediately notify the chairman of the committee of the filing of the request, and the report on the measure must be filed within seven calendar days (excluding days on which the House is not in session) after the day on which the request is filed. This does not apply to a report of the Committee on Rules with respect to a rule, joint rule, or order of business of the House or to the reporting of a resolution of inquiry addressed to the head of an executive department.

AVAILABILITY OF REPORTS AND HEARINGS

A measure or matter reported by a committee (except the Committee on Rules in the case of a resolution providing a rule, joint rule, or order of business) may not be considered in the House until the third calendar day (excluding Saturdays, Sundays, and legal holidays unless the House is in session on those days) on which the report of that committee on that measure has been available to the Members of the House. This rule is subject to certain exceptions including resolutions providing for certain privileged matters and measures declaring war or other national emergency. However, it is in order to consider a report from the Committee on Rules on the same day it is reported that proposes only to waive this availability requirement. If hearings were held on a measure or matter so reported, the committee is required to make every reasonable effort to have those hearings printed and available for distribution to the Members of the House prior to the consideration of the measure in the House. Committees are also required, to the maximum extent feasible, to make their publications available in electronic form. A general appropriation bill reported by the Committee on Appropriations may not be considered until printed committee hearings and a committee report thereon have been available to the Members of the House for at least three calendar days (excluding Saturdays, Sundays, and legal holidays unless the House is in session on those days).

NOTES AND QUESTIONS

1. Does the fact that committee reports are written by staff undercut their probative force as legislative history?

2. Why is a section-by-section analysis necessary? Shouldn't the text of a bill be so drafted as to be self-explanatory?

3. What purpose is served by the "Ramseyer" and "Cordon" rules?

4. What probative force should minority and additional views be afforded as legislative history? Of Executive communications regarding the bill?

5. Are committee reports best characterized as analytical, persuasive, or partisan documents? Does your answer depend on the report's disclosure of which members voted for or against the measure or amendment?

6. In considering a constitutional challenge to a statute, what weight should a court give to a statement in the report citing the specific powers granted to Congress in the Constitution to enact the proposed measure?

7. If a committee report is unavailable at the time the House votes on the measure, does that negate its probative force as legislative history?

8. For a tabular presentation of House rules concerning committee reports, see JUDY SCHNEIDER, HOUSE COMMITTEE REPORTS: REQUIRED CONTENTS (January 17, 2003).

H. OBTAINING CONSIDERATION

As the following excerpts indicate, the House and Senate procedures for getting a reported bill to the floor for consideration and debate differ substantially.

CHRISTOPHER M. DAVIS,
LEGISLATIVE PROCEDURES AND THE LEGISLATIVE AGENDA
IN THE HOUSE OF REPRESENTATIVES
12–15, 19–23, 25 (August 7, 2003)

When a House committee reports a bill — that is, when it returns the bill to the control of the full House with a recommendation that the bill be passed, with or without amendments — the bill normally is referred to one of two calendars. According to clause 1 of Rule XIII, authorization, appropriations, and tax bills are placed on the Union Calendar; other public bills appear on the House Calendar. The two calendars taken together may be thought of as a list of bills that have survived committee scrutiny and are now available for consideration on the floor by the full House. If the bills that are introduced can be said to constitute a *possible* agenda for the House the bills on these two calendars constitute a *potential* floor agenda.[4] Each reported bill has been studied and found worthy by the House's designated committee experts. At this stage,

---

[4] Minor and emergency bills are the only ones that often reach the House floor without prior committee action. If a bill has been referred to committee, the House may not consider it until the committee reports it or is discharged from further consideration of the bill. The committee may be discharged by unanimous consent when possible or through the more elaborate procedures of Rule XV when necessary.

the agenda problem for the House becomes one of transforming this potential agenda into a *prospective* agenda of bills on which floor action is expected in the near term, and finally, into the *actual* agenda or schedule for the daily conduct of business.

The various legislative committees of the House can consider bills simultaneously, but the bills they report must be taken up on the House floor one at a time. Some bills on the calendar die at the end of each Congress for lack of time for floor consideration, so a selection process is unavoidable. A mechanical answer would be to call bills to the floor in the order in which they appear on the calendars, which is the order in which they are reported from committee. However, this procedure would not permit necessary differentiations between the critical and the insignificant, nor would it ensure timely action on bills that confront deadlines such as the beginning of the new fiscal year for appropriations bills. Some more discriminating procedure is required.

At one extreme, agenda decisions could be delegated to a single leader, and between roughly 1890 and 1910, it could be argued without much exaggeration that the Speaker enjoyed such power as the elected leader of the majority party. But this is no longer the case. At the other extreme, decisions affecting the floor agenda could require the unanimous concurrence of all Members; in daily practice, the Senate's rules encourage reliance on procedures that approach this limit. Generally speaking, the rules of the House seek the middle ground of majority control. Although the specific procedures to be discussed are varied and rather complicated, they are permeated by a single principle: when the votes of a simple numerical majority are sufficient to pass a bill, the decision to consider it also can be controlled by the same majority.

Privileged Business Under House Rules

The rules of the House provide for arranging the floor agenda by applying the concept of "privileged" business. In brief, a bill that is privileged may be called up for consideration on the floor out of its order on the House or Union Calendar. To put it somewhat differently, privileged business may interrupt the daily order of business that is listed in the House's rules. In fact, this order of business under clause 1 of Rule XIV is never followed, save for the routine proceedings such as the morning prayer, the saying of the pledge of allegiance, and approval of the Journal at the beginning of each day's session. Virtually all legislative business that is transacted on the House floor is an interruption of the regular order of business and is privileged by virtue of House rules, by vote of the House, or by unanimous consent. In practice, a bill that does gain privilege by one of these means cannot be considered on the floor; a motion to consider it may not interrupt the regular order of business and, therefore, is not in order. Thus, House rules affect the floor agenda by designating certain classes of bills as privileged and by establishing procedures by which other bills become privileged.

General Privilege. The rules grant privilege to bills and resolutions on certain subjects and for certain purposes, but only if those measures have been reported by the appropriate committees. Under clause 5(a) of Rule XIII, for example, privilege extends to general appropriations bills, to budget resolutions and budget reconciliation bills, and to House resolutions concerning changes in House rules, the conduct of Representatives and House employees, election challenges affecting Representatives, and certain expenditures for House operations. These matters generally concern either the integrity and proceedings of the House itself or the performance of what is usually considered to be the core constitutional power of Congress — the "power of the purse."

It is in order for the committee that has reported one of these privileged bills or resolutions to call it up for action on the floor at any time that another matter is not already under consideration. However, a variety of other matters also are privileged, including conference reports on legislative disagreements between the House and Senate, certain Senate amendments to House bills, and bills that the President has vetoed. Furthermore, House rules do not establish a fixed and certain order of precedence among all privileged matters; if each of two Representatives wishes to call up a privileged bill or other matter, the rules do not always determine which of them is to be recognized first. The effect of this situation is to leave some important discretion to the Speaker in arranging a specific order of business from among the various matters that enjoy privileged access to the House floor.

Putting the exercise of this discretion aside for the moment, the grant of general privilege by House rules has the effect of moving privileged bills from the potential agenda of bills on the Union and House Calendars to the prospective agenda of bills that can be expected to come to the floor in the near future.[5] But the rules do not require that privileged bills be considered, though they usually are. By one means or another, a numerical majority on the floor usually has an opportunity to vote to block consideration of a bill, thereby avoiding the need to vote for or against it on its merits. Such a vote is rarely necessary, however, because even privileged bills are not called up for floor action unless there is good reason to expect that the House is prepared to pass them. For these bills, unlike bills that are not privileged, the question affecting their fate usually becomes when, not whether, they will be considered on the floor.

Among the legislative measures that can become law, general appropriation measures and budget reconciliation bills are the only ones that frequently reach the floor by virtue of their general privilege under House rules. The rules do not grant such favored status to most bills. Instead, the rules include a number of devices by which the vast majority of non-privileged bills that the House considers are made in order. In the case of general appropriations bills and the other matters that are generally privileged, the House has determined over the years that privilege should extend to them as a class — because of their subjects and without regard to their specific provisions. Two additional devices to be discussed also are designed to facilitate floor action on certain limited classes of legislation — private bills and bills affecting the District of Columbia. There are five other devices by which bills are moved from the potential to the prospective agenda on a case-by-case basis, because of their individual merits and circumstances, not because of the general nature of the subjects they address.

These seven devices may be summarized as follows:

1. Motions to discharge House committees from further consideration of bills they have not reported, making discharged bills eligible for floor considerations;

2. Procedures known as Calendar Wednesday, by which committees may call up nonprivileged bills they have reported but which have not reached the House floor by more conventional routes;

3. Special procedures for considering bills concerning the District of Columbia;

4. Procedures for the call of a special calendar of private bills affecting specific individuals or entities;

5. Procedures for the call of the "Corrections Calendar" for bills that enjoy widespread support in the House;

6. Procedures known as suspension of the rules for expeditious consideration of relatively noncontroversial bills; and

7. Special rules adopted by the House, at the recommendation of its Rules Committee, that provides for consideration of individual, nonprivileged, bills.

These devices are not equally important, nor are they employed with equal frequency. Some are well-suited to relatively minor bills; others are used to consider more controversial bills. In a sense, the first six of these procedures are alternatives to the seventh, which usually is the most complicated and time-consuming, because it is

---

[5] House rules generally require that the written committee report on a bill, even a privileged bill, be available for three days before the bill may be considered on the floor. This delay permits time for Representatives and their staffs to become familiar with the committee's recommendations before they are debated.

through the Rules Committee that the most important nonprivileged bills usually reach the floor . . . .

   . . . .

Special Rules Affecting the Order of Business

The procedures discussed to this point are not applicable to most of the major bills that House committees report each Congress. These bills are not generally privileged under House rules, nor are they supported by large enough majorities to be passed under an expediting procedure such as suspension of the rules. Thus, these procedures are not sufficient to fully resolve the problem of transforming the large potential agenda of reported bills into the smaller prospective agenda of bills that are likely to reach the floor.

For this purpose, the House also has looked for the past century to one of its committees, the Committee on Rules. Like the other standing committees, the Rules Committee has jurisdiction over a class of measures, primarily bills and resolutions affecting House rules. But this committee also is authorized to report House resolutions that, if adopted by the House, affect the order of business on the floor. These resolutions, which also are known as rules or special rules, are privileged and so may be considered by the House at any time that another matter is not already pending. Because of both their provisions and their privilege, special rules constitute the critical link between most major legislation on the House and Union Calendars and the House's actual floor agenda.

A special rule usually begins by providing that, upon adoption of the resolution, the Speaker may declare the House resolved into the Committee of the Whole House on the State of the Union for the consideration of a particular bill designated by the resolution . . . . In the absence of this provision, the Speaker would have no such authority because the bill at issue presumably is not privileged and, therefore, the regular order of business could not be interrupted to consider it in Committee of the Whole (except by unanimous consent). Adoption of the special rule concerning a bill has the effect of making the bill itself in order for consideration.[6]

Once the Rules Committee reports a special rule, it remains for the House to decide by majority vote whether to accept it or reject it. The special rule itself is debated for as much as an hour and it may even be amended, although with difficulty. The Rules Committee proposes moving individual bills from the potential floor agenda to the prospective agenda, but the House is not bound to accept these recommendations. The voting majority on the floor retains negative agenda control. The House usually cannot avoid considering a Rules Committee proposal but the majority may reject it (although this does not happen very often for reasons that will be discussed).

The Rules Committee also can exercise a certain degree of negative agenda control. The authority of the committee is not restricted to recommending the order in which the House should consider the bills reported by the other House committees. The Rules Committee also has the option of not acting — of declining to report the special rule that a bill may require if it is to reach the floor. The committee has often been characterized as a "traffic cop," regulating and directing the flow of legislative traffic to the floor. This metaphor is apt in some respects, but it also has one serious deficiency. The traffic cop decides when a car may pass, but not whether it may pass if its driver is obeying the "rules of the road." By contrast, the Rules Committee is not obliged to allow all bills to come to the floor; it may decide instead that individual bills do not merit floor consideration at all. If the committee fails to report a special rule for a bill, or fails to act promptly, the prospects for that bill becoming law fall precipitously.

---

[6] Different forms of special rules are reported for other purposes, such as waiving points of order against conference reports.

The committee that reported the bill may resort to the Calendar Wednesday procedure, but Calendar Wednesday rarely is invoked in part because it is not difficult to prevent passage of a bill that is brought to the floor in this way. Alternatively, the bill's proponents may attempt to discharge the committee from further consideration of a special rule that would make the bill in order, but discharge petitions rarely have been successful. Thus, since much of the legislative activity in the House focuses on bills that are not privileged and that are too controversial to pass under suspension of the rules (with limited debate, no floor amendments, and a two-thirds vote required for passage) or by call of the Corrections Calendar, the position of the Rules Committee in arranging the floor agenda is absolutely pivotal.

In view of the importance of its decisions, how the Rules Committee makes these decisions requires attention. When one of the other committees reports a bill that does not enjoy enough support to pass under suspension of the rules of by use of the Corrections Calendar, the committee's chairman requests a hearing before the Rules Committee. If the committee obliges (and it need not do so), Representatives appear before it to speak for or against the bill. During the hearing, Rules Committee members may inquire into the merits of the legislation as well as into when and how it should be considered on the floor. The committee then decides, by majority vote, whether to grant a rule and, if so, what its provisions should be. Like any other committee, the Rules Committee bases its decisions on the views of its own members and on their perception of what a majority of the House is prepared to support. But in the contemporary House, the actions of this committee also have been shaped by its unique relationship with the House's majority party leadership.

Today this relationship is cooperative, but it has not always been so. In fact, the changes in this relationship during the 20th century have been at the heart of some of the most important developments that have taken place within the House.[7] At the beginning of this century, the Speaker also served as chairman of the Rules Committee and appointed its other members (as well as the chairmen and members of all other committees). Consequently, he and his allies controlled the committee and its decisions, and the flow of legislation to the floor. If the Speaker did not look with favor on a bill, it was all but certain to perish from Rules Committee inaction. The Calendar Wednesday procedure was adopted in 1909 to assuage critics of the Speaker's power; nevertheless, he soon was stripped of his chairmanship and appointment powers. This was truly a historic moment for the House, because the result was a fundamental redistribution of power from the Speaker and the majority party leadership to the standing committees and their chairmen.

The seniority system became the basis for much of the power of House committees and especially their chairmen. In search of a stable alternative to appointments by the Speaker, the House came to rely more and more on the length of continuous committee service by majority party Representatives as the criterion for selecting chairmen. Once appointed to committees, Representatives usually could remain on them as long as they wished and as long as they were members of the House. If they were members of the majority party, they could eventually expect to become chairman if they remained on their committees longer than any of their party colleagues. As a result, the seniority system tended to insulate committees from the short term influence of elections as well as from the efforts of party leaders to draw their members together in support of a party program for legislation. And nowhere were the consequences of seniority more pronounced than on the Rules Committee.

Although the Democrats were the majority party in the House for all but four years between the mid-1930s and 1960, the Rules Committee could be dominated during most of that period by a coalition of Republicans and conservative Democrats. Although the

---

[7] On the history of the Rules Committee, see U.S. Congress, House Committee on Rules, *A History of the Committee on Rules*, committee print, 97th Cong., 2d sess. (1983).

Democrats enjoyed a nominal majority on the committee, their control over committee decisions was far from certain. The chairman of the Rules Committee during much of the 1950s has been credited with being one of the driving forces behind a bipartisan "conservative coalition" that could stymie the Democratic majority by refusing to report special rules. If this report has been written 40 years ago, it could very well have concluded that effective agenda control rested in the hands of this coalition, when it chose to exercise it, over which the leaders of the majority party had no real control and only uncertain influence.

This situation began to change in 1961 when the House voted narrowly to increase the size of the Rules Committee, giving the Democrats a tenuous one-vote majority on which it could rely more often than not. In 1975, the Democratic majority in the House changed its party rules to tie the Rules Committee more firmly to the party majority acting through its leader, the Speaker. Whereas a party committee nominated new members to other committees, subject to approval by all the Democrats meeting in a caucus, it was the Speaker who nominated the Democratic members of the Rules Committee. Because there now were more than twice as many Democrats as Republicans on the committee, the effect of these changes was to transform the relationship between the committee and the majority party. With rare exceptions, the Rules Committee became allied with the Speaker and the other majority party leaders. Although the Speaker could not dictate committee decisions, he and the committee's Democratic members tended to share the same policy goals and a common desire to use the committee's powers to promote them.

Now that the utility of these arrangements has become well-established, they are likely to be preserved, no matter which party holds a majority of seats in the House. Rule 12B of the House Republican Conference for the 105th Congress authorizes the Speaker to nominate the chairman and other Republican members of the Rules Committee, subject to approval by the Republican Conference. Should the conference reject one of these nominations, the Speaker is to make another one. In other words, the Republican Speaker, like his Democratic predecessors, can ensure that a working majority of the committee will be responsive to the party leadership's priorities and to its short-term agenda preferences and strategic interests.

From the perspective of this report, these developments were critical because of their implications for majority control of the floor agenda. The majority party leadership selects more than a majority of the members of the Rule Committee, who in turn make decisions that meet the needs and interests of their party colleagues who can constitute a working majority on the floor.

The Rules Committee provides an excellent vantage point from which to look again at the implications for agenda-setting in the House of the organization of national parties generally and in Congress specifically. The House has relied heavily on the seniority system for allocating committee chairmanships in part because doing so has avoided the possibility of factional conflicts within the majority party. The Speaker lost his authority to appoint and reappoint majority party members to committees when a significant faction within his own party rebelled and joined forces with the minority party. The presumption that a Representative who serves on a committee may remain on that committee protects the interests of Members individually against the preferences of their party collectively.

This arrangement would not be as acceptable if there were consistently a coherent party position that Representatives were expected to support. But it has been acceptable in the House where party positions often have tended to emerge, if at all, from a weighing of what most party members in the House are willing to support, as they calculate their own electoral interests and as they evaluate national interests and balance them against constituency interests. When majority party unity is particularly strong, Members may delegate to its leaders more de facto authority over the selection of committee chairmen, even in violation of the seniority norm, and over appointments to fill committee vacancies. When unity is weaker, majority party leaders are likely to exercise less unilateral control over these decisions.

Changing the relationship between the Rules Committee and the majority party's leaders in the House narrowed the gap between agenda control by majority vote and agenda control by the majority party. Because members of the committee now are effectively chosen by the party leadership, their interests and decisions are likely to coincide, more often than not, with the preferences of most of their party colleagues. When there is significant opposition on the floor to a special rule, the House tends to divide along party lines, and the outcome usually turns on the number of Members from each party who vote with most of the Members from the other.

In sum, the Rules Committee is the key instrument through which the House makes its agenda decisions affecting most major bills. Without a special rule from the committee, a bill that is not privileged cannot reach the floor for passage by majority vote (except through the rarely successful discharge and Calendar Wednesday procedures). The House accepts or rejects the committee's recommendations by majority vote, and thereby retains the power to refuse a bill a place on the floor agenda. Changes in the committee's membership and the procedures for selecting its members have made the committee more regularly and predictably responsive to the agenda preferences of the majority party, whether Republican or Democrat. The committee always has been reluctant to propose a bill for the floor agenda that a majority might oppose. In the House today, the committee also is reluctant to refuse a special rule for a bill when support for it centers in the majority party. Such a bill may not reach the floor until the committee and party leaders can assemble the majority vote needed to pass it. But, the Rules Committee has become an ally of, not a potential obstacle to, control of the floor agenda by the majority party.

. . . .

Once the Rules Committee reports a special rule, it is privileged for floor consideration, as is any bill made in order by the standing rules or by a special rule the House already has adopted. However, the Speaker retains an important degree of discretion in arranging these matters into a daily and weekly schedule that meets the responsibilities of the House and the interests of his party. As noted earlier, a variety of bills and other matters are privileged for floor consideration. In some cases, they are of equal privilege. Thus, the Speaker may exercise discretion in deciding the order in which they are to be considered. If one Representative seeks to call up a privileged matter, the Speaker may decline to recognize him or her if there is another Representative on the floor who can be recognized instead to bring up some other matter that is at least equally privileged (and who, therefore, has an equal right to be recognized).

It is rarely necessary, however, for the Speaker to actually use his control over recognition on the floor to control the flow of legislative business. Scheduling decisions generally are made within the majority party through consultations by the Speaker and other party leaders with the appropriate committee and subcommittee leaders. A probable schedule for the week then is announced on the floor by a majority party spokesman. Representatives of the minority party also may be consulted. They may inquire about the status of certain bills, and they may complain that some bills are being held back while others are being propelled to the floor prematurely. But the minority has little effective recourse, other than to attempt to defeat the special rules providing for consideration of the bills they oppose.

JUDY SCHNEIDER,
PROVISIONS OF SPECIAL RULES IN THE HOUSE:
AN EXAMPLE OF A TYPICAL OPEN RULE
1–3 (November 10, 2004)

This report includes a typical example of a simple open rule that the House Committee on Rules may report to govern House floor action on a bill that is not otherwise privileged for consideration. This resolution has been divided into five parts . . . .

This first part of the rule makes the bill in order for floor consideration by authorizing the Speaker to transform the House into the Committee of the Whole to consider that bill. Without this authority, a motion for the same purpose would not be in order; it would not be privileged to interrupt the regular daily order of business on the House floor.

The second part waives a reading of the bill. It also governs general debate on the bill by setting the amount of time for the debate, by dividing control of this time, usually between the chairman and ranking minority member of the committee that reported the bill, and by requiring that all general debate be relevant to the subject of the bill.

The third part merely states that the bill shall be read for amendment and that each Member may speak for five minutes on each amendment. By implication, this part also means that the bill is to be read for amendment one section at a time. Further, as each section is read, Members may offer to it whatever amendments they wish, so long as those amendments satisfy the House's rules and precedents — for example, the requirement that amendments must be germane. This part is what makes this special rule an open rule; it leaves the bill fully open to amendments that otherwise would be in order.

The fourth part provides for the Committee of the Whole, after disposing of the last amendment, to transform itself back into the House, and report the bill to the House with whatever amendments the Committee of the Whole adopted. This provision eliminates the need for the House to vote on a motion to achieve the same result. The Committee of the Whole does not vote on the bill as a whole, and the committee may not actually amend the bill, it only makes recommendations to the House about amendments.

The fifth and final part of the rule expedites final House passage of the bill by precluding almost all debate in the House and all other actions except those necessary for the House to vote on the amendments the Committee of the Whole recommended and to dispose of one motion to recommit the bill to a standing committee. That motion to recommit may include instructions containing a proposed amendment to the bill.

A Typical "Open" Rule

RESOLUTION

Resolved, That at any time after the adoption of this resolution the Speaker may, pursuant to clause 19(b) of rule XXIII, declare the House resolved into the Committee of the Whole House on the State of the Union for the consideration of the bill (H.R. 2230) to amend the Civil Right Act of 1957 to extend the life of the Civil Rights Commission, and for other purposes, and the first reading of the bill shall be dispensed with. After general debate, which shall be confined to the bill and shall continue not to exceed one hour, to be equally divided and controlled by the chairman and ranking minority member of the Committee on the Judiciary, the bill shall be read for amendment under the five-minute rule. At the conclusion of the consideration of the bill for amendment, the Committee shall rise and report the bill to the House with such amendments as may have been adopted and the previous question shall be considered as ordered on the bill and amendments thereto to final passage without intervening motion except one motion to recommit.

NOTES AND QUESTIONS

1. Under a typical open rule, one hour of general debate is permitted on major legislation. Is the House truly a deliberative body?

2. "Five different rules may be chosen to govern debate on the House floor. An open rule allows any member to offer an amendment. A modified open rule requires that amendments be printed in the Congressional Record. A structured rule allows three or more amendments to be considered; a modified closed rule allows only one or two. A closed rule prohibits any amendments not recommended by the committee that sent the bill to the floor. Any type of rule may be self-executing meaning that specific amendments can be included as part of it without needing to be voted on separately." Thomas E. Mann, Molly Reynolds & Nigel Holmes, *Could Congress Be Waking Up?* N.Y. TIMES, Jan. 19, 2008, p. A19 cols. 1–2.

3. Some rules are restrictive in that they limit or preclude the freedom of members to offer germane amendments to the bill. ROGER H. DAVIDSON & WALTER J. OLESZEK, CONGRESS AND ITS MEMBERS 244 (9th ed., 2004). Why would party leaders seek such rules?

4. What opportunities does Rules Committee consideration offer a legislative advocate seeking to defeat a bill reported from a substantive committee?

ROBERT B. DOVE,
ENACTMENT OF A LAW 16 (n.d.)

Considering Measures on the Senate Floor

The Senate's Majority and Minority Leaders, as the spokesmen for their parties, and in consultation with their respective policy committees, implement and direct the legislative schedule and program.

Most measures are passed either on the call of the Calendar or by unanimous consent procedure. The more significant and controversial matters are considered, when possible, under unanimous consent agreements limiting debate and controlling time on the measure, amendments thereto, and debatable motions relating to it. This is done because otherwise debate is unlimited. Measures may be brought up on motion by a simple majority vote if they have been on the Calendar one legislative day. Such a motion to proceed is usually made by the Majority Leader or his designee and is usually debatable. The motion to proceed to the consideration of a measure on the Calendar is usually only made if there has been objection to a unanimous consent request to proceed to its consideration.

On highly controversial matters, the Senate frequently has to resort to cloture to work its will. Under Rule XXII, if three-fifths of the Senators duly chosen and sworn (60 if the Senate is at full membership of 100) vote in the affirmative, further debate on the question shall be limited to no more than one hour for each Senator, and the time for consideration of the matter shall be limited to 30 additional hours, unless increased by another three-fifths vote. On a measure or motion to amend the Senate Rules, it takes two-thirds of the Senators present and voting, a quorum being present, to invoke cloture.

Under Rule VIII, which governs the consideration of bills on the call of the Senate Calendar, there is supposed to be a Calendar call each day at the end of the morning business. Under current practice, however, this very rarely occurs; instead, the Calendar is usually called, if at all, pursuant to a unanimous consent order. Rule VII makes a call of the Calendar mandatory on Monday if the Senate had adjourned after its prior sitting. This requirement may only be waived by unanimous consent, and it has become the regular practice of the leadership to request that the requirement be waived.

NOTES AND QUESTIONS

1. Unanimous consent agreements circumvent the Senate's formal rules. They are necessitated by the Senate's tradition of unlimited debate. "In effect, these accords are a voluntary form of cloture." ROGER H. DAVIDSON & WALTER J. OLESZEK, CONGRESS AND ITS MEMBERS 250 (9th ed., 2004).

2. Consider the following example of a unanimous consent agreement:

S. 27

2. *Ordered*, That on either Monday, March 10, 2001, or Monday, March 26, 2001, at a time to be determined by the Majority Leader, after consultation with the Democratic Leader, the Rules and Administration Committee be immediately discharged from consideration of S.27, a bill to amend the Federal Election Campaign Act of 1971 to provide bipartisan campaign reform, as introduced, and that the Senate proceed to its immediate consideration.

Ordered further, That following the reporting of S.27 by the Clerk, the bill become the pending business to the exclusion of all other business, except for a motion to temporarily postpone consideration of the pending legislation made by the Republican Leader, following approval of the Democratic Leader; and that no call for the regular order serve to displace this item, except one made by the Republican Leader, after approval of the Democratic Leader.

Ordered further, That when a first degree amendment is offered, there be up to 3 hours for debate only with the time to be evenly divided in the usual form, after which a motion to table may be made; that if a motion to table fails, the amendment then be fully debatable and amendable; that if a motion to table is not made at the expiration of the 3 hours, a vote occur on the amendment, without any intervening action, motion, or debate, provided that no points of order be considered as having been waived by this agreement.

S.J. RES. 4

3. *Ordered*, That during or immediately following disposition of the McCain-Feingold bill, S. 27, the Senate proceed to the consideration of S.J. Res. 4, proposing an amendment to the Constitution of the United States relating to contributions and expenditures intending to affect elections, that it become the pending business, and that no amendments be in order to S.J. Res. 4.

Ordered further, That there be 5 hours debate thereon, with 2 hours under the control of the Senator from South Carolina (Mr. Hollings); 2 hours under the control of the Senator from Utah (Mr. Hatch), or his designee; and 1 hour, to be equally divided between the Republican and Democratic Leaders or their designees.

Ordered further, That upon the use or yielding back of time, the Senate, without intervening action, motion or debate, proceed to vote on passage of S.J. Res. 4.

U.S. Senate, Calendar of Business, 107th Cong., 1st Sess., March 14, 2001, 4. Are such agreements the functional equivalents of special rules from the House Rules Committee, keeping in mind that they are usually privately negotiated rather than heard in public session as in the House?

3. What is the impact on the legislative process of the fact that 60 votes are necessary to pass controversial legislation in the Senate?

4. Given the fact that the Senate is malapportioned by constitutional design as measured by the equipopulation standard, how democratic is the legislative process in the national legislature as compared with state or local legislative bodies which are subject to the equipopulation standard?

5. If you were an advocate of controversial legislation such as gun control measures, which legislative forum, local, state, or national offers the best prospect of success? Why?

I. FLOOR CONSIDERATION AND DEBATE

1. Introduction

ELIZABETH RYBICKI & STANLEY BACH,
THE LEGISLATIVE PROCESS ON THE HOUSE FLOOR: AN INTRODUCTION
1–8 (October 2, 2003)

A complicated body of rules, precedents, and practices governs the legislative process on the floor of the House of Representatives. The official manual of House rules is more than a thousand pages long and is supplemented by more than 25 volumes of precedents, with more volumes to be published in coming years. Yet there are two reasons why gaining a fundamental understanding of the House's legislative procedures is not as difficult as the sheer number and size of these documents might suggest.

First, the ways in which the House applies its rules are relatively predictable, at least in comparison with the Senate. Some rules certainly are more complex and more difficult to interpret than others, but the House does tend to follow similar procedures under similar circumstances. Even the ways in which the House frequently waives, supplants, or supplements its regular rules with special, temporary procedures generally fall into a relatively limited number of recognizable patterns.

Second, underlying most of the rules that Representatives may invoke and the procedures the House may follow is a fundamentally important premise — that a majority of Members ultimately should be able to work their will on the floor. While House rules generally do recognize the importance of permitting any minority, partisan or bipartisan, to present its views and sometimes to propose its alternatives, the rules do not enable that minority to filibuster or use other devices to prevent the majority from prevailing without undue delay.* This principle provides an underlying coherence to the various specific procedures that are discussed briefly in this report.

The Nature of the Rules

Article I of the Constitution imposes a few restrictions on House (and Senate) procedures — for example, requirements affecting quorums and roll call votes — but otherwise the Constitution authorizes each house of Congress to determine for itself the "Rules of its Proceedings" (Article 1, Section 5).

This grant of authority has several important implications. First, the House can amend its rules unilaterally; it need not consult with either the Senate or the President. Second, the House is free to suspend, waive, or ignore its rules whenever it chooses to do so. By and large, the Speaker or whatever Representative is presiding usually does not enforce the rules at his or her own initiative. Instead, Members must protect their own rights and interests by making points of order whenever they believe that the rules are about to be violated. In addition, House rules include several formal procedures for waiving or suspending certain other rules, and almost any rule can be waived by unanimous consent. Thus, the requirements and restrictions discussed in this report

---

* This premise is not characteristic of Senate rules and procedures, and this difference most clearly distinguishes between the general approaches that the two chambers traditionally have taken to the legislative process.

apply only if the House chooses to enforce them.

The House and the Committee of the Whole

Actually much of the legislative process on the floor occurs not "in the House," but in a committee of the House known as the Committee of the Whole (formally, the Committee of the Whole House on the State of the Union). Every Representative is a member of the Committee of the Whole, and it is in this Committee, meeting in the House chamber, that major bills usually are debated and amended before being passed or defeated by the House itself. Most bills first are referred to, considered in, and reported by a standing committee of the House before coming to the floor. In much the same way, once bills do reach the floor, many of them then are referred to a second committee, the Committee of the Whole, for further debate and for the consideration of amendments.

The Speaker presides over meetings of the House but not over meetings of the Committee of the Whole. Instead, he appoints another member of the majority party to serve as the chair of the Committee of the Whole during the time the Committee is considering a particular bill or resolution. In addition, the rules that apply in Committee of the Whole are somewhat different from those that govern meetings of the House itself. The major differences are discussed in the following sections of this report. In general, the combined effect of these differences is to make the procedures in Committee of the Whole — especially the procedures for offering and debating amendments — considerably more flexible than those of the House.

Limitations on Debate

If for no other reason than the size of its membership, the House has found it necessary to limit the opportunities for each Representative to participate in floor deliberations. Whenever a Member is recognized to speak on the floor, there always is a time limit on his or her right to debate. The rules of the House never permit a Representative to hold the floor for more than one hour. Under some parliamentary circumstances, there are more stringent limits, with Members being allowed to speak for no more than 5, 20, or 30 minutes.

Furthermore, House rules sometimes impose a limit on how long the entire membership of the House may debate a motion or measure. Many bills and resolutions, for instance, are considered under a package of procedures called "suspension of the rules" (discussed later in this report), that limits all debate on a measure to a total of 40 minutes. Under other conditions, when there is no such time limit imposed by the rules, the House (and to some extent, the Committee of the Whole as well) can impose one by simple majority vote. These debate limitations and debate-limiting devices generally prevent a minority of the House from using opportunities for delay to thwart the will of the majority.

House rules also limit debate in other important respects. First, all debate on the floor must be germane to whatever legislative business the House is conducting. Representatives may speak on other subjects only in "one-minute" speeches made at the beginning of each day's session, "special order" speeches occurring after the House has completed its legislative business for the day, and during "morning hour" debates that are scheduled on certain days. Second, all debate on the floor must be consistent with certain rules of courtesy and decorum. For example, a Member should not question or criticize the motives of a colleague or offer assessments of actions by or in the Senate.

Five Modes of Consideration

There is no one single set of procedures that the House always follows when it considers a public bill or resolution on the floor. Instead, there are five different modes of consideration, or different packages of procedural rules, that the House uses. In some cases, House rules require that certain kinds of bills be considered in certain ways. By various means, however, the House chooses to use whichever mode of consideration is most appropriate for a given bill. Which of these modes the House uses depends on such factors as the importance and potential cost of the bill and the amount of controversy over its provisions and merits. The differences among these packages of procedures rest largely on the balance that each strikes between the opportunities for Members to debate and propose amendments, on the one hand, and the ability of the House to act promptly, on the other.

Under Suspension of the Rules

The House frequently resorts to a package of procedures that enables it to act quickly on bills that enjoy overwhelming but not unanimous support. Although this package is called "suspension of the rules," clause 1 of Rule XV provides for these procedures as an alternative to the other modes of consideration. The essential components of suspension of the rules are (1) a 40-minute limit on debate, (2) a prohibition against floor amendments, and (3) a two-thirds vote for passage.

On every Monday and Tuesday, and often during the closing days of a session, the Speaker may, if he chooses, recognize Members to move to suspend the rules and pass a particular bill (or take some other action, such as agreeing to the Senate's amendments to a House bill). In the 108th Congress, these motions may be entertained on Wednesdays as well. Once such a motion is made, the motion and the bill itself together are debatable for a total of only 40 minutes. Half of the time is controlled by the Representative making the motion, often the chair of the committee with jurisdiction over the bill; the other half usually is controlled by the ranking minority member of the committee (or sometimes the subcommittee) of jurisdiction, especially when he or she opposes the motion. The motion may propose to pass the bill with certain amendments, but no Member may propose an amendment from the floor.

During the debate, the two Members who control the time yield parts of it to other Members who wish to speak. At the end of the 40 minutes, a single vote occurs on suspending the rules and simultaneously passing the bill. If two-thirds of the Members present vote "Aye" the motion is agreed to and the bill is passed. If the motion fails, the House may debate the bill again at another time, perhaps under another mode of consideration that permits floor amendments and more debate and that requires only a simple majority vote for passage.

The House frequently considers several suspension motions on the same day, which could result in a series of electronically recorded votes taking place at 40-minutes intervals. For the convenience of the House, therefore, clause 8 of Rule XX permits the Speaker to postpone electronic votes that Members have demanded on motions to suspend the rules until a later time on the same day or the following day. When the votes do take place, they are "clustered," occurring one after the other without intervening debate.

To avoid having these procedures used to consider bills that merit a more elaborate process of debate and amendment, Rule 28 of the House Republican Conference directs the Speaker not to recognize a Member to move to suspend the rules and pass a bill if that bill would make or authorize appropriations, or provide direct or indirect loan commitments or guarantees, of more than $100 million for any fiscal year, unless a majority of the elected Republican leadership authorizes him to do so. Although this is not a rule of the House, it still can be effective because the Speaker, who is selected by and accountable to the majority party conference or caucus, has the discretion to decide whether he will recognize a Member to make a suspension motion. In effect, the Conference rule is a constraint on how the Speaker exercises his discretionary authority.

In the House under the Hour Rule

One of the ironies of the legislative process on the House floor is that the House does relatively little business under the basic rules of the House. Instead, most of the debate and votes on amendments to major bills occur in Committee of the Whole. This is largely because of the rule that generally governs debate in the House itself.

The rule controlling debate during meetings of the House (as opposed to meetings of the Committee of the Whole) is clause 2 of Rule XVII, which states in part that "[a] Member, Delegate, or Resident Commissioner may not occupy more than one hour in debate on a question in the House . . . ." In theory, this rule permits each Representative to speak for as much as an hour on each bill, on each amendment to each bill, and on each of the many debatable motions that Members could offer. Thus, there could be more than four hundred hours of debate on each such question, a situation that would make it virtually impossible for the House to function effectively.

In practice, however, this "hour rule" usually means that each measure considered "in the House" is debated by all Members for no more than a total of only one hour before the House votes on passing it. The reason for this dramatic difference between the rule in theory and the effect of the rule in practice lies in the consequences of a motion to order what is called "the previous question."

When a bill or resolution is called up for consideration in the House — and, therefore, under the hour rule — the Speaker recognizes the majority floor manager to control the first hour of debate. The majority floor manager usually is the chair of the committee or subcommittee with jurisdiction over the measure, and most often supports its passage without amendment. This Member will yield part of his or her time to other Members, and may allocate control of half of the hour to the minority floor manager (usually the ranking minority member of the committee or subcommittee). However, the majority floor manager almost always yields to other Representatives "for purposes of debate only." Thus, no other Member may propose an amendment or make any motion during that hour.

During the first hour of debate, or at its conclusion, the majority floor manager invariably moves the previous question. This motion, which is not debatable, asks the House if it is ready to vote on passing the bill. If a majority votes for the motion, no more debate on the bill is in order, nor can any amendments to it be offered; usually the House votes immediately on whether to pass the bill. Only if the House votes not to order the previous question can debate on the bill continue into a second hour, during which the bill may be amended. Thus, Members who want to amend the measure first must convince the House to vote against ordering the previous question. If they are successful, then the Member controlling the second hour of debate may propose an amendment. However, it is very unusual for the House not to vote for the previous question; so the House disposes of most measures considered in the House, under the hour rule, after no more than one hour of debate, and with no opportunity for amendment from the floor.

These are not very flexible and accommodating procedural ground rules for the House to follow in considering most legislation. Debate on a bill usually is limited to one hour, and only one or two Members control this time. Before an amendment to the bill can even be considered, the House first must vote against a motion to order the previous question. For these reasons, most major bills are not considered in the House under the hour rule. Instead, they are considered under a third and more complicated mode of consideration, a package of procedures involving the Committee of the Whole.

In Committee of the Whole and the House

Clause 3 of Rule XVIII requires that most bills affecting Federal taxes and spending be considered in Committee of the Whole before the House votes on passing them. Most other major bills also are considered in this way. Most commonly, the House adopts a resolution, reported by the Rules Committee, that authorizes the Speaker to declare the House resolved into Committee of the Whole to consider a particular bill. In the case of general appropriations bills, however, the Chair of the Appropriations Committee can move that the House resolve into Committee of the Whole to consider such a bill.

General Debate. There are two distinct stages to consideration in Committee of the Whole. First, there is a period for general debate, which most often is limited to an hour.* Each of the floor managers usually controls half the time, yielding parts to other Members who want to participate in the debate. During general debate, the two floor managers and other Members discuss the bill, the conditions prompting the committee to recommend it, and the merits of its provisions. Members may describe and explain the reasons for the amendments that they intend to offer, but no amendments can actually be proposed at this time. During or after general debate, the majority floor manager may move that the Committee rise — in other words, that the Committee transform itself back into the House. When the House agrees to this motion, it may resolve into Committee of the Whole again at another time to resume consideration of the bill. Alternatively, the Committee of the Whole may proceed immediately from general debate to the next stage of consideration, the amending process.

Amending Process. The Committee of the Whole usually considers a bill for amendment section by section or title by title. Amendments to each section or title of the bill are in order after the part they would amend has been read or designated, and before the next section or title is read or designated. Alternatively, the bill may be open to amendment at any point, usually by unanimous consent. The first amendments considered to each part of the bill are those (if any) recommended by the committee that reported it. Thereafter, members of the committee usually are recognized before other Representatives to offer their own amendments. All amendments must be germane to the text they would amend. Germaneness is a subject matter standard more stringent than one of relevancy and reflects a complex set of criteria that have developed by precedent over the years.

The Committee of the Whole only votes on amendments; it does not vote directly on the bill as a whole. And like the standing committees of the House, the Committee of the Whole does not actually amend the bill: it only decides on the amendments that it will propose to the House. The motion to order the previous question may not be made in Committee of the Whole, so Members usually may offer whatever germane amendments they wish, unless prevented from doing so by the terms of a special rule. After voting on the last amendment to the last portion of the bill, the Committee rises and reports the bill back to the House with whatever amendments it has agreed to.

An amendment to a bill is a first-degree amendment. After such an amendment is offered, but before the Committee votes on it, another Member usually may offer a perfecting amendment to make some change in the first degree amendment. A perfecting amendment to a first-degree amendment is a second-degree amendment. After debate, the Committee first votes on the second-degree perfecting amendment and then on the first-degree amendment as it may have been amended. Clause 6 of Rule XVI also provides that a Member may offer a substitute for the first-degree amendment, before or after a perfecting amendment is offered, and this substitute may be amended. Although a full discussion of these possibilities is beyond the scope of this report, it is important to note that the amending process can become complicated, with Members proposing several choices before the Committee votes on any of them.

Debate on amendments in Committee of the Whole is governed by the five-minute rule, not the hour rule that governs debate in the House. The Member offering each

---

* The length of general debate on a bill is determined either by unanimous consent or by adoption of a resolution, reported by the Committee on Rules, that typically affects various aspects of the procedures for considering that bill . . . .

amendment (or the majority floor manager, in the case of a committee amendment) first is recognized to speak for five minutes. Then a Member opposed to the amendment may claim five minutes for debate. Other Members also may speak for five minutes each by offering a motion "to strike the last word." Technically, this motion is an amendment that proposes to strike out the last word of the amendment being debated. But it is a "pro forma amendment" that is offered merely to secure time for debate, and so is not voted on when the five minutes expire. In this way, each Representative may speak for five minutes on each amendment. However, a majority of the Members can vote (or agree by unanimous consent) to end the debate on an amendment immediately or at some specified time.

Final Passage. When the Committee finally rises and reports the bill back to the House, the House proceeds to vote on the amendments the Committee has adopted. It usually approves all these amendments by one vote, though Members can demand separate votes on any or all of them. After a formal and routine stage called third reading and engrossment (when only the title of the bill is read), there is then an opportunity for a Member, usually of the minority party, to offer a motion to recommit the bill to committee. If the House agrees to a simple motion to recommit, which only proposes to return the bill to committee, the bill is normally effectively killed. Instead, motions to recommit frequently include instructions that the committee report the bill back to the House immediately with an amendment that is stated in the motion. If the House agrees to the motion, it then votes on the amendment itself, so a motion to recommit with instructions is really a final opportunity to amend the bill before the House votes on whether to pass it.

Thus, this complicated mode of consideration, which the House uses to consider most major bills, begins in the House with a decision to resolve into Committee of the Whole to consider a particular bill. General debate and the amending process take place in Committee of the Whole, but ultimately it is the House that formally amends and then passes or rejects the bill.

In the House as in Committee of the Whole

A fourth mode of consideration, which the House does not use very often, is a hybrid form that combines features of the procedures that apply in the House under the hour rule and those that apply in Committee of the Whole. This package of procedures, known as the House meeting "as in Committee of the Whole," has evolved by precedent, and none of the House rules explicitly defines its elements. It may be used to consider private bills, and it was used routinely, although only by unanimous consent, to consider bills reported by the Committee on the District of Columbia before the House abolished that committee in 1995.

A measure considered in this way is debated under the five-minute rule; the hour rule does not apply, nor is there a period for general debate. The majority floor manager secures time to make his opening statement on the bill by moving to strike the last word, that is, the last word of the bill. All other Members who want their own time to speak use the same device. The bill is open to amendment at any point; it is not read for amendment, as are bills being amended under the five-minute rule in Committee of the Whole. But like procedures in the House under the hour rule, the majority floor manager may move the previous question on an individual amendment or on the bill and all amendments to it. Votes on amendments are final because they occur in the House itself. After acting on the last amendment and ordering the bill engrossed and read the third time (by title only), the House votes on final passage.

By Call of the Corrections Calendar

Finally, in 1995, the House created a new set of procedures in clause 6 of Rule XV for considering bills that have been reported from committees and that the Speaker decides to place on the Corrections Calendar. This special calendar was instituted to give the House a convenient and efficient way to pass legislation to correct misapplications and misinterpretations of existing law. However, at the initiative of the Speaker, any bill that been reported favorably from committee may be considered under these procedures.

On the second and fourth Tuesdays of each month, the Speaker may direct the Clerk to call up a bill on the Corrections Calendar. The membership then considers it in the House, under the hour rule. The previous question is ordered automatically after the first hour of debate; no floor amendments can be offered except committee amendments or amendments proposed by the majority floor manager. A three-fifths vote is required to pass the bill. If a bill fails to receive that majority, however, it remains on the House or Union Calendar and may be brought up again under one of the House's other procedures that only requires a simple majority vote for passage.

NOTES AND QUESTIONS

1. Given the time constraints under which the House operates, should debate in the Committee of the Whole be afforded great probative force as legislative history? Does that depend on whether the remarks are made by the floor manager for the winning coalition? By the proponent of a successful floor amendment? How about debate on a measure passed under suspension of the rules? A measure passed under the one-hour rule?

2. What inference can be taken from the fact that a measure was passed by call of the Corrections Calendar?

3. Suppose that a section of the bill affecting your client is never mentioned in floor debate. Does that strengthen the probative force of the explanation of that section in the Committee Report?

What if there is a substantial disparity, adverse to your client's interests, between the Committee report explanation and the remarks of the floor manager?

4. What probative force should be given to floor debate by the opponents of the bill? Should that depend on whether the remarks concern the general policies projected by the bill or focus on the wording of a particular section of the measure?

5. If a bill is recommitted with instructions and the bill is later passed in the same session, is the floor debate before recommittal still of probative force?

6. If a bill passed in the 108th Congress does not become law in that session, does the floor debate still have probative force if the identical measure becomes law in the 110th Congress?

JUDY SCHNEIDER,
AMENDMENTS ON THE HOUSE FLOOR:
SUMMARY OF MAJOR RESTRICTIONS
(August 22, 2003)

The opportunities for Representatives to offer floor amendments to a bill or resolution depends on the procedures by which the House considers the measure. In summary:

- After general debate on a bill in *Committee of the Whole*, Members may offer whatever amendments they choose if (1) those amendments comply with applicable House rules and precedents, some of which are identified below, (2) Members offer their amendments at the appropriate times, and (3) the House has not adopted a special rule that prohibits consideration of some or all amendments to the bill. An amendment also can be proposed in a recommittal motion that is offered in the House after the Committee of the Whole completes action on the bill and reports it back to the House.

- *In the House, under the one-hour rule,* an amendment can be offered only by the Member who controls the floor or if that Member yields to a colleague for the purpose of offering an amendment. If the House votes to order the previous question on a bill after no more than one hour of debate, as it usually does, the effect of that vote is to prevent any floor amendments, except for an amendment that may be incorporated into a motion to recommit the bill to committee.

- Under *suspension of the rules*, no floor amendments are in order. However, the Member offering the suspension motion may include amendments in the motion. If so, that Member moves to suspend the rules and pass the bill as amended. The House cannot vote separately on any such amendments.

- When a bill is considered from *the Corrections Calendar*, no amendments to it are in order except amendments recommended by the committee of jurisdiction and amendments offered by that committee's chair or a designee.

General Restrictions on Amendments

The House's rules and precedents impose certain restrictions that apply generally to House floor amendments, regardless of the procedure under which they are offered.

In general, for example, an amendment is not in order (1) if the amendment is not in writing at the time it is offered; (2) if the amendment is in the third degree — i.e., it is an amendment to an amendment to an amendment; (3) if the House already has acted on an identical amendment; (4) if the amendment only proposes to re-amend a portion of the bill that already has been amended; (5) if the amendment affects different parts of the bill and actually constitutes two or more amendments that can be offered *en bloc* only by unanimous consent; or (6) if the amendment is not offered at the time the Committee of the Whole is considering amendments only to the section or title of the bill that the amendment would affect. This list is not exhaustive, and there are exceptions to some of these general restrictions. For instance, an amendment to a substitute for an amendment is not considered to be a third degree amendment. Also, an amendment may re-amend something that already has been amended if it does so in the process of amending a larger part of the text in question.

The Germaneness Requirement

In addition to such general restrictions, clause 7 of House Rule XVI also requires that each amendment must be germane to the text it would amend. This principle can be difficult to apply in practice.

Volumes 10 and 11 of *Deschler-Brown Precedents of the House of Representatives* devote almost 2,000 pages to the germaneness rule and its application. To be germane, it is not sufficient that the amendment be relevant to the bill the House is considering or even to the section or title of the bill that the amendment would change. It is possible for an amendment to be relevant without satisfying the technical standards of germaneness.

In the commentary that follows the text of the germaneness rule in the *House Rules and Manual*, the House parliamentarian identifies three tests of germaneness: *subject matter, fundamental purpose,* and *committee jurisdiction.* To be germane: (1) "[a]n amendment must relate to the subject matter under consideration;" (2) "[t]he fundamental purpose of an amendment must be germane to the fundamental purpose of the bill;" and (3) "[a]n amendment when considered as a whole should be within the jurisdiction of the committee reporting the bill."

None of these tests is always conclusive, nor is one of them necessarily more controlling than the others. Furthermore, an amendment may satisfy all three of these tests and still not be germane. To help explain this possibility, the parliamentarian also elaborates several principles of germaneness, including the following: (1) "[o]ne individual proposition may not be amended by another individual proposition even though the two belong to the same class;" and (2) "[a] specific subject may not be amended by a provision general in nature, even when of the class of the specific subject"; but (3) "[a] general subject may be amended by specific propositions of the same class."

JAMES V. SATURNO, AMENDMENTS IN THE HOUSE: TYPES AND FORMS
(November 18, 2004)

Distinctions Among Amendments

The amending process is central to the consideration of legislation by the House of Representatives, and the rules, practices, and precedents that underlie this process frequently depend on distinguishing among amendments based on their type and form. Simply put, not all amendments are equal in a procedural sense, and the form or type of amendment frequently determines what further amendments may be offered, and therefore what alternatives the House may choose among. For more information on legislative process, see [www.crs.gov/products/guides/guidehome.shtml].

Degrees of Amendments

A fundamental aspect of the amending process in the House is that it is limited to two degrees. Amendments may be offered to the measure under consideration (first-degree), and to amendments to the measure (second-degree). A second-degree amendment may only be offered while the first-degree amendment to which it is offered is pending, and the House must vote on any second-degree amendments before it votes on a pending first-degree amendment, as it may have been amended. That is, any second-degree amendment that is agreed to is incorporated into a first-degree amendment before that first-degree amendment is voted on.

House Rule XVI, clause 6 provides that "it also shall be in order to offer a further amendment by way of substitute." Such a substitute is treated as a first-degree amendment, presumably because it is offered in the form of an alternative to the original first-degree amendment rather than an amendment to it. Like the original first-degree amendment, this one also is subject to second-degree amendments. Rule XVI also provides that second-degree amendments to the original first-degree amendment must be voted on before pending second-degree amendments to the first-degree substitute. A first-degree substitute, as it may have been amended, must be voted on prior to a vote on the original first-degree amendment, as it may have been amended.

Only one second-degree amendment may be pending at a time to any first-degree amendment. Additional second-degree amendments, however, may be offered subsequently if other conditions permit.

The degree of an amendment will have an impact on the application of the germaneness requirement imposed by Rule XVI, clause 7. Since the definition of germaneness is dependent on the specific propositions involved, first-degree amendments must be germane to the measure, while second-degree amendments must be germane to the first-degree amendment to which they are offered.

Forms of Amendments

Amendments may also be distinguished by whether they are posed in the form of (1) a motion to strike out some existing text from a measure (or from a first-degree amendment); (2) a motion solely to insert some new text into a measure (or into a first-degree amendment); or (3) a motion both to strike out some existing text and insert something new (in either a measure or a first-degree amendment).

Scope of Amendments

A third way to distinguish among amendments is by their scope. The procedural scope of an amendment is defined in relation to the text the amendment would effect, and not indicative of any substantive policy changes that would result from the proposed amendment. An amendment is a substitute if it would replace all of a pending text. Generally, a perfecting amendment is one that inserts text or replaces less than a complete text.

Although they are rarely referred to as such, first-degree amendments that are drafted to amend some portion of a measure (but less than the entire measure) are perfecting amendments. Likewise, second-degree amendments that are drafted to amend some portion of a first-degree amendment are perfecting amendments.

As provided by Rule XVI, clause 6, a substitute for a first-degree amendment is in order and will likewise be treated as a first-degree amendment. The substitute, as it may have been amended, will be voted on prior to a vote on the original first-degree amendment, as it may have been amended.

A special case arises when a substitute is offered in the form of a motion to strike out everything in a measure after the enacting clause (or the resolving clause, in the case of a resolution) and insert a different text. This is known as an amendment in the nature of a substitute, and is rarely offered without protection under a special rule reported by the Rules Committee. Because committees frequently report their recommendations to the House in this form, Members typically focus their consideration on the substitute and special rules typically provide that the substitute be treated as "an original bill for the purpose of amendment." This language means that the amendment in the nature of a substitute will not be treated as a first-degree amendment; instead two degrees of amendment will be allowed as though the amendment in the nature of a substitute were the text of the measure.

NOTES AND QUESTIONS

1. Floor amendments do not normally carry with them the paper trail of legislative history that accompanies the text of the bill reported by the committee. *See Fullilove v. Klutznick*, 448 U.S. 448 (1980) (discussing a floor amendment creating minority business enterprise set-asides in federally funded public contracts). Accordingly, the scope of source material for legislative history may be limited to the truncated debate permissible under the five-minute rule. This is particularly true when the House approves an amendment in the nature of a substitute which jettisons the entire text reported by the committee.

2. Successful motions to strike or to insert language in the bill should be particularly salient even for interpreters who question the probative force of legislative history.

The "germaneness" requirement imposed by the House on its work product marks an important difference with the Senate's practices as the following excerpt indicates.

CHARLES W. JOHNSON,
HOW OUR LAWS ARE MADE
39–42 (2003)

The rules of procedure in the Senate differ to a large extent from those in the House. The Senate relies heavily on the practice of obtaining unanimous consent for actions to be taken. For example, at the time that a bill is reported, the Majority Leader may ask unanimous consent for the immediate consideration of the bill. If the bill is of a noncontroversial nature and there is no objection, the Senate may pass the bill with little or no debate and with only a brief explanation of its purpose and effect. Even in this instance, the bill is subject to amendment by any Senator. A simple majority vote is necessary to carry an amendment as well as to pass the bill. If there is any objection, the report must lie over one legislative day and the bill is placed on the calendar.

Measures reported by standing committees of the Senate may not be considered unless the report of that committee has been available to Senate Members for at least two days (excluding Sundays and legal holidays) prior to consideration of the measure in the Senate. This requirement, however, may be waived by agreement of the Majority and Minority leaders and does not apply in certain emergency situations.

In the Senate, measures are brought up for consideration by a simple unanimous consent request, by a complex unanimous consent agreement, or by a motion to proceed to the consideration of a measure on the calendar. A unanimous consent agreement, sometimes referred to as a "time agreement", makes the consideration of a measure in order and often limits the amount of debate that will take place on the measure and lists the amendments that will be considered. The offering of a unanimous consent request to consider a measure or the offering of a motion to proceed to the consideration of a measure is reserved, by tradition, to the Majority Leader.

Usually a motion to consider a measure on the calendar is made only when unanimous consent to consider the measure cannot be obtained. There are two calendars in the Senate, the Calendar of Business and the Executive Calendar. All legislation is placed on the Calendar of Business and treaties and nominations are placed on the Executive Calendar. Unlike the House, there is no differentiation on the Calendar of Business between the treatment of: (1) bills raising revenue, general appropriation bills, and bills of a public character appropriating money or property; and (2) other bills of a public character not appropriating money or property.

The rules of the Senate provide that at the conclusion of the morning business for each "legislative day" the Senate proceeds to the consideration of the calendar. In the Senate, the term "legislative day" means the period of time from when the Senate adjourns until the next time the Senate adjourns. Because the Senate often "recesses" rather than "adjourns" at the end of a daily session, the legislative day usually does not correspond to the 24-hour period comprising a calendar day. Thus, a legislative day may cover a long period of time — from days to weeks, or even months. Because of this and the modern practice of waiving the call of the calendar by unanimous consent at the start of a new legislative day, it is rare to have a call of the calendar. When the calendar is called, bills that are not objected to are taken up in their order, and each Senator is entitled to speak once and for five minutes only on any question. Objection may be interposed at any stage of the proceedings, but on motion the Senate may continue consideration afer the call of the calendar is completed, and the limitations on debate then do not apply.

On any day (other than a Monday that begins a new legislative day), following the announcement of the close of morning business, any Senator, usually the Majority Leader, obtaining recognition may move to take up any bill out of its regular order on the calendar. The five-minute limitation on debate does not apply to the consideration of a bill taken up in this manner, and debate may continue until the hour when the Presiding Officer of the Senate "lays down" the unfinished business of the day. At that point consideration of the bill is discontinued and the measure reverts back to the Calendar of Business and may again be called up at another time under the same conditions.

When a bill has been objected to and passed over on the call of the calendar it is not necessarily lost. The Majority Leader, after consulting the Minority Leader, determines the time at which the bill will be considered. At that time, a motion is made to consider the bill. The motion is debatable if made after the morning hour.

Once a Senator is recognized by the Presiding Officer, the Senator may speak for as long as the Senator wishes and loses the floor only when the Senator yields it or takes certain parliamentary actions that forfeit the Senator's right to the floor. However, a Senator may not speak more than twice on any one question in debate on the same legislative day without leave of the Senate. Debate ends when a Senator yields the floor and no other Senator seeks recognition, or when a unanimous consent agreement limiting the time of debate is operating.

On occasion, Senators opposed to a measure may extend debate by making lengthy speeches or a number of speeches at various stages of consideration intended to prevent or defeat action on the measure. This is the tactic known as "filibustering". Debate, however, may be closed if 16 Senators sign a motion to that effect and the motion is carried by three-fifths of the Senators duly chosen and sworn. Such a motion is voted on one hour after the Senate convenes, following a quorum call on the next day after a day of session has intervened. This procedure is called "invoking cloture". In 1986, the Senate amended its rules to limit "post-cloture" consideration to 30 hours. A Senator may speak for not more than one hour and may yield all or a part of that time to the majority or minority floor managers of the bill under consideration or to the Majority or Minority leader. The Senate may increase the time for "post-cloture" debate by a vote of three-fifths of the Senators duly chosen and sworn. After the time for debate has expired, the Senate may consider only amendments actually pending before voting on the bill.

While a measure is being considered it is subject to amendment and each amendment, including those proposed by the committee that reported the bill, is considered separately. Generally, there is no requirement that proposed amendments be germane to the subject matter of the bill except in the case of general appropriation bills or where "cloture" has been invoked. Under the rules, a "rider", an amendment proposing substantive legislation to an appropriation bill, is prohibited. However, this prohibition may be suspended by two-thirds vote on a motion to permit consideration of such an amendment on one day's notice in writing. Debate must be germane during the first three hours after business is laid down unless determined to the contrary by unanimous consent or on motion without debate. After final action on the amendments the bill is ready for engrossment and the third reading, which is by title only. The Presiding Officer then puts the question on the passage and a voice vote is usually taken although a yea-and-nay vote is in order if demanded by one-fifth of the Senators present. A simple majority is necessary for passage. Before an amended measure is cleared for its return to the House of Representatives, or a unamended measure is cleared for enrollment, a Senator who vote with the prevailing side, or who abstained from voting, may make a motion within the next two days to reconsider the action. If the measure was passed without a recorded vote, any Senator may make the motion to reconsider. That motion is usually tabled and its tabling constitutes a final determination. If, however, the motion is granted, the Senate, by majority vote, may either affirm its action, which then becomes final, or reverse it.

The original engrossed House bill, together with the engrossed Senate amendments, if any, or the original engrossed Senate bill, as the case may be, is then returned to the House with a message stating the action taken by the Senate. Where the Senate has adopted amendments, the message requests that the House concur in them.

NOTES AND QUESTIONS

1. Floor debate on a bill in the Senate may not be temporally compressed and focused as it is in the House. And so, matter relevant to a bill's legislative history may appear in the Congressional Record, which is published on a calendar day basis, over a period of weeks or months. That is because the term "day" in Senate Rules VII and VIII means "legislative day," not calendar day. Indeed, in 1980, the Senate convened on January 3, recessed from day to day and did not adjourn until June 12. "For that 162-day period, the Senate remained on the same legislative day of January 3, 1980." CHARLES TIEFER, CONGRESSIONAL PRACTICE AND PROCEDURE 550 (1989).

2. Does the sometimes sporadic and disjointed nature of the process of floor debate in the Senate reduce its probative force as legislative history?

3. What strategic possibilities are open to a legislative advocate by virtue of the general rule that amendments in the Senate need not be germane to the bill? *See* TIEFER, *supra* Note 1 at 584–93.

4. Suppose that a Senator successfully attaches a nongermane amendment consisting of a bill already passed by the House to a Senate bill. Would the Committee Report on the measure passed by the House have probative force as legislative history?

J. CONFERENCE COMMITTEES: THE "THIRD HOUSE"

When the House and the Senate pass similar bills with conflicting texts, these legislative differences are resolvable only by further legislative action. The following report, prepared by the Congressional Research Service, discusses the ways of achieving final action on amended bills. Almost every piece of major legislation travels the paths indicated in the report. Particular attention should be paid to the discussion of Conference Committees. The work product of Conference Committees is so significant that they are often referred to as the "Third House" of the legislative branch. *See generally* DAVID J. VOGLER, THE THIRD HOUSE: CONFERENCE COMMITTEES IN THE U.S. CONGRESS (1971).

**ELIZABETH RYBICKI & STANLEY BACH,
RESOLVING LEGISLATIVE DIFFERENCES IN CONGRESS: CONFERENCE
COMMITTEES AND AMENDMENTS BETWEEN THE HOUSES**
1–28, 33, 37–38 (CRS Report 98-686, updated April 4, 2007)

INTRODUCTION

The process of resolving the legislative differences that arise between the House of Representatives and the Senate is one of the most critical stages of the legislative process. It is also potentially one of the most complicated. Each chamber continues to be governed by its own rules, precedents, and practices; but at this stage, each house also must take into account the preferences and, to some extent, the procedures of the other . . . .

THE NEED FOR RESOLUTION

Before Congress can submit a bill or joint resolution to the President for his approval or disapproval, the Senate and the House of Representatives must agree on each and every provision of that measure.[2]

It is not enough for both houses to pass versions of the same measure that are comparable in purpose but that differ in certain technical or even minor details; the House and Senate must agree on identical legislative language. Nor is it enough for the two chambers to approve separate bills with exactly the same text; the House and Senate both must pass the same bill. In sum, both chambers of Congress must pass precisely the same measure in precisely the same form before it can become law.[3]

Each of these requirements — agreement on the identity of the measure (e.g., HR. 1 or S. 1), and agreement on the text of that measure — is considered in turn in the following sections of this report.

---

[2] Each house may interpret the same legislative language differently; these differences sometimes emerge from a comparison of House and Senate committee reports and floor debates. Deliberate ambiguity in the language of legislation can be used to promote agreement between the two chambers.

[3] This requirement also applies to joint resolutions proposing constitutional amendments and to concurrent resolutions, even though neither are sent to the White House for the President's signature or veto. House and Senate resolutions, on the other hand, do not require action by "the other body." Throughout this report, the terms "bill" and "measure" are used interchangeably to refer to all bills and resolutions on which House and Senate differences are to be resolved.

Selection of the Measure

Because both chambers must pass the same measure before it can become law, at some point during the legislative process the House must act on a Senate bill or the Senate must act on a House bill. Congress usually meets this requirement without difficulty or controversy. In some cases, however, selecting the measure may require some parliamentary ingenuity and can have policy and political consequences.

After either house debates and passes a measure, it sends (or "messages") that bill to the other chamber. If the second house passes the first house's bill without any amendments, the legislative process is completed: both houses have passed the same measure in the same form.[4] If the second house passes the bill with one or more amendments, both chambers have acted on the same measure; now they must resolve the differences between their respective versions of the text if the measure is to become law.

In most cases, either the House or the Senate can be the first chamber to act. However, the Constitution requires that all revenue measures originate in the House, and the House traditionally has insisted that this prerogative extends to appropriations as well as tax measures.[5] Thus, the House normally acts first on such a measure, and consequently, it is a House-numbered bill or joint resolution that Congress ultimately presents to the President for enacting appropriations or tax laws.

In some cases, the proponents of a measure may decide that one house or the other should act first. For example, a bill's supporters may first press for floor action in the chamber where they think the measure enjoys greater support. They may hope that success in one house may generate political momentum that will help the measure overcome the greater opposition they expect in the second chamber. Alternatively, one house may defer floor action on a bill unless and until it is passed by the other, where the measure is expected to encounter stiff opposition. The House leadership, for example, may decide that it is pointless for the House to invest considerable time, and for Representatives to cast possibly unnecessary and politically difficult votes, on a controversial bill until after an expected Senate filibuster on a comparable Senate bill has been avoided or overcome.

As these considerations imply, major legislative proposals frequently are introduced in both houses — either identical companion bills or bills that address the same subject in rather different ways. If so, the appropriate subcommittees and committees of the House and Senate may consider and report their own measures on the same subject at roughly the same time. Thus, when one house passes and sends a bill to the other, the second chamber may have its own bill on the same subject that has been (or is soon to be) reported from committee and available for floor consideration. In such cases, the second chamber often acts initially on its own bill, rather than the bill received from the other house.[6]

This is particularly likely to happen when the committee of the second house reports a bill that differs significantly in approach from the measure passed by the first

---

[4] In this report, terms such as "first chamber" and "second house" are used to refer only to the order in which the House and Senate complete initial floor action on a measure.

[5] From time to time, Senate committees and even the Senate as a whole may take some action on a Senate appropriations or tax measure. However, on the infrequent occasions when the Senate has passed such a bill and sent it to the House, the House often has returned it to the Senate on the ground that the bill infringed on the House's constitutional prerogatives, as interpreted by the House. The resolutions that the House has adopted for this purpose often are called "blue slip" resolutions.

[6] This may occur for strategic or institutional as well as procedural reasons, as when the House refuses to consider a Senate bill that the House finds to be in violation of its constitutional prerogative to originate revenue measures. Also, the two houses may prefer to retain the House or Senate bill number if one is more familiar than the other to the bills' supporters outside of Congress.

chamber. The text selected for floor consideration generally sets the frame of reference within which debate occurs and amendments are proposed. In most cases, the House or Senate modifies, but does not wholly replace, the legislative approach embodied in the bill it considers. It is usually advantageous, therefore, for a committee to press for floor consideration of its approach, rather than the approach proposed by the other house.

In large part for this reason, the House (or the Senate) often acts on its own bill even though it has already received the other chamber's bill on the same subject. Under these circumstances, however, it would not be constructive for the House to pass its bill and then send it to the Senate. If the House were to do so, then each chamber would have in its possession a bill passed by the other, but both chambers would not have acted on the same measure. To avoid this potential problem, the second house often acts initially on its own bill, and then it also acts on the other chamber's bill on the same subject. The usual practices of the House and Senate for doing so differ slightly.

The House customarily debates, amends, and passes the House bill and, immediately thereafter, takes up the counterpart Senate bill. The floor manager then moves to "strike out all after the enacting clause" of the Senate bill (the opening lines of every bill — "Be it enacted by the Senate and House of Representatives of the United States of America in Congress assembled") and replace the stricken text with the full text of the House bill as just passed. The House often agrees by unanimous consent to consider the Senate bill and approves the House substitute routinely. The Senate bill, as amended, then is passed by voice vote or without objection, and the House lays its own bill on the table (which disposes of it adversely).

In some cases, the special rule under which a house bill is considered also includes provisions for such action on the Senate bill. For instance, a special rule may state:

> After the passage of H.R. 1, it shall be in order to take from the Speaker's table the bill S. 1 and to move to strike out all after the enacting clause of the said Senate bill and insert in lieu thereof the provisions contained in H.R. 1 as passed by the House.

In this way, the House actually passes two bills on the same subject and with identical provisions, but it is the Senate bill (which both chambers now have passed) that is the subject of further action.

The Senate acts in a comparable fashion, although it usually does not pass its own bill. Instead, the Senate debates and amends its bill, and agrees to third reading and engrossment of the bill, as amended.[7] The Senate then takes up the House bill by unanimous consent, strikes out all after the enacting clause, inserts the amended text of the Senate bill, and passes the House bill, as it has been amended by the Senate's amendment in the nature of a substitute. The Senate bill that was debated and amended is never actually passed; after passing the House bill, the Senate indefinitely postpones further proceedings on its own bill.

If the first house's bill has been referred to committee in the second chamber and is still there, it is first necessary to discharge the committee from further consideration of the bill. This also is normally accomplished routinely, either by unanimous consent or, in the House, pursuant to the provisions of a special rule. To avoid the need for this action, the Speaker often leaves a Senate bill on "the Speaker's table," instead of referring it to the appropriate House committee, if there is reason to expect the House will soon act on a companion House bill. Similarly, a House bill may be taken up on the Senate floor without first being referred to committee when a companion Senate bill has been reported from committee and is on the Senate's legislative calendar.

By these devices, the House and Senate arrange to act on the same bill, even if they have passed that measure with fundamentally different texts. In most cases, these

---

[7] Third reading and engrossment is a technical and noncontroversial stage in both houses that marks the conclusion of the amending process and precedes the vote on final passage.

arrangements are noncontroversial and routine. Under some circumstances, however, complications and difficulties can arise.

The House operates under a rule which requires that all amendments must be germane to the measure being considered; the Senate does not.[8] Unless the Senate imposes a germaneness requirement on itself by unanimous consent (which it often does), most measures are subject to whatever nongermane floor amendments Senators wish to offer. Consequently, the Senate may select a House bill on one subject as a convenient "vehicle" and amend it to include provisions on other, unrelated subjects. Sometimes the use of unrelated legislative vehicles is accepted by both the House and the Senate as a useful, or even necessary, device to cope with different political and parliamentary conditions prevailing in the two chambers. Although such situations are relatively unusual, problems sometimes arise that make neutral vehicles useful for resolving them.

During the 95th Congress, for example, President Carter submitted a massive proposal for major new national energy legislation. The Democratic leadership of the House chose to consider the President's entire program in a single bill, and eventually the House passed H.R. 8444. In the Senate, on the other hand, the Democratic majority leadership concluded that an omnibus bill would inspire a filibuster that probably could not be broken; consequently, the Senate debated and amended five separate bills that collectively dealt with the same subjects as H.R. 8444.

A dilemma now arose. If the Senate passed its five bills and sent them to the House, the House would face different bills on different aspects of the President's program, which was precisely the situation the House had sought to avoid by consolidating the various proposals in H.R. 8444. Yet if the Senate attempted to pass the House bill, the feared filibuster was likely to develop. To resolve the dilemma, the Senate selected four neutral vehicles: minor House bills that had been awaiting Senate action. To each of these bills the Senate added the texts of one or more of its energy bills as well as provisions of the single House bill (H.R. 8444). It was on these bills that the House and Senate eventually resolved their differences over national energy legislation, even though the four bills originally had been for the relief of Jack R. Misner and Joe Cortina, and to suspend import duties on competition bobsleds and luges for the Lake Placid Winter Olympic Games and on certain doxorubicin hydrochloride antibiotics. In this instance, then, selecting the measure was complicated by the differing situations in the two houses, and was arranged through the use of four unrelated vehicles.[9]

Resorting to such convoluted procedures is unusual. Normally, the selection of the measure is arranged routinely, as the House and Senate proceed toward the more difficult task of resolving their differences over the substance, not the form, of legislation.

TWO METHODS OF RESOLUTION

Once the House and Senate have passed different versions of the same measure, there are basically two methods they can use to resolve the differences between their versions.

One method involves a conference committee — a panel of members representing each house that attempts to negotiate a version acceptable to chambers. Most major bills are sent to conference committees.

The other method makes a conference committee unnecessary by relying instead on amendments between houses — Senate amendments to the House position, or House

---

[8] Senate rule require floor amendments to be germane only when offered to general appropriations bills or budget measures, or after the Senate has invoked cloture.

[9] Once the conferees completed their work, the House agreed to an unusual special rule under which it cast one vote to approve all four conference reports.

amendments to the Senate position, or both. The two houses shuttle the measure back and forth between them, each chamber proposing an alternative to the position of the other or insisting on its own position, in the hope that both houses eventually will agree on the same position.

The essential nature of each method can be described relatively simply. However, potential complications abound. Occasionally, some combination of the two methods may be used. For example, the House and Senate may begin the process of resolving their differences by amending each other's amendments. Then they may decide to go to conference if the first method is not totally, or even partially, successful. Alternatively, the two houses may decide immediately to create a conference committee that is able to resolve some, but not all, of the differences between their two versions. If so, the two chambers may accept whatever agreements the conferees have reached, and then attempt to deal with the remaining disagreements through an exchange of amendments between the houses.

Under some circumstances, the process can become even more complicated. Certain patterns of action are most common, but the possible variations make the procedures at this stage of the legislative process the most difficult to predict with any assurance. Moreover, either house may refuse to act at anytime and at any stage of this process, and if that chamber remains adamant in its refusal to act, the measure dies.

In general, the House or Senate cannot take any action by either method unless it is in formal possession of the "page" — the official copies of the measure and whatever amendments, motions, and accompanying messages have been approved by the House and Senate. In attempting to resolve their differences, the two chambers act sequentially, not simultaneously.

Although most major legislation is considered by a conference committee, amendments between the houses are best discussed first.

AMENDMENTS BETWEEN THE HOUSES

The need to resolve differences arises when one house passes a measure that the second chamber subsequently passes with one or more amendments.[10] It is these amendments that create the differences between the two houses. The differences may be resolved by one chamber accepting the amendments of the other or by proposing new amendments that the other house agrees to accept.

Within limits to be discussed, the measure may be sent back and forth between the House and Senate, each house amending the amendments of the other, in the hope that one chamber will agree to the proposals from the other. When the amending opportunities are exhausted, one house must accept the position of the other or the bill can die for lack of agreement. Alternatively, at any stage during this process either house can request a conference, thereby proposing to use the other method for resolving their differences. (Then, if the conference is not totally successful, it may be necessary to return once again to amendments between the houses.)

The second chamber's amendments to the bill are the text that is subject to amendments between the houses, and that text may be amended in two degrees.[11]

---

[10] Note that, at this point, both houses have agreed to everything in the text except the portion amended by the second chamber. Thereafter, neither chamber should propose changes in portions of the text to which both have agreed.

[11] A measure normally can be amended in two degrees on the House or Senate floor. An amendment offered to the text of the measure itself is an amendment in the first degree. While a first degree amendment is pending (that is, after it has been offered but before it has been voted on), an amendment may be offered to the amendment. Such an amendment to a pending amendment is an amendment in the second degree. Although more complicated situations may arise, both chambers generally prohibit third degree amendments. (In the House, however, a substitute for a first degree amendment is amendable.) Roughly the same principles

Assume that the House has passed H.R. 1 and the Senate has passed the same bill with an amendment. When the Senate sends the bill back to the House, the House may amend the Senate amendment — technically, the House concurs in the Senate amendment with a House amendment. This House amendment to the Senate amendment is a first-degree amendment.

When the Senate receives from the House the bill with the House amendment to the Senate amendment, the Senate may concur in the House amendment to the Senate amendment. If the Senate does so, the differences between the chambers have been resolved. Alternatively, the Senate may amend the House amendment — technically, the Senate concurs in the House amendment to the Senate amendment with a further Senate amendment. This further Senate amendment is a second-degree amendment.

When the bill and the accompanying papers (that is, the various House and Senate amendments and messages) are returned to the House, that chamber may not propose a further amendment. That would be a prohibited amendment in the third degree.[12] The House may concur in the final Senate amendment, in which case the differences are resolved, or it may disagree to the Senate amendment. (Note that this is the first point at which disagreement has been expressed; a later section of this report discusses the importance of reaching the stage of disagreement.)

If the House disagrees to the final Senate amendment (or to any Senate amendment at some earlier stage), the Senate may recede from its amendment and concur in the last position offered by the House (thereby achieving agreement), or the Senate may insist on its amendment. In turn, if both chambers are adamant, the House may insist on its disagreement, the Senate may adhere to its amendment, and the House finally may adhere to its disagreement.[13] If this stage is reached, the bill is almost certain to die unless one house or the other recedes from its last position. (This same sequence of events can begin in the Senate, with the subsequent actions of the chambers reversed.)

The two houses may reach agreement at any stage of this process if one chamber concurs in the amendment of the other or recedes from its own amendment. Alternatively, stalemate could be reached more quickly — for instance, if the chambers refuse to alter their original positions and proceed directly through the stages of disagreement, insistence, and adherence, bypassing the intermediate stages at which they could offer new proposals in the form of first- and second-degree amendments between the houses.

Fortunately, the House and Senate rarely reach the point of insistence and then adherence. It is even rather unusual for there to be second-degree amendments between the houses (for instance, for the House to concur in the Senate amendment to the House amendment to a Senate bill with a further House amendment). Most often, the House and Senate either reach agreement at an earlier stage or they choose instead to submit their differences to a conference committee.

CONSIDERATION OF SENATE AMENDMENTS BY THE HOUSE

The House may consider on the floor a House-passed measure with Senate amendments under several circumstances: (1) instead of sending the bill to a conference committee, (2) in the process of sending it to conference, or (3) after the measure has been considered by a conference. This section discusses House action on Senate

---

apply to amendments between the houses. For more detailed descriptions of these procedures, see CRS Report 98-853, *The Amending Process in the Senate*, by Betsy Palmer and CRS Report 98-995, *The Amending Process in the House of Representatives*, by Christopher M. Davis and Stanley Bach.

[12] The House or Senate may consider a third degree amendment by unanimous consent. In the House, it also may be considered under suspension of the rules pursuant to a special rule.

[13] The terms "recede," "insist," and "adhere" have technical meanings in the legislative process. When the House or Senate "recedes," it withdraws from a previous position or action. To "insist" and to "adhere" have essentially the same meaning but are terms used at different stages of the process.

amendment either instead of or before consideration in conference. House actions on Senate amendments after conference are discussed in later sections of this report on amendments in true and technical disagreement.

A bill that the House has passed and that the Senate has amended and returned to the House usually remains at "the Speaker's table" until it is taken up again on the House floor. It may be referred to a House committee at the discretion of the Speaker, but referral to committee is not mandatory and rarely occurs. The Speaker is most likely to refer the bill to committee if the Senate amendments are major in scope and nongermane in character, and especially if the Senate amendments would fall within the jurisdiction of a House committee that had not considered the bill originally.[14]

At this stage of the legislative process, the bill and the Senate amendments to it are not privileged for floor consideration by the House — in other words, it is not in order for the House to consider the Senate amendments to the bill — unless the Senate amendments do not include any authorization, appropriation, or revenue provisions that House rules requires to be considered in Committee of the Whole. The bill and Senate amendments become privileged for House floor consideration only after the House has reached the stage of disagreement.

The only motion that can be made on the House floor at this stage is a motion to go to conference with the Senate. This motion can take two forms. If the Senate has passed a House bill with Senate amendments, the motion proposes that the House disagree to the Senate amendments and request or agree to a conference with the Senate. If the Senate has disagreed to House amendments to a Senate bill and returned the bill to the House, the motion proposes instead that the House insist on its amendments and request or agree to a conference. In either case, the motion is entertained at the Speaker's discretion, and may be made only at the direction of the committee (or committees) with jurisdiction over the subject of the measure. The same result is achieved far more often by unanimous consent.

If the Senate Amendment requires consideration in Committee of the Whole, it is not in order to move to concur in the Senate amendments (thereby reaching agreement), or to move to concur in the Senate amendments with House amendments (thereby proposing a new House position to the Senate). However, such actions frequently are taken by unanimous consent. The House floor manager may ask unanimous consent, for instance, to take the bill, H.R. 1, with Senate amendments thereto from the Speaker's table and concur in the Senate amendments. Another Member, generally a minority-party member of the committee of jurisdiction, often reserves the right to object, usually only for the purpose of asking the floor manager to explain the purpose of the request and the content of the Senate amendments. Their discussion usually establishes that the Senate amendments are either desirable or minor and, in any case, are acceptable to the Representatives who know and care the most about the measure. The reservation of objection then is withdrawn; the unanimous consent request is accepted, and the differences between the House and Senate are thereby resolved. In similar fashion, the House may — again by unanimous consent — concur in some or all of the Senate amendments with House amendments.

It bears repeating that, if there is objection to a unanimous consent request to concur in Senate amendments (with or without House amendments), no motion to that effect can be made if the amendments require consideration in Committee of the Whole. However, at least two alternatives are available. First, the Speaker may recognize the floor manager to move to suspend the rules and concur in the Senate amendments (again, with or without House amendments). Motions to suspend the rules may be considered, at the discretion of the Speaker, on a Monday or Tuesday, or on a Wednesday through April 9, 2003. The Speaker also may entertain motions to suspend

---

[14] The same applies to a Senate bill with Senate amendments to House amendments, and to a House bill with Senate amendments to House amendments to Senate amendments.

the rules on other days by unanimous consent or pursuant to a special rule. Such a motion is debatable for forty minutes, it is not amendable, and it requires support from two-thirds of the Members present and voting. Second, the Rules Committee may report, and the House may agree to, a special rule making in order a motion to concur (with or without amendments). In fact, the special rule even may be drafted in such a way that the vote to agree to the rule is also the vote to concur in the Senate amendments. Such a resolution is known as a self-executing rule, and may take the following form:

> *Resolved*, That immediately upon the adoption of this resolution the bill (H.R. 1), together with the Senate amendments thereto, is taken from the Speaker's table to the end that the Senate amendments be, and the same are hereby, agreed to.

There are additional rules and precedents concerning the consideration of certain Senate amendments in Committee of the Whole, the germaneness of House amendments to Senate amendments, and the relative precedence of the motion to concur and the motion to concur with amendments. However, these rules and precedents are not often invoked at this stage of House proceedings because the measure and the Senate amendments are either sent directly to conference or they are disposed of by a means that waives these rules and precedents — unanimous consent, suspension of the rules, or special rules. Some of these possibilities are far more likely to arise during House floor action on Senate amendments in true or technical disagreement, and they are discussed in later sections on those subjects.

CONSIDERATION OF HOUSE AMENDMENTS BY THE SENATE

When the Senate receives a bill with House amendments, it normally is held at the desk. The motion to proceed to consideration of the amendments is privileged and, therefore, not debatable. (The motion to proceed normally is debatable.) Moreover, the consideration of these amendments suspends, but does not displace. the pending or unfinished business. Paragraph 3 of Rule VII provides:

> The Presiding Officer may at any time lay, and it shall be in order for a Senator to move to lay, before the Senate, any bill or other matter sent to the Senate by the President or the House of Representatives for appropriate action allowed under the rules and any question pending at that time shall be suspended for this purpose. Any motion so made shall be determined without debate.

Normally, the majority leader asks the presiding officer to lay before the Senate the House message on a bill; such a message may state that the House has passed a certain Senate bill with amendments that are stated in the message. The message also may inform the Senate that the House has requested a conference. Once the Senate has agreed to consider House amendments, the House amendments themselves are amendable.

After some explanation of the Senate bill and the House amendments, the majority leader or the majority floor manager of the bill usually moves or asks unanimous consent (1) that the Senate concur in the House amendments, or (2) that the Senate concur in the House amendments with Senate amendments, or (3) that the Senate disagree to some or all of the House amendments and either request or agree to a conference with the House. Any of these motions is debatable and, therefore, is subject to being filibustered. Whichever proposal is made, however, it is likely to be accepted by the Senate without serious opposition.

Thus, the Senate may act on House amendments at virtually any time, even if a major bill is under consideration, both because the House amendments are privileged business and also because they normally are disposed of quickly (so that the Senate's consideration of the pending bill is not interrupted for long). It usually is not necessary to call up the House amendments by use of nondebatable motions they usually are considered by unanimous consent. But unanimous consent probably is made easier to obtain by the knowledge that the nondebatable motion is in order (and, therefore, that extended debate is not possible).

These Senate practices effectively obviate a variety of parliamentary options that are available for acting on House amendments. For example, a motion to agree to a House amendment has precedence over (and may be offered while there is pending) a motion to disagree and go to conference. But a motion to agree to the House amendment with an amendment has precedence over the motion to agree, and a motion to refer the House amendments to a committee of the Senate has precedence over both the motion to agree and the motion to disagree.

Fortunately, the complexities that these options can create arise very infrequently because House amendments normally are not called up on the Senate floor until after a process of consultations and negotiations that is so characteristic of the Senate. The majority and minority floor managers can be expected to consult with each other and to decide if the House amendments are acceptable or if the two Senators can agree on amendments to those House amendments. Whatever agreement the floor managers reach also is discussed with other interested Senators in the hope of achieving general concurrence. If such concurrence is reached, it is reflected in an expeditious floor decision to agree to the House amendments, with or without amendments. If concurrence cannot be reached, the Senators involved normally decide to resolve the disagreements among themselves (as well as with the House) in conference, rather than through a complicated series of motions and amendments offered on the Senate floor.

THE INFORMAL ALTERNATIVE TO CONFERENCE

If the House and Senate versions of a measure are submitted to conference, the conference committee must meet formally and, if it resolves some or all of the differences between the houses, prepare both a conference report and a joint explanatory statement. To avoid these and other requirements, the two chambers may use the process of sending amendments between the houses as an informal alternative that achieves much the same purpose and result as would a conference committee.

The purpose of a conference committee is to negotiate a settlement of the legislative differences between the two chambers. But these negotiations do not have to take place in the official setting of a conference committee meeting. They also can occur through informal discussions among the most interested Representatives and Senators and their staffs. If such informal discussions are successful, their results can be embodied in an amendment between the houses.

As the second house nears or reaches completion of floor action on a measure, the staffs of the respective House and Senate committees are likely to be comparing the two versions of the bill and seeking grounds for settling whatever differences exist. After initial staff discussions, the House and Senate committee leaders themselves may become involved. If these informal and unofficial conversations appear productive, they may continue until a tentative agreement is reached, even though no conference committee has yet been created. If the tentative agreement proves acceptable to other interested Representatives and Senators, a conference committee may be unnecessary.

Instead, when the bill with the second house's amendments has been returned to the first chamber, the majority floor manager may. under the appropriate rules or practices of that house, call up the bill and propose that the House or Senate (as the case may be) concur in the second chamber's amendments with some amendments. He or she then describes the differences between the House and Senate versions of the measure and explains that the proposed amendments represent a compromise that is agreeable to the interested members of both houses. The floor managers may express their confidence that, if the first house accepts the amendments, the other chamber also will accept them.

If the first house does agree to the amendments, the second chamber then considers and agrees to them as well, under its procedures for considering amendments of the "other body." In this way, the differences between the House and Senate are resolved through the kind of negotiations for which conference committees are created, but without resort to a formal conference committee.

This informal alternative to conference is useful when the bill at issue is not particularly controversial, when the differences between the House and Senate versions are relatively minor, or when the end of a session approaches. It is far less likely to be successful, or even attempted, when there are significant differences between House and Senate approaches to major issues, and when there is time to discuss them at length.

THE STAGE OF DISAGREEMENT

Since the purpose of conference committees is to resolve legislative disagreement between the House and Senate, it follows that there can be no conference committee until there is disagreement — until the House and Senate formally state their disagreement to each other's positions. A chamber reaches this stage either by formally insisting on its own position or by disagreeing to the position of the other house, and so informing the other house. Once the House or Senate reaches the stage of disagreement, it cannot then agree to (concur in) a position of the other chamber, or agree with an amendment, without first receding from its disagreement.

The stage of disagreement is an important threshold. Before this threshold is reached, the two chambers presumably are still in the process of reaching agreement. Thus, amendments between the houses, as an alternative to conference, are couched in terms of one chamber concurring in the other's amendments, or concurring in the other's amendments with amendments. For example, when the House concurs in Senate amendments with House amendments, the House does so because it does not accept the Senate amendments — in fact, it disagrees with them. But the House does not state its disagreement explicitly and formally at this stage because crossing the threshold of disagreement has significant procedural consequences, especially in the House.

Whereas House amendments are always privileged in the Senate, most Senate amendments are not privileged in the House before the House has reached the stage of disagreement. Moreover, the order of precedence among certain motions is reversed in the House (but not in the Senate) after the stage of disagreement has been reached. Before the stage of disagreement, the order of precedence among motions in both chambers favors motions that tend to perfect the measure further; after the stage of disagreement in the House, the order of precedence is reversed, with precedence being given to motions that tend to promote agreement between the chambers. Before the stage of disagreement, for example, a motion to concur with an amendment has precedence over a motion to concur, after the stage of disagreement in the House, a motion to recede and concur has precedence over a motion to recede and concur with an amendment.

The precedence among motions before and after the stage of disagreement can become important during the process of exchanging amendments between the houses. It is most likely to matter after a conference committee has reported and the House and Senate are considering amendments in true or technical disagreement. For this reason, a more detailed discussion of the subject is reserved to the sections on such amendments.

ARRANGING FOR A CONFERENCE

If the differences between the House and Senate cannot be resolved through the exchange of amendments between the houses, two possibilities remain. First, stalemate can lead to the death of the legislation if both chambers remain adamant. Or second, the two houses can agree to create a conference committee to discuss their differences and seek a mutually satisfactory resolution. In fact, major bills usually are sent to a conference committee, either after an unsuccessful attempt to resolve the differences through amendments between the houses or without such an attempt having even being made.

The process of arranging for a conference can begin as soon as the second house passes the bill at issue, either with one or more amendments to parts of the measure or with a single amendment in the nature of a substitute that replaces the entire text approved by the first chamber. The second house then may simply return the bill, with its amendments, to the first chamber if there is reason to believe that the first house might accept the amendments, or that amendments between the houses can be used successfully as an informal alternative to conference. It also may do so if the second house wishes to act first on an eventual conference report, because the chamber that asks for a conference normally acts last on the conference report.

Alternatively, and more commonly, the second house may pass the bill and immediately insist on its amendments and also request a conference with the first chamber. By insisting on its amendments, the second chamber reaches the stage of disagreement. The bill, the second house' s amendments, and the message requesting a conference, then are returned to the first house. The first house is not obliged to disagree to the second chamber's amendments and agree to the requested conference. The first house also has the options, for example, of refusing to act at all or concurring in the second chamber amendments, with or without amendments. When one chamber requests a conference, however, the other house normally agrees to the request.

If the second chamber just returns the bill and its amendments to the first house without insisting on its amendments, the first house may disagree to the amendments and request a conference. The bill, the amendments, and the message requesting the conference then are returned to the second chamber, which usually insists on its amendments (thereby reaching the stage of disagreement) and agrees to the conference.

Thus, there are essentially two direct routes to conference. (There are more indirect routes, of course, if an attempt is first made to resolve the differences through an exchange of amendments.) The second house may begin the process by insisting on its amendments and requesting the conference. If this does not occur, the first house then may begin the process by disagreeing to the second chamber's amendments and requesting the conference itself. The first route is likely to be followed when the need for a conference is a foregone conclusion.

However. strategic considerations also may influence how the Senate and House agree to go to conference, especially in view of the convention that the chamber which asks for the conference normally acts last on the conference report. With this in mind, proponents of the legislation may prefer one route to the other. For example, House or Senate conferees can avoid the possibility of facing a motion in one house to recommit the conference report (with or without instructions) if they have arranged for the other house to act first on the report.[15] By the same token, if Senate opponents are expected to filibuster the conference report, proponents may prefer for the Senate to agree to a House request for a conference, so that the Senate will act first on the report. This arrangement avoids compelling Representatives to cast difficult votes for or against a conference report that may not reach a vote in the Senate. On the other hand, a bill's supporters could prefer that the House agree to the conference and then vote first on the report, with the hope that a successful House vote might improve the prospects for later success on the Senate floor.

---

[15] This possibility is discussed in the section on floor consideration of conference reports.

SELECTION OF CONFEREES

After either house requests or agrees to a conference, it usually proceeds immediately to select conferees, or managers as they also may be called. The selection of conferees can be critically important, because it is this group — sometimes a small group — of Representatives and Senators who usually determine the final form and content of major legislation.

In the House, clause 11 of Rule I authorizes the Speaker to appoint all members of conference committees, and gives him certain guidelines to follow:

> The Speaker shall appoint all select, joint, and conference committees ordered by the House. At any time after an original appointment, the Speaker may remove Members, Delegates, or the Resident Commissioner from, or appoint additional Members. Delegates, or the Resident Commissioner to, a select or conference committee. In appointing Members, Delegates, or the Resident Commissioner to conference committees, the Speaker shall appoint no less than a majority who generally supported the House position as determined by the Speaker, shall name Members who are primarily responsible for the legislation, and shall, to the fullest extent feasible, include the principal proponents of the major provisions of the bill or resolution passed or adopted by the House.

These guidelines carry weight as admonitions but they necessarily give the Speaker considerable discretion, and his exercise of this discretion cannot be challenged on the floor through a point of order.

In the Senate, the presiding officer is almost always authorized to appoint "the managers on the part of the Senate." Should the Senate fail to give the presiding officer this authority, however, Senators would elect their conferees. A motion to elect certain Senators as conferees is both debatable and amendable.

Before the formal announcement of conferees in each chamber, a process of consultation takes place that vests great influence with the chairman and the ranking minority member of the committee (and sometimes the subcommittee) that had considered the bill originally. These Representatives and Senators almost always serve as conferees. Furthermore, they usually play an influential, and often a controlling, role in deciding the number of conferees from their respective chambers, the party ratio among these conferees, and which of their committee colleagues shall be appointed to the conference committee. In the House, the Speaker often accepts without change the list developed by the House committee leaders; the presiding officer in the Senate always does so.

If the bill at issue had been considered by more than one committee in either house, all the involved chairmen and ranking minority members from that chamber normally participate in determining its roster of conferees, and the conferees usually are drawn from both or all of those committees. In such cases, the party leaders in each house are more likely to become involved in the selection process — in determining the total number of House or Senate conferees and the division of conferees between or among the committees of jurisdiction, as well as in choosing individual members to serve. From time to time, the Speaker also exercises his authority to appoint a Representative who offered a key successful floor amendment, even if he or she is not on the committee(s) that reported the legislation.

In some cases — and especially in cases of multiple committee jurisdiction — House or Senate conferees maybe appointed for limited purposes: for example, only for the consideration of Title I of the House version, or only for the consideration of a particular (and possibly nongermane) Senate amendment. Such conferees are expected to limit their participation in the conference to consideration of the matters for which they are appointed. This practice protects the preponderant influence in conference of the appropriate House and Senate standing committees.

Each house determines for itself the size of its delegation to the conference committee. The House and Senate need not select equal numbers of conferees, and they frequently do not. However, unequal numbers of House and Senate managers do not affect the formal power of either house in conference decisions. The conference report requires approval by a majority of the House conferees and a majority of the Senate conferees, rather than a majority of all conferees. Each house usually appoints an odd number of conferees to avoid tie votes.

Two developments concerning the selection of conferees are noteworthy. First, conference committees have generally increased in size. Second, seniority on committee has become a somewhat less controlling factor in the selection of conferees. More members, and more junior members, have been appointed to conference committees during recent Congresses. In addition to giving more members an opportunity to participate in this stage of the legislative process, increasing the number of conferees also increases the likelihood that a house's conference delegation will more accurately reflect the distribution of policy positions within the chamber as a whole (which can make it more difficult for the conferees to reach agreement).

Also contributing to these trends has been the comparatively high rate of turnover among Representatives and Senators in recent years, and the institutional changes that have distributed positions of influence more widely among members and somewhat reduced the importance of seniority. Another contributing factor has been the number of omnibus bills, such as the budget reconciliation bills of recent years, that have touched on the jurisdictions of numerous House and Senate committees. All the affected standing committees have a natural interest in being represented on the conference committees that consider such bills. The result has been some large conferences; the conference committee on the Omnibus Budget Reconciliation Act of 1981 included a total of more than 250 Senators and Representatives.

INSTRUCTING CONFEREES

After the House or Senate decides to go to conference (either by requesting the conference or agreeing to a request from the other house), its conferees usually are appointed immediately. Between these two steps, however, both houses have an opportunity (although usually only a momentary opportunity) to move to instruct the conferees.[16] For example, the managers may be instructed to insist on the position of their house on a certain matter, or even to recede to the position of the other house.

A primary reason is that instructions are not binding. They are only admonitions, or advisory expressions of position or preference. No point of order lies in either the House or the Senate against a conference report on the ground that conferees did not adhere to the instructions they received.

In the Senate, a motion to instruct is debatable and amendable. In the House, such a motion is debated under the one-hour rule, and a germane amendment to the instructions is in order only if the House does not order the previous question during or at the end of the first hour of debate. In neither house can conferees be instructed to take some action that exceeds their authority. In the House, clause 7 of Rule XXII also bars instructions that "include argument." Only one valid motion to instruct is in order in the House before its conferees are named, whether or not the motion is agreed to; but if a motion to instruct is ruled out of order, another motion to instruct may be made.

Under the precedents of the House, a member of the minority party is entitled to recognition to move to instruct. The Speaker normally looks first to senior minority party members of the committee that reported the measure at issue. This recognition practice can he used to try to control the instructions that are proposed; for example,

---

[16] Because the motion to instruct may be made only before the conferees are named, it is less likely to be viewed as a challenge to the intentions of the members appointed as managers.

instructions on one subject may be precluded if the ranking minority member seeks recognition to offer a motion to instruct on another subject.[17]

Successful motions to instruct are relatively uncommon for essentially the same reason they are never binding. Conferences are negotiating sessions in which the conferees appointed by each house meet to discuss their differences and arrange a suitable compromise. To impose binding instructions on them would be to limit their discretion and flexibility, and possibly to reduce the likelihood of a successful conference. Members can view even nonbinding instructions as restricting conferees' latitude, politically if not procedurally. For these reasons, prospective conferees generally oppose being instructed, and some members are inclined to vote against motions to instruct even though they may agree with the content of the instructions.

From time to time, however, the House (more often than the Senate) does vote to instruct its conferees. In some cases, Representatives may question whether their conferees are likely to give sufficient priority to upholding the House position on a certain matter in disagreement. This concern may arise, for example, if the matter in question was included in the House version of the bill by a floor amendment that many of the prospective conferees opposed. In other cases, instructions may be welcomed by House managers as evidence of strong House support for a position the conferees wish to maintain in conference.

In either case, a successful motion to instruct is a form of advance notice to House and Senate conferees that a conference report inconsistent with the instructions may not receive majority support on the House floor. Depending on the circumstances, this notice maybe directed to House conferees, or it may be used by them to convince Senate conferees that the House delegation must stand firm on the subject of the instructions if the conference report is to be approved by the House.

In the House, but not in the Senate, motions to instruct also are in order after House conferees have been appointed but have failed to report an agreement.[18] Clause 7(c)(l) of House Rule XXII provides in part:

> A motion to instruct managers on the part of the House, or a motion to discharge all managers on the part of the House and to appoint new conferees, shall be privileged —
>
> > (A) after a conference committee has been appointed for 20 calendar days and 10 legislative days without making a report . . . .

By precedent, more than one proper motion to instruct is in order when made pursuant to this clause, and the minority party does not enjoy preferential recognition in offering such motions. According to clause 7(c)(2), the Speaker "may designate a time in the legislative schedule on that legislative day for consideration" of the motion to instruct.

The right to instruct under Rule XXII can be used to urge conferees in one policy direction or another, perhaps in an effort to break a logjam in conference. Under these circumstances, instructions maybe welcomed, or even sought, by House conferees to test the sentiment of the House or, more likely, to demonstrate the strength of House opinion to the Senate.

---

[17] However, the House may amend the instructions (if it has not already ordered the previous question on the motion). Such an amendment must be germane to the House or Senate versions of the bill, but not necessarily to the instructions to which the amendment is proposed.

[18] It is possible for Senate conferees to be instructed by resolution while a bill is in conference.

RESTRICTIONS ON THE AUTHORITY OF CONFEREES

In principle, there are significant restrictions on the kinds of policy agreements that House conferees can accept. In practice, however, these restrictions are not as stringent as they might seem at first.

Because conference committees are created to resolve disagreements between the House and Senate, the authority of House conferees is limited to the matters in disagreement between the two houses. House conferees have no authority to change matters that are not in disagreement — that is, either matters that appear in the House and Senate versions of the measure in identical form, or matters that were not submitted to the conference in either the House or the Senate version.

Furthermore, as House conferees consider each matter in disagreement, their authority is limited by the scope of the differences between the House and Senate positions on that matter. The House's managers may agree on the House position, the Senate position, or some middle ground. But they may not include a provision in a conference report that does not fall within the range of options defined by the House position at one extreme and the Senate position at the other. If, for example, the House proposes to appropriate $1 billion for a certain purpose and the Senate proposes $2 billion instead, the House conferees may agree on $1 billion or $2 billion or any intermediate figure. But they may not agree on a figure that is less than $1 billion or more than $2 billion. To do so would exceed the scope of the differences between the House and Senate positions on that matter in disagreement.

The concept of "scope" relates to specific differences between the House and Senate versions of the same measure, not to the implications or consequences of these differences. Thus, House conferees on a general appropriations bill may agree on the higher (or lower) of the House and Senate positions on each appropriation item, even though the sum of their agreements is higher (or lower) than the total sum proposed in either the House or the Senate version of the bill (unless the two versions explicitly state such a total). Also, if one house proposes to amend some existing law and the other chamber does not, the scope of the differences over this matter generally is bounded by the proposed amendments, on the one hand, and the pertinent provisions of existing law, on the other. Thus, the House conferees may agree on the proposed amendments or on alternatives that are closer to existing law.

Thus, there are significant restrictions on the authority of House conferees: their authority is restricted by the scope of the differences between the House and Senate over the matters in disagreement between them.[19] However, it is far easier to make this statement than to apply it in all cases. It becomes much more difficult to define the scope of the differences when the differences are qualitative, not quantitative as in the example above. Moreover, how difficult it is to define the scope of the differences also depends on how the second chamber to act on the measure has cast the matters in disagreement.

If one house takes up a measure from the other and passes the measure with a series of amendments to the first chamber's text, then the matters in disagreement in conference are cast in terms of two or more discrete amendments approved by the second house to pass the bill. These amendments usually are numbered for convenient reference. The two versions of the measure can be compared side by side to identify the provisions that are identical in both versions and those that are the subject of disagreements. Therefore, it is possible to identify both the matters in disagreement and the House and Senate positions on each of them.

However, the second chamber that acts on a measure typically casts its version in the form of an amendment in the nature of a substitute for the entire text passed by the first

---

[19] Clause 5 of House Rule XXII also restricts the authority of House conferees to include certain kinds of Senate amendments in conference reports on general appropriations bills. These restrictions are discussed in the section on amendments in technical disagreement.

house. In such cases, only one amendment is submitted to conference, even though that single amendment may encompass any number of specific differences between the House and Senate versions of the measure. In fact, the text of the bill as passed by one house and the text of the other house's amendment in the nature of a substitute may embody wholly different approaches to the subject of the measure. The two versions may be organized differently and may address the same subject in fundamentally different ways.

Second house substitutes make it much harder, if not impractical, to specifically identify each matter in disagreement and the scope of the differences over that matter. When a second chamber substitute is in conference, therefore, the conferees must have somewhat greater room for maneuver. Technically, the House and Senate are in disagreement over the entire text of the measure; substantively, the policy disagreements may be almost as profound. In such cases, the conferees resolve the differences between the House and Senate by creating a third version of the measure — a conference substitute for both the version originally passed by the first house and the amendment in the nature of a substitute approved by the second house.

This latitude may be necessary, but it also means that the conference substitute could take the form of a third and new approach to the subject at hand — an approach that had not been considered on the floor of either house. To inhibit such a result, clause 9 of House Rule XXII states that:

> Whenever a disagreement to an amendment has been committed to a conference committee, the managers on the part of the House may propose a substitute that is a germane modification of the matter in disagreement. The introduction of any language presenting specific additional matter not committed to the conference committee by either House does not constitute a germane modification of the matter in disagreement. Moreover, a conference report may not include matter not committed to the conference committee by either House and may not include a modification of specific matter committed to the conference committee by either or both Houses if that modification is beyond the scope of that specific matter as committed to the conference committee.

Notwithstanding this specificity, determining whether a conference substitute includes some new "matter" is far more difficult than determining whether the conferees' agreement on an appropriation for a program falls within the scope of the differences between the funding levels originally proposed by the House and Senate.

If the House conferees have exceeded their authority in any one respect in agreeing to a conference report, that report as a whole is tainted and so is subject to a point of order on the House floor. [20] However, there are at least three reasons why it is relatively unusual for a point of order to be made and sustained against a conference report. First, House conferees are aware of the limits within which they are to negotiate, and they usually try not to exceed their authority. Second, conferees frequently are presented with second chamber substitutes and, in those cases, they have somewhat greater discretion in the agreements they can reach.

Third, even if the House managers propose a conference report that exceeds their authority, there are several ways in which they can protect their report against being subject to a point of order on the House floor. If the conferees were negotiating over separate numbered amendments and their agreement concerning one or more of the amendments is beyond their authority, they can report those amendments back to the House and Senate as amendments in technical disagreement. However, conferees may not report back in disagreement on part of an amendment in the nature of a substitute. Alternatively, the House can approve a conference report by a two-thirds vote under suspension of the rules, a procedure which does not allow points of order to he made on

---

[20] Conference reports also are subject to points of order if they violate certain provisions of the Budget Act.

the floor. Finally, and perhaps most important in current practice, the House Rules Committee may propose that the House approve a special rule waiving any or all points of order against a conference report and against its consideration.

Even if a conference report is ruled out of order, it may then be possible to propose precisely the same agreements that were contained in the report in the form of amendments between the houses (if the amendments are not in the third degree and do not contain non-germane matter).

The Senate's rules and precedents embody roughly the same principles regarding restrictions on the authority of its conferees. Paragraphs 2 and 3 of Senate Rule XXVIII state that:

> 2. Conferees shall not insert in their report matter not committed to them by either House, nor shall they strike from the bill matter agreed to by both Houses. If new matter is inserted in the report, or if matter which was agreed to by both Houses is stricken front the bill, a point of order may be made against the report, and if the point of order is sustained, the report is rejected or shall be recommitted to the committee of conference if the House of Representatives has not already acted thereon.

> 3. (a) In any case in which a disagreement to an amendment in the nature of a substitute has been referred to conferees, it shall be in order for the conferees to report a substitute on the same subject matter, but they may not include in the report matter not committed to them by either House. They may, however, include in their report in any such case matter which is a germane modification of subjects in disagreement.

> (b) In any case in which the conferees violate subparagraph (a) the conference report shall be subject to a point of order.

Furthermore, the Senate's procedures do not include effective ways to waive these rules, except for the rarely used motion to suspend the rules by a two-thirds vote.

Historically, the Senate has interpreted its rules and precedents affecting the content of conference reports in ways that grant conferees considerable latitude in reaching agreements with the House. According to *Riddick's Senate Procedure*, for example, a "conference report may not include new 'matter entirely irrelevant to the subject matter,' not contained in the House- or Senate-passed versions of a measure as distinct from a substitute therefor."[21] And regarding conference substitutes, Senate precedents state that, "in such cases, they [the conferees] have the entire subject before them with little limitation placed on their discretion, except as to germaneness, and they may report any germane bill."[22]

Under current practice, the Senate takes a commonsense approach to deciding whether new matter is sufficiently relevant to constitute "a germane modification of subjects in disagreement" (Rule XXVIII, paragraph 3(a)).

CONFERENCE PROCEDURES AND REPORTS

Rules of procedure guide and constrain the legislative activities of both the House and Senate. So it is striking that there are almost no rules governing procedure in conference. The members of each conference committee can select their own chairman. They also can decide for themselves whether they wish to adopt any formal rules governing such matters as debate, quorums, proxy voting, or amendments, but usually they do not. The only rules imposed by the two houses governing conference committee meetings concern approval of the conference report and open meetings.

A majority of the House managers and a majority of the Senate managers must

---

[21] *Riddick's Senate Procedure*, p. 484.

[22] *Ibid.*, p. 463.

approve and sign the conference report. Decisions are never made by a vote among all the conferees combined. All votes take place within the House delegation and within the Senate delegation. This is why there is no requirement or necessity for the two houses to appoint the same number of conferees; five Senate conferees, for example, enjoy the same formal collective power in conference as 25 House conferees.

Until the mid-1970s, conference meetings were almost always closed to the public; now they are open unless a specific decision is made to close part or all of a meeting. Paragraph 6 of Senate Rule XXVIII states that:

> Each conference committee between the Senate and the House of Representatives shall be open to the public except when managers of either the Senate or the House of Representatives in open session determine by a rollcall vote of a majority of those managers present, that all or part of the remainder of the meeting on the day of the vote shall be closed to the public.

The comparable House rule is even more stringent. Clause 12 of House Rule XXII requires a majority vote on the House floor to close part or all of a conference meeting. In other words, House conferees cannot vote to close a conference committee meeting unless they have been authorized to do so by a specific rollcall vote of the House. This difference between House and Senate rules has not been a source of public contention because efforts to close conferences normally are made only when they must deal with national security matters. When House managers want the authority to close part or all of a formal conference meeting, they usually offer a motion to this effect at the time the House arranges to go to conference.

In the 110th Congress, the House agreed to impose additional requirements on conference meetings. According to the new language added to clause 12 of Rule XXII, managers "should endeavor to ensure" that meetings only occur if every House manager has been given notice and an opportunity to attend. It also explicitly states that all matters in disagreement are open to discussion at a conference meeting. The new subparagraphs responded to the complaints of some conferees in the 108th and 109th Congresses that they were excluded from conference committee meetings. Other Members argued at the time that bicameral negotiators commonly hold informal discussions, in small or large groups, and that a highly flexible negotiation process is necessary to reach a compromise. It is not clear what impact the new requirements of clause 12 will have on conference committee practice because the House has yet to determine what constitutes a "meeting" of the conference under the new provisions.

If a point of order is made and sustained on the House floor that conferees met in violation of clause 12 (or that they never met at all), the conference report is rejected and the House is considered to have requested a further conference with the Senate.

Few other rules govern conference proceedings nor do conference committees often vote to establish their own rules. Instead, they generally manage without them. This absence of rules reflects the basic nature of the conference committee as a negotiating forum in which the negotiators should be free to decide for themselves how to proceed most effectively.

In some cases, conferences are rather formal. One delegation puts a proposal on the table; the other delegation considers it and responds with a counter proposal. In other cases, conferences resemble free-form discussions in which the issues and the matters in disagreement are discussed without any apparent agenda or direction until the outlines of a compromise begin to emerge. In recent years, conferences on massive omnibus bills have even created "sub-conferences" to seek agreements which then can be combined into a single conference report.

Sometimes customary practices develop among members of House and Senate committees who meet with each other regularly in conference. For example, they may alternate the chairmanship from one conference to the next between the committee or subcommittee chairmen from each house. Conference bargaining also can be facilitated by preliminary staff work. Staff may prepare side-by-side comparisons of the House and Senate versions so that the conferees can understand more easily how the two houses dealt with the same issues or problems.[23] Furthermore, senior staff may engage in preliminary negotiations among themselves, seeking agreements acceptable to their principals, so that the members themselves can concentrate on the more intractable disagreements.

When the conferees reach full agreement, staff prepare a conference report which indicates how each amendment in disagreement has been resolved. For example, the report may propose that the Senate recede from certain of its amendments to the House bill, that the House recede from its disagreement to certain other Senate amendments, and that the House recede from its disagreement to the remaining Senate amendments and concur in each with a House amendment (the text of which is made part of the report). When the conferees have considered a single amendment in the nature of a substitute, the report proposes that the House which originated the bill recede from its disagreement to the other house's substitute, and concur in that amendment in the nature of a substitute with a substitute amendment that is the new version of the bill on which the conference committee has agreed.

Two copies of the conference report must be signed by a majority of House conferees and a majority of Senate conferees. No additional or minority views may be included in the report . . . .

The conference report itself is not the most informative document, because it does not describe the nature of the disagreements that confronted the conferees. Therefore, the rules of both houses require that a conference report be accompanied by a joint explanatory statement. According to paragraph 4 of Senate Rule XXVIII, this statement is to be "sufficiently detailed and explicit to inform the Senate as to the effect which the amendments or propositions contained in such report will have upon the measure to which those amendments or propositions relate." Clause 7(d) of House Rule XXII contains a comparable requirement. Normally, this joint explanatory statement summarizes the House, Senate, and conference positions on each amendment in disagreement (or each provision, in the case of second chamber and conference substitutes). The statement also is prepared in duplicate and signed by majorities of both House and Senate conferees.

The house that agreed to the conference normally acts first on the conference report.[24] Because this is an established practice, not a requirement of either House or Senate rules, the order of consideration can be reversed, if that is strategically advantageous. For example, the House may wish to delay acting on a report until after the Senate has voted on it because of the possibility that the report may fall victim to a Senate filibuster. Alternatively, Senate conferees may agree that the House should act first if the report is likely to enjoy greater support in the House, in the belief (or hope) that the House vote will increase the prospects for approving the report in the Senate.[25]

Also, the first house to consider a conference report has the option of voting to recommit the report to conference. If and when either house agrees to the report, the effect of that vote is to discharge that house's conferees, so there no longer is a conference committee to which the report can be recommitted. Therefore, the second house to consider the report does not have the option of recommitting it; it only may

---

[23] The preparation of such documents is not required, but they are particularly useful to help conferees identify and compare the corresponding House and Senate provisions of large and complex bills. These "side by sides", as they often are called, sometimes are available from the House or Senate committee of jurisdiction. However, they are not generally available for public distribution to the same extent as House and Senate reports and documents, for example.

[24] This practice is stated in Section XLVI of Jefferson's Manual.

[25] Rather than violate the customary order for considering conference reports, the same end can be achieved by arranging for one house to request the conference instead of agreeing to a request by the other.

accept or reject the report. Sometimes, therefore, the supporters of a bill arrange for one house or the other to act first on the conference report in order to avoid the possibility of a successful recommittal motion. Whatever the case may be, the conferees must see to it that the house they want to act first takes the papers out of the conference.

If conferees cannot agree on any of the amendments before them, or if they cannot agree on all matters encompassed by one house's bill and the other's substitute, they may report back in disagreement. The House and Senate then can seek a resolution of the differences either through a second conference or through an exchange of amendments and motions between the houses. Conferees also may report in total disagreement if they have reached an agreement on a bill and a second chamber substitute which, in some respect, violates their authority. In such a case, their disagreement is technical, not substantive. After the House receives or the Senate agrees to the report in disagreement, the conferees' actual agreement is presented as a floor amendment to the amendment in disagreement, at which point considerations of the conferees' authority no longer apply. Alternatively, the conferees may submit their report to the House and Senate even though it violates their authority in one or more respects, and then, in the House, the Rules Committee can propose and the House can adopt a resolution protecting the report against points of order.

FLOOR CONSIDERATION OF CONFERENCE REPORTS

A conference report may be presented or filed at almost any time the House or Senate is in session, but not when the Senate is in executive session or when the House has resolved into Committee of the Whole. The Senate may consider the report immediately. The House is less likely to do so because of the layover and availability requirements that apply to conference reports under House rules.

In the House, conference reports are subject to a three day "layover" requirement. Clause 8(a) of Rule XXII prohibits consideration of a conference report until the third day (usually excluding weekends and legal holidays) after the report and joint explanatory statement has been available in the *Congressional Record*. These requirements do not apply during the last six days of a session.[26] In addition, copies of the report and the statement must be available for at least two hours before consideration of the report begins. Clause 2(b) applies the same requirements and conditions to amendments reported from conference in disagreement. However, the House may waive these restrictions by adopting a resolution reported from the Rules Committee for that purpose.[27]

A conference report that meets the availability requirements is considered as having been read when called up for consideration in the House. If a report does not meet one or more of the requirements but is called up by unanimous consent, it must be read. However, the House normally agrees by unanimous consent to have the joint explanatory statement read instead of the report, and then it also agrees to dispense with the reading of the statement.

Conference reports are highly privileged in the House, and may be called up at almost any time that another matter is not pending. When called up, the report is considered in the House (not in Committee of the Whole), under the one-hour rule. Clause 8(d) of Rule XXII requires that this hour be equally divided between the majority and minority

---

[26] In contemporary practice, adjournment resolutions usually are not approved until very shortly before the adjournment takes place. This often makes it impossible to know when the "last six days" begin. To achieve the same end, the House may adopt, as the end of the session approaches, a resolution reported from the Rules Committee that triggers certain provisions of House rules and waives others for the duration of the session.

[27] Such a resolution always is in order, notwithstanding the usual requirement that a two-thirds vote is necessary for the House to consider a resolution from the Rules Committee on the same day the resolution is reported.

parties, not necessarily between proponents and opponents. The two floor managers normally explain the agreements reached in conference and then yield time to other Members who wish to speak on the report. If both floor managers support the report, a Member who opposes it is entitled to claim control of one-third of the time for debate. Before a second hour of debate can begin, the majority floor manager moves the previous question. If agreed to, as it invariably is, this motion shuts off further debate and the House immediately votes on agreeing to the conference report.

Any points of order against a conference report in the House must be made or reserved before debate on the report begins (or before the joint explanatory statement is read). A conference report can be protected against one or more points of order if the Rules Committee reports and the House adopts a resolution waiving the applicable rules, or if the report is considered under suspension of the rules.

The Senate has no layover rule governing consideration of conference reports. However, paragraph 1 of Senate Rule XXVIII requires that a conference report must be "available on each Senator's desk" before the Senate may consider it. The report and accompanying statement normally are not printed in the Senate section of the *Record* if they have been printed in the House section. Conference reports also normally are printed only as House documents. Conference reports are privileged in the Senate. The motion to consider a report on the Senate floor is in order at most times,[28] and it is not debatable. The Senate's usual practice is to take up conference reports by unanimous consent at times arranged in advance among the floor and committee leaders. Under a standing order the Senate adopted at the close of the 106th Congress in December 2000, the reading of a conference report no longer is required if the report "is available in the Senate."

When considered on the Senate floor, a conference report is debatable under normal Senate procedures; it is subject to extended debate unless the time for debate is limited by unanimous consent or cloture. Paragraph 5 of Senate Rule XXVIII states that, if time for debating a conference report is limited (presumably by unanimous consent), that time shall be equally divided between the majority and minority parties, not necessarily between proponents and opponents of the report. Consideration of a conference report by the Senate suspends, but does not displace, any pending or unfinished business; after disposition of the report, that business again is before the Senate.

A point of order may be made against a conference report at any time that it is pending on the Senate floor (or after all time for debate has expired or has been yielded back, if the report is considered under a time agreement). The Senate has no procedures for waiving points of order comparable to waivers by special rule in the House. Senate rules do include a procedure for suspending the rules by a two-thirds vote, but this procedure is used very infrequently. However, points of order rarely are made against conference reports on the Senate floor, in part because of the Senate's generous interpretation of its conferees' authority. If a point of order is sustained against a conference report in the Senate, Rule XXVIII provides that "the report shall be recommitted to the committee of conference if the House of Representatives has not already acted thereon."

Conference reports may not be amended on the floor of either house. Conferees are appointed to negotiate over the differences between the versions of the same bill that the two houses have passed; the delegations return to their respective chambers with identical recommendations in the form of a report that proposes a package settlement of all these differences. The House and Senate may accept or reject the settlement but they may not amend it directly. If conference reports were amendable, the process of resolving bicameral differences would be far more tortuous and possibly interminable.

As noted in previous sections, the house that agrees to the request for a conference

---

[28] Several exceptions — for example, while the *Journal* is being read or a quorum call is in progress — are listed in paragraph I of Rule XXVIII.

normally acts first on the report. The first chamber to act may vote to agree or not agree to the report, or it may agree to a preferential motion to recommit the report to conference, with or without non-binding instructions. Successful recommittal motions are quite unusual, in part because such an action implies that the conferees should and could have reached a more desirable compromise. If the first house agrees to the report, the second house only has the options of approving or disapproving the report. At this stage, the report cannot be recommitted. A vote by either house to agree to a conference report has the effect of automatically discharging its conferees and disbanding the conference committee; thus, there is no conference committee to which the second house could recommit the report.

The defeat of a conference report in either house may kill the legislation, but only if no further action is taken, such as requesting a second conference or proposing a new position through an amendment between the houses. For lack of time, a second conference may not be practical near the end of a Congress, when many conference reports are considered.

The vote to agree to a conference report normally completes that house's action on the measure, assuming the other house also approves the report. However, some conference reports, especially those on general appropriations bills, may be accompanied by one or more amendments in either true or technical disagreement. Furthermore, House rules include special procedures for coping with conference report provisions, originating in the Senate, that would not have been germane floor amendments to the bill in the House. These possibilities are discussed in separate sections that follow.

AMENDMENTS IN TRUE DISAGREEMENT

It is generally in the interests of both the House and Senate managers and their parent chambers for the conferees to reach full agreement. Each house already has passed a version of the legislation and has entrusted the responsibility for resolving its differences with the other house to members who usually were actively involved in developing and promoting the measure. Nonetheless, conferees sometimes cannot reach agreement on all the amendments in disagreement. In such a case, the conferees may return to the House and Senate with a partial conference report dealing with the amendments on which they have reached agreement, but excluding one or more amendments that remain in disagreement. The result is complicated and potentially confusing procedural possibilities that, fortunately, do not often arise in current practice . . . .

AMENDMENTS IN TECHNICAL DISAGREEMENT

As discussed in earlier sections of this report, there are important restrictions on the content of conference reports. Conferees may deal only with the matters that are in disagreement between the House and Senate, and they must resolve each of these matters by reaching an agreement that is within the scope of the differences between the House and Senate positions. If a conference report violates these restrictions in any one respect, the entire report is subject to a point of order.[29]

Yet conferees sometimes find it desirable or necessary to exceed their authority. For example, changing circumstances may make it imperative for Congress to appropriate more money for some program than either the House or the Senate initially approved. Or the conferees may decide that a bill should include provisions on a subject that was not included in the version passed by either house. In such cases, the conferees may be able to achieve their purpose, without subjecting their report to a point of order, by

---

[29] As discussed earlier, however, the Senate interprets its rules in a way that gives its conferees considerable latitude, and the House can waive points of order by adopting a special rule for that purpose.

using the device of amendments in disagreement. In doing so, they take advantage of the fact that the restrictions that apply to provisions of conference reports do not govern amendments between the houses.

If the conferees wish to exceed their authority in resolving one of the amendments in disagreement, they can exclude this amendment from the conference report; instead, they present to the House and Senate a partial conference report and an amendment in disagreement. This is called an amendment in technical disagreement. There is no substantive disagreement between the House and Senate conferees; they report the amendment in disagreement only for technical reasons — to avoid the restrictions that apply to conference reports . . . .

SOME CONCLUDING OBSERVATIONS

Describing conference committees as bargaining forums implies an element of competition between the House and Senate. Each house passes its own version of a bill and expects its managers to defend that version in conference. The conferees wish to return to their parent chamber and assert that their report preserves the essential features of their house's version of the bill — that the other body gave more ground in conference.

Which house most often wins in conference? Observers and students of Congress have attempted to answer this question from time to time, using methods ranging from case studies to statistical analyses. Perhaps it is not surprising that the results have been inconsistent and inconclusive. The answer to "Who wins in conference?" depends on the answer to another question: "What do the various participants want to win in conference?" And answering the latter question requires an understanding of Members' motives and intentions that cannot always be discerned accurately from the public record.

If a conference committee accepts the Senate's positions (or relatively minor modifications of them) on three out of every four of the matters in disagreement, has the Senate "won"? There are at least three reasons to be skeptical. First, not all matters in disagreement are of equal significance. The matters on which the House prevailed, though fewer in number, may define and shape the essential character of the legislation; whereas the greater number of matters on which the Senate prevailed may be less important, individually and even collectively, in determining the scope and effect of the legislation.

Second, the conferees from each house almost certainly are not equally committed to defending every element of their chamber's version of the legislation.

One or both houses may include provisions that are bargaining positions, rather than fixed legislative objectives. If one house, for instance, has passed a "weak" version of a bill, the other house may pass a version that is "stronger" than it really wishes or expects to be enacted, in anticipation of conference negotiations that will reach some middle ground.

It also can be tempting for the floor manager of a bill to express no opposition to colleagues' amendments when they are offered on the floor if accepting the amendments will induce their sponsors to vote for the bill without costing the votes of other members. This is a particularly attractive option in the Senate where Senators may offer nongermane amendments on unrelated subjects about which they feel strongly. As a result, the managers can take into conference a number of amendments that they are prepared to trade in return for more substantively important concessions from the other house.

Third, it is a considerable oversimplification to think of each house's delegation to a conference as a single unit or even as a group of individuals with the same goals. It is often said that conferees are to defend the positions of their house. However, all Representatives and Senators have individual legislative goals; each conferee can be

expected to be more concerned about certain provisions in his or her house's version of the bill than about others. And at least some of the conferees usually prefer some of the provisions of the other house's version. In short, as each decision is made in conference, some conferees from each house win, and others lose.

NOTES AND QUESTIONS

1. What weight should an interpreter of a statute give the following matters:

a) evidence from committee reports or floor debate that the language of the statute is "deliberately ambiguous."

b) comparison of the text of an amendment passed by one house with the text of the unamended measure passed by the other body.

c) comparison of the text of a Senate amendment with the text of a House amendment to which the Senate concurs.

d) instructions to House conferees.

e) "side by side" comparisons of House and Senate versions prepared by staff.

f) the conference report.

g) the joint explanatory statement.

h) a provision in the Senate bill omitted in the conference report.

2. What weight should an interpreter of a statute give to following matters:

a) an explanation of House amendments to a Senate bill given by the Senate majority leader.

b) an explanation of Senate amendments to a House bill given by the chair of the House committee of jurisdiction.

c) floor debate in the Senate by a non-member of the committee that reported the measure concerning instructions to the Senate conferees.

d) a colloquy between the two floor managers in the House explaining the agreement reached in conference concerning a particular provision in the bill.

e) statements in floor debate by a Member opposing the report concerning a particular provision in the bill.

3. For further information, see, generally, LAWRENCE D. LONGLEY & WALTER J. OLESZEK, BICAMERAL POLITICS: CONFERENCE COMMITTEE IN CONGRESS (1989); Wayne L. Francis, *Floor Procedures and Conference Committees in State Legislatures, in* JOEL H. SIBLEY, ED., 2 ENCYCLOPEDIA OF THE AMERICAN LEGISLATIVE SYSTEM 721–30 (1994).

K. ENROLLMENT

ROBERT B. DOVE,
ENACTMENT OF A LAW 24 (n.d.)

When the two Houses reach a complete agreement . . . the papers are delivered to the Enrolling Clerk of the House where the bill originated. The Enrolling Clerk prepares a copy of the bill in the form as finally agreed upon by the two Houses and sends it to the Government Printing Office for "enrollment," which means historically "written on parchment." The original papers of the bill are retained in the files of the originating House until the end of a Congress, when they are sent to the National Archives.

Upon receipt of an enrolled bill from the Government Printing Office, either the Secretary of the Senate or the Clerk of the House endorses it, certifying where the bill originated.

CHARLES W. JOHNSON,
HOW OUR LAWS ARE MADE
50–51 (2003)

The preparation of the enrolled bill is a painstaking and important task because it must reflect precisely the effect of all amendments, either by way of deletion, substitution, or addition, agreed to by both bodies. The enrolling clerk of the House, with respect to bills originating in the House, receives the original engrossed bill, the engrossed Senate amendments, the signed conference report, the several messages from the Senate, and a notation of the final action by the House, for the purpose of preparing the enrolled copy. From these documents, the enrolling clerk must meticulously prepare for presentation to the President the final form of the bill as it was agreed to by both Houses. On occasion, as many as 500 amendments have been adopted, each of which must be set out in the enrollment exactly as agreed to, and all punctuation must be in accord with the action taken.

The enrolled bill is printed on parchment paper and certified by the Clerk of the House stating that the bill originated in the House of Representatives. A bill originating in the Senate is examined and certified by the Secretary of the Senate. A House bill is then examined for accuracy by the Clerk. When he is satisfied with the accuracy of the bill, he attaches a slip stating that it finds the bill truly enrolled and sends it to the Speaker of the House for signature. All bills, regardless of the body in which they originated, are signed first by the Speaker and then by the Vice President of the United States, who, under the Constitution, serves as the President of the Senate. The President pro tempore of the Senate may also sign enrolled bills. The Speaker of the House may sign enrolled bills whether or not the House is in session. The President of the Senate may sign bills only while the Senate is actually sitting but advance permission is normally granted to sign during a recess or after adjournment. If the Speaker or the President of the Senate is unable to sign the bill, it may be signed by an authorized Member of the respective House. After both signatures are affixed, a House bill is returned to the Clerk for presentation to the President for action under the Constitution. A Senate bill is presented to the President by the Secretary of the Senate.

ROBERT B. DOVE,
ENACTMENT OF A LAW 24–25 (n.d.)

An error discovered in a bill after the legislative steps in its passage have been completed may be corrected by authority of a concurrent resolution, provided the bill has not yet been approved by the President. If the bill has not been enrolled, the error may be corrected in the enrollment; if it has been enrolled and signed by the Presiding Officers of the two Houses, or by the Speaker, such action may be rescinded by a concurrent resolution agreed to by the two Houses, and the bill correctly re-enrolled if it has been presented to the President, but not acted upon by him, he may be requested by a concurrent resolution to return it to the Senate or the House for correction. If, however, the President has approved the bill, and it has thereby become a law, any amendment thereof can only be made by the passage of another bill, which must take the same course as the original.

The juridical force attributed to an enrolled bill will be explored at the end of Section L. of this chapter and in Chapter 4.

L. PUBLICATION

CHARLES W. JOHNSON,
HOW OUR LAWS ARE MADE
53–55 (2003)

One of the important steps in the enactment of a valid law is the requirement that it shall be made known to the people who are to be bound by it. There would be no justice if the state were to hold its people responsible for their conduct before it made known to them the unlawfulness of such behavior. In practice, our laws are published immediately upon their enactment so that the public will be aware of them.

If the President approves a bill, or allows it to become law without signing it, the original enrolled bill is sent from the White House to the Archivist of the United States for publication. If a bill is passed by both Houses over the objections of the President, the body that last overrides the veto transmits it. It is then assigned a public law number, and paginated for the Statutes at Large volume covering that session of Congress. The public and private law numbers run in sequence starting anew at the beginning of each Congress and are prefixed for ready identification by the number of the Congress. For example, the first public law of the 108th Congress is designated Public Law 108-1 and the first private law of the 108th Congress is designated Private Law 108-1. Subsequent laws of this Congress also will contain the same prefix designator.

SLIP LAWS

The first official publication of the statute is in the form generally known as the "slip law". In this form, each law is published separately as an unbound pamphlet. The heading indicates the public and private law number, the date of approval, and the bill number. The heading of the slip law for a public law also indicates the United States Statutes at Large citation. If the statute has been passed over the veto of the President, or has become law without the President's signature because he did not return it with objections, an appropriate statement is inserted instead of the usual notation of approval.

The Office of the Federal Register, National Archives and Records Administration prepares the slip laws and provides marginal editorial notes giving the citations to laws mentioned in the text and other explanatory details. The marginal notes also give the United States Code classifications, enabling the reader immediately to determine where the statute will appear in the Code. Each slip law also includes an informative guide to the legislative history of the law consisting of the committee report number, the name of the committee in each House, as well as the date of consideration and passage in each House, with a reference to the Congressional Record by volume, year, and date. A reference to presidential statements relating to the approval of a bill or the veto of a bill when the veto was overridden and the bill becomes law is included in the legislative history as a citation to the Weekly Compilation of Presidential Documents.

Copies of the slip laws are delivered to the document rooms of both Houses where they are available to officials and the public. They may also be obtained by annual subscription or individual purchase from the Government Printing Office and are available in electronic form. Section 113 of title I of the United States Code provides that slip laws are competent evidence in all the federal and state courts, tribunals, and public offices.

STATUTES AT LARGE

The United States Statutes at Large, prepared by the Office of the Federal Register, National Archives and Records Administration, provide a permanent collection of the laws of each session of Congress in bound volumes. The latest volume containing the laws of the first session of the 107th Congress is number 116 in the series. Each volume contains a complete index and a table of contents. A legislative history appears at the end of each law. There are also extensive marginal notes referring to laws in earlier volumes and to earlier and later matters in the same volume.

Under the provisions of a statute originally enacted in 1895, these volumes are legal evidence of the laws contained in them and will be accepted as proof of those laws in any court in the United States.

The Statutes at Large are a chronological arrangement of the laws exactly as they have been enacted. The laws are not arranged according to subject matter and do not reflect the present status of an earlier law that has been amended. The laws are organized in that manner in the code of laws.

UNITED STATES CODE

The United States Code contains a consolidation and codification of the general and permanent laws of the United States arranged according to subject matter under 50 title headings, largely in alphabetical order. It sets out the current status of the laws, as amended, without repeating all the language of the amendatory acts except where necessary. The Code is declared to be prima facie evidence of those laws. Its purpose is to present the laws in a concise and usable form without requiring recourse to the many volumes of the Statutes at Large containing the individual amendments.

The Code is prepared by the Law Revision Counsel of the House of Representatives. New editions are published every six years and cumulative supplements are published after the conclusion of each regular session of the Congress. The Code is also available in electronic format on CD-ROM and the Internet.

Twenty-four of the 50 titles have been revised and enacted into positive law, and one title has been eliminated by consolidation with another title. Titles that have been revised and enacted into positive law are legal evidence of the law and may be updated by direct amendment. Eventually all the titles will be revised and enacted into positive law.

NOTES AND QUESTIONS

1. The U.S. Congress has not passed a complete statement of general and permanent law repealing all prior law since 1873. TOBIAS A. DORSEY, LEGISLATIVE DRAFTER'S HANDBOOK 52 (2006). By way of contrast, some state legislatures enact a revision or codification of statute law providing "a well organized and clarified statement of the complete body of the effective legislation of the state" after every session the legislature. Jefferson B. Fordham & Carroll C. Moreland, *Pennsylvania's Statutory Imbroglio: The Need of Statutory Law Revision*, 108 U. PA. L. REV. 1093, 1094 (1960).

And so, whereas an Ohio lawyer or legislative drafter can rely on the Ohio Revised Code as conclusive evidence of the law in force, a practitioner seeking to establish the authoritative text of a Federal statute may have to resolve conflicts among published versions of the law. DORSEY, *supra* at 55–56.

2. The U.S. Code stipulates the relative authority of official publications.

A slip law is "competent" evidence of the law. 1 U.S.C. § 113. The U.S. Code is "prima facie" evidence of the law as to unrevised titles of the code. 1 U.S.C. § 204. The Statutes at Large is legal evidence of the law. 1 U.S.C. § 112. Any conflict between the Statutes at Large and the U.S. Code is resolved in favor of the former. *See Stephan v. United States*, 319 U.S. 423 (1943); *United States National Bank of Oregon v. Independent Insurance Agents*, 508 U.S. 439 (1993).

What if there is a discrepancy between the Statutes at Large and the enrolled bill? *Field v. Clark*, 143 U.S. 649 (1891), gives controlling force to the enrolled bill. Why?

3. What if there is a discrepancy between the enrolled bill and the text presented to the chief executive for approval? *Compare People ex rel. Dezettel v. Lueders*, 283 Ill. 287, 119 N.E. 339 (1918), *with Rice v. Lonoke-Cabot Road Improvement District*, 142 Ark. 454, 221 S.W. 179 (1920). What are the policy arguments for and against invalidating the statute?

Chapter 4
DUE PROCESS OF LAWMAKING

INTRODUCTION

Legislative process and procedure play a significant role in the day to day activities of national, state, and local legislative bodies. When we think of the notion of procedural due process, however, we do not normally have in mind restraints that apply to the decision making processes of legislative bodies. Indeed, it is settled law that the trappings of procedural due process, e.g., notice and an opportunity to be heard, are inapplicable to "legislative" decisions. As Justice Holmes expressed the matter in the leading case:

> Where a rule of conduct applies to more than a few people it is impracticable that every one should have a direct voice in its adoption. The Constitution does not require all public acts to be done in town meeting or assembly of the whole. General statutes within the state power are passed that affect the person or property of individuals, sometimes to the point of ruin, without giving them a chance to be heard. Their rights are protected in the only way that they can be in a complex society, by their power, immediate or remote, over those who make the rule.

Bi-Metallic Investment Co. v. State Board of Equalization, 239 U.S. 441, 445–46 (1915).

This chapter has to do with federal and state constitutional provisions that structure and condition the framework within which the legislature performs its constitutional functions. These materials are gathered together under the heading "due process of lawmaking." *See generally* Hans A. Linde, *Due Process of Law Making*, 55 NEB. L. REV. 197 (1976). We have done so in order to draw attention to the extent to which legislatures are designed to be rule-bound and rule-oriented institutions of governance.

A key feature in the evolution of state legislatures is the entrenchment in state constitutions of rules of legislative practice and procedure. The purpose of these provisions is clear in light of their history. In early state constitutions, the legislature is typically afforded broad autonomy: "The Senate shall . . . determine its own rules of proceedings"; "The House of Representatives shall . . . settle the rules and orders of proceeding in their own house." Despite such language, the incorporation of rules of parliamentary law into the constitution began early on. This tendency is illustrated by the constitutional history of Pennsylvania. The earliest Pennsylvania Constitution, the "radical" constitution of 1776, contained several provisions designed to assure openness, deliberation, and accountability in governance by the unicameral legislature: a two-thirds quorum requirement for doing business, a provision calling for open sessions, weekly printing of votes and proceedings during session including recording "the yeas and nays on any question, vote or resolution where any two members require it"; and a provision requiring a formal enacting clause for all laws.

The distrust of the legislature, seen by Jacksonian democrats as an engine for churning out special privileges for interest groups, produced a wave of constitution making in half of the states between 1845 and 1855. These reformers created "a blueprint for the due process of deliberative, democratically accountable government."

These process reforms continued through the period 1864–1879, during which thirty-seven states wrote and ratified new constitutions. As G. Alan Tarr summarized these developments:

> In 1835 Alexis de Tocqueville observed that "the legislature of each state is faced by no power capable of resisting it." But beginning in the 1830s, state constitution makers sought to impose limits on these supreme legislatures. Initially, their restrictions focused on the process of legislation. Some state constitutions required extraordinary majorities to adopt certain types of

legislation, under the assumption that it would be more difficult to marshal such majorities for dubious endeavors. Others imposed procedural restrictions designed to prevent duplicity and promote greater openness and deliberation, assuming that greater transparency in the legislative process would deter legislative abuses or at least increase accountability for them. Thus, state constitutions mandated that all bills be referred to the committee, that they be read three times prior to enactment, that their titles accurately describe their contents, that they embrace a single subject, that they not be altered during their passage so as to change their original purpose, and so on. Other provisions required that the amendment or revision of laws not proceed by mere reference to their titles, that statutes be phrased in plain language, that taxing and spending measures be enacted only by recorded vote, and, most importantly, that no special laws be enacted where general law was possible. By the end of the nineteenth century, most state constitutions included several of these procedural requirements.

G. Alan Tarr, Understanding State Constitutions 118–19 (1998).

Most state constitutions, therefore, do not follow the Federal model, which has little to say about lawmaking procedures.[1] Instead, like Pennsylvania, they incorporate most of the procedural norms that emerged during the nineteenth century. At the drafting phase, each bill must contain a title that "clearly expresses" the subject matter of the body of the proposed law. In addition to the notice function of the title, each bill, except appropriations, is restricted to "one subject" in order to forestall logrolling and to focus the legislature's attention on discrete policy issues. Values of notice and clarity are furthered by the rule that bills that amend or cross-reference existing laws must include the amended or referenced legislation in their text. Particular rules apply to drafting appropriations measures to ensure notice and bar logrolling.

Constitutional rules were designed to fix accountability and to enhance participation and deliberation. The state house is directly accountable for originating revenue bills. The committee system is recognized and strengthened by the requirement that all bills be referred to a committee and printed. To prevent surprise and foster public notice, no bill could be altered or amended on its passage through either chamber so as to change its original purpose, and every bill must be read at length and printed before the final vote. Principles of accountability and majority rule are embedded in the requirement that a majority of each chamber cast a recorded vote on every bill, and that the presiding officer of each chamber authenticate by signature the fact that the measure was approved, and the fact of signing must be entered in the journal.

Procedural constraints on the state legislature modify both the plenary-power principle and the specific constitutional text granting the legislature the power to determine its rules and proceedings. Procedural constraints seem to embody a historical and retrospective approach to state constitution making by entrenching the results of yesteryear's controversies. Alternatively, one can view procedural constraints as a collective effort by the people of the several states over a period of two centuries to entrench principles of notice, deliberation, and accountability into the legislative process by stipulating rules of due process for legislative bodies.

In many states, judges have refused to enforce all but a few of these procedural constraints. That is because a number of state courts adhere to the *"enrolled bill" rule*, which prevents any evidence outside the text of the enrolled bill itself from being introduced as evidence showing constitutional violations of rules governing the process

---

[1] *But see* Adrian Vermeule, *The Constitutional Law of Congressional Procedure*, 71 U. Chi. L. Rev. 361 (2004); Aaron-Andrew P. Bruhl, *Using Statutes to Set Legislative Rules: Entrenchment, Separation of Powers, and the Rules of Proceedings Clause*, 19 J.L. & Pol. 345 (2003); John C. Roberts, *Are Congressional Committees Constitutional?: Radical Textualism, Separation of Powers, and the Enactment Process*, 52 Case West. Res. L. Rev. 489 (2001).

of enactment. Thus, rules concerning drafting such as the single subject and clear title rules are reviewable, because a violation can be determined from the text of the enactment. But violations of majority vote, referral to committee, printing and reading, limited session, no alteration of original purpose, and similar procedural rules are unchallengeable in a jurisdiction adhering to the enrolled bill rule. The pros and cons of the enrolled bill rule as well as various modifications and exceptions to that rule all share the same policy vice — state courts, not constitution makers, are making fundamental decisions about the enforceability of constitutional norms. Even without the enrolled bill rule, a state court can refuse to enforce procedural rules by holding that judicial intervention violates separation of powers doctrine.

This section explores the application and enforcement of these types of constitutional legislative procedure provisions.

A. DRAFTING STATUTES — FORM, NOTICE, AND CLARITY AS CONSTITUTIONALLY MANDATED POLICIES

1. Creating and Terminating Statute Law

a. Bill or Resolution

SCUDDER v. SMITH
200 A. 601 (Pa. 1938)

Opinion by Mr. Justice Maxey.

Two taxpayers bills were filed in the Dauphin County Court . . . against Ralph H. Smith, E.J. Thompson, Michael C. Chervenck, Jr., John E. McCone and William H. Godfrey, who were appointed to act as a commission to investigate the lubricating oil and gasoline business of the Commonwealth of Pennsylvania, and against the Auditor General and the State Treasurer of the Commonwealth. The complaint was directed against a joint resolution approved April 29, 1937, P.L. 540, which purported to create a commission to investigate the oil industry in Pennsylvania, and against an amending act, called No. 545, approved July 2, 1937, P.L. 2704. The prayer of both bills was for a decree: (a) restraining the defendants purporting to act as a commission under this legislation from contracting or attempting to contract any debts on the part of the Commonwealth; (b) restraining the defendants, the Auditor General and the State Treasurer, from approving for payment any bills, and from paying out of the treasury of the Commonwealth any sums purported to be appropriated by this joint resolution and the amending act; and (c) restraining the defendants purporting to act as a commission from taking any proceedings whatsoever pursuant to the authority conferred upon them by the said joint resolution and the amending act.

The facts set forth in the bills are as follows: The legislature of Pennsylvania, in its regular session in 1937 approved, what it designated, "A Joint Resolution," which purported to create a commission to investigate the "operation of the oil industry in this Commonwealth with special reference to the adequate, efficient and mechanical supplying of lubricating oils and materials to the people of this Commonwealth; conferring upon the commission full power to issue subpoenas, requiring the commission to make a report of its findings to the Governor together with its recommendations as to such regulating legislation . . . ; authorizing the commission to employ counsel and employees; and making an appropriation" of $5,000. The amending act increased the appropriation to $50,000, and provided the procedure and punishment of persons refusing to comply with the Commission's subpoena.

The first question posed is: What is a legislative "Joint Resolution?" Is it a "law" within the meaning of section 1 of Article III of the Constitution of Pennsylvania, or is it what the legislature itself denominated it, "A Joint Resolution," a form of legislative expression recognized in section 26 of this same Article?

The legislative measure here is designated "A Joint Resolution." Section 1 of this legislation begins, "Be it resolved, etc." The amendatory Act No. 545, enacted two months later by this same legislature, showed no intention to treat these words as carelessly chosen, because it refers to it as *"the joint resolution* approved the 29th day of April, 1937, . . . " (italics supplied) and reiterates in at least three other places in this amendatory act that it is "a joint resolution." The legal phraseology designating the passage of a law by *bill* uniformly has been "Be it enacted, etc.," the same phraseology this Assembly so deliberately used in the enactment of the amendatory Act No. 545. That this was intended to be a joint resolution by the Assembly we have no doubt. Here was an express declaration of the intent of the legislature to "resolve" and not to "enact."

Section 1 of Article III of the Constitution provides: "No law shall be passed except by Bill, and no Bill shall be so altered or amended on its passage through either House as to change its original purpose." In the *Southwark Bank v. The Commonwealth*, 26 Pa. 446, 450, this court said: "A bill is the draft or form of an act presented to the legislature, but not enacted. An 'act' is the appropriate term for it after it has been acted on by, and passed, the legislature. It is then something more than a draft or form. It has a legal existence as 'an act' of the legislative body, because it becomes a law, without further action from any other branch of the government, if the executive take no measures to prevent it." A "Bill" has been defined to be "a form or draft of a law presented to a legislature for enactment": Webster's New International Dictionary. A "Joint Resolution" has been defined by the same authority to be "A resolution adopted jointly by the two branches of a legislative body." A "resolution" by the same authority has been defined as "A formal expression of the opinion or will of an official body or a public assembly, adopted by vote; as a legislative resolution." When the Constitution provided that "no law shall be passed except by bill," it meant by "a form or draft of a law submitted to the legislature for enactment"; it did not recognize a mere "formal expression of opinion" as adequate to the *creation of a law*. The fact that the joint resolution went through the *mode of passage* prescribed by the Constitution for bills, does not supply the constitutional deficiencies of its conception. The purpose of the constitutional requirements relating to the enactment of *laws* was to put the members of the Assembly and *others interested, on notice*, by the title of the measure submitted, so that they might vote on it with circumspection. What was attempted to be done by the sponsors of this challenged measure was something utterly alien to the proper subject matter of a "joint resolution." Its deceptive nomenclature is fatal to its validity as a *law*.

This "joint resolution" first purports to create a Commission to investigate the oil industry in Pennsylvania. It confers certain authority upon this Commission, giving it unlimited inquisitorial power by the process of subpoena *upon any person*. It subjects such person in the event of wilful neglect or refusal to testify or produce books, records, papers or documents, "to the penalties provided by the Laws of the Commonwealth in such cases." By Section 4, it contains an appropriation which is to be used to pay the Commission's expenses. The subject matter of this joint resolution is legislative in its nature. It is not a mere formal expression of legislative opinion. Fatal to the Attorney General's contention that this legislative expression is a law, is Article III, Section 1 of our Constitution, which declares that "no law shall be passed except by bill." Clearly the requirements of Section 15 of the same Article that "all appropriations must be passed by bill" cannot be construed to mean that appropriations can be passed by joint resolution as in this case. This "joint resolution" was not a bill and its adoption by the legislature and approval by the Governor did not make it a *law* . . . .

NOTES AND QUESTIONS

1. Why do state taxpayers have standing to challenge the investigating commission's actions? Under similar circumstances federal taxpayers would not. *See* Comment, *Taxpayers' Suits: Statutory Barriers and Pecuniary Constraints*, 59 TEMP. L.Q. 951 (1986).

2. Doesn't the court's decision exalt form over function? If the joint resolution was treated with all the procedural niceties which are constitutionally required by a bill, shouldn't the joint resolution be seen as the functional equivalent of a bill? *See State ex rel. Brewster v. Knapp*, 102 Kan. 701, 171 P. 639 (1918).

3. The federal Constitution, Article I, Section 7, Clause 3 provides as follows:

> Every order, resolution, or vote to which the Concurrence of the Senate and House of Representatives may be necessary . . . shall be presented to the President of the United States: and before the same shall take effect, shall be approved by him or being disapproved by him, shall be repassed by two thirds of the Senate and the House of Representatives, according to the rules and limitations prescribed in the case of a bill.

Are joint resolutions a permissible form of making federal law?

4. In *Moran v. La Guardia*, 1 N.E.2d 961 (N.Y. 1936), the New York Court of Appeals held that an existing law could not be *repealed* by a joint resolution, but would require a bill, properly enacted:

MORAN v. LA GUARDIA
270 N.Y. 450, 1 N.E.2d 961 (1936)

FINCH, J. This is an appeal from an order denying a peremptory mandamus order directed to the authorities of the city of New York commanding them in effect to restore salaries to the pre-emergency level.

The Appellate Division affirmed the denial and gave leave to appeal to this court.

The question arises through the application of a patrolman to compel restoration of his salary to $3,000 per annum, less his pension deductions, whereas at the present time he is receiving $2,810, less the pension deductions.

The patrolman contends that the salary paid him should be the mandatory amount imposed upon the city in accordance with an act of the Legislature (Laws of 1929, ch. 202) following a referendum. The city contends, on the other hand, that the Legislature, by law enacted (Laws of 1982, ch. 637) permitted the city to reduce these salaries and that this later law is still in force. Section 1 of this so-called economy act declared that a temporary emergency existed requiring its enactment and that its provisions are to apply "until the legislature shall find their further operation unnecessary."

At first the Legislature passed a bill to repeal this law which was vetoed by the Governor. Next the Legislature sought to accomplish the same result by means of a joint resolution.

The sole question thus presented by this proceeding is whether the Legislature can terminate this economy legislation by concurrent resolution or whether for such termination there is required a legislative enactment. The answer to that question depends upon the construction to be given to the words "until the legislature shall find their further operation unnecessary."

A concurrent resolution of the Legislature is not effective to modify or repeal a statutory enactment. (*Matter of Leach*, 115 Misc. Rep. 660; *aff'd.*, 197 App. Div. 702; *aff'd.*, 232 N.Y. 600) To repeal or modify a stature requires a legislative act of equal dignity and import. Nothing less than another statute will suffice. A concurrent resolution of the two houses is not a statute. (*People ex rel. Argus Co. v. Palmer*, 12

Misc. Rep. 392; *aff'd*, 146 N.Y. 406) A concurrent resolution, unlike a statute, is binding only on the members and officers of the legislative body. It resembles a statute neither in its mode of passage nor in its consequences. The form of a bill is lacking and readings are not required. It does not have to lie on the desks of members of the Legislature for three legislative days. (N.Y. Const., art. III § 15.) But more important, its adoption is complete without the concurrent action of the Governor, or lacking this, passage by a two-thirds vote of each house of the Legislature over his veto. Thus a joint resolution may be adopted by a mere majority of the Legislature without action by the Governor or notice to the public, whereas the enactment of a statute requires action by three distinct bodies and at least three days' notice to the public. As has been well said: "In the exercise of this vast power, [of the Legislature] according to the fundamental idea and constitution of parliament, the concurrence of the three distinct bodies of which it is composed, each acting by itself, and independent of the others, is necessary. No two of them acting together, much less one alone, can make a law." (Cushing on Elements of the Law and Practice of Legislative Assemblies in the United States, § 707; *People v. Bowen*, 21 N.Y. 517)

In addition to the objection that in general a concurrent resolution may not repeal a statute duly enacted we have here also as a part of this economy law precise language which negatives the contention of petitioner. As noted the economy bill itself provided for its continued operation until the Legislature should find it unnecessary. Ordinarily when we contemplate action by the Legislature we have in mind a statutory enactment. Before we hold that a statute may be terminated or repealed by some act other than a repealing statute we must at least find a clearly expressed provision to that effect embodied in the law thus to be terminated.

In *Matter of Koenig v. Flynn* (258 N.Y. 292; *aff'd*, 285 U.S. 375) it was held that action by the Legislature meant action by both houses and the Governor. The language involved was "shall be prescribed in each State by the Legislature thereof." (U.S. Const. Art. I, § 4.) There is striking similarity between the terms "prescribed . . . by the Legislature" and the terms of the statute in the case at bar " . . . until the legislature shall find . . . ."

The conclusion at which we have arrived is strengthened also by noting that when the Legislature wished to provide for the termination of an emergency by joint resolution it has so expressly stated. In the legislation concerning the Insurance and Banking Laws of 1933 the provisions were as follows: "The period of the emergency herein provided for shall be from the date of the taking effect of this act until such date as the legislature may, by joint resolution, designate to be the termination thereof, or, if the legislature be not in session, the date so designated by a proclamation of the governor." (Chs. 40, 41.)

The divergence in the language used in the above statute as compared with the language used in the statute in the case at bar refutes the contention of the petitioner. The express language providing for the termination of that statute by joint resolution negatives a finding that the same result should be reached in the case at bar by implication after disregarding the ordinary meaning of the language used.

Not only reason but authority demonstrate that the joint resolution upon which is based the application of petitioner does not constitute action by the Legislature and cannot result in the repeal of the so-called economy bill.

It follows that the order appealed from should be affirmed, with costs.

CROUCH, J. (dissenting).

Gathering wisdom or at least technique from an abundance of experience in emergency legislation, the Legislature in enacting chapters 40 and 41 of the Laws of 1933, relating to the powers of the Superintendent of Insurance and of the Banking Board, provided that the period of emergency with which it was then concerned should continue "until such date as the legislature may, by joint resolution, designate to be the terminate thereof." There can be no question that those statutes would be put an end to by the passage of a joint or concurrent resolution.

When the economy act was passed in 1932 (Laws of 1932, ch. 637), the Legislature realized that it was making a law which could be constitutionally justified only by the continued existence of a certain state of facts. (*Cf.* NY. Const., art XII, § 2; *Chastleton Corp. v. Sinclair*, 264 U.S. 543; *Home Building & Loan Assn. v. Blaisdell*, 290 U.S. 398, 442.) It deemed that such a state of facts then existed. It could not foresee how long it would continue to exist. It, therefore, provided at the very outset of the statute as follows:

> "Section 1. It is hereby declared that a temporary emergency exists requiring the enactment of the following provisions, and their application *until the legislature shall find their further operation unnecessary.*"

The question here is a very simple one. Read in the light of the circumstances under which the statute was enacted, did the language used disclose a legislative intent that its provisions should continue to apply until the law was repealed by another law, or until the Legislature, in its fact-finding capacity, should "find" that they were no longer necessary? If termination by a repealing law was intended, the words used are singularly inappropriate and the provision itself is superfluous. The Legislature in its law-making capacity had the power, without any reservation, to pass a repealing statute at any time. The only possible purpose of the provision was to enable the Legislature, by a fact-finding embodied in a joint resolution, to put an end to the act when, in its judgment, the justifying emergency had passed. If the language used here is less sophisticated, it is no less clear in meaning than the language used to the same end in later statutes.

The order appealed from should be reversed.

NOTES AND QUESTIONS

1. If the New York state constitution flatly prohibits repeal of a statute by a joint resolution, why does the court qualify its holding by saying that "before we hold that a statute may be terminated or repealed by some act other than a repealing statute we must at least find a clearly expressed provision to that effect embodied in the law thus to be terminated"?

2. Of what conceivable relevance is the court's reference to the Insurance and Banking Laws as an aid to interpreting a statute having to do with reducing the salaries of city employees?

3. Isn't the dissent correct when it interprets the legislation in question as conditional upon the existence of a temporary emergency? Justice Crouch sees the statute as taking the form "if a then b," that is, if there is an economic emergency, then the city is authorized to reduce salaries. When the legislature declares that there is no longer an emergency, the factual predicate for the conditional law disappears, suspending its operation until the legislature renews its finding.

4. Should the court take into account the fact that this joint resolution was passed when the state legislature failed to override the governor's veto of a repealing statute?

5. See, generally, Jacob E. Gersen, *Temporary Legislation*, 74 U. Chi. L. Rev. 247 (2007).

b.   Legislative Procedure Requirements

The following is an example of part of an act showing the title, an enacting clause, a short title provision, and a definitions section:

1973 REGULAR SESSION
SUBSTANCE ABUSE SERVICES ACT
PUBLIC ACT NO. 56
SENATE BILL NO. 568

AN ACT to create the office of substance abuse services; to prescribe powers and duties; to create an advisory commission; to create a committee; to provide prevention, treatment and rehabilitation services for individuals dependent upon or abusing alcohol or drugs; to provide for coordinating agencies and local advisory councils; to provide for the licensure of approved treatment-rehabilitation and prevention programs; to provide for the confidentiality of certain records; to abolish certain agencies and boards; and to repeal certain acts and parts of acts.

The People of the State of Michigan enact:

M.C.L.A. § 325.711

Sec. 1. This act shall be known and may be cited as the "substance abuse services act".

M.C.L.A. § 325.712

Sec. 2. As used in this act:

(a) "Administrator" means the administrator of the office of substance abuse services.

(b) "Commission" means the advisory commission on substance abuse services as created in section 7.

(c) "Director" means the director of the department of public health.

(d) "Department" means the department of public health.

(e) "Office" means the office of substance abuse services as created in section 3.

(f) "Substance abuse" means the taking of alcohol or drugs at dose level that place an individual's social, economic, psychological and physical welfare in potential hazard . . . .

The federal enacting clause provision, 1 U.S.C. § 101, is as follows:

§ 101. Enacting clause

The enacting clause of all Acts of Congress shall be in the following form: "Be it enacted by the Senate and House of Representatives of the United States of America in Congress assembled."

On numerous occasions, an otherwise valid law has been struck down because of noncompliance with the enacting clause requirement. *See, e.g., Vaughn & Ragsdale Co. v. State Bd. of Equalization*, 109 Mont. 52, 96 P.2d 420 (1939); *People v. Dettenthaler*, 118 Mich. 595, 77 N.W. 450 (1898). As demonstrated above by the constitutional provisions and statutes, the clause lends little or nothing of substance to the act in question. What policies underlie this formalism?

The Supreme Court of Georgia invalidated an amendment to an existing act because of the lack of an enacting clause in the amendatory act. In holding that the prior act remained unchanged, the court discussed the effect of such an omission:

On March 30, 1967 the Governor approved what is termed the "Appellate Practice Act of 1965 Amended. No. 114 (House Bill No. 157)." Section 3 thereof states, in part, "An appeal shall not be dismissed nor consideration thereof refused because of failure of the court reporter to file the transcript of evidence and proceedings within the time allowed by law or order of court, unless it affirmatively appears from the record that such failure was caused by the appellant." This purported amendment contains no enacting clause and the question arises whether this omission invalidates this purported amendment so that the Appellate Practice Act of 1965 as previously amended remains unchanged by it.

A study of this question reveals that, "All written laws, in all times and in all countries, whether in the form of decrees issued by absolute monarchs, or statutes enacted by king and council, or by a representative body, have, as a rule, expressed upon their face the authority by which they were promulgated or enacted. The almost unbroken custom of centuries has been to preface laws with a statement in some form declaring the enacting authority." *Sjoberg v. Security Sav. Etc. Assn.*, 73 Minn. 203, 75 N.W. 1116, 72 Am. St. Rep. 616; 50 Am. Jur. 132, § 153. It is interesting to note that the use of an enacting clause first appeared in the Acts of Parliament in 1433 and from the year 1445 it has continued to be a regular part of English statutes. HOLDSWORTH, "A HISTORY OF ENGLISH LAW" (1909), Vol. II, p. 366. "The enacting clause is that portion of a statute which gives it jurisdictional identity and constitutional authenticity. The form is almost completely standardized beginning with, 'Be it enacted by,' and concluding with an identification of the legislative body from which the act emanates. The constitutions of forty-four [now 46] states specify the form of the enacting clause. Only the constitutions of Delaware, Georgia, Pennsylvania, and Virginia, as well as the Constitution of the United States, are silent on the point . . . [and] Congress, by statute [Act of Feb. 25, 1871, c. 71, 16 Stat. 431, 1 U.S.C.A. § 21] has provided a specific form of enacting clause." Sutherland on Statutory Construction (3rd Ed. 1943), vol. 1, p. 315, § 1801.

"The purpose of an enacting clause is to establish the act; to give it permanence, uniformity and certainty; to afford evidence of its legislative, statutory nature, and to secure uniformity of identification, and thus prevent inadvertence, possible mistake, and fraud." 82 C.J.S. Statutes § 65c (2), p. 104. See *Coley v. Henry*, 42 Ga. 61. Although it might be argued that an enacting clause is a mere matter of form, a relic of antiquity, and serves no useful purpose, we think it is essential for the reasons just cited. Traditionally, the General Assembly of Georgia has used an enacting clause.

Joiner v. State, 223 Ga. 367, 155 S.E.2d 8 (1967).

NOTES AND QUESTIONS

1. Does the court's insistence on the use of an enacting clause necessarily advance the purposes it cites? Do authenticating procedures adequately serve such purposes?

2. Could removal or amendment of a bill's enacting clause be used as a tactical weapon by its opponents?

3. Should there by any difference between the validity of a law with a defective enacting clause and a law without a clause altogether? *See* SUTHERLAND, STATUTORY CONSTRUCTION Vol. 1A, § 19.03 (4th ed. 1985).

4. The Georgia Constitution does not require an enacting clause. Doesn't the court's decision impose an unwarranted extraconstitutional restraint on the legislature's ability to make policy in whatever form it chooses?

c.   Subject — Title, and Related Procedure Provisions

PENNSYLVANIANS AGAINST GAMBLING EXPANSION FUND, INC.
v. COMMONWEALTH
877 A.2d 383 (Pa. 2005)

CHIEF JUSTICE CAPPY.

In this matter, we are asked to resolve, *inter alia*, numerous facial constitutional challenges to the regularity of the procedures employed by the General Assembly in enacting Act 2004-71, The Pennsylvania Race Horse Development and Gaming Act (the "Gaming Act" or the "Act"). 4 Pa.C.S. § 1101 *et seq.* . . . For the reasons that follow, we sustain the Gaming Act, with the exception of certain collateral provisions which can be stricken in light of the Gaming Act's severability provision.

At the outset, it is important to make clear that we are neither passing on the wisdom of the substantive provisions of this Act nor on whether gaming in general is in the best interests of the citizens of our Commonwealth. These decisions are for the General Assembly. We are only considering the discrete legal issues that have been raised for our review primarily regarding the constitutionality of the procedure by which the General Assembly passed this piece of legislation.

. . . .

The Complaint, as well as the brief of Petitioners, sets forth the material facts regarding House Bill 2330 of 2004 ("HB 2330") and the process by which that bill became the Gaming Act. Specifically, HB 2330 was introduced on February 3, 2004. It was titled "An Act Providing for the Duties of the Pennsylvania State Police Regarding Criminal History Background Reports for Persons Participating in Harness or Horse Racing." At this point in time, the bill dealt exclusively with the Pennsylvania State Police providing support to the State Harness and Horse Racing Commissions by performing criminal history checks and the verification of fingerprints of applicants for licensure under the Race Horse Industry Reform Act of 1981. It was one page in length. (H.B. 2330 Printer's No. 3251).

Thereafter, the bill went through three considerations in the House and two considerations in the Senate. In the last consideration in the Senate on Thursday, July 1, 2004, the content of the bill was amended. Additionally, the bill's title was changed to express the multiple amendments made to the bill. These amendments were extensive, increasing the length of the bill from one page to 145 pages which included seven chapters and 86 sections. The bill as amended included the creation of the Pennsylvania Gaming Control Board ("Gaming Control Board" or "Board"), the issuance of gambling licenses authorizing the creation of a variety of slot machine casinos, the generation and distribution of revenues from the licenses, the creation of numerous funds including the Gaming Fund, the Pennsylvania Horse Race Fund, the Gambling and Economic Development and Tourism Fund, the Property Tax Relief Fund as well as a Compulsive and Problem Gambling Treatment Fund. Additionally, the amended bill contained a chapter regarding administration and enforcement and provided for exclusive jurisdiction in our Court regarding disputes over the issuance of licenses and challenges to the Gaming Act.

On Saturday, July 3, 2004, the bill as amended was submitted to the House for a vote on a committed basis; the amended bill was passed and was signed in the House. The next day, on Sunday, July 4, 2004, the bill was signed in the Senate. On Monday, July 5, 2004, Governor Edward Rendell signed the bill into law as Act 71 of 2004.

Approximately five months later, on December 10, 2004, Petitioners filed their Complaint in which they alleged that the Gaming Act is unconstitutional since it was passed in violation of Article III, Sections 1, 3, 4, 6, and 10 of the Pennsylvania Constitution and is an unconstitutional delegation of power to the Gaming Control Board . . . .

. . . .

Section I

Petitioners' first set of challenges to the Gaming Act involves Article III of our Constitution relating to legislation. Article III can be viewed as a constellation of constitutional requirements that govern various aspects of the legislative enactment procedure. Each of these provisions was born in a time in which Pennsylvanians were experiencing rapid growth economically and "'wrenching' social change . . . ." K. GORMLEY, THE PENNSYLVANIA CONSTITUTION, § 3.6[a], p. 61 (2003). An enormous growth in the corporate form of business organization led to significant concentrations of wealth and the corruption of numerous legislators. *Id.* at 62. Corruption took the form of special laws legislation, logrolling[7] and arbitrary favoritism and was met with a demand for reform. *Id.* The Constitutional Convention of 1872–73 was convened to reform corrupt legislative behavior, and to this end, the result was the constitutional strictures contained in Article III. *See* R. BRANNING, PENNSYLVANIA CONSTITUTIONAL DEVELOPMENT 37 (1960). Thus, while these changes to the Constitution originated during a unique time of fear of tyrannical corporate power and legislative corruption, these mandates retain their value even today by placing certain constitutional limitations on the legislative process.

Section I (A)

Specifically, Article III, § 3 of our Pennsylvania Constitution sets forth dual mandates for the General Assembly which prohibit the passing of a bill that contains more than one subject and requires that the subject be clearly expressed in its title. The focus of Petitioners' primary challenge is Section 3's single subject requirement.

> *No bill shall be passed containing more than one subject*, which shall be clearly expressed in its title, except a general appropriation bill or a bill codifying or compiling the law or a part thereof.

PA. CONST. art. III, § 3 (emphasis supplied).

Petitioners merge their arguments regarding single subject and clearly expressed title. This is not necessarily surprising, as in *City of Philadelphia*, our Court indicated that these twin requirements are interrelated in that they both proscribe introducing measures into bills without providing reasonable notice of the same. *City of Philadelphia*, 838 A.2d at 586. Although interrelated, and Petitioners address these two aspects of Article III, Section 3 together in their brief, we will parse the arguments and consider the twin directives separately.

With respect to the single subject requirement, Petitioners argue that, in interpreting Article III, Section 3, in *City of Philadelphia*, our Court set forth the relevant standard to be utilized in determining whether the process by which a piece of legislation has been enacted withstands constitutional challenge. In sum, Petitioners maintain that the amendments to a bill must be "germane" to the bill's subject. Whether the subject matter is viewed as the Commonwealth's "Racehorse Industry" or "Pennsylvania Horse Racing Industry Development and Other Gaming," Petitioners assert that the germaneness test is not met and that by changing the bill to encompass more than one subject, the General Assembly violated Article III, Section 3.

Respondents counter that the Gaming Act does not violate Article III, Section 3 because the amendment made to HB 2330 was germane to the general subject of the bill.

---

[7] "Logrolling" is the practice of "embracing in one bill several distinct matters, none of which could singly obtain the assent of the legislature, and procuring its passage by combining the minorities who favored the individual matters to form a majority that would adopt them all." Charles W. Rubendall II, *The Constitution and the Consolidated Statutes*, 80 DICK L. REV. 118, 120 (1975).

Respondents offer that amendments to bills are permissible when the amendments are germane to and do not wholly change the general subject of the bill. Indeed, Respondents state that it is expected that legislation will be transformed during the enactment process. According to Respondents, courts have traditionally taken a broad view of the overall subject of a bill. Unlike the legislation at issue in *City of Philadelphia*, in which the vast subject of "municipalities" was rejected as overly broad for constitutional purposes, here, all provisions of the Gaming Act relate to the single subject of regulating gaming.

Our analysis of Petitioners' first constitutional challenge begins with our recent decision in *City of Philadelphia*. A scant two years ago, our Court engaged in an in-depth analysis of the aim and application of Article III, Section 3 to certain legislation. Justice Saylor, writing for a unanimous Court, set forth a detailed discussion of the purpose behind Section 3 as well as the evolution of the jurisprudential treatment of this section.

In broad terms, Article III's aim was to "place restraints on the legislative process and encourage an open, deliberative, and accountable government." *City of Philadelphia*, 838 A.2d at 585 (quoting *Pennsylvania AFL-CIO ex rel. George v. Commonwealth*, 563 Pa. 108, 757 A.2d 917, 923 (2000)). More specifically, Section 3 was designed to curb the practice of inserting into a single bill a number of distinct and independent subjects of legislation and purposefully hiding the real purpose of the bill. *City of Philadelphia*, 838 A.2d at 586. Related thereto, the single subject requirement prohibits the attachment of riders that could not become law as is, to popular legislation that would pass. An additional benefit of the Section 3 requirements is that there will be a greater probability that a bill containing a single topic will be more likely to receive a considered review than a multi-subject piece of legislation. *Id.*, citing Millard H. Ruud, *No Law Shall Embrace More Than One Subject*, 42 MINN. L.REV. 389, 391 (1958) (offering that an additional purpose served by the one-subject rule is to facilitate orderly legislative procedure). As we indicated in *City of Philadelphia*, the single subject requirement proscribed the inclusion of provisions into legislation without allowing for "fair notice to the public and to legislators of the existence of the same." *City of Philadelphia*, 838 A.2d at 587. Thus, reasonable notice is the keystone of Article III, Section 3.

While recognizing the importance of Section 3, we acknowledged that bills are frequently subject to amendments as they proceed through the legislative process and not every supplementation of new material is violative of the Constitution. Thus, "where the provisions added during the legislative process assist in carrying out a bill's main objective or are otherwise 'germane' to the bill's subject as reflected in its title," the requirements of Article III, Section 3 are met. *Id.* Article III, Section 3 must have, however, some limits on germaneness, for otherwise virtually all legislation — no matter how diverse in substance — would meet the single-subject requirement, rendering the strictures of Section 3 nugatory. As stated by our Court in *Payne v. School Dist. of Coudersport Borough*, 168 Pa. 386, 31 A. 1072, 1074 (1895), "no two subjects are so wide apart that they may not be brought into a common focus, if the point of view be carried back far enough." Thus, defining the constitutionally-valid topic too broadly would render the safeguards of Section 3 inert. Conversely, the requirements of Section 3 must not become a license for the judiciary to "exercise a pedantic tyranny" over the efforts of the Legislature. *City of Philadelphia*, 838 A.2d at 588 (citing *Estate of Rochez*, 511 Pa. 620, 515 A.2d 899, 902 (1986)). Indeed, "[f]ew bills are so elementary in character that they may not be subdivided under several heads . . . ." *Payne*, 31 A. at 1074.

In light of this tension, as well as the purpose of Article III, Section 3, our focus in *City of Philadelphia* fell upon whether there was a single unifying subject to which all of the provisions of the act are germane. *City of Philadelphia*, 838 A.2d at 589. While acknowledging that exercising deference by hypothesizing a reasonably broad topic was appropriate, to some degree, in determining whether the bill passed constitutional muster, *id.* at 588, the vast subject of "municipalities" stretched the concept of a single topic beyond the breaking point. Indeed, it was not apparent how the diverse subject-matter had a logical or legislative nexus to each other. *Id.* at 589. Finding that, as virtually all of local government is a municipality, the proposed subject was simply too broad to qualify for single subject status for purposes of Article III, Section 3. Thus, we struck the statute as constitutionally infirm.

In contrast to *City of Philadelphia,* in the matter *sub judice* there is a single unifying subject — the regulation of gaming. The single topic of gaming does not encompass the limitless number of subjects which could be encompassed under the heading of "municipalities." Specifically, HB 2330 sets forth the legislative intent of regulating gaming, creates the Gaming Control Board, establishes policies and procedures for gaming licenses for the installation and operation of slot machines, enacts provisions to assist Pennsylvania's horse racing industry through other gaming, and provides for administration and enforcement of the gaming law, including measures to insure the integrity of the operation of slot machines.

Section I(B)

Yet, one particular aspect Petitioners' argument regarding the single subject requirement warrants further discussion. Petitioners contend that the bill's distribution of monies represents additional "subjects" contained in the bill which are unrelated to the development of what Petitioners consider to the be the alleged single subject — "development of the 'horse race industry.'" Petitioners' Brief at p. 36. Specifically, Petitioners point to the disbursement of funds to a variety of entities therein which they claim is strong evidence of the bill containing unconstitutionally disparate subjects.

. . . .

The next question we must answer is whether the provisions for distribution to the Volunteer Fire Company Grant Program and relative to the Forest Reserves Municipal Financial Relief Law which we have found to be invalid may be severed from the other provisions in Chapter 14. In making this determination, we first recognize the General Assembly's clear and expressly stated intention that the invalidity of any provision of the Act "shall not affect other provisions or applications . . . ." 4 Pa.C.S. § 1902(a). Moreover, we are cognizant of the rule that unconstitutional provisions should be severed from their constitutional counterparts unless we determine that the valid provisions are "so essentially and inseparably connected with, and so depend upon, the void provision or application, that it cannot be presumed the General Assembly would have enacted the remaining valid provisions without the void one" or that the "remaining valid provisions, standing alone, are incomplete and incapable of being executed in accordance with the legislative intent." *Commonwealth v. Mockaitis,* 575 Pa. 5, 834 A.2d 488, 502 (2003) (citing 1 Pa.C.S. § 1925).

We find that the above-discussed provisions are severable from the remainder of the Act. First, as they are not germane to the single subject of the regulation of gaming, they are clearly not essentially and inseparably connected with the rest of the Act. Second, the remaining valid provisions are certainly capable of being executed in accordance with legislative intent in the absence of this limited number of disbursement provisions.[14]

. . . .

---

[14] As a separate matter, we acknowledge that there are significant policy justifications militating against severance on a finding of a violation of the single-subject provision in circumstances where logrolling may have occurred. *See, e.g.,* Martha J. Dragich, *State Constitutional Restrictions on Legislative Procedure: Rethinking the Analysis of Original Purpose, Single Subject, and Clear Title Challenges,* 38 HARV. J. ON LEGIS. 103, 161 (2001) (positing that, unless a reviewing court can discern that provisions outside the primary subject matter of legislation did not serve as an inducement for passage of the enactment, the court should strike the entire statute) . . . .

Section II

In addition to the single subject requirement, Article III, § 3, as noted above, also mandates that the subject of the bill must be clearly expressed in its title:

> No bill shall be passed containing more than *one subject, which shall be clearly expressed in its title*, except a general appropriation bill or a bill codifying or compiling the law or a part thereof.

PA. CONST. art. III, § 3 (emphasis supplied).

Petitioners first submit that the title of the one-page bill must be referred to in determining whether the current title is constitutionally defective. Petitioners then compare the title of HB 2330 as originally drafted with the new title as amended by the Senate. Combining concepts relating to clear expression of title with single subject and the overarching concept of germaneness, Petitioners assert that the "obliteration of the title and purpose of the 1-page act is fatal to the constitutionality of the amendment and removes any possibility that the amendment is germane to the purpose and subject of the 1-page act . . . ." Petitioners' Brief at p. 31. Similarly, Petitioners maintain that "the change in titles, . . . conclusively shows that § 1 and § 3 of Article III forbidding amendments which change a bill's purpose and deal with more than one subject have been violated." *Id.*

Respondents argue that Article III, Section 3 requires that the title of a law indicate its contents so that the members of the General Assembly can vote on the legislation with circumspection. In sum, Respondent's agree that Article III, Section 3 prohibits a title from being deceptive. Respondents offer that as long as the title of the law indicates its contents, the bill satisfies its constitutional requirement of placing members of the General Assembly on notice so that they can vote on the legislation with consideration of its circumstances and consequences. Thus, according to Respondents, a violation of Article III, Section 3 occurs "only when (1) the legislators were actually deceived as to the act's contents at the time of passage; or (2) that the title on its face is such that no reasonable person would have been on notice as to the act's contents." *See, e.g.,* Respondent Commonwealth of Pennsylvania's Brief at p. 12.

Applying this standard, Respondents maintain that there is no evidence that the title of HB 2330 was deceptive. There is no assertion that legislators actually were deceived as to the contents of HB 2330. Furthermore, the final title put reasonable persons on notice as to the contents of the Gaming Act. Thus, there was no constitutional violation of Article III, Section 3's clear title requirement.

As originally introduced, HB 2330 was entitled:

> AN ACT PROVIDING FOR THE DUTIES OF THE PENNSYLVANIA STATE POLICE REGARDING CRIMINAL HISTORY BACKGROUND REPORTS FOR PERSONS PARTICIPATING IN HARNESS OR HORSE RACING

The Senate amended the title of the bill prior to passage and in doing so, as pointed out by Petitioners, incorporated no part of the original title:

> AMENDING TITLE 4 (AMUSEMENTS) OF THE PENNSYLVANIA CONSOLIDATED STATUTES, AUTHORIZING CERTAIN RACETRACK AND OTHER GAMING; PROVIDING FOR REGULATION OF GAMING LICENSEES, ESTABLISHING AND PROVIDING FOR THE POWERS AND DUTIES OF THE PENNSYLVANIA GAMING CONTROL DEPART- MENT OF REVENUE, THE DEPARTMENT OF HEALTH, THE OFFICE OF ATTORNEY GENERAL, THE PENNSYLVANIA STATE POLICE, AND THE PENNSYLVANIA LIQUOR CONTROL BOARD; ESTABLISH- ING THE STATE GAMING FUND, THE PENNSYLVANIA RACE HORSE DEVELOPMENT FUND, THE PENNSYLVANIA GAMING ECONOMIC DEVELOPMENT AND TOURISM FUND, THE COMPULSIVE PROB-

LEM GAMBLING TREATMENT FUND AND THE PROPERTY TAX RELIEF FUND; PROVIDING FOR ENFORCEMENT; IMPOSING PENALTIES; MAKING APPROPRIATIONS; AND MAKING RELATED REPEALS.

As noted above, Article III, Section 3, mandates that the single subject contained in a bill must be "clearly expressed in its title . . . ." In *Scudder v. Smith*, 331 Pa. 165, 200 A. 601 (1938), we emphasized that the purpose of the clear title requirement was to "put the members of the Assembly and others interested on notice, by the title of the measure submitted, so they might vote on it with circumspection." *Scudder*, 200 A. at 604. "In essence, Article III, Section 3 prohibits legislative draftsmen from proposing acts with titles calculated to mislead and deceive . . . [and] assures against the practice of the intentional masking of acts with misleading or 'omnibus' titles." *Estate of Rochez*, 515 A.2d at 902.

Our case law interpreting this constitutional provision also makes clear, however, that it is only reasonable notice that is required. We have held that while the Constitution requires that the title of the bill be clear, it "does not require a title to be an index or synopsis of an act's contents." *Id.; McSorley v. Fitzgerald*, 359 Pa. 264, 59 A.2d 142 (1948); *see also DeWeese v. Weaver*, 824 A.2d 364, 372 (Pa. Cmwlth. 2003) (explaining that "[t]he title serves as a signal not a précis of the bill's contents."). Indeed, to require the title to catalogue every provision of a bill might not only make the title unworkably long, but might foster the very problems that the requirement was meant to prevent.

Based upon the purpose behind the clear expression of title requirement, as well as the practical realization that a title does not need to express each and every subtopic contained in the bill, we set forth the burden one must meet in order to sustain a constitutional challenge to the expression of title. "[O]ne who seeks to declare a title unconstitutional under this provision must demonstrate either (1) that the legislators and the public were actually deceived as to the act's contents at the time of passage, or (2) that the title on its face is such that no reasonable person would have been on notice as to the act's contents." *Estate of Rochez*, 515 A.2d at 902. Stated another way, a title will be held to be constitutional if it puts a reasonable person on notice of the general subject matter of the act. *Ewalt v. Pennsylvania Turnpike Commission*, 382 Pa. 529, 115 A.2d 729 (1955).

Looking at the title of the Gaming Act, and comparing the substance of the Act to its title, we believe that Petitioners have failed as a matter of law to show that the title is violative of Article III, Section 3. There is no allegation that any legislator actually was deceived as to the contents of HB 2330. Furthermore, the title passes constitutional muster as it clearly puts a reasonable person on notice of the general subject matter of the Act. Specifically, the Act covers a variety of subtopics regarding the subject of gaming: the Gaming Control Board; Licensees; Revenues, including the establishment of a number of funds; administration and enforcement of the provisions of the Act; making appropriations, and repealing certain acts and parts of acts. Each of these primary subtopics is set forth in the title by clear expression.

Therefore, with the strong presumption regarding the constitutionality of legislation and considering the constitutionality of the Act with all doubts being resolved in favor of a finding of constitutionality, we hold that as a matter of law, the title of the Gaming Act puts reasonable persons on notice of the subject matter contained therein, and therefore, does not run afoul of the clear expression of title requirement found in Article III, Section 3 of our Constitution.

Section III

Next, Petitioners contend that the Gaming Act violates the "change in original purpose" prohibition of Article III, Section 1 of our Constitution. Specifically, Petitioners offer that case law suggests that Article III, Section 1 is aimed at deterring confusion, misconduct, and deception. Petitioners' Brief at p. 37. Both the original title and the amended title are deceptive, according to Petitioners, and the deception is evidenced by the "means by which this bill was hastily pushed through both the Houses of the General Assembly . . . ." Petitioners' Brief at p. 38. Related thereto, Petitioners assert that the House "was disenfranchised to the extent that virtually the entire bill could only be amended if the House rules were first suspended by a two-thirds majority vote of all members — a fact which resulted in the House being unable to amend this bill in any manner." Petitioners' Brief at p. 38. In sum, Petitioners argue that it is "the 'ramrod' element of this bill [that] provides the confusion and deception element . . . ." Petitioners' Brief at p. 39.

Suggesting that there is a lack of case law on Article III, Section 1, Petitioners point to case law from other jurisdictions in which legislation was found to be unconstitutional when an amendment to a bill changed its original purpose. *See, e.g., Advisory Opinion No. 331*, 582 So.2d 1115 (Ala. 1991); *Barclay v. Melton*, 339 Ark. 362, 5 S.W.3d 457 (1999); *Black Hawk Consol. Mines Co. v. Gallegos*, 52 N.M. 74, 191 P.2d 996 (N.M. 1948). Thus, because the General Assembly made numerous changes to the original bill that dealt with fingerprinting at racetracks, and according to Petitioners, changed the specific original purpose of the bill, it is violative of Article III, Section 1.

Respondents answer that the Gaming Act does not violate Article III, Section 1 because the original purpose of HB 2330 remained the same from inception to passage — to regulate gaming. While the bill was amended materially and expanded to contain additional topics, they all were related to the broad and original purpose of regulating gaming. Respondents maintain that our Court has been hesitant to strike legislation due to an alleged change in purpose. Recognizing that the legislative process often requires material changes to legislation during its passage, Respondents contend that our Court has held that an Article III, Section 1 challenge will be rejected if "the bill in final form, with a title that clearly stated its contents, was presented to each house for its consideration and adoption." *Consumer Party v. Commonwealth*, 510 Pa. 158, 507 A.2d 323, 335 (1986). The Gaming Act, according to Respondents, clearly passes this test, and even if the initial and finally passed versions of the bill are compared, the purpose, at its origin and final passage, were both to regulate gaming.

Article III, Section 1 provides that in passage through the legislative bodies, a bill shall not be altered or amended to change its original purpose:

> No law shall be passed except by bill, and no bill shall be so altered or amended, on its passage through either House, as to change its original purpose.

PA. CONST. art III, § 1.

Contrary to Petitioners' assertions, our Court has spoken to the meaning of Article III, Section 1 and offered an analysis to be engaged in when considering a constitutional challenge based on this provision in *Consumer Party v. Commonwealth*, 510 Pa. 158, 507 A.2d 323 (1986). In that decision, the Court was faced with an attack on legislation that, as originally introduced, proposed changes to county codes relating to county officials of counties of the third through eighth classes. After submission to a committee, the legislation was amended significantly to contain substantially different provisions relating to the salaries and compensation of certain Commonwealth officials.

A unanimous Court, while stressing the mandatory nature of Article III, Section 1, set a very high bar for finding a violation of this provision. Our Court recognized the practical realities of passing legislation and narrowly focused the inquiry. It reached its decision that Article III, Section 1 was not violated, not by comparing the original purpose to the purpose at final passage, but by considering only the bill at final passage. Consistent with this concentration, our Court inquired as to whether the legislation put the members of the General Assembly and others interested on notice so that they could "act with circumspection." *Id.* at 335. As stated by the Court, "here the bill in final form with a title that clearly stated its contents, was presented to each house for its consideration and adoption. Under these circumstances, there is no basis for sustaining a challenge under Article III, Section 1." *Id.*

The Court went on to address the challengers' contention, like that argued by Petitioners *sub judice*, that the procedure utilized deprived other interested parties of notice and prevented members of the Legislature from voting with circumspection. The Court rejected this argument, focusing solely on the alleged deceptive nature of the final legislation:

> As noted the title and content of the legislation in final form were in no way deceptive. We will not assume that the majority of members in each house voting in favor of this legislation did not fully understand this piece of legislation . . . . *Implicitly, appellants are seeking to extend the language of Article III, section 1 to provide for a sufficient time frame during consideration of the measure in its ultimate form for communication between the constituency and the legislator before a vote is taken. There is nothing in the language of Article III, section 1 that would support such an interpretation.*

Id. (emphasis supplied).

Thus, the Court strictly limited its review in a challenge brought pursuant to Article III, Section 1 by viewing the title of the legislation and its content in final form. Ultimately, the Court found that the legislation did not violate Article III, Section 1.

This limited construct employed by the Court in *Consumer Party*, however, has not always been strictly and faithfully followed by our lower courts. Indeed, the Commonwealth Court has considered a challenge under Article III, Section 1 by comparing the initial and finally passed versions of a piece of legislation. *See Common Cause v. Commonwealth*, 710 A.2d 108 (Pa. Cmwlth. 1998), *aff'd*, 562 Pa. 632, 757 A.2d 367 (2000). Furthermore, scholarship has criticized the narrow approach taken in *Consumer Party*. Robert F. Williams, *Statutory and Constitutional Interpretation: State Constitutional Limits on Legislative Procedure: Legislative Compliance and Judicial Enforcement*, 48 U. Pitt. L. Rev. 797, 815 (1987) (suggesting that *Consumer Party* unduly narrowed the scope of the constitutional restriction by focusing on deception and failed to recognize the broader purpose of preserving a "regularized legislative procedure").

Upon closer inspection of our now close to twenty-year-old decision, we find that the analysis offered in *Consumer Party* resembles the analysis set forth for reviewing challenges under Article III, Section 3 and fails to give full significance to the language employed in the constitutional provision itself — "change its original purpose." This verbiage certainly suggests a comparative analysis, that is, some form of comparison between an "original" purpose and a final purpose to determine whether an unconstitutional alteration or amendment has occurred so as to change the original purpose of the bill. It also suggests an aim broader than just ensuring that the title and contents of the final bill are not deceptive, but also includes a desire for some degree of continuity in object or intention. Accordingly, we believe that the language adopted by the conventioneers, as well as their purpose in adopting Article III, Section 1 counsel towards, and are best served by, an analytical construct that involves comparison between the original purpose and the final purpose of the bill, as well as consideration of whether the final bill and title are deceptive.

Thus, we now hold that a court entertaining a challenge to legislation under Article III, Section 1 must conduct a two-part inquiry. First, the court will consider the original purpose of the legislation and compare it to the final purpose and determine whether there has been an alteration or amendment so as to change the original purpose. Second, a court will consider, whether in its final form, the title and contents of the bill are deceptive.

Regarding the determination of the original purpose of the legislation, we recognize the realities of the legislative process which can involve significant changes to legislation in the hopes of consensus, *see Consumer Party* at 334, and the "expectation" that legislation will be transformed during the enactment process. *Pennsylvania School Boards Ass'n.*, 805 A.2d at 489. Furthermore, our Court is loathe to substitute our judgment for that of the legislative branch under the pretense of determining whether an unconstitutional change in purpose of a piece of legislation has occurred during the course of its enactment. *See Consumer Party; Common Cause*, 668 A.2d at 198. For these reasons, we believe that the original purpose must be viewed in reasonably broad terms.

Consistent with our suggestion in *City of Philadelphia*, it is helpful for a reviewing court to hypothesize, based upon the text of the statute, as to a reasonably broad original purpose. *City of Philadelphia*, 838 A.2d at 588. Given this approach of considering a reasonably broad original purpose, the General Assembly is given full opportunity to amend and even expand a bill, and not run afoul of the constitutional prohibition on an alteration or amendment that changes its original purpose. The original purpose is then compared to the final purpose and a determination is made as to whether an unconstitutional alteration or amendment, on its passage through either house, has taken place so as to change its original purpose.

Regarding the second prong of this analysis, it will be for the court to determine whether in its final form, the title and contents of the bill are deceptive. If the legislation passes both the purpose comparison and deception inquiries, it will pass constitutional muster.

Applying this construct to the facts of the case, we first consider the original purpose of the bill, and do so in reasonably broad terms; we then compare the original purpose to the final purpose to determine if the purpose has changed. As introduced, HB 2330 provided the State Police with the power and duty to perform criminal background checks on, and identify through conducting fingerprinting, those applicants seeking a license from the State Horse Racing and State Harness Racing Commissions. Considering the original purpose in reasonably broad terms, we believe that here, and in this instance akin to our finding above regarding a single unifying subject, the original purpose of the bill was to regulate gaming. As finally passed, although significantly amended and expanded, we find that the primary objective of the legislation was to regulate gaming. *See* 4 Pa.C.S. § 1102(1). Based on the above, we conclude that the bill was not altered or amended to change its original purpose.

As to the second prong of the analysis, we consider whether the title and the content of the bill in final form were deceptive. Consistent with our finding above regarding the sufficiency of the title, we find that the final title was not deceptive. It placed reasonable persons on notice of the subject of the bill. Furthermore, we find that while amendments to HB 2330 were substantive and came at the end of the consideration cycle, the contents of the bill were not deceptive.

Thus, recognizing that a statute must be upheld unless it clearly, palpably, and plainly violates the Constitution, we hold, as a matter of law, that the process by which HB 2330 became law did not violate Article III, Section 1's prohibition on alteration of amendment so as to change the original purpose of the bill.

Section IV

Petitioners assert in the fourth count of the Complaint that the Gaming Act violated Article III, Section 4 of the Pennsylvania Constitution, entitled "Consideration of Bills." Article III, Section 4 states that:

> *Every bill shall be considered on three different days in each House.* All amendments made thereto shall be printed for the use of the members before the final vote is taken on the bill and before the final vote is taken, upon written request addressed to the presiding officer of either House by at least twenty-five percent of the members elected to that House, any bill shall be read at

length in that House. No bill shall become a law, unless on its final passage the vote is taken by yeas and nays, the names of the persons voting for and against it are entered on the journal, and a majority of the members elected to each House is recorded thereon as voting in its favor.

PA. CONST., art. III, § 4 (emphasis supplied).

Petitioners have alleged that the version of HB 2330 that was considered in each House was completely different from the bill that was amended and changed upon third consideration in the Senate and sent to the House for final passage or concurrence. They claim that the final form of the bill that was considered was so fundamentally different from the bill that was previously considered on five readings that it was effectively a different bill. They contend that the form of the bill that was considered on the last day was not considered on three separate occasions by each house in violation of Article III, Section 4.

Respondents filed preliminary objections to the fourth count, asserting that the Gaming Act received readings on three separate days in the House and the Senate as required. Respondents assert that Article III, Section 4 does not require the Legislature to reconsider a bill after amendment.

As noted above, the Gaming Act was introduced as HB 2330 on February 3, 2004. The bill received its first reading in the House on March 16, 2004. The second reading was on March 17, 2004, and the third reading was on March 22, 2004. The Clerk of the House then presented the bill to the Senate. The bill received its first reading in the Senate on March 23, 2004, and its second reading on March 29, 2004. The bill subsequently was amended and received its third reading on July 1, 2004.

"[A]n amended bill need not be referred to committee and considered on those separate days if the amendments are germane to, and do not wholly change, the general subject of the bill." *Pennsylvania AFL-CIO v. Commonwealth of Pennsylvania*, 691 A.2d 1023, 1037 (Pa. Cmwlth. 1997) (citations omitted), *aff'd*, 563 Pa. 108, 757 A.2d 917 (2000). As Petitioners claim that Article III, Section 4 was violated because the substance of the bill had been altered by the amendments, they must necessarily establish that Article III, Section 1 or 3 had been violated. Petitioners have failed to establish a violation of Article III, Section 1 or 3, except as noted above, and the record demonstrates that the bill was read on three separate occasions in each house. Thus, with the exception of the provisions noted above, we find that Petitioners have failed to state a claim that Article III, Section 4 was violated.

Section V

In the fifth count of the Complaint, Petitioners have asserted that the Gaming Act violated Article III, Section 6 because the Act repealed Section 493(29) of the Liquor Code, 47 P.S. § 4-493(29), and 18 Pa. C.S. § 5513(a) of the Crimes Code, but failed to contain the text of the sections to be repealed . . . .

Article III, Section 6, relating to "revival and amendment of laws," states that:

[n]o law shall be revived, amended, or the provisions thereof extended or conferred, by reference to its title only, but so much thereof as is revived, amended, extended or conferred shall be re-enacted and published at length.

PA. CONST., art. III, § 6.

Our Court has suggested as a general proposition that one of "the purpose[s] of Section 6 of the Constitution, along with other provisions pertaining to legislation in Article III of the Constitution, was to provide full notice and publicity to all proposed legislative enactments, and thus to prevent the passage of 'sneak' legislation." *L.J.W. Realty Corp. v. Philadelphia*, 390 Pa. 197, 134 A.2d 878, 882 (1957). "The constitution does not make the obviously impracticable requirement that every act shall recite all other acts that its operation may incidentally affect, either by way of repeal, modification, extension or supply.' " *Id.*

Nevertheless, by its terms, Section 6 suggests more than just mere notice of alterations of other legislative enactments in some general sense. As we stated in *Commonwealth v. Hallberg*, 374 Pa. 554, 97 A.2d 849 (1953):

> [t]he object of the Constitutional provision . . . is obvious, namely, to enable both the legislators themselves and all persons interested in the legislation to see exactly the changes made between the existing law and the re-enactment, without the necessity of referring to the former for comparison . . . , whereas if the portion to be abrogated were simply deleted, it would be impossible to determine whether such deletion represented an actual legislative intention to abrogate such part of the law or was due to a mere error or oversight in the publication of the amendatory legislation. We are strengthened in this conclusion by the well-known, uniform practice, long existent, of legislative draftsmen thus to place in brackets all parts of an existing law intended to be abrogated, as well as by the general understanding that such abrogation is to be deemed to occur only when so indicated.

Id. at 851–52 (citation omitted).

Thus, we hold that Article III, Section 6 requires, with regard to a directed, specific repealer, the effectuation of which is not otherwise apparent from the associated bill, that as much of the law that is expressly repealed by the bill must be published at length. In this way, legislators may see the elimination of particular existing legislative provisions, from the face of a pending bill, without having to refer to the existing piece of legislation for comparison. Here, HB 2330 amended Section 493 of the Liquor Code by specifically repealing subsection 29 of that section. Section 493 was not republished in HB 2330. Based upon the above, we find that Article III, Section 6 requires that at a minimum, subsection 29 of Section 493 should have been set forth in its entirety with brackets surrounding the text of subsection 29 indicating its repeal.

Section 1903(a)(2), which references potential inconsistencies between the bill and the Crimes Code, does not violate the requirements of Article III, Section 6, however, as this section is simply implementing a general repeal of any inconsistent legislation. Indeed, in light of section (b), enacting a general repealer of all inconsistent statutes, subsection (a)(2) is arguably superfluous. Thus, we hold that Section 1903(a)(1) of the Act which attempted to repeal Section 493(29) of the Liquor Code is violative of Article III, Section 6 and therefore, is invalid. Further, we find that Section 1903(a)(2) of the Act did not violate the requirements of Article III, Section 6.

Section VI

Petitioners have alleged in the sixth count of their complaint that the enactment of the bill violated Article III, Section 10. Article III, Section 10 provides that "[a]ll bills for raising revenue shall originate in the House of Representatives but the Senate may propose amendments as in other bills." PA. CONST. art. III, § 10. Petitioners claim that, although the bill originated in the House, it never became a revenue bill until it was amended on its fifth and last legislative reading in the Senate. They argue that neither the General Assembly, nor the public had notice of the contents of HB 2330, and that the General Assembly did not have the opportunity to vote with circumspection.

Respondents assert that the bill complied with the requirements of Article III, Section 10 because it originated in the House of Representatives and, in any event, was not a revenue-raising bill. They contend that any amendments to the bill, including those relating to revenues generated by gaming regulation, did not transform the bill regulating gaming into a revenue bill. Respondents further offer that the constitutional provision is a procedural directive, and that any alleged failure to comply with the directive does not present a justiciable question, citing *Mikell v. Philadelphia School District*, 359 Pa. 113, 58 A.2d 339 (1948).

We will first address Respondents' non-justiciability argument and their reliance upon *Mikell*. In *Mikell*, the plaintiff sought to enjoin the enforcement of an act that amended the Public School Code by imposing a personal property tax upon residents of first class school districts for public school purposes. The plaintiff challenged the act as a revenue-raising measure that had originated in the Senate in violation of Article III, Section 14 of the Pennsylvania Constitution of 1874. Article III, Section 14 was identical to Article III, Section 10 of our current Constitution.

We rejected the plaintiff's claim that Article III, Section 14 had been violated, finding that the act was not a revenue-raising measure. We explained that "[t]o qualify as a bill within the purview of the cited constitutional provision, at least the revenue derived from the tax imposed should be coverable into the treasury of the exacting sovereign for its own general governmental uses, and that is not the situation in the present instance." *Mikell*, 58 A.2d at 341. The personal property tax was imposed for the maintenance of the public school system, rather than for the Commonwealth's governmental purposes.

We observed that:

> there can be no suggestion that any part of the tax imposed by the Act will be used for the State's governmental purposes . . . . [T]he impost is laid upon personal property of residents of designated school districts and the taxes collected will be used for public school purposes within such districts. The Act so stipulates. It is true that the described personal property is directly made taxable by the Act, but the annual levy, within the statutorily specified maximum and minimum limits, is a matter for the independent action of the respective boards of public education of the designated districts.

Id. at 343.

We determined that there was an additional barrier to plaintiff's challenge to the enactment of the personal property tax because "[t]he clause concerning the place of origin of a bill for raising revenue is a procedural directive and not a substantive interdict" and thus, was non-justiciable. *Id.* at 345.

> The provision in question could not reasonably be deemed other than directory. It is not a denial of the Senate's power as a coordinate and essential branch of the legislature. Indeed, a further clause of the same Article and Section expressly confirms the Senate's own important function and discretion in the due enactment of revenue legislation. Specifically, "the Senate may propose amendments as in other bills": Art. III, Sec. 14 [1874]. In pursuance of its appropriate power in such regard, the Senate may amend a House revenue bill even to the extent of striking out everything following the enacting clause and substituting therefore a bill of its own creation. It follows, therefore, that a revenue statute, once enacted, is not inherently defective simply because the bill originated in the Senate and was passed first by that body.

Id. at 344. "A failure of the legislature to follow a directory provision of the Constitution, respecting the introduction and passage of legislation, does not present a justiciable question, and in no event, does it impair the validity of a duly certified enactment." *Id.*

In this case, Petitioners acknowledge that the *Mikell* analysis would preclude this Court from addressing their constitutional challenge based upon Article III, Section 10. They submit, however, that when a bill raising revenue by applying a tax *de facto* originates in the Senate under the circumstances presented here, Article III, Section 10 lends additional support for striking down the statute as unconstitutional. Petitioners' challenge to the bill premised upon Article III, Section 10 must stand on its own, however.

Although the parties primarily focus upon this Court's analysis in *Mikell*, which narrowly construed the authority of the judiciary to review constitutional challenges to enrolled bills, subsequent decisions reflect an evolving approach by our Court to the application of the non-justiciability doctrine. First, in *Consumer Party*, we determined that any "mandatory" provision of Article III would be enforceable, particularly where the parties agree on the relevant facts. *Consumer Party*, 507 A.2d at 333–34. Furthermore, a constitutional provision is mandatory when it "clearly sets forth the manner in which something shall be done," so that "that procedure must be followed to the exclusion of all others." *City of Philadelphia*, 838 A.2d at 581. Indeed, in *City of Philadelphia*, we recognized that *Consumer Party* modified the *Mikell* abstention doctrine:

> while this Court did for many years adhere to a strict doctrine preventing it from considering matters of form in the passage of legislation, *see Kilgore [v. Magee]*, 85 Pa. [401] at 412 (stating that, "when a law has been passed and approved and certified in due form, it is no part of the duty of the judiciary to go behind the law as duly certified to inquire into the observance of form in its passage."); *Mikell v. School Dist. of Phila.*, 359 Pa. 113, 123–27, 58 A.2d 339, 344–46 (1948); *Perkins v. City of Phila.*, 156 Pa. 539, 554, 568, 27 A. 356, 362 (1893); WOODSIDE, PA. CONSTITUTIONAL LAW, at 348 ("The courts will not go back of the signatures of [the presiding officers and the Governor] to determine whether the bill was enacted in compliance with the constitutional requirements."), this rule has been modified in recent years so that the appropriateness of judicial abstention now depends upon the situation presented. *See generally Pennsylvania Sch. Bds. Ass'n*, 569 Pa. [436] at 454, 805 A.2d [476] at 486–87; *Consumer Party [of Pa. v. Commonwealth]*, 510 Pa. [158] at 177, 507 A.2d [323] at 333; David B. Snyder, Note, *The Rise and Fall of the Enrolled Bill Doctrine in Pennsylvania*, 60 TEMPLE L.Q. 315, 326 (1986). In *Consumer Party*, most notably, this Court explained that, although the need to exercise restraint in deference to a co-equal branch of government often militates in favor of abstention, "the countervailing concern is our mandate to insure that government functions within the bounds of constitutional prescription." *Consumer Party*, 510 Pa. at 177, 507 A.2d at 333.

Id., 838 A.2d at 580.

Applying the analysis articulated in *City of Philadelphia*, we find that the Constitution clearly states that "[a]ll bills for raising revenue shall originate in the House . . . ." PA. CONST. art. III, § 10. As the parties have agreed upon the relevant facts, we determine that the claim is justiciable.

Turning to the merits of the dispute, we find that the bill did not violate the requirements of Article III, Section 10. In essence, Petitioners claim that the bill was a revenue-raising bill that originated *de facto* in the Senate. Regardless of whether Petitioners' characterization of the bill is correct, the bill in fact originated in the House and the proposal of amendments thereto by the Senate was permissible. Petitioners have failed to establish that Article III, Section 10 was violated.

. . . .

Conclusion

. . . .

As our decision is based on procedural grounds arising from the Constitution and the adequacy of legislative direction to the Gaming Control Board and not any absolute substantive proscription, it is obviously without prejudice to the Legislature's ability to cure the defects, via subsequent amendments that are consistent with this opinion.

NOTES AND QUESTIONS

1. Does the trade-off of votes to gain additional support for measures involving multiple matters, or "logrolling," involve advantages greater than those possible through the use of multiple bills? Is the use of one bill more attractive because of the efficiency of incorporating trade-offs between members? Does this limitation on subject matter have additional significance for the chief executive who must determine whether to approve or veto legislation?

2. Should the entire law as amended be invalidated? What is the rationale for doing so?

B. PROCESSES OF ENACTMENT — CONSTITUTIONALIZING RULES OF LEGISLATIVE PROCEDURE AND JURISDICTION

1.   Origination Clause

UNITED STATES v. MUNOZ-FLORES
495 U.S. 385 (1990)

JUSTICE MARSHALL delivered the opinion of the Court.

This case raises the question whether 18 U.S.C. § 3013, which requires courts to impose a monetary "special assessment" on any person convicted of a federal misdemeanor, was passed in violation of the Origination Clause of the Constitution. That Clause mandates that "[a]ll Bills for raising Revenue shall originate in the House of Representatives." U.S. Const., Art. I, § 7, cl. 1 . . . . On the merits, we hold that the special assessment statute does not violate the Origination Clause because it is not a "Bil[l] for raising Revenue."

I

In June 1985, German Munoz-Flores was charged with aiding the illegal entry of aliens into the United States. He subsequently pleaded guilty to two misdemeanor counts of aiding and abetting aliens to elude examination and inspection by immigration officers. The Magistrate sentenced respondent to probation and ordered him to pay a special assessment of $25 on each count under the then-applicable version of 18 U.S.C. § 3013 (1982 ed. Supp. V). Pet. for Cert. 27a–28a.

Respondent moved to correct his sentence, asserting that the special assessments were unconstitutional because Congress has passed § 3013 in violation of the Origination Clause.

. . . .

III

Both parties agree that "revenue bills are those that levy taxes in the strict sense of the word, and are not bills for other purposes which may incidentally create revenue." *Twin City Bank v. Nebeker*, 167 U.S. 196, 202, 17 S. Ct. 766, 769, 42 L. Ed. 134 (1897) (citing 1 J. STORY, COMMENTARIES ON THE CONSTITUTION § 880, pp. 610–611 (3d ed. 1858)). The Court has interpreted this general rule to mean that a statute that creates a particular governmental program and that raises revenue to support that program, as opposed to a statute that raises revenue to support government generally, is not a "Bil[l] for raising Revenue" within the meaning of the Origination Clause. For example, the Court in *Nebeker* rejected an Origination Clause challenge to what the statute denominated a "tax" on the circulating notes of banking associations. Despite its label, "[t]he tax was a means for effectually accomplishing the great object of giving to the people a currency . . . . There was no purpose by the act or by any of its provisions to raise revenue to be applied in meeting the expenses or obligations of the Government." *Nebeker, supra,* at 203, 17 S. Ct., at 769. The Court reiterated the point in *Millard v. Roberts,* 202 U.S. 429, 26 S. Ct. 674, 50 L. Ed. 1090 (1906), where it upheld a statute that levied property taxes in the District of Columbia to support railroad projects. The Court rejected an Origination Clause claim, concluding that "[w]hatever taxes are imposed are but means to the purposes provided by the act." *Id.,* at 437, 26 S. Ct., at 675.

This case falls squarely within the holdings in *Nebeker* and *Millard.* The Victims of Crime Act of 1984 established a Crime Victims Fund, 98 Stat. 2170, 42 U.S.C. § 10601(a) (1982 ed., Supp. II), as a federal source of funds for programs that compensate and assist crime victims. *See* § 10601(d) (allocating moneys among programs); § 10602 (delineating eligible compensation programs); § 10603 (delineating eligible assistance programs). The scheme established by the Act includes various mechanisms to provide money for the Fund, including the simultaneously enacted special assessment provision at issue in this case. § 10601(b)(2). Congress also specified, however, that if the total income to the Fund from all sources exceeded $100 million in any one year, the excess would be deposited in the general fund of the Treasury. § 10601(c)(l). Although nothing in the text of the legislative history of the statute explicitly indicates whether Congress expected that the $100 million cap would ever be exceeded, in fact it never was. The Government reports that the first and only excess occurred in fiscal year 1989, when the cap stood at $125 million and receipts were between $133 million and $134 million, Brief for United States 21, n. 21, a claim respondent does not dispute, Brief for Respondent 19, n. 16.

Moreover, only a small percentage of any excess paid into the general treasury can be attributed to the special assessments. The legislative history of the special assessment provision indicates that Congress anticipated that "substantial amounts [would] not result" from that source of funds. S. Rep. No. 98-497, p. 13 (1984). Reality has accorded with Congress' prediction. *See* U.S. Dept. of Justice, Office for Victims of Crime, Office of Justice Programs, Victims of Crime Act of 1984: A Report to Congress by the Attorney General 12 (1988) (§ 3013 revenues accounted for four percent of all deposits into the Fund received by United States Attorneys' Offices for fiscal year 1987). Four percent of a minimal and infrequent excess over the statutory cap is properly considered "incidenta[l]."

As in *Nebeker* and *Millard,* then, the special assessment provision was passed as part of a particular program to provide money for that program — the Crime Victims Fund. Although any excess was to go to the Treasury, there is no evidence that Congress contemplated the possibility of a substantial excess, nor did such an excess in fact materialize. Any revenue for the general Treasury that § 3013 creates is thus "incidenta[l]" to that provision's primary purpose. This conclusion is reinforced, not undermined, by the Senate Report that respondent claims establishes that § 3013 is a "Bil[l] for raising Revenue." That Report reads: "The purpose of imposing nominal assessment fees is to generate needed income to offset the cost of the [Crime Victims Fund]. Although substantial amounts will not result, these additional amounts will be helpful in financing the program *and will constitute new income for the Federal government.*" S. Rep. No. 98-497, *supra,* at 13–14 (emphasis added). Respondent's reliance on the emphasized portion of the quoted passage avails him nothing. Read in its entirety, the passage clearly evidences Congress' intent that § 3013 provide funds primarily to support the Crime Victims Fund.

Respondent next contends that even if § 3013 is directed entirely to providing support for the Crime Victims Fund, it still does not fall within the ambit of *Nebeker* or *Millard.* Respondent accurately notes that the § 3013 assessments are not collected for the benefit of the payors, those convicted of federal crimes. He then contends, citing *Nebeker* and *Millard*, that any bill that provides for the collection of funds is a revenue bill unless it is designed to benefit the persons from whom the funds are collected. Respondent misreads *Nebeker* and *Millard*. In neither of those cases did the Court state that a bill *must* benefit the payor to avoid classification as a revenue bill. Indeed, had the Court adopted such a caveat, the Court in *Nebeker* would have found the statute to be unconstitutional. There, the Court expressly identified the "people" generally rather than the banking associations required to pay the tax, as the beneficiaries of the system of currency at issue. 167 U.S., at 203, 17 S. Ct., at 769. It nevertheless found that the bill was not a revenue bill, stating that a bill creating a discrete governmental program and providing sources for its financial support is not a revenue bill simply because it creates revenue, a holding that was reaffirmed by *Millard. See supra*, at 1971. Thus, the beneficiaries of the bill are not relevant.

Section 3013 is not a "Bil[l] for raising Revenue." We therefore need not consider whether the Origination Clause would require its invalidation if it *were* a revenue bill. *Nebeker*, 167 U.S., at 203, 17 S. Ct., at 769 (holding consideration of origination question "unnecessary" in light of finding that bill was not a revenue bill).

IV

We hold that this case does not raise a political question and is justiciable. Because the bill at issue here was not one for raising revenue, it could not have been passed in violation of the Origination Clause. The contrary judgment of the Court of Appeals is reversed, and the case is remanded for further proceedings consistent with this opinion.

So ordered.

JUSTICE STEVENS, with whom JUSTICE O'CONNOR joins, concurring in the judgment.

In my opinion, a bill that originated unconstitutionally may nevertheless become an enforceable law if passed by both Houses of Congress and signed by the President. I therefore believe that it is not necessary to decide whether 18 U.S.C. § 3013 was passed in violation of the Origination Clause.

I

The Origination Clause appears in Article I, § 7 of the Constitution, which describes the procedures that the two Houses of Congress and the President shall follow when enacting laws. The Origination Clause is the first of three Clauses in that Section. The Clause provides that "All Bills for raising Revenue shall originate in the House of Representatives," but it does not specify what consequences follow from an improper origination.

The immediately following Clause, however, does speak to consequences. The second Clause of § 7 says, among other things, that "Every Bill which shall have passed the House of Representatives and the Senate, shall, before it becomes a Law, be presented to the President of the United States." An improperly originated bill passed by both Houses would seem to be within a class comprising "Every" bill passed by both Houses, and it therefore seems reasonable to assume that such an improperly originated bill is among those that "shall . . . be presented to the President." The Clause further states that if the President returns to Congress a bill presented to him, and if two-thirds of each House thereafter approve the bill, "it shall become a Law." No exception to this categorical statement is made for bills improperly originated.

The second Clause of § 7 later provides that "any Bill" not acted upon by the President within 10 days "shall be a Law, in like Manner as if he had signed it." In this instance, one express exception is made: if Congress adjourns before the 10-day period expires, the bill "shall not be a Law." Again, no exception is made for bills improperly originated.

It is fairly inferred from this language that some bills may become law even if they are improperly originated. It does not, however, necessarily follow that the bill now at issue became law even if improperly originated. That bill is not governed by the provisions just discussed, because it was signed by the President, and hence did not become law by virtue of either Presidential inaction or the override of a veto. The language in § 7 dealing with bills signed by the President speaks in terms of necessary, rather than sufficient, conditions: the Clause states only that bills must be presented to the President, and that if "he approves he shall sign it." The Clause does not say that any bill signed by the President becomes law, although it does later say that a bill not acted upon becomes law "in like Manner as if he had signed it." In my view, the sufficiency of the procedural conditions in the second Clause is reasonably supplied by implication. I accordingly interpret § 7 to provide that even an improperly originated bill becomes law if it meets the procedural requirements specified later in that section.

II

My reading of the text of § 7 is supported by examination of the Constitution's purposes. I agree with the Court that the purpose of the Origination Clause is to give the most " 'immediate representatives of the people' " — Members of the House, directly elected and subject to ouster every two years — an "effectual weapon" for securing the interest of their constituents. *Ante*, at 1971, quoting The Federalists No. 58, p. 359 (C. Rossiter ed. 1961). For four reasons, I believe that examination of this purpose supports the view that the binding force of an otherwise lawfully enacted bill is not vitiated by an Origination Clause violation.

First, the House is in an excellent position to defend its origination power. A bill that originates in the Senate, whether or not it raises revenue, cannot become law without the assent of the House. The House is free to rely upon the Origination Clause to justify its position in a debate with the Senate, regardless of whether constitutional concerns alone drive the House's position. *See* Bessette & Tulis, *The Constitution, Politics, and the Presidency* 8–16, in The Presidency in the Constitutional Order (J. Bessette & J. Tulis, eds., 1981) (discussing ways, aside from judicial enforcement, in which the Constitution shapes political behavior). The Senate may expect that an improperly originated bill will confront a coalition in the House, composed of those who oppose the bill on substantive grounds and those who would favor it on substantive grounds but regard the procedural error as too important to ignore. Taxes rarely go unnoticed at the ballot box, and there is every reason to anticipate that Representatives subject to reelection every two years will jealously guard their power over revenue-raising measures.[2]

Second, the House has greater freedom than does the judiciary to construe the Origination Clause wisely.[3]

The House may, for example, choose to interpret "Bills for raising Revenue" by

---

[2] The Court properly observes that the house has an interest in upholding "the *entire* Constitution, not just those provisions that protect its institutional prerogatives." *Ante*, at 1969 (emphasis in the original). I agree. It is, however, true that even if the House should mistake its constitutional interest generally, it is unlikely to mistake its more particular interest in being powerful: that specific interest is instrumental to any broader conception the House might have of its duties and interests.

Nevertheless, the Court is again correct to say that the possibility of legislative enforcement does not supply a prudential, nonconstitutional justification for abstaining from constitutional interpretation. *Ante*, at 1969–1970. My point is rather that this possibility is relevant to the substantive task of interpreting § 7 itself.

[3] Respondents observe that the House "has not assumed that it is the final arbiter of the Origination Clause," but has instead "looked to court decisions for guidance in determining whether to return bills to the Senate." Brief for Respondent 11. Although respect for our power of judicial review is a constitutional necessity in the ordinary case, it is not clear that the House's deference is either necessary or wise with respect to this issue. Indeed, a decision by this Court to pass upon Origination Clause questions may be an unfortunate

invoking a test that turns largely upon the substantive economic impact of the measure on society as a whole, or may determine the House of origination by identifying the legislators who were most responsible for the content of the final version of the bill. If employed by the House, rather than the judiciary, inquiries so searching obviously create no tension between enforcement of the Origination Clause and the democratic principle of the legislative process — a principle which the Clause itself is designed to serve. The House may also examine evidence, including informal private disclosures, unavailable (or incomprehensible) to the judiciary.

Third, the House is better able than this Court to judge the prejudice resulting from an Origination Clause violation, and so better able than this Court to judge what corrective action, if any, should be taken. The nature of such a power may be comprehended by analogy to our own recognition that constitutional defect in courtroom procedure does not necessarily vitiate the outcome of that procedure. *See Chapman v. California*, 386 U.S. 18, 87 S. Ct. 824, 17 L. Ed. 2d 705 (1967). I see no reason to believe that a defect in statehouse procedure cannot also be harmless: a tax originated in the Senate may nevertheless reflect the views of the people as interpreted by the House, whether because of a coincidence in the judgment of the two branches or because the House directly influenced the Senate's labor. The House's assent to an improperly originated bill is unlikely to be given if its Members believe that the procedural defect harmed the bill's substance. Yet, it would be difficult to imagine how this Court could reasonably assess the prejudice resulting from any particular Origination Clause violation. On my interpretation of § 7, the Constitution confides this responsibility to the House of Representatives instead. One consequence of this interpretation is that an expansive construction of the Clause by the House need not impose spurious formalities, since spurious violations may be ignored.

Fourth, the violation complained of by respondent is unlike those constitutional problems which we have in the past recognized as appropriate for judicial supervision.[4]

This case is not one involving the constitutionality of statutes alleged to effect prospective alterations in the constitutional distribution of power. *See INS v. Chadha*, 462 U.S. 919, 103 S. Ct. 2764, 77 L. Ed. 2d 317 (1983); *Bowsher v. Synar*, 478 U.S. 714, 106 S. Ct. 3181, 92 L. Ed. 2d 583 (1986); *Morrison v. Olson*, 487 U.S. 654, 108 S. Ct. 2597, 101 L. Ed. 2d 569 (1988). No defect in the representative process threatens to impede a democratic solution to the problem at issue. *See Powell v. McCormack*, 395 U.S. 486, 89 S. Ct. 1944, 23 L. Ed. 2d 491 (1969); *Reynolds v. Sims*, 377 U.S. 533, 84 S. Ct. 1362, 12 L. Ed. 2d 506 (1964). No claim is made that this statute deals with subjects outside the sweep of congressional power, *see Garcia v. San Antonio Metropolitan Transit Authority*, 469 U.S. 528, 105 S. Ct. 1005, 83 L. Ed. 2d 1016 (1985), or that the statute abrogates the substantive and procedural guarantees of the Bill of Rights, *see e.g., Buckley v. Valeo*, 424 U.S. 1, 96 S. Ct. 612, 46 L. Ed. 2d 659 (1976). Nor, finally, does respondent contend that the Constitution has been violated because action has been taken in derogation of structural bulwarks designed either to safeguard groups specially in need of judicial protection, or to tame the majoritarian tendencies of American politics more generally. *See Chadha, supra; Powell, supra; United States v. Carolene Products*, 304 U.S. 144, 152 n.4, 58 S. Ct. 778, 783–84 n.4, 82 L. Ed. 1234 (1938); *Hampton v. Mow Sun Wong*, 426 U.S. 88, 96 S. Ct. 1895, 48 L. Ed. 2d 495 (1976). Indeed, this case presents perhaps the weakest imaginable justification for judicial invalidation of a statute: respondent contends that the judiciary must intervene in order to protect a power of the most majoritarian body in the Federal Government, even

---

inducement to the House to forbear from an independent inquiry into the interpretive issues posed by the Clause.

[4] This observation bears upon the plausibility of an interpretation of the Origination Clause that effectively insulates origination problems from judicial review. *See Cohens v. Virginia*, 6 Wheat. 264, 384–85, 5 L. Ed. 257 (1821).

though that body has an absolute veto over any effort to usurp that power. The democratic structure of the Constitution ensures that the majority rarely if ever needs such help from the judiciary.[5]

These considerations reinforce my construction of the text of § 7 and lead me to conclude that the statute before us is law regardless of whether it was improperly originated. As a practical matter, this reading of the Constitution precludes judicial review of alleged violations of the Origination Clause. It is up to the House of Representatives to enforce that provision by refusing its consent to any revenue bills that originate in the Senate. The Court's holding, however, may itself be not too far removed from such a consequence: the Court's essential distinction between revenues allocated to particular programs and those allocated to the General Treasury, *ante*, at 1972, tends to convert the Origination Clause into a formal accounting requirement, so long as the House consents.

In all events, I think that both a literal and a practical interpretation of the Origination Clause is consistent with the conclusion that a revenue bill becomes a law whenever it is passed by both Houses of Congress and duly signed by the President. Accordingly, I concur in the Court's judgment.

NOTES AND QUESTIONS

1. Which style of interpretation, literal or purposive, seems better adapted to dealing with constitutional provisions relating to legislative procedure? Which style is adopted by the majority opinion? By the concurrence?

2. Are the familiar arguments against judicial activism persuasive when the question of enforcement of constitutional rules of legislative procedure is presented? Is a holding that a statute failed to comply with constitutionally prescribed procedural restraints less intrusive than a holding that the statute violates a substantive constitutional right?

3. Why would the federal and state constitutions require that revenue raising measures originate in the House? *See* J. Michael Medina, *The Origination Clause in the American Constitution: A Comparative Survey*, 23 Tulsa L.J. 165 (1987).

C. JUDICIAL REVIEW AND JUSTICIABILITY

FIELD v. CLARK
143 U.S. 649 (1892)

Mr. Justice Harlan delivered the opinion of the court.

Duties were assessed and collected, according to the rates established by what is known as the Tariff Act of October 1, 1890, on woollen dress goods, woollen wearing apparel and silk embroideries, imported by Marshall Field & Co.; on silk and cotton laces imported by Boyd, Sutton & Co.; and on colored cotton cloths imported by Herrman, Sternbach & Co. 26 Stat. 567, c. 1244, § 1.

The importers severally protested against the assessment upon the ground that the act was not a law of the United States . . . .

---

[5] I agree with the Court that the Origination Clause is intended to "safeguard liberty." *Ante*, at 1971. Indeed, this must be true, in a general sense, of almost every constitutional provision, since the Constitution aims to "secure the Blessings of Liberty." U.S. Const., Preamble. Of course, the Constitution aims as well to create a government able to "promote the general Welfare," but liberty and welfare should ultimately coincide.

I also believe, however, that some constitutional provisions are designed to protect liberty in a more specific sense: they protect the rights of individuals as against the majority. Other provisions give the majority sufficient power to act effectively, within limits. In this sense, the First Amendment secures liberty in a way that the Origination Clause does not.

The appellants question the validity of the act of October 1, 1890, upon three grounds to be separately examined.

First. The seventh section of article one of the Constitution of the United States provides: "All bills for raising revenue shall originate in the House of Representatives, but the Senate may propose or concur with amendments as on other bills . . . ."

The Revised Statutes provide that "whenever a bill, order, resolution or vote of the Senate and House of Representatives, having been approved and signed by the President, or not having been returned by him with his objections, becomes a law or takes effect, it shall forthwith be received by the Secretary of State from the President; and whenever a bill, order, resolution or vote is returned by the President with his objections, and, on being reconsidered, is agreed to be passed, and is approved by two-thirds of both houses of Congress, and thereby becomes a law or takes effect, it shall be received by the Secretary of State from the President of the Senate or Speaker of the House of Representatives in whichsoever house it shall last have been so approved, and he shall carefully preserve the originals." Sec. 204.

The original enrolled act in question, designated on its face. "H.R. 9416," was received at the Department of State October 1, 1890, and, when so received, was attested by the signatures of Thomas B. Reed, Speaker of the House of Representatives, and Levi P. Morton, Vice-President of the United States and President of the Senate, and had thereon these endorsements:

"Approved October 1st, 1890.Benj. Harrison."

"I certify that this act originated in the House of Representatives.

"Edw. McPherson, *Clerk.*"

It is made the duty of the Secretary of State to furnish to the Congressional Printer "a correct copy of every act and joint resolution, as soon as possible after its approval by the President, or after it has become a law in accordance with the Constitution without such approval." That duty was performed by the Secretary of State with respect to the act in question, and the act appears in the volume of statutes published and distributed under the authority of the United States. Rev. Stat. §§ 210, 3803, 3805, 3807, 3808.

The contention of the appellants is, that this enrolled act, in the custody of the Secretary of State, and appearing, upon its face, to have become a law in the mode prescribed by the Constitution, is to be deemed an absolute nullity, in all its parts, because — such is the allegation — it is shown by the Congressional record of proceedings, reports of committees of each house, reports of committees of conference, and other papers printed by authority of Congress, and having reference to house bill 9416, that a section of the bill, as it finally passed, was not in the bill authenticated by the signatures of the presiding officers of the respective houses of Congress, and approved by the President. The section alleged to have been omitted was as follows:

"SEC. 30. That on all original and unbroken factory packages of smoking and manufactured tobacco and snuff, held by manufacturers or dealers at the time the reduction herein provided for shall go into effect, upon which the tax has been paid, there shall be allowed a drawback or rebate of the full amount of the reduction, but the same shall not apply in any case where the claim has not been presented within sixty days following the date of reduction; and such rebate to manufacturers may be paid in stamps at the reduced rate; and no claim shall be allowed or drawback paid for a less amount than five dollars. It shall be the duty of the Commissioner of Internal Revenue, with the approval of the Secretary of the Treasury, to adopt such rules and regulations and to prescribe and furnish such blanks and forms as may be necessary to carry this section into effect. For the payment of the rebates provided for in this section there is hereby appropriated any money in the Treasury not otherwise appropriated."

The argument, in behalf of the appellants, is, that a bill, signed by the Speaker of the House of Representatives and by the President of the Senate, presented to and approved by the President of the United States, and delivered by the latter to the Secretary of State, as an act passed by Congress, does not become a law of the United States if it had not in fact been passed by Congress. In view of the express requirements of the Constitution the correctness of this general principle cannot be doubted. There is no authority in the presiding officers of the House of Representatives and the Senate to attest by their signatures, nor in the President to approve, nor in the Secretary of State to receive and cause to be published, as a legislative act, any bill not passed by Congress.

But this concession of the correctness of the general principle for which the appellants contend does not determine the precise question before the court; for it remains to inquire as to the nature of the evidence upon which a court may act when the issue is made as to whether a bill, originating in the House of Representatives or the Senate, and asserted to have become a law, was or was not passed by Congress. This question is now presented for the first time in this court. It has received, as its importance required that it should receive, the most deliberate consideration. We recognize, on one hand, the duty of this court, from the performance of which it may not shrink, to give full effect to the provisions of the Constitution relating to the enactment of laws that are to operate wherever the authority and jurisdiction of the United States extend. On the other hand, we cannot be unmindful of the consequences that must result if this court should feel obliged, in fidelity to the Constitution, to declare that an enrolled bill, on which depend public and private interests of vast magnitude, and which has been authenticated by the signatures of the presiding officers of the two houses of Congress, and by the approval of the President, and been deposited in the public archives, *as an act of Congress*, was not in fact passed by the House of Representatives and the Senate, and therefore did not become a law.

The clause of the Constitution upon which the appellants rest their contention that the act in question was never passed by Congress is the one declaring that "each house shall keep a journal of its proceedings, and from time to time publish the same, except such parts as may in their judgment require secrecy; and the yeas and nays of the members of either house on any question shall, at the desire of one-fifth of those present, be entered on the journal." Art. 1, sec. 5. It was assumed in argument that the object of this clause was to make the journal the best, if not conclusive, evidence upon the issue as to whether a bill was, in fact, passed by the two houses of Congress. But the words used do not require such interpretation. On the contrary, as Mr. Justice Story has well said, "the object of the whole clause is to insure publicity to the proceedings of the legislature, and a correspondent responsibility of the members to their respective constituents. And it is founded in sound policy and deep political foresight. Intrigue and cabal are thus deprived of some of their main resources, by plotting and devising measures in secrecy. The public mind is enlightened by an attentive examination of the public measures; patriotism, and integrity, and wisdom obtain their due reward; and votes are ascertained, not by vague conjecture, but by positive facts . . . . So long as known and open responsibility is valuable as a check or an incentive among the representatives of a free people, so long a journal of their proceedings and their votes, published in the face of the world, will continue to enjoy public favor and be demanded by public opinion." 1 Story, Constitution, §§ 840, 841.

In regard to certain matters, the Constitution expressly requires that they shall be entered on the journal. To what extent the validity of legislative action may be affected by the failure to have those matters entered on the journal, we need not inquire. No such question is presented for determination. But it is clear that, in respect to the particular mode in which, or with what fulness, shall be kept the proceedings of either house relating to matters not expressly required to be entered on the journals; whether bills, orders, resolutions, reports and amendments shall be entered at large on the journal, or only referred to and designated by their titles or by numbers; these and like matters were left to the discretion of the respective houses of Congress. Nor does any clause of that instrument, either expressly or by necessary implication, prescribe the mode in which the fact of the original passage of a bill by the House of Representatives and the

Senate shall be authenticated, or preclude Congress from adopting any mode to that end which its wisdom suggests. Although the Constitution does not expressly require bills that have passed Congress to be attested by the signatures of the presiding officers of the two houses, usage, the orderly conduct of legislative proceedings and the rules under which the two bodies have acted since the organization of the government, require that mode of authentication.

The signing by the Speaker of the House of Representatives, and by the President of the Senate, in open session, of an enrolled bill, is an official attestation by the two houses of such bill as one that has passed Congress. It is a declaration by the two houses, through their presiding officers, to the President, that a bill, thus attested, has received, in due form, the sanction of the legislative branch of the government, and that it is delivered to him in obedience to the constitutional requirement that all bills which pass Congress shall be presented to him. And when a bill, thus attested, receives his approval, and is deposited in the public archives, its authentication as a bill that has passed Congress should be deemed complete and unimpeachable. As the President has no authority to approve a bill not passed by Congress, an enrolled act in the custody of the Secretary of State, and having the official attestations of the Speaker of the House of Representatives, of the President of the Senate, and of the President of the United States, carries, on its face, a solemn assurance by the legislative and executive departments of the government, charged, respectively, with the duty of enacting and executing the laws, that it was passed by Congress. The respect due to coequal and independent departments requires the judicial department to act upon that assurance, and to accept, as having passed Congress, all bills authenticated in the manner stated: leaving the courts to determine, when the question properly arises, whether the act, so authenticated, is in conformity with the Constitution.

It is admitted that an enrolled act, thus authenticated, is sufficient evidence of itself — nothing to the contrary appearing upon its face — that it passed Congress. But the contention is, that it cannot be regarded as a law of the United States if the journal of either house fails to show that it passed in the precise form in which it was signed by the presiding officers of the two houses, and approved by the President. It is said that, under any other view, it becomes possible for the Speaker of the House of Representatives and the President of the Senate to impose upon the people as a law a bill that was never passed by Congress. But this possibility is too remote to be seriously considered in the present inquiry. It suggests a deliberate conspiracy to which the presiding officers, the committees on enrolled bills and the clerks of the two houses must necessarily be parties, all acting with a common purpose to defeat an expression of the popular will in the mode prescribed by the Constitution. Judicial action based upon such a suggestion is forbidden by the respect due to a coordinate branch of the government. The evils that may result from the recognition of the principle that an enrolled act, in the custody of the Secretary of State, attested by the signatures of the presiding officers of the two houses of Congress, and the approval of the President, is conclusive evidence that it was passed by Congress, according to the forms of the Constitution, would be far less than those that would certainly result from a rule making the validity of Congressional enactments depend upon the manner in which the journals of the respective houses are kept by the subordinate officers charged with the duty of keeping them.

The views we have expressed are supported by numerous adjudications in this country, to some of which it is well to refer. In *Pangborn v. Young*, 32 N.J. Law (3 Vroom) 29, 37, the question arose as to the relative value, as evidence of the passage of a bill, of the journals of the respective houses of the legislature and the enrolled act authenticated by the signatures of the speakers of the two houses and by the approval of the governor. The bill there in question, it was alleged, originated in the house and was amended in the Senate, but, as presented to and approved by the governor, did not contain all the amendments made in the Senate. Referring to the provision in the constitution of New Jersey, requiring each house of the legislature to keep a journal of its proceedings — which provision is in almost the same words as the above clause quoted from the Federal Constitution — the court, speaking by Chief Justice Beasley, said that it was impossible for the mind not to incline to the opinion that the framers of the Constitution, in exacting the keeping of the journals, did not design to create records that were to be the ultimate and conclusive evidence of the conformity of legislative action to the constitutional provisions relating to the enactment of laws. In the nature of things, it was observed, these journals must have been constructed out of loose and hasty memoranda made in the pressure of business and amid the distractions of a numerous assembly. The Chief Justice said: "Can any one deny that, if the laws of the State are to be tested by a comparison with these journals, so imperfect, so unauthenticated, that the stability of all written law will be shaken to its very foundation? Certainly no person can venture to say that many of our statutes, perhaps some of the oldest and most important, those which affect large classes of persons or on which great interests depend, will not be found defective, even in constitutional particulars, if judged by this criterion . . . . In addition to these considerations, in judging of consequences, we are to remember the danger under the prevalence of such a doctrine to be apprehended from the intentional corruption of evidences of this character. It is scarcely too much to say that the legal existence of almost every legislative act would be at the mercy of all persons having access to these journals; for it is obvious that any law can be invalidated by the interpolation of a few lines or the obliteration of one name and the substitution of another in its stead. I cannot consent to expose the state legislation to the hazards of such probable error or facile fraud. The doctrine contended for on the part of the evidence has no foundation, in my estimation, on any considerations of public policy." The conclusion was, that upon grounds of public policy, as well as upon the ancient and well settled rules of law, a copy of a bill bearing the signatures of the presiding officers of the two houses of the legislature and the approval of the governor, and found in the custody of the Secretary of State, was conclusive proof of the enactment and contents of a statute, and could not be contradicted by the legislative journals or in any other mode . . . .

In *Sherman v. Story*, 30 California, 253, 275, the whole subject was carefully considered. The court, speaking through Mr. Justice Sawyer, said: "Better, far better, that a provision should occasionally find its way into the statute through mistake, or even fraud, than that every act, state and national, should at any and all times be liable to be put in issue and impeached by the journals, loose papers of the legislature and parol evidence. Such a state of uncertainty in the statute laws of the land would lead to mischiefs absolutely intolerable . . . . The result of the authorities in England and in the other States clearly is, that, at common law, whenever a general statute is misrecited, or its existence denied, the question is to be tried and determined by the court as a question of law — that is to say, the court is bound to take notice of it, and inform itself the best way it can; that there is no plea by which its existence can be put in issue and tried as a question of fact; that if the enrollment of the statute is in existence, the enrollment itself is the record, which is conclusive as to what the statute is, and cannot be impeached, destroyed or weakened by the journals of Parliament or any other less authentic or less satisfactory memorials; and that there has been no departure from the principles of the common law in this respect in the United States, except in instances where a departure has been grounded on, or taken in pursuance of, some express constitutional or statutory provision requiring some relaxation of the rule, in order that full effect might be given to such provisions; and in such instances the rule has been relaxed by judges with great caution and hesitation, and the departure has never been extended beyond an inspection of the journals of both branches of the legislature." . . .

The case of *Gradner v. The Collector*, 6 Wall. 499, 511, was relied on in argument as supporting the contention of the appellants.

The question there was as to the time when an act of Congress took effect; the doubt, upon that point, arising from the fact that the month and day, but not the year, of the approval of the act by the President appeared upon the enrolled act in the custody of the Department of State. This omission, it was held, could be supplied in support of the act from the legislative journals. It was said by the court: "We are of opinion, therefore, on principle as well as authority, that whenever a question arises in a court of law of the existence of a statute, or of the time when a statute took effect, or of the precise terms of a statute, the judges who are called upon to decide it have a right to resort to any source of information which in its nature is capable of conveying to the judicial mind a clear and satisfactory answer to such question; always seeking first for that which in its nature is most appropriate, unless the positive law has enacted a different rule." There was no question in that case as to the existence or terms of a statute, and the point in judgment was that the time when an admitted statute took effect, not appearing from the enrolled act, could be shown by the legislative journals. It is scarcely necessary to say that that case does not meet the question here presented . . . .

We are of opinion, for the reasons stated, that it is not competent for the appellants to show, from the journals of either house, from the reports of committees or from other documents printed by authority of Congress, that the enrolled bill designated H.R. 9416, as finally passed, contained a section that does not appear in the enrolled act in the custody of the State Department.

D & W AUTO SUPPLY v. DEPARTMENT OF REVENUE
602 S.W.2d 420 (Ky. 1980)

STEPHENS, JUSTICE.

The ultimate question to be decided on this appeal is the constitutionality of KRS 224.905–.970, commonly called the "Litter Control Act," which was enacted by the 1978 regular session of the Kentucky General Assembly. In arriving at our decision we must, perforce, reconsider the validity of a long line of decisions of this court which created and nurtured the so-called "enrolled bill" doctrine.

. . . .

The Act in question is essentially an anti-littering statute. Its stated purposes are to consolidate and promote statewide programs for the reduction of litter and littering; to recover and recycle waste materials; to establish publicity as well as educational and motivational campaigns to build and sustain public awareness of the litter problem; and to create a litter-free ethic among Kentuckians. KRS 224.905, 224.930. The Kentucky Department for Natural Resources and Environmental Protection is given the responsibility of administering the Act. KRS 224.915.

To fund the efforts of state government in carrying out the purposes and mandates of this enactment, the legislature determined that a portion of that cost should be borne by those industries whose products are "reasonably related to the litter problem." KRS 224.955(1). Sixteen specific categories of products are listed as examples of what is intended to be assessed, but, under the specific terms of the Act, the list is not exclusive. KRS 224.955(1)(a)–(p) . . . .

The Act was initially introduced in the Kentucky House of Representatives and, as it wound its way through the legislative process, was known and identified as House Bill 253. It appears conclusively in the record that when House Bill 253 came before that body for final action, it "passed" by a vote of 48 "ayes" and 43 "nays."

Appellants make several arguments in challenging the validity of the Act: (1) The Act is unconstitutional because it did not receive a majority of 51 votes in the House, as is mandated by section 46 of the Kentucky Constitution for an appropriations bill . . . .

Section 46 of the Kentucky Constitution sets out certain procedures that the legislature must follow before a bill can be considered for final passage. In addition, that section mandates that no bill shall become law unless "it receives the votes of at least two-fifths of the members elected to each House, and a majority of the members voting," with the following exception: "Any act or resolution for the appropriation of money or the creation of debt shall, on its final passage, *receive the votes of a majority of all the members elected to each house.*" Kentucky Constitution sec. 46 (emphasis added).

It is conceded by all parties and clearly established by the record that the Litter Control Act, HB 253 of the 1978 regular session of the Kentucky General Assembly, received only 48 votes on its final passage in the House of Representatives. Since there are 100 members of that House, if the Act is an appropriation, its passage did not comply with a clear constitutional mandate.

It is not seriously argued by the appellees that KRS 224.905–.970 does not contain an appropriation . . . .

Under both the legislative definition and the judicial definition, it is clear that the Litter Control Act is an appropriation act and falls within the aegis of section 46 of the Kentucky Constitution.

At this point, logic suggests that the decision of this Court is obvious, viz, since the Act makes an appropriation and since it received less than 51 votes in the House, it is violative of the Kentucky Constitution. However, we are immediately confronted with the huge stumbling block of what is described as the "enrolled bill" doctrine.

HB 253 was signed by the presiding officers of the House of Representatives, and was certified by the Clerk of the House as conforming with all House procedural rules and, in effect, as conforming with all constitutional requirements. Under the enrolled bill doctrine as it now exists in Kentucky, a court may not look behind such a bill, enrolled and certified by the appropriate officers, to determine if there are any defects.

> From every point of reason, therefore, we are convinced that the enrolled bill, when attested by the presiding officers as the law requires, must be accepted by the courts as the very bill adopted by the legislature, and that its mode of enactment was in conformity to all constitutional requirements. When so authenticated, it imports absolute verity, and is unimpeached by the [legislative] journals.

Lafferty v. Huffman, 99 Ky. 80, 35 S.W. 123, 126 (1896). Thus spake Judge Hazelrigg in enunciating the enrolled bill doctrine.

Section 46 of the Kentucky Constitution requires that the final vote on a bill be taken by "yeas" and "nays." In *Lafferty*, passage of the law in question violated this provision, yet the bill was properly enrolled and approved by the governor. In declining to look behind the law to determine the propriety of its enactment, the court enunciated three reasons for adopting the enrolled bill rule. First, the court was reluctant to scrutinize the processes of the legislature, an equal branch of government. Second, reasons of convenience prevailed, which discouraged requiring the legislature to preserve its records and anticipated considerable complex litigation if the court ruled otherwise. Third, the court acknowledged the poor record-keeping abilities of the General Assembly and expressed a preference for accepting the final bill as enrolled, rather than opening up the records of the legislature. Since 1896, this court has concurred in the reasoning applied in *Lafferty*, regardless of what procedural or constitutional defects have been alleged and proved.

Kentucky is not alone in adherence to the enrolled bill doctrine. At least 19 of our sister states follow the rule which conclusively presumes the validity of a bill passed by the legislature and signed by the legislative officers. *See* I C. SANDS, SUTHERLAND STATUTORY CONSTRUCTION sec. 15.03 et seq. (4th ed. 1972); 82 C.J.S. *Statutes* sec. 83 (1953); 72 Am. Jur. 2d *Statutes* sec. 90 (1974); and 4 A.L.R.2d 978 (1949).

Nowhere has the rule been adopted without reason, or as the result of judicial whim. There are four historical bases for the doctrine. (1) An enrolled bill was a "record" and, as such, was not subject to attack at common law. (2) Since the legislature is one of the three branches of government, the courts, being co-equal, must indulge in every presumption that legislative acts are valid. (3) When the rule was originally formulated, record-keeping of the legislatures was so inadequate that a balancing of equities required that the final act, the enrolled bill, be given efficacy. (4) There were theories of convenience as expressed by the Kentucky court in *Lafferty*.

The rule is not unanimous in the several states, however, and it has not been without its critics. From an examination of cases and treatises, we can summarize the criticism as follows: (1) Artificial presumptions, especially conclusive ones, are not favored. (2) Such a rule frequently (as in the present case) produces results which do not accord with facts or constitutional provisions. (3) The rule is conducive to fraud, forgery, corruption and other wrongdoings. (4) Modern automatic and electronic record-keeping devices now used by legislatures remove one of the original reasons for the rule. (5) The rule disregards the primary obligation of the courts to seek the truth and to provide a remedy for a wrong committed by any branch of government.

In light of these considerations, we are convinced that the time has come to re-examine the enrolled bill doctrine.[2]

This court is not unmindful of the admonition of the doctrine of *stare decisis*. The maxim is "Stare decisis et non quieta movere," which simply suggests that we stand by precedents and not disturb settled points of law. Yet, this rule is not inflexible, nor is it of such a nature as to require perpetuation of error or illogic. As we stated in *Daniel's Adm'r v. Hoofnel*, 287 Ky. 834, 155 S.W.2d 469, 471–72 (1941) (citations omitted):

> The force of the rule depends upon the nature of the question to be decided and the extent of the disturbance of rights and practices which a change in the interpretation of the law or the course of judicial opinions may create. Cogent considerations are whether there is clear error and urgent reasons "for neither justice nor wisdom requires a court to go from one doubtful rule to another," and whether or not the evils of the principle that has been followed will be more injurious than can possibly result from a change.

Certainly, when a theory supporting a rule of law is not grounded on facts, or upon sound logic, or is unjust, or has been discredited by actual experience, it should be discarded, and with it the rule it supports.

It is clear to us that the major premise of the *Lafferty* decision, the poor record-keeping of the legislature, has disappeared. Modern equipment and technology are the rule in record-keeping by our General Assembly. Tape recorders, electric typewriters, duplicating machines, recording equipment, printing presses, computers, electronic voting machines, and the like remove all doubts and fears as to the ability of the General Assembly to keep accurate and readily accessible records.

It is also apparent that the "convenience" rule is not appropriate in today's modern and developing judicial philosophy. The fact that the number and complexity of lawsuits may increase is not persuasive if one is mindful that the overriding purpose of our judicial system is to discover the truth and see that justice is done. The existence of difficulties and complexities should not deter this pursuit and we reject any doctrine or presumption that so provides.

Lastly, we address the premise that the equality of the various branches of government requires that we shut our eyes to constitutional failings and other errors of our coparceners in government. We simply do not agree. Section 26 of the Kentucky Constitution provides that any law contrary to the constitution is "void." The proper exercise of judicial authority requires us to recognize any law which is unconstitutional and to declare it void. Without belaboring the point, we believe that under section 228 of the Kentucky Constitution it is our obligation to "support . . . the Constitution of

---

[2] The 1980 General Assembly made its own examination of the doctrine, and enacted legislation providing for review of an enrolled bill in the limited situation where the *language* of the bill as enrolled differs materially from the language of the bill as passed by the legislature. House Bill 84.

this Commonwealth." We are sworn to see that violations of the constitution — by any person, corporation, state agency or branch of government — are brought to light and corrected. To countenance an artificial rule of law that silences our voices when confronted with violations of our constitution is not acceptable to this court.

We believe that a more reasonable rule is the one which Professor Sutherland describes as the "extrinsic evidence" rule. I Sutherland, *supra*, at sec. 15.06. Other jurisdictions have embraced this rule, which we hereby adopt as the law of this case and future cases. Under this approach there is a *prima facie* presumption that an enrolled bill is valid, but such presumption may be overcome by clear, satisfactory and convincing evidence establishing that constitutional requirements have not been met.

We therefore overrule *Lafferty v. Huffman* and all other cases following the so-called enrolled bill doctrine, to the extent that there is no longer a conclusive presumption that an enrolled bill is valid. With regard to the present case, we declare KRS 224.905–.970, the "Litter Control Act," void as violative of section 46 of the Kentucky Constitution.

. . . .

ROBERT F. WILLIAMS, STATE CONSTITUTIONAL LIMITS ON LEGISLATIVE PROCEDURE: LEGISLATIVE COMPLIANCE AND JUDICIAL ENFORCEMENT,
17 Publius 106–12 (1987), *reprinted in*
48 University of Pittsburgh Law Review 797 (1987)[*]

Judicial Approaches to Enforcing State Constitutional Restrictions on Legislative Procedure

State courts have developed a surprisingly wide range of approaches to enforcing restrictions on legislative procedure under circumstances where an act does not carry "its death warrant in its hand." Even within single jurisdictions, one can detect inconsistent doctrines and a lack of continuity over time. These widely varying judicial doctrines reflect what are essentially political decisions, made in the context of adjudicating actual controversies, about the extent of judicial enforcement of state constitutional norms.

The range of approaches can be viewed as a continuum. At one end of the continuum is the "enrolled bill rule" . . . . This is marked by judicial passivity and complete deference to the legislative enactment.[71] At the other end is the "extrinsic evidence rule," characterized by judicial activism and recognition of the written constitution as a binding source of law. In between these two extremes are three intermediate approaches to judicial enforcement. All of these have been developed by the courts as they have been called on by litigants to interpret and enforce state constitutional restrictions on legislative procedure . . . .

The Enrolled Bill Rule

The enrolled bill rule is also referred to as the "conclusive presumption rule" because when it is operative, it prevents any evidence, other than the final enrolled bill itself, from being produced to show constitutional violations occurring during the process of enactment.[73]

---

[*] Copyright © 1987 by *Publius: The Journal of Federalism*. Reprinted with permission.

[71] Norman J. Singer, Statutes and Statutory Construction, Vol. 1 (4th ed.; Wilmette, Ill.: Callaghan and Co., 1985), pp. 609–611.

[73] *Ibid.* p. 609. This approach was adopted by the U.S. Supreme Court in 1892. *See Field v. Clark*, 143 U.S. 649, 669–80 (1892). There are, of course, relatively few procedural challenges to federal statutes . . . . For an

In his 1977 commentary on the revised Texas Constitution, George Braden asserted that the enrolled bill rule was the majority view.[74] The most common argument advanced in favor of the rule is the separation of powers doctrine. Because the legislature is a coordinate branch of government, the argument contends that the courts should not question the validity of its certified (enrolled) acts by going behind them to determine compliance with constitutional limitations. Another argument relies on the need for finality with respect to the validity of statutes, and the need for citizens to rely on such finality. These arguments inevitably leave it to the legislature itself to determine whether there has been compliance with limitation contained in the state constitution . . . .

Braden advocates the enrolled bill rule . . . . He states, "In any event, the members are fully capable of enforcing the rule, and it is their sole responsibility to do so under the enrolled bill doctrine." Texas continues to follow the enrolled bill rule, which has been in effect in civil cases since *Williams v. Taylor* in 1892. The court in *Williams* refused to invalidate a statute even though the legislative journals showed that the bill had not been reported out of committee within three days of final adjournment, in violation of Article 3, Section 32 of the Texas Constitution.

The Supreme Court of Washington recently reaffirmed the enrolled bill rule in *Citizens Council Against Crime v. Bjork*.[80] In continuing to apply the rule, the Court cited earlier Washington precedents and also stated:

> An additional reason of public policy which supports the [enrolled bill] doctrine is that it is necessary in order that people may rely upon the statutes as setting forth the laws which have been enacted by the legislature. If the enrolled bill were not taken as conclusive evidence that it was regularly and constitutionally enacted, Judge John P. Hoyt (who had served as President of the Constitutional Convention) said, it would be practically impossible for the courts even to determine what was the law, and would render it absolutely impossible for the average citizen to ascertain that of which he must at his peril take notice.

The end result of the "finality argument" is that people have laws that they can rely on; but that have no guarantee that those laws were enacted constitutionally. Furthermore, as the experience of states which follow the "journal entry rule" or "extrinsic evidence rule" shows, the unfavorable consequences that Judge Hoyt foresaw have not come to pass.

The "Slightly Modified" Enrolled Bill Rule

If the enrolled bill rule is placed at the far left of the continuum, the current rule in New Mexico can be placed only a short step to the right of it. After observing the enrolled bill rule since 1915, the New Mexico Supreme Court carved out a narrow exception in 1974.[83] The court struck down the statutes in question, enacted after the sixtieth calendar day of the legislative session in violation of Article 4, Section 5 of the New Mexico Constitution. The justices held that courts may examine "the question of whether or not the act or bill purportedly passed by the Legislature within the constitutional time limitation was in truth and in fact passed within that limitation." The

---

exploration of the English antecedents of the enrolled bill rule, see William H. Lloyd, *Pylkinton's Case and Its Successors*, UNIVERSITY OF PENNSYLVANIA LAW REVIEW 69 (November 1920): 20–34.

[74] GEORGE D. BRADEN, THE CONSTITUTION OF THE STATE OF TEXAS, AN ANNOTATED AND COMPARATIVE ANALYSIS (Austin: Texas Advisory Commission on Intergovernmental Relations, 1977), Vol. 1, p. 121.

[80] 84 Wash. 2d 891, 529 P.2d 1072 (1975).

[83] *Dillon v. King*, 87 N.M. 79, 529 P.2d 745 (1974) (overruling *Earnest, Trav. Auditor v. Sargent, Auditor*, 20 N.M. 427, 150 P. 1018 (1915)).

court explicitly held that its decision was to be prospective only, and only applicable to alleged violations of Article 4, Section 5 where "[T]he conclusive legal presumption that ordinarily attaches to enrolled bills simply would not attach."

Acknowledging the separation of powers clause in the New Mexico Constitution, and disclaiming any intention of "even suggesting to the Legislature how it should conduct its affairs," the court concluded that "[i]t is nevertheless our function to say what the law is and what the Constitution means." The court clearly stated that it did "not intend to herald the complete demise of the enrolled bill rule."

The court's arguments as to why it should look behind the enrolled bill to determine compliance with Article 4, Section 5 are persuasive. It noted that "[t]here is not the slightest doubt that the legislators are duty bound to comply with this constitutional directive." Of course, legislators are duty bound to comply with all constitutional directives. The New Mexico court still seems to leave the enrolled bill rule in place for challenges asserting that a bill "was altered or amended during its passage so as to change its original purpose." A violation of this or other provisions would arguably be as unconstitutional as if it had been passed after the constitutionally allotted time for the legislative session had come to an end. Why the court considered only violations of Article 4, Section 5 to be egregious enough to warrant an exception to the enrolled bill rule remains unexplained. All the arguments advanced in support of this exception seem equally applicable to abolishing the enrolled bill rule altogether.

The Modified Enrolled Bill Rule

On another step to the right of the continuum lies the "modified enrolled bill rule" adopted by the Supreme Court of South Dakota in 1936.[89] Under this rule, the enrolled bill is conclusive evidence of proper enactment except when an alleged violation concerns a provision for which the constitution specifically requires that a journal entry be made. Only under these narrow circumstances will the court look to the journals to determine whether a challenged act was passed improperly.

The court's latest consideration of the rule came in 1974.[90] One of the alleged improprieties was that the bill was not "read twice, by number and title once when introduced, and once upon final passage" as required by Article 3, Section 17. The court held that "[t]he modified enrolled bill rule precluded plaintiffs from introducing evidence of the legislature's failure to comply with the requirements of Article 3, Section 17, because a journal entry noting compliance with that section is not *expressly required* by the Constitution." Even though the journals showed that the bill never got a first reading, the journals did not lack any of the required entries on the day the bill was considered and passed. Therefore, the court held that the enrolled bill became conclusive proof of its proper enactment.

The weakness of the modified enrolled bill rule was exposed by Justice Frank Henderson in his dissenting opinion. That is, the rule effectively insulates even intentional violations of the constitution from judicial review, even if the violation appears on the face of the journals, unless the violation occurs with respect to one of the limited exceptions where a specific journal entry is required by the constitution. Henderson favored adoption of the "journal entry rule." In support of his view, Henderson cited Article 3, Section 13, which mandates that "each house shall keep a journal of its proceedings." He also cited the rules apparently followed by the

---

[89] The rule was enunciated in *Barnsdall Refining Corporation v. Welsh*, 64 S.D. 647, 269 N.W. 853 (1936). The rule is discussed in Marion R. Smyser, *Constitutional Limitations on the Enactment of Statutes in South Dakota*, South Dakota Law Review 25 (Winter 1980): 33–35.

[90] *Independent Community Bankers Assoc. v. South Dakota*, 346 N.W.2d 737 (S.D. 1984). Ohio recently adopted the modified enrolled bill rule in a thoughtful opinion. *Hoover v. Bd. of County Commissioners*, 19 Ohio St. 3d 1, 482 N.E.2d 575 (1985).

neighboring states of Minnesota and Michigan. He concluded that, "making laws is the State Legislature's business, but protecting the Constitution is this Court's business. Viewing an enrolled bill as conclusive and blessing it as legal is to forsake, oftentimes, the truth."

The Journal Entry Rule

The middle of the continuum is represented by the "journal entry rule." This rule allows a court to consider an evidence appearing in the legislative journals to help determine the validity of a statute which has been challenged on constitutional grounds, with the enrolled bill being considered only *prima facie* valid.

One state that follows the journal entry is Florida. In a 1983 case,[97] a Florida drug trafficking statute was challenged on the grounds that it had not been properly read before passage as required by Article 3, Section 7. The trial court had considered extrinsic evidence (voice recordings of the legislative proceedings and transcripts generated from those recordings) to contradict the journals. The journals indicated that both houses of the legislature had properly read the bills before their enactment.

In continuing to follow the journal entry rule, the Florida Supreme Court held that the legislative journals were the only evidence "superior in dignity" to enrolled bills. The rationale for the court's holding, and the basis of the journal entry rule, is that the legislative journals are considered to be "public records" because the constitution mandates that they be kept. Under this view, the journals are at least as reliable as the enrolled bill as evidence of what procedure the legislature actually followed, or did not follow, in enacting legislation. Indeed, in Florida, if there is a conflict between an act and the journal, the journal controls.

The court did list some specific exceptions where extrinsic evidence might be used to impeach the journals: for example, where "clear and legally sufficient allegations of fraud are presented" or when it is alleged that actions were taken by a legislature after it ceased to be a duly constituted legislature. Absent a challenge based on circumstances like these, the legislative journals are the only evidence that can be used to overcome the presumption of constitutionality afforded to enrolled bills in states which, like Florida, follow the journal entry rule.

The Extrinsic Evidence Rule

At the right end of the continuum is the "extrinsic evidence rule." This rule "accords the enrolled bill a prima facie presumption of validity but permits an attack by clear, satisfactory and convincing evidence establishing that the constitutional requirements have not been met."[105] This rule was adopted by the Supreme Court of Kentucky in 1980,[106] in a challenge based on Section 46 of the Kentucky Constitution. Although the journals indicated, and all parties conceded, that only 48 votes in a 100-member house were cast in favor of a bill containing an appropriation, Section 46 sets out certain procedures, including: "Any act or resolution for the appropriation of money or the creation of debt shall, on its final passage, receive the votes of a majority of all members elected to each house."

This case gave the Supreme Court of Kentucky the change it apparently was looking

---

[97] *State v. Kaufman*, 430 So. 2d 904 (1983). Rhode Island also follows the journal entry rule. *See State Terminal Corp. v. General Scrap Iron Inc.*, 107 R.I. 24, 264 A.2d 334 (1970). *See also* Elizabeth Hunter Cobb, *Judicial Review of the Legislative Enactment Process: Louisiana's "Journal Entry Rule,"* Louisiana Law Review 41 (Summer 1981) 1187–1200.

[105] Singer, Statutes and Statutory Construction, pp. 617–618.

[106] *D & W Auto Supply v. Dept. of Revenue*, 602 S.W.2d 420 (Ky. 1980). The extrinsic evidence rule is also followed by Illinois. *See Yarger v. Board of Regents of Regency Universities*, 98 Ill. 2d 259, 456 N.E.2d (1983). *See also Jensen v. Matheson, supra*, note 96 (Maughan, J., dissenting).

for to reexamine, and abandon, the enrolled bill rule which had been in effect there since 1896. Before abandoning the enrolled bill rule, the court examined the four historical bases of the doctrine and the criticisms of the rule. A major argument the court advanced in favor of adopting the extrinsic evidence rule was that it is the "sworn duty of the courts under Section 26 of the Kentucky Constitution to see that violations of the constitution . . . are brought to light and corrected." The court stated, "[t]o countenance an artificial rule of law that silences our voices when confronted with violations of our constitution is not acceptable to this court." The court concluded that the extrinsic evidence rule is "a more reasonable rule," and one that will best allow the court to fulfill its obligation to "support the Constitution of the Commonwealth."

Conclusion

It should now be obvious, from this brief review, that there is a wide range of judicial attitudes toward enforcing state constitutional restrictions on legislative procedure.[110] Litigants seeking an adjudication of a statute's invalidity on the basis of procedural defects are not neutral, good-government watchdogs seeking enforcement of the state constitution as an abstract value. They are, rather, directly affected by, and opposed to, the challenged statute's substantive outcome and are seeking a procedural "handle" to avoid its consequences. They appear to be seeking a judicial windfall after losing in the legislature. This may be what leads to judicial ambivalence about enforcing constitutional restrictions on legislative procedure.

The question still remains whether, in the absence of legislative adherence and executive enforcement (which may be common with respect to controversial statutes), courts should enforce apparently mandatory requirements of the written constitution. These are basic questions of justiciability and the judicial function in constitutional interpretation and enforcement.

NOTES AND QUESTIONS

1. In the Origination Clause case, *United States v. Munoz-Flores, supra,* the Court held that an alleged violation of that clause is justiciable. Does *Munoz-Flores* tacitly overrule *Field v. Clark, supra?*

2. Is the enrolled bill rule akin to the "political question" doctrine? *See generally* Nat Stern, *The Political Question Doctrine in State Courts,* 35 S.C. L. Rev. 405 (1984).

3. A lengthy debate in the 1872–1873 Pennsylvania Constitutional Convention concerning the question of judicial enforceability of legislative procedural requirements in the state constitution was illuminating, but inconclusive. The Legislation Committee had recommended the inclusion of the following provision in the legislative article:

> Any bill passed in disregard of the provisions and directions prescribed in this article shall be void and of no effect; and when the validity of any law passed by the Legislature is questioned in any court of record, it shall be competent for such court to inspect the Journals of either House, and if it does not appear thereon that all the forms of legislation, in both Houses, as hereinbefore prescribed, have been observed in the passage of such law, the same shall be adjudged by such court to be void.

2 Debates of the Convention to Amend the Constitution of Pennsylvania, 1872–1873, at 758. A debate followed, during which the delegates fully discussed the pros and cons of judicial enforcement, together with alternatives, such as enforcement by the executive branch. *Ibid.* at 758–97. At the conclusion of the debate, the Convention simply voted not to accept the recommended language. *Ibid.* at 797.

---

[110] Justice Hans A. Linde of Oregon has noted: "When a law is promulgated without compliance with the rules of legitimate lawmaking, is it not a law? Remarkably, we have no coherent national doctrine on this fundamental question." Hans A. Linde, *Due Process of Lawmaking,* Nebraska Law Review 55 (1976): 242.

4. Study the following New Jersey statute. Would you recommend the adoption of this statute in an enrolled bill rule jurisdiction? In a journal entry rule jurisdiction? Would the statute be constitutional?

NEW JERSEY STATUTES ANNOTATED, Tit. 1, Ch. 7
CHAPTER 7. JUDICIAL ANNULMENT OF LAWS OR JOINT RESOLUTIONS

1:7-1. Direction by governor to attorney general to institute proceeding; application by attorney general

If, at any time within one year after any law or joint resolution has been filed with the Secretary of State pursuant to sections 1:2-5, 1:2-6 or 1:2-7 of this Title, the Governor has reason to believe that any such law or joint resolution was not duly passed by both houses of Legislature, or approved by the Governor or otherwise made effective as law in the manner required by the Constitution, he may direct the Attorney-General to apply to the Appellate Division of the Superior Court, to have the law or joint resolution adjudged void. Thereupon the Attorney-General shall prepare, sign and prosecute the application.

1:7-2. Summary hearing of application; witnesses; depositions; notices

The court, on the application, shall inquire summarily into the circumstances and may, for that purpose, order witnesses to be subpoenaed and sworn and their depositions taken and such notice to be given of the taking of depositions and the hearing before the court, by publication or otherwise, as it deems just.

1:7-3. Hearings; adjudging law or resolution void

After a full hearing the court may, if satisfied that the constitutional and statutory provisions relating to the enactment and approval of laws and joint resolutions have not been complied with, adjudge the law or joint resolution or any part thereof to be void.

1:7-4. Application by citizens; procedure thereon

Any two citizens of the State may, within the time prescribed by section 1:7-1 of this Title, present to the Appellate Division of the Superior Court an application, such as is authorized by said section 1:7-1 to be presented by the Attorney-General, and the court shall proceed thereon in the manner provided by sections 1:7-2 and 1:7-3 of this Title. The applicants may prosecute the application, and the Attorney-General may, if required so to do by the Governor, defend on behalf of the State.

1:7-5. Participation by citizens in proceedings

Any citizen of The State may, when an application is presented under authority of either section 1:7-1 or section 1:7-4 of this Title, appear before the court, in defense and subpoena and examine and cross-examine witnesses.

1:7-6. Judgment of invalidity; copy for and proclamation by governor; operation and effect

If in any application authorized in this chapter, the court shall adjudge any law or joint resolution, or any part thereof, to be void, the clerk of the court shall thereupon make a true copy of the judgment, certify the same under his hand and seal of the court and deliver the copy to the Governor or person administering the government, who shall issue his proclamation under the great seal of the State, setting forth such judgment. The proclamation shall be filed, published and printed with the laws as other proclamations are required to be filed, published and printed, and shall be judicially noticed and received in evidence in all courts of the State in the same manner and to the same extent that the law or joint resolution therein specified would have been if such judgment had not been made. No law or joint resolution, or part thereof, adjusted void shall, after the entry of such judgment as provided in this chapter, be judicially noticed or received in evidence by any of the courts of the State.

1:7-7. Costs, fees and expenses of proceedings

When an application presented under authority of section 1:7-4 of this Title is dismissed the court shall allow and tax the costs and necessary expenses of the Attorney-General, including a fee to the Attorney-General of not to exceed five hundred dollars ($500.00) in any one case, and shall order the payment thereof by such citizens, and payment thereof may be enforced by execution.

For a discussion of New Jersey's statute, see J.A.C. Grant, *New Jersey's "Popular Action" In Rem to Control Legislative Procedure*, 4 RUTGERS L. REV. 391 (1950).

D. BICAMERAL PASSAGE AND EXECUTIVE PRESENTMENT

IMMIGRATION & NATURALIZATION SERVICE v. CHADHA
462 U.S. 919 (1983)

CHIEF JUSTICE BURGER delivered the opinion of the Court.

[These cases] challenge . . . the constitutionality of the provision in § 244(c)(2) of the Immigration and Nationality Act, 66 Stat. 216, as amended, 8 U.S.C. § 1254(c)(2), authorizing one House of Congress, by resolution, to invalidate the decision of the Executive Branch, pursuant to authority delegated by Congress to the Attorney General of the United States, to allow a particular deportable alien to remain in the United States.

I

Chadha is an East Indian who was born in Kenya and holds a British passport. He was lawfully admitted to the United States in 1966 on a nonimmigrant student visa. His visa expired on June 30, 1972. On October 11, 1973, the District Director of the Immigration and Naturalization Service ordered Chadha to show cause why he should not be deported for having "remained in the United States for a longer time than permitted." App. 6. Pursuant to § 242(b) of the Immigration and Nationality Act (Act), 8 U.S.C. § 1252(b), a deportation hearing was held before an Immigration Judge on January 11, 1974. Chadha conceded that he was deportable for overstaying his visa and the hearing was adjourned to enable him to file an application for suspension of deportation under § 244(a)(1) of the Act, 8 U.S.C. § 1254(a)(1). Section 244(a)(1), at the time in question, provided:

> "As hereinafter prescribed in this section, the Attorney General may, in his discretion, suspend deportation and adjust the status to that of an alien lawfully admitted for permanent residence, in the case of an alien who applies to the Attorney General for suspension of deportation and —

> "(1) is deportable under any law of the United States except the provisions specified in paragraph (2) of this subsection; has been physically present in the United States for a continuous period of not less than seven years immediately preceding the date of such application, and proves that during all of such period he was and is a person of good moral character; and is a person whose deportation would, in the opinion of the Attorney General, result in extreme

hardship to the alien or to his spouse, parent, or child, who is a citizen of the United States or an alien lawfully admitted for permanent residence."[1]

After Chadha submitted his application for suspension of deportation, the deportation hearing was resumed on February 7, 1974. On the basis of evidence adduced at the hearing, affidavits submitted with the application, and the results of a character investigation conducted by the INS, the Immigration Judge, on June 25, 1974, ordered that Chadha's deportation be suspended. The Immigration Judge found that Chadha met the requirements of § 244(a)(1): he had resided continuously in the United States for over seven years, was of good moral character, and would suffer "extreme hardship" if deported.

Pursuant to § 244(c)(1) of the Act, 8 U.S.C. § 1254(c)(1), the Immigration Judge suspended Chadha's deportation and a report of the suspension was transmitted to Congress. Section 244(c)(1) provides:

"Upon application by any alien who is found by the Attorney General to meet the requirements of subsection (a) of this section the Attorney General may in his discretion suspend deportation of such alien. If the deportation of any alien is suspended under the provisions of this subsection, a complete and detailed statement of the facts and pertinent provisions of law in the case shall be reported to the Congress with the reasons for such suspension. Such reports shall be submitted on the first day of each calendar month in which Congress is in session."

Once the Attorney General's recommendation for suspension of Chadha's deportation was conveyed to Congress, Congress had the power under § 244(c)(2) of the Act, 8 U.S.C. § 1254(c)(2), to veto[2] the Attorney General's determination that Chadha should not be deported. Section 244(c)(2) provides:

"(2) In the case of an alien specified in paragraph (1) of subsection (a) of this subsection —

"if during the session of the Congress at which a case is reported, or prior to the close of the session of the Congress next following the session at which a case is reported, either the Senate or the House of Representatives passes a resolution stating in substance that it does not favor the suspension of such deportation, the Attorney General shall thereupon deport such alien or authorize the alien's voluntary departure at his own expense under the order of deportation in the manner provided by law. If, within the time above specified, neither the Senate nor the House of Representatives shall pass such a resolution, the Attorney General shall cancel deportation proceedings."

. . . .

On December 12, 1975, Representative Eilberg, Chairman of the Judiciary Subcommittee on Immigration, Citizenship, and International Law, introduced a resolution opposing "the granting of permanent residence in the United States to [six] aliens," including Chadha. H. Res. 926, 94th Cong., 1st Sess.; 121 Cong. Rec. 40247 (1975). The resolution was referred to the House Committee on the Judiciary. On December 16,

---

[1] Congress delegated the major responsibilities for enforcement of the Immigration and Nationality Act to the Attorney General. 8 U.S.C. § 1103(a). The Attorney General discharges his responsibilities through the Immigration and Naturalization Service, a division of the Department of Justice. *Ibid.*

[2] In constitutional terms, "veto" is used to describe the President's power under Art. I, § 7, of the Constitution. *See* Black's Law Dictionary 1403 (5th ed. 1979). It appears, however, that congressional devices of the type authorized by § 244(c)(2) have come to be commonly referred to as a "veto." *See, e.g.,* Martin, *The Legislative Veto and the Responsible Exercise of Congressional Power,* 68 VA. L. REV. 253 (1982); Miller & Knapp, *The Congressional Veto: Preserving the Constitutional Framework,* 52 IND. L.J. 367 (1977). We refer to the congressional "resolution" authorized by § 244(c)(2) as a "one-House veto" of the Attorney General's decision to allow a particular deportable alien to remain in the United States.

1975, the resolution was discharged from further consideration by the House Committee on the Judiciary and submitted to the House of Representatives for a vote. 121 Cong. Rec. 40800. The resolution had not been printed and was not made available to other Members of the House prior to or at the time it was voted on. *Ibid.* So far as the record before us shows, the House consideration of the resolution was based on Representative Eilberg's statement from the floor that

> "[i]t was the feeling of the committee, after reviewing 340 cases, that the aliens contained in the resolution [Chadha and five others] did not meet these statutory requirements, particularly as it relates to hardship; and it is the opinion of the committee that their deportation should not be suspended." *Ibid.*

The resolution was passed without debate or recorded vote.[3] Since the House action was pursuant to § 244(c)(2), the resolution was not treated as an Art. I legislative act; it was not submitted to the Senate or presented to the President for his action.

After the House veto of the Attorney General's decision to allow Chadha to remain in the United States, the Immigration Judge reopened the deportation proceedings to implement the House order deporting Chadha. Chadha moved to terminate the proceedings on the ground that § 244(c)(2) is unconstitutional . . . .

. . . .

III

A

We turn now to the question whether action of one House of Congress under § 244(c)(2) violates strictures of the Constitution. We begin, of course, with the presumption that the challenged statute is valid. Its wisdom is not the concern of the

---

[3] It is not at all clear whether the House generally, or Subcommittee Chairman Eilberg in particular, correctly understood the relationship between H. Res. 926 and the Attorney General's decision to suspend Chadha's deportation. Exactly one year previous to the House veto of the Attorney General's decision in this case, Representative Eilberg introduced a similar resolution disapproving the Attorney General's suspension of deportation in the case of six other aliens. H. Res. 1518, 93d Cong., 2d Sess. (1974). The following colloquy occurred on the floor of the House:

> "Mr. WYLIE. Mr. Speaker, further reserving the right to object, is this procedure to expedite the ongoing operations of the Department of Justice, as far as these people are concerned. Is it in any way contrary to whatever action the Attorney General has taken on the question of deportation; does the gentleman know?
>
> "Mr. EILBERG. Mr. Speaker, the answer is no to the gentleman's final question. These aliens have been found to be deportable and the Special Inquiry Officer's decision denying suspension of deportation has been reversed by the Board of Immigration Appeals. We are complying with the law since all of these decisions have been referred to us for approval or disapproval, and there are hundreds of cases in this category. In these six cases however, we believe it would be grossly improper to allow these people to acquire the status of permanent resident aliens.
>
> "Mr. WYLIE. In other words, the gentleman has been working with the Attorney General's office?
>
> "Mr. EILBERG. Yes.
>
> "Mr. WYLIE. This bill then is in fact a confirmation of what the Attorney General intends to do?
>
> "Mr. EILBERG. The gentleman is correct insofar as it relates to the determination of deportability which has been made by the Department of Justice in each of these cases.
>
> "Mr. WYLIE. Mr. Speaker, I withdraw my reservation of objection." 120 Cong. Rec. 41412 (1974).

Clearly, this was an obfuscation of the effect of a veto under § 244(c)(2). Such a veto in no way constitutes "a confirmation of what the Attorney General intends to do." To the contrary, such a resolution was meant to overrule and set aside, or "veto," the Attorney General's determination that, in a particular case, cancellation of deportation would be appropriate under the standards set forth in § 244(a)(1).

courts; if a challenged action does not violate the Constitution, it must be sustained:

"Once the meaning of an enactment is discerned and its constitutionality determined, the judicial process comes to an end. We do not sit as a committee of review, nor are we vested with the power of veto." *TVA v. Hill*, 437 U.S. 153, 194–95 (1978).

By the same token, the fact that a given law or procedure is efficient, convenient, and useful in facilitating functions of government, standing alone, will not save it if it is contrary to the Constitution. Convenience and efficiency are not the primary objectives — or the hallmarks — of democratic government and our inquiry is sharpened rather than blunted by the fact that congressional veto provisions are appearing with increasing frequency in statutes which delegate authority to executive and independent agencies:

"Since 1932, when the first veto provision was enacted into law, 295 congressional veto-type procedures have been inserted in 196 different statutes as follows: from 1932 to 1939, five statutes were affected; from 1940–49, nineteen statutes; between 1950–59, thirty-four statutes; and from 1960–69, forty-nine. From the year 1970 through 1975, at least one hundred sixty-three such provisions were included in eighty-nine laws." Abourezk, *The Congressional Veto: A Contemporary Response to Executive Encroachment on Legislative Prerogatives*, 52 IND. L. REV. 323, 324 (1977).

See also Appendix to Justice White's dissent, *post*, at 1003.

Justice White undertakes to make a case for the proposition that the one-House veto is a useful "political invention," *post*, at 972, and we need not challenge that assertion. We can even concede this utilitarian argument although the long-range political wisdom of this "invention" is arguable. It has been vigorously debated, and it is instructive to compare the views of the protagonists. *See, e.g.*, Javits & Klein, *Congressional Oversight and the Legislative Veto: A Constitutional Analysis*, 52 N.Y.U. L. REV. 455 (1977), *and* Martin, *The Legislative Veto and the Responsible Exercise of Congressional Power*, 68 VA. L. REV. 253 (1982). But policy arguments supporting even useful "political inventions" are subject to the demands of the Constitution which defines powers and, with respect to this subject, sets out just how those powers are to be exercised.

Explicit and unambiguous provisions of the Constitution prescribe and define the respective functions of the Congress and of the Executive in the legislative process. Since the precise terms of those familiar provisions are critical to the resolution of these cases, we set them out verbatim. Article I provides:

"All legislative Powers herein granted shall be vested in a Congress of the United States, which shall consist of a Senate *and* House of Representatives" Art. I, § 1. (Emphasis added.)

"Every Bill which shall have passed the House of Representatives *and* the Senate, *shall*, before it becomes a law, be presented to the President of the United States . . . ." Art. I, § 7, cl. 2. (Emphasis added.)

"*Every* Order, Resolution, or Vote to which the Concurrence of the Senate and House of Representatives may be necessary (except on a question of Adjournment) *shall be* presented to the President of the United States; and before the Same shall take Effect, *shall be* approved by him, or being disapproved by him, *shall be* repassed by two thirds of the Senate and House of Representatives, according to the Rules and Limitations prescribed in the Case of a Bill." Art. I, § 7, cl. 3. (Emphasis added.)

These provisions of Art. I are integral parts of the constitutional design for the separation of powers. We have recently noted that "[t]he principle of separation of powers was not simply an abstract generalization in the minds of the Framers: it was woven into the document that they drafted in Philadelphia in the summer of 1787."

Buckley v. Valeo, 424 U.S., at 124. Just as we relied on the textual provision of Art. II, § 2, cl. 2, to vindicate the principle of separation of powers in *Buckley*, we see that the purposes underlying the Presentment Clauses, Art. I, § 7, cls. 2, 3, and the bicameral requirement of Art. I, § 1, and § 7, cl. 2, guide our resolution of the important question presented in these cases. The very structure of the Articles delegating and separating powers under Arts. I, II, and III exemplifies the concept of separation of powers, and we now turn to Art. I.

B

The Presentment Clauses

The records of the Constitutional Convention reveal that the requirement that all legislation be presented to the President before becoming law was uniformly accepted by the Framers. Presentment to the President and the Presidential veto were considered so imperative that the draftsmen took special pains to assure that these requirements could not be circumvented. During the final debate on Art. I, § 7, cl. 2, James Madison expressed concern that it might easily be evaded by the simple expedient of calling a proposed law a "resolution" or "vote" rather than a "bill." 2 Farrand 301–302. As a consequence, Art. I, § 7, cl. 3, *supra*, at 945–946, was added. 2 Farrand 304–305.

The decision to provide the President with a limited and qualified power to nullify proposed legislation by veto was based on the profound conviction of the Framers that the powers confered on Congress were the powers to be most carefully circumscribed. It is beyond doubt that lawmaking was a power to be shared by both Houses and the President. In The Federalist No. 73 (H. Lodge ed. 1888), Hamilton focused on the President's role in making laws:

> "If even no propensity had ever discovered itself in the legislative body to invade the rights of the Executive, the rules of just reasoning and theoretic propriety would of themselves teach us that the one ought not to be left to the mercy of the other, but ought to possess a constitutional and effectual power of self-defence." *Id.*, at 458.

See also The Federalist No. 51. In his Commentaries on the Constitution, Joseph Story makes the same point. 1 J. Story, Commentaries on the Constitution of the United States 614–615 (3d ed. 1858).

The President's role in the lawmaking process also reflects the Framers' careful efforts to check whatever propensity a particular Congress might have to enact oppressive, improvident, or ill-considered measures. The President's veto role in the legislative process was described later during public debate on ratification:

> "It establishes a salutary check upon the legislative body, calculated to guard the community against the effects of faction, precipitancy, or of any impulse unfriendly to the public good, which may happen to influence a majority of that body.

> ". . . The primary inducement to conferring the power in question upon the Executive is, to enable him to defend himself; the secondary one is to increase the chances in favor of the community against the passing of bad laws, through haste, inadvertence, or design." The Federalist No. 73, *supra*, at 458 (A. Hamilton).

See also The Pocket Veto Case, 279 U.S. 655, 678 (1929); *Myers v. United States*, 272 U.S. 52, 123 (1926). The Court also has observed that the Presentment Clauses serve the important purpose of assuring that a "national" perspective is grafted on the legislative process:

"The President is a representative of the people just as the members of the Senate and of the House are, and it may be, at some times, on some subjects, that the President elected by all the people is rather more representative of them all than are the members of either body of the Legislature whose constituencies are local and not countrywide . . . ." *Myers v. United States, supra,* at 123.

C

Bicameralism

The bicameral requirement of Art. I, §§ 1, 7, was of scarcely less concern to the Framers than was the Presidential veto and indeed the two concepts are interdependent. By providing that no law could take effect without the concurrence of the prescribed majority of the Members of both Houses, the Framers reemphasized their belief, already remarked upon in connection with the Presentment Clauses, that legislation should not be enacted unless it has been carefully and fully considered by the Nation's elected officials. In the Constitutional Convention debates on the need for a bicameral legislature, James Wilson, later to become a Justice of this Court, commented:

"Despotism comes on mankind in different shapes, sometimes in an Executive, sometimes in a military, one. Is there danger of a Legislative despotism? Theory & practice both proclaim it. If the Legislative authority be not restrained, there can be neither liberty nor stability; and it can only be restrained by dividing it within itself, into distinct and independent branches. In a single house there is no check, but the inadequate one, of the virtue & good sense of those who compose it." 1 Farrand 254.

Hamilton argued that a Congress comprised of a single House was antithetical to the very purposes of the Constitution. Were the Nation to adopt a Constitution providing for only one legislative organ, he warned:

"[W]e shall finally accumulate, in a single body, all the most important prerogatives of sovereignty, and thus entail upon our posterity one of the most execrable forms of government that human infatuation ever contrived. Thus we should create in reality that very tyranny which the adversaries of the new Constitution either are, or affect to be, solicitous to avert." The Federalist No. 22, p. 135 (H. Lodge ed. 1888).

This view was rooted in a general skepticism regarding the fallibility of human nature later commented on by Joseph Story:

"Public bodies, like private persons, are occasionally under the dominion of strong passions and excitements; impatient, irritable, and impetuous . . . . If [a legislature] feels no check but its own will, it rarely has the firmness to insist upon holding a question long enough under its own view, to see and mark it in all its bearings and relations on society." 1 STORY, *supra,* at 383–384.

These observations are consistent with what many of the Framers expressed, none more cogently than Madison in pointing up the need to divide and disperse power in order to protect liberty:

"In republican government, the legislative authority necessarily predominates. The remedy for this inconveniency is to divide the legislature into different branches; and to render them, by different modes of election and different principles of action, as little connected with each other as the nature of their common functions and their common dependence on the society will admit." The Federalist No. 51, p. 324 (H. Lodge ed. 1888) (sometimes attributed to "Hamilton or Madison" but now generally attributed to Madison).

See also The Federalist No. 62.

However familiar, it is useful to recall that apart from their fear that special interests could be favored at the expense of public needs, the Framers were also concerned, although not of one mind, over the apprehensions of the smaller states. Those states feared a commonality of interest among the larger states would work to their disadvantage; representatives of the larger states, on the other hand, were skeptical of a legislature that could pass laws favoring a minority of the people. *See* 1 Farrand 176–177, 484–491. It need hardly be repeated here that the Great Compromise, under which one House was viewed as representing the people and the other the states, allayed the fears of both the large and small states.

We see therefore that the Framers were acutely conscious that the bicameral requirement and the Presentment Clauses would serve essential constitutional functions. The President's participation in the legislative process was to protect the Executive Branch from Congress and to protect the whole people from improvident laws. The division of the Congress into two distinctive bodies assures that the legislative power would be exercised only after opportunity for full study and debate in separate settings. The President's unilateral veto power, in turn, was limited by the power of two-thirds of both Houses of Congress to overrule a veto thereby precluding final arbitrary action of one person. *See id.*, at 99–104. It emerges clearly that the prescription for legislative action in Art. I, §§ 1, 7, represents the Framers' decision that the legislative power of the Federal Government be exercised in accord with a single, finely wrought and exhaustively considered, procedure.

IV

The Constitution sought to divide the delegated powers of the new Federal Government into three defined categories, Legislative, Executive, and Judicial, to assure, as nearly as possible, that each branch of government would confine itself to its assigned responsibility. The hydraulic pressure inherent within each of the separate Branches to exceed the outer limits of its power, even to accomplish desirable objectives, must be resisted.

Although not "hermetically" sealed from one another, *Buckley v. Valeo*, 424 U.S., at 121, the powers delegated to the three Branches are functionally identifiable. When any Branch acts, it is presumptively exercising the power the Constitution has delegated to it. *See J. W. Hampton & Co. v. United States*, 276 U.S. 394, 406 (1928). When the Executive acts, he presumptively acts in an executive or administrative capacity as defined in Art. II. And when, as here, one House of Congress purports to act, it is presumptively acting within its assigned sphere.

Beginning with this presumption, we must nevertheless establish that the challenged action under § 244(c)(2) is of the kind to which the procedural requirements of Art. I, § 7, apply. Not every action taken by either House is subject to the bicameralism and presentment requirements of Art. I. *See infra*, at 955, and nn. 20, 21. Whether actions taken by either House are, in law and fact, an exercise of legislative power depends not on their form but upon "whether they contain matter which is properly to be regarded as legislative in its character and effect." S. Rep. No. 1335, 54th Cong., 2d Sess., 8 (1897).

Examination of the action taken here by one House pursuant to § 244(c)(2) reveals that it was essentially legislative in purpose and effect. In purporting to exercise power defined in Art. I, § 8, cl. 4, to "establish an uniform Rule of Naturalization," the House took action that had the purpose and effect of altering the legal rights, duties, and relations of persons, including the Attorney General, Executive Branch officials and Chadha, all outside the Legislative Branch. Section 244(c)(2) purports to authorize one House of Congress to require the Attorney General to deport an individual alien whose deportation otherwise would be canceled under § 244. The one-House veto operated in these cases to overrule the Attorney General and mandate Chadha's deportation; absent the House action, Chadha would remain in the United States. Congress has *acted* and its action has altered Chadha's status.

The legislative character of the one-House veto in these cases is confirmed by the character of the congressional action it supplants. Neither the House of Representatives nor the Senate contends that, absent the veto provision in § 244(c)(2), either of them, or both of them acting together, could effectively require the Attorney General to deport an alien once the Attorney General, in the exercise of legislatively delegated authority, had determined the alien should remain in the United States. Without the challenged provision in § 244(c)(2), this could have been achieved, if at all, only by legislation requiring deportation. Similarly, a veto by one House of Congress under § 244(c)(2) cannot be justified as an attempt at amending the standards set out in § 244(a)(1), or as a repeal of § 244 as applied to Chadha. Amendment and repeal of statutes, no less than enactment, must conform with Art. I.

The nature of the decision implemented by the one-House veto in these cases further manifests its legislative character. After long experience with the clumsy, time-consuming private bill procedure, Congress made a deliberate choice to delegate to the Executive Branch, and specifically to the Attorney General, the authority to allow deportable aliens to remain in this country in certain specified circumstances. It is not disputed that this choice to delegate authority is precisely the kind of decision that can be implemented only in accordance with the procedures set out in Art. I. Disagreement with the Attorney General's decision on Chadha's deportation — that is, Congress' decision to deport Chadha — no less than Congress' original choice to delegate to the Attorney General the authority to make that decision, involves determinations of policy that Congress can implement in only one way; bicameral passage followed by presentment to the President. Congress must abide by its delegation of authority until that delegation is legislatively altered or revoked.

Finally, we see that when the Framers intended to authorize either House of Congress to act alone and outside of its prescribed bicameral legislative role, they narrowly and precisely defined the procedure for such action. There are four provisions in the Constitution, explicit and unambiguous, by which one House may act alone with the unreviewable force of law, not subject to the President's veto:

(a) The House of Representatives alone was given the power to initiate impeachments. Art. I, § 2, cl. 5;

(b) The Senate alone was given the power to conduct trials following impeachment on charges initiated by the House and to convict following trial. Art. I, § 3, cl. 6;

(c) The Senate alone was given final unreviewable power to approve or to disapprove Presidential appointments. Art. II, § 2, cl. 2;

(d) The Senate alone was given unreviewable power to ratify treaties negotiated by the President. Art. II, § 2, cl. 2.

Clearly, when the Draftsmen sought to confer special powers on one House, independent of the other House, or of the President, they did so in explicit, unambiguous terms. These carefully defined exceptions from presentment and bicameralism underscore the difference between the legislative functions of Congress and other unilateral but important and binding one-House acts provided for in the Constitution. These exceptions are narrow, explicit, and separately justified; none of them authorize the action challenged here. On the contrary, they provide further support for the conclusion that congressional authority is not to be implied and for the conclusion that the veto provided for in § 244(c)(2) is not authorized by the constitutional design of the powers of the Legislative Branch.

Since it is clear that the action by the House under § 244(c)(2) was not within any of the express constitutional exceptions authorizing one House to act alone, and equally clear that it was an exercise of legislative power, that action was subject to the standards prescribed in Art. I. The bicameral requirement, the Presentment Clauses, the

President's veto, and Congress' power to override a veto were intended to erect enduring checks on each Branch and to protect the people from the improvident exercise of power by mandating certain prescribed steps. To preserve those checks, and maintain the separation of powers, the carefully defined limits on the power of each Branch must not be eroded. To accomplish what has been attempted by one House of Congress in this case requires action in conformity with the express procedures of the Constitution's prescription for legislative action: passage by a majority of both Houses and presentment to the President.

The veto authorized by § 244(c)(2) doubtless has been in many respects a convenient shortcut; the "sharing" with the Executive by Congress of its authority over aliens in this manner is, on its face, an appealing compromise. In purely practical terms, it is obviously easier for action to be taken by one House without submission to the President; but it is crystal clear from the records of the Convention, contemporaneous writings and debates, that the Framers ranked other values higher than efficiency. The records of the Convention and debates in the states preceding ratification underscore the common desire to define and limit the exercise of the newly created federal powers affecting the states and the people. There is unmistakable expression of a determination that legislation by the national Congress be a step-by-step, deliberate and deliberative process.

The choices we discern as having been made in the Constitutional Convention impose burdens on governmental processes that often seem clumsy, inefficient, even unworkable, but those hard choices were consciously made by men who had lived under a form of government that permitted arbitrary governmental acts to go unchecked. There is no support in the Constitution or decisions of this Court for the proposition that the cumbersomeness and delays often encountered in complying with explicit constitutional standards may be avoided, either by the Congress or by the President. *See Youngstown Sheet & Tube Co. v. Sawyer*, 343 U.S. 579 (1952). With all the obvious flaws of delay, untidiness, and potential for abuse, we have not yet found a better way to preserve freedom than by making the exercise of power subject to the carefully crafted restraints spelled out in the Constitution.

V

We hold that the congressional veto provision in § 244(c)(2) is severable from the Act and that it is unconstitutional. Accordingly, the judgment of the Court of Appeals is

Affirmed.

JUSTICE POWELL, concurring in the judgment.

The Court's decision, based on the Presentment Clauses, Art. I, § 7, cls. 2 and 3, apparently will invalidate every use of the legislative veto. The breadth of this holding gives one pause. Congress has included the veto in literally hundreds of statutes, dating back to the 1930' s. Congress clearly views this procedure as essential to controlling the delegation of power to administrative agencies. One reasonably may disagree with Congress' assessment of the veto's utility, but the respect due its judgment as a coordinate branch of Government cautions that our holding should be no more extensive than necessary to decide these cases. In my view, the cases may be decided on a narrower ground. When Congress finds that a particular person does not satisfy the statutory criteria for permanent residence in this country it has assumed a judicial function in violation of the principle of separation of powers. Accordingly, I concur only in the judgment.

I

A

The Framers perceived that "[t]he accumulation of all powers legislative, executive and judiciary in the same hands, whether of one, a few or many, and whether hereditary, self appointed, or elective, may justly be pronounced the very definition of tyranny." The Federalist No. 47, p. 324 (J. Cooke ed. 1961) (J. Madison). Theirs was not a baseless fear. Under British rule, the Colonies suffered the abuses of unchecked executive power that were attributed, at least popularly, to a hereditary monarchy. *See* Levi, *Some Aspects of Separation of Powers*, 76 COLUM. L. REV. 369, 374 (1976); The Federalist No. 48. During the Confederation, the States reacted by removing power from the executive and placing it in the hands of elected legislators. But many legislators proved to be little better than the Crown. "The supremacy of legislatures came to be recognized as the supremacy of faction and the tyranny of shifting majorities. The legislatures confiscated property, erected paper money schemes, [and] suspended the ordinary means of collecting debts." Levi, *supra*, at 374–375.

One abuse that was prevalent during the Confederation was the exercise of judicial power by the state legislatures. The Framers were well acquainted with the danger of subjecting the determination of the rights of one person to the "tyranny of shifting majorities." Jefferson observed that members of the General Assembly in his native Virginia had not been prevented from assuming judicial power, and " '[t]hey have accordingly *in many* instances *decided rights* which should have been left to *judiciary controversy.*' " The Federalist No. 48, *supra*, at 336 (emphasis in original) (quoting T. JEFFERSON, NOTES ON THE STATE OF VIRGINIA 196 (London ed. 1787)). The same concern also was evident in the reports of the Council of the Censors, a body that was charged with determining whether the Pennsylvania Legislature had complied with the State Constitution. The Council found that during this period "[t]he constitutional trial by jury had been violated; and powers assumed, which had not been delegated by the Constitution . . . . [C]ases belonging to the judiciary department, frequently [had been] drawn within legislative cognizance and determination." The Federalist No. 48, at 336–337

It was to prevent the recurrence of such abuses that the Framers vested the executive, legislative, and judicial powers in separate branches. Their concern that a legislature should not be able unilaterally to impose a substantial deprivation on one person was expressed not only in this general allocation of power, but also in more specific provisions, such as the Bill of Attainder Clause, Art. I, § 9, cl. 3. As the Court recognized in *United States v. Brown*, 381 U.S. 437, 442 (1965), "the Bill of Attainder Clause was intended not as a narrow, technical . . . prohibition, but rather as an implementation of the separation of powers, a general safeguard against legislative exercise of the judicial function, or more simply — trial by legislature." This Clause, and the separation-of-powers doctrine generally, reflect the Framers' concern that trial by a legislature lacks the safeguards necessary to prevent the abuse of power.

. . . .

NOTES AND QUESTIONS

1. Doesn't this decision exalt form over function? The same Congress that created administrative agencies unforeseen by the Framers of the Constitution can surely invent ways to check the bureaucracy's natural tendency to aggrandize its powers.

2. Note that the discretion conferred on the Attorney General is in the nature of an equitable power to mitigate the hardships which would result from strict application of the statutory rule in a specific case. Is Mr. Justice Powell right to characterize such a decision as essentially judicial rather than legislative? Would it be unconstitutional for the Congress to pass a statute waiving residency requirements for naturalization which applied only to a particular person? Suppose the Attorney General rejected Chadha's hardship petition. Would it be unconstitutional for Congress to enact a statute overriding the Attorney General's decision?

3. Prior to *Chadha*, Congress had enacted many types of statutory congressional vetoes: 1) concurrent resolutions of approval or disapproval; 2) single-house resolutions of approval or disapproval; 3) committee votes; 4) subcommittee votes; 5) joint committee votes; 6) orders of a committee chair. *See* Cooper & Harley, *The Legislative Veto: A Policy Analysis*, 10 CONG. AND THE PRESIDENCY 3, 6–9 (1983). Can any of these devices pass muster after *Chadha*?

4. See *Harris v. Shanahan*, 192 Kan. 183, 387 P.2d 771 (1963).

5. For a case discussing the mechanics of presenting a passed bill to the President when overseas, see *Eber Bros. Wine and Liquor v. United States*, 337 F.2d 624 (Ct. Cl. 1964). Judge Whitaker of the Court of Claims concluded:

> No action was taken by Congress to present the Bill of the President other than delivery of it to the White House. But the President had notified Congress that he would not accept this as the equivalent of personal delivery to him. Since he had the right to insist on presentation to him in person, it must be held that it was not "presented to the President" prior to his return to this country on September 7, 1959. He vetoed it within 10 days thereafter. In my opinion it never became law.

6. In *King v. Cuomo*, 613 N.E.2d 950 (N.Y. 1993), the Court of Appeals held that the legislative practice of "recalling" a passed bill by the Assembly and Senate violates the presentment clause of the state constitution, N.Y. Const. Art. IV, § 7. In *Campaign for Fiscal Equity, Inc. v. Marino*, 661 N.E.2d 1372 (N.Y. 1995), the Court of Appeals held that the presentment clause mandates delivery to the Governor of bills passed, thus invalidating the legislative practice of "withholding" bills from the Governor.

7. Several state supreme courts have also wrestled with the legislative veto question. *See* L. Harold Levinson, *The Decline of the Legislative Veto: Federal/State Comparisons and Interactions*, 17 PUBLIUS 115 (1987). For example, the West Virginia Supreme Court held, *inter alia*, that a statute which required the approval of a joint legislative rulemaking committee before any agency rule or regulation could take effect unconstitutionally invaded the powers of the executive branch of state government. *State ex rel. Barker v. Manchin*, 279 S.E.2d 622 (W. Va. 1981). Should the U.S. Supreme Court have adopted the West Virginia analysis in *Chadha*? The legislative veto was upheld in *Mead v. Arnell*, 117 Idaho 548, 789 P.2d 1139 (1990).

8. What steps can Congress take to control executive actions? *See* Frederick M. Kaiser, *Congressional Control of Administrative Actions in the Aftermath of the Chadha Decision*, 36 ADMIN. L. REV. 239 (1984).

9. For a discussion of the abuses of a state government based on a unicameral legislature and no executive veto, described by Chief Justice Burger and Justice Powell, see Robert F. Williams, *The State Constitutions of the Founding Decade: Pennsylvania's Radical 1776 Constitution and Its Influences on American Constitutionalism*, 62 TEMP. L. REV. 541 (1989).

10. In 1984, the voters in Iowa added article III, section 40 to their constitution:

> The general assembly may nullify an adopted administrative rule of a state agency by the passage of a resolution by a majority of all of the members of each house of the general assembly.

New Jersey added a similar mechanism in 1992. Could there be any state or federal constitutional challenge to such provisions?

E. LOCAL AND SPECIAL LEGISLATION

In addition to provisions controlling the form or procedure for enacting legislation, covered earlier, many state constitutions contain provisions that limit the power of the legislature to pass certain legislation. One type of restriction concerns local and special laws. Not all statutes actually apply to each person in the jurisdiction. Often an act will define a class of persons to be affected in a specified manner. At times the class defined is so narrow that it applies to only a handful of people; in other instances, the effect of a law is limited to a small geographical area. There is an obvious potential for abuse in such legislation. Federal concepts of equal protection may apply to restrain laws that impose upon or unduly favor a selected class. Equivalent protections to assure that no area or class is given preference over others in the state are provided by provisions in most state constitutions. In drafting legislation, therefore, consideration often must be given to the description of the class of persons affected by the statute or the locations in which it will apply, to insure that the definition is not irrationally narrow or unconstitutionally broad.

The policy reasons for disfavoring local and special laws can be considered in the context of the following cases. Are there circumstances in which local laws can serve a valid state purpose? What exceptional conditions warrant special legislative measures? How can such circumstances be described and are there ways to protect against abuse? Can prohibitions against local and special laws be avoided by delegating to a state agency the power to promulgate and enforce its own regulations when and where it deems best? Can generalized descriptions be tailored to apply to only a few? Efforts to avoid such prohibitions have not suffered from any lack of ingenuity.

SAMPLE CONSTITUTIONAL PROVISIONS

1. Michigan Constitution of 1963, Article 4 Local or special acts.
Sec. 29.

The legislature shall pass no local or special act in any case where a general act can be made applicable, and whether a general act can be made applicable shall be a judicial question. No local or special act shall take effect until approved by two-thirds of the members elected to and serving in each house and by a majority of the electors voting thereon in the district affected. Any act repealing local or special acts shall require only a majority of the members elected to and serving in each house and shall not require submission to the electors of such district.

2. Oklahoma Constitution, Ar5ticle 5

§ 32. Special and local laws — Notice of intended introduction

No special or local law shall be considered by the Legislature until notice of the intended introduction of such bill or bills shall first have been published for four consecutive weeks in some weekly newspaper published of general circulation in the city or county affected by such law, stating in substance the contents thereof, and verified proof of such publication filed with the Secretary of State.

3. New York Constitution, Article 3

§ 17. [Cases in which private or local bills shall not be passed]

The legislature shall not pass a private or local bill in any of the following cases:

Changing the names of persons.

Laying out, opening, altering, working or discontinuing roads, highways or alleys, or for draining swamps or other low lands.

Locating or changing county seats.

Providing for changes of venue in civil or criminal cases.

Incorporating villages.

Providing for election of members of boards of supervisors.

Selecting, drawing, summoning or empaneling grand or petit jurors.

Regulating the rate of interest on money.

The opening and conducting of elections or designating places of voting.

Creating, increasing or decreasing fees, percentages or allowances of public officers, during the term for which said officers are elected or appointed.

Granting to any corporation, association or individual the right to lay down railroad tracks.

Granting to any private corporation, association or individual any exclusive privilege, immunity or franchise whatever.

Granting to any person, association, firm or corporation, an exemption from taxation on real or personal property.

Providing for the building of bridges, except over the waters forming a part of the boundaries of the state, by other than a municipal or other public corporation or a public agency of the state.

4. Pennsylvania Constitution, Article 3

Section 32.

The General Assembly shall pass no local or special law in any case which has been or can be provided for by general law and specifically the General Assembly shall not pass any local or special law:

1. Regulating the affairs of counties, cities, townships, wards, boroughs or school districts:

2. Vacating roads, town plats, streets or alleys:

3. Locating or changing county seats, erecting new counties or changing county lines:

4. Erecting new townships or boroughs, changing township lines, borough limits or school districts:

5. Remitting fines, penalties and forfeitures, or refunding moneys legally paid into the treasury:

6. Exempting property from taxation:

7. Regulating labor, trade, mining or manufacturing:

8. Creating corporations, or amending, renewing or extending the charters thereof: Nor shall the General Assembly indirectly enact any special or local law by the partial repeal of a general law; but laws repealing local or special acts may be passed.

5. Alabama Constitution, Article 4

Sec. 110. Definition of general, local and special laws.

A general law within the meaning of this article is a law which applies to the whole state; a local law is a law which applies to any political subdivision or subdivisions of the state less than the whole; a special or private law within the meaning of this article is one which applies to an individual, association, or corporation.

NOTES AND QUESTIONS

1. What vice do these constitutional provisions attempt to prohibit? Are the constitutional drafters of these articles primarily concerned with provincialism on the part of legislators, or are they attempting to analogize to concepts of equal protection under the law? What concepts do these different articles have in common?

2. The Michigan constitutional provision states that "whether a general act can be made applicable shall be a judicial question." What does this mean? Is a decision by the legislature concerning the applicability of a general act constitutionally suspect? Must the legislature obtain judicial approval of local or special acts?

3. The Oklahoma provision requires that a notice of a proposed special or local law be published in the affected locality. Does this solve the problems associated with such laws? Is this appeal to self-interest a better enforcement mechanism than leaving enforcement to later litigation? Does it matter that the proposed special or local law is a benefit and not a burden for the affected city or county?

4. What are the advantages of listing the situations in which "private or local" laws cannot be passed, as in the New York constitutional provision? Is a legislative determination that a bill does not fall within a prohibited category conclusive on the New York courts? Could a bill that does not fall into one of the listed categories still be considered a "private or local" bill in New York?

5. Does Pennsylvania's "hybrid" text, which combines a general prohibition with a laundry list of specific prohibitions, seem preferable to the Michigan or New York models?

6. Is the Alabama provision preferable to a case by case determination by the judiciary concerning how to define a general, local, or special law?

ANDERSON v. BOARD OF COUNTY COMMISSIONERS
OF COUNTY OF CLOUD
77 Kan. 721, 95 P. 587 (1908)

The opinion of the court was delivered by PORTER, J.:

In April 1907, the board of county commissioners of Cloud county appropriated the sum of $8000 for the purpose of removing and rebuilding a bridge across the Republican river, and afterward proceeded to let the work by contract to the Western Bridge and Construction Company. The plaintiff, who is the owner of a 640-acre farm in Cloud county, brought suit to enjoin the proceedings. The court refused to grant a temporary injunction, and the plaintiff brings the case here for review.

The facts are not disputed. The bridge in question is located upon a regularly established road, which leads north from the city of Concordia across the Republican river. The road is known as the "McCrary road," and crosses the plaintiff's farm. That portion of plaintiff's land where his buildings are located is an island, by reason of there being a branch of the Republican river south of his improvements which has its upper opening in the river above the bridge and connects again with the river below. The bridge therefore furnishes the only means of getting to and from that portion of his farm on which his improvements are located. It is alleged that its removal would cause irreparable injury to the plaintiff. The bridge was built in 1903, at a cost of $10,000. In the opinion of the board there is a necessity for its removal, on account of a change in the channel of the river, which has left it practically useless. The question of removing it and of appropriating money and issuing bonds to pay for the expense has never been submitted at any election to the voters of the county.

It is admitted that the board is without power or authority in the premises except as conferred upon it by chapter 72 of the Laws of 1907, for the reason that the expense of removing the bridge and building a new one will exceed the sum which the board is allowed to appropriate for such purposes without a vote of the people; that it is the intention of the board to remove the bridge to another road across the river a mile west of its present location; and that for the purpose of meeting the expense thereof the commissioners intend to issue and sell the bonds of the county without submitting the proposition to the voters of the county at an election.

The sole contention is that the act of the legislature under which the board is proceeding is unconstitutional. The title of the act reads as follows:

> An act to provide for the erection and maintenance of a bridge, and removal of a bridge, or bridges, across the Republican river, in the vicinity of Concordia, Cloud county, Kansas, and to authorize the board of county commissioners of said county to issue bonds to provide funds for payment of the same.

The first section provides:

> That the board of county commissioners of Cloud county, Kansas, be and are hereby authorized and empowered, in their discretion, to erect and maintain such bridge or bridges for the use of the public across the Republican river and its various channels and cut-offs in the vicinity of the city of Concordia, Cloud county, Kansas, at such points as may be by said board of county commissioners selected; and to remove and relocate any bridge heretofore or hereafter erected by said county and which, by reason of changes in the channel of said river, has, in the opinion of said board, become useless to the general public. (Laws 1907, ch. 72, § 1.)

Section 2 empowers the board to issue the bonds of the county in such amount as may be necessary to meet the expense of such removal and erection, not exceeding the total amount of $15,000. Section 3 provides that the bonds shall not be sold for less than par, and authorizes the registry of the bonds and provides for their payment and cancelation. Section 4 authorizes the county commissioners to levy a tax annually to pay the interest on the bonds and create a sinking-fund for their final redemption. Section 5 provides that none of the restrictions in any former statute shall apply to or in any way affect the issuance of bonds under this act.

The ground upon which the validity of the act is assailed is that it is a special act, and for that reason repugnant to the second clause of section 17 of article 2 of the constitution. By its express terms the act is special and applies to Cloud county alone. From 1859, when the constitution was adopted, until the amendment of 1906 the language of section 17 of article 2 read as follows:

> All laws of a general nature shall have a uniform operation throughout the state; and in all cases where a general law can be made applicable, no special law shall be enacted. (Gen. Stat. 1901, § 135.)

In the early case of *State of Kansas ex rel. Johnson v. Hitchcock*, 1 Kan. 178, 81 Am. Dec. 503, this provision was construed and the rule declared that it was for the legislature to determine whether its purposes could or could not be expediently accomplished by a general law. That rule has never been departed from by the court in construing the second clause of the foregoing provision. (*Rambo v. Larrabee*, 67 Kan. 634, 73 Pac. 915, and cases cited.) This constitutional limitation is based upon the theory that the state is a unit, to be governed throughout its length and breadth on all subjects of common interest by the same laws, and that these laws should be general in their application and uniform in their operation. When it was adopted the evil effects of special legislation enacted at the behest of private individuals or local communities were well understood and appreciated. The makers of the constitution were confronted with the experience of the older states, which had demonstrated that legislatures were wholly unable to withstand the constant demands for private grants of power and special privilege. The same year that our constitution was adopted the conditions in Illinois had reached such a stage that, in the language of the supreme court, the mischiefs of special legislation were "beyond recovery or remedy." (*Johnson v. Joliet and Chicago Railroad Company*, 23 Ill. 202, 207.) In the case just cited Mr. Justice Breese said:

> It is too late now to make this objection, since, by the action of the general assembly under this clause, special acts have been so long the order of the day, and the ruling passion with every legislature which has convened under the constitution, until their acts of this description fill a huge and misshapen volume, and important and valuable rights [are] claimed under them. The clause has been wholly disregarded, and it would now produce far-spread ruin to declare

such acts unconstitutional and void. (Page 207.)

. . . .

In 1878 the supreme court of New Jersey, construing a similar constitutional provision, declined to adopt the construction that the determination of the legislature to the effect that a general law could not be made applicable was binding upon the courts, and in the case of *Pell v. Newark*, 40 N.J. Law 71, 29 Am. Rep. 266, used this language:

It cannot be adopted by the courts without abandoning one of the most important branches of jurisdiction committed to them by the constitution. That the legislature would act in good faith, must be presumed; purity of motive and a desire to keep within the prescribed limitations must be conceded to its members at all times; but that the people should have deliberately framed and imbedded in their organic law an amendment to prohibit special legislation where general laws might be passed, and, at the same time, should have intended to put legislative action beyond review, where there was a clear infraction of the prohibition, is a proposition to which it seems impossible to assent. The mere form in which a law is enacted cannot be conclusive of the question. (Page 81.)

The foregoing quotations indicate some of the many reasons that might have been urged in support of the other theory of constitutional construction if this court had seen fit to adopt that theory when the case of *State of Kansas ex rel. Johnson v. Hitchcock, supra*, was before it. More than one-half of the states of the Union have sought to curb the growing evils of special legislation by constitutional prohibitions. And the courts in construing provisions similar in language to our section 17 of article 2 as it read before the recent amendment have almost uniformly held it to be the province solely of the legislature to determine when a general law can be made applicable. Whether the rule adopted in *State of Kansas ex rel. Johnson v. Hitchcock* was sanctioned by the better reason, it undoubtedly was supported by the weight of authority. In many of the states the constitutional limitation is coupled with a specific enumeration of subjects with respect to which special laws are expressly forbidden. This is true of the constitutions of all of the newer states, and the same plan has been adopted in some of the older states by amendment.

. . . .

. . . The experience of those states which have attempted thus to solve the problem has demonstrated that it is impossible to anticipate the various subjects upon which this kind of legislation will be demanded. The fact that the people have not attempted in our constitution to enumerate any of the specific subjects upon which the legislature shall not pass special laws has the effect necessarily to expand rather than to limit the scope of the provision as it reads.

The inherent vice of special laws is that they create preferences and establish irregularities. As an inevitable consequence their enactment leads to improvident and ill-considered legislation. The members whose particular constituents are not affected by a proposed special law became indifferent to its passage. It is customary, on the plea of legislative courtesy, not to interfere with the local bill of another member; and members are elected and re-elected on account of their proficiency in procuring for their respective districts special privileges in the way of local or special laws. The time which the legislature would otherwise devote to the consideration of measures of public importance is frittered away in the granting of special favors to private or corporate interests or to local communities. Meanwhile, in place of a symmetrical body of statutory law on subjects of general and common interest to the whole people, we have a wilderness of special provisions whose operation extends no further than the boundaries of the particular school district or township or county to which they were made to apply. For performing the same services the sheriff or register of deeds or probate judge of one county receives an entirely different compensation from that received by the same officer of another county. The people of one community of the state are governed as to many subjects by laws wholly different from those which apply to other localities. Worse still, rights and privileges which should only result from the decree of a court of competent jurisdiction, after a full hearing and notice to all parties in interest, are conferred upon individuals and private corporations by special acts of the legislature without any pretense of investigation as to the merits or of notice to adverse parties. Commenting upon the evils of special legislation, Mr. Samuel P. Orth, in the *Atlantic Monthly* for January, 1906, used this language:

> The Romans recognized the distinction between private bills and laws. To them, special laws were *privilegia* or *constitutionis privilegia*. In England they used to say when a public bill was passed: *Le roi le veult,* — it is the king's wish; and of a private measure: *Soit fait comme il est desire,* — let it be granted as prayed for.
>
> Here is the gist of the matter: a public law is a measure that affects the welfare of the state as a unit; a private law is one that provides an exception to the public rule. The one is an answer to a public need, the other an answer to a private prayer. When it acts upon a public bill, a legislature legislates; when it acts upon a private bill, it adjudicates. It passes from the function of a lawmaker to that of a judge. It is transformed from a tribune of the people into a justice shop for the seeker after special privilege. (Page 69.)

It has been estimated that fully one-half of the laws enacted by the state legislatures in recent years have been special laws. Since 1859 the rapid growth of cities and towns has produced so many changes in social and economic conditions, and added so much to the complex necessities of local communities, that the demand upon legislatures for this species of class legislation has increased and the evil effects have multiplied. The legislature of 1905, which differed in this respect but little from its predecessors, passed no less than twenty-five special acts relating to bridges, and thirty-five fixing the fees of officers in various counties and cities. Out of a total of 527 chapters, more than half are special acts. This does not include appropriation laws, which from their nature are inherently special. The first act passed by this legislature declared a certain young woman the adopted child and heir at law of certain persons. Others changed the names of individuals. Many granted valuable rights and privileges to private corporations. Hundreds granted special favors to municipal corporations, and many others conferred special privileges upon individuals. Such were the conditions which induced the people at the general election in 1906 to change the constitution by adopting the amendment to section 17 of article 2. The amendment was submitted by the legislature of 1905 (Laws 1905, ch. 543, § 1) and reads as follows, the amendatory part being italicized:

> All laws of a general nature shall have a uniform operation throughout the state; and in all cases where a general law can be made applicable no special law shall be enacted; *and whether or not a law enacted is repugnant to this provision of the constitution shall be construed and determined by the courts of the state.*

The only change is to require the courts to determine, as a judicial question, whether in a given case this provision has been complied with by the legislature. The amendment adds nothing to the mandatory character of the provision. As it read originally it was mandatory, and the validity of every law enacted by the legislature since the adoption of the constitution may be said to have depended upon a strict compliance with it. Under the construction adopted by the court, however, the way was open for the legislature to disregard both the spirit and the letter of the provision, and, as we have attempted to show, both have been honored more in the breach than in the observance. It is apparent that had this section as originally adopted provided that the courts should determine the question, or had a different rule of construction been adopted by the court, many laws must necessarily have been declared invalid because repugnant to the provision.

Constitutions are the work, not of legislatures or of the courts, but of the people. The people give, and the people take away, constitutional provisions. The adoption of the amendment must be regarded as the sober, second thought of the people upon the subject, and as an emphatic declaration of their determination to strike at the root of the evil and to rely upon the vigilance of the courts to restrain the action of the legislature in the future. The legislature no longer has the power of finally determining either that a proposed law will have uniform operation throughout the state or that a local condition exists which require a special law. A cursory glance through the bulky volume of the Session Laws of the legislature of 1907 indicates that the adoption of the amendment has not served any good purpose unless the action of the courts shall give to it the effect which the people intended.

As observed, the provision has not been altered except to take from the legislature and give to the courts the final determination of the question whether a given act of the legislature is repugnant to its terms; it still recognizes the necessity for some special legislation; it is still a limitation and not a prohibition. Without some special laws state governments could not exist. An appropriation law, however general in its terms, is necessarily special. A law changing the boundaries of a judicial district is a special law, but one which may be required at any time, and to enact a general law upon the subject might accomplish more evil than good. Again, conditions sometimes arise and emergencies are created which require the enactment of special legislation. The mere mention of the subject in the constitution is a recognition of this necessity.

What is the attitude which the courts must take in respect to this subject since the amendment?

. . . .

. . . It will be the duty of the courts to determine the question without reference to anything the legislature has declared, either in the act in question or in other acts.

It is obvious that the amendment has the effect to destroy the force of some of the former decisions of this court as precedents. The general canon of statutory construction which makes it the duty of courts to uphold the validity of a law if it is possible to do so can have no application in the future where an act is assailed as repugnant to this provision, however much that principle may apply to objections falling under other provisions of the constitution.

The constitution expressly forbids special laws where a general law can be made to apply. When a special law is passed, therefore, the legislature necessarily determines in the first instance that a general law cannot be made to apply. But their determination is not final. There is, of course, a presumption that public officers have discharged their duties properly, and every act of the legislature is presumed to be valid until there is a judicial determination to the contrary. But when a special law has been enacted and its validity is assailed in the courts the question is to be finally determined by the courts as a judicial question, uncontrolled by the determination of the legislature. The courts must determine the question as other purely judicial questions are determined, by reference to the nature of the subject; not upon proof of facts or conditions, but upon the theory that judicial notice supplies the proof of what courts are bound to know, and that courts must be aware of those things which are within the common knowledge, observation and experience of men generally.

The first clause of this section of the constitution involves the question of classification, which it is apparent does not enter into the present case. Here there will doubtless remain in the future an ample field upon which lawyers may contend and courts and judges differ. It may be said in passing, however, that it will be the duty of the courts, when that question arises, to apply the established tests to determine whether an attempted classification by the legislature is a proper one, based upon some apparently natural reason suggested by necessity and occasioned by a real difference in the situation and circumstances of the class to which it applies, or whether it is arbitrary or capricious and excludes from its provisions some persons, localities or things to which it would naturally apply except for its own limitations. It may be said, however, that it will not become the duty of the courts to invent reasons for upholding a law which is repugnant to either clause of this provision.

It requires no argument or discussion to demonstrate that the special act in question violates the constitution. To enact a general law on the subject, giving to boards of county commissioners in every county in the state authority to build or remove bridges, appropriate funds and issue bonds to meet the expense thereof under such restrictions and limitations upon their authority in the premises as the legislature may deem wise and salutary, would not require more than ordinary skill in the science of legislation.

We are not concluded either way by the fact that a general law on the subject was in existence when a special act was passed. That fact, however, serves as an apt illustration of the adaptability of a general law upon the subject, and as an argument against the necessity for a special law. It is argued that the local conditions in Cloud county are such as to authorize an exception to be made and to require this special act. It appears that the bridge which the board was intending to remove was built in the first place by authority of a special law enacted in 1903 (Laws 1903, ch. 102); that the claims for a special law at that time were that the river had abandoned its channel and left a former bridge useless. Everybody knows that the rivers of the Missouri valley frequently change their course and create conditions similar to those which existed in Cloud county in 1906. The experience of Cloud county in this respect differs from that of many other counties in the state, if at all, only in the extent to which that county has suffered. From twenty-five to thirty special laws of this nature have been passed by almost every legislature for years, and practically the same reasons urged for their enactment. No reason can be suggested why a general law upon the subject could not be made to apply; with a uniform operation throughout the state, wherever similar conditions are likely to arise. In fact, the only suggestion made as to why the general law already in existence authorizing the erection of bridges is not sufficient to meet the conditions is that in the opinion of the members of the board the voters would defeat any proposition submitted. This amounts to a confession that in the act in question there inhere the vices which the amendment was designed to prevent. To hold that the reasons suggested are sufficient to warrant a special law would raise again the lid of Pandora's box only to permit its evils to escape. It follows, therefore, that the act must be declared void.

The judgment is reversed and the cause remanded for further proceedings.

NOTES AND QUESTIONS

1. Why did the Kansas constitution have to be amended before the state supreme court would undertake judicial review of a mandatory provision of the state constitution? Does the absence of a provision explicitly calling for judicial review in the Oklahoma, New York, or Pennsylvania constitutions mean that courts in those states should be bound by the legislature's characterization of a law as general?

2. The Kansas Supreme Court reads the text in light of its purposes. What purposes does the prohibition against local or special legislation serve?

3. Is the practice of legislative courtesy as described by the Kansas Supreme Court constitutionally suspect? *See Sylvester v. St. Landry Parish Police Jury*, 461 So. 2d 534 (La. App. 1984) (arbitrary and capricious for local governing body to abandon road in deference to opinion of local legislator residing in area where road is located).

DEARBORN v. BOARD OF SUPERVISORS
275 Mich. 151, 266 N.W. 304 (1936)

Fead, J.

Plaintiffs, municipal corporations in Wayne County, filed petition for declaration of rights, particularly praying that Act No. 131, Pub. Acts 1935, providing for representation of cities upon county boards of supervisors, be declared unconstitutional. The court held the law valid.

Under 1 Comp. Laws 1929, § 2263, governing home rule cities, a graduated scale of representation of cities upon boards of supervisors, based upon population, was provided. Act No. 131 reenacts section 2263 but adds a proviso which raises the question in the case:

Provided, That in counties whose cities shall have a total representation upon their board of supervisors of seventy-five or more representatives under the aforesaid provisions, the number of representatives of cities on the board of supervisors in such counties on and after the Tuesday following the second Monday in April, in the year nineteen hundred thirty-six, shall be as follows: Cities having less than fifteen thousand population shall have one representative on the board of supervisors of the county; cities having over fifteen thousand and not more than thirty thousand population shall have two representatives; cities having over thirty thousand and not more than sixty thousand population, shall have three representatives; cities having over sixty thousand and not more than one hundred thousand, shall have four representatives; cities having over one hundred thousand and not more than five hundred thousand population, shall be entitled to one additional representative for each additional fifty thousand population or fraction thereof; cities having five hundred thousand or more population shall be entitled to such number of representatives as will give such cities a representation equal to fifty-seven per cent. of the total number of representatives on the board of supervisors from all the cities and townships of such county, and for any fraction resulting in the determination of the number representing fifty-seven per cent. such city shall be entitled to one additional representative.

It is conceded that Wayne County is the only county in the state which has 75 or more city members on its board of supervisors and Detroit is the only city having 500,000 or more population. The Wayne County Board of Supervisors has 151 members, of which Detroit has 79, a proportion of about 52 per cent. Under the proviso the total membership would be 83, Detroit with 47 members, or 57 per cent., and the proportionate representation of all plaintiffs would be reduced.

Plaintiffs contend the act (proviso) is invalid on several grounds, but we need consider only one — that it violates article 5, § 30, of the Constitution of 1908 [now article 4, § 29, of the Constitution of 1963 — Eds.]:

Sec. 30. The legislature shall pass no local or special act in any case where a general act can be made applicable, and whether a general act can be made applicable shall be a judicial question. No local or special act, excepting acts repealing local or special acts in effect January one, nineteen hundred nine and receiving a two-thirds vote of the legislature shall take effect until approved by a majority of the electors voting thereon in the district to be affected.

. . . .

The first test to be applied is whether population has a reasonable relation to the purpose of the statute. In *Mulloy v. Wayne County Board of Supervisors*, 246 Mich. 632, 635, the distinction is pointed out:

Clearly, because of its provision as to population, the act applies to Wayne County only. If it is a reasonable and logical basis of classification, considering the subject of legislation, unquestionably a specified population may be made the test of the applicability of a general legislative act; and under such conditions the act will not be construed to be invalid as local legislation. *Hayes v. Auditor General*, 184 Mich. 39. But where the subject of legislation is such that population has no obvious relation to the purpose sought to be accomplished, an attempt to make the application of the legislative act dependent on population is unwarranted and amounts to local legislation. *Attorney General, ex rel. Dingeman v. Lacy*, 180 Mich. 329 . . . .

. . . .

The second test of a general law, based upon population, is that it shall apply to all other municipalities if and when they attain the statutory population. It must have — "an open end through which cities are automatically brought within its operation when they attain the required population." . . .

. . . .

The constitutional provision cannot be circumvented by the subterfuge of couching a law in general terms. The statute must meet the tests through practical operation of its provisions. In *Mulloy v. Board of Supervisors, supra*, the act was held invalid because its terms could not be squared with automatic application to other counties as they should reach the provided population.

The probability or improbability of other counties or cities reaching the statutory standard of population is not the test of a general law. In the above cases the acts were sustained as general upon the hypothesis that other municipalities would attain the provided population. By the same token, it must be assumed here that other counties will have boards of supervisors with 75 city members and other cities in Wayne County and elsewhere will have 500,000 population. Unless the act works under such conditions, it is a local, not a general act.

It may be conceded that the proviso in Act No. 131 is general in the respect that it would apply to any county which shall attain 75 or more city members of the board of supervisors. But in other respects it has not the earmarks of a general law, designed to operate statewide and under possible future as well as present actual conditions.

The 57 per cent. clause is not a reasonable use of population as a basis of a general law. It establishes an absolute representation on the board, regardless of the relative population of the favored city to that of the county at large, and of the number and size of other cities in the county. The absolute standard imports a local act, based upon things as they are, and may be held reasonable only in a present, known situation. It is repugnant to the theory of a general law which operates upon things as they may be in the future.

In any event, the lack of indicia of a general law is conclusively shown by the failure of the act to provide for the possibility that two cities in the same county may have a population of 500,000 or over. Under the terms of the statute each would be entitled to 57 per cent. of the membership of the board.

It is said to be the purpose of the proviso to reduce the size of the board of supervisors in Wayne County because it is unwieldy. A laudable purpose does not validate unconstitutional means. The Constitution provides a method of attaining local objects through legislation with referendum to the people of the locality, in accord with the principle of local self-government. If a local benefit is sought without referendum, the law must be general in both terms and operation.

We must find that, in purpose and legal effect, Act No. 131 is a local act and is in violation of the Constitution because it does not provide for a referendum.

Decree will be reversed, but without costs, and one may be entered declaring the act invalid.

NORTH, C.J., and WIEST, BUTZEL, BUSHNELL, EDWARD M. SHARPE, POTTER, and TOY, JJ., concurred.

NOTES AND QUESTIONS

1. The court quotes extensively from *Mulloy*, which concerned a statute limiting the time in which a county could attain the population requirement of the statute. Thus, the statute was unconstitutional because it was not "open ended." Is *Mulloy* really applicable? Does the statute here arguably meet the "open-ended" test?

2. The court says that "the probability or improbability of other counties or cities reaching the statutory standard of population is not the test of a general law." Why

shouldn't that be the test? Are all these rationales simply ingenious attempts to avoid the clear intent of the constitutional provision?

3. What justification is there for an "open-ended" test? Was the court concerned with a proviso that apparently froze the present relative populations or was it concerned because the statute used a purported population criterion but in fact allocated to one city, Detroit, full control of the county government without proportional representation and by an arbitrary fifty-seven percent standard?

4. Would the decision have been different if the act in question had conflicted with a general law of Michigan? Where a local act has been approved by the voters, is this ratification a sufficient protection so that it should control over a conflicting general law? Although the court has jurisdiction to determine what is a general law and whether it is sufficient, shouldn't the court defer to the legislature on at least the second question?

5. Given the "laudable purpose" of reducing the number of commissioners, what language would have been effective while still providing for later qualifications?

6. In 1939, the Michigan legislature provided for the creation of the Huron-Clinton Metropolitan Authority for planning, developing, owning and maintaining parks in five southeastern counties in the Detroit metropolitan area. The validity of this legislation was reviewed in *Huron-Clinton Metro. Auth. v. Boards of Supvrs.*, 300 Mich. 1, 1 N.W.2d 430 (1942):

> We are not in accord with respondents' contention that Act. No. 147, Pub. Acts 1939 [authorizing creation of the Authority] is violative of the state constitution (1908), art. 5, § 30 [now art. 4, § 29 — Eds.], which provides that the legislature shall not pass a local or special act "where a general act can be made applicable, and whether a general act can be made applicable shall be a judicial question." This Court might well take judicial notice that there are conditions prevalent in the designated metropolitan area which create a pressing demand for the accomplishment of the purposes of this act, and that these conditions do not prevail in any other section of the State and in all seeming probability never will. But aside from judicial notice of such conditions, there is sufficient alleged in the petition filed herein which is not traversed to justify the conclusion that conditions exist in the designated metropolitan area, and not elsewhere in the State, which afford ample justification for local legislation. While not conclusive, the fact that in its context the legislature designated the enactment as a "local act" is a circumstance which the Court may well consider in reaching its judicial conclusion . . . .
>
>   . . . .
>
> As local legislation Act No. 147, Pub. Acts 1939, was properly submitted for approval "by a majority of the electors voting thereon in the district to be affected."

Was the court here simply exercising its authority under the Michigan Constitution to determine "whether a general act can be made applicable"? Is this why the court took judicial notice of certain metropolitan conditions? How did the legislature's labeling the act "local" affect this determination? Would an open-ended description of the five counties have been sufficient to avoid the need for local approval as a "general" law?

7. Which approach is sounder — the loose scrutiny of classifications by reference to population or the stricter approach adopted by the Michigan Supreme Court in the instant case? Which approach better serves the purposes of such provisions as enunciated by the Kansas Supreme Court in *Anderson v. Board of Cty. Comm'rs of the Cty. of Cloud*?

8. Article III, section 20 of the Pennsylvania Constitution provides as follows:

> The legislature shall have power to classify counties, cities, boroughs, and school districts according to population, and all laws passed relating to each

class . . . shall be deemed general legislation within the meaning of this constitution.

Would this provision change the result in the instant case?

Is it possible to enact a statute classifying by population which contravenes the Pennsylvania Constitution's prohibition against local or special legislation? *See Allegheny County. v. Monzo*, 509 Pa. 26, 500 A.2d 1096 (1985).

BENDERSON DEVELOPMENT CO. v. SCIORTINO
236 Va. 136, 372 S.E.2d 751 (1988)

RUSSELL, JUSTICE.

This appeal challenges Virginia's Sunday-closing laws. The challenge is based upon the prohibitions against "special laws" contained in the Constitution of Virginia. Eight corporations doing business in Virginia Beach (six retail merchants and two real estate development companies operating shopping centers) (the plaintiffs), filed a motion for declaratory judgment in the circuit court. They alleged that they are compelled to close their retail stores in the City of Virginia Beach every Sunday due to the Sunday-closing laws, with which they comply. At the same time, they say, a number of their competitors selling identical products are exempt from the operation of those laws and therefore do business in Virginia Beach on Sundays, to the plaintiffs' great competitive disadvantage.

Although they raise additional federal constitutional questions, the plaintiffs' primary contention is that the Sunday-closing laws, as applied to them, constitute special legislation violating Article IV, sections 14 and 15, of the Constitution of Virginia . . . .

Virginia has had a Sunday observance law since at least 1610, *Mandell v. Haddon*, 202 Va. 979, 988, 121 S.E.2d 516, 523 (1961), and during the Colonial period, probably was subject to English Sunday laws dating from the thirteenth century. *Bonnie BeLo v. Commonwealth*, 217 Va. 84, 85, 225 S.E.2d 395, 396 (1976). During the Colonial period, these laws had a religious purpose, requiring every man and woman to " 'repair in the morning to the divine service.' " *Mandell*, 202 Va. at 988, 121 S.E.2d at 523 (citation omitted). During the Revolutionary War, in 1779, a Sunday-closing law was substituted which had an entirely secular purpose. It simply prohibited all Sunday labor or business except for "work of necessity or charity." 12 Hen. Stat. 336, 337 (1779). The purpose of the law was merely to provide a common day of rest "to prevent the physical and moral debasement which comes from uninterrupted labor." *Mandell*, 202 Va. at 988, 121 S.E.2d at 524 (citations omitted).

In 1974, the General Assembly completely rewrote the Sunday-closing law. The 1974 law, which has been frequently amended, forms the basis of present Code § 18.2-341. It contains a general prohibition against Sunday labor but grants blanket exemptions to all transactions conducted by over 60 "industries or businesses" now grouped in 22 categories of exemptions. In addition to exemptions of the basic industries of agriculture, mining, and manufacturing, exemptions also cover retail stores which may engage in the sale of every conceivable kind of merchandise. The General Assembly has, on numerous occasions, added additional, and frequently broader, exemptions to those contained in the original 1974 enactment. One of these, covering "festival market places," permits a local governing body to designate, on a case-by-case basis, any privately-owned shopping center as exempt from the Sunday-closing law if it is the site of a public "gathering" and more than 50% of its sales area "is used for otherwise exempt activities." If the property is publicly-owned, even though leased for commercial use, the 50% requirement does not apply.

In 1974, the legislature enacted Code § 15.1-29.5, which permitted cities and counties, upon a favorable referendum vote, to remove themselves entirely from the operation of the Sunday-closing law. By employing this local option provision, the counties of Albemarle, Arlington, Buchanan, Chesterfield, Culpeper, Fairfax, Fauquier, Frederick, Gloucester, Grayson, Henrico, James City, King George, Loudoun, Mecklenburg, Orange, Page, Prince George, Prince William, Pulaski, Smyth, Spotsylvania, Stafford, Tazewell, Warren, and York, as well as the cities of Alexandria, Bristol, Charlottesville, Falls Church, Fredericksburg, Hopewell, Petersburg, Radford, Richmond, Waynesboro, Williamsburg, and Winchester, have chosen to remove themselves from the operation of the Sunday-closing law.

According to the undisputed facts, approximately 50% of all employed persons in Virginia work in counties and cities in which the Sunday laws are not in force. Nearly 57% of all employed persons in Virginia work in statutorily exempt businesses and industries. The parties agree that approximately 80% of Virginia workers are exempt from the operation of the law for one reason or the other.

Further, the General Assembly, as a part of the 1974 revision of the Sunday laws, enacted Code §§ 40.1-28.1 through 40.1-28.5. These provisions require employers to allow each nonmanagerial employee at least 24 consecutive hours of rest in each week. § 40.1-28.1. Such employees may choose Sunday as a day of rest as a matter of right, § 40.1-28.2, and sabbatarians may choose Saturday, § 40.1-28.3.

Code § 40.1-28.5, however, provides that the foregoing laws "shall not apply to persons engaged in any of the industries or businesses enumerated in § 18.2-341(a)(1) through (19), except (15) ['sale of food, ice and beverages']." Thus, employees in any of the other 60 or more businesses and industries exempted by the referenced subsections may be denied a day of rest by their employers.

We upheld the 1974 Sunday-closing law against a constitutional challenge based upon the Equal Protection clause of the Fourteenth Amendment to the Federal Constitution in *Malibu Auto Parts v. Commonwealth*, 218 Va. 467, 237 S.E.2d 782 (1977). There, citing similar holdings by the Supreme Court of the United States in *McGowan v. Maryland*, 366 U.S. 420, 81 S. Ct. 1101, 6 L. Ed. 2d 393 (1961) (Maryland's Sunday-closing law not violation of Equal Protection clause), and *Gallagher v. Crown Kosher Market*, 366 U.S. 617, 81 S. Ct. 1122, 6 L. Ed. 2d 536 (1961) (Massachusetts' Sunday-closing law not violation of Equal Protection clause), we noted that the statute applies, within the areas subject to it, " 'to all who are similarly situated or engaged in the same kind of business.' " *Malibu Auto Parts*, 218 Va. at 471, 237 S.E.2d at 785 (quoting *Mandell*, 202 Va. at 922, 121 S.E.2d at 526). With regard to the lack of uniformity of application or enforcement of the law in different jurisdictions, we relied on the holding in *McGowan* that " 'territorial uniformity is not a constitutional prerequisite.' " *Malibu Auto Parts*, 218 Va. at 471, 237 S.E.2d at 785 (quoting *McGowan*, 366 U.S. at 427).

Although the plaintiffs here argue that the Sunday-closing law, as applied to them, denies them the "equal protection of the laws," we adhere to our decision in *Malibu Auto Parts* and hold that the statutory scheme successfully withstands scrutiny under equal-protection analysis.

Amici curiae, on brief, argue that the foregoing holding should end our inquiry because this Court, in some of its earlier decisions, has sometimes analyzed statutes under both the special-laws prohibitions of the Virginia Constitution and the Equal Protection clause of the Federal Constitution as though the two were substantially the same. *See, e.g., Standard Drug v. General Electric*, 202 Va. 367, 117 S.E.2d 289 (1960); *Public Finance Corp. v. Londeree*, 200 Va. 607, 106 S.E.2d 760 (1959); *Avery v. Beale*, 195 Va. 690, 80 S.E.2d 584 (1954).

It is true that for a long period of our history, the Equal Protection clause was interpreted by both federal and state courts in language that bore marked similarities to the analysis we made of statutes under the special-laws prohibition contained in the Virginia Constitution. But the two are not the same. The Fourteenth Amendment to the Federal Constitution, of which the Equal Protection clause is a part, was declared ratified in 1868, during the period of Reconstruction. Its purpose was the prevention of racial discrimination by state legislatures. Although it was, in later years, extended to apply to other kinds of state legislation, the Supreme Court of the United States has, based upon considerations of federalism, been markedly deferential to state laws which make economic classifications, when those laws have been challenged on Equal Protection grounds. *See, e.g., Whalen v. Roe*, 429 U.S. 589, 97 S. Ct. 869, 51 L. Ed. 2d 64 (1977); *New Orleans v. Dukes*, 427 U.S. 297, 96 S. Ct. 2513, 49 L. Ed. 2d 511 (1976); *Lehnhausen v. Lake Shore Auto Parts Co.*, 410 U.S. 356, 93 S. Ct. 1001, 35 L. Ed. 2d 351 (1973); *Ferguson v. Skrupa*, 372 U.S. 726, 83 S. Ct. 1028, 10 L. Ed. 2d 93 (1963). *McGowan v. Maryland*, for instance, held that Maryland's Sunday-closing law would offend the Equal Protection clause "only if the classification rests on grounds *wholly* irrelevant to the achievement of the State's objective." 366 U.S. at 425, 81 S. Ct. at 1105 (emphasis added). On the other hand, federal equal-protection analysis as applied to "suspect classifications," has become far more stringent than analysis of economic legislation. *See, e.g., Palmore v. Sidoti*, 466 U.S. 429, 104 S. Ct. 1879, 80 L. Ed. 2d 421 (1984); *Rogers v. Lodge*, 458 U.S. 613, 102 S. Ct. 3272, 73 L. Ed. 2d 1012 (1982).

By contrast, the special-laws prohibitions contained in the Virginia Constitution are aimed squarely at economic favoritism, and have been so since their inception. Article IV, § 14, of the Virginia Constitution, provides, in pertinent part:

> The General Assembly shall not enact any local, special, or private law in the following cases:
>
> . . . .
>
> (12) Regulating labor, trade, mining, or manufacturing . . . .
>
> . . . .
>
> (18) Granting to any private corporation . . . any special . . . right, privilege or immunity.

Article IV, § 15, Va. Const., provides, in pertinent part:

> In all cases enumerated in the preceding section, . . . the General Assembly shall enact general laws. Any general law shall be subject to amendment or repeal, but the amendment or partial repeal thereof shall not operate directly or indirectly to enact, and shall not have the effect of enactment of, a special, private, or local law.
>
> . . . .
>
> No private corporation, association, or individual shall be specially exempted from the operation of any general law, nor shall a general law's operation be suspended for the benefit of any private corporation, association, or individual.

The foregoing provisions were first adopted as part of §§ 63 and 64 of the Constitution of 1902. They were carried forward into the present Constitution with no substantial change. Their purpose was to correct the perception that the General Assembly, in the nineteenth century, devoted an excessive amount of its time to the furtherance of private interests, *see* I A. Howard, Commentaries on the Constitution of Virginia, 536–37 (1974), and to counter the "sway that moneyed interests were seen to hold over state legislatures at the turn of the century." *Id.* at 543 (relating specifically to Va. Const. art. IV, § 14 (12), quoted above). "Taken together, the pervading philosophy of Article IV, sections 14 and 15 reflects an effort to avoid favoritism, discrimination, and inequalities in the application of the laws." *Id.* at 549. *See also Martin's Ex'rs v. Commonwealth*, 126 Va. 603, 611–12, 102 S.E. 77, 81 (1920); *Winfree v. Riverside Cotton Mills*, 113 Va. 717, 722, 75 S.E. 309, 311 (1912).

As noted above, under the Equal Protection clause, both state and federal courts will uphold state laws which make economic classifications "unless 'the classification rests on grounds *wholly* irrelevant to the achievement of the State's objective,'" *McGowan*, 366 U.S. at 425, 81 S. Ct. at 1105, or unless the law "is so unrelated to the achievement of a legitimate purpose that it appears irrational," *Ballard v. Commonwealth*, 228 Va. 213,

217, 321 S.E.2d 284, 286 (1984), *cert. denied*, 470 U.S. 1085, 105 S. Ct. 1848, 85 L. Ed. 2d 146 (1985). On the other hand, the test for statutes challenged under the special-laws prohibitions in the Virginia Constitution is that they must bear "a reasonable and substantial relation to the object sought to be accomplished by the legislation." *Mandell*, 202 Va. at 991, 121 S.E.2d at 525.

Although all legislative enactments are entitled to a presumption of constitutionality, we have not hesitated to invalidate laws found, upon careful consideration, to violate the prohibitions against special laws . . . .

Accordingly, we do not think that the equal-protection analysis which we made of the Sunday-closing law in *Malibu Auto Parts* is dispositive of the present case . . . . The present case requires us to analyze the Sunday-closing law, in light of the constitutional prohibitions against special laws, for the first time.

In proceeding to a special-laws analysis of the Sunday-closing statutory scheme as it is now applied, we return to the tests by which we analyzed its statutory predecessor in *Mandell v. Haddon*. According the law the presumption of constitutionality to which it is entitled, we first inquire whether it "affects all persons similarly situated or engaged in the same business throughout the State without discrimination." *Mandell*, 202 Va. at 991, 121 S.E.2d at 525. The answer is obviously no. The law affects only those businesses, in those localities which remain subject to it, which cannot fit themselves within some 60 exemptions. Do the exempt categories confine themselves to "works of necessity under the modern day conception of things"? *Id.* at 990, 121 S.E.2d at 525. An inspection of the statutory exemptions makes plain that their aim was far broader. Is its scope sufficient to "close a great majority of stores" throughout the Commonwealth? *Id.* Its present scope is sufficient to close only a small minority of stores in Virginia. Merchandise of every kind can be purchased in every county and city on Sunday.

Finally and crucially, we must inquire: does the statutory scheme, as applied, bear "a reasonable and substantial relationship to the object sought to be accomplished by the legislation"? *Id.* at 991, 121 S.E.2d at 525. That object is the same as the object of all Sunday-closing laws since 1779: to provide the people of Virginia a common day of rest "to prevent the physical and moral debasement which comes from uninterrupted labor." *Id.* at 988, 121 S.E.2d at 524. Plainly, the answer is no. The statute covers only about 20% of the employed persons in the Commonwealth. Further, in those jurisdictions currently covered by the law, employers engaged in the approximately 60 businesses or industries exempted by the act's provisions may deny their employees a weekly day of rest. Most employees in jurisdictions subject to Sunday-closing law are exposed to such a requirement, if their employers should see fit to impose it. Ironically, employees in jurisdictions *not* subject to the Sunday-closing law may not be compelled to work on Sunday. We conclude that the present statutory scheme, as presently applied, fails to pass each of the tests we articulated in *Mandell* to distinguish general laws from special laws.

The plaintiffs make no contention that the General Assembly, in enacting the present Sunday-closing laws in 1974, or in repeatedly amending them thereafter, had any intent to practice invidious discrimination against them, or against anyone. The laws appear facially to be reasonably related to the attainment of the legislative goal. Further, a set of facts can be conceived which would reasonably justify each of the exemptions appended to the statute. Indeed, we cannot say that the entire statutory scheme, or any of its component parts considered alone, creates a classification which rests *wholly* on grounds unrelated to the attainment of the legislative goal. This is the principal reason we upheld the law against an equal-protection challenge in *Malibu Auto Parts*, and now reaffirm that holding.

But the plaintiffs do not make a facial attack on the Sunday-closing law. Rather, they argue that it is a special law *as applied*. They contend that a statutory scheme, which began its life as a general law, has become, by application, a special law by attrition: through subsequent piece-meal steps, each proper in itself, which reduced the ambit of the law to a very few businesses. Among these steps, they point to the local-option feature and the fact that over half the population of the Commonwealth has utilized it to escape the law's effects entirely; to the construction we necessarily gave the law in *Bonnie BeLo;* to the repeated acts of the General Assembly creating additional and broader exemptions culminating in an exemption for nearly any shopping center a local governing body might decide to favor; and finally, to the difficulty of enforcement resulting in prosecutions only on "private complaint." We agree that none of these steps was in itself improper in any respect, but we further agree that their combined effects have reduced the application of a general law to the kind of special legislation prohibited by Article IV, sections 14 and 15 of the Virginia Constitution.

The framers of Section 64 of the Constitution of 1902 (now art. IV, § 15, quoted above) were well aware of the danger that a general law might be converted into a special law by subsequent events, and to that end provided specific protections against such changes, whether accomplished by amendment, partial repeal, exemption, or suspension of a general law "for the benefit of any private corporation, association, or individual." *Id.* In *Martin's Exr's v. Commonwealth,* 126 Va. at 612, 102 S.E. at 80, we said: "Though an act be general in form, if it be special in purpose and *effect,* it violates the spirit of the constitutional prohibition." (Emphasis added). We also observed: "an arbitrary separation of persons, places, or things of the same general class, so that some of them will and others of them will not be affected by the law, is of the essence of special legislation." *Id.* at 610, 102 S.E. at 79.

In earlier decisions, we have held unconstitutional laws which were general when first enacted, but were rendered special by subsequent amendment. *County Bd. of Sup'rs v. Am. Trailer Co.,* 193 Va. 72, 68 S.E.2d 115 (1951); *Quesinberry v. Hull,* 159 Va. 270, 165 S.E. 382 (1932). As demonstrated by the present case, general laws may be rendered special in their application by a combination of several factors, of which legislative amendment may be but one. Because the power of judicial review is the only protection which exists against legislation which has become unconstitutional as applied, our role is not limited to examining the effect of legislative amendments. When the application of a law is fairly challenged under the Constitution, it is our duty to examine its actual effect upon those subject to it, regardless of the origin of the factors which combine to produce that effect. Having thus examined the Sunday-closing laws as applied to the plaintiffs in this case, we conclude that they are special laws, and are therefore unconstitutional and void.

NOTES AND QUESTIONS

1. Equal protection jurisprudence and case law concerning local or special legislation address a similar problem — the validity of the legislature's classificatory schemes.

Is there any reason why state supreme courts shouldn't follow federal equal protection precedents when determining whether a challenged classification is constitutionally permissible? What result in the instant case if the statute were tested against federal equal protection standards?

2. Within the body of a statute, exceptions, exemptions, and provisos are commonly used to qualify the broad sweep of a general rule enunciated in the statute. For example, a prohibition against racial discrimination in the rental of housing might be qualified by an exception for owner-occupied housing with less than five units. Are exceptions, exemptions, and provisos now constitutionally vulnerable in Virginia?

3. Statutes are subject to continuous reconsideration through amendment and repeal which refines and sharpens their scope. Can you advise a client, based on your reading of the instant case, when and under what circumstances that process of legislative tinkering will result in unconstitutional special legislation?

4. Many observers regard the legislative text as a deal whose substantive content owes more to the pulling and hauling of special interest groups than to a principled effort to define and implement the public interest. What implications, if any, should this viewpoint have on judicial review of legislation challenged as local or special?

5. Does this case cast doubt on the common practice of mitigating the effect of new legislation on settled expectations by including a "grandfather clause" exempting certain persons from its coverage? Suppose the city of Alexandria bans food vending in its downtown area but exempts those who have been previously licensed to do so. What result? What if Virginia bans food vending anywhere in the Commonwealth but exempts those previously licensed by Virginia cities to do so?

F. REVISION AND CODIFICATION

JEFFERSON B. FORDHAM & CARROLL C. MORELAND, PENNSYLVANIA'S STATUTORY IMBROGLIO: THE NEED OF STATUTE LAW REVISION,
108 University of Pennsylvania Law
Review1093, 1094–95, 1100, 1103–08, 1111–14 (1960)[*]

Revision in General

Although the official language of a legislative act is to be found in the enrolled bill, usually on file in the office of the secretary of state, each state has always published the acts of each legislative session at the conclusion of the session so that the laws could be readily obtained and consulted. But consultation of the large number of volumes of session laws which accumulate over the years is impracticable, if not impossible. Various methods have been adopted to make the accumulated legislative material available in usable and up-to-date form. The most elementary method — one no longer used — is the republication in chronological order of all general statutes in force. A more common method today is the republication of all sections of the general statutes in force, arranged by broad general subjects. Such a publication is properly referred to as a compilation, although this usage is not uniform throughout the United States.

Compilations, even when prepared under the direction of the legislature, are only prima facie evidence of the law inasmuch as they are not enacted as the law. The most familiar example of such a compilation is the first edition of the *United States Code*. Unofficial compilations, such a *Purdon's Pennsylvania Statutes Annotated*, have no authority other than usage, although a state may "legalize" such a work as was done, for example, in Maryland.

A third and much more effective method is the one frequently referred to as a codification or revision, although here again usage in this country is not uniform. As used in this Article, revision refers to enactment of the entire body of general and permanent statute law in improved, simplified style and in orderly arrangement. It involves the harmonizing of the language of the entire body of statutory law and the elimination of duplications, contradictions, obsolete provisions, redundant and verbose expressions, acts or parts of acts judicially declared invalid and provisions of law impliedly repealed. It does not make changes in the substance and effect of existing law, but merely provides a well-organized and clarified statement of the complete body of the effective legislation of the state. It requires enactment by the legislature to become effective and upon enactment becomes the law. Any pre-existing general and permanent statutes which are neither included nor preserved by saving clause are repealed.

What we have been describing is, in substance, a process of consolidation of laws, whose function is to bring together the existing general and permanent legislation which is to be continued in force and not to achieve substantive changes. Such is the

---

[*] Copyright 1960 by the University of Pennsylvania Law Review. Reprinted by permission.

problem of language, though, that some changes may be wrought unintentionally in an effort to improve style and expression. This is not likely to be a matter of substantial moment, especially if the revisors exercise restraint and care and if the revision expressly declares that no changes in substance are intended.

The Single-Subject Problem

A constitutional provision that "no bill, except general appropriation bills, shall be passed containing more than one subject, which shall be clearly expressed in the title" is not unique . . . . Thirty-eight other state constitutions now have similar provisions, although five, those of Louisiana, Michigan, New Jersey, Virginia and West Virginia, use the word "object" rather than "subject." Ten of these thirty-eight states have specifically exempted general revisions from this stricture. Michigan, on the other hand, prohibits a general revision of the laws. The South Carolina and Missouri constitutions have one-subject provisions but expressly call for revisions at least every ten years. Florida exempts general revisions only from the necessity of being read three times, and Maryland refers to amending the "Code of laws of this State."

Frequent attacks have been made on the constitutionality of codifications or revisions passed in the face of single-subject restrictions. The leading case, though not the earliest in the field, is *Central of Ga. Ry. v. State*,[49] where the constitutionality of the Georgia Code of 1895 was challenged. The Georgia legislature, by Act of December 19, 1893, conferred on the code commissioners the power to "codify and arrange in systematic and condensed form the laws now in force in Georgia, from whatever source derived." The report of the commissioners was examined and approved by a joint committee of both houses of the legislature which passed an "adopting act" on December 16, 1895. This act, entitled "an Act to approve, adopt, and make of force the Code of laws prepared under the direction and by authority of the General Assembly . . . ," declared in its first section that "the Code of laws prepared under its authority by John L. Hopkins, Clifford Anderson and Joseph R. Lamar, and revised, fully examined and identified by the certificate of its joint committee, and recommended and reported for adoption, and with the Acts passed by the General Assembly of 1895 added thereto by the codifiers, be, and at the same is, hereby adopted and made of force as the Code of Georgia." It was contended that this adopting act violated article III, section 7, paragraph 8 of the constitution, which provided that "no law or ordinance shall pass which refers to more than one subject-matter, or contains matter different from what is expressed in the title thereof." The court noted that the purpose of the latter provision was to prevent a repetition of the fraud of the "Yazoo Act" of 1795; the object was to prevent surreptitious, not comprehensive, legislation. As to the one-subject provision, the court said:

> An act, however, adopting a code, or a system of laws, obviously does not fall within any of the classes of mischiefs which this restriction in the constitution was intended to remedy. No one need be misled by a title to an act which declares that its purpose is to adopt a certain code, or system of laws; nor is there anything in such an act to occasion any alarm that it would pass contrary to the wishes of the people by virtue of improper combinations among members of the legislature. What the constitution looks to is unity of purpose. It does not mean by one subject-matter only such subjects as are so simple that they can not be subdivided into topics; but it matters not how many subdivisions there may thus exist in a statute or how many different topics it may embrace, yet if they all can be included under one general comprehensive subject which can be clearly indicated by a comprehensive title, such matter can be constitutionally embodied in a single act of the legislature.

---

[49] 104 Ga. 831, 31 S.E. 531 (1898).

The court concluded that there was unity of subject — namely, the adoption of a code . . . .

The trend noted by the Georgia court in 1898 has gained force. Since that time, the highest courts of thirteen states have had before them the constitutionality of complete revisions under constitutions which restrict bills to one subject and which do not exempt revisions from that restriction; in no case has the revision been declared unconstitutional.

. . . .

The constitutional requirement with respect to the title presents no problem. A short statement which identifies the subject in general terms is enough. It has been said that the requirement is met if the title will lead a reasonably inquiring mind into the body of the act, or if the title gives notice of the subject dealt with so that a reasonably inquiring state of mind would lead one to examine the body of the act . . . . [A] bulk formal revision, such as is contemplated by this Article, is not at odds with the purpose of the single-subject provision. When the revision of the entire body of the statutory law of a state is the subject of a bill, there is not likelihood of log-rolling: everything that is to be the law is in the bill — literally or by reference — and there is not the practical setting for a combination of legislators formed for the purpose of passing an act containing sections which might not stand on their own merit. Nor could one be misled by such a title as Kentucky employed: "an Act revising the statute laws of the Commonwealth, enacting the revised statutes as the law of the Commonwealth, repealing all prior statute laws of a general and public nature, and prescribing the effective date of this Act."

If a codification or revision is but a consolidation, the plurality of subject objection is on its weakest footing, for in a consolidation no change in substantive policy is intended. A code enactment, on the other hand, may involve substantive changes in the law as in the *Central of Georgia* case. Such changes, scattered through a proposed code, would be acted upon by the legislature as part of a package and would not be the subject of independent legislative consideration. While this would hardly involve log-rolling in its traditional sense, it would not allow independent action on disparate subjects on their particular merits.

It could be urged, even as to a consolidation with the force of law, that the repeal of various disparate statutory provisions would involve plurality of subject matter even though the "code" would otherwise have but the unitary purpose of consolidation. This is a point; but the situation is not the same as repeal in a new law of related pre-existing legislation. Nevertheless, the repeal is a part of a unitary plan of identifying and continuing in consolidated form the general and permanent legislation which is neither obsolete nor defective. A "code" clearly intended to be comprehensive would have the effect of repealing any pre-existing statutory material left out, either by express repealers or, in their absence, by implication.

The Pennsylvania Commission on Constitutional Revision has proposed that section 3 of article III be amended to exempt codification of existing law from the one-subject requirement, in order to remove "any doubt that it is permissible to adopt an official code, bringing together the entire body of Commonwealth statutory law of a general and permanent nature."

The Revision Process

. . . .

It seems that the preparation of a plan for the order, classification and arrangement of a code should take precedence over the identification and assembling of the existing statute law, inasmuch as the plan provides a framework within which existing legislation can be arranged as it is identified and assembled . . . .

The master file of all general statutes which may still be in force is commonly called the statute plant. The selection of statutes to be included in the plant is a crucial step which marks the bounds of the revision. In order to ensure that all laws actually in force are contained in the statute plant, it is desirable to include all those with respect to which there is doubt as to current force, noting them for future independent review by the revising agency.[86] In compiling the statute plant, resort must be had to the enrolled bills in the office of the secretary of state or other custodian as the authoritative expressions of the statute law . . . .

The sections in a division under the plan are arranged in a tentative order, thus bringing the work to the stage of intensive, section-by-section review and editorial treatment . . . . Each revisor examines and acts upon every section in his assigned materials, taking into account implied repeals or amendments and judicial decisions as to the validity of statutory provisions. This process involves, to a substantial degree, the exercise of editorial judgment. It is important that repeals by implication be identified and their effect determined. Obviously, what is commonly described as an implied repeal may in substance be an amendment. Only so much of an earlier act as cannot be squared with a later one is repealed by implication unless the part repealed is a crucial provision without which the remainder of the act could not be given rational effect.

The elimination of "unconstitutional" material presents problems. Should the revisors be authorized to carry their work to the point of cutting out acts or provisions which they consider unconstitutional even though the issue has not been adjudicated? Apparently this was done in Kentucky at least as to formal constitutional defects, such as pluralness of subject matter. The major objection to such a procedure is that it involves the exercise by the revisors of a judicial function or, put more accurately, it is the making by the revisors of a prediction as to what the courts would do on questions of constitutional interpretation.

In cases where there has been an adjudication of unconstitutionality, the effect of the decision must be considered. In some instances there may be large gray areas as where a court refuses, on constitutional grounds, to enforce a particular provision of an act applicable to the challenging party but finds it unnecessary to determine whether the remainder of the act is separable. The holding of an act unconstitutional, moreover, does not erase it from the statute books. If the adverse decision is later overruled, the act can be enforced without reenactment. The revisor, however, does not have to stand on his own judgment as to these matters — he can always recommend repeals of statutes which he has classified as unconstitutional.[96]

Assuming a broad enough grant of authority to the revising agency, the editorial work may go well beyond matters of form, such as spelling, capitalization, punctuation, and the elimination of needless verbiage (for example, "null and" in "null and void"), to include the combination of repetitious sections, the breaking-up of long multitopic sections, the resolution of conflicts between sections, the deletion of obsolete sections, and the exclusion of provisions appropriate only to an original enactment, such as legislative titles, enacting and effective date clauses, temporary provisions and saving clauses. The editorial work should include the conforming of referential language to the revision structure: references in particular laws to "this act" or "this law" must give way to references to "this chapter," and references to offices and agencies should be brought up to date in order to reflect changes in the governmental structure. An editorial team faced with these tasks will need guidance as to matters involving the exercise of judgment on legal questions, as well as on matters of form, style and accuracy of reference; it thus behooves the revision agency to provide, at a relatively early stage, a manual or set of rules for the guidance of the revision team.

The proposal that a revision agency be authorized to redraft legislation to conform to

---

[86] *See* Cullen, *Mechanics of Statutory Revision — A Revisor's Manual*, 24 Ore. L. Rev. 1, 3–5 (1944).

[96] E.g., Ohio Laws 1947, at 25, 27–28, 239; Ohio Laws 1949, at 202. Campbell, *Continuous Code Revision in Ohio*, 11 Ohio St. L.J. 533, 539 (1950).

judicial interpretation has been the subject of discussion. It is patent that such redrafting is not needed in order to obviate any question with respect to whether or not the revision will actually be governed by previous judicial interpretation — if substantive change is not contemplated in the revision, and none is actually made in the language used, the effect of revision is simply to continue the pre-existing law, and prior interpretations would be unaffected. Because of the limitations of human understanding and the vagaries of semantics, there is a danger that in changing the language of pre-existing legislation so as to give judicial interpretations express recognition in the revised statutes, unintended changes in substance will be made. On the whole, it is not evident that any substantial benefit is gained from an attempt to make the revised statutes take express account of judicial interpretation, and there are possibilities of actual loss from such an attempt.

NOTES AND QUESTIONS

1. Does the subject-title rule forbid the state legislature from enacting a code in the European sense — "a comprehensive statutory embodiment of the principles of private law"?

2. The subject-title rule of the Pennsylvania constitution was changed to read as follows:

> No law shall be passed containing more than one subject, which shall be clearly expressed in its title, except a general appropriation bill or a bill codifying or compiling the law or a part thereof.

Pennsylvania Constitution, art. 3, § 3.

Does this language give the legislature power to enact a bulk revision of statute law? For an argument that it does not, see William E. Zeiter, *Introduction to the Pennsylvania Consolidated Statutes*, 1 PA. CONS. STAT. 16, at 18–19.

3. For another discussion of these problems, see W.L. Jenks, *History of Michigan Constitutional Prohibition Prohibiting General Revision of the Law*, 19 MICH. L. REV. 615 (1921).

4. The consequences of failure to revise are nicely illustrated by the following excerpts from *Stephan v. United States*, 319 U.S. 423 (1943):

> PER CURIAM.
>
> This case is before us on an application for the allowance of a direct appeal as of right from a judgment of the district court sentencing applicant to death, it being contended that such an appeal may be taken pursuant to the section appearing in the United States Code (1940 edition) as § 681 of Title 18. The application was presented to Mr. Justice Reed, and by him referred to the full Court . . . . A similar application has been denied by the trial judge on the ground, among others, that the section relied on to establish the jurisdiction of this Court has been repealed. 49 F. Supp. 897.
>
> Stephan . . . now contends that, in addition to the appellate review which he has already obtained, he is entitled to an appeal as of right from the district court directly to this Court, in view of the provisions of 18 U.S.C. § 681, which in terms authorizes such an appeal "in all cases of conviction of crime the punishment of which provided by law is death, tried before any court of the United States."
>
> This section of the Code has its origin in § 6 of the Act of February 6, 1889, 25 Stat. 655, 656, which granted a writ of error as of right from this Court to any federal trial court "in all cases of conviction of crime the punishment of which provided by law is death." This provision preceded the creation of circuit courts of appeals by the Act of March 3, 1891, 26 Stat. 826. *See United States v. Rider*, 163 U.S. 132, 138. Section 5 of the latter Act provided that appeals be taken from

district courts (or the existing circuit courts) directly to this Court in six specified classes of cases, one of which was "In cases of conviction of a capital or otherwise infamous crime"; and by § 6 it was provided that the circuit courts of appeals should exercise appellate jurisdiction "in all cases other than those provided for in the preceding section of this act, unless otherwise provided by law."

The Act of January 20, 1897, 29 Stat. 492, withdrew from this Court and transferred to the circuit courts of appeals appellate jurisdiction in criminal cases not capital. This was accomplished by deleting, from the clause of § 5 of the Act of March 2, 1891, just quoted, the phrase "or otherwise infamous," so that the direct appeal to this Court was preserved only "in cases of conviction of a capital crime."

Section 5 remained in that form until the enactment of the Judicial Code. Act of March 3, 1911, 36 Stat. 1087. Section 238 of the Judicial Code (36 Stat. 1157), which in connection with § 236 (36 Stat. 1156) defined the jurisdiction of this Court on direct appeals from district courts, set forth the substance of § 5 of the Act of March 3, 1891, except that it omitted the clause providing for appeals from the trial court to this Court "in cases of conviction of a capital crime." This omission was not accidental, but deliberate, and its purpose was to withdraw the jurisdiction of this Court to entertain a direct appeal from a district court in a capital case. This may be seen from the notes of the Revisers, which state:

"The only change made in the section is in striking out the words 'in cases of conviction of a capital crime.' The effect of this is to take from the Supreme Court jurisdiction in capital cases and to transfer the jurisdiction it now possesses to the circuit courts of appeals." S. Rep. No. 388, Part 1, 61st Cong., 2d Sess., p. 77; and also H.R. Doc. No. 783, Part 1, 61st Cong., 2d Sess., p. 81.

Consistently with this purpose, § 128 of the Judicial Code provided (36 Stat. 1133) that "The circuit courts of appeals shall exercise appellate jurisdiction . . . in all cases other than those in which appeals and writs of error may be taken direct to the Supreme Court, as provided in section two hundred and thirty-eight, unless otherwise provided by law." And § 297 directed (36 Stat. 1169) that "all other Acts and parts of Acts, in so far as they are embraced within and superseded by this Act, are hereby repealed."

Such a plain purpose, established both by language of the Judicial Code and its legislative history, cannot be ignored. Our appellate jurisdiction is defined by statute . . . and it is evident that since 1911 the statutes have not authorized a direct appeal to this Court in capital cases. The fact that the words of 18 U.S.C. § 681 have lingered on in the successive editions of the United States Code is immaterial. By 1 U.S.C. § 54(a), the Code establishes "prima facie" the laws of the United States. But the very meaning of "prima facie" is that the Code cannot prevail over the Statutes at Large when the two are inconsistent. Cf. *Warner v. Goltra*, 293 U.S. 155, 161; *Cloverleaf Co. v. Patterson*, 315 U.S. 148, 164, n.16.

Accordingly the application for leave to appeal is denied, and the stay heretofore granted is vacated.

So ordered.

STATE ex rel. PEARCY v. CRIMINAL COURT OF MARION COUNTY
274 N.E.2d 519 (Indiana 1971)

HUNTER, JUDGE.

. . . [O]n September 8, 1971, the Prosecutor of Marion County filed his "Response and Objection in Two Paragraphs to Defendant's Motion to Sentence Under Acts of 1971"; alleging that Public Law 155 is unconstitutional, in part . . . .

. . . .

It is the contention of the Prosecutor of Marion County that Public Law No. 155 of the Acts of 1971 is unconstitutional, as being violative of Art. 4, § 19 of the Constitution of the State of Indiana, which provides:

> Subject matter and title — Amendments. — Every act, amendatory act or amendment of a code shall *embrace but one subject and matters properly connected therewith;* which subject shall be expressed in the title. But if any subject shall be embraced in an act, amendatory act or amendment of a code, which shall not be expressed in the title, such act, amendatory act or amendment of a code shall be void only as to so much thereof as shall not be expressed in the title. The requirements of this paragraph shall not apply to original enactments of codifications of laws.

> Every amendatory act and every amendment of a code shall identify the original act or code, as last amended, and the sections or subsections amended shall be set forth and published at full length. The identification required by this paragraph may be made by citation reference. (As amended November 8, 1960.) (Our emphasis.)

It should be noted that the last sentence of the first paragraph of Art. 4, § 19 indicates that this section will not apply to original codifications of laws. The sentence reads as follows:

> The requirements of this paragraph shall not apply to original enactments of codifications of laws.

Amicus Curiae suggests

> . . . that unless the Indiana Code of 1971 (so-called) is held to be a codification covered by the exception in Article 4, Section 19, that exception is rendered meaningless. That exception was added by the 1960 amendment to the Constitution. Before 1960, Article 4, Section 19 provided:

> > "Every act shall embrace but one subject and matters properly connected therewith; which subject shall be expressed in the title. But if any subject shall be embraced in the title, such act shall be void only as to so much thereof as shall not be expressed in the title."

However, the so called Indiana Code of 1971 is not of the class of codes referred to in that sentence. The above sentence has reference to *single subjects* which are enacted from time to time as *"original enactments"* and which contain in a codified form matters properly connected to that single general subject. Examples are the Probate Code, the Uniform Commercial Code, The Uniform Consumer Credit Code, etc. Each example has but one "subject." It is the product of a commission study of one general subject, culminating in the proposed enactment of a particular code containing all the pre-existing laws pertaining to such single subject.

The suggestion made by *Amicus Curiae* seems to indicate that the only significant change in language by the 1960 amendment was the addition of the last sentence of the first paragraph as amended and as hereinbefore set forth. *Amicus Curiae*, however, apparently overlooked the inclusion of other very significant language in said amendment. For example, in the first sentence of the first paragraph we find the words "amendatory act *or* amendment of *a code*," and in the second sentence of said paragraph the inclusion of the words "amendatory act or amendment of *a code*." The language of the exception relied upon by *Amicus Curiae* is found in the last sentence, to wit: "the requirements of this paragraph shall not apply to original enactments of codifications of laws." Readily apparent [are] the significant plural designations in said last sentence. It is a reasonable construction to interpret such plurals as referring to a series of separate codes each containing a single general subject and matters properly connected therewith, thus giving meaning to the two prior references in the paragraph to "*a code*" expressed in each instance in the singular. Also the 1960 amendment added *a second paragraph* and continued the singular designation with the words "a code" and "code" followed by the last sentence therein authorizing "identification by citation reference" to the sections and subsections of amendatory acts and amendments to an original act or "code."

An examination of the Indiana "Code" of 1971 readily reveals that it contains a multitude of widely varying subjects. Although there is language contained therein which might be unrealistically and unrestrainedly stretched to reach the conclusion that this assembling and grouping constitutes an original enactment of a code, it is in reality nothing more than an *official* comprehensive compilation of all of the legislative Acts, just as Burns Annotated Statutes is a similar private compilation of the same laws. Moreover, the "code" recognizes that each of its provisions is dependent upon some Act of the Indiana General Assembly, for we find continuous reference therein to "Source." Thus, the so called Code is only a comprehensive compilation of the viable existing statutory law of this State. Hence, each and every viable statute or section thereof contained therein, shall remain in effect unless or until repealed or amended by an Act of the General Assembly which satisfies the title and single subject requirements of Art. 4, § 19. We reach such conclusion in order to give force and effect to the purpose of each provision of Art. 4, § 19. Finding no ambiguities therein we deem it unnecessary to turn to decisions of other states which were based on dissimilar constitutional provisions.

In summation, all enactments, other than original enactments of codifications of laws as defined by this opinion, must satisfy the title and single subject matter requirements set forth in the first paragraph of Art. 4, § 19. Further, every amendatory act or amendment of a code must meet the identification requirements of the second paragraph in addition to the provisions of the first paragraph of said section. The second paragraph thereof permits such identification to be made by citation reference. Thus identification requirements are satisfied by reference to the corresponding section of the Official Indiana Compilation of 1971. By such interpretation and construction of Art. 4, § 19 we give full meaning to each and every provision thereof, as well as preserve the efficacy of the Indiana Compilation.

Public Law No. 155 is entitled:

> An Act to amend I.C. 1971 11-2-1 concerning penal officers, employees, and length of sentences of convicts.

This Act was approved April 16, 1971, and became effective September 3, 1971. This Act, which sets the salary (compensation) for a physician, clerk, deputy warden, and a moral instructor in penal institutions, and denotes criminal activity by prison personnel and penalties therefor, also contains the following material, purportedly mandatory upon and directed to the sentencing court:

> The term of service and imprisonment of every convict shall commence from the day of his conviction and sentence. Provided, however, that the sentencing court, in the case of conviction for any felony or misdemeanor; shall order that the convicted person be credited with all of his actual time spent in imprisonment prior to trial. Such order shall be credited with statutory good time diminution of his sentence for time so served prior to imprisonment; . . . .

It is the contention of the Prosecuting Attorney that there is no rational unity existing between the provisions relating to penal institution employees and the provisions relating to length and diminution of sentences.

We are in agreement with this contention. Public Law 155 is clearly double and embraces two subjects which are not properly connected. There is no apparent relation between the subject of prison officials and employees and the subject of the length and diminution of sentences of convicts, and none is disclosed in either the title or body of Public Law 155. Therefore, Public Law 155, in its entirety, is in violation of Art. 4, § 19, and is ineffective as an amendment to IC 1971, 11-2-1-1 (Acts of 1857, c. 56, s. 6).

Since the time of the 1960 amendment to Art. 4, § 19 of the Constitution of the State of Indiana, there is no requirement that the subject matter of the amendatory act be expressed in the title of the original act, but only in the title to the amendatory act itself. However, this does not mean that a section of an original act may be amended to include matters which are totally unrelated to the subject of the original section. Even though the title to the amendatory act might meet the test of the 1960 version of Art. 4, § 19, it is also necessary that the amendatory language bear some relationship to the subject of the section amended.

The last sentence of IC 1971, 11-2-1-1 (Acts of 1857, c. 56, s. 6), has also been challenged so we must next direct our attention to this issue. The last sentence of the original act is as follows:

> The term of service and imprisonment of every convict shall commence from the day of his conviction and sentence.

Clearly the term of service and imprisonment of convicts is in no way connected to the salaries or discipline of penal officials or personnel nor is it related to the title of the Act. Therefore, we hold that portion of the Act to be unconstitutional in violation of Art. 4, § 19.

. . . .

NOTES AND QUESTIONS

1. Doesn't the language of article 4, section 19 of the Indiana Constitution permit the enactment of "matters properly connected with" codes?

2. How would you characterize the Indiana Supreme Court's interpretation of the exemption from the subject-title rule for "original enactments or codifications of laws"? Is it strict or purposive? Should all exemptions from constitutional requirements of form be strictly construed?

3. Are you persuaded that the terms "code" and "codification" ought to be interpreted as the court does? What about the court's distinction between "compilation" and "codification"? Can a "compilation" ever qualify as a "code" within the meaning of the Indiana Constitution?

4. An authoritative discussion of the issues raised by this case is provided by F. Reed Dickerson, *The Sad Story of Superbill, or What Happened to the Indiana Code of 1971?*, 5 IND. LEGAL F. 250 (1972).

JONES v. CHRISTINA
184 So. 2d 181 (Fla. 1966)

DREW, JUSTICE.

. . . .

The trial court, in a common-law action, denied a motion by non-resident defendants, made in reliance on F.S. § 46.01, F.S.A. as amended by Ch. 63-572, Laws of Florida, 1963, to dismiss or transfer for improper venue. The defendants contended that the amendment removed the provision of § 46.01 F.S.A. which had rendered it inapplicable to non-residents. The denial of the motion was predicated on a holding by the trial court that the amendment in question was unconstitutional inasmuch as the subject of the amendatory statute is not adequately expressed in its title and the statute in question dealt with more than one subject contrary to the provisions of Article III, Section 16, of the Florida Constitution, F.S.A.[1]

_____

[1] Section 10. Each law enacted in the Legislature shall embrace but one subject and matter properly connected therewith, which subject shall be briefly expressed in the title, and no law shall be amended or

. . . .

Ch. 63-572, Laws of Florida, 1963 was a revisor's bill titled:

An Act correcting, amending and repealing certain Sections of the Florida Statutes pursuant to Section 16.44, Florida Statutes, in accordance with the revisor's notes attached hereto showing changes made and reason therefor.

Section 12 read:

46.01. Where suits may be begun. — Suits shall be begun only in the county (or if the suit is in the justice of the peace court in the justice's district) where the defendant resides, or where the cause of action accrued, or where the property in litigation is located.

This amendment did not include the second paragraph of § 46.01 which had read:

If brought in any county or justice district where the defendant does not reside, the plaintiff, or some person in his behalf, shall make and file with the complaint, an affidavit that the suit is brought in good faith, and with no intention to annoy the defendant. This section shall not apply to suits against non-residents.

The revisor's note for § 12 was:

Section 46.01, Florida Statutes, is amended to eliminate the second paragraph which requires an affidavit of good faith. This requirement is obsolete and superfluous in view of rule 1.5(a)[5] of the rules of civil procedure [30 F.S.A.].

The statutory revision power given to the attorney general was intended only for the purification of the statutory law; and not to make changes in the substantive law without express legislative action. The revisor's notes which must, by statute, accompany his bills, give his reason for each recommended change and are an integral part of a revisor's bill and must be considered in any interpretation of it. The revisor's note here clearly established that the intent of the legislature in accepting the amendment proposed by the revisor to F.S. § 46.01, F.S.A. and passing it as Ch. 63-572, Laws of Florida, 1963 was to eliminate the affidavit requirement, not to make this section applicable to non-resident defendants. This interpretation of legislative intent is reinforced by the revisor's bill enacted by the next-ensuing session of the legislature as Ch. 65-1, Laws of 1965, which added to F.S. § 46.01, F.S.A. the following:

This section shall not apply to suits against non-residents.

Since the clear legislative intent was merely to eliminate the required affidavit and we are bound to effectuate that demonstrated intent, all other portions of § 46.01 remained unchanged by Ch. 63-572 and the section is of no avail to non-residents.

The judgment of the trial court and the decision of the District Court were predicated on the proposition that the questioned act violated Art. III, Section 16, of the Florida Constitution because "the subject of the statute is not adequately expressed in the title and the statute dealt with more than one subject." The quoted language is from the judgment of the trial court which language was approved in the decision and judgment of the District Court which added the additional reason that said act ". . . constituted, in part, the actual repeal of an important rule of procedural law without giving notice of such repeal or the particular subject in the title of the act."

Our conclusion that, construing the act *with the revisor's notes*, the only change made was the elimination of the required affidavit — leaving the act in all other respects intact, effectively disposes of the concluding observation of the District Court quoted above.

As to the other point, viz, that the mandatory requirements of Art. III, Section 16,

---

revised by reference to its title only; but in such case the act, as revised, or section, as amended, shall be re-enacted and published at length.

[5] (a) Pleadings to be signed by Attorney . . . .

Florida Constitution, were not observed, this provision is inapplicable to revisor's bills where, necessarily, many subjects must be dealt with in one bill at regular intervals if the basic purpose of continuing revision is to be accomplished. The revisor's notes are essentially a part of each such bill and each must be construed in the light of such notes which are the explanation for deletions, purification, rearrangements, consolidations and matters of that nature which enable the legislature to keep the statute laws of this State constantly up to date in books of reasonable size. This system has worked well for the past quarter century and has been [one] of the greatest contributions to the effective administration of justice in this State.

There may be — as suggested by the District Court — some difference in the enactment of an entire code and a revisor's bill but the difference is not of substance so far as this question is concerned. This Court has long held that Art. III, Sec. 16, is not applicable to complete revisions.[10] The reasons stated in these decisions are even more cogent when applied to revisor's bills. We hold that Chapter 63-572 was validly enacted.

That portion of the decision of the District Court of Appeal holding the subject statute unconstitutional is reversed but, for the reasons herein set forth, the judgment of that court affirming the trial court's action is

Affirmed.

NOTES AND QUESTIONS

1. What are the overriding purposes of statutory revision? Are those purposes fulfilled or defeated by the Florida Supreme Court's holding?

2. What research techniques are necessary to uncover arguments such as these?

G. THE NATURE AND SCOPE OF LEGISLATURE'S INVESTIGATIVE AND INFORMATIONAL POWERS

The nature of the legislative process requires a constant influx of facts in order for federal and state lawmakers to exercise its legislative powers. The availability of compulsion is necessary to assure congressional access to relevant information. The power to issue subpoenas to compel testimony and production of documents is analogous to that in judicial proceedings, raising questions as to the extent that court procedures should be emulated in legislative hearings. Since the scope of legislative investigations is potentially very broad — relating to the need for legislation on any subject — problems of violation of the individual's constitutionally guaranteed rights may arise. What rights do individuals have in legislative fact-finding proceedings? How are these rights to be balanced against the legislature's need for access to relevant facts? What is the attorney's role as a political and legal advisor in these hearings, and what tactics are available to the attorney in representing the client's interest?

The nature of this legislative power and the danger of violations of individual rights is discussed in *Watkins v. United States*, 354 U.S. 178, 187 (1957):

We start with several basic premises on which there is general agreement. The power of the Congress to conduct investigations is inherent in the legislative process. That power is broad. It encompasses inquiries concerning the administration of existing laws as well as proposed or possibly needed statutes. It includes surveys of defects in our social, economic or political system for the purpose of enabling the Congress to remedy them. It comprehends probes into departments of the Federal Government to expose corruption, inefficiency or waste. But broad as is this power of inquiry, it is not unlimited. There is no general authority to expose the private affairs of individuals without justification in terms of the functions of the Congress. This was freely conceded

---

[10] *Mathis v. State*, 1893, 31 Fla. 291, 12 So. 681; *Martin v. Johnson*, 1894, 33 Fla. 287, 14 So. 725.

by the Solicitor General in his argument of this case. Nor is the Congress a law enforcement or trial agency. These are functions of the executive and judicial departments of government. No inquiry is an end in itself; it must be related to and in furtherance of a legitimate task of the Congress. Investigations conducted solely for the personal aggrandizement of the investigators or to "punish" those investigated are indefensible.

It is unquestionably the duty of all citizens to cooperate with the Congress in its efforts to obtain the facts needed for intelligent legislative action. It is their unremitting obligation to respond to subpoenas, to respect the dignity of the Congress and its committees and to testify fully with respect to matters within the province of proper investigation. This, of course, assumes that the constitutional rights of witnesses will be respected by the Congress as they are in a court of justice. The Bill of Rights is applicable to investigations as to all forms of governmental action. Witnesses cannot be compelled to give evidence against themselves. They cannot be subjected to unreasonable search and seizure. Nor can the First Amendment freedoms of speech, press, religion, or political belief and association be abridged.

Legislative investigations involve examinations of the activities of the other branches of government. Such investigations create the potential for conflict between the branches and involve issues of political philosophy and power. The historical importance given to such legislative investigations is expressed in *United States v. Rumely*, 345 U.S. 41, 43 (1953):

We are asked to recognize the penetrating and pervasive scope of the investigative power of Congress. The reach that may be claimed for that power is indicated by Woodrow Wilson's characterization of it:

"It is the proper duty of a representative body to look diligently into every affair of government and to talk much about what it sees. It is meant to be the eyes and the voice, and to embody the wisdom and will of its constituents. Unless Congress have and use every means of acquainting itself with the acts and the disposition of the administrative agents of the government, the country must be helpless to learn how it is being served; and unless Congress both scrutinize these things and sift them by every form of discussion, the country must remain in embarrassing, crippling ignorance of the very affairs which it is most important that it should understand and direct. The informing function of Congress should be preferred even to its legislative function." Wilson, Congressional Government 303.

How do the concepts of executive privilege, prosecutorial discretion and safeguarding of judicial proceedings interact with this view? To what extent can the thought processes of administrators be subjected to inquiry? At what point does this "informing" function become one of "exposure"?

In *Cusack v. Howlett*, 44 Ill. 2d 233, 254 N.E.2d 506 (1969), the Illinois Supreme Court considered the power of a special House committee to investigate allegations of judicial impropriety by a member or members of the Supreme Court. Justice Schaefer noted:

Although it is impossible to define with precision the limits of legislative power, the authority of legislative investigating committees to ask questions and compel answers, in order to acquire the information necessary for informed legislative action, was regarded as essential by the British Parliament and has been so regarded from the outset by the Congress of the United States. Nevertheless, the exercise of the power in specific instances has never ceased to give rise to heated legislative debate and to difficult judicial determinations. *See* Landis, *Constitutional Limitations on the Congressional Power of Investigation*, 40 HARV. L.R. 152.

The court concluded that the investigation was improper because the "authority to remove judicial officers by legislative address that was formerly given to the legislative department of the government has now been given to the judicial department . . . ."

THOMAS I. EMERSON,
THE SYSTEM OF FREEDOM OF EXPRESSION
247-54 (1970)*

Legislative investigating committees have always played an important role in American political life. The scope and intensity of their operations have steadily increased as the function of the legislature has shifted from formulating policy and initiating legislation to approving proposals of the executive branch, overseeing the government bureaucracy, and generally registering public opinion. The New Deal had given considerable impetus to the growth of the legislative investigating committee, using it to expose the operation of the securities markets, the public utility holding companies, labor spies and professional strikebreakers, lobbyists, and other features of our economic and social institutions that seemed to need reform . . . .

Beginning with the creation of the Dies Committee in 1938, legislative investigating committees started to probe into political opinions and associations, first in government and then throughout the country. For many years this form of investigation commenced with Communist Party membership and activities, and spread from there in a widening circle into other shades of unpopular opinion. More recent committees have been concerned with "subversive influences" in the civil-rights movement, the "black revolution," and the New Left.

The extension of legislative investigations to the field of political expression has been accompanied by a significant advance in the technique and scope of operations of the committees. Legislative investigating committees generally have greatly improved their methods of investigation, their presentation of material, and their ability to command public attention. Equally important, they have taken on the characteristics of a permanent bureaucracy. With more funds available, larger staffs, organized on a continuing basis, they have become established institutions with a life and direction of their own . . . .

. . . A major part of legislative fact finding is concerned with the collection of general information genuinely designed to throw light on pending legislation. The material sought and obtained consists of statistical data, reports of scientific studies, analysis of comparative legislation, the opinions of experts, and the views of interested parties. Witnesses are voluntary, appearing upon invitation or by their own request, and no element of compulsion is present. Another large segment of legislative investigation involves inquiry into some phase of the operations or policies of the executive branch. Here the probe may concern more specific facts or relate to specific individuals, but it is directed toward action, or to opinions freely given and defended. The problems for a system of freedom of expression arise in a relatively narrow area in which the legislative committee is seeking information about the political opinions, attitudes or associations of particular individuals. Since the information sought relates to unorthodox or unpopular positions these proceedings become adversary or adjudicative in nature, rather than broadly legislative. The subject matter is expression, not action, and the social interest in the name of which the right of expression is invaded is usually the interest in internal security.

Nearly all the major controversies that have raged over interference with freedom of expression by Federal legislative investigations have arisen out of the operations of three committees. These have been the House Committee on Un-American Activities, now the House Committee on Internal Security; the Subcommittee on Internal Security of the Senate Judiciary Committee, which has functioned under the chairmanship of

---

Senators McCarran, Jenner and Eastland; and the Subcommittee on Investigations of the Senate Committee on Government Operations, as it operated during the Eisenhower administration under Senator Joseph McCarthy. At the State and local level, also, virtually all the problems have emanated from particular committees of similar design and attitude. Many other types of legislative investigating committee can, and occasionally do, raise issues that touch on freedom of expression. Most committee hearings of the adversary or adjudicatory type also present serious issues of other individual rights. Yet, the conflict between legislative investigations and freedom of expression has concerned only a very small fraction of the legislative fact-finding process.

. . . .

The question for consideration here is to what extent the law and legal institutions can protect the system of freedom of expression against interference by legislative investigating committees. Several general observations should be made at the outset. In the first place the efforts of the courts to limit the functioning of legislative investigating committees have been largely confined to those aspects of committee operations that involve the use of compulsory process to obtain testimony or other evidence. When a legislative committee undertakes to compel a person to appear before it and answer questions, or produce documentary evidence, or attempts to obtain the records of an association, procedures for review of such committee action are available in the courts, at least at some stage. But other features of the committee's operation, such as its power to send investigators in search of information, to conduct hearings if the evidence is produced voluntarily, or to issue reports, have been considered largely beyond the capacity of courts to review. Most of the discussion, therefore, will relate to judicial supervision over the use of compulsory procedures to obtain information.

In the second place, even within this narrow area of judicial supervision, the formulation of theory by which to control the scope of legislative committee investigation is beset with difficulties. By its very nature an investigation has no precise limits that can be readily defined in advance of the outcome. It may be necessary to exceed the tentatively prescribed boundaries in order to ascertain them, or to understand the full scope of the problem, or to check out provisional answers. The court is thus confronted with a complex doctrinal problem at the outset of its deliberations.

Thirdly, the institutional techniques available for accommodating opposing interests in this area are not well designed to carry out that task effectively. The judiciary is particularly reluctant to interfere with the legislative branch at this stage in its operations. The interposition of judicial review in the middle of an on-going investigation raises some difficult problems. Methods of adequately protecting the witness, without at the same time seriously interrupting the investigation, have been slow to evolve.

. . . .

A major portion of the legislative investigating power rests upon the authority of the legislature or its committees to compel the production of evidence, either oral or documentary. That authority can be exercised in two ways. A refusal to appear and answer questions or to produce documents can be punished directly by the legislature itself, or by either house, as a contempt of the legislature. Under this procedure the offender is adjudged guilty or not guilty by vote of the legislative body and, if guilty, is taken into custody and held in confinement by officials of the legislature. He cannot be held, however, beyond the end of the legislative session. This procedure, it can be seen, is cumbersome and time-consuming for the legislature, as well as limited by the length of the legislative term. The more usual method of enforcing the legislative power to compel production of evidence is through passage of a statute making it an offense punishable through regular court procedures for any person to refuse to comply with the legislative mandate. Thus the existing Federal statute on the subject, Section 192 of Title 2 of the U.S. Code, makes it a misdemeanor, punishable by a fine of not more than

$1000 or less than $100 and imprisonment for not less than one month or more than twelve months, for any person who, "having been summoned as a witness by authority of either House of Congress to give testimony or to produce papers upon any matter under inquiry before either House . . . willfully makes default, or who, having appeared, refuses to answer any question pertinent to the question under inquiry." Under either procedure, it is now well established, the courts may review the contempt issue, through habeas corpus proceedings in cases of direct citation for contempt and through the usual methods if the statute has been invoked. Thus the courts have ultimate jurisdiction to decide whether the legislative power to compel evidence has been validly exerted.

The validity of the exercise of legislative authority depends in the first instance, in theory at least, upon whether that authority may be found within the affirmative powers of the legislature to require the production of evidence. The established doctrine is that, while the legislature may not compel the production of evidence merely for its own sake, it does have constitutional power to do so in aid of any of its functions. These functions include not only the primary one of enacting laws, but also such ancillary powers as judging the election of its members, expelling or disciplining members, impeaching government officials, approving appointments (in the case of the Senate), and such implied functions as protecting its own integrity by punishing those who would attempt to bribe its members. The potential range of these functions is so broad that any attempt to limit the scope of legislative investigation by a narrowing construction of the basic affirmative power poses serious difficulties. Even the Federal Congress, operating under the doctrine of enumerated powers, may investigate in aid of the spending power, the appropriating power, the power to assure the States a republican form of government, perhaps even the amending power. The State legislatures are not confined by anything except the possibility of conflict with Federal power. To forge a connection between the obtaining of information on virtually any subject and possible legislation is therefore not a difficult task. The suspicion that the connection is a spurious one, designed only as a cover for probing into other areas, can be translated into a legal prohibition only if the courts are willing to delve into the recesses of legislative motives, a task they normally shrink from undertaking.

A second limitation upon legislative investigating powers derives not from seeking the outermost limits of the affirmative power but from looking to specific constitutional limitations, such as those embodied in the Bill of Rights, which cut across and limit the affirmative power at the point where the two conflicting principles intersect. The main task in limiting the legislative investigating power in the interests of freedom of expression is to formulate rules for applying the constitutional limitations found in the First Amendment. A cluster of other constitutional doctrines can be employed for the same purpose; so can various nonconstitutional techniques of statutory construction or procedural niceties . . . .

NOTES AND QUESTIONS

1. Should the legislature be prevented from inquiring into political opinions and associations? To what extent can such inquiries be justified on practical grounds? Were the political opinions of anti-Vietnam war activists relevant to legislative action? Were their actions relevant? Would inquiry without use of compulsory process be more acceptable? Does such voluntary testimony nevertheless create problems for those whose opinions or actions are described by others?

2. Can doctrinal rules for the conduct of hearings, defining the constitutionally permissible scope of inquiry, be fashioned by courts for general application in advance of proceedings?

When an individual has been subpoenaed or others have been subpoenaed to testify or produce documents that affect the individual's interests, an initial concern may be whether the committee can be prevented from enforcing the subpoena. The following materials raise a number of issues relevant to this question.

At what point in the process of legislative hearings is it appropriate for a court to become involved? Is a legislative finding of contempt required? Can an attempt at character assassination be forestalled by seeking injunctions against holding the hearing, calling witnesses, or restricting the scope of questions asked? How should courts protect citizens' rights during the hearing?

EASTLAND v. UNITED STATES SERVICEMEN'S FUND
421 U.S. 491 (1975)

MR. CHIEF JUSTICE BURGER delivered the opinion of the Court.

We granted certiorari to decide whether a federal court may enjoin the issuance by Congress of a subpoena *duces tecum* that directs a bank to produce the bank records of an organization which claims a First Amendment privilege status for those records on the ground that they are the equivalent of confidential membership lists. The Court of Appeals for the District of Columbia Circuit held that compliance with the subpoena "would invade the constitutional rights" of the organization, and that judicial relief is available to prevent implementation of the subpoena.

I

In early 1970 the Senate Subcommittee on Internal Security was given broad authority by the Senate to "make a complete and continuing study and investigation of . . . the administration, operation and enforcement of the Internal Security Act of 1950 . . . ." S.Res. 341, 91st Cong., 2d Sess., 116 Cong.Rec. 3419 (January 30, 1970). The authority encompassed discovering the "extent, nature and effect of subversive activities in the United States," and the resolution specifically directed inquiry concerning "infiltration by persons who are or may be under the control of foreign governments . . . ." *Ibid.*

Pursuant to that mandate the Subcommittee began an inquiry into the activities of respondent herein, the United States Servicemen's Fund, Inc. (USSF).

USSF describes itself as a nonprofit membership corporation supported by contributions. Its stated purpose is "to further the welfare of persons who have served or are presently serving in the military." To accomplish its declared purpose USSF has engaged in various activities directed at United States servicemen. It established "coffeehouses" near domestic military installations, and aided the publication of "underground" newspapers for distribution on American military installations throughout the world. The coffeehouses were meeting places for servicemen, and the newspapers were specialized publications which USSF claims dealt with issues of concern to servicemen. Through these operations USSF attempted to communicate to servicemen its philosophy and attitudes concerning United States involvement in South East Asia. USSF claims the coffeehouses and newspapers "became the focus of dissent and expressions of opposition within the military toward the war in Southeast Asia."

In the course of its investigation of USSF, the Subcommittee concluded that a prima facie showing had been made of the need for further investigation, and it resolved that appropriate subpoenas, including subpoenas *duces tecum* could be issued. Petitioner Eastland, a United States Senator, is, as he was then, Chairman of the Subcommittee. On May 28, 1970, pursuant to the above authority, he signed a subpoena *duces tecum*, issued on behalf of the Subcommittee, to the bank where USSF has an account. The subpoena commanded the bank to produce on June 4, 1970:

> "any and all records appertaining to or involving the account or accounts of [USSF]. Such records to comprehend papers, correspondence, statements, checks, deposit slips and supporting documentation, or microfilm thereof within [the bank's] control or custody or within [its] means to produce."

From the record it appears the subpoena was never actually served on the bank. In any event, before the June 4, 1970, return date, USSF and two of its members brought this action to enjoin implementation of the subpoena *duces tecum.*

The complaint named as defendants Chairman Eastland, eight other Senators, the Chief Counsel to the Subcommittee, and the bank. The complaint charged that the authorizing resolutions and the Subcommittee's actions implementing them were an unconstitutional abuse of the legislative power of inquiry, that the "sole purpose" of the Subcommittee investigation was to force "public disclosure of beliefs, opinions, expressions and associations of private citizens which may be unorthodox or unpopular," and that the "sole purpose" of the subpoena was to "harass, chill, punish and deter [USSF and its members] in their exercise of their rights and duties under the First Amendment and particularly to stifle the freedom of the press and association guaranteed by that Amendment." The subpoena was issued to the bank rather than to USSF and its members, the complaint claimed, "in order to deprive [them] of their right to protect their private records, such as the sources of their contributions, as they would be entitled to do if the subpoena had been issued against them directly." The complaint further claimed that financial support to USSF is obtained exclusively through contributions from private individuals, and if the bank records are disclosed, "much of that financial support will be withdrawn, and USSF will be unable to continue its constitutionally protected activities."

For relief USSF and its members, the respondents, sought a permanent injunction restraining the members of the Subcommittee and its Chief Counsel from trying to enforce the subpoena by contempt of Congress or other means and restraining the bank from complying with the subpoena.

. . . .

We conclude the actions of the Senate Subcommittee, the individual Senators, and the Chief Counsel are protected by the Speech or Debate Clause of the Constitution, Art. I, § 6, cl. 1, and are therefore immune from judicial interference. We reverse.

. . . .

II

The question to be resolved is whether the actions of the petitioners fall within the "sphere of legislative activity." If they do, the petitioners "shall not be questioned in any other Place" about those activities since the prohibitions of the Speech or Debate Clause are absolute . . . .

Without exception, our cases have read the Speech or Debate Clause broadly to effectuate its purposes. *Kilbourn v. Thompson,* 103 U.S. 168, 204 (1881); *United States v. Johnson,* 383 U.S. 169, 179 (1966); *Powell v. McCormack,* 395 U.S. 486, 502–503 (1969); *United States v. Brewster,* 408 U.S. 501, 508–509 (1972); *Gravel v. United States,* 408 U.S. 606, 617–618 (1972); . . . The purpose of the Clause is to insure that the legislative function the Constitution allocates to Congress may be performed independently.

. . . .

The applicability of the Clause to private civil actions is supported by the absoluteness of the terms "shall not be questioned," and the sweep of the terms "in any other Place." In reading the Clause broadly we have said that legislators acting within the sphere of legitimate legislative activity "should be protected not only from the consequences of litigation's results but also from the burden of defending themselves." *Dombrowski v. Eastland, supra,* 387 U.S., at 85. Just as a criminal prosecution infringes upon the independence which the Clause is designed to preserve, a private civil action, whether for an injunction or damages, creates a distraction and forces Members to divert their time, energy, and attention from their legislative tasks to defend the litigation. Private civil actions also may be used to delay and disrupt the legislative function. Moreover, whether a criminal action is instituted by the Executive Branch, or a civil action is brought by private parties, judicial power is still brought to bear on Members of Congress and legislative independence is imperiled. We reaffirm that once it is determined that Members are acting within the "legitimate legislative sphere" the Speech or Debate Clause is an absolute bar to interference.

III

In determining whether particular activities other than literal speech or debate fall within the "legitimate legislative sphere" we look to see whether the activities are "done in a session of the House by one of its members in relation to the business before it." *Kilbourn v. Thompson, supra*, 103 U.S., at 204. More specifically, we must determine whether the activities are:

> "an integral part of the deliberative and communicative processes by which Members participate in committee and House proceedings with respect to the consideration and passage or rejection of proposed legislation or with respect to other matters which the Constitution places within the jurisdiction of either House." *Gravel v. United States*, 408 U.S. 606, 625 (1972).

The power to investigate and to do so through compulsory process plainly falls within that definition. This Court has often noted that the power to investigate is inherent in the power to make laws because "[a] legislative body cannot legislate wisely or effectively in the absence of information respecting the conditions which the legislation is intended to affect or change." *McGrain v. Daugherty*, 273 U.S. 135, 175 (1927); *United States v. Rumely*, 345 U.S. 41, 46 (1953). Issuance of subpoenas such as the one in question here has long been held to be a legitimate use by Congress of its power to investigate . . . .

It also has been held that the subpoena power may be exercised by a committee acting, as here, on behalf of one of the Houses. Without such power the subcommittee may not be able to do the task assigned to it by Congress . . . .

We have already held that the "act of authorizing an investigation pursuant to which . . . materials were gathered" is an integral part of the legislative process. *Doe v. McMillan*, 412 U.S. 306, 313 (1973). The issuance of a subpoena pursuant to an authorized investigation is similarly an indispensable ingredient of lawmaking; without it our recognition that the "act of authorizing" is protected would be meaningless . . . .

The particular investigation at issue here is related to and in furtherance of a legitimate task of Congress. On this record the pleadings show that the actions of the Members and the Chief Counsel fall within the "sphere of legitimate legislative activity." The Subcommittee was acting under an unambiguous resolution from the Senate authorizing it to make a complete study of the "administration, operation, and enforcement of the Internal Security Act of 1950 . . . ." S. Res. 341, 91st Cong., 2d Sess., 116 Cong. Rec. 3419 (January 30, 1970). That grant of authority is sufficient to show that the investigation upon which the Subcommittee had embarked concerned a subject on which "legislation could be had." *McGrain v. Daugherty*, 273 U.S., at 177 . . . .

The propriety of making USSF a subject of the investigation and subpoena is a subject on which the scope of our inquiry is narrow. "The courts should not go beyond the narrow confines of determining that a committee's inquiry may fairly be deemed within its province." *Tenney v. Brandhove, supra*, 341 U.S., at 378 (1950).

Even the most cursory look at the facts presented by the pleadings reveals the legitimacy of the USSF subpoena. Inquiry into the sources of funds used to carry on activities suspected by a Subcommittee of Congress to have a potential for undermining the morale of the armed forces is within the legitimate legislative sphere. Indeed, the complaint here tells us that USSF operated on or near military and naval bases, and that its facilities became the "focus of dissent" to declared national policy. Whether USSF activities violated any statute is not relevant; the inquiry was intended to inform

Congress in an area where legislation may be had. USSF asserted it does not know the sources of its funds; in light of the Senate authorization to the Subcommittee to investigate "infiltration by persons who are or may be under the control of foreign governments," . . . and in view of the pleaded facts, it is clear that the subpoena to discover USSF's bank records "may fairly be deemed within [the Subcommittee's] province." *Tenney v. Brandhove, supra.*

We conclude that the Speech or Debate Clause provides complete immunity for the Members for issuance of this subpoena. We draw no distinction between the Members and the Chief Counsel. In *Gravel, supra,* we made it clear that "the day-to-day work of such aides is so critical to the Members' performance that they must be treated as [the Members'] alter egos . . . ." Here the complaint alleges that the "Subcommittee members and staff caused the . . . subpoena to be issued . . . under the authority of Senate Resolution 366 . . . ." The complaint thus does not distinguish between the activities of the Members and those of the Chief Counsel. Since the Members are immune because the issuance of the subpoena is "essential to legislating" their aides share that immunity.

IV

Respondents rely on language in *Gravel v. United States, supra,* 408 U.S., at 621:

> "[N]o prior case has held that Members of Congress would be immune if they executed an invalid resolution by themselves carrying out an illegal arrest, or if, in order to secure information for a hearing, themselves seized property or invaded the privacy of a citizen. Neither they nor their aides should be immune from liability or questioning in such circumstances."

From this respondents argue that the subpoena works an invasion of their privacy, and thus cannot be immune from judicial questioning. The conclusion is unwarranted. The quoted language from *Gravel* referred to actions which were *not* "essential to legislating." 408 U.S., at 621. For example, the arrest by the Sergeant-At-Arms was held unprotected in *Kilbourn v. Thompson, supra,* because it was not "essential to legislating." Quite the contrary is the case with a routine subpoena intended to gather information about a subject on which legislation may be had.

Respondents also contend that the subpoena cannot be protected by the speech or debate immunity because the "sole purpose" of the investigation is to "force public disclosure of beliefs, opinions, expressions and associations of private citizens which may be unorthodox or unpopular." Respondents view the scope of the privilege too narrowly. Our cases make clear that in determining the legitimacy of a congressional act we do not look to the motives alleged to have prompted it. In *Brewster, supra,* we said "the Speech or Debate Clause protects against inquiry into acts that occur in the regular course of the legislative process *and into the motive for those acts.*" *Id.,* at 525 (emphasis added). And in *Tenney v. Brandhove* we said that, "[t]he claim of an unworthy purpose does not destroy the privilege." 341 U.S., at 377. If the mere allegation that a valid legislative act was undertaken for an unworthy purpose would lift the protection of the Clause then the Clause simply would not provide the protection historically undergirding it. "In times of political passion, dishonest or vindictive motives are readily attributed to legislative conduct and as readily believed." *Tenney v. Brandhove, supra,* 341 U.S., at 379. The wisdom of congressional approach or methodology is not open to judicial veto. Nor is the legitimacy of a congressional inquiry to be defined by what it produces. The very nature of the investigative function — like any research — is that it takes the searchers up some "blind alleys" and into nonproductive enterprises. To be a valid legislative inquiry there need be no predictable end result.

Finally, respondents argue that the purpose of the subpoena was to "harass, chill, punish and deter them" in the exercise of their First Amendment rights, . . . and thus that the subpoena cannot be protected by the Clause. Their theory seems to be that once it is alleged that First Amendment rights may be infringed by congressional action the judiciary may intervene to protect those rights; the Court of Appeals seems to have subscribed to that theory. That approach, however, ignores the absolute nature of the speech or debate protection and our cases which have broadly construed that protection:

> "Congressmen and their aides are immune from liability for their actions within the 'legislative sphere,' *Gravel v. United States, supra,* at 624–625, even though their conduct, if performed in other than legislative contexts would in itself be unconstitutional or otherwise contrary to criminal or civil statutes." *Doe v. McMillan, supra,* at 312–313.

For us to read the Clause as respondents suggest would create an exception not warranted by the language, purposes or history of the Clause. Respondents make the familiar argument that the broad protection granted by the Clause creates a potential for abuse. That is correct, and in *Brewster, supra,* we noted that the risk of such abuse was "the conscious choice of the Framers buttressed and justified by history." 408 U.S., at 516. Our consistently broad construction of the Speech or Debate Clause rests on the belief that it must be so construed to provide the independence which is its central purpose.

This case illustrates vividly the harm that judicial interference may cause. A legislative inquiry has been frustrated for nearly five years during which the Members and their aide have been obliged to devote time to consultation with their counsel concerning the litigation, and have been distracted from the purpose of their inquiry. The Clause was written to prevent the need to be confronted by such "questioning" and to forbid invocation of judicial power to challenge the wisdom of Congress' use of its investigative authority.

Reversed and remanded.

Mr. Justice Marshall, with whom Mr. Justice Brennan and Mr. Justice Stewart join, concurring in the judgment.

. . . .

I write today only to emphasize that the Speech and Debate Clause does not entirely immunize a congressional subpoena from challenge by a party not in a position to assert his constitutional rights by refusing to comply with it.

. . . .

Mr. Justice Douglas, dissenting.

I would affirm the judgment below.

The basic issues in this case were canvassed by me in *Tenney v. Brandhove,* 341 U.S. 367, 381–383 (1951) (dissenting opinion), and by the Court in *Dombrowski v. Eastland,* 387 U.S. 82 (1967), in an opinion which I joined. Under our federal regime that delegates, by the Constitution and Acts of Congress, awesome powers to individuals, those powers may not be used to deprive people of their First Amendment or other constitutional rights. It is my view that no official, no matter how high or majestic his or her office, who is within the reach of judicial process, may invoke immunity for his actions for which wrongdoers normally suffer. There may be few occasions when, on the merits, it would be appropriate to invoke such a remedy. But no regime of law that can rightfully claim that name may make trustees of these vast powers immune from actions brought by people who have been wronged by official action. *See Watkins v. United States,* 354 U.S. 178, 198 (1957).

NOTES AND QUESTIONS

1. Why does the Court resolve this suit through the Speech or Debate Clause? The Court goes to great length to show that the actions of the committee were within the "sphere of legislative activity." Is that the issue? Can't the issue, in fact, be viewed with equal justification as one involving the scope of protection to be afforded to First Amendment "fundamental rights"? Should the Speech or Debate Clause be read to protect members of Congress from charges of abuse of legislative process? Does the Clause prevent the Court from preserving other constitutionally derived rights, *i.e.*, of free speech and association? Can the problem be reached by holding the person serving the subpoena outside the protections of the Speech or Debate Clause? Can the issue be raised by trying to enjoin the bank from complying with the subpoena?

2. In *Hentoff v. Ichord*, 318 F. Supp. 1175 (D.D.C. 1970), District Judge Gesell enjoined the public printing and distribution of a Report entitled "Limited Survey of Honoraria Given Guest Speakers for Engagements at Colleges and Universities" which listed the names of persons characterized by the Committee on Internal Security of the House of Representatives as "Pied Pipers of pernicious propaganda." In granting the injunction, the court concluded:

> If a report has no relationship to any existing or future proper legislative purpose and is issued solely for sake of exposure or intimidation, then it exceeds the legislative function of Congress; and where publication will inhibit free speech and assembly, publication and distribution in official form at government expense may be enjoined. This is such a report.

> The Court recognizes that an injunction against public printing and distribution of the Report, except through the *Congressional Record*, will not prevent distribution and discussion of the so-called "blacklist." There are limits to judicial power just as there are limits to congressional committee action under our tripartite form of government.

Does the district court's holding survive the *Eastland* decision?

3. The scope of Speech or Debate Clause's grant of immunity has been enunciated in a variety of contexts, including a grand jury investigation. *See, e.g., Gravel, supra.*

Another leading case involved a Federal bribery prosecution. The Supreme Court in *United States v. Brewster*, 408 U.S. 501 (1972), discussed the scope of immunity for "legislative acts."

A former U.S. Senator had been indicted for accepting a bribe to deliver a certain speech in the Senate. The District Court had dismissed the prosecution against the Senator, deciding that he was immune under the Speech or Debate Clause. Chief Justice Burger delivered the opinion of the Court:

> The immunities of the Speech or Debate Clause were not written into the Constitution simply for the personal or private benefit of Members of Congress, but to protect the integrity of the legislative process by insuring the independence of individual legislators . . . .

> . . . .

> [*United States v. Johnson*, 388 U.S. 1969 (1966)] . . . stands as a unanimous holding that a Member of Congress may be prosecuted under a criminal statute provided that the government's case does not rely on legislative acts or the motivation for legislative acts. A legislative act has consistently been defined as an act generally done in Congress in relation to the business before it. In sum, the Speech or Debate Clause prohibits inquiry only into those things generally said or done in the House or the Senate in the performance of official duties and into the motivation for those acts.

> It is well known, of course, that Members of the Congress engage in many activities other than the purely legislative activities protected by the Speech or Debate Clause. These include a wide range of legitimate "errands" performed for constituents, the making of appointments with government agencies, assistance in securing government contracts, preparing so-called "news letters" to constituents, news releases, and speeches delivered outside the Congress. The range of these related activities has grown over the years. They are

performed in part because they have come to be expected by constituents, and because they are a means of developing continuing support for future elections. Although these are entirely legitimate activities, they are political in nature rather than legislative, in the sense that term has been used by the Court in prior cases. But it has never been seriously contended that these political matters, however appropriate, have the protection afforded by the Speech or Debate Clause. Careful examination of the decided cases reveals that the Court has regarded the protection as reaching only those things "generally done in a session of the House by one of its members in relation to the business before it," *Kilbourn v. Thompson*, [103 U.S. 168, 204 (1881)], or things "said or done by him, as a representative, in the exercise of the functions of that office," *Coffin v. Coffin*, 4 Mass. 1, 27 (1808).

. . . .

In no case has this Court ever treated the Clause as protecting all conduct *relating* to the legislative process. In every case thus far before this Court, the Speech or Debate Clause has been limited to an act which was clearly a part of the legislative process — the *due* functioning of the process . . . .

. . . .

We would be closing our eyes to the realities of the American political system if we failed to acknowledge that many non-legislative activities are an established and accepted part of the role of a Member, and are indeed "related" to the legislative process. But if the Executive may prosecute a Member's attempt, as in *Johnson*, to influence another branch of the Government in return for a bribe, its power to harass is not greatly enhanced if it can prosecute for a promise relating to a legislative act in return for a bribe. We therefore see no substantial increase in the power of the Executive and Judicial Branches over the Legislative Branch resulting from our holding today. If we underestimate the potential for harassment, the Congress, of course, is free to exempt its Members from the ambit of federal bribery laws, but it has deliberately allowed the instant statute to remain on the books for over a century.

. . . [T]he purpose of the Speech or Debate Clause is to protect the individual legislator, not simply for his own sake, but to preserve the independence and thereby the integrity of the legislative process. But financial abuses, by way of bribes, perhaps even more than Executive power, would gravely undermine legislative integrity and defeat the right of the public to honest representation . . . .

. . . .

Taking a bribe is, obviously, no part of the legislative process or function; it is not a legislative act. It is not, by any conceivable interpretation, an act performed as a part of or even incidental to the role of a legislator. It is not an "act resulting from the nature, and in the execution, of the office." Nor is it a "thing said or done by him, as a representative, in the exercise of the functions of that office," 4 Mass. at 27. Nor is inquiry into a legislative act or the motivation for a legislative act necessary to a prosecution under this statute or this indictment. When a bribe is taken, it does not matter whether the promise for which the bribe was given was for the performance of a legislative act as here or, as in *Johnson*, for use of a Congressman's influence with the Executive Branch. And an inquiry into the purpose of a bribe "does not draw in question the legislative acts of the defendant member of Congress or his motives for performing them." [*United States v. Johnson*], 383 U.S., at 185, 15 L. Ed. 2d, at 691.

. . . .

The only reasonable reading of the Clause, consistent with its history and purpose, is that it does not prohibit inquiry into activities that are casually or incidentally related to legislative affairs but not a part of the legislative process itself. Under this indictment and these statutes no such proof is needed.

We hold that under this statute and this indictment, prosecution of appellee is not prohibited by the Speech or Debate Clause . . . .

Are you satisfied that the *Brewster* precedent is congruent with the *Eastland* decision?

4. A problem similar to that experienced by the plaintiff in *Eastland* can arise when data otherwise confidential under government statutes or common law trade secret doctrine is provided by a third party to a congressional committee either by request or under subpoena. Should a legislative committee be able to obtain confidential data without directly procuring it from the person to whom it belongs?

This issue arose in *Ashland Oil, Inc. v. Federal Trade Comm'n*, 548 F.2d 977 (D.C. Cir. 1976):

PER CURIAM:

This action was brought by Ashland Oil, Inc. to enjoin the Federal Trade Commission from transferring information obtained from Ashland to the House Subcommittee on Oversight and Investigation of the Committee on Interstate and Foreign Commerce. The Subcommittee Chairman, Rep. John E. Moss, intervened. The information in question consists of Ashland's reserve estimates for all its natural gas leases and contracts on federal lands. All parties concede this information is a "trade secret" of great competitive value to Ashland. It is also of great interest to the Subcommittee for whatever light it may cast on the causes of the current natural gas shortage. *See generally FTC v. Texaco*, 170 U.S. App. D.C. 323, 517 F.2d 137 (1975), *vacated and rehearing en banc ordered* (Feb. 6, 1976).

Judge Corcoran denied Ashland's request for preliminary and permanent injunctive relief in a comprehensive opinion. 409 F.Supp. 297 (1976). Ashland's central argument is that experience shows that if the information is made available to Congress, it will inevitably be "made public." This in turn is alleged to violate the prohibition in 15 U.S.C. § 46(f) against the FTC's "mak[ing] public" trade secrets. Judge Corcoran rejected this argument on the grounds that "the courts must presume that the committees of Congress will exercise their powers responsibly and with due regard for the rights of affected parties," 409 F.Supp. at 308. Concluding that Ashland's showing was insufficient to overcome this presumption, the court held that no likelihood of irreparable injury warranting an injunction had been established, *id.*, 309.

We affirm, . . .

I

No substantial showing was made that the materials in the possession of the FTC will necessarily be "made public" if turned over to Congress. Therefore, we need not decide what application, if any, 15 U.S.C. § 46(f) might have if it were evident that Congress intended to "make public" trade secrets. At a minimum, we think it is clear that absent such a showing, 15 U.S.C. § 46(f) does not preclude the FTC from transmitting trade secrets to Congress pursuant either to subpoena or formal request.

Ashland managed to enjoin, at least temporarily, the handing over of the data to the committee by the FTC. Could the court have intervened to prevent disclosure by the committee once the data had been handed over? Could the Congressmen themselves have been enjoined from disclosing the data? Would *Gravel* prevent re-publication of the data by news media?

5. In light of *Eastland*, does the Speech or Debate Clause confer an immunity from civil discovery procedures? *See MINPECO, S.A. v. Commodity Services, Inc.*, 844 F.2d

856 (D.C. Cir. 1988) (quashing subpoena for information and documents directed at congressional subcommittee); *Brown and Williamson Tobacco Co. v. Williams*, 62 F.3d 408, 423 (D.C. Cir. 1995) (broad discovery of documents in Congressional files that came from third parties refused; irrelevant that documents were stolen and privileged); *Miller v. Transamerican Press, Inc.*, 709 F.2d 524 (9th Cir. 1983) (former member of Congress cannot be compelled to testify about circumstances under which he placed material in the Congressional Record).

6. *Eastland* indicates it may be difficult at times to directly challenge a committee's action. If data is subpoenaed from a disinterested party, it may not be willing to risk contempt proceedings to test the committee's right to access to the information. A suit against the committee seeking to enjoin the demand requires asking the court to intervene in a situation where congressional immunity controls. The issue may be differently decided, however, if the court is being asked to enforce contempt proceedings arising from failure to provide Congress with the data; the court might be less willing to lend itself to enforcement of congressional action that would violate the private person's constitutional or statutory rights.

7. Subsequent to *Eastland*, in *United States v. American Tel. & Tel. Co.*, 419 F. Supp. 454 (D.D.C. 1976), the court enjoined a third party, AT&T, from producing evidence to a congressional committee based on the Executive's claim of privilege relating to a perceived threat to national security. The court attempted to balance the competing interests resulting from the House subcommittee's subpoena for information on electronic and telephone surveillance authorized by the Attorney General. The court recognized that enjoining AT&T was equivalent in practical terms to quashing the committee's subpoena. It held, distinguishing *Eastland*, that the Speech or Debate Clause did not limit judicial evaluation of congressional investigative authority where competing constitutional powers (executive privilege) were involved.

      Gasch, District Judge.

This is an action brought on behalf of the Executive Branch of the United States seeking to restrain the American Telephone & Telegraph Company (hereinafter AT & T) from disclosing to the Subcommittee on Oversight and Investigations of the House Committee on Interstate and Foreign Commerce, pursuant to a subpoena of that Subcommittee, certain documents, the delivery of which the President has determined "would involve unacceptable risks of disclosure of extremely sensitive foreign intelligence and counterintelligence information and would be detrimental to the national defense and foreign policy of the United States."

. . . .

The intervenor, Chairman Moss, ostensibly participating in this action on behalf of the Subcommittee, has taken the position that the Speech or Debate Clause of the Constitution is an absolute bar to judicial interference with a Congressional subpoena issued pursuant to a legitimate legislative investigation. The Speech or Debate Clause in Art. I, Section 6 of the Constitution provides "for any Speech or Debate in either House, [the Senators and Representatives] shall not be questioned in any other Place."

The plaintiff has taken the position that this action should be considered one seeking solely to restrain a private entity, AT & T, from releasing documents in its possession. In this way, plaintiff argues, the Court need not consider the applicability of the Speech or Debate Clause, since the immunity of that constitutional provision runs only to members of Congress and their close aides when defending against a lawsuit, and does not afford any protection to a private entity such as AT & T. This argument is advanced so that the Court can avoid dealing with a constitutional confrontation between two of the three branches of our Government. But to take this avenue would be to place form over substance. The effect of any injunction entered by this Court enjoining the release of materials by AT & T to the Subcommittee would have the same effect as if this Court were to quash the Subcommittee's subpoena. In this sense the action is one against the power of the Subcommittee and should be treated as such, assuming that Representative Moss has authority to speak for the Subcommittee.

The Court is thus faced with a conflict between two substantial and fundamental components of our Constitutional system. On the one hand is the power of the Congress to investigate in aid of the legislative function . . . .

Moreover, the Supreme Court has written that the policies expressed in the Speech or Debate Clause are designed "to forbid invocation of judicial power to challenge the wisdom of Congress' use of its investigative authority." *Eastland v. United States Servicemen's Fund*, 421 U.S. 491, 511 (1975).

On the other hand is the authority of the Executive to invoke the claim of privilege concerning matters of national security, foreign affairs or national defense, where the Executive determines disclosure would be inimical to those interests. The courts have accorded great deference to the Executive's judgment in this area . . . .

The Court accepts the position of the intervenor that the subpoenaed materials are sought pursuant to a legitimate legislative investigation. Contrary to the intervenor's argument, however, the Court's inquiry cannot conclude at this point. The legislative authority to investigate is not absolute. In our system of government the Constitution is supreme, but no one portion of the Constitution is sacrosanct. Here, the nature, the extent and the relative importance of the power of one coordinate branch of government must be balanced against that of the other. Neither can be considered in a vacuum.

This balancing of the powers and needs of the constituent branches of government has been considered by the courts in somewhat similar circumstances . . . . Such balancing is *not* precluded by the decision in *Eastland v. United States Servicemen's Fund*, 421 U.S. 491 (1975). In *Servicemen's Fund* there was no countervailing interest at stake of the magnitude of that involved here. The absolute language used by the Court in *Servicemen's Fund* should be considered in the light of the facts of that case: a private party challenging the Congressional investigatory power. Mr. Justice Marshall in his concurrence in *Servicemen's Fund* (in which he was joined by two other Justices) elaborated on the scope of the *Servicemen's Fund* decision:

> "I write today only to emphasize that the Speech or Debate Clause does not entirely immunize a congressional subpoena from challenge by a party not in a position to assert his constitutional rights by refusing to comply with it . . . . The Speech or Debate Clause cannot be used to avoid meaningful review of constitutional objections to a subpoena simply because the subpoena is served on a third party. Our prior cases arising under the Speech and Debate Clause indicate only that a Member of Congress or his aide may not be called upon to defend a subpoena against constitutional objection, and not that the objection will not be heard at all." *Id.*, at 455, 458–59.

8. In *United States v. House of Representatives of the United States*, 556 F. Supp. 150 (D.D.C. 1983), the Reagan administration sought a declaratory judgment to determine whether the Environmental Protection Administrator's refusal to release certain documents to a congressional subcommittee was justified by a claim of executive privilege. What result under *Eastland*?

9. In *United States v. Nixon*, 418 U.S. 683 (1974), the Supreme Court rejected a generalized claim of executive privilege protecting the confidentiality of Presidential communications in the context of a judicial subpoena sought by defendants in an ongoing criminal prosecution. The Court observed:

Absent a claim of need to protect, military, diplomatic, or sensitive national security secrets, we find it difficult to accept the argument that even the very important interest in the confidentiality of Presidential communications is significantly diminished by production for an in camera inspection that a district court will be obliged to provide.

Id. at 684.

In *Senate Select Committee on Presidential Campaign Activities v. Nixon*, 498 F.2d 725 (D.C. Cir. 1974), the District of Columbia Circuit Court of Appeals balanced a generalized claim of executive privilege against the interests that would be served by disclosure to the committee in refusing to enforce a congressional subpoena directing the President to deliver certain tapes and documents. Can the district court's decision in *United States v. House of Representatives of the United States, supra*, be squared with the D.C. Circuit's decision? Can the D.C. Circuit's decision be squared with *Eastland, supra*?

10. For historical materials on legislative investigations, see ARTHUR M. SCHLESINGER, JR. & ROGER BRUNS, EDS., CONGRESS INVESTIGATES, 1792–1974 (1975). For a treatise-like presentation of the issues, see JOHN C. GRABOWSKI, CONGRESSIONAL INVESTIGATIONS (1988). For a brief, practical approach, see Joseph L. Rauh & Daniel H. Pollitt, *Right to and Nature of Representation Before Congressional Committees*, 45 MINN. L. REV. 853 (1961).

11. For a pre-*Eastland* consideration of an action to block a state legislative investigation, see *Goldman v. Olson*, 286 F. Supp. 35 (W.D. Wis. 1968).

HUTCHINSON v. PROXMIRE
443 U.S. 111 (1979)

MR. CHIEF JUSTICE BURGER delivered the opinion of the Court.

We granted certiorari, ___ U.S. ___ (1978), to resolve three issues: (1) Whether a Member of Congress is protected by the Speech or Debate Clause of the Constitution, Art. I, § 6, against suits for allegedly defamatory statements made by the Member in press releases and newsletters; (2) Whether petitioner Hutchinson is either a "public figure" or a "public official," thereby making applicable the "actual malice" standard of *New York Times v. Sullivan*, 376 U.S. 254 (1964); and (3) Whether respondents were entitled to summary judgment.

Ronald Hutchinson, a research behavioral scientist, sued respondents, William Proxmire, a United States Senator, and his legislative assistant, Morton Schwartz, for defamation arising out of Proxmire's giving what he called his "Golden Fleece" award. The "award" went to federal agencies that had sponsored Hutchinson's research. Hutchinson alleged that in making the award and publicizing it nationwide, respondents had libeled him, damaging him in his professional and academic standing, and had interfered with his contractual relations. The District Court granted summary judgment for respondents and the Court of Appeals affirmed.

We reverse and remand to the Court of Appeals for further proceedings consistent with this opinion.

I

Respondent Proxmire is a United States Senator from Wisconsin. In March 1975 he initiated the "Golden Fleece of the Month Award" to publicize what he perceived to be the most egregious examples of wasteful governmental spending. The second such award, in April 1975, went to the National Science Foundation, the National Aeronautics and Space Administration, and the Office of Naval Research, for spending almost half a million dollars during the preceding seven years to fund Hutchinson's research.

At the time of the award, Hutchinson was director of research at the Kalamazoo State Mental Hospital . . . . When the research department at Kalamazoo State Mental Hospital was closed in June 1975, Hutchinson became research director of the Foundation for Behavioral Research, a nonprofit organization. The research funding was transferred from the hospital to the foundation.

The bulk of Hutchinson's research was devoted to the study of emotional behavior. In particular, he sought an objective measure of aggression, concentrating upon the behavior patterns of certain animals, such as the clenching of jaws when they were exposed to various aggravating stressful stimuli. The National Aeronautics and Space Agency and the Navy were interested in the potential of this research for resolving problems associated with confining humans in close quarters for extended periods of time in space and undersea exploration.

The Golden Fleece Award to the agencies that had sponsored Hutchinson's research was based upon research done for Proxmire by Schwartz. While seeking evidence of wasteful governmental spending, Schwartz read copies of reports that Hutchinson had prepared under grants from NASA. Those reports revealed that Hutchinson had received grants from the Office of Naval Research, the National Science Foundation, and the Michigan State Department of Mental Health. Schwartz also learned that other federal agencies had funded Hutchinson's research. After contacting a number of federal and state agencies, Schwartz helped to prepare a speech for Proxmire to present in the Senate on April 18, 1975; the text was then incorporated into an advance press release, with only the addition of introductory and concluding sentences. Copies were sent to a mailing list of 275 members of the news media throughout the United States and abroad.

Schwartz telephoned Hutchinson before releasing the speech to tell him of the award; Hutchinson protested that the release contained an inaccurate and incomplete summary of his research. Schwartz replied that he thought the summary was fair.

In the speech Proxmire described the federal grants for Hutchinson's research, concluding with the following comment:[3]

"The funding of this nonsense makes me almost angry enough to scream and kick or even clench my jaws. It seems to me it is outrageous.

"Dr. Hutchinson's studies should make the taxpayers as well as his monkeys grind their teeth. In fact, the good doctor has made a fortune from his monkeys and in the process made a monkey out of the American taxpayer.

"It is time for the Federal Government to get out of this 'monkey business.' In view of the transparent worthlessness of Hutchinson's study of jaw-grinding and biting by angry or hard-drinking monkeys, it is time we put a stop to the bite Hutchinson and the bureaucrats who fund him have been taking of the taxpayer." 121 Cong. Rec. 10803 (1975).

In May 1975, Proxmire referred to his Golden Fleece Awards in a newsletter sent to about 100,000 people whose names were on a mailing list that included constituents in Wisconsin as well as persons in other states. The newsletter repeated the essence of the speech and the press release. Later in 1975, Proxmire appeared on a television interview program where he referred to Hutchinson's research, though he did not mention Hutchinson by name.

---

[3] Proxmire is not certain that he actually delivered the speech on the Senate floor. He said that he might have merely inserted it into the Congressional Record, App., at 220–221. In light of that uncertainty, the question arises whether a nondelivered speech printed in the Congressional Record is covered by the Speech or Debate Clause. This Court has never passed on that question and neither the District Court nor the Court of Appeals seemed to think it was important. Nevertheless, we assume, without deciding, that a speech printed in the Congressional Record carries immunity under the Speech or Debate Clause as though delivered on the floor.

The final reference to the research came in a newsletter in February 1976. In that letter Proxmire summarized his Golden Fleece Awards of 1975. The letter did not mention Hutchinson's name, but it did report:

> "— The NSF, the Space Agency, and the Office of Naval Research won the 'Golden Fleece' for spending jointly $500,000 to determine why monkeys clench their jaws.

> . . . .

> "All the studies on why monkeys clench their jaws were dropped. No more monkey business." App., at 168–171.

After the award was announced, Schwartz, acting on behalf of Proxmire, contacted a number of the federal agencies that had sponsored the research. In his deposition he stated that he did not attempt to dissuade them from continuing to fund the research but merely discussed the subject. Hutchinson, by contrast, contends that these calls were intended to persuade the agencies to terminate his grants and contracts.

II

On April 16, 1976, Hutchinson filed this suit in United States District Court in Wisconsin. In Count I he alleges that as a result of the actions of Proxmire and Schwartz he has "suffered a loss of respect in his profession, has suffered injury to his feelings, has been humiliated, held up to public scorn, suffered extreme mental anguish and physical illness and pain to his person. Further, he has suffered a loss of income and ability to earn income in the future." Count II alleges that the respondents' conduct has interfered with Hutchinson's contractual relationships with supporters of his research. He later amended the complaint to add an allegation that his rights of privacy and peace and tranquility have been infringed.

Respondents moved for a change of venue and for summary judgment. In their motion for summary judgment they asserted that all of their acts and utterances were protected by the Speech or Debate Clause. In addition, they asserted that their criticism of the spending of public funds was privileged under the free speech clause of the First Amendment. They argued that Hutchinson was both a public figure and a public official, and therefore would be obliged to prove the existence of "actual malice." Respondents contended that the facts of this case would not support a finding of actual malice.

Without ruling on venue, the District Court granted respondents' motion for summary judgment. 431 F. Supp. 1311 (W.D. Wis. 1977). In so ruling, the District Court relied on both grounds urged by respondents. It reasoned that the Speech or Debate Clause afforded absolute immunity for respondents' activities in investigating the funding of Hutchinson's research, for Proximire's speech in the Senate, and for the press release covering the speech. The court concluded that the investigations and the speech were clearly within the ambit of the Clause. The press release was said to be protected because it fell within the "informing function" of Congress. To support its conclusion the District Court relied upon cases interpreting the franking privilege granted to Members by statute. See 39 U.S.C. § 3210.

Although the District Court referred to the "informing function" of Congress and to the franking privilege, it did not base its conclusion concerning the press release on those analogies. Instead, the District Court held that the "press release, in a constitutional sense, was no different than would have been a television or radio broadcast of his speech from the Senate floor." 431 F. Supp., at 1325. That the District Court did not rely upon the "informing function" is clear from its implicit holding that the newsletters were not protected.

. . . .

The Court of Appeals affirmed, holding that the Speech or Debate Clause protected the statements made in the press release and in the newsletters. 579 F.2d 1027 (CA7

1978). It interpreted *Doe v. McMillan*, 412 U.S. 306 (1973), as recognizing a limited protection for the "informing function" of Congress and concluded that distribution of both the press release and the newsletters did not exceed what was required for legislative purposes. 579 F.2d, at 1033. The follow-up telephone calls and the statements made by Proxmire on television and radio were not protected by the Speech or Debate Clause; they were, however, held by the Court of Appeals to be protected by the First Amendment.[10]

. . . .

The purpose of the Speech or Debate Clause is to protect Members of Congress "not only from the consequences of litigation's results but also from the burden of defending themselves." *Dombrowski v. Eastland*, 387 U.S. 82, 85 (1967). *See also Eastland v. United Servicemen's Fund*, 421 U.S. 491, 503 (1975). If the respondents have immunity under the Clause, no other questions need be considered for they may "not be questioned in any other place."

. . . .

IV

In support of the Court of Appeals holding that newsletters and press releases are protected by the Speech or Debate Clause, respondents rely upon both historical precedent and present-day congressional practices. They contend that impetus for the Speech or Debate Clause privilege in our Constitution came from the history of parliamentary efforts to protect the right of members to criticize the spending of the Crown and from the prosecution of a Speaker of the House of Commons for publication of a report outside of Parliament. Respondents also contend that in the modern day very little speech or debate occurs on the floor of either House; from this they argue that press releases and newsletters are necessary for Members of Congress to communicate with other Members. For example, in his deposition Proxmire testified:

> "I have found in 19 years in the Senate that very often a statement on the floor of the Senate or something that appears in the Congressional Record misses the attention of most members of the Senate, and virtually all members of the House, because they don't read the Congressional Record. If they are handed a news release, or something, that is going to call it to their attention . . . ." App., at 220.

Respondents also argue that an essential part of the duties of a Member of Congress is to inform constituents, as well as other Members, of the issues being considered.

The Speech or Debate Clause has been directly passed on by this Court relatively few times in 190 years. *Eastland v. United Servicemen's Fund, supra; Doe v. McMillan*, 412 U.S. 306 (1973); *Gravel v. United States*, 408 U.S. 606 (1972); *United States v. Brewster*, 408 U.S. 501 (1972); *Dombrowski v. Eastland, supra; United States v. Johnson*, 383 U.S. 169 (1966); *Kilbourn v. Thompson*, 103 U.S. 168 (1881). Literal reading of the Clause would, of course, confine its protection narrowly to a "Speech or Debate *in* either

---

[10] Respondents did not cross-petition; neither did they argue that the Speech or Debate Clause protected the follow-up telephone calls made by Schwartz to governmental agencies or the television and radio interviews of Proxmire. Instead, respondents relied only upon the protection afforded by the First Amendment. In light of our conclusion, *infra*, that Hutchinson is not a public figure, respondents would nevertheless be entitled to raise the Speech or Debate Clause as an alternative ground for supporting the judgment. From our conclusion, *infra*, that the Speech or Debate Clause does not protect the republication of libelous remarks, it follows that libelous remarks in the follow-up telephone calls to executive agencies and in the television and radio interviews are not protected. Regardless of whether and to what extent the Speech or Debate Clause may protect calls to federal agencies seeking information, it does not protect attempts to influence the conduct of executive agencies or libelous comments made during the conversations. *Cf. United States v. Johnson*, 383 U.S., at 172; *United States v. Brewster*, 408 U.S., at 512–513.

House." But the Court has given the Clause a practical rather than a strictly literal reading which would limit the protection to utterances made within the four walls of either Chamber. Thus, we have held that committee hearings are protected, even if held outside the Chambers; committee reports are also protected. *Doe v. McMillan, supra; Gravel v. United States, supra. Cf. Coffin v. Coffin,* 4 Mass. 1, 27–28 (1808).

The gloss going beyond a strictly literal reading of the Clause has not, however, departed from the objective of protecting only legislative activities. In Thomas Jefferson's view,

> "[The privilege] is restrained to things done in the House in a Parliamentary course . . . . For [the Member] is not to have privilege contra morem parliamentarium, to exceed the bounds and limits of his place and duty." T. JEFFERSON, A MANUAL OF PARLIAMENTARY PRACTICE 20 (1854), reprinted in THE COMPLETE JEFFERSON 704 (S. Padover ed. 1943).

One of the draftsmen of the Constitution, James Wilson, expressed a similar thought in lectures delivered between 1790 and 1792 while he was a Justice of this Court. He rejected Blackstone's statement, 1 W. BLACKSTONE, COMMENTARIES 164, that Parliament's privileges were preserved by keeping them indefinite:

> "Very different is the case with regard to the legislature of the United States . . . . The great maxims, upon which our law of parliament is founded, are defined and ascertained in our constitutions. The arcana of privilege, and the arcana of prerogative, are equally unknown to our system of jurisprudence." 2 THE WORKS OF JAMES WILSON 35 (J. Andrews ed. 1896).[12]

In this respect Wilson was underscoring the very purpose of our Constitution — *inter alia*, to provide *written* definitions of the powers, privileges, and immunities granted rather than rely on evolving constitutional concepts identified from diverse sources as in English law. Like thoughts were expressed by Joseph Story, writing in the first edition of his Commentaries on the Constitution in 1833:

> "But this privilege is strictly confined to things done in the course of parliamentary proceedings, and does not cover things done beyond the place and limits of duty." *Id.,* § 863, at 329.

Cf. Coffin v. Coffin, 4 Mass. 1, 34 (1808).

In *United States v. Brewster,* 408 U.S. 501 (1972), we acknowledged the historical roots of the Clause going back to the long struggle between the English House of Commons and the Tudor and Stuart monarchs when both criminal and civil processes were employed by crown authority to intimidate legislators. Yet we cautioned that the Clause must be interpreted in light of the American experience, and in the context of the American constitutional scheme of government rather than the English parliamentary system . . . . [T]heir Parliament is the supreme authority, not a coordinate branch. Our speech or debate privilege was designed to preserve legislative independence, not supremacy. 408 U.S., at 508.

Nearly a century ago, in *Kilbourn v. Thompson,* 103 U.S. 168, 204 (1881), this Court held that the Clause extended "to things generally done *in a session* of the House by one of its members *in relation to the business before it.*" (Emphasis added.) More recently we expressed a similar definition of the scope of the Clause:

> "Legislative acts are not all-encompassing. The heart of the Clause is speech or debate in either House. Insofar as the Clause is construed to reach other matters, *they must be an integral part of the deliberative and communicative processes* by which Members participate *in committee and House proceedings*

---

[12] *But see* T. JEFFERSON, MANUAL OF PARLIAMENTARY PRACTICE 15–16 (1854), *reprinted in* THE COMPLETE JEFFERSON 702 (S. Padover ed. 1943) (quoting BLACKSTONE with approval).

with respect to the consideration and passage or rejection of proposed legislation or with respect to other matters which the Constitution places within the jurisdiction of either House. As the Court of Appeals put it, the courts have extended the privilege to matters beyond pure speech or debate in either House, but 'only when necessary to prevent indirect impairment of such deliberations.'" *Gravel v. United States, supra*, at 625 (quoting *United States v. Doe*, 455 F.2d 753, 760 (1st Cir. 1972) (emphasis added).

Cf. Doe v. McMillan, supra, at 313–314, 317; *United States v. Brewster, supra*, at 512, 515–516, 517–518; *Long v. Ansell*, 293 U.S. 76, 82 (1934).

Whatever imprecision there may be in the term "legislative activities," it is clear that nothing in history or in the explicit language of the Clause suggests any intention to create an absolute privilege from liability or suit for defamatory statements made outside the Chamber. In *Brewster, supra*, at 507, we observed:

> "The immunities of the Speech or Debate Clause were not written into the Constitution simply for the personal or private benefit of Members of Congress, but to protect the integrity of the legislative process by insuring the independence of individual legislators."

Claims under the Clause going beyond what is needed to protect legislative independence are to be closely scrutinized. In *Brewster* we took note of this:

> "The authors of our Constitution were well aware of both the need for the privilege *and the abuses that could flow from too sweeping safeguards*. In order to preserve other values, they wrote the privilege so that it tolerates and protects behavior on the part of Members not tolerated and protected when done by other citizens, *but the shield does not extend beyond what is necessary to preserve the integrity of the legislative process.*" *Id.*, at 517 (emphasis added).

Indeed, the precedents abundantly support the conclusion that a Member may be held liable for republishing defamatory statements originally made in either House. We perceive no basis for departing from that long-established rule.

Justice Story in his Commentaries, for example, explained that there was no immunity for republication of a speech first delivered in Congress:

> "Therefore, although a speech delivered in the house of commons is privileged, and the member cannot be questioned respecting it elsewhere; *yet, if he publishes his speech, and it contains libellous matter, he is liable to an action and prosecution therefor, as in common cases of libel.* And the same principles seem applicable to the privilege of debate and speech in congress. No man ought to have a right to defame others under colour of a performance of the duties of his office. And if he does so *in the actual discharge of his duties in congress, that furnishes no reason, why he should be enabled through the medium of the press to destroy the reputation, and invade the repose of other citizens.* It is neither within the scope of his duty, nor in furtherance of public rights, or public policy. Every citizen has as good a right to be protected by the laws from malignant scandal, and false charges, and defamatory imputations, as a member of congress has to utter them in his seat."[13] J. STORY, COMMENTARIES

---

[13] Story acknowledged the arguments to the contrary: "It is proper, however, to apprise the learned reader that it has been recently denied in congress by very distinguished lawyers, that the privilege of speech and debate in congress does not extend to publication of his speech. And they ground themselves upon an important distinction arising from the actual differences between English and American legislation. In the former, the publication of the debates is not strictly lawful, except by license of the house. In the latter, it is a common right, exercised and supported by the direct encouragement of the body. This reasoning deserves a very attentive examination." J. STORY, COMMENTARIES ON THE CONSTITUTION § 863, at 329–330 (1833).

At oral argument counsel for respondents referred to a note in the fifth edition of the Commentaries saying

ON THE CONSTITUTION, § 863, at 329 (1833) (emphasis added).

See also L. CUSHING, ELEMENTS OF THE LAW AND PRACTICE OF LEGISLATIVE ASSEMBLIES IN THE UNITED STATES OF AMERICA 604, at p. 244 (2d ed. 1863).

Story summarized the state of the common law at the time the Constitution was drafted, recalling that Parliament had by then succeeded in its struggle to secure freedom of debate. But the privilege did not extend to republication of libellous remarks even though first made in Parliament. Thus, in *Rex v. Lord Abingdon*, 1 Esp. 225, 170 Eng. Rep. 337 (N.P. 1794), Lord Chief Justice Kenyon rejected Lord Abingdon's argument that parliamentary privilege protected him from suit for republication of a speech first made in the House of Lords:

> "[A]s to the words in question, had they been spoken in the House of Lords, and confined to its walls, [the] Court would have had no jurisdiction to call his Lordship before them, to answer for them as an offence; but . . . in the present case, the offence was the publication under his authority and sanction, and at his expense: . . . a member of Parliament had certainly a right to publish his speech, but that speech should not be made the vehicle of slander against any individual; if it was, it was a libel . . . ." *Id.*, at 228, 170 Eng. Rep., at 338.

A similar result was reached in *Rex v. Creevey*, 1 M. & S. 273, 105 Eng. Rep. 102 (K.B. 1813).

In *Gravel v. United States*, 408 U.S. 606, 622–626 (1972), we recognized that the doctrine denying immunity for republication had been accepted in the United States:

> "[P]rivate publication by Senator Gravel . . . was in no way essential to the deliberations of the Senate; nor does questioning as to the private publication threaten the integrity or independence of the Senate by impermissibly exposing its deliberations to executive influence." *Id.*, at 625.

We reaffirmed that principle in *Doe v. McMillan*, 412 U.S. 306, 314–315 (1973):

> "A Member of Congress may not with impunity publish a libel from the speaker's stand in his home district, and clearly the Speech or Debate Clause would not protect such an act even though the libel was read from an official committee report. The reason is that republishing a libel under such circumstances is not an essential part of the legislative process and is not part of that deliberative process 'by which Members participate in committee and House proceedings.'" (Quoting from *Gravel v. United States*, 408 U.S. 606, 625 (1972)).[14]

We reach a similar conclusion here. A speech by Proxmire in the Senate would be wholly immune and would be available to other Members of Congress and the public in the Congressional Record. But neither the newsletters nor the press release was "essential to the deliberations of the Senate" and neither was part of the deliberative process.

Respondents, however, argue that newsletters and press releases are essential to the

---

that the Speech or Debate Clause protected the circulation to constituents of copies of speeches made in Congress. Tr. of Oral Arg. 43. In attributing the note to Story counsel made an understandable mistake. As explained in the preface to the fifth edition, that note was added by the editor, Melville Bigelow. The note does not appear in Story's first edition. Moreover, it is clear from the text of the note and the sources cited, that Bigelow did not mean that there was an absolute privilege for defamatory remarks contained in a speech mailed to constituents as there would be if the mailing was protected by the Speech or Debate Clause. Instead, he suggested that there was a qualified privilege, akin to that for accurate newspaper reports of legislative proceedings.

[14] It is worth noting that the Rules of the Senate forbid disparagement of other Members on the floor. Senate Rule XIX (April 1979). *See also* T. JEFFERSON, MANUAL OF PARLIAMENTARY PRACTICE 40–41 (1854), *reprinted in* THE COMPLETE JEFFERSON 714–715 (S. Padover ed. 1943).

functioning of the Senate; without them, they assert, a Senator cannot have a significant impact on the other Senators. We may assume that a Member's published statements exert some influence on other votes in the Congress and therefore have a relationship to the legislative and deliberative process. But in *Brewster, supra,* at 512, we rejected respondents' expansive reading of the Clause:

> "It is well known, of course, that Members of the Congress engage in many activities other than the purely legislative activities protected by the Speech or Debate Clause. These include . . . preparing so-called 'news letters' to constituents, news releases, and speeches delivered outside the Congress."

There we went on to note that *Johnson* had carefully distinguished between what is only "related to the due functioning of the legislative process," and what constitutes the legislative process entitled to immunity under the Clause:

> "In stating that those things [Johnson's attempts to influence the Department of Justice] 'in no wise related to the due functioning of the legislative process' were *not* covered by the privilege, the Court did not in any sense imply as a corollary that everything that 'related' to the office of a Member was shielded by the Clause. Quite the contrary, in *Johnson* we held, citing *Kilbourn v. Thompson, supra,* that only acts generally done in the course of the process of enacting legislation were protected.
>
>   . . . .
>
> "In no case has this Court ever treated the Clause as protecting all conduct relating to the legislative process.
>
>   . . . .
>
> "In its narrowest scope, the Clause is a very large, albeit essential, grant of privilege. It has enabled reckless men to slander [by speech or debate] and even destroy others with impunity, but that was the conscious choice of the Framers." *Id.,* at 513–516. (Emphasis in original; citations omitted.)

We are unable to discern any "conscious choice" to grant immunity for defamatory statements scattered far and wide by mail, press, and the electronic media.

Respondents also argue that newsletters and press releases are privileged as part of the "informing function" of Congress. Advocates of a broad reading of the "informing function" sometimes tend to confuse two uses of the term "informing." In one sense, Congress informs itself collectively by way of hearings of its committees. It was in that sense that Woodrow Wilson used "informing" in a statement quoted by respondents. In reality, Wilson's statement related to congressional efforts to learn of the activities of the Executive Branch and administrative agencies; he did not include wideranging inquiries by individual Members on subjects of their choice. Moreover, Wilson's statement itself clearly implies a distinction between the *informing* function and the *legislative* function:

> "Unless Congress have and use every means of acquainting itself with the acts and the disposition of the administrative agents of the government, the country must be helpless to learn how it is being served; and unless Congress both scrutinize these things and sift them by every form of discussion, the country must remain in embarrassing, crippling ignorance of the very affairs which it is most important that it should understand and direct. The informing function of Congress should be preferred even to its legislative function . . . . [T]he only really self-governing people is that people which discusses and interrogates its administration." W. Wilson, Congressional Government 303 (1885).

It is in this narrower Wilsonian sense that this Court has employed "informing" in previous cases holding that congressional efforts to inform itself through committee hearings are part of the legislative function.

The other sense of the term, and the one relied upon by respondents, perceives it to be the duty of Members to tell the public about their activities. Valuable and desirable as it may be in broad terms, the transmittal of such information by individual Members in order to inform the public and other Members is not a part of the legislative function or the deliberations that make up the legislative process.[15]

As a result, transmittal of such information by press releases and newsletters is not protected by the Speech or Debate Clause.

Doe v. McMillan, 412 U.S. 306 (1973), is not to the contrary. It dealt only with reports from congressional committees, and held that Members of Congress could not be held liable for voting to publish a report. Voting and preparing committee reports are the individual and collective expressions of opinion within the legislative process. As such, they are protected by the Speech or Debate Clause. Newsletters and press releases, by contrast, are primarily means of informing those outside the legislative forum; they represent the views and will of a single Member. It does not disparage either their value or their importance to hold that they are not entitled to the protection of the Speech or Debate Clause.

V

Since *New York Times v. Sullivan*, 376 U.S. 254 (1964), this Court has sought to define the accommodation required to assure the vigorous debate on public issues that the First Amendment was designed to protect while at the same time affording protection to the reputations of individuals . . . .

. . . .

Hutchinson did not thrust himself or his views into public controversy to influence others. Respondents have not identified such a particular controversy; at most, they point to concern about general public expenditures. But that concern is shared by most and relates to most public expenditures; it is not sufficient to make Hutchinson a public figure. If it were, everyone who received or benefited from the myriad public grants for research could be classified as a public figure — a conclusion that our previous opinions have rejected. The "use of such subject-matter classifications to determine the extent of constitutional protection afforded defamatory falsehoods may too often result in an improper balance between the competing interests in this area." *Time, Inc. v. Firestone, supra*, at 456.

Moreover, Hutchinson at no time assumed any role of public prominence in the broad question of concern about expenditures. Neither his applications for federal grants nor his publications in professional journals can be said to have invited that degree of public attention and comment on his receipt of federal grants essential to meet the public figure level. The petitioner in *Gertz v. Robert Welch, Inc.*, [418 U.S. 323 (1974),] had published books and articles on legal issues; he had been active in local community affairs. Nevertheless, the Court concluded that his activities did not make him a public figure.

Finally, we cannot agree that Hutchinson had such access to the media that he should be classified as a public figure. Hutchinson's access was limited to responding to the announcement of the Golden Fleece Award. He did not have the regular and continuing access to the media that is one of the accouterments of having become a public figure.

We therefore reverse the judgment of the Court of Appeals and remand the case to the Court of Appeals for further proceedings consistent with this opinion.

Reversed and remanded.

---

[15] Provision for the use of the frank, 39 U.S.C. § 3210, does not alter our conclusion. Congress, by granting franking privileges, stationery allowances, and facilities to record speeches and statements for radio broadcast cannot expand the scope of the Speech or Debate Clause to render immune all that emantes via such helpful facilities.

. . . .

Mr. Justice Brennan, dissenting.

I disagree with the Court's conclusion that Senator Proxmire's newsletters and press releases fall outside the protection of the speech or debate immunity. In my view, public criticism by legislators of unnecessary governmental expenditures, whatever its form, is a legislative act shielded by the Speech or Debate Clause. I would affirm the judgment below for the reasons expressed in my dissent in *Gravel v. United States*, 408 U.S. 606, 648 (1972) (Brennan, J., dissenting).

NOTES AND QUESTIONS

1. What happened to the Court's willingness, enunciated in *Gravel*, to read the Speech or Debate Clause "in view of the complexities of the modern legislative process"? If one extends the Speech or Debate Clause privilege to aides who are unmentioned in the text, why not read the privilege in light of the evolving mores of the legislative branch, as Jefferson recommended in his comment cited in the majority opinion?

2. Proxmire was a member of the Appropriations Committee, the committee that determines the expenditure of government monies. What meaningful alternatives aside from the press release does he have to communicate his concerns about the subject matter which was intimately connected to his legislative duties? Are you troubled by the fact that Senator Proxmire can make a speech in the Senate which is duly reported in the Congressional Record but cannot respond to a constituent's question in a meeting in Milwaukee as to why he made that speech without exposing himself to tort liability? Isn't explaining an integral part of decisionmaking?

3. Isn't the pressure (as a result of such nationwide publicity) which their constituents may exert on his colleagues to vote to control government inefficiency one of the most significant means Proxmire has to generate legislative support? If so, should it be considered legislative activity? If he had inserted his statements in the *Congressional Record* and then sent copies of that portion of the *Record* to his constituents, would a different result have been justified?

4. Does the Court adequately consider the increased importance of Congress' informational function in this era of electronic communications? For instance, are broadcasts by radio and television of floor debates and committee proceedings within the immunity provided by the Clause? If so, is there a sufficient distinction between such media exposure and that involving statements during personal television appearances or by press releases?

5. In March of 1980, Senator Proxmire announced a $10,000 settlement from his own funds with Dr. Hutchinson and admitted that some of his 1975 statements were incorrect. A Senate Rules Committee aide said that the Senator's legal defense cost taxpayers $124,351. International Herald Tribune, March 26, 1980, at 3, col. 1–2.

6. In *Dickey v. CBS, Inc.*, 387 F. Supp. 1332 (E.D. Pa. 1975), the court drew a distinction between legislative and political activities. The case involved a libel suit against the television network which had broadcast statements made by Representative Williams. Dickey gave Williams notice of the taking of dispositions and Williams sought a protective order and moved to quash the subpoena. In denying the motion to quash, the court stated:

> Precisely because the delivery of a speech by a Congressman outside the Congress is a political, not a legislative activity, it is not entitled to the protection of the Speech or Debate Clause. To be sure, some might think that this conclusion is based on an overly restrictive definition of "legislative activity."

. . . .

. . . As a matter of logic, one could argue that a Congressman who reads verbatim from an official committee report is performing a "legislative" function, that is, informing his constituents. The majority of the Supreme Court, however, has held differently and negated that theory when it stated in *Doe v. McMillan, supra,* that "[a] Member of *Congress* may not with impunity publish a libel from the speaker's stand in his home district, and clearly the Speech or Debate Clause would not protect such an act even though the libel was read from an official committee report." 412 U.S. at 314, 93 S. Ct. at 2025. Liability would attach to the Congressman because "republishing a libel in such circumstances is not an essential part of the legislative process and is not part of that deliberative process 'by which members participate in committee and House proceedings.' *Gravel v. United States, supra,* [408 U.S.] at 625, at 2627 of 92 S. Ct." *Doe v. McMillan, supra,* 412 U.S. at 314–15, 93 S. Ct. at 2026. The Speech or Debate Clause does not "immunize those who publish and distribute otherwise actionable materials beyond the reasonable requirements of the legislative function." *Id.* at 315–316, 93 S. Ct. at 2026.

. . . .

. . . For the purpose of this motion to quash, I can see no significant difference between a speech outside Congress and a television appearance outside Congress. Because that appearance of Congressman Williams was political rather than legislative, it was not protected by the Speech or Debate Clause, and he would be subject to criminal or civil liability for anything he said or did during that appearance.

Id. at 1335–36.

7. If C-Span broadcasts a member's speech which contains arguably actionable remarks, can it be sued, even though the member is immune? Is C-Span an "aide" to both houses of Congress?

8. One attempt to define the scope of legislative activities was Senate Bill S.1314, entitled the "Congressional Free Speech Act of 1973," that was introduced in 1973 by Senator Ervin and others to resolve some of the questions of what constitutes legitimate legislative activity:

SEC. 2. As used in this Act:

(1) the term "legislative activity" means any activity relating to the due functioning of the legislative process and carrying out the obligations a Member of Congress owes to the Congress and to his constituents and shall include, but not be limited to speaking, debating, or voting in committee or on the floor of Congress, receipt of information for use in legislative proceedings, any conduct in committee related to the consideration of legislation or related to the conduct of an investigation, speeches, or publications outside of Congress informing the public on matters of national or local importance, and the motives and decisionmaking process leading to the above activity or leading to the decision not to engage in the above activity;

(2) the term "Member" means a present or former Member of Congress;

(3) the term "aide" means any person who assists a Member in his performance of legislative activity; and

(4) the term "protected legislative activity" means legislative activity performed by a Member or by an aide on behalf of the Member while he was a Member of Congress.

Legislative Immunity Generally

SEC. 3. No court or grand jury shall inquire of a Member or an aide either directly or indirectly into the protected legislative activities of a Member in a criminal proceeding without the Member's consent.

S.1314 expands the immunity to be read into the Speech or Debate Clause by the courts. Should all speeches that fulfill an informational function be included within the sphere of legislative immunity? What problems are raised by this proposed statute?

9. In *Hoellen v. Annunzio*, 468 F.2d 522 (7th Cir. 1972), *cert. denied*, 412 U.S. 953 (1973), an injunction had been granted to stop Representative Annunzio from using his franking privilege for mass mailings to persons he did not presently represent, who lived in a new district where he planned to be a candidate. Annunzio claimed the mailing of questionaires was official business and inquiry into his motives was contrary to the Speech or Debate Clause. The court rejected these claims and upheld the injunction, stating:

> Defendant's reliance on the Speech or Debate Clause as foreclosing inquiry into his motivation assumes that the mailing was a legislative act. But, as the district court clearly recognized, the Supreme Court's recent decision in *United States v. Brewster*, 408 U.S. 501, 92 S. Ct. 2531, 33 L. Ed. 2d 507, requires rejection of that assumption. Although a Congressman's motivation for a legislative act may not be questioned, the clause does not preclude consideration of his motive in the determination of whether a particular mailing was "upon official business" within the meaning of § 3210.

Id. at 527.

Why is this dissemination of information not "official business"? Does the case mean that a representative can never seek opinions from outside his constituency? Would his actions have been proper, but for the fact that Annunzio was mailing to persons not presently in his district? Are these mailings significantly different in character from the press releases in *Hutchinson*?

BISHOP v. WAYNE CIRCUIT JUDGE
237 N.W.2d 465 (Mich. 1976)

FITZGERALD, J. Defendant Wayne Circuit Judge appeals from an order of the Court of Appeals quashing a subpoena. The subpoena directed plaintiff, a state senator, to give a pretrial discovery deposition and to produce certain documents in connection with a civil action which had been assigned to defendant. The issue before us is whether, on the facts of this case, we should judicially construe an exception for intra-session adjournments to this state's constitutional provision granting senators and representatives immunity "from civil arrest and civil process *during sessions of the legislature* and for five days next before the commencement and after the termination thereof."[1] (Emphasis supplied.)

The action out of which arose the instant complaint for superintending control was brought by one Walter Benkert and a non-profit corporation, Michigan Association for Consumer Protection, for themselves and all persons similarly situated. Named as defendants in that suit were the Michigan State Police, its Director, Col. George Halverson, and Governor William G. Milliken. The complaint alleged that the state police, acting at the request of a state legislator,[2] had conducted investigations of the named plaintiffs. It requested that such investigations be permanently enjoined, and that the fruits thereof be produced before the court for destruction. Defendants therein, through the attorney general, answered the complaint, admitting the following: that the state police had been contacted by a state legislator to conduct an investigation of the named plaintiffs; that the scope of the Benkert investigation included his background and relationship with MACP; that the scope of the investigation of MACP

---

[1] Const. 1963, art. 4, § 11.

[2] Since identified by the class-action plaintiffs, in an amended complaint, to be one other than plaintiff Bishop.

included its background, finances, objectives and membership. Defendants pleaded no contest to the allegation that the state police had exceeded its statutory authority in conducting these investigations.

In connection with the above action, on August 30, 1974, the plaintiffs therein caused to be served on plaintiff Bishop a subpoena directing him to appear at a certain law office at 11:30 a.m. on September 5, 1974, to testify and produce documents. On September 5, plaintiff Bishop filed a motion supported by affidavit in the trial court requesting that the subpoena be quashed on the grounds *inter alia* that he was privileged from civil process. The motion was denied by defendant who reasoned that, although the Legislature had convened on the second Wednesday in January 1974 and had not as of the date of the purported service adjourned its regular session *sine die*, nevertheless the Senate had recessed from July 13 until September 17. Consequently, it was defendant's opinion that plaintiff was "on free time" and should be available to testify.

In quashing the subpoena, the Court of Appeals cited Const. 1963, art. 4, § 11, and *Auditor General v. Wayne Circuit Judge*, 234 Mich. 540; 208 N.W. 696 (1926). In that case . . . the policy underlying the immediate predecessor of article 4, § 11, was articulated as follows:

> "This is a too narrow view of the situation. The idea back of the constitutional provision was to protect the legislators from the trouble, worry and inconvenience of court proceedings during the session, and for a certain time before and after, so that the State could have their undivided time and attention in public affairs. Mr. Culver, as principal defendant, had the right to make a defense to the garnishee proceeding. In the present case the garnishee proceeding succeeded in doing just what the constitutional provision was created to avoid. It harassed the legislator, drove him to make a defense in the garnishee proceeding, and deprived him of the means of subsistence pending the balance of the session. We think the case clearly comes within the constitutional inhibition." 234 Mich. 541–542.

In the case at bar, rather than argue that plaintiff is not being subjected to civil process, it is contended that the privilege should not apply during intra-session adjournments. In actuality, the term "adjournment" in this sense more properly partakes of the nature of a "recess" in the legislative session.

Article 4, § 13, of our Constitution, in pertinent part, reads:

> "The legislature shall meet at the seat of government on the second Wednesday in January of each year at twelve o'clock noon. *Each regular session shall adjourn without delay, on a day determined by concurrent resolution*, at twelve o'clock noon." (Emphasis added.)

We are of the opinion that the word "sessions" in article 4, § 11, includes the regular session as defined in article 4, § 13, and the special session of article 4, § 28; article 5, § 15. Thus, we decline the invitation to define "sessions" as meaning only "working sessions" when the Legislature is actually sitting.

Constituent contact, research, committee assignments, and other legislative business are not always confined to days when the Legislature is actually sitting. Under defendant's "free time" exception, the legislator asserting the privilege could spend as much time and effort convincing the process-issuing court that he was about the public's business and therefore immune as he would subjecting himself to process. The policy which underlies the privilege and which is aimed at the potential as well as actual distraction from public duty would suffer. The Constitution specifies the period during which the privilege applies. If there is to be a judicial determination that the privilege must give way, our inquiry should be focused on whether the need for process in the individual case is compelling.

Defendant contends, with merit, that consistent late December *sine die* adjournments could result in immunity continued from one regular session to the next, and therefore could totally frustrate access to the judicial process. This Court is mindful that unreasonably long periods of immunity could, in a hypothetical case not before us, amount to a denial of due process, particularly if the legislator were an essential party to the litigation. The need of a wife for a judgment of divorce[4] or of a child for a decree of support[5] may compel a legislator's participation in the judicial process. It is conceivable that immunity unreasonably extended could result in a loss of a cause of action without a judicial tempering of the privilege, such as a rule tolling the statute of limitations during the period of inability to pursue process.[6] However, we are also mindful that we deal with a privilege created not by statute, but by our Constitution. Today, we decide the scope of the privilege on the facts before us. As to other facts "[c]hoice may prudently be postponed until choice becomes essential."

In this case, there is no indication that the testimony of plaintiff Bishop is crucial to the maintenance of suit or that facts sought to be discovered from him are unavailable through other sources. From the Benkert pleadings it appears that the need advanced in opposition to the specific constitutional privilege here at issue is that of discovery from a non-party in a civil case to prove a point not in dispute. In the Benkert action, it was conceded that the investigations had been requested by a member of the legislature and that the investigations were beyond the statutory authority of the state police.

We therefore hold that the constitutional privilege from civil process obtains when the legislature is in regular session, as defined in art. 4, § 13, that this case on its facts does not advance due process interests sufficient to outweigh that privilege, and that the Court of Appeals did not err in quashing the subpoena.

Affirmed. No costs, a public question.

KAVANAGH, C.J., and WILLIAMS, LEVIN, COLEMAN and LINDEMER, JJ., concurred with FITZGERALD, J.

RYAN, J., took no part in the decision of this case.

NOTES AND QUESTIONS

1. Given the state constitutional principles involved, is the court correct in asserting that it might, in other situations, compel a legislator's participation in judicial proceedings during legislative sessions? If the Senator's testimony were critical, what factors should the court consider in determining whether, on the basis of federal due process considerations, to override the state constitutional protections afforded the legislator?

2. Should the immunity be applicable to legislators who are attorneys? Note the references in footnotes 4 and 5.

3. What differences are there between prohibiting service of process and avoiding participation as a party, witness or attorney once voluntarily involved in the proceeding? Are the distinctions realistic given the underlying rationale for the concept of legislative immunity?

4. It would seem to be technically possible for the sessions plus five-day periods to extend throughout the year, thereby permitting a Michigan legislator to avoid service of process entirely. Does that factor argue for strictly construing the provision so that it would apply only to working sessions? Could the court avoid injustice by extending the

---

[4] *See Granai v. Witters, Longmoore, Akley & Brown*, 123 Vt. 468; 194 A.2d 391 (1963), which involved an action for divorce and where the statutory privilege applied to legislators as party or attorney.

[5] *See Thurmond v. Superior Court of the City & County of San Francisco*, 66 Cal. 2d 836; 59 Cal. Rptr. 273; 427 P.2d 985 (1967), which involved a paternity action and where the statutory privilege extended to legislators as attorney.

[6] *See Seamans v. Walgren*, 82 Wash. 2d 771; 514 P.2d 166 (1973).

applicable statute of limitations, as suggested by the reference to the State of Washington decision?

5. An interesting problem may arise regarding the scope of state immunity in federal civil or criminal actions. In *In re Grand Jury Proceedings*, 563 F.2d 577, 582 (3d Cir. 1977), the court held that state constitutional provisions do not prevent federal prosecutions of legislators for acts immunized by state law. In *Tenney v. Brandhove*, 341 U.S. 367, 376 (1951), the Court recognized a common-law doctrine of legislative immunity sufficient to prevent a federal lawsuit for damages otherwise protected by state law. Note, *Protection of State Legislative Activity from Federal Prosecution: Common-Law and Constitutional Immunity*, 58 B.U. L. REV. 469 (1978), presents arguments for extension of such a common-law immunity to federal criminal prosecutions.

6. *See generally* Steven F. Huefner, *The Neglected Value of the Legislative Privilege in State Legislatures*, 45 WM. & MARY L. REV. 221 (2003); Paul E. Salamanca & James E. Keller, *The Legislative Privilege to Judge the Qualifications, Elections, and Returns of Members*, 95 KY. L.J. 241 (2006–07).

Chapter 5

THE EXECUTIVE ROLES IN LEGISLATION

A. EXECUTIVE VETO POWER

ROBERT B, DOVE,
ENACTMENT OF A LAW 25 (n.d.)

The President, under the Constitution, has 10 days (Sundays excepted) after the bill has been presented to him in which to act upon it. If the subject matter of the bill is within the jurisdiction of a department of the Government, or affects its interests in any way, he may in the meantime, at his discretion, refer the bill to the head of that department for investigation and a report thereon. The report of such official may serve as an aid to the President in reaching a decision about whether or not to approve the bill.

OFFICE OF MANAGEMENT AND BUDGET,
CIRCULAR NO. A.19
(revised September 20, 1979)

10. Enrolled Bills. Under the Constitution, the President has 10 days (including holidays but excluding Sundays) to act on enrolled bills after they are presented to him. To assure that the President has the maximum possible time for consideration of enrolled bills, agencies shall give them top priority.

a. Initial OMB action. OMB will obtain facsimiles of enrolled bills from the Government Printing Office and immediately forward one facsimile to each interested agency, requesting the agency's views and its recommendation for Presidential action.

b. Agency action. Each agency receiving such a request shall immediately prepare a letter presenting its views and deliver it in duplicate to OMB not later than two days (including holidays but excluding Sundays) after receipt of the facsimile. OMB may set different deadlines as dictated by circumstances. Agencies shall deliver these letters by special messenger to OMB.

c. Preparation of enrolled bill letters.

(1) Agencies' letters on enrolled bills are transmitted to the President and should be written so as to assist the President in reaching a decision. Each letter should, therefore, be complete in itself and should not, as a general rule, incorporate earlier reports by reference.

(2) Agencies' letters on enrolled bills are privileged communications, and agencies shall be guided accordingly in determining their content.

(3) Because of the definitive nature of Presidential action on enrolled bills, agency letters shall be signed by a Presidential appointee.

(4) Agencies' letters shall contain:

(a) An analysis of the significant features of the bill including changes from existing law. OMB staff will advise the agencies on which one should write the detailed analysis of the bill where more than one agency is substantially affected;

(b) a comparison of the bill with the Administration proposals, if any, on the same subject;

(c) comments, criticisms, analyses of benefits and shortcomings, or special considerations that will assist the President in reaching a decision;

(d) identification of any factors that make it necessary or desirable for the President to act by a particular date;

(e) an estimate of the first-year and recurring costs or savings and the relationship of the estimates to those previously incorporated in the President's budgetary program;

(f) an estimate of the additional number of personnel required to implement the bill; and

(g) a specific recommendation for approval or disapproval by the President.

(5) Agencies recommending disapproval shall submit with their letters a proposed veto message or memorandum of disapproval, in quadruplicate, prepared on legal-size paper and double-spaced. Such messages or memoranda should be finished products in form and substance that can be used by the President without further revision.

(6) Agencies may wish to recommend issuance of a signing statement by the President. Agencies so recommending shall submit with their letters a draft of such statement, in the same form and quantity as required for a proposed veto message. In some cases, OMB may request an agency to prepare a draft signing statement.

(7) Agencies' letters on private bills shall cite, where appropriate, precedents that support the action they recommend or that need to be distinguished from the action recommended.

d. Subsequent OMB action. OMB will transmit agencies' letters to the President, together with a covering memorandum, not later than the fifth day following receipt of the enrolled bill at the White House.

ROBERT B. DOVE,
ENACTMENT OF A LAW 25–26 (n.d.)

If the President does approve it, he signs the bill, giving the date, and transmits this information by messenger to the Senate or the House, as the case might be. In the case of revenue and tariff bills, the hour of approval is usually indicated. The enrolled bill is delivered to the Archivist of the United States, who designates it as a public or private law, depending upon its purpose, and gives it a number. Public and private laws are numbered separately and serially. An official copy is sent to Government Printing Office to be used in making the so-called slip law print.

In the event the President does not desire to approve a bill, but is unwilling to veto it, he may, by not returning it within the 10-day period after it is presented to him, permit it to become a law without his approval. The Archivist makes an endorsement on the bill that having been presented to the President of the United States for his approval and not having been returned to the House of Congress in which it originated within the time prescribed by the Constitution, it has become a law without his approval.

Where the 10-day period extends beyond the date of the final adjournment of Congress, the President may, within that time approve and sign the bill, which thereby becomes a law. If, however, in such a case, the President does not approve and sign the bill before the expiration of the ten-day period, it fails to become a law. This is what is known as a pocket veto. The United States Court of Appeals, in the case of *Kennedy v. Sampson*, 511 F.2d 430 (D.C. Cir., 1974), held that a Senate bill could not be pocket-vetoed by the President during an "intrasession" adjournment of Congress to a day certain for more than three days, where the Secretary of the Senate had been authorized to receive Presidential messages during such adjournment. In the case of *Barnes v. Kline*, 759 F.2d 21 (D.C. Cir., 1985), the Court held the same with regard to an intersession adjournment.

If the President does not favor a bill and vetoes it, he returns it to the House of origin without his approval, together with his objections thereto (referred to as the "veto message."). It should be noted that after the final adjournment of the 94th Congress, 1st session, the President returned two bills, giving Congress the opportunity to reconsider and "override" the vetoes.

The constitutional provision for reconsideration by the Senate is met, under the precedents, by the reading of the veto message, spreading it on the Journal, and adopting a motion (1) to act on it immediately, (2) to refer it, with the accompanying papers, to a standing committee, (3) to order that it lie on the table, to be subsequently considered, or (4) to order its consideration postponed to a definite day. The House's procedures are much the same.

If, upon reconsideration by either House, the House of origin acting first, the bill does not receive a two-thirds vote, the President's veto is sustained and the bill fails to become a law.

If a bill which has been vetoed is passed upon reconsideration by the first House by the required two-thirds vote, an endorsement to this effect is made on the back of the bill, and it is then transmitted, together with the accompanying message, to the second House for its action thereon. If likewise reconsidered and passed by that body, a similar endorsement is made thereon. The bills, which has thereby been enacted into law, is not again presented to the President, but is delivered to the Administrator of the General Services Administration for deposit in the Archives, and is printed, together with the attestations of the Secretary of the Senate and the Clerk of the House of its passage over the President's veto.

1. The Presidential Veto

CONSTITUTION OF THE UNITED STATES
Art. 1, § 7

Section 7. All Bills for raising Revenue shall originate in the House of Representatives; but the Senate may propose or concur with Amendments as on other Bills.

Every Bill which shall have passed the House of Representatives and the Senate, shall, before it becomes a Law, be presented to the President of the United States; If he approve he shall sign it, but if not he shall return it, with his Objections to that House in which it shall have originated, who shall enter the Objections at large on their Journal, and proceed to reconsider it. If after such Reconsideration two thirds of that House shall agree to pass the Bill, it shall be sent, together with the Objections, to the other House, by which it shall likewise be reconsidered, and if approved by two thirds of that House, it shall become a Law. But in all such Cases the Votes of both Houses shall be determined by Yeas and Nays, and the Names of the Persons voting for and against the Bill shall be entered on the Journal of each House respectively. If any Bill shall not be returned by the President within ten Days (Sundays excepted) after it shall have been presented to him, the Same shall be a Law, in like Manner as if he had signed it, unless the Congress by their Adjournment prevent its Return, in which Case it shall not be a Law.

Every Order, Resolution, or Vote to which the Concurrence of the Senate and House of Representatives may be necessary (except on a question of Adjournment) shall be presented to the President of the United States; and before the Same shall take Effect, shall be approved by him, or being disapproved by him, shall be repassed by two thirds of the Senate and House of Representatives, according to the Rules and Limitations prescribed in the Case of a Bill.

CHARLES J. ZINN,
THE VETO POWER OF THE PRESIDENT,
12 Federal Rules Decisions 207 (1951)

I. THE BACKGROUND AND NATURE OF THE VETO POWER

The idea of the veto in one form or another has existed in organized government since before the Christian era. It has ranged in scope from an unqualified and unlimited nullification of executive as well as legislative acts to the moderated delaying form affecting only legislative acts which prevails under our own Constitution. It is essentially a protective device, customarily exercised on behalf of the people but occasionally invoked for the sole benefit of the person wielding it, the chief magistrate himself.

A modern law dictionary defines it as —

> the refusal of assent by the executive officer whose assent is necessary to perfect a law which has been passed by the legislative body, and the message which is usually sent to such body by the executive, stating such refusal and the reasons therefor. It is either absolute or qualified, according as the effect of its exercise is either to destroy the bill finally, or to prevent its becoming law unless again passed by a stated proportion of votes or with other formalities. Or the veto may be merely suspensive.

. . . .

II. THE IMPORTANCE OF THE VETO
POWER IN OUR POLITICAL ECONOMY

It is almost impossible to overevaluate or exaggerate the importance of the Presidential veto power in our political economy. Woodrow Wilson considered it beyond all comparison his most formidable prerogative. It was his opinion that the President is no greater than his prerogative of veto makes him.

Bryce points out that while the strength of the Congress consists in its authority to pass statutes, the strength of the President consists in his right to veto them. His real strength, the rampart from behind which he can resist the aggression of the Legislature, is in ordinary times this veto power. It is his most potent weapon and admirably adapted to thwart or mitigate the tyranny of a legislative majority.

The veto power is, in fact, in the nature of an appeal to the people by the President. It was given to him to enable him to protect himself from the encroachments of the Legislature. Drawing their inferences from history and reason, the framers of the Constitution believed that in a free government the tendency was for the legislature to absorb all its powers. They sought to prevent this disastrous effect by dividing it into two Houses and by investing the Executive with all the powers requisite for a free execution of the laws and granting him the prerogative of at least a suspensive negative over the legislative acts.

. . . .

A "Legislative" Function of the President

Notwithstanding some slight areas of overlapping of functions the political structure erected by the Constitution maintains the explicit and definite separation of the three branches of government. Furthermore — aside from the quasi-legislative nature of Executive orders, proclamations, and Executive agreements, none of which is mentioned in the Constitution — the President is granted no specific function with respect to legislation other than that provided for in article I, section 7.

Of course, the treaty-making power under article II (the Executive article) may be interpreted as a legislative function because the advice and consent of one branch of the

Legislature is required, and because treaties constitute part of the supreme law of the land.

The exercise of the veto power is patently a legislative act although the President is not a member of either House of Congress, being associated with the Legislature for the special purpose of arresting its action by his disapproval. The Supreme Court has said in *La Abra Mining Company v. United States* that —

> undoubtedly the President when approving bills passed by Congress may be said to participate in the enactment of laws which the Constitution requires him to execute.

Wilson observed that the President is powerful rather as a branch of the Legislature than as the titular head of the executive.

In its character as a legislative act on the part of the Executive the importance of the veto power must not be minimized. Where the Constitution deviates from the pattern of vesting all legislative powers in the Congress to the extent that it grants the Executive a single legislative function, that grant may be made precise and unambiguous by legislation.

THE DIFFICULTY OF OVERRIDING

The importance of the Presidential power is enhanced by the difficulty in securing a sufficient number of votes in both Houses of the Legislature to override a veto. Unless the required number can be mustered, the action of the President remains effective and the proposed legislation fails. His will prevails over that of any number of legislators short of two-thirds of each House. Not a single bill was passed over the Presidential veto during the first 50 years of the Republic.

Requirement for Two-Thirds Vote

The Constitution provides that if, after reconsideration of a bill returned by the President, two-thirds of the House in which it originated agree to pass it, the bill shall be sent to the other House where it shall likewise be considered and if approved by two-thirds thereof it shall become a law.

. . . .

Thus, if a bill which originated in the Senate is returned by the President to that body and as few as 17 Senators, constituting more than one-third of those present, vote to sustain the veto, the bill is defeated regardless of a possible unanimity in favor of the bill on the part of the other body.

. . . .

Political Complexion of the Congress

A legislator who has voted for a bill upon its initial consideration frequently becomes reluctant to vote for the overriding of its veto by a President of his own political party. Without intending any reflection upon the integrity of the Congress it may be said that the merit of the particular legislation sometimes seems to be overlooked in the light of a vote which may be considered as a rebuke to the President. The withholding of Executive approval appears to clothe the bill with a significance which was not evident in the first instance. Of course, the added significance is on many occasions more real than apparent in view of the contents of the message of disapproval setting forth the President's objections, in which event the exercise of the veto power fully justifies the wisdom of the founding fathers in providing it.

Because of the almost equal strength of the two major parties there is rarely a two-thirds majority of either House in the hands of one party.

Whatever the reason, the difficulty of obtaining sufficient votes to override the President's veto is manifest from even a cursory glance at the statistics. Barely 6 percent of all bills returned without approval during the first 78 Congresses have been passed over the President's veto. The power which has resulted in the negativing of almost 1,000 bills (not including pocket vetoes) during that period is certainly not a negligible one.

III. THE CONSTITUTIONAL PROVISIONS

The word "veto" does not appear in any of the provisions of the Constitution, having apparently been avoided studiously in the debates of the Convention. The authority for the President's function in this respect is found in the legislative article of that document, Article I, Section 7.

. . . .

LACK OF STATUTORY IMPLEMENTATION

On many occasions attempts have been made by Members of Congress to enact legislation modifying or curtailing the President's veto power. These efforts in almost all instances have taken the form of proposed amendments to the Constitution and have met with no success.

It seems particularly surprising, therefore, that so important a power which has been so widely discussed should not have been the subject of legislation designed to supply definitions of the terms or to provide a modus operandi for carrying out the intentions of the framers of the Constitution. However, a thorough examination of the United States Code and the Statutes at Large reveals no existing legislation on the subject. It has never been suggested that this failure to enact any legislation on the subject is due to a lack of authority on the part of the Congress to implement the constitutional provisions. Nevertheless, it has not exercised this function, with the result that the constitutional provisions stand alone, with less than a half-dozen significant judicial decisions construing them.

. . . .

INADEQUACY OF JUDICIAL INTERPRETATION

The Supreme Court has handed down important decisions in cases involving the Presidential veto power on only five occasions.

The first of these decisions, rendered in 1899,[15] involved the question of the President's authority to approve bills within the 10-day constitutional period although the Congress was in recess on the day his approval was given to the bill. It was held that he could constitutionally do so.

Twenty years later the Supreme Court held that two-thirds of a quorum of each House was sufficient to pass a bill over the President's disapproval.[16] After an interval of 10 years the Court decided the famous Pocket Veto case,[17] holding that a bill not approved by the President within the 10-day constitutional period did not become law because the Congress had adjourned sine die at the end of the first session of a Congress. Shortly thereafter the Court held that the President is authorized to approve a bill during the constitutional 10-day period although the Congress had in the meantime adjourned sine die.[18] It was not until 1938 that the Court held that the return of a bill disapproved by the President was not prevented by a recess of 3 days or less on the part

---

[15] *La Abra Silver Mining Co. v. United States*, 175 U.S. 423, 20 S. Ct. 168, 44 L. Ed. 223.

[16] *Missouri Pac. R. Co. v. Kansas* (1919), 248 U.S. 276, 39 S. Ct. 93, 63 L. Ed. 239.

[17] *Okanogan v. United States* (1929), 279 U.S. 655, 49 S. Ct. 463, 73 L. Ed. 894.

[18] *Edwards v. United States* (1932), 286 U.S. 482, 52 S. Ct. 627, 76 L. Ed. 1239.

of the House in which the bill originated during which the other House remained in session.[19]

. . . .

THE BASIS FOR NONAPPROVAL

The exercise of the veto power has been described as an interesting commentary upon the expectations of the framers of the Constitution; it has not followed the course set for it in the Convention but has worked out a path different in direction and extent from that prophesied.

The early Presidents seemed loath to exercise the power save on what they considered constitutional grounds. In a letter to Edmund Pendleton in 1793, George Washington stated:

> You do me no more than Justice when you suppose that from motives of respect to the Legislature (and I might add from my interpretation of the Constitution) I give my Signature to many Bills with which my Judgment is at variance. In declaring this, however, I allude to no particular Act. From the nature of the Constitution, I must approve all the parts of a Bill, or reject it in toto. To do the latter can only be Justified upon the clear and obvious ground of propriety; and I never had such confidence in my own faculty of judging as to be over tenacious of the opinions I may have imbided in doubtful cases.

Jefferson, who did not exercise the veto power during his two terms of office, expressed similar sentiments.

During the second session of the Fiftieth Congress, in 1889, Senator Davis stated in the Senate:

> It is as clear as anything, from the debates when the Constitution was formed, that the veto power was only to be exercised to veto unconstitutional legislation.

On the other hand it has been argued that the President does not have the right to exercise his veto on the grounds of unconstitutionality, for to do so is the assumption of a right to decide a question which should be left to the judicial branch. President Taft expressed his disagreement with this latter view in his veto message on the Webb Kenyon bill in the Sixty-second Congress. He declared later that he had much less hesitation in vetoing the bill than the Court should have in declaring it unconstitutional.

In his veto message on the renewal of the charter of the Bank of the United States, President Jackson declared that it was as much the duty of the Congress and the President to decide upon the constitutionality of a bill as it is for the Court when it may be brought before it for judicial decision.

Although a Presidential veto has never been successfully challenged other than by being overridden by two-thirds of each House, the divergence of views as to the basis for the exercise of the power could be resolved by the Congress by proper legislation in keeping with the letter and spirit of the Constitution.

PRESIDENTIAL MEMORANDA ON APPROVAL

An interesting question is raised by the practice indulged in on occasion by several of the Presidents of writing a memorandum containing an exposition of their views, and even of their interpretation of certain parts of the bill, at the time of affixing their signatures of approval.

The Constitution provides merely that if the President approves a bill he shall sign it; if not he shall return it with his reasons for disapproving it. There is no specific provision

---

[19] *Wright v. United States* (1938), 302 U.S. 583, 58 S. Ct. 395, 82 L. Ed. 439.

authorizing him to change any provision of the bill or to assign any interpretation of its meaning.

In 1830 President Jackson interpolated the following words over his signature on an original enrolled bill:

> I approve this bill, and ask a reference to my communication to Congress of this date, in relation thereto.

The message to Congress explained that he wished to be understood as having approved the bill with the understanding that a road authorized by one section of the bill was not to be extended beyond the limits of the Territory of Michigan.

A few years later, a select committee of the House of Representatives submitted a report on the propriety of President Tyler's action in filing with a bill an exposition of his reasons for signing it. The report was severely critical of the action of both Presidents, declaring that President Jackson's action was in substance an objection to one section of the bill and in form an approval of the bill, and that such form of proceeding was unwarranted by the Constitution. The committee concluded that President Tyler's action also was unwarranted by the Constitution.

Most recently President Truman, in approving the Hobbs Anti-Racketeering Act and the Portal-to-Portal Act sent messages to Congress construing certain of the provisions of the relative acts.

In the New York Times of May 16, 1947, Arthur Krock, the columnist, suggested that these messages would become an essential part of the legislative history to which the Court might refer in the event it is called upon to construe either statute. Professor Corwin strongly demurs from this view, pointing out that a Presidential message which was not before the Congress when the bill was being considered by that body could not assist in determining its purpose in passing the bill; and that the legislative intent is to be derived only from the action of the Congress in which the Constitution vests "all legislative powers granted herein." This view is probably too narrow.

The intent of such a memorandum must be assumed to be to aid the courts and administrative officials in interpreting the act when called upon to do so. In recent years the legislative history of statutes has become an increasingly important source of information for purposes of construction by the judiciary and the executive departments and agencies. More and more, recourse is being had to committee hearings, reports, and debates, as aids to arriving at "the legislative intent." Executive communications transmitting proposed bills to the Congress are another source of useful information for determining the purposes of such bills.

Inasmuch as the courts have not had occasion, in construing a statute, to advert to a Presidential memorandum made at the time of approving it, we do not have the benefit of a judicial evaluation of such memoranda as aids in construction — nor even of their constitutional validity. However, so long as the President does not interpolate any new matter in the bill itself there seems to be no constitutional basis for objecting to his expounding his views with respect to the bill. It is an accepted and occasionally useful practice, particularly as an aid to administrative interpretation, for the President to express his views regarding existing statutes, either with or without the support of an opinion by the Attorney General. The expression of such opinion is not less consistent with the Constitution merely because made at the time of approving the bill in question. Whether it has any value as an aid to judicial construction is a matter which must be determined by the courts in each case and depends upon the ambiguity in the law and the scope of the President's views. They would generally not be as persuasive as regular items of legislative history but might be helpful as cumulative evidence of legislative intent if not inconsistent with statements in the committee reports and other elements of the history, including any Executive communication transmitting the proposed legislation to the Congress. In many instances they would have no greater value than statements made in congressional debate on the bill, and may be considered as a form of extension of that debate. Clearly they should not be used as an implied partial veto.

The broadest significance given by a State court to the action of the governor at the time of approving a bill is found in Washington where the constitution permits the veto of separate items. The supreme court of Washington held that —

> the governor, when acting upon bills passed by both houses of the legislature, is a part of the legislature, and acting in a legislative capacity, and we cannot therefore consider the intent of the house and the senate apart from the intent of the governor.

These aids to statutory construction are available only to assist the courts in clarifying ambiguities in the language used in the law. The President could not thereby change the plain meaning of a statute any more than he could make any physical changes or corrections on the original enrolled bill. The latter action on the part of the King of England, as pointed out earlier, was not sanctioned by the Parliament and led to the limitation of his veto power.

It was more particularly the action of Presidents Jackson and Tyler in adding notations to the original bills, rather than the expression of their views, that brought down the wrath of the House of Representatives. The President's signature is the exclusive evidence admitted by the Constitution of his approval; and all additions of extraneous matter can "be regarded in no other light than a defacement of the public records and archives." The committee deemed the action injurious to the public interest and protested against it and against its ever being repeated or adduced as a precedent.

See generally *Symposium: The Last Word? The Constitutional Implications of Presidential Signing Statements*, 16 Wm. & Mary Bill Rts. J. 131 (2007).

ARTHUR S. MILLER,
CONGRESSIONAL POWER TO DEFINE THE
PRESIDENTIAL POCKET VETO POWER
25 Vanderbilt Law Review 557, 558–60 (1972)*

The constitutional arrangements of article I, section 7 evidence the concern of the framers that power should be checked and balanced in its assertion, and that a mechanism be provided to cabin the several branches of government and minimize the friction that results when they abrade one another. Thus we see a procedure recited for the course of normal expectation — the mechanism for a return veto, whereby the President returns disapproved legislation to the house of origin, together with his reasons for disapproval. This type of veto allows the Congress to reconsider the legislation; if two-thirds of a quorum of both houses so vote, the bill becomes law over the President's objections. The "return veto" reflects the framers' distrust of executive power, particularly their rejection of the absolute veto power enjoyed by George III over acts of Parliament.

This mechanism eloquently testifies to two primary concerns: first, that the Congress, assumed to be closer to the people, ordinarily will have the last word; and, secondly, that the fullest debate and consideration will be expended upon those bills that occasion disagreement between legislative and executive branches. The President is required to state his reasons for disapproval, and Congress, in attempting to muster the extraordinary two-thirds majority needed to override, must presumably rethink and redebate the measure convincingly. The victor in this struggle is the people. In the usual course of lawmaking, when the President and Congress agree on the bill, the people receive a law assented to by the two branches representing a national constituency. It is assumed that the approved bill represents, as well as anything can, the "national will." When the two branches disagree, the people will be assured of an even fuller debate, trading, and brokerage that also will elicit the "national will."

---

* Reprinted with permission from Vanderbilt Law Review.

The provisions for two special circumstances in the remainder of article I, section 7 represent remedies for breach of faith by one or the other of the branches. First is a provision that if the President does not return a bill within ten days (Sundays excepted), failing either to approve or disapprove it, it becomes law "in like Manner as if he had signed it." Clearly, this provision was inserted to obviate the possibility that executive inaction could frustrate the legislative will. For the President, then, there is provided a real incentive to return a bill of which he disapproves, in hopes that his stated reasons for disapproving and the normal working of partisan politics will prevent muster of the extraordinary majority needed to override. This check on executive temptation can be seen as supportive of the clearly preferred return veto process set out first in Article I, Section 7. The language of the phrase is explicit, and has not, to date, occasioned controversy; the President has ten days (Sundays excepted) to consider the measure, and if he does nothing in that ten days the bill becomes law. Our problem arises under the second provision, which establishes a remedy for congressional abuse of the process. The last sentence of clause 2 permits the pocket veto — "an entirely different category from the ordinary veto" — which empowers the President to halt the promulgation of an act of Congress because he has not had his constitutional ten days to consider the act.

Presidents have principally employed the pocket veto at the end of a session of Congress, but there have been instances in which pocket vetoes were used during brief recesses of Congress. This use of the pocket veto power during recesses short of adjournments *sine die* presents serious questions concerning the separation of powers. As Senator Charles Mathias put it, "[T]he question that is raised in its boldest form is whether the executive branch, through the vehicle of the pocket veto, has usurped the powers of the legislative branch, or perhaps even more boldly whether the President, by use of the pocket veto, has circumvented the orderly legislative process of sending a vetoed bill back to Congress for its final consideration . . . . [T]he time is ripe to make a final determination of its proper limits and boundaries and settle this question . . . ." Senator Sam J. Ervin has said that "a 'pocket' veto during a short recess of Congress within a session is tantamount to an absolute veto, which is contrary to the intent of the Framers of the Constitution."

It is clear that Congress might be tempted to enact a law without subjecting it to the risks of presidential veto. Here the remedy is to kill the proposed law if "the Congress by their Adjournment prevent its Return." This provision assures the President his constitutional ten days for consideration and provides an incentive for Congress to hew to the preferred procedure and to depend upon electoral ire and fear of override to induce presidential approval. The crux of the controversy lies within the generality of the constitutional phrase "unless the Congress by their Adjournment prevent its Return." Unhappily, the language of this phrase has not been accepted as explicit, particularly the words "Adjournment" and "prevent its Return."

KENNEDY v. JONES
412 F. Supp. 353 (D.D.C. 1976)

SIRICA, DISTRICT JUDGE.

The above entitled matter is presently before the Court on defendants' Motion To Dismiss and plaintiff's opposition in response thereto.

Plaintiff is a United States Senator from the Commonwealth of Massachusetts. Defendant Jones is the Chief of White House Records and defendant Sampson is the Administrator of the General Services Administration.

In this action plaintiff is seeking this Court to declare that two bills passed by Congress, H.R. 10511 and H.R. 14225, became validly enacted laws of the United States in accordance with Article I, Section 7, Clause 2 of the Constitution, and requests that this Court order defendants to publish these bills as laws pursuant to 1 U.S.C. §§ 106a, 112 and 113.

Defendants have moved to dismiss this case, arguing that plaintiff lacks standing to bring this action and that the controversy is moot since Congress has subsequently passed, and the President has signed into law, legislation identical to the bills in question here.

I

The first bill in dispute, H.R. 10511, is an amendment to the Urban Mass Transportation Act of 1964. It was passed by the Congress and presented to the President on December 22, 1973, the day that Congress adjourned the first session of the 93rd Congress *sine die*. On January 4, 1974, the President issued a memorandum of disapproval announcing that he would withhold his signature from the bill. He did not return the bill to Congress. Rather, the President took the position that it had been effectively "pocket vetoed" under the provisions of Article I of the Constitution. Relying upon this position, defendants did not, and have not as yet, published the bill as a law of the United States contending that it was properly vetoed.

On January 29, 1974, plaintiff filed this suit claiming that the President's attempt to "pocket veto" a bill during a *sine die* adjournment of Congress was improper; that the President's failure to either sign or return the bill to Congress within ten days caused the bill to automatically become law; and that, since the bill automatically became law, defendants had a nondiscretionary ministerial duty to publish the bill as a law of the United States.

Seven months later, in August of 1974, Congress passed S. 3066 which contained provisions essentially identical to the provisions of H.R. 10511, and which the President signed into law on August 22, 1974. Defendants published S. 3066 as a law of the United States, Public Law 93-383, 88 Stat. 633.

II

The second bill at issue is H.R. 14225, an aid-to-the-handicapped bill which was passed by Congress on October 16, 1974. At the conclusion of the following day, October 17, 1974, the day on which the bill was presented to the President, Congress adjourned for thirty-one days for Congressional elections, authorizing the Clerk of the House of Representatives to receive messages from the President during that period. On October 29, 1974, the President returned the bill with objections, stating that the withholding of his signature prevented the bill from becoming law, once again relying upon the "pocket veto" provision of the Constitution.

On November 20, 1974, apparently in disregard of the President's attempted "pocket veto," Congress voted to override the veto of H.R. 14225. Plaintiff was one of those voting to override the veto. Defendants Jones and Sampson, relying upon the President's position did not publish H.R. 14225 as a law of the United States.

Congress passed H.R. 17503, which contained provisions essentially identical to those of H.R. 14225, on November 26, 1974. The President signed this new bill into law on December 7, 1974, and it was published by the defendants as Public Law 93-516, 88 Stat. 1617.

Plaintiff amended his original complaint in this case on March 24, 1975 to include H.R. 14225, alleging that both bills that the President attempted to "pocket veto" should have been published by defendants as laws of the United States . . . .

. . . .

It is clear to the Court that the plaintiff is not merely asking for an advisory opinion, but that a clear controversy does indeed exist. As Judge Waddy stated at the district court level in *Kennedy v. Sampson:*

 . . . [T]he complaint in this action clearly demonstrates that the requisite elements of a "case" or "controversy" are present within the meaning of Article

III of the Constitution. Contrary to the suggestion in the defendants' State-ment, plaintiff seeks no advisory opinion from this Court. Plaintiff sponsored, supported, and voted for S. 3418 in the Senate. The action of the President in disapproving S. 3418 and the injury to plaintiff caused by the refusal of the defendants to perform their ministerial, nondiscretionary duties in reliance upon that action provide exactly the sort of clear concreteness, precise framing of questions, adversary argument, conflicting and demanding interests, and necessity for decision that have always been regarded as meeting the Article III requirement for the exercise of Federal judicial power. (364 F. Supp. 1075, 1081, 1082 *aff'd*, 511 F.2d 430)

This same reasoning is applicable to the facts of the instant case. And the fact that Congress saw fit to enact subsequent legislation covering the same subject area as that of the bills in dispute does not serve to alter the fact that a clear controversy exists. To date the defendants have not published H.R. 10511 and H.R. 14225 as laws and it is their failure to perform this duty which is in contest here.

Also, this is not a case in which the relief requested has been obtained by the plaintiff, thus rendering the dispute moot. Here plaintiff requests a declaratory judgment that the bills became law in accordance with the provisions of the Constitution and seeks a mandatory injunction requiring the defendants to publish the bills as law. This relief has not been obtained and the case is not moot on this basis.

Based on the foregoing, it is the opinion of the Court that this case is not moot and that a justiciable controversy exists. It is, therefore, by the Court this 19th day of January, 1976,

ORDERED that the defendants' Motion to Dismiss in the above entitled matter be, and the same hereby is, denied.

ORDER

The Court having considered the plaintiff's supplemental complaint and plaintiff's motion for summary judgment, and the entire file in this case; and the defendants having filed a statement of consent to entry of judgment with the Court on April 13, 1976, it appears to the Court that the plaintiff is entitled to entry of judgment.

It is therefore this 21st day of April, 1976.

ORDERED that plaintiff's motion for summary judgment be, and the same hereby is, granted; and it is

FURTHER ORDERED that judgment be entered for the plaintiff in the above entitled matter.

NOTES AND QUESTIONS

1. In Senator Kennedy's article on the pocket veto power, Edward M. Kennedy, *Congress, the President and the Pocket Veto*, 63 VA. L. REV. 355 (1977),[*] *Jones* is described as a major congressional victory over presidential authority:

> *Jones* is a major cutback on the pocket veto power. By agreeing to summary judgment, the executive branch conceded that the President may not constitu-tionally pocket veto a bill during a thirty-one-day intrasession adjournment, which far exceeds the five-day adjournment held in *Sampson* not to activate the pocket veto power. Because present intrasession adjournments of Congress rarely exceed thirty-one days, *Jones* makes a constitutional intrasession pocket veto highly unlikely. The Ford Administration's acceptance of the view — implied by the rationale of *Sampson* — that the pocket veto power is

---

[*] Reprinted with permission from Virginia Law Review and Fred B. Rothman & Co.

inapplicable to intersession adjournments of Congress was even more important. After *Sampson* and *Jones*, the pocket veto power appears clearly constitutional only with regard to a *sine die* adjournment after the final session of a Congress. In effect, *The Pocket Veto Case* has been confined to its facts, and the intersession pocket veto has become an obsolete relic.

Id. at 377.

Does *Jones* leave open the possibility that some intrasession pocket vetoes will be sustained by the courts?

2. Should the pocket veto power be characterized as a vital tool of the President, or as a stopgap provision of the Constitution designed to fill in the correct procedure for an unlikely but possible situation which might arise? Was it likely that the framers of the Constitution contemplated that the "pocket veto" would be used during intrasession adjournments? Did the framers anticipate that intrasession adjournments would even occur?

CHARLES J. ZINN,
THE VETO POWER OF THE PRESIDENT
12 Federal Rules Decisions 207 (1951)

X. THE ITEM VETO

Since the Civil War the question has on numerous occasions been raised as to whether or not the President has or should have the power to disapprove one or more portions of a bill while approving the balance.

The record of debates in the Constitutional Convention does not disclose any discussion of this problem at that time, the chief concern of the delegates having been whether the veto should be exercised by the President alone, and what proportion of the Congress should be required to override it. As finally adopted the veto clause of the Constitution provided that —

> Every Bill . . . shall . . . be presented to the President . . . ; If he approve he shall sign it, but if not he shall return it . . . .

That language seems to afford the President only two alternatives — either sign or return the bill.

Apparently these alternatives were quite satisfactory until the second half of the nineteenth century as there is no evidence of agitation prior to that time for the exercise of an item veto on the part of the President.

However, when the Confederate States adopted their provisional Constitution on February 8, 1861, they included a provision permitting their President to veto any appropriation or appropriations, and approve any other appropriation or appropriations in the same bill. The permanent Constitution adopted the following month contained substantially the same provision.

Among the States, Georgia was the first, in 1865, to include a similar provision for its Governor in its fifth constitution ratified on November 7, 1865, followed soon thereafter by Texas in 1866. At the present time, with the exception of North Carolina (whose Governor has no veto power) and eight other States,[3] all the States have constitutional provisions permitting the governor to veto items in appropriation bills.

In addition, the Governors of California and Massachusetts and several other States may reduce items in such bills, while the Governors of South Carolina and Washington may veto sections of any bill, under their constitutions.

During the Civil War the Congress commenced the practice of adding legislative

---

[3] Indiana, Iowa, Maine, Nevada, New Hampshire, Rhode Island, Tennessee, and Vermont.

"riders" to appropriation bills, thereby imposing its will upon the President without an opportunity to exercise his veto power other than by disapproving the necessary appropriations as well. Impelled by this practice, President Grant in his message to the Forty-third Congress recommended a constitutional amendment "to authorize the Executive to approve of so much of any measure passing the two Houses of Congress as his judgment may dictate, without approving the whole, the disapproved portion or portions to be subject to the same rules as now." Presidents Hayes and Arthur subsequently made similar recommendations, limited, however, to appropriation bills.

The first of numerous proposals to amend the Constitution for the purpose of giving the President an item-veto power in one form or another was introduced in 1876 by Representative Faulkner, of West Virginia. With only one exception these proposed amendments, however, received no favorable action by a congressional committee, the exception being a resolution to authorize the President to veto items in appropriation bills which was reported favorably by the Senate Judiciary Committee in 1884. The Senate as a whole did not consider the resolution.

It has apparently been generally assumed that such power could be conferred upon the President by constitutional amendment alone.

This assumption and all the proposals are apparently based upon the proposition as stated above that under the Constitution the President has only two alternatives. That interpretation is predicated upon a definition of the term "bill" as meaning one legislative instrument.

CLINTON v. CITY OF NEW YORK
524 U.S. 417 (1998)

Justice Stevens delivered the opinion of the Court.

The Line Item Veto Act (Act), 110 Stat. 1200, 2 U.S.C. § 691 et seq. (1994 ed., Supp. II), was enacted in April 1996 and became effective on January 1, 1997. The following day, six Members of Congress who had voted against the Act brought suit in the District Court for the District of Columbia challenging its constitutionality. On April 10, 1997, the District Court entered an order holding that the Act is unconstitutional. *Byrd v. Raines*, 956 F. Supp. 25 (D.D.C. 1997). In obedience to the statutory direction to allow a direct, expedited appeal to this Court, *see* §§ 692(b)–(c), we promptly noted probable jurisdiction and expedited review, 520 U.S. 1194, 117 S. Ct. 1489, 137 L. Ed. 2d 699 (1997). We determined, however, that the Members of Congress did not have standing to sue because they had not "alleged a sufficiently concrete injury to have established Article III standing," *Raines v. Byrd*, 521 U.S. 811, —, 117 S. Ct. 2312, 2322, 138 L. Ed. 2d 849 (1997); thus, "in . . . light of [the] overriding and time-honored concern about keeping the Judiciary's power within its proper constitutional sphere," *id.*, at —, 117 S. Ct., at 2318, we remanded the case to the District Court with instructions to dismiss the complaint for lack of jurisdiction.

Less than two months after our decision in that case, the President exercised his authority to cancel one provision in the Balanced Budget Act of 1997, Pub.L. 105-33, 111 Stat. 251, 515, and two provisions in the Taxpayer Relief Act of 1997, Pub.L. 105-34, 111 Stat. 788, 895–896, 990–993. Appellees, claiming that they had been injured by two of those cancellations, filed these cases in the District Court. That Court again held the statute invalid, 985 F. Supp. 168, 177–182 (1998), and we again expedited our review, 522 U.S. 1144, 118 S. Ct. 1123, 140 L. Ed. 2d 172 (1998). We now hold that these appellees have standing to challenge the constitutionality of the Act and, reaching the merits, we agree that the cancellation procedures set forth in the Act violate the Presentment Clause, Art. I, § 7, cl. 2, of the Constitution.

I

We begin by reviewing the canceled items that are at issue in these cases.

Section 4722(c) of the Balanced Budget Act

Title XIX of the Social Security Act, 79 Stat. 343, as amended, authorizes the Federal Government to transfer huge sums of money to the States to help finance medical care for the indigent. *See* 42 U.S.C. § 1396d(b). In 1991, Congress directed that those federal subsidies be reduced by the amount of certain taxes levied by the States on health care providers.[1] In 1994, the Department of Health and Human Services (HHS) notified the State of New York that 15 of its taxes were covered by the 1991 Act, and that as of June 30, 1994, the statute therefore required New York to return $955 million to the United States. The notice advised the State that it could apply for a waiver on certain statutory grounds. New York did request a waiver for those tax programs, as well as for a number of others, but HHS has not formally acted on any of those waiver requests. New York has estimated that the amount at issue for the period from October 1992 through March 1997 is as high as $2.6 billion.

Because HHS had not taken any action on the waiver requests, New York turned to Congress for relief. On August 5, 1997, Congress enacted a law that resolved the issue in New York's favor. Section 4722(c) of the Balanced Budget Act of 1997 identifies the disputed taxes and provides that they "are deemed to be permissible health care related taxes and in compliance with the requirements" of the relevant provisions of the 1991 statute.[2]

On August 11, 1997, the President sent identical notices to the Senate and to the House of Representatives canceling "one item of new direct spending," specifying § 4722(c) as that item, and stating that he had determined that "this cancellation will reduce the Federal budget deficit." He explained that

"§ 4722(c) would have permitted New York 'to continue relying upon impermissible provider taxes to finance its Medicaid program' and that '[t]his preferential treatment would have increased Medicaid costs, would have treated New York differently from all other States, and would have established a costly precedent for other States to request comparable treatment.' "[3]

Section 968 of the Taxpayer Relief Act

A person who realizes a profit from the sale of securities is generally subject to a capital gains tax. Under existing law, however, an ordinary business corporation can acquire a corporation, including a food processing or refining company, in a merger or stock-for-stock transaction in which no gain is recognized to the seller, *see* 26 U.S.C. §§ 354(a), 368(a); the seller's tax payment, therefore, is deferred. If, however, the purchaser is a farmers' cooperative, the parties cannot structure such a transaction because the stock of the cooperative may be held only by its members, *see* 26 U.S.C.

---

[1] Medicaid Voluntary Contribution and Provider-Specific Tax Amendments of 1991, Pub.L. 102–234, 105 Stat. 1793, 42 U.S.C. § 1396b(w).

[2] Section 4722(c) provides:

"(c) WAIVER OF CERTAIN PROVIDER TAX PROVISIONS. — Notwithstanding any other provision of law, taxes, fees, or assessments, as defined in section 1903(w)(3)(A) of the Social Security Act (42 U.S.C. 1396b(w)(3)(A)), that were collected by the State of New York from a health care provider before June 1, 1997, and for which a waiver of the provisions of subparagraph (B) or (C) of section 1903(w)(3) of such Act has been applied for, or that would, but for this subsection require that such a waiver be applied for, in accordance with subparagraph (E) of such section, and, (if so applied for) upon which action by the Secretary of Health and Human Services (including any judicial review of any such proceeding) has not been completed as of July 23, 1997, are deemed to be permissible health care related taxes and in compliance with the requirements of subparagraphs (B) and (C) of section 1903(w)(3) of such Act." 111 Stat. 515.

[3] App. to Juris. Statement 63a–64a (Cancellation No. 97–3). The quoted text is an excerpt from the statement of reasons for the cancellation, which is required by the Line Item Veto Act. *See* 2 U.S.C. § 691a (1994 ed., Supp. II).

§ 521(b)(2); thus, a seller dealing with a farmers' cooperative cannot obtain the benefits of tax deferral.

In § 968 of the Taxpayer Relief Act of 1997, Congress amended § 1042 of the Internal Revenue Code to permit owners of certain food refiners and processors to defer the recognition of gain if they sell their stock to eligible farmers' cooperatives.[4] The purpose of the amendment, as repeatedly explained by its sponsors, was "to facilitate the transfer of refiners and processors to farmers' cooperatives."[5] The amendment to § 1042 was one of the 79 "limited tax benefits" authorized by the Taxpayer Relief Act of 1997 and specifically identified in Title XVII of that Act as "subject to [the] line item veto."[6]

On the same date that he canceled the "item of new direct spending" involving New York's health care programs, the President also canceled this limited tax benefit. In his explanation of that action, the President endorsed the objective of encouraging "value-added farming through the purchase by farmers' cooperatives of refiners or processors of agricultural goods,"[7] but concluded that the provision lacked safeguards and also "failed to target its benefits to small-and-medium-size cooperatives."[8]

II

Appellees filed two separate actions against the President[9] and other federal officials challenging these two cancellations. The plaintiffs in the first case are the City of New York, two hospital associations, one hospital, and two unions representing health care

---

[4] Section 968 of the Taxpayer Relief Act of 1997 amended 26 U.S.C. § 1042 by adding a new subsection (g), which defined the sellers eligible for the exemption as follows:

"(2) QUALIFIED REFINER OR PROCESSOR. — For purposes of this subsection, the term 'qualified refiner or processor' means a domestic corporation —

"(A) substantially all of the activities of which consist of the active conduct of the trade or business of refining or processing agricultural or horticultural products, and

"(B) which, during the 1-year period ending on the date of the sale, purchases more than one-half of such products to be refined or processed from —

"(i) farmers who make up the eligible farmers' cooperative which is purchasing stock in the corporation in a transaction to which this subsection is to apply, or

"(ii) such cooperative." 111 Stat. 896.

[5] H.R.Rep. No. 105-148, p. 420 (1997); see also 141 Cong. Rec. S18739 (Dec. 15, 1995) (Senator Hatch, introducing a previous version of the bill, stating that it "would provide farmers who form farmers cooperatives the opportunity for an ownership interest in the processing and marketing of their products"); ibid. (Senator Craig, cosponsor of a previous bill, stating that "[c]urrently, farmers cannot compete with other business entities . . . in buying such [processing] businesses because of the advantages inherent in the tax deferrals available in transactions with these other purchases"; bill "would be helpful to farmers cooperatives"); App. 116–117 (Letter from Congresspersons Roberts and Stenholm (Dec. 1, 1995)) (congressional sponsors stating that a previous version of the bill was intended to "provide American farmers a more firm economic footing and more control over their economic destiny. We believe this proposal will help farmers, through their cooperatives, purchase facilities to refine and process their raw commodities into value-added products. . . . It will encourage farmers to help themselves in a more market-oriented environment by vertically integrating. If this legislation is passed, we are confident that, 10 years from now, we will look on this bill as one of the most beneficial actions Congress took for U.S. farmers").

[6] § 1701, 111 Stat. 1101.

[7] App. to Juris. Statement 71a (Cancellation No. 97-2). On the day the President canceled § 968, he stated: "Because I strongly support family farmers, farm cooperatives, and the acquisition of production facilities by co-ops, this was a very difficult decision for me." App. 125. He added that creating incentives so that farmers' cooperatives can obtain processing facilities is a "very worthy goal." Id., at 130.

[8] App. to Juris. Statement 71a (Cancellation No. 97-2). Section 968 was one of the two limited tax benefits in the Taxpayer Relief Act of 1997 that the President canceled.

[9] In both actions, the plaintiffs sought a declaratory judgment that the Line Item Veto Act is unconstitutional and that the particular cancellation was invalid; neither set of plaintiffs sought injunctive relief against the President.

employees. The plaintiffs in the second are a farmers' cooperative consisting of about 30 potato growers in Idaho and an individual farmer who is a member and officer of the cooperative. The District Court consolidated the two cases and determined that at least one of the plaintiffs in each had standing under Article III of the Constitution.

Appellee New York City Health and Hospitals Corporation (NYCHHC) is responsible for the operation of public health care facilities throughout the City of New York. If HHS ultimately denies the State's waiver requests, New York law will automatically require[10] NYCHHC to make retroactive tax payments to the State of about $4 million for each of the years at issue. 985 F.Supp., at 172. This contingent liability for NYCHHC, and comparable potential liabilities for the other appellee health care providers, were eliminated by § 4722(c) of the Balanced Budget Act of 1997 and revived by the President's cancellation of that provision. The District Court held that the cancellation of the statutory protection against these liabilities constituted sufficient injury to give these providers Article III standing.

Appellee Snake River Potato Growers, Inc. (Snake River) was formed in May 1997 to assist Idaho potato farmers in marketing their crops and stabilizing prices, in part through a strategy of acquiring potato processing facilities that will allow the members of the cooperative to retain revenues otherwise payable to third-party processors. At that time, Congress was considering the amendment to the capital gains tax that was expressly intended to aid farmers' cooperatives in the purchase of processing facilities, and Snake River had concrete plans to take advantage of the amendment if passed. Indeed, appellee Mike Cranney, acting on behalf of Snake River, was engaged in negotiations with the owner of an Idaho potato processor that would have qualified for the tax benefit under the pending legislation, but these negotiations terminated when the President canceled § 968. Snake River is currently considering the possible purchase of other processing facilities in Idaho if the President's cancellation is reversed. Based on these facts, the District Court concluded that the Snake River plaintiffs were injured by the President's cancellation of § 968, as they "lost the benefit of being on equal footing with their competitors and will likely have to pay more to purchase processing facilities now that the sellers will not [be] able to take advantage of section 968's tax breaks." *Id.*, at 177.

On the merits, the District Court held that the cancellations did not conform to the constitutionally mandated procedures for the enactment or repeal of laws in two respects. First, the laws that resulted after the cancellations "were different from those consented to by both Houses of Congress." *Id.*, at 178.[11] Moreover, the President violated Article I "when he unilaterally canceled provisions of duly enacted statutes." *Id.*, at 179.[12] As a separate basis for its decision, the District Court also held that the Act

---

[10] *See, e.g.*, N.Y. Pub. Health Law § 2807-c(18)(e) (Supp.1997–1998) ("In the event the secretary of the department of health and human services determines that the assessments do not . . . qualify based on any such exclusion, then the exclusion shall be deemed to have been null and void . . . and the commissioner shall collect any retroactive amount due as a result . . . . Interest and penalties shall be measured from the due date of ninety days following notice from the commissioner"); § 2807-d(12) (1993) (same); § 2807-j(11) (Supp.1997–1998) (same); § 2807-s(8) (same).

[11] As the District Court explained: "These laws reflected the best judgment of both Houses. The laws that resulted after the President's line item veto were different from those consented to by both Houses of Congress. There is no way of knowing whether these laws, in their truncated form, would have received the requisite support from both the House and the Senate. Because the laws that emerged after the Line Item Veto are not the same laws that proceeded through the legislative process, as required, the resulting laws are not valid." 985 F.Supp., at 178–179.

[12] "Unilateral action by any single participant in the law-making process is precisely what the Bicameralism and Presentment Clauses were designed to prevent. Once a bill becomes law, it can only be repealed or amended through another, independent legislative enactment, which itself must conform with the requirements of Article I. Any rescissions must be agreed upon by a majority of both Houses of Congress. The President cannot single-handedly revise the work of the other two participants in the lawmaking process, as

"impermissibly disrupts the balance of powers among the three branches of government." *Ibid.*

. . . .

IV

The Line Item Veto Act gives the President the power to "cancel in whole" three types of provisions that have been signed into law: "(1) any dollar amount of discretionary budget authority; (2) any item of new direct spending; or (3) any limited tax benefit." 2 U.S.C. § 691(a) (1994 ed., Supp. II). It is undisputed that the New York case involves an "item of new direct spending" and that the Snake River case involves a "limited tax benefit" as those terms are defined in the Act. It is also undisputed that each of those provisions had been signed into law pursuant to Article I, § 7, of the Constitution before it was canceled.

The Act requires the President to adhere to precise procedures whenever he exercises his cancellation authority. In identifying items for cancellation he must consider the legislative history, the purposes, and other relevant information about the items. *See* 2 U.S.C. § 691(b) (1994 ed., Supp. II). He must determine, with respect to each cancellation, that it will "(i) reduce the Federal budget deficit; (ii) not impair any essential Government functions; and (iii) not harm the national interest." § 691(a)(3)(A). Moreover, he must transmit a special message to Congress notifying it of each cancellation within five calendar days (excluding Sundays) after the enactment of the canceled provision. *See* § 691(a)(3)(B). It is undisputed that the President meticulously followed these procedures in these cases.

A cancellation takes effect upon receipt by Congress of the special message from the President. *See* § 691b(a). If, however, a "disapproval bill" pertaining to a special message is enacted into law, the cancellations set forth in that message become "null and void." *Ibid.* The Act sets forth a detailed expedited procedure for the consideration of a "disapproval bill," *see* § 691d, but no such bill was passed for either of the cancellations involved in these cases.[24] A majority vote of both Houses is sufficient to enact a disapproval bill. The Act does not grant the President the authority to cancel a disapproval bill, *see* § 691(c), but he does, of course, retain his constitutional authority to veto such a bill.[25] The effect of a cancellation is plainly stated in § 691e, which defines the principal terms used in the Act. With respect to both an item of new direct spending and a limited tax benefit, the cancellation prevents the item "from having legal force or effect." 2 U.S.C. §§ 691e(4)(B)–(c) (1994 ed., Supp. II).[26] Thus, under the plain text of the statute, the two actions of the President that are challenged in these cases prevented one

---

he did here when he vetoed certain provisions of these statutes." *Ibid.*

[24] Congress failed to act upon proposed legislation to disapprove these cancellations. *See* S. 1157, H.R. 2444, S. 1144, and H.R. 2436, 105th Cong., 1st Sess. (1997). Indeed, despite the fact that the President has canceled at least 82 items since the Act was passed, *see* Statement of June E. O' Neill, Director, Congressional Budget Office, Line Item Veto Act After One Year, The Process and Its Implementation, before the Subcommittee on Legislative and Budget Process of the House Committee on Rules, 105th Cong., 2d Sess. (Mar. 11–12, 1998), Congress has enacted only one law, over a Presidential veto, disapproving any cancellation, *see* Pub.L. 105-159, 112 Stat. 19 (1998) (disapproving the cancellation of 38 military construction spending items).

[25] *See* n. 29, *infra.*

[26] The term "cancel," used in connection with any dollar amount of discretionary budget authority, means "to rescind." 2 U.S.C. § 691e(4)(A). The entire definition reads as follows:

   "The term 'cancel' or 'cancellation' means —

   "(A) with respect to any dollar amount of discretionary budget authority, to rescind;

   "(B) with respect to any item of new direct spending —

   "(i) that is budget authority provided by law (other than an appropriation law), to prevent such budget authority from having legal force or effect;

section of the Balanced Budget Act of 1997 and one section of the Taxpayer Relief Act of 1997 "from having legal force or effect." The remaining provisions of those statutes, with the exception of the second canceled item in the latter, continue to have the same force and effect as they had when signed into law.

In both legal and practical effect, the President has amended two Acts of Congress by repealing a portion of each. "[R]epeal of statutes, no less than enactment, must conform with Art. I." *INS v. Chadha,* 462 U.S. 919, 954, 103 S. Ct. 2764, 2785–2786, 77 L. Ed. 2d 317 (1983). There is no provision in the Constitution that authorizes the President to enact, to amend, or to repeal statutes. Both Article I and Article II assign responsibilities to the President that directly relate to the lawmaking process, but neither addresses the issue presented by these cases. The President "shall from time to time give to the Congress Information on the State of the Union, and recommend to their Consideration such Measures as he shall judge necessary and expedient . . . ." Art. II, § 3. Thus, he may initiate and influence legislative proposals.[27] Moreover, after a bill has passed both Houses of Congress, but "before it become[s] a Law," it must be presented to the President. If he approves it, "he shall sign it, but if not he shall return it, with his Objections to that House in which it shall have originated, who shall enter the Objections at large on their Journal, and proceed to reconsider it." Art. I, § 7, cl. 2.[28] His "return" of a bill, which is usually described as a "veto,"[29] is subject to being overridden by a two-thirds vote in each House.

There are important differences between the President's "return" of a bill pursuant to Article I, § 7, and the exercise of the President's cancellation authority pursuant to the Line Item Veto Act. The constitutional return takes place before the bill becomes law; the statutory cancellation occurs after the bill becomes law. The constitutional return is of the entire bill; the statutory cancellation is of only a part. Although the Constitution expressly authorizes the President to play a role in the process of enacting statutes, it is silent on the subject of unilateral Presidential action that either repeals or amends parts of duly enacted statutes.

There are powerful reasons for construing constitutional silence on this profoundly important issue as equivalent to an express prohibition. The procedures governing the enactment of statutes set forth in the text of Article I were the product of the great

---

"(ii) that is entitlement authority, to prevent the specific legal obligation of the United States from having legal force or effect; or

"(iii) through the food stamp program, to prevent the specific provision of law that results in an increase in budget authority or outlays for that program from having legal force or effect; and

"(C) with respect to a limited tax benefit, to prevent the specific provision of law that provides such benefit from having legal force or effect." 2 U.S.C. § 691e(4) (1994 ed., Supp. II).

[27] *See* 3 J. STORY, COMMENTARIES ON THE CONSTITUTION OF THE UNITED STATES § 1555, p. 413 (1833) (Art. II, § 3, enables the President "to point out the evil, and to suggest the remedy").

[28] The full text of the relevant paragraph of § 7 provides:

"Every Bill which shall have passed the House of Representatives and the Senate, shall, before it become a Law, be presented to the President of the United States; If he approve he shall sign it, but if not he shall return it, with his Objections to that House in which it shall have originated, who shall enter the Objections at large on their Journal, and proceed to reconsider it. If after such Reconsideration two thirds of that House shall agree to pass the Bill, it shall be sent, together with the Objections, to the other House, by which it shall likewise be reconsidered, and if approved by two thirds of that House, it shall become a Law. But in all such Cases the Votes of both Houses shall be determined by Yeas and Nays, and the Names of the Persons voting for and against the Bill shall be entered on the Journal of each House respectively. If any Bill shall not be returned by the President within ten Days (Sundays excepted) after it shall have been presented to him, the Same shall be a Law, in like Manner as if he had signed it, unless the Congress by their Adjournment prevent its Return, in which Case it shall not be a Law."

[29] "In constitutional terms, 'veto' is used to describe the President's power under Art. I, § 7, of the Constitution." *INS v. Chadha,* 462 U.S. 919, 925, n.2, 103 S. Ct. 2764, 2771, n.2, 77 L. Ed. 2d 317 (1983) (citing BLACK'S LAW DICTIONARY 1403 (5th ed. 1979)).

debates and compromises that produced the Constitution itself. Familiar historical materials provide abundant support for the conclusion that the power to enact statutes may only "be exercised in accord with a single, finely wrought and exhaustively considered, procedure." *Chadha*, 462 U.S., at 951, 103 S. Ct., at 2784. Our first President understood the text of the Presentment Clause as requiring that he either "approve all the parts of a Bill, or reject it in toto."[30] What has emerged in these cases from the President's exercise of his statutory cancellation powers, however, are truncated versions of two bills that passed both Houses of Congress. They are not the product of the "finely wrought" procedure that the Framers designed.

At oral argument, the Government suggested that the cancellations at issue in these cases do not effect a "repeal" of the canceled items because under the special "lockbox" provisions of the Act,[31] a canceled item "retain[s] real, legal budgetary effect" insofar as it prevents Congress and the President from spending the savings that result from the cancellation. Tr. of Oral Arg. 10.[32] The text of the Act expressly provides, however, that a cancellation prevents a direct spending or tax benefit provision "from having legal force or effect." 2 U.S.C. §§ 691e(4) (B)–(c). That a canceled item may have "real, legal budgetary effect" as a result of the lockbox procedure does not change the fact that by canceling the items at issue in these cases, the President made them entirely inoperative as to appellees. Section 968 of the Taxpayer Relief Act no longer provides a tax benefit, and § 4722(c) of the Balanced Budget Act of 1997 no longer relieves New York of its contingent liability.[33] Such significant changes do not lose their character simply because the canceled provisions may have some continuing financial effect on the Government.[34] The cancellation of one section of a statute may be the functional equivalent of a partial repeal even if a portion of the section is not canceled.

---

[30] 33 Writings of George Washington 96 (J. Fitzpatrick ed., 1940); *see also* W. Taft, The Presidency: Its Duties, Its Powers, Its Opportunities and Its Limitations 11 (1916) (stating that the President "has no power to veto part of a bill and let the rest become a law"); *cf.* 1 W. Blackstone, Commentaries *154 ("The crown cannot begin of itself any alterations in the present established law; but it may approve or disapprove of the alterations suggested and consented to by the two houses").

[31] The lockbox procedure ensures that savings resulting from cancellations are used to reduce the deficit, rather than to offset deficit increases arising from other laws. *See* 2 U.S.C. §§ 691c(a)–(b); *see also* H.R. Conf. Rep. No. 104-491, pp. 23–24 (1996). The Office of Management and Budget (OMB) estimates the deficit reduction resulting from each cancellation of new direct spending or limited tax benefit items and presents its estimate as a separate entry in the "pay-as-you-go" report submitted to Congress pursuant to § 252(d) of the Balanced Budget and Emergency Deficit Control Act of 1985 (or "Gramm-Rudman-Hollings Act"), 2 U.S.C. § 902(d). *See* § 691c(a)(2)(A) (1994 ed., Supp. II); *see also* H.R. Conf. Rep. No. 104-491, at 23. The "pay-as-you-go" requirement acts as a self-imposed limitation on Congress' ability to increase spending and/or reduce revenue: if spending increases are not offset by revenue increases (or if revenue reductions are not offset by spending reductions), then a "sequester" of the excess budgeted funds is required. *See* 2 U.S.C. §§ 900(b), 901(a)(1), 902(b), 906(l). OMB does not include the estimated savings resulting from a cancellation in the report it must submit under §§ 252(b) and 254 of the Balanced Budget and Emergency Deficit Control Act of 1985, 2 U.S.C. §§ 902(b), 904. *See* § 691c(a)(2)(B). By providing in this way that such savings "shall not be included in the pay-as-you-go balances," Congress ensures that "savings from the cancellation of new direct spending or limited tax benefits are devoted to deficit reduction and are not available to offset a deficit increase in another law." H.R. Conf. Rep. No. 104-491, at 23. Thus, the "pay-as-you-go" cap does not change upon cancellation because the canceled item is not treated as canceled. Moreover, if Congress enacts a disapproval bill, "OMB will not score this legislation as increasing the deficit under pay as you go." *Ibid.*

[32] The Snake River appellees have argued that the lockbox provisions have no such effect with respect to the canceled tax benefits at issue. Because we reject the Government's suggestion that the lockbox provisions alter our constitutional analysis, however, we find it unnecessary to resolve the dispute over the details of the lockbox procedure's applicability.

[33] Thus, although "Congress's use of infelicitous terminology cannot transform the cancellation into an unconstitutional amendment or repeal of an enacted law," Brief for Appellants 40–41 (citations omitted), the actual effect of a cancellation is entirely consistent with the language of the Act.

[34] Moreover, Congress always retains the option of statutorily amending or repealing the lockbox

V

The Government advances two related arguments to support its position that despite the unambiguous provisions of the Act, cancellations do not amend or repeal properly enacted statutes in violation of the Presentment Clause. First, relying primarily on *Field v. Clark*, 143 U.S. 649, 12 S. Ct. 495, 36 L. Ed. 294 (1892), the Government contends that the cancellations were merely exercises of discretionary authority granted to the President by the Balanced Budget Act and the Taxpayer Relief Act read in light of the previously enacted Line Item Veto Act. Second, the Government submits that the substance of the authority to cancel tax and spending items "is, in practical effect, no more and no less than the power to 'decline to spend' specified sums of money, or to 'decline to implement' specified tax measures." Brief for Appellants 40. Neither argument is persuasive.

In *Field v. Clark*, the Court upheld the constitutionality of the Tariff Act of 1890. Act of Oct. 1, 1890, 26 Stat. 567. That statute contained a "free list" of almost 300 specific articles that were exempted from import duties "unless otherwise specially provided for in this act." 26 Stat. 602. Section 3 was a special provision that directed the President to suspend that exemption for sugar, molasses, coffee, tea, and hides "whenever, and so often" as he should be satisfied that any country producing and exporting those products imposed duties on the agricultural products of the United States that he deemed to be "reciprocally unequal and unreasonable . . . " 26 Stat. 612, quoted in *Field*, 143 U.S., at 680, 12 S. Ct., at 500. The section then specified the duties to be imposed on those products during any such suspension. The Court provided this explanation for its conclusion that § 3 had not delegated legislative power to the President:

"Nothing involving the expediency or the just operation of such legislation was left to the determination of the President . . . . [W]hen he ascertained the fact that duties and exactions, reciprocally unequal and unreasonable, were imposed upon the agricultural or other products of the United States by a country producing and exporting sugar, molasses, coffee, tea or hides, it became his duty to issue a proclamation declaring the suspension, as to that country, which Congress had determined should occur. He had no discretion in the premises except in respect to the duration of the suspension so ordered. But that related only to the enforcement of the policy established by Congress. As the suspension was absolutely required when the President ascertained the existence of a particular fact, it cannot be said that in ascertaining that fact and in issuing his proclamation, in obedience to the legislative will, he exercised the function of making laws . . . . It was a part of the law itself as it left the hands of Congress that the provisions, full and complete in themselves, permitting the free introduction of sugars, molasses, coffee, tea and hides, from particular countries, should be suspended, in a given contingency, and that in case of such suspensions certain duties should be imposed." *Id.*, at 693, 12 S. Ct., at 504–505.

This passage identifies three critical differences between the power to suspend the exemption from import duties and the power to cancel portions of a duly enacted statute. First, the exercise of the suspension power was contingent upon a condition that did not exist when the Tariff Act was passed: the imposition of "reciprocally unequal and unreasonable" import duties by other countries. In contrast, the exercise of the cancellation power within five days after the enactment of the Balanced Budget and Tax Reform Acts necessarily was based on the same conditions that Congress evaluated when it passed those statutes. Second, under the Tariff Act, when the President determined that the contingency had arisen, he had a duty to suspend; in contrast, while it is true that the President was required by the Act to make three determinations before he canceled a provision, *see* 2 U.S.C. § 691(a)(A) (1994 ed., Supp. II), those

---

provisions and/or the Gramm-Rudman-Hollings Act, so as to eliminate any lingering financial effect of canceled items.

determinations did not qualify his discretion to cancel or not to cancel. Finally, whenever the President suspended an exemption under the Tariff Act, he was executing the policy that Congress had embodied in the statute. In contrast, whenever the President cancels an item of new direct spending or a limited tax benefit he is rejecting the policy judgment made by Congress and relying on his own policy judgment.[35] Thus, the conclusion in *Field v. Clark* that the suspensions mandated by the Tariff Act were not exercises of legislative power does not undermine our opinion that cancellations pursuant to the Line Item Veto Act are the functional equivalent of partial repeals of Acts of Congress that fail to satisfy Article I, § 7.

The Government's reliance upon other tariff and import statutes, discussed in *Field*, that contain provisions similar to the one challenged in Field is unavailing for the same reasons.[36] Some of those statutes authorized the President to "suspen[d] and discontinu[e]" statutory duties upon his determination that discriminatory duties imposed by other nations had been abolished. *See* 143 U.S., at 686–687, 12 S. Ct., at 502–503 (discussing Act of Jan. 7, 1824, ch. 4, § 4, 4 Stat. 3, and Act of May 24, 1828, ch. 111, 4 Stat. 308).[37] A slightly different statute, Act of May 31, 1830, ch. 219, § 2, 4 Stat. 425, provided that certain statutory provisions imposing duties on foreign ships "shall be repealed" upon the same no-discrimination determination by the President. *See* 143 U.S., at 687, 12 S. Ct., at 503; *see also id.*, at 686, 12 S. Ct., at 502–503 (discussing similar tariff statute, Act of Mar. 3, 1815, ch. 77, 3 Stat. 224, which provided that duties "are hereby repealed," "[s]uch repeal to take effect . . . whenever the President" makes the required determination).

The cited statutes all relate to foreign trade, and this Court has recognized that in the foreign affairs arena, the President has "a degree of discretion and freedom from statutory restriction which would not be admissible were domestic affairs alone involved." *United States v. Curtiss-Wright Export Corp.*, 299 U.S. 304, 320, 57 S. Ct. 216, 221, 81 L. Ed. 255 (1936). "Moreover, he, not Congress, has the better opportunity of knowing the conditions which prevail in foreign countries." *Ibid.*[38] More important, when enacting the statutes discussed in Field, Congress itself made the decision to suspend or repeal the particular provisions at issue upon the occurrence of particular events subsequent to enactment, and it left only the determination of whether such events occurred up to the President.[39] The Line Item Veto Act authorizes the President himself to effect the repeal of laws, for his own policy reasons, without observing the procedures set out in Article I, § 7. The fact that Congress intended such a result is of

---

[35] For example, one reason that the President gave for canceling § 968 of the Taxpayer Relief Act was his conclusion that "this provision failed to target its benefits to small- and medium-size cooperatives." App. to Juris. Statement 71a (Cancellation No. 97-2); *see* n. 8, *supra*. Because the Line Item Veto Act requires the President to act within five days, every exercise of the cancellation power will necessarily be based on the same facts and circumstances that Congress considered, and therefore constitute a rejection of the policy choice made by Congress.

[36] The Court did not, of course, expressly consider in *Field* whether those statutes comported with the requirements of the Presentment Clause.

[37] *Cf.* 143 U.S., at 688, 12 S. Ct., at 503 (discussing Act of Mar. 6, 1866, ch. 12, § 2, 14 Stat. 4, which permitted the President to "declare the provisions of this act to be inoperative" and lift import restrictions on foreign cattle and hides upon a showing that such importation would not endanger U.S. cattle).

[38] Indeed, the Court in *Field v. Clark*, 143 U.S. 649, 12 S. Ct. 495, 36 L. Ed. 294 (1892), so limited its reasoning: "in the judgment of the legislative branch of the government, it is often desirable, if not essential for the protection of the interests of our people, against the unfriendly or discriminating regulations established by foreign governments, . . . to invest the President with large discretion in matters arising out of the execution of statutes relating to trade and commerce with other nations." *Id.*, at 691, 12 S. Ct., at 504.

[39] *See also J.W. Hampton, Jr., & Co. v. United States*, 276 U.S. 394, 407, 48 S. Ct. 348, 351, 72 L. Ed. 624 (1928) ("Congress may feel itself unable conveniently to determine exactly when its exercise of the legislative power should become effective, because dependent on future conditions, and it may leave the determination of such time to the decision of an Executive").

no moment. Although Congress presumably anticipated that the President might cancel some of the items in the Balanced Budget Act and in the Taxpayer Relief Act, Congress cannot alter the procedures set out in Article I, § 7, without amending the Constitution.[40]

Neither are we persuaded by the Government's contention that the President's authority to cancel new direct spending and tax benefit items is no greater than his traditional authority to decline to spend appropriated funds. The Government has reviewed in some detail the series of statutes in which Congress has given the Executive broad discretion over the expenditure of appropriated funds. For example, the First Congress appropriated "sum[s] not exceeding" specified amounts to be spent on various Government operations. *See, e.g.*, Act of Sept. 29, 1789, ch. 23, § 1, 1 Stat. 95; Act of Mar. 26, 1790, ch. 4, § 1, 1 Stat. 104; Act of Feb. 11, 1791, ch. 6, 1 Stat. 190. In those statutes, as in later years, the President was given wide discretion with respect to both the amounts to be spent and how the money would be allocated among different functions. It is argued that the Line Item Veto Act merely confers comparable discretionary authority over the expenditure of appropriated funds. The critical difference between this statute and all of its predecessors, however, is that unlike any of them, this Act gives the President the unilateral power to change the text of duly enacted statutes. None of the Act's predecessors could even arguably have been construed to authorize such a change.

VI

Although they are implicit in what we have already written, the profound importance of these cases makes it appropriate to emphasize three points.

First, we express no opinion about the wisdom of the procedures authorized by the Line Item Veto Act. Many members of both major political parties who have served in the Legislative and the Executive Branches have long advocated the enactment of such procedures for the purpose of "ensur[ing] greater fiscal accountability in Washington." H.R. Conf. Rep. 104-491, p. 15 (1996).[41] The text of the Act was itself the product of much debate and deliberation in both Houses of Congress and that precise text was signed into law by the President. We do not lightly conclude that their action was unauthorized by the Constitution.[42] We have, however, twice had full argument and briefing on the question and have concluded that our duty is clear.

Second, although appellees challenge the validity of the Act on alternative grounds, the only issue we address concerns the "finely wrought" procedure commanded by the

---

[40] The Government argues that the Rules Enabling Act, 28 U.S.C. § 2072(b), permits this Court to "repeal" prior laws without violating Article I, § 7. Section 2072(b) provides that this Court may promulgate rules of procedure for the lower federal courts and that "[a]ll laws in conflict with such rules shall be of no further force or effect after such rules have taken effect." *See Sibbach v. Wilson & Co.*, 312 U.S. 1, 10, 61 S. Ct. 422, 425, 85 L. Ed. 479 (1941) (stating that the procedural rules that this Court promulgates, "if they are within the authority granted by Congress, repeal" a prior inconsistent procedural statute); *see also Henderson v. United States*, 517 U.S. 654, 664, 116 S. Ct. 1638, 1644, 134 L. Ed. 2d 880 (1996) (citing § 2072(b)). In enacting § 2072(b), however, Congress expressly provided that laws inconsistent with the procedural rules promulgated by this Court would automatically be repealed upon the enactment of new rules in order to create a uniform system of rules for Article III courts. As in the tariff statutes, Congress itself made the decision to repeal prior rules upon the occurrence of a particular event-here, the promulgation of procedural rules by this Court.

[41] *Cf.* TAFT, THE PRESIDENCY, *supra* n. 30, at 21 ("A President with the power to veto items in appropriation bills might exercise a good restraining influence in cutting down the total annual expenses of the government. But this is not the right way").

[42] *See Bowsher*, 478 U.S., at 736, 106 S. Ct., at 3192–3193 (Stevens, J., concurring in judgment) ("When this Court is asked to invalidate a statutory provision that has been approved by both Houses of the Congress and signed by the President, particularly an Act of Congress that confronts a deeply vexing national problem, it should only do so for the most compelling constitutional reasons").

Constitution. *Chadha*, 462 U.S., at 951, 103 S. Ct., at 2784. We have been favored with extensive debate about the scope of Congress' power to delegate law-making authority, or its functional equivalent, to the President. The excellent briefs filed by the parties and their amici curiae have provided us with valuable historical information that illuminates the delegation issue but does not really bear on the narrow issue that is dispositive of these cases. Thus, because we conclude that the Act's cancellation provisions violate Article I, § 7, of the Constitution, we find it unnecessary to consider the District Court's alternative holding that the Act "impermissibly disrupts the balance of powers among the three branches of government." 985 F. Supp., at 179.[43]

Third, our decision rests on the narrow ground that the procedures authorized by the Line Item Veto Act are not authorized by the Constitution. The Balanced Budget Act of 1997 is a 500-page document that became "Public Law 105-33" after three procedural steps were taken: (1) a bill containing its exact text was approved by a majority of the Members of the House of Representatives; (2) the Senate approved precisely the same text; and (3) that text was signed into law by the President. The Constitution explicitly requires that each of those three steps be taken before a bill may "become a law." Art. I, § 7. If one paragraph of that text had been omitted at any one of those three stages, Public Law 105-33 would not have been validly enacted. If the Line Item Veto Act were valid, it would authorize the President to create a different law-one whose text was not voted on by either House of Congress or presented to the President for signature. Something that might be known as "Public Law 105-33 as modified by the President" may or may not be desirable, but it is surely not a document that may "become a law" pursuant to the procedures designed by the Framers of Article I, § 7, of the Constitution.

If there is to be a new procedure in which the President will play a different role in determining the final text of what may "become a law," such change must come not by legislation but through the amendment procedures set forth in Article V of the Constitution. *Cf. U.S. Term Limits, Inc. v. Thornton*, 514 U.S. 779, 837, 115 S. Ct. 1842, 1871, 131 L. Ed. 2d 881 (1995).

The judgment of the District Court is affirmed.

It is so ordered.

JUSTICE KENNEDY, concurring.

[Sections I & II of Justice Kennedy's opinion have been deleted.]

III

. . . .

The Presentment Clause requires, in relevant part, that "[e]very Bill which shall have passed the House of Representatives and the Senate, shall, before it becomes a Law, be presented to the President of the United States; If he approve he shall sign it, but if not he shall return it," U.S. Const., Art. I, § 7, cl. 2. There is no question that enactment of the Balanced Budget Act complied with these requirements: the House and Senate passed the bill, and the President signed it into law. It was only after the requirements of the Presentment Clause had been satisfied that the President exercised his authority under the Line Item Veto Act to cancel the spending item. Thus, the Court's problem with the Act is not that it authorizes the President to veto parts of a bill and sign others into law, but rather that it authorizes him to "cancel" — prevent from "having legal force or effect" — certain parts of duly enacted statutes.

Article I, § 7 of the Constitution obviously prevents the President from cancelling a

---

[43] We also find it unnecessary to consider whether the provisions of the Act relating to discretionary budget authority are severable from the Act's tax benefit and direct spending provisions. We note, however, that the Act contains no severability clause; a severability provision that had appeared in the Senate bill was dropped in conference without explanation. H.R. Conf. Rep. No. 104-491, at 17, 41.

law that Congress has not authorized him to cancel. Such action cannot possibly be considered part of his execution of the law, and if it is legislative action, as the Court observes, "repeal of statutes, no less than enactment, must conform with Art. I." *Ante,* at 2103, quoting from *INS v. Chadha,* 462 U.S. 919, 954, 103 S. Ct. 2764, 2785, 77 L. Ed. 2d 317 (1983). But that is not this case. It was certainly arguable, as an original matter, that Art. I, § 7 also prevents the President from cancelling a law which itself authorizes the President to cancel it. But as the Court acknowledges, that argument has long since been made and rejected. In 1809, Congress passed a law authorizing the President to cancel trade restrictions against Great Britain and France if either revoked edicts directed at the United States. Act of Mar. 1, 1809, § 11, 2 Stat. 528. Joseph Story regarded the conferral of that authority as entirely unremarkable in *The Orono,* 18 F. Cas. 830, No. 10,585, (CCD Mass. 1812). The Tariff Act of 1890 authorized the President to "suspend, by proclamation to that effect" certain of its provisions if he determined that other countries were imposing "reciprocally unequal and unreasonable" duties. Act of Oct. 1, 1890, § 3, 26 Stat. 612. This Court upheld the constitutionality of that Act in *Field v. Clark,* 143 U.S. 649, 12 S. Ct. 495, 36 L. Ed. 294 (1892), reciting the history since 1798 of statutes conferring upon the President the power to, inter alia, "discontinue the prohibitions and restraints hereby enacted and declared," *id.,* at 684, 12 S. Ct., at 501–502, "suspend the operation of the aforesaid act," *id.,* at 685, 12 S. Ct., at 502, and "declare the provisions of this act to be inoperative," *id.,* at 688, 12 S. Ct., at 503.

As much as the Court goes on about Art. I, § 7, therefore, that provision does not demand the result the Court reaches. It no more categorically prohibits the Executive reduction of congressional dispositions in the course of implementing statutes that authorize such reduction, than it categorically prohibits the Executive augmentation of congressional dispositions in the course of implementing statutes that authorize such augmentation — generally known as substantive rulemaking. There are, to be sure, limits upon the former just as there are limits upon the latter — and I am prepared to acknowledge that the limits upon the former may be much more severe. Those limits are established, however, not by some categorical prohibition of Art. I, § 7, which our cases conclusively disprove, but by what has come to be known as the doctrine of unconstitutional delegation of legislative authority: When authorized Executive reduction or augmentation is allowed to go too far, it usurps the nondelegable function of Congress and violates the separation of powers.

It is this doctrine, and not the Presentment Clause, that was discussed in the *Field* opinion, and it is this doctrine, and not the Presentment Clause, that is the issue presented by the statute before us here. That is why the Court is correct to distinguish prior authorizations of Executive cancellation, such as the one involved in *Field,* on the ground that they were contingent upon an Executive finding of fact, and on the ground that they related to the field of foreign affairs, an area where the President has a special "degree of discretion and freedom," *ante,* at 2106 (citation omitted). These distinctions have nothing to do with whether the details of Art. I, § 7 have been complied with, but everything to do with whether the authorizations went too far by transferring to the Executive a degree of political, law-making power that our traditions demand be retained by the Legislative Branch.

. . . .

For the foregoing reasons, I respectfully dissent.

Justice Breyer, with whom Justice O'Connor and Justice Scalia join as to Part III, dissenting.

[Sections I & II have been omitted.]

III

The Court believes that the Act violates the literal text of the Constitution. A simple syllogism captures its basic reasoning:

Major Premise: The Constitution sets forth an exclusive method for enacting, repealing, or amending laws. *See ante*, at 2103.

Minor Premise: The Act authorizes the President to "repea[l] or amen[d]" laws in a different way, namely by announcing a cancellation of a portion of a previously enacted law. *See ante*, at 2102–2103.

Conclusion: The Act is inconsistent with the Constitution. *See ante*, at 2108.

I find this syllogism unconvincing, however, because its Minor Premise is faulty. When the President "canceled" the two appropriation measures now before us, he did not repeal any law nor did he amend any law. He simply followed the law, leaving the statutes, as they are literally written, intact.

To understand why one cannot say, literally speaking, that the President has repealed or amended any law, imagine how the provisions of law before us might have been, but were not, written. Imagine that the canceled New York health care tax provision at issue here, Pub.L. 105-33, § 4722(c), 111 Stat. 515 (quoted in full *ante*, at 2095, n. 2), had instead said the following:

> Section One. Taxes . . . that were collected by the State of New York from a health care provider before June 1, 1997 and for which a waiver of provisions [requiring payment] have been sought . . . are deemed to be permissible health care related taxes . . . provided however that the President may prevent the just-mentioned provision from having legal force or effect if he determines x, y and z. (Assume x, y and z to be the same determinations required by the Line Item Veto Act).

Whatever a person might say, or think, about the constitutionality of this imaginary law, there is one thing the English language would prevent one from saying. One could not say that a President who "prevent[s]" the deeming language from "having legal force or effect," *see* 2 U.S.C. § 691e(4)(B) (1994 ed., Supp. II), has either repealed or amended this particular hypothetical statute. Rather, the President has followed that law to the letter. He has exercised the power it explicitly delegates to him. He has executed the law, not repealed it.

It could make no significant difference to this linguistic point were the italicized proviso to appear, not as part of what I have called Section One, but, instead, at the bottom of the statute page, say referenced by an asterisk, with a statement that it applies to every spending provision in the act next to which a similar asterisk appears. And that being so, it could make no difference if that proviso appeared, instead, in a different, earlier-enacted law, along with legal language that makes it applicable to every future spending provision picked out according to a specified formula. *See, e.g.,* Balanced Budget and Emergency Deficit Control Act of 1985 (Gramm-Rudman-Hollings Act), Pub.L. 99-177, 99 Stat. 1063, 2 U.S.C. § 901 et seq. (enforcing strict spending and deficit-neutrality limits on future appropriations statutes); *see also* 1 U.S.C. § 1 (in "*any* Act of Congress" singular words include plural, and vice versa) (emphasis added).

But, of course, this last-mentioned possibility is this very case. The earlier law, namely, the Line Item Veto Act, says that "the President may . . . prevent such [future] budget authority from having legal force or effect." 2 U.S.C. §§ 691(a), 691e(4)(B) (1994 ed., Supp. II). Its definitional sections make clear that it applies to the 1997 New York health care provision, *see* 2 U.S.C. § 691e(8), just as they give a special legal meaning to the word "cancel," 2 U.S.C. § 691e(4). For that reason, one cannot dispose of this case through a purely literal analysis as the majority does. Literally speaking, the President has not "repealed" or "amended" anything. He has simply executed a power conferred upon him by Congress, which power is contained in laws that were enacted in compliance with the exclusive method set forth in the Constitution. *See Field v. Clark*, 143 U.S. 649, 693, 12 S. Ct. 495, 504–505, 36 L. Ed. 294 (1892)

(President's power to raise tariff rates *"was a part of the law itself, as it left the hands of Congress"* (emphasis added)).

Nor can one dismiss this literal compliance as some kind of formal quibble, as if it were somehow "obvious" that what the President has done "amounts to," "comes close to," or is "analogous to" the repeal or amendment of a previously enacted law. That is because the power the Act grants the President (to render designated appropriations items without "legal force or effect") also "amounts to," "comes close to," or is "analogous to" a different legal animal, the delegation of a power to choose one legal path as opposed to another, such as a power to appoint.

To take a simple example, a legal document, say a will or a trust instrument, might grant a beneficiary the power (a) to appoint property "to Jones for his life, remainder to Smith for 10 years so long as Smith . . . etc., and then to Brown," or (b) to appoint the same property "to Black and the heirs of his body," or (c) not to exercise the power of appointment at all. *See, e.g.,* 5 W. BOWE & D. PARKER, PAGE ON LAW OF WILLS § 45.8 (rev.3d ed.1962) (describing power of appointment). To choose the second or third of these alternatives prevents from taking effect the legal consequences that flow from the first alternative, which the legal instrument describes in detail. Any such choice, made in the exercise of a delegated power, renders that first alternative language without "legal force or effect." But such a choice does not "repeal" or "amend" either that language or the document itself. The will or trust instrument, in delegating the power of appointment, has not delegated a power to amend or to repeal the instrument; to the contrary, it requires the delegated power to be exercised in accordance with the instrument's terms. *Id.,* § 45.9, at 516–518.

The trust example is useful not merely because of its simplicity, but also because it illustrates the logic that must apply when a power to execute is conferred, not by a private trust document, but by a federal statute. This is not the first time that Congress has delegated to the President or to others this kind of power-a contingent power to deny effect to certain statutory language. *See, e.g.,* Pub.L. 95-384, § 13(a), 92 Stat. 737 ("Section 620(x) of the Foreign Assistance Act of 1961 *shall be of no further force and effect* upon the President's determination and certification to the Congress that the resumption of full military cooperation with Turkey is in the national interest of the United States and [other criteria]") (emphasis added); 28 U.S.C. § 2072 (Supreme Court is authorized to promulgate rules of practice and procedure in federal courts, and "[a]ll laws in conflict with such rules *shall be of no further force and effect*") (emphasis added); 41 U.S.C. § 405b (subsection (a) requires the Office of Federal Procurement Policy to issue "[g]overnment-wide regulations" setting forth a variety of conflict of interest standards, but subsection (e) says that "if the President determine[s]" that the regulations "would have a significantly adverse effect on the accomplishment of the mission" of government agencies, "the requirement [to promulgate] the regulations . . . *shall be null and void*") (emphasis added); Gramm-Rudman-Hollings Act, § 252(a)(4), 99 Stat. 1074 (authorizing the President to issue a "final order" that has the effect of *"permanently cancell[ing]"* sequestered amounts in spending statutes in order to achieve budget compliance) (emphasis added); Pub.L. 104-208, 110 Stat. 3009-695 ("Public Law 89-732 [dealing with immigration from Cuba] *is repealed* . . . upon a determination by the President . . . that a democratically elected government in Cuba is in power") (emphasis added); Pub.L. 99-498, § 701, 100 Stat. 1532 (amending § 758 of the Higher Education Act of 1965) (Secretary of Education "may" sell common stock in an educational loan corporation; if the Secretary decides to sell stock, and "if the Student Loan Marketing Association acquires from the Secretary" over 50 percent of the voting stock, "section 754 [governing composition of the Board of Directors] *shall be of no further force or effect*") (emphasis added); Pub.L. 104-134, § 2901(c), 110 Stat. 1321-160 (President is "authorized to suspend the provisions of the [preceding] proviso" which suspension may last for entire effective period of proviso, if he determines suspension is "appropriate based upon the public interest in sound environmental management . . . [or] the protection of national or locally-affected interests, or protection of any cultural, biological or historic resources").

All of these examples, like the Act, delegate a power to take action that will render statutory provisions "without force or effect." Every one of these examples, like the present Act, delegates the power to choose between alternatives, each of which the statute spells out in some detail. None of these examples delegates a power to "repeal" or "amend" a statute, or to "make" a new law. Nor does the Act. Rather, the delegated power to nullify statutory language was itself created and defined by Congress, and included in the statute books on an equal footing with (indeed, as a component part of) the sections that are potentially subject to nullification. As a Pennsylvania court put the matter more than a century ago: "The legislature cannot delegate its power to make a law; but it can make a law to delegate a power." *Locke's Appeal*, 72 Pa. 491, 498 (1873).

In fact, a power to appoint property offers a closer analogy to the power delegated here than one might at first suspect. That is because the Act contains a "lockbox" feature, which gives legal significance to the enactment of a particular appropriations item even if, and even after, the President has rendered it without "force or effect." *See* 2 U.S.C. § 691c; *see also ante*, at 2104, n. 31 (describing lockbox); *but cf.* Letter from Counsel for Snake River Cooperative, dated Apr. 29, 1998 (available in Clerk of Court's case file) (arguing "lockbox" feature inapplicable here due to special provision in Balanced Budget Act of 1997, the constitutionality and severability of which have not been argued). In essence, the "lockbox" feature: (1) points to a Gramm-Rudman-Hollings Act requirement that, when Congress enacts a "budget-busting" appropriation bill, automatically reduces authorized spending for a host of federal programs in a pro rata way; (2) notes that cancellation of an item (say, a $2 billion item) would, absent the lockbox provision, neutralize (by up to $2 billion) the potential "budget busting" effects of other bills (and therefore potentially the President could cancel items in order to "save" the other programs from the mandatory cuts, resulting no net deficit reduction); and (3) says that this "neutralization" will not occur (i.e., the pro rata reductions will take place just as if the $2 billion item had not been canceled), so that the canceled items truly provide additional budget savings over and above the Gramm-Rudman-Hollings regime. *See generally* H.R. Conf. Rep. No. 104-491, pp. 23–24 (1996) (lockbox provision included "to ensure that the savings from the cancellation of [items] are devoted to deficit reduction and are not available to offset a deficit increase in another law"). That is why the Government says that the Act provides a "lockbox," and why it seems fair to say that, despite the Act's use of the word "cancel," the Act does not delegate to the President the power truly to cancel a line item expenditure (returning the legal status quo to one in which the item had never been enacted). Rather, it delegates to the President the power to decide how to spend the money to which the line item refers — either for the specific purpose mentioned the item, or for general deficit reduction via the "lockbox" feature.

These features of the law do not mean that the delegated power is, or is just like, a power to appoint property. But they do mean that it is not, and it is not just like, the repeal or amendment of a law, or, for that matter, a true line item veto (despite the Act's title). Because one cannot say that the President's exercise of the power the Act grants is, literally speaking, a "repeal" or "amendment," the fact that the Act's procedures differ from the Constitution's exclusive procedures for enacting (or repealing) legislation is beside the point. The Act itself was enacted in accordance with these procedures, and its failure to require the President to satisfy those procedures does not make the Act unconstitutional.

. . . .

[Section IV is omitted]

V

In sum, I recognize that the Act before us is novel. In a sense, it skirts a constitutional edge. But that edge has to do with means . . . . represent an experiment that may, or may not, help representative government work better. The Constitution, in my view, authorizes Congress and the President to try novel methods in this way. Consequently, with respect, I dissent.

NOTES AND COMMENTS

1. Does this case basically turn on applying a canon of construction: the canon of negative implication (expresso unius est exclusio alterius), to Art. 1, § 7 and Art. 2, § 3 of the Constitution? Is there more or less justification for applying that canon to these parts of the Constitution than to the Qualifications Clause cases, *Powell vs. McCormick, supra,* and *U.S. Term Limits vs. Thornton, supra?*

2. Justice Breyer says that the challenged statute represents "an experiment that may, or may not, help representative government work better" and that the Constitution "authorizes Congress and the President to try novel methods in this way." If Justice Breyer had served on the Court when *Chadha, supra,* was decided should he, in light of these views, have dissented? Should the Court always defer to the political branches of government when they enter into procedural deals which the political branches believe facilitate the aims of representative government?

3. Is the majority right in its view that even the mechanisms of the lawmaking process, when entrenched in the constitutional text, embody weighty and significant policy concerns? What, in your opinion, might these concerns be?

4. For an insightful and entertaining application of game theory to Article 1, § 7 of the Constitution, see William Eskridge, Jr. & John Ferejohn, *The Article 1, Section 7 Game,* 80 Geo. L.J. 523 (1992).

2.   The Gubernatorial Veto

TYPICAL STATE VETO PROVISIONS

Most states give their governors the veto power, including the item veto, but limit the item veto to appropriation bills. Some of these, including California, empower the governor to eliminate *or reduce* an item of appropriation:

California Constitution, Article IV, Section 12

[Article IV]

Section 12

(b) The Governor may reduce or eliminate one or more items of appropriation while approving other portions of a bill. He shall append to the bill a statement of the items reduced or eliminated with the reasons for his action. The Governor shall transmit to the house originating the bill a copy of his statement and reasons. Items reduced or eliminated shall be separately reconsidered and may be passed over the Governor's veto in the same manner as bills.

In other states, such as New York, the governor may eliminate but may not reduce appropriation items:

New York Constitution, Article IV, Section 7

[Article IV]

Section 7

. . . If any bill presented to the governor contain several items of appropriation of money, he may object to one or more of such items while approving of the other portion of the bill. In such case he shall append to the bill, at the time of signing it, a statement of the items to which he objects; and the appropriation so objected to shall not take effect. If the legislature be in session, he shall transmit to the house in which the bill originated a copy of such statement, and the items objected to shall be separately reconsidered. If on reconsideration one or more of such items be approved by two-thirds of the members elected to each house, the same shall be part of the law, notwithstanding the objections of the governor. All the provisions of this section, in relation to bills not approved by the governor, shall apply in cases in which he shall withhold his approval from any item or items contained in a bill appropriating money.

A few states give their governors broader item veto power:

Washington Constitution, Article III, Section 12

[Article III]

Section 12

. . . If any bills presented to the governor contain several sections or appropriation items, he may object to one or more sections or appropriation items while approving other portions of the bill: *Provided*, That he may not object to less than an entire section, except that if the section contain one or more appropriation items he may object to any such appropriation item or items. In case of objection he shall append to the bill, at the time of signing it, a statement of the section or sections, appropriation item or items to which he objects and the reasons therefor; and the section or sections, appropriation item or items so objected to shall not take effect unless passed over the governor's objection, as hereinbefore provided.

Oregon Constitution, Article V, Section 15a

[Article V]

Section 15a. Single item and emergency clause veto.

The Governor shall have power to veto single items in appropriation bills, and any provision in new bills declaring an emergency, without thereby affecting any other provision of such bill.

In some states, the governor has veto power but no item veto:

Indiana Constitution, Article V, Section 14

[Article V]

§ 14. Bills signed or vetoed. —

Every bill which shall have passed the General Assembly shall be presented to the Governor. The Governor shall have seven days after the day of presentment to act upon such bill.

(1) He may sign it, in which event it shall become a law.

(2) He may veto it:

(a) In the event of a veto while the General Assembly is in session, he shall return such bill, with his objections, within 7 days of presentment, to the House in which it originated, which House shall enter the objections at large upon its journals and proceed to reconsider the bill. If, after such reconsideration, a majority of all the members elected to that House shall approve the bill, it shall be sent, with the Governor's objections, to the other House, by which it shall likewise be reconsidered and, if approved by a majority of all the members elected to that House, it shall be a law. If such bill is not so returned by the Governor within 7 days of presentment, it shall be a law notwithstanding such veto.

(b) In the event of a veto after final adjournment of a session of the General Assembly, or during a temporary adjournment of a session, such bill shall be returned by the Governor to the House in which it originated on the first day that the General Assembly is in session after such adjournment, which House shall proceed in the same manner as with a bill vetoed before adjournment. If such bill is not so returned, it shall be a law notwithstanding such veto.

(3) He may refuse to sign or veto such bill in which event it shall become a law without his signature on the eighth day after presentment to the Governor.

Every bill presented to the Governor which is signed by him or on which he fails to act within said seven days after presentment shall be filed with the Secretary of State within ten days of presentment. The failure to so file shall not prevent such a bill from becoming a law.

In the event a bill is passed over the Governor's veto, such bill shall be filed with the Secretary of State without further presentment to the Governor: Provided, That in the event of such passage over the Governor's veto in the next succeeding General Assembly, the passage shall be deemed to have been the action of the General Assembly which initially passed such bill.

For an exhaustive study of the veto in one state, see FRANK W. PRESCOTT & JOSEPH F. ZIMMERMAN, THE POLITICS OF THE VETO OF LEGISLATION IN NEW YORK STATE (2 vols. 1980).

The general "all-or-nothing" quality of the veto power began to cause significant problems in the area of gubernatorial review of appropriation bills, which often include many, even hundreds, of appropriations of government funds for various programs. As a response to this problem, the "item veto" was devised, whereby the governor could disapprove of items or parts of appropriation bills. Interestingly, it first appeared in the provisional constitution of the Confederate States, adopted on February 8, 1861. Subsequently, the item veto mechanism, with some variations, has been adopted in the constitutions of more than forty states. House Comm. on Rules, 99th Cong., 2d Sess., Item Veto: State Experience and its Application to the Federal Situation 201–02 (Comm. Print 1986).

RICHARD BRIFFAULT,
THE ITEM VETO: A PROBLEM IN STATE SEPARATION OF POWERS,
2 EMERGING ISSUES IN STATE CONSTITUTIONAL LAW 85 (1989)[*]

. . . This paper does not take a position on former President Reagan's proposal that the federal government follow the states and give the President item veto authority.[5] Instead, it is intended only to suggest that there is one lesson to be learned from the state item veto experience: whatever the veto's successes in dealing with budget problems,[6] by empowering the executive to veto a part of a bill, the item veto opens up a set of knotty legal and conceptual difficulties.[7]

---

[*] Copyright © 1989, National Association of Attorneys General. Reprinted with permission.

[5] For an extensive discussion and critique of President Reagan's item veto proposal, see *Symposium on the Line-Item Veto*, 1 NOTRE DAME J. OF LAW, ETHICS & PUB. POLICY 157-283 (1985).

[6] That success is debatable. *See, e.g.*, Gosling, *Wisconsin Item-Veto Lessons*, 46 PUB. ADMIN. REV. 292 (1986) (finding that over six Wisconsin budget biennial periods nearly 60 percent of items vetoes were motivated by policy consideration and only 18 percent involved concern over cost or budgetary impact; and that the highest percentage budget reduction attributed to the item veto in any biennium was 2.5 percent, while in one period the saving was well under 1 percent).

[7] By one estimate there have been nearly 120 item veto cases since the 1890's, with the pace of litigation

I. *The Item Veto in State Constitutional Law*

The item veto, although unknown to the federal Constitution, plays an important role in executive-legislative relations at the state level. Immediately after the Civil War, states began to amend their constitutions to allow governors to veto items in an appropriation bill without having to veto the whole bill. By World War I, most states had adopted the item veto. Today, forty-three states provide for the item veto, including every state admitted to the Union since the Civil War. The last state to have authorized the item veto was Iowa, which adopted it in 1968. No state that adopted the item veto has ever rescinded it.

The item veto represents the coming together of three widespread state constitutional policies: the rejection of legislative logrolling; the imposition of fiscal restrictions on the legislature; and the strengthening of the governor's role in budgetary matters. In other words, the item veto is at the confluence of the policies underlying the single-subject rule, the balanced budget requirement, and the executive budget.

. . . .

Although the states display a nationwide commitment to the item veto, there is considerable interstate variation with respect to the scope of the governor's item veto power. These variations are partially a matter of differences in state constitutional texts, but seem even more to relate to differences among state supreme courts over questions of constitutional interpretation, and to differences in state institutional traditions.

Thus, states have disagreed over how to define an appropriation and what constitutes an appropriations bill; whether a governor may veto items within an appropriation or must veto the entire lump sum; whether the governor may reduce as well as disallow an item; whether the governor may veto non-monetary items; whether the governor may veto conditions, provisos or restrictions on appropriations without vetoing the appropriation itself; and whether the governor may exercise the veto power in a manner which changes the policy the legislature intended to enact.

All of these disputes have a common theme — how to assure the governor authority broad enough to consider and determine each item of appropriation separately without giving the governor unwarranted legislative power. In other words, how is the item veto and the power it gives to the governor to be integrated into the traditional concepts of the appropriate role of the executive and the legislature?

. . . .

In defining an "appropriation bill," as in defining an "item," state courts have had to grapple with the uncertainties of language in a setting that has powerful implications for the distribution of power between the executive and the legislature. The item veto is a fundamental component of the state approach to budget-making and to the adoption of balanced budgets, but it also raises complex questions not found in the federal system, about the proper relationship between the executive and the legislature — as well as about the role of the judiciary in resolving these executive-legislative disputes. The very purpose of the item veto is at odds with traditional notions of separation of powers. Although the item veto has long been a part of the state budget process, it still fits uncertainly in our state constitutional systems.

The item veto is not simply a mechanical device for increasing executive control over the budget by reducing fiscal imbalances. Rather, by altering the role of the executive in the enactment of laws, the item veto opens questions about basic structural arrangements. Similarly, the item veto forces courts to think closely about the

---

accelerating since 1970. R. Moe, Prospects for the Item Veto at the Federal Level: Lessons from the States (1988) . . . .

relationship of the parts of a bill to each other and to the bill as a whole, and to consider the degree to which the executive's power to unravel legislative packages conflicts with our customary notions of legislative intent and the way in which legislatures reach agreement. If Congress, driven by fiscal concerns, should decide to give serious attention to the state item veto as a model for the federal constitution, Congress should also give comparable attention to the questions of interpretation and allocation of law-making responsibility that result when the item veto is grafted onto the longstanding federal system of separation of powers.

WOOD v. STATE ADMINISTRATIVE BOARD
238 N.W. 16 (Mich. 1931)

FEAD, J.

Plaintiffs filed bill to enjoin the State officers from expending money under the general appropriation law of 1931, House Enrolled Act No. 248 (Act No. 334, Pub. Acts 1931), on the claim that it, or parts of it, had not been properly enacted. Defendants, without answering, moved to dismiss the bill, and the court has certified six questions for decision.

The act contains a large number of specific appropriations for the various State departments, officers, institutions, and projects. After passage by both houses of the legislature, it was presented to the governor on June 5th. On June 17th the governor transmitted to the house of representatives, which received it of record June 18th, a message to the effect that he had qualifiedly approved the act, but had reduced many of the specific appropriations in amount, without, however, disapproving any of such items *in toto*. The bill, as qualifiedly approved, was not returned to the house with the message, but was filed in the office of the secretary of State. It was not again passed by the legislature. The legislature had adjourned on May 22d to June 18th, held sessions on June 18th and 19th, and adjourned without day on June 19th.

. . . .

Question No. 3.

"Can the governor reduce specific items in an appropriation bill?"

The answer is "No."

Under both the Constitutions of 1850 and 1908, the governor was given general power to veto bills. In the Constitution of 1908, art. 5, § 37, the provision was added:

"The governor shall have power to disapprove of any item or items of any bill making appropriations of money embracing distinct items; and the part or parts approved shall be the law; and the item or items disapproved shall be void, unless repassed according to the rule and limitations prescribed for the passage of other bills over the executive veto."

Neither in the debates in the Constitutional Convention (1 Debates, pp. 493, 494), nor in the Address to the People (2 Debates, p. 1423), was it suggested that the power given the governor by section 37 includes authority to reduce an appropriation item. The debates centered upon extending the general veto power to cover distinct items in appropriation bills so the governor could eliminate an unapproved item and escape the serious alternative of legally approving such item or vetoing the whole bill. In this State the general veto power never has included and does not include the authority to modify a bill or disapprove it in part. Had the Constitutional Convention intended to enlarge such power as applied to items in an appropriation bill, presumably it would have used apt language to do so.

The veto power is a legislative function, although it is not affirmative and creative, but is strictly negative and destructive. It cannot be exercised by the executive except through constitutional grant. By Constitution, art. 4, § 1, in harmony with American political theory, the State government is divided into the three historic departments, the legislative, executive, and judicial, and by section 2 it is declared that:

> "No person belonging to one department shall exercise the powers properly belonging to another, except in the cases expressly provided in this Constitution."

This historical and constitutional division of the powers of government forbids the extension, otherwise than by explicit language or necessary implication, of the powers of one department to another. The language of section 37 must be read with all intendments against enlargement beyond its plain words. And if it were ambiguous, the doubt should be resolved in favor of the traditional separation of governmental powers and the restricted nature of the veto.

But the language of the provision is not ambiguous. The power of the governor under it, like the general veto power, is to approve or disapprove. Neither the language of the section nor its purpose carries necessary implication of power to reduce an item in amount, nor, in the ordinary use of words, would such a construction be justified.

. . . .

Question No. 4.

If the court holds that the governor cannot reduce items, then the following questions are to be decided:

(a)   Is such attempted partial veto of specific items a nullity, or
(b)   Does it veto those items, or
(c)   The tax clause not being correspondingly reduced, does it invalidate the whole appropriation bill?

Under the facts here, the action of the governor in reducing the items, being without warrant of constitutional power, was a complete nullity and did not affect the bill in any way, either as an approval or disapproval of any such items. *Peebly v. Childers, supra; Fergus v. Russel, supra; Mills v. Porter, supra; Lukens v. Nye*, 156 Cal. 498 (105 Pac. 593, 36 L.R.A. [N.S.] 244, 20 Ann. Cas. 158); *State v. Holder*, 76 Miss. 158 (23 South. 643). But had the bill been returned to the originating house with such reductions, it would have constituted a veto of the objected items.

Question No. 5.

Did the appropriation bill as passed by the legislature become a law on account of the failure of the governor to return the bill itself to the house of representatives along with his veto message?

The decisive part of this question will be answered later.

Question No. 6.

Does the fact that the legislature adjourned from May 22d to June 18th and thereby prevented the governor from returning the said House Enrolled Act No. 248 to the house in session until June 18th, or 11 days after its presentation to him, constitute the prevention of return by adjournment provided by section 36, art. 5 of the Constitution, and thereby cause so much of said bill as was not properly signed by the governor on June 17th to fail of enactment under said constitutional provision?

The answer is "No."

Constitution, art. 5, § 36, with the provision indicated in the question in italics, reads in part:

> "Sec. 36. Every bill passed by the legislature shall be presented to the governor before it becomes a law. If he approve, he shall sign it; if not, he shall

return it with his objections to the house in which it originated, which shall enter the objections at large upon its journal and reconsider it. On such reconsideration, if two-thirds of the members elected agree to pass the bill, it shall be sent with the objections to the other house, by which it shall be reconsidered. If approved by two-thirds of the members elected to that house, it shall become a law . . . . *If any bill be not returned by the governor within ten days, Sundays excepted, after it has been presented to him, it shall become a law in like manner as if he had signed it, unless the legislature, by adjournment, prevents its return, in which case it shall not become a law.*"

The weight of State authority seems to be that it is only the final adjournment of the legislature which prevents return of a bill on veto and that a temporary adjournment does not. 64 A.L.R. 1446, note. Plaintiffs, however, rest strongly on the recent case of *Okanogan Indians v. United States*, 279 U.S. 655 (49 Sup. Ct. 463, 64 A.L.R. 1434), the "Pocket Veto Case," in which it was held, both upon reasoning and long governmental practice, that adjournment of the first regular session of a congress prevents return of a bill to it, although congress continues in existence for another session.

. . . .

Undoubtedly the reasoning of the court supports plaintiffs' contention that any adjournment of the originating house, overnight, week-end, or otherwise, prevents return of a bill to it during such recess. The constitutional provisions are identical, and, while there is some difference in facts, attempt to distinguish the *Okanogan* from the instant case would be fruitless.

As the question is new in this State, we are at liberty and under duty to adopt the line of authority and reasoning which seems soundest. And we do not feel justified in applying the doctrine of the *Okanogan Case* to State legislation, because it would introduce into what was designed as a simple, practical, and definitely operating provision for executive disapproval of bills, an element disturbing or destructive of such constitutional power.

. . . .

. . . A construction which permits the legislature to impair the executive power of veto, whether active or "pocket," or which gives rise to a situation concerning a bill as to which the effect of either executive or legislative action or inaction is not stated in the Constitution, manifestly is untenable.

. . . .

We must reject the *Okanogan Case* doctrine because we cannot hold that the originating house may destroy the executive power of veto by preventing return through its adjournment, or that adjournment of such house is adjournment of the legislature permitting "pocket veto." The alternative is that return of a bill may be made to a house, although it is not in actual session. There is no difficulty about such procedure, because, under the Constitution, each house must organize with officers, and return may be made to the proper officer as well when the house is at recess as when it is in actual session. And this construction is necessary to render the constitutional plan complete in operation and prevent uncertainty and confusion as to the important question of when a bill becomes a law.

Does temporary adjournment of both houses prevent return on veto? If only the language of the Constitution be consulted, it will be found that while temporary adjournments of the respective houses are recognized, from day to day by less than a quorum, three days or less on action of a house, and more than three days with consent of the other house (Constitution, art. 5, §§ 14, 18), it recognizes no temporary adjournment of the legislature, but provides only for its adjournment without day on concurrent resolution (article 5, § 13). The language would seem to support the view that the legislature itself may adjourn only without day.

If, however, the section be construed, as it should be, as a practical, workable part of the enactment of legislation, and in accordance with its evident purpose, and to effectuate its obvious object, the right of the legislature, as distinguished from its component branches, to temporarily adjourn is unimportant. Return of a bill on veto is not merely a matter of ceremony between executive and legislative branches of the government. It is an act of the executive, (a) to unequivocally evidence his disapproval of the bill, and thereby (b) to confer jurisdiction on the legislature to make the bill a law in spite of his disapproval. It was carefully and skilfully designed to obviate uncertainty as to such disapproval and jurisdiction. The provision that a bill shall finally fail if the legislature, by adjournment, prevents such return is, in practical effect, a sort of penalty imposed upon the legislature for depriving the governor of the power of active veto. Where the adjournment is one which neither prevents the act of return nor requires the imposition of the penalty, the provision is not applicable.

The legislature holds one regular session. Each house is organized for the session. Temporary adjournments do not disrupt or interrupt the legislature or an organized house. Each constitutes a constitutional entity throughout the session. So, the governor may transmit the bill to the originating house through its officers and thus unequivocally evidence his disapproval. As temporary adjournment provides for further session of the legislature, its jurisdiction to pass the bill over his veto is retained.

. . . .

Returning to question No. 5, and as indicated by the foregoing discussion, the answer to that part of it reading, "Did the appropriation bill as passed by the legislature become a law?" is "Yes." The disputed items not having been approved by the governor, the entire bill became law as passed by the legislature because the governor did not return the bill to the originating house within the required time and the legislature did not prevent its return by adjournment.

BUTZEL, C.J., and CLARK, POTTER, SHARPE, and NORTH, JJ., concurred with FEAD, J.

NOTES AND QUESTIONS

1. The court in *Wood* seems to hold that the reduction of the amount of specific appropriations is an inherently legislative function not granted to the governor by the state constitution. Would this apply as well in the case where the governor increased specific appropriation amounts? Is the governor's action unconstitutional because he did not veto or approve the modified provisions, or because he effectively vetoed the provisions and substituted his own provisions?

2. The court held that the governor's actions in no way affected the bill. Is there a presumption which favors a bill's validity? Why?

3. Although the state and federal constitutional provisions regarding veto were identical, the court rejected the square holding of *The Pocket Veto Case* by saying that "adjournment" referred only to "final adjournment." Are there policy reasons that would favor opposite results in the state and federal contexts?

4. How does *Wood* square with *Kennedy*? If *The Pocket Veto Case* were presented today would it be decided differently?

5. *United States v. Mandel*, 415 F. Supp. 1025 (D. Md. 1976), in which the conviction was later reversed on other grounds, involved a mail fraud and antiracketeering prosecution against the governor of Maryland for allegedly receiving payment for approving a bill. Mandel claimed legislative immunity because of his legislative function in approving or vetoing bills. The court conceded that certain conduct might come under the legislative immunity doctrine, stating:

> It can scarcely be questioned that the functions of approving or vetoing bills and recommending matters for legislation would, if performed by a legislator or the legislature, be legislative acts entitled to protection under the doctrine of legislative immunity. Nor can it be doubted that the states under our federal scheme have, within broad constitutional limits, the exclusive power to allocate

the functions of the executive, judicial, and legislative powers as they wish. But neither of those observations settle the question whether legislative immunity attaches to legislative acts performed by someone not in the legislative branch.

Id. at 1031. However, the court concluded,

> . . . [T]he denial of the privilege afforded by the doctrine of legislative immunity under the circumstances of this case will not contravene the purposes behind the privilege. The Court is aware of no significant public interest which would be served by the recognition of the privilege in this criminal proceeding. Accordingly, the Court finds that defendant Mandel is not entitled to invoke legislative privilege or immunity in this proceeding.

Should legislative immunity be applicable to executive acts in aid of legislation? Is proposing legislation or vetoing it the type of activity the legislative immunity was meant to protect? Is the calling of a special session?

WELSH v. BRANSTAD
470 N.W.2d 644 (Iowa 1991)

CARTER, JUSTICE.

The Governor of Iowa has appealed from a judgment which invalidated the exercise of the item vetoes of portions of three appropriation bills enacted by the General Assembly . . . .

II. *The Legislation Which Was Vetoed*

The three pieces of legislation which were the subjects of the challenged item vetoes were totally unrelated. We briefly describe the portions of those acts which are the subject of the present controversy.

. . . .

C. *S.F. 520, section 1(8).* The act designated as S.F. 520 contained a series of appropriations to the department of economic development for the fiscal year beginning July 1, 1989, and ending June 30, 1990. These appropriations related to salaries, tourism promotion programs, national marketing programs, and export trade activities. The appropriation for export trade activities was contained in subsection 8 of section 1 of S.F. 520. This legislation, as enacted by the legislature, provided as follows:

Export trade activities

For international trade activities including a program to encourage and increase participation in trade shows and trade missions by providing financial assistance to businesses for a percentage of their costs of participating in trade shows and trade missions, by providing the lease/sublease of showcase space in existing world trade centers, by providing temporary office space for foreign buyers, international prospects, and potential reverse investors, and by providing other promotional and assistance activities, including salaries and support for not more than the following full-time equivalent positions:

. . . . $400,000

. . . . FTEs 0.25

As a condition, limitation, and qualification, any official Iowa trade delegation led by the governor which receives financial or other support from the appropriation in this subsection shall be represented by a bipartisan delegation of the executive council or their designees. Notwithstanding section 8.39, funds appropriated by this subsection shall not be subject to transfer.

1989 Iowa Acts ch. 308, § 1(8) (emphasis added). The Governor item vetoed that portion of the bill which we have italicized.

. . . .

V. *Validity of Item Veto of S.F. 520*

Our determination of the validity of the item veto exercised with respect to S.F. 520 calls into play the "unrelated rider" characterization espoused in *Colton*, 372 N.W.2d at 190–91. We recognized in that case, as concomitant principles, that, on the one hand, the Governor may not selectively strike words and phrases from "conditions inextricably linked to an appropriation," and, on the other hand, the legislature may not block item veto by attaching "unrelated riders" to an appropriation. *Id.* at 190–91. Our recognition of this distinction forces us to decide whether the requirement for nonpartisan executive counsel (sic) representation on foreign trade delegations financed by appropriations contained in S.F. 520 was an "unrelated rider" tacked on to the appropriation.

In urging that the mandate for nonpartisan executive council representation was an "unrelated rider," the Governor asserts that the attachment of this requirement constituted "inappropriate" legislative drafting. This argument may stem from our use of quoted language in *Colton* which mentions "matter[s] of general legislation more appropriately dealt with in a separate enactment." *Id.* at 191 (quoting *Henry v. Edwards*, 346 So. 2d 153, 158 (La. 1977)). The absence of a useful frame of reference for determining when and how it is "appropriate" in the legislative sense to combine fiscal legislation with substantive provisions affecting the objects of the expenditures causes us to reject this test. We believe, rather, that the line must be drawn solely on the basis of whether the vetoed provision effectively qualified the subject, purpose, or amount of the appropriation either quantitatively or qualitatively.

Viewed in this light, the "unrelated rider" characterization recognized in *Colton* is but a restatement of the observations which this court made in its initial item veto case of *State ex rel. Turner*, 186 N.W.2d at 150. In *Turner* section 4 of an appropriations act specified that a particular appropriation could be used for overtime pay but not for capital improvements. Section 5 of the same bill provided that the permanent resident engineers' offices of the state highway commission should not be moved from their present locations. In holding that the provisions of section 5 were subject to item veto we stated:

> It should be noted section 5 places no prohibition against the use of any moneys appropriated by the act for the moving of permanent resident engineers' offices presently established by the defendant commission. Had such language [been] used . . . we are impelled to the view that section 5 would have in such case been a proviso or condition upon the expenditure of the funds appropriated, but lacking such phraseology it obviously is not.

Id.

By analogy to *State ex rel. Turner*, the issue with respect to the item veto of S.F. 520 is whether the words "[a]s a condition, limitation, and qualification" impact upon the appropriation or whether they are a separate and unrelated piece of legislation affecting the composition of foreign trade delegations. We find the latter to be the case. The language with respect to bipartisan executive council representation on Iowa export trade delegations does not suggest that the amount or purpose of the appropriated funds would be affected if, for some reason, that provision was ignored. Consequently, we hold that this provision was properly subject to item veto and that the district court erred in concluding that it was not.

NOTES AND QUESTIONS

1. What alternative remedies are available if the governor is not permitted to use the item veto to remove unrelated riders? *See Brown v. Firestone*, 382 So. 2d 654 (Fla. 1980).

2. In 1988, the Wisconsin Supreme Court upheld the governor's veto of phrases, digits, letters, and word fragments so as to create new numbers, words, and sentences in the general appropriation bill. *State ex rel. Wisconsin Senate v. Thompson*, 144 Wis. 2d 429, 424 N.W.2d 385 (1988). In 1990, the people of Wisconsin adopted an amendment to the item veto provision, Article V, Section 10(1)(c): "(c) In approving an appropriation bill in part, the governor may not create a new word by rejecting individual letters in the words of the enrolled bill."

This is a very rare *reduction* in gubernatorial power by constitutional amendment.

3. A federal constitutional challenge, by legislators, to the Wisconsin item veto provision was rejected in *Risser v. Thompson*, 930 F.2d 549 (7th Cir. 1991).

4. For an exhaustive review of the state experience and an evaluation of its adaptability to the federal government, see HOUSE COMM. ON RULES, 99TH CONG., 2D SESS., ITEM VETO: STATE EXPERIENCE AND ITS APPLICATION TO THE FEDERAL SITUATION (Comm. Print 1986).

Two recent commentators on the question of adopting the item veto at the federal level cautioned:

> [T]he granting of item veto authority to the President may fundamentally alter the constitutional balance between Congress and the President.
>
> The "state analogy" suffers from a number of serious deficiencies. The item veto exercised by the governors of many states is sustained by a governmental design unique to the states and cannot be severed from it. State constitutions differ dramatically from the federal Constitution, especially in their distribution of executive and legislative powers. There is a much greater state bias against legislatures than exists at the national level. State budget procedures differ substantially from federal procedures. Appropriations bills in the states are structured to facilitate item vetoes by governors. Appropriations bills passed by Congress contain few items. Finally, state judges have experienced severe problems in developing a coherent and principled approach to monitoring the scope of item veto power. Many of those problems would be duplicated and possibly compounded at the federal level.
>
> More fundamentally, the adoption of what might appear to be a relatively modest reform proposal could result in a radical redistribution of constitutional power. The item veto has significance beyond the budgetary savings that may, or may not, be realized. At stake are the power relationships between the executive and legislative branches, the exercise of Congress' historic power over the purse, and the relative abilities of each branch to establish budgetary priorities.

Louis Fisher & Neal Devins, *How Successfully Can the States' Item Veto Be Transferred to the President?*, 75 GEO. L.J. 159 (1986).

5. For earlier discussions of the item veto at the federal level, see Note, *Separation of Power: Congressional Riders and the Veto Power*, 6 U. MICH. J.L. REF. 735 (1973); Note, *The Legislative Rider and the Veto Power*, 26 GEO. L.J. 954 (1938); Note, *The Item Veto in the American Constitutional System*, 25 GEO. L.J. 166 (1936).

6. Is the veto power executive or legislative in nature?

The states of Alabama, Illinois, Massachusetts, Montana, New Jersey, South Dakota, and Virginia have further refined the gubernatorial veto to provide for a "conditional" or "amendatory" veto. For example, Article VI, section 10(2) of the Montana Constitution provides:

> (2) The governor may return any bill to the legislature with his recommendation for amendment. If the legislature passes the bill in accordance with the governor's recommendation, it shall again return the bill to the governor for his

reconsideration. The governor shall not return a bill for amendment a second time.

Note the range of issues a provision like this raises, and read the next case with these in mind.

CONTINENTAL ILLINOIS NATIONAL BANK & TRUST CO. v. ZAGEL
78 Ill. 2d 387, 401 N.E.2d 491 (1979)

UNDERWOOD, JUSTICE.

. . . Both complaints seek a declaratory judgment that the Illinois replacement tax act (Pub. Act 81-1SS-1, effective August 14, 1979, hereinafter referred to as the Act) is invalid.

. . . On June 30, 1979, the General Assembly passed house Bill 2569, which was an earlier version of the Act. Subsequently, the Governor exercised an amendatory veto over House Bill 2569 and the General Assembly in a special session approved his recommendations on August 6, 1979. Upon the Governor's certification of the General Assembly's actions, the Act became law on August 14, 1979.

. . . .

The petitioners assert that the Act is unconstitutional on several grounds. First, petitioners maintain that the Governor's exercise of his amendatory veto power exceeded the bounds of section 9(e) of article IV of the 1970 Illinois Constitution, which provides:

> The Governor may return a bill together with specific recommendations for change to the house in which it originated. The bill shall be considered in the same manner as a vetoed bill but the specific recommendations may be accepted by a record vote of a majority of the members elected to each house. Such bills shall be presented again to the Governor and if he certifies that such acceptance conforms to his specific recommendations, the bill shall become law. If he does not so certify, he shall return it as a vetoed bill to the house in which it originated.

The Governor employed the amendatory veto to make the following recommendations: (1) reduction of the increase in the yearly corporate income tax from the 2.85% provided in House Bill 2569 to 2.5% for the period following January 1, 1981; (2) special provisions for taxpayers' returns affected by the rate change in the middle of a tax year; and (3) consistent treatment in the computation of base income and filing of returns for partnerships and subchapter S corporations. Only the first recommendation is challenged. Arguing that this recommendation involved more than a minor or technical change of House Bill 2569, petitioners maintain that the Governor's use of the veto power was unconstitutional. We disagree.

The extent of the Governor's amendatory veto power under section 9(e) of article IV was examined by this court in *People ex rel. Klinger v. Howlett* (1972), 50 Ill. 2d 242, 249, 278 N.E.2d 84. There, it was concluded that section 9(c)'s authorization of "specific recommendations for change" did not include the substitution of a completely new bill through the exercise of the amendatory veto power. While noting the existence of such words of limitation in the records of the constitutional convention as "corrections" and "precise corrections," a significant exchange in the debates was also noted. In response to Delegate Netsch's question: "Then was it the Committee's thought that the conditional veto would be available only to correct technical errors?," a committee member answered, "No Ma'am." (50 Ill. 2d 242, 249, 278 N.E.2d 84, 88.) The absence of further clarification, of course, leaves unclear the drafter's intent as to the precise scope of the amendatory veto power.

While recognizing that constitutional debates often assist in comprehending the purpose of unclear constitutional provisions, we have emphasized that "the true inquiry concerns the understanding of its provisions by the voters who, by their vote, have given life to the product of the convention." . . . Even less by way of inference is required to ferret out public understanding of section 9(e) of article IV, since the voters themselves have addressed the very question we now consider. By resolution of the General Assembly, a proposal for amending section 9(e) was submitted to the voters in 1974. That proposal would have altered the opening sentence of section 9(e) to read: "The Governor may return a bill together with specific recommendations for the correction of technical errors or matters of form to the House in which it originated." (H.J. Res. Const. Amend. 7, 78th Gen. Assem.) This amendment was rejected by the voters in the 1974 referendum. When this public rejection of the proposed restriction is viewed along with the somewhat imprecise interpretation by the delegates, it is clear that section 9(e) of article IV was not intended by the voters to restrict the amendatory veto power to a proofreading device. Although the point beyond which the amendatory veto power does not extend is not as clear from the constitutional debates or referendum, that point is not, in our judgment, reached here. The specific recommendations made by the Governor regarding House Bill 2569 contain no change in the fundamental purpose of the legislation, nor are they so substantial or so expansive as to render his use of the veto power violative of section 9(e) of article IV.

. . . .

NOTES AND QUESTIONS

1. Does the amendatory veto represent a further refinement of the executive veto? Does it provide a power the governor did not already have? Does it, in fact, reduce the incentive for the governor to give her attention to legislation before it passes? All of these issues are addressed in Jack R. Van Der Slik, *Reconsidering the Amendatory Veto in Illinois*, 8 N. Ill. U. L. Rev. 753 (1988).

2. In all but a few states, except for the item veto, the governor must exercise the veto in an "all-or-nothing" fashion. In other words, he or she must either accept or reject a bill as a package, without being able to approve certain sections while rejecting others. One of the few exceptions to this rule is in Washington. *See* Timothy P. Burke, *The Partial Veto Power: Legislation by the Governor*, 49 Wash. L. Rev. 603 (1974); Note, *Washington's Partial Veto Power: Judicial Construction of Article III, Section 12*, 10 U. Puget Sound L. Rev. 699 (1987); *Washington State Motorcycle Dealers Ass'n v. State*, 111 Wash. 2d 667, 763 P.2d 442 (1968). This has led the Washington Supreme Court to say: "In effect, the Governor holds one-third of the votes." *Washington Fed'n of State Emps. v. State*, 682 P.2d 869, 874 (Wash. 1984).

B. CONSTITUTIONALLY MANDATED LIMITED LEGISLATIVE SESSION; LIMITATION OF SUBJECT MATTER TO GOVERNOR'S CALL

A number of states operationalize the "citizen legislature" concept by limiting the duration of the legislative session. Consider the next case in light of the institutional competence of the judiciary to enforce such restrictions.

STATE ex rel. HECK'S DISCOUNT CENTERS v. WINTERS
147 W. Va. 861, 132 S.E.2d 374 (1963)

Calhoun, Judge:

By this original proceeding in prohibition, the relators, Heck's Discount Centers, Inc., a corporation, and Pic-Way Shoes of West Virginia, a corporation, seek to prohibit the respondents, Honorable Ernest E. Winters, judge of the Court of Common Pleas of Cabell County, and Honorable Russell Dunbar, prosecuting attorney of that county, from proceeding to trial on certain indictments pending against the relators.

The basic question presented to this Court for decision is the constitutionality of Chapter 37, Acts of the Legislature, Regular Session, 1963, by which the legislature undertook to repeal Code, 1931, 61-8-17 and 18, as amended, and to enact in lieu thereof certain new provisions. The purpose of the new act was to amend and reenact the statutes of this state which inhibit certain acts and activities "on a Sabbath day." The amendatory act inhibits certain acts and activities "on the first day of the week, commonly known and designated as Sunday," and provides for more severe punishment.

The primary ground urged in support of the contention of unconstitutionality is the assertion that the amendatory act was passed after the legislative session had terminated by operation of law.

. . . .

Constitution, Article VI, Section 18, provides in part: "Regular sessions of the Legislature shall commence on the second Wednesday of January of each year . . . ." Accordingly, the legislature convened on January 9, 1963, for the regular session.

A portion of Article VI, Section 22 of the Constitution is as follows: "The regular session of the Legislature . . . shall not exceed sixty days . . . . All regular sessions may be extended by the concurrence of two-thirds of the members elected to each house." A joint resolution for extension of the session, pursuant to that provision, was proposed but failed to pass.

A portion of Article VI, Section 51, Sub-Section D of the Constitution is as follows: "If the 'Budget Bill' shall not have been finally acted upon by the Legislature three days before the expiration of its regular session, the governor may, and it shall be his duty to issue a proclamation extending the session for such further period as may, in his judgment, be necessary for the passage of such bill; but no other matter than such bill shall be considered during such extended session except a provision for the cost thereof." The governor extended the session for three days for budgetary purposes.

In the light of the constitutional provisions referred to above, the legislature had no constitutional right, power or authority to pass, and was inhibited by the Constitution from passing any law after midnight of the sixtieth day of its session, except enactments relating to the budget.

. . . .

It is common knowledge that over a period of years the legislature has undertaken from time to time to circumvent the constitutional provision which limits the length of a regular session, and that on occasions it has undertaken to prolong its sessions by the mere expedient of stopping the clock. In *Capito v. Topping*, 65 W. Va. 587, 593, 64 S.E. 845, 847, the Court referred to the "common practice of staying the hands of the clock to enable the Legislature to effect an adjournment apparently within the time fixed by the Constitution for the expiration of the term . . . ."

Doubtless it is a fact that the legislature of this state is not unique in having indulged in that practice. It is a fact, nevertheless, that when a regular legislative session ends by operation of law by reason of the expiration of the period fixed by the Constitution for its duration, the legislature becomes *functus officio* and ceases to have the legislative power accorded to it while in lawful, constitutional session.

. . . .

From prior decisions of this Court it appears that a bill duly enrolled, authenticated and approved is presumed to be correct but the courts may look to the journals of the legislature and to other official records to determine whether such an act was passed in accordance with constitutional requirements. If the legislative journals of either house of the legislature disclose on their face an omission, ambiguity or conflict in relation to the question of compliance with or failure to comply with constitutional requirements, resort may be had by a court to extrinsic evidence for the purpose of resolving such omission, ambiguity or conflict.

. . . .

We believe that we are warranted in the assertion that, by brief and oral argument, counsel for the proponents of the constitutionality of the amendatory act admit tacitly, though not expressly, that such act was passed after the session was terminated by operation of law. In their petition, the relators specifically allege that the act was voted upon and passed after midnight on the night of March 9–10. In their answer the respondents make no denial of such allegation except by reliance upon the legislative journal of March 9. The entire case in behalf of the respondents on this question of constitutionality is based on reliance upon the legislative journal.

With the prohibition petition there was filed as an exhibit and made a part of the petition an affidavit by Honorable C. A. Blankenship, Clerk of the House of Delegates. In that affidavit he stated that on the evening of March 9, 1963, "he was directed by the Speaker of the House of Delegates, the Honorable Julius W. Singleton, Jr., to stop the clock, this being the official clock of the House of Delegates," and that the act in question "was passed when the official clock was stopped at 11:28 P.M., but the actual time was 12:15 or 12:18 A.M., March 10, 1963." The allegation of the petition that the official clock was stopped has not been denied or contradicted by answer, affidavit or otherwise.

In both the *Armbrecht* case and the *Heston* case, the legislative journals indicated, in clear, unambiguous language, that adjournment occurred on a date when the legislature was constitutionally authorized to be in session. No ambiguity in that respect appeared. On the contrary, the journal of the House of Delegates for March 9, 1963, does not contain a clear, unequivocal or unambiguous declaration or pronouncement of the date and hour of adjournment. The language employed in the journal of the house for that day is as follows: "*Stating that according to the clock in the House Chamber it was now 11:58 P.M.*, Mr. Brotherton moved that the House of Delegates adjourn until 12:00 noon, Monday, March 11, 1963." (Emphasis supplied.) This language is contrasted with the following unequivocal, unambiguous declaration contained in the House journal for Monday, March 11, 1963: "At 6:55 P.M., on motion of Mr. Brotherton, the House of Delegates adjourned *sine die*." We believe, therefore, that the House journal for Saturday, March 9, 1963, omitted to disclose an affirmative declaration in clear, unambiguous language, that the adjournment was within the sixty-day period prescribed by the Constitution.

Courts of this state may take judicial notice of the journals of either house of the legislature. *State v. Heston*, 137 W. Va. 375, pt. 1 syl., 71 S.E.2d 481. From the journal of the House of Delegates for March 9, 1963, the sixtieth day of the session, it is fairly obvious that various members of that body, who opposed the enactment involved in this case, proceeded by concert of action to cause the journal of that day's proceedings to demonstrate, in conformity with prior pronouncements by this Court, that the act here in question was considered for passage and voted upon after midnight of the night of March 9–10.

The bill here in question is described in the journal as "Eng. Com. Sub. for Senate Bill No. 125." At page 162 of the House journal appears the following remark by Delegate J.S. Barker: "The clock was stopped at eleven thirty and I want that in the record." As disclosed by the journal at the same page, Mr. Barker stated: "I voted against this bill at twelve seventeen according to my watch and I checked the time, Eastern Standard time, before I voted."

According to the journal at page 161, Delegate Simonton stated: "This carnival trick of stopping the clock, now showing eleven thirty, and by every other member's watch in this House right now it is at least fifteen after, is something that I, as a citizen, just simply cannot swallow."

The following remarks of Delegate Cann appear at page 163 of the journal: "Mr. Speaker, the clock in the House chamber now shows eleven-thirty. That clock has so shown that time for one hour and five minutes. At the time that I rose in opposition to

Eng. Com. Sub. for Senate Bill No. 125, that bill had not been voted on at that time by the House of Delegates of the West Virginia Legislature. I announced that it was twelve minutes after twelve."

According to the journal at page 163, Delegate Bailey stated: "Mr. Speaker, I would like to explain my vote on Eng. Com. Sub. for Senate Bill No. 125 at twelve-fifteen on March 10, 1963, the clock on the wall showing eleven-thirty."

As disclosed by page 170 of the House journal, Delegate Auvil stated: "Mr. Speaker, I believe that by passing Eng. Com. Sub. for Senate Bill 125, the Sunday Blue Law, fifteen minutes after the hour of twelve, Sunday morning, March 10, 1963, that we have mocked the legislative process."

The following remark by Delegate Gentile appears at page 173 of the House journal: "I voted for the bill. The time on my watch was 12:15 A.M., March 10, 1963."

The following appears at page 158 of the House journal: "Mr. Kidd stated that according to his watch it was now 12:05 A.M., Sunday, March 10, 1963, and inquired of the Speaker as to the correct time. The Speaker stated that according to the clock in the House Chamber it was now 11:28 P.M., Saturday, March 9, 1963." At page 159 of the House journal, the following appears in relation to the bill involved in this case:

> Mr. White then moved that the report of the Committee of Conference be adopted.
>
> Mr. Simonton raised the point of order that it was now after 12:00 midnight, March 9, 1963, and for this reason the House could not constitutionally further consider the legislation.
>
> Which point of order was overruled by the Presiding Officer.

According to page 177 of the House journal, Delegate Slonaker stated that "action was taken" on the bill in question and others after midnight.

The following appears on pages 178 and 179 of the House journal:

> Mr. Nuzum explained his vote on Eng. Com. Sub. for S. B. No. 125, and while occupying the floor, asked certain members to yield for questions.
>
> Concluding his explanation and questioning Mr. Nuzum requested that his explanation and questions and answers be incorporated in the Journal.
>
> The Speaker stated that under the rules the gentleman was entitled to have his explanation included in the Journal, and that the answers to his questions could be included with the consent of the members giving the answers.
>
> The gentleman answering the questions joined in the request.
>
> The explanation, questions and answers were as follows:

Mr. Nuzum. Mr. Speaker, I would like to explain my vote on Eng. Com. Sub. for S.B. No. 125.

I call your attention to Section 22, Article VI of the Constitution, dealing with length of legislative sessions.

The gentleman from Hampshire has made the point, but I call attention to the provision of this section providing that "All regular sessions may be extended by the concurrence of two thirds of the members elected to each House."

Now, Mr. Speaker, would the gentleman from Marion yield for a question?

The Speaker. The gentleman from Marion indicates he will yield.

Mr. Nuzum. Mr. Watson, do you have a watch?

Mr. Watson. Yes, sir.

Mr. Nuzum.   What time does your watch show?

Mr. Watson.   I've got nine after one.

Mr. Nuzum.   Would the gentleman from Wood yield?

Mr. Nuzum.   Mr. Simonton, do you have a watch?

Mr. Simonton.   Yes, sir.

Mr. Nuzum.   What time does your watch show?

Mr. Simonton.   My watch shows six after one.

Mr. Nuzum.   Will the gentleman from Gilmer yield?

Mr. Kidd.   Yes, sir.

Mr. Nuzum.   What time does your watch show?

Mr. Kidd.   Eleven minutes after.

Mr. Nuzum.   Will the gentleman from Mingo yield?

Mr. Nuzum.   What time does your watch show?

Mr. Gentile.   Eleven after one.

Mr. Nuzum.   Will the gentleman from Fayette (Mr. Myles) yield?

Mr. Nuzum.   Mr. Myles, do you have a watch?

Mr. Myles.   Yes, sir.

Mr. Nuzum.   What time does your watch say?

Mr. Myles.   I can't see it but the clock on the wall says four minutes till twelve on March 9, 1963.

Mr. Nuzum.   You can't see your watch?

Mr. Myles.   No, sir. It's covered up with my shirt sleeve.

From the journal of the House of Delegates for March 9, 1963, it appears affirmatively and without contradiction that the official clock was stopped at approximately 11:28 P.M., and that it remained stopped for a considerable period of time. It likewise appears affirmatively and without substantial contradiction that the bill in question was voted upon after the hour of midnight and at approximately 12:15 or 12:18 A.M., on Sunday, March 10, 1963. Perhaps the only portion of the House journal for March 9, 1963, which tends to disclose that the bill was voted upon before midnight is the following which appears at page 173: "Mr. Myles. Mr. Speaker, I wish to explain my vote on Eng. Com. Sub. for S. B. No. 125, which was passed Saturday night, March 9, 1963, at approximately 11:29 P.M." In that connection we bear in mind that it appears from the journal that the official clock was stopped at approximately 11:29 P.M., and that Mr. Myles is the same member of the House who stated that he could not see his watch because it was covered by his shirt sleeve.

Considering, as a whole, the journal of the House of Delegates for March 9, 1963, certainly it is an understatement to assert that it fails to disclose without omission, ambiguity or conflict that the bill in question was voted upon before midnight on the night of March 9–10, 1963.

In addition to the affidavit of the Clerk of the House of Delegates referred to previously, two other affidavits were filed as exhibits with and made a part of the prohibition petition. One of these, by Honorable C. Donald Robertson, Attorney General of the State of West Virginia, stated that on the evening of March 9, 1963, he was present in the chamber of the House of Delegates. That fact appears from the journal itself. The affidavit states further that the official clock was "stopped at 11:28 P.M."; that the bill in question was "taken up and considered for passage" at 12:05 A.M., March 10, 1963;

and that, following debate, the bill "was passed at approximately 12:18 A.M. on March 10, 1963." A similar affidavit by Ivor F. Boiarsky, a member of the House of Delegates from Kanawha County, was filed with and made a part of the prohibition petition. It states that the official clock was stopped at 11:28 P.M., and that the bill in question "was not voted upon by any member of the 1963 House of Delegates with regard to its passage, until March 10, 1963."

Considering the journal of the House of Delegates for March 9, 1963, in its entirety, the undenied allegations of the prohibition petition and the three affidavits filed as exhibits with and made a part of the petition, the Court holds that it clearly appears that the bill in question was not voted upon on the question of its passage or enactment until the early morning of Sunday, March 10, 1963, when the 1963 regular session had ceased and terminated by passage of time and by operation of law; and that, therefore, Chapter 37, Acts of the Legislature, Regular Session, 1963, is unconstitutional, void and a nullity.

. . . .

For reasons stated, a writ is awarded to prohibit the respondents from the further prosecution or trial of the pending indictments against the relators under the provisions of the challenged statute or any other statute relating to the subject matter of such indictments.

Writ awarded.

NOTES AND QUESTIONS

1. Admittedly there was overwhelming evidence of the late hour of passage here. But, isn't the court's standard of a journal "omission, ambiguity or conflict" that would allow resort to the journals too much of an invitation to dissenting legislators? Once having opened the door to extrinsic evidence, what types of evidence should it accept and how should the court resolve conflicts?

2. What is the purpose of limiting the length of a legislative session? How does that purpose relate to a policy that would require nullifying a law simply because it was passed 18 minutes late?

3. Are these kinds of provisions akin to those which require referral to committee in that they are designed to force the legislature into a deliberative mode such that hasty, ill-considered legislation will be discouraged? Are courts the appropriate vehicle for enforcing such curbs on the legislature?

Many state constitutions have provisions permitting the governor to call the legislature into special session to consider urgent matters; at such sessions, however, these provisions usually limit the legislation that can be enacted to only that specified in the governor's message. Occasionally disputes arise concerning the scope that such provisions permit the legislature.

What happens if the governor has submitted a bill, but the legislature makes major revisions in the nature of the bill? Clearly the governor cannot restrict the legislature to a "yes-no" response to his proposal, but how far can the legislature deviate from the governor's topic? Can the governor define his topic so as to limit the options of the legislature? Can the executive restrict the legislature by specifying the means to be used to deal with the problems it is to consider?

STATE TAX COMMISSION v. PREECE
266 P.2d 757 (Utah 1954)

CROCKETT, JUSTICE.

We are asked to determine the constitutionality of a statute enacted by the 1953 Special Session of the Utah Legislature which raised the excise tax on cigarettes from 2¢ to 4¢ per pack and allocated the revenue derived therefrom to the Uniform School Fund.

Pursuant to its duty of collecting such taxes, the Tax Commission requisitioned necessary stamps. The defendant, Sherman J. Preece, State Auditor, upon the advice of the attorney general, wilfully refused to comply with the requisition. He contends that the act referred to was not within the purview of the agenda of the Special Session as presented by the governor. This action was brought to compel the auditor to comply with the plaintiff's request.

It is not open to question that unless such act was included within the subject matter presented to the Special Session by the governor it would be invalid. In support of his position that although the governor recommended the adoption of a school financing program which would entail increased costs, that this neither expressly nor by necessary implication embraced the imposition of a tax on cigarettes, the attorney general makes two contentions: First, that other means of meeting such costs were available without the imposition of any new taxes by the state; and second, that any increased taxes resulting from the new financing program would be a property tax.

The parties hereto cite authorities representing widely divergent views: From the extreme on the one hand, that the subject matter must be restricted very narrowly within the confines of the governor's words; to the opposite, that anything reasonably incidental to, or even apparently within the scope of the subject would be within the governor's call. Exemplary of the first class of cases, which are relied on by the defendant, are: *Smith v. Curran*, which held unconstitutional an act validating bonds not covered by sufficient popular vote, which had been enacted by a special session called by a message which included "validation of bonds issued by a municipality under *sufficient* popular vote." The Michigan court, in the above case, said: "While the governor, within the range of a 'subject,' may not restrict the legislature, he has the authority to limit the subject according to his conception of the need for legislation." In *State ex rel. National Conservation Exposition Co. v. Woollen* the governor's call stated ". . . appropriations of the public monies as may be deemed necessary and proper to maintain the state's institutions, offices and departments." The court struck down a legislative appropriation to a corporation for the purpose of presenting an exposition, on the grounds that the corporation was not a State Department or office and therefore not within the subject matter before the Special Session, the court observing: "The governor has power, under the Constitution, to limit the subjects which they may consider, and in order to do this he may define the subject so as to make it broad or narrow, according to his conception of his public duty."

Another case of similar import which defendants point to as controlling in principle, is *Sims v. Weldon*, wherein the basic facts, except the substance of the governor's call, further detail of which will hereinafter be given, are very similar to those of our case. The governor's proclamation made reference to the fact that "the financial distress of the public schools of the state has compelled me to convene you . . ." and expressly directed attention to income taxes and a severance tax. A tax imposed upon cigarettes and cigars was held not within the call.

Doubt is cast upon the soundness of the ruling in the *Sims* case just referred to by reason of the fact that the same jurisdiction in the later case of *McCarroll v. Clyde Collins Liquors* went about as far to the opposite extreme of giving a liberal interpretation to the language of the message as any we have found. However, it should be noted that the call there referred to no specific tax, it simply stated the purpose of providing "additional facilities for tubercular patients . . . and to provide funds therefor"; an act levying excise taxes on liquor was upheld as within the call, under the broad rule that "the General Assembly may consider not only the legislation specifically mentioned . . . but such other legislation as may necessarily or incidentally arise out of that call . . . ."

The rule just stated is urged by plaintiff in support of their argument that the governor opened up the subject of school finance and methods of raising funds which includes taxation. Other cases cited by them are: *Baldwin v. State:* The purpose stated was to reduce taxes, but instead the legislature increased taxes; the act was upheld as within the purpose; *Commonwealth ex rel. Schnader v. Liveright:* The message specified the enactment of unemployment relief, a bill granting relief to the poor was upheld as not outside the proclamation; and *Timmer v. Talbot* in which the call related to rectifying difficulties encountered by Federal Loan Agencies in financing installment mortgages on *livestock and produce* which the legislature used as a basis of a bill covering *all mortgages of goods and chattels.* In holding the bill within the purview of the proclamation the court said: "The guiding principle in sustaining legislation of a special session is that it be germane to, or within, the apparent scope of the subjects which have been designated as proper fields for legislation."

Perusal of the authorities touching upon the legislative prerogative under calls to special session leads to the conclusion that although the extreme cases either way seem to be irreconcilable, there is no disagreement as to the proposition that while the legislature must confine itself to the subject matter submitted, it is not required to follow the views of the governor as to the means it uses to accomplish the objectives stated in the subject set before them, the conflict is not so much in the statement of the rule as it is as to whether a narrow or a broad interpretation will be given to the terms "subject matter" or "purpose" for which the special session is called.

The language of our constitutional provision is explicit — Sec. 6, Art. VII provides:

> On extraordinary occasions, the Governor may convene the Legislature by proclamation, in which shall be stated the purpose for which the Legislature is to be convened, and it shall transact no legislative business except that for which it was especially convened, or such other legislative business as the Governor may call to its attention while in session . . . .

The interdiction "shall transact no legislative business except . . ." plainly evidences the intent that legislation should, in the main, be done at regular sessions and that special sessions are to be called only when there is some special need therefor and that matters considered should be limited to the essentials designated by the governor. The reasons underlying such restriction undoubtedly were conservation of the time and effort of legislators and other state officials, considerations of economy, and that the public have notice of the legislation to be considered.

In considering what was the *purpose* the governor called to the attention of the legislature, we must look to the entire context of his message, notwithstanding the fact that he expressly denied any desire that the state impose any new or higher taxes. In his letter announcing his intention to deliver it, he characterized the message as being ". . . on the subject of school retirement and finance"; and similarly in its first paragraph as "a message on the all important subjects of school retirement, finance and taxation"; and proceeding to the "specific proposals I have to make . . . ," he recommended the enactment of certain previously prepared measures which would put into effect a program devised by the Legislative Council which increased the funds available under the state supported school finance plan.

. . . .

Realization by the governor that it was up to the legislature to find the means of providing this money seems clearly manifest. He not only called the subject to their attention but he made suggestions to them as how they should handle it as evidenced by the following expressions:

> Any discussion of further increase in finances, however, must be related to our present tax burden and what we can afford.

> The only way the increased levy on property can be postponed or avoided is to provide more money in the uniform school fund from other sources.

> As to the source of the funds, I recommend that they be obtained by borrowing from the appropriation of $2,157,000 that was made in the regular

session to the school building fund . . . . The borrowing of $935,000 from the school building fund would not be out of order.

. . . .

He also recommended the adoption of legislation by which the local districts would levy higher taxes resulting in more funds coming into the State Uniform School Fund; and further to a plan to allocate such funds to the districts on the basis of the increase of current year's enrollment over that of the previous year, with respect to which he stated: "A bill has been prepared based on these factors which will provide an additional $935,000 to eligible school districts for this year."

It seems clear that the governor's objective was to avoid the imposition of any new state tax and to see that the added expense of the new program was supported from other sources, primarily by the local districts, as these comments show: "There are certain requisites to a changed financing law that will be met in my proposal including better equalization among the districts and greater local responsibility and control. It is essential that we increase local board responsibilities, . . . if we are ever to bring taxing and spending into line. Those who decide on expenditure policies should bear the political responsibility for raising the necessary funds."

The governor's suggestions as to the ways and means of handling the added cost of financing the schools may have been helpful and even desirable. However, we are in no wise concerned with the wisdom thereof, nor of the legislation which was actually passed, but only with whether the legislature acted within its constitutional powers in imposing a tax on cigarettes.

It cannot be disputed that the principal purpose of the Special Session was to relieve the condition of financial distress existing in our public school system. In attempting to do so, the legislature, for the most part, adopted the proposals of the Legislative Council, which were also recommended by the governor. However, they did not "borrow" the $935,000 from the school building reserve fund as he suggested, but rather took the sum of $1,525,000 from the mine occupation tax reserve fund. There is no suggestion that this deviation from the governor's suggestion rendered that act invalid. And in order to provide additional needed funds, they passed the cigarette tax, which is here challenged.

We do not regard the question herein presented as being whether the governor may limit the subject matter of his call by specifying a particular portion within a general subject without opening the entire subject to litigation. We do not disagree with the attorney general's contention that he may do so, if he does so expressly, and if it does not result in infringing upon the legislative prerogatives by attempting to dictate policy to them.

We believe that the message here was of sufficient breadth that it presented the problem of school financing and the providing of funds therefor. Normally it is both the duty and responsibility of the legislature to determine how this shall be done. We are then confronted with the question whether the governor can call a Special Session to deal with the subject of financing our public schools, and by limiting the agenda to definite proposals as to how it shall be handled, formulate the policy with respect thereto. The answer to this proposition is found in the quite universally accepted rule, hereinbefore stated, which we approve: That while the governor may limit the legislative agenda as to the purpose or subject matter to be considered, he cannot restrict it as to the means it pursues in solving a problem presented as a subject for legislative action. It is true, of course, that the governor may make such recommendations as he sees fit, but these are not binding on the legislature; they may exercise their discretion in following the recommendations or seek alternative methods in dealing with the "subject" presented.

In further support of the conclusion reached herein it is pertinent to observe that the authorities on statutory construction, without exception, hold that if any doubt exists as to the constitutionality of a statute, such doubt should be resolved in favor of the act of the legislature. Sutherland, in speaking of the constitutionality of measures passed by special sessions under constitutional provisions similar to our own says: "In determining whether the legislative action conforms to the governor's call, the constitutional provisions should be strictly construed in favor of the legislative power, and a statute enacted during an extraordinary session should be presumed to be constitutional." In *State ex rel. National Conservation Exposition Co. v. Woollen* the Court said: "It is agreed . . . that the presumption is always in favor of the constitutionality of an act, and that any piece of legislation so under consideration should be within the call, if it can be done by any reasonable construction."

We hold that passing the cigarette tax was within the purview of the subject matter presented to the legislature by the governor. The writ directing the auditor to have prepared and delivered the stamps requisitioned by the Tax Commission is granted.

NOTES AND QUESTIONS

1. Should it make any difference if the governor "approves" the legislation by signing it? See *Beard v. Stanley*, 218 Miss. 192, 67 So. 2d 263 (1953), where the court seemed to rely on this fact. Is the broader issue of adequate notice to the public-at-large avoided by this approach?

2. An extensive dissent in *Preece* points out that the governor specified that no increase in taxes should be considered at the session. The issue was to be reallocation of existing funds. Should the governor be permitted to so restrict the legislature? A concurring opinion points out that it would be rather difficult to consider financing issues separate from questions of raising monies by taxes.

3. In this instance the governor vetoed the bill, but was overridden. Is his veto action relevant?

4. When making a call for a Special Session, must the governor open up the whole subject or can he limit action to one phase of the subject? Can related tax issues always be considered at such sessions since most laws have financial consequences?

5. Texas courts have taken the position that the enrolled act is conclusive, so they will not inquire further into the governor's proclamation. *See W.T. Waggoner Estate v. Gleghorn*, 370 S.W.2d 786, 789 (1963).

Part IV

STATUTORY INTERPRETATION ARGUMENTS AND APPROACHES

INTRODUCTION

Legislation affects every area of law as well as virtually every activity in modern day society. Consequently, facility in the interpretation of legislation is a necessary skill for lawyers, because it enables them to perform the essential function of applying statutes to particular situations. A knowledge of interpretation techniques is also important in guiding the adoption of legislation through the legislative process, for the wise drafter will consider in advance the possible interpretation of any proposed legislation.

The role of the attorney as advisor and advocate is to assist the client in pursuing a course of action that meets the client's needs. Persuading administrative agencies and courts to interpret a statute in favor of the client's interests may be required where potentially relevant, but equivocal, language occurs. In planning for corporate, business, and tax matters, attorneys must interpret a statute and accompanying regulations to advise their clients as to how the provisions may apply. In matters involving proceedings in administrative regulation and criminal law, attorneys must argue an interpretive viewpoint before the presiding jurist. In all circumstances where statutory construction is at issue, attorneys need to possess the requisite skill in interpretation to be effective.

The judge's role in statutory interpretation is to determine the application of a statute to the circumstances before the court. This judicial function differs from common-law adjudication, because it requires the judiciary to apply a type of law with legislative, rather than judicial, origins. In this relationship, the legislature is supreme, but interpretation of statutes is a legitimate judicial function. Where conflicting meanings are attributed to a statute, the legislative rationale for its enactment will often become a key element in its interpretation. This process of determining why the legislature enacted a particular law can be a complex one. The appropriate scope of the court's inquiry — from simply the words themselves to the historical record of the statute's enactment, for instance — has generated much controversy.

The past generation has produced renewed judicial and academic attention to these debates. This Part will point out some of the problems encountered in the interpretation of legislation, and some of the approaches courts have adopted to solve them. These attempts to deal with what is always an after-the-fact exercise — what did the legislature mean when it used the arguably ambiguous language — are extensively examined. These efforts to resolve conflicts should be carefully evaluated by those who would resort to them. The shorthand expressions of interpretative techniques, such as the various canons and rules of statutory construction, need to be understood in context. Their continuing vitality may be an expression of their validity or simply their usefulness in avoiding more difficult issues. In any event, everyone concerned with statutory provisions, and this means all lawyers, must be not only conversant and facile in the use of these techniques but also aware of the inherent conflicts that have produced a counterthrust for each technique. While one may be cynical about their use, knowledge of these techniques of statutory interpretation is still important both to support specific interpretations and to assist legislative drafters in avoiding the creation of unnecessary interpretation problems.

No single technique of statutory interpretation will be adequate to resolve all types of interpretation problems. None of the techniques, nor a combination of them, necessarily lead to a "correct" answer. The chapters in this Part are intended to convey the rich variety of different approaches to the problem of statutory interpretation, which, as the immediately following materials indicate, have been necessary since the advent of statutes.

The leading treatise on statutory interpretation, STATUES AND STATUTORY CONSTRUC-TION, is now in its sixth edition, having appeared originally in 1896. The seventh edition of at least one volume has appeared. This multivolume set is edited by Professor Norman J. Singer, updated each year, contains excerpts from leading law review articles, and provides detailed coverage of virtually all approaches to statutory interpretation.

For very good single volume sources, see WILLIAM N. ESKRIDGE, JR., PHILIP P. FRICKEY & ELIZABETH GARRETT, LEGISLATION AND STATUTORY INTERPRETATION (2000); MICHAEL SINCLAIR, GUIDE TO STATUTORY INTERPRETATION (2000).

ARISTOTLE,
RHETORIC[*]

First, then, let us take laws and see how they are to be used in persuasion and dissuasion, in accusation and defense. If the written law tells against our case, clearly we must appeal to the universal law, and insist on its greater equity and justice. We must argue that the juror's oath "I will give my verdict according to my honest opinion" means that one will not simply follow the letter of the written law. We must urge that the principles of equity are permanent and changeless, and that the universal law does not change either, for it is the law of nature, whereas written laws often do change. This is the bearing of the lines in Sophocles' *Antigone*, where Antigone pleads that in burying her brother she had broken Creon's law, but not the unwritten law:

> Not of to-day or yesterday they are,
>
> But live eternal: (none can date their birth.)
>
> Not I would fear the wrath of any man,
>
> (And brave Gods' vengeance) for defying these.[71]

We shall argue that justice indeed is true and profitable, but that sham justice is not, and that consequently the written law is not, because it does not fulfil the true purpose of law. Or that justice is like silver, and must be assayed by the judges, if the genuine is to be distinguished from the counterfeit. Or that the better a man is, the more he will follow and abide by the unwritten law in preference to the written. Or perhaps that the law in question contradicts some other highly-esteemed law, or even contradicts itself. Thus it

---

[*] [Bk. 1, Chap. 15.]

[71] Sophocles, Antigone, 456.

may be that one law will enact that all contracts must be held binding, while another forbids us ever to make illegal contracts. Or if a law is ambiguous, we shall turn it about and consider which construction best fits the interests of justice or utility, and then follow that way of looking at it. Or if, though the law still exists, the situation to meet which it was passed exists no longer, we must do our best to prove this and to combat the law thereby. If however the written law supports our case, we must urge that the oath "to give my verdict according to my honest opinion" is not meant to make the judges give a verdict that is contrary to the law, but to save them from the guilt of perjury if they misunderstand what the law really means. Or that no one chooses what is absolutely good, but every one what is good for himself.[1] Or that not to use the laws is as bad as to have no laws at all. Or that, as in the other arts, it does not pay to try to be cleverer than the doctor: for less harm comes from the doctor's mistakes than from the growing habit of disobeying authority. Or that trying to be cleverer than the laws is just what is forbidden by those codes of law that are accounted best . . . .

NOTES AND QUESTIONS

1. The view that different interpretive strategies are rhetorical devices aimed at making a bad case seem better is a very old one, as this excerpt from Aristotle indicates. Is a decision making process dominated by the adversary system predestined to create a set of indeterminate, endlessly shifting claims and counterclaims, or are there valid neutral principles of interpretation?

2. James F. Simon, The Antagonists 223 (1989):

Hugo Black waited in his chambers, secure in the knowledge that his and Earl Warren's political backgrounds would make a close personal and professional collaboration inevitable. Soon enough, Warren asked, to recommend a book on opinion writing. Black enthusiastically recommended Aristotle's *On Rhetoric*, a single ancient volume on the art of analyzing and making arguments. Earl Warren followed Black's advice that day and on many days to come.

3. Remember that Athenian advocates argued to lay judges, not professionals. Won't professional judges see through the kind of arguments described by Aristotle, or reject them out of hand as based on appeals to emotion rather than to reason? Has the emergence of a professional judiciary led to the creation of a science of interpretation?

4. Could the legislature bring the war of words to an end simply by enacting a statute which would codify the principles of statutory interpretation that courts and other officials are permitted to use? *See* McKinney's Consolidated Laws of New York, vol. 1 (1971).

ALAN WATSON, ed.,
THE DIGEST OF JUSTINIAN,
VOLUME 1, BOOK 1. STATUTES,
SENATUS CONSULTA, AND LONG-ESTABLISHED CUSTOM 11–13 (1985)[*]

1 PAPINIAN, *Definitions*, *book 1:* A statute is a communal directive, a resolution of wise men, a forcible reaction to offenses committed either voluntarily or in ignorance, a communal covenant of the state.

. . . .

---

[1] *sc.*, and our written laws, which were made for us, may not reach the abstract ideal of perfection, but they probably suit us better than if they did.

[*] From *The Digest of Justinian* edited by Alan Watson. Copyright © 1985, University of Pennsylvania Press. Reprinted with permission.

12 JULIAN, *Digest, book 15:* It is not possible for every point to be specifically dealt with either in statutes or in *senatus consulta;* but whenever in any case their sense is clear, the president of the tribunal ought to proceed by analogical reasoning and declare the law accordingly.

13 ULPIAN, *Curule Aediles' Edict, book 1:* For, as Pedius says, whenever some particular thing or another has been brought within statute law, there is good ground for other things which further the same interest to be added in supplementation, whether this be done by [juristic] interpretation or *a fortiori* by judicial decision.

17 CELSUS, *Digest, book 26:* Knowing laws is not a matter of sticking to their words, but a matter of grasping their force and tendency.

18 CELSUS, *Digest, book 29:* Statutes ought to be given the more favorable interpretation, whereby their intendment is saved.

19 CELSUS, *Digest, book 33:* When there is an ambiguity in a statute, that sense is to be preferred which avoids an absurdity, especially when by this method the intendment of the act is also secured.

20 JULIAN, *Digest, book 55:* It is not possible to find an underlying reason for everything which was settled by our forebears.

21 NERATIUS, *Parchments, book 6:* Accordingly, it is not right to go ferreting after the motives behind the things which are settled as law. To do otherwise is to subvert many present certainties.

24 CELSUS, *Digest, book 8:* It is not lawyer-like practice to give judgment or to state an opinion on the basis of one particular part of a statute without regard to the whole.

25 MODESTINUS, *Replies, book 8:* It is not allowable under any principle of law or generous maxim of equity that measures introduced favorably to men's interests should be extended by us through a sterner mode of interpretation on the side of severity and against those very interests.

26 PAUL, *Questions, book 4:* It is not an innovation to reconcile earlier laws with later ones.

27 TERTULLIAN, *Questions, book 1:* Accordingly, because the practice is to read earlier laws in the light of later ones, we ought always to deem it already inherent in statutes that they refer also to those persons and those things which may at any time turn out analogous [with persons and things expressly referred to].

28 PAUL, *Lex Julia et Papia, book 5:* But later laws also refer to earlier ones, unless they contradict them; there are many proofs of this.

29 PAUL, *Lex Cincia, sole book:* It is a contravention of the law if someone does what the law forbids, but fraudulently, in that he sticks to the words of the law but evades its sense.

30 ULPIAN, *Edict, book 4:* Fraud on the statute is practiced when one does that which the statute does not wish anyone to do, yet which it has failed expressly to prohibit.

. . . .

37 PAUL, *Questions, book 1:* If a question should arise about the interpretation of a statute, what ought to be looked into first is the law that the *civitas* had previously applied in cases of the same kind. For custom is the best interpreter of statutes.

38 CALLISTRATUS, *Questions, book 1:* In fact, our reigning Emperor Severus has issued a rescript to the effect that in cases of ambiguity arising from statute law, statutory force ought to be ascribed to custom or to the authority of an unbroken line of similar judicial decisions.

NOTES AND QUESTIONS

1. These excerpts from Justinian lie at the roots of the civil law tradition in interpretation: Do you see them as rhetorical tricks which clever advocates manipulate to obtain an interpretation favorable to their client's interest? Or are they genuine efforts to grapple with the intellectual difficulties posed by the task of interpretation?

2. If you were drafting a statute on statutes which sought to codify the canons of statutory interpretation, which of the above-excerpted canons would you include? Which would you reject? Which do you find irrelevant to our modern age?

CARLOS E. GONZALEZ, REINTERPRETING STATUTORY INTERPRETATION, 74 N. Car. L. Rev. 593 (1996)*

II. NORMATIVE THEORIES OF STATUTORY INTERPRETATION

Statutory interpretation theories are divisible into three main families: textual, intentional, and dynamic. Pure textual theories hold the words and only the words of statutes as legitimate guides to discerning statutory meaning. Pure intentional theories attempt to interpret legal texts in accord with the intentions or purposes of the enacting Congress. Under pure dynamic theories, the meaning of statutes can change over time and circumstance; statutes are interpreted with an eye toward shaping statutory law in light of changing social and contextual conditions. Of course, actual interpretive approaches, whether advanced as theories or practiced by judges, are often hybrids of the three. For example, a hybrid approach might follow the plain meaning of the text; if the text is unclear, the purpose or intention of certain relevant actors may be consulted; finally, if the first two steps yield a determinate interpretation that would be unjust or anachronistic, the court may develop a novel interpretation aimed at doing justice or updating the law.

Each of the three theoretical families can be associated with underlying conceptions of what statutes are, or of their role or function, and also with normative accounts of the proper structural relationship between courts and legislatures. Both descriptive theories of statutes and normative ideas regarding the court-legislature relationship serve as underlying yet often unstated premises in arguments supporting different normative theories of statutory interpretation. The pure textualist considers statutes to be commands from the sole politically legitimate statutory law-creating body. The role of the judge is simply to apply that command verbatim. Interpretation that goes beyond statutory text operates in an extra-legal domain. Thus, when applying the legislative command, judges should rely only on a statute's text to determine the meaning of the command. The pure intentionalist views statutes only as evidence of the true law, which is the intention of the enacting legislature, or alternatively the personified purpose of the statute. The role of the judge in interpreting statutes is simply to effectuate the legislative intent or statutory purpose. The judge ought to use the inscribed words of a statute as guide posts in the search for intent or purpose, but should give statutory text no weight independent of legislative intent or statutory purpose. The pure dynamicist thinks of statutes as mere starting points in the politically legitimate statutory law-creating process, which extends from the point of congressional enactment, through the agency process, to litigation in courts, and possibly back to the beginning with reconsideration by Congress. For the pure dynamicist the normative role of courts is to update statutory law in light of the other actors in the process, a changed legal landscape, shifting majoritarian sentiments, or altered underlying assumptions.

Note the following key distinction between the textual and intentional approaches on the one hand, and the dynamic approaches on the other hand: The former two view statutes as laws created in the past, and somehow fixed or unchanging; the latter views statutes as laws always changing, never solidified, or never at a state of rest or completion. Under both textual and intentional approaches to statutory interpretation, the task is to discover what the law already is, while under dynamic approaches the task is to shape law from the mass of politically legitimate legal material available.

UNIFORM STATUTE AND RULE CONSTRUCTION ACT (1995)
14 UNIFORM LAWS ANNOTATED (POCKET PART) 83 (1999)*

§ 18 Principles of Construction; Presumption.

(a) A statute or rule is construed, if possible, to:

(1) give effect to its objective and purpose;
(2) give effect to its entire text; and
(3) avoid an unconstitutional, absurd, or unachievable result.

(b) A statue that is intended to be uniform with those of other States is construed to effectuate that purpose with respect to the subject of the statute.

(c) The presumption that a civil statute in derogation of the common law is construed strictly does not apply to a statute of this [State].

Comment

. . . .

As discussed hereafter, this Act provides a process to be followed by the construer in construing a statute or rule rather than embracing any particular theory of construction.

Theories of Construction

A particular theory of construction is not adopted, by this Act, in part, because of the state of the law on statutory construction and, in part, because ". . . American courts have no intelligible, generally accepted and consistently applied theory of statutory construction." Henry M. Hart, Jr., and Albert M. Sacks, *The Legal Process; Basic Problems in Making Application of Law*, 1169, (William N. Eskridge and Philip P. Frickey, eds., Foundation Press, 1994). A careful review of state court opinions discloses that the rules of statutory construction are not rules in the same sense as are other rules of law, such as the rule imposing strict liability on a manufacturer of goods. It is not clear whether this status of the law is due to the basic inadequacy and contradictory nature of the many and often contradictory rules of statutory construction, the imprecision of language, the inclination of some to start with the answer instead of the question, other factors, or some combination of these factors.

Although none of them are embraced by this Act, there are four generally recognized historic theories of statutory construction. These are, in historical order: the Mischief rule, the Equity of Statute Rule, the Plain Meaning Rule, and the Golden Rule.

The Mischief rule or Purpose Approach was early articulated in *Heydon's Case*, 3 Co. 7a, 76 Eng. Rep. 637 (Exchequer 1584). Under this rule the construer first identifies the mischief or deficiencies of the common law and the remedy provided by the legislature and then adopts the construction that will suppress the mischief and

---

* Reprinted by permission.

advance the remedy. With an understanding of the true reason for the remedy in mind, the words of the text are expanded or contracted from their usual meaning to carry out the legislative purpose. There is no need to first find the text ambiguous or uncertain before obtaining from other sources an understanding of the purpose of the statute.

The Equity of the Statute Rule makes the statute's purpose, true reason for it, or the equity of the statute paramount. Unlike in the Mischief Rule or Purpose Approach, the construer is not restricted by the text in carrying out the statute or rule's purpose. Sometimes it requires a construction not within the literal meaning of the text. *Baker v. Jacobs*, 23 A. 588 (Vt. 1891). That case involved a statute that entitled a losing party to a new trial if the prevailing party gave any juror "victuals or drink" by way of treat. The prevailing party gave several jurors cigars by way of treat. In affirming the order granting a new trial, the court stated that "We do not deem it necessary to decide whether tobacco falls within the strict meaning of the terms 'victuals or drink,' as has been ingenuously argued by the defendants' counsel." 23 A. at 588. This approach is now little used.

The Plain Meaning Rule has several aspects. It is strongly literal. In its pure form, it precludes resort to any other sources of legislative intent or purpose if the meaning of the text or rule is plain from the text; only if it is ambiguous may the construer resort to the other sources. A common formulation is that "where there is no ambiguity in the words, there is no room for construction." Chief Justice Marshall in *United States v. Wiltberger*, 5 Wheat. 76, 5 L. Ed. 73, 92 (1820). The Comment to Section 13 MSCA embraces this view.

Most state courts claim that they follow the Plain Meaning Rule, although it has many formulations and is often stated differently in opinions of the same court. Most commentators have criticized its use for various reasons, including that it has often been used to frustrate the apparent intent of the legislature. Thus, a court may find, or not find, an ambiguity, depending on the result it desires. Arthur W. Murphy, *Old Maxims Never Die: The "Plain Meaning Rule" and Statutory Interpretation in the "Modern" Federal Courts*, 75 COLUM. L. REV. 1299 (1975); E. Russell Hopkins, *The Literal Canon and the Golden Rule*, XV CANADIAN BAR REV. 689–692 (1937); Hon. Felix Frankfurter, *Some Reflections on Reading Statutes*, 47 COLUM. L. REV. 527 (1947). That appellate courts often divide almost equally as to whether a particular text is ambiguous has furthered doubts about the way this approach is used. Another criticism is that the strict plain meaning rule requires a court to make a threshold finding of the existence of an ambiguity before all the information that the court needs to make an informed judgement is presented to it.

Although it was thought that the Plain Meaning Rule had received the death blow in the federal courts over 50 years ago in *United States v. American Trucking Ass'n*, 310 U.S. 534 (1940), the United States Supreme Court has recently stated that a version of it was followed. Philip P. Frickey, *From the Big Sleep to the Big Heat: The Revival of Theory in Statutory Construction*, 77 MINN. L. REV. 241, 254 (1992).

The Golden Rule or Baron Parke's Rule provides that if the unambiguous or literal meaning of the statute leads to an absurd or unjust result or even an inconsistency in the statute, the construer should search further for the correct meaning of the statute and construe it so as to avoid the absurd or unjust result. This may simply be a way to demonstrate that the text is ambiguous so that the construer may go beyond the specific word or phrase in question in its search for legislative intent.

There has been a great revival in interest in theories of statutory construction in the last two decades. The relative role of the text and other evidence of the legislative intent or purpose is a major concern of most of this literature. The plain meaning advocates or textualists insist on confining construction to the plain import of the words. The intentionalists or purpose adherents rely to a major extent on the intention or purpose of the statute. Some of them engage in "imaginative reconstruction" in order to understand the conditions existing at the time of the enactment so as to better understand the language. Judge Richard A. Posner would put the construer in the shoes of those who enacted the statute to find out how they would have resolved the problem, especially as to a situation apparently overlooked by the statute. This is the approach used in *Baker v. Jacobs*, 23 A. 588 (Vt. 1891), the Vermont Equity of the Statute case. Richard A. Posner, *Statutory Interpretation — In the Classroom & in the Courtroom*, 50 U. CHI. L. REV. 800 (1983).

The law and economics theorists advocate a public choice view that statutes are the product of deals made among competing private interest groups with the legislature. They, therefore, urge that the consequence of this agreement is that a statute should be narrowly construed and courts should not fill gaps. *Symposium on Theory of Public Choice*, 74 VA. L. REV. 167–518 (1988).

Another view is that "the statute ought always to be presumed to be the work of reasonable men pursuing reasonable purposes reasonably, unless the contrary is made unmistakably to appear." Henry M. Hart, Jr., & Albert M. Sacks, *The Legal Process: Basic Problems in the Making and Application of Law*, 1125 (William N. Eskridge, Jr. and Philip P. Frickey, eds., Foundation Press, 1994). A statute therefore is to be construed accordingly. *Id.* at 1374–1380. *See also* Philip P. Frickey, *From Big Sleep to Big Heat: The Revival of Theory in Statutory Construction*, 77 MINN. L. REV. 241, 249 (1992); Reed Dickerson, *The Fundamentals of Legal Drafting* (2d ed. 1986).

Dynamic statutory interpretation is another theory advocated by some writers. Its advocates urge that as the societal, legal, and constitutional context of a statute changes, the interpretation of the statute may change. William N. Eskridge, Jr., *Dynamic Statutory Interpretation*, 135 PENN. L. REV. 1479 (1987); Paul Brest, *The Misconceived Quest for the Original Understanding*, 60 B.U. L. REV. 204 (1980). Others insist this is improper.

Most writers would probably agree that there is a consensus that statutory construction is an art and not a science, but that the construer should conscientiously seek the legislature's view and not the construer's view.

The Construction Process

Instead of embracing any particular theory of construction, this Act adopts a process to be followed by the construer when seeking to construe a statute or rule . . . .

The context of a statute or rule includes the section of the statute or rule in which the word or phrase appears, the entire statute, code, or rule of which the section is part, other statutes or rules on the same subject, and the facts and circumstances of the matter before the construer. The general legal environment, whether economic, political, social, or other, in which the statute or rule functions is also part of the context. For example, if the statute or rule in question functions in the legal environment of regulation of employment relations, that context must be considered. Any of these contexts may suggest the need to accommodate the meaning of the word or phrase to a particular context.

. . . .

In construing a statute or rule, the initial and primary focus is on the text. But its meaning may not be certain until the construer considers the context and the facts before the construer. For example, if a workers' compensation statute calculates the weekly benefit to be paid upon the basis of the average "weekly wages" paid to the injured employee in the 12 weeks preceding the injury, the question is what are "wages" for the purpose of the statute. The weekly payment by the employer of $280 (40 hours x $7.00) to a worker is certainly "wages." "Payment" as used in the statute is, therefore, included in the core meaning of the word "wages." What, however, if there is also a payment by the employer to an insurance company for the worker's fringe benefits, such as health care? This payment is certainly "compensation" but probably not "wages." What of tips regularly paid to a waiter? When the tip is placed on a credit card it is paid to the waiter by the employer. Whether the tip in that case is wages is not certain on the face of the statute. Depending on which fact situation of the three is before the construer, the meaning of "wages" is respectively certain, probably certain, and uncertain.

On the other hand, there are statutes or rules where the text is inherently unclear, at least if the literal meaning of the text is considered. A classic example is the Canadian provincial statute that requires drug stores to "close every evening at 10:30 p.m." The question presented is: When could a drug store reopen? At 10:31 p.m., 12:01 a.m., 7:30 a.m. or some other time? The statute literally provides no answer. If the construer, however, determines the purpose that the statute apparently was intended to serve, it might conclude that reopening at 10:31 p.m. or even 12:01 a.m. is not permitted.

The lack of clarity sometimes is not apparent until after all the factors have been considered. It is, therefore, anticipated that an advocate will present to the construer at the beginning of the inquiry all of the materials the advocate considers relevant but the construer will select, consider, and weigh only those materials and aids it considers to be relevant, valid, or persuasive to the inquiry. Because all the materials will be in writing, no oral testimony is anticipated as being necessary. At the end of the review the construer may conclude that only the text itself is pertinent or it may find that other aids to construction are relevant in ascertaining the intent of the enacting body.

It is recognized that construers often consider and weigh various aids to construction and it is not the intent of this Act to restrict full judicial inquiry. It is intended that a construer seriously seeking to carry out the legislative objectives be given considerable discretion to select and weigh those aids to construction that are considered relevant and helpful.

NOTES AND QUESTIONS

1. Henry Hart and Albert Sacks made a famous observation many years ago: "The hard truth of the matter is that American courts have no intelligible, generally accepted, and consistently applied theory of statutory interpretation." HENRY M. HART, JR. & ALBERT M. SACKS, THE LEGAL PROCESS: BASIC PROBLEMS IN THE MAKING AND APPLICATION OF LAW 1169 (William N. Eskridge, Jr. and Philip P. Frickey, eds., 1994).

As you read and analyze the materials in this Part, consider whether there could be *a* "generally accepted, and consistently applied theory of statutory interpretation." Rather, possibly the approach must be contextual, and case-by-case, depending on the type of statute involved (for example, criminal, civil, tax, remedial, etc.), the type of statutory interpretation issue involved (meaning of a term or phrase, gap, overlapping provisions, etc.), and the nature and specificity of available legislative history, evolution of the statutory text or prior judicial interpretations.

2. For other useful considerations of the differing approaches to statutory interpretation, see GEORGE COSTELLO, STATUTORY INTERPRETATION: GENERAL PRINCIPLES AND RECENT TRENDS (Congressional Research Service Report for Congress 2006); J. Clark Kelso & Charles Kelso, *Statutory Interpretation: Four Theories in Disarray*, 53 SMU L. REV. 81 (2000); William S. Blatt, *Interpretative Communities: The Missing Element in Statutory Interpretation*, 95 NW. U. L. REV. 629 (2001); John M. Walker, Jr., *Judicial Tendencies in Statutory Interpretation: Differing Views on the Role of the Judge*, 58 NYU ANN. SURV. AM. L. 203 (2001); WILLIAM D. POPKIN, STATUTES IN COURT: THE HISTORY AND THEORY OF STATUTORY INTERPRETATION (1999).

PROBLEM

You are an associate in a law firm where your clients include a number of residents of "life care" communities. The partner to whom you report has told you that questions have arisen as to the eligibility for homestead tax rebates of these clients, under a statute in Pennsylvania, where you practice and they reside. This statute has just been enacted, and it provides:

> Every citizen and resident of this State shall be entitled, annually, to a homestead rebate on a dwelling house and the land upon which such dwelling house is situated, or on a dwelling house assessed as real estate situated on land owned by another or others which constitutes the place of his domicile and which is owned and used by him as his principal residence . . . . The said requirement of ownership shall be satisfied by the holding of the beneficial interest where the legal title thereto is held by another for the benefit of the said citizen and resident, or for a resident shareholder in a cooperative or mutual housing corporation as defined herein.

> A person who is a tenant for life or a tenant under a lease for 99 years or more . . . shall be deemed to be an owner for the purpose of this act.

There are, of course, no cases under this statute yet, but New Jersey has an identical statute and the following litigation took place under that act:

MILLS v. EAST WINDSOR TWP.
422 A.2d 819 (N.J. Tax Ct. 1980)

CONLEY, J.T.C.

This proceeding involves homestead tax rebates claimed by residents of a retirement community for the years 1977, 1978 and 1979. The retirement community, known as Meadow Lakes, is located in Mercer County, partly in East Windsor Township and partly in the Borough of Hightstown. Rebate applications were filed by approximately 350 residents of Meadow Lakes with the tax assessors of the two taxing districts for 1977 and 1978. All applications were denied . . . . The issue presented by this litigation is whether the residents of the Meadow Lakes retirement community have a sufficient ownership interest in their respective residences to be entitled to homestead tax rebates for the years in issue.

. . . .

As a precondition to becoming a resident at Meadow Lakes, each plaintiff signed a residence agreement with Presbyterian Homes. The agreement is particularly significant in the present case. The agreement covers all aspects of residence in the retirement community and provides in part that the rights of the resident under the agreement "do not include any proprietary interest in the property or assets of the Corporation or any membership in the Corporation." The agreement also provides that Presbyterian Homes will provide total care to the resident for the rest of his or her life in return for the payment of an initial capital fee and subsequent monthly fees, unless the agreement is terminated under certain specified circumstances . . . .

At trial, plaintiffs presented the testimony of the vice-president for finance of Presbyterian Homes. He stated that in the 14-year history of Meadow Lakes it has been the intent of both new residents and the corporation that a resident will stay at and be cared for at Meadow Lakes for life. During the period only 95 residents of a total of approximately 900 have left the community during their lifetimes . . . .

Plaintiffs place primary reliance upon the term "tenant for life" in the second paragraph . . . . They concede that they do not have "formal legal life estates in the Medford Lakes realty," but they contend that it was the intent of the Legislature to grant homestead tax rebates to residents of retirement communities whose rights are as set forth in the agreement between Presbyterian Homes and plaintiffs.

The Director contends that the Homestead Rebate Act must be strictly construed and that plaintiffs are not entitled to rebates because they do not fall squarely within the terms of the statutory language . . . . These cases all recite the following proposition:

The fundamental approach of our statutes is that ordinarily all property shall bear its just and equal share of the public burden of taxation. As the existence of government is a necessity, taxes are demanded and received in order for government to function [citation omitted]. Statutes granting exemption from taxation represent a departure and consequently they are most strongly construed against those claiming exemption. The burden of proving a tax-exempt status is upon the claimant. [47 N.J. at 363]

This rule is particularly cogent in the context of local government finance and local property taxation. In that context finite local budgets are funded by revenues raised by the imposition of the requisite tax rate upon an existing ratable base . . . .

The homestead tax rebate exists in a different context. It is not a tax exemption. The rebate program has no effect on local budgets or local tax rates . . . . The actual payment is made by the State from gross income tax revenues on deposit in the Property Tax Relief Fund . . . .

The appropriate rule of statutory construction to be applied to the Homestead Rebate Act is that of the "equity of the statute." This principle was explained in the following language in *Dvorkin v. Dover Tp.*, 29 N.J. 303 (1959):

> . . . [W]hen the lawgiver's intent is in doubt, the court "ought to interpret the law to be what is more consonant to equity and least inconvenient." *Kerlin's Lessee v. Bull*, 1 Dall. 175, 1 U.S. 175, 1 L.Ed. 88 (Sup. Ct. Pa. 1786); *Associates of Jersey Company v. Davison*, 29 N.J.L. 415, 424 (E. & A. 1860). This is the doctrine of "equity of the statute" which found expression in *Eyston v. Studd*, 2 Plowd. 459 A, 75 Eng. Rep. (1574), and from which flows the constructional aid that has taken firm roots in our jurisprudence — that the spirit of the legislative direction prevails over its terms. *See Horack, Sutherland Statutory Construction* (3d ed. 1943), §;§ 6001 to 6007; *McCaffrey, Statutory Construction*, § 4, p. 8 (1953).

> . . . [T]he "equity of the statute" rule does not, when properly applied, substitute the judicial for the legislative will, but rather in the consideration of all the material elements reaches the result probably intended by the draftsman had he anticipated the situation at hand. [at 315]

This rule is especially pertinent with regard to statutes with "sweeping social objectives" . . . . It is therefore necessary to examine the overall purpose and thrust of the homestead rebate program in order to determine how the Legislature would treat residents of retirement communities such as Meadow Lakes if the issue were squarely presented to that body.

. . . .

The present case deals with the entitlement of senior citizens to homestead rebates. The Legislature in recent years has been supportive of the needs and concerns of the State's senior citizens. Specifically with regard to taxation, the Legislature has granted additional benefits to senior citizens whenever the Constitution has permitted such special treatment . . . .

The history of the Homestead Rebate Act itself is also instructive in that the Legislature has only increased the availability of rebates and has never restricted them. The Legislature amended the act three times to make it clear that certain persons were intended to be granted rebates . . . .

These considerations oblige us to conclude that if the Legislature were to consider squarely the status of retirement community residents, it would treat them for purposes of the act the same as "tenants for life" and accordingly as eligible for the rebate. We so hold. In doing so we are aware that the residence agreement states that the rights of the resident "do not include any proprietary interest in the property or assets of the Corporation or any membership in the Corporation," and that the agreement may be terminated in a number of circumstances . . . . When the Legislature amended the Homestead Rebate Act to include resident shareholders in cooperatives and mutual housing corporations, the Governor upon signing the bills issued a statement that the legislation "recognizes that co-op owners should be treated as home owners in view of the substantial investment they have in their property." The same reasoning supports a determination that rebates should be made available to plaintiffs, who are domiciliaries of New Jersey and who reside in homes in which they have a substantial investment. Although plaintiffs do not possess an ownership interest in Meadow Lakes, the spirit of the Homestead Rebate Act indicates that they should be treated as owners for purposes of the act. Equity and common sense require this result.

MACMILLAN v. DIRECTOR, DIVISION OF TAXATION
434 A.2d 620 (N.J. App. Div. 1981)

FRITZ, P.J.A.D.

Never more than here did an appeal tend to demonstrate the capacity of hard facts to make bad law. The sole question involved is the eligibility of retirement community residents for tax rebates under the Homestead Rebate Act, N.J.S.A. 54:4-3.80 *et seq.* The opinion of the tax court judge in *Mills v. East Windsor Tp.* appears at 176 N.J. Super. 271 (Tax Ct. 1980) . . . .

We respect the demonstrated humanity of the tax court judge. We are not sufficiently insensitive to demean his concern for "common sense" or his reach for the "equity of the statute" principle. We are not sufficiently bold to gainsay stubbornly his conviction that "if the Legislature were [today] to consider squarely the status of retirement community residents it would treat them for purposes of the act the same as 'tenants for life' and accordingly as eligible for the rebate."

But we remain judges and as such cannot succumb to the humanistic pressures or substitute our concern in place of the legislative design. Indeed, we may not even permit ourselves the luxury of liberal construction — or, as a matter of fact, any construction — if the words of the statute plainly convey the legislative intent, as we are persuaded they do here. We must enforce the legislative will as written. *Dacunzo v. Edgye*, 19 N.J. 443, 451 (1955). We certainly may not supply a provision no matter how confident we are of what the Legislature would do if it were to reconsider today. *Stamboulos v. McKee*, 134 N.J. Super. 567 (App. Div. 1975). "Construing" or "interpreting" a clear and unambiguous statute is simply not permissible.

More significant than the result in any one case is the wear of the forbidden practice on the doctrine of separation of powers. *Watt v. Franklin*, 21 N.J. 274, 277 (1956). To the extent the executive or the judiciary superimposes its judgement on the clearly expressed will of the Legislature, we threaten the doctrine itself and its function as a viable control on our government of laws.

Restraint is particularly essential in tax matters . . . .

The tax court judge distinguishes between a tax exemption and a tax rebate. He points out that no local tax revenues are diverted and that actual payment is made from gross income tax revenues on deposit in the Property Tax Relief Fund. The distinction is technical . . . .

Nor should we lose sight of the fact that answers so clear and necessary in our view that they tempt us to embellish must be equally clear to the many fine minds in the Legislature, the body charged with determining the necessity in any event. We may, of course, draw the attention of the Legislature to the result (*Dacunzo v. Edgye, supra*, 19 N.J. at 454) and this seems to be an entirely appropriate situation in which to do that.

We are not insensitive to the many persuasions which moved the tax court judge and which are here urged by respondents. As is pointed out in *Mills, supra*, these residents

> . . . are by no means transient or seasonal residents of New Jersey. They have almost invariably sold their homes and invested their savings in a capital fee

paid to the retirement community. These fees range from $20,000 to $65,000. Plaintiffs and other residents of retirement communities certainly have more invested in their "homes" than do tenants of apartments, who at least would be entitled to homestead credits against the gross income tax. [176 N.J. Super. at 282]

But the fact remains that the statute is outspoken and unambiguous. The statutory scheme is clear. The legislation requires a proprietary interest which, it expressly details, is satisfied only by: legal or beneficial ownership; a tenancy for life or for 99 years or more; possession and entitlement thereto under an executory contract or under an agreement with a leading institution which holds title as security, or as resident shareholdership in a cooperative or mutual housing corporation. N.J.S.A. 54:4-3.80. The tax court judge recognized, as is the fact, that the "life-care" residents (*Onderdonk v. Presbyterian Homes of N.J.*, 85 N.J. 171 (1981)) do not have a proprietary interest in their place of residence . . . . We do not lack sympathy or appreciation for his concern. We simply do not agree with his judgement for we are convinced that neither he nor we may thus preempt the legislative function.

MACMILLAN v. DIRECTOR, DIVISION OF TAXATION
445 A.2d 397 (N.J. 1982)

PER CURIAM.

The judgement is affirmed substantially for the reasons expressed in the opinion of the Appellate Division, reported at 180 N.J. Super. 175 (1981).

PASHMAN, J., dissenting.

I would reverse the Appellate Division judgement substantially for the reasons stated by Judge Conley writing for the Tax court below, *Mills v. East Windsor Tp.*, 176 N.J. Super. 271 (Tax Ct. 1980). I add several observations.

. . . .

I agree that where the plain language of a statute suggests a certain result and there are no indications of legislative intent to the contrary, the Court's job is clear. However that is not this case. Words take meaning from their context. Failure to consider relevant statutory policies and statutory history may cause courts to frustrate rather than implement the legislative will. The plain meaning rule does not compel us to view the statutory language out of context. Nor does it require us to ignore the history of the statute, its scope and its relation to other legislative enactments. As Justice Handler said in *Unemployed-Employed Council of N.J., Inc. v. Horn*, 85 N.J. 646, 655 (1981), "statutory language must be read perceptively and sensibly with a view toward fulfilling the legislative intent."

Judges invented the rule that tax exemptions are strictly construed because they presumed that legislatures intend all citizens to pay their fair share of taxes. We use the rule because, as a general matter, it is probably a good statement of what the Legislature wants us to do. However, the rule is merely a presumption; the ultimate inquiry remains legislative intent. When other indications show that the Legislature intended a broad interpretation of a tax exemption, it is not our role to thwart the legislative purpose by mechanically applying traditional rules of construction.

In this case, there is ample evidence that the Legislature intended the property rebate to be liberally construed to include "life-care" residents. As the Tax Court noted, the Legislature has made property tax relief available on a broad scale to comply with the constitutional mandate to use the income tax to grant property tax relief. N.J. Const. (1947), Art. VIII, § 1, ¶¶ 5, 7; 176 N.J. Super. at 278–79. It has also amended the statute several times, progressively broadening the categories of persons benefitted by the rebate. *Id.* at 280. Moreover, in recent years the Legislature has given special attention to the needs of the State's senior citizens. It has repeatedly granted them special tax benefits. *Id.* at 279–80. This is a further indication of a legislative desire to include plaintiffs within the scope of the statute.

As a practical matter, plaintiffs have *de facto* life tenancies. Virtually all make large down payments. The overwhelming majority of residents stay for the remainder of their lives. During the 14-year history of Meadow Lakes, for example, the corporation has attempted to terminate the residency of only two persons out of a total of approximately 900. The small technical differences between life-care contracts and life tenancies as such do not suggest any reason for granting rebates only to the latter.

All the residents of life-care facilities are elderly. They enter these communities for companionship, care and peace of mind. The unique contractual and property interests involved are designed to satisfy those needs. I do not believe the Legislature intended to exclude life-care residents from the property tax rebate merely because they had the good sense to avail themselves of an innovative living arrangement. The special needs that impel the elderly to enter life-care communities should not be frustrated by special burdens.

Finally, I respectfully reject the Appellate Division assertion that in construing statutes, judges must not "succumb to the humanistic pressures . . . ," 180 N.J. Super. at 177. We should presume that the Legislature acts with such considerations in mind. There is simply no good reason to believe the Legislature intended the harsh and inequitable result of excluding the elderly residents of life-care communities from the statute's coverage. I fully agree with Judge Conley that extension of the rebate to these plaintiffs not only furthers the legislative design, but is based on "equity and common sense." 176 N.J. Super. at 282. I therefore dissent.

In preparation for the development of your legal opinion, review the different approaches to statutory interpretation reflected in this portfolio of cases. Identify the approaches, arguments, and counter arguments that are reflected in the New Jersey litigation and develop arguments under the new, identical Pennsylvania statute. Would you want to know if the Pennsylvania statute was modeled directly on the New Jersey statute?

Chapter 6

APPROACHES TO STATUTORY INTERPRETATION BASED ON STATUTORY TEXT

INTRODUCTION

There is a wide variety of statutory interpretation techniques that are based on the text of the statute under consideration, or upon the text of related statutes. These are grouped together in this chapter.

A. THE "PLAIN MEANING" RULE

CAMINETTI v. UNITED STATES
242 U.S. 470 (1917)

MR. JUSTICE DAY delivered the opinion of the court:

These three cases were argued together, and may be disposed of in a single opinion. In each of the cases there was a conviction and sentence for violation of the so-called White Slave Traffic Act of June 25, 1910 (36 Stat. at L. 825, chap. 395, Comp. Stat. 1913, § 8813), the judgments were affirmed by the circuit courts of appeals, and writs of certiorari bring the cases here.

In the Caminetti Case, the petitioner was indicted in the United States district court for the northern district of California, upon the 6th day of May, 1913, for alleged violations of the act. The indictment was in four counts, the first of which charged him with transporting and causing to be transported, and aiding and assisting in obtaining transportation for a certain woman from Sacramento, California, to Reno, Nevada, in interstate commerce, for the purpose of debauchery, and for an immoral purpose, to wit, that the aforesaid woman should be and become his mistress and concubine. As to the first count, defendant was found guilty and sentenced to imprisonment for eighteen months and to pay a fine of $1,500. Upon writ of error to the United States circuit court of appeals for the ninth circuit, that judgment was affirmed. 136 C.C.A. 147, 220 Fed. 545.

. . . .

It is contended that the act of Congress is intended to reach only 'commercialized vice,' or the traffic in women for gain, and that the conduct for which the several petitioners were indicted and convicted, however reprehensible in morals, is not within the purview of the statute when properly construed in the light of its history and the purposes intended to be accomplished by its enactment. In none of the cases was it charged or proved that the transportation was for gain or for the purpose of furnishing women for prostitution for hire, and it is insisted that, such being the case, the acts charged and proved, upon which conviction was had, do not come within the statute.

It is elementary that the meaning of a statute must, in the first instance, be sought in the language in which the act is framed, and if that is plain, and if the law is within the constitutional authority of the lawmaking body which passed it, the sole function of the courts is to enforce it according to its terms . . . .

Where the language is plain and admits of no more than one meaning, the duty of interpretation does not arise, and the rules which are to aid doubtful meanings need no discussion. *Hamilton v. Rathbone*, 175 U.S. 414, 421, 44 L. Ed. 219, 222, 20 Sup. Ct. Rep. 155. There is no ambiguity in the terms of this act. It is specifically made an offense to knowingly transport or cause to be transported, etc., in interstate commerce, any woman or girl for the purpose of prostitution or debauchery, or for 'any other immoral purpose,' or with the intent and purpose to induce any such woman or girl to become a prostitute or to give herself up to debauchery, or to engage in any other immoral practice.

Statutory words are uniformly presumed, unless the contrary appears, to be used in their ordinary and usual sense, and with the meaning commonly attributed to them. To cause a woman or girl to be transported for the purposes of debauchery, and for an immoral purpose, to wit, becoming a concubine or mistress . . . would seem by the very statement of the facts to embrace transportation for purposes denounced by the act, and therefore fairly within its meaning.

While such immoral purpose would be more culpable in morals and attributed to baser motives if accompanied with the expectation of pecuniary gain, such considerations do not prevent the lesser offense against morals of furnishing transportation in order that a woman may be debauched, or become a mistress or a concubine, from being the execution of purposes within the meaning of this law. To say the contrary would shock the common understanding of what constitutes an immoral purpose when those terms are applied, as here, to sexual relations.

In *United States v. Bitty*, 208 U.S. 393, 52 L. Ed. 543, 28 Sup. Ct. Rep. 396, it was held that the act of Congress against the importation of alien women and girls for the purpose of prostitution 'and any other immoral purpose' included the importation of an alien woman to live in concubinage with the person importing her. In that case this court said:

> All will admit that full effect must be given to the intention of Congress as gathered from the words of the statute. There can be no doubt as to what class was aimed at by the clause forbidding the importation of alien women for purposes of 'prostitution.' It refers to women who, for hire or without hire, offer their bodies to indiscriminate intercourse with men. The lives and example of such persons are in hostility to 'the idea of the family, as consisting in and springing from the union for life of one man and one woman in the holy estate of matrimony; the sure foundation of all that is stable and noble in our civilization; the best guaranty of that reverent morality which is the source of all beneficent progress in social and political improvement.' *Murphy v. Ramsey*, 114 U.S. 15, 45, 29 L. Ed. 47, 57, 5 Sup. Ct. Rep. 747 . . . . Now the addition in the last statute of the words, 'or for any other immoral purpose,' after the word 'prostitution,' must have been made for some practical object. Those added words show beyond question that Congress had in view the protection of society against another class of alien women other than those who might be brought here merely for purposes of 'prostitution.' In forbidding the importation of alien women 'for any other immoral purpose,' Congress evidently thought that there were purposes in connection with the importations of alien women which, as in the case of importations for prostitution, were to be deemed immoral. It may be admitted that, in accordance with the familiar rule of ejusdem generis, the immoral purpose referred to by the words 'any other immoral purpose' must be one of the same general class or kind as the particular purpose of 'prostitution' specified in the same clause of the statute. 2 Lewis's Sutherland, Stat. Constr. § 423, and authorities cited. But that rule cannot avail the accused in this case; for the immoral purpose charged in the indictment is of the same general class or kind as the one that controls in the importation of an alien woman for the purpose strictly of prostitution. The prostitute may, in the popular sense, be more degraded in character than the concubine, but the latter none the less must be held to lead an immoral life, if any regard whatever be had to the views that are almost universally held in this country as to the relations which may rightfully, from the standpoint of morality, exist between man and woman in the matter of sexual intercourse.

This definition of an immoral purpose was given prior to the enactment of the act now under consideration, and must be presumed to have been known to Congress when it enacted the law here involved. (See the sections of the act[1] set forth in the margin.)

But it is contended that though the words are so plain that they cannot be misapprehended when given their usual and ordinary interpretation, and although the sections in which they appear do not in terms limit the offense defined and punished to acts of 'commercialized vice,' or the furnishing or procuring of transportation of women for debauchery, prostitution, or immoral practices for hire, such limited purpose is to be attributed to Congress and engrafted upon the act in view of the language of § 8 and the report which accompanied the law upon its introduction into and subsequent passage by the House of Representatives.

In this connection, it may be observed that while the title of an act cannot overcome the meaning of plain and unambiguous words used in its body (*United States v. Fisher*, 2 Cranch 358, 386, 2 L. Ed. 304, 313 . . . .) the title of this act embraces the regulation of interstate commerce 'by prohibiting the transportation therein for immoral purposes of women and girls, and for other purposes.' It is true that § 8 of the act provides that it shall be known and referred to as the 'White Slave Traffic Act,' and the report accompanying the introduction of the same into the House of Representatives set forth the fact that a material portion of the legislation suggested was to meet conditions which had arisen in the past few years, and that the legislation was needed to put a stop to a villainous interstate and international traffic in women and girls. Still, the name given to an act by way of designation or description, or the report which accompanies it, cannot change the plain import of its words. If the words are plain, they give meaning to the act,

---

[1] Sections 2, 3, and 4 of the act are as follows:

Sec. 2. That any person who shall knowingly transport or cause to be transported, or aid or assist in obtaining transportation for, or in transporting, in interstate or foreign commerce, or in an territory or in the District of Columbia, any woman or girl for the purpose of prostitution or debauchery, or for any other immoral purpose, or with the intent and purpose to induce, entice, or compel such woman or girl to become a prostitute or to give herself up to debauchery, or to engage in any other immoral practice; or who shall knowingly procure or obtain, or cause to be procured or obtained, or aid or assist in procuring or obtaining, any ticket or tickets, or any form of transportation or evidence of the right thereto, to be use by any woman or girl in interstate or foreign commerce, or in any territory or the District of Columbia, in going to any place for the purpose of prostitution or debauchery, or for any other immoral purpose, or with the intent or purpose on the part of such person to induce, entice, or compel her to give herself up to the practice of prostitution, or to give herself up to debauchery, or any other immoral practice, whereby any such woman or girl shall be transported in interstate or foreign commerce, or in any territory or the District of Columbia, shall be deemed guilty of a felony, and upon conviction thereof shall be punished by a fine not exceeding five thousand dollars, or by imprisonment of not more than five years, or by both such fine and imprisonment, in the discretion of the court,

Sec. 3. That any person who shall knowingly persuade, induce, entice, or coerce, or cause to be persuaded, induced, enticed, or coerced, or aid or assist in persuading, inducing, enticing, or coercing any woman or girl to go from one place to another in interstate or foreign commerce, or in any territory or the District of Columbia, for the purpose of prostitution or debauchery, or for any other immoral purpose, or with the intent and purpose on the part of such person that such woman or girl shall engage in the practice of prostitution or debauchery, or any other immoral practice, whether with or without her consent, and who shall thereby knowingly cause or aid or assist in causing such woman or girl to go and to be carried or transported as a passenger upon the line or route of any common carrier or carriers in interstate or foreign commerce, or any territory or the District of Columbia, shall be deemed guilty of a felony and on conviction thereof shall be punished by a fine of not more than five thousand dollars, or by imprisonment for a term not exceeding five years, or by both such fine and imprisonment, in the discretion of the court.

Sec. 4. That any person who shall knowingly persuade, induce, entice or coerce any woman or girl under the age of eighteen years, from any state or territory of the District of Columbia, with the purpose and intent to induce or coerce her, or that she shall be induced or coerced to engage in prostitution or debauchery, or any other immoral practice, and shall in furtherance of such purpose knowingly induce or cause her to go and to be carried or transported as a passenger in interstate commerce upon the line or route of any common carrier or carriers, shall be deemed guilty of a felony, and on conviction thereof shall be punished by a fine of not more than ten thousand dollars, or by imprisonment for a term not exceeding ten years, or by both such fine and imprisonment, in the discretion of the court.

and it is neither the duty nor the privilege of the courts to enter speculative fields in search of a different meaning.

Reports to Congress accompanying the introduction of proposed laws may aid the courts in reaching the true meaning of the legislature in cases of doubtful interpretation . . . . But, as we have already said, and it has been so often affirmed as to become a recognized rule, when words are free from doubt they must be taken as the final expression of the legislative intent, and are not to be added to or subtracted from by considerations drawn from titles or designating names or reports accompanying their introduction, or from any extraneous source. In other words, the language being plain, and not leading to absurd or wholly impracticable consequences, it is the sole evidence of the ultimate legislative intent. *See Mackenzie v. Hare*, 239 U.S. 299, 308, 60 L. Ed. 297, 300, 36 Sup. Ct. Rep. 106.

The fact, if it be so, that the act as it is written opens the door to blackmailing operations upon a large scale, is no reason why the courts should refuse to enforce it according to its terms, if within the constitutional authority of Congress. Such considerations are more appropriately addressed to the legislative branch of the government, which alone had authority to enact and may, if it sees fit, amend the law. *Lake County v. Rollins*, 130 U.S. 662, 32 L. Ed. 1060, 9 Sup. Ct. Rep. 651.

. . . .

Mr. Justice McKenna, dissenting:

Undoubtedly, in the investigation of the meaning of a statute we resort first to its words, and, when clear, they are decisive. The principle has attractive and seemingly disposing simplicity, but that it is not easy of application, or, at least, encounters other principles, many cases demonstrate. The words of a statute may be uncertain in their signification or in their application. If the words be ambiguous, the problem they present is to be resolved by their definition; the subject matter and the lexicons become our guides. But here, even, we are not exempt from putting ourselves in the place of the legislators. If the words be clear in meaning, but the objects to which they are addressed be uncertain, the problem then is to determine the uncertainty. And for this a realization of conditions that provoked the statute must inform our judgment. Let us apply these observations to the present case.

The transportation which is made unlawful is of a woman or girl 'to become a prostitute or to give herself up to debauchery, or to engage in any other immoral practice.' Our present concern is with the words 'any other immoral practice,' which, it is asserted, have a special office. The words are clear enough as general descriptions; they fail in particular designation; they are class words, not specifications. Are they controlled by those which precede them? If not, they are broader in generalization and include those that precede them, making them unnecessary and confusing. To what conclusion would this lead us? 'Immoral' is a very comprehensive word. It means a dereliction of morals. In such sense it covers every form of vice, every form of conduct that is contrary to good order. It will hardly be contended that in this sweeping sense it is used in the statute. But, if not used in such sense, to what is it limited and by what limited? If it be admitted that it is limited at all, that ends the imperative effect assigned to it in the opinion of the court. But not insisting quite on that, we ask again, By what is it limited? By its context, necessarily, and the purpose of the statute.

For the context I must refer to the statute; of the purpose of the statute Congress itself has given us illumination. It devotes a section to the declaration that the 'act shall be known and referred to as the "White Slave Traffic Act".' And its prominence gives it prevalence in the construction of the statute. It cannot be pushed aside or subordinated by indefinite words in other sentences, limited even there by the context. It is a peremptory rule of construction that all parts of a statute must be taken into account in ascertaining its meaning, and it cannot be said that § 8 has no object. Even if it gives only a title to the act, it has especial weight. *United States v. Union P. R. Co.*, 91 U.S. 72, 82, 23 L. Ed. 224, 229. But it gives more than a title; it makes distinctive the purpose of the statute. The designation 'white slave traffic' has the sufficiency of an axiom. If apprehended, there is no uncertainty as to the conduct it describes. It is commercialized vice, immoralities having a mercenary purpose, and this is confirmed by other circumstances.

The author of the bill was Mr. Mann, and in reporting it from the House committee on interstate and foreign commerce he declared for the committee that it was not the purpose of the bill to interfere with or usurp in any way the police power of the states, and further, that it was not the intention of the bill to regulate prostitution or the places where prostitution or immorality was practiced, which were said to be matters wholly within the power of the states, and over which the Federal government had no jurisdiction. And further explaining the bill, it was said that the sections of the act had been 'so drawn that they are limited to the cases in which there is an act of transportation in interstate commerce of women for the purposes of prostitution.' And again:

> The White Slave Trade. — A material portion of the legislation suggested and proposed is necessary to meet conditions which have arisen within the past few years. The legislation is needed to put a stop to a villainous interstate and international traffic in women and girls. The legislation is not needed or intended as an aid to the states in the exercise of their police powers in the suppression or regulation of immorality in general. It does not attempt to regulate the practice of voluntary prostitution, but aims solely to prevent panderers and procurers from compelling thousands of women and girls against their will and desire to enter and continue in a life of prostitution.

Cong. Rec. vol. 50, pp. 3368, 3370. In other words, it is vice as a business at which the law is directed, using interstate commerce as a facility to procure or distribute its victims.

In 1912 the sense of the Department of Justice was taken of the act in a case where a woman of 24 years went from Illinois, where she lived, to Minnesota, at the solicitation and expense of a man. She was there met by him and engaged with him in immoral practices like those for which petitioners were convicted. The assistant district attorney forwarded her statement to the Attorney General, with the comment that the element of traffic was absent from the transaction and that therefore, in his opinion, it was not 'within the spirit and intent of the Mann Act.'[1] Replying, the Attorney General expressed his concurrence in the view of his subordinate.[2] Of course, neither the declarations of the report of the committee on interstate commerce of the House nor the opinion of the Attorney General are conclusive of the meaning of the law, but they are highly persuasive. The opinion was by one skilled in the rules and methods employed in the interpretation or construction of laws, and informed, besides, of the conditions to which the act was addressed. The report was by the committee charged with the duty of investigating the necessity for the act, and to inform the House of the results of that investigation, both of evil and remedy. The report of the committee has, therefore, a higher quality than debates on the floor of the House. The representations of the latter may indeed be ascribed to the exaggerations of advocacy or opposition. The report of a

---

[1] 'Careful consideration of the facts and circumstances as related by Miss Cox fails to convince me that her case came within the spirit and intent of the Mann act. The element of traffic is entirely absent from this transaction. It is not a case of prostitution or debauchery and the general words "or other immoral practice" should be qualified by the particular preceding words and be read in the light of the rule of ejusdem generis. This view of the statute is the more reasonable when considered in connection with § 8, where Congress employs the terms "slave" and "traffic" as indicative of its purpose to suppress certain forms of abominable practice connected with the degradation of women for gain.'

[2] 'I agree with your conclusion that the facts and circumstances set forth in your letter and its inclosure do not bring the matter within the true intent of the White Slave Traffic Act, and that no prosecution against Edwards should be instituted in the Federal courts unless other and different facts are presented to you.'

committee is the execution of a duty and has the sanction of duty. There is a presumption, therefore, that the measure it recommends has the purpose it declares and will accomplish it as declared.

This being the purpose, the words of the statute should be construed to execute it, and they may be so construed even if their literal meaning be otherwise. In *Church of the Holy Trinity v. United States*, 143 U.S. 457, 36 L. Ed. 226, 12 Sup. Ct. Rep. 511, there came to this court for construction an act of Congress which made it unlawful for anyone in any of the United States 'to prepay the transportation, or in any way assist or encourage the importation or migration of any alien or aliens, any foreigner or foreigners, into the United States . . . under contract or agreement . . . to perform labor or *service of any kind* [italics mine] in the United States, its territories or the District of Columbia.' The Trinity Church made a contract with one E.W. Warren, a resident of England, to remove to the city of New York and enter its service as rector and pastor. The church was proceeded against under the act and the circuit court held that it applied, and rendered judgment accordingly. 36 Fed. 303.

It will be observed that the language of the statute is very comprehensive, — fully as much so as the language of the act under review, — having no limitation whatever from the context; and the circuit court, in submission to what the court considered its imperative quality, rendered judgment against the church. This court reversed the judgment, and, in an elaborate opinion by Mr. Justice Brewer, declared that 'it is a familiar rule that a thing may be within the letter of the statute and yet not within the statute, because not within its spirit, nor within the intention of its makers.' And the learned justice further said: 'This has been often asserted, and the reports are full of cases illustrating its application.'

It is hardly necessary to say that the application of the rule does not depend upon the objects of the legislation, to be applied or not applied as it may exclude or include good things or bad things. Its principle is the simple one that the words of a statute will be extended or restricted to execute its purpose.

Another pertinent illustration of the rule is *Reiche v. Smythe*, 13 Wall. 162, 20 L. Ed. 566, in which the court declared that if at times it was its duty to regard the words of a statute, at times it was also its duty to disregard them, limit or extend them, in order to execute the purpose of the statute. And applying the principle, it decided that in a tariff act the provision that a duty should be imposed on horses, etc., and other live animals imported from foreign countries should not include canary birds, ignoring the classification of nature. And so again in *Silver v. Ladd*, 7 Wall. 219, 19 L. Ed. 138, where the benefit of the Oregon Donation Act was extended by making the words 'single man' used in the statute mean an unmarried woman, disregarding a difference of genders clearly expressed in the law.

The rule that these cases illustrate is a valuable one and in varying degrees has daily practice. It not only rescues legislation from absurdity (so far the opinion of the court admits its application), but it often rescues it from invalidity, — a useful result in our dual form of governments and conflicting jurisdictions. It is the dictate of common sense. Language, even when most masterfully used, may miss sufficiency and give room for dispute. Is it a wonder, therefore, that when used in the haste of legislation, in view of conditions perhaps only partly seen or not seen at all, the consequences, it may be, beyond present foresight, it often becomes necessary to apply the rule? And it is a rule of prudence and highest sense. It rescues from crudities, excesses, and deficiencies, making legislation adequate to its special purpose, rendering unnecessary repeated qualifications, and leaving the simple and best exposition of a law the mischief it was intended to redress. Nor is this judicial legislation. It is seeking and enforcing the true sense of a law notwithstanding its imperfection or generality of expression.

There is much in the present case to tempt to a violation of the rule. Any measure that protects the purity of women from assault or enticement to degradation finds an instant advocate in our best emotions; but the judicial function cannot yield to emotion — it must, with poise of mind, consider and decide. It should not shut its eyes to the facts of the world and assume not to know what everybody else knows. And everybody knows that there is a difference between the occasional immoralities of men and women and that systematized and mercenary immorality epitomized in the statute's graphic phrase 'white slave traffic.' And it was such immorality that was in the legislative mind, and not the other. The other is occasional, not habitual, — inconspicuous, — does not offensively obtrude upon public notice. Interstate commerce is not its instrument as it is of the other, nor is prostitution its object or its end. It may, indeed, in instances, find a convenience in crossing state lines, but this is its accident, not its aid.

There is danger in extending a statute beyond its purpose, even if justified by a strict adherence to its words. The purpose is studied, all effects measured, not left at random,-one evil practice prevented, opportunity given to another. The present case warns against ascribing such improvidence to the statute under review. Blackmailers of both sexes have arisen, using the terrors of the construction now sanctioned by this court as a help — indeed, the means — for their brigandage. The result is grave and should give us pause. It certainly will not be denied that legal authority justifies the rejection of a construction which leads to mischievous consequences, if the statute be susceptible of another construction.

United States v. Bitty, 208 U.S. 393, 52 L. Ed. 543, 28 Sup. Ct. Rep. 396, is not in opposition. The statute passed upon was a prohibition against the importation of alien women or girls, — a statute, therefore, of broader purpose than the one under review. Besides, the statute finally passed upon was an amendment to a prior statute, and the words construed were an addition to the prior statute, and necessarily, therefore, had an added effect. The first statute prohibited the importation of *any alien woman or girl into the United States for the purpose of prostitution*. The second statute repeated the words and added '*or for any other immoral purpose*.' [italics mine] Necessarily there was an enlargement of purpose, and besides, the act was directed against the importation of foreign corruption, and was construed accordingly. The case, therefore, does not contradict the rule; it is an example of it.

For these reasons I dissent from the opinion and judgment of the court, expressing no opinion of the other propositions in the cases.

I am authorized to say that the CHIEF JUSTICE and MR. JUSTICE CLARKE concur in this dissent.

NOTES AND QUESTIONS

1. From whence does the Court derive the presumption that statutory words "are used in their ordinary and usual sense and with the meaning commonly attributed to them"? Did the defendant, Caminetti, lose because his counsel failed to adduce sufficient evidence to rebut that presumption? If so, what standard of proof had to be met — "clear and convincing evidence," "preponderance" or some other standard?

2. The gist of the dispute in this case centers on the meaning of the phrase "prostitution, or debauchery, or other immoral purpose." Do you agree with the majority that the meaning of this language is "plain" and "free from doubt"? If so, why did the majority invoke the *Bitty* precedent defining the term "immoral purpose" and observe that "this definition of an immoral purpose was given prior to the enactment of the act now under consideration and must be presumed to have been known to Congress when it enacted the law here involved." What evidentiary basis supports this presumption? What evidence concerning the legislative process could Caminetti have addressed to rebut this presumption?

Does the invocation of *Bitty* suggest that the majority viewed this case as falling within the ambit of the principle of *stare decisis*?

Are you persuaded by the dissent's effort to distinguish the force of the *Bitty* precedent?

3. What role does the canon of construction called *ejusdem generis* play in this case? What role should it play?

4. Is the dissent right when it views *Holy Trinity Church* rather than *Bitty* as the more significant precedent for resolving the issues raised in interpreting the White Slave Traffic Act? What standard was applied in *Holy Trinity Church* to rebut the presumption that statutory words are used in their "ordinary and usual sense"? *Holy Trinity Church* is included in the next chapter.

5. Suppose that Caminetti had been engaged in transporting males for the purpose of prostitution. Does the logic of *Silver v. Ladd* cited by the dissent suggest that the court should be free to disregard "a difference of genders clearly expressed in the law"?

6. What deference should be given to the administrative construction of the statute given by the Attorney General cited in the dissent?

7. How would you redraft the statute to make it more precise?

8. For a complete discussion of the background of the Caminetti case, the facts leading up to it and the political situation in which it arose, see DAVID J. LANGUM, CROSSING OVER THE LINE (1994).

ARTHUR W. MURPHY,
OLD MAXIMS NEVER DIE:
THE "PLAIN-MEANING RULE" AND STATUTORY INTERPRETATION
IN THE "MODERN" FEDERAL COURTS,
75 COLUMBIA LAW REVIEW 1299 (1975)[*]

Although there have been occasional heretics,[1] it is an article of faith among American lawyers that the function of a court when dealing with a statute is to ascertain and effectuate the intention of the legislature. Even while recognizing that the task is frequently more easily said than done, courts ritually describe their relationship to the legislature as that of obedient servant. Whether they always mean this is, of course, something else again. In the nineteenth century and well into the twentieth, the real attitude of many courts might more accurately have been described as grudging rather than obedient.[2]

One way in which the courts, consciously or unconsciously, frustrated the intention of the legislature was to apply "the plain meaning rule."[3]

That "rule," at one time asserted to be the dominant approach to legislative interpretation, asserts that:

> . . . where the language of an enactment is clear and construction according to its terms does not lead to absurd or impracticable consequences, the words employed are to be taken as the final expression of the meaning intended.[4]

The plain meaning rule has many formulations, but its essential aspect is a denial of

---

[1] *See, e.g.*, Radin, *Statutory Interpretation*, 43 HARV. L. REV. 863 (1930); Curtis, *A Better Theory of Legal Interpretation*, 3 VAND. L. REV. 407 (1950).

[2] Often they seem to have been challenging the legislature to draft a statute with sufficient clarity to overcome the presumption that the common law was not lightly to be altered. *See* Pound, *Common Law and Legislation*, 21 HARV. L. REV. 383 (1908).

[3] Realistic analysis of the plain meaning doctrine, however, must be based upon full recognition that interpretation according to the literal approach does not involve any effort to discover the "intention of the legislature," in the sense of a meaning or purpose which the draftsmen of a statute ever actually entertained. Jones, *The Plain Meaning Rule and Extrinsic Aids in the Interpretation of Federal Statutes*, 25 WASH. U.L.Q. 2, 6 (1939).

[4] *United States v. Missouri Pac. R.R.*, 278 U.S. 269, 278 (1929).

the need to "interpret" unambiguous language. In its name, courts have refused (or purported to refuse) to test the meaning of a particular provision against the broad purpose of a statute, and even refused to look at such "intrinsic" material as the statute's title or preamble. In the federal courts the most common effect of the rule has been to preclude resort to bits of legislative history such as reports, hearings, and debates. It is that aspect of the rule which is the focus of this Comment.

A vintage example of the rule in operation is the famous decision of the United States Supreme Court in *Caminetti v. United States*.[10] The statutory issue in the case was whether the Mann Act, which forbade the taking of a woman across state lines for purposes of "prostitution or debauchery, or for any other immoral purpose," applied to a case of private, non-commercial vice. Although there was ample evidence in the legislative history that Congress was aiming at the "white slave traffic" and did not intend to cover non-commercial vice, the Supreme Court upheld convictions under the Act.

In rejecting proferred evidence of legislative intent the majority said:

> . . . when words are free from doubt they must be taken as the final expression of the legislative intent, and are not to be added to or subtracted from by considerations drawn from titles or designating names or reports, accompanying their introduction or from any extraneous source . . . . The language being plain, and not leading to absurd or wholly impracticable consequences, it is the sole evidence of the ultimate legislative intent.

The dissent, to no avail, argued that the phrase "for any other immoral purpose" was not so clear and unambiguous as the majority had found. It is worth noting that the minority did not reject the plain meaning rule but argued that the term "any other immoral purpose" was ambiguous and, therefore, that resort to extrinsic materials as an aid to interpretation was permissible.

The plain meaning rule's inconsistency with the search for legislative intent does not need protracted exposition.[15] Nor is it necessary to expend much effort in proving the semantic invalidity of the notion that words — especially words like "immorality" — can have fixed meanings apart from the context in which they are used. As is so often the case, the short answer was given by Judge Learned Hand, when he said that "[t]here is no surer way to misread any document than to read it literally."

Although at one time said to be the mandated approach to legislative history, the plain meaning rule was never as widely practiced as preached. American courts never followed the British practice of forbidding any resort to legislative history, and even under the plain meaning rule there were many ways in which a court could look at legislative history, if it wanted to — by characterizing the words as "ambiguous," by finding that their plain meaning led to "absurd" results, or by using extrinsic aids to "confirm" the plain meaning.

The "rule" was thought to have received a death blow in the United States courts with the decision of the Supreme Court in *United States v. American Trucking Associations*. Mr. Justice Reed, speaking for the majority, said:

> When aid to construction of the meaning of words, as used in the statute, is available, there certainly can be no "rule of law" which forbids its use, however clear the words may appear on "superficial examination."[22]

But just as its vigor in life was overstated, so too, have reports of its death been exaggerated. In decisions of the Supreme Court and lower federal courts one periodi-

---

[10] 242 U.S. 470 (1917).

[15] *See* Jones, *supra* note 3; Nutting, *The Ambiguity of Unambiguous Statutes*, 24 MINN. L. REV. 509 (1940).

[22] 310 U.S. at 545 (footnotes omitted).

cally runs into plain meaning language . . . .

One difficulty in assessing the importance of the plain meaning rule today is that there are a number of cases using language which is very similar to the rule but which seems to mean something very different to the courts. The difficulty is compounded by the courts' practice of indiscriminately citing these cases alongside "pure" plain meaning cases as though all stood for the same thing.

NOTES AND QUESTIONS

1. Would adherence to a plain meaning approach necessarily restrict resort to legislative history in statutory interpretation?

2. *See generally* Russell Holder, *Say What You Mean and Mean What You Say: The Resurrection of Plain Meaning in California Courts*, 30 U.C. DAVIS L. REV. 569 (1997).

UNIFORM STATUTE AND RULE CONSTRUCTION ACT (1995)*

SECTION 19. PRIMACY OF TEXT.

The text of a statute or rule is the primary, essential source of its meaning.

Comment

Source: New.

As stated in the Comment to Section 18, Sections 18, 19, and 20, with their comments, are to be read together and set forth a unified step-by-step process that a construer should follow. The primary focus in that process is always the text.

NOTE ON PLAIN MEANING AND THE NEW TEXTUALISM

In the next Chapter, where the use of legislative history is analyzed, a reemphasis on plain meaning and the "new textualism" that arose in the 1980s as part of an attack on the use of legislative history will be analyzed. To the extent that development is based on "plain meaning," it should be introduced here.

In 1991, Professor Frederick Schauer wrote an article describing the reemergence of the plain meaning doctrine in United States Supreme Court decisions and defending this development "in terms of the use of plain language as a second-best coordinating device for multiple decision makers attempting to reach some methodological consensus in the face of substantive disagreements among them." Frederick Schauer, *Statutory Construction and the Coordinating Function of Plain Meaning*, 1990 SUP. CT. REV. 231, 232 (1991). Schauer argued that because of the extraordinarily wide range of statutory interpretation issues reaching the court, the details of which were not as exciting and stimulating to the Justices as, say, constitutional questions, and because of the press of time and the need to seek some agreement among the Justices, the plain meaning approach has been a second-best method of gaining concensus in lieu of a full-blown investigation of all of the statutory interpretation techniques, including the use of legislative history.

> If these perceptions are correct, then the Justices are faced with a coordi-
> nation problem. Given their lack of expertise about the areas involved, and given
> what seems to be some lack of interest in the areas involved, and given some
> presumed time and related constraints, how are the Justices to achieve some
> degree of agreement? Here the virtues of plain meaning seem more compelling.
> If we take as a given the relative unwillingness of the Justices to get totally
> involved in the detailed ramifications of the cases involved, or take as an

---

* Reprinted with permission.

alternative given the likelihood that were they to do so a great deal of disagreement would result, then the reliance on plain meaning may be a hardly novel suboptimizing second-best solution, a way in which people with potentially divergent views and potentially different understandings of what the context would require may still be able to agree about what the language they all share requires. Plain language may provide some minimal mutual understanding that guards something that is shared in the face of widely disparate political views and social experiences.

All of this presupposes that the Justices have some reason for seeking agreement, if not as to results then at least as to the permissible sources for the inquiry. Here there are a number of different stories that might be told, but at least one would see the Justices as people who both want to agree in fact and want to be seen as people who agree with some frequency. Justice Marshall and Justice Scalia are likely never to agree about affirmative action, but they can agree that December 30 is not the same day as December 31, just as they can agree that an action brought by an insurance company is not the same as one brought against one. But if there is shared agreement among all of the Justices that something shared is worth preserving (and here the increase in reliance on plain meaning from the 1988 Term to the 1989 Term may bear some relationship to the decrease in acrimony from the 1988 Term to the 1989 Term), then the search for some common ground is understandable, and the finding of plain meaning as that common ground, despite all its failings, is understandable as well.

Id., at 254–55.[*]

Schauer's article drew a wide response. Professors Alexander Aleinikoff and Theodore Shaw, for example, challenged Schauer's assertion that there really was a resurgence of plain meaning decision making by the Supreme Court, and disagreed that the Justices (or their law clerks) would not do the hard work to master the statutory context of each case. Finally, they argued that the plain meaning approach can so often lead to results at odds with actual legislative intent that it could not be viewed as a "second-best" alternative. T. Alexander Aleinikoff & Theodore M. Shaw, *The Costs of Incoherence: A Comment on Plain Meaning, West Virginia University Hospitals, Inc. v. Casey, and Due Process of Statutory Interpretation*, 45 VAND. L. REV. 687 (1992). Professor Schauer responded in *The Practice and Problems of Plain Meaning: A Response to Aleinikoff and Shaw*, 45 VAND. L. REV. 715 (1992).

For another defense of the plain meaning approach, see John F. Manning, *Textualism as a Nondelegation Doctrine*, 97 COLUM. L. REV. 673 (1997); *Textualism and the Equity of the Statute*, 101 COLUM. L. REV. 1 (2001).

B.　DICTIONARY ACTS, DICTIONARIES AND WORD USAGE

MUSCARELLO v. UNITED STATES
524 U.S. 125 (1998)

JUSTICE BREYER delivered the opinion of the Court.

A provision in the firearms chapter of the federal criminal code imposes a 5-year mandatory prison term upon a person who "uses or carries a firearm" "during and in relation to" a "drug trafficking crime." 18 U.S.C. § 924(c)(1). The question before us is whether the phrase "carries a firearm" is limited to the carrying of firearms on the person. We hold that it is not so limited. Rather, it also applies to a person who knowingly possesses and conveys firearms in a vehicle, including in the locked glove compartment or trunk of a car, which the person accompanies.

---

[*] Reprinted with permission.

I

The question arises in two cases, which we have consolidated for argument. The defendant in the first case, Frank J. Muscarello, unlawfully sold marijuana, which he carried in his truck to the place of sale. Police officers found a handgun locked in the truck's glove compartment. During plea proceedings, Muscarello admitted that he had "carried" the gun "for protection in relation" to the drug offense, App. in No. 96-1654, p. 10a . . . .

II

A

We begin with the statute's language. The parties vigorously contest the ordinary English meaning of the phrase "carries a firearm." Because they essentially agree that Congress intended the phrase to convey its ordinary, and not some special legal, meaning, and because they argue the linguistic point at length, we too have looked into the matter in more than usual depth. Although the word "carry" has many different meanings, only two are relevant here. When one uses the word in the first, or primary, meaning, one can, as a matter of ordinary English, "carry firearms" in a wagon, car, truck, or other vehicle that one accompanies. When one uses the word in a different, rather special, way, to mean, for example, "bearing" or (in slang) "packing" (as in "packing a gun"), the matter is less clear. But, for reasons we shall set out below, we believe Congress intended to use the word in its primary sense and not in this latter, special way.

Consider first the word's primary meaning. The *Oxford English Dictionary* gives as its *first* definition "convey, originally by cart or wagon, hence in any vehicle, by ship, on horseback, etc." 2 Oxford English Dictionary 919 (2d ed. 1989); *see also* Webster's Third New International Dictionary 343 (1986) (*first* definition: "move while supporting (as in a vehicle or in one's hands or arms)"); The Random House Dictionary of the English Language, Unabridged 319 (2d ed. 1987) (*first* definition: "to take or support from one place to another; convey; transport").

The origin of the word "carries" explains why the first, or basic, meaning of the word "carry" includes conveyance in a vehicle. *See* The Barnhart Dictionary of Etymology 146 (1988) (tracing the word from Latin "carum," which means "car" or "cart"); 2 Oxford English Dictionary, *supra*, at 919 (tracing the word from Old French "carier" and the late Latin "carricare," which meant to "convey in a car"); The Oxford Dictionary of English Etymology 148 (C. Onions ed. 1966) (same); The Barnhart Dictionary of Etymology, *supra*, at 143 (explaining that the term "car" has been used to refer to the automobile since 1896).

The greatest of writers have used the word with this meaning. *See, e.g.,* the King James Bible, 2 Kings 9:28 ("[H]is servants carried him in a chariot to Jerusalem"); *id.,* Isaiah 30:6 ("[T]hey will carry their riches upon the shoulders of young asses"). Robinson Crusoe says, "[w]ith my boat I carry'd away every Thing." D. Defoe, Robinson Crusoe 174 (J. Crowley ed. 1972). And the owners of Queequeg's ship, Melville writes, "had lent him a [wheelbarrow], in which to carry his heavy chest to his boardinghouse." H. Melville, Moby Dick 43 (U. Chicago 1952). This Court, too, has spoken of the "carrying" of drugs in a car or in its "trunk." *California v. Acevedo,* 500 U.S. 565, 572–573 (1991); *Florida v. Jimeno,* 500 U.S. 248, 249 (1991).

These examples do not speak directly about carrying guns. But there is nothing linguistically special about the fact that weapons, rather than drugs, are being carried. Robinson Crusoe might have carried a gun in his boat; Queequeg might have borrowed a wheelbarrow in which to carry, not a chest, but a harpoon. And, to make certain that there is no special ordinary English restriction (unmentioned in dictionaries) upon the use of "carry" in respect to guns, we have surveyed modern press usage, albeit crudely, by searching computerized newspaper databases — both the New York Times database in Lexis/Nexis, and the "US News" database in Westlaw. We looked for sentences in which the words "carry," "vehicle," and "weapon" (or variations thereof) all appear. We found thousands of such sentences, and random sampling suggests that many, perhaps more than one third, are sentences used to convey the meaning at issue here, *i.e.*, the carrying of guns in a car.

. . . .

Now consider a different, somewhat special meaning of the word "carry" — a meaning upon which the linguistic arguments of petitioners and the dissent must rest. The Oxford English Dictionary's *twenty-sixth* definition of "carry" is "bear, wear, hold up, or sustain, as one moves about; habitually to bear about with one." 2 Oxford English Dictionary, *supra*, at 921. Webster's defines "carry" as "to move while supporting," not just in a vehicle, but also "in one's hands or arms." Webster's Third New International Dictionary, *supra*, at 343. And Black's Law Dictionary defines the entire phrase "carry arms or weapons" as

"To wear, bear or carry them upon the person or in the clothing or in a pocket, for the purpose of use, or for the purpose of being armed and ready for offensive or defensive action in case of a conflict with another person." Black's Law Dictionary 214 (6th ed. 1990).

These special definitions, however, do not purport to *limit* the "carrying of arms" to the circumstances they describe. No one doubts that one who bears arms on his person "carries a weapon." But to say that is not to deny that one may *also* "carry a weapon" tied to the saddle of a horse or placed in a bag in a car.

Nor is there any linguistic reason to think that Congress intended to limit the word "carries" in the statute to any of these special definitions. To the contrary, all these special definitions embody a form of an important, but secondary, meaning of "carry," a meaning that suggests support rather than movement or transportation, as when, for example, a column "carries" the weight of an arch. 2 Oxford English Dictionary, *supra*, at 919, 921. In this sense a gangster might "carry" a gun (in colloquial language, he might "pack a gun") even though he does not move from his chair. It is difficult to believe, however, that Congress intended to limit the statutory word to this definition — imposing special punishment upon the comatose gangster while ignoring drug lords who drive to a sale carrying an arsenal of weapons in their van.

We recognize, as the dissent emphasizes, that the word "carry" has other meanings as well. But those other meanings, (*e.g.*, "carry all he knew," "carries no colours"), *see post*, at 6, are not relevant here. And the fact that speakers often do *not* add to the phrase "carry a gun" the words "in a car" is of no greater relevance here than the fact that millions of Americans did *not* see Muscarello carry a gun in his car. The relevant linguistic facts are that the word "carry" in its ordinary sense includes carrying in a car and that the word, used in its ordinary sense, keeps the same meaning whether one carries a gun, a suitcase, or a banana.

Given the ordinary meaning of the word "carry," it is not surprising to find that the Federal Circuit Courts of Appeals have unanimously concluded that "carry" is not limited to the carrying of weapons directly on the person but can include their carriage in a car . . . .

B

We now explore more deeply the purely legal question of whether Congress intended to use the word "carry" in its ordinary sense, or whether it intended to limit the scope of the phrase to instances in which a gun is carried "on the person." We conclude that neither the statute's basic purpose nor its legislative history support circumscribing the scope of the word "carry" by applying an "on the person" limitation.

. . . .

C

We are not convinced by petitioners' remaining arguments to the contrary. First, they say that our definition of "carry" makes it the equivalent of "transport." Yet, Congress elsewhere in related statutes used the word "transport" deliberately to signify a different, and broader, statutory coverage . . . .

As we interpret the statutory scheme, it makes sense. Congress has imposed a variable penalty with no mandatory minimum sentence upon a person who "transports" (or "ships" or "receives") a firearm knowing it will be used to commit any "offense punishable by imprisonment for [more than] . . . one year," § 924(b), and it has imposed a 5-year mandatory minimum sentence upon one who "carries" a firearm "during and in relation to" a "drug trafficking crime," § 924(c). The first subsection imposes a less strict sentencing regime upon one who, say, ships firearms by mail for use in a crime elsewhere; the latter subsection imposes a mandatory sentence upon one who, say, brings a weapon with him (on his person or in his car) to the site of a drug sale.

Second, petitioners point out that, in *Bailey v. United States*, 516 U.S. 137 (1995), we considered the related phrase "uses . . . a firearm" found in the same statutory provision now before us. *See* 18 U.S.C. § 924(c)(1) ("uses or carries a firearm"). We construed the term "use" narrowly, limiting its application to the "active employment" of a firearm. *Bailey*, 516 U.S. at 144. Petitioners argue that it would be anomalous to construe broadly the word "carries," its statutory next-door neighbor.

In *Bailey*, however, we limited "use" of a firearm to "active employment" in part because we assumed "that Congress . . . intended each term to have a particular, non-superfluous meaning." *Id.*, at 146. A broader interpretation of "use," we said, would have swallowed up the term "carry." *Ibid.* But "carry" as we interpret that word does not swallow up the term "use." "Use" retains the same independent meaning we found for it in *Bailey*, where we provided examples involving the displaying or the bartering of a gun. *Ibid.* "Carry" also retains an independent meaning, for, under *Bailey*, carrying a gun in a car does not necessarily involve the gun's "active employment." More importantly, having construed "use" narrowly in *Bailey*, we cannot also construe "carry" narrowly without undercutting the statute's basic objective. For the narrow interpretation would remove the act of carrying a gun in a car entirely from the statute's reach, leaving a gap in coverage that we do not believe Congress intended.

In sum, the "generally accepted contemporary meaning" of the word "carry" includes the carrying of a firearm in a vehicle. The purpose of this statute warrants its application in such circumstances. The limiting phrase "during and in relation to" should prevent misuse of the statute to penalize those whose conduct does not create the risks of harm at which the statute aims.

For these reasons, we conclude that the petitioner's conduct falls within the scope of the phrase "carries a firearm." The decisions of the Court of Appeals are affirmed.

It is so ordered.

JUSTICE GINSBURG, with whom THE CHIEF JUSTICE, JUSTICE SCALIA, and JUSTICE SOUTER, join, dissenting.

. . . .

Without doubt, "carries" is a word of many meanings, definable to mean or include carting about in a vehicle. But that encompassing definition is not a ubiquitously necessary one. Nor, in my judgement, is it a proper construction of "carries" as the term appears in § 924(c)(1). In line with *Bailey* and the principle of lenity the Court has long followed, I would confine "carries a firearm," for § 924(c)(1) purposes, to the undoubted meaning of that expression in the relevant context. I would read the words to indicate not merely keeping arms on one's premises or in one's vehicle, but bearing them in such manner as to be ready for use as a weapon.

  . . . .

B

Unlike the Court, I do not think dictionaries, surveys of press reports, or the Bible tell us, dispositively, what "carries" means embedded in § 924(c)(1). On definitions, "carry" in legal formulations could mean, *inter alia*, transport, possess, have in stock, prolong (carry over), be infectious, or wear or bear on one's person. At issue here is not "carries" at large but "carries a firearm." The Court's computer search of newspapers is revealing in this light. Carrying guns in a car showed up as the meaning "perhaps more than one third" of the time. *Ante*, at 4. One is left to wonder what meaning showed up some two thirds of the time. Surely a most familiar meaning is, as the Constitution's Second Amendment ("keep and *bear* Arms") (emphasis added) and BLACK'S LAW DICTIONARY, at 214, indicate: "wear, bear, or carry . . . upon the person or in the clothing or in a pocket, for the purpose . . . of being armed and ready for offensive or defensive action in a case of conflict with another person."

On lessons from literature, a scan of Bartlett's and other quotation collections shows how highly selective the Court's choices are. *See Ante*, 3–4. If "[t]he greatest of writers" have used "carry" to mean convey or transport in a vehicle, so have they used the hydra-headed word to mean, *inter alia*, carry in one's hand, arms, head, heart, or soul, sans vehicle. Consider, among countless examples:

    "[H]e shall gather the lambs with his arm, and carry them in his bosom." The King James Bible, Isaiah 40:11.

    "And still they gaz'd, and still the wonder grew, That one small head could carry all he knew." O. GOLDSMITH, THE DESERTED VILLAGE, II. 215–216, in THE POETICAL WORDS OF OLIVER GODSMITH 30 (A. Dobson ed. 1949).

    "There's a Legion that never was 'listed, That carries no colours or crest." R. KIPLING, THE LOST REGION, st. 1, in RUDYARD KIPLING'S VERSE, 1885–1918, p. 222 (1920).

    "There is a homely adage which runs, 'Speak softly and carry a big stick; you will go far.;'" T. Roosevelt, Speech at Minnesota State Fair, Sept. 2, 1901, in J. BARTLETT, FAMILIAR QUOTATIONS 575:16 (J. Kaplan ed. 1992).[6]

These and the Court's lexicological sources demonstrate vividly that "carry" is a word commonly used to convey various messages. Such references, given their variety, are not reliable indicators of what Congress meant, in § 924(c)(1), by "carries a firearm."

NOTES AND QUESTIONS

1. For an important survey of the variety of linguistic ambiguity that can appear in statutes, see Clark D. Cunningham, Judith N. Levi, Georgia M. Green & Jeffrey P. Kaplan, *Plain Meaning and Hard Cases*, 103 YALE L.J. 1561 (1994).

2. What are the various sources the *Muscarello* court resorts to in its search for meaning? How legitimate are these sources?

3. *Muscarello* presents one of the classic problems in statutory interpretation:

---

[6] Popular films and television productions provide corroborative illustrations. In "The Magnificent Seven," for example, O'Reilly (played by Charles Bronson) says: "You think I am brave because I carry a gun; well, your fathers are much braver because they carry responsibility, for you, your brothers, your sisters, and your mothers." *See* us.imdb.com/M/search_quotes?for=carry. And in the television series M*A*S*H, Hawkeye Pierce (played by Alan Alda) presciently proclaims: "I will not carry a gun . . . I'll carry your books, I'll carry a torch, I'll carry a tune, I'll carry on, carry over, carry forward, Cary Grant, cash and carry, carry me back to Old Virginia, I'll even 'hari-kari' if you show me how, but I will not carry a gun!" *See* www.geocities.com/Hollywood/8915/mashquotes.html.

ascertaining the *meaning* of a term or phrase used in a statute. We will see this problem reappear throughout these materials on statutory interpretation. Other classic statutory interpretation problems include "gaps," where the statute apparently does not include a provision covering a factual situation apparently within the statute's scope, and "overlap," where more than one statute seems to apply to the same set of facts or circumstances. Try to remain aware of exactly the type of statutory interpretation problem with which you are confronted.

4. What is the underlying rationale for resort to dictionaries in interpreting statutes? *See generally* Note, *Looking it Up: Dictionaries and Statutory Interpretation*, 107 HARV. L. REV. 1437 (1994); A. Raymond Randolph, *Dictionaries, Plain Meaning, and Context in Statutory Interpretation*, 17 HARV. L. & PUB. POL'Y 71 (1994); Lawrence Solan, *When Judges Use the Dictionary*, 68 AM. SPEECH 50 (1993); Ellen Aprill, *The Law of the Word: Dictionary Shopping in the Supreme Court*, 30 ARIZ. ST. L.J. 275 (1998).

5. The *Harvard Law Review* Note "*Looking it Up*," cited above, documented a sharp increase in the United States Supreme Court's reliance on dictionaries, and associated this with a plain meaning approach. Does reliance on dictionaries necessarily reflect an adherence to plain meaning?

6. Analyzing the 1996 United States Supreme Court Term, Professor Jane Schacter concluded that the Court's reliance on dictionaries had declined, but was still significant. Jane S. Schacter, *The Confounding Common Law Originalism in Recent Supreme Court Statutory Interpretation: Implications for the Legislative History Debate and Beyond*, 51 STAN. L. REV. 1, 16 (1998).

ROWLAND v. CALIFORNIA MENS COLONY U.S.
506 U.S. 194 (1993)

JUSTICE SOUTER delivered the opinion of the Court.

Title 28 U.S.C. § 1915, providing for appearances *in forma pauperis*, authorizes federal courts to favor any "person" meeting its criteria with a series of benefits including dispensation from the obligation to prepay fees, costs, or security for bringing, defending, or appealing a lawsuit. Here, we are asked to decide whether the term "person" as so used applies to the artificial entities listed in the definition of that term contained in 1 U.S.C. § 1. We hold that it does not, so that only a natural person may qualify for treatment *in forma pauperis* under § 1915.

I

Respondent California Mens's Colony, Unit II Men's Advisory Council is a representative association of prison inmates organized at the behest of one of the petitioners, the Warden of the Colony, to advise him of complaints and recommendations from the inmates, and to communicate his administrative decisions back to them. The general prison population elects the Council's members.

In a complaint filed in the District Court in 1989, the Council charged the petitioners, state correctional officers, with violations of the Eighth and Fourteenth Amendments in discontinuing their practice of providing free tobacco to indigent inmates. The Council sought leave to proceed *in forma pauperis* under 28 U.S.C. § 1915(a), claiming by affidavit of the Council's Chairman that the Warden forbad the Council to hold funds of its own . . . .

II

A

Both § 1915(a), which the Council invoked in seeking to be excused from prepaying filing fees, and § 1915(d) employ the word "person" in controlling access to four benefits provided by § 1915 and a related statute . . . .

"Persons" were not always so entitled, for the benefits of § 1915 were once available only to "citizens," a term held, in the only two cases on the issue, to exclude corporations. *See Atlantic S.S. Corp. v. Kelley*, 79 F.2d 339, 340 (5th Cir. 1935) (construing the predecessor to § 1915); *Quittner v. Motion Picture Producers & Distributors of America, Inc.*, 70 F.2d 331, 332 (2d Cir. 1934) (same). In 1959, however, Congress passed a one-sentence provision that "section 1915(a) of title 28, United States Code, is amended by deleting the word 'citizen' and inserting in place thereof the word 'person.' " Pub. L. 86-320, 73 Stat. 590. For this amendment, the sole reason cited in the legislative history was to extend the statutory benefits to aliens.

B

The relevant portion of the Dictionary Act, 1 U.S.C. § 1, provides (as it did in 1959) that

> "[i]n determining the meaning of any Act of Congress, unless the context indicates otherwise —
>
> "The wor[d] 'person' . . . include[s] corporations, companies, associations, firms, partnerships, societies, and joint stock companies, as well as individuals."

See 1 U.S.C. § 1 (1958). "Context" here means the text of the Act of Congress surrounding the word at issue, or the texts of other related congressional Acts, and this is simply an instance of the word's ordinary meaning: "[t]he part or parts of a discourse preceding or following a 'text' or passage or a word, or so intimately associated with it as to throw light upon its meaning." WEBSTER'S NEW INTERNATIONAL DICTIONARY 576 (2d ed. 1942). While "context" can carry a secondary meaning of "[a]ssociated surroundings, whether material or mental," *ibid.*, we doubt that the broader sense applies here. The Dictionary Act uses "context" to give an instruction about how to "determin[e] the meaning of a[n] Act of Congress," a purpose suggesting the primary sense. If Congress had meant to point further afield, as to legislative history, for example, it would have been natural to use a more spacious phrase, like "evidence of congressional intent," in place of "context."

If "context" thus has a narrow compass, the "indication" contemplated by 1 U.S.C. § 1 has a broader one. The Dictionary Act's very reference to contextual "indication" bespeaks something more than an express contrary definition, and courts would hardly need direction where Congress had thought to include an express, specialized definition for the purpose of a particular Act; ordinary rules of statutory construction would prefer the specific definition over the Dictionary Act's general one. Where a court needs help is in the awkward case where Congress provides no particular definition, but the definition in 1 U.S.C. § 1 seems not to fit. There it is that the qualification "unless the context indicates otherwise" has a real job to do, in excusing the court from forcing a square peg into a round hole.

The point at which the indication of particular meaning becomes insistent enough to excuse the poor fit is of course a matter of judgement, but one can say that "indicates" certainly imposes less of a burden than, say, "requires" or "necessitates." One can also say that this exception from the general rule would be superfluous if the context "indicate[d] otherwise" only when use of the general definition would be incongruous enough to invoke the common mandate of statutory construction to avoid absurd results.[3] *See, e.g., McNary v. Haitian Refugee Center, Inc.,* 498 U.S. 479 (1991) ("It is presumable that Congress legislates with knowledge of our basic rules of statutory construction"). In fine, a contrary "indication" may raise a specter short of inanity, and with something less than syllogistic force.

III

Four contextual features indicate that "person" in § 1915(a) refers only to individuals, the first being the provision of § 1915(d) that "[t]he court *may* request an attorney to represent any such person unable to employ counsel." (Emphasis added.) This permissive language suggests that Congress assumed the court would in many cases not "request" counsel, *see Mallard v. United States District Court,* 490 U.S. 296, 301–302 (1989) (holding that § 1915(d) does not authorize mandatory appointments of counsel), leaving the "person" proceeding *in forma pauperis* to conduct litigation on his own behalf. Underlying this congressional assumption are probably two others: that the "person" in question enjoys the legal capacity to appear before a court for the purpose of seeking such benefits as appointment of counsel without being represented by professional counsel beforehand, and likewise enjoys the capacity to litigate without counsel if the court chooses to provide none, in the exercise of the discretion apparently conferred by the permissive language. The state of the law, however, leaves it highly unlikely that Congress would have made either assumption about an artificial entity like an association, and thus just as unlikely that "person" in § 1915 was meant to cover more than individuals. It has been the law for the better part of two centuries, for example, that a corporation may appear in the federal courts only through licensed counsel . . . .

The second revealing feature of § 1915(d) is its description of the affidavit required by § 1915(a) as an "allegation of poverty." Poverty, in its primary sense, is a human condition, to be "[w]anting in material riches or goods; lacking in the comforts of life; needy," Webster's New International Dictionary 1919 (2d ed. 1942), and it was in just such distinctly human terms that this Court had established the standard of eligibility long before Congress considered extending *in forma pauperis* treatment from "citizens" to "persons." As we first said in 1948, "[w]e think an affidavit is sufficient which states that one cannot because of his poverty 'pay or give security for the costs . . . and still be able to provide' himself and dependents 'with the necessities of life.' " *Adkins v. E.I. DuPont de Nemours & Co.,* 335 U.S. 331, 339. But artificial entities do not fit this description. Whatever the state of its treasury, an association or corporation cannot be said to "lac[k] the comforts of life," any more than one can sensibly ask whether it can provide itself, let alone its dependents, with life's "necessities." Artificial entities may be insolvent, but they are not well spoke of as "poor." So eccentric a description is not lightly to be imputed to Congress.

The third clue is much like the second. Section 1915(a) authorizes the courts to allow litigation without the prepayment of fees, costs or security "by a person who makes affidavit that he is unable to pay such costs or give security therefor," and requires that the affidavit also "state the nature of the action, defense or appeal and affiant's belief that he is entitled to redress." Because artificial entities cannot take oaths, they cannot make affidavits . . . .

Next, some weight should probably be given to the requirement of § 1915(a) that the affidavit state the "affiant's belief that *he* is entitled to redress" (emphasis added). "He," read naturally, refers to the "affiant" as the person claiming *in forma pauperis* entitlement. If the affiant is an agent making an affidavit on behalf of an artificial entity, however, it would wrench the rules of grammar to read "he" as referring to the entity. Finally, and most significantly, the affidavit requirement cannot serve its deterrent function fully when applied to artificial entities . . . .

---

[3] This rule has been applied throughout history of 1 U.S.C. § 1 and its predecessors . . . .

The fourth clue to congressional understanding is the failure of § 1915 even to hint at a resolution of the issues raised by applying an "inability to pay" standard to artificial entities . . . .

Justice Thomas, with whom Justice Blackmun, Justice Stevens, and Justice Kennedy join, dissenting.

The parties agree that the interpretive point of departure in deciding whether an association is a "person" for purposes of the *in forma pauperis* statute, 28 U.S.C. § 1915, is the first section of the United States Code. The question presented in this case may thus be formulated as follows: Must the presumption codified in 1 U.S.C. § 1 — namely, that "[i]n determining the meaning of any Act of Congress," the word "person" should be construed to include an association — be given effect in determining the meaning of the *in forma pauperis* statute, or has the presumption been overcome because the context "indicates otherwise"? The answer to that question ultimately turns on the meaning of the phrase "unless the context indicates otherwise." In my view, the Court's holding rests on an impermissibly broad reading of that language. I see no basis for concluding that an association is not entitled to *in forma pauperis* status.

The Court states that the word "context" in U.S.C. § 1 "means the text of the Act of Congress surrounding the word at issue, or the texts of other related congressional Acts." *Ante*, 4–5. The Court then goes on to say that the word "indicates" has a broader scope than the word "context"; that it "imposes less of a burden than, say, 'requires' or 'necessitates' "; and that "a contrary 'indication' may raise a specter short of inanity, and with something less than syllogistic force." *Ante*, at 5, 6. I share the Court's understanding of the word "context," I do not share the Court's understanding of the word "indicates," however, because its gloss on that word apparently permits (and perhaps even requires) courts to look beyond the words of a statute, and to consider the policy judgements on which those words may or may not be based. (It certainly enables the Court to do so in this case). I agree that the exception to the rule of construction codified in 1 U.S.C. § 1 is not susceptible of precise definition, and that determining whether "the context indicates otherwise" in any given case is necessarily "a matter of judgement." *Ante*, at 5. Whatever "unless the context indicates otherwise" means, however, it cannot mean "unless there are sound policy reasons for concluding otherwise."

. . . .

II

The Court's holding rests on the view that § 1915 has four "contextual features," *ante*, at 6, indicating that only a natural person is entitled to *in forma pauperis* status. These "features" include a few select words in § 1915 and a number of practical problems that may arise when artificial entities seek to proceed *in forma pauperis*. I do not believe that § 1915 contains any language indicating that an association is not a "person" for purposes of that provision, and I do not think it is appropriate to rely upon what are at bottom policy considerations in deciding whether "the context indicates otherwise." In my view, none of the "contextual features" discussed by the Court, either alone or in combination with the others, can overcome the statutory presumption that an association is a "person."

. . . .

III

Congress has created a rule of statutory construction (an association is a "person") and an exception to that rule (an association is not a "person" if the "context indicates otherwise"), but the Court has permitted the exception to devour the rule. In deciding that an association is not a "person" for purposes of 28 U.S.C. § 1915(a), the Court effectively reads 1 U.S.C. § 1 as if the presumption ran the other way — as if the statute said that "in determining the meaning of any Act of Congress, unless the context indicates otherwise, the word 'person' does *not* include corporations, partnerships, and associations." While it might make sense as a matter of policy to exclude associations and other artificial entities from the benefits of the *in forma pauperis* statute, I do not believe that Congress has done so.

I respectfully dissent.

NOTES AND QUESTIONS

1. What is the difference between a court's reliance on a dictionary and a dictionary act?

2. How does a dictionary act differ from a definition section in a bill?

UNIFORM STATUTE AND RULE CONSTRUCTION ACT (1995)*

SECTION 1. APPLICABILITY.

(a) This [Act] applies to a statute enacted or rule adopted before, on, or after the effective date of this [Act], unless the statute or rule expressly provides otherwise, the context of its language requires otherwise, or the application of this [Act] to the statute or rule would be infeasible.

NIX v. HEDDEN
149 U.S. 304 (1893)

Statement by MR. JUSTICE GRAY:

This was an action brought February 4, 1887, against the collector of the port of New York to recover back duties paid under protest on tomatoes imported by the plaintiff from the West Indies in the spring of 1886, which the collector assessed under "Schedule G. — Provisions," of the tariff act of March 3, 1883, (chapter 121) imposing a duty on "vegetables in their natural state, or in salt or brine, not specially enumerated or provided for in this act, ten per centum ad valorem"; and which the plaintiffs contended came within the clause in the free list of the same act, "Fruits, green, ripe, or dried, not specially enumerated or provided for in this act." 22 Stat. 504, 519.

At the trial the plaintiff's counsel, after reading in evidence definitions of the words "fruit" and "vegetables" from Webster's Dictionary, Worcester's Dictionary, and the Imperial Dictionary, called two witnesses, who had been for 30 years in the business of selling fruit and vegetables, and asked them, after hearing these definitions, to say whether these words had "any special meaning in trade or commerce, different from those read."

One of the witnesses answered as follows: "Well, it does not classify all things there, but they are correct as far as they go. It does not take all kinds of fruit or vegetables; it takes a portion of them. I think the words 'fruit' and 'vegetable' have the same meaning in trade today that they had on March 1, 1883. I understand that the term 'fruit' is applied in trade only to such plants or parts of plants as contain the seeds. There are more vegetables than those in the enumeration given in Webster's Dictionary under the term 'vegetable,' as 'cabbage, cauliflower, turnips, potatoes, peas, beans, and the like,' probably covered by the words 'and the like.' "

The other witness testified: "I don't think the term 'fruit' or the term 'vegetables' had, in March, 1883, and prior thereto, any special meaning in trade and commerce in this country different from that which I have read here from the dictionaries."

The plaintiff's counsel then read in evidence from the same dictionaries the definitions of the word "tomato."

The defendant's counsel then read in evidence from Webster's Dictionary the

---

* Reprinted with permission.

definitions of the words "pea," "egg plant," "cucumber," "squash," and "pepper."

The plaintiff then read in evidence from Webster's and Worcester's dictionaries the definitions of "potato," "turnip," "parsnip," "cauliflower," "cabbage," "carrot," and "bean."

No other evidence was offered by either party. The Court, upon the defendant's motion, directed a verdict for him, which was returned, and judgment rendered thereon. The plaintiffs duly excepted to the instruction, and sued out this writ of error.

. . . .

Mr. Justice Gray, after stating the facts in the foregoing language, delivered the opinion of the Court.

The single question in this case is whether tomatoes, considered as provisions, are to be classed as "vegetables" or as "fruit," within the meaning of the tariff act of 1883.

The only witnesses called at the trial testified that neither "vegetables" nor "fruit" had any special meaning in trade or commerce different from that given in the dictionaries, and that they had the same meaning in trade today that they had in March, 1883.

The passages cited from the dictionaries define the word "fruit" as the seed of plants, or that part of plants which contains the seed, and especially the juicy, pulpy products of certain plants, covering and containing the seed. These definitions have no tendency to show that tomatoes are "fruit," as distinguished from "vegetables," in common speech, or within the meaning of the tariff act.

There being no evidence that the words "fruit" and "vegetables" have acquired any special meaning in trade or commerce, they must receive their ordinary meaning. Of that meaning the Court is bound to take judicial notice, as it does in regard to all words in our own tongue; and upon such a question dictionaries are admitted, not as evidence, but only as aids to the memory and understanding of the Court. *Brown v. Piper*, 91 U.S. 37, 42; *Jones v. United States*, 137 U.S. 202, 216, 11 S. Ct. 80; *Nelson v. Cushing*, 2 Cush. 519, 532, 533; *Page v. Fawcet*, 1 Leon. 242; Tayl. Ev. (8th Ed.) §§ 16, 21.

Botanically speaking, tomatoes are the fruit of a vine, just as are cucumbers, squashes, beans, and peas. But in the common language of the people, whether sellers or consumers of provisions, all these are vegetables which are grown in kitchen gardens, and which, whether eaten cooked or raw, are, like potatoes, carrots, parsnips, turnips, beets, cauliflower, cabbage, celery, and lettuce, usually served at dinner in, with, or after the soup, fish, or meats which constitute the principal part of the repast, and not, like fruits generally, as dessert.

The attempt to class tomatoes as fruit is not unlike a recent attempt to class beans as seeds, of which Mr. Justice Bradley, speaking for this Court, said: "We do not see why they should be classified as seeds, any more than walnuts should be so classified. Both are seeds, in the language of botany or natural history, but not in commerce nor in common parlance. On the other hand in speaking generally of provisions, beans may well be included under the term 'vegetables.' As an article of food on our tables, whether baked or boiled, or forming the basis of soup, they are used as a vegetable, as well when ripe as when green. This is the principal use to which they are put. Beyond the common knowledge which we have on this subject, very little evidence is necessary, or can be produced." *Robertson v. Salomon*, 130 U.S. 412, 414, 9 S. Ct. 559.

Judgment affirmed.

NOTES AND QUESTIONS

1. Should the courts ever rely on a technical definition that can be established only with difficulty, that is, with special proof? Is the Court's distinction between "ordinary meaning" or "common knowledge" and dictionary definitions an appropriate resolution in most cases? Should the dictionary definition of a word be given equal weight with that word's easily established technical definition? When a legislature intends a word to be interpreted technically, or as a term of art, should this not be spelled out with particularity or in a definitional section?

2. What effect might the fact that one of the parties was the government tax collector have had on the case?

3. Is there any reason to believe the legislature meant to use the ordinary meaning of words rather than the dictionary meaning? Does the continuous change in contemporary language create somewhat out-of-date dictionaries? Was a judicial rule used as a means of determining legislative intent or was it a device to fill a gap which had occurred? Would a legislature ever intend a word to be interpreted according to "ordinary meaning" or "common knowledge" as opposed to the dictionary definition of that word? Is the dictionary definition not in fact the "ordinary or popularly accepted meaning"?

UNIFORM STATUTE AND RULE CONSTRUCTION ACT (1995)*

§ 2 Common and Technical Usage.

Unless a word or phrase is defined in the statute or rule being construed, its meaning is determined by its context, the rules of grammar, and common usage. A word or phrase that has acquired a technical or particular meaning in a particular context has that meaning if it is used in that context.

C. REFERENTIAL LEGISLATION: INTERPRETING STATUTORY CROSS REFERENCES

UNIFORM STATUTE AND RULE CONSTRUCTION ACT (1995)*

§ 12 Incorporation by Reference.

  (a) A statute or rule that incorporates by reference another statute of this [State] incorporates a later enactment or amendment of the other statute.
  (b) A statute that incorporates by reference a rule of this [State] does not incorporate a later adoption or amendment of the rule.
  (c) A rule that incorporates by reference another rule of this [State] incorporates a later adoption or amendment of the other rule.
  (d) A statute or rule that incorporates by reference a statute or rule of another jurisdiction does not incorporate a later enactment or adoption or amendment of the other statute or rule.

ERNEST E. MEANS,
STATUTORY CROSS REFERENCES —
THE "LOOSE CANNON" OF STATUTORY CONSTRUCTION IN FLORIDA,
9 FLORIDA STATE UNIVERSITY LAW REVIEW 1 (1981)*

I. *Introduction*

Considering the flood of legislation passed in recent years by state legislatures and Congress, it is becoming less and less likely that the practitioner can ever afford to ignore statutory materials in researching a legal problem. But once the Florida

---

practitioner turns to the Florida Statutes, the likelihood is that he will encounter, in the text of the law consulted, at least one specific reference to some other provision of Florida law. Of the approximately 16,000 sections making up the Florida Statutes, some 5,500 contain such references. In all, there are about 13,000 specific references to other provisions of the Florida Statutes.

Statutory cross referencing is by no means peculiar to Florida or modern times. It appeared in legislation of the English Parliament as early as the thirteenth century and was commonly utilized in the early years of the Canadian provinces and the American colonies.[3]

At the present time, other states apparently rely on statutory cross references to about the same extent as Florida.

CITY OF WARRENSBURG v. BOARD OF REGENTS OF CENTRAL MISSOURI STATE UNIVERSITY
562 S.W.2d 340 (Mo. 1978)

HENDLEY, JUDGE.

This is an action by the City of Warrensburg (City) seeking a money judgment against the Board of Regents of Central Missouri State University (University) for city imposed sales taxes not collected but allegedly due the City upon sales made (or services rendered) by the University . . . . The University appealed, contending, inter alia, that sales made by it are exempt from the provisions of the sales tax ordinances by reason of the provisions of sections of state statutes, and, therefore, it was not required to and did not collect the tax and is not liable therefor . . . .

The authority of cities to enact ordinances imposing a 1% Sales tax comes from the City Sales Tax Act. Subsection 1(2) of § 94.540, RSMo 1969, relating to exemptions, adopts by reference the exemption provisions of § 144.040, one of the sections of the state Sales Tax Law. Subsection 1(2) of § 94.540 is, in pertinent part, as follows:

"1. The following provisions shall govern the collection by the director of revenue of the tax imposed by sections 94.500 to 94.570: . . .

"(2) All exemptions granted to agencies of government, organizations, persons and to the sale of certain articles and items of tangible personal property and taxable services under the provisions of sections 144.010 to 144.510, RSMo, are hereby made applicable to the imposition and collection of the tax imposed by sections 94.500 to 94.570."

When the City Sales Tax Act was adopted, § 144.040 read as follows:

"In addition to the exemptions under section 144.030 there shall also be exempted from the provisions of sections 144.010 to 144.510, all *sales made by or to* religious, charitable, eleemosynary institutions, penal institutions and industries operated by the department of penal institutions or *educational institutions supported by public funds* or by religious organizations, in the conduct of the regular religious, charitable, eleemosynary, penal or educational functions and activities, and all sales made by or to a state relief agency in the exercise of relief functions and activities." (Emphasis added.)

Section 144.040 was amended in 1971 by dividing it into two subsections and by making changes in the extent or breadth of coverage of the exemption of certain institutions. One change, said by the City to be crucial here, is that the exemption of an "institution of higher education supported by public funds" was narrowed by limiting it

---

[3] Poldervaart, *Legislation by Reference — A Statutory Jungle*, 38 IOWA L. REV. 705, 706 (1953), citing to Statute of Westminster II, c.11 (1285); Read, *Is Referential Legislation Worth While?* 25 MINN. L. REV. 261, 262 (1941).

to sales made to such institution, so that sales made by such an institution were no longer exempt.

The University contends that the exemption provisions of § 144.040 adopted in 1969 by subsection 1(2) of § 94.540 and thereby made a part of the City Sales Tax Act was not changed by the 1971 amendment of § 144.040. In other words, the University argues that the adoption of specific provisions of a law includes only those provisions as they exist at the time of adoption; that it does not include later modifications of those provisions by amendment of the law adopted, absent a clear expression in the adopting law that it was also intended thereby to adopt any subsequent amendment of those provisions.

This court said in *State v. Rogers*, 253 Mo. 399, 161 S.W. 770, at p. 772 (1913):

> "When a reference statute specifically designates the section or article of the statute of which it is made a part, such reference statute will not be changed or modified by any subsequent change in the statute to which it refers . . . . [W]here the reference statute pertains only to a method of procedure and refers generally to some statute which defines how certain things may be done, such reference statute will be expanded, modified, or changed every time the statute referred to is changed by the Legislature." *See also Gaston v. Lamkin*, 115 Mo. 20, 33, 21 S.W. 1100, 1103 (banc 1893).

The court stated the rule succinctly in *Crohn v. Kansas City Home Telephone Co.*, 131 Mo. App. 313, 109 S.W. 1068 at l.c. 1070 (1908): "An act adopting by reference the whole or a portion of another statute means the law as existing at the time of adoption, and does not adopt any subsequent addition thereto or modification thereof."

In *Hassett v. Welch*, 303 U.S. 303, 58 S. Ct. 559, 82 L. Ed. 858 (1938) the court resorted to the use of this canon of construction in a case involving the construction of a taxing statute, stating the canon to be: " 'Where one statute adopts the particular provisions of another by a specific and descriptive reference to the statute or provisions adopted, the effect is the same as though the statute or provisions adopted had been incorporated bodily into the adopting statute . . . . Such adoption takes the statute as it exists at the time of adoption and does not include subsequent additions or modifications of the statute so taken unless it does so by express intent.' "[7]

There can be no doubt here as to which provisions of the state Sales Tax Law § 94.540, Subsection 1(2) intended to adopt and make applicable to the imposition and collection of the sales tax authorized by the City Sales Tax Act. It adopted the *exemption* provisions. It did so by making "specific and descriptive reference" to those "particular provisions." This adoption was of such nature that it did not include any subsequent amendment of those provisions. Therefore, the exemption provisions of the City Sales Tax Act were not affected by and remain the same as they were before the 1971 amendment of § 144.040. It follows that the sales tax ordinances enacted in 1971 effective January 1, 1972, also were not affected by the 1971 amendment of § 144.040. The University is exempt from the imposition and collection of the city sales tax on all sales made *by or to it*.

NOTES AND QUESTIONS

1. Was there any indication that the legislators who amended the state sales tax law in 1971 knew they might be affecting the referencing statute by amending the referenced statute? Was there any evidence that the legislators who adopted the city sales tax law *intended* only to adopt the cross-referenced statute as it stood at that point in time? Does it make sense to have different exemptions under the state sales tax law and the city sales tax law?

2. What are the implications of this problem for the use of codified statutes?

---

[7] 303 U.S. at 314, 58 S. Ct. at 564, quoting Lewis Sutherland on Statutory Construction, 2d ed., Vol. II, pp. 707–8.

3. The *City of Warrensburg* case reflects a *judicial* response to the problem of interpreting referential statutes. Consider the following *statutory* approaches to the cross-referencing problem:

> When an act adopts the provisions of another law by reference it also adopts by reference any subsequent amendments of such other law, except where there is clear legislative intention to the contrary.

Minn. Stat. Ann. § 645.31, subd. 2 (1980).

> When one statute refers to another either by general or by specific reference or designation, the reference shall extend to and include, in addition to the statute to which reference was made, amendments thereto and statutes enacted expressly in lieu thereof unless a contrary intent is expressed specifically or unless the amendment to, or the statute enacted in lieu of, the statute referred to is substantially different in the nature of its essential provisions from what the statute to which reference was made was when the statute making the reference was enacted.

Or. Rev. Stat. § 174.060 (1969).

4. How are legislators who are voting on amendments to statutes to know whether such statutes have been adopted by reference into earlier statutes, and that therefore they are making changes to other statutes without notice, deliberation or debate?

5. Which is the best institution of government to resolve questions about the meaning of changes to cross-referenced statutes, the legislature or the courts? Should the courts continue to decide cases under the *City of Warrensburg* approach to force the legislature to consider the effect on cross-referencing statutes of amendments to referenced statutes? Should cases like *City of Warrensburg* be reconsidered by the courts themselves, or are they binding under the doctrine of *stare decisis*?

ERNEST E. MEANS,
STATUTORY CROSS REFERENCES —
THE "LOOSE CANNON" OF STATUTORY CONSTRUCTION IN FLORIDA,
9 FLORIDA STATE UNIVERSITY LAW REVIEW 1, 29 (1981)[*]

By requiring the legislature to take precautions to avoid legislating blindly whenever it amends an existing law that may have been referenced by another statute, the proposed solution would place a new and relatively heavy responsibility upon the Florida Legislature. Fortunately, as a result of recent technical developments, the Florida Legislature is well equipped to handle this added responsibility.

The technical development referred to is the ability of the Florida Legislature to search the text of the Florida Statutes electronically. Since 1973, the full text of the statutes has been in computer memory and subject to search by electronic procedures. A Florida Statutes section number constitutes a numeric word and can be instantly located wherever it appears in the text of the Florida Statutes with absolute accuracy. Presumably, then, if the legislature adopts the proposed rule of construction, it would also adopt procedures by which all references to sections being amended or repealed would be routinely located and analyzed. The purpose of this analysis would be to determine whether the amendment or repeal would have undesirable consequences in any of the sections in which the provision had previously been cross referenced.

In re COMMITMENT OF EDWARD S.
118 N.J. 118, 570 A.2d 917 (1990)

WILENTZ, C.J.

Edward S., having been found not guilty of murder by reason of insanity, was committed to the New Jersey State Forensic Hospital for the Criminally Insane. The issue in this case is whether subsequent hearings to determine whether he should be freed or remain committed may be open to the public or must be *in camera*. We hold that the statutory mandate requiring that such hearings be *in camera* where a civil committee is involved does not apply to one committed following a verdict of not guilty by reason of insanity (NGI committees).

. . . .

The question, therefore, is whether the Legislature in passing this new civil commitment law in 1987 intended this requirement, without qualification, of an *in camera* hearing to extend to NGI committees' hearings as a result of the reference in the earlier criminal statutes that an NGI be "treated as a person civilly committed," which reference was passed at a time when the right to an *in camera* hearing was qualified by the good cause exception.

. . . .

IV

We hold that the statutes governing the disposition of NGI defendants, N.J.S.A. 2C:4-8 and -9, should not be construed to incorporate the absolute requirement of *in camera* hearings found in the new law enacted in 1987, N.J.S.A. 30:4-27.1 to -27.23. More precisely, we hold that when the Legislature adopted the new law concerning civil commitments, it did not intend the absolute *in camera* requirement to apply to NGI commitments.

The question of statutory interpretation when one statute, i.e., N.J.S.A. 2C:4-8 and -9, incorporates all or part of another statute by reference, can be a difficult one.[6]

The general rule is that when a statute incorporates another by specifically referring to it by title or section number, only the precise terms of the incorporated statute as it then exists become part of the incorporating statute; absent language to the contrary, subsequent amendments to the incorporated statute have no effect on the incorporating statute. Indeed, even repeal of the incorporated statute does not ordinarily affect the incorporating statute. The latter remains in force just as it would if the referenced words had been written directly into it. On the other hand, if a statute, instead of incorporating the terms of another statute, incorporates a general body of law, the rule is that subsequent changes in that body of law do become part of the incorporating statute. N. Singer, 2A *Sutherland Statutory Construction*, § 51.07; 51.08 (Sands 4th ed.

---

[6] We note here that Article IV, § VII, paragraph 5 of the State Constitution deals with this matter. The section provides that, "No act shall be passed which shall provide that any existing law, or any part of the act or which shall enact that any existing law, or part thereof, shall be applicable, except by inserting in such act." This provision has been interpreted to forbid the incorporation by reference of a substantive right or duty but not of a procedural or enforcement mechanism. *See Port of New York Auth. v. Heming*, 34 N.J. 144, 153, 167 A.2d 609, *cert. denied, appeal dismissed*, 367 U.S. 487, 81 S. Ct. 1676, 6 L. Ed. 2d 1241 (1961) [and cases cited therein]; *State v. Cruz*, 76 N.J. Super. 325, 328, 184 A.2d 528 (App. Div. 1962). Alternately, the provision has been read to forbid legislation not "complete in self," but to permit incorporation of "auxiliary laws on the subject." *State v. Cruz, supra*, 76 N.J. Super. at 328, 184 A.2d 528 (*quoting Eggers v. Kenny*, 15 N.J. 107, 124[,] 104 A.2d 10 (1954)); *see State in Interest of L.M.*, 229 N.J. Super. 88, 101–102, 550 A.2d 1252 (App. Div. 1988). We do not address the constitutional issue here because the parties did not raise it, and because a decision either way would not change our conclusion, *i.e.*, if the constitutional provision invalidates the incorporation, our conclusion is unaffected since we hold there is no incorporation intended insofar as an absolute requirement of in camera hearings for NGI committees is concerned; if, on the other hand, the constitutional prohibition does not apply, our conclusion is unaffected, having been reached without regard to it.

1984 & Supp. 1989) (hereinafter *Sutherland*).

Although cases citing this rule, or canon of statutory construction, go back more than a hundred years, they say little or nothing about its rationale.[7] Nevertheless, the reason for the rule is easily surmised. Thus, where a statute refers specifically to another statute by title or section number, there is no reason to think its drafters meant to incorporate more than the provision specifically referred to. Nor is there any reason to think repeal of the incorporated statute indicates any intention to negate the incorporating statute, which may bear on an entirely different subject. Reference to a general body of law implies more, however, if only because there are likely to be facets of that law beyond those immediately occupying the Legislature's attention. Incorporating that general body of law then implies a judgment that the overall policies governing the incorporated law should likewise govern the statute incorporating it. On this assumption, it makes sense to incorporate new developments in that body of law into the incorporating statute as well.

The case law supports this understanding. Courts citing the rule have often modified it to conform to legislative intent. Thus where "[the surface specificity of the incorporating language dissolve[d] upon close judicial scrutiny," *Director, Office of Workers' Compensation v. Peabody Coal Co.*, 554 F.2d 310, 324 (7th Cir. 1977), courts have treated the specific reference as a general one.

At first glance, the case at bar seems to present the opposite problem. The criminal law regarding NGIs refers, on its face, to the general law regarding civil committees. It requires that the NGI committee "be treated as a person civilly committed" (N.J.S.A. 2C:4-8(3)), and that his case "shall be specifically reviewed as provided by the law governing civil commitments." N.J.S.A. 2C:4-9d. However, these provisions were inserted to conform to judicial rulings that mandated *substantially* equal, not identical, treatment of NGIs and civil committees. Moreover, the Legislature has repeatedly qualified this requirement of uniform treatment with provisions requiring differential treatment of these groups.

In these circumstances, classifying the reference as "specific" or "general" can only be misleading. The real and unavoidable task is to determine whether the Legislature intended this substantially equal treatment to include the same unqualified right to an "*in camera*" hearing. Here given the policy considerations involved, we do not believe that the Legislature intended that an NGI committee, where the charge was murder, having obtained an acquittal through testimony in open court that he was insane and presumably most dangerous, at least at the time of the offense, could shortly thereafter be released and join society on the basis of closed proceedings that found that he was either sane or not dangerous.

NOTES AND QUESTIONS

1. Is the court primarily concerned with the intent of the legislature for the referencing statute, on the one hand, or the intent of the legislature when it amended the referenced statute? Is there any indication that the legislature knew of the referencing statue when it amended the referenced statute?

2. Is the court in *Edward S.* applying a rule of law or an aid to interpretation? What about the court in *City of Warrensburg*?

---

[7] . . . The rule regarding the interpretation of general references apparently originated in an 1859 Florida case, *Jones v. Dexter*, 8 Fla. 276. *See* discussion in Read, *supra*, at 272–73.

PALM BEACH COUNTY NATIONAL UTILITY CO. v. PALM BEACH COUNTY HEALTH DEPARTMENT
390 So. 2d 115 (Fla. App. 1980)

BERANEK, JUDGE.

. . . .

A statute or regulation may adopt by reference another statute or regulation. Once adopted by specific reference, the subsequent repeal of the initial statute will not have the effect of rendering void the latter adoption by reference unless a contrary intent clearly appears. *Overstreet v. Blum*, 227 So. 2d 197 (Fla. 1969). Florida follows the general rule which distinguishes between adoption by specific reference and adoption by general reference. If adopted by general reference, the rule is to the contrary of that applied to adoptions by specific reference and the subsequent repeal of the regulation renders the adoption by reference unenforceable. *Reino v. State*, 352 So. 2d 853 (Fla. 1977). In this case we hold that the State regulation was adopted by general reference rather than adopted by specific reference.

NOTES AND QUESTIONS

1. How does this approach compare with New Jersey's?

2. What are the implications of this view of *repeals* for the use of codified statutes?

3. What legislative research techniques are necessary to deal with the problems of interpreting referential legislation?

D. INTERPRETING STATUES *IN PARI MATERIA*

DEARBORN TOWNSHIP CLERK v. JONES
335 Mich. 658, 57 N.W.2d 40 (1953)

BUSHNELL, J. This is an appeal by defendants from a declaratory decree in which it was ordered that each of the defendants be certified as a candidate for nomination for office, at the ensuing primary election, on only 1 party ticket.

Petitions were filed with William H. Thorne, the township clerk, by defendant Howard F. Jones as a candidate for the Democratic nomination for the office of township supervisor. Later a group of citizens presented petitions for Jones for nomination on the ticket of the Republican party. Similar groups filed petitions on behalf of defendant Robert Claude Jendron for nomination as a candidate on both the Democratic and Republican tickets for the office of township trustee. Petitions were also filed for defendant Carl H. Roth for nomination as a candidate of both of these parties for the office of township treasurer. The township clerk, acting upon the advice of counsel, notified Jones that the petitions which he had personally filed designating himself as a candidate for the Democratic nomination would be accepted, but that the petitions naming him as a candidate for the Republican nomination would be rejected. Jendron and Roth were each notified that they must determine upon which ticket they would stand for their respective nominations. In response to these notices each of the defendants demanded that their names be printed on the primary election ballots as candidates for nomination by both the Democratic and Republican parties.

A declaratory decree was sought by the clerk under the provisions of C.L. 1948, §§ 691.501–691.507 (Stat. Ann. §§ 27.501–27.507).

. . . .

Primaries for the selection of nominees for township offices are provided for in chapter 9 of part 3 of the election law. (C.L. 1948, § 163.1 *et seq.* [Stat. Ann. § 6.225 *et seq.*], as last amended by P.A. 1952, No. 247.) Section 6 of this chapter, as amended by P.A. 1951, No. 191, provides for separate party ballots for "each political party or organization" in the township. This chapter does not contain any specific prohibition against the names of candidates appearing on more than 1 party or organization ballot. Because of this legislative silence defendants insist that the trial judge erred in ordering that each could be certified as a candidate for nomination upon only 1 party ballot.

It is elementary that statutes *in pari materia* are to be taken together in ascertaining the intention of the legislature, and that courts will regard all statutes upon the same general subject matter as part of 1 system.

> "In the construction of a particular statute, or in the interpretation of any of its provisions, all acts relating to the same subject, or having the same general purpose, should be read in connection with it, as together constituting one law."
> *Remus v. City of Grand Rapids*, 274 Mich. 577, 581.

This rule of construction was applied in recent election cases. *See Foster v. Board of Education of School District No. 10, Delta Township, Eaton County*, 326 Mich. 272, and *People ex rel. Angel v. Smith*, 328 Mich. 323, 330. In the *Remus* case we had the problem of reconciling certain inconsistencies in the general tax law. There we found not only that the history of the statute added light to the determination of the controlling question of legislative intent, but that certain sections, when read in connection with other sections, performed a like function.

Here we must reconcile certain inconsistencies in the general election law, *i.e.*, the omission from chapter 9 of part 3 of a specific prohibition against filing petitions for the same person as a candidate for the same office on different political party tickets, with the mandatory provisions of chapter 7 of part 4. The pertinent sections of the latter chapter are 9, 10 and 11, which, according to section 12, are applicable to township elections. Section 9, which is C.L. 1948, § 177.9, as amended by P.A. 1951, No. 192 (Stat. Ann. 1951 Cum. Supp. § 6.353), requires the board of election commissioners to print on the ballots, or place on the voting machines, when used, the names of the certified candidates. The mandatory requirement is that the name of no candidate shall be placed or printed in more than 1 column on the ballot for the same office. Section 10 of the same chapter requires a person who has been nominated for the same office by 2 or more parties, to select the party column in which he desires his name to be printed or placed. Section 11 states how the ballot shall be prepared in the event of the failure or refusal of the person to so elect. To carry appellants' contention to its logical conclusion could possibly result in the nomination of each of them on more than 1 party ticket at the primary, and thus thwart any opposition in the ensuing election. The history of the development of the election law of this state and a consideration of those statutes presently in effect clearly indicate that it was the intention of the legislature, even though not specifically spelled out in the primary election part of the law, that names of a person should appear on the primary election ballots as a candidate of only 1 political party or organization. Any other holding would be repugnant to other parts of the general election law.

Appellants argue that, in the absence of express statutory language on this question, we must look to the basic law of the state. A constitutional argument based upon section 1 of article 2 of the Constitution of 1908 is then made. This section reads:

> "All political power is inherent in the people. Government is instituted for their equal benefit, security and protection."

The case of *Public Schools of the City of Battle Creek v. Kennedy*, 245 Mich. 585, is cited for the proposition that this inherent power remains, except as delegated by Constitution or statute. It is proposed, therefore, that we should hold that, since the right of a person to seek public office cannot be tested by the yardstick of political affiliation (*see Attorney General v. Board of Councilmen of the City of Detroit*, 58 Mich. 213 [55 Am. Rep. 675]) the electors should not be restricted in their right to nominate a person as a candidate on more than 1 political ticket.

Consideration of the various provisions of the general election law and the discussion in *Attorney General ex rel. Connolly v. Reading*, 268 Mich. 224, requires rejection of this argument. If the people desire to eliminate party designation of candidates, dispense with the responsibility of political parties for their selection, and substitute therefor systems in vogue elsewhere, that policy is one for legislative determination in the light of constitutional restrictions.

The decree is affirmed. A public question being involved, no costs will be allowed.

DETHMERS, C.J., and ADAMS, BUTZEL, CARR, and REID, JJ., concurred.

SHARPE and BOYLES, JJ., did not participate in this opinion.

NOTES AND QUESTIONS

1. Does the doctrine of *in pari materia* assume a certain degree of consistency in statutory materials? Does the doctrine also presume a high level of thoroughness in the legislature's researching of existing legislation? How would a persistent judicial application of this doctrine effect legislative drafting?

2. Is it possible the legislature decided there was nothing inappropriate about having an election determined at the primary stages? Did the court assume inconsistency with the general election law? Does it make a difference if voters in the state are not preregistered by party and can "cross-over" to vote for candidates of either party?

3. The appellants argued the Constitution of Michigan provides that all political power is inherent in the people except for those instances where it is delegated by statute. Since there was no statute expressly prohibiting a person from being a candidate on more than one party ticket, the appellants contended they still had that right. The court rejected their argument, stating such a construction would be repugnant to other parts of the general election law. In effect, is not appellants' argument that, when the legislature has not specifically considered an issue, it is not possible to determine a contrary legislative intent? The court, on the other hand, ascertained the intent of the legislature by reading the election statutes *in pari materia*. Which approach is more appropriate? Does reading statutes *in pari materia* always involve the creative application of laws by courts?

4. This case presents the problem of an apparent gap in a statute. Is the presence of such a gap always easy to perceive? As noted in Question 2 above, is it possible that the legislature intended to enact the statute as it was written?

5. Professor Eric Lane criticized the use of the *in pari materia* canon in Eric Lane, *Legislative Process and its Judicial Renderings: A Study in Contrast*, 48 U. PITT. L. REV. 639, 657–58 (1987).

JONES v. UNITED STATES
526 U.S. 227 (1999)

JUSTICE SOUTER delivered the opinion of the Court.

This case turns on whether the federal carjacking statute, 18 U.S.C. § 2119, as it was when petitioner was charged, defined three distinct offenses or a single crime with a choice of three maximum penalties, two of them dependent on sentencing factors exempt from the requirements of charge and jury verdict. We think the better reading is of three distinct offenses, particularly in light of the rule that any interpretive uncertainty should be resolved to avoid serious questions about the statute's constitutionality.

I

In December 1992, petitioner, Nathaniel Jones, and two others, Oliver and McMillan, held up two men, Mutanna and Mardaie. While Jones and McMillan went through the victims' pockets, Oliver stuck his gun in Mutanna's left ear, and later struck him on the head . . . .

A grand jury in the Eastern District of California indicted Jones and his two accomplices on two counts: using or aiding and abetting the use of a firearm during and in relation to a crime of violence, in violation of 18 U.S.C. § 924(c), and carjacking or aiding and abetting carjacking, in violation of 18 U.S.C. § 2119, which then read as follows:

> "Whoever, possessing a firearm as defined in section 921 of this title, takes a motor vehicle that has been transported, shipped, or received in interstate or foreign commerce from the person or presence of another by force and violence or by intimidation, or attempts to do so, shall —

> "(1) be fined under this title or imprisoned not more than 15 years, or both,

> "(2) if serious bodily injury (as defined in section 1365 of this title) results, be fined under this title or imprisoned not more than 25 years, or both, and

> "(3) if death results, be fined under this title or imprisoned for any number of years up to life, or both." 18 U.S.C. § 2119 (1988 ed., Supp. V).

The indictment made no reference to the statute's numbered subsections and charged none of the facts mentioned in the latter two, and at the arraignment the Magistrate Judge told Jones that he faced a maximum sentence of 15 years on the carjacking charge. App. 4–5, 7. Consistently with this advice, the District Court's subsequent jury instructions defined the elements subject to the Government's burden of proof by reference solely to the first paragraph of § 2119, with no mention of serious bodily injury. *Id.*, at 10. The jury found Jones guilty on both counts.

The case took a new turn, however, with the arrival of the presentence report, which recommended that petitioner be sentenced to 25 years for the carjacking because one of the victims had suffered serious bodily injury. The report noted that Mutanna had testified that Oliver's gun caused profuse bleeding in Mutanna's ear, and that a physician had concluded that Mutanna had suffered a perforated eardrum, with some numbness and permanent hearing loss. *Id.*, at 15–16, 60 F.3d, at 554. Jones objected that the 25-year recommendation was out of bounds, since serious bodily injury was an element of the offense defined in part by § 2119(2), which had been neither pleaded in the indictment nor proven before the jury. App. 12–13. The District Court saw the matter differently and, based on its finding that the serious bodily injury allegation was supported by a preponderance of evidence, imposed a 25-year sentence on the carjacking count, *ibid.*, together with a consecutive 5-year sentence for the firearm offense, 60 F.3d, at 549.

. . . .

II

Much turns on the determination that a fact is an element of an offense rather than a sentencing consideration, given that elements must be charged in the indictment, submitted to a jury, and proven by the Government beyond a reasonable doubt . . . .

Accordingly, some statutes come with the benefit of provisions straightforwardly addressing the distinction between elements and sentencing factors. *See McMillan v. Pennsylvania*, 477 U.S. 79, 85–86 (1986) (express identification of statutory provision as sentencing factor). Even without any such help, however, § 2119 at first glance has a look to it suggesting that the numbered subsections are only sentencing provisions. It begins with a principal paragraph listing a series of obvious elements (possession of a firearm, taking a motor vehicle, connection with interstate commerce, and so on). That paragraph comes close to standing on its own, followed by sentencing provisions, the first of which, subsection (1), certainly adds no further element. But the superficial impression loses clarity when one looks at the penalty subsections (2) and (3). These not only provide for steeply higher penalties, but condition them on further facts (injury, death) that seem quite as important as the elements in the principal paragraph (*e.g.*, force and violence, intimidation). It is at best questionable whether the specification of facts sufficient to increase a penalty range by two-thirds, let alone from 15 years to life, was meant to carry none of the process safeguards that elements of an offense bring with them for a defendant's benefit. The "look" of the statute, then, is not a reliable guide to congressional intentions, and the Government accordingly advances two, more subtle structural arguments for its position that the fact specified in subsection (2) is merely a sentencing factor.

Like the Court of Appeals, the Government stresses that the statute's numbered subsections do not stand alone in defining offenses, most of whose elements on anyone's reckoning are set out in the statute's opening paragraph. This integrated structure is said to suggest that the statute establishes only a single offense . . . . The text alone does not justify any confident inference. But statutory drafting occurs against a backdrop not merely of structural conventions of varying significance, but of traditional treatment of certain categories of important facts, like the degree of injury to victims of crime, in relation to particular crimes. If a given statute is unclear about treating such a fact as element of penalty aggravator, it makes sense to look at what other statutes have done, on the fair assumption that Congress is unlikely to intend any radical departures from past practice without making a point of saying so.

We engaged in just such an enquiry this past Term in *Almendarez-Torres*, where we stressed the history of treating recidivism as a sentencing factor, and noted that, with perhaps one exception, Congress had never clearly made prior conviction an offense element where the offense conduct, in the absence of recidivism, was independently unlawful. 523 U.S., at 230. Here, on the contrary, the search for comparable examples more readily suggests that Congress had separate and aggravated offenses in mind when it employed the scheme of numbered subsections in § 2119. Although Congress has explicitly treated serious bodily injury as a sentencing factor, *see, e.g.*, 18 U.S.C. § 2262(b)(2) (interstate violation of a protection order); § 248(b)(2) (free access to clinic entrances; bodily injury), it has unmistakably identified serious bodily injury as an offense element in any number of statutes, *see, e.g.*, 10 U.S.C. § 928(b)(2) (assault by a number of the armed forces); 18 U.S.C. § 37(a)(1) (violence at international airports); § 1091(a)(2) (genocide). The likelihood that Congress understood injury to be an offense element here follows all the more from the fact that carjacking is a type of robbery, and serious bodily injury has traditionally been treated, both by Congress and by the state legislatures, as defining an element of the offense of aggravated robbery. As the Government acknowledges, Brief for United States 20–21, and n.8, Congress modeled the federal carjacking statute on several other federal robbery statutes. [4] One of them, 18 U.S.C. § 2118 (robbery involving controlled substances), clearly makes causing serious bodily injury an element of the offense . . . . A second model, § 2113 (bank robbery), as the Government concedes, *see* Brief for United States 17, makes related facts of violence, that is, assault and jeopardizing life by using a dangerous weapon, elements defining an aggravated form of that type of robbery. *See* §§ 2113(d), (e); *cf. Almendarez-Torres, supra*, at 231 (citing bank robbery statute as example of statute establishing greater and lesser included offenses); *McMillan*, 477 U.S. at 88 (contrasting § 2113(d) with provision defining a sentencing enhancement).

When pressed at oral argument, the Government proved unable to explain why Congress might have chosen one treatment of serious bodily harm or violence in defining two of the three offenses it used as its models for § 2119 and a different treatment in writing the carjacking statute itself, *see* Tr. Of Oral Arg. 41–44, and we are unable to imagine a convincing reason ourselves. We thus think it fair to say that, as in the earlier

---

[4] Legislative history identifies three such models. *See* H.R. Rep. No. 102-851, pt. 1, p. 17 (1992) ("The definition of the offense tracks the language used in other federal robbery statutes (18 U.S.C. §§ 2111, 2113, 2118)"). One of them, 18 U.S.C. § 2111 (robbery in areas of federal maritime or territorial jurisdiction), lacks aggravated forms of the offense altogether, and thus is not on point here.

robbery statutes, so in the carjacking statute, Congress probably intended serious bodily injury to be an element defining an aggravated form of the crime.

State practice bolsters the conclusion. Many States use causation of serious bodily injury or harm as an element defining a distinct offense of aggravated robbery . . . . While the state practice is not, admittedly, direct authority for reading the federal carjacking statute, it does show that in treating serious bodily injury as an element, Congress would have been treading a well-worn path.

. . . .

III

While we think the fairest reading of § 2119 treats the fact of serious bodily harm as an element, not a mere enhancement, we recognize the possibility of the other view. Any doubt that might be prompted by the arguments for that other reading should, however, be resolved against it under the rule, repeatedly affirmed, that "where a statute is susceptible of two constructions, by one of which grave and doubtful constitutional questions arise and by the other of which such questions are avoided, our duty is to adopt the latter." . . .

In sum, the Government's view would raise serious constitutional questions on which precedent is not dispositive. Any doubt on the issue of statutory construction is hence to be resolved in favor of avoiding those questions. This is done by construing § 2119 as establishing three separate offenses by the specification of distinct elements, each of which must be charged by indictment, proven beyond a reasonable doubt, and submitted to a jury for its verdict. The judgement of the Court of Appeals is accordingly reversed, and the case is remanded for proceedings consistent with this opinion.

It is so ordered.

JUSTICE KENNEDY, with whom THE CHIEF JUSTICE, JUSTICE O'CONNOR, and JUSTICE BREYER join, dissenting.

. . . .

Before it departs on its troubling constitutional discussion, the Court analyzes the text of § 2119. This portion of the Court's opinion, it should be acknowledged, is careful and comprehensive. In my submission, however, the analysis suggests the presence of more interpretative ambiguity than in fact exists and reaches the wrong result. Like the Court, I begin with the textual question.

. . . .

I

In addition, the plain reading of § 2119 is reinforced by common patterns of statutory drafting. For example, in one established statutory model, Congress defines the elements of an offense in an initial paragraph ending with the phrase "shall be punished as provided in" a separate subsection. The subsection provides for graded sentencing ranges, predicated upon specific findings (such as serious bodily injury or death). *See, e.g.,* 8 U.S.C. § 1324(a)(1). Section 2119 follows a similar logic. It is true that clauses (1)–(3) are not separated into a separate subsection, thus giving rise to the textual problem we must resolve. Congress does not always separate sentencing factors into separate subsections, however. *See, e.g.,* 18 U.S.C. § 1347 (1994 ed., Supp. III) (health-care fraud; enhanced penalties if the violation "results in serious bodily injury" or "results in death"). As with statutes like § 1324, the structure of § 2119 suggests a design which defines the offense first and the punishment afterward.

In addition, there is some significance in the use of the active voice in the main paragraph and the passive voice in clauses (2) and (3) of § 2119. In the more common practice, criminal statutes use the active voice to define prohibited conduct. *See, e.g.,* 18 U.S.C. § 1116 (1994 ed., Supp. III) ("[w]hoever kills or attempts to kill"); 18 U.S.C.

§ 2114 ("assaults," "robs or attempts to rob," "receives, possesses, conceals, or disposes"); Tex. Penal Code Ann. § 29.03(a)(1), (2) (1994) (aggravated robbery; "causes serious bodily injury," or "uses or exhibits a deadly weapon"); cf. 18 U.S.C. § 248(b) (setting forth, as sentencing factors, "if bodily injury results," and "if death results"); United States Sentencing Commission, Guidelines Manual § 2B3.1(b)(3) (Nov. 1998) (robbery guideline; "[i]f any victim sustained bodily injury").

These drafting conventions are not absolute rules. Congress uses active language in phrasing sentencing factors in some instances. See, e.g., 18 U.S.C. § 2262(b)(3) (1994 ed., Supp. III) ("if serious bodily injury to the victim results or if the offender uses a dangerous weapon during the offense"). Nevertheless, the more customary drafting conventions support, rather than contradict, the interpretation that § 2119 sets forth but one offense.

The Court offers specific arguments regarding these background considerations, each deserving of consideration and response.

. . . .

In short, even indulging the Court's assumptions, the federal robbery statutes do not support the conclusion that § 2119 contains three substantive offenses. Rather, all four statutes employ similar language to define the elements of a basic robbery-type offense. It is in this sense that § 2119 is modeled on §§ 2111, 2113, and 2118.

. . . .

The Court's final justification for its reading of § 2119 rests on state practice. Of course, the Court cannot argue that States do not take factors like serious bodily injury into account at sentencing; as discussed above, they do. Instead, the Court says many States have created a distinct offense of aggravated robbery, requiring proof of serious bodily injury or harm. This is unremarkable. The laws reflect nothing more than common intuition that a forcible theft, all else being equal, is more blameworthy when it results in serious bodily injury or death. I have no doubt Congress was responding to this same intuition when it added clauses (2) and (3) to § 2119. Recognizing the common policy concern, however, gives scant guidance on the question before us: whether Congress meant to give effect to the policy by making serious bodily injury and death elements of distinct offenses or by making them sentencing factors. I agree with the Court that these state statutes are not direct authority for the issue presented here. *Ante*, at 10.

The persuasive force of the Court's state-law citation is further undercut by the structural differences between those laws and § 2119. Ten of the thirteen statutes cited by the Court follow the same pattern. One statutory section sets forth the elements of the basic robbery offense. Another section (captioned "Aggravated robbery" or "Robbery in the first degree") incorporates the basic robbery offense (either by explicit cross-reference or by obvious implication), adds the bodily or physical injury element (in the active voice), and then provides that the aggravated crime is subject to a higher penalty set forth elsewhere (*e.g.*, "a class A felony"). Two of the remaining three statutes, N.Y. Penal Law § 160.15 (McKinney 1988), and Ky. Rev. Stat. Ann. § 515.020 (Michie 1990), deviate from this pattern in only minor respects while the third, N.H. Rev. Stat. Ann. § 636:1 (1996), has a singular structure.

Had Congress wished to emulate this state practice in detail, one might have expected it to structure § 2119 in a similar manner to the majority model. *Cf.* 18 U.S.C. §§ 2113(e), (d). It did not do so. This suggests to me either (i) that Congress chose a different structure than utilized by the States in order to show its intent to treat "serious bodily injury" as a sentencing factor, or (ii) that Congress simply did not concentrate on state practice in deciding whether "serious bodily injury" should be classed as an element or a sentencing factor. Neither possibility sustains the Court's interpretation of § 2119.

NOTES AND QUESTIONS

1. How is the approach used by the majority in *Jones* different from interpreting statutes *in pari materia*? Is it in fact different?

> Statutes dealing with a variety of subjects may begin to cluster around some common value judgement. Recognizing this reality, a court is warranted in finding evidence of legislative intent under a given act by reference to what legislators have done regarding like subjects under other acts.

> . . . .

> The statutory text is basic and central. But if law is to be a vital force in society, the text usually must be seen as part of a flow of policy-making activity that originates before the text is voted and continues after it is on the books.

J.W. Hurst, Dealing With Statutes 45, 46 (1982).

3. Judge Learned Hand referred to related statutes as throwing "a cross light" on other statutes. *See United States v. Hutcheson*, 312 U.S. 219 (1941) ("A later statute in pari materia was considered to throw a cross light upon the Anti-Trust Acts."). *United States v. Aluminum Co. of America*, 148 F.2d 416, 429 (2d Cir. 1945). *See also Great Northern Ry. Co. v. United States*, 315 U.S. 262, 277 (1942) ("It is settled that subsequent legislation may be considered to assist in the interpretation of prior legislation on the same subject.").

For a more recent formulation by Justice Brennan, see *Andrus v. Allard*, 444 U.S. 51, 62 (1979) ("related statutes may sometimes shed light upon a previous enactment").

4. Professor Jane Schacter analyzes this technique of statutory interpretation in *The Confounding Common Law Originalism in Recent Supreme Court Statutory Interpretation: Implications for the Legislative History Debate and Beyond*, 51 Stan. L. Rev. 1, 31–33 (1998).

E.   STATUTORY CONFLICT

UNIFORM STATUTE AND RULE CONSTRUCTION ACT (1995)*

§ 10 Irreconcilable Statutes or Rules.

(a) If statutes appear to conflict, they must be construed, if possible, to give effect to each. If the conflict is irreconcilable, the later enacted statute governs. However, an earlier enacted specific, special, or local statute prevails over a later enacted general statute unless the context of the later enacted statute indicates otherwise.

. . . .

(c) If a statute is a comprehensive revision of the law on a subject, it prevails over previous statutes on the subject whether or not the revision and the previous statutes conflict irreconcilably.

. . . .

---

1. The Last Enacted; Discretionary Versus Nondiscretionary Statutes

ELY v. VELDE
451 F.2d 1130 (4th Cir. 1971)

Appellants, who are residents of the Green Springs area of Louisa County, Virginia, brought an action to halt the proposed funding and construction in their neighborhood of a Medical and Reception Center ("Center") for Virginia prisoners. To this end, they sought to enjoin appellees Richard W. Velde and Clarence M. Coster, Associate Administrators of the Law Enforcement Assistance Administration ("LEAA"),[1] from allocating to Virginia $775,000 of federal funds for the construction of the Center.[2]

. . . .

The Complaint of the residents in the District Court alleges that the National Environmental Policy Act of 1970 ("NEPA") requires both the LEAA and the State of Virginia to (1) take into account, in the funding and location of the Center, the possible effects the Center might have on the Green Springs natural environment and (2) prepare an "impact statement" detailing these possible effects, before proceeding with the funding and construction of the Center.[4]

A further claim of the residents was that the National Historic Preservation Act ("NHPA") requires the LEAA and the State of Virginia to consider the effect the proposed Center will have on certain historic properties in Green Springs, and to afford an opportunity to the Advisory Council on Historic Preservation to comment on the undertaking.[6]

Since none of the procedures outlined by NHPA and NEPA was observed in

---

[1] The LEAA is an agency created by the Omnibus Crime Control and Safe Streets Act of 1968, 42 U.S.C. § 3701, *et seq.*, charged with the administration of that Act, including the approval and allocation of federal grants to the states for various law enforcement purposes. *See* 42 U.S.C. §§ 3711, 3751–69.

[2] This sum is part of a "block grant" of $4,150,000 to be used by the State of Virginia for a variety of purposes. For an explanation of the term "block grant" *see* note 8, *infra*.

[4] Enacted in 1970, NEPA expresses a strong federal policy in favor of preserving the natural environment, including our "historic and cultural heritage." 42 U.S.C. § 4331. To this end, Congress has directed that "to the fullest extent possible" all laws, regulations and policies of the United States should be interpreted and administered in accordance with the policies of NEPA. 42 U.S.C. § 4332(1).

In addition to this generalized command, NEPA also imposes specific procedural requirements on "all agencies of the Federal Government." They must, in connection with "other major federal actions significantly affecting the quality of the human environment," prepare a detailed statement of the impact the proposed action will have on the environment, including a discussion of alternatives to the proposed action. 42 U.S.C. § 4332(1)(C).

Prior to the making of such an "impact statement," the agency involved must consult with and obtain the comments of any other federal agency "which has jurisdiction by law or special expertise with respect to any environmental impact involved." *Id.*

[6] NHPA, enacted into law in 1966, reflects the congressional desire "that the historical and cultural foundations of the Nation should be preserved . . . in order to give a sense of orientation to the American people . . . ." 16 U.S.C. § 470. The Act provides for the creation and maintenance of a "National Register" by the Secretary of the Interior. This National Register is a list of "districts, sites, buildings, structures, and objects significant in American history, architecture, archeology, and culture." 16 U.S.C. § 470a.

Prior to the expenditure of any federal funds in an undertaking which might have an effect on anything listed in the National Register, the head of the federal agency concerned must: (1) take such effect into account in approving the funds to be spent and (2) afford an opportunity to the Advisory Council on Historic Preservation to comment in regard to the undertaking. 16 U.S.C. § 470f.

The Advisory Council on Historic Preservation, created by NHPA, advises the President and Congress, as well as state and federal agencies on matters relating to historic preservation. 16 U.S.C. § 470j.

deciding upon the funding and location of the Center, the appellants charge the appellees with a violation of these two statutes.

In defense of its admitted failure to comply with NHPA and NEPA, the LEAA relies upon certain provisions in Title I of the Omnibus Crime Control and Safe Streets Act of 1968 ("Safe Streets Act"), pursuant to which the grant here at issue was approved. Its position is that the Safe Streets Act prohibits any interference or control of the states by the federal government in the spending of grants, except as expressly authorized by the statute.[8]

Thus the LEAA claims it may not look beyond its governing statute and is prohibited, in approving grants, from reading into that statute the requirements of NHPA and NEPA.

. . . .

I

The Green Springs area is aptly described in the District Court's opinion:

Green Springs is an area of land consisting of approximately 10,000 acres located in the Western part of Louisa County. It is a uniquely historical and architecturally significant rural community in that almost all of the homes were built in the nineteenth century and have been maintained in substantially the same condition ever since. Three of the homes, Boswell's Tavern, Hawkwood and Westend, are on the National Register for Historic Places, as provided in [NHPA].

The proposed Center will consist of at least four concrete-faced buildings, a thirty-foot guard tower and a surrounding fence. It will, in addition, contain parking facilities for 150 cars. Appellee Brown estimated that the Center would use 40,000 gallons of water per day to support its projected population of 400 to 500 inmates and 74 correctional officers.

The above facts would seem to warrant the application of the procedural requirements of both NHPA and NEPA. While neither the LEAA nor the Virginia Department of Welfare and Institutions complied with these two Acts, the Virginia agency seems to have given consideration to factors such as soil and water requirements. These factors are indeed "environmental" in a sense, but other environmental or cultural factors — the very ones accented in NHPA and NEPA — were not taken into account by either of the agencies in the decisions concerning the Center.

In assessing the residents' claims, the District Court thought it was faced with an irreconcilable conflict between the Safe Streets Act on the one hand and NHPA and NEPA on the other. The Court sought to resolve the problems arising from the supposed conflict by applying two familiar rules of statutory construction. First, since the Safe Streets Act was enacted *after* NHPA, the Court held that the later expression

---

[8] The Safe Streets Act, which was passed in 1968, is an effort to "assist State and local governments in strengthening and improving law enforcement at every level by national assistance." 42 U.S.C. § 3701. To do so, the Act provides for planning grants to subsidize the formulation of comprehensive law enforcement plans for each state. *See* 42 U.S.C. §§ 3721–25. Once a state has submitted its comprehensive plan to the LEAA, and the LEAA finds that the plan "conforms with the purposes and requirements of [the Safe Streets Act]," the state then becomes eligible to receive action grants to carry out its comprehensive plan. 42 U.S.C. § 3733. At this stage, there are two types of action grants available, "block" grants and "discretionary" grants. Block grants are allocated to all eligible states solely on the basis of population and without regard to need. Discretionary grants, on the other hand, are "allocated as the [LEAA] shall determine." 42 U.S.C. § 3766.

Eighty-five percent of the money appropriated by Congress for law enforcement action grants is given to the states in the form of block grants. Discretionary grants comprise the remaining fifteen percent. *Id.*

of Congress must prevail, thus precluding consideration of historic and cultural factors as prescribed by the earlier NHPA.

However, as between NEPA and the Safe Streets Act, the District Court departed from the rule it previously applied and attributed prevailing force to the Safe Streets Act, despite the fact that NEPA was the later enactment. The Court accepted the LEAA's interpretation which turned on an odd reading of the language of NEPA that commands all federal agencies to observe the procedural duties it imposes "to the fullest extent possible." The argument advanced was that this phrase made the statute "discretionary," while the duty of the LEAA to make grants was claimed to be "non-discretionary." Reasoning from this categorization of NEPA as "discretionary" and the Safe Streets Act as "nondiscretionary," the Court was persuaded to apply the rule of construction that in case of conflict, a discretionary statute must yield to a nondiscretionary one.

II

We reject the appellees' basic assumption that the Safe Streets Act is irreconcilable with NHPA and NEPA.

The rules of thumb urged by the LEAA — namely that a later enactment controls earlier legislation and that a discretionary command must yield to a mandatory one — can be useful as aids in statutory construction. But they represent a last resort, to be invoked only when it is impossible to avoid a collision between two statutes and to effectuate both. Where reconciliation is possible, these rules of thumb do not come into play.

Normally there is a strong presumption against one statute repealing or amending another by implication. *United States v. Welden*, 377 U.S. 95, 102–03, n.12, 84 S. Ct. 1082, 12 L. Ed. 2d 152 (1964); *United States v. Borden Co.*, 308 U.S. 188, 198–99, 60 S. Ct. 182, 84 L. Ed. 181 (1939) (there must be a "positive repugnancy between the new law and the old"). This circuit has similarly applied this approach several times. *See, e.g., Fanning v. United Fruit Co.*, 355 F.2d 147 (4th Cir. 1966). "When two statutes present an apparent conflict, the proper approach is to ascertain the purposes underlying both enactments, not to dispose of the problem by a mechanical rule." 355 F.2d at 149.

. . . .

Close examination of the purposes and policies of the Safe Streets Act reveals no real antagonism to NHPA and NEPA such as would prevent effectuation of all three statutes.

The LEAA insists that it is not obliged to comply — indeed it may not comply — with NHPA and NEPA because it has been disabled, when approving block grants, from imposing any conditions not found in the Safe Streets Act itself. Support for this proposition is claimed in the language and the policy inherent in the Safe Streets Act.

In 42 U.S.C. § 3733, Congress specified that:

> The [LEAA] *shall make grants* under this chapter to a State planning agency if such agency has on file with the [LEAA] an approved comprehensive State plan . . . which conforms with the purposes and requirements of this chapter. (Emphasis added.)

In addition, 42 U.S.C. § 3757 provides that grant funds under the Safe Streets Act can be withheld only if the LEAA finds that there has been a "substantial failure" of the grantee to comply with (1) the Safe Streets Act, (2) regulations and guidelines promulgated by the LEAA, or (3) the state comprehensive plan itself. The LEAA maintains that these two sections specify the only criteria that the states can be required to meet before they become entitled to a block grant. Thus, it is argued, the permissible areas of inquiry with regard to the states' plans are similarly restricted.

The LEAA urges that its reading of the Safe Streets Act is required by the unique policy underlying that Act. Characterizing this policy as a "hands off" approach to federal financial assistance to the states, the LEAA cites several statements by congressional proponents of the Safe Streets Act as indicative of an intention that the federal government play as small a role as possible in the individual states' spending of allotted funds. Finally, the LEAA places additional reliance on 42 U.S.C. § 3766(a):

> Nothing contained in this chapter or any other Act shall be construed to authorize any department, agency, officer, or employee of the United States to exercise any direction, supervision, or control over any police force or any other law enforcement agency of any state or political subdivision thereof.

Reliance in the present case is misplaced, for it is plain that the LEAA has overdrawn the "hands off" policy of the Safe Streets Act. Properly read, neither the Act's language nor its policy prohibits or excuses compliance with NHPA and NEPA.

III

The genesis of the "hands off" approach lies in considerations more subtle than a simple desire to give the states more latitude in the spending of federal money. The dominant concern of Congress apparently was to guard against any tendency towards federalization of local police and law enforcement agencies. Such a result, it was felt, would be less efficient than allowing local law enforcement officials to coordinate their state's overall efforts to meet unique local problems and conditions. Even more important than Congress' search for efficiency and expertise was its fear that overbroad federal control of state law enforcement could result in the creation of an Orwellian "federal police force."

The above-quoted section 3766(a), which forbids federal control over local police and law enforcement agencies, was the congressional solution for these problems. The legislative history reflects the congressional purpose to shield the routine operations of local police forces from ongoing control by the LEAA — a control which conceivably could turn the local police into an arm of the federal government.

. . . .

Congress could well have been justified in its concern and was reasonable in its reaction — the adoption of section 3766(a). However, in the absence of unmistakable language to the contrary, we should hesitate to read the congressional solution to one problem — protection of local police autonomy — so broadly as unnecessarily to undercut solutions adopted by Congress to preserve and protect other societal values, such as the natural and cultural environment. It is not to be assumed lightly that Congress intended to cancel out two highly important statutes without a word to that effect.

It is our conclusion that Congress, in enacting the Safe Streets Act, did not intend to forbid the LEAA from considering NHPA and NEPA. An LEAA requirement, in every comprehensive state plan and grant application, of enough information to assess the environmental and cultural impact of the proposed plan or grant, would not remotely approach the apprehended "control over any police force or other law enforcement agency." The instant case presents a prime example. The decision as to the location of the proposed Center is far removed from the everyday activities of state and local police in Virginia. Moreover, it is a decision which, once made, would not invite continued supervision and control by the LEAA. This could not conceivably constitute a step towards the establishment of a "federal police force." The object of the "hands off" policy in the Safe Streets Act would not be frustrated by LEAA's compliance with NHPA and NEPA.

. . . .

Concluding, as we do, that the "hands off" character of the Safe Streets Act is not as sweeping as the LEAA contends, it follows that NHPA, with its unequivocal command to "any federal agency," must be complied with by the LEAA.

We conclude further that NEPA, no less than NHPA, must be followed here. The LEAA misconstrues the import of the language "to the fullest extent possible," found in NEPA. The quoted language does not render the procedural requirements of NEPA "discretionary." Rather, the words are an injunction to all federal agencies to exert utmost efforts to apply NEPA to their own operations. In short, the phrase "to the fullest extent possible" reinforces rather than dilutes the strength of the prescribed obligations.

NOTES AND QUESTIONS

1. Was one of the flaws in the reasoning of the district court its use of the canon of "the last enacted" to establish priority between two statutes which dealt with entirely different subject matters? Should the canons of "the last enacted" and "the non-discretionary controls the discretionary" be limited in use to situations where the conflicting statutes are *in pari materia*? If these canons can be used in situations where conflicting statutes govern unrelated subject matters, is there a substantial risk that eventually many statutes will be "amended or repealed by implication"?

2. Note how the district court used the doctrine of "the last enacted" to give the Safe Streets Act priority over the NHPA, but discarded this rule in giving priority to the Safe Streets Act over the NEPA. Do such canons give courts too much latitude in deciding which statutes take priority in the case of conflict? Can the canons be abused by courts that use them to justify decisions made on other, often unstated, grounds?

2.   The Specific Controls the General

Another canon of statutory construction which is used when there is a conflict between statutes is that "a specific statute will be given effect over a more general one applicable to the same situation." Again, there must be an actual conflict before recourse to the canon is appropriate. The canon appears to be logically sound upon a cursory examination, but considerable difficulty in application of the canon can occur in several situations. For instance, when the general statute was enacted later, how is a court to resolve the conflict between this and the previous canon, "the last enacted"? Is the problem not a result of an oversight by the drafters in failing to recognize the conflict between specific and general statutes? As devices for resolving conflicts where legislative intent must be presumed without the availability of other evidence, this canon and the preceding ones have little apparent justification in either fact or logic. No legislature would knowingly pass a statute intending it to conflict with an existing statute!

PREISER v. RODRIGUEZ
411 U.S. 475 (1973)

Syllabus

Respondents were state prisoners who had elected to participate in New York's conditional-release program, by which a prisoner serving an indeterminate sentence may earn up to 10 days per month good-behavior-time credits toward reduction of his maximum sentence. For in-prison disciplinary reasons the good-time credits of each were canceled. Each respondent brought a civil rights action under 42 U.S.C. § 1983, in conjunction with a habeas corpus action, claiming that his credits were unconstitutionally canceled and seeking their restoration. The District Court in each case viewed the habeas corpus claim merely as an adjunct to the civil rights action, thus obviating the need for exhaustion of state remedies, and on the merits ruled for the respondent, a ruling that in each case entitled him to immediate release on parole. The Court of Appeals consolidated the actions and affirmed. *Held:* When a state prisoner challenges the fact or duration of his physical imprisonment and by way of relief seeks a determination that he is entitled to immediate release or a speedier release, his sole federal remedy is a writ of habeas corpus.

(a) Although the broad language of § 1983 seems literally to apply, Congress' enactment of the specific federal habeas corpus statute, with its requirement that a state prisoner exhaust state remedies, was intended to provide the exclusive means of relief in this type of situation.

. . . .

Opinion by Mr. Justice Stewart.

. . . .

Although conceding that they could have proceeded by way of habeas corpus, the respondents argue that the Court of Appeals was correct in holding that they were nonetheless entitled to bring their suits under § 1983 so as to avoid the necessity of first seeking relief in a state forum. Pointing to the broad language of § 1983, they argue that since their complaints plainly came within the literal terms of that statute, there is no justifiable reason to exclude them from the broad remedial protection provided by that law. According to the respondents, state prisoners seeking relief under the Civil Rights Act should be treated no differently from any other civil rights plaintiffs, when the language of the Act clearly covers their causes of action.

The broad language of § 1983, however, is not conclusive of the issue before us. The statute is a general one, and, despite the literal applicability of its terms, the question remains whether the specific federal habeas corpus statute, explicitly and historically designed to provide the means for a state prisoner to attack the validity of his confinement, must be understood to be the exclusive remedy available in a situation like this where it so clearly applies. The respondents' counsel acknowledged at oral argument that a state prisoner challenging his underlying conviction and sentence on federal constitutional grounds in a federal court is limited to habeas corpus. It was conceded that he cannot bring a § 1983 action, even though the literal terms of § 1983 might seem to cover such a challenge, because Congress has passed a more specific act to cover that situation, and, in doing so, has provided that a state prisoner challenging his conviction must first seek relief in a state forum, if a state remedy is available. It is clear to us that the result must be the same in the case of a state prisoner's challenge to the fact or duration of his confinement, based, as here, upon the alleged unconstitutionality of state administrative action. Such a challenge is just as close to the core of habeas corpus as an attack on the prisoner's conviction, for it goes directly to the constitutionality of his physical confinement itself and seeks either immediate release from that confinement or the shortening of its duration.

In amending the habeas corpus laws in 1948, Congress clearly required exhaustion of adequate state remedies as a condition precedent to the invocation of federal judicial relief under those laws. It would wholly frustrate explicit congressional intent to hold that the respondents in the present case could evade this requirement by the simple expedient of putting a different label on their pleadings. In short, Congress has determined that habeas corpus is the appropriate remedy for state prisoners attacking the validity of the fact or length of their confinement, and that specific determination must override the general terms of § 1983.

The policy reasons underlying the habeas corpus statute support this conclusion. The respondents concede that the reason why only habeas corpus can be used to challenge a state prisoner's underlying conviction is the strong policy requiring exhaustion of state remedies in that situation — to avoid the unnecessary friction between the federal and state court systems that would result if a lower federal court upset a state court conviction without first giving the state court system an opportunity to correct its own constitutional errors.

. . . .

Mr. Justice Brennan, with whom Mr. Justice Douglas and Mr. Justice Marshall join, dissenting.

. . . .

At bottom, the Court's holding today rests on an understandable apprehension that the no-exhaustion rule of § 1983 might, in the absence of some limitation, devour the exhaustion rule of the habeas corpus statute. The problem arises because the two statutes necessarily overlap. Indeed, every application by a state prisoner for federal habeas corpus relief against his jailers could, as a matter of logic and semantics, be viewed as an action under the Ku Klux Klan Act to obtain injunctive relief against "the deprivation," by one acting under color of state law, "of any rights, privileges, or immunities secured by the Constitution and laws" of the United States. 42 U.S.C. § 1983. To prevent state prisoners from nullifying the habeas corpus exhaustion requirement by invariably styling their petitions as pleas for relief under § 1983, the Court today devises an ungainly and irrational scheme that permits some prisoners to sue under § 1983, while others may proceed only by way of petition for habeas corpus. And the entire scheme operates in defiance of the purposes underlying both the exhaustion requirement of habeas corpus and the absence of a comparable requirement under § 1983.

I

At the outset, it is important to consider the nature of the line that the Court has drawn. The Court holds today that "when a state prisoner is challenging the very fact or duration of his physical imprisonment, and the relief he seeks is a determination that he is entitled to immediate release or a speedier release from that imprisonment, his sole federal remedy is a writ of habeas corpus." But, even under the Court's approach, there are undoubtedly some instances where a prisoner has the option of proceeding either by petition for habeas corpus or by suit under § 1983.

. . . .

In sum, the absence of an exhaustion requirement in § 1983 is not an accident of history or the result of careless oversight by Congress or this Court. On the contrary, the no-exhaustion rule is an integral feature of the statutory scheme. Exhaustion of state remedies is not required precisely because such a requirement would jeopardize the purposes of the Act. For that reason, the imposition of such a requirement, even if done indirectly by means of a determination that jurisdiction under § 1983 is displaced by an alternative remedial device, must be justified by a clear statement of congressional intent, or, at the very least, by the presence of the most persuasive considerations of policy. In my view, no such justification can be found.

NOTES AND QUESTIONS

1. In *Preiser*, the Court states that "the broad language of § 1983 seems literally to apply," yet rules the section inapplicable. Does use of the canon add anything of significance to the Court's analysis? Is the policy consideration for exhaustion of state remedies inherent in concepts of habeas corpus simply elevated over the considerations underlying the 1866 statute — § 1983?

2. Is the 1948 revision of the habeas corpus law as compared to the 1866 date of § 1983 of any relevance? Given the more extensive nature of federal legislative history, should not the Court have some evidence that Congress intended the later law to apply? The fact that § 1983 was dormant for about 100 years may indicate the reason for the conflict. Does that fact, therefore, make invalid any assumption of legislative intent on the conflict?

3. The federal Magnuson-Moss Warranty Act is a consumer-protection statute providing a cause of action in court that is unwaivable. On the other hand, the Federal Arbitration Act instructs courts to honor arbitration clauses in contracts. On this apparent conflict, see Andrew P. Lamis, *The New Age of Artificial Legal Reasoning as Reflected in the Judicial Treatment of the Magnuson-Moss Act and the Federal Arbitration Act*, 15 Loy. Consumer L. Rev. 173 (2003); Daniel G. Lloyd, *The Magnuson-Moss Warranty Act v. The Federal Arbitration Act: The Quintessential Chevron Case*, 16 Loy. Consumer L. Rev. 1 (2003); Mace E. Gunter, *Can Warrantors Make an End Run? The Magnuson-Moss Act and Mandatory Arbitration in Written Warranties*, 34 Ga. L. Rev. 1483 (2000).

3. Note on Repeals

When legislation is repealed, the courts may subsequently face problems of statutory interpretation. Most of these problems involve the precise definition of what has been eliminated by the repealing act. These questions occur because legislatures seldom undertake a comprehensive review of the laws in force before enacting new legislation. Consequently, they are often unaware that a bill under consideration contradicts one or more previously enacted statutes.

It is imperative to note the distinction between repeal and amendment. An act is amended when a portion is added to it, or when a portion is withdrawn and another is substituted for it. A repeal, in contrast, is the elimination of an act or any number of its sections without replacing them by provisions having the same or similar effect.

There are two types of repealing statutes: those which recognize an inconsistency and describe the prior enactments to be eliminated are "express"; those giving no indication that inconsistencies with prior enactments exist are "implied."

An express repeal requires that one be able to identify those statutes to be eliminated through their description in the repealing act. Generally, if a description is sufficient to lead one to the prior enactment the repeal will be effective. Following somewhat naturally, to the extent that there is a specific repeal, "the existence of a specific repealer is considered to be some evidence of an intent that further repeals by implication are not intended by the legislature." *Buffum v. Chase National Bank of City of New York*, 192 F.2d 58 (7th Cir. 1951).

Implied repeals create complex problems for the courts. Judges are often faced with the arduous task of reviewing legislative history to determine the scope and purpose of the repealing legislation, a job they must feel the legislature should have performed. Such a search will usually be limited to repeals of provisions involving the subject matter under consideration by the legislature, but, obviously, at times, a fine line must be drawn. Before finding an implied repeal, the courts must also overcome a presumption that the legislature enacts a consistent body of law. *See, e.g., Stevens v. Biddle*, 298 F. 209 (8th Cir. 1924). This presumption has been described as follows:

(1) The "cardinal rule" is that repeal by implication is disfavored.

(2) When two acts cover the same subject, or otherwise appear to involve a possible inconsistency, the aim is to give effect to both if possible.

(3) The intent of the legislature to repeal must be "clear and manifest."

(4) The intent of the legislature is to be ascertained by accepted rules of statutory construction.

(5) A repeal by implication obtains only to the extent necessary.

(6) There are two well-settled categories of repeals by implication — (1) where provisions in the two acts are in irreconcilable conflict, the later act to the extent of the conflict constitutes an implied repeal of the earlier one; and (2) if the later act covers the whole subject of the earlier one and is clearly intended as a substitute, it will operate similarly as a repeal of the earlier act.

46 U. Colo. L.R. at 306 (1974).

The concept of implied repeals surfaced in two cases involving federal legislation. In the most recent, *T.V.A. v. Hill*, 435 U.S. 902 (1978), defendant's argument was that an appropriation act granting funds to be used for a dam constituted an implied repeal of provisions in the previously enacted Endangered Species Act, which would otherwise have required discontinuance of the work. The Supreme Court firmly rejected this argument in an opinion by Chief Justice Burger, who pointed out the disfavored status of the concept and its inappropriateness in the circumstances. The Court's opinion is set forth later in this Chapter. In contrast, an earlier opinion in *Friends of the Earth v. Armstrong*, 485 F.2d 1 (10th Cir. 1973), held that subsequent federal appropriations legislation refusing funds for a protective bulwark around the Rainbow Bridge National Monument to prevent its erosion from flooding created by the construction of a downstream dam impliedly repealed a prior statute that had made the protective work a condition precedent to completion of the dam. This decision has been strongly criticized for misinterpreting the contrary federal legislative history. That case is also set forth later in this Chapter.

Repeals also can occur when legislation is amended or comprehensively revised. After an amendatory act is passed, some courts have held that provisions of the original which are irreconcilable with the amendment are impliedly repealed. Courts have thought such repeals even more appropriate where the subject matter in an amended section is inconsistent with the provisions in that same section in the original. *See, e.g., Marine Trust Co. v. Kenngott*, 175 Misc. 362, 22 N.Y.S.2d 869 (1940). The logic of these positions can easily be rebutted, however, since a presumption exists that the legislature was cognizant, at least, of the provisions of the act it was amending. Presumably, it would have specified and expressly repealed sections thought to be inconsistent with the amendments.

When a legislature undertakes a comprehensive revision of a particular subject, some courts have found this to manifest a strong intent to repeal all existing law on that subject. *Orange City Water Co. v. Town of Orange City*, 255 So. 2d 257 (Fla. 1971). Evidence that the legislature intended such a revision has been discerned in the title of an act or the advisory committee's notes for a code.

As all these examples suggest, implied repeals can only be sustained by straining to find a basis for imputing legislative intent. The necessity for this action may suggest the invalidity of the exercise.

Another problem encountered is interpreting the effect of a repeal of what was, itself, a repealing provision. Blackstone stated the common-law answer to this problem as follows:

> If a statute, that repeals another, is itself repealed afterwards, the first statute is hereby revived, without any formal words for that purpose. So when the statutes of 26 and 35 Hen. VIII., declaring the king to be the supreme head of the church, were repealed by a statute 1 and 2 Philip and Mary, and this latter statute was afterwards repealed by an act of 1 Eliz., there needed not any express words of revival in Queen Elizabeth's statute, but these acts of King Henry were implied and virtually revived.

1 BLACKSTONE'S COMMENTARIES 90.

Several states and the United States (1 U.S.C. § 109) have enacted legislation abrogating the common-law rule. In these jurisdictions, a previously repealed law cannot be revived by eliminating the repealing provision.

F.   SUBSTANTIVE LEGISLATION BY APPROPRIATIONS ACT

Legislation by appropriation occurs when Congress changes substantive law through passage of an appropriations bill, rather than through a substantive enactment. Appropriations committees, however, are not delegated authority by the body to consider substantive legislation; the committee's authority extends only to allocation of funds, through determinations of subcommittees that are organized around functional budget areas. Distribution of funds to various activities within its area of concern is a subcommittee's only real responsibility. Overall budget amounts by functional area are now established, in advance, on the basis of resolutions initiated by the budget committees in each house. The enactment of the new budget process has substantially limited the appropriations committee's role.

The effect of congressional organization by committees is that not only does the committee have no authority to act on matters outside its delegated role, its members generally lack the expertise that would justify such action. These facts thus make recourse to an appropriation act's legislative history of questionable value with respect to interpreting the effect of the appropriations act on other substantive legislation.

Despite the limited authority of appropriations committees, appropriations bills when enacted are law and can affect other legislation. Floor amendments or "riders" can be attached to appropriations bills, just as with other legislation, since Congressional enactments are not limited to one subject as is required by some state constitutions. To preclude the possibility of members' attempting to bypass the normal allocation of committee responsibilities by attaching amendments to appropriations acts, the rules of both houses permit a member to raise a point of order to provisions that make a change in substantive law.

There are several exceptions to the current point of order procedures such as those authorized by current House Rule XXI. Provisions which reduce or limit expenditures authorized in the substantive act (a "retrenchment") are not subject to a point of order under an exception known as the Holman Rule. Additionally, a waiver of Rule XXI can be obtained from the Rules Committee for a specific bill, although any subsequent substantive amendments would still be subject to a point of order.

One of the major objections to such riders is that they are not subject to hearings or committee deliberations. In recent years, issues that the substantive committees would not consider have been tacked onto appropriations acts by cutting off funds for federally funded abortions, supersonic transports, the Vietnam War and bussing of school children.

Provisions that reduce or limit funds are not subject to a point of order (under the Holman Rule) even if the effect is to totally delete a program. The effect, however, will only be for the period covered by the annual appropriations bill, and the activity can be funded in the next year or by a Supplemental Appropriations Act.

Senate Rule XVI(4) is analogous to House Rule XXI(2).

IN EFFECT, A SEPARATE SYSTEM: THE "TWO-CONGRESS" THEORY

These materials are based primarily on the Congressional appropriations process. It used to be the preserve of insiders and technicians. Few realized that the budgeting and appropriations process was "the life-blood of government, the medium through which flowed the essential life-support systems of public policy." AARON WILDAVSKY, THE NEW POLITICS OF THE BUDGETARY PROCESS vii (1988). Repeated fiscal crises at the national, state, and local government levels have brought stories about the budget and appropriations process to the focus of public attention. Although the materials in this edition are primarily oriented toward the workings of the federal government, students are encouraged to familiarize themselves with the diverse mechanisms for translating policy choices into dollars in the state and subordinate jurisdictions in which they intend to practice.

The public is most familiar with that portion of the legislature's work product which makes substantive policy. For example, the Legal Services Corporation Act, 42 U.S.C. § 2996 et seq., establishes a federally funded program of legal assistance to the poor. Not everyone is aware, however, that before a cent can be spent pursuant to this law, a separate law must be enacted which appropriates funds to carry out the substantive program embodied in the Legal Services Corporation Act.

This two-step procedure is the authorization-appropriations process. This process institutionalizes a division of labor within Congress between authorizing committees (the judiciary committee, for example), which have legislative jurisdiction over substantive programs, and the appropriations subcommittee for the Justice Department, which has legislative jurisdiction over providing funding for these programs.

Thus, an authorizing committee is defined as "a standing committee of the House or Senate with legislative jurisdiction over the subject matter of those laws . . . that set up or continue the legal operations of Federal programs or agencies." Authorizing legislation is "substantive legislation enacted by Congress that sets up or continues the legal operation of a Federal program or agency . . . or sanctions a particular type of obligation or expenditure within a program." U.S. General Accounting Office, A Glossary of Terms Used in the Federal Budget Process 39 (3d ed. 1981). An appropriation act is "a statute, under the jurisdiction of the House and Senate Committees on Appropriations that generally provides authorization for Federal agencies to incur obligations and to make payments out of the Treasury for specified purposes." *Id.* at 35. "Authorization" is used in two senses in the foregoing quotations. The "authorizations" on which an "authorizing committee" performs its legislative role are programming tasks which set the contents of bills and laws within its substantive jurisdiction. The "authorization" to spend, under appropriations committees' jurisdiction, on the other hand, is "permission," *e.g.* permission to a federal agency to draw money from the Treasury and spend it. The term "federal agency" should be understood in its broadest sense.

Since authorizing legislation normally precedes appropriations legislation, the workings of the authorization-appropriations process may be conveniently conceptualized by the "two-Congress theory," which treats the authorizing function as if it were performed by a different legislature from the one that carries out the appropriations function.

For a useful description of the appropriations process, see generally, Louis Fisher, *The Authorization-Appropriation Process in Congress: Formal Rules and Informal Practices*, 29 CATH. U. L. REV. 51 (1979); Kenneth W. Dam, *The American Fiscal Constitution*, 44 U. CHI. L. REV. 271 (1977).

Under the "two-Congress" theory, after the first legislature completes its task and a new government program becomes law with the signature of the President, a second legislative process begins which may significantly change the substantive and temporal shape of the new program or even prevent it from ever coming into existence. The participants are the same and the procedures are very similar. This "second legislature," nevertheless, is quite separate and sometimes acts as if it had no relationship to the body that created the programs.

The factor that differentiates and defines the work of these two congresses is the committee system. While one committee is responsible for substantive legislation in a particular field, an entirely different committee, generally composed of entirely different members and often possessed of a different philosophy, is responsible for providing funds for that same legislation. This divergence is true even though most members will serve on one authorizing committee and some of them will also be on an appropriations subcommittee, but seldom is there any overlap of substantive area between the two.

Although the development of regulatory legislation is an important function of Congress, the creation and funding of federal programs constitutes an even more important part of the work that Congress performs. Moreover, even regulatory programs require funds to operate. Congress determines the actual level of funding for a program by a separate appropriations act enacted after the measure creating the program has become law. Those who work for enactment of any governmental program or activity through the legislative process soon learn that their job is not completed simply because they have succeeded in the "first legislature." Often an effort equivalent to that required initially to obtain authorization for a program must be undertaken in order to get it funded.

The typical order of action that proceeds enactment of a program is a familiar one. The measure is initiated in the appropriate legislative subcommittee in either house. Subcommittees designated for particular substantive areas evaluate programs and determine their cost. The subcommittee then prepares a report and refers the bill to the whole committee, which, in turn, studies the bill and reports it to the whole house. Once approved by Congress and signed by the President, these bills become the authorizing legislation for a specific program. For the related funding permission, the process is similar except the measure generally starts as part of the President's annual budget structured under rules first set forth in the Budget and Accounting Act of 1921 and processed under the Congressional Budget and Impoundment Control Act of 1974. The President's Budget is split up for processing by the respective appropriations subcommittee having funding jurisdiction for an act or program.

The executive branch agency that will be responsible for administering the program now becomes more visibly involved. The agency studies the legislation and develops plans to implement the new program. Hearings may again be held at the subcommittee level, usually with testimony from the administering agency, but this time before an appropriations subcommittee. This second bill is the appropriations bill. It specifies how much money is to be made available by the Treasury to carry out the purposes of the first act. Such amounts may be less than that authorized, but they essentially cannot exceed the authorization. From the subcommittee, the bill goes to the full committee, the entire house, the other house, and is presented to the President as before.

The procedure for considering appropriations bills is much the same as that for considering authorizations. One of the important differences, however, lies in the interrelation of the actions of the two houses. Traditionally, all appropriations bills originate in the House of Representatives. Most of the initial work and study must necessarily be done there. The Senate, therefore, often functions as sort of a court of appeals. Supporters of programs that were cut from appropriations bills in the House press their case in the Senate. The Senate also examines the appropriation bills to determine if cuts should be made from the House version.

While bills containing authorizations tend to focus on one program or a group of related programs, appropriations bills almost always group together programs by the same administrative agency and often combine appropriations for several different agencies in one bill. Since large amounts of money, a multitude of programs, and a considerable range of conflicting public policy considerations are thus involved in each appropriations bill, there is room for a great deal of disagreement whenever questions of priority arise. Serious dispute between the two chambers on several aspects of virtually every appropriations bill is almost preordained. Conference committees established to resolve these differences hold considerable power in molding federal policy and programs and determining the funding for them. The Conference committee serves as the court of last resort following up on the Senate' s role as an appeals court.

The "Two Congress" procedure gives the chief executive additional power. Unlike the governors of some states, the President does not have the power to "item veto" certain aspects of an appropriations bill while approving the remainder. Nevertheless, the President has power to veto or threaten to veto the entire bill if he objects to specific parts of it. The appropriations process gives the President two opportunities to impose his policy choices.

The following cases indicate the problems that have been created because of the congressional appropriations procedures. These situations have presented difficult cases for the courts to resolve because of the need to consider the effect of internal congressional procedures in order to determine the legislative intent where it is contended that a statutory conflict has occurred.

FRIENDS OF THE EARTH v. ARMSTRONG
485 F.2d 1 (10th Cir. 1973)

Before LEWIS, CHIEF JUDGE, and HILL, SETH, HOLLOWAY, McWILLIAMS, BARRETT and DOYLE, CIRCUIT JUDGES, sitting en banc.

SETH, CIRCUIT JUDGE.

These suits were commenced in the United States District Court for the District of Columbia, and transferred to the District of Utah. They are in the nature of mandamus, and seek also injunctive and declaratory relief. The initial defendants were the Secretary of the Interior and the Commissioner of the Bureau of Reclamation. The plaintiffs seek to have these officials take such action as may be necessary to prevent the water being impounded in Lake Powell from spreading into any part of Rainbow Bridge National Monument.

The plaintiffs are Friends of the Earth, a nonprofit membership corporation organized under the laws of New York . . . .

The trial court, D.C., 360 F. Supp. 165, entered a judgment and decree granting plaintiffs' motion for summary judgment. This decree ordered the defendant officials to take action to have the waters from Lake Powell withdrawn from within the boundaries of Rainbow Bridge National Monument, and to prevent in the future such encroachment.

The defendants and intervening defendants have taken this appeal. The decree of the District Court was stayed pending an expedited hearing of this court sitting en banc on the appeal of the case on its merits.

This case reaches us on the issue of whether or not the trial court was correct in holding that certain provisions of the Colorado River Storage Project Act of 1956 (43 U.S.C. § 620), and especially sections 1 and 3 thereof prohibit any water from Lake Powell entering any part of the Rainbow Bridge National Monument.

The record shows that the water enters the Monument when the water level in Lake Powell reaches 3,606 feet above mean sea level. The plaintiffs did not assert a claim based upon the possibility of physical damage to the Rainbow Bridge itself, but relied upon the statutory provisions in the Colorado River Storage Project Act.

We must conclude that the trial court was in error, and the case must be reversed.

Rainbow Bridge National Monument:

This Monument was created by Presidential Proclamation in 1910, and is a square tract of 160 acres in the southernmost portion of Utah between the Colorado River Canyon and the Arizona state line. The Monument has been visited by few people in past years because of its isolated location. It is a very important Monument and contains a unique work of nature. Rainbow Bridge itself is an impressive natural sandstone arch of great size extending across the inner gorge or cut of Bridge Creek within a larger canyon. Within and under the span, the inner gorge of Bridge Creek is seventy to seventy-five feet deep and extends below the lower base or abutment of the arch. It has steep, rocky, shelving, sandstone sides . . . .

As the level of Lake Powell rises, the water, of course, backs up the side canyons including that of Bridge Creek. When the water level in the Lake reaches 3,606 feet above mean sea level, the reservoir water has moved up the bed of Bridge Creek to a point at the outer boundary of the 160-acre tract of land comprising Rainbow Bridge National Monument. At any higher level the water enters the Monument within the creek bed at the bottom of the deep Bridge Canyon. When the water level of Lake Powell reaches the level of 3,700 feet above sea level, which is the maximum design capacity for Glen Canyon Dam, the reservoir water will be standing in the inner gorge of the creek under the Rainbow Bridge Arch. At this level the water will there have a depth of about forty-eight feet, but will not rise enough to get out of the gorge or to reach the base of the Rainbow Bridge Arch since this point is some twenty-five feet above that level. The water, however, would then be well within the boundaries of the Monument although confined in the inner gorge of the creek.

. . . [T]he water level is subject to frequent and wide variations. This results in an unsightly deposition of sediments and debris, as well as a conspicuous staining of the rocks at the various water levels all through the reservoir area.

. . . .

Glen Canyon Dam:

This Dam is on the Colorado River near the Arizona-Utah boundary and was built in the period 1957 to 1964 . . . .

. . . .

The power facilities at the Dam are designed to generate a large amount of electricity to provide additional power to the Southwest, and to the Pacific Coast. This power generation was considered by Congress at length in the hearings conducted on the proposed construction of the Dam, both as to the availability of the additional power, and the revenue to be derived from its sale. The planned quantity of electricity which was to be generated and the revenues therefrom were predicated upon the Dam being utilized to its maximum design capacity, and this would also provide a firm source on an annual basis.

. . . .

The Statutes:

. . . In 1956 Congress passed the comprehensive Colorado River Storage Act (43 U.S.C. § 620 et seq.; Public Law 485, 84th Cong.2d Sess.) . . . .

. . . .

As part of the Storage Act, Congress included the two following provisions which are in issue here. The record shows this was done in response to the objections made by some conservation groups. Thus Congress in the Storage Act (43 U.S.C. § 620) included a proviso in section 1:

> "That as part of the Glen Canyon Unit the Secretary of the Interior shall take adequate protective measures to preclude impairment of the Rainbow Bridge National Monument."

There was also included in section 3 the following:

> "It is the intention of Congress that no dam or reservoir constructed under the authorization of this Act shall be within any national park or monument."

. . . As construction of Glen Canyon Project proceeded, Congress passed annually the appropriation acts for construction of Glen Canyon Dam itself. These will be hereinafter considered, and are of great significance to the issues raised.

In 1968 Congress passed the Colorado River Basin Project Act (43 U.S.C. § 1501 et seq.). This was to further carry out the Colorado River water development. This Act is significant here because it was considered after Glen Canyon Dam was completed. In the Colorado River Basin Project Act at 43 U.S.C. § 1521(a), provision having been made for construction of the Central Arizona Project in the Lower Basin, it was provided that the full capacity of the aqueduct supplying water to this project could not be used unless Lake Powell was full or releases are made from Lake Powell to prevent the reservoir from exceeding the elevation of 3,700 feet or when water is released pursuant to other provisions of the Act. The Act elsewhere directs that the projects be operated to maintain as nearly as practicable active storage in Lake Mead equal to active storage in Lake Powell. This attempted equality, and the limitation on capacity of the aqueduct, is again based on the operation of Lake Powell to maximum capacity . . . .

The provisions of the Project Act of 1968 (43 U.S.C. § 1501 et seq.) are important in that they directed the Secretary of the Interior to adopt a specific plan for the operation of the reservoirs built pursuant to the 1956 Storage Act. These operating criteria were to insure that the provisions of both the Colorado River Compact and the Upper Basin Compact were carried out; and further, that the treaty deliveries to Mexico were given the proper priority. These criteria were adopted and reported to Congress.

. . . .

From the above description of the legislation, it is apparent that Lake Powell is an important element or link in the Colorado River water and power development. It cannot be considered alone as all the existing projects in the Upper Basin, and the planned ones, are interrelated and interdependent. The projects have different purposes and functions, but are dependent on Lake Powell to provide basic storage necessary to fulfill the delivery requirements to the downstream states and Mexico, especially in dry years. If these requirements can be so met by use of this storage, the upper states can develop the water allocated to them for irrigation and other projects. If this storage is reduced by a limitation on the level of Lake Powell, some projects built, and some authorized, are at least impaired. This interrelation created by the comprehensive plan for development is rather delicate and can be disturbed if the capacity of by far the largest storage or regulating unit is reduced significantly. The total development plan was given extensive consideration by water experts and by Congress. *See* 84 Cong. 1st Sess. (1955), S. Report 128, and 84th Cong. 2d Sess. (1956), House Report 1087. The repayment schedules and power revenues were also fully integrated into the plan. *See* 2 U.S. Code Cong. & Admin. News, 84th Cong. 2d Sess. (1956) 2352–59. This in turn all relates to the above two quoted sections inserted in the Storage Act and about which the issues revolve.

Action by Congress Following the Storage Act:

The provisions contained in the Colorado River Storage Act (43 U.S.C. § 620 et seq.) quoted above which direct the Secretary to take protective measures as to Rainbow Bridge National Monument could not be a more specific reference. It is clearly and solely directed to the extension of Lake Powell water into the Monument. This had been considered at great length during extensive hearings, and was an issue to which the several conservation groups had directed the attention of the members of Congress by a long and vigorous campaign. *See* House Report No. 1087, 84th Cong. 2d Sess. (1956). There were at the time of enactment of the Storage Act no specific plans or cost estimates as to these protective works or measures referred to in section 1. With the inclusion of this provision, with additions to section 3, and with the elimination of the Echo Park Project, the conservation groups, or some of them, apparently withdrew their objections to the Act.

As quoted above, Congress inserted in the Storage Act, in section 3 thereof, the language upon which the plaintiffs place great reliance. It reads:

"It is the intention of Congress that no dam or reservoir constructed under the authorization of this Act shall be within any national park or monument."

This reference is general and all-inclusive as contrasted to the section 1 reference to Rainbow Bridge National Monument. This is a clear and direct expression of the intent of Congress, but is made in the absence of any direct prohibition or affirmative directive. This is again in contrast with section 1; however, we do not consider this factor to be of particular significance, and will assume the section 3 language to be a direct prohibition directed to the appropriate officials.

These two provisions were inserted in the context of plans for the Glen Canyon Dam which included a designed maximum water level of 3,700 feet above sea level. This is apparently the reason for the specific directive in section 1 to the Secretary to take protective measures as to Rainbow Bridge National Monument. It was apparent, and it was discussed, that water would be in the Monument at the designed level. Thus it was obvious from the start that water would be backed up into the Monument if nothing further were done. Of course, the record shows that nothing further was done, and the water has so entered the outer boundaries of the Monument.

As indicated above, there were no firm plans or cost estimates for protective works as there were for all the other aspects of the Glen Canyon Project, when Congress enacted the Storage Act in 1956. Construction began soon after and continued into 1964.

The action taken by Congress after passage of the Storage Act demonstrates a repeal of sections 1 and 3 thereof. The record shows that in 1960, in reference to the 1961 Public Works Appropriation Bill, House Report No. 1634 (86th Cong. 2d Sess.), the budget estimate for Glen Canyon Unit was reduced by $3,500,000. The House Committee Report stated in part:

> "Glen Canyon Unit — An appropriation of $23,535,000 is recommended, a reduction of $3,500,000 in the budget estimate of $27,035,000. This action deletes the funds programmed for protection of the Rainbow Bridge National Monument. It has been estimated that the total cost of protecting this Bridge would be in a vicinity of $20,000,000. Access to this national monument will not be affected by the construction of Glen Canyon dam and reservoir, in fact it will be improved to some extent. *The geological examination report on the problem indicates clearly that there will be no structural damage to Rainbow Bridge by the reservoir waters beneath it.* The Committee sees no purpose in undertaking an additional expenditure in the vicinity of $20,000,000, in order to build the complicated structures necessary to provide the protection contemplated." (Emphasis added).

The $3,500,000 was the request by the Commissioner to begin the protective works for the Monument.

The Senate Committee, on the same Appropriation Act, reached the same conclusion (S. Report No. 1763, 86th Cong. 2d Sess.), and reported in part:

> "The recommendation of the committee is in accord with the House action of disallowing all funds requested for the initiation of construction of facilities to protect the Rainbow Bridge National Monument."

And added:

> "In taking this action the committee has considered the findings of the Geological Survey that the impoundment of water in Glen Canyon Reservoir [Lake Powell] will not result in any structural damage to the Rainbow Bridge."

The deletion of funds by Congress for protective works was fully considered at committee hearings on the 1961 Appropriation Act. It may be noted that Glen Canyon Dam was then several years from completion.

The matter was again considered during the hearings and in the reports for the 1962 Public Works Appropriation Act (*see* 87th Cong. 1st Sess., House Report No. 1125, and Senate Report No. 1097). Requested funds for protective works were again disallowed. The Senate Report No. 1097 explained why — that no damage would result and the costs were too great.

In the 1962 Appropriation Act, this proviso was inserted:

> "Provided, That no part of the funds herein appropriated shall be available for construction or operation of facilities to prevent waters of Lake Powell from entering any National Monument."

Thus the funds specifically requested for protective works by the Commissioner were again disallowed, and of greater significance, the express prohibition as to use of funds was thus added. At hearings again the matter was fully considered.

In 1963 the Secretary of the Interior raised the issue of protective works for Rainbow Bridge before Congress although no formal budget request had been made for them. References in the hearings were made as to the changes in the law, and the Secretary was advised that protective works would not be considered. *See* 87th Cong. 2d Sess. House Subcommittee Hearings on Appropriations, Public Works Appropriations, 1963, Part 3. Also see the Senate Hearings on Public Works Appropriations for 1963.

In the years after 1963 the Secretary did not make further formal requests for funds for protective works. However, all subsequent Appropriation Acts for public works to 1973 carry the same prohibition quoted above. Thus the proviso appeared in some twelve separate Acts, and was considered and enacted during virtually all stages of construction of Glen Canyon Dam and thereafter.

The Appropriation Act for 1972, referred to above, for the Upper Colorado River Storage Project (P.L. 92-134), was considered during the latter part of 1971 and in 1972. This Act contained the same proviso that funds be not used for protective works, and it is of interest that water from Lake Powell was within the boundaries of Rainbow Bridge National Monument continuously from May 15, 1971, to September 15, 1972, and from October 20, 1972, to January 1, 1973.

The record thus demonstrates affirmatively that Congress evaluated the consequences of water encroachment into Rainbow Bridge National Monument, and the difficulty, unsightliness of the protective dam, pumps, and tunnel, and the costs, and made a choice. The resultant specific prohibition as to the use of funds for protective works in the face of the inevitable water advance in the stream bed under the Bridge has overridden the expression of intent in section 3 of the Storage Act as to Rainbow Bridge, and has overriden the specific reference to Rainbow Bridge in section 1 thereof. This indicates that Congress reached the decision not to modify the planned operation of the Glen Canyon Dam nor to authorize protective works to be built . . . .

. . . .

Considering the legislation passed by Congress with reference directly to Lake Powell and which also was predicated upon its use to capacity, together with committee reports directed specifically to the matters here concerned, there is a firm directive by Congress as to Rainbow Bridge National Monument specifically and as to Lake Powell. We have affirmative statements of position by Congress as to the two sections of the Storage Act in issue. This is all in the larger context of prior expressions of the concern of Congress for National Parks and Monuments, and the long series of legislative acts relative to such an important and urgent subject. The position of Congress as to such subjects has thus been made clear, and there resulted somewhat of a collision between such concern and the other important and urgent subject of the implementation of the Colorado River Compacts. This was resolved by Congress, not without some pain and suffering, as described above.

The Authorities:

The basic statutory provisions in the Storage Act (43 U.S.C. § 620 et seq.) with which we are concerned were inserted, as described above, in sections 1 and 3 of the comprehensive statute for the Colorado River Development. These provisions have there remained, but Congress has made them a nullity by the contrary provisions in the many appropriation acts which are supported by its declared reasons set forth in the formal committee reports.

Appropriation acts are just as effective a way to legislate as are ordinary bills relating to a particular subject. An appropriation act may be used to suspend or to modify prior Acts of Congress. In the case before us, there is both the denial of budget requests for the protective works, and also there is the direct prohibition against the use of money for such purposes. In addition, the committee reports described the considerations examined and evaluated by Congress and the reasons for the action taken. This is thus not really a situation of repeal by implication as in *Posadas v. National City Bank*, 296 U.S. 497, 56 S. Ct. 349, 80 L. Ed. 351, but more a reversal of a previous position after considering it fully in the public hearings and after the members apparently came to the conclusion that the protective works would be more detrimental than the presence of water in the Monument. The committee reports indicate it was concluded there would be no physical damage to the Rainbow Bridge itself. This "repeal," if it should be called that, thus was straightforward, direct, and after hearings on the subject.

The Supreme Court, in *United States v. Dickerson*, 310 U.S. 554, 60 S. Ct. 1034, 84 L. Ed. 1356, considered a proviso in an appropriation act that the funds in that or any other appropriation acts could not be used to pay reenlistment allowances. There was a specific statute providing for such allowances. The Court said:

"There can be no doubt that Congress could suspend or repeal the authorization contained in Section 9; and it could accomplish its purpose by an amendment to an appropriation bill, or otherwise."

. . . However, in the case before us the above description of the explanations in the committee reports, and in the legislation itself compel us to say that the provisions in the Storage Act were repealed. The facts in this case present more and stronger reasons for reaching the same result as reached in *United States v. Dickerson* [*supra*].

This case at issue here is significant, and different, however, from the cited cases, in that it does not involve a money provision in both statutes. Instead there is a reference to, and consideration of, what action should be taken with reference to the National Monument in which Congress had expressed concern, and the subsequent money legislation which could or could not have resolved the initial concern. The record shows that Congress evaluated the issues and reached a decision. This is sufficiently well documented in committee reports and otherwise to dictate the conclusion here reached. As the Court said in *Dickerson*:

"The meaning to be ascribed to an Act of Congress can only be derived from a considered weighing of every relevant aid to construction."

In addition to the Appropriation Acts, we have considered the other Acts of Congress, described above, which concerned other dams and projects within the scope of the Storage Act in reaching our conclusions.

. . . .

The plaintiffs argue that the Dam and the Lake should be operated by the Bureau of Reclamation at a reduced level, and the Lake not be filled at any time above the 3,606 foot level. This is basically what the trial court directed. This argument, and the remedy sought, is directed to the executive branch and assumes that the above quoted provisions of the Storage Act be taken by such officials as originally enacted and without regard to what Congress may have since done.

Under such a position, the facilities at Glen Canyon, as related to others in the overall system, would be used to about one-half the design capacity. This in our opinion is contrary to the intention and to the directives of Congress. We have indicated above that the entire development was a balanced system or plan, considered as such by Congress, and so approved. To so radically change the effectiveness of the principal regulating reservoir is to prevent the attainment of the objectives of the Colorado River Compacts, and to prevent the fulfillment of the objectives of the Colorado River Storage Act and the Colorado River Basin Project Act.

. . . .

In conclusion on the argument that Glen Canyon Dam should be operated at less than capacity, we again refer to the portion of this opinion which considers the elimination by Congress of provision for protective works for Rainbow Bridge, and to the termination by Congress, as to Rainbow Bridge, of the application of the general wording in section 3 of the Storage Act. This left the project as planned at the time Congress approved it, and this was to the full extent of its design capacity as now constructed in all respects.

The officials of the Bureau of Reclamation who are charged with the operation of Glen Canyon Dam and Lake Mead have so operated the Dams, and this is correct. There was included a specific admonition by Congress to them that the power generation facilities be operated at their most productive rate (43 U.S.C. § 620f).

. . . .

Thus, it is ordered that the judgment of the trial court is vacated and set aside . . . .

. . . .

LEWIS, CHIEF JUDGE, with whom HILL, CIRCUIT JUDGE, joins, dissenting:

This case brings to the court the necessity of considering several aspects of the continuing controversy between two ideologies, each desirable when viewed in isolation but necessarily clashing in practical application. In particular, the subject matter of the case involves whether the national welfare is best served by maximum conservation and industrial utility of the waters of the Colorado River or whether the national interest requires a modified use so as to protect the natural environment of the area designated as the Rainbow Bridge National Monument. So stated, the issue is a classic one for congressional consideration and not for judicial determination. And since I firmly believe that the posture of the case itself does not bring the controversy within the orbit of judicial concern, I must dissent. A majority of the court is, however, in agreement that Congress has already performed its full function and has clearly indicated that the present national interest requires maximum potential industrial use of the water of Lake Powell as contained back of the Glen Canyon Dam. To reach this result the majority must and does hold that sections 1 and 3 of the Colorado River Storage Act of 1956 (43 U.S.C. § 620, et seq., Public Law 485, 84 Cong. 2d Sess.) have been repealed by implication or so modified as to be impotent under the express wording of the statutes as they still exist in the law. But however viewed[,] I consider the action of the majority to be a deep trespass upon the prerogatives of Congress and a clear and dangerous violation of the doctrine of separation of powers.

Section 1 of the cited Act provides:

> "That as part of the Glen Canyon Unit the Secretary of the Interior shall take adequate protective measures to preclude impairment of the Rainbow Bridge National Monument."

This section makes specific reference to the Rainbow Bridge National Monument but, as the main opinion recognizes, is completely severable in context from section 3, later discussed. However the majority places considerable emphasis upon the repeated refusal of Congress to provide funds for the Secretary of the Interior to implement section 1 as a supporting argument that section 3 has been repealed by implication. I do not agree. Congress authorizes many projects which die aborning from lack of funding or are not immediately implemented by funding. It is not for the courts to deny the validity of the statutory authorization simply from lack of funding. And that is particularly true in the case at bar. As pointed out in the main opinion, funding under section 1 has been specifically negated as to Rainbow Bridge Monument, to me a clear expression of Congress' recognition that section 1 is viable. The majority appears to recognize this in part and would seem to take some of the language contained in the appropriation acts as authority for holding that it is the present intent of Congress to protect only Rainbow Bridge and not the surrounding Monument area. In any event the decision breathes new life into protecting the Bridge proper and designates an allowable depth under the Bridge of fifty-five feet of water as the maximum to be tolerated, retaining jurisdiction for ten years apparently as guardian of the Bridge proper. Perhaps current events have persuaded the majority to impose this restriction. This year's run-off is extremely high and is now in progress. The capacity of Lake Powell has been or soon will be attained through the Glen Canyon Dam reaching its holding capacity. Water is now beneath the Bridge and is expected to reach a depth of forty-eight feet as estimated and the unexpected may occur. The protective order of the main opinion is understandable to me. But such extraordinary judicial action is without precedent and invades the legislative and administrative fields of authority. It is not for this court to say that the Bridge proper is to be protected from the waters of Lake Powell but that the Rainbow Bridge National Monument should not be so protected. Nor should this court volunteer to police the control of Lake Powell waters for a period of ten years or any other period for any purpose whatsoever, absent the necessity of using the injunctive power to enforce an act of Congress and then only under the most extraordinary circumstances. And I consider my views in this regard to be not only applicable to section 1 of the Act but also clearly applicable to section 3. 43 U.S.C. § 620b provides in pertinent part:

> "It is the intention of Congress that no dam or reservoir constructed under the authorization of this chapter shall be within any national park or monument."

This mandate from Congress is not limited in any way to the problem at Rainbow Bridge. The statute is not ambiguous and indeed, it is seldom that Congress deems it necessary to so specifically spell out its intention. The legislative history of the Colorado Storage Act indicates that the inclusion of section 3 was necessary to assure its enactment. Congressman Aspinall (Colo.), then a leading proponent of the Storage Act, in reporting the amended project bill, said "And may I here and now advise the committee that the sponsors of the legislation promise and agree with the Members of the House that they shall keep their agreement with the conservationists of the Nation in this particular." Mr. Aspinall commented further on this "agreement" as follows:

> ". . . We have entered into an agreement with the conservationists to the effect that we would not trespass upon any national park or national monument area in the construction of projects authorized under the provisions of this bill. I mention this because of a colloquy relative to the position of the Sierra Club. Since that time, I have talked to Mr. Brower, the Director of the Club, and he has assured me within the last 20 minutes that their opposition is withdrawn provided we place and keep within this bill the provisions that we will not trespass upon the national park or national monument areas."

Ultimately the Conference Report of the two Houses stated:

> "The matter of retaining intact our national park system was an important issue in the consideration by Congress of this legislation. The House approved bill — (1) deleting the Echo Park Storage unit, (2) requiring 'protective measures to preclude impairment of the Rainbow Bridge National Monument' and (3) expressing the 'intention of Congress that no dam or reservoir constructed under the authorization of this act shall be within any national park or monument,' . . . makes clear the intention of the House that there be no invasion or impairment of the national park system by the works authorized to be constructed under this legislation. The conference committee upheld the House position and adopted the House-approved language."

We start then with an original congressional mandate, not expressly repealed by any subsequent Congress, that *no* reservoir shall be within *any* national monument and the undisputed fact that the Rainbow Bridge National Monument is now flooded even under the Bridge and [end] with the judicial sanction of repeal by implication. To me, the judicial words "repealed by implication," by very definition, carry heavy overtones of erosion into the doctrine of separation of powers. So, too, the chosen words contained in the main opinion "reversal of a previous position" describe an equally dangerous judicial aggression.

Congress has not failed to amend or repeal the subject legislation through inadvertence. Eight different bills have been presented to the United States Congress during the past thirteen years in an attempt to amend the limiting language found in sections 1 and 3 of the Act. Senator Moss has introduced six bills, all identical in nature, to amend section 3 by deleting "[i]t is the intention of Congress that no dam or reservoir constructed under the authorization of the Act shall be within any national park or monument." Senator Bennett and Representative McKay of Utah have each introduced a bill attempting to repeal the limiting language found in the Act. None of these bills has been reported out of committee, evidencing a lack of broad-based support for their passage in the Congress.

Furthermore, the very fact that these Congressmen felt it necessary to introduce amending legislation indicates, at least on their part, no assurance that Congress has in any manner repealed the sections in question. Quite to the contrary, remarks of both Senator Bennett and Senator Moss contained in the Congressional Record manifest a belief that direct repeal is necessary.

The Supreme Court has consistently stated that judicial interpretation is disfavored as a means of establishing a repeal of legislation. In one case only has repeal by implication been upheld. *Mathews v. United States*, 123 U.S. 182, 8 S. Ct. 80, 31 L. Ed. 127. Such implied repeal has been rejected in a multitude of cases . . . .

In simple summation the court has done that which the Congress has many times refused to do and has, to all practical effect, enacted legislation which is actually pending before Congress for its consideration. Such judicial action is unprecedented and while the decision may be heralded by some as a good pragmatic solution to a difficult and controversial problem this is not a judicial prerogative. Current events in other unrelated fields indicate that more problems are created than solved by a softening of the basic concept of a firm and strict application of the doctrine of separation of powers.

I would affirm.

NOTES AND QUESTIONS

1. What is the effect of the statement in the appropriations bill forbidding any funds appropriated from being used to stop the flooding of Rainbow Monument? Why do the majority and dissenting opinions seize on this negative pronouncement to support their positions? Would the result have been different had Congress simply failed to provide an appropriation for this purpose without comment? Was what Congress did an explicit repeal of the prohibition against flooding the Monument?

2. The majority states that, "An appropriations act may be used to suspend or modify prior Acts of Congress." Does the court's view recognize the distinctions between the appropriations process and the process by which authorizing legislation is passed? Given the congressional allocation of responsibility to committees, if expertise on this topic resides in the Interior Committee, why should the Appropriations Committee, whose expertise is in budget matters, have the power to impliedly repeal enacted legislation? Is the Appropriations Committee's power limited to controlling the budget? Under the Rules of each house, only attempts by an appropriations committee to initiate legislation that deals with substantive matters is subject to a point of order and deletion of the provision on objection. What is the policy behind this rule? Should the courts take notice of informal congressional procedures? Is the recognition of the validity of substantive committee reports a recognition of such internal legislative matters?

3. Does the majority opinion ignore a crucial fact by not discussing the numerous attempts by Congress to repeal the legislation protecting the Rainbow Monument? How much should a court read into a refusal to enact a repealing provision in such circumstances?

4. What effect does the "compromise" that was critical in providing support to pass the original Act authorizing the dam have on the interpretation of the provision at issue?

5. The majority opinion refers to the *specific prohibition* in the appropriations bill as overriding the "expression of intent in section 3" and the "specific reference to the Rainbow Bridge in section 1."

Can this holding be explained by the following arguments?

A) A specific statute will be given effect over a more general one applicable to the same situation.

B) A later enacted statute will control a prior one when there is irreconcilable conflict between them.

6. Is there a difference between applying either of these rules and simply repealing sections 1 and 3 of that Act by implication? Why does the court apparently find it necessary to specifically deny that this is a case of repeal by implication?

7. In *Brooks v. Dewar*, 313 U.S. 354 (1941), repealed appropriations were held to have authorized administrative actions for which there was no substantive basis in the act being funded. The Court felt that floor statements gave further support for its rationale. The substantive legislation, the Taylor Grazing Act, required the Secretary of the Interior to issue renewable term permits with fees adjusted to individual costs. In fact, the Secretary had been issuing permits at uniform fees per head of livestock grazed. The Court held the appropriation acts ratified the new fee structure since there was "plentiful and varied information" on the Secretary's practices before Congress and the Appropriations Committee.

Presumably, the applicability of an appropriations act to prior legislation can be resolved on the basis of general principles of legislative interpretation and with recourse to legislative history. Does an appropriations committee's repeated appropriation of funds for a program where the agency that administers it has modified the substantive legislation, constitute a legislative act that justifies the assumption that the whole body ratifies the administrative practices, and thus, implicitly, the substantive legislation? How is a compiler of laws to document the relationship between the two statutes? Is it appropriate to assume the substantive committee has knowledge of and has acquiesced in the changes? Shouldn't the appropriations act make specific reference to the amended substantive legislation if a modification of the latter is intended? How does each house's rule on the availability of points of orders for substantive changes affect the analysis on these questions?

Brooks also raises a number of other issues. How much weight should an agency's "self-serving" testimony at the hearings be given in such circumstances? If there is a clear difference of opinion on a matter between the substantive and appropriations committees, should the court take notice of that fact in determining the application of appropriations acts to substantive matters? Would it be significant if the substantive committee held oversight hearings and took no action?

8. Appropriations committees are more likely to have an annual review of administrative actions in reassessing the need for funding; substantive committees may not necessarily take annual action unless the substantive act requires annual authorization of funds. Authorizations may be indefinite or for five-year periods. What effects might proposals for "sunset" legislation that requires reauthorization of each program within a set time (*e.g.*, five years) to prevent automatic death of the program have on the relationship between appropriations and authorizing committees?

9. A result contrary to *Brooks* occurred in *National Wildlife Federation v. Andrus*, 440 F. Supp. 1245 (D.C. Cir. 1977). In *Andrus*, the government had argued that annual appropriation of funds for a Navajo Indian Irrigation Project for a three-year period along with statements on the floor in support of the changes were sufficient to authorize a change in the facility's location and an increase in its size when construction of the original facility became impractical. The court held the new plans were too substantial a deviation from the originally approved facility to withstand challenge by the environmental group, stating at 1250:

    . . . References to the power plant, buried as they are amid many other
    proposals related to NIIP, hardly seem sufficient to alert Congress to the

possibility that it is being asked to appropriate funds for an unauthorized project.

In *City of Los Angeles v. Adams*, 556 F.2d 40 (D.C. Cir. 1977), the court considered the propriety of the Federal Aviation Administration's (FAA) allocation of funds under the Airport and Airway Development Act of 1970, 49 U.S.C. § 1714. Funds were to be apportioned to certain airports based on the number of passengers served by the airports, population of the state in which they were located, and other factors. The appropriations measure designed to implement the section involved substantially less money than authorized by the substantive act. The FAA decided to allocate the money on a priority basis rather than by the apportionment scheme of the substantive act. The court held that the legislation apportionment scheme must be followed. It held that the appropriations act did not modify the substantive act solely because a smaller allocation was made than was originally envisioned, reiterating the doctrine that repeal by implication is disfavored.

Questions about the relevance of appropriations acts to the issue of an administering agency's adherence to statutory requirements are not likely to arise often, since the issue must affect someone's vital interests to justify a suit. To what extent are such issues likely to be raised in Congress? Which members are likely to have knowledge of the discrepancy?

10. In *Associated Electric Coop. v. Morton*, 507 F.2d 1167 (D.C. Cir. 1974), the court rejected an attempt to use subsequent appropriations acts and statements in the Appropriations Committee's reports to show a ratification of administrative changes by the Secretary of the Interior in the setting of electrical charges that were beyond the authority granted in the substantive act.

How relevant to the government's position were supportive statements in the Appropriations Committee reports? Are such sources sufficient to constitute "plentiful information" so as to provide an awareness that changes in substantive acts are intended?

11. Use of appropriation acts to infer congressional assent to the Vietnam War was rejected in *Mitchell v. Laird*, 488 F.2d 611 (D.C. Cir. 1973), where the court stated at 615:

> . . . [W]e regard the Constitution as contemplating various forms of Congressional assent, and we do not find any authority in the courts to require Congress to employ one rather than another form, if the form chosen by Congress be in itself constitutionally permissible. That conclusion, however, leaves unanswered the further question whether the particular forms which the Government counsel at our bar refer to as having been used by Congress in the Indo-China war are themselves of that character which makes them *in toto*, if not separately, a constitutionally permissible form of assent.

> The overwhelming weight of authority, including some earlier opinions by the present writer, holds that the appropriation, draft extension, and cognate laws enacted with direct or indirect reference to the Indo-China war, (and which have been acutely and comprehensively analyzed by Judge Judd in *Berk v. Laird* [317 F. Supp. 715 (E.D.N.Y. 1970)]) did constitute a constitutionally permissible form of assent. *Massachusetts v. Laird* [451 F.2d 26 (1st Cir. 1971)], *Orlando v. Laird* [443 F.2d 1039 (2d Cir. 1971)], *Berk v. Laird, supra*, and *United States v. Sisson*, 294 F. Supp. 511 (D. Mass. 1968). Judge Tamm is content to adhere to that line of authority.

> But Chief Judge Bazelon and I now regard that body of authority as unsound. It is, of course, elementary that in many areas of the law appropriations by Congress have been construed by the courts as involving Congressional assent to, or ratification of, prior or continuing executive action originally undertaken without Congressional legislative approval. Without a pause to cite

or to examine in detail the vast body of cases involving such construction, it is more relevant to emphasize the special problem which is presented when one seeks to spell out from military appropriation acts, extensions of selective service laws, and cognate legislation the purported Congressional approval or ratification of a war already being waged at the direction of the President alone. This court cannot be unmindful of what every schoolboy knows: that in voting to appropriate money or to draft men a Congressman is not necessarily approving of the continuation of a war no matter how specifically the appropriation or draft act refers to that war. A Congressman wholly opposed to the war's commencement and continuation might vote for the military appropriations and for the draft measures because he was unwilling to abandon without support men already fighting. An honourable, decent, compassionate act of aiding those already in peril is no proof of consent to the actions that placed and continued them in that dangerous posture. We should not construe votes cast in pity and piety as though they were votes freely given to express consent. Hence Chief Judge Bazelon and I believe that none of the legislation drawn to the court's attention may serve as a valid assent to the Vietnam war.

Where there is no substantive legislation to the contrary, *i.e.*, there is only an absence of legislative authority not a contrary provision, should appropriation of funds be sufficient to authorize such action? Could a point of order under House Rule XXI, which makes "changing existing law" subject to challenge, be taken in such circumstances?

In *AT & SF v. Callaway*, 382 F. Supp. 610 (D.D.C. 1974), *vacated on other grounds*, 431 F. Supp. 722 (D.D.C. 1977), the court reviewed proposed action by the Army Corps of Engineers to rebuild and enlarge a lock on the Mississippi River near Alton, Illinois. Under 33 U.S.C. § 5, the Corps was authorized to draw expenses for upkeep and repair of waterways, and a report was made to Congress stating that monies were required under this statute for the Alton project. Funds were then appropriated. Later it became evident that the project was not a "repair," but instead involved a substantial increase in lock capacity, a course of action (new construction) which required congressional authorization (*see* 33 U.S.C. § 401). No point of order under Rule XXI was raised against the appropriation, however. The court stated: "the fact that no point of order was raised to the recent appropriation is not indicative of authorization." 382 F. Supp. at 620.

12. Should an appropriations act be considered a sufficient basis to authorize condemnations? The general condemnation statute, 40 U.S.C. § 257, allows condemnation only where authorized by another source. In a situation where no substantive authorization existed, but there was only a general appropriations act for the National Park Service setting aside funds for "the acquisition of lands . . . ," two courts have held the appropriations act sufficient authorization for condemnation. *United States v. Kennedy*, 278 F.2d 121 (9th Cir. 1960); *United States v. 0.37 Acres of Land*, 414 F. Supp. 470 (D. Mont. 1976).

13. For additional references, see *Legislative Bargains and the Doctrine of Repeal by Implication*, 46 U. Colo. L. Rev. 289 (1973); Howard E. Walker, *Appropriating Act Repeals by Implication — A Prior Substantive Enactment*, 54 B.U. L. Rev. 457 (1974); Felicity Hannay, *Rainbow Bridge*, 4 Ecol. L.Q. 385 (1974); Jay D. Christensen, *Friends of the Earth v. Armstrong*, 71 Utah L. Rev. 808 (1973).

TENNESSEE VALLEY AUTHORITY v. HILL
437 U.S. 153 (1978)

Mr. Chief Justice Burger delivered the opinion of the Court.

The questions presented in this case are (a) whether the Endangered Species Act of 1973 requires a court to enjoin the operation of a virtually completed federal dam — which had been authorized prior to 1973 — when, pursuant to authority vested in him by Congress, the Secretary of the Interior has determined that operation of the dam would eradicate an endangered species; and (b) whether continued congressional appropriations for the dam after 1973 constituted an implied repeal of the Endangered Species Act, at least as to the particular dam.

I

The Little Tennessee River originates in the mountains of northern Georgia and flows through the national forest lands of North Carolina into Tennessee, where it converges with the Big Tennessee River near Knoxville. The lower 33 miles of the Little Tennessee takes the river' s clear, free-flowing waters through an area of great natural beauty. Among other environmental amenities, this stretch of river is said to contain abundant trout. Considerable historical importance attaches to the areas immediately adjacent to this portion of the Little Tennessee's banks. To the south of the river's edge lies Fort Loudon, established in 1756 as England's southwestern outpost in the French and Indian War. Nearby are also the ancient sites of several native American villages, the archeological stores of which are to a large extent unexplored.[1] These include the Cherokee towns of Echota and Tennase, the former being the sacred capital of the Cherokee Nation as early as the 16th century and the latter providing the linguistic basic from which the State of Tennessee derives its name.

In this area of the Little Tennessee River the Tennessee Valley Authority, a wholly owned public corporation of the United States, began constructing the Tellico Dam and Reservoir Project in 1967, shortly after Congress appropriated initial funds for its development. Tellico is a multipurpose regional development project designed principally to stimulate shoreline development, generate sufficient electric current to heat 20,000 homes, provide flatwater recreation and flood control, as well as improve economic conditions in "an area characterized by underutilization of human resources and outmigration of young people." Hearings before a Subcommittee of the House Committee on Appropriations, 94th Cong., 2d Sess., at 261. Of particular relevance to this case is one aspect of the project, a dam which TVA determined to place on the Little Tennessee, a short distance from where the river's waters meet with the Big Tennessee. When fully operational, the dam would impound water covering some 16,500 acres — much of which represents valuable and productive farmland — thereby converting the river's shallow, fast-flowing waters into a deep reservoir over 30 miles in length.

The Tellico Dam has never opened, however, despite the fact that construction has been virtually completed and the dam is essentially ready for operation. Although Congress has appropriated monies for Tellico every year since 1967, progress was delayed, and ultimately stopped, by a tangle of lawsuits and administrative proceedings. After unsuccessfully urging TVA to consider alternatives to damming the Little Tennessee, local citizens and national conservation groups brought suit in the District Court, claiming that the project did not conform to the requirements of the National Environmental Policy Act of 1969 (NEPA), 42 U.S.C. § 4331 *et seq.* After finding TVA to be in violation of NEPA, the District Court enjoined the dam's completion pending the filing of an appropriate Environmental Impact Statement. *Environmental Defense Fund v. Tennessee Valley Authority*, 339 F. Supp. 806 (ED Tenn. 1972), *aff'd*, 468 F.2d 1164 (CA6 1972). The injunction remained in effect until late 1973, when the District Court concluded that TVA's final Environmental Impact Statement for Tellico was in compliance with the law. *Environmental Defense Fund v. Tennessee Valley Authority*, 371 F. Supp. 1004 (ED Tenn. 1973), *aff'd*, 492 F.2d 466 (6th Cir. 1974).

A few months prior to the District Court's decision dissolving the NEPA injunction,

---

[1] This description is taken from the opinion of the District Judge in the first litigation involving the Tellico Dam and Reservoir Project. *Environmental Defense Fund v. Tennessee Valley Authority*, 339 F. Supp. 806, 808 (ED Tenn. 1972). In his opinion, "all of these benefits of the present Little Tennessee River Valley will be destroyed by impoundment of the river . . . ." *Ibid.* The District Judge noted that "[t]he free-flowing river is the likely habitat of one or more of seven rare or endangered species." *Ibid.*

a discovery was made in the waters of the Little Tennessee which would profoundly affect the Tellico Project. Exploring the area around Coytee Springs, which is about seven miles from the mouth of the river, a University of Tennessee ichthyologist, Dr. David A. Etnier, found a previously unknown species of perch, the snail darter, or *Percina Imostoma tanasi.* This three-inch, tannish-colored fish, whose numbers are estimated to be in the range of 10,000 to 15,000, would soon engage the attention of environmentalists, the TVA, the Department of the Interior, the Congress of the United States, and ultimately the federal courts, as a new and additional basis to halt construction of the dam.

Until recently the finding of a new species of animal life would hardly generate a cause celebre. This is particularly so in the case of darters, of which there are approximately 130 known species, eight to 10 of these having been identified only in the last five years. The moving force behind the snail darter's sudden fame came some four months after its discovery, when the Congress passed the Endangered Species Act of 1973, 87 Stat. 884, 16 U.S.C. § 1531 *et seq.* 1976 ("Act"). This legislation, among other things, authorizes the Secretary of the Interior to declare species of animal life "endangered" and to identify the "critical habitat" of these creatures. When a species or its habitat is so listed, the following portion of the Act — relevant here — becomes effective:

> "The Secretary [of the Interior] shall review other programs administered by him and utilize such programs in furtherance of the purposes of this Act. All other Federal departments and agencies shall, in consultation with and with the assistance of the Secretary, utilize their authorities in furtherance of the purposes of this Act by carrying out programs for the conservation of endangered species and threatened species listed pursuant to section 4 of this Act and *by taking such action necessary to insure that actions authorized, funded, or carried out by them do not jeopardize the continued existence of such endangered species and threatened species or result in the destruction or modification of habitat of such species* which is determined by the Secretary, after consultation as appropriate with the affected States, to be critical." 16 U.S.C. § 1536 (emphasis added).

In January 1975, the respondents in this case and others petitioned the Secretary of the Interior to list the snail darter as an endangered species. After receiving comments from various interested parties, including TVA and the State of Tennessee, the Secretary formally listed the snail darter as an endangered species on November 10, 1975. 40 Fed. Reg. 47505–47506; *see* 50 C.F.R. § 17.11(I). In so acting, it was noted that "the snail darter is a living entity which is genetically distinct and reproductively isolated from other species." 40 Fed. Reg., at 47505. More important for the purposes of this case, the Secretary determined that the snail darter apparently lives only in that portion of the Little Tennessee River which would be completely inundated by the reservoir created as a consequence of the Tellico Dam's completion. *Id.*, at 47506. The Secretary went on to explain the significance of the dam to the habitat of the snail darter:

> "[T]he snail darter occurs only in the swifter portions of shoals over clean gravel substrate in cool, low-turbidity water. Food of the snail darter is almost exclusively snails which require a clean gravel substrate for their survival. *The proposed impoundment of water behind the proposed Tellico Dam would result in total destruction of the snail darter's habitat." Ibid.* (emphasis added).

Subsequent to this determination, the Secretary declared the area of the Little Tennessee which would be affected by the Tellico Dam to be the "critical habitat" of the snail darter. 41 Fed. Reg. 13926–13928; *see* 50 C.F.R. § 17.81. Using these determinations as a predicate, and notwithstanding the near completion of the dam, the Secretary declared that pursuant to § 7 of the Act, "all Federal agencies must take such action as is necessary to insure that actions authorized, funded, or carried out by them do not result in the destruction or modification of this critical habitat area." 41 Fed. Reg., at 13928; 50 C.F.R., at § 17.81(b). This notice, of course, was pointedly directed at TVA and clearly aimed at halting completion or operation of the dam.

During the pendency of these administrative actions, other developments of relevance to the snail darter issue were transpiring. Communication was occurring between the Department of the Interior's Fish and Wildlife Service and TVA with a view toward settling the issue informally. These negotiations were to no avail, however, since TVA consistently took the position that the only available alternative was to attempt relocating the snail darter population to another suitable location. To this end, TVA conducted a search of alternate sites which might sustain the fish, culminating in the experimental transplantation of a number of snail darters to the nearby Hiwassee River. However, the Secretary of the Interior was not satisfied with the results of these efforts, finding that TVA had presented "little evidence that they have carefully studied the Hiwassee to determine whether or not" there were "biological and other factors in this river that [would] negate a successful transplant." 40 Fed. Reg., at 47506.

Meanwhile, Congress had also become involved in the fate of the snail darter. Appearing before a Subcommittee of the House Committee on Appropriations in April 1975 — some seven months before the snail darter was listed as endangered — TVA representatives described the discovery of the fish and the relevance of the Endangered Species Act to the Tellico Project . . . . At that time TVA presented a position which it would advance in successive forums thereafter, namely, that the Act did not prohibit the completion of a project authorized, funded, and substantially constructed before the Act was passed. TVA also described its efforts to transplant the snail darter, but contended that the dam should be finished regardless of the experiment's success. Thereafter, the House Committee on Appropriations, in its June 20, 1975 report, stated the following in the course of recommending that an additional $29 million be appropriated for Tellico:

> "The *Committee* directs that the project, for which an environmental impact statement has been completed and provided the Committee, should be completed as promptly as possible . . . ." H.R. Rep. No. 94-319, 94th Cong., 1st Sess., 76 (1975). (Emphasis added.)

Congress then approved the TVA general budget, which contained funds for continued construction of the Tellico Project.[14]

In December 1975, one month after the snail darter was declared an endangered species, the President signed the bill into law. Public Works for Water and Power Development and Energy Research Appropriations Act, 1976, 89 Stat. 1035, 1047.

In February 1976, pursuant to § 11(g) of the Endangered Species Act, 16 U.S.C. § 1540(g), respondents filed the case now under review, seeking to enjoin completion of the dam and impoundment of the reservoir on the ground that those actions would violate the Act by directly causing the extinction of the species *Percina Imostoma tanasi*. The District Court denied respondent's request for a preliminary injunction and set the matter for trial. Shortly thereafter the House and Senate held appropriations hearings which would include discussions of the Tellico budget.

At these hearings, TVA Chairman Wagner reiterated the agency's position that the Act did not apply to a project which was over 50% finished by the time the Act became effective and some 70 to 80% complete when the snail darter was officially listed as endangered. It also notified the Committees of the recently filed lawsuit's status and

---

[14] TVA projects generally are authorized by the Authority itself and are funded — without the need for specific congressional authorization — from lump sum appropriations provided in yearly budget grants. *See* 16 U.S.C. §§ 831c(j) and 831z.

reported that TVA's efforts to transplant the snail darter had "been very encouraging." Hearings on Public Works for Water and Power Development and Energy Research and Appropriation Bill, 1977, before a Subcommittee of the House Committee on Appropriations, 94th Cong., 2d Sess., Part 5, 261–262 (1976); Hearings on Public Works for Water and Power Development and Energy Research Appropriations Bill, 1977, before a Subcommittee of the Senate Committee on Appropriations, 94th Cong., 2d Sess., Part 4, 3096–3099 (1976).

Trial was held in the District Court on April 29 and 30, 1976, and on May 25, 1976, the court entered its memorandum opinion and order denying respondents their requested relief and dismissing the complaint. The District Court found that closure of the dam and the consequent impoundment of the reservoir would "result in the adverse modification, if not complete destruction, of the snail darter's critical habitat," making it "highly probable" that "the continued existence of the snail darter" would be "jeopardize[d]." *Hill v. Tennessee Valley Authority*, 419 F. Supp. 753, 757 (ED Tenn. 1976). Despite these findings, the District Court declined to embrace the plaintiff's position on the merits: that once a federal project was shown to jeopardize an endangered species, a court of equity is compelled to issue an injunction restraining violation of the Endangered Species Act.

In reaching this result, the District Court stressed that the entire project was then about 80% complete and, based on available evidence, "there [were] no alternatives to impoundment of the reservoir, short of scrapping the entire project." 419 F. Supp., at 758. The District Court also found that if the Tellico Project was permanently enjoined, "[s]ome $53 million would be lost in nonrecoverable obligations," 419 F. Supp., at 759, meaning that a large portion of the $78 million already expended would be wasted. The court also noted that the Endangered Species Act of 1973 was passed some seven years after construction on the dam commenced and that Congress had continued appropriations for Tellico, with full awareness of the snail darter problem. Assessing these various factors, the District Court concluded:

"At some point in time a federal project becomes so near completion and so incapable of modification that a court of equity should not apply a statute enacted long after inception to produce an unreasonable result . . . . Where there has been an irreversible and irretrievable commitment of resources by Congress to a project over a span of almost a decade, the Court should proceed with a great deal of circumspection." 419 F. Supp., at 760.

To accept the plaintiffs' position, the District Court argued, would inexorably lead to what it characterized as the absurd result of requiring "a court to halt impoundment of water behind a fully completed dam if an endangered species were discovered in the river on the day before such impoundment was scheduled to take place. We cannot conceive that Congress intended such a result." 419 F. Supp., at 763.

Less than a month after the District Court decision, the Senate and House Appropriations Committees recommended the full budget request of $9 million for continued work on Tellico. See S. Rep. No. 94-960, 94th Cong., 2d Sess., 96 (1976); H. R. Rep. No. 94-1223, 94th Cong., 2d Sess., 83 (1976). In its report accompanying the appropriations bill, the Senate Committee stated:

"During subcommittee hearings, TVA was questioned about the relationship between the Tellico project's completion and the November 1975 listing of the snail darter (a small three-inch fish which was discovered in 1973) as an endangered species under the Endangered Species Act. TVA informed the Committee that it was continuing its efforts to preserve the darter, while working towards the scheduled 1977 completion date. TVA repeated its view that the Endangered Species Act did not prevent the completion of the Tellico project, which has been under construction for nearly a decade. The subcommittee brought this matter, as well as the recent U.S. District Court's decision upholding TVA's decision to complete the project, to the attention of the full

Committee. *The Committee does not view* the Endangered Species Act as prohibiting the completion of the Tellico project at its advanced stage and directs that this project be completed as promptly as possible in the public interest." S. Rep. No. 94-960, *supra*, at 96. (Emphasis added.)

On June 29, 1976, both Houses of Congress passed TVA's general budget, which included funds for Tellico; the President signed the bill on July 12, 1976. Public Works for Water and Power Development and Energy Research Appropriations Act, 1977, Pub. L. 94-355, 90 Stat. 889, 899.

Thereafter, in the Court of Appeals, respondents argued that the District Court had abused its discretion by not issuing an injunction in the face of "a blatant statutory violation." *Hill v. Tennessee Valley Authority*, 549 F.2d 1064, 1069 (CA6 1977). That court agreed, and on January 31, 1977 it reversed, remanding "with instructions that a permanent injunction issue halting all activities incident to the Tellico Project which may destroy or modify the critical habitat of the snail darter." 549 F.2d, at 1075. The Court of Appeals directed that the injunction "remain in effect until Congress, by appropriate legislation, exempts Tellico from compliance with the Act or the snail darter has been deleted from the list of endangered species or its critical habitat materially redefined." *Ibid.*

The Court of Appeals accepted the District Court's finding that closure of the dam would result in the known population of snail darters being "significantly reduced if not completely extirpated." 549 F.2d, at 1069. TVA, in fact, had conceded as much in the Court of Appeals, but argued that "closure of the Tellico Dam, as the last stage of a 10-year project, falls outside the legitimate purview of the Act if it is rationally construed." 549 F.2d, at 1070. Disagreeing, the Court of Appeals held that the record revealed a prima facie violation of § 7 of the Act, namely that TVA had failed to take "such action necessary to insure" that its "actions" did not jeopardize the snail darter or its critical habitat.

The reviewing court thus rejected TVA's contention that the word "actions" in § 7 of the Act was not intended by Congress to encompass the terminal phases of ongoing projects. Not only could the court find no "positive reinforcement" for TVA's argument in the Act's legislative history, but such an interpretation was seen as being "inimical to . . . its objectives." 549 F.2d, at 1070. By way of illustration, that court pointed out that "the detrimental impact of a project upon an endangered species may not always be clearly perceived before construction is well underway." *Ibid.* Given such a likelihood, the Court of Appeals was of the opinion that TVA's position would require the District Court, sitting as a chancellor, to balance the worth of an endangered species against the value of an ongoing public works measure, a result which that court was not willing to accept. Emphasizing the limits on judicial power in this setting, the court stated:

"Current project status cannot be translated into a workable standard of judicial review. Whether a dam is 50 percent or 90 percent completed is irrelevant in calculating the social and scientific costs attributable to the disappearance of a unique form of life. Courts are ill-equipped to calculate how many dollars must be invested before the value of a dam exceeds that of the endangered species. Our responsibility under § 1540(g)(1)(A) is merely to preserve the status quo where endangered species are threatened, thereby guaranteeing the legislative or executive branches sufficient opportunity to grapple with the alternatives." 549 F.2d, at 1071.

As far as the Court of Appeals was concerned, it made no difference that Congress had repeatedly approved appropriations for Tellico, referring to such legislative approval as an "advisory opinion" concerning the proper application of an existing statute. In that court's view, the only relevant legislation was the Act itself, "the meaning and spirit" of which was "clear on its face." 549 F.2d, at 1072.

Turning to the question of an appropriate remedy, the Court of Appeals ruled that the

District Court had erred by not issuing an injunction. While recognizing the irretrievable loss of millions of dollars of public funds which would accompany injunctive relief, the court nonetheless decided that the Act explicitly commanded precisely that result:

> "It is conceivable that the welfare of an endangered species may weigh more heavily upon the public conscience, as expressed by the final will of Congress, than the writeoff of those millions of dollars already expended for Tellico in excess of its present salvageable value." 549 F.2d, at 1074.

Following the issuance of the permanent injunction, members of TVA's Board of Directors appeared before Subcommittees of the House and Senate Appropriations Committees to testify in support of continued appropriations for Tellico. The subcommittees were apprised of all aspects of Tellico's status, including the Court of Appeal's decision. TVA reported that the dam stood "ready for the gates to be closed and the reservoir filled," Hearings on Public Works for Water and Power Development and Energy Research Appropriation Bill, 1978, before a Subcommittee of the House Committee on Appropriations, 95 Cong., 1st Sess., Part 4, 234 (1977), and requested funds for completion of certain ancillary parts of the project, such as public use areas, roads and bridges. As to the snail darter itself, TVA commented optimistically on its transplantation efforts, expressing the opinion that the relocated fish were "doing well and ha[d] reproduced." *Id.*, at 235, 261–262.

Both appropriations committees subsequently recommended the full amount requested for completion of the Tellico Project. In its June 2, 1977 report, the House Appropriations Committee stated:

> "It is *the Committee's view* that the Endangered Species Act was not intended to halt projects such as these in their advanced stage of completion, and [the Committee] strongly recommends that these projects not be stopped because of misuse of the Act." H.R. Rep. No. 95-379, 95th Cong., 1st Sess., 104. (Emphasis added.)

As a solution to the problem, the House Committee advised that TVA should cooperate with the Department of the Interior "to relocate the endangered species to another suitable habitat so as to permit the project to proceed as rapidly as possible." *Id.*, at 11. Toward this end, the committee recommended a special appropriation of $2 million to facilitate relocation of the snail darter and other endangered species which threatened to delay or stop TVA projects. Much the same occurred on the Senate side, with its Appropriations Committee recommending both the amount requested to complete Tellico and the special appropriation for transplantation of endangered species. Reporting to the Senate on these measures, the Appropriations Committee took a particularly strong stand on the snail darter issue:

> "This *committee has not viewed* the Endangered Species Act as preventing the completion and use of these projects which were well under way at the time the affected species were listed as endangered. If the act has such an effect which is contrary to *the Committee's understanding* of the intent of Congress in enacting the Endangered Species Act, funds should be appropriated to allow these projects to be completed and their benefits realized in the public interest, the Endangered Species Act notwithstanding." S. Rep. No. 95-301, 95th Cong., 1st Sess., 99 (1977). (Emphasis added.)

TVA's budget, including funds for completion of Tellico and relocation of the snail darter, passed both Houses of Congress and was signed into law on August 7, 1977. Public Works for Water and Power Development and Energy Research Appropriations Act, 1978, Pub. L. 95–96, 91 Stat. 797.

We granted certiorari, 434 U.S. 954, 98 S. Ct. 478, 54 L. Ed. 2d 312 (1977), to review the judgment of the Court of Appeals.

II

We begin with the premise that operation of the Tellico Dam will either eradicate the known population of snail darters or destroy their critical habitat. Petitioner does not now seriously dispute this fact. In any event, under § 4(a)(1) of the Act, 16 U.S.C. § 1533(a)(1), the Secretary of the Interior is vested with exclusive authority to determine whether a species such as the snail darter is "endangered" or "threatened" and to ascertain the factors which have led to such a precarious existence. By § 4(d) Congress has authorized — indeed commanded — the Secretary to "issue such regulations as he deems necessary and advisable to provide for the conservation of such species." 16 U.S.C. § 1533(d). As we have seen, the Secretary promulgated regulations which declared the snail darter an endangered species whose critical habitat would be destroyed by creation of the Tellico Reservoir. Doubtless petitioner would prefer not to have these regulations on the books, but there is no suggestion that the Secretary exceeded his authority or abused his discretion in issuing the regulations. Indeed, no judicial review of the Secretary's determinations has even been sought and hence the validity of his actions are not open to review in this Court.

Starting from the above premise, two questions are presented: (a) would TVA be in violation of the Act if it completed and operated the Tellico Dam as planned?; (b) if TVA's actions would offend the Act, is an injunction the appropriate remedy for the violation? For the reasons stated hereinafter, we hold that both questions must be answered in the affirmative.

(A)

It may seem curious to some that the survival of a relatively small number of three-inch fish among all the countless millions of species extant would require the permanent halting of a virtually completed dam for which Congress has expended more than $100 million. The paradox is not minimized by the fact that Congress continued to appropriate large sums of public money for the project, even after congressional appropriations committees were apprised of its apparent impact upon the survival of the snail darter. We conclude, however, that the explicit provisions of the Endangered Species Act require precisely that result.

One would be hard pressed to find a statutory provision whose terms were any plainer than those in § 7 of the Endangered Species Act. Its very words affirmatively command all federal agencies "to *insure* that actions *authorized, funded,* or *carried out* by them do not *jeopardize* the continued existence" of an endangered species or "*result* in the destruction or modification of habitat of such species . . . ." 16 U.S.C. § 1536. (Emphasis added.) This language admits of no exception. Nonetheless, petitioner urges, as do the dissenters, that the Act cannot reasonably be interpreted as applying to a federal project which was well under way when Congress passed the Endangered Species Act of 1973. To sustain that position, however, we would be forced to ignore the ordinary meaning of plain language. It has not been shown, for example, how TVA can close the gates of the Tellico Dam without "carrying out" an action that has been "authorized" and "funded" by a federal agency. Nor can we understand how such action will "*insure*" that the snail darter's habitat is not disrupted. Accepting the Secretary's determinations, as we must, it is clear that TVA's proposed operation of the dam will have precisely the opposite effect, namely the *eradication* of an endangered species.

Concededly, this view of the Act will produce results requiring the sacrifice of the anticipated benefits of the project and of many millions of dollars in public funds. But examination of the language, history and structure of the legislation under review here indicates beyond doubt that Congress intended endangered species to be afforded the highest of priorities.

. . . .

Notwithstanding Congress' expression of intent in 1973, we are urged to find that the continuing appropriations for Tellico Dam constitute an implied repeal of the 1973 Act, at least insofar as it applies to the Tellico Project. In support of this view, TVA points to the statements found in various House and Senate appropriations committees' reports; as described in Part I, *supra*, those reports generally reflected the attitude of the *committees* either that the Act did not apply to Tellico or that the dam should be completed regardless of the provisions of the Act. Since we are unwilling to assume that these latter committee statements constituted advice to ignore the provisions of a duly enacted law, we assume that these committees believed that the Act simply was not applicable in this situation. But even under this interpretation of the committees' actions, we are unable to conclude that the Act has been in any respect amended or repealed.

There is nothing in the appropriations measures, as passed, which state that the Tellico Project was to be completed irrespective of the requirements of the Endangered Species Act. These appropriations, in fact, represented relatively minor components of the lump sum amounts for the *entire* TVA budget.[35] To find a repeal of the Endangered Species Act under these circumstances would surely do violence to the "cardinal rule . . . that repeals by implication are not favored." *Morton v. Mancari*, 417 U.S. 535, 549, 94 S. Ct. 2474, 2482, 41 L. Ed. 2d 290 (1974), quoting *Posadas v. National City Bank*, 296 U.S. 497, 503, 56 S. Ct. 349, 352, 80 L. Ed. 351 (1936). In *Posadas* this Court held, in no uncertain terms, that "the intention of the legislature to repeal must be clear and manifest." *Ibid. See Georgia v. Pennsylvania R. Co.*, 324 U.S. 439, 456–457, 65 S. Ct. 716, 725–726, 89 L. Ed. 1051 (1945) ("Only a clear repugnancy between the old and the new [law] results in the former giving [a]way . . ."); *United States v. Borden Co.*, 308 U.S. 188, 198–199, 60 S. Ct. 182, 188, 84 L. Ed. 181 (1939) ("[I]ntention of the legislature to repeal must be clear and manifest . . . . [A] positive repugnancy [between the old and the new laws]"); *Wood v. United States*, 41 U.S. 342, 363, 10 L. Ed. 987 (1842) ("[T]here must be a positive repugnancy . . ."). In practical terms, this "cardinal rule" means that "[i]n the absence of some affirmative showing of an intention to repeal, the only permissible justification for a repeal by implication is when the earlier and later statutes are irreconcilable." *Mancari, supra*, 417 U.S. at 550, 94 S. Ct. at 2482.

The doctrine disfavoring repeals by implication "applies with full vigor when . . . the subsequent legislation is an *appropriations* measure." *Committee for Nuclear Responsibility v. Seaborg*, 149 U.S. App. D.C. 380, 382, 463 F.2d 783, 785 (1971) (emphasis added); *Environmental Defense Fund v. Froehlke*, 473 F.2d 346, 355 (CA8 1972). This is perhaps an understatement since it would be more accurate to say that the policy applies with even *greater* force when the claimed repeal rests solely on an appropriations act. We recognize that both substantive enactments and appropriations measures are "acts of Congress," but the latter have the limited and specific purpose of providing funds for authorized programs. When voting on appropriations measures, legislators are entitled to operate under the assumption that the funds will be devoted to purposes which are lawful and not for any purpose forbidden. Without such an assurance, every appropriations measure would be pregnant with prospects of altering substantive legislation, repealing by implication any prior statute which might prohibit the expenditure. Not only would this lead to the absurd result of requiring Members to review exhaustively the background of every authorization before voting on an appropriation, but it would flout the very rules the Congress carefully adopted to avoid this need. House Rule XXI(2), for instance, specifically provides:

> "No appropriation shall be reported in any general appropriation bill, or be in order as an amendment thereto, for any expenditure not previously autho-

---

[35] The appropriations Acts did not themselves identify the projects for which the sums had been appropriated; identification of these projects requires reference to the legislative history. *See supra*, at 2287 n. 14. Thus, unless a Member scrutinized in detail the committee proceedings concerning the appropriations, he or she would have no knowledge of the possible conflict between the continued funding and the Endangered Species Act.

rized by law, unless in continuation of appropriations for such public works as are already in progress. *Nor shall any provision in any such bill or amendment hereto changing existing law be in order.*" (Emphasis added.)

See also Standing Rules of the Senate, Rule 16.4. Thus, to sustain petitioner's position, we would be obliged to assume that Congress meant to *pro tanto* repeal § 7 of the Act by means of a procedure expressly prohibited under the rules of Congress.

Perhaps mindful of the fact that it is "swimming upstream" against a strong current of well-established precedent, TVA argues for an exception to the rule against implied repealers in a circumstance where, as here, appropriations committees have expressly stated their "understanding" that the earlier legislation would not prohibit the proposed expenditure. We cannot accept such a proposition. Expressions of committees dealing with requests for appropriations cannot be equated with statutes enacted by Congress, particularly not in the circumstances presented by this case. First, the appropriations committees had no jurisdiction over the subject of endangered species, much less did they conduct the type of extensive hearings which preceded passage of the earlier endangered species acts, especially the 1973 Act. We venture to suggest that the House Committee on Merchant Marine and Fisheries and the Senate Committee on Commerce would be somewhat surprised to learn that their careful work on the substantive legislation had been undone by the simple — and brief — insertion of some inconsistent language in appropriations committees' reports.

Second, there is no indication that Congress as a whole was aware of TVA's position, although the appropriations committees apparently agreed with petitioner's views. Only recently in *SEC v. Sloan*, 436 U.S. 103, 98 S. Ct. 1702, 56 L. Ed. 2d 148 (1978), we declined to presume general congressional acquiescence in a 34-year-old practice of the SEC, despite the fact that the Senate committee *having jurisdiction over the Commission's activities* had long expressed approval of the practice. Mr. Justice Rehnquist, speaking for the Court, observed that we should be "extremely hesitant to presume general congressional awareness of the Commission's construction based only upon a few isolated statements in the thousands of pages of legislative documents." *Id.*, at ___, 98 S. Ct., at 1713. *A fortiori*, we should not assume that petitioner's views — and the appropriations committees' acceptance of them — were any better known, especially when the TVA is not the agency with primary responsibility for administering the Endangered Species Act. Quite apart from the foregoing factors, we would still be unable to find that in this case "the earlier and later statutes are irreconcilable," *Mancari, supra*, 417 U.S. at 551, 94 S. Ct. at 2483; here it is entirely possible "to regard each as effective." *Id.*, at 550, 94 S. Ct. at 2482. The starting point in this analysis must be the legislative proceedings leading to the 1977 appropriations since the earlier funding of the dam occurred prior to the listing of the snail darter as an endangered species. In all successive years, TVA confidently reported to the appropriations committees that efforts to transplant the snail darter appeared to be successful; this surely gave those committees some basis for the impression that there was no direct conflict between the Tellico Project and the Endangered Species Act. Indeed, the special appropriation for 1978 of $2 million for transplantation of endangered species supports the view that the committees saw such relocation as the means whereby collision between Tellico and the Endangered Species Act could be avoided. It should also be noted that the reports issued by the Senate and House Appropriations Committees in 1976 came within a month of the District Court's decision in this case, which hardly could have given the Members cause for concern over the possible applicability of the Act. This leaves only the 1978 appropriations, the reports for which issued after the Court of Appeals' decision now before us. At that point very little remained to be accomplished on the project; the committees understandably advise TVA to cooperate with the Department of the Interior "to relocate the endangered species to another suitable habitat so as to permit the project to proceed as rapidly as possible." H.R. Rep. No. 95-379, 95th Cong., 1st Sess., at 11. It is true that the *committees* repeated their earlier expressed "view" that the Act did not prevent completion of the Tellico Project.

Considering these statements in context, however, it is evident that they "represent only the personal views of these legislators," and "however explicit, cannot serve to change the legislative intent of Congress expressed before the Act's passage." *Regional Rail Reorganization Cases*, 419 U.S. 102, 132, 95 S. Ct. 335, 353, 42 L. Ed. 2d 320 (1974).

. . . .

Affirmed.

NOTES AND QUESTIONS

1. The majority opinion in *Hill* holds that there was no implied repeal of the Endangered Species Act by the appropriation acts and that the former Act was unambiguous on its face, therefore requiring cessation of the dam's construction. Would it have made a difference to the Court if the appropriations acts themselves had identified the Tellico dam? Is there any significance to the fact that TVA projects were authorized and funded without the need for specific congressional authorization from lump sum annual budget amounts? (*See* n. 14, Opinion.)

2. For purposes of evaluating legislative history to ascertain legislative intent, are members of Congress likely to assume in appropriating funds for a project that the project is authorized by existing laws? *See Environmental Defense Fund v. Froehlke*, 473 F.2d 346, 355 (8th Cir. 1972).

3. Note the reliance the *Hill* Court placed on House Rule XXI which can be used to prevent an amendment in an appropriations bill which changes existing law. What is the rationale behind Rule XXI?

4. *Hill* reinforces the general doctrine that repeal by implication is disfavored, especially where the vehicle is an appropriations act. After *Hill*, should subsequent appropriation measures ever be construed to impliedly repeal a previous authorizing act? In view of the nature of congressional organization, should appropriations acts have the power to explicitly repeal a substantive act? Does the *Armstrong* case still have vitality after *Hill*? Can *Armstrong* be distinguished on the basis that another substantive act (the 1968 Colorado River Basin Project Act) enacted after the original 1956 substantive act and also after the appropriation acts in question, could be construed to have countermanded the prohibition against allowing periodic backwater buildups from the dam?

Professor Stephen Ross made the following observation about *TVA v. Hill*:

> Some canons may both accurately describe congressional behavior and reflect judicial norms of how legislation should be read. For example, in *Tennessee Valley Authority v. Hill*, 437 U.S. 153, 191–92 (1978), the Supreme Court held that appropriations measures will be presumed not to amend substantive statutes. This presumption reflects both an understanding of Congress's intent, based on House and Senate rules prohibiting substantive legislation on appropriation bills, and normative arguments that statutes should be construed to limit casual, ill-considered, or interest-driven measures that may be easier to attach to appropriations statutes.

Stephen F. Ross, *Where Have You Gone, Karl Llewellyn? Should Congress Turn Its Lonely Eyes To You?* 45 Vand. L. Rev. 561, 563 n.12 (1992).

5. Several days after the Supreme Court's decision in *TVA v. Hill*, a Tennessee congressman introduced an amendment to the Public Works Appropriations Bill which stated: "Provided that $1.8 million be appropriated to complete the Tellico Dam." Representative Dingell, the ranking majority member of the Subcommittee on Fisheries and Wildlife Conservation, and the original author of Section 7, raised a point of order under House Rule XXI. Prior to the ruling from the Chair, however, Dingell withdrew his point of order remarking, that upon a close reading of the amendment, it was evident that it in no way attempted to affect substantive law. The amendment was then approved as was the entire appropriations bill.

What would have been the effect of the amendment upon the Endangered Species Act had the bill not been vetoed? Can congressional intent to amend the Endangered Species Act be assumed because of the vast publicity that was given to the Court's decision?

Should Dingell's remarks be deemed conclusive as to whether the amendment should be construed as an implied repeal? How significant is it that Dingell was the ranking member and former Chairman of the committee, and the author of the critical provision in the Endangered Species Act of 1973? What language should be necessary in an appropriations act in order to effect an implied repeal? Is it possible to avoid a point of order if the language is clear?

6. Rules of the 105 Congress, House Doc. #104-272, 104th Cong 2nd Sess.:

Ramseyer Rule: XIII, clause 3(e):

Germaneness within appropriations is covered under Rule XXI, clause 2(b)

"No provision changing existing law shall be reported in a general appropriations bill, including a provision making the availability of funds contingent on the receipt or possession of information not required by existing law for the period of the appropriation . . . ."

However, although a point of order may lie, on political grounds it may not be asserted in any given circumstance.

7. Justice Powell in dissent argued that *Hill* was not

[a] case where Congress, without explanation or comment upon the statute in question, merely has voted apparently inconsistent financial support in subsequent appropriations acts. Testimony on this precise issue was presented before congressional committees, and the committee reports for three consecutive years addressed the problem and affirmed their understanding of the original congressional intent. We cannot assume — as the Court suggests — that Congress, when it continued each year to approve the recommended appropriations was unaware of the contents of the supporting committee reports. All this amounts to strong corroborative evidence that the interpretation of § 7 as not applying to completed or substantially completed projects reflects the initial legislative intent. *See, e.g., Fleming v. Mohawk Wrecking & Lumber Co.*, 331 U.S. 111, 116, 67 S. Ct. 1129, 1132, 91 L. Ed. 1375 (1947); *Brooks v. Dewar*, 313 U.S. 354, 61 S. Ct. 979, 85 L. Ed. 1399 (1941).

437 U.S. at 210.

Should appropriation committee reports be considered an appropriate source of legislative history for a statute that is not within the appropriation committee's area of expertise? Are such reports more relevant for purposes of determining legislative intent where the interpretation is of the statute for which the appropriations are sought? Should appropriation acts ever be considered to apply to the "initial legislative intent" of the prior substantive or authorizing provision as Powell suggests?

8. For coverage of this case, its aftermath, and its broader context, see KENNETH M. MURCHISON, THE SNAIL DARTER CASE: TVA VERSUS THE ENDANGERED SPECIES ACT (2007).

ROBERTSON v. SEATTLE AUDUBON SOCIETY
503 U.S. 429 (1992)

JUSTICE THOMAS delivered the opinion of the Court.

In this case we must determine the operation of § 318 of the Department of the Interior and Related Agencies Appropriations Act, 1990.

I

This case arises out of two challenges to the Federal Government's continuing efforts to allow the harvesting and sale of timber from old-growth forests in the Pacific Northwest. These forests are home to the northern spotted owl, a bird listed as threatened under the Endangered Species Act of 1973, 16 U.S.C. § 1531 *et seq.* (1998 ed. and Supp. II), since June 1990. *See* 55 Fed. Reg. 26114. Harvesting the forests, say environmentalists, would kill the owls. Restrictions on harvesting, respond local timber industries, would devastate the region's economy.

. . . .

In response to this ongoing litigation, Congress enacted § 318 of the Department of the Interior and Related Agencies Appropriations Act, 1990, 103 Stat. 745, popularly known as the Northwest Timber Compromise. The Compromise established a comprehensive set of rules to govern harvesting within a geographically and temporarily limited domain. By its terms, it applied only to "the thirteen national forests in Oregon and Washington and [BLM] districts in western Oregon known to contain northern spotted owls." § 318(I). It expired automatically on September 30, 1990, the last day of Fiscal Year 1990, except that timber sales offered under § 318 were to remain subject to its terms for the duration of the applicable sales contracts. § 318(k).

The Compromise both required harvesting and expanded harvesting restrictions. Subsections (a)(1) and (a)(2) required the Forest Service and the BLM respectively to offer for sale specified quantities of timber from the affected lands before the end of Fiscal Year 1990. On the other hand, subsections (b)(3) and (b)(5) prohibited harvesting altogether from various designated areas within those lands, expanding the applicable administrative prohibitions and then codifying them for the remainder of the fiscal year. In addition, subsections (b)(1), (b)(2) and (b)(4) specified general environmental criteria to govern the selection of harvesting sites by the Forest Service. Subsection (g)(1) provided for limited, expedited judicial review of individual timber sales offered under § 318.

This controversy centers around the first sentence of subsection (b)(6)(A), which stated in part:

> "[T]he Congress hereby determines and directs that management of areas according to subsections (b)(3) and (b)(5) of this section on the thirteen national forests in Oregon and Washington and Bureau of Land management lands in western Oregon known to contain northern spotted owls is adequate consideration for the purpose of meeting the statutory requirements that are the basis for the consolidated cases captioned *Seattle Audubon Society et al. v. F. Dale Robertson*, Civil No. 89-160 and *Washington Contract Loggers Assoc. et al. v. F. Dale Robertson*, Civil No. 89-99 (order granting preliminary injunction) and the case *Portland Audubon Society et al. v. Manuel Lujan, Jr.*, Civil No. 87-1160-FR."

. . . .

After § 318 was enacted, both the *Seattle Audubon* and *Portland Audubon* defendants sought dismissal, arguing that the provision had temporarily superseded all statutes on which the plaintiffs' challenges had been based. The plaintiffs resisted on the ground that the first sentence of subsection (b)(6)(A), because it purported to direct the results in two pending cases, violated Article III . . . .

The Ninth Circuit . . . held that the first sentence of § 318(b)(6)(A) "does not, by its plain language, repeal or amend the environmental laws underlying this litigation," but rather "directs the court to reach a specific result and make certain factual findings under existing law in connection with two [pending] cases." *Id.*, at 1316. Given that interpretation, the court held the provision unconstitutional under *United States v. Klein*, 80 U.S. (13 Wall.) 128, 20 L. Ed. 519 (1872), which it construed as prohibiting

Congress from "direct[ing] . . . a particular decision in a case, without repealing or amending the law underlying the litigation." 914 F.2d, at 1315. The Ninth Circuit distinguished this Court's decision in *Pennsylvania v. Wheeling & Belmont Bridge Co.*, 59 U.S. (18 How.) 421, 15 L. Ed. 435 (1856), which it construed as permitting Congress to "*amend or repeal* any law, even for the purpose of ending pending litigation." 914 F.2d, at 1315 (emphasis in original).

. . . .

II

The first sentence of subsection (b)(6)(A) provided that "management of areas according to subsections (b)(3) and (b)(5) . . . is adequate consideration for the purpose of meeting the statutory requirements that are the basis for [*Seattle Audubon*] and [*Portland Audubon*]." The Ninth Circuit held that this language did not "amend" any previously existing "laws," but rather "direct[ed]" certain "factual findings" and "specific result[s]" under those laws. 914 F.2d, at 1316. Petitioners interpret the provision differently. They argue that subsection (b)(6)(A) replaced the legal standards underlying the two original challenges with those set forth in subsections (b)(3) and (b)(5), without directing particular applications under either the old or the new standards. We agree.

We describe the operation of subsection (b)(6)(A) by example. The plaintiffs in both cases alleged violations of MBTA § 2, 16 U.S.C. § 703, which makes it unlawful to "kill" or "take" any "migratory bird." Before the Compromise was enacted, the courts adjudicating these MBTA claims were obliged to determine whether the challenged harvesting would "kill" or "take" any northern spotted owl, within the meaning of § 2. Subsection (b)(6)(A), however, raised the question whether the harvesting would violate different prohibitions — those described in subsections (b)(3) and (b)(5). If not, then the harvesting would constitute "management . . . according to" subsections (b)(3) and (b)(5), and would therefore be deemed to "mee[t]" MBTA § 2 regardless of whether or not it would cause an otherwise prohibited killing or taking. Thus under subsection (b)(6)(A), the agencies could satisfy their MBTA obligations in either of two ways: by managing their lands so as neither to "kill" nor "take" any northern spotted owl within the meaning of § 2, or by managing their lands so as not to violate the prohibitions of subsections (b)(3) and (b)(5). Subsection (b)(6)(A) operated identically as well upon all provisions of NEPA, NFMA, FLPMA and OCLA that formed "the basis for" the original lawsuits.

We conclude that subsection (b)(6)(A) compelled changes in law, not findings or results under old law. Before subsection (b)(6)(A) was enacted, the original claims would fail only if the challenged harvesting violated none of five old provisions. Under subsection (b)(6)(A), by contrast, those same claims would fail if the harvesting violated neither of two new provisions. Its operation, we think, modified the old provisions. Moreover, we find nothing in subsection (b)(6)(A) that purported to direct any particular findings of fact or applications of law, old or new, to fact . . . . A statutory directive binds *both* the executive officials who administer the statute *and* the judges who apply it in particular cases — even if (as is usually the case) Congress fails to preface its directive with an empty phrase like "Congress . . . directs that." Here, we fail to see how inclusion of the "Congress . . . directs that" preface undermines our conclusion that what Congress directed — to agencies and courts alike — was a change in law, not specific results under old law.

. . . .

. . . To the extent that subsection (b)(6)(A) affected the adjudication of the cases, it did so by effectively modifying the provisions at issue in those cases.

In the alternative, the Ninth Circuit held that subsection (b)(6)(A) "could not" effect an implied modification of substantive law because it was embedded in an appropriations measure. See 914 F.2d, at 1317. This reasoning contains several errors. First, although repeals by implication are especially disfavored in the appropriations context, *see, e.g., TVA v. Hill*, 437 U.S. 153, 190 (1978), Congress nonetheless may amend substantive law in an appropriations statute, as long as it does so clearly. *See, e.g., United States v. Will*, 449 U.S. 200, 222 (1980). Second, because subsection (b)(6)(A) provided *by its terms* that compliance with certain new law constituted compliance with certain old law, the intent to modify was not only clear, but express. Third, having determined that subsection (b)(6)(A) would be unconstitutional unless it modified previously existing law, the court then became obliged to impose that "saving interpretation," 914 F.2d, at 1317, as long as it was a "possible" one. *See NLRB v. Jones & Laughlin Steel Corp.*, 301 U.S. 1, 30 (1937) ("[A]s between two possible interpretations of a statute, by one of which it would be unconstitutional and by the other valid, our plain duty is to adopt that which will save the act").

We have no occasion to address any broad question of Article III jurisprudence. The Court of Appeals held that subsection (b)(6)(A) was unconstitutional under *Klein* because it directed decisions in pending cases without amending any law. Because we conclude that subsection (b)(6)(A) *did* amend applicable law, we need not consider whether this reading of *Klein* is correct.

NOTES AND QUESTIONS

1. Can the holding in this case be squared with the Supreme Court's approach in *TVA v. Hill*? What about the presumption discussed by Professor Ross?

2. For a critical assessment of substantive amendments in appropriations legislation, see Sandra Beth Zellmer, *Sacrificing Legislative Integrity at the Altar of Appropriations Riders: A Constitutional Crisis*, 21 HARV. ENVIRON. L. REV. 457 (1997).

3. Florida Const., art. III, § 12 provides that:

> Laws making appropriations for salaries and other current expenses of the state shall contain provisions on no other subject.

What result in the instant case if the Florida provision were applicable? How would such a provision have influenced the reasoning in the following Washington case? Does the Florida provision simply shift the battleground as to what is a "current expense"? Can you think of a reason why "current expenses" should be protected from appropriation riders, but long-term capital expenses should not?

FLANDERS v. MORRIS
88 Wash. 2d 183, 558 P.2d 769 (1977)

HUNTER, ASSOCIATE JUSTICE.

Lois Flanders, petitioner in this original mandamus action, is 28 years old, unemployed and in need. Therefore she is entitled to public assistance under the codified public assistance laws of this state: RCW 74.08.025, .04.005(6), (13), and .08.040. However, the supplemental appropriations bill for the 1975–1977 biennium, House Bill 1624 (Laws of 1975, 2nd Ex. Sess., ch. 133, p. 472) contains a provision which limits general, non-continuing public assistance to persons who, if single, are at least 50 years old. Under this law, she is ineligible for assistance . . . . The two constitutional provisions upon which this legislation is challenged are Const. art. 2, § 19, and Const. art. 2, § 37. Const. art. 2, § 19 provides that "No bill shall embrace more than one subject, and that shall be expressed in the title." Const. art. 2, § 37 provides that "No act shall ever be revised or amended by mere reference to its title, but the act revised or the section amended shall be set forth at full length."

Petitioner contends that the action of the legislature in this instance, that of including in a budget bill a new limitation on public assistance eligibility, is offensive to both these provisions of our constitution. Petitioner argues that section 17, subsection 10 of House Bill 1624, is legislation of a substantive nature, amendatory of existing public assistance law, and as such was improperly enacted. The legislature should be required to pass a separate act, which would be codified as an amendment to existing law. Petitioner argues that although the legislature has the power to authorize expenditures in an appropriations bill, and customarily does place limitations on the expenditure of public monies under the title of the appropriations bill, such a title is not sufficient to encompass conditions which amount to substantive changes in the law.

. . . .

Section 17, subsection 10 of the bill, challenged by petitioner, provides in pertinent part:

General assistance for unemployed, employable persons may be provided in accordance with eligibility requirements and standards established by the department to an applicant who:

(a) Meets the eligibility requirements of RCW 74.08.025; and

(b) Is a resident of the State of Washington; and

(c) Is either:

(i) A single person who is fifty years of age or over; or

(ii) A married couple . . . .

Tracing the history of the above quoted provision, we find that it epitomizes the very type of legislation that the two cited constitutional provisions were designed to protect against. We refer to two previous attempts unsuccessfully made to create such an age limitation on public assistance.

First, the Department of Social and Health Services promulgated a regulation. It was struck down by this court as in excess of the agency's administrative authority and in conflict with existing statutes. *Fecht v. Department of Social & Health Serv.*, 86 Wash. 2d 109, 542 P.2d 780 (1975). Subsequent to Fecht Senate Bill 3278 attempted to enact the same limitation under the title:

AN ACT Relating to public assistance; and adding new sections to Chapter 26, Laws of 1959, and to Chapter 74.08, RCW.

The bill was twice voted down in House Committee, and therefore never enacted.

Thus, a law which could not pass on its own merit, under a proper title, became law by being slipped into a 45-page appropriations bill. Aside from the problem of whether legislators were properly put on notice by the title that such a provision was contained within, there is the additional problem that even if they were, they would feel somewhat constrained to reject that single provision. Frequently the appropriations bill is the result of a free conference committee. As such it must be voted on in its entirety and cannot be amended. See Rule 12, 1975 Joint Rules of the Senate and House of Representatives. It is obvious why a legislator would hesitate to hold up the funding of the entire state government in order to prevent the enactment of a certain provision, even though he would have voted against it if it had been presented as independent legislation.

Article 2, section 19 of our state constitution has a dual purpose: (1) to prevent "logrolling," or pushing legislation through by attaching it to other necessary or desirable legislation, and (2) to assure that the members of the legislature and the public are generally aware of what is contained in proposed new laws. In *State ex rel. Washington Toll Bridge Authority v. Yelle*, 54 Wash. 2d 545, 550–51, 342 P.2d 588, 591 (1959), we . . . held that the inclusion in an appropriations act of a provision authorizing the State Highway Commission to annually divert proceeds from a certain excise tax to the Toll Bridge Authority was violative of both article 2, section 19, and article 2, section 37, of our state constitution. We reasoned that the provision was an amendment to existing law, and also that it was legislation of a general and continuing nature lasting beyond the biennium, which went beyond limiting disbursements or qualifying the appropriations. We found it to be a substantive enactment which did not constitutionally belong in an appropriations bill, going on to define such a bill as follows, quoting from *State ex rel. Blakeslee v. Clausen*, 85 Wash. 260, 272, 148 P. 28 (1915):

> . . . An appropriation bill is not a law in its ordinary sense. It is not a rule of action. It has no moral or divine sanction. It defines no rights and punishes no wrongs. It is purely *lex scripta*. It is a means only to the enforcement of law, the maintenance of good order, and the life of the state government. Such bills pertain only to the administrative functions of government . . . .

State ex rel. Washington Toll Bridge Authority v. Yelle, 54 Wash. 2d 545, 551, 342 P.2d 588, 592 (1959).

An appropriations bill which "defines no rights" certainly cannot abolish or amend existing law. It cannot add restrictions to public assistance eligibility and still be said to define no rights. The proper legislative procedure is to enact separate, independent, properly titled legislation.

Clearly, greater latitude must be granted the legislature in enacting multisubject legislation under the appropriations bill title than any other, since the purpose of appropriations bills is to allocate monies for the state's multitudinous and disparate needs. The fact that many states exempt appropriations bills from the subject-title restriction in their constitutions makes clear the difficulty involved in conforming such legislation to the requirement and still getting the job done. *See generally* 1A C. Sands, Sutherland Statutory Construction § 17.01 (4th ed. 1972). We have frequently stated that a title need not be an index to the contents of a bill. Where the title to any act expresses a single general subject or purpose, all matters which are naturally and reasonably connected with it, or any measure which will further its purpose, will be held to be germane . . . .

However, even construing the title and subject of this appropriations bill most liberally, the provision must be found to be in violation of article 2, section 19, of our state constitution. The title is not sufficiently broad to apprise the public of an uncodified change in the substantive law. Neither can such an amendment to the public assistance laws be said to be germane to the subject.

We next deal with the constitutional challenge made under Const. art. 2, § 37. The reason for requiring amendatory legislation to set out the statute in full was stated in the 1959 *Washington Toll Bridge Authority* case, quoting from *State ex rel. Gebhardt v. Superior Court*, 15 Wash. 2d 673, 685, 131 P.2d 943, 949 (1942):

> The section of our constitution above referred to was undoubtedly framed for the purpose of avoiding confusion, ambiguity, and uncertainty in the statutory law through the existence of separate and disconnected legislative provisions, original and amendatory, scattered through different volumes or different portions of the same volume. Such a provision, among other things, forbids amending a statute simply by striking out or inserting certain words, phrases, or clauses, a proceeding formerly common, through which laws became complicated and their real meaning often difficult of ascertainment. The result desired by such a provision is to have in a section as amended a complete section, so that no further search will be required to determine the provisions of such section as amended.

Another important purpose of Const. art. 2, § 37, not mentioned above, is the necessity of insuring that legislators are aware of the nature and content of the law which is being amended and the effect of the amendment upon it. 1A Sutherland, Statutory Construction, § 22.16.

For 37 years, the statutory law of this state has provided for public assistance on the basis of need with no age restriction. The new restriction is clearly an amendment to RCW 74.04.005, adding to the restrictions already enumerated there. However, the statute will never reflect this change but will continue to read as it always has, with no age restriction. One seeking the law on the subject would have to know one must look under an "appropriations" title in the *uncodified* session laws to find the amendment. The fact that the budget bill is not codified strikes at the very heart and purpose of Const. art. 2, § 37.

. . . .

. . . There are other provisions in the very appropriations bill before us which the Governor criticized as substantive legislation improperly enacted. The following is an excerpt from the Governor's letter to the House of Representatives upon signing House Bill 1624:

> I take this opportunity also to point out my concern over the recent trend by legislative drafters of incorporating substantive legislation into budget bills. One example of such drafting is found in Section 17, subsection (6), which relates to accounting procedures on claims by public assistance vendors, and another in subsection (7), which deals with average lengths of stay of persons receiving aid under the medical assistance program. I believe that provisions such as these involve policy considerations that should be dealt with by the Legislature in separate bills, rather than inserting them into budget bills, where substantive changes in policy will not receive adequate study and consideration, and where they tend to create confusion for the appropriation provisions of the budget bill. While I am not vetoing these and other similar items, I strongly urge the Legislature to put an end to this kind of drafting.

We realize that in certain instances the legislature must place conditions and limitations on the expenditures of monies, but to the extent that such conditions or limitations have the effect of modifying or amending the general law they are unconstitutional enactments. An appropriations bill may not constitutionally be used for the enactment of substantive law which is in conflict with the general law as codified. Hence, we declare the challenged provision a nullity.

NOTES AND QUESTIONS

1. What makes this case different from *Robertson v. Seattle Audubon Soc'y*? Is it that the Washington state constitution contains procedural restraints on lawmaking that have no parallel in the federal Constitution? Or does the state supreme court have a different view of appropriations acts?

Note that there is no textual basis in the Washington state constitution, by contrast to Florida's, for differentiating appropriations acts from other laws.

2. Could the Washington governor veto provisions such as those that were challenged in this case? Could governors in other states? Review *Welsh v. Branstad* in Chapter 5, Section [A][2].

Chapter 7

LEGISLATIVE INTENT, PURPOSE, CONTEXT, AND HISTORY

A. LEGISLATIVE INTENT, PURPOSE, AND CONTEXT

The division of the American system of government into three branches has brought general acceptance of the proposition that the role of the judiciary is not to create law, but to interpret it. Indeed, it rarely happens that a court has the last word regarding a statute's vitality. The legislature or an administering agency will usually make that ultimate decision.

Legislation is not enacted for judges, but for those who are to be affected by it. To facilitate understanding by those affected, statutory language should be as plain and simple as possible. The difficulty comes in applying the words of a general statute to specific situations which are inevitably unanticipated. Courts developed a "plain meaning" rule that justified ignoring legislative history when the meaning of the words was clear. That there is a "plain" meaning to a statute is questionable, however, and once the meaning is challenged, the doctrine simply becomes a justification for the court's decision. The doctrine's weakness became increasingly apparent and it was fully discredited by the 1940s. Statutory interpretation became based increasingly on legislative history.

Once several possible meanings have been ascribed to statutory language, a common starting point for an interpreter is to find the legislative goals behind the statute. These goals have often been classified as either "legislative intent" or "legislative purpose." The definitions of these terms have not been applied consistently, as the materials which follow will demonstrate. Ideally, determining the legislative goals aids in formulating a broad statutory policy; this in turn can clarify ambiguities and can limit or expand the reach of particular provisions in the context of specific factual situations.

Questions can be raised about such searches for meaning. Consider whether any inquiry into legislative goals is appropriate. British practice, for instance, until recently rejected any source for interpretation save the statute itself. And, if ambiguity of language is a precondition to the inquiry, can ambiguity, as such, be defined? As an example of the confusion that has evolved, the "absurd" or "illogical result" doctrine can be used to justify an inquiry into a statute's meaning despite its clear language.

This search for legislative goals entails significant conceptual problems. How can a diverse and multiple membership have "an intent" when members often have varied motives for passage of legislation? The threshold question in interpreting the language of a statute is whether or not to look to these legislative goals, and the next question is how these goals are ascertained. The inquiries are interrelated, however, for only if goals can be reasonably determined are they relevant in interpretation. Part of the rationale for the British denying the relevance of legislative goals in their interpretation inquiries is the difficulty in finding such legislative motivations.

A search for legislative goals necessarily requires a knowledge of the legislative process. One must understand the organizational structure of the legislature in order to assess where in the legislative process the most accurate indications of its goals can be found. For example, are floor colloquies more or less indicative of legislative goals than statements in committee reports? What is the relevance of dissenting statements by members opposing legislative action? What significance is to be accorded both statements and votes in the various political maneuvers that may be involved in a bill's passage? Consideration of such questions is important in weighing the importance of items reflecting the history of the enacting process. A knowledge of legislative process and the body's organization is equally critical in determining such issues as whether statements of individual legislators are representative of the whole body.

REPORTER'S NOTE TO EYSTON v. STUDD
2 Plowden 459, 465, 75 E.R. 688, 695–96 (1574)

. . . It is not the words of the law, but the internal sense of it which makes the law, and our law, (like all others) consists of two parts, viz. of body and soul, the letter of the law is the body of the law, and the sense and reason of the law is the soul of the law . . . . And the law may be resembled to a nut, which has a shell and a kernel within, the letter of the law represents the shell, and the sense of it the kernel, and as you will be no better for the nut if you make use only of the shell, so you will receive no benefit by the law, if you rely only upon the letter, and as the fruit and profit of the nuts lies in the kernel, and not in the shell, so the fruit and profit of the law consists in the sense more than in the letter. And it often happens that when you know the letter, you know not the sense, for sometimes the sense is more confined and contracted than the letter, and sometimes it is more large and extensive. And equity, which in Latin is called equitas, enlarges or diminishes the letter according to its discretion . . . . And this correction of the general words is much used in the law of England . . . .

HEYDON'S CASE
3 Co. 7a, 76 Eng. Rep. 637 (Exchequer 1584)

. . . And it was resolved by them, that for the sure and true interpretation of all statutes in general (be they penal or beneficial, restrictive or enlarging of the common law,) four things are to be discerned and considered: —

1st. What was the common law before the making of the Act.

2nd. What was the mischief and defect for which the common law did not provide.

3rd. What remedy the Parliament hath resolved and appointed to cure the disease of the commonwealth.

And, 4th. The true reason of the remedy; and then the office of all the Judges is always to make such construction as shall suppress the mischief, and advance the remedy, and to suppress subtle inventions and evasions for continuance of the mischief, and *pro privato commodo*, and to add force and life to the cure and remedy, according to the true intent of the makers of the Act, *pro bono publico* . . . .

NOTES AND QUESTIONS

1. *Eyston v. Studd* and *Heydon's Case* are among the foundational cases in Anglo-American statutory interpretation. They reflect, respectively, the origins of consideration of the "spirit" of a statute (*Eyston*) and the "purpose" approach (*Heydon*).

2. For a survey of the history of statutory interpretation, see William S. Blatt, *The History of Statutory Interpretation: A Study in Form and Substance*, 6 Cardozo L. Rev. 799 (1985).

3. In the materials that follow, watch for these perspectives to emerge repeatedly, and contrast them with the "plain meaning" approach.

F. REED DICKERSON,
STATUTORY INTERPRETATION:
A PEEK INTO THE MIND AND WILL OF A LEGISLATURE,
50 Indiana Law Journal 206, 206–07 (1975)*

Introduction

One of the most fundamental, and at the same time elusive, concepts in the interpretation and application of statutes is that of legislative intent.

---

* Reprinted with permission from Indiana Law Journal and Fred B. Rothman & Co.

The appeal of the concept is strong. In the division of responsibilities represented by the constitutional separation of powers, the legislature calls the main policy turns and the courts must respect its pronouncements. In such a relationship, it would seem clear that so far as the legislature has expressed itself by statute, the courts should try to determine as accurately as possible what the legislature intended to be done . . . .

RICHARD I. NUNEZ,
THE NATURE OF LEGISLATIVE INTENT AND THE USE OF LEGISLATIVE DOCUMENTS AS EXTRINSIC AIDS TO STATUTORY INTERPRETATION: A RE-EXAMINATION,
9 CALIFORNIA WESTERN LAW REVIEW 128–31 (1972)*

Having drafted and interpreted numerous pieces of legislation and observed a state legislature "making up its mind," I have slowly reached the conclusion that the concept of legislative intent, as discussed in the legal profession, is a fiction. A convenient legal fiction, and perhaps necessary to help smooth over the rough or thin spots in a statute, but a fiction nevertheless.

After a review of the literature on legislative intent and on the use of extrinsic aids to ascertain legislative intent, I came to realize that much of the confusion surrounding the concept of legislative intent, even among scholars, is caused by the misconception that legislative intent is a single entity which must be proven to exist or not exist. In truth, there is not one, but three legislative intents, two of which can usually be proven to exist, while one is most often created by legal fiction. The purpose of this article is to lay out in a systematic pattern the three legislative intents and to issue a warning regarding the use of legislative documents as extrinsic aids in finding specific legislative intent.

I. The Nature of Legislative Intent

The necessity of hunting for legislative intent arises under two circumstances: first, when an administrator or court cannot read the statute and grasp its simple meaning because of shoddy draftsmanship or language errors, and second, when the statute is understandable but the case at hand was not anticipated at the time the statute was enacted. In either situation, whether due to defective drafting or unexpected problems, the search for legislative intent is a search for some evidence, intrinsic or extrinsic, that can be used as the basis for the statement: "The legislature intended . . . ." Once this intent is discovered, the problem at hand can be solved.

A more precise examination reveals that the concept of legislative intent subdivides into three major categories. The three intents, ranked from the most general to the most specific, are:

(1) Legislative intent concerning solution to a general social problem. For example, a statute enacted in response to the pollution problem is not intended to be used with respect to other social problems in which pollution plays an insignificant role. Mr. Justice Cardozo, speaking of the importance of the larger social problem, stated that "the meaning of a statute is to be looked for, not in any single section, but in all the parts together and *in their relation to the end in view*."

(2) Legislative intent concerning the general purposes of a specific statute. For example, a Selective Service statute intended to recruit men for military service is not intended to be employed to suppress political dissent. "[T]he *general purpose* is a more important aid to the meaning than any rule which grammar or formal logic may lay down."

(3) Legislative intent concerning the meaning of a specific statutory word or phrase. It is this category that is usually thought of when the words "legislative intent" are

---

* Reprinted with permission from California Western Law Review.

debated. There is often a need to know whether the statute covers the particular case in mind, or whether the administrator possesses the specific power he wishes to exercise. Because most of the debate in the profession is focused upon this single category of legislative intent, the debaters are pressed to prove the existence or nonexistence of this single category of intent. If, in the debate, the concept of intent in this category is rejected, then all legislative intent is apparently rejected, and the legislative process appears as a mindless operation.

At the beginning of each debate on the existence or nonexistence of legislative intent, we should start with these questions: Which intent? At what level of generality? Are we interested in the larger social policy, the general purpose of the statute, or the meaning of specific words?

It is possible for a legislature to have a clear and discernible intent concerning the social policy and the general purpose of the statute, and yet not have devoted a single moment of thought to the specific meaning of a word or phrase. Among the documents there may be evidence of specific intent; most often there is none. If the specific legislative intent does not exist and yet we act as though it does, we are acting upon a legal fiction. And even when legislative intent exists on a higher level of generality, it is still likely to be a legal fiction when applied to a word or phrase.

Where does the researcher turn for evidence of legislative intent? Simply answered: Anywhere. Chief Justice Marshall stated: "Where the mind labors to discover the design of the legislature, it seizes everything from which aid can be derived . . . ." Mr. Justice Frankfurter was almost as broad, asking only that the evidence be relevant: "If the purpose of construction is the ascertainment of meaning, nothing that is logically relevant should be excluded."

Such statements open up a wide range of evidence that can be brought forward to "prove" the legislative intent. However, all evidence is not equally reliable. Evidence can be grouped into three major categories which vary in degree of reliability; statisticians would say these categories were based on the "hardness" of the evidence. The "hardest" evidence is internal evidence derived from within the statute itself, such as the definition section, the preamble, or the explicit recitals of policy. This is the type of evidence Mr. Justice Holmes relied upon: "We do not inquire what the legislature meant; we ask only what the statute means."

The second category of evidence is legislative evidence, such as transcripts of debates, minutes of committee hearings and reports of legislative investigating committees . . . .

The last category, the "softest" evidence, is non-legislative evidence, which is evidence not produced by the legislative process, and generally includes journal articles, restatements of the law, and acquiescences in known administrative interpretations.

These categories of evidence can be combined with the previously discussed categories of legislative intent as follows:

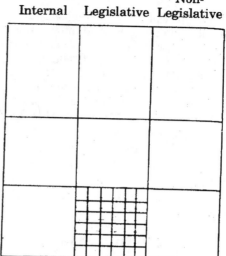

NATURE OF LEGISLATIVE INTENT	TYPE OF EVIDENCE		
	Internal	Legislative	Non-Legislative
Concerns Solution of General Social Problem			
Concerns General Purpose of the Statute			
Concerns Meaning of a Specific Statutory Provision			

The purpose of this table is to lay out in a systematic manner the three legislative intents, ranked on levels of generality, together with the categories of evidence, ranked on the reliability or "hardness" of the evidence, used to prove the existence of the legislative intent. In the legal profession, debate tends to wander up and down the list of legislative intents and across the categories of evidence without distinction. The remainder of this article will focus upon the use of legislative documents to prove the legislative intent behind a specific word or phrase in a statute (shaded area in the table).

. . . .

When searching for the meaning of a word or phrase, one must also keep in mind the nature of the legislative process that produced the troublesome language within the statute. The essential nature of the legislative process is compromise, bargain and consensus. Legislatures often resort to vagueness in language in order to obtain agreement among the widest number of legislators, or to avoid thorny issues that would be exposed were exactness demanded. In the legislature, vagueness keeps the process moving. Justice Frankfurter colorfully described this situation: "The Court no doubt must listen to the voice of Congress. But often Congress cannot be heard clearly because its speech is muffled." Thus, a subsequent attempt to read into a statute an exact meaning when exactness was purposefully avoided can only be described as a legal fiction. The aim of this warning is to point out that legislative documents have no inherent value as evidence of legislative intent.

III. *Conclusion*

This article aims neither to ridicule the concept of legislative intent, nor to persuade others to abandon the search. Rather, the purpose is to prevent confusion by pointing out the various kinds of legislative intent and to sound a note of caution in the use of legislative documents to prove specific legislative intent.

If, to construe a statute, it is necessary to rely upon a legal fiction, so be it; but let us acknowledge the fiction squarely. Legal fictions are necessary in law; like imaginary bridges, they carry us over weak spots in legal arguments. But we must be cautious that one legal fiction, legislative intent, not be asked to bear more than it is able to support.

NOTES AND QUESTIONS

1. An empirical study of legislators' use of written materials in Massachusetts, Oregon, and Indiana classified information sources as follows: 1) insiders (a legislator's colleagues and staff members); 2) middle range (interest groups and representatives of executive agencies); and 3) outsiders (constituents, officials of other units of government, the mass media and academics). The study then identified the following subprocesses in legislative decisionmaking: the development of legislation; persuasion; and voting decisions. Christopher Z. Mooney, *Information Sources in State Legislative Decision Making*, 16 LEGIS. STUD. Q. 445, 447, 449 (1991).

2. Which sources of written information would you expect to have been used the most in developing legislation? In persuasion? In voting decisions? Why?

3. Which sources should be given the most weight in statutory interpretation? Which should be excluded?

4. Do Professor Mooney's researches strengthen, undermine, or refine the points made in the Nunez article?

J.W. HURST: DEALING WITH STATUTES (1982)[*]

"THE INTENTION OF THE LEGISLATURE"

The standard criterion for proper interpretation of a statute is to find "the intention of the legislature." In 1930 Max Radin denied the validity of this formula in a challenge which has become a modern classic. He argued that the canon pursued a fiction; a legislative body in fact had no common intent, and could have none. Alternatively, he contended that if search revealed an actual legislative intent, that intent carried no legal title to govern application of the statute. Radin pursued his argument in extreme terms. But the uncompromising character of his analysis makes it a useful instrument to bring into focus basic matters of fact and questions of principle in dealing with statutes.

To Radin the idea that in voting a particular text into the statute book the legislature had a "series of pictures in mind," one of which was the particular situation now in issue, was a "transparent and absurd fiction."

. . . .

Of course we use a fiction if we speak of the legislature as if it were a being of one mind. But so durable a fiction endures because it has a use validated by experience. This formula reminds all who deal with a statute that they are operating in a field of law in which they are not free to define public policy simply according to their own judgment.

. . . .

In this light reference to legislative intention, insofar as it invokes a legal fiction, nonetheless serves useful functions for a lawyer. In his role as counselor of a client, the formula admonishes him that he will not serve the client well if he disdains such objective limits of the law as the statute may indicate. As an advocate, he can invoke the formula to curb the will of the administrator or judge who seems inclined to give rein to his own preferences at the client's expense in disregard of statutory guidelines. As negotiator for his client he can draw on the formula to check the policy pretensions of his opposite number on the other side of the bargaining table. To public officers the formula stands as a ready reminder of their obligations under the separation of powers:

---

that, as *Heydon's Case* declared (1584), having sought to learn "what remedy the Parliament hath resolved and appointed to cure the disease of the commonwealth" and what be "the true reason of the remedy", then "the office of all the judges is always to make such construction [as] . . . to add force and life to the cure and remedy, according to the true intent of the makers of the Act, *pro bono publico.*"

Radin presents two solid objections to the reality of a discoverable legislative intention. First, that a statutory text of any substantial generality will normally prove capable of embracing too many and too diverse situations to allow lawmakers to foresee them all. Second, that legislators are too numerous and bring too many different perceptions and desires to their task to allow them to come to shared choices.

> The chances that of several hundred men each will have exactly the same determinate situations in mind as possible reductions of a given determinable, are infinitesimally small. The chance is still smaller that a given determinate, the litigated issue, will not only be within the minds of all these men but will be certain to be selected by all of them as the present limit to which the determinable should be narrowed.

To appraise Radin's two points in light of typical patterns of legislative behavior helps us to locate points of effective power in the legislative process.

Radin puts his many-situations objection in a way that in large measure begs the question. The question posed by the search for legislative intent he says is, "Did the legislator in establishing this determinable [the general proposition set out in the statutory text] have a series of pictures in mind, one of which was this particular determinate [the specific situation to which someone proposes to apply the statute]?" In effect he asks us to accept that legislative intent could have reality only in a fashion analogous to a reel of motion picture film — a succession of little frames, each freezing the image of a specific, focused condition of facts. In his statement of the problem, legislative intent can exist relevant to the particular occasion for which someone would invoke the statute only if that occasion has its specific counterpart in one of the frames of the reel of pictures the legislators ran through their minds as they decided whether to pass the bill before them. But this approach defines away the problem, rather than coming to grips with it.

Of course due to variety and change in human affairs it will often be true that the legislators did not forecast the particular condition or set of facts to which someone now suggests applying the statute. But they may well supply sufficient specifications to provide a discernible frame of reference within which the situation now presented quite clearly fits, even though it represents in some degree a new condition of affairs unknown to the lawmakers . . . .

There is another range within which legislators can hold and adopt common purposes. There is a type of policy choice that looms large in the law, but that Radin blandly ignores when he asks us to accept his "series of pictures" as the only sense in which legislators could share intentions. Lawmakers can join in declaring general goals they want legal agencies to pursue, or a general range of means they want agencies to employ. The Sherman Act provides a stellar example. Its sweeping ban on "every contract, combination in the form of trust or otherwise, or conspiracy in restraint of trade or commerce among the several states or with foreign nations" perhaps goes to the verge of being unconstitutional for vagueness. Its legislative history adds little specificity to its definition, and its generality amounts to delegating broad authority to judges to spell out the particular content of its policy. However, the Act manifested a real intent that the federal government assume some positive responsibility to check self-destructive tendencies in interstate markets, and to act to keep competition alive.

. . . .

Radin's second major objection to the possible existence of shared legislative intent is that there are many legislators, who must be expected to foresee different particular situations that might arise within a statutory formula, and to make different choices as to which situations would be included. This objection ignores the core reality of the division of labor in producing legislation. A statute is normally the product of the focused effort and detailed attention of a relatively few individuals involved in the legislative process — of sponsors, members of the relevant legislative committees, and the staff of the sponsors or committees. The committee is the key workplace of the legislature, as is recognized in the primacy judges give to committee reports as admissible evidence of legislative intent. If statutory text, with or without supporting legislative history, is capable of conveying a persuasive message from those thus specially involved, realism does not require looking further to find that a legislative intent exists and is known. To take this course does not ignore the general membership of the legislature. Again, if doctrine is to fit reality — and Radin advances his analysis as a contribution to a realistic jurisprudence — we should note that normally the role of the general membership is a cautionary, residual one, to promote responsible work by the specialists. Sponsors, committee members, and supporting staff have to do their particular work with the knowledge that at some point their product must pass the test of a vote by the whole body. Though only a few members may in fact vote on many bills, the process stands open for critics to rally a larger turnout; thus the limited circle that works up the bill must make such choices and adjustments as they calculate will pass muster before the larger body or not unduly arouse opposition there.

In both of the principal objections to the reality of legislative intent Radin's analysis lacks realism in proportion as he implicitly treats each enactment as an isolated episode. In fact statute books show important lines of continuity and development of public policy. The effect of successive attention to like problem areas and of cumulative effort of successive groups of legislative specialists is often to sharpen the focus and build the detailed content of lines of statute law . . . .

Beyond this argument against the reality of legislative intent, Radin seeks to persuade us that if there is such a thing as a discoverable intent of the legislature, it has no legal claim to be binding. This conclusion he derives from the "specialized function" of legislators:

> That function is not to impose their will even within limits on their fellow-citizens, but to "pass statutes", which is a fairly precise operation. That is, they make statements in general terms of undesirable and desirable situations, from which flow certain results. As a rule, the statements must be made in the words of a specified language. A statute made in Latin at the present time is no statute, although the intention of the legislature can be as well or as ill made out from Latin as from English . . . . When the legislature has uttered the words of a statute, it is *functus officio*, not because of the Montesquieuean separation of powers, but because that is what legislating means. The legislature might also be a court and an executive, but it can never be all three things simultaneously.

Much of this argument seems either legally wrong or beside the point. Of course people do not elect legislators "to impose their will" in any individualistic or arbitrary sense. But they do elect legislators to make choices designed to promote what legislators can reasonably deem to be the public interest. Some of these choices may be general, as in the Sherman Act; some may be quite specific, as in the line items of appropriations bills. In either instance they are choices given the force of law because they are made by a special body delegated to do so by a legally legitimated process of selection. Both to supervise the legislators and to adapt everyday behavior to the frame of public policy thus provided, people need to know what their delegates intend by the choices they have voted into the statute books . . . .

The basic difficulty with Radin's argument is that he treats a statute as though it were a value-neutral tool to be used by lawyers, administrators, or judges for particular ends of their choosing, within the ample room he finds usually allowed by the minimum and maximum extension of statutory texts. He apparently would approve of the use of statutes much as a carpenter uses a saw or a hammer, choosing the instrument most efficient to what the user wants to accomplish. This attitude surfaces when he observes that the "purpose" of a statute need not be identified with "the actual purpose entertained by those who framed it or voted it"; in that sense "purpose" is the same as "intention," presenting the same difficulties that "this purpose is practically undiscoverable and would be irrelevant if discovered."

. . . .

But a statute is not a "thing," a tool carrying in itself no obligation on the user in choosing the product for which he uses it . . . . In contrast, a statute embodies a choice of values carrying obligations on those within its governance, backed by the force of the state. Under our constitutional arrangement of official powers, legislators may legitimately thus set guiding or limiting frames of action for other people. Because the statute's function is to make authoritative value determinations, fulfillment of the function is impossible without inquiry as to what values and what order of values the legislators had in mind. Inevitably those who put statutes to use must exercise considerable discretionary judgment on specifics that the legislators have not directly resolved. Also, they must exercise cautious wisdom in consulting materials outside the statutory text. But in the end the presence of the statute tells them that they deal with an area of public policy where not their value choices but those of a distinct body are to set the course.

NOTES AND QUESTIONS

1. Max Radin's article, *Statutory Interpretation*, 43 Harv. L. Rev. 863 (1930), stimulated a number of responses. *See, e.g.*, F. Reed Dickerson, *Statutory Interpretation: A Peek Into the Mind and Will of a Legislature*, 50 Ind. L.J. 206, 207–17 (1975).

2. Both Nunez and Hurst refer to the concept of legislative intent as a legal fiction, albeit a convenient (Nunez) and useful (Hurst) one. As you have already seen and will continue to see in this Part, a good deal of the practice of statutory interpretation is based on legal fiction. You should learn to recognize these fictions when you see them and to know when you are using them yourself. Possibly, one might conclude, the increasing level of fiction used by an advocate may bear a direct relationship to the level of desperation felt by the advocate.

3. For an exhaustive argument that courts often do, and ought to, interpret statutes in accord with the preference of the *current*, rather than the *enacting*, legislature, see Einer Elhauge, *Preference-Estimating Statutory Default Rules*, 102 Colum. L. Rev. 2027, 2162 (2002).

UNIFORM STATUTE AND RULE CONSTRUCTION ACT (1995)*

§ 18. Principles of Construction; Presumption

(a) A statute or rule is construed, if possible, to:

(1) give effect to its objective and purpose;

. . . .

NOTE ON LEGISLATIVE PURPOSE

An essential part of the context of every statute is its purpose. Every statute must be conclusively presumed to be a purposive act. The idea of

---

a statute without an intelligible purpose is foreign to the idea of law and inadmissible.

The meaning of a statute is never plain unless it fits with some intelligible purpose. Any judicial opinion which finds a plain meaning in a statute without consideration of its purpose, condemns itself on its face. The opinion is linguistically, philosophically, legally, and generally ignorant. It is deserving of nothing but contempt. (There are lots of opinions of this kind being handed down every day by both English and American courts.)

The first task in the interpretation of any statute (or of any provision of a statute) is to determine what purpose ought to be attributed to it. The principal problem in the development of a workable technique of interpretation is the formulation of accepted and acceptable criteria for the attribution of purpose.

Deciding what purpose ought to be attributed to a statute is often difficult. But at least three things about it are always easy. (a) The statute ought always to be presumed to be the work of reasonable men pursuing reasonable purposes reasonably, unless the contrary is made unmistakably to appear. (b) The general words of a statute ought never to be read as directing an irrational pattern of particular applications. (c) What constitutes an irrational pattern of particular applications ought always to be judged in the light of the overriding and organizing purpose.

HENRY M. HART JR. & ALBERT M. SACKS, THE LEGAL PROCESS 1124–25 (William N. Eskridge, Jr. & Philip P. Frickey eds., 1994).

INTRODUCTION TO CASES

In light of the preceding articles, examine the following cases to see how well judges follow the theoretical concepts. In each case try to determine whether resort to legislative goals by the court is required, and what options are available to the court in attempting to resolve ambiguities.

Keep the following questions in mind as you read through the cases. What emphasis is placed on ascertaining legislative goals in each case? Does the court distinguish between intent and purpose? How consistent with Nunez's conceptual framework is the court's analysis of the legislative history before it? What sources of legislative history are used, and how reliable is each source? How available is the legislative history utilized? Does the court distinguish between extrinsic and intrinsic legislative history and, if so, to what purpose? What role do judges' assumptions regarding legislative knowledge and process play in the court's analysis? How convincing is the court's analysis and conclusion with respect to the meaning of the language at issue? Is there an underlying rationale for the decision apart from the court's reference to discerned legislative goals?

STILLWELL v. STATE BAR
29 Cal. 2d 119, 173 P.2d 313 (1946)

SPENCE, JUSTICE.

Petitioner's application to the Committee of Bar Examiners of the State Bar for certification to this court for admission and a license to practice law in this state, without examination, pursuant to the provisions of sections 6060 and 6060.5 of the Business and Professions Code was denied by the Committee of Bar Examiners of the State Bar for the sole reason that before entering the armed forces he took an examination for admission to the bar of another state. In this proceeding petitioner seeks an order that he be admitted, without examination, to membership in the State Bar and to practice law in the courts of the State of California.

The facts are not in dispute. Petitioner was graduated from the Law School of Washington University, St. Louis, Missouri, on June 10, 1941, being awarded an LL.B. degree. Washington University is accredited by the examining committee of the State Bar of California. Thereafter, petitioner took and passed the State of Missouri bar examination and was admitted to practice before the courts of that state by the Supreme Court of Missouri on August 9, 1941. On or about July 21, 1942, petitioner took up residence in Los Angeles, California, and on November 5, 1943, entered the United States Marine Corps at Los Angeles. He received an honorable discharge from that service on July 8, 1946. He has never taken a California bar examination.

Prior to the enactment this year of section 6060.5 of the Business and Professions Code, it was necessary that an applicant for admission to practice law should comply with the provisions of section 6060 unless he could qualify as an out-of-state attorney with four years' practice under section 6062 of said code. The requirements of section 6060 remain in force, except as modified by section 6060.5, and the requirements of section 6060 are, among others, (1) that the applicant shall "Have passed a final bar examination given by the examining committee" of The State Bar (subd. h), and (2) that the applicant shall "Have been a bona fide resident of this State for at least three months immediately prior to the date of his final bar examination." (Subd. d.)

The recent 56th (1st extraordinary) Session of the Legislature of this state passed an act to add section 6060.5 to the Business and Professions Code, chapter 65, pertaining to the admission on motion, without examination of certain classes of law school graduates. The proposed legislation was approved by the governor on March 2, 1946. It reads as follows:

> 6060.5. The provisions of subdivisions (d) and (h) of Section 6060 do not apply to any person who, after September 16, 1940, and prior to the termination of hostilities between the United States and the nations with which the United States is now at war as determined by Act of Congress or Proclamation of the President, has graduated from a law school accredited by the examining board and who after such graduation served in the armed forces of the United States *before taking an examination for admission to the bar,* nor to any person who, after September 16, 1940 satisfactorily completed at least two years of study at a law school then accredited by the examining board and whose legal education was thereafter interrupted by his service in the armed forces of the United States, and who subsequently graduates from a law school accredited by the examining board. The provisions of this section shall not apply to any person who enters the armed forces of the United States after the effective date of this section, nor to any person who at the time of entering the armed forces was not a bona fide resident of this State.
>
> This section shall remain in effect until the ninety-first day after final adjournment of the Fifty-eighth Regular Session of the Legislature. While this section is in effect it shall supersede any existing provisions of law which are in conflict with this section; but such provisions are not repealed by this section and after this section is no longer effective shall have the same force as though this section had not been enacted. (Emphasis added.)

Owing to the limited duration of his practice, petitioner cannot comply with section 6062 of the Business and Professions Code providing for the admission of out-of-state attorneys. Therefore, in order to be admitted to practice law in this state he must qualify under sections 6060 and 6060.5. On May 20, 1946, petitioner believing that he did so qualify filed with respondent Committee of Bar Examiners an application for certification for admission on motion without examination. Such application was denied for the sole reason that petitioner "took an examination for admission to the bar after graduation and before serving in the armed forces." Thereafter, petitioner requested a reconsideration of the committee's action and on August 15, 1946, the committee determined that its former action be sustained.

In response to an order to show cause, respondents take the position that the phrase "examination for admission to the bar" in section 6060.5 has no specific or sole reference to the California bar, but refers to an examination for admission to any bar. On the other hand petitioner argues that he is entitled to admission under the act, inasmuch as he did not, prior to entering the armed forces, take an examination for admission to the California bar. We find ourselves in accord with petitioner's construction of section 6060.5, both as a result of the plain language of the section read in conjunction with section 6060, and as a result of a consideration of the purpose and object sought to be accomplished by enactment of the legislation.

Section 6060.5 is in effect but an amendment, of temporary duration, to section 6060, which deals in its entirety with qualifications for admission to the bar of this state, as does the whole of article 4, division 3, chapter 4 of the Business and Professions Code. The new section supersedes, but does not repeal, subdivisions (d) and (h) of section 6060 to the extent that there is a conflict. In other words the two pieces of legislation coexist, their application depending upon the individual circumstances of each particular applicant.

It may be presumed that the Legislature, in passing the amendatory legislation, had in mind the original act (see *Robbins v. Omnibus R. Co.*, 32 Cal. 472, 474; 1 Sutherland on Statutory Construction, 3d Ed., § 1933), and it is a well-established rule of construction that when a word or phrase has been given a particular scope or meaning in one part or portion of a law it shall be given the same scope and meaning in other parts or portions of the law. *Coleman v. City of Oakland*, 110 Cal. App. 715, 295 P. 59; *Ransome-Crummey Co. v. Woodhams*, 29 Cal. App. 356, 156 P. 62. It seems plain that the context of the temporary amendatory legislation should be interpreted consistently with the original and permanent legislation. Thus under subdivision (h) of section 6060 an applicant must have taken and passed a California bar examination given by the examining committee, but under section 6060.5 if he served in the armed forces of the United States before taking the California bar examination, and otherwise qualifies under section 6060.5, subdivision (h) does not apply. Similarly, under subdivision (d) of section 6060, an applicant must have been a resident of this state for at least three months prior to the date of "his final bar examination" in this state, but, pursuant to section 6060.5, if he has not taken such an examination prior to entering the armed forces, he must instead have been a bona fide resident of this state at the time of entering the armed forces. If the Legislature did not have in mind any certain bar and did not intend that reference be made to the specific bar designated in section 6060, surely it would not have used the wording "the bar" in the phrase "examination for admission to the bar," but would have chosen a more generic or indefinite term such as "a bar," "any bar," or "bar of any state."

Even if the meaning of the legislation were not plain we would arrive at the same result as above set forth by ascertaining the intent of the Legislature through the purpose and object sought to be accomplished . . . .

Where language is susceptible of more than one meaning, it is the duty of the courts to accept that intended by the framers of the legislation, so far as its intention can be ascertained . . . .

. . . As hereinbefore mentioned, section 6060.5 was enacted during the recent 1946 extraordinary session of the Legislature, called by the governor for the stated purpose of consideration of matters affecting veterans. It is a part of a broad program in this state and as such should be liberally construed, in so far as reasonably possible, so as to effectuate its object . . . .

The manifest purpose of section 6060.5 is to aid those residents of California, who, because of disturbed conditions and their service to their country during time of war, did not have the normal opportunity to take the examination for admission to the California bar at a time of their own choosing and within a reasonable time after graduation from law school. To require them now to take such an examination would be to impose a hardship that would not have been encountered except for such service. It seems clear that the members of the class intended to be benefitted are the California veterans, that is, those who were bona fide residents of this state at the time of entering the armed forces. The requirement that an applicant should have entered the armed forces before taking an examination for admission to the bar, would seem to be to eliminate from the benefits of the act those law school graduates who had shown themselves, in examinations taken prior to the assumption of military duties, to be unqualified for the practice of law in this state. The Legislature might also, with some reason, have eliminated those who took examinations and failed to qualify elsewhere, but respondents' construction would penalize those residents of our state who industriously undertook and successfully passed examinations outside this state. Such construction would exclude from the class benefitted many lifetime California residents who attended law schools of eastern universities with the intention of returning to California to practice, provided that they happened to take the bar examinations of other states before returning to California. It does not cast a different light on the picture that petitioner and perhaps some others were not residents of California when they took examinations elsewhere. Petitioner had become such a resident at the time he entered the armed forces, as required by the act, and presumably his preparation for the taking of a California bar examination was thwarted. We are of the opinion that petitioner comes within the class intended to be benefitted by section 6060.5 and that he is entitled to the relief demanded.

It is therefore ordered that petitioner be admitted to membership in the State Bar of California and to practice in the courts of this state upon the payment of the fees and the taking of the oath required by law.

GIBSON, C.J., and SHENK, EDMONDS, CARTER, TRAYNOR, and SCHAUER, JJ., concurred.

NOTES AND QUESTIONS

1. In his article, Nunez states that legal "debate tends to wander up and down the list of legislative intents and across the categories of evidence without distinction." If the *Stillwell* court had been compelled to categorize the evidence it used, would it have been more cautious in its pronouncement of the legislative purpose? What type of evidence, if any, did the court use in ascertaining the purpose of the legislature in enacting section 6060.5? How clear was the evidence? Where would the evidence and the type of purpose determined fit into Nunez's matrix? Does fitting the evidence into the grid help us determine the reliability of the inference which was drawn?

2. The court determined the meaning of an ambiguous word by first determining the purpose of the legislature and then relating that purpose to the specific word. Is the practice of determining specific legislative intent from a general legislative purpose a valid method of statutory interpretation? Dickerson says that the concept of legislative purpose (that is, the general purpose of a statute) "provides a strong temptation to perform the bootstrap operation of formulating a 'legislative purpose' with one eye on the situation to which it is to be applied." 50 IND. L.J. at 230. Are his concerns applicable to *Stillwell*?

3. The court determined that the manifest purpose of section 6060.5 was to aid those California residents who did not have normal opportunities to take the California bar because of the disruption caused by the war and their service to the country. Considering the fact that Stillwell had lived in California well over a year before he entered the Marine Corps and that he had been admitted to the bar in Missouri, does this purpose necessarily include him within the scope of the statute? If the legislature had introduced section 6060.5 with the statement "This statute is to aid those whose legal education was interrupted by the war," would the statute more clearly apply to Stillwell? Would a purpose clause providing: "This statute is to benefit those who, because of the war, were unable to become a member of the legal profession in the normal course of events" provide more clarity? Finally, is there a significant difference between these alternative purposes and one which states: "This statute is to benefit veterans who have served their country during the war"?

4. The court rejected an interpretation of the statute by the bar committee. What kind of evidence would the bar's version constitute in Nunez's chart? Is it any stronger than the evidence the court used?

5. If Stillwell had been a resident of California for three years before entering the service, instead of 15 months, and had he not taken any bar, would the court still have been justified in its result? At what point would his delay in taking the California bar preclude him from receiving the benefits of the statute? Would a different result have emerged if the court had investigated all of the implications of the statute's "manifest" legislative purpose?

6. Dickerson refers to two basic functions that courts perform with respect to statutes: (1) the cognitive function which essentially is the process of determining the meaning of a statute; and (2) the creative function which is the application of a statute to a situation where no clear solution to the issue before the court emerges from the statute itself. 50 IND. L.J. at 221. Which of these functions was the court performing in *Stillwell*? Can determination of legislative purpose be helpful to the courts in their performance of both functions? How important is a determination of Nunez's specific legislative intent to the courts in performing their creative function?

UNITED STATES v. GERKEN
182 F. Supp. 738 (E.D.N.Y. 1966)

ZAVATT, DISTRICT JUDGE.

This is a case of first impression in which the defendant moves to dismiss the one-count indictment which charges him with a violation of 18 U.S.C. § 220 as follows:

> The Grand Jury Charges:
>
> That on or about the 24th day of April 1957, within the Eastern District of New York, the defendant, C. William Gerken, who was then and there a vice president of the Security National Bank of Long Island, the deposits of which bank were insured by the Federal Deposit Insurance Corporation, did knowingly, wilfully and unlawfully receive a fee, commission and thing of value from a corporation for endeavoring to procure a loan for such corporation from a bank whose deposits were insured by the Federal Deposit Insurance Corporation, to wit: that he did receive Two Thousand Seven Hundred Fifty Dollars ($2,750.00) from the Huntington Station Realty Corp. for endeavoring to procure a loan from the Riverhead Savings Bank in the amount of Two Hundred Seventy-five Thousand Dollars ($275,000.00) for the benefit of said corporation.

The defendant contends that no violation of § 220 is charged because the money which he received from the Huntington Station Realty Corp. was not received for endeavoring to procure a loan for that corporation from the bank of which he was an officer. The Government contends that the language of § 220 is so broad as to include a transaction such as is set forth in the indictment. It is the Government's contention that no officer of a bank whose deposits are insured by the Federal Deposit Insurance Corporation may lawfully receive a fee, commission or thing of value from a borrower for procuring or endeavoring to procure for that borrower a loan from any bank whose deposits are insured by the Federal Deposit Insurance Corporation, regardless of whether or not the person procuring such a loan is an officer of the lender bank; that it is sufficient that this person be an officer of a bank whose deposits are so insured to bring him within the ambit of § 220.

Prior to the 1948 revision of Title 18 U.S.C., the acts now proscribed by 18 U.S.C. § 220 were covered by three separate sections of Title 12, to wit: sections 595, 1125 and

1315. They were then consolidated into 18 U.S.C. § 220, with minor changes, to read as follows:

§ 220. Receipt of commissions or gifts for procuring loans

Whoever, being an officer, director, employee, agent, or attorney of a member bank of the Federal Reserve System, of a Federal intermediate credit bank, or of a National Agricultural Credit Corporation, except as provided by law, stipulates for or receives or consents or agrees to receive any fee, commission, gift, or thing of value, from any person, firm, or corporation, for procuring or endeavoring to procure for such person, firm, or corporation, or for any other person, firm, or corporation, from any such bank or corporation, any loan or extension or renewal of loan or substitution of security, or the purchase or discount or acceptance of any paper, note, draft, check, or bill of exchange by any such bank or corporation, shall be fined not more than $5,000 or imprisoned not more than one year, or both.

The language of 12 U.S.C. § 595 leaves no doubt that an officer of a member bank committed no offense thereunder if he received a fee, commission, gift or other thing of value for procuring or endeavoring to procure a loan by a bank other than the member bank of which he was an officer. The phrase "such member bank" in that section clearly refers to the member bank of which the person charged is an officer. 12 U.S.C. §§ 1125 and 1315 applied respectively to officers of a Federal intermediate credit bank and a National Agricultural Credit Corporation. The phrase "any such corporation" which appeared in both of these sections clearly refers back to the Federal intermediate credit bank or the National Agricultural Credit Corporation, as the case may be, of which the person charged was an officer. The language of these two sections leaves no doubt that such an officer committed no offense thereunder if he received a fee, commission, gift or thing of value for procuring or endeavoring to procure a loan for a person by either one of such corporate institutions other than the institution of which he was an officer.

When the consolidation of these three sections of Title 12 into section 220 of Title 18 was under consideration by Congress in 1948, the Committee on the Judiciary of the House of Representatives filed a report to accompany the House bill (H.R. 3190) in which it is crystal clear that the 1948 revision was made solely for the purposes of consolidation and with no intention to enlarge the scope of those three sections so as to make the 1948 revision applicable to persons to whom they had not had [sic] previously been applicable. The Committee on the Judiciary stated that "verbal changes were made for style purposes." H.R. Rep. No. 304, 80th Cong., 1st Sess. A21 (1947). As of the effective date of the 1948 revision of Title 18, § 220 thereof did not apply to an officer of a bank other than an officer "of a member bank" of the "Federal Reserve System." The Federal Deposit Insurance Act, 12 U.S.C., c. 16, §§ 1814 and 1815, requires every bank that is a member of the Federal Reserve System to be insured under the Federal Deposit Insurance Act. Non-member banks (National or State) may become insured banks. A National non-member bank must apply and receive certification by the Comptroller of the Currency. A State non-member bank must apply to and receive the approval of the Board of Directors of the Federal Reserve System.

In 1950, 18 U.S.C. § 220 was amended to read as follows:

§ 220. Receipt of commissions or gifts for procuring loans

Whoever, being an officer, director, employee, agent, or attorney of any bank, the deposits of which are insured by the Federal Deposit Insurance Corporation, of a Federal intermediate credit bank, or of a National Agricultural Credit Corporation, except as provided by law, stipulates for or receives or consents or agrees to receive any fee, commission, gift, or thing of value, from any person, firm or corporation, for procuring or endeavoring to procure for such person, firm, or corporation, or for any other person, firm, or corporation, from any such bank or corporation, any loan or extension or renewal of loan or substitution of security, or the purchase or discount or acceptance of any paper, note, draft, check, or bill of exchange by any such bank or corporation, shall be fined not more than $5,000 or imprisoned not more than one year or both.

This amendment made the section applicable to officers of non-member banks whose deposits are insured by the Federal Deposit Insurance Corporation. The only change in language effected by the 1950 amendment was to substitute "any bank, the deposits of which are insured by the Federal Deposit Insurance Corporation" for "a member bank of the Federal Reserve System." Nothing in the legislative history of this 1950 amendment suggests an intention on the part of Congress to enlarge the scope of section 220 beyond making it applicable to officers of non-member banks just as it was previously applicable to officers of member banks. *See* H. Rep. No. 2564, 81st Cong., 2d Sess., U.S. Cong. & Adm. News, p. 3765 (1950).

"There is no more likely way to misapprehend the meaning of language — be it in a constitution, a statute, a will or a contract — than to read the words literally, forgetting the object which the document as a whole is meant to secure. Nor is a court ever less likely to do its duty than when, with an obsequious show of submission, it disregards the overriding purpose because the particular occasion which has arisen, was not foreseen." L. Hand, J., in *Central Hanover Bank & Trust Co. v. Commissioner*, 159 F.2d 167, 169 (2d Cir. 1947). This profound scholar who writes so pithily and incisively seeks what he has called "the full heart" and not merely the written words "for words are such temperamental things that the surest way to lose their essence is to take them at their face. Courts must reconstruct the past solution imaginatively in its setting and project the purposes which inspired it upon the concrete occasions which arise from their decision." L. Hand, *The Contribution of an Independent Judiciary to Civilization* in Jurisprudence in Action 228 (1953). The late Judge Frank expressed the same thought when he criticized "the one-word-one-meaning fallacy based on the false assumption that each verbal symbol refers to one and only one specific subject." Frank, Courts on Trial 299 (1949). We know from the Bible that the letter killeth and the spirit giveth life. The meaning of a sentence in a statute "is to be felt rather than to be proved," said Holmes, J., in *United States v. Johnson*, 1911, 221 U.S. 488, 496, 31 S. Ct. 627, 55 L. Ed. 823. Judge Learned Hand affords us a share of his wisdom when he urges judges "not to make a fortress out of the dictionary; but to remember that statutes always have some purpose or object to accomplish, whose sympathetic and imaginative discovery is the surest guide to their meaning." *Cabell v. Markham*, 2 Cir., 1945, 148 F.2d 737, 739. *See also* Frederick J. De Sloove're, *The Equity and Reason of a Statute*, 21 Corn. L.Q. 591 (1936).

The decision of this motion requires the court to break the crust of the verbiage in which § 220 is encased; to track the thread of purpose in search of the meaning which the legislature attempted to express. In this process, the tyranny of literalness is of little help — and more often a hindrance. By considering the legislative history we may find a rational content to the words quite different from what they appear to have as "plain words." The legislative history of a statute often suggests confinement of the mere words to the general purpose of the legislative scheme. *See United States v. Witkovich*, 1957, 353 U.S. 194, 199, 77 S. Ct. 779, 782, 1 L. Ed. 2d 765.

Mr. Justice Frankfurter illuminates some guide posts along the route of statutory interpretation of criminal provisions of the law. He reminds us:

> Generalities about statutory construction help us little. They are not rules of law but merely axioms of experience . . . . They do not solve the special difficulties in construing a particular statute. The variables render every problem of statutory construction unique . . . . For that reason we may utilize, in construing a statute not unambiguous, all the light relevantly shed upon the words and the clause and the statute that express the purpose of Congress . . . . Particularly is this so when we construe statutes defining conduct which entail stigma and penalties and prison. Not that penal statutes are not

subject to the basic consideration that legislation like all other writings should be given, insofar as the language permits, a commonsensical meaning. But when choice has to be made between two readings of what conduct Congress has made a crime, it is appropriate, before we choose the harsher alternative, to require that Congress should have spoken in language that is clear and definite. We should not derive criminal outlawry from some ambiguous implication.

United States v. Universal C.I.T. Credit Corp., 1952, 344 U.S. 218, 221–22, 73 S. Ct. 227, 229, 97 L. Ed. 260.

On December 31, 1949, of a total of 14,687 operating commercial and mutual savings banks in the United States, 13,628 were institutions whose deposits were insured. U.S. Code Cong. & Adm. News, p. 3766 (1950). The Government would have the court so construe section 220 that an attorney for one insured bank could not receive a fee for procuring a loan for a client by any one of the banking institutions throughout the United States so insured, no matter how remotely situated from his bank client, without becoming a criminal.

The legislative history of 18 U.S.C. § 220 plus the unreasonable and absurd consequences to which the interpretation urged by the Government would lead, satisfy the court that the indictment in the instant case does not allege a crime within the meaning of the statute.

The defendant's motion to dismiss the indictment is granted. Settle an order within 10 days.

NOTES AND QUESTIONS

1. Is it not clear that the activity of the defendant fell within the scope of activities that the statute sought to correct? Must all statutes be read in light of the purpose of the statute or should the purpose be determined only when a statute is ambiguous or difficult to apply to the facts? What kind of "evidence" did the court use? Where would it fit into the Nunez grid?

2. The court says that nothing in the 1950 amendment suggests an intention on the part of Congress to enlarge the scope of section 220. Is the following excerpt from the House Report on the 1950 Amendment of any assistance in interpreting the statute?

SECTION 4 OF THE BILL

This section amends section 220, title 18, U.S.C., to prohibit any officer, director, employee of, or attorney or agent for, an insured bank from receiving fees or gifts for procuring loans. At present section 220 of title 18, U.S.C., is applicable only to banks which are members of the Federal Reserve System.

House Rep. No. 2564, 1950 U.S. Code Cong. Service 3765.

Is the absence of any extrinsic indication that the legislature meant to change the effect of a statute a sufficient basis for deciding that no change was intended? What would the court have done in this case had there been no prior statutes from which to reason?

3. The "plain meaning rule" was almost totally destroyed in 1940. Was one of the functions of the "plain meaning rule" to limit judicial power? Did the court in this case usurp some of the powers of Congress by looking for a legislative purpose when the meaning was clear?

BAILEY v. UNITED STATES
516 U.S. 137 (1995)

JUSTICE O'CONNOR delivered the opinion of the Court.

These consolidated petitions each challenge a conviction under 18 U.S.C. § 924(c)(1). In relevant part, that section imposes a 5-year minimum term of imprisonment upon a person who "during and in relation to any crime of violence or drug trafficking crime . . . uses or carries a firearm." We are asked to decide whether evidence of the proximity and accessibility of a firearm to drugs or drug proceeds is alone sufficient to support a conviction for "use" of a firearm during and in relation to a drug trafficking offense under 18 U.S.C. § 924(c)(1).

I

In May 1989, petitioner Roland Bailey was stopped by police officers after they noticed that his car lacked a front license plate and an inspection sticker. When Bailey failed to produce a driver's license, the officers ordered him out of the car. As he stepped out, the officers saw Bailey push something between the seat and the front console. A search of the passenger compartment revealed one round of ammunition and 27 plastic bags containing a total of 30 grams of cocaine. After arresting Bailey, the officers searched the trunk of his car where they found, among a number of items, a large amount of cash and a bag containing a loaded 9-mm. pistol.

Bailey was charged on several counts, including using and carrying a firearm in violation of 18 U.S.C. § 924(c)(1). A prosecution expert testified at trial that drug dealers frequently carry a firearm to protect their drugs and money as well as themselves. Bailey was convicted by the jury on all charges, and his sentence included a consecutive 60-month term of imprisonment on the § 924(c)(1) conviction.

. . . .

II

Section 924(c)(1) requires the imposition of specified penalties if the defendant, "during and in relation to any crime of violence or drug trafficking crime . . . uses or carries a firearm." Petitioners argue that "use" signifies active employment of a firearm. Respondent opposes that definition and defends the proximity and accessibility test adopted by the Court of Appeals. We agree with petitioners, and hold that § 924(c)(1) requires evidence sufficient to show an *active employment* of the firearm by the defendant, a use that makes the firearm an operative factor in relation to the predicate offense.

This case is not the first one in which the court has grappled with the proper understanding of "use" in § 924(c)(1). In *Smith*, we faced the question whether the barter of a gun for drugs was a "use," and concluded that it was. *Smith v. United States*, 508 U.S. 223 (1993). As the debate in *Smith* illustrated, the word "use" poses some interpretational difficulties because of the different meanings attributable to it. Consider the paradoxical statement: "I *use* a gun to protect my house, but I've never had to *use* it." "Use" draws meaning from its context, and we will look not only to the word itself, but also to the statute and the sentencing scheme, to determine the meaning Congress intended.

We agree with the majority below that "use" must connote more than mere possession of a firearm by a person who commits a drug offense. *See* 36 F.3d, at 109; *accord, United States v. Castro-Lara, supra,* at 983; *United States v. Theodoropoulos,* 866 F.2d 587, 597–598 (3d Cir. 1989); *United States v. Wilson,* 884 F.2d 174, 177 (5th Cir. 1989). Had Congress intended possession alone to trigger liability under § 924(c)(1), it easily could have so provided. This obvious conclusion is supported by the frequent use of the term "possess" in the gun-crime statutes to describe prohibited gun-related conduct. *See, e.g.,* §§ 922 (g), 922(j), 922(k), 922(o)(1), 930(a), 930(b).

Where the Court of Appeals erred was not in its conclusion that "use" means more than mere possession, but in its standard for evaluating whether the involvement of a firearm amounted to something more than mere possession. Its proximity and accessibility standard provides almost no limitation on the kind of possession that would be criminalized; in practice, nearly every possession of a firearm by a person engaged in drug trafficking would satisfy the standard, "thereby eras[ing] the line that the statutes, and the courts, have tried to draw." *United States v. McFadden, supra,* at 469 (Breyer, C.J., dissenting). Rather than requiring actual use, the District of Columbia Circuit would criminalize "simpl[e] possession with a floating intent to use." 36 F.3d, at 121 (Williams, J., dissenting) . . . .

An evidentiary standard for finding "use" that is satisfied in almost every case by evidence of mere possession does not adhere to the obvious congressional intent to require more than possession to trigger the statute's application.

This conclusion — that a conviction for "use" of a firearm under § 924(c)(1) requires more than a showing of mere possession — requires us to answer a more difficult question. What must the Government show, beyond mere possession, to establish "use" for the purpose of the statute? We conclude that the language, context, and history of § 924(c)(1) indicate that the Government must show active employment of the firearm.

. . . .

We assume that Congress used two terms because it intended each term to have a particular, nonsuperfluous meaning. While a broad reading of "use" undermines virtually any function for "carry," a more limited, active interpretation of "use" preserves a meaningful role for "carries" as an alternative basis for a charge. Under the interpretation we enunciate today, a firearm can be used without being carried, *e.g.,* when an offender has a gun on display during a transaction, or barters with a firearm without handling it; and a firearm can be carried without being used, *e.g.,* when an offender keeps a gun hidden in his clothing throughout a drug transaction.

This reading receives further support from the context of § 924(c)(1). As we observed in *Smith,* "using a firearm" should not have a "different meaning in 924(c)(1) than it does in § 924(d)." 508 U.S. at 235 (Slip op., at 11). *See also United Savings Assn. v. Timbers of Inwood Forest Assocs., Ltd.,* 484 U.S. 365, 371 (1988) ("A provision that may seem ambiguous in isolation is often clarified by the remainder of the statutory scheme"). Section 924(d)(1) provides for the forfeiture of any firearm that is "used" or "intended to be used" in certain crimes. In that provision, Congress recognized a distinction between firearms "used" in commission of a crime and those "intended to be used," and provided for forfeiture of a weapon even before it had been "used." In § 924(c)(1), however, liability attaches only to cases of actual use, not intended use, as when an offender places a firearm with the intent to use it later if necessary. The difference between the two provisions demonstrates that, had Congress meant to broaden application of the statute beyond actual "use," Congress could and would have so specified, as it did in § 924(d)(1).

. . . .

The example given above — "I *use* a gun to protect my house, but I've never had to *use* it" — shows that "use" takes on different meanings depending on context. In the first phrase of the example, "use" refers to an ongoing, inactive function fulfilled by a firearm. It is this sense of "use" that underlies the Government's contention that "placement for protection" — *i.e.,* placement of a firearm to provide a sense of security or to embolden — constitutes a "use." It follows, according to this argument, that a gun placed in a closet is "used," because its mere presence emboldens or protects its owner. We disagree. Under this reading, mere possession of a firearm by a drug offender, at or near the site of a drug crime or its proceeds or paraphernalia, is a "use" by the offender, because its availability for intimidation, attack, or defense would always, presumably, embolden or comfort the offender. But the inert presence of a firearm, without more, is not enough to trigger § 924(c)(1). Perhaps the nonactive nature of this asserted "use" is clearer if a synonym is used: storage. A defendant cannot be charged under § 924(c)(1) merely for storing a weapon near drugs or drug proceeds. Storage of a firearm, without its more active employment, is not reasonably distinguishable from possession.

. . . .

The test set forth by the Court of Appeals renders "use" virtually synonymous with "possession" and makes any role for "carry" superfluous. The language of § 924(c)(1), supported by its history and context, compels the conclusion that Congress intended "use" in the active sense of "to avail onself of." To sustain a conviction under the "use" prong of § 924(c)(1), the Government must show that the defendant actively employed the firearm during and in relation to the predicate crime.

NOTES AND QUESTIONS

1. Compare this case with *Muscarello v. United States* in Chapter 6[B]. Is there a difference in the Court's focus on *intent* (as demonstrated by context) here and its focus on *meaning* in *Muscarello*?

2. What does the Court mean when it states that "A provision that may seem ambiguous in isolation is often clarified by the remainder of the statutory scheme"? What approach to interpreting statutes does this view support?

3. Is the Court's desire to avoid an interpretation that would render the word "use" superfluous based on a canon of statutory interpretation?

B. LEGISLATIVE HISTORY

Since the main source of legislative goals is the legislative history, and the legislative history is derived from the legislative process, an understanding of the legislative process and its context is essential to an understanding and determination of legislative goals. As stated by Professor Stewart:

> In interpreting statutes judges must surely address the question of how legislative decisions are actually made. Every theory of statutory interpretation betrays an implicit model, real or idealized, of the legislative process.

11 HARV. J. LEGIS. 539, 553–54 (1974).

The legislative context is a function of variable human behavior, and almost defies quantification. The relevant factors in the circumstances include such matters as the legislative procedure, the legislature's form of organization and self-government, outside influences resulting from social pressures, the interactions of the executive and the judiciary, party politics and the political strategies of individuals, as well as issues related to internal power struggles. These factors, discussed in some detail in Chapter 5, will affect the result of the enactment process in any particular situation. An awareness of these considerations is important in assessing the relevance and weight to be accorded any specific item reflecting legislative history.

1. Congressional Legislative History

The Congress is unique among legislatures in this country for the completeness of its legislative history, although some states do maintain more than a pro forma record of their respective legislative proceedings. The Congress, however, maintains a Congressional Record of all of its activities. Indeed, the Record not only records actual proceedings, but also contains a large quantity of remarks and articles that were inserted without actually having been read. One may ask whether the Record is primarily intended to accurately record events as they happen, or whether it is a forum for members of Congress to present their views on proposed legislation.

NOTE

To properly assess each source of legislative history, consider who is speaking or whose document it is. Consider also at what point in the legislative process the speech is made or the document produced, and what purpose the speech or document serves. The questions previously posed regarding the reliability and origin of each source of legislative history are also relevant here. Below is a partial list of sources of legislative history as well as factors that may be helpful in determining the reliability of these sources:

1. Floor debate.

2. Planned colloquy.

3. Prepared statements on submission of a bill, in committee hearings and at the time of floor debates.

4. Revised and amended statements.

5. Statements in committees by the relevant executive branch administrators.

6. Committee reports.

7. Transcripts of discussions at committee hearings.

8. Statements and submissions by interested persons, both local or state government and private parties.

9. Committee debates on "mark-up" of bills.

10. Conference committee reports.

11. Analysis of bills by legislative counsel.

12. Analysis of bills by relevant executive departments.

13. Amendments accepted or rejected.

14. Actions on and discussions about separate bills on the same topic, offered by each house, or in contrast to a similar composite bill.

15. Executive branch messages and proposals whether from the President, cabinet secretaries or from independent agencies.

16. Prior relevant administrative action or judicial decisions, with or without congressional acknowledgment.

17. Other subsequent or prior legislation, especially conflicting acts.

18. Recorded votes.

19. The status of the person speaking, *i.e.*, a sponsor, committee chairman, floor leader, etc.

20. Actions taken and reports, hearings and debates on prior related legislation.

WILLIAM ESKRIDGE,
THE NEW TEXTUALISM,
37 UCLA Law Review 621, 636 (1990)*

C. *Hierarchy of Sources in the Court's Use of Legislative History*

Given the foregoing discussion, the Court is not at a loss in having much material from which imaginatively to reconstruct a legislative history. Sometimes all the sources point to the same interpretive answer, which makes the Court highly confident of its resolution. Other times the different sources will point in different directions. As a result, the Court has worked out a rough hierarchy of evidence to resolve conflicts. The hierarchy is based upon the comparative reliability of each source: How likely does this source reflect the views or assumptions of the enacting Congress? Is there a danger of strategic manipulation by individual Members or biased groups seeking to "pack" the legislative history? How well-informed is the source? The figure below, which Professor Frickey and I have developed in teaching Legislation at the University of Minnesota

---

School of Law and at the Georgetown University Law Center (respectively),[58] reflects this hierarchy.

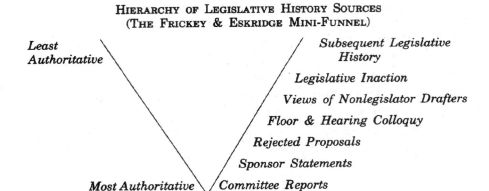

**HIERARCHY OF LEGISLATIVE HISTORY SOURCES
(THE FRICKEY & ESKRIDGE MINI-FUNNEL)**

Least Authoritative

Subsequent Legislative History

Legislative Inaction

Views of Nonlegislator Drafters

Floor & Hearing Colloquy

Rejected Proposals

Sponsor Statements

Most Authoritative *Committee Reports*

NOTES AND QUESTIONS

1. As you work with legislative history materials, consider this hierarchy of sources.

2. For considerations of nonlegislative sources of "legislative history," see Allison C. Giles, Note, *The Value of Nonlegislators' Contributions to Legislative History*, 79 GEO. L.J. 359 (1990); Kathryn M. Dessayer, Note, *The First Word: The President's Place in Legislative History*, 89 MICH. L. REV. 399 (1990); Marc N. Garber & Kurt A. Wimmer, *Presidential Signing Statements as Interpretations of Legislative Intent: An Executive Aggrandizement of Power*, 24 HARV. J. ON LEGIS. 363 (1987); William D. Popkin, *Judicial Use of Presidential Legislative History: A Critique*, 66 IND. L.J. 699 (1991).

3. For a consideration of the types of arguments made from legislative history, see William N. Eskridge, Jr., *Legislative History Values*, 66 CHI.-KENT L. REV. 365 (1990).

UNIFORM STATUE AND RULE CONSTRUCTION ACT (1995)[*]

§ 20. Other Aids to Construction

. . . .

(c) If, after considering the text of a statute or rule in light of Sections 2 through 7, Section 18, the context in which the statute or rule is applied, and the aids to construction in subsections (a) and (b), the meaning of the text or its application is uncertain, the following aids to construction may be considered in ascertaining the meaning of the text:

    (1) the circumstances that prompted the enactment or adoption of the statute or rule;

    (2) the purpose of a statute or rule as determined from the legislative or administrative history of the statute or rule;

    (3) the history of other legislation on the same subject;

---

[58] *See* Eskridge & Frickey, *Statutory Interpretation as Practical Reasoning*, 42 STAN. L. REV. 319, 353 (1990), which uses a similar funnel-shaped diagram to discuss the pull of text, legislative history, purpose, and evolutive considerations in statutory interpretation. The figure in the text is an adaptation of this diagram to a theory of legislative history.

[*] Reprinted with permission.

(4)   legislative or rule-making materials, including proposed or adopted amendments, preambles, statements of intent or purpose, findings of fact, notes indicating source, contemporaneous documents prepared as a part of the legislative or rule-making process, fiscal notes, and committee reports; [and]

(5)   the record of legislative or administrative agency debates and hearings [; and

(6)   written or printed materials that are not legislative materials].

(d) In ascribing weight to the materials listed in subsection (c), greater weight must be given to materials that:

(1)   are shown by the record to have been considered by the legislature or administrative agency before passage or adoption than to materials not shown by the record to have been so considered;

(2)   were available to the legislature or administrative agency before passage or adoption than to materials not so available;

(3)   formed the basis for the language in the statute or rule than to materials that did not do so; and

(4)   were not revised after they were considered by the legislature or administrative agency than to materials that were so revised.

COMMISSIONER v. ACKER
361 U.S. 87 (1959)

[The question presented in this case was whether the failure to file a declaration of estimated income tax subjected taxpayers not only to the penalty for failure to file a declaration under section 294(d)(1)(A) of the 1939 Code, but also subjected them to a further penalty for the filing of a substantial underestimate of their tax under section 294(d)(2). The majority held that the second penalty did not apply, as the failure to file a declaration was not equivalent to a filed declaration estimating zero tax. The dissent which follows objects to the failure of the majority to recognize the effect of certain legislative documents. — Eds.]

MR. JUSTICE FRANKFURTER, whom MR. JUSTICE CLARK and MR. JUSTICE HARLAN join, dissenting.

English courts would decide the case as it is being decided here. They would do so because English courts do not recognize the relevance of legislative explanations of the meaning of a statute made in the course of its enactment. If Parliament desires to put a gloss on the meaning of ordinary language, it must incorporate it in the text of legislation. *See* Plucknett, A Concise History of the Common Law (5th ed.), 330–36; Amos, *The Interpretation of Statutes*, 5 CAMB. L.J. 163; Davies, *The Interpretation of Statutes*, 35 COL. L. REV. 519; Lord Haldane in *Viscountess Rhondda's Claim*, [1922] 2 A.C. 339, 383–84. Quite otherwise has been the process of statutory construction practiced by this Court over the decades in scores and scores of cases. Congress can be the glossator of the words it legislatively uses either by writing its desired meaning, however odd, into the text of its enactment, or by a contemporaneously authoritative explanation accompanying a statute. The most authoritative form of such explanation is a congressional report defining the scope and meaning of proposed legislation. The most authoritative report is a Conference Report acted upon by both Houses and therefore unequivocally representing the will of both Houses as the joint legislative body.

No doubt to find failure to file a declaration of estimated income to be a "substantial underestimate" would be to attribute to Congress a most unlikely meaning for that phrase in § 294(d)(2) *simpliciter*. But if Congress chooses by appropriate means for expressing its purpose to use language with an unlikely and even odd meaning, it is not for this Court to frustrate its purpose. The Court's task is to construe not English but congressional English. Our problem is not what do ordinary English words mean, but what did Congress mean them to mean. "It is said that when the meaning of language is plain we are not to resort to evidence in order to raise doubts. That is rather an axiom of experience than a rule of law, and does not preclude consideration of persuasive evidence if it exists." *Boston Sand & Gravel Co. v. United States*, 278 U.S. 41, 48.

Here we have the most persuasive kind of evidence that Congress did not mean the language in controversy, however plain it may be to the ordinary user of English, to have the ordinary meaning. These provisions were first enacted in the Current Tax Payment Act of 1943, c. 120, 57 Stat. 126, as additions to § 294(a) of the Internal Revenue Code of 1939. The Conference Report, H.R. Conf. Rep. No. 510, p. 56, and the Senate Report, S. Rep. No. 221, p. 42, both gave the provision dealing with substantial underestimation of taxes the following gloss:

> "In the event of a failure to file any declaration where one is due, the amount of the estimated tax for the purposes of this provision will be zero."

The revision of the section eight months later by the Revenue Act of 1943, c. 63, 58 Stat. 21, did not affect its substance, and this provision, therefore, continued to carry the original gloss. While the Court adverts to this congressional definition, it disregards its controlling significance.

NOTES AND QUESTIONS

1. In *Acker*, Justice Frankfurter states that the most authoritative form of explanation accompanying a statute is a Conference Report. After reading the articles regarding legislative intent, *supra*, is it accurate to say that a Conference Report unequivocally represents the will of both Houses? Are some of the policy considerations behind the former English rule of not looking at the legislative gloss on a statute applicable? In 1993, the House of Lords relaxed the rule prohibiting resort to Parliamentary history in *Pepper v. Hart*, 1 All E.R. 42 (1993). *See* T. St. J.N. Bates, *The Contemporary Use of Legislative History in the United Kingdom*, 54 CAMBRIDGE L.J. 127 (1995).

2. Is it true that Congress can make a word or phrase mean anything it wants to through clever use of legislative history? Should Congress have this power? Is there a contrary policy which favors interpretation of words according to their "natural," technical, or ordinary meaning? What legitimate purpose is served by distinguishing English from "congressional English"? Is it the courts' job to correct Congress' use of English? When there is a mistake in a statute, should the courts correct it? Does the answer depend upon the nature of the mistake? Should there be a formalized procedure to handle problems like this? If there is not a clearcut mistake, but an ambiguity, is the answer any different?

3. In the majority opinion in *Acker*, the Court referred to two arguments of the Tax Commissioner regarding the legislative history behind the statute. The Commissioner first introduced a Senate Report and a Conference Report, both supporting his construction of the statute. The Court dismissed these reports by saying that they "pertained to the forerunner of the section with which we are not confronted, and not to that section itself." The Commissioner then argued that since Congress amended the 1939 Tax Code several times without ever changing the statute in question, it approved of the administrative interpretation given to the statute by the Commissioner. The Court also dismissed this contention as immaterial, for Congress could not expand or add to the statute by impliedly approving the interpretation. How convincing is the Court's analysis?

4. For an insightful consideration of the special problems in interpreting federal tax statutes, see Michael Livingston, *Congress, the Courts, and the Code: Legislative History and the Interpretation of Tax Statutes*, 69 TEX. L. REV. 819 (1991).

CHURCH OF THE HOLY TRINITY v. UNITED STATES
143 U.S. 457 (1892)

Mr. Justice Brewer delivered the opinion of the court.

Plaintiff in error is a corporation, duly organized and incorporated as a religious society under the laws of the State of New York. E. Walpole Warren was, prior to September, 1887, an alien residing in England. In that month the plaintiff in error made a contract with him, by which he was to remove to the city of New York and enter into its service as rector and pastor; and in pursuance of such contract, Warren did so remove and enter upon such service. It is claimed by the United States that this contract on the part of the plaintiff in error was forbidden by the act of February 26, 1885, the penalty prescribed by that act . . . .

The first section describes the act forbidden, and is in these words:

> "*Be it enacted by the Senate and House of Representatives of the United States of America in Congress assembled,* That from and after the passage of this act it shall be unlawful for any person, company, partnership, or corporation, in any manner whatsoever, to prepay the transportation, or in any way assist or encourage the importation or migration of any alien or aliens, any foreigner or foreigners, into the United States, its Territories, or the District of Columbia, under contract or agreement, parol or special, express or implied, made previous to the importation or migration of such alien or aliens, foreigner or foreigners, to perform labor or service of any kind in the United States, its Territories, or the District of Columbia."

It must be conceded that the act of the corporation is within the letter of this section, for the relation of rector to his church is one of service, and implies labor on the one side with compensation on the other. Not only are the general words labor and service both used, but also, as it were to guard against any narrow interpretation and emphasize a breadth of meaning, to them is added "of any kind;" and, further, as noticed by the Circuit Judge in his opinion, the fifth section, which makes specific exceptions, among them professional actors, artists, lecturers, singers and domestic servants, strengthens the idea that every other kind of labor and service was intended to be reached by the first section. While there is great force to this reasoning, we cannot think Congress intended to denounce with penalties a transaction like that in the present case. It is a familiar rule, that a thing may be within the letter of the statute and yet not within the statute, because not within its spirit, nor within the intention of its makers. This has been often asserted, and the reports are full of cases illustrating its application. This is not the substitution of the will of the judge for that of the legislator, for frequently words of general meaning are used in a statute, words broad enough to include an act in question, and yet a consideration of the whole legislation, or of the circumstances surrounding its enactment, or of the absurd results which follow from giving such broad meaning to the words, makes it unreasonable to believe that the legislator intended to include the particular act . . . . The reason of the law in such cases should prevail over its letter. The common sense of man approves the judgment mentioned by Puffendorf, that the Bolognian law which enacted "that whoever drew blood in the streets should be punished with the utmost severity," did not extend to the surgeon who opened the vein of a person that fell down in the street in a fit. The same common sense accepts the ruling, cited by Plowden, that the statute of 1st Edward II., which enacts that a prisoner who breaks prison shall be guilty of felony, does not extend to a prisoner who breaks out when the prison is on fire, "for he is not to be hanged because he would not stay to be burnt" . . . .

. . . .

Again, another guide to the meaning of a statute is found in the evil which it is designed to remedy; and for this the court properly looks at contemporaneous events, the situation as it existed, and as it was pressed upon the attention of the legislative body. *United States v. Union Pacific Railroad,* 91 U.S. 72, 79. The situation which called for this statute was briefly but fully stated by Mr. Justice Brown when, as District Judge, he decided the case of *United States v. Craig*, 28 Fed. Rep. 795, 798: "The motives and history of the act are matters of common knowledge. It had become the practice for large capitalists in this country to contract with their agents abroad for the shipment of great numbers of an ignorant and servile class of foreign laborers, under contracts, by which the employer agreed, upon the one hand, to prepay their passage, while, upon the other hand, the laborers agreed to work after their arrival for a certain time at a low rate of wages. The effect of this was to break down the labor market, and to reduce other laborers engaged in like occupations to the level of the assisted immigrant. The evil finally became so flagrant that an appeal was made to Congress for relief by the passage of the act in question, the design of which was to raise the standard of foreign immigrants, and to discountenance the migration of those who had not sufficient means in their own hands, or those of their friends, to pay their passage."

It appears, also, from the petitions, and in the testimony presented before the committees of Congress, that it was this cheap unskilled labor which was making the trouble, and the influx of which Congress sought to prevent. It was never suggested that we had in this country a surplus of brain toilers, and, least of all, that the market for the services of Christian ministers was depressed by foreign competition. Those were matters to which the attention of Congress, or of the people, was not directed. So far, then, as the evil which was sought to be remedied interprets the statute, it also guides to an exclusion of this contract from the penalties of the act.

A singular circumstance, throwing light upon the intent of Congress, is found in this extract from the report of the Senate Committee on Education and Labor, recommending the passage of the bill: "The general facts and considerations which induce the committee to recommend the passage of this bill are set forth in the Report of the Committee of the House. The committee report the bill back without amendment, although there are certain features thereof which might well be changed or modified, in the hope that the bill may not fail of passage during the present session. Especially would the committee have otherwise recommended amendments, substituting for the expression 'labor and service,' whenever it occurs in the body of the bill, the words 'manual labor' or 'manual service,' as sufficiently broad to accomplish the purposes of the bill, and that such amendments would remove objections which a sharp and perhaps unfriendly criticism may urge to the proposed legislation. The committee, however, believing that the bill in its present form will be construed as including only those whose labor or service is manual in character, and being very desirous that the bill become a law before the adjournment, have reported the bill without change." 6059, Congressional Record, 48th Congress. And, referring back to the report of the Committee of the House, there appears this language: "It seeks to restrain and prohibit the immigration or importation of laborers who would have never seen our shores but for the inducements and allurements of men whose only object is to obtain labor at the lowest possible rate, regardless of the social and material well-being of our own citizens and regardless of the evil consequences which result to American laborers from such immigration. This class of immigrants care nothing about our institutions, and in many instances never even heard of them; they are men whose passage is paid by the importers; they come here under contract to labor for a certain number of years; they are ignorant of our social condition, and that they may remain so they are isolated and prevented from coming into contact with Americans. They are generally from the lowest social stratum, and live upon the coarsest food and in hovels of a character before unknown to American workmen. They, as a rule, do not become citizens, and are certainly not a desirable acquisition to the body politic. The inevitable tendency of their presence among us is to degrade American labor, and to reduce it to the level of the imported pauper labor." Page 5359, Congressional Record, 48th Congress.

We find, therefore, that . . . the evil which was intended to be remedied, the circumstances surrounding the appeal to Congress, the reports of the committee of each house, all concur in affirming that the intent of Congress was simply to stay the influx of this cheap unskilled labor.

But beyond all these matters no purpose of action against religion can be imputed to any legislation, state or national, because this is a religious people. This is historically true. From the discovery of this continent to the present hour, there is a single voice making this affirmation . . . . These, and many other matters which might be noticed, add a volume of unofficial declarations to the mass of organic utterances that this is a Christian nation. In the face of all these, shall it be believed that a Congress of the United States intended to make it a misdemeanor for a church of this country to contract for the services of a Christian minister residing in another nation? . . . It is the duty of the courts, under those circumstances, to say that, however broad the language of the statute may be, the act, although within the letter, is not within the intention of the legislature, and therefore cannot be within the statute.

NOTES AND QUESTIONS

1. Is Justice Brewer's reliance on legislative history convincing? What about his reliance on the conclusion that this is a "Christian nation"? *See generally* Steven K. Green, *Justice David Josiah Brewer and the "Christian Nation" Maxim*, 63 ALB. L. REV. 427 (1999).

2. Professor Adrian Vermeule provides an exhaustive analysis of the factual context of *Holy Trinity Church* as well as the legislative history of the statute in question. Interestingly, he concludes that Justice Brewer actually misread the legislative history, and that despite early indications that only manual labor was to be covered, that position was later abandoned in favor of a broader prohibition. *See* Adrian Vermeule, *Legislative History and the Limits of Judicial Competence: The Untold Story of Holy Trinity Church*, 50 STAN. L. REV. 1833 (1998). Professor Vermeule draws some conclusions that are relevant to the debate over the use of legislative history that is covered later in this Chapter. For a strongly contrary view, see Carol Chomsky, *Unlocking the Mysteries of Holy Trinity: Spirit, Letter and History in Statutory Interpretation*, 100 COLUM. L. REV. 901 (2000).

UNITED STEELWORKERS OF AMERICA v. WEBER
443 U.S. 193 (1979)

MR. JUSTICE BRENNAN delivered the opinion of the Court.

Challenged here is the legality of an affirmative action plan — collectively bargained by an employer and a union — that reserves for black employees 50% of the openings in an in-plant craft training program until the percentage of black craft workers in the plant is commensurate with the percentage of blacks in the local labor force. The question for decision is whether Congress, in Title VII of the Civil Rights Act of 1964 as amended, 42 U.S.C. § 2000e, left employers and unions in the private sector free to take such race-conscious steps to eliminate manifest racial imbalances in traditionally segregated job categories. We hold that Title VII does not prohibit such race-conscious affirmative action plans.

I

In 1974 petitioner United Steelworkers of America (USWA) and petitioner Kaiser Aluminum & Chemical Corporation (Kaiser) entered into a master collective-bargaining agreement covering terms and conditions of employment at 15 Kaiser plants. The agreement contained, *inter alia*, an affirmative action plan designed to eliminate conspic[u]ous racial imbalances in Kaiser's then almost exclusively white craft work forces. Black craft hiring goals were set for each Kaiser plant equal to the percentage of blacks in the respective local labor forces. To enable plants to meet these goals, on-the-job training programs were established to reach unskilled production workers —

black and white — the skills necessary to become craft workers. The plan reserved for black employees 50% of the openings in these newly created in-plant training programs.

This case arose from the operation of the plan at Kaiser's plant in Gramercy, La. Until 1974 Kaiser hired as craft workers for that plant only persons who had had prior craft experience. Because blacks had long been excluded from craft unions,[1] few were able to present such credentials. As a consequence, prior to 1974 only 1.83% (five out of 273) of the skilled craft workers at the Gramercy plant were black, even though the work force in the Gramercy area was approximately 39% black.

Pursuant to the national agreement Kaiser altered its craft hiring practice in the Gramercy plant. Rather than hiring already trained outsiders, Kaiser established a training program to train its production workers to fill craft openings. Selection of craft trainees was made on the basis of seniority, with the proviso that at least 50% of the new trainees were to be black until the percentage of black skilled craft workers in the Gramercy plant approximated the percentage of blacks in the local labor force. *See* 415 F. Supp. 761, 764.

During 1974, the first year of the operation of the Kaiser-USWA affirmative action plan, 13 craft trainees were selected from Gramercy's production work force. Of these, 7 were black and 6 white. The most junior black selected into the program had less seniority than several white production workers whose bids for admission were rejected. Thereafter one of those white production workers, respondent Brian Weber, instituted this class action in the United States District Court for the Eastern District of Louisiana.

The complaint alleged that the filling of craft trainee positions at the Gramercy plant pursuant to the affirmative action program had resulted in junior black employees receiving training in preference to more senior white employees, thus discriminating against respondent and other similarly situated white employees in violation of §§ 703(a)[2] and (d)[3] of Title VII. The District Court held that the plan violated Title VII, entered a judgment in favor of the plaintiff class, and granted a permanent injunction

---

[1] Judicial findings of exclusion from crafts on racial grounds are so numerous as to make such exclusion a proper subject for judicial notice. *See, e.g., United States v. International Union of Elevator Constructors,* 538 F.2d 1012 (3d Cir. 1976); *Associated General Contractors of Massachusetts v. Alshuler,* 490 F.2d 9 (1st Cir. 1973); *Southern Illinois Builders Association v. Ogilve,* 471 F.2d 680 (7th Cir. 1972); *Contractors Association of Eastern Pennsylvania v. Secretary of Labor,* 442 F.2d 159 (3d Cir. 1971); *Local 53 of International Association of Heat & Frost, etc. v. Vogler,* 407 F.2d 1047 (5th Cir. 1969); *Buckner v. Goodyear,* 339 F. Supp. 1108 (N.D. Ala. 1972), *aff'd without opinion,* 476 F.2d 1287 (5th Cir. 1973). *See also* United States Commission on Civil Rights, The Challenge Ahead: Equal Opportunity in Referral Unions 58–94 (1976), (summarizing judicial findings of discrimination by craft unions); G. Myrdal, An American Dilemma (1944) 1079–1124; R. Marshall and V. Briggs, The Negro and Apprenticeship (1967); S. Spero and A. Harris, The Black Worker (1931); United States Commission on Civil Rights, Employment 97 (1961), State Advisory Committee, United States Commission on Civil Rights, 50 States Report 209 (1961); Marshall, *The Negro in Southern Unions,* in The Negro and the American Labor Movement (ed. Jacobson, Anchor 1968) p. 145; App., 63, 104.

[2] Section 703(a), 42 U.S.C. § 2000e-2(a), provides:

"(a) It shall be an unlawful employment practice for an employer —

"(1) to fail or refuse to hire or to discharge any individual, or otherwise to discriminate against any individual with respect to his compensation, terms, conditions, or privileges of employment, because of such individual's race, color, religion, sex, or national origin; or

"(2) to limit or classify his employees or applicants for employment in any way which would deprive or tend to deprive any individual of employment opportunities or otherwise adversely affect his status as an employee, because of such individual's race, color, religion, sex, or national origin."

[3] Section 703(d), 42 U.S.C. § 2000e-2(d), provides:

"It shall be an unlawful employment practice for any employer, labor organization, or joint labor-management committee controlling apprenticeship or other training or retraining, including on-the-job training programs to discriminate against any individual because of his race, color, religion, sex, or national origin in admission to, or employment in, any program established to provide apprenticeship or other training."

prohibiting Kaiser and the USWA "from denying plaintiffs, Brian F. Weber and all other members of the class, access to on-the-job training programs on the basis of race." 415 F. Supp. 761 (1976). A divided panel of the Court of Appeals for the Fifth Circuit affirmed, holding that all employment preferences based upon race, including those preferences incidental to bona fide affirmative action plans, violated Title VII's prohibition against racial discrimination in employment. 563 F.2d 216 (1978). We granted certiorari. 439 U.S. 1045 (1979). We reverse.

II

We emphasize at the outset the narrowness of our inquiry. Since the Kaiser-USWA plan does not involve state action, this case does not present an alleged violation of the Equal Protection Clause of the Constitution. Further, since the Kaiser-USWA plan was adopted voluntarily, we are not concerned with what Title VII requires or with what a court might order to remedy a past proven violation of the Act. The only question before us is the narrow statutory issue of whether Title VII *forbids* private employers and unions from voluntarily agreeing upon bona fide affirmative action plans that accord racial preferences in the manner and for the purpose provided in the Kaiser-USWA plan. That question was expressly left open in *McDonald v. Santa Fe Trail Trans. Co.*, 427 U.S. 273, 281 n.8 (1976) which held, in a case not involving affirmative action, that Title VII protects whites as well as blacks from certain forms of racial discrimination.

Respondent argues that Congress intended in Title VII to prohibit all race-conscious affirmative action plans. Respondent's argument rests upon a literal interpretation of §§ 703(a) and (d) of the Act. Those sections make it unlawful to "discriminate . . . because of . . . race" in hiring and in the selection of apprentices for training programs. Since, the argument runs, *McDonald v. Santa Fe Trail Trans. Co., supra*, settled that Title VII forbids discrimination against whites as well as blacks, and since the Kaiser-USWA affirmative action plan operates to discriminate against white employees solely because they are white, it follows that the Kaiser-USWA plan violates Title VII.

Respondent's argument is not without force. But it overlooks the significance of the fact that the Kaiser-USWA plan is an affirmative action plan voluntarily adopted by private parties to eliminate traditional patterns of racial segregation. In this context respondent's reliance upon a literal construction of §§ 703(a) and (d) and upon *McDonald* is misplaced. *See McDonald v. Santa Fe Trail Trans. Co., supra*, at 281 n.8. It is a "familiar rule, that a thing may be within the letter of the statute and yet not within the statute, because not within its spirit, nor within the intention of its makers." *Holy Trinity Church v. United States*, 143 U.S. 457, 459 (1892). The prohibition against racial discrimination in §§ 703(a) and (d) of Title VII must therefore be read against the background of the legislative history of Title VII and the historical context from which the Act arose. *See Train v. Colorado Public Interest Research Group*, 426 U.S. 1, 10 (1976); *Woodworkers v. NLRB*, 386 U.S. 612, 620 (1967); *United States v. American Trucking Assns.*, 310 U.S. 534, 543–544 (1940). Examination of those sources makes clear that an interpretation of the sections that forbade all race-conscious affirmative action would "bring about an end completely at variance with the purpose of the statute" and must be rejected. *United States v. Public Utilities Comm'n*, 345 U.S. 295, 315 (1953). *See Johansen v. United States*, 343 U.S. 427, 431 (1952); *International Union v. Juneau Spruce Corp.*, 342 U.S. 237, 243 (1952); *Texas & Pacific R. Co. v. Abilene Oil Co.*, 204 U.S. 426 (1907).

Congress' primary concern in enacting the prohibition against racial discrimination in Title VII of the Civil Rights Act of 1964 was with "the plight of the Negro in our economy." 110 Cong. Rec. 6548 (remarks of Sen. Humphrey). Before 1964, blacks were largely relegated to "unskilled and semi-skilled jobs." *Id.*, at 6548 (remarks of Sen. Humphrey); *id.*, at 7204 (remarks of Sen. Clark); *id.*, at 7279–7280 (remarks of Sen.

Kennedy). Because of automation the number of such jobs was rapidly decreasing. *See* 110 Cong. Rec., at 6548 (remarks of Sen. Humphrey); *id.*, at 7204 (remarks of Sen. Clark). As a consequence "the relative position of the Negro worker [was] steadily worsening. In 1947 the non-white unemployment rate was only 64 percent higher than the white rate; in 1962 it was 124 percent higher." *Id.*, at 6547 (remarks of Sen. Humphrey). *See also id.*, at 7204 (remarks of Sen. Clark). Congress considered this a serious social problem. As Senator Clark told the Senate:

> "The rate of Negro unemployment has gone up consistently as compared with white unemployment for the past 15 years. This is a social malaise and a social situation which we should not tolerate. That is one of the principal reasons why this bill should pass." *Id.*, at 7220.

Congress feared that the goals of the Civil Rights Act — the integration of blacks into the mainstream of American society — could not be achieved unless this trend were reversed. And Congress recognized that that would not be possible unless blacks were able to secure jobs "which have a future." *Id.*, at 7204 (remarks of Sen. Clark). *See also id.*, at 7279–7280 (remarks of Sen. Kennedy). As Senator Humphrey explained to the Senate:

> "What good does it do a Negro to be able to eat in a fine restaurant if he cannot afford to pay the bill? What good does it do him to be accepted in a hotel that is too expensive for his modest income? How can a Negro child be motivated to take full advantage of integrated educational facilities if he has no hope of getting a job where he can use that education?" *Id.*, at 6547.
>
> . . . .
>
> "Without a job, one cannot afford public convenience and accommodations. Income from employment may be necessary to further a man's education, or that of his children. If his children have no hope of getting a good job, what will motivate them to take advantage of educational opportunities?" *Id.*, at 6552.

These remarks echoed President Kennedy's original message to Congress upon the introduction of the Civil Rights Act in 1963:

> "There is little value in a Negro's obtaining the right to be admitted to hotels and restaurants if he has no cash in his pocket and no job." *Id.*, at 11159.

Accordingly, it was clear to Congress that "the crux of the problem [was] to open employment opportunities for Negroes in occupations which have been traditionally closed to them," *id.*, at 6548 (remarks of Sen. Humphrey), and it was to this problem that Title VII's prohibition against racial discrimination in employment was primarily addressed.

It plainly appears from the House Report accompanying the Civil Rights Act that Congress did not intend wholly to prohibit private and voluntary affirmative action efforts as one method of solving this problem. The Report provides:

> "No bill can or should lay claim to eliminating all of the causes and consequences of racial and other types of discrimination against minorities. There is reason to believe, however, that national leadership provided by the enactment of Federal legislation dealing with the most troublesome problems *will create an atmosphere conducive to voluntary or local resolution of other forms of discrimination.*" H.R. Rep. No. 914, 88th Cong., 1st Sess. (1963), at 18. (Emphasis supplied.)

Given this legislative history, we cannot agree with respondent that Congress intended to prohibit the private sector from taking effective steps to accomplish the goal that Congress designed Title VII to achieve. The very statutory words intended as a spur or catalyst to cause "employers and unions to self-examine and to self-evaluate their employment practices and to endeavor to eliminate, so far as possible, the last vestiges of an unfortunate and ignominious page in this country's history," *Albemarle v. Moody*, 422 U.S. 405, 418 (1975), cannot be interpreted as an absolute prohibition against all private, voluntary, race-conscious affirmative action efforts to hasten the elimination of such vestiges.[4] It would be ironic indeed if a law triggered by a Nation's concern over centuries of racial injustice and intended to improve the lot of those who had "been excluded from the American dream for so long," 110 Cong. Rec., at 6552 (remarks of Sen. Humphrey), constituted the first legislative prohibition of all voluntary, private, race-conscious efforts to abolish traditional patterns of racial segregation and hierarchy.

Our conclusion is further reinforced by examination of the language and legislative history of § 703(j) of Title VII.[5] Opponents of Title VII raised two related arguments against the bill. First, they argued that the Act would be interpreted to *require* employers with racially imbalanced work forces to grant preferential treatment to racial minorities in order to integrate. Second, they argued that employers with racially imbalanced work forces would grant preferential treatment to racial minorities, even if not required to do so by the Act. *See* 110 Cong. Rec. 8618–8619 (remarks of Sen. Sparkman). Had Congress meant to prohibit all race-conscious affirmative action, as respondent urges, it easily could have answered both objections by providing that Title VII would not require or *permit* racially preferential integration efforts. But Congress did not choose such a course. Rather Congress added § 703(j) which addresses only the first objection. The section provides that nothing contained in Title VII "shall be interpreted to *require* any employer . . . to grant preferential treatment . . . to any group because of the race . . . of such . . . group on account of" a de facto racial imbalance in the employer's work force. The section does *not* state that "nothing in Title VII shall be interpreted to *permit*" voluntary affirmative efforts to correct racial imbalances. The natural inference is that Congress chose not to forbid all voluntary race-conscious affirmative action.

The reasons for this choice are evident from the legislative record. Title VII could not have been enacted into law without substantial support from legislators in both Houses who traditionally resisted federal regulation of private business. Those legislators demanded as a price for their support that "management prerogatives and union freedoms . . . be left undisturbed to the greatest extent possible." H.R. Rep. No. 914, 88th Cong., lst Sess., Pt. 2 (1963), at 29. Section 703(j) was proposed by Senator Dirksen to allay any fears that the Act might be interpreted in such a way as to upset this compromise. The section was designed to prevent § 703 of Title VII from being interpreted in such a way as to lead to undue "Federal Government interference with

---

[4] The problem that Congress addressed in 1964 remains with us. In 1962 the non-white unemployment rate was 124% higher than the white rate. *See* 110 Cong. Rec. 6547 (remarks of Sen. Humphrey). In 1978 the black unemployment rate was 129% higher. *See* Monthly Labor Review, U.S. Department of Labor Bureau of Labor Statistics 78 (Mar. 1979).

[5] Section 703(j) of Title VII, 42 U.S.C. § 2000e-2(j), provides:

"Nothing contained in this subchapter shall be interpreted to require any employer, employment agency, labor organization, or joint labor-management committee subject to this subchapter to grant preferential treatment to any individual or to any group because of race, color, religion, sex, national origin of such individual or group on account of an imbalance which may exist with respect to the total number or percentage of persons of any race, color, religion, sex, or national origin employed by any employer, referred or classified for employment by any employment agency or labor organization, or admitted to, or employed in, any apprenticeship or other training program, in comparison with the total number or percentage or persons of such race, color, religion, sex, or national origin in any community, State, section, or other area, or in the available work force in any community, State, section, or other area."

Section 703(j) speaks to substantive liability under Title VII, but it does not preclude courts from considering racial imbalance as evidence of a Title VII violation. *See Teamsters v. United States*, 431 U.S. 324, 339–340, n.20 (1977). Remedies for substantive violations are governed by § 706(g), 42 U.S.C. § 2000e-5(g).

private businesses because of some Federal employee's ideas about racial balance or imbalance." 110 Cong. Rec., at 14314 (remarks of Sen. Miller).[6] *See also id.*, at 9881 (remarks of Sen. Allott); *id.*, at 10520 (remarks of Sen. Carlson); *id.*, at 11471 (remarks of Sen. Javits); *id.*, at 12817 (remarks of Sen. Dirksen). Clearly, a prohibition against all voluntary, race-conscious, affirmative action efforts would disserve these ends. Such a prohibition would augment the powers of the Federal Government and diminish traditional management prerogatives while at the same time impeding attainment of the ultimate statutory goals. In view of this legislative history and in view of Congress' desire to avoid undue federal regulation of private businesses, use of the word "require" rather than the phrase "require or permit" in § 703(j) fortifies the conclusion that Congress did not intend to limit traditional business freedom to such a degree as to prohibit all voluntary, race-conscious affirmative action.[7]

We therefore hold that Title VII's prohibition in §§ 703(a) and (d) against racial discrimination does not condemn all private, voluntary, race-conscious affirmative action plans.

III

We need not today define in detail the line of demarcation between permissible and impermissible affirmative action plans. It suffices to hold that the challenged Kaiser-USWA affirmative action plan falls on the permissible side of the line. The purposes of the plan mirror those of the statute. Both were designed to break down old patterns of racial segregation and hierarchy. Both were structured to "open employment opportunities for Negroes in occupations which have been traditionally closed to them." 110 Cong. Rec. 6548 (remarks of Sen. Humphrey).[8]

At the same time the plan does not unnecessarily trammel the interests of the white employees. The plan does not require the discharge of white workers and their replacement with new black hires. *Cf. McDonald v. Santa Fe Trail Trans. Co., supra.* Nor does the plan create an absolute bar to the advancement of white employees; half of those trained in the program will be white. Moreover, the plan is a temporary measure; it is not intended to maintain racial balance, but simply to eliminate a manifest racial imbalance. Preferential selection of craft trainees at the Gramercy plant will end

---

[6] Title VI of the Civil Rights Act of 1964, considered in *University of California Regents v. Bakke*, 438 U.S. 265 (1978), contains no provision comparable to § 703(j). This is because Title VI was an exercise of federal power over a matter in which the Federal Government was already directly involved: the prohibitions against race-based conduct contained in Title VI governed "program[s] or activit[ies] receiving Federal financial assistance." 42 U.S.C. § 2000d. Congress was legislating to assure federal funds would not be used in an improper manner. Title VII, by contrast, was enacted pursuant to the Commerce power to regulate purely private decisionmaking and was not intended to incorporate and particularize the commands of the Fifth and Fourteenth Amendments. Title VII and Title VI, therefore, cannot be read *in pari materia*. See 110 Cong. Rec. 8315 (1964) (remarks of Sen. Cooper). *See also id.*, at 11615 (remarks of Sen. Cooper).

[7] Respondent argues that our construction of § 703 conflicts with various remarks in the legislative record. *See, e.g.*, 110 Cong. Rec. 7213 (Sens. Clark and Case); *id.*, at 7218 (Sens. Clark and Case); *id.*, at 6549 (Sen. Humphrey); *id.*, at 8921 (Sen. Williams). We do not agree. In Senator Humphrey's words, these comments were intended as assurances that Title VII would not allow establishment of systems "to *maintain* racial balance in employment," *id.*, at 11848. They were not addressed to temporary, voluntary, affirmative action measures undertaken to eliminate manifest racial imbalance in traditionally segregated job categories. Moreover, the comments referred to by respondent all preceded the adoption of § 703(j), 42 U.S.C. § 2000e-2(j). After § 703(j) was adopted congressional comments were all to the effect that employers would not be *required* to institute preferential quotas to avoid Title VII liability, *see, e.g., id.*, at 12819 (remarks of Sen. Dirksen); *id.*, at 13079–13080 (remarks of Sen. Clark); *id.*, at 15876 (remarks of Rep. Lindsay). There was no suggestion after the adoption of § 703(j) that wholly voluntary, race-conscious, affirmative action efforts would in themselves constitute a violation of Title VII . . . .

[8] *See* n.1 *supra*. This is not to suggest that the freedom of an employer to undertake race-conscious affirmative action efforts depends on whether or not his effort is motivated by fear of liability under Title VII.

as soon as the percentage of black skilled craft workers in the Gramercy plant approximates the percentage of blacks in the local labor force. *See* 415 F. Supp. 761, 763.

We conclude, therefore, that the adoption of the Kaiser-USWA plan for the Gramercy plant falls within the area of discretion left by Title VII to the private sector voluntarily to adopt affirmative action plans designed to eliminate conspicuous racial imbalance in traditionally segregated job categories.[9] Accordingly, the judgment of the Court of Appeals for the Fifth Circuit is

Reversed.

MR. JUSTICE POWELL and MR. JUSTICE STEVENS took no part in the consideration or decision of this case.

MR. JUSTICE BLACKMUN, concurring.

While I share some of the misgivings expressed in Mr. Justice Rehnquist's dissent, *post,* concerning the extent to which the legislative history of Title VII clearly supports the result the Court reaches today, I believe that additional considerations, practical and equitable, only partially perceived, if perceived at all, by the 88th Congress, support the conclusion reached by the Court today, and I therefore join its opinion as well as its judgment.

Strong considerations of equity support an interpretation of Title VII that would permit private affirmative action to reach where Title VII itself does not. The bargain struck in 1964 with the passage of Title VII guaranteed equal opportunity for white and black alike, but where Title VII provides no remedy for blacks, it should not be construed to foreclose private affirmative action from supplying relief. It seems unfair for respondent Weber to argue, as he does, that the asserted scarcity of black craftsmen in Louisiana, the product of historic discrimination, makes Kaiser's training program illegal because it ostensibly absolves Kaiser of all Title VII liability. Brief for Respondents 60. Absent compelling evidence of legislative intent, I would not interpret Title VII itself as a means of "locking in" the effects of segregation for which Title VII provides no remedy. Such a construction, as the Court points out, *ante,* at 9, would be "ironic," given the broad remedial purposes of Title VII.

The dissent, while it focuses more on what Title VII does not require than on what Title VII forbids, cites several passages that appear to express an intent to "lock in" minorities. In mining the legislative history anew, however, the dissent, in my view, fails to take proper account of our prior cases that have given that history a much more limited reading than that adopted by the dissent. For example, in *Griggs v. Duke Power Co.,* 401 U.S. 424, 434–436, and n.11 (1971), the Court refused to give controlling weight to the memorandum of Senators Clark and Case which the dissent now finds so persuasive. *See post,* at 21–24. And in quoting a statement from that memorandum that an employer would not be "permitted . . . to prefer Negroes for future vacancies," *post,* at 22, the dissent does not point out that the Court's opinion in *Teamsters v. United States,* 431 U.S. 324, 349–351 (1977), implies that that language is limited to the protection of established seniority systems. Here seniority is not in issue because the craft training program is new and does not involve an abrogation of pre-existing seniority rights. In short, the passages marshaled by the dissent are not so compelling as to merit the whip hand over the obvious equity of permitting employers to ameliorate the effects of past discrimination for which Title VII provides no direct relief.

. . . [I]f the Court has misperceived the political will, it has the assurance that because the question is statutory Congress may set a different course if it so chooses.

MR. CHIEF JUSTICE BURGER, dissenting.

---

[9] Our disposition makes unnecessary consideration of petitioners' argument that their plan was justified because they feared that black employees would bring suit under Title VII if they did not adopt an affirmative action plan. Nor need we consider petitioners' contention that their affirmative action plan represented an attempt to comply with Executive Order 11246.

The Court reaches a result I would be inclined to vote for were I a Member of Congress considering a proposed amendment of Title VII. I cannot join the Court's judgment, however, because it is contrary to the explicit language of the statute and arrived at by means wholly incompatible with long-established principles of separation of powers. Under the guise of statutory "construction," the Court effectively rewrites Title VII to achieve what it regards as a desirable result. It "amends" the statute to do precisely what both its sponsors and its opponents agreed the statute was *not* intended to do.

. . . .

Oddly, the Court seizes upon the very clarity of the statute almost as a justification for evading the unavoidable impact of its language. The Court blandly tells us that Congress could not really have meant what it said, for a "literal construction" would defeat the "purpose" of the statute — at least the congressional "purpose" as five Justices divine it today. But how are judges supposed to ascertain the *purpose* of a statute except through the words Congress used and the legislative history of the statute's evolution? One need not even resort to the legislative history to recognize what is apparent from the face of Title VII — that it is specious to suggest that § 703(j) contains a negative pregnant that permits employers to do what §§ 703(a) and (d) unambiguously and unequivocally *forbid* employers from doing. Moreover, as Mr. Justice Rehnquist's opinion — which I join — conclusively demonstrates, the legislative history makes equally clear that the supporters and opponents of Title VII reached an agreement about the statute's intended effect. That agreement, expressed so clearly in the language of the statute that no one should doubt its meaning, forecloses the reading which the Court gives the statute today.

. . . .

Until today, I had thought the Court was of the unanimous view that "discriminatory preference for any group, minority or majority, is precisely and only what Congress has proscribed" in Title VII. *Griggs v. Duke Power Co.*, 401 U.S. 424, 431 (1971). Had Congress intended otherwise, it very easily could have drafted language allowing what the Court permits today. Far from doing so, Congress expressly *prohibited* in § 703(a) and (d) the discrimination against Brian Weber the Court approves now. If "affirmative action" programs such as the one presented in this case are to be permitted, it is for Congress, not this Court, to so direct.

. . . .

Mr. Justice Rehnquist, with whom The Chief Justice joins, dissenting.

. . . .

The operative sections of Title VII prohibit racial discrimination in employment *simpliciter*. Taken in its normal meaning, and as understood by all Members of Congress who spoke to the issue during the legislative debates, *see infra*, this language prohibits a covered employer from considering race when making an employment decision, whether the race be black or white . . . .

. . . It may be that one or more of the principal sponsors of Title VII would have preferred to see a provision allowing preferential treatment of minorities written into the bill. Such a provision, however, would have to have been expressly or impliedly excepted from Title VII's explicit prohibition on all racial discrimination in employment. There is no such exception in the Act. And a reading of the legislative debates concerning Title VII, in which proponents and opponents alike uniformly denounced discrimination in favor of, as well as discrimination against, Negroes, demonstrates clearly that any legislator harboring an unspoken desire for such a provision could not possibly have succeeded in enacting it into law.

. . . .

Introduced on the floor of the House of Representatives on June 20, 1963, the bill — H. R. 7152 — that ultimately became the Civil Rights Act of 1964 contained no compulsory provisions directed at private discrimination in employment. The bill was promptly referred to the Committee on the Judiciary, where it was amended to include Title VII. With two exceptions, the bill reported by the House Judiciary Committee contained §§ 703(a) and (d) as they were ultimately enacted. Amendments subsequently adopted on the House floor added § 703's prohibition against sex discrimination and § 703(d)'s coverage of "on the job training."

After noting that "[t]he purpose of [Title VII] is to eliminate . . . discrimination in employment based on race, color, religion, or national origin," the Judiciary Committee's report simply paraphrased the provisions of Title VII without elaboration. H.R. Rep. No. 914, 88th Cong., 1st Sess., 26 (1963) (hereinafter H.R. Rep.). In a separate Minority Report, however, opponents of the measure on the Committee advanced a line of attack which was reiterated throughout the debates in both the House and Senate and which ultimately led to passage of § 703(j). Noting that the word "discrimination" was nowhere defined in H.R. 7152, the Minority Report charged that the absence from Title VII of any reference to "racial imbalance" was a "public relations" ruse and that "the administration intends to rely upon its own construction of 'discrimination' as including the lack of racial balance . . . ." H.R. Rep., at 67–68. To demonstrate how the bill would operate in practice, the Minority Report posited a number of hypothetical employment situations, concluding in each example that the employer "*may be forced to hire according to race*, to 'racially balance' those who work for him *in every job classification* or be in violation of Federal law." *Id.*, at 69 (emphasis in original).

. . . .

Thus, the battle lines were drawn early in the legislative struggle over Title VII, with opponents of the measure charging that agencies of the federal government such as the Equal Employment Opportunity Commission (EEOC), by interpreting the word "discrimination" to mean the existence of "racial imbalance," would "require" employers to grant preferential treatment to minorities, and supporters responding that the EEOC would be granted no such power and that, indeed, Title VII prohibits discrimination "in favor of workers because of their race." Supporters of H.R. 7152 in the House ultimately prevailed by a vote of 290 to 130, and the measure was sent to the Senate to begin what became the longest debate in that body's history.

B

The Senate debate was broken into three phases: the debate on sending the bill to Committee, the general debate on the bill prior to invocation of cloture, and the debate following cloture.

1

When debate on the motion to refer the bill to Committee opened, opponents of Title VII in the Senate immediately echoed the fears expressed by their counterparts in the House, as is demonstrated by the following colloquy between Senators Hill and Ervin:

"Mr. ERVIN. I invite attention to . . . Section [703(a)] . . . .

"I ask the Senator from Alabama if the Commission could not tell an employer that he had too few employees, that he had limited his employment, and enter an order, under [Section 703(a)], requiring him to hire more persons, not because the employer thought he needed more persons, but because the Commission wanted to compel him to employ persons of a particular race.

"Mr. HILL. The Senator is correct. That power is written into the bill. The employer could be forced to hire additional persons . . . ." 110 Cong. Rec. 4764 (1964).

Senator Humphrey, perhaps the primary moving force behind H. R. 7152 in the Senate, was the first to state the proponents' understanding of Title VII. Responding to a political advertisement charging that federal agencies were at liberty to interpret the word "discrimination" in Title VII to require racial balance, Senator Humphrey stated: "[T]he meaning of racial or religious discrimination is perfectly clear . . . . [I]t means a distinction and treatment given to different individuals because of their different race, religion, or national origin." *Id.*, at 5423.[16]

Stressing that Title VII "does not limit the employer's freedom to hire, fire, promote, or demote for any reasons — or no reasons — so long as his action is not based on race," Senator Humphrey further stated that "nothing in the bill would permit any official or court to require any employer or labor union to give preferential treatment to any minority group." *Ibid.*[17]

After 17 days of debate the Senate voted to take up the bill directly, without referring it to a committee. *Id.*, at 6455. Consequently, there is no Committee Report in the Senate.

2

Formal debate on the merits of H.R. 7152 began on March 30, 1964. Supporters of the bill in the Senate had made elaborate preparations for this second round. Senator Humphrey, the Majority Whip, and Senator Kuchel, the Minority Whip, were selected as the bipartisan floor managers on the entire civil rights bill. Responsibility for explaining and defending each important title of the bill was placed on bipartisan "captains." Senators Clark and Case were selected as the bipartisan captains responsible for Title VII. Vass, *Title VII: Legislative History*, 7 B.C. INDUS. & COM. L. REV. 431, 444–445 (1966) (hereinafter Title VII: Legislative History).

In the opening speech of the formal Senate debate on the bill, Senator Humphrey addressed the main concern of Title VII' s opponents, advising that not only does Title VII not require use of racial quotas, *it does not permit* their use. "The truth," stated the floor leader of the bill, "is that this title forbids discriminating against anyone on account of race. This is the simple and complete truth about title VII." 110 Cong. Rec. 6549 (1964). Senator Humphrey continued:

> "Contrary to the allegations of some opponents of this title, there is nothing in it that will give any power to the Commission or to any courts to require hiring, firing, or promotion of employees in order to meet a racial 'quota' or to achieve a certain racial balance.
>
> "That bugaboo has been brought up a dozen times; but it is nonexistent. In

---

[16] This view was reiterated two days later in the "Bipartisan Civil Rights Newsletter" distributed to the Senate on March 19 by supporters of H.R. 7152:

> "3. Defining discrimination: Critics of the civil rights bill have charged that the word 'discrimination' is left undefined in the bill and therefore the door is open for interpretation of this term according to 'whim or caprice.' . . .
>
> "There is no sound basis for uncertainty about the meaning of discrimination in the context of the civil rights bill. It means a distinction in treatment given to different individuals because of their different race, religion, or national origin." 110 Cong. Rec. 7477 (1964).

[17] Earlier in the debate, Senator Humphrey had introduced a newspaper article quoting the answers of a Justice Department "expert" to the "ten most common objections to Title VII." Insofar as is pertinent here, the article stated:

> "Objection: The law would empower Federal 'Inspectors' to require employers to hire by race. White people would be fired to make room for Negroes. Seniority rights would be destroyed . . . .
>
> "Reply: The bill requires no such thing. The five-member Equal Employment Opportunity Commission that would be created would have no powers to order anything . . . .
>
> ". . . The bill would not authorize anyone to order hiring or firing to achieve racial or religious balance. An employer will remain wholly free to hire on the basis of his needs and of the job candidate's qualifications. What is prohibited is the refusal to hire someone because of his race or religion. Similarly, the law will have no effect on union seniority rights." 110 Cong. Rec. 5095 (1964).

fact, *the very opposite is true. Title VII prohibits discrimination.* In effect, it says that race, religion, and national origin are not to be used as the basis for hiring and firing. Title VII is designed to encourage hiring on the basis of ability and qualifications, not race or religion." *Ibid.* (emphasis added).

At the close of his speech, Senator Humphrey returned briefly to the subject of employment quotas: "It is claimed that the bill would require racial quotas for all hiring, when in fact it provides that race shall not be a basis for making personnel decisions." *Id.*, at 6553.

Senator Kuchel delivered the second major speech in support of H.R. 7152. In addressing the concerns of the opposition, he observed that "[n]othing could be further from the truth" than the charge that "Federal inspectors" would be empowered under Title VII to dictate racial balance and preferential advancement of minorities. *Id.*, at 6563. Senator Kuchel emphasized that seniority rights would in no way be affected by Title VII: "Employers and labor organizations could not discriminate *in favor of or against* a person because of his race, his religion, or his national origin. In such matters . . . the bill now before us . . . is color-blind." *Id.*, at 6564 (emphasis added).

A few days later the Senate's attention focused exclusively on Title VII, as Senators Clark and Case rose to discuss the title of H.R. 7152 on which they shared floor "captain" responsibilities. In an interpretative memorandum submitted jointly to the Senate, Senators Clark and Case took pains to refute the opposition's charge that Title VII would result in preferential treatment of minorities. Their words were clear and unequivocal:

> "There is no requirement in title VII that an employer maintain a racial balance in his work force. On the contrary, any deliberate attempt to maintain a racial balance, whatever such a balance may be, would involve a violation of title VII because maintaining such a balance would require an employer to hire or to refuse to hire on the basis of race. It must be emphasized that discrimination is prohibited as to any individual." *Id.*, at 7213.[18]

Of particular relevance to the instant case were their observations regarding seniority rights. As if directing their comments at Brian Weber, the Senators said:

> "Title VII would have no effect on established seniority rights. Its effect is prospective and not retrospective. Thus, for example, if a business has been discriminating in the past and as a result has an all-white working force, when the title comes into effect the employer's obligation would be simply to fill future vacancies on a nondiscriminatory basis. He would not be obliged — or *indeed*

---

[18] In obvious reference to the charge that the word "discrimination" in Title VII would be interpreted by federal agencies to mean the absence of racial balance, the interpretative memorandum stated:

"[Section 703] prohibits discrimination in employment because of race, color, religion, sex, or national origin. It has been suggested that the concept of discrimination is vague. In fact it is clear and simple and has no hidden meanings. To discriminate is to make a distinction, to make a difference in treatment *or favor*, and those distinctions or differences in treatment *or favor* which are prohibited by [Section 703] are those which are based on any five of the forbidden criteria: race, color, religion, sex, or national origin." 110 Cong. Rec. 7213 (1964) (emphasis added).

Earlier in his speech, Senator Clark introduced a memorandum prepared at his request by the Justice Department with the purpose of responding to criticisms of Title VII leveled by opponents of the measure, particularly Senator Hill. With regard to racial balance, the Justice Department stated:

"Finally, it has been asserted that title VII would impose a requirement for 'racial balance.' This is incorrect. There is no provision . . . in title VII . . . that requires or authorizes any Federal agency or Federal court to require preferential treatment for any individual or any group for the purpose of achieving racial balance . . . . No employer is required to maintain any ratio of Negroes to whites . . . . On the contrary, any deliberate attempt to maintain a given balance would almost certainly run afoul of title VII because it would involve a failure or refusal to hire some individual because of his race, color, religion, sex, or national origin. What title VII seeks to accomplish, what the civil rights bill seeks to accomplish is equal treatment for all." *Id.*, at 7207.

permitted — to fire whites in order to hire Negroes, *or to prefer Negroes for future vacancies, or, once Negroes are hired, to give them special seniority rights at the expense of the white workers hired earlier.*" *Ibid.* (emphasis added).[19]

Thus with virtual clairvoyance the Senate's leading supporters of Title VII anticipated precisely the circumstances of this case and advised their colleagues that the type of minority preference employed by Kaiser would violate Title VII's ban on racial discrimination. To further accentuate the point, Senator Clark introduced another memorandum dealing with common criticisms of the bill, including the charge that racial quotas would be imposed under Title VII. The answer was simple and to the point: "Quotas are themselves discriminatory." *Id.*, at 7218.

. . . On May 25, Senator Humphrey again took the floor to defend the bill against "the well-financed drive by certain opponents to confuse and mislead the American people." *Id.*, at 11846. Turning once again to the issue of preferential treatment, Senator Humphrey remained faithful to the view that he had repeatedly expressed:

"The title does not provide that any preferential treatment in employment shall be given to Negroes or to any other persons or groups. It does not provide that any quota systems may be established to maintain racial balance in employment. In fact, *the title would prohibit preferential treatment for any particular group*, and any person, whether or not a member of any minority group, would be permitted to file a complaint of discriminatory employment practices." *Id.*, at 11848 (emphasis added).

While the debate in the Senate raged, a bipartisan coalition under the leadership of Senators Dirksen, Mansfield, Humphrey, and Kuchel was working with House leaders

---

[19] A Justice Department memorandum earlier introduced by Senator Clark, *see* n.18, *supra*, expressed the same view regarding Title VII's impact on seniority rights of employees:

"Title VII would have no effect on seniority rights existing at the time it takes effect . . . . This would be true even in the case where owing to discrimination prior to the effective date of the title, white workers had more seniority than Negroes . . . . [A]ssuming that seniority rights were built up over a period of time during which Negroes were not hired, these rights would not be set aside by the taking effect of title VII. Employers and labor organizations would simply be under a duty not to discriminate against Negroes because of their race." 110 Cong. Rec. 7207 (1964).

The interpretation of Title VII contained in the memoranda introduced by Senator Clark totally refutes the Court's implied suggestion that Title VII would prohibit an employer from discriminating on the basis of race in order to *maintain* a racial balance in his work force, but would permit him to do so in order to *achieve* racial balance. *See ante*, at 13, and n.7.

The maintain-achieve distinction is analytically indefensible in any event. Apparently, the Court is saying that an employer is free to *achieve* a racially balanced work force by discriminating against whites, but that once he has reached his goal, he is no longer free to discriminate in order to maintain that racial balance. In other words, once Kaiser reaches its goal of 39% minority representation in craft positions at the Gramercy plant, it can no longer consider race in admitting employees into its on-the-job training programs, even if the programs become as "all-white" as they were in April 1974.

Obviously, the Court is driven to this illogical position by the glaring statement, quoted in text, of Senators Clark and Case that "any deliberate attempt to *maintain* a racial balance . . . would involve a violation of Title VII because *maintaining* such a balance would require an employer to hire or to refuse to hire on the basis of race." 110 Cong. Rec. 7123 (1964) (emphasis added). Achieving a certain racial balance, however, no less than maintaining such a balance, would require an employer to hire or to refuse to hire on the basis of race. Further, the Court's own conclusion that Title VII's legislative history, coupled with the wording of § 703(j), evinces a congressional intent to leave employers free to employ "private, voluntary, race-conscious affirmative action plans," *ante* at 12, is inconsistent with its maintain-achieve distinction. If Congress' primary purpose in enacting Title VII was to open employment opportunities previously closed to Negroes, it would seem to make little difference whether the employer opening those opportunities was achieving or maintaining a certain racial balance in his work force. Likewise, if § 703(j) evinces Congress' intent to permit imposition of race-conscious affirmative action plans, it would seem to make little difference whether the plan was adopted to achieve or maintain the desired racial balance.

and representatives of the Johnson Administration on a number of amendments to H.R. 7152 designed to enhance its prospects of passage. The so-called "Dirksen-Mansfield" amendment was introduced on May 26 by Senator Dirksen as a substitute for the entire House-passed bill. The substitute bill, which ultimately became law, left unchanged the basic prohibitory language of §§ 703(a) and (d), as well as the remedial provisions in § 706(g). It added, however, several provisions defining and clarifying the scope of Title VII's substantive prohibitions. One of those clarifying amendments, § 703(j), was specifically directed at the opposition's concerns regarding racial balancing and preferential treatment of minorities, providing in pertinent part: "Nothing contained in [Title VII] shall be interpreted to require any employer . . . to grant preferential treatment to any individual or to any group because of the race . . . of such individual or group on account of" a racial imbalance in the employer's work force. 42 U.S.C. § 2000e-2(j) . . . .

. . . .

. . . In light of Title VII's flat prohibition on discrimination "against any individual . . . because of such individual's race," § 703(a), 42 U.S.C. § 2000e-2(a), such a contention would have been, in any event, too preposterous to warrant response. Indeed, speakers on both sides of the issue, as the legislative history makes clear, recognized that Title VII would tolerate no *voluntary* racial preference, whether in favor of blacks or whites . . . . The complaint consistently voiced by the opponents was that Title VII, particularly the word "discrimination," would be *interpreted*s by federal agencies such as the Equal Employment Opportunity Commission to *require* the correction of racial imbalance through the granting of preferential treatment to minorities. Verbal assurances that Title VII would not require — indeed, would not permit — preferential treatment of blacks having failed, supporters of H.R. 7152 responded by proposing an amendment carefully worded to meet, and put to rest, the opposition's charge. Indeed, unlike §§ 703(a) and (d), which are by their terms directed at entities — *e.g.*, employers, labor unions — whose actions are restricted by Title VII's prohibitions, the language of § 703(j) is specifically directed at entities — federal agencies and courts — charged with the responsibility of interpreting Title VII's provisions.

In light of the background and purpose of § 703(j), the irony of invoking the section to justify the result in this case is obvious. The Court's frequent references to the "voluntary" nature of Kaiser's racially discriminatory admission quota bear no relationship to the facts of this case. Kaiser and the Steelworkers acted under pressure from an agency of the Federal Government, the Office of Federal Contract Compliance, which found that minorities were being "underutilized" at Kaiser's plants. *See* n.2, *supra.* That is, Kaiser's work force was racially imbalanced. Bowing to that pressure, Kaiser instituted an admissions quota preferring blacks over whites, thus confirming that the fears of Title VII's opponents were founded. Today § 703(j), adopted to allay those fears, is invoked by the Court to uphold imposition of a racial quota under the very circumstances that the section was intended to prevent.

. . . .

On June 9, Senator Ervin offered an amendment that would entirely delete Title VII from the bill. In answer to Senator Ervin's contention that Title VII "would make the members of a particular race special favorites of the laws," *id.*, at 13079, Senator Clark retorted:

"The bill does not make anyone higher than anyone else. It establishes no quotas. It leaves an employer free to select whomever he wishes to employ . . . .

"All this is subject to one qualification, and that qualification, is to state: 'In your activity as an employer . . . you must not discriminate because of the color of a man's skin . . . .'

"That is all this provision does . . . . It merely says, 'When you deal in

interstate commerce, you must not discriminate on the basis of race . . . .' "
Id., at 13030.

The Ervin amendment was defeated, and the Senate turned its attention to an amendment proposed by Senate Cotton to limit application of Title VII to employers of at least 100 employees. During the course of the Senate's deliberations on the amendment, Senator Cotton had a revealing discussion with Senator Curtis, also an opponent of Title VII. Both men expressed dismay that Title VII would prohibit preferential hiring of "members of a minority race in order to enhance their opportunity":

> "Mr. CURTIS. Is it not the opinion of the Senator that any individuals who provide jobs for a class of people who have perhaps not had sufficient opportunity for jobs should be commended rather than outlawed?
>
> "Mr. COTTON. Indeed it is." *Id.*, at 13036.

Thus in the only exchange on the Senate floor raising the possibility that an employer might wish to reserve jobs for minorities in order to assist them in overcoming their employment disadvantage, both speakers concluded that Title VII prohibits such, in the words of the Court, "voluntary, private, race-conscious efforts to abolish traditional patterns of racial segregation and hierarchy." *Ante*, at 9. Immediately after this discussion, both Senator Dirksen and Senator Humphrey took the floor in defense of the 25-employee limit contained in the Dirksen-Mansfield substitute bill, and neither Senator disputed the conclusions of Senators Cotton and Curtis. The Cotton amendment was defeated.

3

On June 10 the Senate, for the second time in its history, imposed cloture on its members. The limited debate that followed centered on proposed amendments to the Dirksen-Mansfield substitute. Of some 24 proposed amendments, only 5 were adopted.

. . . .

Later that day, June 19, the issue was put to a vote, and the Dirksen-Mansfield substitute bill was passed.

C

The Act's return engagement in the House was brief. The House Committee on Rules reported the Senate version without amendments on June 30, 1964. By a vote of 289 to 126, the House adopted House Resolution 789, thus agreeing to the Senate's amendments of H.R. 7152. Later that same day, July 2, the President signed the bill and the Civil Rights Act of 1964 became law.

. . . .

Our task in this case, like any other case involving the construction of a statute, is to give effect to the intent of Congress. To divine that intent, we traditionally look first to the words of the statute and, if they are unclear, then to the statute's legislative history . . . .

. . . By going not merely *beyond*, but directly *against* Title VII's language and legislative history, the Court has sown the wind. Later courts will face the impossible task of reaping the whirlwind.

RONALD DWORKIN,
HOW TO READ THE CIVIL RIGHTS ACT,
The New York Review of Books, December 20, 1979, Vol. 26, No. 20, at 37–43[*]

Weber was not a simple case to decide . . . .

Burger and Rehnquist thought that the language of 703(a) of Title VII was so precise and unambiguous that there was no need for the Court to do more than read the statute . . . .

Weber required the Court to decide the question it had left open in *McDonald*. If it were clear that "discriminate . . . because of . . . race" was used in the neutral sense, it would have made no sense for the Court to leave open the question of whether it applied to affirmative action. The majority in *Weber* was right, both as a matter of ordinary language and precedent: the question of how Title VII should be interpreted cannot be answered simply by staring at the words Congress used.

. . . .

How is a court to choose between two justifications for a statute, each of which fits the statute and finds a basis in political opinion? Of course, if one of these justifications has been attached to the statute as an institutionalized intention, through some legislative convention of the sort described earlier, then the court must apply that justification even though it prefers another. If the legislative history shows that while one justification had great support among a number of legislators, the other went unnoticed or was rejected by all who noticed it, then that might well be some evidence that the second does not, after all, reflect any widespread political opinion. But in most hard cases testing whether a statute applies in controversial circumstances, when there are two justifications available that point in opposite directions, both justifications will fit well enough both the text of the statute and the political climate of the day, and neither will be attached to the statute by convention.

Weber was such a case. In these cases I see no procedure for decision — no theory of legislation — other than this: one justification for a statute is better than another, and provides the direction for coherent development of the statute, if it provides a more accurate or more sensitive or sounder analysis of the underlying moral principles. So judges must decide which of the two competing justifications is superior as a matter of political morality, and apply the statute so as to further that justification. Different judges, who disagree about morality, will therefore disagree about the statute. But that is inevitable, and if each judge faces the moral decision openly, an informed public will be in a better position to understand and criticize them than if the moral grounds of decision lie hidden under confused arguments about nonexistent legislative intents.

It is no use protesting that this procedure allows judges to substitute their own political judgment for the judgment of elected representatives of the people. That protest is doubly misleading. It suggests, first, that the legislators have in fact made a judgment so that it is wrong for the judges to displace that judgment. But if there is no institutionalized intention, no pertinent collective understanding, and two competing justifications, there is no such judgment. Second, the protest suggests that judges have some way to decide such a case that does *not* require them to make a political judgment. But there simply is no such procedure, except a method that leaves the decision to chance, like flipping a coin.

NOTES AND QUESTIONS

1. Justice Rehnquist makes his argument on the basis of his reading of the legislative history. How proper is his use of legislative documents? In his parade of statements during congressional debate, does he adequately distinguish between those statements prior to and after cloture when Section 703(j) was added to the bill? Is such an event a proper basis for distinguishing between the statements made in debate?

2. How appropriate is Rehnquist's use of the following types of legislative history?

a. The Minority Report of the House Judiciary Committee.

b. The exchange between Senators Ervin and Hill.

c. The "Bipartisan Civil Rights Newsletter."

d. The newspaper article introduced by Senator Humphrey.

e. The Clark-Case Interpretative Memorandum.

f. The Justice Department memorandum introduced by Senator Clark.

g. Senator Clark's "another memorandum."

h. The "Dirksen-Mansfield" amendment, substituted for the entire House-passed bill.

i. The clarifying amendment, Section 703(j).

j. Senator Ervin's amendment rejected on June 9.

k. Senator Cotton's amendment rejected on June 9.

l. The institution of cloture on June 10.

m. That 5 of 24 amendments then pending were adopted.

3. Several Justices suggested that Congress could or should amend the 1964 Act if the Court did not accurately reflect congressional intent in its decision. Is that a realistic assumption? Professor Dworkin in his article suggested that "It seems unlikely that Congress would now pass legislation either explicitly condoning or explicitly forbidding affirmative action in employment, at least so long as that issue remains politically as volatile as it is now."

4. In the context of the enactment of the 1964 Act, how feasible would the inclusion of a useful preamble have been?

5. How does one adequately distinguish Dworkin's concept of *institutional intention* from his "collective understanding"? What sources are used to establish each theory?

6. How is a congressional "convention" established and what evidence is appropriate to demonstrate its acceptance?

7. Is one legislator's contradiction of a spokesman's statement a sufficient basis for rejection of that supporting statement as a basis for institutional intention, especially when the provision being discussed is then passed? If overwhelming support occurs for the bill, does this statement then constitute evidence of a collective understanding?

8. Earl M. Maltz concludes that *Weber* represents a case of judicial underenforcement of a statute — "the refusal of the judiciary to apply statutory commands in situations that the enacting legislature clearly intended to cover." Earl M. Maltz, *Rhetoric and Reality in the Theory of Statutory Interpretation: Underenforcement, Overenforcement, and the Problem of Legislative Supremacy*, 71 B.U. L. Rev. 767, 782 (1991). Do you agree? Professor Maltz provides an important discussion of the distinction between underenforcement and overenforcement.

9. In 1999, the New Jersey Supreme Court confronted a situation where a plaintiff brought an age discrimination claim alleging his employment was terminated because he was *young. See Bergen Commercial Bank v. Sisler*, 723 A.2d 944 (N.J. 1999) (upholding the claim). Is this a similar problem to that faced the court in *Weber*?

PHILIP P. FRICKEY,
WISDOM ON *WEBER*,
74 TUL. L. REV. 1169 (2000)*

The Supreme Court issued its decision in *Weber* on June 27, 1979. Surprisingly, a five-member majority coalesced, and it voted to overturn the Fifth Circuit (in effect vindicating Judge Wisdom's dissenting vote below) by holding that the Kaiser/Steelworkers apprenticeship program did not violate Title VII. Justice Brennan's majority opinion was joined by the other three Justices who voted with him in *Bakke* to uphold the admissions program at issue, although, as discussed below, Justice Blackmun only grudgingly stayed with this group. The critical fifth vote for Justice Brennan's opinion came from Justice Stewart, who had been a member of the bloc of four Justices in *Bakke* who had voted to invalidate the admissions program in that case. Chief Justice Burger and Justice Rehnquist, who had also been part of that bloc, dissented in *Weber*.

One might hope that Justice Stewart's apparent flip-flop could be traced to the drafting of an overwhelmingly persuasive opinion by Justice Brennan. Regrettably, however, the Brennan opinion in *Weber* is a June opinion in more than date. With all due respect for Justice Brennan, a man I admired both for his sense of justice and his legal acumen, the opinion is a failure: it so lacks persuasive methodological power as to raise questions, to which we will eventually turn, about the Court's candor in identifying the real reasons why five Justices voted as they did.

The opinion got off to an inauspicious start by failing to trace Weber's claim to any specific statutory prohibition. To be sure, it noted that the complaint prepared by Fontham for Weber alleged that the apprenticeship program violated sections 703(a) and (d) of Title VII, and the opinion dutifully quoted these provisions in footnotes. But that was not merely the beginning, it was also the end of Justice Brennan's interest in the actual words of the prohibitions of Title VII. Justice Brennan accused Weber of relying upon a "literal interpretation" of these provisions, but never stopped to parse the statutory words so that the reader could evaluate how "literally" they supported his claim. Justice Brennan's apparent lack of interest in the statutory text was confirmed by how quickly he concluded that Weber's "reliance upon a literal construction of" these provisions was "misplaced" because it was trumped by a " 'familiar rule, that a thing may be within the letter of the statute and yet not within the statute, because not within its spirit, nor within the intention of its makers.' " Justice Brennan's ultimate argument was that the legislative history and historical context of Title VII demonstrated that an interpretation of Title VII prohibiting affirmative action would " 'bring about an end completely at variance with the purpose of the statute' and [therefore] must be rejected." For Justice Brennan, the purpose of Title VII was to open employment doors to historically disadvantaged minorities, and fostering that purpose required rejecting Weber's claim.

To be fair to Justice Brennan, his lack of interest in statutory text was not idiosyncratic. During the era of *Weber*, the Court had reached a consensus that the touchstone of statutory meaning was legislative intent. The briefs in the case marshaled arguments from the legislative history and paid little attention to statutory text standing alone, reflecting the views of skilled advocates concerning what actually was of interest to the Justices. Nonetheless, even judged within its nontextual times, the majority opinion in *Weber* was ineffective. Frankly, this is one of the reasons why it is such a good teaching case for my colleagues and I who use it to introduce the problem of statutory interpretation: first-year law students, with a little prodding, can do a better job.

Recall that Justice Brennan avoided the statutory text by invoking the proposition that the unenacted purpose or spirit of a law may trump the plain meaning of its text.

For this approach, Justice Brennan cited a nearly century-old precedent, *Church of the Holy Trinity v. United States*. I tell my students that the Holy Trinity move is what you do when the statutory text is hopelessly against you. It is sort of like the Hail Mary pass in football. One might guess from all this that the text of Title VII essentially precluded the result that Justice Brennan wanted and so he needed a supervening principle that allowed him to escape its clutches. That was not the case, however.

Although the prohibitions of Title VII do lend obvious support to Weber's claim, in my judgment the statute lacks crystalline clarity. Parsed carefully, the three provisions cited by Justice Brennan say essentially the following concerning the *Weber* circumstances. First, section 703(a)(1) of Title VII makes it illegal "to discriminate against any individual with respect to his . . . terms, conditions, or privileges of employment, because of such individual's race." Second, section 703(a)(2) also makes it illegal "to limit, segregate, or classify . . . employees . . . in any way which would deprive or tend to deprive any individual of employment opportunities . . . because of such individual's race." Third, in this context, section 703(d) makes it illegal "for any employer, labor organization, or joint labor-management committee controlling apprenticeship or other training or retraining, including on-the-job training programs to discriminate against any individual because of his race . . . in admission to, or employment in, any program established to provide apprenticeship or other training."

To be sure, all three provisions have language that can be rather easily read as invalidating the Kaiser/Steelworkers apprenticeship program. In a sense, though, that is as much an analytical problem for Weber as a benefit. If the statute is to have textual integrity, it should not have provisions that overlap each other in varying degrees of specificity and varying breadths of coverage. When I teach this case to my first-year law students, I ask them to pick the provision that they believe should apply. They always pick section 703(d), because it squarely deals with apprenticeship programs. These students intuit the policy behind the long-standing canon of statutory interpretation that when two statutory provisions overlap or conflict, the specific trumps the general.

If I were the attorney for Kaiser or the Steelworkers, I would be delighted to concede that the governing provision is section 703(d). The reason is that this provision, along with the more generally worded section 703(a)(1), uses the term "discriminate against any individual . . . because of . . . race." Although it may not seem so at first glance, this phrase may be ambiguous, as suggested below. If I were an attorney arguing for the legality of the plan, I would want to run as far away as possible from the other provision, section 703(a)(2), which does not use the word "discriminate" and contains more general language prohibiting classifying employees on the basis of race.

If, as I suggest, the most apt provision is section 703(d) because it squarely deals with apprenticeship programs, then one can argue that its key term, "discriminate" on the basis of race, does not inexorably include what Kaiser and the Steelworkers agreed to do. Arguably, not every consideration of race, not even every consideration of race that disadvantages someone because of his or her own race, is "discrimination."

In my own desk dictionary, which was copyrighted in 1968 and thus is roughly contemporaneous with Title VII, the first definition for "discriminate" is "[t]o act toward someone or something with partiality or prejudice: to discriminate against a minority; to discriminate in favor of one's friends." The second definition is "[t]o draw a clear distinction; distinguish; to discriminate between good and evil." The first definition speaks of invidious discrimination, such as that practiced against African-Americans throughout much of American history. The second definition speaks of drawing a clear distinction. My colleague Jim Chen, who creates vivid labels of legal concepts for his students, calls the first definition "the Boss Hogg definition of discrimination" and the second one "the Audrey Hepburn definition of discrimination."

Weber clearly prevails under the second definition, but not the first. He was not excluded from the apprenticeship program because of invidious prejudice against white people. The message he received was not that he was less a human being than others because of his race, that he was not fit to associate with the dominant group because he was inferior or loathsome. To be sure, his potential earning capacity and employment opportunities were frustrated, and no doubt he was extremely upset. In press accounts, he reportedly felt "cheated." We can all understand and sympathize; his complaint is hardly that of a racist. We can even imagine that Congress might have thought that such frustration of potential on account of race, even if well-intentioned to redress significant problems in traditionally segregated jobs like craft work, amounted to the drawing of such a clear distinction on the basis of race, our second definition of discrimination, and had such potential for racial friction that it should be illegal, just as invidious discrimination against African-Americans is illegal. But can we be sure that Congress intended both definitions of "discriminate," not just the first one? In my judgment, the text of section 703(d) is ambiguous on this point. If what I say has merit, Justice Brennan could have gotten a lot of mileage out of this analysis, thereby reducing the apparent result orientation of his *Weber* opinion.

Of course, there is ambiguity, and then there is ambiguity. Even if you grant some force to what I say, it may still be the case that a fair-minded reading of Title VII makes it cut, say, sixty/forty in favor of Weber. But that is far removed from Justice Brennan's apparent admission that the statute was one-hundred percent unambiguous in Weber's favor, requiring the judicial Heimlich maneuver of the Holy Trinity move to dislodge text supposedly choking the spirit out of the statute.

With today's law students, I often find a failure, at first blush, to appreciate the two potential ways in which "discriminate" can be defined. One reason may be that the word itself has evolved over the past four decades. Professor Chen has a desk dictionary, copyrighted in 1990, that gives the Audrey Hepburn definition of "discriminate" as the first one and the Boss Hogg definition as the second. This tiny example suggests an ambiguity about plain meaning, if you will: which dictionary should we prefer? Or should we simply say that literal meaning only gets us so far in judging the meaning of a statute? Notice that, if that seems plausible, we have reached that conclusion by textual analysis, not textual avoidance à la Brennan.

One would expect that the dissenting Justices would have attacked the Brennan majority opinion in *Weber* for failing to acknowledge the importance of statutory text. Oddly, the attack was oblique, not frontal. The major dissenting opinion in the case, by Justice Rehnquist, did assert that the apprenticeship program was "flatly prohibited by the plain language of Title VII," but like Justice Brennan, Justice Rehnquist never seriously grappled with what the text actually said, possible nuance and all. Even more fundamentally, Justice Rehnquist largely operated within the same interpretive paradigm as Brennan, for Rehnquist stated that the Court's "task in this case, like any other case involving the construction of a statute, is to give effect to the intent of Congress." Justice Rehnquist surely believed that supposedly plain statutory textual meaning was the best evidence of legislative intent, but by conflating textual meaning and legislative intent into one package, he was inviting a long, and somewhat inconclusive, battle over what the legislative history revealed.

Indeed, both the Brennan majority opinion and the Rehnquist dissent devoted extensive attention to the legislative history of Title VII. In a nutshell, Justice Brennan marshaled quotations from the legislative history to support his conclusion that the primary purpose of Title VII was to open doors to historically disadvantaged peoples. One might easily grant him the point and remain unconvinced about his rejection of Weber's argument, however, for it simply begs the question of what means Congress chose to effectuate this purpose: the narrow means of outlawing racial distinctions that harm racial minorities or the broader means of outlawing all racial distinctions. Similarly, Justice Rehnquist marshaled many quotations in support of the general proposition that Title VII was to prohibit all discrimination on account of race, even discrimination against nonminorities, but that again begs the question whether "discrimination" means something narrower (invidious discrimination) or broader (any distinction based on race).

The debate about legislative history produced a wonderful irony. Justice Brennan pounced on an amendment to Title VII in the Senate that added section 703(j), which provides that nothing in the statute "shall be interpreted to require any employer . . . to grant preferential treatment . . . to any group because of" its race to correct racial imbalance in the workforce. Had Congress intended to disallow what Kaiser and the Steelworkers had done, according to Brennan, it would have used the word "permit" rather than "require." Here Justice Brennan, who fled any consideration of the text of Title VII's prohibitions, clung for dear life to the literal language of a proviso. Justice Rehnquist, too, had a bit of a dilemma here: he had to flee the apparent plain meaning of the clause in favor of its spirit of color blindness, his own mini-Trinity move.

In the last analysis, however, because of the methodological weakness of the Brennan opinion, there was force to Justice Rehnquist's heated assertions that the majority opinion was an example of Orwellian doublespeak, "a tour de force reminiscent not of jurists such as Hale, Holmes, and Hughes, but of escape artists such as Houdini." Chief Justice Burger, in a short dissent, joined in the Rehnquistian chorus, accusing the majority of engaging in "judicially unauthorized, [even] intellectually dishonest means" to achieve a result it believed was desirable. Even by the standards of Supreme Court Justices, to whom Justice Oliver Wendell Holmes supposedly once referred as "nine scorpions in a bottle," this is harsh language about persons who, after all, remain colleagues in a small-group decisional setting for the foreseeable future.

When methodological weakness is combined with perhaps the hottest social issue of our time, affirmative action, especially when racial quotas are involved, one can expect more than the usual reaction to a Supreme Court opinion. Justice Rehnquist played the "quota card" in his dissent, calling the racial quota "a creator of castes, a two-edged sword that must demean one in order to prefer another." Justice Rehnquist intimated that, whatever Title VII was intended to do, it was not designed to foster, instead of undermine, caste.

In conservative circles the condemnation of the *Weber* outcome was swift and loud. Even Judge Gee, who had written the majority opinion for the Fifth Circuit in favor of Weber, got into the act. When the case arrived on remand from the Supreme Court on its way to the district court, Judge Gee wrote a remarkable statement expressing his strong belief that the majority of the Supreme Court was mistaken and had not just wrongly, but dangerously, taken the nation in a direction of race consciousness rather than color blindness. Judge Gee wrote: "Subordinate magistrates such as I must either obey the orders of higher authority or yield up their posts to those who will." "I obey," he continued, "since in my view the action required of me by the Court's mandate is only to follow a mistaken course and not an evil one," although in context you get the sense that he thought the question was a close one.

As I mentioned at the beginning of the Lecture, my interest in *Weber*, as a law professor concerned with statutory interpretation, is not so much in the outcome as in the methodology. Although I cannot prove it, and lectures like these are great places to make unprovable assertions, I believe that *Weber* has had a remarkable impact upon the methodology of statutory interpretation. I recall as a young lawyer hearing a senior partner at my firm, a sort of "lawyer's lawyer" who was by no means a conservative, opining to the effect that if the only defense of the outcome in *Weber* was Brennan's, then the Court should have simply given up on affirmative action. In my judgment, *Weber*, or more precisely, the conservative reaction to *Weber*, has provided much fuel for the remarkable evolution in conservative statutory methodology we have seen since the early 1980s.

Indeed, if pressed to put the case most strongly, I would suggest that *Weber* is the case most responsible for the widespread consideration and, in some circles, the embrace, of two key elements of the new textualism promoted by Justice Scalia that are inconsistent with both the Brennan and the Rehnquist approaches in *Weber*. The first is that the only "law" we have is statutory text: statutory interpretation is supposed to be undertaken as a matter of discerning the outcome most capable with the ordinary meaning and integrity of statutory text, perhaps filtered through established canons of statutory interpretation. The second is that legislative intent is essentially a myth. As two journalists once put it, how can Congress, an entity with two bodies and 535 heads, have any collective intent? To be sure, the law engages in legal fictions when it is functional to do so, but the new textualism maintains that "legislative intent" is a dysfunctional fiction that should be jettisoned. A corollary is that the use of legislative history in statutory interpretation is a waste of time at best and, at worst, an activity so manipulable that it is much more like looking over a crowd and picking out your friends than it is an objective historical recreation of what legislators collectively were contemplating.

These methodological transformations were manifest when the Court revisited the *Weber* issue in 1987, in *Johnson v. Transportation Agency, Santa Clara County, California*. A majority of the Court, again in an opinion by Justice Brennan, reaffirmed *Weber* and even extended its holding to authorize affirmative action any time there was a "manifest imbalance" or underrepresentation of a protected class under Title VII, racial minorities or women, for example, in a particular work category. The case fractured the Justices in a variety of interesting ways. Again, Justice Brennan had a bare majority of five Justices. Justices Marshall and Blackmun, who had been with him in *Weber*, remained with him in *Johnson*. But Justice White, who had joined Brennan's majority opinion in *Weber*, dissented in *Johnson* and urged the overruling of *Weber*. For Justice White, *Weber* concerned an apprenticeship program that was legal because it had been designed "to remedy the intentional and systematic exclusion of blacks by the employer and the unions from certain job categories," not on the much broader ground that the program simply was intended to overcome a manifest racial imbalance in the workforce. Justice Powell, who had not taken part in *Weber*, silently provided the fourth vote for Brennan in *Johnson*. The crucial fifth vote came from Justice Stevens, who also had not participated in *Weber* and who, you may recall, had concluded in *Bakke* that Title VI of the Civil Rights Act required color blindness. For Justice Stevens, the issue was whether he should adhere to a decision "that is at odds with my understanding of the actual intent of the authors of the legislation." He agreed to do so, essentially concluding that the law was well settled: he said that *Weber* is "an important part of the fabric of our law" and that there is an important "public interest in 'stability and orderly development of the law.'" Justice O'Connor concurred in the judgment on narrower grounds similar to those articulated by Judge Wisdom in the court of appeals back in the *Weber* case.

Justice Scalia, joined by Chief Justice Rehnquist and to a great extent by Justice White, dissented in *Johnson*. His dissenting opinion avoided the missed opportunities found in the Rehnquist dissent eight years earlier in *Weber*. He stressed the apparent plain meaning of the statutory text and the slippery nature of the Holy Trinity move Justice Brennan used in *Weber* to avoid it. He did not trouble himself with quotations from the legislative history, merely indicating that Justice Rehnquist's dissent had "convincingly demonstrated" that, even if one should pretend to believe in such things as the spirit of the statute, whatever that spirit was for Title VII, it could not have been the one invoked by Justice Brennan.

My concern about *Weber* is not the outcome, which has allowed employers and unions to take steps to improve the lot of racial minorities and women in the workforce. As a policy matter, I am untroubled by that result. As someone interested in legal methodology, my concern is that the majority opinion seems so flimsy and result-oriented. Indeed, one Justice in the majority in *Weber* expressed concerns at the time. Justice Blackmun began his concurring opinion in *Weber* this way:

> While I share some of the misgivings expressed in Mr. Justice Rehnquist's dissent concerning the extent to which the legislative history of Title VII clearly supports the result the Court reaches today, I believe that additional considerations, practical and equitable, only partially perceived, if perceived at all, by the 88th Congress, support the conclusion reached by the Court today . . . .

Justice Blackmun took his guidance in these regards from Judge Wisdom's dissenting opinion in the court of appeals. A consideration of this and related factors illuminates what was really going on in *Weber*.

. . . .

As mentioned earlier, Justice Blackmun was dubious about how solidly the legislative history supported the majority's theory. He was much more attracted to Judge Wisdom's theory, articulated in his dissent below, that the apprenticeship program was justified not on the basis of arguably dubious, and certainly reconstructed and rather hypothetical, legislative intent, but rather on the basis that Kaiser was engaged in affirmative action to remedy arguable violations of Title VII.

The Wisdom "arguable violation" theory[126] is attractive to me for many reasons. I think it more honestly recognizes what was really going on in *Weber*. It makes sense to assume that Kaiser would not have embarked upon an expensive, and legally questionable, apprenticeship program unless it viewed the consequences of maintaining the status quo an even greater legal risk. Kaiser had two significant problems. First, it had federal inspectors breathing down its neck, worrying about whether the shockingly low number of African-Americans in craft work at Gramercy made Kaiser in violation of the federal executive order requiring nondiscrimination by federal contractors. Second, it faced potential legal liability to African-Americans themselves. Eight years before *Weber*, in *Griggs v. Duke Power Co.*, the Supreme Court (with Justice Brennan not participating) had unanimously held that Title VII not only prohibits intentional discrimination against racial minorities, it also invalidates barriers to minority employment that, although neutral with respect to race, have a statistically significant exclusionary racial effect and cannot be justified by business necessity. Kaiser's former requirement that only applicants with experience in craft work would be considered for craft openings was precisely the sort of prerequisite to employment rendered legally dubious by *Griggs*, for it produced the extraordinarily segregated craft workforce at Kaiser and there were presumably other means, such as an apprenticeship program, to ensure Kaiser a supply of able craft workers. This is not to say that the former requirement necessarily violated Title VII, as interpreted in *Griggs*. When this problem is combined with the pressures flowing from the executive order concerning federal contracting, however, one gets a much better sense of Kaiser's motivations. It is difficult to consider its motivations a simple matter of private sector volunteerism, an example of private ordering designed to remedy societal discrimination.

Earlier, I suggested that one element missing from the Brennan/Rehnquist exchange in *Weber* was careful consideration of the statutory text. We are now ready to consider another important perspective that was missing. In the Brennan/Rehnquist debate, both sides were ossified in supposedly neutral inquiries reconstructing the probable intent of the 1964 Congress, a body of 535 people that had ceased to exist a decade and a half before. Neither admitted to any evaluation of the current perspective, the facts of this case, as a perspective filtered through developments after 1964.

Judge Wisdom in the court of appeals had filled this vacuum concerning this postenactment perspective. Because Judge Wisdom had been instrumental in developing the theory of disparate impact embraced in *Griggs*, he must have well understood the problem Kaiser faced. In 1969, two years before *Griggs* was decided, Judge Wisdom

---

[126] *See Weber v. Kaiser Aluminum & Chem. Corp.*, 563 F.2d 216, 230–34 (5th Cir. 1977) (Wisdom, J., dissenting), *rev'd sub nom. United Steelworkers of Am. v. Weber*, 443 U.S. 193 (1979).

had written an influential decision for the Fifth Circuit in *Local 189, United Paperworkers v. United States*, in which he reached the Griggs conclusion that facially neutral job rules that perpetuate the effects of past discriminatory practices are presumptively invalid under Title VII. A year later, the United States Court of Appeals for the Fourth Circuit in *Griggs* disagreed, creating a split in the courts of appeals on the issue that led to Supreme Court review. Judge Soboleff of the Fourth Circuit had dissented in *Griggs*, relying upon Judge Wisdom's analysis and identifying him by name in support of the contrary position. The Supreme Court decision in *Griggs* vindicated the Wisdom/Soboleff vision of the breadth of Title VII's reach in favor of historically disadvantaged minorities.

. . . .

Like Justice Brennan's result later in the Supreme Court, Judge Wisdom's solution was to allow private ordering by management and unions. But unlike Justice Brennan, Judge Wisdom wanted the plan to be tailored to the facts that suggested affirmative action was sensible in context. He wrote: "If an affirmative action plan, adopted in a collective bargaining agreement, is a reasonable remedy for an arguable violation of Title VII, it should be upheld."

Unlike both Justices Brennan and Rehnquist in *Weber*, Judge Wisdom did not maintain, with a straight face, that the 1964 Congress foresaw and precisely decided the issue in one way or the other. The vantage point of Wisdom, if you will, was not from 1964 looking forward, but from the late 1970s looking backward. The vantage point of Wisdom was not to maintain that the meaning of law was inexorably fixed at some point by static materials (statutory text and legislative intent) such that in, say, 1965 any sensible court would have reached one decision or the other. Frankly, as Justice Blackmun suggested in his concurring opinion embracing the vantage point of Wisdom, Justice Rehnquist had the better of those arguments. Instead, Judge Wisdom in effect maintained that the vantage point of the late 1970s should count as well. For him, the role of the judge was a synthetic one, attempting to mediate the influences of statutory text, original legislative context, and current context, including social and legal evolution since 1964. His "arguable violation" theory is just such an attempt at mediating a variety of competing sources of legal legitimacy rather than privileging one to the exclusion of all the others.

The vantage point of Wisdom also has candor supporting it. It is no surprise to anyone familiar with the individual philosophies of William Brennan and William Rehnquist that they would disagree in *Weber*. Indeed, in the world of political science, scholars have long maintained that personal judicial ideology accounts for Supreme Court voting patterns far better than any other explanation. We law professors hope that there is more to it than that, that the process also involves such factors as legal doctrine and precedent; the desire to articulate rules of law of a sufficiently abstract quality so that they can be applied fairly neutrally in the future, even when the judge would rather not do so; the moderating pressures inherent in multimember courts and the opinion-writing process; the judge's desire to have legitimacy and respect in the legal interpretive community, a community in which there is a fairly widely shared value in the rule of law rather than the rule of judges; and so on. However one comes out on this, though, I think the reasonable judgment is that virtually no person is capable of deciding a question like the one in *Weber* by blanking her mind to all developments over the subsequent fifteen years and mechanically applying statutory text and objectively reconstructed legislative intent, finding self-satisfaction in the role of automaton rather than human being. And I think if we found such a person, most of us would be scared to death to give that person the power of the judge, the authority to exercise the coercive power of the state.

NOTES AND QUESTIONS

1. Reread the *Weber* opinions with these thoughts in mind.

2. Do you agree that the statutory terms had plausible, alternative definitions?

3. Daniel B. Rodriguez and Barry Weingast have analyzed legislative history in the context of the Civil Rights Act of 1964 and cases like *Weber*:

> It is necessary to distinguish between cheap talk — that is, communication that is costless for the speaker to make and that is unverifiable and therefore untrustworthy — and costly signaling — communication where the speaker pays a price for inaccuracies. The point of this distinction is that, in contrast to cheap talk, costly signals can be trusted; they therefore more accurately reflect the intent of those legislators whose support was most critical to securing assent to the final bill. For example, speeches made at the introduction legislation are ordinarily cheap talk. This stage occurs before any of the legislative compromises necessary to pass the act and, therefore, cannot reflect the critical compromise provisions in the final act. Indeed, since so many more bills are introduced than are ever passed, these speeches involve fair amounts of hyperbole about grand goals and aspirations rather than accurate portrayals of either the introduced legislative details or projections of those provisions likely to pass. Similarly, discussions in news conferences or memoirs after the legislation's creation are cheap talk: legislators typically do not pay a price for inaccurate assessments of the legislation in these circumstances.

> In contrast, discussions on the floor of the legislative chamber that focus on the meaning of critical compromises offered in amendments are costly signals. Because they risk losing the votes of the moderates, ardent supporters pay a large price for attempts to downplay or inaccurately describe the compromise during floor debates preceding acceptance of the compromise. The same holds for committee reports. If these reports fail to describe accurately the compromises made in committee, members whose support was necessary to pass the bill from the committee to the floor may work against the bill's passage, thus discouraging moderates from signing on to the legislation.

> Another implication of the theory of legislative rhetoric is that the legislative record contains multiple, side-by-side interpretations of an act. Ardent supporters, on cheap talk occasions, typically propound expansionary readings of the act. Yet moderates, emphasizing their compromises, focus on the act's limitations; ardent supporters, on costly signal occasions after the compromises but before an act's passage, will also accurately describe the act's limits. The theory of legislative rhetoric also implies that statements by ardent supporters in costly signaling settings may well contradict their statements in cheap talk settings. These multiple and potentially contradictory statements therefore require careful attention to sort out trustworthy from untrustworthy information.

> While the focus of the theory of legislative rhetoric is positive, there is a normative conclusion. In the real world, courts reinforce legislator incentives and efforts at spin control by using legislative history selectively. In particular, courts are drawn under traditional theories of interpretation toward the "winner's history"; that is, they tend to look more closely at legislative statements of authors, sponsors, and other ardent supporters of legislation, on the not-implausible grounds that these legislators were most important to the development of the legislation.

> The theory of legislative rhetoric suggests that this traditional approach is

flawed because it is based upon an erroneous depiction of the legislative process. Rather, given the structure of legislative coalitions and the strategic incentives of legislators, the proper task of courts is to sort out the various different and often contradictory statements made about the act over an often long and complicated legislative process. In the end, our prescription flips the typical approach to interpreting legislative history by steering attention away from the expressed views of ardent supporters toward those of pivotal, moderate legislators and the ardent supporters' costly signals.

Daniel B. Rodriguez & Barry R. Weingast, *The Paradox of Expansionist Statutory Interpretations*, 101 Nw. U. L. Rev. 1207, 1220–22 (2007). *See also* Daniel B. Rodriguez & Barry R. Weingast, *The Positive Political Theory of Legislative History: New Perspectives on the 1964 Civil Rights Act and its Interpretation*, 151 U. Penn. L. Rev. 1417 (2003).

Can you distinguish the cheap talk from the costly signaling in *Weber*?

DANIEL A. FARBER & PHILIP P. FRICKEY, LEGISLATIVE INTENT AND PUBLIC CHOICE,
74 Virginia Law Review 423, 437–43 (1988)*

IMAGINE a country where laws are usually the unpredictable results of shifting coalitions and arbitrary agendas. Legislative committees produce official reports that purport to explain those laws, but are actually concocted by staff members and lobbyists to deceive courts about the meaning of the statutes. After statutes are passed, legislators contrive to smuggle their personal interpretations of the laws into later committee reports and debates dealing with other matters. Courts foolishly give credence to this deceptive evidence of a legislative intent that itself is little more than a legal fiction; moreover, the courts sometimes even elevate counterfeit legislative history above the duly enacted language of the law itself. Only by jettisoning the whole idea of legislative intent can judges escape this chamber of illusions.

This scenario is only a slight caricature of how legislative intent is viewed by several prominent judges appointed by President Reagan. Although no one judge would agree that everything in our opening paragraph is true, it is an accurate synthesis of their collective writings. These judges, including most notably Justice Antonin Scalia, have advocated a radical reassessment of the concept of legislative intent.

. . . .

II. *Legislative Intent and Legislative History*

One time-honored source of legislative intent is the legislative history of the statute. Recently, however, Justice Scalia has roundly attacked the current judicial practice of routinely considering legislative history. He has asserted that even if legislative intent is a coherent concept, legislative history provides an exceedingly poor documentary record of it. This assault upon the use of legislative history in statutory interpretation is premised on the notion that legislative history is the product of legislators at their worst — promoting private interest deals, strategically posturing to mislead judges, or abdicating all responsibility to their unelected staffs (who presumably either have their own political agendas or randomly run amok). The relationship between this vision of the legislative process and the assumptions of public choice theory is obvious.

Justice Scalia's attack began when he sat on the United States Court of Appeals for the District of Columbia Circuit. In *Hirschey v. Federal Energy Regulatory Commission*,[56] then-Judge Scalia discussed a House committee report concerning

---

[56] 777 F.2d 1 (D.C. Cir. 1985).

amendments to a federal statute. The report noted a split in the courts of appeals concerning the interpretation of certain statutory language unaffected by the amendments and stated that the approach taken by the Ninth Circuit was incorrect. Judge Scalia was unimpressed:

> It is most interesting that the House Committee rejected the interpretation of the Ninth Circuit, and perhaps that datum should be accorded the weight of an equivalently unreasoned law review article. But the authoritative, as opposed to the persuasive, weight of the Report depends entirely upon how reasonable it is to assume that the rejection was reflected in the law which *Congress* adopted. I frankly doubt that it is ever reasonable to assume that the details, as opposed to the broad outlines of purpose, set forth in a committee report come to the attention of, much less are approved by, the house which enacts the committee's bill. And I think it time for courts to become concerned about the fact that routine deference to the detail of committee reports, and the predictable expansion in that detail which routine deference has produced, are converting a system of judicial construction into a system of committee-staff prescription.[58]

At first glance, much of this language seems unexceptional . . . .

Upon closer inspection, however, Judge Scalia's dictum in *Hirschey* contains some extraordinary elements. The last sentence quoted above refers to "a system of committee-staff prescription." This is a rather stark judicial impeachment of the legislative process — Judge Scalia is, in effect, asserting that legislators have abdicated important responsibilities to staff members, who routinely connive to subvert the judicial function by planting their (not even their legislators') subjective desires about statutory meaning into committee reports, hoping that their ideas will blossom later in judicial opinions. To support these assertions, Judge Scalia attached a footnote to the excerpt quoted above presenting an anecdote from the Senate floor.

From the footnote it would appear that Senator Robert Dole, the committee chair who was managing floor consideration of a tax bill, admitted under sharp fire from Senator William Armstrong that he had not even read the entire committee report, much less written any of it, that the report was prepared wholly by staff, and that senators, including committee members, had little opportunity to object to the report's contents.[60]

---

[58] *Hirschey*, 777 F.2d at 7–8 (Scalia, J., concurring) (footnote omitted) (emphasis added).

[60] The footnote, in its entirety, read as follows:

> Several years ago, the following illuminating exchange occurred between members of the Senate, in the course of floor debate on a tax bill:

Mr. ARMSTRONG	. . . .My question, which may take [the chairman of the Committee on Finance] by surprise, is this: Is it the intention of the chairman that the Internal Revenue Service and the Tax Court and other courts take guidance as to the intention of Congress from the committee report which accompanies this bill?
Mr. DOLE.	I would certainly hope so . . . .
Mr. ARMSTRONG.	Mr. President, will the Senator tell me whether or not he wrote the committee report?
Mr. DOLE.	Did I write the committee report?
Mr. ARMSTRONG.	Yes.
Mr. DOLE.	No, the Senator from Kansas did not write the committee report.
Mr. ARMSTRONG.	Did any Senator write the committee report?
Mr. DOLE.	I have to check.
Mr. ARMSTRONG.	Does the Senator know of any Senator who wrote the committee report?
Mr. DOLE.	I might be able to identify one, but I would have to search. I was here all during the time it was written, I might say, and worked carefully with the staff as they worked . . . .

It turns out, however, that in context the exchange between Armstrong and Dole was more benign than Judge Scalia's presentation might suggest. Indeed, what Judge Scalia seemingly characterized as a gross malfunction of the legislative process was in reality an admirable performance — in Senator Armstrong's own evaluation.[61] The Armstrong-Dole colloquy demonstrates that staffs prepare committee reports, that legislators do

Mr. ARMSTRONG.   Mr. President, has the Senator from Kansas, the chairman of the Finance Committee, read the committee report in its entirety?

Mr. DOLE.   I am working on it. It is not a bestseller, but I am working on it.

Mr. ARMSTRONG.   Mr. President, did members of the Finance Committee vote on the committee report?

Mr. DOLE.   No.

Mr. ARMSTRONG.   Mr. President, the reason I raise the issue is not perhaps apparent on the surface, and let me just state it: . . . The report itself is not considered by the Committee on Finance. It was not subject to amendment by the Committee on Finance. It is not subject to amendment now by the Senate.

. . . .

. . . If there were matter within this report which was disagreed to by the Senator from Colorado or even by a majority of all Senators, there would be no way for us to change the report. I could not offer an amendment tonight to amend the committee report.

. . . [F]or any jurist, administrator, bureaucrat, tax practitioner, or others who might chance upon the written record of this proceeding, let me just make the point that this is not the law, it was not voted on, it is not subject to amendment, and we should discipline ourselves to the task of expressing congressional intent in the statute.

Id. (citing 128 Cong. Rec. S8659 (daily ed. July 19, 1982)).

[61] One might assume, based on the excerpt from the Congressional Record, *see supra* note 60, that Senator Armstrong considered specific language in the committee report to be inconsistent with the language of the bill, that he believed that committee staff had run amok in preparing the report, that he felt powerless to make an effective objection, and that he more generally found Dole's work as chairman slovenly. In fact, the context was quite different. Just prior to the colloquy quoted by Judge Scalia, Armstrong made a number of statements to the contrary. First, he noted that he was a member of the Finance Committee and supported the bill in the form it was reported, although he did plan to propose some amendments concerning aspects of the bill that he found "distasteful." 128 Cong. Rec. 16914–15 (1982). As a member of the committee, presumably he had good access to committee staff, as well as the responsibility to rein them in if they acted improperly. Second, and also just prior to the language quoted by Judge Scalia, Armstrong heaped praise upon Dole's work as committee chairman. *See id.* at 16918 (In getting a majority of the committee to agree to the bill within a necessarily short time frame, Dole showed "a degree of legislative perspicacity, management, and statesmanship that is rare. In fact, in my experience and observation it has never been excelled.").

Based on what Judge Scalia presented, one might also think that this was a simple bill and that staff wrote into the report matter that could easily have been inserted in the bill. In fact, the bill was a huge and highly complicated piece of tax legislation that ran seventy pages in the Congressional Record! Perhaps no senator had read the entire committee report — but how many likely read the entire bill?

Next, one might examine what Judge Scalia deleted internally in the quotation used in his footnote. First, after stating "I would certainly hope so" to Armstrong's question about whether the committee report should guide interpretation of the statute, Dole continued: "plus not only the committee report but hopefully in the debate on certain compliance provisions that we will probably have lengthy discussions on the next few days." *Id.* This language suggests that Dole, Armstrong, and everyone else understood that senators had other methods of creating somewhat authoritative legislative history or of decreasing the authoritativeness of a committee report.

Second, after reporting that he had "worked carefully with the staff as they worked" on the report, Dole continued: "As I recall, during the July 4 recess there were about five different working groups of staff from both parties, the joint committee, and the Treasury working on different provisions." *Id.* Needless to say, these remarks rebut the appearance — created by Judge Scalia's editing, not by Armstrong's remarks — that low-level, irresponsible staff prepared the report in a setting hostile to the representation and consideration of different points of view.

Finally, following Armstrong's comment that the report "is not subject to amendment now by the Senate," Armstrong clearly stated why he made these remarks. *Id.* We reproduce his statement, putting the portions not included by Judge Scalia in italics:

not formally ratify language in reports, and that at least one senator — Armstrong — hoped courts in the interpretive exercise would not treat language in reports on a par with, or more important than, statutory language. The colloquy provides no support, however, for Judge Scalia's assertion about "committee-staff prescription" of judicial functions.

. . . .

A realistic appreciation of the legislative process does raise doubts about how reliably legislative history represents legislative intentions, even assuming that those "unenacted" intentions are useful for interpretation. Much legislative history, in context, may be what Charles Curtis called "the ashcans of the legislative process,"[74] bits and fragments of thought (or the lack thereof) that cannot fairly be regarded as saying anything reliable about the meaning to be accorded the statute. As Judge Scalia suggested in Hirschey, the legislative body as a whole is unlikely to pay much attention to the minutia found in legislative history.[75] *Moreover, a committee report may contain material that simply lacked the political force to make its way into the statute.*[76]

Perhaps even more worrisome is that judicial interpretation of a statute will be skewed by legislative history planted just for that purpose.[77]

I became aware recently of the practice which I think honestly is a most injudicious practice in which some courts have in fact relied upon committee report language as if it were a statute.

I only wish the record to reflect that this is not statutory language. It is not before us. If there were matter within this report which was disagreed to by the Senator from Colorado or even by a majority of all Senators, there would be no way for us to change the report. I could not offer an amendment tonight to amend the committee report.

I only wish to put that in the RECORD. I am not leaning in any particular direction. It is not my purpose at this moment to remonstrate about any particular language in the committee report. But for any jurist, administrator, bureaucrat, tax practitioner, or others who might chance upon the written record of this proceeding, let me just make the point that this is not the law, it was not voted on, it is not subject to amendment, and we should discipline ourselves to the task of expressing congressional intent in the statute.

Having made that point I do not wish to belabor it, but I might just add this footnote: I expect to make the same point with respect to other committee reports as they come down the pike and at some stage I may implement a scheme which I have long had in mind which is to offer language to a bill — I do not intend to do it on this particular bill — to simply endorse or reject specifically the language of committee reports.

What I find is that so often these committee reports are treated not only as if they were a statute, but as if they were something better than statutes, as if they somehow superseded statutory enactment and particularly in the case of tax law I think that is a very dangerous practice.

So on this quiet and otherwise uneventful evening, I thought I would make that point.

Id. at 16918–19.

. . . .

Thus, Senator Armstrong was expressing a general concern about courts using committee reports as if they were statutes — or "something better than statutes" — which is a legitimate concern. *See infra* text accompanying notes 100-04 [not reproduced here — Eds.]. This exchange cannot properly be viewed as a case study of actual committee report abuse.

[74] C. Curtis, It's Your Law 52 (1954).

[75] *See Hirschey*, 777 F.2d at 8 (Scalia, J., concurring).

[76] *See* Lane, *Legislative Process and its Judicial Renderings: A Study in Contrast*, 48 U. Pɪᴛᴛ. L. Rᴇᴠ. 639, 659 (1987) (quoting speech by Judge Abner Mikva); *see also* Mikva, *Reading and Writing Statutes*, 48 U. Pɪᴛᴛ. L. Rᴇᴠ. 627, 631 (1987) (explaining purposes committee reports serve other than explaining the text of the statute). Karl Llewellyn once remarked, "I think any aspect of legislative history may be useful, and should be looked at, for what it is worth; thus, the contrived 'friendly colloquy' deserves attention, frequently, as evidence of what was carefully left out of the bill." K. Llewellyn, The Common Law Tradition: Deciding Appeals 529 (1960).

[77] *See* Wasby, *Legislative Materials as an Aid to Statutory Interpretation: A Caveat*, 12 J. Pᴜʙ. L. 262, 267–68 (1963). Notwithstanding Senator Armstrong's comments, *supra* note 61, many members of Congress

Several things seem to distinguish the Scalia-led attack upon the use of legislative history from its forbears. First, Justice Scalia and his followers indulge in some doubtful factual assumptions. For example, Judge Kozinski's assertion that "few if any legislators read the reports"[79] is mere unsupported assertion, if it is not flatly incorrect. To the contrary, according to a principal study of congressional policymaking procedures, legislators outside the committee and their staffs focus primarily on the report, not the bill itself.[25]

The important factor is whether the public officials have abdicated their decision-making responsibilities to staff. When Justice Scalia's own example of committee-report abuse is placed in proper context, it does not support his fear of "committee-staff prescription." No doubt there are instances in which congressional staff exceed their appropriate role; however, what their role should be is surely the primary concern of the legislative rather than the judicial branch. In short, Justice Scalia and others have not established the universal truth of legislator abuse of legislative history or of congressional staff overreaching, have not given the legal community any effective way of identifying either in particular instances, and have not demonstrated any reason why change in judicial use of legislative history would "reform" congressional processes.

. . . .

In short, American public law has quite properly recognized that statutory meaning is necessarily greatly influenced by statutory context. Legislative history is part of that context, and some aspects of it — such as committee reports — will frequently represent the most intelligent exposition available of what the statute is all about. Legislative history is, after all, merely evidence of intent . . . .

Moreover, to the extent that the technical findings of public choice theory — rather than simply the rejection of the public-interest theory of legislation generally — have anything to say regarding Justice Scalia's suggestions, they probably cut against him. Political science has long stressed the overarching influence of legislative committees on legislative outcomes. Traditionally, committee power was attributed to the committee's roles as legislative "gatekeeper" and "policy incubator," to its expertise and agenda control, and to reciprocal deference among committees. Recently, public choice scholarship has suggested that a critical element explaining the demonstrable committee power in Congress is the frequent existence of an ex post committee veto. Briefly, even if the standing committee's proposal is modified on the floor of the legislature, the committee will later have great influence on the final outcome if (1) a conference committee on the bill is necessary (because it did not pass both houses of Congress in identical form), and (2) the standing committee essentially populates and controls the

---

are probably well aware of the judicial use of legislative history for purposes of statutory interpretation. *See, e.g.*, K. Kofmehl, Professional Staffs of Congress 119 (3d ed. 1977); Moorhead, *A Congressman Looks at the Planned Colloquy and Its Effect in the Interpretation of Statutes*, 45 A.B.A.J. 1314 (1959).

[79] *See supra* note 72.

[25] This reliance is described as follows:

Reports are directed primarily at members of the House and Senate and seek to persuade the membership to endorse the committee's recommendations when it comes up for a vote on the floor. For some members, or their staff aides, the report is the only document they read before deciding how to vote on an issue. The report, therefore, is the principal official means of communicating a committee decision to the entire chamber.

W. Oleszek, Congressional Procedures and the Policy Process 94 (2d ed. 1984) (footnote omitted). Oleszek noted that reports also provide guidance to courts and administrative agencies later called upon to interpret the statute. *See id.* at 97 n.32.

Similarly, Eric Redman, a former Senate aide, observed that committee reports provide information to courts and the Executive about legislative intent and then stated that "[w]ithin the Senate itself, reports are important chiefly because many Senators read nothing else before deciding how to vote on a particular bill. A good report, therefore, does more than explain — it also persuades." E. Redman, The Dance of Legislation 140 (1973).

conference committee. Both of these contingencies occur for nearly all major bills in Congress.[95]

The presence of an ex post veto strengthens the committee's ex ante gatekeeping and proposal powers (for example, it makes little sense to use a discharge petition to dislodge a bill from committee if the members of that committee are likely to control the conference committee down the road).

Although this recent public choice scholarship suggests little in particular about committee reports, it does indicate that the search for a coherent understanding of a statute must include a careful examination of the work of the relevant committees. That work will be reflected, albeit imperfectly, in the reports, which legislators and staff are likely to read more carefully than the bill itself and therefore may represent part of the congressional understanding of the statute's purpose and meaning. Thus recent public choice scholarship, as well as longstanding political science understandings of congressional committee power, supports the traditional presumption that "very likely most [members of Congress] knew only of the general purpose [of a bill], relied for the details on members who sat on the committees particularly concerned, and were quite willing to adopt these committees' will on subordinate points as their own."[97]

. . . .

That judges can effectively use legislative history does not, of course, ensure that they always do so. We acknowledge that judicial opinions sometimes appear more mechanical than reflective. In particular, today's standard Supreme Court opinion interpreting a statute brooks little uncertainty: it argues with a straight face that all relevant sources of meaning unambiguously point in the same direction. Moreover, the Court sometimes seemingly misuses legislative history, exalting it above the statute itself. These techniques do not necessarily reveal the true paths taken by judges in reaching results; instead, they may be explainable as wooden pieces of advocacy, rather than persuasive pieces of justification. Perhaps they are also understandable as (transparent) devices to "objectify" the opinion by making it appear that Congress, rather than the courts, made the controversial policy choices.

THE NEW YORK STATE BAR ASSOCIATION COMMITTEE ON FEDERAL LEGISLATION, COMMITTEE REPORT: LEGISLATING STATUTORY INTERPRETATION: THE "LEGISLATIVE HISTORY" PROVISION OF THE CIVIL RIGHTS ACT OF 1991,
65 N.Y.S.B.J. 44 (Jan. 1993)[*]

I. Introduction

The Civil Rights Act of 1991 (the "Act") was enacted on November 21, 1991. One of the more hotly-contested portions of this important legislation involved the extent to which the Act would codify the "disparate impact" doctrine enunciated by the Supreme Court in *Griggs v. Duke Power Co.* Under that doctrine, a claim of discrimination in the workplace may be based merely upon a showing that a specific business practice of the employer, while facially neutral, had a disproportionately adverse affect on a protected

---

[95] *See id.* at 94–95. For criticism and defense of this analysis, *see Why Are Congressional Committees Powerful?*, 81 AM. POL. SCI. REV. 929–45 (1987) (criticism by Keith Krehbiel and response by Kenneth Shepsle and Barry Weingast).

[97] H. Friendly, *supra* note 87, at 216.

[*] The New York State Bar Association Committee on Federal Legislation, Committee Report: Legislating Statutory Interpretation: The "Legislative History" Provision of the Civil Rights Act of 1991, 65 N.Y.S.B.J. 44 (Jan. 1993). Copyright 1993 by New York State Bar Journal. All Rights Reserved.

group. If such a showing is made by the employee, *Griggs* and its progeny hold that the burden shifts to the employer to show that the practice was "job related" and satisfied some "business necessity."

As might be imagined, the debate concerning this aspect of the Act was conducted by both sides with a passion and Congressional reports, documents, statements, prints, hearing testimony and floor debates were filled with favorable and unfavorable reactions to the preliminary versions of the legislation that ultimately was enacted. Notwithstanding this extensive body of research and analysis — normally referred to as the "legislative history" — Section 105(b) of the Act endeavors to circumscribe the legislative history of the disparate impact portion of the Act to a one-page "interpretive memorandum," which was inserted into the Congressional Record shortly before the legislation's enactment.

This report comments on the wisdom and practicality of the effort made in Section 105(b) to permit a review of legislative history in construing and applying the Act, but to limit that review to a single document.

II. Relevant Provisions

Section 105(b) of the Act provides:

> No statements other than the interpretive memorandum appearing at Vol. 137 Congressional Record S 15276 (daily ed. Oct. 25, 1991) shall be considered legislative history of, or relied upon in any way as legislative history in construing or applying, any provision of this Act that relates to Wards Cove-Business necessity/cumulation/alternative business practice.

The "interpretive memorandum" that is referred to in Section 105(b), which is dated October 25, 1991, provides, in its entirety:

> The final compromise on S. 1745 agreed to by several Senate sponsors, including Senators DANFORTH, KENNEDY and DOLE, and the Administration states that with respect to Wards Cove-Business necessity/cumulation/ alternative business practice — the exclusive legislative history is as follows:
>
> > The terms "business necessity" and "job related" are intended to reflect the concepts enunciated by the Supreme Court in *Griggs v. Duke Power Co.*, 401 U.S. 424 (1971), and in the other Supreme Court decisions prior to *Wards Cove Packing Co. v. Antonio*, 490 U.S. 642 (1989).
>
> > When a decision-making process includes particular, functionally-integrated practices which are components of the same criterion, standard, method of administration, or test, such as the height and weight requirements designed to measure strength in *Dothard v. Rawlinson*, 433 U.S. 321 (1977), the particular, functionally-integrated practices may be analyzed as one employment practice.[6]

. . . .

IV. Conclusion

Regardless of why Congress chose to place language that purports to be important to an understanding of the Act in the Congressional Record rather than in the Act itself, bill drafting by such indirection creates a distinctly negative impression of backroom dealing and manipulation. Is it really conceivable, for example, that all of the legislators who voted in favor of the Act were familiar both with the contents of the interpretive memorandum and with the enormity of detail that was being excluded by that memorandum from the Act's legislative history?

We view the effort made in Section 105(b) of the Act to limit the scope of legislative

---

[6] 137 Cong. Rec. S 15276, *reprinted in* 1991 U.S. Code Cong. & Admin. News 549, 767.

history review as misplaced. Whether it be a court that is deciding a Title VII action, an employer or employee who is either litigating a Title VII claim or weighing the ramifications of certain business practices, or an attorney or legal commentator who is attempting accurately to characterize the provisions of the Act, if the reader of the legislation finds ambiguous any provision thereof, he or she should be permitted, and encouraged, to review and analyze all of the available records, memoranda, testimony and other documents and information that led to the agreement among both houses of Congress and the President to enact this significant piece of legislation.

NOTES AND QUESTIONS

1. Does this congressional attempt to limit the range of available legislative history reflect an example of the tactic Senator Armstrong described in his colloquy with Senator Dole, excerpted in the preceding Farber and Frickey article?

2. In *Jenkins v. City of Grenada, Mississippi*, 813 F. Supp. 443, 448 n.9 (N.D. Miss 1993), the court noted in passing the preceding criticism of the Congress' attempt to limit legislative history.

3. For a careful look at the actual legislative process in Congress, see Victoria F. Nourse & Jane S. Schacter, *The Politics of Legislative Drafting: A Congressional Case Study,* 77 N.Y.U. L. Rev. 575 (2002).

EXCURSUS ON PUBLIC CHOICE THEORY AND
STATUTORY INTERPRETATION

A functional explanation of any given pattern of behavior takes the following form: "the consequences of some behavior or social arrangement are essential elements of the causes of that behavior."[1] When we ask why the legislature as an institution created this or that statute, we normally receive an explanation couched in terms of the statute's anticipated impact on American society.

Public choice theory is a functional explanation of legislative behavior which answers the why question with another question — cui bono, who will benefit? Public choice theorists give a wide range of answers to this question. At a constitutional level, for example, laws benefit everyone. Constitutions delineate a framework within which citizens can organize themselves to deliberate about the common good and make collective choices.[2] A constitution can be regarded as a perfect example of a pure public good. A pure public good has two salient characteristics: 1) jointness of supply; and 2) the impossibility or inefficiency of excluding others from consumption once it has been supplied to some members of the community.[3] Jointness of supply is a property of the production or cost function of the public good. This joint supply characteristic necessitates a cooperative decision if the good is to be provided efficiently. The exclusion criterion highlights the "free rider" problem. It makes no sense for an individual to incur the transaction and bargaining costs necessary to secure the provision of pure public goods, like statutes, since each individual will benefit from its supply without regard to whether and in what proportion he or she has contributed to its production. As a result, pure public goods are unlikely to be provided by the market. Furthermore, the market generates externalities. An externality occurs when the consumption or production activity of one actor has an unintended impact on the utility or consumption function of another. When externalities arise with large numbers of individuals, government economizes on the transaction and bargaining costs of obtaining information on individual preferences regarding public goods and externalities. However, government may be used to engineer redistributive goals as

---

[1] ARTHUR STINCHCOMBE, CONSTRUCTING SOCIAL THEORIES 80 (1968).

[2] JAMES M. BUCHANAN & GORDON TULLOCK, THE CALCULUS OF CONSENT (1962).

[3] This discussion leans heavily on DENNIS C. MUELLER, PUBLIC CHOICE II (1989).

well as to achieve allocative efficiency in the market. When it does so, government action is likely to be skewed in the direction of redistributive activities which benefit well-organized special interest groups.[4] These interest groups coalesce around policies which are likely to yield a surplus for their constituencies in excess of the transaction and bargaining costs incurred in influencing the legislative process. The free rider problem makes it unlikely that the broader public will organize itself to influence public policy. Hence, statutory law will increasingly embody transactions in which a narrowly focused group extracts benefits from the public as a whole and allocates those benefits within that interest group. Where there is a proliferation of interest groups, a statute is likely to reflect a deal, a compromise between competing predators seeking to extract rents from the commonwealth.

To the extent that public choice theory speaks to the problem of interpretation, those influenced by it would presumably draw a distinction between enactments which serve private interests and those which are public-regarding.[5] Private interest statutes would be confined narrowly, whereas public interest statutes would presumably receive a more welcome reception. It is unclear how public choice theorists or anyone else who purports to do so can devise neutral criteria for the identification and sorting of statutes into public versus private interest oriented. What is sound public policy to some is pork barrel legislation to others.

In *Begier v. Internal Revenue Service*, 496 U.S. 53, 110 S. Ct. 2258 (1990), the Court decided whether the Bankruptcy Act permitted a trustee in bankruptcy to recover from the IRS withholding and excise taxes which had already been paid over to the IRS prior to bankruptcy. In concluding that the trustee could not recover such taxes, the court relied on legislative history.

BEGIER v. INTERNAL REVENUE SERVICE
496 U.S. 53 (1990)

JUSTICE SCALIA, concurring in the judgment.

Representative Edwards, the House floor manager for the bill that enacted the Bankruptcy Code, said on the floor that "[t]he courts should permit the use of reasonable assumptions" regarding the tracing of tax trustfunds. 124 Cong. Rec. 32417 (1978). We do not know that anyone except the presiding officer was present to hear Representative Edwards. Indeed, we do not know for sure that Representative Edwards' words were even uttered on the floor rather than inserted into the Congressional Record afterwards. If Representative Edwards did speak these words, and if there were others present, they must have been surprised to hear him talking about the tracing of 26 U.S.C. § 7501 tax trust funds, inasmuch as the bill under consideration did not relate to the Internal Revenue Code but the Bankruptcy Code, and contained no provision even mentioning trust-fund taxes. Only the Senate bill, and not the House proposal, had mentioned trust-fund taxes — and even the former had said nothing whatever about the *tracing* of tax trustfunds. *See* S. 2266, 95th Cong., 2d

---

[4] MANCUR OLSON, THE LOGIC OF COLLECTIVE ACTION (1965); ANTHONY DOWNS, AN ECONOMIC THEORY OF DEMOCRACY (1957); ELMER E. SCHATTSCHNEIDER, THE SEMI-SOVEREIGN PEOPLE (1960).

[5] This distinction appears in Frank H. Easterbrook, *Statutes' Domains*, 50 U. CHI. L. REV. 533 (1983). Easterbrook has been associated with public choice theory. His writings about statutory interpretation have been treated in the academy as presumptive evidence of what a public choice theorist would say about such matters.

See also William N. Eskridge, Jr., *Politics Without Romance: Implications of Public Choice Theory for Statutory Interpretation*, 74 VA. L. REV. 275 (1988); Daniel A. Farber & Philip P. Frickey, *The Jurisprudence of Public Choice*, 65 TEX. L. REV. 873 (1987); Daniel A. Farber & Philip P. Frickey, *Legislative Intent and Public Choice*, 74 VA. L. REV. 423 (1988); Jonathan R. Macey, *Promoting Public-Regarding Legislation Through Statutory Interpretation: An Interest Group Model*, 86 COLUM. L. REV. 223 (1986); DANIEL A. FARBER & PHILIP P. FRICKEY, LAW AND PUBLIC CHOICE: A CRITICAL INTRODUCTION (1990).

Sess., § 541 (1978). Only the Senate *Committee Report* on the *unenacted* provision of the Senate bill had discussed that subject. *See* S. Rep. No. 95-1106, p. 33 (1978).

Nonetheless, on the basis of Representative Edwards' statement today's opinion concludes that "[t]he courts are *directed*" (presumably it means directed by the entire Congress, and not just Representative Edwards) "to apply 'reasonable assumptions' to govern the tracing of funds." *Ante*, at 12 (emphasis added). I do not agree. Congress conveys its directions in the Statutes at Large, not in excerpts from the Congressional Record, much less in excerpts from the Congressional Record that do not clarify the text of any pending legislative proposal.

Even in the absence of direction to do so, however, I certainly think we should apply reasonable assumptions to govern the tracing of funds. Unfortunately, that still does not answer the question before us here. One "traces" a fund only after one identifies the fund in the first place. The problem here is not "following the res" of the tax trust, but identifying the res to begin with. Seeking to come to grips with this point, the Court once again resorts to legislative history, this time even farther afield. It relies upon the House Report on what later became 11 U.S.C. § 547, which says:

> "A payment of withholding taxes constitutes a payment of money held in trust under Internal Revenue Code § 7501(a), and thus will not be a preference because the beneficiary of the trust, the taxing authority, is in a separate class with respect to those taxes, if they have been properly held for payment, as they will have been if the debtor is able to make the payments." H.R. Rep. No. 95-595, p. 373 (1977).

The Court decides this case by "adopting" "a literal reading" of the above language. *Ante*, at 12. I think it both demeaning and unproductive for us to ponder whether to adopt literal or not-so-literal readings of Committee Reports, as though they were controlling statutory text . . . . It was certainly thoughtful of whoever drafted the report to try to clear up the issue of what kind of an estate, legal or equitable, the debtor possesses in trust-fund taxes that are paid, but that discussion is a kind of legislative-history "rider" that even the most ardent devotees of legislative history should ignore.

If the Court had applied to the text of the statute the standard tools of legal reasoning, instead of scouring the legislative history for some scrap that is on point (and therefore ipso facto relevant, no matter how unlikely a source of congressional reliance or attention), it would have reached the same result it does today.

NOTES AND QUESTIONS

1. What does Justice Scalia mean when he refers to the "standard tools of legal reasoning"? What is a "legislative history 'rider' "?

2. Why shouldn't a court or advocate look to legislative history?

3. See Abner Mikva & Eric Lane, *The Muzak of Justice Scalia's Revolutionary Call to Read Unclear Statutes Narrowly*, 53 SMU L. Rev. 121 (2000).

IMMIGRATION & NATURALIZATION SERVICE v. CARDOZA-FONSECA
480 U.S. 421 (1987)

JUSTICE STEVENS delivered the opinion of the Court.

Since 1980, the Immigration and Nationality Act has provided two methods through which an otherwise deportable alien who claims that he will be persecuted if deported can seek relief. Section 243(h) of the Act, 8 U.S.C. § 1253(h), requires the Attorney General to withhold deportation of an alien who demonstrates that his "life or freedom would be threatened" on account of one of the listed factors if he is deported. In *INS v. Stevic*, 467 U.S. 407 (1984), we held that to qualify for this entitlement to withholding of deportation, an alien must demonstrate that "it is more likely than not that the alien would be subject to persecution" in the country to which he would be returned. *Id.*, at

429–430. The Refugee Act of 1980, 94 Stat. 102, also established a second type of broader relief. Section 208(a) of the Act, 8 U.S.C. § 1158(a), authorizes the Attorney General, in his discretion, to grant asylum to an alien who is unable or unwilling to return to his home country "because of persecution or a well-founded fear of persecution on account of race, religion, nationality, membership in a particular social group, or political opinion." § 101(a)(42), 8 U.S.C. § 1101(a)(42).

In *Stevic*, we rejected an alien's contention that the § 208(a) "well-founded fear" standard governs applications for withholding of deportation under § 243(h). Similarly, today we reject the Government's contention that the § 243(h) standard, which requires an alien to show that he is more likely than not to be subject to persecution, governs applications for asylum under § 208(a). Congress used different, broader language to define the term "refugee" as used in § 208(a) than it used to describe the class of aliens who have a right to withholding of deportation under § 243(h).

. . . .

III

The message conveyed by the plain language of the Act is confirmed by an examination of its history. Three aspects of that history are particularly compelling: The pre-1980 experience under § 203(a)(7), the only prior statute dealing with asylum; the abundant evidence of an intent to conform the definition of "refugee" and our asylum law to the United Nations Protocol to which the United States has been bound since 1968; and the fact that Congress declined to enact the Senate version of the bill that would have made a refugee ineligible for asylum unless "his deportation or return would be prohibited by § 243(h)."

. . . .

JUSTICE SCALIA, concurring in the judgment.

I agree with the Court that the plain meaning of "well-founded fear" and the structure of the Immigration and Nationality Act (Act) clearly demonstrate that the "well-founded fear" standard and the "clear probability" standard are not equivalent. I concur in the judgment rather than join the Court's opinion, however, for two reasons. First, despite having reached the above conclusion, the Court undertakes an exhaustive investigation of the legislative history of the Act. *Ante*, at 432–443. It attempts to justify this inquiry by relying upon the doctrine that if the legislative history of an enactment reveals a " 'clearly expressed legislative intention' contrary to [the enactment's] language," the Court is required to "question the strong presumption that Congress expresses its intent through the language it chooses." *Ante*, at 432, n.12. Although it is true that the Court in recent times has expressed approval of this doctrine, that is to my mind an ill-advised deviation from the venerable principle that if the language of a statute is clear, that language must be given effect — at least in the absence of a patent absurdity . . . . Judges interpret laws rather than reconstruct legislators' intentions. Where the language of those laws is clear, we are not free to replace it with an unenacted legislative intent.

Even by its own lights, however, the Court's explication of the legislative history of the Act is excessive. The INS makes a number of specific arguments based upon the legislative history of the Act. It would have sufficed, it seems to me, for the Court to determine whether these specific arguments establish a "clearly expressed legislative intent" that the two standards be equivalent. I think it obvious that they do not, as apparently does the Court. That being so, there is simply no need for the lengthy effort to ascertain the import of the entire legislative history. And that effort is objectionable not only because it is gratuitous. I am concerned that it will be interpreted to suggest that similarly exhaustive analyses are generally appropriate (or, worse yet, required) in cases where the language of the enactment at issue is clear . . . .

NOTES AND QUESTIONS

1. In 1983, Judge Patricia Wald observed:

Two preliminary observations may be made. First, although the Court still refers to the "plain meaning" rule, the rule has effectively been laid to rest. No occasion for statutory construction now exists when the Court will *not* look at the legislative history. When the plain meaning rhetoric is invoked, it becomes a device not for ignoring legislative history but for shifting onto legislative history the burden of proving that the words do not mean what they appear to say. Second, the Court has greatly expanded the types of materials and events that it will recognize in the search for congressional intent. Floor debates and hearings, for example, are now routinely cited, as is evidence that the legislature did not act to override or alter administrative or judicial interpretation at either the time of passage or later.

Yet, despite this enlarged view of legislative history, the Supreme Court's recent opinions indicate that legislative history is rarely the determinative factor in statutory construction. While plain meaning rule does not preclude a detailed examination of legislative history its invocation almost invariably signals that the legislative history will not meet the burden of rebutting the reading of the text that is "readily apparent" to the author of the opinion. Even when a majority is not inclined to presume a clear meaning from the statutory language, other presumptions are likely to compete with and outweigh the construction suggested by the legislative history.

Patricia M. Wald, *Some Observations on the Use of Legislative History in the 1981 Supreme Court Term*, 68 Iowa L. Rev. 195 (1983). Does Justice Scalia's concurrence in *Cardoza-Fonseca* indicate a different approach?

2. For a thorough discussion of *Cardoza-Fonseca*, see William N. Eskridge, *The New Textualism*, 37 UCLA L. Rev. 621 (1990). Eskridge notes:

Justice Scalia's new textualism is a radical, as opposed to marginal, critique. It is a bold rethinking of the Court's role. Partly because of its analytical boldness, and partly because Justice Scalia is an intellectually aggressive member of the Court, the critique has already changed the Court's practice in statutory interpretation cases. Particularly during the last two Terms, the Court has been much more willing to ignore legislative history, has been slightly more reluctant to deviate from the apparent meaning of the statutory text, and has relied more heavily than before on structural arguments and canons of statutory interpretation.

Id. at 624–25. *See also* Patricia M. Wald, *The Sizzling Sleeper: The Use of Legislative History in Construing Statutes in the 1988–1989 Term of the United States Supreme Court*, 39 Am. U.L. Rev. 277 (1990); Michael H. Koby, *The Supreme Court's Declining Reliance on Legislative History: The Impact of Justice Scalia's Critique*, 36 Harv. J. Legis. 369 (1999); Charles Tiefer, *The Reconceptualization of Legislative History in the Supreme Court*, 2000 Wis. L. Rev. 205 (2000).

3. In *Wisconsin Public Intervenor v. Mortier*, 501 U.S. 597 (1991), the Court resolved a question of statutory interpretation unanimously. Justice Scalia wrote a single concurrence criticizing the Court's assessment of legislative history. In a footnote, joined by eight Justices, the Court stated:

As for the propriety of using legislative history at all, common sense suggests that inquiry benefits from reviewing additional information rather than ignoring it. As Chief Justice Marshall put it, "[w]here the mind labours to discover the design of the legislature, it seizes every thing from which aid can be derived." *United States v. Fisher*, 2 Cranch 358, 386 (1805). Legislative history materials are not generally so misleading that jurists should never employ them in a good-faith effort to discern legislative intent. Our precedents demonstrate that the Court's practice of utilizing legislative history reaches well into its past. *See, e.g., Wallace v. Parker*, 6 Pet. 680, 687–690 (1832). We suspect that the practice will likewise reach well into the future.

501 U.S. at 610 n.4.

4. After this 1991 rebuff by the Court, Justice Scalia has continued his critique, often in concurring opinions. *See, e.g., Conroy v. Aniskoff*, 507 U.S. 511, 518 (1993) (Scalia, J., concurring):

> The Court begins its analysis with the observation: "The statutory command in § 525 is unambiguous, unequivocal, and unlimited." *Ante*, at 3. In my view, discussion of that point is where the remainder of the analysis should have ended. Instead, however, the Court feels compelled to demonstrate that its holding is consonant with legislative history, including some dating back to 1917 — *a full quarter century* before the provision at issue was enacted. That is not merely a waste of research time and ink; it is a false and disruptive lesson in the law. It says to the bar that even an "unambiguous [and] unequivocal" statute can never be dispositive; that, presumably under penalty of malpractice liability, the oracles of legislative history, far into the dimmy past, must always be consulted. This undermines the clarity of law, and condemns litigants (who, unlike us, must pay for it out of their own pockets) to subsidizing historical research by lawyers.

> The greatest defect of legislative history is its illegitimacy . . . . But not the least of the defects of legislative history is it indeterminacy. If one were to search for an interpretive technique that, *on the whole*, was more likely to confuse than to clarify, one could hardly find a more promising candidate than legislative history. And the present case nicely proves that point.

> Judge Harold Leventhal used to describe the use of legislative history as the equivalent of entering a crowded cocktail party and looking over the heads of the guests for one's friends. If I may pursue that metaphor: The legislative history of § 205 of the Soldiers' and Sailors' Civil Relief Act contains a variety of diverse personages, a selected few of whom — its "friends" — the Court has introduced to us in support of its result. But there are many other faces in the crowd, most of which, I think, are set against today's result.

> . . . .

> I confess that I have not personally investigated the entire legislative history — or even that portion of it which relates to the four statutes listed above. The excerpts I have examined and quoted were unearthed by a hapless law clerk to whom I assigned the task. The other Justices have, in the aggregate, many more law clerks than I, and it is quite possible that if they all were unleashed upon this enterprise they would discover, in the legislative materials dating back to 1917 *or earlier*, many faces friendly to the Court's holding. Whether they would or not makes no difference to me — and evidently makes no difference to the Court, which gives lipservice to legislative history but does not trouble to set forth and discuss the foregoing material that others found so persuasive. In my view, that is as it should be, except for the lipservice. The language of the statute is entirely clear, and if that is not what Congress meant then Congress has made a mistake and Congress will have to correct it. We should not pretend to care about legislative intent (as opposed to the meaning of the law), lest we impose upon the practicing bar and their clients obligations that we do not ourselves take seriously.

UNITED STATES v. ESTATE OF ROMANI
523 U.S. 517 (1998)

JUSTICE STEVENS delivered the opinion of the Court.

The federal priority statute, 31 U.S.C. § 3713(a), provides that a claim of the United States Government "shall be paid first" when a decedent's estate cannot pay all of its debts. The question presented is whether that statute requires that a federal tax claim be given preference over a judgment creditor's perfected lien on real property even though such a preference is not authorized by the Federal Tax Lien Act of 1966, 26 U.S.C. § 6321 *et seq.*

. . . .

I

On January 25, 1985, the Court of Common Pleas of Cambria County, Pennsylvania, entered a judgment for $400,000 in favor of Romani Industries, Inc., and against Francis J. Romani. The judgment was recorded in the clerk's office and therefore, as a matter of Pennsylvania law, it became a lien on all of the defendant's real property in Cambria County. Thereafter, the Internal Revenue Service filed a series of notices of tax liens on Mr. Romani's property. The claims for unpaid taxes, interest, and penalties described in those notices amounted to approximately $490,000.

When Mr. Romani died on January 13, 1992, his entire estate consisted of real estate worth only $53,001. Because the property was encumbered by both the judgment lien and the federal tax liens, the estate's administrator sought permission from the Court of Common Pleas to transfer the property to the judgment creditor, Romani Industries, in lieu of execution. The Federal Government acknowledged that its tax liens were not valid as against the earlier judgment lien; but, giving new meaning to Franklin's aphorism that "in this world nothing can be said to be certain, except death and taxes," it opposed the transfer on the ground that the priority statute (§ 3713) gave it the right to "be paid first."

The Court of Common Pleas overruled the Government's objection and authorized the conveyance. The Superior Court of Pennsylvania affirmed, and the Supreme Court of the State also affirmed. 547 Pa. 41, 688 A.2d 703 (1997). That court first determined that there was a "plain inconsistency" between § 3713, which appears to give the United States "absolute priority" over all competing claims, and the Tax Lien Act of 1966, which provides that the federal tax lien "shall not be valid" against judgment lien creditors until a prescribed notice has been given. *Id.*, at 45, 688 A.2d, at 705. Then, relying on the reasoning in *United States v. Kimbell Foods, Inc.*, 440 U.S. 715, 99 S. Ct. 1448, 59 L. Ed. 2d 711 (1979), which had noted that the Tax Lien Act of 1966 modified the Federal Government's preferred position in the tax area and recognized the priority of many state claims over federal tax liens, *id.*, at 738, 99 S. Ct., at 1463–1464, the court concluded that the 1966 Act had the effect of limiting the operation of § 3713 as to tax debts.

. . . .

III

The text of the priority statute on which the Government places its entire reliance is virtually unchanged since its enactment in 1797. As we pointed out in *United States v. Moore*, 423 U.S. 77, 96 S. Ct. 310, 46 L. Ed. 2d 219 (1975), not only were there earlier versions of the statute, but "its roots reach back even further into the English common law," *id.*, at 80, 96 S. Ct., at 313. The sovereign prerogative that was exercised by the English Crown and by many of the States as "an inherent incident of sovereignty," *ibid.*, applied only to unsecured claims. As Justice Brandeis noted in *Marshall v. New York*, 254 U.S. 380, 384, 41 S. Ct. 143, 145, 65 L. Ed. 315 (1920), the common-law priority "[did] not obtain over a specific lien created by the debtor before the sovereign undertakes to enforce its right." Moreover, the statute itself does not create a lien in favor of the United States. Given this background, respondent argues that the statute should be read as giving the United States a preference over other unsecured creditors but not over secured creditors.

. . . .

There are sound reasons for treating the Tax Lien Act of 1966 as the governing statute when the Government is claiming a preference in the insolvent estate of a delinquent taxpayer. As was the case with the National Bank Act, the Transportation Act of 1920, and the Bankruptcy Act of 1898, the Tax Lien Act is the later statute, the more specific statute, and its provisions are comprehensive, reflecting an obvious attempt to accommodate the strong policy objections to the enforcement of secret liens. It represents Congress' detailed judgment as to when the Government's claims for unpaid taxes should yield to many different sorts of interests (including, for instance, judgment liens, mechanic's liens, and attorney's liens) in many different types of property (including, for example, real property, securities, and motor vehicles). *See* 26 U.S.C. § 6323. Indeed, given our unambiguous determination that the federal interest in the collection of taxes is paramount to its interest in enforcing other claims, *see United States v. Kimbell Foods, Inc.*, 440 U.S., at 733–735, 99 S. Ct., at 1461–1462, it would be anomalous to conclude that Congress intended the priority statute to impose greater burdens on the citizen than those specifically crafted for tax collection purposes.

. . . .

The Government emphasizes that when Congress amended the Tax Lien Act in 1966, it declined to enact the American Bar Association's proposal to modify the federal priority statute, and Congress again failed to enact a similar proposal in 1970. Both proposals would have expressly provided that the Government's priority in insolvency does not displace valid liens and security interests, and therefore would have harmonized the priority statute with the Tax Lien Act. *See* Hearings on H.R. 11256 and 11290 before the House Committee on Ways and Means, 89th Cong., 2d Sess., 197 (1966) (hereinafter Hearings); S. 2197, 92d Cong., 1st Sess. (1971). But both proposals also would have significantly changed the priority statute in many other respects to follow the priority scheme created by the bankruptcy laws. *See* Hearings, at 85, 198; Plumb 10, n.53, 33–37. The earlier proposal may have failed because its wide-ranging subject matter was beyond the House Ways and Means Committee's jurisdiction. *Id.*, at 8. The failure of the 1970 proposal in the Senate Judiciary Committee — explained by no reports or hearings — might merely reflect disagreement with the broad changes to the priority statute, or an assumption that the proposal was not needed because, as Justice Story had believed, the priority statute does not apply to prior perfected security interests, or any number of other views. Thus, the Committees' failures to report the proposals to the entire Congress do not necessarily indicate that any legislator thought that the priority statute should supersede the Tax Lien Act in the adjudication of federal tax claims. They provide no support for the hypothesis that both Houses of Congress silently endorsed that position.

The actual measures taken by Congress provide a superior insight regarding its intent. As we have noted, the 1966 amendments to the Tax Lien Act bespeak a strong condemnation of secret liens, which unfairly defeat the expectations of innocent creditors and frustrate "the needs of our citizens for certainty and convenience in the legal rules governing their commercial dealings." 112 Cong. Rec. 22227 (1966) (remarks of Rep. Byrnes); *cf. United States v. Speers*, 382 U.S. 266, 275, 86 S. Ct. 411, 416, 15 L. Ed. 2d 314 (1965) (referring to the "general policy against secret liens"). These policy concerns shed light on how Congress would want the conflicting statutory provisions to be harmonized:

> "Liens may be a dry-as-dust part of the law, but they are not without significance in an industrial and commercial community where construction and credit are thought to have importance. One does not readily impute to Congress

the intention that many common commercial liens should be congenitally unstable." E. Brown, The *Supreme Court, 1957 Term-Foreword: Process of Law*, 72 HARV. L. REV. 77, 87 (1958) (footnote omitted).

In sum, nothing in the text or the long history of interpreting the federal priority statute justifies the conclusion that it authorizes the equivalent of a secret lien as a substitute for the expressly authorized tax lien that Congress has said "shall not be valid" in a case of this kind.

The judgment of the Pennsylvania Supreme Court is affirmed.

. . . .

JUSTICE SCALIA, concurring in part and concurring in the judgment.

I join the opinion of the Court except that portion which takes seriously, and thus encourages in the future, an argument that should be laughed out of court. The Government contended that 31 U.S.C. § 3713(a) must have priority over the Federal Tax Lien Act of 1966, because in 1966 and again in 1970 Congress "failed to enact" a proposal put forward by the American Bar Association that would have subordinated § 3713(a) to the Tax Lien Act, citing hearings before the House Committee on Ways and Means, and a bill proposed in, but not passed by, the Senate. *See* Brief for United States 25–27, and n.10 (citing American Bar Association, Final Report of the Committee on Federal Liens 7, 122–124 (1959), contained in Hearings on H.R. 11256 and 11290 before the House Committee on Ways and Means, 89th Cong., 2d Sess., 85, 199 (1966); S. 2197, 92d Cong., 1st Sess. (1971)). The Court responds that these rejected proposals "provide no support for the hypothesis that both Houses of Congress silently endorsed" the supremacy of § 3713, *ante*, at 1488, because those proposals contained other provisions as well, and might have been rejected because of those other provisions, or because Congress thought the existing law already made § 3713 supreme. This implies that, if the proposals had not contained those additional features, or if Members of Congress (or some part of them) had somehow made clear in the course of rejecting them that they wanted the existing supremacy of the Tax Lien Act to subsist, the rejection *would* "provide support" for the Government's case.

That is not so, for several reasons. First and most obviously, Congress cannot express its will by a *failure* to legislate. The act of refusing to enact a law (if that can be called an act) has utterly no legal effect, and thus has utterly no place in a serious discussion of the law. The Constitution sets forth the only manner in which the Members of Congress have the power to impose their will upon the country: by a bill that passes both Houses and is either signed by the President or repassed by a supermajority after his veto. Art. I, § 7. Everything else the Members of Congress do is either prelude or internal organization. Congress can no more express its will by not legislating than an individual Member can express his will by not voting.

Second, even if Congress *could* express its will by not legislating, the will of a later Congress that a law enacted by an earlier Congress should bear a particular meaning is of no effect whatever. The Constitution puts Congress in the business of writing new laws, not interpreting old ones. "[L]ater enacted laws . . . do not declare the meaning of earlier law." *Almendarez-Torres v. United States*, 523 U.S. 224, 237, 118 S. Ct. 1219, 1227, 140 L. Ed. 2d 350 (1998); *id.*, at 269–270, 118 S. Ct., at 1243 (Scalia, J., dissenting) ("This later amendment can of course not cause [the statute] to have meant, at the time of petitioner's conviction, something different from what it then said"). If the *enacted* intent of a later Congress cannot change the meaning of an earlier statute, then it should go without saying that the later *unenacted intent* cannot possibly do so. It should go without saying, and it should go without arguing as well.

I have in the past been critical of the Court's using the so-called legislative history of an enactment (hearings, committee reports, and floor debates) to determine its meaning. *See, e.g., Conroy v. Aniskoff*, 507 U.S. 511, 518–528, 113 S. Ct. 1562, 1566–1572, 123 L. Ed. 2d 229 (1993) (Scalia, J., concurring in judgment); *United States v. Thompson/*

Center Arms Co., 504 U.S. 505, 521, 112 S. Ct. 2102, 2111–2112, 119 L. Ed. 2d 308 (1992) (Scalia, J., concurring in judgment); *Blanchard v. Bergeron*, 489 U.S. 87, 98–100, 109 S. Ct. 939, 946–948, 103 L. Ed. 2d 67 (1989) (Scalia, J., concurring in part and concurring in judgment). Today, however, the Court's fascination with the files of Congress (we must consult them, because they are there) is carried to a new silly extreme. Today's opinion ever-so-carefully analyzes, not legislative history, but the history of legislation-that-never-was. If we take this sort of material seriously, we require conscientious counsel to investigate (at clients' expense) not only the hearings, committee reports, and floor debates pertaining to the history of the law at issue (which is bad enough), but to find, and then investigate the hearings, committee reports, and floor debates pertaining to, later bills on the same subject that were never enacted. This is beyond all reason, and we should say so.

NOTES AND QUESTIONS

1. Is it ever relevant to consider a legislature's failure to enact a law or amendment? What if the proposal is fully considered in committee, debated on the floor and then defeated?

2. This case presents the problem of statutory conflict or overlap. What other techniques are available to lawyers to argue, and for courts to decide, which statute applies?

3. After Justice Scalia began his attack on the use of legislative history, both the Congress and the executive branch reexamined its use. *See* Statutory Interpretation and the Uses of Legislative History, *Hearings Before the Subcommittee on Courts, Intellectual Property, and the Administration of Justice of the House Committee on the Judiciary*, 101st Cong., 2d Sess. 97–127 (1990); Office of Legal Policy, Using and Misusing Legislative History: A Re-evaluation of the Status of Legislative History in Statutory Interpretation (1989).

4. For Justice Stephen Breyer's views on legislative history, prior to his nomination to the United States Supreme Court, see Stephen Breyer, *On the Uses of Legislative History in Interpreting Statutes*, 65 S. Cal. L. Rev. 845 (1992).

5. For an article contending that the Michigan Supreme Court has begun to follow Justice Scalia's approach, see Maura D. Corrigan & J. Michael Thomas, *"Dice Loading" Rules of Statutory Interpretation*, 59 N.Y.U. Ann. Surv. Am. L. 231 (2003).

EXXON MOBIL CORP. v. ALLAPATTAH SERVICES, INC.
125 S. Ct. 2611 (2005)

Justice Kennedy delivered the opinion of the Court.

These consolidated cases present the question whether a federal court in a diversity action may exercise supplemental jurisdiction over additional plaintiffs whose claims do not satisfy the minimum amount-in-controversy requirement, provided the claims are part of the same case or controversy as the claims of plaintiffs who do allege a sufficient amount in controversy. Our decision turns on the correct interpretation of 28 U.S.C. § 1367. The question has divided the Courts of Appeals, and we granted certiorari to resolve the conflict . . . .

We hold that, where the other elements of jurisdiction are present and at least one named plaintiff in the action satisfies the amount-in-controversy requirement, § 1367 does authorize supplemental jurisdiction over the claims of other plaintiffs in the same Article III case or controversy, even if those claims are for less than the jurisdictional amount specified in the statute setting forth the requirements for diversity jurisdiction . . . .

. . . .

It follows from this conclusion that the threshold requirement of § 1367(a) is satisfied in cases, like those now before us, where some, but not all, of the plaintiffs in a diversity action allege a sufficient amount in controversy. We hold that § 1367 by its plain text overruled *Clark* and *Zahn* and authorized supplemental jurisdiction over all claims by diverse parties arising out of the same Article III case or controversy, subject only to enumerated exceptions not applicable in the cases now before us.

C

The proponents of the alternative view of § 1367 insist that the statute is at least ambiguous and that we should look to other interpretative tools, including the legislative history of § 1367, which supposedly demonstrate Congress did not intend § 1367 to overrule *Zahn*. We can reject this argument at the very outset simply because § 1367 is not ambiguous. For the reasons elaborated above, interpreting § 1367 to foreclose supplemental jurisdiction over plaintiffs in diversity cases who do not meet the minimum amount in controversy is inconsistent with the text, read in light of other statutory provisions and our established jurisprudence. Even if we were to stipulate, however, that the reading these proponents urge upon us is textually plausible, the legislative history cited to support it would not alter our view as to the best interpretation of § 1367.

Those who urge that the legislative history refutes our interpretation rely primarily on the House Judiciary Committee Report on the Judicial Improvements Act. H.R. Rep. No. 101-734 (1990) (House Report or Report). This Report explained that § 1367 would "authorize jurisdiction in a case like *Finley*, as well as essentially restore the pre-*Finley* understandings of the authorization for and limits on other forms of supplemental jurisdiction." House Report, at 28. The Report stated that § 1367(a) "generally authorizes the district court to exercise jurisdiction over a supplemental claim whenever it forms part of the same constitutional case or controversy as the claim or claims that provide the basis of the district court's original jurisdiction," and in so doing codifies *Gibbs* and fills the statutory gap recognized in *Finley*. House Report, at 28–29, and n. 15. The report then remarked that § 1367(b) "is not intended to affect the jurisdictional requirements of [§ 1332] in diversity-only class actions, as those requirements were interpreted prior to *Finley*," citing, without further elaboration, *Zahn* and *Supreme Tribe of Ben-Hur v. Cauble*, 255 U.S. 356 (1921). House Report, at 29, and n.17. The Report noted that the "net effect" of § 1367(b) was to implement the "principal rationale" of *Kroger*, House Report, at 29, and n.16, effecting only "one small change" in pre-*Finley* practice with respect to diversity actions: § 1367(b) would exclude "Rule 23(a) plaintiff-intervenors to the same extent as those sought to be joined as plaintiffs under Rule 19." House Report, at 29. (It is evident that the report here meant to refer to Rule 24, not Rule 23).

As we have repeatedly held, the authoritative statement is the statutory text, not the legislative history or any other extrinsic material. Extrinsic materials have a role in statutory interpretation only to the extent they shed a reliable light on the enacting Legislature's understanding of otherwise ambiguous terms. Not all extrinsic materials are reliable sources of insight into legislative understandings, however, and legislative history in particular is vulnerable to two serious criticisms. First, legislative history is itself often murky, ambiguous, and contradictory. Judicial investigation of legislative history has a tendency to become, to borrow Judge Leventhal's memorable phrase, an exercise in " 'looking over a crowd and picking out your friends.' " *See* Wald, *Some Observations on the Use of Legislative History in the 1981 Supreme Court Term*, 68 Iowa L. Rev. 195, 214 (1983). Second, judicial reliance on legislative materials like committee reports, which are not themselves subject to the requirements of Article I, may give unrepresentative committee members — or, worse yet, unelected staffers and lobbyists both the power and the incentive to attempt strategic manipulations of legislative history to secure results they were unable to achieve through the statutory text. We need not comment here on whether these problems are sufficiently prevalent to render legislative history inherently unreliable in all circumstances, a point on which

Members of this Court have disagreed. It is clear, however, that in this instance both criticisms are right on the mark.

First of all, the legislative history of § 1367 is far murkier than selective quotation from the House Report would suggest. The text of § 1367 is based substantially on a draft proposal contained in a Federal Court Study Committee working paper, which was drafted by a Subcommittee chaired by Judge Posner. Report of the Subcommittee on the Role of the Federal Courts and Their Relationship to the States 567–568 (Mar. 12, 1990), reprinted in Judicial Conference of the United States, 1 Federal Courts Study Committee Working Papers and Subcommittee Reports (July 1, 1990). While the Subcommittee explained, in language echoed by the House Report, that its proposal "basically restores the law as it existed prior to *Finley*," Subcommittee Working Paper, at 561, it observed in a footnote that its proposal would overrule *Zahn* and that this would be a good idea, Subcommittee Working Paper, at 561, n. 33. Although the Federal Courts Study Committee did not expressly adopt the Subcommittee's specific reference to *Zahn*, it neither explicitly disagreed with the Subcommittee's conclusion that this was the best reading of the proposed text nor substantially modified the proposal to avoid this result. Study Committee Report, at 47–48. Therefore, even if the House Report could fairly be read to reflect an understanding that the text of § 1367 did not overrule *Zahn*, the Subcommittee Working Paper on which § 1367 was based reflected the opposite understanding. The House Report is no more authoritative than the Subcommittee Working Paper. The utility of either can extend no further than the light it sheds on how the enacting Legislature understood the statutory text. Trying to figure out how to square the Subcommittee Working Paper's understanding with the House Report's understanding, or which is more reflective of the understanding of the enacting legislators, is a hopeless task.

Second, the worst fears of critics who argue legislative history will be used to circumvent the Article I process were realized in this case. The telltale evidence is the statement, by three law professors who participated in drafting § 1367, *see* House Report, at 27, n.13, that § 1367 "on its face" permits "supplemental jurisdiction over claims of class members that do not satisfy section 1332's jurisdictional amount requirement, which would overrule [*Zahn*]. [There is] a disclaimer of intent to accomplish this result in legislative history . . . . It would have been better had the statute dealt explicitly with this problem, and the legislative history was an attempt to correct the oversight." Rowe, Burbank, & Mengler, *Compounding or Creating Confusion About Supplemental Jurisdiction? A Reply to Professor Freer*, 40 Emory L.J. 943, 960, n.90 (1991). The professors were frank to concede that if one refuses to consider the legislative history, one has no choice but to "conclude that section 1367 has wiped *Zahn* off the books." *Ibid.* So there exists an acknowledgment, by parties who have detailed, specific knowledge of the statute and the drafting process, both that the plain text of § 1367 overruled *Zahn* and that language to the contrary in the House Report was a post hoc attempt to alter that result. One need not subscribe to the wholesale condemnation of legislative history to refuse to give any effect to such a deliberate effort to amend a statute through a committee report.

In sum, even if we believed resort to legislative history were appropriate in these cases — a point we do not concede — we would not give significant weight to the House Report. The distinguished jurists who drafted the Subcommittee Working Paper, along with three of the participants in the drafting of § 1367, agree that this provision, on its face, overrules *Zahn*. This accords with the best reading of the statute's text, and nothing in the legislative history indicates directly and explicitly that Congress understood the phrase "civil action of which the district courts have original jurisdiction" to exclude cases in which some but not all of the diversity plaintiffs meet the amount in controversy requirement.

No credence, moreover, can be given to the claim that, if Congress understood § 1367 to overrule *Zahn*, the proposal would have been more controversial. We have little sense whether any Member of Congress would have been particularly upset by this result. This is not a case where one can plausibly say that concerned legislators might not have realized the possible effect of the text they were adopting. Certainly, any competent legislative aide who studied the matter would have flagged this issue if it were a matter of importance to his or her boss, especially in light of the Subcommittee Working Paper. There are any number of reasons why legislators did not spend more time arguing over § 1367, none of which are relevant to our interpretation of what the words of the statute mean.

. . . .

JUSTICE STEVENS, with whom JUSTICE BREYER joins, dissenting.

Justice Ginsburg's carefully reasoned opinion . . . demonstrates the error in the Court's rather ambitious reading of this opaque jurisdictional statute. She also has demonstrated that "ambiguity" is a term that may have different meanings for different judges, for the Court has made the remarkable declaration that its reading of the statute is so obviously correct — and Justice Ginsburg's so obviously wrong — that the text does not even qualify as "ambiguous." . . . Because ambiguity is apparently in the eye of the beholder, I remain convinced that it is unwise to treat the ambiguity *vel non* of a statute as determinative of whether legislative history is consulted. Indeed, I believe that we as judges are more, rather than less, constrained when we make ourselves accountable to all reliable evidence of legislative intent. *See Koons Buick Pontiac GMC, Inc. v. Nigh*, 543 U.S. slip op., at 2 and n.1 (Stevens, J., concurring).

The legislative history of 28 U.S.C. § 367 provides powerful confirmation of Justice Ginsburg's interpretation of that statute. It is helpful to consider in full the relevant portion of the House Report, which was also adopted by the Senate . . . .

Not only does the House Report specifically say that § 1367 was not intended to upset *Zahn v. International Paper Co.*, 414 U.S. 291 (1973), but its entire explanation of the statute demonstrates that Congress had in mind a very specific and relatively modest task — undoing this Court's 5-to-4 decision in *Finley v. United States*, 490 U.S. 545 (1989). In addition to overturning that unfortunate and much-criticized decision, the statute, according to the Report, codifies and preserves the "the pre-*Finley* understandings of the authorization for and limits on other forms of supplemental jurisdiction," House Report, at 28, with the exception of making "one small change in pre-*Finley* practice," *id.*, at 29, which is not relevant here.

The sweeping purpose that the Court's decision imputes to Congress bears no resemblance to the House Report's description of the statute. But this does not seem to trouble the Court, for its decision today treats statutory interpretation as a pedantic exercise, divorced from any serious attempt at ascertaining congressional intent . . . .

The Court's reasons for ignoring this virtual billboard of congressional intent are unpersuasive. That a subcommittee of the Federal Courts Study Committee believed that an earlier, substantially similar version of the statute overruled *Zahn*, . . . only highlights the fact that the statute is ambiguous. What is determinative is that the House Report explicitly rejected that broad reading of the statutory text. Such a report has special significance as an indicator of legislative intent. In Congress, committee reports are normally considered the authoritative explication of a statute's text and purposes, and busy legislators and their assistants rely on that explication in casting their votes . . . .

The Court's second reason — its comment on the three law professors who participated in drafting § 1367 . . . — is similarly off the mark. In the law review article that the Court refers to, the professors were merely saying that the text of the statute was susceptible to an overly broad (and simplistic) reading, and that clarification in the House Report was therefore appropriate. *See* Rowe, Burbank, & Mengler, *Compounding or Creating Confusion About Supplemental Jurisdiction? A Reply to Professor Freer*, 40 Emory L.J. 943, 960, n.90 (1991). Significantly, the reference to

Zahn in the House Report does not at all appear to be tacked-on or out of place; indeed, it is wholly consistent with the Report's broader explanation of Congress' goal of overruling *Finley* and preserving pre-*Finley* law. To suggest that these professors participated in a "deliberate effort to amend a statute through a committee report," . . . reveals an unrealistic view of the legislative process, not to mention disrespect for three law professors who acted in the role of public servants. To be sure, legislative history can be manipulated. But, in the situation before us, there is little reason to fear that unholy conspiracy of "unrepresentative committee members," . . . law professors, and "unelected staffers and lobbyists," . . . endeavored to torpedo Congress' attempt to overrule (without discussion) two longstanding features of this Court's diversity jurisprudence.

After nearly 20 pages of complicated analysis, which explores subtle doctrinal nuances and coins various neologisms, the Court announces that § 1367 could not reasonably be read another way . . . . That conclusion is difficult to accept. Given Justice Ginsburg's persuasive account of the statutory text and its jurisprudential backdrop, and given the uncommonly clear legislative history, I am confident that the majority's interpretation of § 1367 is mistaken. I respectfully dissent.

NOTES AND QUESTIONS

1. Do you agree with Justice Stevens that judges are "more, rather than less, constrained when we make ourselves accountable to all reliable evidence of legislative intent"? Would Justice Scalia agree?

2. How often do you think there would be, as in this case, actual evidence of an apparent "deliberate effort to amend a statute through a committee report"? Was this an example of, in Justice Scalia's terminology, a "legislative history rider"?

3. The members of the Court provided detailed analysis of the federal subject matter jurisdiction implications of the alternative readings of 28 U.S.C. § 1367, which are not reproduced here. These forms of analysis supplemented the plain meaning and legislative history analysis presented here.

4. For a consideration of *Allapattah*'s approach to statutory interpretation, see Debra Lyn Bassett, *Statutory Interpretation in the Context of Federal Jurisdiction*, 76 Geo. Wash. L. Rev. 52 (2007).

SCHIAVO v. SCHIAVO
403 F.3d 1223 (11th Cir. 2005)

Per Curiam:

Plaintiffs have appealed the district court's denial of their motion for a temporary restraining order to require the defendants to transport Theresa Marie Schindler Schiavo to a hospital to reestablish nutrition and hydration and for any medical treatment necessary to sustain her life, and to require the state court judge defendant to rescind his February 25, 2005 order directing removal of nutrition and hydration from Schiavo and to restrain him from issuing any further orders that would discontinue nutrition and hydration.[1] After notice and a hearing, the district court entered a careful order which is attached as an Appendix to this opinion. Plaintiffs have also petitioned this Court to grant the same injunctive relief under the All Writs Act, 28 U.S.C. § 1651(a).

Although we ordinarily do not have jurisdiction over appeals from orders granting or

---

[1] Our dissenting colleague says that "the denial of Plaintiffs' request for an injunction frustrates Congress's intent, which is to maintain the status quo." Dissenting Op. at 1237. The status quo is that Mrs. Schiavo is not receiving nutrition and hydration. The plaintiffs do not want the status quo maintained. They want this Court or the district court to issue an injunction affirmatively requiring the respondents to change the status quo by bringing about the surgical procedure necessary to reinsert the feeding tube into Mrs. Schiavo.

denying temporary restraining orders, in circumstances such as these, "when a grant or denial of a TRO might have a serious, perhaps irreparable, consequence, and can be effectually challenged only by immediate appeal, we may exercise appellate jurisdiction." . . .

The district court correctly stated the four factors to be considered in determining whether temporary restraining or preliminary injunctive relief is to be granted, which are whether the movant has established: (1) a substantial likelihood of success on the merits; (2) that irreparable injury will be suffered if the relief is not granted; (3) that the threatened injury outweighs the harm the relief would inflict on the non-movant; and (4) that entry of the relief would serve the public interest. *See Ingram*, 50 F.3d at 900; *Siegel v. LePore*, 234 F.3d 1163, 1176 (11th Cir.2000) (en banc). Requests for emergency injunctive relief are not uncommon in federal court and sometimes involve decisions affecting life and death. Controlling precedent is clear that injunctive relief may not be granted unless the plaintiff establishes the substantial likelihood of success criterion. *See Siegel*, 234 F.3d at 1176; *see also Grupo Mexicano de Desarrollo v. Alliance Bond Fund, Inc.*, 527 U.S. 308, 339, 119 S. Ct. 1961, 1978, 144 L. Ed. 2d 319 (1999) ("Plaintiffs with questionable claims would not meet the likelihood of success criterion.").

. . . .

Applying those factors, the district court determined that the last three weighed in favor of granting the temporary restraining order. The court reasoned that because those three factors were met, plaintiffs only had to show a substantial case on the merits. After analyzing each of plaintiffs' claims, the district court concluded they had failed to show a substantial case on the merits as to any of the claims.

. . . .

The principal theme of plaintiffs' argument against the district court's denial of a temporary restraining order is that Pub. L. No. 109-3, which Congress enacted to enable them to bring this lawsuit, mandates that injunctive relief be granted to enable them to have a full trial on the merits of their claims. Pub. L. No. 109-3 is an extraordinary piece of legislation, and it does many things. Defendants contend that the legislation is so extraordinary that it is unconstitutional in several respects. We need not decide that question. For purposes of determining whether temporary or preliminary injunctive relief is appropriate, we indulge the usual presumption that congressional enactments are constitutional. *United States v. Morrison*, 529 U.S. 598, 607, 120 S. Ct. 1740, 1748, 146 L. Ed. 2d 658 (2000); *Benning v. Georgia*, 391 F.3d 1299, 1303 (11th Cir. 2004). It is enough for present purposes that in enacting Pub.L. No. 109-3 Congress did not alter for purposes of this case the long-standing general law governing whether temporary restraining orders or preliminary injunctions should be issued by federal courts.

There is no provision in Pub. L. No. 109-3 addressing whether or under what conditions the district court should grant temporary or preliminary relief in this case. There is no more reason in the text of the Act to read in any special rule about temporary or preliminary relief than there would be to read in a special rule about deciding the case before trial on Fed. R. Civ. P. 12(b)(6) or summary judgment grounds. Not only that, but Congress considered and specifically rejected provisions that would have mandated, or permitted with favorable implications, the grant of the pretrial stay. There is this enlightening exchange in the legislative history concerning the Senate bill that was enacted:

Mr. LEVIN.   Mr. President, I rise to seek clarification from the majority leader about one aspect of this bill, the issue of whether Congress has mandated that a Federal court issue a stay pending determination of the case.

Mr. FRIST.   I would be pleased to help clarify this issue.

Mr. LEVIN.   Section 5 of the original version of the Martinez bill conferred jurisdiction on a Federal court to hear a case like this, and then stated that the Federal court "shall" issue a stay of State court proceedings pending determination of the Federal case. I was opposed to that provision because I believe Congress should not mandate that a Federal judge issue a stay. Under longstanding law and practice, the decision to issue a stay is a matter of discretion for the Federal judge based on the facts of the case. The majority leader and the other bill sponsors accepted my suggestion that the word "shall" in section 5 be changed to "may."

The version of the bill we are now considering strikes section 5 altogether. Although nothing in the text of the new bill mandates a stay, the omission of this section, which in the earlier Senate-passed bill made a stay permissive, might be read to mean that Congress intends to mandate a stay. I believe that reading is incorrect. The absence of any state [sic] provision in the new bill simply means that Congress relies on current law. Under current law, a judge may decide whether or not a stay is appropriate.

Does the majority leader share my understanding of the bill?

Mr. FRIST.   I share the understanding of the Senator from Michigan, as does the junior Senator from Florida who is the chief sponsor of this bill. Nothing in the current bill or its legislative history mandates a stay. I would assume, however, the Federal court would grant a stay based on the facts of this case because Mrs. Schiavo would need to be alive in order for the court to make its determination. Nevertheless, this bill does not change current law under which a stay is discretionary.

Mr. LEVIN.   In light of that assurance, I do not object to the unanimous consent agreement under which the bill will be considered by the Senate. I do not make the same assumption as the majority leader makes about what a Federal court will do. Because the discretion of the Federal court is left unrestricted in this bill, I will not exercise my right to block its consideration.

151 Cong. Rec. S3099-100 (daily ed. Mar. 20, 2005) (colloquy between Sens. Levin & Frist).

This enlightening exchange does not contradict the plain meaning of Pub. L. No. 109-3, but instead reinforces it. Plainly, Congress knew how to change the law to favor these plaintiffs to the extent that it collectively wished to do so. That is what the changes it did make, including those to standing law, the *Rooker-Feldman* doctrine, and abstention, demonstrate. When Congress explicitly modifies some pre-existing rules of law applicable to a subject but says nothing about other rules of law, the only reasonable reading is that Congress meant no change in the rules it did not mention. The dissent characterizes the language of the Act as clear. It is on this point: the language of the Act clearly does not purport to change the law concerning issuance of temporary or preliminary relief.

To interpret Pub. L. No. 109-3 as requiring that temporary or preliminary relief be entered regardless of whether it is warranted under pre-existing law would go beyond reading into the Act a provision that is not there. It would require us to read into the Act a provision that Congress deliberately removed in order to clarify that pre-existing law did govern this issue.

NOTES AND QUESTIONS

1. Compare the federal statute involved in this case with the one involved in *Robertson v. Seattle Audubon Society*, in Chapter 6F. What are the differences?

2. Is the legislative history in *Schaivo* evidence of specific or general legislative intent?

3. What would have (should have?) happened if the legislative history did contradict the plain meaning of the statute?

In *Monell v. Department of Social Servs. of N.Y.*, 436 U.S. 658 (1978), the Court overruled a decision, *Monroe v. Pape*, it had followed for 17 years. *Monroe* had held that a municipality was not, under 42 U.S.C. § 1983, a "person" who could be liable for damages for depriving individuals of certain federally protected rights. The *Monroe* holding was based on the refusal of Congress to adopt, in 1871, an amendment that would have had the effect of including units of local governments in the definition of "person." The *Monell* Court found they had misinterpreted the legislative history in *Monroe v. Pape* and upon reexamination, in particular of the floor debates, that concluded § 1983 properly applied to municipal corporations.

MONELL v. DEPARTMENT OF SOCIAL SERVICES OF NEW YORK
436 U.S. 658 (1978)

Mr. Justice Brennan delivered the opinion of the Court.

Petitioners, a class of female employees of the Department of Social Services and the Board of Education of the City of New York, commenced this action under 42 U.S.C. § 1983 in July 1971. The gravamen of the complaint was that the Board and the Department had as a matter of official policy compelled pregnant employees to take unpaid leaves of absence before such leaves were required for medical reasons . . . .

The suit sought injunctive relief and back pay for periods of unlawful forced leave. Named as defendants in the action were the Department and its Commissioner, the Board and its Chancellor, and the City of New York and its Mayor . . . .

. . . .

We granted certiorari in this case . . . to consider

> Whether local governmental officials and/or local independent school boards are "persons" within the meaning of 42 U.S.C. § 1983 when equitable relief in the nature of back pay is sought against them in their official capacities?

Pet. for Cert. 8.

. . . .

[The Supreme Court had acknowledged that *Monroe v. Pape*, 365 U.S. 167, 5 L. Ed. 2d 492, 81 S. Ct. 473 (1961), would give the defendants immunity from this suit. — Eds.]

. . . [W]e now overrule *Monroe v. Pape* . . . , insofar as it holds that local governments are wholly immune from suit under § 1983.

I

In *Monroe v. Pape*, we held that "Congress did not undertake to bring municipal corporations within the ambit of [§ 1983]." 365 U.S. at 187, 5 L. Ed. 2d 492, 81 S. Ct. 473. The sole basis for this conclusion was an inference drawn from Congress' rejection of the "Sherman amendment" to the bill which became the Civil Rights Act of 1871, 17 Stat. 13 — the precursor of § 1983 — which would have held a municipal corporation liable for damage done to the person or property of its inhabitants by *private* persons "riotously and tumultuously assembled." Cong. Globe, 42d Cong., 1st Sess., 749 (1871) (hereinafter "Globe"). Although the Sherman amendment did not seek to amend § 1 of the Act, which is now § 1983, and although the nature of the obligation created by that amendment was vastly different from that created by § 1, the Court nonetheless concluded in *Monroe* that Congress must have meant to exclude municipal corporations from the coverage of § 1 because " 'the House [in voting against the Sherman amendment] had solemnly decided that in their judgment Congress had no constitutional power to impose any *obligation* upon county and town organizations, the mere instrumentality for the administration of state law.' " 365 U.S., at 190, 5 L. Ed. 2d 492, 81 S. Ct. 473 (emphasis added), quoting Globe, at 804 (Rep. Poland). This statement, we thought, showed that Congress doubted its "constitutional power . . . to impose *civil liability* on municipalities," 365 U.S., at 190, 5 L. Ed. 2d 492, 81 S. Ct. 473 (emphasis added), and that such doubt would have extended to any type of civil liability.

A fresh analysis of debate on the Civil Rights Act of 1871, and particularly of the case law which each side mustered in its support, shows, however, that *Monroe* incorrectly equated the "obligation" of which Representative Poland spoke with "civil liability."

A.

An Overview

There are three distinct stages in the legislative consideration of the bill which became the Civil Rights Act of 1871. On March 28, 1871, Representative Shellabarger, acting for a House select committee, reported H.R. 320, a bill "to enforce the provisions of the Fourteenth Amendment to the Constitution and for other purposes." H.R. 320 contained four sections. Section 1, now codified as 42 U.S.C. § 1983, was the subject of only limited debate and was passed without amendment. Sections 2 through 4 dealt primarily with the "other purpose" of suppressing Ku Klux Klan violence in the southern states. The wisdom and constitutionality of these sections — not § 1, now § 1983 — was the subject of almost all congressional debate and each of these sections was amended. The House finished its initial debates on H.R. 320 on April 7, 1871 and one week later the Senate also voted out a bill. Again, debate on § 1 of the bill was limited and that section was passed as introduced.

Immediately prior to the vote on H.R. 320 in the Senate, Senator Sherman introduced his amendment. This was *not* an amendment to § 1 of the bill, but was to be added as § 7 at the end of the bill. Under the Senate rules, no discussion of the amendment was allowed and, although attempts were made to amend the amendment, it was passed as introduced. In this form, the amendment did *not* place liability on municipal corporations, but made any inhabitant of a municipality liable for damage inflicted by persons "riotously or tumultuously assembled."

The House refused to acquiesce in a number of amendments made by the Senate, including the Sherman amendment, and the respective versions of H.R. 320 were therefore sent to a conference committee. Section 1 of the bill, however, was not a subject of this conference since, as noted, it was passed verbatim as introduced in both Houses of Congress.

. . . .

The first conference substitute [which imposed civil liability on municipalities for violations of the act by their citizens,] passed the Senate but was rejected by the House. House opponents, within whose ranks were some who had supported § 1, thought the federal government could not, consistent with the Constitution, obligate municipal corporations to keep the peace if those corporations were neither so obligated nor so authorized by their state charters. And, because of this constitutional objection, opponents of the Sherman amendment were unwilling to impose damage liability for nonperformance of a duty which Congress could not require municipalities to perform . . . .

Because the House rejected the first conference report a second conference was called and it duly issued its report. The second conference substitute for the Sherman amendment abandoned municipal liability and, instead, made "any person or persons having knowledge [that a conspiracy to violate civil rights was afoot], and having power to prevent or aid in preventing the same," who did not attempt to stop the same, liable to any person injured by the conspiracy. The amendment in this form was adopted by both Houses of Congress and is now codified as 42 U.S.C. § 1986.

The meaning of the legislative history sketched above can most readily be developed by first considering the debate on the report of the first conference committee. This debate shows conclusively that the constitutional objections raised against the Sherman amendment — on which our holding in *Monroe* was based, *see supra*, at 664 — would not have prohibited congressional creation of a civil remedy against state municipal corporations that infringed federal rights. Because § 1 of the Civil Rights Act does not state expressly that municipal corporations come within its ambit, it is finally necessary to interpret § 1 to confirm that such corporations were indeed intended to be included within the "persons" to whom that section applies.

B.

Debate on the First Conference Report

. . . .

House opponents of the Sherman amendment — whose views are particularly important since only the House voted down the amendment — did not dispute [the] claim that the Fourteenth Amendment created a federal right to protection, . . . but they argued that the local units of government upon which the amendment fastened liability were not obligated to keep the peace at state law and further that the federal government could not constitutionally require local governments to create police forces, whether this requirement was levied directly, or indirectly by imposing damages for breach of the peace on municipalities . . . .

. . . .

Finally, the very votes of those Members of Congress, who opposed the Sherman amendment but who had voted for § 1, confirm that the liability imposed by § 1 was something very different from that imposed by the amendment. Section 1 without question could be used to obtain a damages judgment against state or municipal *officials* who violated federal constitutional rights while acting under color of law. However, for *Prigg-Dennison-Day** purposes, as Blair and others recognized, there was no distinction of constitutional magnitude between officers and agents — including corporate agents — of the state: both were state instrumentalities and the state could be impeded no matter over which sort of instrumentality the federal government sought to assert its power. *Dennison* and *Day*, after all, were not suits against municipalities but against *officers* and Blair was quite conscious that he was extending these cases by applying them to municipal corporations. Nonetheless, Senator Thurman, who gave the most exhaustive critique of § 1 — *inter alia*, complaining that it would be applied to state officers, *see* Globe, at 217 — and who opposed both § 1 and the Sherman amendment, the latter on *Prigg* grounds, agreed unequivocally that § 1 was constitutional. Those who voted for § 1 must similarly have believed in its constitutionality despite *Prigg, Dennison*, and *Day*.

---

* [*Prigg v. Pennsylvania*, 16 Pet. 539, 10 L. Ed. 1060 (1842); *Kentucky v. Dennison*, 24 How. 66, 16 L. Ed. 717 (1861); *Collector v. Day*, 11 Wall. 113, 20 L. Ed. 122 (1871). — Eds.]

C.

Debate on § 1 of the Civil Rights Bill

From the foregoing discussion, it is readily apparent that nothing said in debate on the Sherman amendment would have prevented holding a municipality liable under § 1 of the Civil Rights Act for its own violations of the Fourteenth Amendment. The question remains, however, whether the general language describing those to be liable under § 1 — "any person" — covers more than natural persons. An examination of the debate on § 1 and application of appropriate rules of construction shows unequivocally that § 1 was intended to cover legal as well as natural persons.

Representative Shellabarger was the first to explain the function of § 1:

[Section 1] not only provides a civil remedy for persons whose former condition may have been that of slaves, but also to all people where, under color of state law, they or any of them may be deprived of rights to which they are entitled under the Constitution by reason and virtue of their national citizenship.

Globe App., at 68.

By extending a remedy to all people, including whites, § 1 went beyond the mischief to which the remaining sections of the 1871 Act were addressed. Representative Shellabarger also stated without reservation that the constitutionality of § 2 of the Civil Rights Act of 1866 controlled the constitutionality of § 1 of the 1871 Act, and that the former had been approved by "the supreme courts of at least three states of this Union" and by Mr. Justice Swayne, sitting on circuit, who had concluded " 'We have no doubt of the constitutionality of every provision of this act.' " Globe App. 68 . . . .

. . . .

In both Houses, statements of the supporters of § 1 corroborated that Congress, in enacting § 1, intended to give a broad remedy for violations of federally protected civil rights. Moreover, since municipalities through their official acts, could equally with natural persons create the harms intended to be remedied by § 1, and, further, since Congress intended § 1 to be broadly construed, there is no reason to suppose that municipal corporations would have been excluded from the sweep of § 1 . . . .

One need not rely on this inference alone, however, for the debates show that Members of Congress understood "persons" to include municipal corporations.

Representative Bingham, for example, in discussing § 1 of the bill, explained that he had drafted § 1 of the Fourteenth Amendment with the case of *Barron v. Baltimore*, 7 Pet. 243, 8 L. Ed. 672 (1834), especially in mind. "In [that] case the *city* had taken private property for public use, without compensation . . . , and there was no redress for the wrong . . . ." Globe App., at 84 (emphasis added). Bingham's further remarks clearly indicate his view that such takings by cities, as had occurred in *Barron*, would be redressable under § 1 of the bill. *See id.*, at 85. More generally, and as Bingham's remarks confirm, § 1 of the bill would logically be the vehicle by which Congress provided redress for takings, since that section provided the only civil remedy for Fourteenth Amendment violations and that Amendment unequivocally prohibited uncompensated takings. Given this purpose, it beggars reason to suppose that Congress would have exempted municipalities from suit, insisting instead that compensation for a taking come from an officer in his individual capacity rather than from the government unit that had the benefit of the property taken.

In addition, by 1871, it was well understood that corporations should be treated as natural persons for virtually all purposes of constitutional and statutory analysis . . . .

. . . .

That the "usual" meaning of the word person would extend to municipal corporations is also evidenced by an Act of Congress which had been passed only months before the Civil Rights Act was passed. This Act provided that

> "in all acts hereafter passed . . . the word 'person' may extend and be applied to bodies politic and corporate . . . unless the context shows that such words were intended to be used in a more limited sense."

Act of Feb. 25, 1871, ch. 71 § 2, 16 Stat. 431. Municipal corporations in 1871 were included within the phrase "bodies politic and corporate" and, accordingly, the "plain meaning" of § 1 is that local government bodies were to be included within the ambit of the persons who could be sued under § 1 of the Civil Rights Act. Indeed, a Circuit Judge, writing in 1873 in what is apparently the first reported case under § 1, read the Dictionary Act in precisely this way in a case involving a corporate plaintiff and a municipal defendant . . . .

II

Our analysis of the legislative history of the Civil Rights Act of 1871 compels the conclusion that Congress *did* intend municipalities and other local government units to be included among those persons to whom § 1983 applies . . . .

. . . .

MR. JUSTICE POWELL, concurring.

This Court traditionally has been hesitant to overrule prior constructions of statutes or interpretations of common-law rules. "*Stare decisis* is usually the wise policy." *Burnet v. Coronado Oil & Gas Co.*, 285 U.S. 393, 406, 76 L. Ed. 815, 52 S. Ct. 443 (1932) (Brandeis, J., dissenting), but this cautionary principle must give way to countervailing considerations in appropriate circumstances. I concur in the Court's view that this is not a case where we should "place on the shoulders of Congress the burden of the Court's own error." *Girouard v. United States*, 328 U.S. 61, 70, 90 L. Ed. 1084, 66 S. Ct. 826 (1946).

Finally, if we continued to adhere to a rule of absolute municipal immunity under § 1983, we could not long avoid the question whether "we should, by analogy to our decision in *Bivens v. Six Unknown Fed. Narcotics Agents*, 403 U.S. 388, 29 L. Ed. 2d 619, 91 S. Ct. 1999 (1971), imply a cause of action directly from the Fourteenth Amendment which would not be subject to the limitations contained in § 1983 . . . ." *Mt. Healthy City Board of Ed. v. Doyle*, 429 U.S. 274, 278, 50 L. Ed. 2d 471, 97 S. Ct. 568 (1977). One aspect of that inquiry would be whether there are any "special factors counselling hesitation in the absence of affirmative action by Congress," *Bivens, supra*, at 396, such as an "explicit congressional declaration that persons injured by a [municipality] may not recover money damages . . . , but must instead be remitted to another remedy, equally effective in the view of Congress," *id.*, at 397 . . . . In light of the Court's persuasive reexamination in today's decision of the 1871 debates, I would have difficulty inferring from § 1983 "an explicit congressional declaration" against municipal liability for the implementation of official policies in violation of the Constitution. Rather than constitutionalize a cause of action against local government that Congress intended to create in 1871, the better course is to confess error and set the record straight, as the Court does today.

. . . .

NOTES AND QUESTIONS

1. The *Monroe* decision rested on congressional rejection of an amendment. Does the *Monell* decision provide any lessons with respect to the validity of recourse to consideration of such actions for purposes of ascertaining legislative intent? Based on Powell's concurrence, what is the Court now saying: that the Sherman Amendment did not really do what the Court initially had thought it would do, that it was not germane

at all, or that other evidence reflects that Congress did not understand the amendment to have the effect of including municipalities within the term "person"?

2. What are the inherent deficiencies in a court's effort to assess, as was attempted in *Monell*, the motives for a congressional body's rejection of an amendment so as to use that determination as evidence of legislative intent? Does use of such an analysis require one to assume a solitary objective for the legislative action?

3. Is not the "Dictionary Act" of February 25, 1871, which defines "person" to include municipalities, dispositive of the issue before the Court in *Monell*? Does this represent a more authoritative basis for the Court's conclusion than the other items of legislative history discussed?

4. One of the issues the Court had to face was the possible application of *stare decisis* to its prior decision. Do the majority's posture on *stare decisis* and the discussions by Rehnquist on this issue provide any useful tests? How is one to determine whether the reexamination meets Harlan's test as set forth in *Monroe*? In any event, is the Court not a bit cavalier about its statement that Congress can correct the Court's mistakes? Could the reopening of debate on what is still an emotional issue allow changes far more significant than simply resolving the subject of the Court's concern? Should not the Court, to be consistent, also expect Congress to correct an error, whether or not the mistake was that of the Court? How is Congress to tell whose mistake it was? These questions of *stare decisis* in statutory interpretation cases, together with *Monell*'s discussion, are treated directly in Chapter 9, Section A.

5. Can the Court's reversal of this long-standing interpretation and its rejection of *stare decisis* be explained in part by its fear of potentially broader liability exposure for municipalities if this case had been decided the other way? As Justice Powell points out in his concurring opinion, the doctrine of the *Bivens* case (403 U.S. 388 (1971)) would have justified permitting suit against a municipality simply on the authority of the Fourteenth Amendment, without congressional midwifery. From this perspective, is not *Monell* a choice of the lesser of two evils for those who would have been otherwise willing to permit municipalities a continued exemption from liability, since § 1983 at least contains some structuring of the procedures and specification of the grounds for such suits?

6. Is it possible to make a distinction between an amendment and a conscious substitution of the conflicting language of one House's version for the other? In *Southern Pac. Transp. Co. v. Usery*, 539 F.2d 386 (5th Cir. 1976), the court discounted the interpretive value of the floor debate and gave more weight to the choice of the Senate over the House version of a bill:

> The conference committee recognized the difference in language and consciously chose the Senate version. Since the legislative process — the process by which Congress arrived at the statutory language — is often a better guide than the interpretations of individual legislators or committee reports, . . . we attach some weight to the substitution of the Senate version for that passed by the House.

Id. at 391. The next line of the opinion, however, raises the question whether the court was substituting something only slightly invalid for something more invalid:

> And although the Senate's language remains less than pellucid, the conscious and deliberate substitution of that language for the House version tending more clearly toward an industry-wide exemption *strongly suggests* that the statute as passed contemplates a narrower kind of exemption.

Id. at 391 (emphasis added).

7. In a subsequent session of the legislature, if an amendment is proposed to an existing act, should its failure to pass be used in interpreting the original act? Does it make any difference whether the amendment is proposed in the same or a different legislative session? Can the intent of the legislature be presumed from a failure to change an existing law? Should it make any difference if there has been an intervening court decision that the amendment would have obviated?

8. In *City of Ingleside v. Johnson*, 537 S.W.2d 145 (Tex. Civ. App. 1976), the court held:

> There are decisions holding that in construing a statute, rejected amendments, or rejected alternative legislation, should not be considered, or at least should be given little weight, since the courts can have no means of knowing the real reasons that influenced the legislature in such rejection. In any event, the rejection of an amendment, or the elimination of words from a bill before its passage, is not conclusive of the bill's inapplicability to the matters included in such amendment or described by such words.

Id. at 153.

In *People for Environmental Progress v. Leisz*, 373 F. Supp. 589 (C.D. Cal. 1974), however, a somewhat different position was taken:

> We recognize that changes in a statute in the course of enactment must be observed with caution in determining legislative intent. However, rejection of specific provisions is in our view more significant, may be properly considered and is most persuasive in the circumstances here found.

Id. at 592.

Are these positions irreconcilable? Should the court look to the specific circumstances of rejected alternative legislation before deciding what weight it is to be given? Should the answer depend on the availability and content of the statute's legislative history?

9. In *Williams v. Justice Court*, 230 Cal. App. 2d 87, 40 Cal. Rptr. 724 (1964), appellants contended that search warrants under which illegal pinball machines had been seized were void because of noncompliance with California Penal Code sections 1523 and 1529. These sections required that seized property be brought immediately before a magistrate, a procedure which had not been followed. The court found the warrants lawful, however, because of 1957 amendments incorporated in sections 1528 and 1536, which directed that property be retained by the seizing officer. The court held that these sections, being later expressions of legislative intent, should take precedence over earlier inconsistent sections.

Appellants had argued that section 1529 was amended in 1961, four years *after* sections 1528 and 1536, and that the requirement of bringing seized property before a magistrate had been reiterated at that time. Therefore, the appellants argued, section 1529 was the latest expression of legislative intent and should control.

The court rejected this argument by noting that the 1961 amendment to section 1529 was purely mechanical, leaving the pertinent part unchanged. Since only part of a statute was amended, the court regarded the unchanged portion as a continuation of existing law. As a result, the court held the 1961 change manifested no legislative intent to alter sections 1528 and 1536; these sections continued to control.

10. In *In re Wallace W*, 634 A.2d 53 (Md. 1993), the defendant was charged with violating a statute prohibiting the unauthorized use of listed livestock and vehicles, followed by "or property whatsoever." In overturning the conviction for unauthorized use of a student's purse, the court noted:

> In 1918, the Maryland Legislature added the language, "including motor vehicle as defined in the laws of this State relating to such," to § 349. *See* Ch. 422 of the Acts of 1918. In 1979, the Legislature further amended the unauthorized use statute by adding "boat, craft, [and] vessel" to the property covered by the statute. *See* ch. 552 of the Acts of 1979. The latter amendment was for "the purpose of prohibiting the unauthorized use of boats." *Id.* These two amendments were made despite the fact that the unauthorized use statute always included the phrase, "or property whatsoever." The unauthorized use statute

now covers "any horse, mare, colt, gelding, mule, ass, sheep, hog, ox or cow, or any carriage, wagon, buggy, cart, *boat, craft, vessel*, or any other vehicle *including motor vehicle as defined in the laws of this State relating to such*, or property whatsoever . . . ." § 349 (emphasis added).

If the Legislature believed that "property whatsoever" meant any and all property, then these two amendments were unnecessary. For instance, if boats were always covered by the statute under the "property whatsoever" provision, an amendment for "the purpose of prohibiting the unauthorized use of boats" was entirely superfluous. Rather than deem this amendment mere surplusage, it is more reasonable to believe that, in 1979, the Legislature expanded the statute's limited coverage to vehicles that travel by water in addition to those that travel on land. Similarly, in 1918, the Legislature obviously wanted to assure that the statute covered motor vehicles as well as those vehicles traditionally drawn by animals.

Id., at 58.

JANE S. SCHACTER,
THE CONFOUNDING COMMON LAW ORIGINALISM IN RECENT SUPREME COURT STATUTORY INTERPRETATION: IMPLICATIONS FOR THE LEGISLATIVE HISTORY DEBATE AND BEYOND,
51 STAN. L. REV. 1 (1998)[*]

INTRODUCTION

It is common, even mundane, to observe that the Supreme Court's approach to statutory interpretation has become increasingly "textualist" in character — that is, more oriented to statutory language and the assertedly "objective" meaning of statutory text than to the collective subjective intent behind the legislation. A principal piece of evidence marshaled in support of this characterization is a decline in the Court's use of legislative history in construing federal laws. Because committee reports, floor statements, and other materials generated during the legislative process traditionally appear in statutory interpretation opinions as evidence of the controlling legislative intent, the Court's declining use of these materials in construing ambiguous statutory provisions has generally been taken to signal a move away from "intentionalism" and toward the "new textualism" associated most prominently with Justice Antonin Scalia. Justice Scalia, legislative history's most conspicuous critic,[3] vigorously challenges the legitimacy of legislative history as an "authoritative indication" of statutory meaning.[4] Because Scalia and others claim that the judicial search for legislative intent in general, and the use of legislative history as evidence of that intent in particular, is inconsistent with the constitutionality prescribed roles of both the courts and Congress, the legislative history question has spilled over the confines of statutory interpretation into a larger debate about institutional characteristics and roles.

The embattled character of legislative history in the Supreme Court has been widely viewed as a proxy for the rise of the "new textualism," and has therefore commanded extended scholarly attention. Most of this commentary has been normative in nature,

---

[3] Scalia is not the lone judicial voice against legislative history. Judges Frank Easterbrook, Alex Kozinski, and James Buckley, and former Judge Kenneth Starr have also taken positions against the use of legislative history. *See* Kenneth W. Starr, *Observations About the Use of Legislative History*, 1987 DUKE L.J. 371, 377; Nicholas S. Zeppos, *Justice Scalia's Textualism: The "New" New Legal Process*, 12 CARDOZO L. REV. 1597, 1599 (1991).

[4] *See* ANTONIN SCALIA, A MATTER OF INTERPRETATION 29–30 (1997).

weighing the strengths and weaknesses of the major critiques of legislative history. A smaller body of work has ventured into empirical terrain and has charted the declining use of legislative history in the Supreme Court by examining the Court's statutory cases and noting the trend away from citing committee reports, floor debates, and other sources reflecting the statutory background.

In this paper, I pursue a somewhat different path — what I think of as empirically-informed normative analysis. My point of departure is the 45 statutory interpretation decisions in the October 1996 Term of the Supreme Court. As in previous empirical studies by Professor Thomas Merrill and Judge Patricia Wald, I use the statutory interpretation opinions in a recent Supreme Court Term to assess the extent to which legislative history continues to figure prominently in the Court's interpretive approach. Unlike these other analyses, however, I also use the cases to analyze the extent to which the Court uses a broad range of *other* interpretive resources in these opinions. My purpose in doing so is to generate a picture of the Court's interpretive practices that is more textured and nuanced than one based on citations to legislative history alone, and to use this richer empirical portrait to assess the critiques of legislative history in the context of the Court's demonstrated interpretive practices . . . .

In the end, I draw three principal conclusions. First, when measured against other empirical analyses, the 1996 Term reflects some resurgence in the use of legislative history and an apparent decline in another benchmark of the new textualism — citations to the dictionary. Second, and more interesting, there are significant features in the Court's interpretive jurisprudence that confound the interpretive divides that structure so much contemporary scholarship. It is standard, for example, to distinguish among different forms of originalism in statutory construction, and to draw an important line between "textualism" on the one hand, and "intentionalism" or "purposivism" on the other. Similarly, in his recent book, Justice Scalia set textualism, his preferred brand of originalism, against its asserted opposite — the common law mode. My analysis of the recent opinions suggests that these categories are far too stylized to capture the Court's interpretive practices which, in fact, cut across these familiar categories. I argue that the idea of "common law originalism" better describes the approach taken in the Court's recent opinions, and that it describes equally well cases that do and do not cite legislative history. In fact, the profile of legislative history cases and nonlegislative history cases is strikingly similar. In both groups of cases from the 1996 Term, the Court's methodology is "originalist" in that it uses statutory language as an interpretive anchor and focal point. At the same time, however, this methodology bears significant traces of the common law form because it draws from an array of *judicially*-created sources to delineate the range of plausible textual meanings and then to select from among them. Across the range of the Term's cases, I argue, this approach best describes the Justices' opinions, whether they or others would characterize their approach as "textualist," "intentionalist," or otherwise. In charting this common law originalism, I place special emphasis on the Justices' consistent use of what I call judicially-selected policy norms, and I argue that previous accounts of statutory interpretation have failed to identify and appreciate the significance of these norms.

Third, when situated within the empirical context created by the study, the critique of legislative history does not fare well. Given what common law originalism entails, and what the Justices are regularly doing in statutory interpretation cases, it is difficult to sustain the basic premises of the attack on legislative history. Moreover, if the common law originalism that I find characteristic of the Term's cases has staying power, it will have significant implications for statutory interpretation more generally. It will suggest that instead of taking at face value the lines between "textualism" and either "intentionalism," "purposivism," "dynamic interpretation," or interpretation in a common law mode, we should acknowledge both the limitations in those lines and the substantial residual policymaking discretion retained by judges marching under any interpretive banner. Shifting the focus in this way suggests that the use of legislative history and other interpretive resources should be assessed not for their capacity to reveal accurately a singularly correct original meaning, but instead for their ability to advance the more eclectic, policy-oriented process of assigning meaning to ambiguous legislative directives.

. . . .

In analyzing the 45 interpretive decisions from the 1996 Term, I sought not only to determine the frequency with which the Court cites legislative history, but also to generate a full picture of both the range of interpretive resources and the frequency with which the Court employs them when deciding what federal statutes mean. I included the following nine interpretive resources in my analysis: (1) the statutory language at issue in the case; (2) legislative history (including committee reports, statements and other information in the Congressional Record, or other material generated in the legislative process through which the law was enacted); (3) other statutes (state or federal), or other sections of the same statute at issue in the case; (4) judicial opinions (including previous decisions by the Supreme Court or other federal or state courts); (5) canons of construction; (6) administrative materials (including federal regulations or policy statements, letters or advisory opinions written by agency officials, and agency adjudicatory decisions); (7) secondary sources (including law review and newspaper articles, treatises, other books, and policy reports); (8) dictionaries (whether general or legal); and (9) miscellaneous other. I did not include briefs as a category of interpretive resources because they are advocacy documents that differ in kind from the other resources I tracked . . . .

These nine categories reflect familiar judicial resources for statutory interpretation. In addition, I have identified and included in the analysis an additional interpretive resource used by the Court with striking frequency in the Term's cases, but not established in the study of statutory interpretation. I call this category "judicially-selected policy norms." One important strain of these norms appears in opinions that argue that a particular interpretation should be embraced or rejected because of the potential policy consequences that would be produced. Other opinions simply invoke a policy norm as the relevant one to guide the Court in selecting from among the proffered readings of the statute. These norms appear in different ways in the cases, but are unified by a defining characteristic: they are nonoriginalist. They reflect the Justices' own invocation of policy values that are grounded in neither the text of the statute nor the legislative history or any other claim about intended legislative design.

. . . .

The frequent use of these judicially-selected norms stands in sharp contrast to the rhetoric that appears in several of the Term's opinions decrying the dangers of judicial policymaking in the guise of interpretation. Moreover, although the use of judicially-selected policy norms is in clear tension with the rhetorical claims of textualism, these norms cut across the methodological divides on the Court. The professed textualists displayed no reluctance to make arguments of this kind. Despite his attack on the use of "common law" methods in statutory interpretation, Justice Scalia, for example, wrote several opinions in which he selected a policy norm and argued against an interpretation that would undermine the norm. Similarly, Justice Thomas is often regarded as sympathetic to textualism, but he also freely used judicially-selected policy norms in several opinions. And arguments of this kind appear repeatedly in cases that cite no legislative history.

. . . .

A. *Implications for the Critiques of Legislative History*

Recall that the critiques of legislative history are institutional in nature, focusing on the ways in which the use of legislative history in statutory interpretation assertedly distorts the appropriate institutional roles of the courts and Congress, respectively. The interpretive patterns that emerge in the opinions studied call into question significant aspects of both the judicial and legislative critiques of legislative history.

1. *Implications for the judicial critique of legislative history.*

The central argument of the judicial critique is that the use of legislative history enables an undesirable brand of "judicial activism" because the volume and variability of a statute's legislative history permits judges to make selective, strategic use of that history while professing to defer to Congress by honoring its intent. The common law originalism that characterizes the opinions studied undermines this argument in several ways.

First, the study illustrates with detail and texture that the terrain of "judicial activism" ranges far beyond legislative history . . . . Value-laden, judicially-created interpretive resources are used regularly. Second, the similar profiles of the legislative history and nonlegislative history cases suggest that it is problematic to target the use of legislative history for special disapproval on judicial activism grounds. The absence of legislative history hardly translates into the presence of judicial "restraint." Conversely, the use of legislative history does not seem, in any systematic way, to make an interpretive opinion more vulnerable to a charge of judicial activism. The opinions that do not consult legislative history generally make use of the same judicially-created resources like precedent, policy norms, and canons of construction at comparable rates as the opinions consulting legislative history . . . . Cases that do and do not cite legislative history are equally likely to use judicially-shaped policy norms.

Third, given the prevalent usage of judicially-selected policy norms in the opinions studied, we might conclude that the failure to consult legislative history is actually the more activist move, for it gives the judge more power to shape the policy objectives of the statute unilaterally, unconstrained by policy priorities or goals that may have been expressed by legislators. Indeed, from the standpoint of judicial activism concerns, there is something perverse about a rule that would license judges to invoke policy considerations of their own making, secondary sources, and canons of construction, yet prohibit them from distilling and considering what relevant policy concerns may appear in the deliberative record generated by the legislators who drafted and debated the bill. This is particularly so given that . . . statutes are ambiguous for many reasons. Several of the Term's cases involved questions and ambiguities that would not have been reasonably foreseen even by a conscientious statutory drafter, and many of these ambiguities can only be resolved by making one or another value-laden choice. If we regard it as inevitable that statutory interpretation must often be informed by some policy sense about the statute or the consequences of choosing one reading over another, then the important questions become: What policy sense? Chosen by whom? Consultation of the written legislative record is one way — certainly not the only way, as the opinions reflect — to bring policy concerns to bear on the interpretive enterprise. Moreover, a judicial decision to categorically disregard legislative history is, after all, a *judicial* decision about who decides what is relevant to statutory meaning, and is, in that sense, difficult to reconcile with a strong conception of judicial restraint.

NOTES AND QUESTIONS

1. Professor Schacter points to the Court's use of judge-made factors in its statutory interpretation decisions. The next chapter provides a direct focus on many such judicially created factors.

2. Can you identify judicially-selected policy norms that were applied in cases you have studied so far? What about Justice Brewer's conclusion, in *Holy Trinity Church*, that Congress would not have intended to interfere with our "Christian nation"?

3. Professor Schacter notes that sometimes statutes contain ambiguities that could not be foreseen, and "can only be resolved by making one or another value-laden choice." Does this remind you of the *Weber* case, and the comments Dworkin made about that case?

ADRIAN VERMEULE,
LEGISLATIVE HISTORY AND THE LIMITS
OF JUDICIAL COMPETENCE:
THE UNTOLD STORY OF *HOLY TRINITY CHURCH*,
50 STAN. L. REV. 1833 (1998)[*]

. . . .

Holy Trinity sharply poses the question whether intentionalists can establish that legislative history increases the accuracy of judicial determinations of legislative intent. After all, in *Holy Trinity* the Court would have captured the legislative intent more accurately by deciding solely in accordance with the Court's own understanding of the text than it did by *also* considering (and misreading) the legislative history. This is not to say that the legislative history in *Holy Trinity* proves unreliable or unhelpful when read as a whole, without significant constraints of time or background information. In that sense, the legislative history provides valuable confirmation of the legislative intention evidenced by the statutory text. But that valuable confirmation was available only if the Court has gotten the legislative history right. As the case actually developed, the structural and contingent constraints under which the Court did its work caused it to form a less accurate assessment of legislative intent by looking at the legislative history than it would have achieved by not looking at it.

B. *A Thesis Concerning Legislative History*

Accordingly, one thesis that arises from *Holy Trinity* might be put this way: Imagine a court faced with an indefinite set of statutory interpretation cases. Assume that in each instance Congress and the President formed a collective intention about the meaning of the statutory text at issue. Also assume that in each case the legislative history, taken as a whole, provides reliable evidence of that intention — in the sense that an ideal interpreter who is knowledgeable about the legislative process and who suffers no constraints of time or information would, on reading all of the relevant legislative-history materials, correctly discern that collective intention. In other words, assume away the textualist argument against legislative history, insofar as that argument is based on the legislative process. Is there now any reason to question judicial resort to legislative history?

Perhaps. Unlike an ideal interpreter, courts *do* operate under significant constraints of time, information, and expertise. In certain circumstances, those constraints may cause courts to mistake the import of the legislative history, just as a court presiding in a bench trial might, for various reasons, issue erroneous factual findings even if the evidence reliably reflected the events that are the subject of the suit. Moreover, courts might mishandle legislative history with sufficient frequency and gravity that courts relying principally on statutory text (as well as canons of construction, judicial precedent, and other standard sources of interpretation) might achieve *more* accurate approximations of the legislature's intent over the whole run of future cases than would courts that admit legislative history as an interpretive source.

This possibility at first seems remote. Intuition suggests that, whatever the risks of error in judicial use of legislative history, adding legislative history to the standard sources of text, precedent, and canons of construction would surely move interpreters closer to the genuine legislative intent than would an approach that relied solely on those other sources. After all, legislative history provides courts with additional information about legislative intent, indeed with information that (unlike judicial precedent and most canons of construction) is at least generated within the legislature.

But it is not the case that more information always and necessarily produces more accurate decisionmaking than does less information. As subsequently discussed, a range of legal rules rests on the premise that certain special types of additional information may prove particularly distortive, inflammatory, or burdensome when considered by a decisionmaker with limited capacity to absorb and evaluate the information. Such information may not only fail to improve the accuracy of the decision made by the constrained decisionmaker, but may decrease it, relative to a decision made without the distorting information. It is at least possible, then that distortive features of legislative history might interact with structural constraints of the adjudicative process in a manner that decreases, rather than increases, judicial accuracy in the determination of legislative intent.

To be sure, any argument in support of this possibility represents a quasi-empirical assessment that is, in practice, hardly subject to rigorous proof or disproof. Yet the implicit assumption of intentionalism — that resort to legislative history *enhances* judicial accuracy — rests on precisely the same sort of unprovable assessment. Any attempt to prove that legislative history either increases or reduces judicial accuracy over an aggregate set of cases would require, at minimum, full examination of the statutes, legislative histories, and resulting judicial opinions in a fair sample of all the statutory cases decided in the federal system both before and after *Holy Trinity*. The practical impossibility of proof, however, does not in principle bar an informed prediction that resort to legislative history reduces judicial accuracy. An argument in support of such a prediction could take the form of reasoned inferences about the interaction between legislative history and discernible structural and institutional constraints that govern the adjudicative process. Legal rules that restrict decisionmakers' access to information in order to enhance accuracy often rest not on empirical proof in any strong sense, but rather on similar informed assessments of institutional structure and performance under alternative decisionmaking regimes.

The following considerations suggest that the interaction between distinctive features of legislative history and structural constraints of the adjudicative process may indeed cause legislative history to reduce rather than increase judicial accuracy. There is no reason to think that judicial error in the interpretation of legislative history occurs randomly, either in the sense that error in particular cases occurs without any cause or in the sense that, over the whole set of cases, errors are proportionally distributed in favor of the various types of parties or the various types of legal claims. Rather, judicial error in the interpretation of legislative history arises from predictable causes and has predictable effects. In the abstract, two types of errors occur: errors of information and errors of evaluation. Errors of information occur when the court lacks, or fails to seek, full information about the materials in the legislative history. Perhaps the court's attempts to generate a complete set of such information have failed, or the court has relied on the parties to bring all relevant information to its attention and they have failed to do so; perhaps some mix of the two possibilities has occurred. Errors of evaluation occur when the court acts with a full set of information, but mistakes the significance of material in the legislative history due to constraints of time, background expertise, or other resources. For example, the court's lack of familiarity with the legislative process, or the press of judicial business, might cause it to overestimate or underestimate the weight due to a particular item of legislative history.

These general considerations do not provide reason to question judicial resort to legislative history in particular unless there is some alternative to its use. Even proof that use of a particular source poses severe risks of adjudicative error is irrelevant if there is no conceivable alternative to that source. In many domains, judges must consider and evaluate complex and voluminous information, sources, and arguments, and are thought competent to do so. Moreover, any accuracy-related critique of legislative history must provide reason to believe that courts are *especially* prone to err in their evaluation of legislative history. After all, errors of information and evaluation can occur with respect to many different sources. Litigants may fail to reference, or courts to find through independent research, relevant statutory texts, judicial precedents, or canons of construction; and even if those sources are introduced, the court may misjudge their weight or meaning in any particular case. The possibility of error hardly justifies skepticism of a particular source unless there is some distinctive risk that courts will err in evaluating that source.

Even on these terms, however, there is a plausible case that legislative history indeed warrants skepticism. First, in statutory interpretation, unlike other areas in which a particular source creates risks of adjudicative error, there is a conceivable alternative to the use of legislative history. Because statutory interpretation, on any account, takes into consideration many interpretive sources — statutory text, judicial precedent, and canons of construction, to name a few — it is at least possible to exclude legislative history while leaving in place other sources from which adjudication can proceed, whether or not it is attractive to do so. Second, legislative history is a source with unique characteristics. In particular, as described below, legislative history is distinctively voluminous and heterogeneous in comparison to other interpretive sources. The interaction of those characteristics with structural features of the adjudicative process creates a distinctive risk that judges will mishandle legislative history, even if an unconstrained interpreter would find that the legislative history accurately reflects congressional intent.

NOTES AND QUESTIONS

1. How does Professor Vermeule's critique of the use of legislative history compare with Justice Scalia's? Does this critique focus on limitations of *judicial* competence rather than *legislative* decisionmaking? What is the difference?

2. Does Professor Vermeule share Justice Scalia's faith in the "standard tools of legal reasoning"?

3. Professor Vermeule's position is based on the premise that the court in *Holy Trinity Church* misread the legislative history. For a contrary view, *see* William N. Eskridge, Jr. *Textualism, The Unknown Ideal*, 96 MICH. L. REV. 1509, 1533–42 (1998) (reviewing ANTONIN SCALIA, A MATTER OF INTERPRETATION: FEDERAL COURTS AND THE LAW (1997)).

4. For another contrary view, *see* Carol Chomsky, *Unlocking The Mysteries of Holy Trinity: Spirit, Letter and History in Statutory Interpretation*, 100 COLUM. L. REV. 901 (2000).

16 THE SUPREME COURT OF THE UNITED STATES: HEARINGS AND REPORTS ON SUCCESSFUL AND UNSUCCESSFUL NOMINATIONS OF SUPREME COURT JUSTICES BY THE SENATE JUDICIARY COMMITTEE 1916–1990,
pp. 130–132, DAVID H. SOUTER

Senator DECONCINI. Let me turn to another subject, Judge. Over the last few terms of the Supreme Court, almost 50 percent of the Supreme Court cases have involved issues of statutory interpretation. Your judicial experience has been in a State court, so you have not had much exposure to cases of Federal statutory interpretation, and that is why I would like to as a few questions.

I did notice in the committee's questionnaire, you stated,

"The foundation of judicial responsibility in statutory interpretation is respect for the enacted text and for the legislative purpose that may explain a text that is unclear."

Based on that response to what extent do you believe the legislative history should be taken into consideration, if you were sitting on the Supreme Court interpreting a statute passed by the Congress?

Judge SOUTER. Senator, I am very much aware, in answering or in approaching an answer to that question, about the great spectrum of evidence that gets grouped under the umbrella of legislative history. It seems to me that the one general rule — and it is a truism to state it, but the one general rule that I can state is, when we look to legislative history in cases where the text is unclear, we at least have got to look to reliable legislative history.

When we are looking to legislative history on an issue of statutory construction, what we are doing is gathering evidence, and the object of gathering evidence for statutory interpretation is ultimately not in any way different from the object of gathering evidence of extraneous fact in a courtroom.

We are trying to establish some kind of standard of reliability, in this case to know exactly what was intended. And what we want to know is, to the extent we can find it out, is whether, aside from the terms of the statute itself, there really is a reliable guide to an institutional intent, not just a spectrum of subjective intent. I suppose a vague statute can get voted on by five different Senators for five different reasons, so that if we are going to look to pure subjectivity, we are going to be in trouble.

What we are looking for is an intent which can be attributed to the institution itself, and, therefore, what we are looking for is some index of intended meaning, perhaps signaled by adoption or by, at the very least, an informed acquiescence that we can genuinely point to and say this represents not merely the statement of one committee member or committee staffer or one person on the floor, but in fact to an institution or to a sufficiently large enough number of the members of that institution, so that we can say they probably really do stand as surrogates for all those who voted for it.

Senator DECONCINI. So, in looking at legislative history, I take it from that, the amount, the intensity of it, those that are associated with the subject matter are of importance in a judge's interpretation?

Judge SOUTER. Yes, indeed.

Senator DECONCINI. More so than if it can be distinguished that someone merely put something in the record, because it appeared that it was the right place to put it in, but had no history in that legislation themselves.

Judge SOUTER. Yes, sir.

Senator DECONCINI. What other sources should a judge rely on in a statutory construction case outside the statutes and legislative history?

Judge SOUTER. Well, there is a kind of, I suppose, broad principle of coherence that we look to. The fact is we so frequently speak of interpreting sections of statutes. What we are really obligated to is to interpret whole statutes. We should not be interpreting a statutory section, without looking at the entire statute that we are interpreting.

One of the things that I have found — and I do not know particularly why I learned it, but I found one thing on the New Hampshire Supreme Court which has stood me in pretty good stead, and that is when I get a statutory interpretation issue in front of me, I read the brief, I listen to the argument. But if I am going to write that opinion, I sit down, I tell my law clerks to sit down, but I do it myself before I am done, and I just sit there and I read the whole statute. Fortunately, I do not have to construe the Internal Revenue Code, in which case I would be in serious trouble with that methodology. But within reason, I try to read the whole statute, and I am amazed at the number of times when I do that, I will find a clear clue in some other section that nobody has bothered to cite to me in a brief.

We are trying to come up with statutory coherence, not with just a bunch of pinpoints in individual sections. So, the first thing to do, in a very practical way, is to read the whole statute.

It is beyond the intent of your question, of course, to get into constitutional issues, but we do know it is accepted statutory interpretation that if we have a choice between two possible meanings, one of which raises a serious constitutional issue and one of which does not, it is responsible to take the latter, and, of course, we looked at that.

Senator DECONCINI. Judge, the term, textualism, has been used to describe a judge who attempts to limit the statutory interpretation to the text and ignores the legislative history. You explained what you do, and such an approach really fails to take into consideration, I think, the necessity — although I have never been a judge, I have certainly had a lot of association and argued enough cases where I have felt at least the judges have listened to legislative history propounded on both sides of it, maybe not always coming to the same conclusion.

The fact that the matter is passed by a legislative body — often, those of us in those bodies are not clear ourselves as to the absolute interpretation or how it is going to be applied by the regulators or the bureaucracy that must implement our statutes.

TRAIN v. COLORADO PUBLIC INTEREST RESEARCH GROUP, INC.
426 U.S. 1 (1976)

Mr. Justice Marshall delivered the opinion of the Court.

The issue in this case is whether the Environmental Protection Agency (EPA) has the authority under the Federal Water Pollution Control Act (FWPCA), as amended in 1972, 86 Stat. 816, 33 U.S.C. § 1251 et seq. (1970 ed., Supp. IV), to regulate the discharge into the Nation's waterways of nuclear waste materials subject to regulation by the Atomic Energy Commission (AEC) and its successors under the Atomic Energy Act of 1954 (AEA). 68 Stat. 919, as amended, 42 U.S.C. § 2011 et seq. In statutory terms, the question is whether these nuclear materials are "pollutants" within the meaning of the FWPCA.

I

Respondents are Colorado-based organizations and Colorado residents who claim potential harm from the discharge of radioactive effluents from two nuclear plants — the Fort St. Vrain Nuclear Generating Station and the Rocky Flats nuclear weapons components plant. These facilities are operated in conformity with radioactive effluent standards imposed by the AEC pursuant to the Atomic Energy Act. The dispute in this case arises because the EPA has disclaimed any authority under the FWPCA to set standards of its own to govern the discharge of radioactive materials subject to regulation under the AEA. Respondents, taking issue with the EPA's disclaimer of authority, brought this suit against petitioners . . . . They sought a declaration that the definition of a "pollutant" under the FWPCA encompasses all radioactive materials, including those regulated under the terms of the AEA, and an injunction directing the EPA and its Administrator to regulate the discharge of all such radioactive materials.

. . . .

II

Since 1946, when the first Atomic Energy Act was passed, 60 Stat. 755, the Federal Government has exercised control over the production and use of atomic energy through the AEC — replaced since the commencement of this litigation by the Nuclear Regulatory Commission (NRC) and the Energy Research and Development Administration (ERDA). Under the AEA, private parties are permitted to engage in the production of atomic energy for industrial or commercial purposes, but only in accordance with licenses issued by the AEC (NRC) in the furtherance of the purposes of the Act. 42 U.S.C. § 2133.

The comprehensive regulatory scheme created by the AEA embraces the production, possession, and use of three types of radioactive materials — source material,[2] special nuclear material,[3] and byproduct material.[4]

. . . .

The FWPCA established a regulatory program to control and abate water pollution, stating as its ultimate objective the elimination of all discharges of "pollutants" into the navigable waters by 1985. In furtherance of this objective, the FWPCA calls for the achievement of effluent limitations that require applications of the "best practicable control technology currently available" by July 1, 1977, and the "best available technology economically achievable" by July 1, 1983. 33 U.S.C. § 1311(b) (1970 ed., Supp. IV). These effluent limitations are enforced through a permit program. The discharge of "pollutants" into water is unlawful without a permit issued by the Administrator of the EPA or, if a State has developed a program that complies with the FWPCA, by the State. 33 U.S.C. §§ 1311(a), 1342 (1970 ed., Supp. IV).

The term "pollutant" is defined by the FWPCA to include, inter alia, "radioactive materials."[7] But when the Administrator of the EPA adopted regulations governing the permit program, 40 CFR, pt. 125 (1975), he specifically excluded source, byproduct, and special nuclear materials — those covered by the AEA — from the program upon his understanding of the relevant legislative history of the FWPCA:

> "The legislative history of the Act reflects that the term 'radioactive materials' as included within the definition of 'pollutant' in section 502 of the Act covers only radioactive materials which are not encompassed in the definition of source, byproduct, or special nuclear materials as defined by the Atomic Energy Act of 1954, as amended, and regulated pursuant to the latter Act. Examples of radioactive materials not covered by the Atomic Energy Act and, therefore, included within the term 'pollutant' are radium and accelerator produced isotopes." 40 CFR § 125.1(y) (1975) (citations omitted).

It was the Administrator's exclusion of source, byproduct, and special nuclear materials from the permit program, and consequent refusal to regulate them, that precipitated the instant lawsuit. The question we are presented with, then, is whether source, byproduct, and special nuclear materials are "pollutants" within the meaning of the FWPCA.

III

The Court of Appeals resolved the question exclusively by reference to the language of the statute. It observed that the FWPCA defines "pollution" as "the man-made or

---

[2] "The term 'source material' means (1) uranium, thorium, or any other material which is determined by the Commission pursuant to the provisions of section 2091 of this title to be source material; or (2) ores containing one or more of the foregoing materials, in such concentration as the Commission may by regulation determine from time to time." 42 U.S.C. § 2014(z).

[3] "The term 'special nuclear material' means (1) plutonium, uranium enriched in the isotope 233 or in the isotope 235, and any other material which the Commission, pursuant to the provisions of section 2071 of this title, determines to be special nuclear material, but does not include source material; or (2) any material artificially enriched by any of the foregoing, but does not include source material." 42 U.S.C. § 2014(aa).

[4] "The term 'byproduct material' means any radioactive material (except special nuclear material) yielded in or made radioactive by exposure to the radiation incident to the process of producing or utilizing special nuclear material." 42 U.S.C. § 2014(e).

[7] "The term 'pollutant' means dredged spoil, solid waste, incinerator residue, sewage, garbage, sewage sludge, munitions, chemical wastes, biological materials, radioactive materials . . . . This term does not mean (A) 'sewage from vessels' within the meaning of section 1322 of this title; or (B) water, gas, or other material which is injected into a well to facilitate production of oil or gas . . . ."

man-induced alteration of the chemical, physical, biological, and radiological integrity of water." 33 U.S.C. § 1362(19) (1970 ed., Supp. IV). And it noted that the reference to "radioactive materials" in the definition of "pollutant" was without express qualification or exception, despite the fact that the overall definition of "pollutant" does contain two explicit exceptions. The court concluded from this analysis of the language that by the reference to "radioactive materials" Congress meant all radioactive materials. The court explained:

> "In our view, then, the statute is plain and unambiguous and should be given its obvious meaning. Such being the case, . . . we need not here concern ourselves with the legislative history of the 1972 Amendments. In this regard we would note parenthetically that in our view the legislative history of the 1972 Amendments is conflicting and inconclusive. Be that as it may, in the case before us there is no need to address ourselves to the ofttimes difficult task of ascertaining legislative intent through legislative history. Here, the legislative intent is clearly manifested in the language of the statute itself, and we need not resort to legislative history." 507 F.2d, at 748 (citations omitted).

To the extent that the Court of Appeals excluded reference to the legislative history of the FWPCA in discerning its meaning, the court was in error. As we have noted before: "When aid to construction of the meaning of words, as used in the statute, is available, there certainly can be no 'rule of law' which forbids its use, however clear the words may appear on 'superficial examination.' " *United States v. American Trucking Assns.*, 310 U.S. 534, 543–544 (1940) (footnotes omitted). *See Cass v. United States*, 417 U.S. 72, 77–79 (1974). *See generally* Murphy, *Old Maxims Never Die: The "Plain-Meaning Rule" and Statutory Interpretation in the "Modern" Federal Courts*, 75 Col. L. Rev. 1299 (1975). In this case, as we shall see, the legislative history sheds considerable light on the question before the Court.

. . . .

IV

The legislative history of the FWPCA speaks with force to the question whether source, byproduct, and special nuclear materials are "pollutants" subject to the Act's permit program. The House Committee Report was quite explicit on the subject:

> "The term 'pollutant' as defined in the bill includes 'radioactive materials.' *These materials are those not encompassed in the definition of source, byproduct, or special nuclear materials as defined by the Atomic Energy Act of 1954, as amended, and regulated pursuant to that Act. 'Radioactive materials' encompassed by this bill are those beyond the jurisdiction of the Atomic Energy Commission.* Examples of radioactive material not covered by the Atomic Energy Act, and, therefore, included within the term 'pollutant,' are radium and accelerator produced isotopes." H.R. Rep. No. 92-911, p. 131 (1972), 1 Leg. Hist. 818 (emphasis added).[10]

The definition of "pollutant" in the House version of the bill, H.R. 11896, 92d Cong., 2d Sess., § 502(6) (1972), 1 Leg. Hist. 1068, contained the same broad reference to "radioactive materials" as did the definition in the Senate bill, S. 2770, 92d Cong., 1st Sess., § 502(f) (1971), 2 Leg. Hist. 1697, and the bill ultimately enacted as the FWPCA; for our purposes the definitions are identical. Moreover, the House version of the bill contained the provision now codified as § 1311(f), banning the discharge of radiological warfare agents and high-level radioactive waste "[n]otwithstanding any other provisions

---

[10] Citations to "Leg. Hist." refer to a two-volume Committee print for the Senate Committee on Public Works, A Legislative History of the Water Pollution Control Act Amendments of 1972, 93d Cong., 1st Sess. (1973).

of this Act." H.R. 11896, *supra*, § 301(e), 1 Leg. Hist. 965. Thus, the House Committee, describing the import of the precise statutory language with which we are concerned, cautioned that the definition of "pollutant" did not include those radioactive materials subject to regulation under the AEA.

. . . .

. . . A colloquy on the Senate floor between Senator Pastore, the Chairman of the Joint Committee on Atomic Energy, and Senator Muskie, the FWPCA's primary author, provides a strong indication that Congress did not intend the FWPCA to alter the AEC's control over the discharge of source, byproduct, and special nuclear materials. Senator Pastore, referring to the need to define what materials are "subject to control requirements" under the FWPCA, noted that the definition of "pollutant" included the words "radioactive materials." 2 Leg. Hist. 1265. The following exchange then took place:

"MR. PASTORE.   . . ."My question is this: Does this measure that has been reported by the committee in any way affect the existing law, that is, the existing Atomic Energy Act of 1954, insofar as the regulatory powers of the AEC are concerned with reference to radioactive material?

"MR. MUSKIE.   It does not; and it is not the intent of this act to affect the 1954 legislation.

"MR. PASTORE.   In other words, this bill does not change that feature of the Atomic Energy Act in any regard?

"MR. MUSKIE.   That is correct.

"MR. PASTORE.   I thank the Senator.

"MR. MUSKIE.   May I say in addition, that legislation (sic) dealing with the setting of effluent limitations as they involve nuclear powerplants is now pending in the courts. The Senator is aware of that litigation.

"MR. MUSKIE.   "For example, a recent decision of the U.S. Court of Appeals for the Eighth Circuit, in the case of Northern States Power and Light versus Minnesota, raises the issue. I would like to point out that the committee considered speaking specifically to that decision, but chose to remain silent so as not to prejudice the decision or any appeal from it.

"MR. PASTORE.   Yes. As a matter of fact, that decision held that the Federal Government did pre-empt in this field under existing law. That is the opinion, and we hope this legislation does not change that opinion in any way, and does not affect existing law. That is all I am concerned with.

"MR. MUSKIE.   The Senator is correct in his evaluation of the legislation on that point." *Id.*, at 1265–1266.

Respondents contend that this colloquy "merely reiterates that the FWPCA does not alter the regulatory authority of the AEC" over source, byproduct, and special nuclear materials. Brief for Respondents 40–41. The exchange, they assert, says nothing about the EPA's authority to regulate the same materials. The discussion is consistent, they claim, with their position that the AEC must defer to the EPA in the setting of effluent limitations for AEA-regulated materials — that, for example, NRC licenses must conform to permits issued under the FWPCA. We disagree.

The thrust of Senator Muskie's assurances that the FWPCA would not "in any way affect" the regulatory powers of the AEC was, we think, that the AEC was to retain full authority to regulate the materials covered by the AEA, unaltered by the exercise of regulatory authority by any agency under the FWPCA. This conclusion is reinforced by

Senator Muskie's reference to the case of *Northern States Power Co. v. Minnesota*, 447 F.2d 1143 (CA8 1971). In that case, which was subsequently affirmed summarily by this Court, 405 U.S. 1035 (1972), the Eighth Circuit had held that the AEA created a pervasive regulatory scheme, vesting exclusive authority to regulate the discharge of radioactive effluents from nuclear power plants in the AEC, and pre-empting the States from regulating such discharges. The absence of any room for a state role under the AEA in setting limits on radioactive discharges from nuclear power plants stands in sharp contrast to the scheme created by the FWPCA, which envisions the development of state permit programs, 33 U.S.C. §§ 1342(b), (c) (1970 ed., Supp. IV), and allows the States to adopt effluent limitations more stringent than those required or established under the FWPCA. 33 U.S.C. § 1370 (1970 ed., Supp. IV). *See also* 33 U.S.C. §§ 1311(b)(1)(C), 1314(b), 1316(c), 1341(a)(1) (1970 ed., Supp. IV). Senator Muskie's specific assurance to Senator Pastore that the FWPCA would not affect existing law as interpreted in *Northern States* can only be viewed, we think, as an indication that the exclusive regulatory scheme created by the AEA for source, byproduct, and special nuclear materials was to remain unaltered.

In the course of the House's consideration of the FWPCA, an unsuccessful attempt was made to alter the AEA's scheme for regulating the discharge of the radioactive materials involved in this case. Representative Wolff proposed to amend what is now 33 U.S.C. § 1370 (1970 ed., Supp. IV), which gives States the authority to set more stringent limits on the discharge of pollutants, by adding a paragraph giving the States the authority to regulate the discharge of radioactive wastes from nuclear power plants. The debate on that amendment and its defeat by a 3-to-1 vote provide solid support for the conclusion that the FWPCA's grant of regulatory authority to the EPA and the States did not encompass the control of AEA-regulated materials.

. . . .

Representative McCormack, a Member of the House Committee on Public Works and Chairman of the House Science and Astronautics Committee's Task Force on Energy Research and Development, urged the amendment's defeat in similar terms. After noting the inadvisability of "throwing away" the AEC's "meticulous work" in the area of safety in favor of state regulation, *id.*, at 550, he concluded:

> "[I]t is obvious from the report by the House Committee on Public Works for this bill, and from the committee report from the other body that this bill does not impact directly upon the Atomic Energy Act of 1954. This bill applies only to radioactive materials not covered by the Atomic Energy Act of 1954 and, as such, the amendment is not relevant to this bill at all." *Id.*, at 551.[16]

Respondents urge that the Wolff amendment was addressed only to the question of the States' regulatory authority, and that its defeat did not reflect any intent to foreclose regulation of source, byproduct, and special nuclear materials by the EPA. We do not agree that the House's consideration of the Wolff amendment leaves room for EPA regulation. Several of the opponents of the amendment were quite explicit in their reliance upon the House Committee Report's statement that radioactive materials subject to AEA regulation were excluded from the coverage of the FWPCA. Neither Representative Wolff nor Representative Frenzel took issue with that interpretation in the course of the debate on their amendment, and indeed it is arguable that their amendment was premised on the assumption that source, byproduct, and special nuclear materials were wholly beyond the scope of the FWPCA. If these materials were covered by the Act — that is, if they were "pollutants" — the amendment was wholly superfluous, for the unamended provision that is now 33 U.S.C. § 1370 (1970 ed., Supp. IV) would permit the states to regulate their discharge. But regardless of the underlying assumptions of the sponsors of the Wolff amendment, the interpretation respondents

---

[16] *See also id.*, at 546–547 (remarks of Rep. Holifield); 553 (remarks of Rep. Hosmer); 553 (remarks of Rep. Clausen); 557 (remarks of Rep. Harsha).

would place upon its defeat is unacceptable. As respondents would have it, the House expressed an intent to permit EPA regulation of the materials in question, but to preclude state regulation of the same materials under the FWPCA. That result could find no basis in the language of the Act. In our view, then, the House's consideration and rejection of the Wolff amendment offers additional support for the interpretation stated in the House Committee Report that source, byproduct, and special nuclear materials are beyond the reach of the FWPCA.

The House's rather explicit statement of intent to exclude AEA-regulated materials from the FWPCA was unchallenged by the Conference Committee, which simply retained the same reference to "radioactive materials" contained in both the House and Senate bills. S. Conf. Rep. No. 92-1236, p. 144 (1972), 1 Leg. Hist. 327. Representative Harsha, a ranking member of the Conference Committee, explained the import of the Conference Committee action as follows:

> "The conference report does not change the original intent as it was made clear in the colloquy between Senators Muskie and Pastore in the course of the debate in the other body. I also note that an amendment to H.R. 11896 was offered on March 28, 1972, which would have overturned the Northern States Power against Minnesota case."

. . . .

V

If it was not clear at the outset, we think it abundantly clear after a review of the legislative materials that reliance on the "plain meaning" of the words "radioactive materials" contained in the definition of "pollutant" in the FWPCA contributes little to our understanding of whether Congress intended the Act to encompass the regulation of source, byproduct, and special nuclear materials. To have included these materials under the FWPCA would have marked a significant alteration of the pervasive regulatory scheme embodied in the AEA. Far from containing the clear indication of legislative intent that we might expect before recognizing such a change in policy, *cf. United States v. United Continental Tuna Corp.*, 425 U.S. 164, 168–169 (1976), the legislative history reflects, on balance, an intention to preserve the pre-existing regulatory plan.

We conclude, therefore, that the "pollutants" subject to regulation under the FWPCA do not include source, byproduct, and special nuclear materials, and that the EPA Administrator has acted in accordance with his statutory mandate in declining to regulate the discharge of such materials.

The judgment of the Court of Appeals is

Reversed.

NOTES AND QUESTIONS

1. According to Justice Scalia's expressed views about legislative history, how might he have addressed the problem confronted by the *Train* Court? How does the outcome fit with Judge Wald's observations? Having read Senator DeConcini's questioning of Justice Souter, how would the senator view the outcome in *Train*? What about Justice Souter?

2. Wasn't the EPA Administrator's interpretation of the FWPCA entitled to deference? See the lower court's opinion in *Train*, 507 F.2d 748 (10th Cir. 1974). This issue of statutory interpretation is treated in Chapter 7, Section B.

2. Post-enactment Legislative History

The next materials involve cases where courts have considered events occurring after a statute's enactment as part of the legislative history used to interpret the statute. How does after-the-fact legislative history fit into the chain of reasoning which links legislative history to statutory interpretation? Whatever may be the problems with the reliability of legislative history in general to determine legislative goals, they are compounded in the case of after-the-fact history. Consider how useful and reliable this type of history is in statutory interpretation. Can a legislature bar a subsequent legislature from amending an act without nullifying the whole act? Is an amendment by a later legislature a total reenactment?

Some examples of after-the-fact legislative history that courts have been asked to consider in assessing the meaning of the original legislation are:

Amendment of a statute by a subsequent legislature.

Amendment of a statute after it has been subject to judicial or administrative construction.

An affidavit of a congressman after enactment of a law.

A post-enactment colloquy.

Post-enactment comments of legislators placed in the record.

NEW YORK STATE DEPARTMENT OF SOCIAL SERVICES v. DUBLINO
413 U.S. 405 (1973)

MR. JUSTICE POWELL delivered the opinion of the Court.

The question before us is whether the Social Security Act of 1935 bars a state from independently requiring individuals to accept employment as a condition for receipt of federally funded aid to families with dependent children. More precisely, the issue is whether that part of the Social Security Act known as the federal Work Incentive Program, preempts the provisions of the New York Social Welfare Law, McKinney's Consol. Laws, c. 55, commonly referred to as the New York Work Rules. A brief description of both the state and federal programs will be necessary.

The Work Rules were enacted by New York in 1971 as part of Governor Rockefeller's efforts to reorganize the New York Welfare Program. Their aim, as explained by the Governor, is to encourage "the young and able-bodied, temporarily in need of assistance through no fault of their own, to achieve the education and the skills, the motivation and the determination that will make it possible for them to become increasingly self-sufficient, independent citizens who can contribute to and share in the responsibility for their families and our society."

To achieve this, the Work Rules establish a presumption that certain recipients of public assistance are employable and require those recipients to report every two weeks to pick up their assistance checks in person; to file every two weeks a certificate from the appropriate public employment office stating that no suitable employment opportunities are available; to report for requested employment interviews; to report to the public employment office the result of a referral for employment; and not to fail willfully to report for suitable employment, when available. In addition to establishing a system of referral for employment in the private sector of the economy, the Work Rules permit the establishment of public works projects in New York's social service districts. Failure of "employable" persons to participate in the operation of the Work Rules results in a loss of assistance.

Like the Work Rules, the federal Work Incentive Program (WIN) is designed to help individuals on welfare "acquire a sense of dignity, self-worth, and confidence which will flow from being recognized as a wage-earning member of society . . . ," 42 U.S.C.A. § 630. The program was enacted as part of the 1967 amendments to the Social Security Act, whereby states were required to incorporate the Work Incentive

Program into their AFDC plans. 42 U.S.C.A. § 602(a)(19), § 630 *et seq.* Every state AFDC plan must provide that certain "employable" individuals, as a condition for receiving aid, shall register for manpower services, training, and employment under regulations promulgated by the Secretary of Labor. 42 U.S.C.A. § 602(a)(19)(A). Available services, to be provided by the State, must include "such health, vocational rehabilitation, counseling, child care, and other such supportive services as are necessary to enable such individuals to accept employment or receive manpower training . . . ." 42 U.S.C.A. § 602(a)(19)(G). After the required services have been provided, the State must certify to the Secretary of Labor those individuals who are ready for employment or training programs. 42 U.S.C.A. §§ 602(a)(19)(G), 632, 633. Employment consists both of work in the regular economy and participation in public service programs. 42 U.S.C.A. §§ 630, 632, 633. As with the Work Rules, cooperation in WIN is necessary for employable individuals to continue to receive assistance.

In the court below, appellees, New York public assistance recipients subject to the Work Rules, challenged those Rules as violative of several provisions of the Constitution and as having been preempted by the WIN provisions of the Federal Social Security Act. The three-judge District Court rejected all but the last contention. 348 F. Supp. 290 (1972). On this point, it held that "for those in the AFDC program, WIN preempts" the New York Work Rules. *Id.*, at 297. As this holding not only affected the continued operation of the New York rules but raised serious doubts as to the viability of the supplementary work programs in 22 states, we set the cause for argument, 409 U.S. 1123, 93 S. Ct. 940, 35 L. Ed. 2d 255 (1973). We now reverse this holding.

I

. . . .

This Court has repeatedly refused to void state statutory programs, absent congressional intent to preempt them.

> "If Congress is authorized to act in a field, it should manifest its intention clearly. It will not be presumed that a federal statute was intended to supersede the exercise of the power of the state unless there is a clear manifestation of intention to do so. The exercise of federal supremacy is not lightly to be presumed." *Schwartz v. Texas*, 344 U.S. 199, 202–03, 73 S. Ct. 232, 235, 97 L. Ed. 231 (1952).

If Congress intended to preempt state plans and efforts in such an important dimension of the AFDC program as employment referrals for those on assistance, such intentions would in all likelihood have been expressed in direct and unambiguous language. No such expression exists however, either in the federal statute or in the committee reports.[15]

Appellees argue, nonetheless, that Congress intended to preempt state work programs because of the comprehensive nature of the WIN legislation, its legislative history,[16] and the alleged conflicts between certain sections of the state and federal laws. We do not agree. We reject, to begin with, the contention that preemption is to be inferred merely from the comprehensive character of the federal work incentive provisions, 42 U.S.C. § 602(a)(19), § 630 *et seq.* The subjects of modern social and

---

[15] No express intention to eliminate co-existing state work programs appears either at the time of the original 1967 enactment of the WIN program, *see* S. Rep. No. 744, 90th Cong., 1st Sess., at 26, 145–57; H.R. Rep. No. 1030, 90th Cong., 1st Sess., at 58–59, U.S. Code Cong. & Admin. News 1967, p. 2834, or at the time of the 1971 amendments.

[16] The court below also asserted that the legislative history was supportive of a preemptive intent, 348 F. Supp., at 297, but no legislative history is cited for that proposition.

regulatory legislation often by their very nature require intricate and complex responses from the Congress but without Congress necessarily intending its enactment as the exclusive means of meeting the problem, *cf. Askew v. American Waterways*, 411 U.S. 325, 93 S. Ct. 1590, 36 L. Ed. 2d 280 (1973). Given the complexity of the matter addressed by Congress in the federal work incentive program, a detailed statutory scheme was both likely and appropriate, completely apart from any questions of preemptive intent. This would be especially the case when the federal work incentive provisions had to be sufficiently comprehensive to authorize and govern programs in states which had no welfare work requirements of their own as well as cooperatively in states with such requirements.

Appellees also rely, as did the District Court, on the legislative history as supporting the view that "the WIN legislation is addressed to all AFDC recipients, leaving no employable recipients to be subject to state work rules." Brief, p. 29. The Court below pointed to no specific legislative history as supportive of its conclusion. Appellees do cite fragmentary statements which we find unpersuasive. Reliance is placed, for example, on a statement in the report of the House Ways and Means Committee on the WIN legislation as follows:

> "Under your committee's bill, states would be required to develop a program *for each appropriate* relative and dependent child which would assure, to the maximum extent possible, that each individual would enter the labor force, *in order to become self-sufficient*. To accomplish this, the states would have to assure that *each* adult in the family, and each child over age 16 who is not attending school is given, when appropriate, employment counseling, testing and job training."

(Emphasis supplied by appellees.) H.R. Rep. No. 544, 90th Cong., 1st Sess., at 16 (1967). At best, this statement is ambiguous as to a possible congressional intention to supersede all state work programs.[19] "Appropriateness," as used in the Committee

---

[19] Perhaps the most revealing legislative expressions confirm, subsequent to enactment, a congressional desire to preserve supplementary state work programs, not to supersede them. In the wake of the invalidation of the New York Work Rules by the three-judge District Court, members of the New York congressional delegation became concerned that the court had misconstrued the intent of Congress. The following colloquy occurred between Senator Buckley of New York and Senator Long of Louisiana, Chairman of the Finance Committee which considered the WIN program prior to approval by the Senate:

"Mr. Buckley: Was it ever the intention of Congress at that time to have the provisions of the WIN statutes preempt the field of employment and training for ADC recipients?

"Mr. Long: I did not have that in mind . . . .

"Mr. Buckley: . . . So far as the distinguished chairman is concerned, was it ever the intention of at least this body to have a preemption in the field?

"Mr. Long: It was never our intention to prevent a State from requiring recipients to do something for their money if they were employable . . . ." 118 Cong. Rec. S. 18492, Oct. 17, 1972.

In the House of Representatives, a similar dialogue took place between Congressman Carey of New York and Congressman Mills, Chairman of the House Ways and Means Committee, which considered the WIN program:

"Mr. Carey: My specific question for the chairman has to do with the intent of the Congress in authorizing the WIN program in 1967 and in amendments to that program in subsequent years. It is my understanding that Congress intended, through the WIN program, merely to assist the states in the critical area of guiding able-bodied welfare recipients toward self-sufficiency — and not to supersede individual state programs designed to achieve the same end. Under this interpretation, New York and other states could operate their own programs as supplementary to the Federal WIN program. Is my understanding of the congressional intent in this area correct?

"Mr. Mills: I agree with the interpretation of my friend, the gentleman from New York, on the matter, so long as the state program does not contravene the provisions of federal law." 118 Cong. Rec., H. 10212, Oct. 17, 1972.

Report, may well mean "appropriateness" solely within the scope and confines of the WIN program. Furthermore, the language employed by Congress in enacting the WIN program must be considered in conjunction with its operational scope and level of funding, which, as will be shown, is quite limited with respect to the total number of employable AFDC recipients, Part II, *infra*.

In sum, our attention has been directed to no relevant argument which supports, except in the most peripheral way, the view that Congress intended, either expressly or impliedly, to preempt state work programs. Far more would be required to show the "clear manifestation of [congressional] intention" which must exist before a federal statute is held "to supersede the exercise" of state action . . . .

II

Persuasive affirmative reasons exist in this case which also strongly negate the view that Congress intended, by the enactment of the WIN legislation, to terminate all existing state work programs and foreclose additional state cooperative programs in the future. We note, first, that the WIN program itself was not designed on its face to be all embracing.

. . . .

It is evident that WIN is a partial program which stops short of providing adequate job and training opportunities for large numbers of state AFDC recipients. It would be incongruous for Congress on the one hand to promote work opportunities for AFDC recipients and on the other to prevent states from undertaking supplementary efforts toward this very same end. We cannot interpret federal statutes to negate their own stated purposes.

. . . .

Moreover, the Department of Health, Education, and Welfare, the agency of government responsible for administering the Federal Social Security Act — including reviewing of state AFDC programs — has never considered the WIN legislation to be preemptive. HEW has followed consistently the policy of approving state plans containing welfare work requirements so long as those requirements are not arbitrary or unreasonable. Congress presumably knew of this settled administrative policy at the time of enactment of WIN, when 21 states had welfare work programs. Subsequent to WIN's passage, HEW has continued to approve state work requirements. Pursuant to such approval, New York has received federal grants in aid for the operation of its AFDC plan, including its work provisions. In interpreting this statute, we must be mindful that "the construction of a statute by those charged with its execution should be followed unless there are compelling indications that it is wrong . . . ." *Red Lion Broadcasting Co. v. FCC*, 395 U.S. 367, 381, 89 S. Ct. 1794, 1802, 23 L. Ed. 2d 371 (1969); *Dandridge v. Williams*, 397 U.S. 471 at 481–482, 90 S. Ct. 1153 at 1159–1160, 25 L. Ed. 2d 491 (1970). In this case, such indications are wholly absent.

New York, furthermore, has attempted to operate the Work Rules in such a manner as to avoid friction and overlap with the WIN program. Officials from both the State Department of Labor and a local Social Service Department testified below that every AFDC recipient appropriate for a WIN program was first referred there, that no person was to be referred to the state program who was participating in a WIN program, and that only if there was no position available for him under WIN, was a recipient to be referred for employment pursuant to state statute. Where coordinate state and federal efforts exist within a complementary administrative framework, and in the pursuit of common purposes, the case for federal preemption becomes a less persuasive one.

III

We thus reverse the holding below that the federal work incentive program preempts the New York Work Rules. Our ruling establishes the validity of a state work program as one means of helping AFDC recipients return to gainful employment. We do not resolve, however, the question of whether some particular sections of the Work Rules might contravene the specific provisions of the Federal Social Security Act.

MR. JUSTICE MARSHALL, with whom MR. JUSTICE BRENNAN joins, dissenting.

Because the Court today ignores a fundamental rule for interpreting the Social Security Act, I must respectfully dissent. As we said in *Townsend v. Swank*, 404 U.S. 282, 286, 92 S. Ct. 502, 505, 30 L. Ed. 2d 448 (1971), "in the absence of congressional authorization for the exclusion clearly evidenced from the Social Security Act or its legislative history, a state eligibility standard that excludes persons eligible for assistance, under federal AFDC standards violates the Social Security Act and is therefore invalid under the Supremacy Clause." . . . The New York Work Rules fall squarely within this statement; they clearly exclude persons eligible for assistance under federal standards, and it could hardly be maintained that they did not impose additional conditions of eligibility. Thus, according to the rules of interpretation we have heretofore followed, the proper inquiry is whether the Social Security Act or its legislative history clearly show congressional authorization for state employment requirements other than those involved in the federal Work Incentive Program.

The answer is that neither the Act nor its legislative history show such an authorization. The only relevant work-related conditions of eligibility in the Act are found at 42 U.S.C. § 602(a)(19) (Supp. I, 1971). In addition to exempting certain persons from registration for and participation in the federal WIN Program, the Act permits states to disregard the needs of persons otherwise eligible for assistance who "have refused without good cause to participate under a work incentive program- . . . or . . . to accept employment in which he is able to engage." 42 U.S.C. § 602(a)(19)(F) (Supp. I, 1971). The Act thus makes actual refusal to participate in a WIN Program or to accept employment a permissible ground for denying assistance. In contrast, New York has adopted the none-too-subtle technique of "deeming" persons not to have accepted employment because they have not, for example, obtained a certain certificate from the local employment office every two weeks. "Deeming" is a familiar legal device to evade applicable requirements by saying that they have been satisfied when they have not in fact been satisfied. But the federal requirement, which the state may not alter without clear congressional authorization, requires an actual refusal to participate in a WIN Program or to accept employment, not a refusal to participate in some other program or a fictitious refusal of employment.

The legislative history of the Social Security Act confirms this interpretation, for whenever Congress legislated with respect to work requirements, it focused on actual refusals to accept employment or to participate in certain special programs clearly authorized by Congress. At no time has Congress authorized states to adopt other work-referral programs or to make refusal to participate in such programs a condition of eligibility, even under the guise of "deeming" such a refusal a refusal to accept employment.

At its inception, the program of aid to dependent children was designed to lessen somewhat the burden of supporting such children . . . .

. . . .

Until 1961, then, the sole emphasis of the Social Security Act's provisions for assistance to dependent children was on preserving the integrity of the family unit. In that year, Congress expanded the definition of dependent child to include children deprived of parental support by reason of the unemployment of a parent. 42 U.S.C. § 607. Families with two parents present could, for the first time, receive assistance, and one parent could leave the home to work without impairing the integrity of the family unit. Congress therefore required states participating in the program for aid to families with an unemployed parent to deny assistance under this provision to individuals who refused to accept bona fide offers of employment. Pub. L. 87-31, 75 Stat. 76 (1961). Refusal of actual offers of employment was clearly the contemplated condition. *See* S. Rep. No. 165, 87th Cong., 1st Sess., at 3 (1961), U.S. Code Cong. & Admin. News 1961, p. 1716. Congress then developed this concept, permitting states to establish "Community Work and Training Programs" of work on public projects, Pub. L. 87-543, 76 Stat. 172, 186 (1962), repealed by Pub. L. 90-248, 81 Stat. 892 (1968). Refusal to accept a work assignment on such a project without good cause would be a ground for denial of public assistance. *See* H.R. Rep. No. 1414, 87th Cong., 2d Sess., at 15 (1962), U.S. Code Cong. & Admin. News 1962, p. 1943.

When Congress established the Work Incentive Program, it did not abandon its previous policies. Recipients of public assistance could be required only to accept bona fide offers of employment or placement in specified programs. There is no indication whatsoever in the legislative history that Congress intended to permit states to deny assistance because potential recipients had refused to participate in programs not supervised by the Secretary of Labor, as WIN Programs are. The parameters of the WIN Program were designed to accommodate Congress' dual interests in guaranteeing the integrity of the family and in maximizing the potential for employment of recipients of public assistance. Without careful federal supervision, of the sort contemplated by the delegation to the Secretary of Labor to establish testing and counseling services and to require that states designed employability plans, 81 Stat. 885, state work programs might upset the accommodation that Congress sought. The Work Incentive Program was thus a carefully coordinated system, whose individual parts fit into an integrated whole. It is hardly surprising that Congress did not expressly or impliedly authorize states to develop independent work programs, since the WIN Program represented Congress' recognition that such programs had to be kept under careful scrutiny if the variety of goals Congress sought to promote were to be achieved. I believe that the Court seriously misconceives the purposes of the federal programs of public assistance, in its apparent belief that Congress had the sole purpose of promoting work opportunities, a purpose that precluding additional state programs would negate. *Ante*, pp. 2515–16.

Instead, Congress has consistently indicated its desire to adopt programs that will enhance the employability of recipients of public assistance while maintaining the integrity of families receiving assistance. A work-referral program can do this only if it is regulated, both as to the persons required to participate and as to the terms on which they must participate. And Congress has consistently recognized that such regulation requires close federal supervision of work programs. In my view, this course of legislation, which is not mentioned by the Court, is neither "ambiguous," "fragmentary," nor "peripheral," *ante*, pp. 2514–15. No matter how it is viewed, however, one cannot fairly say that the Social Security Act or its legislative history clearly evidences congressional authorization for making participation in state work programs a condition of eligibility for public assistance.

The policy of clear statement in *Townsend* serves a useful purpose. It informs legislators that, if they wish to alter the accommodations previously arrived at in an Act of major importance, they must indicate clearly that wish, since what may appear to be minor changes of narrow scope may in fact have ramifications throughout the administration of the Act. A policy of clear statement insures that Congress will consider those ramifications,[11] but only if it is regularly adhered to.

---

[11] In this connection, I cannot let pass without comment *the extraordinary use the Court makes of legislative "history,"* in relying on exchanges on the floor of the House and Senate that occurred *after* the decision by the District Court in this case. *Ante*, n.19. Although reliance on floor exchanges has been criticized in this Court, *Schwegmann Bros. v. Calvert Distillers Corp.*, 341 U.S. 384, 395–97, 71 S. Ct. 745, 751–52, 95 L.

Finally, it is particularly appropriate to require clear statement of authorization to impose additional conditions of eligibility for public assistance. Myths abound in this area. It is widely yet erroneously believed, for example, that recipients of public assistance have little desire to become self-supporting. *See, e.g.,* L. Goodwin, Do the Poor Want to Work? 5, 51–52, 112 (1972). Because the recipients of public assistance generally lack substantial political influence, state legislators may find it expedient to accede to pressures generated by misconceptions. In order to lessen the possibility that erroneous beliefs will lead state legislators to single out politically unpopular recipients of assistance for harsh treatment, Congress must clearly authorize states to impose conditions of eligibility different from the federal standards. As we observed in *King v. Smith*, 392 U.S. 309, 318–19, 88 S. Ct. 2128, 2134, 20 L. Ed. 2d 1118 (1968), this rule leaves the states with "considerable latitude in allocating their AFDC resources, since each state is free to set its own standard of need and to determine the level of benefits by the amount of funds it devotes to the program." The Court today quotes this observation but misses its import. The states have latitude to adjust benefits in the two ways mentioned, but not by imposing additional conditions of eligibility. When across-the-board adjustments like those are made, legislators cannot single out especially unpopular groups for discriminatory treatment.

For these reasons, I would affirm the judgment of the District Court.

NOTES AND QUESTIONS

1. The Court in *Dublino* stated that a clear manifestation of congressional intent must exist before a federal statute is held to supersede the exercise of state action. Should a court even have to look for evidence in legislative history to find such a manifestation? To the extent that legislative history is examined, should a court ever look further than the final committee report?

2. The dissent views the work rules as a set of *eligibility standards* which exclude persons otherwise eligible under federal standards. The majority views the case as a question of preemption and the rules as a *supplementary program.* According to the dissent, Congress must clearly authorize state employment requirements which differ from federal standards. The majority says that a federal program will not preempt a state program unless there is a clear manifestation of congressional intent to do so. Are not both the majority and the dissent using an *absence* of legislative history to arrive at their conclusions? Can reasoning on the basis of the absence of a "clearly" expressed intent be used to justify almost any desired conclusion?

3. In footnote 19, the majority refers to a colloquy between Senators Buckley and Long which occurred after a lower court's invalidation of the work rules. What factors prevent such a colloquy from being persuasive evidence? In his article, Nunez states that one of the barriers to finding legislative intent is often created by lobbyists and legislators opposed to the bill. Is that caveat possibly applicable here? In footnote 11 of his dissenting opinion, Justice Marshall states his objections to the use of a post-enactment colloquy to determine legislative intent. What other arguments are there against this practice? The statute in question was amended in 1967, while the Supreme

---

Ed. 1035 (1951) (Jackson, J., concurring), there is some force to the more generally accepted proposition that such exchanges, particularly when sponsors of a bill or committee chairmen are involved, are relevant to a determination of the purpose Congress sought to achieve in enacting the bill. *United States v. St. Paul, M. & M. R. Co.,* 247 U.S. 310, 318, 38 S. Ct. 525, 528, 62 L. Ed. 1130 (1918). For legislators know how legislative history is made, and they ought to be aware of the importance of floor exchanges. If they disagree with the interpretation placed on the bill in such exchanges, they may offer amendments or vote against it. Thus, Congress, in enacting a statute, may fairly be taken to have endorsed the interpretations offered in such exchanges. None of this is true of post-enactment floor exchanges, which have no bearing on pending legislation and to which a disinterested legislator might well pay scant attention. If Senator Buckley or Representative Carey wished to have a congressional expression of intent on the issue of preemption, they were not barred from introducing legislation.

Court relied on statements made in 1972 to determine legislative intent. Is it not probable, given the five-year lapse, that legislators who voted on the 1967 Amendment were no longer in Congress, and therefore not in a position to enter objections to the interpretation relied on by the Supreme Court?

4. The Court stated that the Department of Health, Education and Welfare had never considered WIN legislation to be preemptive and had followed a consistent pattern of approving state plans containing welfare work requirements, so long as those requirements were not arbitrary or unreasonable. Does the presumption of the Court that Congress knew of the HEW policy have any factual basis? Does the fact that 21 states had such programs strengthen the presumption?

5. The Court also says that the construction of a statute by the agency charged with its execution should be followed unless there are compelling indications that it is wrong. Does the basis for this rule lie in the fact that an administrative agency has been involved with a statute from its enactment, and is therefore closer to the source of congressional intent, while the court only gets involved when there is a dispute — often after many years have passed? If the administrative agency was wrong in the beginning, however, does continuation of a mistake give legitimacy to its interpretation? Or is the rule based upon an assumption that Congress would correct an erroneous interpretation of an agency? If so, are there other factors that might have influenced congressional action to correct the administrative position? What avenues of control over such administrative rules does Congress have?

6. On the problem that *Dublino* addressed, see James J. Brudney, *Congressional Commentary on Judicial Interpretations of Statutes: Idle Chatter or Telling Response?*, 93 MICH. L. REV. 1 (1994).

7. Another example of a court's use of "after-the-fact" legislative history occurred in *NLRB v. Business Mach. & Office Appliance Mechanics Conf. Bd., I.U.E., Local 459*, 228 F.2d 553 (2d Cir. 1955). In his opinion, Judge Lumbard used statements by the principal sponsor of the Taft-Hartley Act (Senator Taft), made two years subsequent to enactment, to support the court's interpretation of a provision in the Act. Taft's statements described the "spirit of the Act" and endorsed a district court's interpretation of the legislative history of the provision. Is it any more justifiable to use such post-enactment statements by a legislator simply because the statement "approves" of a court's interpretation?

The court in *Local 459* also seemed to rely on the fact that President Eisenhower, seven years after the provision's enactment, had given Congress a message that suggested Congress change the Act to make the earlier court's interpretation "explicit." How much weight should be given to a presidential recommendation that Congress amend a statute to conform to a prior judicial interpretation? Does the President's action weaken or enhance the argument for the interpretation he supported?

8. In *Regional Rail Reorganization Act Cases*, 419 U.S. 102 (1975), the Court was considering the validity of a scheme Congress had designed for resolving the takeover and reorganization of a number of bankrupt railroads. One issue was whether the 1973 Rail Act permitted recovery in a suit under the Tucker Act for any shortfall between the liquidation value of the railroads and the compensation they (and ultimately their creditors) would receive under the Rail Act. The Tucker Act allows for suit on a claim against the United States for damage arising out of the operation of "any Act of Congress." If such a suit were not available there would be a taking of property without just compensation in violation of the Fifth Amendment and thus the Rail Act might have to be declared void. In response to evidence of legislative intent offered to show that the Rail Act was intended to withdraw the general availability of suit under the Tucker Act the Court commented:

> Finally, reliance is put upon what is referred to as "subsequent legislative history" in the form of statements by congressmen during Oversight Hearings of the House Subcommittee on Transportation and Aeronautics on June 14,

1974, and on an *amicus* brief filed in this Court on behalf of 36 congressmen. But post-passage remarks of legislators, however explicit, cannot serve to change the legislative intent of Congress expressed before the Act's passage. *See, e.g., United States v. Mine Workers of America,* 330 U.S. 258, 282 (1947). Such statements "represent only the personal views of these legislators, since the statements were [made] after passage of the Act." *National Woodwork Manufacturers Assn. v. NLRB,* 386 U.S. 612, 639 n.34 (1967). Moreover, during oral argument before this Court, Representative Adams, spokesman for the congressional group, expressly conceded that circumstances might arise when the Tucker Act remedy would be available:

"QUESTION: So you do anticipate a situation where the Tucker Act would be available?

"MR. ADAMS: Oh, yes. Let's say, for example, that after this is all over — and this is the three-judge court's problem — that if a party comes in and says, you held us beyond the constitutional limit on erosion and at that point we are of the opinion that it went just too long, it was unreasonable, but that is a specific individual case at that point.

"QUESTION: And so the Tucker Act, you think, would be available in that situation?

"MR. ADAMS: Of course. *We did not repeal the Tucker Act."* (Emphasis supplied.)

In sum, we cannot find that the legislative history supports the argument that the Rail Act should be construed to withdraw the Tucker Act remedy. The most that can be said is that the Rail Act is ambiguous on the question. In that circumstance, applicable canons of statutory construction require us to conclude that the Rail Act is not to be read to withdraw the remedy under the Tucker Act. (419 U.S. at p. 132)

In dissent, Justice Douglas noted in a footnote:

The Court properly notes that these post-enactment expressions should be treated with caution, a warning that applies as much to the "relatively spontaneous responses of counsel to equally spontaneous questioning from the Court" (419 U.S. at p. 173, note 15).

Is Justice Douglas correct? Does Congressman Adams' appearance on behalf of 36 congressmen have sufficient authority in this matter, as architect of the Rail Act, so that the Court could have relied on his statements, had they been contemporaneous with its enactment?

Should a distinction be made on the basis of comments made at a hearing session rather than those resulting from floor debate? Is it relevant whether the remarks came in the context of consideration of a related legislative matter? What is the element that makes such statements open to challenges that they are irrelevant and unpersuasive?

9. *See generally* Marc R. Perman, Comment, *Statutory Interpretation in California: Individual Testimony as an Extrinsic Aid,* 15 U.S.F. L. REV. 241 (1981).

OTTO J. HETZEL,
INSTILLING LEGISLATIVE INTERPRETATION SKILLS IN THE CLASSROOM AND THE COURTROOM,
48 UNIVERSITY OF PITTSBURGH LAW REVIEW 663, 685–86 (1987) ᐧ

D. *The Invalidity of Post-Enactment Legislative History*

One final area of interpretive doctrine that suggests the need to provide ample opportunity to examine and assess legislative interpretation techniques relates to the relatively common but inappropriate practice of extending the use of legislative history

---

to actions occurring after enactment of a measure. Such post-enactment legislative history may include use of affidavits or testimony of a legislator in judicial proceedings to explain his or the body's intent in enacting the law, record statements or floor colloquy relating to a previously enacted measure, and assertions in committee reports or statements concerning the body's original intent made in amending an act. While each of these may have been valid items of legislative history had they occurred prior to enactment of the provision they attempt to explain, it should be clear that use of such after-the-fact history is unreliable and should be rejected out of hand. No controls exist. A vote on a measure is not pending. How does one ensure that such later rationalizations are indeed the proper interpretation of the statute, since they were neither apparent nor expressed before enactment? While hindsight may indicate that certain matters should have been clarified, more fully explained and resolved, attempts to do so after enactment should be given *no* weight.

Legislative history is of value in determining intent. By its very nature, however, it does not have the impact of the legislative language on which the vote was taken. Legislative history prior to the taking of a vote is thought to have value because it reflects the sources of information on which those voting relied in casting their vote. Giving any weight to post-enactment history in interpreting a statute is unjustified, because it assigns a value to these expressions that is unrelated to their use by the body. Such utterances are disembodied from the legislative process and therefore are invalid means of ascertaining the reasons for enacting any provision. Since they were not relied upon by the enacting body and cannot easily be counteracted by those who might disagree, no reliability should attach to such statements.

Far too many courts, however, having learned that legislative history has some value, find it difficult to reject completely post-enactment history.[72] Obviously, a legislature acts only through legislation. Any post-enactment rationalization is clearly suspect. Its rejection is similar to the rationale for our unwillingness to hear, let alone accept jurors' subsequent explanations for their actions, or misunderstandings. If not expressed before the vote is taken, too many other factors can influence subsequent expressions of the basis for a legislator's position or his understanding of a provision. Legislators are buffeted by many forces, and the temptation to please all sides by generating new justifications after a vote could be overwhelming at times.

NOTES AND QUESTIONS

1. For other discussions of post-enactment legislative history, see Daniel A. Farber & Philip P. Frickey, *Legislative Intent and Public Choice*, 74 VA. L. REV. 423, 465–68 (1988) (moderately supportive); William N. Eskridge, *The New Textualism*, 37 UCLA L. REV. 621, 636–37 (1990) (moderately supportive); Lawrence C. Marshall, *"Let Congress Do It": The Case for an Absolute Rule of Statutory Stare Decisis*, 88 MICH. L. REV. 177, 193–96 (1989) (opposed); William N. Eskridge, Jr., *Post-Enactment Legislative Signals*, 57 LAW & CONTEMP. PROBS. 75 (Winter, 1994).

2. For Justice Scalia's views, see the following concurring opinion in *Sullivan v. Finkelstein*, 496 U.S. 617, 631 (1990):

JUSTICE SCALIA, concurring in part.

I join the opinion of the Court, except for footnote 8, which responds on the merits to "two arguments based on subsequent legislative history." *Ante*, at 631, n.8.

The legislative history of a statute is the history of its consideration and enactment. "Subsequent legislative history" — which presumably means the *post*-enactment history of a statute's consideration and enactment — is a contradiction in terms. The phrase is used to smuggle into judicial consideration

---

[72] *See, e.g., New York State Dept. of Social Servs. v. Dublino*, 413 U.S. 405, 416 n.19 (1973).

legislators' expressions *not* of what a bill currently under consideration means (which, the theory goes, reflects what their colleagues understood they were voting for), but of what a law *previously enacted* means.

It seems to be a rule for the use of subsequent legislative history that the legislators or committees of legislators whose post-enactment views are consulted must belong to the institution that passed the statute. Never, for example, have I seen floor statements of Canadian MPs cited concerning the meaning of a United States statute; only statements by Members of Congress qualify. No more connection than that, however, is required. It is assuredly *not* the rule that the legislators or committee members in question must have considered, or at least voted upon, the particular statute in question — or even that they have been members of the particular Congress that enacted it. The subsequent legislative history rejected as inconclusive in today's footnote, for example, tells us (according to the Court's analysis) what committees of the 99th and 95th Congresses thought the 76th Congress intended.

In my opinion, the views of a legislator concerning a statute already enacted are entitled to no more weight than the views of a judge concerning a statute not yet passed. In some situations, of course, the expression of a legislator relating to a previously enacted statute may bear upon the meaning of a provision in a bill under consideration — which provision, if passed, may in turn affect judicial interpretation of the previously enacted statute, since statutes *in pari materia* should be interpreted harmoniously. Such an expression would be useful, if at all, not because it was subsequent legislative history of the earlier statute, but because it was plain old legislative history of the later one.

Arguments based on subsequent legislative history, like arguments based on antecedent futurity, should not be taken seriously, not even in a footnote.

3. Judge Richard Posner provided a further observation:

Ordinarily a committee report that is not explaining new or altered statutory language has little significance in the interpretation of a statute. *Public Employees Retirement System v. Betts*, 492 U.S. 158, 109 S. Ct. 2854, 2861, 106 L. Ed. 2d 134 (1989). Suppose a congressional committee issued a report expressing disagreement with a decision by the Supreme Court interpreting a provision of the Sherman Act unchanged since 1890. The report might be persuasive document by virtue of the cogency of its reasoning but it would have no *legislative* significance. Congress legislates by passing bills and sending them to the President for his signature. It does not legislate by issuing committee reports. *Prussner v. United States*, 896 F.2d 218, 228 (7th Cir. 1990) (en banc); *In re Sinclair*, 870 F.2d 1340 (7th Cir. 1989). Post-enactment legislative history (an oxymoron — the history of an event lies in its past, not its future) is sometimes a sneaky device for trying to influence the interpretation of a statute, in derogation of the deal struck in the statute itself among the various interests represented in the legislature. *Covalt v. Carey Canada Inc.*, 860 F.2d 1434, 1438–39 (7th Cir. 1988); *In re Tarnow*, 749 F.2d 464, 467 (7th Cir. 1984). Courts must be careful not to fall for such tricks and thereby upset a legislative compromise.

American Hosp. Ass'n v. NLRB, 899 F.2d 651, 657 (7th Cir. 1990), *aff'd*, 499 U.S. 606, 111 S. Ct. 1539 (1991). How does Judge Posner's view differ from Justice Scalia's?

4. For a state judge's discussion of subsequent legislative history, see *State v. Brantley*, 56 P.3d 1252, 1270–71 (Haw. 2002) (Acoba, J., dissenting).

3. A Caveat

In reading the following materials, keep in mind the realistic alternatives to using legislative history for ascertaining the meaning of statutes as well as the practical advantages of utilizing legislative intent and purpose as an aid in interpreting statutes.

STEPHEN WASBY,
**LEGISLATIVE MATERIALS AS AN AID TO
STATUTORY INTERPRETATION: A CAVEAT,**
12 JOURNAL OF PUBLIC LAW 262 (1963) *

Sufficient attention has not been devoted to the relative probative value of the legislative materials which the courts use, such as committee reports, hearing transcripts, and records of debates, and it is primarily with this point that this article will deal. Situations in which the materials are used to determine the coverage of a particular statute are the concern here. Only materials accompanying a statute through the legislative process will be considered.

It will also be assumed that the materials are at some times actually used by the courts to attain the answer for which they are searching, and not solely as ex post facto rationalization for a position already reached by intuition, considerations of public policy, or some other method. Judges do not make clear the relation of the materials to their decisions, nor with few exceptions do they reveal whether they have any reservations about the use of these materials, generally giving the impression that they accept at face value the documents they examine and cite.

. . . .

The possibilities of misleading evidence are legion. One deception comes from the fact that some records are in a sense too complete, that is, they contain material that does not come to the attention of most of the legislators. The *Congressional Record* is full of inclusions placed there by members of Congress in deference to their constituents, material which may be noticed by congressmen's legislative assistants or clerks but not called to their superiors' attention. Despite the image of Congress, and particularly of the Senate, as a great debating society, in a large number of instances only a few men may be on the floor listening to speeches which in many cases are clearly not part of a debate. If they have not heard the speech, they may have read the material in the Record — or they may not. But the fact that it is in writing does not mean that all who must vote on an issue have seen the material. A further point is that when members of Congress amend their spoken remarks before they appear in print in the *Congressional Record*, then not even those parts of the Record which are purportedly a verbatim account of actual proceedings will be completely accurate.

Judges attempt to rely initially on the bill as passed in final form. However, at times what the legislators vote on is not the bill itself, but a paraphrase which a committee has prepared. There may thus be two versions available to the legislators — the original, complex version, and a much simpler restatement. The judge thus has to try to guess which one was the basis of the legislators' decision. However, the legislators may not have used even the simpler committee version. In the rush at the end of a legislative session, and at other times as well, a legislator may turn to a colleague he perceives as a specialist on the subject under consideration and ask for advice as to how to vote, or at least for information on which the vote will be based. In certain situations, the interpretations of a lobbyist or constituent may be accepted as determinative of the direction of the legislator's vote. As Donald Matthews points out, it is almost impossible to be a "legislative generalist"; legislators specialize and draw on the complementary specializations of their colleagues. Certainly much of this exchanged information is not

* Stephen Wasby, Legislative Materials as an Aid to Statutory Interpretation: A Caveat, 12 J. Pub. L. 262 (1963). Reprinted by permission of the Emory Law Journal of the Emory University School of Law.

part of the written record, which is incomplete to that extent.

. . . .

The committee often does approximate the position of delegate or agent of the legislative body as a whole, doing the latter's work as a substitute for its full consideration of the matter in question. There are many times when the committee becomes, for a particular piece of legislation, a body superior to the rest of the legislature in that its decisions will be approved quickly and without debate by the legislature; the work of the legislature is carried out predominantly in committees, and the body as a whole does not have time to supervise the work of all of them. At other times, the committee does much of the groundwork for the larger body, and provides many of the tentative decisions which the larger body may or may not make final. Much the same pattern is true of subcommittees in relation to the committee of which they are a part. The word of committees must be accepted almost on faith by the legislators in many situations if the work of the legislature is to be accomplished; if the legislature as a whole is to review de novo all the material the committee examined, the value of the committee as a timesaving device would be radically reduced. "The tendency . . . is for the standing committees to set policy that the whole legislature usually follows." Where such simple "rubber stamping" or ratification occurs, it may not be particularly inaccurate for the courts to take the statement of committee members to indicate intent. However, committees are not always representative of the general membership; they are not each a random sample of the larger body, nor are they fractional committees of the whole. They deal with particular subject matter areas, and attract people who have a particular *expertise* or are interested in those areas, in enacting or blocking legislation concerning that topic. When seniority operates, it adds another and extremely important factor distorting the representative character of the committee in relation to the legislature as a whole.

. . . .

What several authors suggest as various functions of committee hearings serve to point out the limitations of using the transcripts as conclusive or even preponderant evidence of committee, or legislative, intent. Truman goes so far as to say that the transmittal of information is probably both the most familiar and "probably the least important" function of the committee hearing. Access to committee members is frequently established before hearings are conducted, and it has been said that if a person needs to appear at a hearing to make his point, one can infer that he carries relatively little weight with the committee. This approaches the view which assumes that all political activity is conducted behind the scenes. While the view is extreme, it has its core of sense. Perhaps the hearing is not the best place for a group to attempt persuasion, particularly when it has access to committee members in other ways.

Possibly a more important function than that of transmitting information is that of making a public record of information already transmitted to committee members. "The hearings themselves, if held, serve as the forum in which all of the conflicting or interlocking claims of fact and of equity, by now thoroughly familiar to all active participants, are publicly recorded." And a still more critical value of the hearing may be to release steam, to operate as a safety valve for the conflicting interests so that pressure will not develop to the point where more serious — and more difficult to control — conflict would occur.

. . . .

If judges take intentions of committees, in so far as these can be determined from the committee documents, as evidence of legislative intent or as an effective substitute for it, on the grounds that committees do much of the work on proposed legislation and that the legislation originates with them, perhaps they should be aware that much of the legislation, at least in the form of draft statutes, arises at a stage prior to committee consideration. For example, the committee may rely on its technical staff to draft a bill for consideration, although this may be done after the committee has decided basically what it intends to include in the legislation. Or the committee may work from a proposal submitted by a lobbyist. In the states, a legislative counsel's office may do the bill-drafting work, or the state bar association may provide a bill-drafting service during legislative sessions.

The man who actually writes the law is not usually a Senator or Representative. He is a lawyer employed either by a government department or by a politically influential group of citizens which is trying to get the law passed . . . . The officials and clients are the people who know what the law is supposed to say, and in whose minds is born the "intention" behind the original choice of words. Only then does it reach a congressional committee which is told what it later will be said to have "intended."

NOTE

It is hardly surprising that some abuses in the recording of legislative history have occurred. One noteworthy example was creation of a 4,500-page record of the budget hearings on the Departments of Labor and Health, Education and Welfare for fiscal 1977. Nothing in the document disturbed the impression it was a verbatim transcription of live hearings. In fact, approximately half of the published "hearings" had been canceled and never held. Prepared texts of the "hearings" were inserted, complete with quoted "remarks" of committee members who were not present. Room numbers of hearing rooms were listed as well as the commencement and adjournment times for the nonexistent hearings.

The hearing record had been praised before the discovery of its actual character as a "complete," unusually timely and well researched committee report of hearings. After challenge, a spokesman asserted that the editing would be done "differently" in the future. *See* H. Smeck Jr., *8-Volume Record of Hearings That Were Never Held Is Published, With Full Quotations, by Senate Panel*, N.Y. TIMES, Oct. 4, 1976, at C-15, col. 1.

The *Congressional Record*, because of its nature as an edited, rather than verbatim, record of floor discussions, has also been abused. Until 1978, there was no distinction made in the Record's pages between speeches which were actually read on the House or Senate floor and those simply inserted without having been read aloud. This situation sometimes created confusion about what had occurred and even generated the macabre — in December, 1972, a Christmas message from Representative Hale Boggs of Louisiana to his House colleagues was contained in the Record two days after his airplane disappeared in Alaska.

More serious difficulties have arisen from the use of inserted statements that were not heard by the body or included in discussions before votes were taken. For example, interpretations of legislation have unwittingly been based on debate which never took place. In such circumstances, no opportunity exists for opposing views to be presented in response nor can objections be made to misstatements. *See* R. Madden, *Changes Are Sought in Congressional Record*, N.Y. TIMES, Oct. 16, 1977, at A-28, col. 1.

Since March, 1978, a large black dot or "bullet" has been placed at the beginning and end of material not actually uttered on the floor. The potential for misleading readers of the Record still exists, however, since a member of Congress need only read the first few sentences of a speech in person and the entire text will appear as if read.

Production of the Record is a major undertaking. As Madden notes:

> It is a $16-million-a-year operation that requires about 800 workers and 100 Linotype machines to produce what is said to be the equivalent of three major metropolitan newspapers overnight for a limited circulation of about 44,000.

> . . . An issue of the Record now averages about 256 pages, with more than 500,000 words. (A weekday issue of The New York Times has about 160,000 words in its news columns.)

Transcripts of the floor proceedings, prepared mostly from the shorthand scribbles of the official reporters of debates working in relays on the floor, are typed in rooms near each chamber, where members or their aides can go to edit their remarks. Couriers begin taking the copy to the printing office about 6 P.M. The aim is to send the first printed copies of the Record back to the Capitol by 7 A.M. About 40 copies are also delivered to the doorsteps of senators and representatives who live in the District of Columbia.

Thomas F. McCormick, the public printer in charge of the printing office, and John J. Boyle, his deputy, estimate that 30 percent of each day's Record is taken down by the official reporters, with the remaining 70 percent consisting of prepared statements and articles to be reprinted from other publications.

The *Congressional Record*, thus, constitutes a timely and valuable source of legislative history, which is extremely useful when it is properly understood.

NOTES AND QUESTIONS

1. In light of the preceding, how do you view the credibility and reliability of congressional legislative history? Does the usefulness of legislative history outweigh the potential of possible deception or manipulation of the legislative record? Is it possible to view legislative history with a presumption of accuracy or truthfulness? Is the primary deficiency of the legislative record misrepresentation of the proceedings as official, or falsification of data? If the former, was the data appropriate for consideration by Congress? Does this usefulness justify inclusion of materials not actually presented on the floor as appropriate for the interpretation of statutes? Does it matter whether the members had access to the "revised" materials before they voted? In assessing the weight or even relevancy of legislative history, how important is access to it (or at least the potential of access) by the voting members?

2. Based on recent changes, how should courts treat "bulleted" parts of the Record? Are these inserted materials any less appropriate for ascertaining legislative intent than non-inserted materials? Will the use of "bullets" be swallowed up by the exception for speeches partially read on the floor? Do you expect that legislators will change their tactics regarding the insertion of materials into the Record due to the new rule? How?

3. Five minutes before the House vote on the 1968 Civil Rights Act, Title VIII Fair Housing, then-Minority Leader Gerald Ford inserted in the *Congressional Record* a lengthy analysis by Minority Counsel on the potential reach of the various provisions in the Title. What effect should such a document have for purposes of ascertaining legislative intent?

4. Is the structure of the legislative record system inherently susceptible to abuse? Are these abuses sufficient to exclude all extrinsic evidence of legislative goals as the English apparently do?

5. What is the major formal purpose of congressional hearings? Is this purpose avoided by publishing the records of hearings which were never held? As the opinion of the committee "holding" the hearings, are such records any less valuable than other hearing records? What significance for legislative history purposes is the maxim that "if the committee hasn't made up its mind prior to the hearing, it don't have one."

6. Considering the huge volume of material printed in it and the speed with which it is made available, one can be amazed that the Record is as accurate as it is.

GREGG v. BARRETT
771 F.2d 539 (D.C. Cir. 1985)

Mikva, Circuit Judge:

Appellants, who are Members of Congress, lawyers and academicians, ask this court to address their contention that the Congressional Record is not properly prepared by the responsible officials of the Congress. The District Court dismissed the complaint brought by appellants on the ground that the Speech or Debate Clause of Art. I, § 6 of the United States Constitution precluded any jurisdiction to hear the complaint. We affirm the dismissal of the complaint, albeit on different but related grounds.

. . . .

The gist of the complaint is that the Congressional Record is not a faithful transcript of what actually is said on the floor of the House and of the Senate. All of the appellants claim that the first amendment warrants their claim. The congressional appellants, for example, insist that they have a constitutional right to transmit an "accurate" report of congressional proceedings to their constituents, and that it is equally important that they receive an accurate transcript so that they can perform their congressional duties. The lawyer appellants claim that they need an accurate record to serve as the legislative history of statutes passed by the Congress.

Although Art. I, § 5, cl. 3 of the United States Constitution requires that "Each House shall keep a Journal of its Proceedings, and from time to time publish the same," these official journals are abbreviated versions of congressional proceedings, recording only major acts taken by the respective Houses. They are separate and distinct from the Congressional Record, the document involved in this action. Prior to 1846, debates in Congress were not officially reported. Private publications, such as the National Intelligence, the Register of Debates, and the Congressional Globe, however, began regularly publishing partial texts of debates. *See* 126 Cong. Rec. 18775, 18776 (1980) (statement of Sen. Byrd) (historical address); McPherson, *Reporting the Debates of Congress*, 28 Q.J. Speech 141, 142–46 (1942).

The transition to official publication began in 1846, when the Senate authorized each member to subscribe for twelve copies of the Congressional Globe; the House followed suit in 1847. The two Houses attempted to contract with private printers to transcribe all debates and to furnish those debates to the Congressional Globe to publish. When these contracts failed, the Government Printing Office took on the responsibility for publishing the Congressional Record, and the House and Senate hired reporters to transcribe their debates. *See* McPherson, *supra*, at 148.

Appellants claim that Congress committed itself to publishing an "accurate" Record, and cite the congressional declaration that: "The Joint Committee on Printing shall control the arrangement and style of the Congressional Record, and while providing that *it shall be a substantially verbatim report of proceedings*, shall take all needed action for the reduction of unnecessary bulk." Act of January 12, 1895, ch. 23, § 13, 28 Stat. 603, codified in 44 U.S.C. § 901 (1982) (emphasis added). Appellants point to other internal rules designed to create an accurate Record; among these is the "bullet rule," which provides: "Only as aid in distinguishing the manner of delivery in order to contribute to the historical accuracy of the Record, statements or insertions in the Record where no part of them was spoken will be preceded and followed by a 'bullet' symbol . . . ." *Laws and Rules of Publication of the Congressional Record*, 130 Cong. Rec. App. (daily ed. Feb. 2, 1984).

The thrust of appellants' complaint is that these rules governing the accuracy of the Record are routinely broken by individual members of Congress. Appellants attached to their complaint a copy of an article by James Nathan Miller, *Congress's License to Lie*, Reader's Digest, Feb. 1983, at 72, written as an open letter to Congress, which details examples of alleged distortion of the Record . . . .

II. *Analysis*

We offer neither criticism nor defense of the congressional practice. Like the philosophy of the Speech or Debate Clause used by the District Court, *Gregg v. Barrett*, 594 F. Supp. 108 (D.D.C. 1984), to reject appellants' claims, our analysis precludes this Court from reviewing congressional practices and procedures when they primarily and directly affect the way Congress does its legislative business.

. . . .

Basically, the congressional appellants seek a more accurate reporting of proceedings in the Record. There are at least two ways that the congressional appellants could achieve this end through resort to the legislative process. First, they could convince other members to insist on enforcement of existing rules. For example, appellants could monitor the Record for inaccuracies and request the consent of the House or Senate to strike out clearly inaccurate passages. The House Rules provide, for example, that in revising his speech, a member may not place a different aspect on the remarks of a colleague. House Rules § 928. A congressional plaintiff, concerned that his remarks or the remarks of a colleague had been distorted by another member in his written submissions to the Record, could move to have that portion of the Record stricken. *Id.* Second, as a more permanent solution, appellants could convince their congressional fellows to adopt a rule of verbatim accuracy, ending all controversy about the extent of permissible distortions of the Record. As the article on which the appellants largely base their claim puts it: "all [Congress] has to do is pass a resolution adopting the practice that has been followed by the Canadian and British parliaments for decades: all words spoken on the floor are recorded verbatim in the *Record*." Miller, *Congress's License to Lie*, Reader's Digest, Feb. 1983, at 87. Similarly, the Advisory Committee on Automation has found that "[i]f, in the future, the leadership should desire a completely verbatim transcript such as is produced in a courtroom, it need only give the word and the changeover will be accomplished." Advisory Committee on Automation and Standardization of Congressional Publications, 95th Cong., 2d Sess., Current Procedures and Production Processes of the Congressional Record 70–71 (Comm. Print 1978).

The court notes that, within the last few months, House Members, including the appellants, have sought and obtained some of the relief which the doctrine of equitable discretion leaves to Congress. After extensive and partisan debate, the House of Representatives agreed to H. Res. 230, the Accuracy in House Proceedings Resolution. 131 Cong. Rec. H6893–97 (daily ed. July 31, 1985). This resolution directs the Joint Committee on Printing to print in the Congressional Record a "substantially verbatim account of remarks actually spoken during the proceedings of the House" in typeface that is clearly distinguishable from the typeface used for "any remarks not actually spoken but inserted under permission to extend remarks." This rule will continue in force for the remainder of the first session of the current Ninety-ninth Congress, and the Committee on House Administration will then report to the House its findings and its recommendation as to whether the rule should be continued. By reaching a provisional political solution and expressly contemplating later evaluation and modification of that solution, Congress underscores the wisdom of this court's non-entanglement in the House's preparation of the Congressional Record.

NOTES AND QUESTIONS

1. Is Judge Mikva correct that the legislative solutions to the problem are realistic? Could there be a judicially-ordered solution?

2. It should be noted that Judge Mikva was himself a member of the Illinois Legislature and, later, a member of Congress before he became a judge. *See generally* Mikva, *Reading and Writing Statutes*, 48 U. Pitt. L. Rev. 627 (1987).

3. Federal Circuit Court Judge Frank Coffin offered the following comments concerning the use of legislative history in an advocacy setting:

There is often some law or legislative history imperfectly reflected in the briefs that can be decisive . . . . I am rarely satisfied with what the parties report as legislative history. Perhaps this skepticism stems from my own days as a legislator, when I listened to many debates and many remarks "for the record" that had absolutely nothing to do with the outcome. I rarely read a complete legislative debate or committee report without gaining insights not found in the briefs.

I recall one appeal where all of the case authority, some seven or eight cases, was unanimous that the legislative history behind a statute commanded a certain result. The result seemed to be at odds with national policy in this area. A search was indicated and proved productive. It revealed that the eighth case relied on the previous seven, the seventh on the previous six, and so on, back to the first decision, a rather conclusory lower court decision based on a few extracts from the legislative debates. Reading the entire debate placed the matter in quite a different light. Our opinion made so bold as to take on all prior authority. The case went to the Supreme Court, where we were affirmed, the Court obviously being just as impressed as we were by a look at the whole legislative history.

FRANK COFFIN, THE WAYS OF A JUDGE 167–68 (1980).

4.   State Legislative History

Unlike Congress, most state legislatures do not keep extensive records of legislative proceedings. This results mostly from concern with the costs of recordkeeping. State legislative records are usually confined to *de minimis* English-style procedural notes and journals, with relatively few arguments presented. State legislative history is commonly inferred by the courts from the following sources:

Judicial constructions of similar statutes in other states;

National debates for uniform statutes;

Presumptions based on reenactment after judicial or administrative interpretation;

Reports of law revision commissions;

Governor's messages or calls to the legislature;

Occasional committee studies;

Amendments offered to statutes or bills; and

Comparisons to language in other statutes of the state.

Finally, state courts often cite preambles and statements of purpose, as well as presumptions and canons of construction applied to the language of the statute itself.

ROBERT M. RHODES, JOHN WESLEY WHITE & ROBERT S. GOLDMAN, THE SEARCH FOR INTENT: AIDS TO STATUTORY CONSTRUCTION IN FLORIDA,
6 FLORIDA STATE UNIVERSITY LAW REVIEW 383, 391–402 (1978)[*]

Florida appellate court cases are noticeably silent on the use of standing committee reports to assess legislative intent. This appears to result from two facts: (1) committee reports on bills are not required by the Florida Senate and House of Representatives, and (2) reports which are prepared are often misplaced and ultimately inaccessible.

Legislative committees in Florida do, however, prepare reports on many bills. Generally, these reports are written to support legislation developed de novo by a committee, although, less frequently, reports are prepared to explain legislation which has been referred to the committee for consideration and recommendation. In many instances, these reports are prepared for use by the committee itself, or for release to the public, and do not appear to be intended to educate or persuade the general membership of the legislature. More often, when the purpose is to persuade the members of the whole body, materials take the form of "fact sheets" or memoranda which are extremely transitory and are rarely retained beyond the time of floor consideration of the bill. When full reports are prepared, there is generally an adequate

---

effort to disseminate the report to interested persons, although it is not unusual for the personnel of the legislative library incidentally or randomly to discover an oversight in providing the library with a copy of a report.

In 1976, the legislature enacted chapter 76–276, which requires the house and the senate to "consider the economic impact . . . legislation will have upon the public and the agencies of government" prior to enactment of any general or special law. Committees of both houses implement this law by preparing "Economic Impact Statements" (EIS). These are generally updated as necessary as bills are amended by various committees and distributed to legislators on the floor. After a bill is passed, a copy of the EIS is filed with the legislative library along with the bill, indexed by bill number.

. . . .

When substantive reports on legislation other than EIS's are received by the legislative library, they are coded by subject matter and are incorporated into the materials held by the library. Although appropriate as a procedure for a legislative reference library, this process does not build productive resources for researching legislative intent.

Whether or not committee reports are filed with the legislative library, committee offices generally retain copies of reports which have been produced on specific legislation, but there is no requirement to do so, and retrieval or location of such reports in committee files several years after enactment may be difficult. Despite conscientious work by the legislative library, one must conclude that retention of reports of standing committees in a manner which might be helpful to research on legislative intent is haphazard at best. These are indeed the most important of extrinsic aids. And lack of adequate access to these reports undoubtedly has contributed to the paucity of appellate decisions relying on these aids.

V. *Reports of Special Committees*

Reports of standing committees at the state level often include only the committee's recommendation regarding a measure. Frequently, however, special committees are created specifically to investigate problem areas and propose legislation. The reports of these committees are generally extensive, and the courts have found them useful aids in construing statutes enacted pursuant to committee recommendation.

> Reliance on . . . the committee reports can be justified in two ways. First, because of their specialization and the concentration of their experience, these committees possess a good deal of expertise in their respective areas. Second, since the legislature establishes the committees for specific purposes, it is reasonable to assume that in voting for the bill the legislature accepts the definition of its purpose promulgated by the committee.[43]

Many states have also established revision commissions to study and recommend legislation. The courts generally treat the reports and comments of these commissions in the same fashion as reports of special committees of the legislature. Similar treatment is often accorded reports and notes of national commissions . . . .

Special or select committees and commissions in Florida are much more likely to present specific reports on proposed legislation than standing committees. Many of the same problems associated with location and retrieval of standing committee reports also apply to reports of special committees or commissions. However, the singular focus of these special groups may make their submittals more formal and visible. Florida appellate courts have not yet relied on a report of special committee or a state

---

[43] Comment, *Statutory Construction — Legislative Use of Extrinsic Aids in Wisconsin*, 1964 Wis. L. Rev. 660, 663–64.

commission to establish legislative intent. However, the cases suggest that the courts would be favorably disposed to rely upon such aids.

VI. *Reports of Conference Committees*

Reports of conference committees become particularly important where the language differs in the versions of similar legislation passed by the two houses. This importance springs from the fact that usually a conference committee recommendation cannot be amended by either house, but must be either accepted or rejected.

Few courts outside the federal system have been presented with conference committee reports. However, when such reports are used, they are likely to receive great weight . . . .

A review of the journals of the Florida Senate and the Florida House of Representatives reveals that reports of conference committees generally take the form of brief letters of transmittal to the officers of the two houses, recommending specific amendments to reconcile the differing versions of the legislation. Little is revealed about explicit legislative intent, although much can be inferred by the adoption of one alternative instead of another. In some instances, comparison summaries are made among the house, senate, and conference committee recommendations. Usually, however, these are informal "fact sheets" revealing very little about intent and they are not systematically retained.

Perhaps the closest thing to a true conference committee report in Florida is the "Letter of Intent" signed by the chairmen of the senate and house committees responsible for appropriations. This letter is prepared collaboratively by the staffs of these committees, purportedly as a result of matters resolved by the respective committees and/or the appropriations conference committee. The letter is usually prepared after adjournment of the legislature. It is not available to the membership of the legislature when voting on final passage of the appropriations bill. Nonetheless, it is a potentially valuable source of information for the courts in determining legislative intent in state fiscal and administrative matters.

VII. *Committee Hearings*

The federal courts are willing to consider records of committee proceedings in construing statutes, but other extrinsic aids (*e.g.* committee reports) may carry more evidentiary weight. Judicial reliance on committee proceedings has been criticized. Wasby points out the dangers of resorting to such materials:

> Although a hearing transcript does provide some indication of the intention of some of the committee members, at best it provides only partial evidence. Hearings may, for example, be held by only those committee members interested in the passage of the legislation, or in its defeat. The questioning of witnesses is not unlikely to be conducted with the aim of eliciting support for the questioner's position or discrediting the statements of hostile or unfavorable witnesses, and the latter may not be as well represented as those taking the majority view, because of invitations the committee has extended to those it already favors.[57]

Nevertheless, courts are likely to continue to consider statements made at committee hearings where the records are available. Certainly, one may assume that judges will exercise reasoned judgment in relying on these materials. The weight attached to committee proceedings as extrinsic aids should vary with their reliability as disclosed by the circumstances of each factual situation.

---

[57] *A Caveat, supra* note 15, at 272.

In Florida, although committee proceedings are almost always taped, these tapes usually are not transcribed. Some committees forward their tapes to the legislative library, where they are retained for an indefinite period. Other committees do not deliver their tapes to the library. Rather, they erase them for re-use or retain them indefinitely. Thus, the researcher interested in Florida legislative committee proceedings must determine: (1) whether the proceeding was taped; (2) if so, whether the tape still exists; and (3) if so, where it is located. In many cases, the difficulties associated with making these determinations are insurmountable. The result is a complete absence of case law in Florida in which committee hearings have been offered to prove legislative intent.

VIII. *Floor Debates*

Courts have generally refused to consider statements made during floor debate as evidence of legislative intent. Various reasons have been advanced for this rule. Some legislators may not have been present during floor debate. Often what is said in debate is for the benefit of constituents only and may be regarded by courts as self-serving. Furthermore, supporters of a controversial measure may fear that too much explanation and discussion will cause its defeat, and thus they attempt to minimize debate. At the federal level, congressmen have been free to amend their remarks before publication, so the record may not accurately reflect the proceedings.

. . . .

Because most states do not maintain records of legislative debates,[73] few state courts have had the opportunity to consider their probative value. In Florida, floor debates in both houses are recorded but are rarely transcribed. Tapes are kept in the offices of the clerk of the house of representatives and the secretary of the senate. Both officers stress, however, that the manner of recordation and storage makes these tapes informal working tools rather than official records of legislative proceedings. Neither house has a formal policy on retention of tapes, although current practice is to retain them indefinitely pending the development of such a policy. Both houses maintain a cooperative attitude toward supplying copies of tapes of floor debates to interested person, and a high-speed tape copying machine has been acquired to facilitate this service.

IX. *Journals*

American courts uniformly utilize legislative journals to track changes in a bill as it proceeds through the enactment process. Florida decisions are in harmony with the other jurisdictions. In *State ex rel. Finlayson v. Amos*, the court consulted the journals and relied on the action taken on amendments:

> It was through no mere inadvertence that the Legislature did this [changed the basis for fixing the price of a license on a given class of vehicle], because the amendment was first considered and adopted in the House, next considered and rejected in the Senate, then considered by a conference committee composed of members from both houses, and thereafter adopted by the Senate upon

[73] A 1971 study by the Council of State Governments reveals that only Connecticut, Guam, Maine, Nebraska, Nevada, New York, Pennsylvania, Puerto Rico, Tennessee, Utah, Vermont[,] the Virgin Islands, and West Virginia "always" maintain verbatim records of house proceedings. In New York, the record is available only to the press; in Utah tape recordings are made and are unavailable to the public for ten years. The Hawaii and New Hampshire Senates are listed as "usually" keeping a verbatim record; Washington "sometimes" keeps house records, and Michigan and North Dakota "rarely" maintain records of debate. Louisiana keeps them "in part." *See* The Council of State Governments, The Book of the States 1970–71, at 70–72 (1971). *See also* Cashmen, *Availability of Records of Legislative Debates*, 24 Rec. A.B. City N.Y. 153 (1969).

recommendation on the conference committee.[78]

Similarly, in *McDonald v. Roland*,[79] the Florida Supreme Court referred to the history of the statute as reflected in the journals:

> [O]riginal House Bill No. 154 was modified in committee by changing the word "shall" throughout section 39.18 of the original bill to "may" and by inserting the word "permissible" in subsections 39.18(2) (f) and 39.18(6) . . . . Thus it appears that in the process of enactment of the provisions relevant to the matter before us, the use of the word "shall," having a normal mandatory meaning and connotation, has been rejected in favor of "may," having a normal meaning of permission. We think, therefore, that the specific purpose and intent of the legislature with respect to section 39.18 is so clear that it must withstand whatever inconsistent general intent may be argued for the Chapter as a whole. Where the legislature has thus advisedly expressed its specific intention, we are not permitted, by the application of a general rule of statutory construction, to read into the resulting statute a contrary meaning and effect which the legislature has manifestly rejected.

So where the legislature adopts language expressed in an amendment to the original bill, the courts consider this persuasive evidence that the original language and its connotation were rejected. Conversely, rejection of a proposed amendment strongly suggests that the language or amendment is inconsistent with the legislative will. Sands adds a note of caution, however. An amendment may be adopted because it clarifies, rather than changes, the intended meaning. On the other hand, the amendment may be rejected because the bill as originally written better expresses the legislative intent.

The disposition of an amendment, then, is not necessarily an unequivocal indicator that only the language ultimately enacted comports with the legislative will. Nevertheless, the use of journals is regarded as reliable in the vast majority of cases. This view will undoubtedly persist.

X. *Post-enactment Statements*

Statements of legislators subsequent to the enactment of a statute are generally disapproved as evidence of legislative intent, whether by affidavit, oral testimony, or otherwise. In the federal courts, such statements are entitled to little or no weight at all. A recent federal case explained the rationale this way:

> Such statements are not offered by way of committee report and are not offered for response by other members of the law-making body. The intent which is helpful in interpreting a statute, is the intent of the legislature and not of one of its members. For purposes of statutory construction, a legislative body can only speak through a statute, with the words that are used in light of the circumstances surrounding its enactment.[84]

Florida is in accord with the majority view in rejecting post enactment statements of legislators . . . .

XI. *Methods of Presentation*

Authorities disagree on the proper method of presenting statutory history to the courts. One view holds that the attorney must present extrinsic data in the trial court to preserve the record, since an appellate court cannot be compelled to consider matters

---

[78] 79 So. 433, 435 (Fla. 1918).

[79] 65 So. 2d 12 (Fla. 1963).

[84] *Epstein v. Resor*, 296 F. Supp. 214, 216 (N.D. Cal. 1969), *aff'd*, 421 F.2d 930 (9th Cir.), *cert. denied*, 398 U.S. 965 (1970); *see United States v. United Mine Workers*, 330 U.S. 258 (1947).

outside the record. On the other hand, courts often consider other judicially noticeable facts for the first time on appeal, and a rigid rule in the case of statutory history seems harsh. Moreover, technical rules of evidence may inhibit the presentation at trial. To add a margin of safety, the lawyer is probably well advised to attempt the introduction of statutory history in the lower court. Any difficulties encountered will then be preserved for appeal.

HATTER v. LANDSBERG
563 A.2d 146 (Pa. Super. 1989)

Opinion by HESTER, J.:

Sandra and Michael Hatter appeal from the order entered by the Philadelphia Court of Common Pleas on June 9, 1988, granting summary judgment to appellee, Dr. Marc Landsberg, and dismissing their complaint. Appellants contend that the trial court erred in dismissing their complaint by misconstruing and misapplying 42 Pa.C.S. § 8305, enacted March 25, 1988, which abolishes causes of action for wrongful birth and wrongful life, and by not permitting them to amend their complaint. We reverse.

. . . .

. . . Appellant filed the present wrongful conception action seeking damages for pre- and post-natal expenses, pain and suffering, and emotional distress for both herself and her husband. A count on behalf of the child in the form of a wrongful life action was not included.

42 Pa.C.S. § 8305 (1988) provides:

(A) Wrongful Birth. — There shall be no cause of action or award of damages on behalf of any person based on a claim that, but for an act or omission of the defendant, a person once conceived would not or should not have been born.

Nothing contained in this subsection shall be construed to provide a defense against any proceeding, charging a health care practitioner with intentional misrepresentation under the act of October 5, 1978 (P.L. 1109, No. 261), known as the Osteopathic Medical Practice Act, the act of December 20, 1985 (P.L. 457, No. 112), known as The Medical Practice Act of 1985, or any other act regulating the professional practices of health care practitioners.

(B) Wrongful Life. — There shall be no cause of action on behalf of any person based on a claim of that person, that, but for an action or omission of the defendant, the person would not have been conceived or once conceived, would or should have been aborted.

Following the completion of discovery, but prior to trial, appellee filed a motion for summary judgment, alleging that the recent enactment of 42 Pa.C.S. § 8305 barred appellants' suit as a matter of law. The trial court granted appellee's motion and stated that summary judgment would have been proper even in the absence of the statute based on current case authority.

It is clear that 42 Pa.C.S. § 8305(B) precludes only an action by a child or his representative for the child's own wrongful life resulting from a negligently performed contraceptive procedure or abortion. Thus, § 8305(B) does not bar this action by appellants for their *own* expenses and pain and suffering resulting from an improperly performed contraceptive procedure. Accordingly, we must determine whether the trial court was correct in determining that § 8305(A) bars such an action.

Appellants argue that the phrase *"once conceived"* in § 8305(A) demonstrates the limited scope of that section and does not bar recovery for costs resulting from negligence occurring prior to conception. Instead, they contend, Section A is directed solely at prohibiting suits for the nonperformance or negligent performance of an abortion. Appellants argue that the legislative history of 42 Pa.C.S. § 8305 clearly indicates that the bar against "wrongful birth" in § 8305(A) does not apply to an action for "wrongful conception," which is an action seeking damages for negligence occurring prior to conception. In support of this argument, appellants cite the following statements by the sponsors of the law in debate in both the Senate and the House on the Senate bill prior to its enactment:

> Senator Rocks: It is not the objective of this legislation to provide immunity to any doctor who does harm to a pregnant woman or to her child, but, rather — and this is the intent of what the wrongful life and wrongful birth legislation is about — to stop a court-engendered policy which views the birth of a child, be that child handicapped or otherwise, a damaging event for which someone should be punished in order to prevent this quality of life ethic from becoming so persuasive that a handicapped child is routinely considered better off dead and of less value than what we would call "a normal child" and to prevent the practice of medicine, especially obstetrics and gynecology, from becoming coerced into accepting eugenic abortion as a condition for avoiding what are particularly wrongful birth lawsuits. As a matter of public policy, the failure to kill an unborn child, handicapped or normal, should never constitute a wrong . . . .

Pa. Senate Leg. 1961 (*March* 22, 1988).

> Senator Rocks: [O]n the facts of the legislation in front of us . . . the physician described with the so-called botched or fully negligent sterilization, nothing in this legislation would prevent an action fully calling into account the negligence of that physician. In fact, that suit would be on the grounds of wrongful conception. It could be brought today and should be brought tomorrow. Nothing in the legislation in front of us deals with that. In that hypothetical situation, while I would hope it would not happen that physician would be fully liable to the fullest extent of the court's decision for both his or her negligence and the financial damages involved.

Pa. Senate Leg. 1963 (*March* 22, 1988).

Similar questions and statements were made in the House:

> MR. McHALE. Thank you, Mr. Speaker. Mr. Speaker, I have a number of questions related to very specific instances that might arise under the terms of this amendment.

> My first question relates to a negligent procedure performed by a doctor prior to conception. And specifically, if a doctor were to negligently perform a contraceptive procedure — for instance, a tubal ligation that was improperly performed — and thereafter the patient were to become pregnant and subsequently gave birth to a child, would your amendment, if adopted, have any impact upon a possible cause of action that could be brought against that physician for the negligent performance of that medical procedure?

> MR. FREIND: The answer to that is no, Mr. Speaker. This would not. In fact, if you look at the language — we were very careful about this — under "Wrongful birth," we say, "there shall be no cause of action or award of damages on behalf of any person based on a claim that, but for an act or omission of the defendant, a person once conceived would not or should not have been born." So it would in no way bar a wrongful conception action.

Pa. House Leg. 307–308 (*February* 24, 1988).

Appellee counters that it is improper for us to consider the legislative history for this statute since the language of the statute is clear and unambiguous in precluding *any damages* resulting from the birth of a child, and the remarks of individual legislators in debate represent only their view and not that of the proposing or enacting body. *See Martin's Estate*, 365 Pa. 280, 74 A.2d 120 (1950); *National Transit Co. v. Boardman*, 328 Pa. 450, 197 A. 239 (1938); *Tarlo's Estate*, 315 Pa. 321, 172 A. 139 (1934); *Zemprelli v.*

Thornburg, 47 Pa. Cmwlth. 43, 407 A.2d 102 (1979); *see also* 1 Pa.C.S. § 1939. We disagree.

Legislative history is relevant in construing a statute when the statute is unclear. *See* 1 Pa.C.S. § 1939. 42 Pa.C.S. § 8305(A) states that it bars an action by *any* person on the basis that *a* person should not have been born. (Emphasis added.) It is unclear from this language whether or not the term "wrongful birth" includes actions for negligent conception, since the damages from negligent conception constitute the expenses and suffering resulting from birth and, thus, also might be construed to fall within the bar. Consequently, we deem the statutory language unclear, and in order to construe it must proceed to ascertain the reason why the act was necessary, the object to be obtained by its passage, the circumstances under which it was enacted, and the mischief that it remedied. 1 Pa.C.S. § 1921(c); *Coretsky v. Board of Comm'rs of Butler*, 520 Pa. 513, 555 A.2d 72 (1989).

Our review of the legislative history indicates that the legislature primarily was concerned with eliminating suits brought by children or their parents in an effort to recover damages for the failure to abort a child or negligently aborting a child. The legislature's expressed overriding concern was to prevent law suits leading to eugenic abortions of deformed or unwanted children. The legislators also specifically state that this legislation was not intended to bar cases of "wrongful conception" resulting from negligently performed sterilization. We therefore find that the trial court improperly granted appellee summary judgment on the basis of 42 Pa.C.S. § 8305(A).

NOTES AND QUESTIONS

1. Are there reasons to feel the same level of concern about the legislative history of state statutes as Justice Scalia expresses about federal statutes?

2. Why would earlier Pennsylvania cases have concluded that "the remarks of individual legislators in debate represent only their view and not that of the proposing or enacting body"?

3. The court cited a *statute* providing that legislative history could be considered, but that statute referred only to comments or reports of commissions which drafted the statute.

4. The Pennsylvania Superior Court did not cite a Pennsylvania Supreme Court case stating that "what is said on the floor of the House or the Senate should not be relied upon in formulating legislative intent." *Commonwealth v. Alcoa Props., Inc.*, 269 A.2d 748, 750 n.1 (Pa. 1970). Do you agree with such a blanket statement?

5. The authors of the Florida article updated it in Robert M. Rhodes & Susan Seereiter, *The Search for Intent: Aids to Statutory Construction in Florida — An Update*, 13 Fla. St. U. L. Rev. 485 (1985).

6. *See also* Jack L. Landau, *Some Observations About Statutory Construction in Oregon*, 32 Williamette L. Rev. 1 (1996); D. O'Connor, *The Use of Connecticut Legislative History in Statutory Construction*, 58 Conn. B.J. 422 (1984); *In re Valerie D.*, 613 A.2d 748, 761–64 (Conn. 1992); Eric Lane, *How to Read a Statute in New York: A Response to Judge Kaye and Some More*, 28 Hofstra L. Rev. 85 (1999).

7. For an excellent fifty-state bibliography on state legislative history, *see* Jose R. Torres & Steve Windsor, *State Legislative Histories: A Select, Annotated Bibliography*, 85 Law Lib. J. 545 (1993). *See also* Mary L. Fisher, Guide to State Legislative and Administrative Materials (1988).

COSTA v. JOSEY
415 A.2d 337 (N.J. 1980)

SCHREIBER, J.

Joseph Costa, as general administrator and administrator ad prosequendum of the estates of Edward J. Flocco, Jr. and his wife Phyllis Flocco, instituted a wrongful death action against the New Jersey Department of Transportation (Department). He charged the Department with having negligently maintained and repaired the center barrier separating the eastbound and westbound traffic on Route 4 in Teaneck, N.J., so that a dangerous condition existed in the roadway. He alleged that as a result the vehicle of the codefendant Albert J. Josey crossed over the barrier and collided with the Floccos' car causing their deaths.

. . . .

In considering the Department's motion for summary judgment, all parties have assumed (1) that the dividing barrier in the roadway was in a dangerous condition at the time of the injury; (2) that the dangerous condition created a reasonably foreseeable risk of the kind of injury which occurred; (3) that the Department had notice of the dangerous condition a sufficient time prior to the injury to have taken measures to correct it; and (4) that the failure to take such action was palpably unreasonable. *See* N.J.S.A. 59:4-2. The Department contends that despite the hazardous condition of its road it is immune from responsibility under N.J.S.A. 59:4-6. That section immunizes a public entity from liability for an injury caused by the plan or design of public property "either in its original construction or any improvement thereto," where the plan or design has been approved in advance of construction by a public employee exercising discretionary authority to give such approval.

The Department's defense is that the initial design contemplated that the divider would be lowered by subsequent resurfacing of the road. We agree with the conclusion in the dissenting opinion . . . that there are material factual disputes over whether the original plan or design of the road contemplated that resurfacing the pavement would reduce the height of the dividing barrier and cover its lower part . . . . Nor are we satisfied on the basis of the moving papers that the subsequent plans for repairing the road constituted an "improvement" to the original construction as distinguished from maintenance. We remain mindful of the principle that on a motion for summary judgment, the movant must exclude any reasonable doubt as to the existence of a factual issue. *Ruvolo v. American Casualty Co.*, 39 N.J. 490, 499, 189 A.2d 204 (1963).[1]

---

[1] The dissent seems to assume that the government is immune from liability under N.J.S.A. 59:4-6 even though its negligent maintenance of property causes the existence of a dangerous condition. Any such assumption is misplaced. That provision only applies to plans or designs of original construction or any "improvement" to the original construction.

When the dangerous condition arises because of the design or plan of the original construction, governmental immunity attaches and remains, even though a dangerous condition may subsequently arise because of the activities of others. However, that does not immunize a governmental body from responsibility for dangerous conditions created by its careless or negligent affirmative acts arising out of its maintenance as distinguished from improvements to its property.

Baldwin v. State, 6 Cal. 3d 424, 491 P.2d 1121, 99 Cal. Rptr. 145 (1972), to which the dissent refers, is irrelevant to the issue in this case. In Baldwin, plans for construction of a highway made no provision for a left-hand turning lane at a certain intersection because at the time traffic conditions did not warrant any such special consideration. Twenty-five years later the traffic pattern had changed so that the failure to have a traffic control at the intersection allegedly resulted in a dangerous condition. In the litigation involving a claim for injuries arising out of an automobile accident at that intersection, the California Supreme Court held that the immunity under the California statute, Cal. Gov't Code § 830.6 (1966), whose language served as a model for our Tort Claims Act, did not apply. The Report of the New Jersey Attorney General's Task Force on Sovereign Immunity (1972) rejected that interpretation and concluded that the plan or design immunity should be perpetual, Report at 223, a position adopted by our Legislature. That proposition does not immunize a public entity for a dangerous condition caused by its careless affirmative acts involving maintenance.

The Department also argues that it is entitled to immunity under N.J.S.A. 59:2-3. That section reads as follows:

a.   A public entity is not liable for an injury resulting from the exercise of judgment or discretion vested in the entity;

b.   A public entity is not liable for legislative or judicial action or inaction, or administrative action or inaction of a legislative or judicial nature;

c.   A public entity is not liable for the exercise of discretion in determining whether or (sic) to seek or whether to provide the resources necessary for the purchase of equipment, the construction or maintenance of facilities, the hiring of personnel and, in general, the provision of adequate governmental services;

d.   A public entity is not liable for the exercise of discretion when, in the face of competing demands, it determines whether and how to utilize or apply existing resources, including those allocated for equipment, facilities and personnel unless a court concludes that the determination of the public entity was palpably unreasonable. Nothing in this section shall exonerate a public entity for negligence arising out of acts or omissions of its employees in carrying out their ministerial functions.

Subdivisions (b), (c) and (d) of N.J.S.A. 59:2-3 do not by their terms cover the action taken here. Neither legislative nor judicial action is implicated (subdivision (b)); nor is discretion in determining whether to provide the funds necessary for the construction or maintenance of the road (subdivision (c)); nor does defendant suggest that a choice among competing demands for existing resources is involved (subdivision (d)).

Subdivision (a) of N.J.S.A. 59:2-3 states broadly that a public entity is not liable for an injury resulting from the exercise of judgment or discretion. However, subdivision (a) should be read in conjunction with the areas of protected discretion expressly outlined in subparagraphs (b), (c) and (d). All the subsections should be read consistently, each with respect to the subject of the others. These subparagraphs are signposts to understanding the nature of immunized discretionary determinations. They suggest that the "exercise of . . . discretion" in N.J.S.A. 59:2-3(a) refers to actual, high-level policymaking decisions involving the balancing of competing considerations. Such decisions have been traditionally entrusted to coordinate branches of government, and courts, utilizing standard tort principles, are ill-equipped to interfere with them. These discretionary determinations likely include such decisions as "whether to utilize the Department's resources and expend funds for the maintenance of (a) road; whether to repair the road by patching or resurfacing; (and) what roads should be repaired . . . ." *Costa v. Josey*, 79 N.J. at 545, 401 A.2d at 531. Once it is determined that a maintenance program involving resurfacing will be undertaken, however, the government will ordinarily be held to the standard of care set forth in N.J.S.A. 59:4-2. Although the exercise of some discretion may still be involved (e.g., the transportation planners may choose one resurfacing plan over another), the immunity rule will protect only basic policy determinations. Such a construction would be in harmony with subparagraphs (b) through (d).

A task force selected by the Attorney General drafted the New Jersey Tort Claims Act. Its Report on Sovereign Immunity, published in May 1972, contained substantial explanatory comment. It is fitting, therefore, that we look to that comment in searching for the legislative intent of N.J.S.A. 59:2-3. The Comment explains that this provision was intended to codify existing law. It cites as examples, *Willis v. Dep't of Conservation & Economic Development*, 55 N.J. 534, 264 A.2d 34 (1970), *Amelchenko v. Freehold Borough*, 42 N.J. 541, 201 A.2d 726 (1964), and *Bergen v. Koppenal*, 52 N.J. 478, 246 A.2d 442 (1968). All three cases, along with *Fitzgerald v. Palmer*, 47 N.J. 106, 219 A.2d 512 (1966), support the principle that only high-level policy determinations are entitled to immunity.

Fitzgerald and *Amelchenko* both involved high-level policy choices. In *Fitzgerald* we rejected a claim that the Highway Department, in constructing a highway overpass, should have built a fence to prevent persons from throwing objects on cars passing below. This was because matters such as "whether a road should have four or six or eight lanes," or should have "dividers, or circles or jughandles for turns, or traffic lights, or traffic policemen," or a certain speed limit "involve discretion . . . and are committed to the judgment of the legislative and executive branches." 47 N.J. at 109–110, 219 A.2d at 514.

In *Amelchenko* we found that a municipality had not breached the duty it owed under N.J.S.A. 40:60-25.5 to a person who fell in an unplowed municipal parking lot several days after a snowstorm. The Court found that the municipal officials' determinations as to which streets and lots to plow and in what order constituted a high-level policy choice. 42 N.J. at 550, 201 A.2d 726.

On the other hand, in *Willis* the Court upheld the cause of action of a three-year-old child who claimed that the traumatic amputation of her arm in feeding sugar to a caged bear was the result of the State's negligence in leaving the cage unattended and in permitting holes to remain in the screening. The Court held that, once the State decided to cage a wild animal, ordinary tort principles would govern the question of the adequacy of suitable safeguards.

The Comment to N.J.S.A. 59:2-3 also indicates that subparagraph (a) provides the broad immunity for discretionary acts adopted by other jurisdictions including California (Cal. Gov't Code § 820.2 (1966)) and by the federal government (Federal Tort Claims Act, 28 U.S.C.A. § 2680(a)). Both the California and the federal statutes contain broadly worded clauses predicating immunity upon the exercise of discretion. Although neither contains clauses of specific restrictive nature similar to subparagraphs (b) through (d) of the New Jersey Act, both statutes have been construed to protect only basic policy decisionmaking.

Since the New Jersey statute was patterned in large measure after the California statute, we turn first to the California law . . . .

. . . .

That the discretionary function immunity should be limited to actual policymaking is further supported by practical considerations. It is apparent that a literal interpretation of the term "discretion" would effectively exempt from the operation of the Tort Claims Act all government action unless it resulted from mere inadvertence. Almost all official conduct, no matter how ministerial, involves the exercise of some judgment and decisionmaking. To construe subsection (a) that broadly, however, would in effect eliminate most of the liability which the Legislature clearly intended to permit when it enacted the statute. Summary judgment on the basis of discretionary immunity under N.J.S.A. 59:2-3 was not warranted.

We reverse and remand for a plenary trial at which all the facts may be fully developed with respect to the applicability of the immunity provisions of N.J.S.A. 59:2-3 and N.J.S.A. 59:4-6.

CLIFFORD, J., dissenting.

. . . .

The plaintiff argues that the resurfacing substantially changed the nature of the divider, transforming it into a vaulting ramp. He charges the Department of Transportation with negligently maintaining and repairing the divider, thereby creating a dangerous condition which caused the accident. The Department defends on the basis of immunity afforded by the New Jersey Tort Claims Act, N.J.S.A. 59:1-1 et seq. (hereafter the Act), particularly plan and design immunity, N.J.S.A. 59:4-6, and discretionary activities immunity, N.J.S.A. 59:3-2.

Immunity is the dominant consideration of the Act. *See, e.g., Malloy v. State*, 76 N.J. 515, 519, 388 A.2d 622 (1978). It is beyond dispute that the legislative intent was to restore the State's tort and contract immunity subject to certain carefully delineated exceptions. *Id.* at 518–19, 388 A.2d 622; N.J.S.A. 59:1-2. To make this as explicit as possible, the Comment to N.J.S.A. 59:2-1 states that the statute is "intended to ensure that any immunity provisions provided in the act or by common law will prevail over the liability provisions."[1]

. . . .

The Act clearly dictates that there is no limitation on the length of protection offered to governmental entities by the statutory immunity of N.J.S.A. 59:4-6. As the Comment states:

> [I]t is intended that the plan or design immunity provided in this section be perpetual. That is, once the immunity attaches no subsequent event or change of conditions shall render a public entity liable on the theory that the existing plan or design of public property constitutes a dangerous condition.

Accordingly, I would affirm.

NOTES AND QUESTIONS

1. Is the Report of the New Jersey Attorney General's Task Force on Sovereign Immunity a piece of "legislative" history? Under the circumstances of this case, what weight should it be given?

2. Review the Eskridge and Frickey "Mini-Funnel" illustrating the "Hierarchy of Legislative History Sources." It presents the "Views of Nonlegislator Drafters" as being not very authoritative. In the context of this case, do you agree? Doesn't it depend on the specific circumstances of the statutory interpretation problems in each case?

3. Compare this case with *Van Horn v. William Blanchard Co.*, in Chapter, 8 Section [B], also concerning the matter of a statute copied from another state.

DILLEHEY v. STATE
815 S.W.2d 623 (Tex. Crim. App. 1991)

MILLER, JUDGE.

. . . .

The issue upon which we granted appellant's petition is whether or not a defendant can appeal from a deferred adjudication probation under the provisions of the article of the Texas Code of Criminal Procedure that authorizes the State's, not the defendant's, right to appeal. Specifically appellant, in an articulate, well reasoned brief seeks relief under the provisions of Article 44.01(j), V.A.C.C.P., which states:

> Nothing in this article is to interfere with the defendant's right to appeal under the procedures of Article 44.02 of this code. The defendant's right to appeal under 44.02 may be prosecuted by the defendant where the punishment assessed is in accordance with subsection (a), Section 3d, Article 42.12 of this code, as well as any other punishment assessed in compliance with art. 44.02 of this code.

Upon initial examination of this sentence, the strict construction utilized by the court of appeals appears to be a fairly logical technical interpretation of the law, particularly regarding the interpretation of the commonplace legal phrase "assessment of punishment", as used in *Hernandez v. State*, 705 S.W.2d 700 (Tex. Cr. App. 1986).

However, research into the legislative intent behind paragraph (j) leads us to a

---

[1] The Comments appended to the statute are taken from the Report of the Attorney General's Task Force on Sovereign Immunity May 1972, and accompanied the Act during its consideration by the legislature. They have the precedential weight and value of legislative history. *See Ellison v. Housing Auth.*, 162 N.J.Super. 347, 353, 392 A.2d 1229 (App.Div.1978) (Comment cited as indicative of legislature's express intention).

completely different result than that reached in the court of appeals.[2]

A legislative history can be researched at the state library on the second floor of the Capitol. Obtaining the legislative history can be accomplished by some or all of the steps illustrated in Appendix A. The technical interpretation of paragraph (j), particularly the interpretation of the phrase "assessment of 'punishment' " advocated by the court of appeals, was simply not what the author of the bill or the author of paragraph (j), or for that matter, the legislature had in mind. We clearly see the intent of the legislature from the following excerpts from the Senate Floor discussions on the constitutional amendment (SJR 34, 1987) allowing the State's right to appeal and the corresponding enabling legislation (specifically, paragraph (j)) (SB 762, 1987). The discussions are between Senator Montford, author of the bill, and Senator Washington, author of paragraph (j).

SJR 34, SECOND READING, SENATE FLOOR

WASHINGTON So other than that situation [a not guilty verdict] the State has an unlimited right of appeal?

MONTFORD Yes.

WASHINGTON All right. Now the defendant has the right to appeal only after conviction, is that right?

MONTFORD Yes.

WASHINGTON So the defendant has to be at risk before he or she has the right to appeal and complain to a higher court with respect to the manner in which the law has been interpreted by the District Court or the County Court at Law?

MONTFORD Yes.

WASHINGTON And this would give a right to the State that the defendant doesn't have.

MONTFORD That right is absolute in terms of the defendant. No, I don't think so. I think the defendant unequivocally has the right of appeal. Period. Unless he or she is found not guilty.

WASHINGTON Unless he received deferred adjudication.

MONTFORD *That's another instance and I indicated to you I would be willing to accept an amendment for clarity on the issue of deferred adjudication.*

WASHINGTON So the law is now that the defendant has to be at risk, that is, the defendant has to be convicted before he/she can complain of any procedural or substantive error committed by the trail court, is that right?

MONTFORD Yes.

SB 762, SECOND READING, SENATE FLOOR

Amendment (paragraph (j)), authored by Sen. Washington, is introduced and read.

WASHINGTON Thank you, Mr. President. Mr. President, Members of the Senate. This amendment is acceptable to the author. It merely provides for the situation which I believe is *a hiatus in the law* right now. A person can appeal, as Senator Montford and I were discussing, if a person enters a plea of guilty or no contest and receives probation, and there has been a legitimate pretrial issue where they've discussed, where the court has ruled on the admissibility of some evidence or some other matter that either or both parties feels may have

---

[2] We note that the Court of Appeals did no research into the legislative history of the bills that culminated in this amendment to the code of criminal procedure. Since it may not be necessary or appropriate to do such research in every case, we are not chiding the court of appeals here. However hindsight teaches us that this was an appropriate case in which to do so.

been dispositive of the case, *this would allow the person to appeal from a deferred adjudication probation the same as they can appeal from a regular probation.* The courts have interpreted provisions of the law now as to now allow a person to be able to appeal on a deferred adjudication where they can appeal from a regular probation and I think the amendment is acceptable.

MONTFORD Amendment is acceptable, Mr. President.

(Emphasis added).

The amendment was adopted *unanimously* viva voce vote (viva voce — "With the living voice . . . signifies voting by speech or outcry", *Blacks Law Dictionary*). All senators were present and answered "yea" to the roll vote on paragraph (j) except for Sen. Truan, who was absent excused. They were aware of, because they were told face to face on the Senate floor, the specific purpose of the addition of Art. 44.01(j). SB 762 passed to engrossment as amended. The 3-day rule was suspended, 3rd reading of SB 762 took place — with no discussion, Bill 762 passed.

The fundamental rule governing the construction of a statute is to ascertain the intent of the legislature in enacting the statute. *Patterson v. State*, 769 S.W.2d 938, 941 (Tex. Cr. App. 1989) (most common rule of statutory construction is for judiciary to attempt to effectuate intent of legislature). Once determined, the intent of the legislature must be enforced by the courts even though it may not be entirely consistent with the strict letter of the statute. *See State v. Terrell*, 588 S.W.2d 784 (Tex. 1979), *Ex Parte Groves*, 571 S.W.2d 888 (Tex. Cr. App. 1978).

We have long honored, as binding evidence of legislative intent, bill analyses and study group reports and legislative council reports and floor debate. *See Studer v. State*, 799 S.W.2d 263 (Tex. Cr. App. 1990). The intent of the legislature when enacting 44.01(j) is clear. The statute is susceptible to a construction that would effectuate the clear intent of the legislature. Where intent is clear, there is no room for further construction. *Patterson, supra*. The legislature, without a single objection, nor any discussion on paragraph (j), clearly spelled out that it intended for defendants placed on deferred adjudication probation to be allowed, under Article 44.01(j), V.A.C.C.P., to immediately appeal rulings on pre-trial motions in compliance with Article 44.02.

It is inherent in the duty of this Court to adhere to interpretations of the law consistent with the intent of the legislature . . . .

APPENDIX A
COMPILING TEXAS LEGISLATIVE HISTORY
at the Legislative Reference Library State Capitol — Austin, Texas

Unlike U.S. legislation, Texas legislative history is not written and must be compiled by the researcher. The following steps should be taken by the researcher;

1. Determine the bill number and the session which enacted the bill.
2. Examine the original bill file.
3. Listen to the tape recordings of the public hearings of committee meetings and debate in the House and Senate.
4. Examine other documents which may be helpful.

Please note that the numbering of the House and Senate bills begins over again during each legislative session.

The bill number is assigned based on whether the bill was introduced in the House or the Senate.

The bill number does not change during the session.

1. DETERMINE THE BILL NUMBER AND THE SESSION WHICH EN-ACTED THE BILL

A. Locate the desired section or article of the law (the statute) in Vernon's Annotated Texas Statues (for criminal law, you can check for the section or article at the end of each section of the Penal code or the end of each article in the Code of Criminal Procedure).

B. The end of the statute has a history note which lists all the changes made to the statute. Locate the citation to the General and Special Laws of Texas (referred to as the session laws).

Example: Acts 1977, 65th Leg., p. 2411, ch. 571

C. SESSION LAWS — (General and Special Laws of Texas). The session laws are the full text of the final (enrolled) version of all of the bills passed by the Legislature in the order they are signed by the Governor. The bills are called acts and are numbered by chapters.

Locate the bill in the session laws by using the citation from the statute to find the volume for the legislative session, the chapter, and/or the page number.

Example: The session laws for 1977, from the 65th Legislature, page 2411, chapter 571.

Look up the chapter in the session laws, and the bill number is shown directly under the chapter number.

Example: Chapter 571

H.B. 2455

Note the House bill number or Senate bill number and the session number.

Examples: House Bill 2455, 65th Session

Senate Bill 387, 69th First Called Session

2. EXAMINE THE ORIGINAL BILL FILE

A. The bill file typically contains the various versions of the bill, the bill analysis, and the fiscal note. Versions of the bill may include the introduced, committee, engrossed, and the final (enrolled) version.

B. The bill analysis is a brief document which gives a short explanation of the bill, and a summary of each section of the bill. The bill analysis is prepared for the committee version of the bill, not the final version of the bill.

C. The Legislative Reference Library has the bill files on microfilm for bills from the 63rd session (1973) to the present. Request assistance in locating the microfilmed bill file from a librarian. You may make photocopies from the bill file.

D. Microfilmed copies of the original bill files for bills from the 63rd (1973) through the 70th (1987) sessions are also available at the Dallas Public Library, (214) 670-1468, and at the Houston Public Library, (713) 236-1313, ask for the Texas Room. E. Bill files dating before 1973 are located in the Archives Division of the State Library (Lorenzo de Zavala Bldg., 12th and Brazos, Austin (512) 463-5480). Bill analyses were *sometimes* prepared for bills dating before 1973.

3. LISTEN TO THE TAPE RECORDINGS OF THE PUBLIC HEARINGS OF COMMITTEE MEETING AND DEBATE IN THE HOUSE AND SENATE

A. Beginning with the 63rd session (1973), the Legislature began tape recording the public hearings held by committees, and the debate in the House or the Senate. (Formal meetings are also *sometimes* taped at the committee chairman's request). In order to listen to the tapes, you will need the dates of these hearings and debates.

B. Locate the bill's history in the House Bill History volume or the Senate Bill History volume for each session. Note whether the committee is from the House or the Senate (indicated by H or S), the name of the committee, and the date(s) of any public hearing or formal meetings held by that committee. Note the dates of the second and third reading (which is when any debate may have taken place) in both the House and the Senate.

C. You may go to the buildings shown below to listen to the tapes, or you may order copies (prepaid unless you are a State agency) of the tapes.

House tapes, 1973-present (512) 463-0489

House Committee Coordinator (Room 110, Reagan Building, 14th & Congress)

Senate tapes, 1973–1976 (512) 463-5480

Archives Division of the Texas State Library (Room 100, Zavala Building, 12th and Brazos)

Senate tapes, 1977-present (512) 463-0430

Senate Staff Services (Room 206, 14th and Trinity)

(The time it takes to get your tapes depends on how busy the staff is at the time. Generally, if the Legislature is out of session, it takes only a week, however, waits of up to two months (for Senate tapes) are not unheard of.)

D. The bill history for bills dating before 1973 is given only in the House and Senate Journals for each session. There is a bill history index in the last volume of each of the Journals for each session. No tape recordings are available. Very little information is available for these bills. There may have been an interim study for major legislation.

4. EXAMINE OTHER DOCUMENTS WHICH MAY BE HELPFUL

A. Legislative Interim Committee Reports

Any reports or studies which may have been made by any standing or special legislative committees during the time period between sessions (the interim) are listed in the card catalog of the Legislative Reference Library. These reports are listed in the card catalog by chairman, title, and subject.

B. House Research Organization (HRO) Bill Analysis

(1) Beginning with the 65th session (1977), the HRO began preparing bill analyses for *some* bills when the bill reached the 2nd reading in the House. The bill analyses are compiled in Daily Floor Reports.

(2) Locate the bill analysis by noting the date of the 2nd reading in the House, which is given in the bill history. Beginning with the 67th session (1981), the last volume of the Reports also has an index giving the date of the bill analysis.

(3) Then locate the bill analysis in the Daily Floor Report on the date indicated. You may photocopy the bill analysis. Some courts have accepted the HRO bill analysis for proving intent.

(4) The Daily Floor Reports are located on the mezzanine in the Documents section of the Legislative Reference Library, call number: L 1801.9 St 94/ (number of the session) d (date of the 2nd reading in the House)

C. Publications from state agencies and commissions

Agency publications often discuss needed changes in law that affect agency operations. A commission may be created to research a particular problem for the Legislature. These publications are listed in the card catalog by name of the agency or commission, title, and subject.

Some publications are also listed in the card catalog by the legislative session and bill number.

Example: Texas. Legislature, 65th. Senate bill 72.

It is a good idea to cross-reference as much as you can. You should cross-reference your bill in the following reference volumes, reports and microfilm to see if you've missed anything. All of the following can be found at the Legislative Reference Library in the Capitol.

1. Senate Bill History (this is the name of a book)
2. Bills by History
3. Bills by Committee
4. Index to Sections Affected
5. Author/Sponsor Index to Bills
6. Detailed Subject Index to Bills
7. House and Senate Journals
8. Bill microfilm
9. HRO Bill Analysis (Daily Floor Reports)
10 Interim Committee Reports

If you get confused or lost in the paper jungle, the librarians are extremely helpful — just ask, they' ll point the way.

BIBLIOGRAPHY

1. Allison, Malinda. *Texas Legislative History: A Manual of Sources*, Legislative Reference Library, 1980.

2. Allison, Malinda, and Hambleton, James. "Research in Texas Legislative History." *Texas Bar Journal*, Mar. 1984, pp. 314–317.

3. Gruben, Karl T. and Hambleton, James E., ed. *Reference Guide to Texas Law and Legal History*, 2nd ed., Austin, Texas. Butterworth Legal Publishers, 1987.

4. Texas Legislative Council. *Guide to Legislative Information*. Report 88-3. Nov. 1988. (Library call number: L 1400.7 In88-3).

The legislative history information guide in this appendix was provided by the Legislative Reference Library, State Capitol Building, Austin, Texas.

5. Interpretation of Initiative Measures

NOTE, THE USE OF EXTRINSIC AIDS IN THE INTERPRETATION OF POPULARLY ENACTED LEGISLATION,
89 COLUMBIA LAW REVIEW 157 (1989)*

Introduction

A remnant of direct democracy survives in the sharing of the power to enact legislation between the people and the legislature in many state constitutions.[1]

This reserved power has been exercised to address a wide range of topics and involves some of the more pressing matters of our day. This last unfiltered voice of the people, however, is being usurped by judicial action under the guise of statutory interpretation. State courts have long ignored reliable extrinsic aids to discern the

---

[1] The states which allow for legislative activity by the people are: Alaska, Arizona, Arkansas, California, Colorado, Florida, Idaho, Illinois, Maine, Massachusetts, Michigan, Missouri, Montana, Nebraska, Nevada, North Dakota, Ohio, Oklahoma, Oregon, South Dakota, Utah, and Washington. The District of Columbia also allows for such action . . . .

intent behind popularly enacted legislation and so the accurate interpretation of these statutes may have suffered.

. . . .

. . . Popularly enacted legislation does not suffer from the problem of nonrecording of state legislative history and, in fact, produces a wide range of extrinsic aids.

Direct initiatives or propositions usually are written by private interest groups to obtain a variety of goals. The proposed text, after a petition drive and campaign, is then either adopted or rejected by a majority of the voters. States that allow passage of legislation by popular vote require that proposed ballot issues receive a requisite number of signatures before the matter may be placed on the ballot. This process does not ensure that voters will read the entirety of a proposed statute. Professional petitioners often secure signatures by canvassing an area such as a shopping center, museum, or other place where people are moving slowly, and frame the proposal in its most favorable light.

After a measure is approved for appearance on the ballot, a voter pamphlet is often prepared and mailed to the registered voters of the state in order to educate the electorate and announce the proposed legislation. Generally the pamphlets are drafted by either a state official, the proponent of a measure, or both the proponent and the main group in opposition. Such pamphlets usually contain the title, a summary description, and the arguments for and against the measure. Frequently, the arguments presented in the pamphlets frame the debate prior to the vote.

Depending on the prominence of the issue, a debate may also occur in the media. Therefore, the public has other sources of information, ranging from news editorials, to paid political announcements, to a legally required printing of the measure in all newspapers of general circulation.[72]

. . . .

The history of popularly enacted statutes, which serves as evidence of intent, differs from traditional legislative history in that the sources on which the court must rely are not products of the majority of those who vote. For this reason, the materials generated in a popular election present special problems involving the weight a court should afford them. The materials in these campaigns often do not reach all of the voters of a state in the way that traditional legislative history reaches all of the legislators. Also, the popular understanding of word meanings and the evil to be remedied by the statute may vary from region to region. These obstacles and others prevent the wholesale adoption of the traditional model to the interpretation of popularly enacted initiatives.

A solution does exist that combines the theory of the traditional model of statutory interpretation with the limitations inherent in the popular initiative . . . . The solution entails dividing the materials generated from an initiative campaign into two distinct categories, based on the materials' known circulation and informed preparation. The first tier includes voter pamphlets, statutory statements of intent, and voter exit polls. The second includes the remainder of materials generated in an initiative election. Given this point of delineation, the more reliable group of materials can be used to create a presumption of the intent of the initiative that is rebuttable by an overwhelming showing from the second category. This second category then acts as a buffer for the shortcomings of the first.

. . . .

---

[72] *See id.* at 57. The material in the media can range from empty slogans to more thoughtful commentary in editorial portions of newspapers and television broadcasts.

WASHINGTON STATE DEPARTMENT OF REVENUE v. HOPPE
82 Wash. 2d 549, 512 P.2d 1094 (1973)

BRACHTENBACH, ASSOCIATE JUSTICE.

While this appeal involves a multitude of issues involving this state's complex scheme of property taxation, a constitutional amendment, an initiative and various statutes, the pivotal question to be answered by this court is the maximum millage rate at which property will be taxed for collection in the calendar year 1973.

. . . .

We venture into the thicket of issues in this case with several fundamental precepts in mind:

. . . .

(4) These rules of construction apply equally to direct legislation by the people as to legislative enactments. *State ex rel. Jones v. Erickson*, 75 Mont. 429, 244 P. 287 (1926).

(5) The collective intent of the people becomes the object of the court's search for "legislative intent" when construing a law adopted by a vote of the people. E. Crawford, The Construction of Statutes § 365 (1940 ed.) p. 745.

(6) Material in the official voters' pamphlet may be considered by the court in determining the purpose and intent of these acts. *Bayha v. PUD*, 2 Wash. 2d 85, 97 P.2d 614 (1939).

The controlling language and limitation of SJR 1 is:

> *[T]he aggregate of all tax levies* upon real and personal property by the state and all taxing districts now existing or hereafter created, *shall not in any year exceed one per centum* of the true and fair value of such property . . . .

(Italics ours.)

The state contends that this limitation means that only those taxes *levied* after the effective date of SJR 1 are so limited. We can find no such meaning in the quoted language. Nowhere does SJR 1 limit itself to levies made at any particular time. But, argues the state, the word levy is a word of art, a word having special meaning; in its narrow, technical sense it refers only to the legislative act of the county in adopting a levy ordinance. The state couples this argument with its assertion that the effective date of SJR 1 was December 7, 1972. Since the original King County levy ordinance was adopted before that date, it would follow that the levy, collectible in 1973, would not be subject to the 1 percent limitation.

Bearing in mind the construction principles cited above, and particularly the rule that words, unless otherwise defined, must be given their usual and ordinary meaning, does the word "levies" have such a usual and ordinary meaning that it can only mean the legislative function of adopting a levy ordinance?

. . . .

It is well established that the word "levy" has a variety of meanings . . . .

If the broad, nontechnical definition were adopted, the levy was not complete on December 7, 1972, since the assessor had not spread the levy on the books against specific property. The existence of broader definitions than that contended for by the state indicates that the intent of SJR 1 could well have been premised upon the belief that it would affect all taxes which had not been spread on the rolls. If December 7th were the controlling date, however, we point out the potentially paradoxical result that a county which had adopted its levy ordinance after December 7th would be subject to the limitation of SJR 1, while a county which passed its ordinance before that date would not.

Finding the language of SJR 1 to be unclear, we turn to the official voters' pamphlet for aid in interpretation. The ballot title speaks of replacing the present 40-mill limit with a new provision under which the maximum allowable rate would be 1 percent of true and fair value. We find no mention in the text of SJR 1 or the official explanation thereof of the idea that no tax relief would be granted until 1974. There is not the slightest hint that a technical interpretation of the word levies would stand in the way of reduced taxes in 1973. Instead, the official statement for SJR 1 is couched in glowing terms of how much the taxpayer will save in regular property levies. It points out the extreme burden and hardship of property taxes which have more than doubled in the 5 years from 1966 to 1971. The reference to 1971 is highly significant; where is the warning that these taxes may be even higher in 1973? The final inspiration for an affirmative vote is this language: "Cast your vote on November 7 to protect your home, farm and business property from excessive taxation."

A conscientious voter who read every word of the text of SJR 1, the ballot title, the official explanation of the effect of the measure and the statement for the proposal would not find a whisper of suggestion that its impact would not be felt until 1974. We refuse to attribute to the average informed voter or even the better-than-average informed voter the legal theory that the proposed amendment hinged on the complex scheme of levying taxes in one year and collecting them in the next year, so that all taxes levied in 1972 were beyond the reach of SJR 1. If that was intended by the drafters of the measure, it would have been simple to say so.

We hold that SJR 1 applies to and sets the limits for the regular property taxes legislatively levied in 1972 and collectible in 1973.

. . . .

Moving to Initiative 44, we note that the ballot title describes it as "An act to limit tax levies on real and personal property by the state, and other taxing districts, except port and power districts, to an aggregate of twenty (20) mills on assessed valuation . . . ." The text of the proposal then sets forth the existing statutory scheme and concludes that ". . . the aggregate of all tax levies upon real and personal property by the state, municipal corporations, taxing districts and governmental agencies, now existing or hereafter created, shall not exceed twenty mills on the dollar of assessed valuation, which assessed valuation shall be fifty percent of the true and fair value of such property in money."

The official explanation of the effect of Initiative 44 is that it is designed to replace the existing statutory limitation on millage which is described as 22 mills with respect to levies made in 1970 through 1972, and 21 mills for subsequent years. The statement for the initiative is that it is a "clean property tax measure . . . . The intent is to 'hold the line' on property taxes until a responsible constitutional limitation is adopted." It points out that there is no conflict between SJR 1 and Initiative 44: "Both are clean, no strings attached, property tax limit measures . . . . Passage of both is double insurance and is compatible."

Our comments about SJR 1 and the content of the voters' pamphlet are equally in point here. Again the possibility that the tax first due on April 30, 1974, is the subject of this "clean, hold the line" measure is so well obscured as to be invisible.

. . . .

We hold that Initiative 44 is applicable to the taxes in question . . . .

UTTER, ASSOCIATE JUSTICE (dissenting).

The conclusion that tax relief measures are not immediately effective is an unpopular one. I believe, however, no other conclusion should be reached. The result of the majority opinion is to invalidate levies passed in 37 counties of this state, in what must have been reliance on the language of the acts in question and our previous cases.

. . . .

Given our recognition in this state that the word "levy" may receive numerous usages depending upon the meaning to be conveyed, no resort to outside authority is needed. The critical error by the majority, however, is not their source, but their purpose. The cases used do demonstrate the word "levy" is subject to numerous meanings, but they do not support a conclusion that the word is ambiguous when used in the context now before us. The mere fact a word may receive multiple meanings does not mean it is ambiguous when used in a particular context and the majority has failed to demonstrate any ambiguity of "levy" here. In this case, the word "levy" is not ambiguous and the majority need not search the legislative history resource of the voters' pamphlet, explaining SJR 1 and Initiative 44, to clarify its meaning . . . .

The voters' pamphlet may be referred to in an effort to determine the general intent of the voters but it fails to provide any justification for altering the meaning to be given "levy" operating in the context of SJR 1, Initiative 44, and RCW 84.52. The majority recites extensively from the pamphlet but fails to show any particular language bearing directly on the meaning of "levy." Rather, all that can be concluded from a reading of the pamphlet is that the voters intended both SJR 1 and Initiative 44 take effect at the next "levy." To construe "levy" to refer to the administrative duties of collection and not the legislative act of enacting the levy is arbitrary and without logical explanation.

Rather than surmising a meaning for "levy" from the voters' pamphlet, we must search its usage in those laws in which it is here to operate (RCW 84.52) and refer to our case law rulings. The majority fails to recognize that Initiative 44 is an amendment to RCW 84.52 and must be understood in that context.

. . . .

Chapter 8

JUDICIALLY CREATED CANONS, ASSUMPTIONS, AND PRESUMPTIONS OF STATUTORY INTERPRETATION

A. CANONS OF STATUTORY INTERPRETATION

In Chapter 6, concerning interpretation based on text, we saw several judge-made canons of interpretation such as those concerning statutes *in pari materia* and interpretation of words according to ordinary meaning. In Chapter 7 we saw the preference Justice Scalia has expressed for the "standard tools of legal reasoning," including canons, over resort to legislative history, as well as Professor Jane Schacter's conclusion that the Supreme Court has continued to apply judge-made policy preferences, including canons. In this Chapter we will look directly at the canons of statutory interpretation.

Judicial decisions have developed a number of canons of construction which courts use as aids in resolving interpretation issues. These canons involve assumptions of a legislative approach in drafting legislation rather than assumptions of legislative consideration. Most of the canons are working rules for interpretation where legislative history is unavailable. One theoretical effect of the uniform application of these doctrines by the courts would be to prod the drafters toward actions consistent with the doctrines. This does not happen in practice, however, since all of these canons are subject to counter-arguments. Thus, neither courts nor drafters consistently observe these conventions. Nevertheless, a thorough working knowledge of the canons is essential, since these doctrines are still used, albeit irregularly.

There are several basic difficulties with relying on such presumptions of legislative intent. Most legislatures have two houses, both of which must pass a bill before it becomes law, but each may concur for its own reasons. Each may desire differing language, resulting in conflicts which must be resolved through a conference committee. Provisions are often the result of compromise, not only between the two legislative houses, but to an even greater extent between the competing interests in each house. Compromises within committees are still subject to amendment on the floor of the particular body. Drafters may try to be specific and accurate, but two words may be used as synonyms at one place, and the same words may be used to indicate different concepts elsewhere in the legislation. The exigencies of obtaining compromise and consensus may overcome desires to abide by general conventions for interpretation; the assumptions of consistent use of language in legislative drafting, therefore, can be severely strained in practice.

KARL N. LLEWELLYN,
REMARKS ON THE THEORY OF APPELLATE DECISION
AND THE RULES OR CANONS ABOUT HOW
STATUTES ARE TO BE CONSTRUED,
3 Vanderbilt Law Review 395 (1950)[*]

[Karl N. Llewellyn provided some perceptions of the uses made of canons which survive to this day. — Eds.]

When it comes to presenting a proposed statutory construction in court, there is an accepted conventional vocabulary. As in argument over points of case law, the accepted convention still, unhappily, requires discussion as if only one single correct meaning could exist. Hence there are two opposing canons on almost every point. An arranged

---

[*] Reprinted with permission from Vanderbilt Law Review.

selection is appended. Every lawyer must be familiar with them all: they are still needed tools of argument. At least as early as Fortescue the general picture was clear, on this, to any eye which would see.

Plainly, to make any canon take hold in a particular instance, the construction contended for must be sold, essentially, by means other than the use of the canon: the good sense of the situation and a *simple* construction of the available language to achieve that sense, by *tenable means, out of the statutory language.*

THRUST	BUT PARRY
1. A statute cannot go beyond its text.	1. To effect its purpose a statute may be implemented beyond its text.
2. Statutes in derogation of the common law will not be extended by construction.	2. Such acts will be liberally construed if their nature is remedial.
3. Statutes are to be read in the light of the common law, and a statute affirming a common-law rule is to be construed in accordance with the common law.	3. The common law gives way to a statute which is inconsistent with it and when a statute is designed as a revision of a whole body of law applicable to a given subject it supersedes the common law.
4. Where a foreign statute which has received construction has been adopted, previous construction is adopted too.	4. It may be rejected where there is conflict with the obvious meaning of the statute or where the foreign decisions are unsatisfactory in reasoning or where the foreign interpretation is not in harmony with the spirit or policy of the laws of the adopting state.
5. Where various states have already adopted the statute, the parent state is followed.	5. Where interpretations of other states are inharmonious, there is no such restraint.
6. Statutes *in pari materia* must be construed together.	6. A statute is not *in pari materia* if its scope and aim are distinct or where a legislative design to depart from the general purpose or policy of previous enactments may be apparent.
7. A statute imposing a new penalty or forfeiture, or a new liability or disability, or creating a new right of action will not be construed as having a retroactive effect.	7. Remedial statutes are to be liberally construed and if a retroactive interpretation will promote the ends of justice, they should receive such construction.
8. Where design has been distinctly stated no place is left for construction.	8. Courts have the power to inquire into real — as distinct from ostensible — purpose.
9. Definitions and rules of construction contained in an interpretation clause are part of the law and binding.	9. Definitions and rules of construction in a statute will not be extended beyond their necessary import nor allowed to defeat intention otherwise manifested.
10. A statutory provision requiring liberal construction does not mean disregard of unequivocal requirements of the statute.	10. Where a rule of construction is provided within the statute itself the rule should be applied.

THRUST	BUT PARRY
11. Titles do not control meaning; preambles do not expand scope; section headings do not change language.	11. The title may be consulted as a guide when there is doubt or obscurity in the body; preambles may be consulted to determine rationale, and thus the true construction of terms; section headings may be looked upon as part of the statute itself.
12. If language is plain and unambiguous it must be given effect.	12. Not when literal interpretation would lead to absurd or mischievous consequences or thwart manifest purpose.
13. Words and phrases which have received judicial construction before enactment are to be understood according to that construction.	13. Not if the statute clearly requires them to have a different meaning.
14. After enactment, judicial decision upon interpretation of particular terms and phrases controls.	14. Practical construction by executive officers is strong evidence of true meaning.
15. Words are to be taken in their ordinary meaning unless they are technical terms or words of art.	15. Popular words may bear a technical meaning and technical words may have a popular signification and they should be so construed as to agree with evident intention or to make the statute operative.
16. Every word and clause must be given effect.	16. If inadvertently inserted or if repugnant to the rest of the statute, they may be rejected as surplusage.
17. The same language used repeatedly in the same connection is presumed to bear the same meaning throughout the statute.	17. This presumption will be disregarded where it is necessary to assign different meanings to make the statute consistent.
18. Words are to be interpreted according to the proper grammatical effect of their arrangement within the statute.	18. Rules of grammar will be disregarded where strict adherence would defeat purpose.
19. Exceptions not made cannot be read in.	19. The letter is only the "bark." Whatever is within the reason of the law is within the law itself.
20. Expression of one thing excludes another. [Quite typically: not "*the other*."]	20. The language may fairly comprehend many different cases where some only are expressly mentioned by way of example.
21. General terms are to receive a general construction.	21. They may be limited by specific terms with which they are associated or by the scope and purpose of the statute.
22. It is a general rule of construction that where general words follow an enumeration they are to be held as applying only to persons and things of the same general kind or class specifically mentioned (*ejusdem generis*).	22. General words must operate on something. Further, *ejusdem generis* is only an aid in getting the meaning and does not warrant confining the operations of a statute within narrower limits than were intended.

THRUST	BUT PARRY
23. Qualifying or limiting words or clauses are to be referred to the next preceding antecedent.	23. Not when evident sense and meaning require a different construction.
24. Punctuation will govern when a statute is open to two constructions.	24. Punctuation marks will not control the plain and evident meaning of language.
25. It must be assumed that language has been chosen with due regard to grammatical propriety and is not interchangeable on mere conjecture.	25. "And" and "or" may be read interchangeably whenever the change is necessary to give the statute sense and effect.
26. There is a distinction between words of permission and mandatory words.	26. Words imparting permission may be read as mandatory and words imparting command may be read as permissive when such construction is made necessary by evident intention or by the rights of the public.
27. A proviso qualifies the provision immediately preceding.	27. It may clearly be intended to have a wider scope.
28. When the enacting clause is general, a proviso is construed strictly.	28. Not when it is necessary to extend the proviso to persons or cases which come within its equity.

NOTES AND QUESTIONS

1. Does Llewellyn seem to feel that canons of construction are less a means of interpreting legislation than a means of justifying the result the court desires? Should the "canons" as doctrine be totally abandoned? Llewellyn added a number of other canons to his "thrust but parry" table in an appendix to THE COMMON LAW TRADITION: DECIDING APPEALS 521 (1960).

2. Many of the leading scholars on legislation reviewed Llewellyn's influential article, and the current thinking about the canons of statutory interpretation, in *Symposium: A Reevaluation of the Canons of Statutory Interpretation*, 45 VAND. L. REV. 529 (1992).

3. In 1983 Professor Robert Weisberg referred to Llewellyn's 1950 article as "fiendishly deconstructive." Robert Weisberg, *The Calabresian Judicial Artist: Statutes and the New Legal Process*, 35 STAN. L. REV. 213, 213 (1983).

4. *See also* John F. Manning, *Legal Realism and the Canons' Revival*, 5 GREEN BAG 2d 283 (2002).

T. ALEXANDER ALEINIKOFF & THEODORE M. SHAW, THE COSTS OF INCOHERENCE: A COMMENT ON PLAIN MEANING, *WEST VIRGINIA UNIVERSITY HOSPITALS, INC. v. CASEY*, AND DUE PROCESS OF STATUTORY INTERPRETATION, 45 VAND. L. REV. 687 (1992)[*]

I. INTRODUCTION

Karl Llewellyn's classic article on the canons of statutory construction, which we rightly celebrate in this Symposium, is too clever by half. To the reader untutored in

---

[*] T. Alexander Aleinikoff, Theodore M. Shaw, The Costs of Incoherence: A Comment on Plain Meaning, *West Virginia University Hospitals v. Casey*, and Due Process of Statutory Interpretation, 45 VAND. L. REV.

the scholarly literature on statutory interpretation, the "thrust but parry" pairing of the canons is a delightful demonstration of how legal argument is structured in a way guaranteed to maintain discretion in the judiciary and to keep lawyers in business. No case involving a statute is clear cut because the canons can lend support to either side. This means that no lawyer is without an argument, and a judge is free to do what he or she thinks "situation sense," natural justice, or economic efficiency demands.

But this rendering of the tools of statutory interpretation really misses the point. The canons are not free-floating rules, snatched out of the air or created on the spot in helter-skelter fashion. They are rules of thumb ("generalizations of experience," Felix Frankfurter called them[2]) for approaching legal texts, and as such, canons have at least two attributes: they summarize common-sensical ways of thinking about language and communication, and they follow from a broader normative theory about the proper way to read statutes. For example, if one starts with a theory that an interpreter ought to read a statute as its drafters would have read it at the time of enactment, then certain rules or guidelines for interpretation become sensible based on our assumptions regarding how legal drafters indicate their intent.

From this perspective, the battle of canons identified by Llewellyn is really an inter-system, not an intra-system, dispute. This is easiest to see if one focuses on "plain meaning" and "intentionalist" or "purposive" theories of interpretation. It is immediately apparent that many of the "thrust but parry" pairs simply represent a canon from one model posed against one from the other. Thus:

> 1. A statute cannot go beyond its text. [plain meaning]
>
> But
>
> To effect its purpose a statute may be implemented beyond its text. [purpose]
>
> . . . .
>
> 12. If the language is plain and unambiguous it must be given effect. [plain meaning]
>
> But
>
> Not when a literal interpretation would lead to absurd or mischievous consequences or thwart manifest purpose. [purpose]
>
> . . . .
>
> 18. Words are to be interpreted according to the proper grammatical effect of their arrangement within the statute. [plain meaning]
>
> But
>
> Rules or grammar will be disregarded where strict adherence would defeat purpose. [purpose]
>
> 19. Exceptions not made cannot be read. [plain meaning]
>
> But
>
> The letter is only the "bark." Whatever is within the reason of the law is within the law itself. [purpose]

So Llewellyn's article should lead us not to despair or ridicule, but rather to a discussion of the more interesting question of the appropriate normative approach, which, in turn, might well dissolve the very oppositions that have made the piece famous.

---

    [2] Felix Frankfurter, *Some Reflections on the Reading of Statutes*, 47 Colum. L. Rev. 527, 544 (1947).

EDWARD L. RUBIN,
MODERN STATUTES, LOOSE CANONS, AND THE LIMITS OF PRACTICAL REASON:
A RESPONSE TO FARBER AND ROSS,
45 Vand. L. Rev. 579, 583–84 (1992)[*]

B. The Problem of Loose Canons

The fact that modern statutes are instructions to implementation mechanisms which operate within a larger scheme of governance indicates why the standard canons of statutory construction are generally useless and occasionally harmful. The canons are decontextualized; they are general statements about the interpretation of statutory language with no consideration of the different types of statutes or the different roles that courts play in relation to these statutes. They are loose canons, showing up at unpredictable times and rolling about in unpredictable directions. Worse than their unpredictability is their oppressive noise and the ever-present danger of explosion. They distract judges from the real task at hand — the determination of the statute's role, and their own role, in the complicated task of modern governance.

A statute's structural features, such as its degree of transitivity, will control the applicability of many standard canons of interpretation. One of the most familiar canons is *ejusdem generis*: "where general words follow an enumeration they are to be held as applying only to persons and things of the same general kind or class specifically mentioned." Jonathan Macey and Geoffrey Miller, in their contribution to this Symposium, give the example of the Labor-Management Reporting and Disclosure Act (LMRDA), which forbids unions to "fine, suspend, expel, or otherwise discipline" members for exercising certain labor-related rights. In *Breininger v. Sheet Metal Workers*, the issue was whether the union, by discriminating against the plaintiff in making job referrals through its hiring hall, was engaged in discipline forbidden by the Act. Applying the rule of *ejusdem generis*, the Supreme Court held that "discipline" referred to sanctions authorized by the union, not "personal vendettas" by union officials. Justice Stevens dissented from this holding, relying on the usage of the term "discipline" in prior Supreme Court cases. This, of course, is another canon of statutory construction; as might be expected, it often leads in an opposite direction from *ejusdem generis*.

Both canons of statutory construction that the Justices invoked in *Breininger* are loose canons. They are incoherent without an understanding of the statute's position in our administrative structure. The initial questions to ask are what implementation mechanism is the legislature addressing and in what terms is that mechanism being addressed. These issues do not turn on legislative intent or any metaphysical assumptions about the thought processes of a collective body. They are determined by the structural features of the statute itself.

STEPHEN F. ROSS,
WHERE HAVE YOU GONE, KARL LLEWELLYN?
SHOULD CONGRESS TURN ITS LONELY EYES TO YOU?
45 Vand. L. Rev. 561, 563 (1992)[*]

II. The Use of Normative Canons

Many commentators have correctly observed that the canons serve a number of functions, but I believe they are best understood as falling into two discrete categories:

descriptive canons and normative canons. Descriptive canons are principles that involve predictions as to what the legislature must have meant, or probably meant, by employing particular statutory language. These canons may be directed to the judiciary expressly by statute or created by the courts themselves. Rules of syntax or grammar, principles that statutory provisions should be read to avoid internal inconsistency or conflict with other enactments, or canons such as *ejusdem generis* are examples of descriptive canons. A judge deploying a descriptive canon is attempting to act as an agent to effectuate congressional intent.

In contrast, normative canons are principles, created in the federal system exclusively by judges, that do not purport to describe accurately what Congress actually intended or what the words of a statute mean, but rather direct courts to construe any ambiguity in a particular way in order to further some policy objective. Judge Wald provided a classic example of a normative canon when she observed that judges often presume "that Congress did not intend to interfere with the traditional power and authority of the states unless it signaled its intention in neon lights."

Especially today, normative canons require careful consideration. They clearly reflect *judicial*, not congressional, policy concerns. . . .

J.W. HURST,
DEALING WITH STATUTES
57–62, 65 (1982)[*]

By the late twentieth century many rules familiar in nineteenth-century opinions and treatises had atrophied or suffered sharply diminished appeal. My concern is with a few which survive in action and continue to figure materially in current handling of statutes. Two main lines of difference emerge. Some rules of construction endure because they reflect specific realities of communication through the legislative process. Most rules inherited from the nineteenth century were of a highly general character. This is the type that has tended to disappear in twentieth-century analysis. Of this kind there are only two notable survivors — the rule enjoining strict construction of statutes in derogation of common law, and the rule requiring strict construction of penal statutes.

The rules of construction that best reflect the realities of legislative process are those that are most consistent with the deference owed the legislature's primacy in policymaking. Three types of rules creating presumptions as to legislative intent especially conform to this attitude: those dealing with word usage, with statutory context, and with legislation bearing on related subjects.

Legislators do not usually invent language; like other people normally they draw on the common stock of communication. Most of the time it is realistic to presume that they intend to follow familiar usage. One basic distinction in regular usage is that between words that connote broad classes of persons, things or situations and those that denote particular times. Thus where a statute uses generic rather than specific words there seems reason to presume that the legislature intends an expansive rather than a restrictive reading. In *Church of the Holy Trinity*, though it found the inferences from the face of the statute rebutted from legislative history, the Supreme Court conceded that there was "great force" to the argument for breadth from the words of the Act. The Act did not forbid the assisted emigration of foreigners to perform carpentry, shoemaking, or any other particular occupations, but rather, the Court noted, "the general words labor and service [are] both used." In contrast, the Court gave full force to what it deemed words of broad categories in holding that the federal Safety Appliance Acts required power brakes on a motor track car used by a section gang in maintaining the railroad right of way: Congress "wrote into the Safety Appliance Acts that their coverage embraced 'all trains, locomotives, tenders, cars, and

---

similar vehicles.' This plain language could not have been more all-inclusive. This Court has construed the language of the Act in its generic sense."

Another presumption with a realistic basis in regular patterns of communication says that if the legislature uses words which have an ordinary meaning, we should assume that it intends them in that meaning unless the contrary is shown. The burden of persuasion is on one who claims that the words should be read in some sense peculiar to a special situation, as with usage particular to a given trade or category of technical or professional knowledge. Thus where a tariff act fixed different rates for "vegetables" and for "fruits" without indicating any specialized meaning for the terms, the Supreme Court appealed to common usage to decide that Congress did not intend to tax tomatoes as "fruit."

However, with all its commonsense appeal, resort to the ordinary meaning of words carries a high risk of begging the real issue in many cases. Words do not have meaning in the abstract. They have meaning with reference only to some subject which those choosing the words mean to address. We cannot answer the question, what is the ordinary meaning of the word "ring" without asking a prior question: Is the speaker talking about a signal from a telephone, an ornament to slip on a finger, an arena under a circus tent? Often the difficult problem is to identify the subject the legislature intends to deal with; if we know that, then the ordinary meaning of the words, used with reference to that subject, is likely to present no serious issue. The majority opinion in *Caminetti v. United States* (1917) shows a classic instance of begging the true question under the deceptive simplicity of appealing to the presumption favoring ordinary meaning. The Mann Act makes it an offense knowingly to transport in interstate commerce any woman "for the purpose of prostitution or debauchery, or for any other immoral purpose." The defendant took a woman across a state line for illicit sex, without payment. The majority had no trouble in finding his conduct within the ban of the Act. . . .

. . . But the fighting issue was precisely whether Congress used the words intending to deal with "sexual relations" or only with commercialized sexual relations. When Congress passed the Mann Act there was unquestionably a "common understanding of what constitutes an immoral purpose," when people were talking about any sexual relations outside of marriage. But that fact provides no evidence whether the subject Congress was addressing was all illicit sex or only illicit sex for pay.

A third presumption that fits the realities of legislative communication is that which enjoins that we read particular words or phrases in the light cast by other parts of the same statute. Legislation of any consequence is typically a complex of parts. It will have components that deal with persons or situations regulated, with the nature of apprehended evils or needs, with goals and the ranking of goals, and with procedures or means to accomplish its objectives. Adjustments, bargains, compromises made in hammering out the final product will likely have explicit or implicit reflections in the different elements built into the statute. We should not romanticize the process of obtaining legislation; it is usually a somewhat rough-and-tumble business, and what emerges is unlikely to be a finely joined piece of cabinet work. Nonetheless, those who draft and shepherd through a measure create some pattern of policy, so that there is ground for presuming that their intent in particulars lies in the relations of those particulars to the surrounding pattern.

A fourth presumption belonging to the general category of rules which carry persuasion because they reflect characteristic legislative operations is that which, in reading the statute immediately in issue, gives weight to material contained in other acts dealing with the same subject or with similar subject matter. A legislature typically acts only when and as someone presses it to act. Hence it is likely to deal at one point of time with less than the whole, potential extent of the issues or choices it confronts. Thus legislative intent may emerge in full definition only through a succession of acts.

. . . .

Judges' readiness to give weight to inferences from the succession of statutory provisions on the same subject or to provisions in other legislation dealing with like subject matter accords with their willingness to take note of amendments dealt with in the course of passage of a bill, and to consider evidence from committee reports, and transcripts of legislative hearings and debates. Arguably, material drawn from what legislators vote into the statute books should be preferred evidence of likely legislative intent; the fact of its enactment carries more persuasive certification of its validity. At least, the tone of judicial opinions is to treat such statute book evidence with respect comparable to that accorded committee reports.

In contrast to rules of construction that reflect familiar patterns of communication or operations in the legislative process are those that explicitly declare broad value preferences not tied to any particular statutory subject matter. . . .

If we regard together uses judges make of statutory text, legislative history, and general rules of construction in the second half of the twentieth century, one approach is clearly dominant, standing in sharp contrast to nineteenth-century treatment of legislation. The twentieth-century emphasis is on coming to a specific focus on a given statute in its full-dimensioned particularity of policy, rather than emphasizing materials or values not immediately connected to that enactment. Courts now seem usually to strive to grasp the distinctive message of statutory words, taken in their own context, with reference to the documented process that produced that particular act, including legislative history deserving credibility, and policy guides supplied by the legislature's successive development of the given policy area and related areas. The twentieth-century emphasis thus is not on broad, standardized formulas, but on custom-built determinations, fashioned out of materials immediate and special to the legislation at issue. It is an approach both more pragmatic and more deferential to the functions of courts under the separation of powers. For our time the single most practical guide to the interpretation of statutes is a caution from Justice Holmes, that "every question of construction is unique, and an argument that would prevail in one case may be inadequate in another."

NOTES AND QUESTIONS

1. For another treatment of the modern use of canons of statutory construction, see CASS SUNSTEIN, AFTER THE RIGHTS REVOLUTION: RECONCEIVING THE REGULATORY STATE 148–57 (1990).

2. Have you been able to see evidence of Holmes' view that "every question of construction is unique" in the materials in this Part on statutory interpretation?

MICHAEL SINCLAIR,
"ONLY A SITH THINKS LIKE THAT": LLEWELLYN'S
"DUELING CANONS," ONE TO SEVEN[*]
50 N.Y.L. SCH. L. REV. 919 (2005–06)

[I]n the field of statutory construction . . . there are "correct," unchallengeable rules of "how to read" which lead in happily variant directions.[1]

I. INTRODUCTION

In 1950 the redoubtable Karl N. Llewellyn launched the most famous of all attacks on canons of construction, a list of twenty-eight pairs of canons having opposite effect.[2] This

---

[*] Copyright 2005 by New York Law School Law Review. Reprinted with permission.

[1] Karl N. Llewellyn, *Remarks on the Theory of Appellate Decision and the Rules or Canons of About How Statutes are to be Construed*, 3 VAND. L. REV. 395, 399 (1950) [hereinafter Llewellyn, *Canons*].

[2] *Id.*

was and has been widely considered by statutory interpretation theorists to be devastating to the legitimacy of canons. Fifteen years ago, *Vanderbilt Law Review* ran a symposium on Llewellyn's attack and it met with uniform approval.[3] Daniel Farber, for example, called Llewellyn's list "fiendishly deconstructive;"[4] Jonathan Macey and Geoffrey Miller said it "derailed" "intellectual debate about the canons for almost a quarter of a century."[5] But there was no detailed examination then, nor has there been since, of the validity or contrariety of Llewellyn's pairings.

In any other discipline one would expect every element of every pair in Llewellyn's list to be scrutinized closely, and the justifications to be laid on the table for examination. We should not accept Llewellyn's list as a "devastating deconstruction" just because of its rhetorical impact. It is like adopting a theory in chemistry on the basis of an extraordinary experiment that nobody ever even tried to replicate. Indeed, the relative stability and longevity of many canons suggest that they are well adapted to their tasks, that a sudden demonstration of their invalidity is likely to be ill-founded. Thus, the contrasting pairs of canons in Llewellyn's list deserve examination.

That is my project: to take each pair in turn and hold it up to scrutiny, to trick out the justifications, and examine the applications to which they have been put. My initial hypothesis was that Llewellyn's pairings might not prove devastatingly inconsistent. The conditions for the proper use of each of the superficially contrary members of a pair, and the justifications for their use, might adequately deflate the dramatic effect of the prima facie contrariety.

. . . .

II. CANONS: AN OVERVIEW

If one is to criticize Llewellyn's use of a verbal formula as insufficiently canonical, one owes an explanation of what a canon is.

Canons are wise saws backed by experience and intuition. They are not law, nor do they claim to be universally binding, but they should have significance greater than a mere cliché. One might see them as having compulsive weight somewhere between homespun sayings and general truths of science or mathematics. That is, "*expressio unius est exclusio alterius*" carries more weight than "A stitch in time saves nine," but less than "Every even number is the sum of two primes."

. . . .

Most general criticisms of canons treat them as fixed, unconditional, formulaic rules to be applied mindlessly at every opportunity.[17] Yet recently, scholars of statutory construction have been arguing for an increase in rigidity and formalism in the use of canons. Adrien Vermeule argues that every judge should adopt and follow a fixed interpretive doctrine;[18] Gary O' Connor argues for a restatement as an authoritative formulation of permissible rules of interpretation;[19] and in the extreme, Nicholas Quinn

---

[3] Symposium: *A Reevaluation of the Canons of Statutory Interpretation*, 45 VAND. L. REV. 529 (1992).

[4] Daniel A. Farber, *The Inevitability of Practical Reason: Statutes, Formalism, and the Rule of Law*, 45 VAND. L. REV. 533 (1992).

[5] Jonathan R. Macey & Geoffrey P. Miller, *The Canons of Statutory Construction and Judicial Preferences*, 45 VAND. L. REV. 647 (1992).

[17] *See, e.g.*, REED DICKERSON, THE INTERPRETATION AND APPLICATION OF STATUTES 234 (1975).

[18] Adrien Vermeule, *Interpretive Choice*, 75 N.Y.U. L. REV. 74 (2000). I have argued that the reasoning on which Vermeule's thesis is based is fallacious. *See* Michael Sinclair, *The Proper Treatment of "Interpretive Choice" in Statutory Decision-Making*, 45 N.Y.L. SCH. L. REV. 389 (2002).

[19] Gary E. O'Connor, *Restatement (First) of Statutory Interpretation*, 7 N.Y.U. J. LEGIS. & PUB. POL'Y 333 (2003).

Rosenkranz argues for the adoption of statue-like rules of interpretation.[20] I hope to show that any attempt to rigidify or formalize canons and their use is fundamentally misguided. The application of a canon depends on its justification. When the conditions presupposed by a canon do not obtain, then it should not be used. Llewellyn himself says so: "Plainly, to make any canon take hold in a particular instance, the construction contended for must be sold, essentially, by means other than the use of the canon."[21] A canon, then, looks more like a formulaic summary of the end result of a process of reasoning, but a process sufficiently commonplace to justify a canonical formula.

. . . .

III. Llewellyn's Pairs

Pair One

THRUST: "A statute cannot go beyond its text."[29]

PARRY: "To effect its purpose a statute may be implemented beyond its text."[30]

Thrust #1: "A statute cannot go beyond its text."

This is not the familiar "Statutes in derogation of the common law will be construed narrowly;" Llewellyn saved that for his second pair. Thrust #1 would be applicable in either of two situations: (i) when two statutes converge as to some requirement, one may not be construed so broadly as to encroach upon the other; or (ii) when the common law is neutral, a statute may not be applied by judicial construction beyond its terms.

. . . .

NOTES AND QUESTIONS

1. Professor Sinclair provides a detailed analysis of Llewellyn's "pairs," based on the authorities cited by Llewellyn at the time he published his article in 1950. Sinclair concludes that the pairs are not so opposite as has been assumed over the years.

2. Part II of Professor Sinclair's analysis appears at 51 N.Y.L. Sch. L. Rev. 1003 (2006–2007).

3. Can you make a practical, advocacy argument based on Professor Sinclair's conclusions?

4. Are you beginning to see that each canon must be considered on its own and not in a "loose" or "decontextualized" manner?

5. For a provocative discussion of canons, or "default rules," see Einer Elhauge, *Preference-Estimating Statutory Default Rules*, 102 Colum. L. Rev. 2027, 2162 (2002). For a response, see Amanda L. Tyler, *Continuity, Coherence, and the Canons*, 99 Nw. U. L. Rev. 1389 (2005).

6. In 1996 the United States Supreme Court noted: "To apply a canon properly one must understand its rationale." *Varity Corp. v. Howe*, 516 U.S. 489, 511 (1996).

7. For an in-depth consideration of the "communis opinio" canon ("it is the common opinion"), see Michael P. Healy, Cummunis Opinio *and the Methods of Statutory Interpretation: Interpreting Law or Changing Law*, 43 Wm. & Mary L. Rev. 539 (2001).

---

[20] Nicholas Quinn Rosenkranz, *Federal Rules of Statutory Interpretation*, 115 Harv. L. Rev. 2085 (2002).

[21] Llewellyn, *Canons, supra* note 1, at 401. To do Llewellyn justice, one should see his list of dueling canons not as a devastating deconstruction, but as a demonstration of this thesis.

[29] Llewellyn, *Canons, supra* note 1, at 401.

[30] *Id.*

1. The Words

Arguably, the most logical starting point in statutory interpretation is with an examination of the words themselves. Indeed, other aids to interpretation are necessary only when the words can be challenged as ambiguous. Of course, even perfectly obvious and clear statutory language can be "interpreted" when the literal result under the statute is "unfair" or "manifestly against the purpose and intent of the legislature," to mention some of the rationales. Most interpretation problems, however, start with consideration of the language used, whether or not other factors will also be evaluated.

As you read the following cases, consider the following questions. Are the canons of construction flexible or rigid? Which should they be? Are the words under consideration actually ambiguous? Could the problem have been solved without resort to the canons? Is the court's interpretation consistent with the legislature's apparent objective? If two canons are applicable but would create contrary results, which should take priority? Are the canons appropriate means for persuading legislative drafters to adopt consistent practices?

a. Expressio Unius

UNITED STATES v. ROBINSON
359 F. Supp. 52 (S.D. Fla. 1973)

MEHRTENS, DISTRICT JUDGE.

This case is before the Court following its remand by the United States Court of Appeals for the Fifth Circuit "for an expedited evidentiary hearing to determine whether the wiretap applications in this case were properly authorized under 18 U.S.C. § 2516(1)."[1]

. . . .

Having reviewed and analyzed the record and the arguments of counsel, this Court has concluded that the three wiretap applications in this case were improperly authorized, resulting in the suppression of all evidence obtained directly or indirectly as a result of the wiretaps. This Court is not unmindful of the worthwhile law enforcement objectives which are thereby frustrated; however, we are a nation of laws, and if we are to continue to be so, the laws which define and limit the legitimate enterprise of government within the scope of precious constitutional protections must be enforced with a vigor no less unrelenting than are those laws which define and limit the legitimate enterprise of individual citizens.

In concluding that the law compels the suppression of the intercepted communications and their fruits in this case, the Court makes the following factual findings:

The then-Attorney General, John N. Mitchell, played no part whatsoever in the three wiretap authorizations in the instant case. In its Supplemental Brief, the government argued that the Attorney General was made aware of the ongoing wiretaps on the Escandar apartment and lobby phones and ratified them. The Court finds that there was no such ratification and even had there been, it hardly would have satisfied the statutory authorization requirement.

At some unspecified time prior to the authorizations in this case, the Attorney

---

[1] 28 U.S.C. § 510 provides as follows:

"The Attorney General may from time to time make such provisions as he considers appropriate authorizing the performance by any other officer, employee, or agency of the Department of Justice of any function of the Attorney General."

For the reasons set out below, the Court has concluded that 28 U.S.C. § 510 has been superseded in wiretap matters by the Congress in 18 U.S.C. § 2516.

General delegated to his Executive Assistant, Sol Lindenbaum, a general authority pursuant to 28 U.S.C. § 510 to authorize wiretap applications in his absence. The record is clear, however, that this delegation was not *ad hoc* but was, at best, general and unproscribed and was, at worst, formally nonexistent.

The three authorization decisions in this case were made by Sol Lindenbaum, the Executive Assistant to the Attorney General. The Court is compelled to this conclusion despite various documents in the record to the contrary, by the most recent affidavits of Lindenbaum and Henry E. Petersen, then Deputy Assistant Attorney General. Apart from these affidavits, the record thoroughly refutes the conclusion they compel. . . .

Having discovered, therefore, that Sol Lindenbaum as Executive Assistant to the Attorney General made the authorization decisions in this case, the Court has reached the legal conclusion that 18 U.S.C. § 2516 forbids the exercise of this function by anyone other than *the Attorney General* personally or one of *the Assistant Attorneys General* personally and then only when specially designated by *the Attorney General. A fortiori,* even had Sol Lindenbaum merely "specially designated" Will Wilson to make the authorization decision and had Henry E. Petersen made that decision for Will Wilson, the legal result would be no different. As 18 U.S.C. § 2516 forbids the authorization power to Sol Lindenbaum, so does it forbid to him the power to specially designate an Assistant Attorney General for that purpose. Likewise, as the statutory scheme forbids the authorization decision by the Executive Assistant to the Attorney General, so does it forbid that decision by a Deputy Assistant Attorney General.

The legal issue before the Court is a simple one. Not only does this Court hold that as a matter of law Sol Lindenbaum may not authorize a wiretap application consistently with the law as passed by Congress, but the majority of courts speaking to this issue reach this same conclusion. One must not lose sight amidst all the debate, which superficially appears to center around a contest of words, that we are dealing here with a power which has, for by far the greatest part of our history, been forbidden to government under all but the very most limited circumstances. We are dealing with an awesome power which strikes directly at the heart of the right to privacy, which has been elevated in other contexts to the highest level of constitutional protection. That the power legitimately exists at all is beyond the understanding of many of our great legal and constitutional minds.

Nevertheless, the Supreme Court has approved, at least in principle, of wiretapping under tightly controlled conditions. Congress has responded both to the need for new effective law enforcement tools and to the tacit and limited acceptance by the Supreme Court of electronic surveillance as such a tool, with Title III of the Omnibus Crime Control and Safe Streets Act of 1968. Title III forbids the interception of electronic communications and provides severe penalties for those who violate the prohibition. Only as an exception in its most narrow sense has Congress provided in Title III for the interception of wire and oral communications as a tool in the investigation of certain offenses for which the need for such interception is particularly acute. The Supreme Court has made it explicit that Title III is to be strictly construed in favor of the rights of the individual.

In 18 U.S.C. § 2516, as well as throughout Title III, Congress has drafted the wiretap law clearly and unambiguously. The words of Section 2516 are themselves plain and definite. Unless we are to disregard entirely longstanding canons of construction which have heretofore been given a high place in our judicial thinking, the words of this statute must be applied as they read.

. . . .

The Court also finds unpersuasive the government's argument that the same Congress which enacted 18 U.S.C.A. § 2516 also enacted 18 U.S.C.A. § 245(a)(1) which expressly forbids subdelegation of the authority to institute prosecution under the Civil Rights Act of 1968. The government reasons that had the same Congress intended to forbid delegation beyond the express terms of the statute, it would have said so in unequivocal terms. This argument must fail, because from the language of § 2516, "the Attorney General, or any Assistant Attorney General specially designated by the Attorney General," it is absolutely clear how far Congress intended that the Attorney General's power of subdelegation in wiretap authorizations should extend. It is a long-recognized rule of statutory construction that the enumeration of specific items implies the exclusion of all others, *expressio unius est exclusio alterius*. The government, itself, quotes with approval from Professor Davis that "differences in statutory language are haphazard and unplanned." Congress certainly could have added the phrase, "which authorization power may not be further delegated," to § 2516, which would likely have satisfied the government's contentions; but in the Court's opinion, any such additional language would have been redundant.

. . . .

Upon consideration of the foregoing, the evidence used to convict the defendants, which has been conceded to have come from these improperly authorized wiretaps, is hereby suppressed.

NATIONAL PETROLEUM REFINERS ASSOCIATION v. FEDERAL TRADE COMMISSION
482 F.2d 672 (D.C. Cir. 1973)

J. Skelly Wright, Circuit Judge.

This case presents an important question concerning the powers and procedures of the Federal Trade Commission. We are asked to determine whether the Commission, under its governing statute, the Trade Commission Act, 15 U.S.C. § 41 *et seq.* (1970), and specifically 15 U.S.C. § 46(g), is empowered to promulgate substantive rules of business conduct or, as it terms them, "Trade Regulation Rules."

. . . .

Appellees argue that since Section 5 mentions only adjudication as the means of enforcing the statutory standard, any supplemental means of putting flesh on that standard, such as rule-making, is contrary to the overt legislative design. But Section 5(b) does not use limiting language suggesting that adjudication alone is the only proper means of elaborating the statutory standard. It merely makes clear that a Commission decision, after complaint and hearing, followed by a cease and desist order, is the way to force an offender to halt his illegal activities. Nor are we persuaded by appellees' argument that, despite the absence of limiting language in Section 5 regarding the role of adjudication in defining the meaning of the statutory standard, we should apply the maxim of statutory construction *expressio unius est exclusio alterius* and conclude that adjudication is the *only* means of defining the statutory standard. This maxim is increasingly considered unreliable . . . for it stands on the faulty premise that all possible alternative or supplemental provisions were necessarily considered and rejected by the legislative draftsmen.

. . . .

. . . We hold that under the terms of its governing statute, 15 U.S.C. § 41 *et seq.*, and under Section 6(g), 15 U.S.C. § 46(g), in particular, the Federal Trade Commission is authorized to promulgate rules defining the meaning of the statutory standards of the illegality the Commission is empowered to prevent. Thus we must reverse the District Court's judgment and remand this case for further proceedings.

It is so ordered.

NOTES AND QUESTIONS

1. Given the general authority of the Attorney General in § 510, would he (and Congress if it were aware of it) be reasonable in relying on that authority to delegate actions to his subordinates? Would the court's argument be more cogently stated as follows: that the specific wiretap provisions control the general delegation provision? Is

not § 2516's language clear? If so, is not the only ambiguity caused by § 510? If that is the case, is reliance on *expressio unius* misplaced? How useful in determining the meaning of the language in § 2516 is the doctrine of looking to parallel statutes, such as § 245(a)(1)? That section was enacted by the same Congress that enacted § 2516, and expressly forbids subdelegation. Does the court effectively counter this argument by referring to the specific rather than the general provision?

2. Is the seemingly clear congressional policy of permitting wiretapping only under extremely close supervision an effective argument in assessing Congress' use of specific designations in § 2516? Was there a desire to limit wiretaps to those the Attorney General personally authorized and directed? If this is the rationale of the court's interpretation, must the Attorney General under § 2516 designate an Assistant Attorney "specially" for each case, or can the designated Assistant Attorney supervise all wiretapping cases? Can several Assistant Attorneys General each be so "specially" designated at any one time?

3. Since all parties seem to agree that "differences in statutory language are haphazard and unplanned," does this fact not argue strongly for rejection of all canons based on assumptions of legislative knowledge?

4. When the Supreme Court considered the interpretation question posed by 18 U.S.C. § 2516(1), it did not mention the *expressio unius* canon. Instead, the Court relied upon the purpose of the statute and an extensive discussion of legislative history. *United States v. Giordano*, 416 U.S. 505, 516–24 (1974). Which approach is preferable: Canons without more or the more expansive inquiry in *Giordano*?

5. In *NPRA v. FTC*, the court says the canon rests on the "faulty premise that all possible alternative or supplemental provisions were necessarily considered and rejected by the legislative draftsmen." Does this mean that use of the canon is never appropriate?

6. To what extent is the canon of *expressio unius* simply reflective of the antipathy of the courts to the legislative process and an effort by courts to restrict the operation of an act to its narrowest permissible limits? Such was stated by Justice Jackson in rejecting application of this canon and that of *ejusdem generis;* he went on to comment:

> However well these rules may serve at times to aid in deciphering legislative intent, they long have been subordinated to the doctrine that courts will construe the details of an act in conformity with its dominating general purpose, will read text in the light of context and will interpret the text so far as the meaning of the words fairly permits so as to carry out in particular cases the generally expressed legislative policy.

Does Jackson's alternative basis for analysis lack somewhat in certainty? Do the canons have continual vitality, in part, because they provide some concrete (if not necessarily valid) basis for deciding a case?

7. Should failure to state other commonly utilized and accepted alternatives ever be sufficient to infer an intent to negate such other options? Could not Congress specify "and by no other means" if limitations were intended? Should the doctrine be overcome where the drafter says "including but not limited to"?

8. In *Sonneman v. Hickel*, 836 P.2d 936 (Ala. 1992), the Court rejected application of the *expressio unius* canon where it would have produced an interpretation of the statute leading to serious constitutional questions.

UNIFORM STATUTE AND RULE CONSTRUCTION ACT (1995)[*]

SECTION 20. OTHER AIDS TO CONSTRUCTION

. . . .

Comment

. . . .

The canon "the statement of one thing implies the exclusion of another" (*Expressio Unius Est Exclusio Alterius*"), is not included in this Act because it has little practical use. It is appropriately used only if the statement, context, and other evidence of legislative intent indicates that the listing in the text is exhaustive; it merely states what is already known — that the text is exhaustive. Sutherland, *Stat. Const.* § 47.25 (5th ed. 1992). Often it is readily apparent that a statement is exhaustive and, if so, use of the canon merely reinforces that conclusion. *See Mercein v. Burton*, 17 Tex. 206 (1856). The canon is merely an aid to determining legislative intent and is not a rule of law. *American Rio Grande Land & Irrigation Co., v. Karle*, 237 S.W. 358 (Tex. Civ. App. 1922). The canon's limitations are noted in *Industrial Trust Co. v. Goldman*, 193 A. 852, 855 (R.I. 1937).

b.   Ejusdem Generis

STATE OF MAINE v. FERRIS
284 A.2d 288 (Me. 1971)

Before Dufresne, C.J., and Webber, Weatherbee, Pomeroy, Wernick and Archibald, JJ.

Weatherbee, Justice.

The State Police obtained a warrant to search the defendant's residence and garage after several months of surveillance and investigation. The police allegedly had probable cause to believe that Mr. Ferris was engaged in illegal bookmaking and pursuant to the search seized evidence of such alleged activity. While executing the search on the defendant's premises, a police officer looked through the window of a car, which defendant had recently parked in the driveway, and observed on the floor slips of paper which appeared to be records of gambling activities. The police subsequently obtained a warrant to search the car and seized the material found therein. . . .

The defendant was indicted on six counts of . . . (bookmaking) and one count of violation of 17 M.R.S.A. § 1811 (possession of gambling implements). . . . The defendant, who had waived jury trial, was found not guilty as to the six counts of bookmaking but guilty as to the violation of 17 M.R.S.A. § 1811. The defendant appealed.

At trial on the charge of violation of 17 M.R.S.A. § 1811 the state introduced 22 exhibits found in the car which witnesses identified as "betting slips" which the witnesses said represented abbreviated handwritten notations of wagers placed on sporting events. The Justice found the possession of these slips to be violative of 17 M.R.S.A. § 1811. . . .

17 M.R.S.A. § 1811 provides:

> No person shall have in his actual or constructive possession any punch board, seal card, slot gambling machine or other implements, apparatus or materials of any form of gambling, and no person shall solicit, obtain or offer to obtain orders for the sale or delivery of any punch board, seal card, slot

---

[*] Reprinted with permission.

gambling machine or other implements, apparatus or material of gambling.

The count of the indictment which charged the defendant with violation of this statute read:

COUNT VII: THE GRAND JURY FURTHER CHARGES: that Ferris P. Ferris, of Waterville, County of Kennebec, State of Maine, did on or about December 12, 1969, at Waterville, County of Kennebec, State of Maine, have in his actual and constructive possession certain gambling implements and materials, to wit: numerous betting slips and records used in relation to illegal wagers on horseraces and sporting events unauthorized by law in violation of 17 M.R.S.A. § 1811. . . .

In interpreting statutes, this Court must effectuate the intention of the legislature. *State v. London*, 156 Me. 123, 162 A.2d 150 (1960). We find the intent of the legislature in enacting this statute was to prohibit the possession or sale of actual gambling devices — those devices or mechanisms the functioning of which determine whether a gambler wins or loses. . . .

In construing the ambiguous use of the general language of the statute we turn to the familiar rule of *ejusdem generis*. When words of enumeration are immediately followed by words of general import the general words, when their use is uncertain, should be governed by the specific. Here, the enumeration of devices specifically prohibited — "punch board, seal card, slot gambling machine" — indicates that in adding the words "other implements, apparatus or materials of any form of gambling" the legislature intended to include only other articles which also have a per se relationship to the determination of the outcome of wagers recognizable from common experience. We hold that the legislature's addition of the general language prohibits the possession of other implements of the same character and class as those gambling devices specifically mentioned. . . .

We agree with the defendant that the possession of the material which the state alleges was seized from him is not prohibited by the statute.

Betting slips and records of betting do not constitute such gambling devices as the legislature has outlawed. Records of such things as amounts wagered, the point spreads, the odds, and the successes and failures of athletic teams or race horses in prior events are aids to the memory of the gambler but not in themselves devices which determine the outcome of the wager. Although such materials may be evidence of illegal gambling or bookmaking they are not implements, apparatus, or materials of gambling which were declared contraband under 17 M.R.S.A. § 1811. . . .

Appeal sustained. Indictment dismissed.

All Justices concurring.

SHORT v. STATE
234 Ind. 17, 122 N.E.2d 82 (1954)

GILKISON, JUDGE.

On April 27, 1953, appellant was charged by affidavit in the Trial Court. Omitting caption, signature, verification and endorsements the affidavit is as follows:

Jess Julian being duly sworn upon his oath says that Robert Maloney Short on or about the 15th day of December, A.D. 1952, at said County and State as affiant verily believed did then and there unlawfully, forcibly and feloniously take from the person of and the possession of Fred C. Luhring, by violence and putting the said Fred C. Luhring in fear, certain personal property, to-wit: Three Thousand dollars ($3,000.00) in lawful and current money of the United States of America of the personal property of said Fred C. Luhring, and while engaged in the commission of said robbery, the said Robert Maloney Short inflicted physical injury upon the person of the said Fred C. Luhring with a soft drink bottle.

Then and there being contrary to the form of the Statute, in such cases made and provided, and against the peace and dignity of the State of Indiana.

. . . .

Appellant invokes the rule of *"Ejusdem Generis"* in interpreting the legislative intent as to that part of section 10-4101 involved in this appeal. That rule, in substance, is that when words of specific or limited signification in a statute are followed by general words of more comprehensive import, the general words are construed to embrace only such things as are of like kind or class with those designated by the specific words, unless a contrary intention is clearly expressed.

. . . .

Notwithstanding the rules noted above, the construction of penal statutes should not be wantonly narrowed so as to exclude the cases that are fairly covered by them. . . . A criminal statute should be interpreted so as to give efficient operation to the expressed intent of the legislature, if reasonably possible.

The statute upon which the prosecution is based is as follows:

> Robbery — Assault and battery with intent to commit robbery — Physical injury inflicted in robbery or attempt — Penalty. — Whoever takes from the person of another any article of value by violence or by putting in fear, is guilty of robbery, and on conviction shall be imprisoned not less than ten (10) years nor more than twenty-five (25) years, and be disfranchised and rendered incapable of holding any office of trust or profit for any determinate period. Whoever inflicts any wound or other physical injury upon any person with any firearm, dirk, stiletto, bludgeon, billy, club, blackjack, or any other deadly or dangerous weapon or instrument while engaged in the commission of a robbery, or while attempting to commit a robbery, shall, upon conviction, be imprisoned in the state prison for life.

Section 10-4101, Burns 1942 Repl.

A soft drink bottle is not designed to be either an offensive or defensive weapon, but the experience of man teaches us that it may be so used. Among other weapons, the use of which is forbidden by the statute are: "bludgeon, billy, club, blackjack." A soft drink bottle could be used in the capacity of either of these weapons, with like results to the victim. If so used in a robbery, it would be *ejusdem generis* with these weapons. It was the evident intent of the legislature to inflict heavy punishment upon anyone engaging in such violence. No error was committed in overruling the motion to quash the affidavit on this ground.

Finding no reversible error in the record, the judgment is affirmed.

EMMERT, J., Dissenting.

The majority opinion correctly states the rule of *ejusdem generis*, and then refuses to follow it. The same is true with the rule construing criminal statutes against the state and in favor of the defendant. Under the rule of *ejusdem generis*, as stated in the majority opinion, generic terms "embrace only such things as are of like kind or class with those designated by the specific words." The affidavit does not charge an injury was inflicted with a deadly and dangerous weapon and instrument, to-wit: a soft drink bottle, so the state asks us to take judicial notice that a soft drink bottle is a deadly or dangerous weapon like a bludgeon, a billy, a club, or a blackjack. This we have no right to do.

NOTES AND QUESTIONS

1. In *Ferris*, could the court have reached the result it did without using the canon? Is there some sort of a condition precedent that should be satisfied before a canon is invoked? Should canons of construction be used as a last resort when no other rationale for interpretation exists or should they be used whenever feasible? If used only where there is no other explanation, does the concept not lose its rationale as a "practice" engaged in by legislatures that courts should recognize?

2. As to the concept of *ejusdem generis*, is it not just as logical to conclude that words of enumeration are broadened in scope when followed by words of general import? Is the court more concerned here because the statute is penal?

3. Is the validity of the rule of *ejusdem generis* dependent upon the legislature's acceptance and adoption of it? Or, is the rule valid because it is based on a universal manner of reasoning? Would the rule be more defensible if the courts and the legislature reached an understanding or a mutual acceptance regarding its use?

4. The purpose of the rule *ejusdem generis* is to limit the meaning of general words which follow a list of specific words. Did the court in *Short* limit or expand the meaning of "deadly or dangerous weapon or instrument" by the use of the rule? Is the dissent not correct in saying the statute should be limited to weapons which are commonly recognized as being deadly or dangerous regardless of their use in a particular situation?

5. In *Short*, the intent of the legislature was to impose greater penalties on robberies involving injury to the victim. Does penalizing the use of weapons accomplish this goal? Was the wording of the statute necessary? How could it have been written to avoid the problem? Should the court rely on rules of construction when the result would be contrary to "logic and common sense"?

6. In *Gooch v. United States*, 297 U.S. 124, 128 (1936), the Court said: "The rule of *ejusdem generis*, while firmly established, is only an instrumentality for ascertaining the correct meaning of words when there is uncertainty. Ordinarily, it limits general terms which follow specific ones to matters similar to those specified; but it may not be used to defeat the obvious purpose of legislation."

7. In *In re Wallace W.*, 634 A.2d 53 (Md. 1993), the defendant who temporarily took another student's purse was charged under a statute prohibiting the unauthorized use of "any horse, mare, colt, buggy, cart, boat, craft, vessel, or any other vehicle including motor vehicle as defined in the laws of this state relating to such, *or property whatsoever*." (emphasis added). The defendant, of course, relied on the *ejusdem generis* canon. The court recognized two exceptions to the "rule"; 1) where the particular words exhaust the class, and therefore the general words following the class of particular words would be rendered meaningless surplusage, and 2) where invoking the canon would subvert the statute's obvious purpose. *Id.* at 56–57. Finding that the statute's particular words did not exhaust the classes of livestock and vehicles, and that there was no clear manifestation of contrary legislative intent, the court applied the canon and overturned the defendant's conviction.

8. A rule closely related to *ejusdem generis* is *noscitur a sociis*, "it is known from its associates." Under this rule, doubtful words or phrases are to take their character from associated words or phrases. How does this rule differ from *ejusdem generis*? Is it simply a more general statement of that rule? "[W]here two or more words are grouped together and ordinarily have a similar meaning, but are not equally comprehensive, the general words will be limited and qualified by the special words." 2 SUTHERLAND STATUTORY CONSTRUCTION 393 (3d ed. 1943). What impact would this rule have on the decision in *Short*?

9. In *Gutierrez v. Ada*, 528 U.S. 250 (2000), the Supreme Court considered whether the Organic Act of Guam's provisions required runoff elections in certain circumstances. It noted:

II

The key to understanding what the phrase "in any election" means is also the most salient feature of the provision in which it occurs. The section contains six express references to an election for Governor and Lieutenant Governor: "The Governor of Guam, together with the Lieutenant Governor, shall be elected . . ."; "[t]he Governor and Lieutenant Governor shall be chosen jointly, by the casting of each voter of a single vote . . ."; "a runoff election shall be held between the candidates for Governor and Lieutenant Governor . . ."; "[t]he first election for Governor and Lieutenant Governor shall be held . . ."; "[t]he Governor and Lieutenant Governor shall be elected every four years . . ."; "[t]he Governor and Lieutenant Governor shall hold office . . . until their successors are elected . . ." 48 U.S.C. § 1422. The reference to "any election" is preceded by two references to gubernatorial election and followed by four. With "any election" so surrounded, what could it refer to except an election for Governor and Lieutenant Governor, the subject of such relentless repetition? To ask the question is merely to apply an interpretive rule as familiar outside the law as it is within, for words and people are known by their companions. *See Gustafson v. Alloyd Co.*, 513 U.S. 561, 575 (1995) "[A] word is known by the company it keeps"); *Jarecki v. G.D. Searle & Co.*, 367 U.S. 303, 307 (1961) ("The maxim *noscitur a sociis*, . . . while not an inescapable rule, is often wisely applied where a word is capable of many meanings in order to avoid the giving of unintended breadth to the Acts of Congress").

. . . .

The second argument supposedly undermining the meaning naturally suggested by association was stressed by the Court of Appeals, which thought that reading "any election" to mean gubernatorial election would render the phrase a nullity and thus offend the rule against attributing redundancy to Congress, *see Kungys v. United States*, 485 U.S. 759, 778 (1988). The fact is that this argument has some force, but not enough. There is no question that the statute would be read as we read it even if the phrase were missing. But as one rule of construction among many, albeit an important one, the rule against redundancy does not necessarily have the strength to turn a tide of good cause to come out the other way.

CIRCUIT CITY STORES, INC. v. ADAMS
532 U.S. 105 (2001)

JUSTICE KENNEDY delivered the opinion of the Court.

Section 1 of the Federal Arbitration Act (FAA or Act) excludes from the Act's coverage "contracts of employment of seamen, railroad employees, or any other class of workers engaged in foreign or interstate commerce." 9 U.S.C. § 1. All but one of the Courts of Appeals which have addressed the issue interpret this provision as exempting contracts of employment of transportation workers, but not other employment contracts, from the FAA's coverage. A different interpretation has been adopted by the Court of Appeals for the Ninth Circuit, which construes the exemption so that all contracts of employment are beyond the FAA's reach, whether or not the worker is engaged in transportation. It applied that rule to the instant case. We now decide that the better interpretation is to construe the statute, as most of the Courts of Appeals have done, to confine the exemption to transportation workers.

I

In October 1995, respondent Saint Clair Adams applied for a job at petitioner Circuit City Stores, Inc., a national retailer of consumer electronics. Adams signed an employment application which included the following provision:

> "I agree that I will settle any and all previously unasserted claims, disputes or controversies arising out of or relating to my application or candidacy for employment, employment and/or cessation of employment with Circuit City, *exclusively* by final and binding *arbitration* before a neutral Arbitrator. By way of example only, such claims include claims under federal, state, and local statutory or common law, such as the Age Discrimination in Employment Act, Title VII of the Civil Rights Act of 1964, as amended, including the amendments of the Civil Rights Act of 1991, the Americans with Disabilities Act, the law of contract and [the] law of tort." App. 13 (emphasis in original).

Adams was hired as a sales counselor in Circuit City's store in Santa Rosa, California.

Two years later, Adams filed an employment discrimination lawsuit against Circuit City in state court, asserting claims under California's Fair Employment and Housing Act, Cal. Govt. Code Ann. § 12900 *et seq.* (1992 and Supp. 1997), and other claims based on general tort theories under California law. Circuit City filed suit in the United States District Court for the Northern District of California, seeking to enjoin the state-court action and to compel arbitration of respondent's claims pursuant to the FAA, 9 U.S.C. §§ 1–16. The District Court entered the requested order. Respondent, the court concluded, was obligated by the arbitration agreement to submit his claims against the employer to binding arbitration. An appeal followed.

. . . .

II

A

Congress enacted the FAA in 1925. As the Court has explained, the FAA was a response to hostility of American courts to the enforcement of arbitration agreements, a judicial disposition inherited from then-longstanding English practice. *See, e.g., Allied-Bruce Terminix Cos. v. Dobson*, 513 U.S. 265, 270–271, 115 S. Ct. 834, 130 L. Ed. 2d 753 (1995); *Gilmer v. Interstate/Johnson Lane Corp.*, 500 U.S. 20, 24, 111 S. Ct. 1647, 114 L. Ed. 2d 26 (1991). To give effect to this purpose, the FAA compels judicial enforcement of a wide range of written arbitration agreements. The FAA's coverage provision, § 2, provides that

> "[a] written provision in any maritime transaction or a contract evidencing a transaction involving commerce to settle by arbitration a controversy thereafter arising out of such contract or transaction, or the refusal to perform the whole or any part thereof, or an agreement in writing to submit to arbitration an existing controversy arising out of such a contract, transaction, or refusal, shall be valid, irrevocable, and enforceable, save upon such grounds as exist at law or in equity for the revocation of any contract." 9 U.S.C. § 2.

We had occasion in *Allied-Bruce, supra*, at 273–277, 115 S. Ct. 834, to consider the significance of Congress' use of the words "involving commerce" in § 2. The analysis began with a reaffirmation of earlier decisions concluding that the FAA was enacted pursuant to Congress' substantive power to regulate interstate commerce and admiralty . . . and that the Act was applicable in state courts and pre-emptive of state laws hostile to arbitration . . . . Relying upon these background principles and upon the evident reach of the words "involving commerce," the Court interpreted § 2 as implementing

Congress' intent "to exercise [its] commerce power to the full." *Allied-Bruce, supra*, at 277, 115 S. Ct. 834.

The instant case, of course, involves not the basic coverage authorization under § 2 of the Act, but the exemption from coverage under § 1. The exemption clause provides the Act shall not apply "to contracts of employment of seamen, railroad employees, or any other class of workers engaged in foreign or interstate commerce." . . .

. . . .

B

Respondent, at the outset, contends that we need not address the meaning of the § 1 exclusion provision to decide the case in his favor. In his view, an employment contract is not a "contract evidencing a transaction involving interstate commerce" at all, since the word "transaction" in § 2 extends only to commercial contracts. *See Craft*, 177 F.3d, at 1085 (concluding that § 2 covers only "commercial deal[s] or merchant's sale[s]"). This line of reasoning proves too much, for it would make the § 1 exclusion provision superfluous. If all contracts of employment are beyond the scope of the Act under the § 2 coverage provision, the separate exemption for "contracts of employment of seamen, railroad employees, or any other class of workers engaged in . . . interstate commerce" would be pointless. *See, e.g., Pennsylvania Dept. of Public Welfare v. Davenport*, 495 U.S. 552, 562, 110 S. Ct. 2126, 109 L. Ed. 2d 588 (1990) ("Our cases express a deep reluctance to interpret a statutory provision so as to render superfluous other provisions in the same enactment"). . . . If, then, there is an argument to be made that arbitration agreements in employment contracts are not covered by the Act, it must be premised on the language of the § 1 exclusion provision itself.

Respondent, endorsing the reasoning of the Court of Appeals for the Ninth Circuit that the provision excludes all employment contracts, relies on the asserted breadth of the words "contracts of employment of . . . any other class of workers engaged in . . . commerce." Referring to our construction of § 2's coverage provision in *Allied-Bruce*-concluding that the words "involving commerce" evidence the congressional intent to regulate to the full extent of its commerce power-respondent contends § 1's interpretation should have a like reach, thus exempting all employment contracts. The two provisions, it is argued, are coterminous; under this view the "involving commerce" provision brings within the FAA's scope all contracts within the Congress' commerce power, and the "engaged in . . . commerce" language in § 1 in turn exempts from the FAA all employment contracts falling within that authority.

This reading of § 1, however, runs into an immediate and, in our view, insurmountable textual obstacle. Unlike the "involving commerce" language in § 2, the words "any other class of workers engaged in . . . commerce" constitute a residual phrase, following, in the same sentence, explicit reference to "seamen" and "railroad employees." Construing the residual phrase to exclude all employment contracts fails to give independent effect to the statute's enumeration of the specific categories of workers which precedes it; there would be no need for Congress to use the phrases "seamen" and "railroad employees" if those same classes of workers were subsumed within the meaning of the "engaged in . . . commerce" residual clause. The wording of § 1 calls for the application of the maxim *ejusdem generis*, the statutory canon that "[w]here general words follow specific words in a statutory enumeration, the general words are construed to embrace only objects similar in nature to those objects enumerated by the preceding specific words." 2A N. Singer, Sutherland on Statutes and Statutory Construction § 47.17 (1991); *see also Norfolk & Western R. Co. v. Train Dispatchers*, 499 U.S. 117, 129, 111 S. Ct. 1156, 113 L. Ed. 2d 95 (1991). Under this rule of construction the residual clause should be read to give effect to the terms "seamen" and "railroad employees," and should itself be controlled and defined by reference to the enumerated categories of workers which are recited just before it; the interpretation of the clause pressed by respondent fails to produce these results.

Canons of construction need not be conclusive and are often countered, of course, by some maxim pointing in a different direction. The application of the rule *ejusdem generis* in this case, however, is in full accord with other sound considerations bearing upon the proper interpretation of the clause. For even if the term "engaged in commerce" stood alone in § 1, we would not construe the provision to exclude all contracts of employment from the FAA. Congress uses different modifiers to the word "commerce" in the design and enactment of its statutes. . . .

It is argued that we should assess the meaning of the phrase "engaged in commerce" in a different manner here, because the FAA was enacted when congressional authority to regulate under the commerce power was to a large extent confined by our decisions. *See United States v. Lopez*, 514 U.S. 549, 556, 115 S. Ct. 1624, 131 L. Ed. 2d 626 (1995) (noting that Supreme Court decisions beginning in 1937 "ushered in an era of Commerce Clause jurisprudence that greatly expanded the previously defined authority of Congress under that Clause"). When the FAA was enacted in 1925, respondent reasons, the phrase "engaged in commerce" was not a term of art indicating a limited assertion of congressional jurisdiction; to the contrary, it is said, the formulation came close to expressing the outer limits of Congress' power as then understood. . . . Were this mode of interpretation to prevail, we would take into account the scope of the Commerce Clause, as then elaborated by the Court, at the date of the FAA's enactment in order to interpret what the statute means now.

A variable standard for interpreting common, jurisdictional phrases would contradict our earlier cases and bring instability to statutory interpretation. The Court has declined in past cases to afford significance, in construing the meaning of the statutory jurisdictional provisions "in commerce" and "engaged in commerce," to the circumstance that the statute predated shifts in the Court's Commerce Clause cases. . . .

The Court's reluctance to accept contentions that Congress used the words "in commerce" or "engaged in commerce" to regulate to the full extent of its commerce power rests on sound foundation, as it affords objective and consistent significance to the meaning of the words Congress uses when it defines the reach of a statute. To say that the statutory words "engaged in commerce" are subject to variable interpretations depending upon the date of adoption, even a date before the phrase became a term of art, ignores the reason why the formulation became a term of art in the first place: The plain meaning of the words "engaged in commerce" is narrower than the more open-ended formulations "affecting commerce" and "involving commerce." *See, e.g., Gulf Oil, supra,* at 195, 95 S. Ct. 392 (phrase "engaged in commerce" "appears to denote only persons or activities within the flow of interstate commerce"). It would be unwieldy for Congress, for the Court, and for litigants to be required to deconstruct statutory Commerce Clause phrases depending upon the year of a particular statutory enactment.

. . . .

In sum, the text of the FAA forecloses the construction of § 1 followed by the Court of Appeals in the case under review, a construction which would exclude all employment contracts from the FAA. While the historical arguments respecting Congress' understanding of its power in 1925 are not insubstantial, this fact alone does not give us basis to adopt, "by judicial decision rather than amendatory legislation," *Gulf Oil, supra,* at 202, 95 S. Ct. 392, an expansive construction of the FAA's exclusion provision that goes beyond the meaning of the words Congress used. While it is of course possible to speculate that Congress might have chosen a different jurisdictional formulation had it known that the Court would soon embrace a less restrictive reading of the Commerce Clause, the text of § 1 precludes interpreting the exclusion provision to defeat the language of § 2 as to all employment contracts. Section 1 exempts from the FAA only contracts of employment of transportation workers.

C

As the conclusion we reach today is directed by the text of § 1, we need not assess the legislative history of the exclusion provision. *See Ratzlaf v. United States*, 510 U.S. 135, 147–148, 114 S. Ct. 655, 126 L. Ed. 2d 615 (1994) ("[W]e do not resort to legislative history to cloud a statutory text that is clear"). We do note, however, that the legislative record on the § 1 exemption is quite sparse. Respondent points to no language in either Committee Report addressing the meaning of the provision, nor to any mention of the § 1 exclusion during debate on the FAA on the floor of the House or Senate. Instead, respondent places greatest reliance upon testimony before a Senate subcommittee hearing suggesting that the exception may have been added in response to the objections of the president of the International Seamen's Union of America. *See* Hearing on 120 S. 4213 and S. 4214 before a Subcommittee of the Senate Committee on the Judiciary, 67th Cong., 4th Sess., 9 (1923). Legislative history is problematic even when the attempt is to draw inferences from the intent of duly appointed committees of the Congress. It becomes far more so when we consult sources still more steps removed from the full Congress and speculate upon the significance of the fact that a certain interest group sponsored or opposed particular legislation. *Cf. Kelly v. Robinson*, 479 U.S. 36, 51, n. 13, 107 S. Ct. 353, 93 L. Ed. 2d 216 (1986) ("[N]one of those statements was made by a Member of Congress, nor were they included in the official Senate and House Reports. We decline to accord any significance to these statements"). We ought not attribute to Congress an official purpose based on the motives of a particular group that lobbied for or against a certain proposal — even assuming the precise intent of the group can be determined, a point doubtful both as a general rule and in the instant case. It is for the Congress, not the courts, to consult political forces and then decide how best to resolve conflicts in the course of writing the objective embodiments of law we know as statutes.

. . . .

JUSTICE STEVENS, with whom JUSTICE GINSBURG and JUSTICE BREYER join, and with whom JUSTICE SOUTER joins as to Parts II and III, dissenting.

JUSTICE SOUTER has cogently explained [*infra*] why the Court's parsimonious construction of § 1 of the Federal Arbitration Act (FAA or Act) is not consistent with its expansive reading of § 2. I join his dissent, but believe that the Court's heavy reliance on the views expressed by the Courts of Appeals during the past decade makes it appropriate to comment on three earlier chapters in the history of this venerable statute.

I

Section 2 of the FAA makes enforceable written agreements to arbitrate "in any maritime transaction or a contract evidencing a transaction involving commerce." 9 U.S.C. § 2. If we were writing on a clean slate, there would be good reason to conclude that neither the phrase "maritime transaction" nor the phrase "contract evidencing a transaction involving commerce" was intended to encompass employment contracts.

The history of the Act, which is extensive and well documented, makes clear that the FAA was a response to the refusal of courts to enforce commercial arbitration agreements, which were commonly used in the maritime context. The original bill was drafted by the Committee on Commerce, Trade, and Commercial Law of the American Bar Association (ABA) upon consideration of "the further extension of the principle of *commercial* arbitration." Report of the Forty-third Annual Meeting of the ABA, 45 A.B.A. Rep. 75 (1920) (emphasis added). As drafted, the bill was understood by Members of Congress to "simply provid[e] for one thing, and that is to give an opportunity to enforce an agreement in *commercial* contracts and *admiralty* contracts."

65 Cong. Rec.1931 (1924) (remarks of Rep. Graham) (emphasis added).[2] It is no surprise, then, that when the legislation was first introduced in 1922, it did not mention employment contracts, but did contain a rather precise definition of the term "maritime transactions" that underscored the commercial character of the proposed bill. Indeed, neither the history of the drafting of the original bill by the ABA, nor the records of the deliberations in Congress during the years preceding the ultimate enactment of the Act in 1925, contain any evidence that the proponents of the legislation intended it to apply to agreements affecting employment.

Nevertheless, the original bill was opposed by representatives of organized labor, most notably the president of the International Seamen's Union of America, because of their concern that the legislation might authorize federal judicial enforcement of arbitration clauses in employment contracts and collective-bargaining agreements. In response to those objections, the chairman of the ABA committee that drafted the legislation emphasized at a Senate Judiciary Subcommittee hearing that "[i]t is not intended that this shall be an act referring to labor disputes, at all," but he also observed that "if your honorable committee should feel that there is any danger of that, they should add to the bill the following language, 'but nothing herein contained shall apply to seamen or any class of workers in interstate and foreign commerce.'" Hearing 9. Similarly, another supporter of the bill, then Secretary of Commerce Herbert Hoover, suggested that "[i]f objection appears to the inclusion of workers' contracts in the law's scheme, it might be well amended by stating 'but nothing herein contained shall apply to contracts of employment of seamen, railroad employees, or any other class of workers engaged in interstate or foreign commerce.'" *Id.*, at 14. The legislation was reintroduced in the next session of Congress with Secretary Hoover's exclusionary language added to § 1 and the amendment eliminated organized labor's opposition to the proposed law.

That amendment is what the Court construes today. History amply supports the proposition that it was an uncontroversial provision that merely confirmed the fact that no one interested in the enactment of the FAA ever intended or expected that § 2 would apply to employment contracts. It is particularly ironic, therefore, that the amendment has provided the Court with its sole justification for refusing to give the text of § 2 a natural reading. Playing ostrich to the substantial history behind the amendment, *see ante*, at 1311 ("[W]e need not assess the legislative history of the exclusion provision"), the Court reasons in a vacuum that "[i]f all contracts of employment are beyond the scope of the Act under the § 2 coverage provision, the separate exemption" in § 1 "would be pointless," *ante*, at 1308. But contrary to the Court's suggestion, it is not "pointless" to adopt a clarifying amendment in order to eliminate opposition to a bill. . . .

The irony of the Court's reading of § 2 to include contracts of employment is compounded by its cramped interpretation of the exclusion inserted into § 1. As proposed and enacted, the exclusion fully responded to the concerns of the Seamen's Union and other labor organizations that § 2 might encompass employment contracts by expressly exempting the labor agreements not only of "seamen" and "railroad employees," but also of *"any other class of workers* engaged in foreign or interstate commerce."

---

[2] Consistent with this understanding, Rep. Mills, who introduced the original bill in the House, explained that it "provides that where there are *commercial* contracts and there is disagreement under the contract, the court can [en]force an arbitration agreement in the same way as other portions of the contract." 65 Cong. Rec., at 11080 (emphasis added). And before the Senate, the chairman of the New York Chamber of Commerce, one of the many business organizations that requested introduction of the bill, testified that it was needed to "enable *business men* to settle their disputes expeditiously and economically, and will reduce the congestion in the Federal and State courts." Hearing on S. 4213 and S. 4214 before a Subcommittee of the Senate Committee on the Judiciary, 67th Cong., 4th Sess., 2 (1923) (Hearing) (emphasis added). *See also id.*, at 1312 (letter of H. Hoover, Secretary of Commerce) ("I have been, as you may know, very strongly impressed with the urgent need of a Federal *commercial* arbitration act. The American Bar Association has now joined hands with the business men of this country to the same effect and unanimously approved" the bill drafted by the ABA committee and introduced in both Houses of Congress (emphasis added)).

9 U.S.C. § 1 (emphasis added). Today, however, the Court fulfills the original — and originally unfounded — fears of organized labor by essentially rewriting the text of § 1 to exclude the employment contracts *solely* of "seamen, railroad employees, or any other class of [*transportation*] workers engaged in foreign or interstate commerce." *See ante*, at 1311. In contrast, whether one views the legislation before or after the amendment to § 1, it is clear that it was not intended to apply to employment contracts at all.

. . . .

It is not necessarily wrong for the Court to put its own imprint on a statute. But when its refusal to look beyond the raw statutory text enables it to disregard countervailing considerations that were expressed by Members of the enacting Congress and that remain valid today, the Court misuses its authority. As the history of the legislation indicates, the potential disparity in bargaining power between individual employees and large employers was the source of organized labor's opposition to the Act, which it feared would require courts to enforce unfair employment contracts. That same concern, as JUSTICE SOUTER points out, *see post*, at 1321, n. 2, underlay Congress' exemption of contracts of employment from mandatory arbitration. When the Court simply ignores the interest of the unrepresented employee, it skews its interpretation with its own policy preferences.

This case illustrates the wisdom of an observation made by Justice Aharon Barak of the Supreme Court of Israel. He has perceptively noted that the "minimalist" judge "who holds that the purpose of the statute may be learned only from its language" has more discretion than the judge "who will seek guidance from every reliable source." Judicial Discretion 62 (Y. Kaufmann transl.1989). A method of statutory interpretation that is deliberately uninformed, and hence unconstrained, may produce a result that is consistent with a court's own views of how things should be, but it may also defeat the very purpose for which a provision was enacted. That is the sad result in this case.

JUSTICE SOUTER, with whom JUSTICE STEVENS, JUSTICE GINSBURG, and JUSTICE BREYER join, dissenting.

. . . .

II

Like some Courts of Appeals before it, the majority today finds great significance in the fact that the generally phrased exemption for the employment contracts of workers "engaged in commerce" does not stand alone, but occurs at the end of a sequence of more specific exemptions: for "contracts of employment of seamen, railroad employees, or any other class of workers engaged in foreign or interstate commerce." Like those other courts, this Court sees the sequence as an occasion to apply the interpretive maxim of *ejusdem generis*, that is, when specific terms are followed by a general one, the latter is meant to cover only examples of the same sort as the preceding specifics. Here, the same sort is thought to be contracts of transportation workers, or employees of transporters, the very carriers of commerce. And that, of course, excludes respondent Adams from benefit of the exemption, for he is employed by a retail seller.

Like many interpretive canons, however, *ejusdem generis* is a fallback, and if there are good reasons not to apply it, it is put aside. *E.g.*, *Norfolk & Western R. Co. v. Train Dispatchers*, 499 U.S. 117, 129, 111 S. Ct. 1156, 113 L. Ed. 2d 95 (1991).[2] There are good reasons here. As Adams argued, it is imputing something very odd to the working of the

---

[2] What is more, the Court has repeatedly explained that the canon is triggered only by uncertain statutory text, *e.g.*, *Garcia v. United States*, 469 U.S. 70, 74–75, 105 S. Ct. 479, 83 L. Ed. 2d 472 (1984); *Gooch v. United States*, 297 U.S. 124, 128, 56 S. Ct. 395, 80 L. Ed. 522 (1936), and that it can be overcome by, *inter alia*, contrary legislative history, *e.g.*, *Watt v. Western Nuclear*, Inc., 462 U.S. 36, 44, n. 5, 103 S. Ct. 2218, 76 L. Ed. 2d 400 (1983). The Court today turns this practice upside down, using *ejusdem generis* to establish that the text is so clear that legislative history is irrelevant. *Ante*, at 1311.

congressional brain to say that Congress took care to bar application of the Act to the class of employment contracts it most obviously had authority to legislate about in 1925, contracts of workers employed by carriers and handlers of commerce, while covering only employees "engaged" in less obvious ways, over whose coverage litigation might be anticipated with uncertain results. It would seem to have made more sense either to cover all coverable employment contracts or to exclude them all. In fact, exclusion might well have been in order based on concern that arbitration could prove to resist an arbitration clause if their prospective employers insist on one.[3] And excluding all employment contracts from the Act's enforcement of mandatory arbitration clauses is consistent with Secretary Hoover's suggestion that the language would respond to any "objection . . . to the inclusion of workers' contracts."

The Court tries to deflect the anomaly of excluding only carrier contracts by suggesting that Congress used the reference to seamen and rail workers to indicate the class of employees whose employment relations it had already legislated about and would be most likely to legislate about in the future. *Ante*, at 1311–1312. This explanation, however, does nothing to eliminate the anomaly. On the contrary, the explanation tells us why Congress might have referred specifically to the sea and rail workers; but, if so, it also indicates that Congress almost certainly intended the catchall phrase to be just as broad as its terms, without any interpretive squeeze in the name of *ejusdem generis*.

The very fact, as the Court points out, that Congress already had spoken on the subjects of sailors and rail workers and had tailored the legislation to the particular circumstances of the sea and rail carriers may well have been reason for mentioning them specifically. But making the specific references was in that case an act of special care to make sure that the FAA not be construed to modify the existing legislation so exactly aimed; that was no reason at all to limit the general FAA exclusion from applying to employment contracts that had not been targeted with special legislation. Congress did not need to worry especially about the FAA's effect on legislation that did not exist and was not contemplated. As to workers uncovered by any specific legislation, Congress could write on a clean slate, and what it wrote was a general exclusion for employment contracts within Congress's power to regulate. The Court has understood this point before, holding that the existence of a special reason for emphasizing specific examples of a statutory class can negate any inference that an otherwise unqualified general phrase was meant to apply only to matters ejusdem generis.[4] On the Court's own reading of the history, then, the explanation for the catchall is not *ejusdem generis;* instead, the explanation for the specifics is *ex abundanti cautela*, abundance of caution, see *Fort Stewart Schools v. FLRA*, 495 U.S. 641, 646, 110 S. Ct. 2043, 109 L. Ed. 2d 659 (1990).

Nothing stands in the way of construing the coverage and exclusion clauses together,

---

[3] Senator Walsh expressed this concern during a subcommittee hearing on the FAA:

"'The trouble about the matter is that a great many of these contracts that are entered into are really not voluntar[y] things at all. . . . It is the same with a good many contracts of employment. A man says, "There are our terms. All right, take it or leave it." Well, there is nothing for the man to do except to sign it; and then he surrenders his right to have his case tried by the court, and has to have it tried before a tribunal in which he has no confidence at all.'" Hearing on S. 4213 et al., at 9.

[4] In *Watt v. Western Nuclear, Inc., supra*, at 44, n. 5, 103 S. Ct. 2218, the Court concluded that the *ejusdem generis* canon did not apply to the words "coal and other minerals" where "[t]here were special reasons for expressly addressing coal that negate any inference that the phrase 'and other minerals' was meant to reserve only substances *ejusdem generis*," namely that Congress wanted "to make clear that coal was reserved even though existing law treated it differently from other minerals."

consistently and coherently. I respectfully dissent.

NOTES AND QUESTIONS

1. Can you explain how an analysis of Congress' *constitutional* power to regulate interstate commerce has relevance in *statutory interpretation*? Does it matter that the Court's interpretation of the commerce power has changed since the statutory enactment?

2. Does the dissenters' reliance on legislative history outweigh the textual and canon-based approach of the majority?

c. The Last Antecedent

Under the doctrine of last antecedent, a qualifying phrase is interpreted as modifying the immediately preceding words or phrases. In *City of Corsicana v. Willman*, 147 Tex. 377, 216 S.W.2d 175 (1948), the court had to construe a provision of a city charter which read:

> The said limits of the City of Corsicana may be extended so as to take in other territory, by ordinance duly passed by the Commission, in the manner and form as prescribed by the general laws of the State of Texas.

Application of the last antecedent doctrine by the *Willman* Court is discussed below.

NOTES AND QUESTIONS

1. Using the last antecedent doctrine, does the qualifying phrase "in the manner and form as prescribed by the general laws of the State of Texas" refer to "limits . . . extended" or "ordinance duly passed"?

2. The *Willman* court said the doctrine of last antecedent is neither controlling nor inflexible and may be rebutted by circumstances. The court concluded the last phrase modified "limits . . . extended" rather than "ordinance . . . passed" because: (a) the laws of Texas contain no provisions dealing with the manner and form of passing city ordinances, and (b) the word "ordinance" was used in a like manner 36 times in the city charter without being similarly qualified.

3. If the authors of the charter intended both of the latter phrases to modify the first phrase, how could they have written the provision so as to avoid confusion?

4. In *Singer v. United States*, 323 U.S. 338 (1945), the defendants were indicted and convicted for conspiracy to aid a third person to evade service in the armed forces. The Selective Training and Service Act listed seven offenses, each set off from the other by commas, and then concluded "or conspire to do *so*." (emphasis added). The question was whether the conspiracy clause only applied to the last enumerated offense (not the offense for which defendants were convicted of conspiring to commit) set off by a comma and appearing right before the conspiracy clause, or, rather, whether the conspiracy clause applied to all of the preceding offenses. The Court, over a strong dissent by Justice Frankfurter, rejected the last antecedent rule and held the conspiracy clause to apply to all seven of the offenses, upholding the convictions.

5. In *United States v. Ron Pair Enterprises, Inc.*, 489 U.S. 235 (1989), the question arose as to whether the United States could receive interest on its tax lien for the period after a bankruptcy petition was filed. Of course, there had been no agreement between the government and the taxpayer about this or anything else. The taxpayer attempted to argue that post-petition interest could not be recovered unless it was provided for in an agreement between the parties. The Supreme Court rejected this argument:

> The relevant phrase in § 506(b) is: "[T]here shall be allowed to the holder of such claim, interest on such claim, and any reasonable fees, costs, or charges provided for under the agreement under which such claim arose." "Such claim"

refers to an oversecured claim. The natural reading of the phrase entitles the holder of an oversecured claim to post-petition interest and, in addition, gives one having a secured claim created pursuant to an agreement the right to reasonable fees, costs, and charges provided for in that agreement. Recovery of postpetition interest is unqualified. Recovery of fees, costs, and charges, however, is allowed only if they are reasonable and provided for in the agreement under which the claim arose. Therefore, in the absence of an agreement, postpetition interest is the only added recovery available.

This reading is also mandated by the grammatical structure of the statute. The phrase "interest on such claim" is set aside by commas, and separated from the reference to fees, costs, and charges by the conjunctive words "and any." As a result, the phrase "interest on such claim" stands independent of the language that follows. "[I]nterest on such claim" is not part of the list made up of "fees, costs, or charges," nor is it joined to the following clause so that the final "provided for under the agreement" modifies it as well. *See Best Repair Co., v. United States*, 789 F.2d, at 1082. The language and punctuation Congress used cannot be read in any other way. By the plain language of the statute, the two types of recovery are distinct.

Id. at 241–42.

d.　"May" and "Shall"; Mandatory or Directory

DOE v. STATEWIDE GRIEVANCE COMMITTEE
694 A.2d 1218 (Conn. 1997)

Katz, Judge.

The sole issue in this certified appeal is whether the failure by the defendant, the statewide grievance committee (committee), to comply with the temporal requirements of General Statutes (Rev. to 1993) § 51-90g(g) . . . deprives the defendant of subject matter jurisdiction to act on a grievance complaint alleging attorney misconduct and, further, deprives the court of subject matter jurisdiction to exercise its inherent authority over attorney conduct. We conclude that it does not.

In June, 1993, misconduct charges against the plaintiff were brought to the attention of the committee. When the committee failed to act within the statutory period, the plaintiff brought this action for injunctive relief in the Superior Court. Determining that the committee's failure to render a decision on a grievance complaint within the prescribed time period was not cause to dismiss the complaint, the trial court rendered judgement denying the plaintiff's request for a permanent injunction against any further action by the committee. The Appellate Court reversed the judgement of the trial court, concluding that the committee's failure to comply with the statutory time period required dismissal of the underlying complaint.

. . . .

We begin with this court's decision in *Statewide Grievance v. Rozbicki, supra*, 211 Conn. 232, 558 A.2d 986, wherein we held that the defendant's failure to act within the time constraints of General Statutes (Rev. to 1987) § 51-90g(c),[8] did not require dismissal of the complaint absent a showing of prejudice. Our decision was premised largely upon the broad supervisory role of the judiciary in governing attorney conduct. We emphasized that "the rules regulating attorney grievance procedures exist within the broader framework of the relationship between attorneys and the judiciary. The practice of law is . . . a profession the main purpose of which is to aid in the doing of

---

[8] General Statutes (rev. to 1987) § 51-90g(c) provided: The subcommittee shall conclude any hearing or hearings and shall render its proposed decision not later than ninety days from the date the panel's determination of probable cause or no probable cause was filed with the state-wide grievance committee. . . .

justice. . . . An attorney as an officer of the court in the administration of justice, is continually accountable to it for the manner in which he exercises the privilege which has been accorded him. . . . This unique position as officers and commissioners of the court . . . casts attorneys in a special relationship with the judiciary and subjects them to its discipline." (Citations omitted; internal quotation marks omitted.) *Id.*, at 237–38, 558 A.2d 986.

. . . .

In *Rozbicki*, we thereafter examined § 51-90g(c) in order to decide whether its time requirements were mandatory and, if so, whether the statutory mandates had been violated and what effect such a violation has on the jurisdiction of the Superior Court. We held that the provision's use of the word "shall" was mandatory, but concluded nevertheless that its violation did not require a dismissal of the complaint.[9] "Both the broader context of the supervisory role of the judiciary in governing attorney conduct, as discussed above, and the language of § 51-90g(c) support the conclusion that the trial court's jurisdiction was not affected by the delay. The operative language on which we focus is . . . the [final] phrase of § 51-90g(c) requiring the grievance committee after subcommittee delay to 'determine the appropriate course of action.' . . . We will not, therefore, construe § 51-90g(c) to require that if the subcommittee has failed to act within the prescribed time, and there is no showing of prejudice, the complaint must be dismissed. Such a construction would impermissibly render the final phrase in § 51-90g(c) a nullity." (Citations omitted; internal quotation marks omitted.) *Id.*, at 242–43, 558 A.2d 986. Accordingly, we concluded that the subcommittee's failure to act within the prescribed time, although a violation of § 51-90g(c), did not mandate dismissal of the complaint.

. . . .

"Well established principles of statutory construction govern our determination of whether a statutory time period is mandatory or directory. Our fundamental objective is to ascertain and give effect to the apparent intent of the legislature. . . . In seeking to discern that intent, we look to the words of the statute itself, to the legislative history and circumstances surrounding its enactment, to the legislative policy it was designed to implement, and to its relationship to existing legislation and common law principles governing the same general subject matter. . . . The test to be applied in determining whether a statute is mandatory or directory is whether the prescribed mode of action is the essence of the thing to be accomplished, or in other words, whether it relates to a matter of substance or a matter of convenience. . . . If it is a matter of substance, the statutory provision is mandatory. If, however, the legislative provision is designed to secure order, system and dispatch in the proceedings, it is generally held to be directory, especially where the requirement is stated in affirmative terms unaccompanied by negative words." (Citations omitted; internal quotation marks omitted.) *Stewart v. Tunxis Service Center*, 237 Conn. 71, 76–77, 676 A.2d 819 (1996).

Looking solely at the words of § 51-90g(g), it would appear that the language requires that the committee "render its decision not later than four months from the date of the panel's determination of probable cause or no probable cause was filed with the state-wide grievance committee." Definitive words, such as "must" or "shall," ordinarily express legislative mandates of a nondirectory nature. . . . We have noted, however, that the use of the word "shall," though significant, does not invariably establish a mandatory duty. . . . Therefore, we turn to the other aforementioned considerations in deciding whether § 51-90g(g) is directory or mandatory.

"One . . . reliable guide in determining whether a statutory provision is directory or

---

[9] Although in *Rozbicki* we used the word "mandatory," our conclusion that, absent a showing of prejudice as a result of the temporal violation, the complaint should not be dismissed, was more consistent with a determination that the time limit was "directory." *See Fidelity Trust Co. v. BVD Associates*, 196 Conn. 270, 278–79, 492 A.2d 180 (1985).

mandatory is whether the failure of the state to comply with its provisions results in either a penalty or a requirement that the state seek an extension of time. *Caron v. Inland Wetlands & Watercourses Commission,* 222 Conn. 269, 273–74, 610 A.2d 584 (1992); *State v. White,* 169 Conn. 223, 238, 363 A.2d 143, *cert. denied,* 423 U.S. 1025, 96 S. Ct. 469, 46 L. Ed. 2d 399 (1975)." *Angelsea Productions, Inc. v. Commission on Human Rights & Opportunities, supra,* 236 Conn. at 695, 674 A.2d 1300. It is noteworthy that the legislature elected not to include either option in the language of § 51-90g(g).

Another guide to interpreting subsection (g) of § 51-90g is to look to other provisions governing the powers and duties of the committee. *See Murchison v. Civil Service Commission,* 234 Conn. 35, 45, 660 A.2d 850 (1995) ("[i]n order to determine the meaning of a statute, we must consider the statute as a whole when reconciling its separate parts in order to render a reasonable overall interpretation"); *University of Connecticut Chapter, AAUP v. Governor,* 200 Conn. 386, 399, 512 A.2d 152 (1986) (statute to be read "as a whole, with a view toward reconciling its separate parts in order to render a reasonable overall interpretation"). As we held in *Statewide Grievance Committee v. Rozbicki, supra,* 211 Conn. at 239, 558 A.2d 986, the failure to comply with the time constraints of § 51-90g(c) does not deprive the court of jurisdiction. Therefore, were we to agree with the plaintiff's interpretation of § 51-90g(g), we would in essence be stating that the committee, in cases in which the subcommittee conducts the hearing, would, after 120 days, have more power in its review of subcommittee delay to assess appropriate action than the Superior Court, in those cases in which the committee has failed, after essentially the same period of time, to assign the complaint for a hearing, would have over such committee delay. Such a pronounced dichotomy between, on the one hand, *allowing* the committee authority to review delay, and, on the other hand, *denying* the court any authority to review delay would be problematic at best. We should not construe statutory language to mandate such a curious result.

Additionally, we note that General Statutes § 51-90h(b) provides that within sixty days after the fourteen day period for the filing of statements in support of or in opposition to the subcommittee's proposed decision, the committee is required to issue a decision. That same subsection also provides, however, that the committee may instead refer the complaint to the same or a different subcommittee for further investigation and a proposed decision, in which event there are no additional time constraints imposed. To interpret § 51-90g(g) as a mandatory and as imposing a jurisdictional constraint, when neither §§ 51-90g(c) nor 51-90h have time constraints that have jurisdictional implications, would be inconsistent and indeed unreasonable. Because we read statutes "with common sense so as to accomplish a reasonable result"; *State v. Chiarizio,* 8 Conn. App. 673, 682, 514 A.2d 370, *cert. denied,* 201 Conn. 809, 515 A.2d 379 (1986); we are inclined, in the face of these other provisions, to reject the plaintiff's invitation to interpret § 51-90g(g) as mandatory in nature and as establishing a jurisdictional constraint.

This inclination is buttressed by the legislative history relative to § 51-90g(g). That history indicates that the revision of attorney discipline procedures in 1986 was influenced by a concern for the public and for expediency in the disciplinary process for the benefit of the public as well as for those facing charges. *See Doe v. Statewide Grievance Committee, supra,* 41 Conn. App. at 683, 677 A.2d 960 (Schaller, J., concurring). It does not, however, reflect an intent to limit judicial branch involvement over attorney grievance complaints. Indeed, not only is there no indication of an intent to limit the jurisdiction of the court, but, to the contrary, the legislators expressed deference to the judiciary. *See* 28 H.R. Proc., Pt. 23, 1985 Sess., pp. 8538–45, 8547–48, 8554–55. Indeed, the legislature in the primary debate recognized that the court is "the ultimate authority as to attorneys, in how they are disciplined." *Id.*, p. 8542, remarks of Representative Richard T. Tulisano. The debate in the House of Representatives reflects concern with judicial independence and the rulemaking authority of the court relative to the attorney disciplinary process, not jurisdictional considerations. *Id.*, pp. 8542–55. Nothing in the legislative history specifically supports a mandatory linguistic interpretation.

It is well settled that statutes are to be read as favoring subject matter jurisdiction, absent a clear indication of legislative intent to limit it. *Ambroise v. William Raveis Real Estate, Inc.*, 226 Conn. 757, 765, 628 A.2d 1303 (1993). There is no such clear indication here. We therefore are brought full circle to the purpose of the comprehensive disciplinary scheme before us. . . . In light of these very strong public policy concerns for attorney accountability, and the need for public confidence in the justice system, it would be improper to interpret § 51-90g(g) to create mandatory jurisdictional limitations that would ultimately undermine the long-standing law regarding the inherent authority of the court to regulate attorney conduct.

BERDON, JUDGE, dissenting.

The majority concludes that the failure of the defendant, the statewide grievance committee (committee), to comply with the time requirements of General Statutes (Rev. to 1993) § 51-90g(g) . . . does not deprive the committee of subject matter jurisdiction to act on a grievance complaint alleging attorney misconduct. In other words, according to the majority, the committee may permissibly pursue a grievance complaint well beyond the four month time limitation specifically provided in § 51-90g(g). I disagree.

I agree with the majority that we have a special obligation with respect to assuring that attorney conduct comports with standards of the practice of law, "a profession the main purpose of which is to aid in the doing of justice . . . ." . . .

In reaching its conclusion, the majority today ignores the mandate in § 51-90g(g), the statute's legislative history and our own rules of practice, and stands the precedent of *Rozbicki* on its head. In other words, according to the majority, "shall" means shall when the court wants it to mean shall, but "shall" does not mean shall when the court is of another mind.[5]

My analysis starts, as the Appellate Court's did, with the plain language of the statute. General Statues (Rev. to 1993) § 51-90g(g) provides in relevant part: "When the committee conducts the hearing or hearings under this section, *it shall render its decision not later than four months* from the date the panel's determination of probable cause or no probable cause was filed with the state-wide grievance committee . . . ." (Emphasis added.) It is undisputed that more than four months elapsed from the time that the local grievance panel filed its determination of no probable cause to the time that the committee referred the matter to a subcommittee. I, like the Appellate Court, conclude that "this language clearly and unambiguously mandates that the committee complete its action within four months." *Doe v. Statewide Grievance Committee*, 41 Conn. App. 671, 676, 677 A.2d 960 (1996). "Where the meaning of a statute . . . is plain and unambiguous, the enactment speaks for itself and there is no occasion to construe it. Its unequivocal meaning is not subject to modification by way of construction." (Internal quotation marks omitted.) *Grievance Committee v. Trantolo*, 192 Conn. 15, 22, 470 A.2d 228 (1984).

Furthermore, even if § 51-90g(g) were ambiguous, the legislative history supports

---

[5] Indeed, the majority's reasoning is reminiscent of the following passage from the book, Through the Looking-Glass, by Lewis Carroll:

"There's glory for you!

"I don't know what you mean by 'glory,' Alice said.

"I meant, 'there's a nice knock down argument for you!'

"But 'glory' doesn't mean 'a nice knock down argument,' Alice objected.

"When *I* use a word," Humpty Dumpty said in a rather scornful tone, "it means just what I choose it to mean — neither more nor less."

(Emphasis in original.) L. Carroll, Through the Looking-Glass (Messner ed. 1982) p. 198.

the conclusion that the legislature intended the time limits in § 51-90g(g) to be mandatory. In 1986, the legislature revised the statute to include the requirement that the committee render its decision within four months of the local panel's determination. Public Acts 1986, No. 86-276, § 8 (P.A. 86-276). In enacting this amendment, the legislature emphasized the importance of the newly-added four month time frame for committee action. "The amendment maintains . . . that if you're going to have a hearing with probable cause, that must be held within four months . . . ." 28 H.R. Proc., Pt. 23, 1985 Sess., p. 8562, remarks of Representative Richard D. Tulisano. As another legislator stated: "Once the determination is made that there is probable cause to continue to a full hearing, at that point within the four months, the hearing would have to take place. . . . One of the complaints of the community has been that it takes too long for this grievance procedure to take place. It is hoped that this would tighten that up." *Id.*, pp. 8529–30, remarks of Representative William L. Wollenberg.

Indeed, the legislature underscored the need to establish rigid guidelines for the investigation of complaints of misconduct in order to bolster public confidence in the process as well as to protect the rights of attorneys who are involved. "[I]t is extremely important at this point that the public know how the system works, that it have some assurance that the standards are going to be laid down and observed consistently, and I think this advances [the statute] by . . . eliminating some of the abuses without itself becoming abusive to those whose professional integrity may be at stake." *Id.*, p. 8561, remarks of Representative Richard Blumenthal. Accordingly, the legislative history reflects that the legislature intended that the committee must render a decision within four months of filing of a complaint.

NOTES AND QUESTIONS

1. Should the dissent's plain meaning approach foreclose the majority's investigation of factors other than the meaning of the word "shall"?

2. How does the mandatory/directory distinction relate to the meaning of "shall" and "may"?

3. In *Rocklite Prods. v. Municipal Ct. for the Los Angeles Dist. of Los Angeles Cty.*, 217 Cal. App. 2d 638, 32 Cal. Rptr. 183 (1963), appellants-defendants in a misdemeanor antitrust action argued for a construction of "may" as mandatory. The prosecution was based on a statute which provided for initiating civil actions "in any court having jurisdiction . . . ." However, it also said criminal antitrust actions "may be brought in the superior court in counties where the defendant resided or did business, or where the offense was committed." The drafter of the statute apparently had used "may" before the three options because there were multiple alternatives. The state initiated a misdemeanor criminal action in a municipal court under a general statute giving municipal courts jurisdiction over misdemeanors. Defendants argued the venue and subject matter jurisdiction provisions of the antitrust law were mandatory, therefore requiring dismissal of an action not filed in the superior court.

The court held the construction of "may" usually allows for discretionary action. "The statute . . . does not, therefore, state a legislative intention to give exclusive jurisdiction to the superior court of all prosecutions [under the Act]." The legislature in the same session had refused to adopt a pending bill exempting antitrust prosecutions from the general statute that gave municipal courts jurisdiction over misdemeanors. Thus, the Court stated: "It cannot be inferred that the legislature intended to do indirectly what it refrained from doing directly."

4. *In re Cartmell's Estate*, 138 A.2d 588 (Vt. 1958), indicates it is possible to construe "may" as mandatory. Is *Rocklite* such a case? Assuming "may" is not usually considered mandatory, should one, as a drafter, ever use it that way? The drafter of the *Rocklite* statute apparently intended exclusive superior court rather than municipal court jurisdiction as evidenced by the rejected companion bill that would have exempted these prosecutions from general municipal court jurisdiction. If the drafter had used "shall" rather than "may," would this have precluded alternative superior court options? Can the problem be avoided by a definitional section in the general statutes on "may" and "shall" applicable to all enactments?

5. Does the legislature's failure to enact the other bill excluding these violations from the municipal court really bolster the *Rocklite* court's decision? Could there not be other reasons for the legislature's inaction?

6. Are there any instances where "shall" should be interpreted as being discretionary? In *Ely v. Verde, supra,* the trial court found the language "shall require compliance . . . to the fullest extent possible" to be discretionary. Would you interpret the phrase "the agency shall, in its discretion, make such rules . . ." as mandatory or discretionary?

7. In light of the inconsistent interpretations of "shall," is there any reason to continue using this word in drafting statutes? Would "must" be an effective alternative?

8. For an interesting analysis of the word "shall" in a state domestic violence mandatory arrest statute, and whether, even though it is mandatory, it creates an "entitlement" of the victim to police enforcement supporting a federal constitutional claim, see *Town of Castle Rock v. Gonzales,* 545 U.S. 748, 758–66 (2005).

UNIFORM STATUTE AND RULE CONSTRUCTION ACT (1995)[*]

SECTION 4. CONSTRUCTION OF "SHALL," "MUST," AND "MAY."

(a)   "Shall" and "must" express a duty, obligation, requirement, or condition precedent.

(b)   "May" confers a power, authority, privilege, or right.

(c)   "May not," "must not," and "shall not" prohibit the exercise of a power, authority, privilege, or right.

Comment

. . . .

The context of a statute or rule may indicate that a "shall" or "must" is directory and not mandatory. See Section 1.

e.   "And" and "Or"

STATE v. HILL
157 So. 2d 462 (La. 1963)

HAMITER, JUSTICE.

John Lee Hill was charged in a bill of information with the violation of L.R.S. 14:285 in that he, on October 17, 1962, unlawfully made a local anonymous telephone call to a named female wherein he used vulgar, obscene, profane, loud [lewd], lascivious and indecent language and threats. On the mentioned date such statute (Act No. 121 of 1958) recited in part: "No person shall engage in or institute a local telephone call, conversation or conference of an anonymous nature and herein use obscene, profane, vulgar, lewd, lascivious or indecent language, suggestions or proposals of an obscene nature and threats of any kind whatsoever."

In a motion for a bill of particulars the defendant requested that he be informed as to (1) the obscene, indecent, etc., language used and (2) the specific threats that he allegedly made. The state responded by saying: (1) Words and proposals to the effect

---

   [*]   Reprinted with permission.

that he desired sexual intercourse with her, and (2) none other than that inherent in the foregoing language.

. . . .

In this case we are presented with the question: Is the language of the statute ("and threats of any kind whatsoever") conjunctive, by reason of which the state is required to prove the use of threats as an element of the crime? If it is not (but rather disjunctive), the words "and threats" contained in the instant bill of information are to be treated as surplusage.

L.R.S. 14:285 was originally enacted as Act 435 of 1954. That statute provided: "No person shall engage in or institute a local telephone call, conversation or conference of an anonymous nature and therein use obscene, profane, vulgar, lewd, lascivious or indecent language, suggestions or proposals." No mention, it is noticed, was made therein of threats. By Act 121 of 1958, as aforestated, the statute was amended by adding: "of an obscene nature and threats of any kind *whatsoever*." (Italics ours.)

This change, we think, was not intended to require that threats of some kind be made in addition to the obscene, etc., language used in order to constitute the crime denounced. Its sole purpose was to forbid as a separate and distinct act the making of threats of any kind in a local anonymous telephone call. Stated another way, the word "and" was used in a disjunctive sense, the aim of the amendment being to enlarge the scope of the prohibitions to include the use of any threats whatsoever, regardless of whether they accompanied language of an obscene, etc., nature.

. . . .

For the reasons assigned the judgment of the District Court is reversed and set aside, the motion to quash is now overruled, and the case is remanded for further proceedings in accordance with law.

EARLE v. ZONING BOARD OF WARWICK
191 A.2d 161 (R.I. 1963)

JOSLIN, JUSTICE.

To adopt the construction urged by petitioners is to equate the disjunctive "or" with the conjunctive "and." The words "or" and "and" are not the equivalent of each other and should not be considered as interchangeable unless reasonably necessary in order to give effect to the intention of the enacting body. *Pedro v. Muratore*, 83 R.I. 123, 113 A.2d 731.

Reference to sec. 6.1.4 of the ordinance which sets forth uses permitted in a heavy commercial district indicates that the local legislative body clearly understands the difference between the disjunctive "or" and the conjunctive "and." The pertinent portion reads as follows: "Retail stores, service establishments and repair shops, the merchandise *and* operations of which are stored or conducted outside a building as customarily as within . . ." (italics ours).

In sec. 6.1.4 the legislative body made clear its intention by the use of the conjunctive "and" that both the storage of the merchandise *and* the conduct of the operations of the business are to be stored or conducted outside a building as customarily as within. In sec. 6.1.3 it equally made clear that it is intended by the use of the disjunctive "or" something different from what it intended by the use of the conjunctive "and" in sec. 6.1.4.

. . . .

NOTES AND QUESTIONS

1. In *Earle*, the court said because the legislature used the disjunctive "or" in one section, it clearly intended to use the conjunctive "and" differently in the next section. If this reasoning had been applied by the court in *State v. Hill*, would the same result have been reached? In *Hill*, the legislature used "or" disjunctively four times and "and" conjunctively once. Should this have been persuasive in determining how the other disputed "and" should be interpreted?

2. Were the courts in *State v. Hill* and *In re Cartmell's Estate, supra,* simply correcting sloppy legislative drafting? Since a criminal statute was involved, was it not important for the court (and others) to know exactly what the elements of the crime were?

3. For a discussion of the debate between drafters who favor the use of "and/or" ("Andorians") and those who oppose such usage ("Anti-Andorians"), see Maurice B. Kirk, *Legal Drafting: The Ambiguity of "And" and "Or,"* 2 TEX. TECH. L. REV. 235 (1971).

F. REED DICKERSON,
THE DIFFICULT CHOICE BETWEEN "AND" AND "OR,"
46 AMERICAN BAR ASSOCIATION JOURNAL 310 (1960)*

One of the difficult problems in writing, particularly in a field such as legal drafting that calls for high precision, is to know when to use "and" and when to use "or." I know several excellent draftsmen who say that they develop mental blocks whenever they meet a complicated situation involving this decision. The lawyers' recent preoccupation with the mysteries of "and/or" has distracted attention from the broader difficulties here.

The reader will wonder why the following analysis ignores the many court decisions construing specific uses of "and" and "or." The answer is that such decisions (being concerned for the most part with misused language) are largely irrelevant to this discussion. Even where they are not irrelevant they carry no official weight. Although the courts are the final arbiters of the meaning of particular litigated documents, their pronouncements are directed in such cases toward extracting the meaning of the whole document when viewed in its proper setting which means overriding any specific inconsistent wording.

The difference between "and" and "or" is usually explained by saying that "and" stands for the conjunctive, connective, or additive and "or" for the disjunctive or alternative. The former connotes "togetherness" and the latter tells you to "take your pick." So much is clear. Beyond this point, difficulties arise.

One difficulty is that each of these two words is on some occasions ambiguous. Thus, it is not always clear whether the writer intends the *inclusive* "or" (A or B, or both) or the *exclusive* "or" (A or B, but not both). This long recognized uncertainty has given rise to the abortive attempt to develop "and/or" as an acceptable English equivalent to the Latin "vel" (the inclusive "or").

What has not been so well recognized is that there is a corresponding, though less frequent, uncertainty in the use of "and." Thus, it is not always clear whether the writer intends the *several* "and" (A and B, jointly or severally) or the *joint* "and" (A and B, jointly but not severally). This uncertainty will surprise some, because "and" is normally used in the former sense. Even so, the authors of documents sometimes intend things to be done jointly or not at all. This idea inheres in the purchase of a pair of shoes (try to buy one shoe separately!) without, however, posing any grammatical problem. On the other hand, a reference to "husbands and wives" may create a grammatical uncertainty as to whether the right, privilege, or duty extends to husbands without wives, and vice versa, or whether it may be enjoyed or discharged only jointly. Where such a doubt exists, it is desirable to recognize and deal with it.

Observation of legal usage suggests that in most cases "or" is used in the inclusive rather than the exclusive sense, while "and" is used in the several rather than the joint

* Reprinted with permission from American Bar Association Journal.

sense. If true, this is significant for legal draftsmen and other writers, because it means that in the absence of special circumstances they can rely on simple "or's" and "and's" to carry these respective meanings. This, incidentally, greatly reduces the number of occasions for using the undesirable expression "and/or" or one of its more respectable equivalents, such as "A or B, or both," or "either or both of the following."

Special circumstances in which it is unsafe to rely on general usage exist, on the other hand, wherever the courts have shown an unfriendly or biased attitude in "interpreting" language. Thus, in drafting a criminal statute, with respect to which the courts are inclined to legislate restrictively under the euphemism of "strict construction," it is safer not to rely on the chance that "or" will be given its normal inclusive reading but to say expressly "shall be fined not more than $5,000 or imprisoned not more than three years, *or both*."

Another and more perplexing difficulty in the use of "and" and "or" is that it is often uncertain, because of a possible conflict between grammar and immediate context, whether the draftsman has attempted an enumeration of people or institutions, on the one hand, or of their characteristics or traits, on the other. Take the phrase "every husband and father." If this is intended as an enumeration of two classes of persons, that fact can be less equivocally expressed by saying "every husband and every father" or, taking another approach, by saying "every person who is either a husband or a father." If, on the other hand, it is intended as an enumeration of characteristics or traits necessary to identify each member to be covered, that alternative can be less equivocally expressed by saying "every person who is both a husband and a father."

Because of the subtlety of the point, it may be desirable to clarify it with an example and explanation that I have used elsewhere:

. . . Compare, for instance, these two provisions:

Provision A:

The security roll shall include —

(1) each person who is 70 years of age or older;

(2) each person who is permanently, physically disabled; *and*

(3) each person who has been declared mentally incompetent.

Provision B:

The security roll shall include each person who —

(1) is 70 years of age or older;

(2) is permanently, physically disabled; *or*

(3) has been declared mentally incompetent.

Although both provisions say exactly the same thing, "and" is necessary to provision *A* because it enumerates three separate classes of persons each of which must be included, whereas "or" is necessary to provision *B* because it names a single class of persons by enumerating its three alternative qualifications for membership.

2. Other Internal Guides

In addition to the words, the face of the statute has other indicia of the meaning a legislature intended, such as punctuation, titles, section or chapter headings, and preambles. Statutory language is rarely good English. Commas, semicolons and colons, etc., extend one sentence over many lines and thoughts. Distinguishing between related and unrelated thoughts in one provision or sentence is a major problem.

Headings and preambles pose different problems. Are they little capsules of legislative intent, or simply an aid to statutory format or layout? Can they limit or expand the scope of the provisions? Can a general rule regarding the use of internal guides in statutory interpretation be formulated?

a.   Punctuation

WEINACHT v. BOARD OF CHOSEN FREEHOLDERS OF BERGEN COUNTY
3 N.J. 330, 70 A.2d 69 (1949)

WACHENFELD, J.

Does R.S. 40:9-3 N.J.S.A., require bids for structural steel and ornamental iron work singly or in combination?

. . . .

R.S. 40:9-3, N.J.S.A., reads as follows:

> "In the preparation of plans and specifications for the erection, construction, alteration or repair of any public building by any political subdivision of this state, when the entire cost of the work will exceed one thousand dollars in amount, the architect engineer or other person preparing the plans and specifications, shall prepare separate plans and specifications for the plumbing and gas fitting, and all kindred work, and of the steam and hot water heating and ventilating apparatus, steam power plants and kindred work, and electrical work, structural steel and ornamental iron work."

. . . .

The respondent contends the omission of a comma after the words "structural steel" indicates a legislative intent to treat structural steel and miscellaneous iron work as a single item, while the appellant asserts the courts are not bound by punctuation marks but may disregard them in the search for the legislative intention, citing *Howard Savings Institution v. City of Newark*, 63 N.J.L. 65, 42 A. 848 (Sup. Ct. 1899). The Supreme Court there held the courts are not bound by punctuation marks or the absence of them. In their search for the intention of the legislature they may disregard punctuation or repunctuate if need be. But this case was reversed by the Court of Errors and Appeals, 63 N.J.L. 547, 44 A. 654, 656 (E. & A. 1899), where Chief Justice Magie said: "The punctuation of a legislative act will not control its evident meaning. But punctuation is one of the means for discovering the legislative intent."

This rule is supported by the text writers, who point out parliamentary enactments originally were not punctuated and thus it was a necessary conclusion that the punctuation subsequently inserted was no part of the act. Today, however, statutes are punctuated prior to submission to the legislature and: "The better rule is that punctuation is a part of the act and that it may be considered in the interpretation of the act but may not be used to create doubt or to distort or defeat the intention of the legislature. When the intent is uncertain, punctuation, if it affords some indication of the true intention, may be looked to as an aid." Sutherland, Statutory Construction, 3d Ed., 1943, Sec. 4939.

So, here, we think, the punctuation affords some indication of the true legislative intent.

The statute requires separate plans and specifications for plumbing and gas fitting, steam and hot water heating and ventilating apparatus, steam power plants and kindred work, and electrical work, which are not here in dispute. The question is as to whether or not structural steel and ornamental iron work must be broken down into two parts, (a) structural steel, and (b) ornamental iron work.

Bearing upon the inquiry is the question whether greater economies would be effected through combined bids or separate bids for these items. The only proof in this respect is an affidavit by the president of the Structural Steel and Ornamental Iron Association of New Jersey submitted by the respondent, in which he says substantial economies will be effected by the use of joint bids, thus making "bids much lower in amounts" and creating a greater number of bidders, "increasing competition considerably, to the benefit of the public."

These allegations are not denied but are attested to by the record, which shows no bids were received for miscellaneous metal work on the first advertisement calling for separate bids but on readvertisement for joint bids five were submitted. This affidavit, together with others, shows the general custom of the trade and of the public bodies advertising for bids has been to regard structural steel and ornamental iron as a single item. One such affidavit lists over two hundred public buildings in New Jersey which have been built in the last twenty years and on which the bids and awards for structural steel and ornamental iron work were made as a single unit. These affidavits are not controverted.

Long established custom or usage is relied upon and given consideration in determining the construction to be placed upon ambiguous statutes unless such custom is plainly at variance with the statute. Such is not the case here.

The punctuation of the statute tends to confirm the thought that the legislature intended to combine the two as a single item. Usually when a series of items is separated by commas, the two concluding items are joined by a conjunction (in this case "and") and the comma is omitted; this does not ordinarily combine the last two items into a single one but leaves undisturbed their status as separate and distinct items along with the ones earlier enumerated. Here, however, in the preceding line the legislature has taken the pains to insert a comma before the word "and" in the phrase "and electrical work." This comma serves to emphasize the fact that the electrical work is a separate and distinct item. No such comma was placed before the word "and" in the phrase "structural steel and ornamental iron work." While it is true the legislature has evidenced an intent to break down the various phases of construction work and require separate bids on each, its intent appears to have been to combine structural steel and ornamental iron work into a single part or unit in such breakdown.

Any doubt remaining is dispelled by the custom in the trade and the history of the adoption of the amendment in 1931 [adding "structural steel and ornamental iron work" to the original statute] which serve to indicate the correctness of the respondent's interpretation as upheld by the Appellate Division.

The judgment below is affirmed.

For affirmance: CHIEF JUSTICE VANDERBILT and JUSTICES CASE, OLIPHANT, WACHEN-FELD, BURLING and ACKERSON — 6.

For reversal: JUSTICE HEHER — 1.

NOTES AND QUESTIONS

1. In *Weinacht*, the court considered the punctuation indicative of "true legislative intent." How convincing is the court's analysis? Could the decision not have gone the other way just as easily? Can an argument be made which would lump together everything after the prior "and" (*i.e.*, electrical work, structural steel and ornamental iron work)?

2. Why does the court rely on industry custom? Is there any indication that the legislature considered and approved of such custom? Is the custom not "plainly at variance with the statute"? Should interpretation of statutory language depend on industry custom?

3. The court notes the statute's construction is contrary to usual rules of punctuation, but defends its position on the basis of the use of the word "and." Does the statute demonstrate a careful use of "and" or a proper use of commas?

4. In *Commonwealth v. Kelly*, 58 N.E. 691 (Mass. 1900), the statute prohibited sale of alcoholic beverages between midnight "and six in the morning; or during the Lord's day, except that . . . an innholder may supply such liquor to guests who have resorted to his house for food or lodgings." The innholder argued that the exception for innholders applied to the midnight to six in the morning provision as well as the Lord's day provision. The court disagreed, because the statute was amended replacing a comma after "morning" with a semicolon. In *Cartmell's Estate, supra*, the court said it is a rule of construction that when the legislature amends a law, it intends to change it, unless a contrary intent appears. In *Kelly*, did the legislature intend the amendment as a change in meaning or simply as a clarification? Is there any way to tell?

5. *See generally* Lance Phillip Timbreza, *The Elusive Comma: The Proper Role of Punctuation in Statutory Interpretation*, 24 QUINNIPIAC L. REV. 63 (2005).

b.   Note on Title, Preamble, Chapter and Section Headings

As has been seen from the *Weinacht* case, *supra*, consideration of the rules of grammar is often helpful to the court in determining legislative intent. Courts sometimes refer to other internal guides for assistance in determining legislative intent as illustrated by the following cases.

(1)   Title

Bellew v. Dedeaux, 240 Miss. 79, 126 So. 2d 249 (1961).

Petitioners appealed their conviction and sentencing for harboring an escaped prisoner on the basis of an ambiguity in the body of the statute. To determine legislative intent, the court referred back to the title and stated:

> The title of the statute . . . defines it as "an Act to make it a felony for any person" etc. and "to provide the penalties for the violation thereof." If there is any uncertainty in the body of an act, the title may be resorted to for the purpose of ascertaining legislative intent and of relieving the ambiguity. . . . Considering the title and the body of the act together it is manifest that the legislature intended for one convicted under the statute to be subject to the stated fine or to imprisonment in the penitentiary.

Conviction was affirmed by the court.

CHURCH OF THE HOLY TRINITY V. UNITED STATES
143 U.S. 457 (1892)

. . . .

Among other things which may be considered in determining the intent of the legislature is the title of the act. We do not mean that it may be used to add or to take from the body of the statute. *Hadden v. The Collector*, 5 Wall. 107, but it may help to interpret its meaning. In the case of *United States v. Fisher*, 2 Cranch 358, 386, Chief Justice Marshall said: "On the influence which the title ought to have in construing the enacting clauses much has been said; and yet it is not easy to discern the point of difference between the opposing counsel in this respect. Neither party contends that the title of an act can control plain words in the body of the statute; and neither denies that, taken with other parts, it may assist in removing ambiguities. Where the intent is plain, nothing is left to construction. Where the mind labors to discover the design of the legislature, it seizes everything from which aid can be derived; and in such case the title claims a degree of notice, and will have its due share of consideration." And in the case of *United States v. Palmer*, 3 Wheat. 610, 631, the same judge applied the doctrine in this way: "The words of the section are in terms of unlimited extent. The words 'any person or persons' are broad enough to comprehend every human being. But general words must not only be limited to cases within the jurisdiction of the State, but also to those objects to which the legislature intended to apply them. Did the legislature intend to apply these words to the subjects of a foreign power, who in a foreign ship may commit murder or robbery on the high seas? The title of an act cannot control its words, but may furnish some aid in showing what was in the mind of the legislature. The title of this act is, 'An act for the punishment of certain crimes against the United States.' It would seem that offences against the United States, not offences against the human race, were the crimes which the legislature intended by this law to punish."

It will be seen that words as general as those used in the first section of this act were by that decision limited, and the intent of Congress with respect to the act was gathered partially, at least, from its title. Now, the title of this act is, "An act to prohibit the importation and migration of foreigners and aliens under contract or agreement to perform labor in the United States, its Territories and the District of Columbia." Obviously the thought expressed in this reaches only to the work of the manual laborer, as distinguished from that of the professional man. No one reading such a title would suppose that Congress had in its mind any purpose of staying the coming into this country of ministers of the gospel, or, indeed, of any class whose toil is that of the brain. The common understanding of the terms labor and laborers does not include preaching and preachers; and it is to be assumed that words and phrases are used in their ordinary meaning. So whatever of light is thrown upon the statute by the language of the title indicates an exclusion from its penal provisions of all contracts for the employment of ministers, rectors and pastors.

(2)   Preamble

Prewitt v. Warfield, 203 Ark. 137, 156 S.W.2d 238 (1941).

This case concerned the method by which county roads were to be laid out and opened. Prior to 1923, by statute, the procedure was solely within the discretion of the county courts. This statute was amended in 1923 to allow citizens to petition to open a new road. Subsequently, the court, without petition, opened a road and appellants charged that the 1923 act superseded the prior statute so that the court, on its own, could no longer open new roads. To determine the validity of this claim, the court looked to the preamble of the 1923 statute:

> Whereas, the amendment, as herein provided to said Act No. 422 of the Acts of 1911 does not repeal any part of Act No. 26 of the Acts of 1871 but simply provides for the additional procedure in the matter, so that either may be followed.

The appellate court relied upon the following rule of statutory construction:

> In construing statutes, it is said that the preamble usually contains the motives and inducements to the making of the act, and resort to the preamble may therefore be useful in ascertaining the causes which lead to the passage of the act. . . .

Thus, the court concluded:

> We think the legislature clearly intended by Act 611 to provide a method whereby application could be made to the county court for the opening of a public road, and did not intend, in any way, to interfere with the county court's authority to lay out roads, as provided in the act of 1911. This was clearly an additional method giving the citizens the right to make application by petition for the laying out of new roads.

(3)   Chapter and Section Headings

New York v. Moleneux, 53 Barb. 9 (N.Y. Sup. Ct. 1968).

The question in *Moleneux* was whether a particular statute contained the procedure for filling a vacancy in the office of Major General of the National Guard. The particular provision was part of a larger act concerning internal administration of the government. On its face, the statute's language clearly embraced the situation, but the section heading limited its application to public officers "other than militia or other town officers."

The court rejected the contention that a section heading is similar to an act's title, useful only in resolving ambiguous language, saying in this situation:

> The inscription to chapter 5 is not in any sense a title to a statute. It forms

a part of the body of the act quite as much as the section cited and it was inserted for the purpose of controlling and limiting the scope and application of the general words used in the chapter. . . . To reject the section headings or to refuse to give effect to them . . . would be to make the law, not to administer it.

NOTES AND QUESTIONS

1. What objectives do each of these devices serve? Are such headings ever "inserted" to control or limit the words in the statute? Does the *Moleneux* court's opinion mean headings cannot *expand* a statute's provisions? In what way should a legislative drafter anticipate courts' possible use of the title, preamble or section headings? Are there any ways to prevent courts from making unintended use of what the drafter intended to be only organizational guides?

2. How reasonable is the court's assumption in *Moleneux* that chapter and section headings that summarize or highlight key parts of provisions can be used to limit or expand the scope of the provisions? What evidence is there that the drafters intended such use? Do titles and headings at least provide good indications of the legislators' general and perhaps specific intent for the material that follows?

3. If it is determined that a statute's organizational guides are not appropriate aids to interpretation is it because the guides were not inserted by the drafters in consideration of their potential effect, or because the legislators did not consider the guides to have significance?

3.   Construction of Penal Statutes

The problem of judicial presumptions as a means of limiting statutory scope is most significant with respect to penal statutes. The doctrine of "strict construction" of such statutes is still used by courts at all levels. Its resiliency is explained by due process notions, which require restricted interpretation because a statute must give adequate notice to the public of the nature of the prohibited act. The presumption was originally generated in an atmosphere of judicial mistrust of all legislation. Does the idea that the words of a penal statute should be narrowly interpreted continue to have validity? A number of questions can be raised about the continued use of the doctrine. Is the issue more properly one of clarity of the expression rather than restricting the scope of the prohibited acts? Are the considerations different for crimes which require no criminal intent? Should the doctrine be applicable to strict liability, or so-called status crimes? Perhaps the classic analysis of the doctrine is contained in the following article.

a.   Strict or Liberal Construction

LIVINGSTON HALL,
STRICT OR LIBERAL CONSTRUCTION OF PENAL STATUTES,
48 HARVARD LAW REVIEW 748 (1935)[*]

III. *The Rationale of the Legal Rules*

The common-law rule requires the strict construction of all penal statutes. The statutory rules, on the other hand, commonly require a liberalized construction of all penal statutes, or, at least, of all those found in the penal code. But the reasons given for the rules, while establishing that *some* penal statutes should be construed strictly, and *some* liberally, do not, and cannot, show that the same rule should be applied to *all* statutes. A brief analysis will make it clear that the result of either rule is a Procrustean

---

bed, necessitating the undue extension, or decapitation, of those unlucky instances of legislative intent which do not naturally fit into the particular rule adopted.

For Strict Construction. Potentially the most serious argument is that the rule is founded "on the plain principle that the power of punishment is vested in the legislative, not in the judicial department." For if this were true, a liberal construction statute would be an unconstitutional delegation of legislative power to the judiciary. But this objection is clearly unsound. Liberal construction does not involve going beyond the intention of the legislature. Want of power to depart from the legislative intent exists as clearly in remedial as in penal statutes; yet this objection has never been urged against a liberal construction of remedial statutes. Where liberal construction statutes have been passed, courts have never raised this objection to their enforcement, and only one court has doubted the power of the legislature to "direct the judiciary in the interpretation of existing statutes."

It has further been claimed that as the state makes the laws, they should be most strongly construed against it. But the contract analogy is weak, for the state is presumably acting in the public interest in enacting criminal statutes, and need not in every case be subjected to a rule of interpretation designed to secure justice between private parties. Nor can the rule be justly defended as a bulwark against tyranny in a country where both executive and legislature are elected by the people; the rule has never achieved the dignity of a constitutional amendment.

Obviously, the original reason for the growth of the rule, to mitigate the extension of capital felonies, no longer applies to all penal statutes, if indeed it was ever of such widespread application; this has often been recognized in states where the rule has been abrogated, and where this argument is still made, it has been limited to those few statutes carrying punishments believed by the courts to be disproportionately severe as compared with the acts sought to be punished.

There remains for consideration only Mr. Justice Holmes' statement in *McBoyle v. United States* that it is "reasonable" for penal statutes to be construed to give "fair warning" of "what the law intends to do if a certain line is passed" in language "that the common world will understand." Why such warning should be needed in murder and theft, two crimes as to which Mr. Justice Holmes himself admits that "it is not likely that a criminal will carefully consider the text of the law before he murders or steals," or especially in transporting stolen property, as in the *McBoyle* case itself, where the offense was clearly a crime under the state laws, and the only question was as to federal prosecution, is far from self-evident. Even if "fair warning" had been called for in the particular case, as it undoubtedly is in many crimes, it was unnecessary to lay down a general rule. Simply because a liberal construction might work injustice in some cases is no proper reason for inflicting on the people the rule of strict construction in all cases.

For Liberal Construction. The argument for liberal construction of non-penal statutes has been put forcibly by Dean Pound nearly 20 years ago in an article concluding: "The public cannot be relied upon permanently to tolerate judicial obstruction or nullification of the social policies to which more and more it is compelled to be committed." This argument is equally applicable to penal statutes, except insofar as "political liberty requires clear and exact definition of the offense." The public is already impatient with the refined, and for practical purposes unnecessary, distinctions embodied in the penal codes. To make Hauptmann's conviction for murder in the first degree turn on whether the window in the nursery was open or shut, with the law until comparatively recently unsettled if the window were partially open, does not commend itself to the average man. Strict construction of such statutes has completed the degradation of the substantive criminal law in his mind, equaled in futility only by the disgraceful pyrotechnics with which the procedure is carried on in a *cause celebre*. An attitude of liberal construction goes far, on the other hand, to make the law appear rational.

Changing conditions of modern civilization, and the growth of scientific knowledge on criminology, render imperative a new approach to the problems of crime. New categories of crimes and criminals cannot always be accurately defined on the first attempt. Shall the new machinery be nullified from the start under the guise of "strict construction," or shall it be carried out liberally in the spirit in which it is conceived? Merely to state the issue is to answer it.

But this does not mean that *all* penal statutes should be liberally construed. Political liberty does require that people should be able to pursue certain types of conduct with definite assurance of the bounds of criminal liability. Carelessly drafted legislation may still require limitation to avoid unforeseen consequences. The doctrine of strict construction often returns like Banquo's ghost to trouble courts committed by legislation and decision to the principle that it has ceased to exist. Doubtless some courts have deliberately ignored their liberal construction statutes, preferring rather to hold to strict construction than to have to apply the new doctrine in all cases, with the inevitable occasional injustice which it would bring. Some compromise is necessary.

UNITED STATES v. R.L.C.
503 U.S. 291 (1992)

JUSTICE SOUTER announced the judgment of the Court.

The provisions of the Juvenile Delinquency Act require the length of official detention in certain circumstances to be limited to "the maximum term of imprisonment that would be authorized if the juvenile had been tried and convicted as an adult." 18 U.S.C. § 5037(c)(1)(B). We hold that this limitation refers to the maximum sentence that could be imposed if the juvenile were being sentenced after application of the United States Sentencing Guidelines.

. . . .

After a bench trial, the District Court found R.L.C. to be a juvenile who had driven the car recklessly while intoxicated and without the owner's authorization, causing [a passenger's] death. R.L.C. was held to have committed an act of juvenile delinquency within the meaning of § 5031, since his acts would have been the crime of involuntary manslaughter in violation of 18 U.S.C. §§ 1112(a) and 1153 if committed by an adult. The maximum sentence for involuntary manslaughter under 18 U.S.C. § 1112(b) is three years. At R.L.C.'s dispositional hearing, the District Court granted the Government's request to impose the maximum penalty for the respondent's delinquency and accordingly committed him to official detention for three years.

Despite the manslaughter statute's provision for an adult sentence of that length, the United States Court of Appeals for the Eighth Circuit, 915 F.2d 320 (1990), vacated R.L.C.'s sentence and remanded for resentencing, after concluding that 36 months exceeded the cap imposed by § 5037(c)(1)(B) upon the period of detention to which a juvenile delinquent may be sentenced. Although the statute merely provides that juvenile detention may not extend beyond "the maximum term of imprisonment that would be authorized if the juvenile had been tried and convicted as an adult," the Court of Appeals read this language to bar a juvenile term longer than the sentence a court could have imposed on a similarly situated adult after applying the United States Sentencing Guidelines. . . . The Court of Appeals therefore concluded that the maximum period of detention to which R.L.C. could be sentenced was 21 months.

. . . .

II

A

The Government suggests a straightforward enquiry into plain meaning to explain what is "authorized." It argues that the word "authorized" must mean the maximum term of imprisonment provided for by the statute defining the offense, since only Congress can "authorize" a term of imprisonment in punishment for a crime. As against the position that the Sentencing Guidelines now circumscribe a trial court's authority, the Government insists that our concern must be with the affirmative authority for imposing a sentence, which necessarily stems from statutory law. It maintains that in any event the Sentencing Commission's congressional authorization to establish sentencing guidelines does not create affirmative authority to set punishments for crime, and that the Guidelines do not purport to authorize the punishments to which they relate.

But this is too easy. The answer to any suggestion that the statutory character of a specific penalty provision gives it primacy over administrative sentencing guidelines is that the mandate to apply the Guidelines is itself statutory. . . . The text is at least equally consistent with treating "authorized" to refer to the result of applying all statutes with a required bearing on the sentencing decision, including not only those that empower the court to sentence but those that limit the legitimacy of its exercise of that power. This, indeed, is arguably the more natural construction.

Plain-meaning analysis does not, then, provide the Government with a favorable answer. The most that can be said from examining the text in its present form is that the Government may claim its preferred construction to be one possible resolution of statutory ambiguity.

B

On the assumption that ambiguity exists, we turn to examine the textual evolution of the limitation in question and the legislative history that may explain or elucidate it. The predecessor of § 5037(c) as included in the Juvenile Justice and Delinquency Prevention Act of 1974 provided that a juvenile adjudged delinquent could be committed to the custody of the Attorney General for a period "not [to] extend beyond the juvenile's twenty-first birthday or the maximum term which could have been imposed on *an adult* convicted of the same offense, whichever is sooner." 18 U.S.C. § 5037(b) (1982 ed.) (emphasis added). In its current form, the statute refers to the "maximum term of imprisonment that would be authorized if *the juvenile* had been tried and convicted as an adult." 18 U.S.C. § 5037(c) (emphasis added). On its face, the current language suggests a change in reference from abstract consideration of the penalty permitted in punishment of the adult offense, to a focused inquiry into the maximum that would be available in the circumstances of the particular juvenile before the court. The intervening history supports this reading.

With the Sentencing Reform Act of 1984 (chapter II of the Comprehensive Crime Control Act of 1984, Pub. L. 98-473, § 214(a), 98 Stat. 2013), § 5037 was rewritten. As § 5037(c)(1)(B), its relevant provision became "the maximum term of imprisonment that would be authorized *by section 3581(b)* if the juvenile had been tried and convicted as an adult." 18 U.S.C. §§ 5037(c)(1)(B), (c)(2)(B)(ii) (1982 ed., Supp. II) (emphasis added). The emphasized language was quickly deleted, however, by the Criminal Law and Procedure Technical Amendments Act of 1986, Pub. L. 99-646, § 21(a)(2), 100 Stat. 3596 (Technical Amendments Act), resulting in the present statutory text, "the maximum term of imprisonment that would be authorized if the juvenile had been tried and convicted as an adult." It thus lost the reference to § 3581(b), which would have guided the sentencing court in identifying the "authorized" term of imprisonment.

R.L.C. argues that this loss is highly significant. Section 3581(b) was and still is part of a classification system adopted in 1984 for use in setting the incidents of punishment for federal offenses by reference to letter grades reflecting their relative seriousness. One provision, for example, sets the maximum period of supervised release for each letter grade. 18 U.S.C. § 3583. Section 3581(b) sets out the maximum term of imprisonment for each letter grade, providing, for instance, that the authorized term of imprisonment for a Class C felony is not more than 12 years, for a Class D not more than 6, and for a Class E not more than 3.

The deletion of the reference to § 3581(b) with its specific catalog of statutory maximums would seem to go against the Government's position. Since, for example, a juvenile who had committed what would have been an adult Class E felony would apparently have been subject to three years of detention, because § 3581(b) "authorized" up to three years of imprisonment for an adult, the deletion of the reference to § 3581(b) would appear to indicate some congressional intent to broaden the range of enquiry when determining what was authorized.

The Government, however, finds a different purpose, disclosed in the section-by-section analysis prepared by the Department of Justice to accompany the bill that became the Technical Amendments Act. . . .

The Government explains that limiting the length of a juvenile detention to that authorized for an adult under § 3581(b) could in some circumstances have appeared to authorize a longer sentence than an adult could have received, when the offense involved was assigned no letter grade in its defining statute. . . . It was to break this tension, according to the Government, that the reference to § 3581(b) was deleted guaranteeing that no juvenile would be given detention longer than the maximum adult sentence authorized by the statute creating the offense. The amendment also, the Government says, left the law clear in its reference to the statute creating the offense as the measure of an "authorized" sentence. This conclusion is said to be confirmed by a statement in the House Report that the amendment "delet[es an] incorrect cross-referenc[e]." H.R. Rep. No. 99-797, p. 21 (1986), which the Government argues, "suggests that no substantive change was intended." Brief for United States 20, n.4.

We agree with the Government's argument up to a point. . . . The legislative history does not prove, however, that Congress intended "authorized" to refer solely to the statute defining the offense despite the enactment of a statute requiring application of the Sentencing Guidelines, a provision that will generally provide a ceiling more favorable to the juvenile than that contained in the offense-defining statute.

Indeed, the contrary intent would seem the better inference. . . .

The point is reinforced by other elements of the legislative history. . . . The legislative history thus reinforces our initial conclusion that § 5037 is better understood to refer to the maximum sentence permitted under the statute requiring application of the Guidelines.[5]

C

We do not think any ambiguity survives. If any did, however, we would choose the construction yielding the shorter sentence by resting on the venerable rule of lenity, see, e.g., United States v. Bass, 404 U.S. 336, 347–348 (1971), rooted in " 'the instinctive distaste against men languishing in prison unless the lawmaker has clearly said they should,' " id., at 348 (quoting H. Friendly, Benchmarks 209 (1967)). While the rule has been applied not only to resolve issues about the substantive scope of criminal statutes, but to answer questions about the severity of sentencing, see Bifulco v. United States, 447 U.S. 381, 387 (1980), its application is unnecessary in this case, since "we have always reserved lenity for those situations in which a reasonable doubt persists about a statute's intended scope even after resort to 'the language and structure, legislative

---

[5] The dissent takes us to task for reliance upon a "technical amendment." But a statute is a statute, whatever its label. Although the critical congressional enactment, the deletion of the reference to § 3581(b), came in the Criminal Law and Procedures Technical Amendments Act, we have applied the usual tools of statutory construction: the language left in the statute after its amendment in 1986 is most naturally read to refer to the term of imprisonment authorized after application of the statute mandating use of the Guidelines. The legislative history of the Technical Amendments Act reinforces this conclusion.

history, and motivating policies' of the statute." *Moskal v. United States*, 498 U.S. ___, (1990) (slip op., at 4) (citation omitted).[6]

. . . .

JUSTICE SCALIA, with whom JUSTICE KENNEDY and JUSTICE THOMAS join, concurring in part and concurring in the judgment.

In my view it is not consistent with the rule of lenity to construe a textually ambiguous penal statute against a criminal defendant on the basis of legislative history. Because Justice Souter's opinion assumes the contrary, I join only Parts I, II-A, and III, and concur in the judgment.

The Court begins its analysis, quite properly, by examining the language of 18 U.S.C. § 5037(c)(1)(B) — which proves to be ambiguous. Reasonable doubt remains, the Court concludes, as to whether the provision refers (i) to the maximum punishment that could be imposed if the juvenile were being sentenced under the United States Sentencing Guidelines (15–21 months) or (ii) to the maximum punishment authorized by the statute defining the offense, *see* 18 U.S.C. § 1112(a) (36 months). *Ante*, at 5. With that conclusion I agree — and that conclusion should end the matter. The rule of lenity, in my view, prescribes the result when a criminal statute is ambiguous: the more lenient interpretation must prevail.

Yet the plurality continues. Armed with its warrant of textual ambiguity, the plurality conducts a search of § 5037's legislative history to determine whether that clarifies the statute. Happily for *this* defendant, the plurality's extratextual inquiry is benign: It uncovers evidence that the "better understood" reading of § 5037 is the more lenient one. *Ante*, at 12. But this methodology contemplates as well a different ending, one in which something said in a Committee Report causes the criminal law to be stricter than the text of the law displays. According to the plurality, "we resort to the [rule of lenity] only when 'a reasonable doubt persists about a statute's intended scope even *after* resort to "the language and structure, legislative history, and motivating policies" of the statute.'" *Ante*, at 12 (quoting *Moskal v. United States*, 498 U.S. ___, ___ (1990) (slip op., at 4)) (citation omitted). I doubt that *Moskal* accurately characterizes the law in this area, and I am certain that its treatment of "the venerable rule of lenity," *ante*, at 12, does not venerate the important values the old rule serves.

The *Moskal* formulation of the rule, in approving reliance on a statute's "motivating policies" (an obscure phrase) seems contrary to our statement in *Hughey v. United States*, 495 U.S. 411, 422 (1990), that "[e]ven [where] the statutory language . . . [is] ambiguous, longstanding principles of lenity . . . preclude our resolution of the ambiguity against [the criminal defendant] on the basis of general declaration of policy in the statute and legislative history." And insofar as *Moskal* requires consideration of

---

[6] Justice Scalia questions the soundness of *Moskal*'s statement that we have reserved lenity for those cases (unlike this one) in which after examining "the . . . structure, legislative history, and motivating policies" in addition to the text of an ambiguous criminal statute, we are still left with a reasonable doubt about the intended scope of the statute's application. But the Court has not in the past approached the use of lenity in the way Justice Scalia would have it.

It is true that the need for fair warning will make it "rare that legislative history or statutory policies will support a construction of a statute broader than that clearly warranted by the text," *Crandon v. United States*, 494 U.S. 152, 160 (1990), and that "general declarations of policy," whether in the text or the legislative history, will not support construction of an ambiguous criminal statute against the defendant. *Hughey v. United States*, 495 U.S. 411, 422 (1990). But lenity does not always require the "narrowest" construction, and our cases have recognized that a broader construction may be permissible on the basis of nontextual factors that make clear the legislative intent where it is within the fair meaning of the statutory language. *See Dixson v. United States*, 465 U.S. 482, 500–501, n.19 (1984). *Cf. McBoyle v. United States*, 283 U.S. 25, 27 (1931) (a criminal statute should be construed in such a way that its language gives "fair warning" to the "common mind"). Whether lenity should be given the more immediate and dispositive role Justice Scalia espouses is an issue that is not raised and need not be reached in this case.

legislative history *at all*, it compromises what we have described to be purposes of the lenity rule. "[A] fair warning," we have said, "should be given to the world in language that the common world will understand, of what the law intends to do if a certain line is passed. To make the warning fair, so far as possible the line should be clear." *McBoyle v. United States*, 283 U.S. 25, 27 (1931). "[T]he rule of lenity ensures the criminal statutes will provide fair warning concerning conduct rendered illegal." *Liparota v. United States*, 471 U.S. 419, 427 (1985). It may well be true that in most cases the proposition that the words of the United States Code or the Statutes at Large give adequate notice to the citizen is something of a fiction, *see McBoyle, supra*, at 27, albeit one required in any system of law; but necessary fiction descends to needless farce when the public is charged even with knowledge of Committee Reports.

Moskal's mode of analysis also disserves the rule of lenity's other purpose: assuring that the society, through its representatives, has genuinely called for the punishment to be meted out. "[B]ecause of the seriousness of criminal penalties, and because criminal punishment usually represents the moral condemnation of the community, legislatures and not courts should define criminal activity," *United States v. Bass*, 404 U.S. 336, 348 (1971). *See also Liparota, supra*, at 427; *United States v. Wiltberger*, 5 Wheat. 76, 95 (1820). The rule reflects, as the plurality acknowledges, " ' "the instinctive distaste against men languishing in prison unless the lawmaker has clearly said they should." ' " *Ante*, at 12 (quoting *Bass, supra*, at 348, and H. Friendly, Benchmarks 209 (1967)). But legislative history can never provide assurance against that unacceptable result. After all, "[a] statute is a statute," *ante*, at 12, n.5, and no matter how "authoritative" the history may be — even if it is that veritable Rosetta Stone of legislative archaeology, a crystal clear Committee Report — one can never be sure that the legislators who voted for the text of the bill were aware of it. The only thing that was authoritatively adopted *for sure* was the text of the enactment; the rest is *necessarily* speculation. Where it is doubtful whether the text includes the penalty, the penalty ought not be imposed. "[T]he moral condemnation of the community," *Bass, supra*, at 348, is no more reflected in the views of a majority of a single committee of congressmen (assuming, of course, they have genuinely considered what their staff has produced) than it is reflected in the views of a majority of an appellate court; we should feel no less concerned about "men languishing in prison" at the direction of the

We have in a number of cases other than *Moskal* done what the plurality has done here: inquired into legislative history and invoked it to support or at least permit the more lenient reading. But only once, to my knowledge, have we relied on legislative history to "clarify" a statute, explicitly found to be facially ambiguous, against the interest of a criminal defendant. In *Dixson v. United States*, 465 U.S. 482, 500–501, n.19 (1984), the Court relied on legislative history to determine that defendants, officers of a corporation responsible for administering federal block grants, were "public officials" within the meaning of 18 U.S.C. § 201(a). The opinion does not trouble to discuss the "fair warning" or "condemnation of the community" implications of its decision, and both of the cases it cites in supposed support of its holding found the statute at hand *not* to be facially ambiguous. . . . I think *Dixson* weak (indeed, utterly unreasoned) foundation for a rule of construction that permits legislative history to satisfy the ancient requirement that criminal statutes speak "plainly and unmistakably," *United States v. Gradwell*, 243 U.S. 476, 485 (1917); *see also Bass, supra*, at 348.

In sum, I would not embrace, as the plurality does, the *Moskal* formulation of this canon of construction, lest lower courts take the dictum to heart. I would acknowledge the tension in our precedents, the absence of an examination of the consequences of the *Moskal* mode of analysis, and the consequent conclusion that *Moskal* may not be good law.

JUSTICE THOMAS, concurring in part and concurring in the judgment.

I agree with Justice Scalia that the use of legislative history to construe an otherwise ambiguous penal statute against a criminal defendant is difficult to reconcile with the rule of lenity. I write separately, however, to emphasize that the rule is not triggered merely because a statute appears textually ambiguous *on its face*. Just last Term, we reaffirmed that the rule operates only " 'at the end of the process' " of construction, *Chapman v. United States*, 500 U.S. ___ , ___ (1991) (slip op., at 9) (quoting *Callanan v. United States*, 364 U.S. 587, 596 (1961)), if ambiguity remains "even after a court has 'seize[d] every thing from which aid can be derived,' " *ibid.* (quoting *United States v. Bass*, 404 U.S. 336, 347 (1971), in turn quoting *United States v. Fisher*, 2 Cranch 358, 386 (1805)). Thus, although we require Congress to enact "clear and definite" penal statutes, *United States v. Universal C.I.T. Credit Corp.*, 344 U.S. 218, 221–222 (1952), we also consult our own "well-established principles of statutory construction," *Gozlon-Peretz v. United States*, 498 U.S. ___ , ___ (1991) (slip op., at 14), in determining whether the relevant text is clear and definite. *See, e.g., id.*, at ___ (slip op., at 8) (applying the rule in *Arnold v. United States*, 9 Cranch 104, 119–120 (1815), that statutes become effective immediately); *Albernaz v. United States*, 450 U.S. 333, 337–342 (1981) (applying the rule in *Blockburger v. United States*, 284 U.S. 299, 304 (1932), to establish the permissibility of multiple punishments).

These cases, I think, demonstrate that we must presume familiarity not only with the United States Code, *see ante* at 2, but also with the United States Reports, in which we have developed innumerable rules of construction powerful enough to make clear an otherwise ambiguous penal statute. *Cf. Chevron U.S.A. Inc. v. Natural Resources Defense Council, Inc.*, 467 U.S. 837, 843, n.9 (1984) ("clear congressional intent" may be discerned by application of "traditional tools of statutory construction"). Like Congress's statutes, the decisions of this Court are law, the knowledge of which we have always imputed to the citizenry. At issue here, though, is a rule that would also require knowledge of committee reports and floor statements, which are not law. I agree with Justice Scalia that there appears scant justification for extending the "necessary fiction" that citizens know the law, *see ante*, at 2–3, to such extra-legal materials.

Justice O'Connor, with whom Justice Blackmun joins, dissenting.

By failing to interpret 18 U.S.C. § 5037(c)(1)(B) in light of the statutory scheme of which it is a part, the Court interprets a "technical amendment" to make sweeping changes to the process and focus of juvenile sentencing. Instead, the Court should honor Congress' clear intention to leave settled practice in juvenile sentencing undisturbed.

. . . .

NOTES AND QUESTIONS

1. What is the difference between Justice Thomas' and Justice Scalia's view of interpreting criminal statutes?

2. For what seems to be a contrary approach, see *State v. Des Marets*, 92 N.J. 62, 455 A.2d 1074 (1983).

3. Should the rule of lenity have any application when criminal statutes are invoked in civil proceedings? *See Crandon v. United States*, 494 U.S. 152, 168 (1990); *United States v. Thompson/Center Arms Co.*, 504 U.S. 505 (1992).

4. In *Muscarello v. United States*, 524 U.S. 125 (1998), considered in Chapter 6[B], the Supreme Court considered the definition of "carries" in the context of a statute providing a mandatory minimum sentence for one who "carries a firearm" during the commission of a drug offense. In the face of a broad definition of "carries" which would include carrying a firearm in the trunk of a car, the defendant sought to rely on the rule of lenity. The majority responded:

> Finally, petitioners and the dissent invoke the "rule of lenity." The simple existence of some statutory ambiguity, however, is not sufficient to warrant application of that rule, for most statutes are ambiguous to some degree. *Cf.*

Smith, 508 U.S., at 239 ("The mere possibility of articulating a narrower construction . . . does not by itself make the rule of lenity applicable"). "The rule of lenity applies only if, 'after seizing everything from which aid can be derived,' . . . we can make 'no more than a guess as to what Congress intended.' " *United States v. Wells*, 519 U.S. 482, 499 (1997) (quoting *Reno v. Koray*, 515 U.S. 50, 64 (1995), *Smith, supra*, at 239, and *Ladner v. United States*, 358 U.S. 169, 178 (1958)). To invoke the rule, we must conclude that there is a " 'grievous ambiguity or uncertainty' in the statute." *Staples v. United States*, 511 U.S. 600, 619, n.17 (1994) (quoting *Chapman v. United States*, 500 U.S. 453 (1991)). Certainly, our decision today is based on much more than a "guess as to what Congress intended," and there is no "grievous ambiguity" here. The problem of statutory interpretation in this case is indeed no different from that in many of the criminal cases that confront us. Yet, this Court has never held that the rule of lenity automatically permits a defendant to win.

5. The origins, rationale, history and application of the rule of lenity are traced, and *R.L.C.* is discussed, in Lawrence M. Solan, *Law, Language, and Lenity*, 40 WM. & MARY L. REV. 57 (1998).

b. California's Response to the Presumption — The Theory and the Practice

In the following materials analyze the approach of California courts to the problem of strict construction of penal statutes. The legislature acted to reverse the presumption, but the issue remains. Why? How could the legislature have been clearer? What factors have made the courts inconsistent in their treatment of the doctrine of strict construction? Is there a noticeable trend in their way of thinking? How "just" are the courts' applications of the doctrine? Is the presence of § 4's counter-instructions as to strict interpretation determinative of the cases' outcomes, or are the decisions unaffected by § 4? Could the same results in each case have been justified without resort to the doctrine? Can one predict with any assurance the status of strict construction of penal statutes in California?

CALIFORNIA PENAL CODE

4 Construction

CONSTRUCTION OF THE PENAL CODE. The rule of the common law, that penal statutes are to be strictly construed, has no application to this Code. All its provisions are to be construed according to the fair import of their terms, with a view to effect its objects and to promote justice.

(Enacted 1872.)

UNIFORM STATUTE AND RULE CONSTRUCTION ACT (1995)*

§ 18 Principles of construction; presumption.

. . . .

Comment

. . . .

The presumption that penal statutes shall be strictly construed is not included in this Act. Like the presumption about statutes in derogation of the common law, this presumption has been expressly rejected by a number of States. Texas rejected it in 1856 and California in 1872. Texas Penal Code Section 1.05(a) (1967); Calif. Penal Code Section 4 (1872). Over a half century ago Livingston Hall, in his article *Strict or Liberal*

---

* Reprinted with permission.

Construction of Penal Statutes, 48 HARV. L. REV. 748 (1935), demonstrated that courts do not consistently apply the presumption. Professor Hall noted that courts have been less willing to apply the presumption if the offense is *malum in se* than if it is merely *malum in prohibitum*. The U.S. Supreme Court, for example, has not applied the presumption consistently. *Compare United States v. Campos-Serrano*, 404 U.S. 293 (1971) (applied), *with Dixson v. United States*, 465 U.S. 482 (1984) (not applied).

Nevertheless, a State that recognizes the presumption that a penal statute shall be strictly construed, and desires to retain that presumption, will need to add an appropriate subsection to this section.

KEELER v. SUPERIOR COURT
2 Cal. 3d 619, 87 Cal. Rptr. 481, 470 P.2d 617 (1970)

MOSK, J. — In this proceeding for writ of prohibition we are called upon to decide whether an unborn but viable fetus is a "human being" within the meaning of the California statute defining murder (Pen. Code, § 187). We conclude that the legislature did not intend such a meaning, and that for us to construe the statute to the contrary and apply it to this petitioner would exceed our judicial power and deny petitioner due process of law.

The evidence received at the preliminary examination may be summarized as follows: Petitioner and Teresa Keeler obtained an interlocutory decree of divorce on September 27, 1968. They had been married for 16 years. Unknown to petitioner, Mrs. Keeler was then pregnant by one Ernest Vogt, whom she had met earlier that summer. She subsequently began living with Vogt in Stockton, but concealed the fact from petitioner. Petitioner was given custody of their two daughters, aged 12 and 13 years, and under the decree Mrs. Keeler had the right to take the girls on alternate weekends.

On February 23, 1969, Mrs. Keeler was driving on a narrow mountain road in Amador County after delivering the girls to their home. She met petitioner driving in the opposite direction; he blocked the road with his car, and she pulled over to the side. He walked to her vehicle and began speaking to her. He seemed calm, and she rolled down her window to hear him. He said, "I hear you're pregnant. If you are you had better stay away from the girls and from here." She did not reply, and he opened the car door; as she later testified, "He assisted me out of the car. . . . [I]t wasn't roughly at this time." Petitioner then looked at her abdomen and became "extremely upset." He said, "You sure are. I'm going to stomp it out of you." He pushed her against the car, shoved his knee into her abdomen, and struck her in the face with several blows. She fainted, and when she regained consciousness petitioner had departed.

Mrs. Keeler drove back to Stockton, and the police and medical assistance were summoned. She had suffered substantial facial injuries, as well as extensive bruising of the abdominal wall. A Caesarian section was performed and the fetus was examined *in utero*. Its head was found to be severely fractured, and it was delivered stillborn. The pathologist gave as his opinion that the cause of death was skull fracture with consequent cerebral hemorrhaging, that death would have been immediate, and that the injury could have been the result of force applied to the mother's abdomen. There was no air in the fetus' lungs, and the umbilical cord was intact.

Upon delivery the fetus weighed five pounds and was 18 inches in length. Both Mrs. Keeler and her obstetrician testified that fetal movements had been observed prior to February 23, 1969. The evidence was in conflict as to the estimated age of the fetus; the expert testimony on the point, however, concluded "with reasonable medical certainty" that the fetus had developed to the stage of viability, *i.e.*, that in the event of premature birth on the date in question it would have had a 75 percent to 96 percent chance of survival.

An information was filed charging petitioner, in count I, with committing the crime of murder (Pen. Code, § 187) in that he did "unlawfully kill a human being, to wit Baby Girl Vogt, with malice aforethought." In count II petitioner was charged with wilful infliction of traumatic injury upon his wife (Pen. Code, § 273d), and in count III, with assault on Mrs. Keeler by means of force likely to produce great bodily injury (Pen. Code, § 245). His motion to set aside the information for lack of probable cause (Pen. Code, § 995) was denied, and he now seeks a writ of prohibition; as will appear, only the murder count is actually in issue. Pending our disposition of the matter, petitioner is free on bail.

I

Penal Code section 187 provides: "Murder is the unlawful killing of a human being, with malice aforethought." The dispositive question is whether the fetus which petitioner is accused of killing was, on February 23, 1969, a "human being" within the meaning of the statute. If it was not, petitioner cannot be charged with its "murder" and prohibition will lie.

Section 187 was enacted as part of the Penal Code of 1872. Inasmuch as the provision has not been amended since that date, we must determine the intent of the legislature at the time of its enactment. But section 187 was, in turn, taken verbatim from the first California statute defining murder, part of the Crimes and Punishments Act of 1850. (Stats. 1850, ch. 99, § 19, p. 231.) Penal Code section 5 (also enacted in 1872) declares: "The provisions of this code, so far as they are substantially the same as existing statutes, must be construed as continuations thereof, and not as new enactments." We begin, accordingly, by inquiring into the intent of the legislature in 1850 when it first defined murder as the unlawful and malicious killing of a "human being."

It will be presumed, of course, that in enacting a statute the legislature was familiar with the relevant rules of the common law, and, when it couches its enactment in common-law language, that its intent was to continue those rules in statutory form. (*Baker v. Baker* (1859) 13 Cal. 87, 95–96; *Morris v. Oney* (1963) 217 Cal. App. 2d 864, 870 [32 Cal. Rptr. 88].) This is particularly appropriate in considering the work of the first session of our legislature: its precedents were necessarily drawn from the common law, as modified in certain respects by the Constitution and by legislation of our sister states.

We therefore undertake a brief review of the origins and developments of the common law of abortional homicide.

. . . .

From that inquiry it appears that by the year 1850 — the date with which we are concerned — an infant could not be the subject of homicide at common law unless it had been born alive.

. . . .

Penal Code section 6 declares in relevant part that "No act or omission" accomplished after the code has taken effect "is criminal or punishable, except as prescribed or authorized by this code, or by some of the statutes which it specifies as continuing in force and as not affected by its provisions, or by some ordinance, municipal, county, or township regulation. . . ." This section embodies a fundamental principle of our tripartite form of government, *i.e.*, that subject to the constitutional prohibition against cruel and unusual punishment, the power to define crimes and fix penalties is vested exclusively in the legislative branch.

. . . .

. . . .

"In this state the common law is of no effect so far as the specification of what acts or conduct shall constitute a crime is concerned. [Citations.] In order that a public offense be committed, some statute, ordinance or regulation prior in time to the commission of the act, must denounce it; likewise with excuses or justifications — if no statutory excuse or justification apply as to the commission of the particular offense, neither the common law nor the so-called 'unwritten law' may legally supply it." (*People v. Whipple* (1929) 100 Cal. App. 261, 262 [279 P. 1008].)

Settled rules of construction implement this principle. Although the Penal Code commands us to construe its provisions "according to the fair import of their terms, with a view to effect its objects and to promote justice" (Pen. Code, § 4), it is clear the courts cannot go so far as to create an offense by enlarging a statute, by inserting or deleting words, or by giving the terms used false or unusual meanings. (*People v. Baker* (1968) 69 Cal. 2d 44, 50 [69 Cal. Rptr. 595, 442 P.2d 675].) Penal statutes will not be made to reach beyond their plain intent; they include only those offenses coming clearly within the import of their language. (*De Mille v. American Fed. of Radio Artists* (1947) 31 Cal. 2d 139, 156 [187 P.2d 769, 175 A.L.R. 382].) Indeed, "Constructive crimes — crimes built up by courts with the aid of inference, implication, and strained interpretation — are repugnant to the spirit and letter of English and American criminal law." (*Ex parte McNulty* (1888) 77 Cal. 164, 168 [19 P. 237].)

Applying these rules to the case at bar, we would undoubtedly act in excess of the judicial power if we were to adopt the People's proposed construction of section 187. As we have shown, the legislature has defined the crime of murder in California to apply only to the unlawful and malicious killing of one who has been born alive. We recognize that the killing of an unborn but viable fetus may be deemed by some to be an offense of similar nature and gravity: but as Chief Justice Marshall warned long ago, "It would be dangerous, indeed, to carry the principle, that a case which is within the reason or mischief of a statute, is within its provisions, so far as to punish a crime not enumerated in the statute, because it is of equal atrocity, or of kindred character, with those which are enumerated." (*United States v. Wiltberger* (1820) 18 U.S. (5 Wheat.) 76, 96 [5 L. Ed. 37, 42].) Whether to thus extend liability for murder in California is a determination solely within the province of the legislature. For a court to simply declare, by judicial fiat, that the time has now come to prosecute under section 187 one who kills an unborn but viable fetus would indeed be to rewrite the statute under the guise of construing it. Nor does a need to fill an asserted "gap" in the law between abortion and homicide — as will appear, no such gap in fact exists — justify judicial legislation of this nature: to make it "a judicial function 'to explore such new fields of crime as they may appear from time to time' is wholly foreign to the American concept of criminal justice" and "raises very serious questions concerning the principle of separation of powers." (*In re Davis* 242 Cal. App. 2d 645, 655–56 & fn. 12 [51 Cal. Rptr. 702].)

The second obstacle to the proposed judicial enlargement of section 187 is the guarantee of due process of law. Assuming *arguendo* that we have the power to adopt the new construction of this statute as the law of California, such a ruling, by constitutional command, could operate only prospectively, and thus could not in any event reach the conduct of petitioner on February 23, 1969.

The first essential of due process is fair warning of the act which is made punishable as a crime.

This requirement of fair warning is reflected in the constitutional prohibition against the enactment of ex post facto laws (U.S. Const., art. I, §§ 9, 10; Cal. Const., art. I, § 16). When a new penal statute is applied retrospectively to make punishable an act which was not criminal at the time it was performed, the defendant has been given no advance notice consistent with due process. And precisely the same effect occurs when such an act is made punishable under a preexisting statute but by means of an unforeseeable *judicial* enlargement thereof. (*Bowie v. City of Columbia* (1964) 378 U.S. 347 [12 L. Ed. 2d 894, 84 S. Ct. 1697].)

. . . .

McComb, J., Peters, J., Tobriner, J., and Peek, J., concurred.

Burke, Acting C.J., dissenting.

. . . .

In my view, we cannot assume that the legislature intended a person such as defendant, charged with the malicious slaying of a fully viable child, to suffer only the mild penalties imposed upon common abortionists who, ordinarily, procure only the miscarriage of a nonviable fetus or embryo. (*See* Comment, Model Penal Code, § 207.11, p. 149 (Tent. Draft No. 9, 1959).) To do so would completely ignore the important common-law distinction between the quickened and unquickened child.

Of course, I do not suggest that we should interpret the term "human being" in our homicide statutes in terms of the common-law concept of quickening. At one time, that concept had a value in differentiating, as accurately as was then scientifically possible, between life and nonlife. The analogous concept of viability is clearly more satisfactory, for it has a well defined and medically determinable meaning denoting the ability of the fetus to live or survive apart from its mother.

The majority opinion suggests that we are confined to common-law concepts, and to the common-law definition of murder or manslaughter. However, the legislature, in Penal Code sections 187 and 192, has defined those offenses for us: homicide is the unlawful killing of a "human being." Those words need not be frozen in place as of any particular time, but must be fairly and reasonably interpreted by this Court to promote justice and to carry out the evident purposes of the legislature in adopting a homicide statute. Thus, Penal Code section 4, which was enacted in 1872 along with sections 187 and 192, provides: "The rule of the common law, that penal statutes are to be strictly construed, has no application to this code. All its provisions are to be construed according to the fair import of their terms, with a view to effect its objects and to promote justice."

. . . .

Penal Code section 4, which abolishes the common-law principle of the strict construction of penal statutes, embodies the doctrine of *Katz v. Walkinshaw*, 141 Cal. 116, and permits this Court fairly to construe the terms of those statutes to serve the ends of justice. Consequently, nothing should prevent this Court from holding that Baby Girl Vogt was a human ("belonging or relating to man; characteristic of man") being ("existence, as opp. to nonexistence; specif. life") under California's homicide statutes.

. . . .

If, as I have contended, the term "human being" in our homicide statutes is a fluid concept to be defined in accordance with present conditions, then there can be no question that the term should include the fully viable fetus.

The majority suggest that to do so would improperly create some new offense. However, the offense of murder is no new offense. Contrary to the majority opinion, the legislature has not "defined the crime of murder in California to apply only to the unlawful and malicious killing of one who has been born alive." . . . Instead, the legislature simply used the broad term "human being" and directed the courts to construe that term according to its "fair import" with a view to effect the objects of the homicide statutes and promote justice. (Pen. Code, § 4.) What justice will be promoted, what objects effectuated, by construing "human being" as excluding Baby Girl Vogt and her unfortunate successors? Was defendant's brutal act of stomping her to death any less an act of homicide than the murder of a newly born baby? No one doubts that the term "human being" would include the elderly or dying persons whose potential for life has nearly lapsed; their proximity to death is deemed immaterial. There is no sound reason for denying the viable fetus, with its unbounded potential for life, the same status.

The majority also suggest that such an interpretation of our homicide statutes would deny defendant "fair warning" that his act was punishable as a crime. . . . Aside from the absurdity of the underlying premise that defendant consulted Coke, Blackstone or Hale before kicking Baby Girl Vogt to death, it is clear that defendant had adequate notice that his act could constitute homicide. Due process only precludes prosecution under a new statute insufficiently explicit regarding the specific conduct proscribed, or under a preexisting statute "by means of an unforeseeable *judicial* enlargement thereof."

Our homicide statutes have been in effect in this state since 1850. The fact that the California courts have not been called upon to determine the precise question before us does not render "unforeseeable" a decision which determines that a viable fetus is a "human being" under those statutes. Can defendant really claim surprise that a 5-pound, 18-inch, 34-week-old, living viable child is considered to be a human being?

. . . .

SULLIVAN, J., concurred.

PEOPLE v. COURTNEY
1 Cal. Rptr. 789 (1959)

FOURT, J. — This is an appeal by Russell Guy Courtney from a judgment wherein he was convicted of pimping and pandering and an appeal by Ardella M. Courtney from a judgment wherein she was convicted of pimping.

. . . .

The woman appellant insists that because section 266h of the Penal Code described pimping in terms of "any male person" that therefore it necessarily follows that no female person can be convicted of pimping. The contrary was established in *People v. Young*, 132 Cal. App. 770, 772 [23 P.2d 524]. The penal statutes are to be construed according to the fair import of their terms with a view to effect its objects and to promote justice. The rule of the common law that penal statutes are to be strictly construed has no application to the Penal Code. (Pen. Code, § 4.)

It was appropriately said in *In re Davis*, 18 Cal. App. 2d 291, 295 [63 P.2d 853]:

". . . the courts are [not] always to be governed by the exact phraseology and literal meaning of every word or phrase employed. The primary rule of intention is to be first applied. . . . In other words, the courts will not blindly follow the letter of a law, when its purpose is apparent, to consequences which are inconsistent with that purpose; and this would seem to be particularly true when the results of a literal interpretation, if adopted, would be absurd, and unjust, and where rights of the public are involved. . . . A thing which is within the intention is as much within the statutes as if it were within the letter . . . ."

Section 266h (pimping) and 266i (pandering) were enacted by the same legislature and should be treated together. (*People v. Jackson*, 30 Cal. 427.) In adopting the section making pandering a crime, the legislature undoubtedly had in mind to discourage the nefarious business of replenishing houses of prostitution with inmates. (*People v. Cimar*, 127 Cal. App. 9, 11–14 [15 P.2d 166, 16 P.2d 139].) Certainly, pimping is equally nefarious. The object of the section is to stop such course of conduct and to discourage prostitution, and justice would seem to dictate that anyone, whether male or female, acting as a pimp should be punished.

The woman appellant further contends that as a female may not directly be charged as a pimp, neither may a female be indirectly prosecuted under section 31 of the Penal Code for taking part in the commission of the crime by a male. Section 31 of the Penal Code reads in part as follows:

"All persons concerned in the commission of a crime, whether it be felony or misdemeanor, and whether they . . . aid and abet in its commission, or, not being present, have advised and encouraged its commission . . . are principals in any crime so committed." (Enacted 1872.)

The *Young* case, *supra* (132 Cal. App. 770), was determined in 1933. Thirteen (13) regular sessions of the legislature have convened since that case and the legislature has never seen fit to change the law. Where a statute has been judicially construed and that construction has not been altered by subsequent legislation it can be presumed that the legislature is aware of the judicial construction and approved of it. (*People v. Hallner*, 43 Cal. 2d 715, 719 [277 P.2d 393]; *People v. Wein*, 50 Cal. 2d 383, 400 [326 P.2d 457].)

. . . .

[*Affirmed.*]

NOTES AND QUESTIONS

1. In his article, Hall argues that one instance where "the doctrine of strict construction provides some measure of needed protection against administrative tyranny" is when old legislation is inapplicable to changed social or economic conditions. Can that argument be turned around? Would this reasoning also apply when a statute is based on dated scientific knowledge? In *Keeler*, was there any danger that an interpretation based on present views of when life begins would result in "administrative tyranny"? The court was concerned that it would create an offense by enlarging the statute. Do you think the legislature of 1850 would have omitted unborn children from the coverage of the statute if they felt an unborn child could be alive? Would the defendant have been denied fair warning if unborn children were included in the statute? If this case had been decided after *Roe v. Wade*, would there have been fair warning that a viable fetus is alive while still unborn?

2. In *Courtney*, the court said that in California the common-law rule "that penal statutes are to be strictly construed has no application to the Penal Code." Given *Keeler*, is this an accurate representation of the situation in California? In *Courtney*, there was precedent for convicting a woman for pimping. The statute concerning liberal construction was used as additional support for the earlier case. In the absence of the earlier case, would the court have been as careful as the court in *Keeler* was, not to extend the words of the statute?

3. For a discussion of the background of *Keeler*, and the legislative process leading to a statute aimed at overruling it, see Comment, *Is the Intentional Killing of an Unborn Child Homicide? California's Law to Punish the Willful Killing of a Fetus*, 2 PAC. L.J. 170 (1971).

4. After *Keeler*, the California Legislature did pass a statute outlawing fetal homicide. For the interpretation questions associated with that new statute, see *People v. Davis*, 872 P.2d 591 (Cal. 1994); Anna Hua Hsu, Case Note, *From Keeler v. Superior Court to People v. Davis: The Definition of Fetal Murder in California*, 23 W. ST. U. L. REV. 219 (1995). No statute was passed banning fetal manslaughter. *People v. Dennis*, 950 P.2d 1035, 1055–58 (Cal. 1998).

5. For a Pennsylvania case similar to *Keeler*, see *Commonwealth v. Booth*, 766 A.2d 843 (Pa. 2001).

4. Statutes in Derogation of the Common Law

The other major area of application of the strict construction principle has been to statutes in derogation of the common law. This judicial attitude toward statutes was introduced in both Chapters 1 and 2. This doctrine arose primarily because judges thought they were better able to establish the law of the land than legislators. *See* Jefferson B. Fordham & Russell L. Leach, *Interpretation of Statutes in Derogation of the Common Law*, 3 VAND. L. REV. 438 (1950).

The doctrine has received much criticism in recent years. The modern trend recognizes the ability of the legislature to make laws which are "good," "just" and "fair." Not only are there policy problems with the doctrine, but constitutional concerns are also involved. Under the constitutional principle of separation of powers, the function of the judiciary is limited to interpretation and application of statutes. Statutory creation is the function of the legislature. Is the strict construction doctrine erroneous because it usurps the principle of the separation of powers?

ALBUQUERQUE HILTON INN v. HALEY
90 N.M. 510, 565 P.2d 1027 (1977)

. . . .

The facts pertinent to disposition are as follows. On September 18, 1974, the plaintiff, Mrs. Haley, arrived in Albuquerque on a Texas International Airlines (TIA) flight. The airline informed her that her luggage had been inadvertently transferred to Los Angeles. Mrs. Haley told TIA that she was staying at the Hilton. The next morning, her retrieved luggage was delivered to the Hilton; a receipt was signed by the desk clerk, the luggage placed on the bell stand and a bellhop called to carry the bags to Mrs. Haley's room. By the time the bellhop arrived, the luggage had disappeared. It has never been found. Mrs. Haley made repeated inquiries at the desk as to the whereabouts of her luggage and was repeatedly informed that it had not yet been delivered. When she finally contacted TIA, she was shown the receipt indicating delivery to the hotel.

Mrs. Haley sued the Hilton for compensatory ($5,000.00) and punitive ($25,000.00) damages, basing her complaint on Hilton's alleged wrongful refusal to return her luggage or compensate her for its loss (Count I) and also for its refusal to assist her as promised in her attempts to locate her luggage (Count II). Nowhere in the complaint do allegations of theft or negligence appear, nowhere does the claim for relief purport to be based on or limited by the hotelkeeper's liability statute, § 49-6-1, *supra*. Hilton moved for partial summary judgment as to any liability beyond the $1,000.00 maximum allowed by that statute. Mrs. Haley's motion in opposition to Hilton's motion claimed that the statute did not apply (1) because it pertained only to loss of property "brought by . . . guests into the hotel" and she had not so brought the missing luggage, and (2) because it worked a deprivation of property without due process of law. The trial court granted Hilton's motion, declared that the hotelkeeper's statute applied to limit liability, awarded Mrs. Haley judgment against Hilton for $1,000.00 accordingly, and granted judgment for Hilton as to any liability in excess of that amount.

. . . .

We decline to adopt the reasoning of the Court of Appeals (Lopez, J.) that the statute only applies to property brought physically into the hotel by the guest or his agent. . . .

The statute in question provides in pertinent part that the liability of hotelkeepers for loss of guests' property is not to exceed the sum of $1,000.00. It is beyond question that the statute is in derogation of the common law rule, which provided sternly that the innkeeper was answerable as an insurer (regardless of absence of negligence) for loss of the goods, money, and baggage of his guest, except for the acts of God, the public enemy or the guest himself. As this court stated long ago [*Horner v. Harvey*, 3 N.M. (Gild.) 307, 309, 5 P. 329, 329–30 (1885)]:

> "The liability of innkeepers is strict, and justly so. . . . The law of civilized countries benignantly protects men away from home, and from those resources with which the denizen or citizen can guard himself from wrong, and protect his property from loss or injury."

. . . .

As a general rule, statutes in derogation of the common law are to be strictly construed. *State v. Chavez*, 70 N.M. 289, 373 P.2d 533 (1962); *El Paso Cat. Loan Co. v. Hunt et al.*, 30 N.M. 157, 228 P. 888 (1924). However, this statute was obviously enacted to ameliorate the effect of the harsh common law rule, and as a remedial statute in derogation of the common law a different rule applies. *In re Gossett's Estate*, 46 N.M. 344, 351, 129 P.2d 56, 60 (1942) sets forth that rule:

> "Where a statute is both remedial and in derogation of the common law it is

usual to construe strictly the question of whether it does modify the common law, but its application should be liberally construed. . . .

"There are three points to be considered in the construction of all remedial statutes; the old law, the mischief, and the remedy; that is, how the common law stood at the making of the act; what the mischief was, for which the common law did not provide; and what remedy the parliament hath provided to cure this mischief. And it is the business of the judges so to construe the act as to suppress the mischief and advance the remedy." 1 Cooley's Blackstone, p. 86.

Applying this rule, it becomes clear that the liberal construction of the statute, the construction which the Legislature obviously intended and which would "suppress the mischief and advance the remedy," should be applied here. This entails looking through the form of the pleadings to the substance of the action and applying the statute to limit defendant's liability.

Under circumstances similar to those involved here the Supreme Court of Hawaii held that an analogous statute applied to limit the defendant hotel's liability for the loss of a guest's mink coat to the $50.00 statutory amount, ruling that [*Minneapolis Fire & Marine Ins. Co. v. Matson Nav. Co.*, 44 Haw. 59, 67, 352 P.2d 335, 340 (1960)]:

"The rule of strict construction does not require or permit a statute 'to be construed so strictly as to defeat the obvious intention of the legislature' (*Johnson v. Southern Pacific Co.*, 196 U.S. 1, 18, 25 S. Ct. 158, 49 L. Ed. 363) and even where strict construction is called for, the words of the statute are to be given their ordinary meaning. *Mann v. Mau*, 38 Haw. 421, 426; *Kamanu v. E.E. Black, Ltd.*, 41 Haw. 442, 459. 'Although a rule of strict construction is applied to a statute in derogation of the common law, it should nevertheless be construed sensibly and in harmony with the purpose of the statute, so as to advance and render effective such purpose and the intention of the legislature. The strict construction should not be pushed to the extent of nullifying the beneficial purpose of the statute, or lessening the scope plainly intended to be given thereto.' " 50 Am. Jur., Statutes, § 404, pp. 428–9.

The trial court did not err in awarding summary judgment on the basis of the statute.

UNIFORM STATUTE AND RULE CONSTRUCTION ACT (1995)*
§ 18 Principles of construction; presumption.

. . . .

(c) The presumption that a civil statute in derogation of the common law is construed strictly does not apply to a statute of this [State].

Comment

. . . .

Subsection (c) rejects what is perhaps the most commonly cited common law presumption — that statutes in derogation of the common law should be strictly construed. In rejecting this presumption, subsection (c) follows legislation taking the same approach adopted many years ago by some States, e.g., Tex. Gov't Code § 312.006 (1988), which was first enacted as part of a 1911 revision. This common law presumption as to the legislative intent was based on an assumption that legislatures had such high regard for the common law that statutes changing the common law should be strictly construed so as to make only those changes that the next of the statute plainly required. If the presumption ever had any basis in fact, the great quantity of legislation changing the common law enacted during the last half century demonstrates it has long been without foundation.

---

* Reprinted with permission.

The presumption that remedial statutes change the common law should be liberally construed seems to compete with the strict construction presumption. Professor Karl N. Llewellyn in his classic article, *Remarks on the Theory of Appellate Decision and the Rules or Canons About How Statutes are to be Construed*, 3 VAND. L. REV. 395, 401 (1950), paired the two presumptions and other similar rules as thrust and parry. He hypothesized that if two equally applicable rules would lead to different results, the choice of rules of the interpretation and not the text of the statute or rule determined the result. His examples may have been instances of a court starting with the answer instead of the question.

RICHARD POSNER, STATUTORY INTERPRETATION — IN THE CLASSROOM AND IN THE COURTROOM,
50 UNIVERSITY OF CHICAGO LAW REVIEW 800, 808–09 (1983)*

. . . Another very popular canon, "remedial statutes are to be construed broadly," goes wrong by being unrealistic about legislative objectives. The idea behind this canon is that if the legislature is trying to remedy some ill, it would want the courts to construe the legislation to make it a more rather than a less effective remedy for that ill. This would be a sound working rule if every statute — at least every statute that could fairly be characterized as "remedial" (which I suppose is every regulatory statute that does not prescribe penal sanctions and so comes under another canon, which I discuss later) — were passed because a majority of the legislators wanted to stamp out some practice they considered to be an evil; presumably they would want the courts to construe the statute to advance that objective. But if, as is often true, the statute is a compromise between one group of legislators that holds a simple remedial objective but lacks a majority and another group that has reservations about the objective, a court that construed the statute broadly would upset the compromise that the statute was intended to embody.

NOTES AND QUESTIONS

1. How is a court, particularly with a state statute, able to determine whether it was a compromise among interest groups?

2. How does Judge Posner's approach comport with the understanding that a statute has the force of law regardless of how close the vote on it was?

3. How would a court's recognition that a statute reflected a compromise affect its resolution of an interpretation issue? *See People ex rel. Chicago Bar Ass'n v. State Bd. of Elections*, 136 Ill. 2d 513, 558 N.E.2d 89, 99–100 (1990) (unconstitutional provisions of statute will not be severed where legislative history reflects an explicit compromise in statute).

4. When interpreting the Worker's Compensation Act, the North Dakota courts liberally construe the provisions of the statute while keeping a close eye on the explicit statutory terms. The North Dakota Supreme Court noted that the Worker's Compensation Act must be liberally construed to promote the ends intended to be secured by its enactment. *Erickson v. North Dakota Workmen's Comp. Bureau*, 123 N.W.2d 292, 294 (N.D. 1963). That same court later cautioned, however, that although the act is to be "liberally construed with the view of extending its benefit provisions to all who can fairly be brought within them . . . liberal construction does not mean we can ignore the terms or the intent of the provisions within the Act." *Effertz v. North Dakota Worker's Comp. Bureau*, 481 N.W.2d 218, 221 (N.D. 1992).

5. *See generally* Blake A. Watson, *Liberal Construction of CERCLA Under the Remedial Purpose Canon: Have the Lower Courts Taken a Good Thing Too Far?* 20

HARV. ENVIRONMENTAL L. REV. 199 (1996). Professor Watson points out that the canon supporting liberal construction of remedial statutes arose from *Heyden's Case* (excerpted in the beginning of Chapter 7), in an era when common law was still dominant, and judges had to incorporate relatively few statutes into that system. He argues the canon should be reconsidered now that statutory law predominates.

> The statutorification of American law and the demise of the derogation canon had consequences for the continued legitimacy and application of the remedial purpose canon. The original justification for this remedial purpose canon — to guide courts faced with the task of integrating statutory enactments into a system of judge-made law — became less relevant in an era where statutory regulation was no longer the exception to the common law rule. The connection between the "mischiefs" and "defects" of the common law and the "remedial" aspect of the statutory enactment likewise was given less emphasis. Instead, the courts began to selectively apply the canon based on the intrinsic "remedial" nature of a statute. In an *ad hoc* manner, certain types of statutes were deemed to be "remedial" and therefore deserving of a liberal construction. This evolution of the remedial purpose canon raised a definitional issue: if the remedial purposes of statutes are no longer judged in reference to the common law, what then are the defining characteristics of a "remedial" statute?

Id., at 232.

6. For an argument that "expansionist" *judicial* interpretation of complex, remedial statutes actually inhibits further *legislative* action, see Daniel B. Rodriguez & Barry R. Weingast, *The Paradox of Expansionist Statutory Interpretations*, 101 NW. U. L. REV. 1207 (2007).

7. *See* Mark L. Mousesian, *Are Statutes Really "Legislative Bargains"? The Failure of the Contract Analogy in Statutory Interpretation*, 76 N.C. L. REV. 1145 (1998).

B. JUDICIAL ASSUMPTIONS OF LEGISLATIVE CONSIDERATION

Often in situations where no legislative record is available, as in state legislative enactments, or where the legislative history does not disclose a legislative intent or purpose, courts will engage in the assumption that the legislature has taken notice of events and circumstances relevant to the legislation in question. In other words, the court will construct a scenario to arrive at explanations for the meaning of legislative provisions. Whether such constructive legislative goals can properly be classified into the intent and purpose categories discussed earlier is an interesting inquiry. Some of the textual canons covered in Chapter 6, such as *in pari materia* and statutory cross-references, are based on judicial assumptions of legislative consideration. We will see this again in the following Chapter 9 where the doctrine of precedent in statutory interpretation cases, which is often based on judicial assumption of legislative acquiescence in earlier interpretations, is analyzed.

The assumptions are that the legislature has considered some external event. Such matters include the language of other statutes, judicial decisions and administrative interpretations. The judicial or administrative determinations are only those that have interpreted legislation. It is assumed the legislature knew of and endorsed the interpretation, since it has not changed the provision or has reenacted that portion of the statute without change. The conceptual basis for these assumptions should be contrasted with the next section, which discusses approaches involving comparisons of several parts of one provision or act. In the latter instance, it is assumed the legislature knows of all relevant statutes and then makes a conscious decision to be consistent.

The problem is that in actuality, a legislature rarely considers the things the court assumes it does, generally leaves no indication if it has done so and certainly does not often so act as a body. One should consider the validity of these assumptions as a form of legislative history. Are they properly a form of (or at least a substitute for) legislative history, are they based on an essentially invalid rationale, and, even so, are they an acceptable device to resolve interpretative issues?

STATE OF NEW JERSEY v. WEISSMAN
73 N.J. Super. 274, 179 A.2d 748 (1962)

Defendant now urges on appeal, for the first time, that plain error was committed by the Court when it allowed the jury to deliberate upon his guilt or innocence when the evidence indicated that Green received marijuana for the purpose of selling the same as his agent, and that the proofs did not establish a sale of narcotics by him to Green. . . .

. . . .

The indictment charges that defendant "did unlawfully sell a narcotic drug, to wit: Marijuana, to one Dolores F. Green, contrary to the provisions of R.S. 24:18-4 [N.J.S.A.]." The cited statute makes it unlawful to "manufacture, possess, have under his control, sell, prescribe, administer, dispense or compound any narcotic drug," except as otherwise authorized by law. This section of our act is identical with its counterpart in the Uniform Narcotic Drug Act, 9B U.L.A., sec. 2, p. 285. The word "sale" has been defined by our legislature to include "barter, exchange or offer therefor, and each such transaction made by any person, whether as principal, proprietor, agent, servant or employee." N.J.S.A. 24:18-2(n). The same definition is included in the uniform act, which adds, however, the word "gift" to the transactions therein enumerated. 9B U.L.A., sec. 1(10), p. 280.

The courts of this state have not heretofore been called upon to construe, in a reported decision, the legislative meaning of "sale" or "sell" as employed in our Narcotic Drug Law. We are not, however, without precedent. The State of Illinois has adopted the Uniform Narcotic Drug Act, and the Supreme Court of that state in *People v. Shannon*, 15 Ill. 2d 494, 155 N.E.2d 578, 580 (1959), in construing their statute, said:

> We interpret the meaning of the word "sale," as defined by the act, to be much broader in scope than that usually given to it in other branches of the law. Admittedly, the defendant took the role of at least an agent, and the act specifically declares an agent in a narcotics transaction to be a seller. We are of the opinion that the definition shows a legislative intent that the act of a person whether as agent, either for the seller or the purchaser, or as a go-between, in such a transaction constitutes a sale.

. . . .

While these opinions, by the highest tribunal of a sister state, are not binding upon this Court, they are of signal import, and we are more or less imperatively obliged to recognize their value as a guiding precedent. A paramount objective of our uniform state laws is the standardization of particular subjects within the United States and, to that end, we should refer to and seriously consider the construction given to comparable statutes in other jurisdictions. *See* 2 Sutherland Statutory Construction (3d ed., Horack, 1943), sec. 5211, p. 557.

. . . .

We are not concerned with semantics but, rather, with legislative intent. If the statutory language is susceptible of two constructions, it is our function to adopt an interpretation that will carry out, not defeat, the manifest objective sought by the legislation. 2 Sutherland, *op. cit.*, sec. 4704, p. 338. "[W]ords used may be expanded or limited according to the manifest reason and obvious purpose of the law. The spirit of the legislative direction prevails over the literal sense of the terms." *Alexander v. N.J. Power & Light Co.*, 21 N.J. 373, 378, 122 A.2d 339, 342 (1956). . . .

It is clear that the legislative design in New Jersey is to eradicate the illegal traffic in narcotic drugs. *State v. Reed*, 34 N.J. 554, 564, 170 A.2d 419 (1961). That was the primary purpose for the adoption of our Narcotic Drug Law in 1933. *Id.* When our

Supreme Court, in discussing R.S. 24:18-4, N.J.S.A. in *Reed*, said:

> The statute was passed as an all-out offensive to combat the drug evil by eliminating sources of supply. Every step in the scheme of illegal distribution was made a violation of section 4.

(P. 564, 170 A.2d p. 425.) [I]t emphatically evinced a judicial policy of interpretation and enforcement consistent with the Illinois decisions, *supra*. . . .

In the case *sub judice* evidence was adduced that defendant delivered and transferred marijuana to Green on several occasions, and that subsequent thereto money was paid by her to him for prior deliveries. Weissman was the moving principal in these insidious transactions in which he made the delivery and for which he received compensation. Under the circumstances of such unlawful episodes, it is immaterial whether Green be characterized as a "buyer," a "purchaser," or an "agent" — she was a recipient of marijuana, and money therefor was passed by her to the party from whom she acquired the illegal drug. We hold, as did the Illinois Supreme Court, that the word "sale" as defined in the Uniform Narcotic Drug Law is broader in scope than the definition usually given to it in other branches of the law, and that the passing of illicit merchandise and money, between the defendant and Green, constituted a sale as comprehended by and within the prohibitions of our narcotic drug laws.

MELBY v. ANDERSON
64 S.D. 249, 266 N.W. 135 (1936)

RUDOLPH and CAMPBELL, JUDGES.

This action, brought by the administratix of the estate of Olaf Melby, deceased, who at the time of his death was a guest passenger in the defendant's car, involves a construction of chapter 147, Laws 1933, the so-called guest statute, which, so far as material here, is as follows: "Provided that no person transferred by the owner or operator of a motor vehicle as his guest without payment for such transportation shall have cause of action for damages against such owner or operator for injury, death or loss, in case of accident, unless such accident shall have been caused by the gross negligence or wilful and wanton misconduct of the owner or operator of such motor vehicle and unless such gross negligence or wilful and wanton misconduct contributed to the injury, death or loss for which the action is brought."

. . . .

[The court reviews a number of guest statutes in other states. — Eds.]

The material portion of the Michigan statute reads as follows: "Provided, however, That no person, transported by the owner or operator of a motor vehicle as his guest without payment for such transportation shall have a cause of action for damages against such owner or operator for injury, death or loss, in case of accident, unless such accident shall have been caused by the gross negligence or wilful and wanton misconduct of the owner or operator of such motor vehicle and unless such gross negligence or wilful and wanton misconduct contributed to the injury, death or loss for which the action is brought."

It will be observed that our statute (chapter 147, Laws 1933) follows the Michigan statute exactly save only that the second word "however" is omitted; the sixth word "transported" reads in our statute "transferred," a very palpable clerical error; and the word "a" before the words "cause of action" in the third line of the Michigan statute as quoted above is omitted in our statute. None of the statutes above cited corresponds in language with the Michigan statute.

Upon a consideration of these statutes, it appears clear beyond question, not only that our legislature adopted the Michigan statute, but also that our legislature did not adopt any other statute, and we do not face here the dilemma suggested in *Pierson v. Minnehaha County* (1910) 26 S.D. 462, 128 N.W. 616, 617, Am. Ann. Cas. 1913B, 386, where the Court points out that at the time of the South Dakota legislative act "there were a number of other states having a similar statute" and inquires, "How is it possible, under such circumstances, for this court to determine, with absolute certainty, from what state our legislature copied or adopted a law?" In the present case an inspection of the existing statutes demonstrates clearly and affirmatively that our legislature did "copy and adopt" the Michigan law and no other.

Before we thus took over the Michigan statute it had been discussed and construed by the Supreme Court of Michigan in at least eleven different cases during a period extending from January, 1931, to January, 1933. . . .

. . . .

Conceding that the prior Michigan interpretation of the statute is not binding upon us "unless we feel that such construction is sound and based upon reason" (*State v. Nelson* (1931) 58 S.D. 562, 237 N.W. 766, 768, 76 A.L.R. 1226), it is nevertheless the general presumption that the South Dakota Legislature intended to enact a law with the meaning that the courts of Michigan had previously placed upon the Michigan statute which our Legislature adopted.

. . . .

A fair statement of the net result of these Michigan cases construing this statute prior to our adoption thereof seems to us about as follows: That "gross negligence," as used in the statute, is really a misnomer, and that the conduct described by those words transcends negligence and is different in kind and amounts to willful, wanton, or reckless misconduct as distinguished from negligence even though spoken of as gross negligence. Its characteristic is willfulness rather than inadvertence. That there is no such thing as "gross negligence" in the sense of great or much negligence, and the term as implied in the statutes does not mean something of a less degree than willful or wanton misconduct. That to create liability under the statute there must be (1) knowledge of a situation requiring the exercise of ordinary care and diligence to avert injury to another; (2) ability to avoid the resulting harm by ordinary care and diligence in the use of the means at hand; (3) omission to use such care and diligence to avert the threatened danger when, to the ordinary mind, it must be apparent that the result is likely to prove disastrous to another.

Practically the same result as a matter of construction of analogous statutes has been reached in other jurisdictions which, as is also true in this jurisdiction, do not recognize degrees of negligence and which are unwilling to define the term gross negligence as being merely more or greater negligence than is implied by the word negligence standing alone without the adjective gross. . . .

We appreciate that the standard of conduct set up by the Michigan Court, as being within the meaning of the statute, is the kind of conduct that we said in *Wittstruck v. Lee*, 62 S.D. 290, 252 N.W. 874, could not as a practical matter be properly determined by a jury as distinguished from negligent conduct. In the *Wittstruck-Lee* case the question involved was whether contributory negligence was a defense which could be pleaded against this kind of conduct of which we are speaking. A holding contrary to that of the *Wittstruck-Lee* case seems to us to tend toward the recognition of the doctrine of comparative negligence in that it in substance (though not in words) encourages the jury to weigh the relative negligence of the plaintiff and defendant in cases where contributory negligence is pleaded in actions for negligent tort. We are opposed to the doctrine of comparative negligence and do not believe the courts ought to try to submit this particular standard of conduct to the jury in ordinary negligence cases. However, in view of the fact that the legislature has seen fit to adopt the Michigan statute, we accept it as such, and with it the construction that had theretofore been placed upon the statute by the Michigan court. The statute applies, of course, only to the so-called guest cases, and in this class of cases there will be no temptation of the jury to weigh the relative negligence because the only question involved will be whether or not the conduct of the defendant is such that it comes within the meaning of the statute.

We conclude, therefore, as follows: This statute was taken from the law of Michigan, and will be construed and interpreted in the light of the Michigan decisions relating to it before our legislature adopted it. Under those decisions, the words "gross negligence" are, for practical purposes, substantially synonymous with the phrase "wilful and wanton misconduct." Willful and wanton misconduct (and gross negligence as it is employed in this statute) means something more than negligence. They describe conduct which transcends negligence and is different in kind and characteristics. They describe conduct which partakes to some appreciable extent, though not entirely, of the nature of a deliberate and intentional wrong. To bring the conduct of the defendant within the prohibition of this statute the jury must find as a fact that defendant intentionally did something in the operation of a motor vehicle which he should not have done or intentionally failed to do something which he should have done under such circumstances that it can be said that he consciously realized that his conduct would in all probability (as distinguished from possibly) produce the precise result which it did produce, and would bring harm to the plaintiff.

. . . .

The judgment appealed from is reversed, and the trial court is directed to enter judgment for the defendant.

All the Judges concur.

NOTES AND QUESTIONS

1. In *Melby*, the court said the general presumption was that the South Dakota legislature intended to enact both the Michigan statute and the interpretation Michigan courts had previously placed on it. Does a legislature actually look at prior judicial interpretations when it adopts the statute of another state? Should evidence of the legislature's inquiry into the other state's judicial interpretations be presented before the court applies the adopted statutes doctrine? Where several states have similar statutes and it is not clear from which one a statute originated, should the court give consideration to judicial interpretations of each of those states' statutes?

2. The court said prior Michigan interpretations would not be binding if the construction was not sound. If the legislature adopted the statute on the basis of these interpretations, should that make any difference? If the *intent* of the legislature is clear, should the court reject it if they feel it is unsound?

3. In 1975, the South Dakota Supreme Court stated that its guest passenger statute, though an "unreasonable social policy," was "compatible with the notion of equal protection" and therefore constitutional. *Behrns v. Burke*, 229 N.W.2d 86, 92, 90 (S.D. 1975). Five months later, the Michigan Supreme Court examined its guest passenger statute and declared it unconstitutional as violative of the equal protection clause of the Michigan Constitution. *Manistee Bank & Trust Co. v. McGowan*, 394 Mich. 655, 232 N.W.2d 636 (1975). What effect should the Michigan Supreme Court decision have on South Dakota's appraisal of its guest passenger statute?

4. In *Weissman*, the court stated that when a Uniform Act is passed, great weight should be given to the harmonious decisions of courts of other states. If the court disagrees with the conclusion of those courts, should it still follow them for the sake of uniformity?

5. For coverage of which Uniform Acts have been adopted by what states, see Uniform Laws Annotated.

6. For interesting discussions of the processes of uniform lawmaking, in the context of the Uniform Commercial Code, see, *e.g.*, Kathleen Patchel, *Interest Group Politics, Federalism, and the Uniform Laws Process: Some Lessons from the Uniform Commercial Code*, 78 MINN. L. REV. 83 (1993); Edward J. Janger, *Predicting When the*

Uniform Law Process Will Fail: Article 9, Capture, and the Race to the Bottom, 83 Iowa L. Rev. 569 (1998); Steven L. Schwarez, A *Fundamental Inquiry Into the Statutory Rulemaking Process of Private Legislatures*, 29 Ga. L. Rev. 909 (1995).

VAN HORN v. WILLIAM BLANCHARD CO.
88 N.J. 91, 438 A.2d 552 (1981)

Clifford, J.

After a bifurcated trial in this negligence action the jury returned a verdict finding plaintiff fifty percent negligent, one defendant thirty percent negligent and a second defendant twenty percent negligent. The trial court molded the verdict and entered judgment in favor of defendants, and thereafter denied plaintiff's motion under R. 4:49-2 to amend the judgment. The Appellate Division affirmed, one judge dissenting, concluding that despite the fact that plaintiff's negligence was not greater than the combined negligence of defendants, recovery was barred under the Comparative Negligence Act, N.J.S.A. 2A:15-5.1 to -5.3.

. . . .

On appeal plaintiff argued that "[i]n multiple defendant cases, in order to avoid harsh and unfair results, the negligence of an individual plaintiff must be compared to the combined negligence of the several tortfeasors." According to plaintiff he was entitled to a judgment on liability inasmuch as his negligence (fifty percent) was not greater than the aggregated negligence (fifty percent) of the two tort feasors.

. . . .

II

The Comparative Negligence Act, L. 1973, C. 146, was the Legislature's response to the harshness of the complete bar to recovery imposed by the rule of contributory negligence. . . . New Jersey has a "modified" comparative negligence system, as distinguished from a "pure" system under which "a plaintiff may recover even if his negligence is greater than the negligence of the adverse tortfeasor," with the recovery "diminished by his degree of contributory negligence." C. Heft & C. Heft, Comparative Negligence Manual § 1.50 (1978).

Section 1 of the Act reads as follows:

> Contributory negligence shall not bar recovery in an action by any person or his legal representative to recover damages for negligence resulting in death or injury to person or property, if such negligence was not greater than the negligence of *the person* against whom recovery is sought, but any damages sustained shall be diminished by the percentage sustained of negligence attributable to the person recovering. [N.J.S.A. 2A:15-5.1 (emphasis added).]

The Legislature's use of the singular "the person" rather than the plural form strongly suggests that the plaintiff's negligence should be compared to the negligence of only one person at a time.

. . . .

The Comparative Negligence Act was taken nearly verbatim from the Wisconsin comparative negligence statute. A legislative enactment patterned after a statute of another state is ordinarily adopted with the prior constructions placed on it by the highest court of the parent jurisdiction. *See* 2A C. Sands, Sutherland Statutory Construction § 52.02 (4th ed. 1973). . . . Hence it is significant that at the time New Jersey adopted the Wisconsin "modified" form of comparative negligence, the individual approach rather than the aggregate system was a fixture in Wisconsin law. *See Schwenn v. Loraine Hotel Co.*, 14 Wis. 2d 601, 111 N.W.2d 495, 499–500 (Wis. 1961). In cases decided after New Jersey had embraced comparative negligence Wisconsin continued to adhere to the principle that the comparison of negligence in multiple defendant cases must be between the plaintiff and each defendant individually. . . . Whereas it is true that Wisconsin flirted with the notion of embracing the aggregate approach, see dictum in *May v. Skelley Oil Co.*, 83 Wis. 2d 30, 264 N.W.2d 574 (1978), the departure was but a momentary aberration, as disclosed by *Reiter v. Dyken*, 95 Wis. 2d 461, 290 N.W.2d 510 (1980).

. . . .

IV

There are public policy considerations supporting both sides of the issue confronting the Court today. We would have difficulty deciding this case on the basis of notions of fairness or the "workability" of the two approaches. However, the unmistakable preference of the Legislature for the individual approach . . . persuades us that any change of our law in this area should come from the legislative rather than the judicial process.[3]

Affirmed.

HANDLER, J., dissenting.

. . . .

The second reason for the Court's conclusion that the New Jersey comparative negligence scheme embraces the individual approach is its belief that determinative weight must be given to the construction placed on the comparative negligence statute of Wisconsin by the courts of that state. It is true that New Jersey's Comparative Negligence Act mirrors Wisconsin's. The majority opinion assumes that in adopting a comparative negligence statute similar to Wisconsin's, our Legislature intended to embrace that state's judicial interpretation of its statute as well.

As a general rule, courts give a legislative enactment patterned after the statute of another state the same construction placed upon it by the highest court of that jurisdiction. See 2A Sutherland, Statutes and Statutory Construction, § 52.02 (4th ed. 1973). New Jersey follows this approach. See *Suter v. San Angelo Foundry & Machine Co.*, 81 N.J. 150, 160 (1979). This rule, of course, is merely a tool for ascertaining the true intention of the Legislature. The judicial decisions of another state are not conclusive evidence of legislative intent. Thus, where the legislature of one state chooses to adopt as part of its laws the statute of another state, the judiciary of the adopting state may, if appropriate, choose to interpret its statute differently from the judicial interpretations of the source state. If there is some doubt that the adopting legislature fully intended to embrace the particular interpretations or applications by the courts of the source state, the courts of the adopting jurisdiction do not have to give greater weight to the originating state's judicial decisions than their intrinsic persuasiveness demands; and this is especially so where the public policies of the adopting state elicit different concerns and invoke priorities that are important or unique to that jurisdiction. . . . *See generally* Dickerson, The Interpretation and Application of Statutes 131–136 (1975).

The assumption that the New Jersey Legislature intended to embrace not only Wisconsin's statute but also its judicial interpretations of that statute is questionable. The majority seemingly takes the view that the New Jersey law does not merely follow but is actually cloned from the Wisconsin statute. While references to the Wisconsin statute are present in the legislative history, there is nothing in that history to indicate that the Legislature, in adopting this statute, considered the central issue presented by this case — whether to employ the aggregate or the individual approach.

---

[3] In fact Senate Bill 1507, introduced on January 9, 1979 and passed by both houses of the Legislature, provided for the aggregate approach. However, the bill was pocket-vetoed by Governor Byrne on February 15, 1980.

In addition, the sponsors' statement accompanying the bill introduced in the Assembly did not refer exclusively to the Wisconsin approach. Rather, it read, in pertinent part: "This State will not be unique if it adopts the law of comparative negligence. Other jurisdictions such as Wisconsin, Arkansas, Georgia, Maine, Florida, Iowa, Mississippi, Nebraska, South Dakota, Puerto Rico, the Canal Zone, the Canadian provinces, etc., have a form of comparative negligence." Assem. No. 665 (Introduced Feb. 7, 1972). Therefore, it seems clear that the sponsors of the bill considered not only the law of Wisconsin but also that of a variety of jurisdictions, some of which adhere to the aggregate approach.

One such state, specifically mentioned by the sponsors, is Arkansas. Though its comparative negligence statute was couched in terms of singular usage, that state adopted the aggregate approach through judicial construction as early as 1962 . . . .

In 1978, the Oklahoma Supreme Court held that the state's comparative negligence statute, then phrased in the singular, should be interpreted to apply an aggregate approach. The court reasoned that its statute was based on the statutory scheme of both Wisconsin and Arkansas and that Arkansas' "aggregate" approach was preferable. *Laubach v. Morgan*, 588 P.2d 1071, 1073 (Okla. 1978).

In opting to follow exactly or literally the Wisconsin judicial interpretation of the Comparative Negligence Act, this Court has abandoned any genuine interpretation of the Act and has walled off its analysis from any considerations of public policy. Yet no compelling argument is made why the decisions of the Wisconsin Supreme Court should be clamped around this State's comparative negligence law like an iron girdle, yielding no breathing room for our own tort law jurisprudence and public policy. In light of a legislative history that does not dictate such a course, our deliberations should be aired fully with reflections of our own public policy and legal traditions.

. . . .

NOTES AND QUESTIONS

1. How would you describe the quality the majority ascribes to the Wisconsin decisions?

2. Why would the majority cite Wisconsin cases decided *after* New Jersey's adoption of the comparative negligence statute? Are such decisions relevant?

3. Reread footnote 3 in the majority decision. Do you agree that the statute passed by the legislature has no relevance?

4. Consider the events that followed the *Van Horn* decision, reproduced next.

JOURNAL OF THE SENATE OF NEW JERSEY 434–35 (1982)

The Secretary read a communication from the Governor who has conditionally vetoed Senate No. 215.

STATE OF NEW JERSEY, EXECUTIVE DEPARTMENT,
September 16, 1982.

SENATE BILL NO. 215 (2nd OCR)

To *the Senate:*

Pursuant to Article V, Section I, Paragraph 14 of the Constitution, I herewith return Senate Bill No. 215 (2nd OCR) with my objections for reconsideration.

This bill provides that a plaintiff in a negligence action may recover damages in any case where his negligence is less than or equal to the combined negligence of multiple defendants, i.e. the aggregate approach to comparative negligence. It overturns the decision in *Van Horn v. William Blanchard Company*, 88 N.J. 91 (1981). In that case, the court, by a 4-3 split, interpreted New Jersey's comparative negligence act to permit the plaintiff to recover only from those defendants who were more negligent than himself, even if in the aggregate his negligence was less than the total percentage fault on the part of all the defendants, i.e., the individual approach.

I endorse this change in the comparative negligence law. I believe that the policy of allocating responsibility among all negligent parties in proportion to their relative fault is more fully achieved as to both plaintiff and defendants under the aggregate approach; and I do not believe that there will be any significant impact upon insurance rates from this change.

The bill as presently drafted, however, suffers from two flaws. . . .

Accordingly, I herewith return Senate Bill No. 215 (2nd OCR) for reconsideration and recommend that it be amended as follows:

. . . .

Respectfully,

/s/ THOMAS H. KEAN

NOTES AND QUESTIONS

1. The New Jersey Legislature accepted the governor's recommended changes and passed the bill. Ch. 191, 1 Acts of the State of New Jersey 786–87 (1982). What does this act say about the *Van Horn* court's view of legislative intent in the 1973 Comparative Negligence Act? Is the 1982 legislative intent indicative of 1973 legislative intent?

2. Consider the governor's role in the enactment of the 1982 legislation.

3. Review *Costa v. Josey* in Chapter 7, also dealing with a statute copied from another state.

UNIFORM STATUTE AND RULE CONSTRUCTION ACT (1995)*
§ 20 Other Aids to Construction

. . . .

(b) In addition to considering the text of a statute or rule in light of Sections 2 through 7, Section 18, the context in which the statute or rule is applied, and the aids to construction in subsection (a), the following aids to construction may be considered in ascertaining the meaning of the text:

    (1) a settled judicial construction in another jurisdiction as of the time a statute or rule is borrowed from the other jurisdiction;

    (2) a judicial construction of the same or similar statute or rule of this or another State;

. . . .

Chapter 9
JUDICIAL INTERPRETATION OF STATUTES AS A MATTER OF INSTITUTIONAL COMPETENCE

To a great extent, the whole matter of statutory interpretation raises questions of institutional competence and distribution of power among the legislature, the judiciary (state and federal), and sometimes the executive. That has been illustrated by the materials covered so far in this Part. This Chapter provides a focus on six areas that specifically implicate these concerns.

A. THE NATURE OF STATUTORY INTERPRETATION PRECEDENTS

UNION ELECTRIC CO. v. ILLINOIS COMMERCE COMMISSION
396 N.E.2d 510 (Ill. 1979)

Ryan, Justice.

These consolidated cases involve the validity of rates established for two public utilities by the Illinois Commerce Commission. The primary issue concerns the elements used by the Commerce Commission in establishing the rate base of each utility. The order of the Commission in each case rejected the "fair value" concept as the appropriate method of determining the rate base and instead computed the rate base by applying the "original cost" method . . . .

Section 30 of the Public Utilities Act (Ill. Rev. Stat. 1975, ch. 1112/3, par. 30) grants to the Commission the power "to ascertain the value of the property" of a public utility. Section 32 of the Act requires that all the rates received by the utility "shall be just and reasonable." Section 36 of the Act provides that the utility is entitled to a "reasonable return on the value of the property of said public utility as found by the Commission." This court, in a series of cases beginning almost 60 years ago, has consistently interpreted "value" in the statute to mean "fair value" and not "original cost."

. . . .

It is well established that the reenactment of a statute which has been judicially construed is in effect an adoption of that construction by the legislature unless a contrary intent appears . . . . In view of the history of the Act and the steadfast adherence by this court for almost 60 years to the present-value method, it is appropriate to paraphrase the language of Mr. Justice Blackmun in *Flood v. Kuhn* . . . . If there are evils in the present-value method which warrant its abandonment in favor of the original-cost method, the change should be by legislation . . . . We invite the legislature's consideration of these two competing methods of computing rate base.

Although it has been argued that mere inaction by the legislature following a judicial construction does not of itself indicate acquiescence (*see* R. Dickerson, The Interpretation and Application of Statutes 255 (1975)), the repeated restatement by this court of the statutory interpretation over an extended period of time strengthens the presumption of acquiescence in the face of inaction by the legislature. (*See, e.g.,* Schaefer, *Precedent and Policy*, 34 U. Chi. L. Rev. 3, 11 (1966).) When we also consider the reenactment of the Act and the several amendments to it without a suggestion of disagreement with this construction, inaction by the legislature strongly suggests agreement. Under these facts it would appear to be an usurpation of legislative power for this court now to abandon the fair-value method and apply the original-cost method. The construction this court has placed upon the Act has in effect become a part of the Act, and a change in that construction by this court would amount to amending the statute. The power to accomplish this does not lie in the courts. *See generally*, R.

Dickerson, The Interpretation and Application of Statutes 252–55 (1975); E. Levi, An Introduction to Legal Reasoning 27–57 (1949); 2A Sutherland, Statutes and Statutory Construction sec. 49.05 (4th ed. 1973); Agusti, *The Effect of Prior Judicial and Administrative Constructions on Codification of Pre-Existing Federal Statutes: The Case of the Federal Securities Code*, 15 HARV. J. LEGIS. 367 (1978); Horack, *Congressional Silence: A Tool of Judicial Supremacy*, 25 TEX. L. REV. 247 (1947); Rogers, *Judicial Reinterpretation of Statutes: The Example of Baseball and the Antitrust Laws*, 14 HOUSTON L. REV. 611 (1977).

As conclusive as we feel *stare decisis* is in the determination of this case, we do not view the rule as being absolute and without exception in all cases where statutes have been construed by the courts. The United States Supreme Court has delineated several areas where prior judicial statutory constructions should not be controlling . . . . Clearly, none of these exceptions are applicable in the cases now before us. We must therefore follow the substantial body of precedent which supports the fair-value method of computing the rate base.

NOTES AND QUESTIONS

1. Do you agree that a change in established statutory interpretation "would amount to amending the statute"?

2. Is there any reason why state courts must follow the United States Supreme Court approach to statutory *stare decisis?*

3. In many states, legislatures are not systematically informed of pertinent judicial interpretations of state statutes. *See* Shirley S. Abrahamson & Robert L. Hughes, *Shall We Dance? Steps for Legislators and Judges in Statutory Interpretation*, 75 MINN. L. REV. 1045 (1991). Judge (formerly Congressman) Abner Mikva has noted that "members of Congress do not even closely follow cases directly involving or interpreting statutes that they have sponsored or in which they have an interest . . . ." Abner J. Mikva, *Reading and Writing Statutes*, 48 U. PITT. L. REV. 627, 630 (1987).

Does this suggest that the presumption be abandoned in favor of some specific evidence, such as reports from the attorney general, revisors of statutes, legislative reference bureaus, or legislative counsel? A detailed state by state survey of state practices is presented by Abrahamson & Hughes, *supra*, at 1059–75.

4. What assumption is the *Union Electric Co.* rule based on? Is this a realistic assumption? Can this assumption be justifiably applied to a codification of existing law? In such a situation, is it reasonable to assume that the legislature studied the case law? How does one go about defining "substantially reenacted"?

5. Should any consideration be given to reenactment after a judicial interpretation? If the legislature is aware of the doctrine, is it reasonable to hold the legislators responsible for taking action to change the statute if they do not like the judicial decision? Are there other factors that may influence a legislator's decision of whether to respond to the judicial interpretation?

GIROUARD v. UNITED STATES
328 U.S. 61 (1946)

In 1943 petitioner, a native of Canada, filed his petition for naturalization in the District Court of Massachusetts. He stated in his application that he understood the principles of the government of the United States, believed in its form of government, and was willing to take the oath of allegiance . . . .

To the question in the application "If necessary, are you willing to take up arms in defense of this country?" he replied, "No (non-combatant) Seventh Day Adventist." He explained that answer before the examiner by saying "It is a purely religious matter with me, I have no political or personal reasons other than that." He did not claim before his Selective Service board exemption from all military service, but only from combatant military duty. At the hearing in the District Court petitioner testified that he was a member of the Seventh Day Adventist denomination, of whom approximately 10,000 were then serving in the armed forces of the United States as non-combatants, especially in the medical corps; and that he was willing to serve in the army but would not bear arms. The District Court admitted him to citizenship. The Circuit Court of Appeals reversed, one judge dissenting. 149 F.2d 760. It took that action on the authority of *United States v. Schwimmer*, 279 U.S. 644; *United States v. Macintosh*, 283 U.S. 605, and *United States v. Bland*, 283 U.S. 636, saying that the facts of the present case brought it squarely within the principle of those cases. The case is here on a petition for a writ of certiorari which we granted so that those authorities might be re-examined.

. . . .

We conclude that the *Schwimmer, Macintosh* and *Bland* cases do not state the correct rule of law.

We are met, however, with the argument that, even though those cases were wrongly decided, Congress has adopted the rule which they announced. The argument runs as follows: Many efforts were made to amend the law so as to change the rule announced by those cases; but in every instance the bill died in committee. Moreover, when the Nationality Act of 1940 was passed, Congress reenacted the oath in its pre-existing form, though at the same time it made extensive changes in the requirements and procedure for naturalization. From this it is argued that Congress adopted and reenacted the rule of the *Schwimmer, Macintosh* and *Bland* cases. *Cf. Apex Hosiery Co. v. Leader*, 310 U.S. 469, 488–489.

We stated in *Helvering v. Hallock*, 309 U.S. 106, 119, that "It would require very persuasive circumstances enveloping Congressional silence to debar this Court from reexamining its own doctrines." It is at best treacherous to find in congressional silence alone the adoption of a controlling rule of law. We do not think under the circumstances of this legislative history that we can properly place on the shoulders of Congress the burden of the Court's own error. The history of the 1940 Act is at most equivocal. It contains no affirmative recognition of the rule of the *Schwimmer, Macintosh* and *Bland* cases. The silence of Congress and its inaction are as consistent with a desire to leave the problem fluid as they are with an adoption by silence of the rule of those cases . . . .

Reversed.

MR. CHIEF JUSTICE STONE, dissenting.

I think the judgment should be affirmed, for the reason that the court below, in applying the controlling provisions of the naturalization statutes, correctly applied them as earlier construed by this Court, whose construction Congress has adopted and confirmed.

. . . .

With three other Justices of the Court I dissented in the *Macintosh* and *Bland* cases, for reasons which the Court now adopts as ground for overruling them. Since this Court in three considered earlier opinions has rejected the construction of the statute for which the dissenting Justices contended, the question, which for me is decisive of the present case, is whether Congress has likewise rejected that construction by its subsequent legislative action, and has adopted and confirmed the Court's earlier construction of the statutes in question. A study of Congressional action taken with respect to proposals for amendment of the naturalization laws since the decision in the *Schwimmer* case, leads me to conclude that Congress has adopted and confirmed this court's earlier construction of the naturalization laws. For that reason alone I think that the judgment should be affirmed.

The construction of the naturalization statutes, adopted by this Court in the three cases mentioned, immediately became the target of an active, publicized legislative attack in Congress which persisted for a period of eleven years, until the adoption of the Nationality Act in 1940. Two days after the *Schwimmer* case was decided, a bill was introduced in the House, H.R. 3547, 71st Cong., 1st Sess., to give the Naturalization Act a construction contrary to that which had been given to it by this Court and which, if adopted, would have made the applicants rejected by this Court in the *Schwimmer, Macintosh* and *Bland* cases eligible for citizenship. This effort to establish by Congressional action that the construction which this Court had placed on the Naturalization Act was not one which Congress had adopted or intended, was renewed without success after the decision in the *Macintosh* and *Bland* cases, and was continued for a period of about ten years.

Thus, for six successive Congresses, over a period of more than a decade, there were continuously pending before Congress in one form or another proposals to overturn the rulings in the three Supreme Court Decisions in question. Congress declined to adopt these proposals after full hearings and after speeches on the floor advocating the change. 72 Cong. Rec. 6966–7; 75 Cong. Rec. 15354–7. In the meantime the decisions of this Court had been followed.

. . . .

Any doubts that such were the purpose and will of Congress would seem to have been dissipated by the reenactment by Congress in 1940 of Paragraphs "Third" and "Fourth" of § 4 of the Naturalization Act of 1906, and by the incorporation in the Act of 1940 of the very form of oath which had been administratively prescribed for the applicants in the *Schwimmer, Macintosh* and *Bland* cases.

. . . .

The Nationality Act of 1940 was a comprehensive, slowly matured and carefully considered revision of the naturalization laws . . . . The modifications in the provisions of Paragraphs "Third" and "Fourth" of § 4 of the 1906 Act show conclusively the careful attention which was given to them.

In the face of this legislative history the "failure of Congress to alter the Act after it had been judicially construed, and the enactment by Congress of legislation which implicitly recognizes the judicial construction as effective, is persuasive of legislative recognition that the judicial construction is the correct one. This is the more so where, as here, the application of the statute . . . has brought forth sharply conflicting views both on the Court and in Congress, and where after the matter has been fully brought to the attention of the public and the Congress, the latter has not seen fit to change the statute." *Apex Hosiery Co. v. Leader*, 310 U.S. 469, 488–9 . . . . In any case it is not lightly to be implied that Congress has . . . delegated to this Court the responsibility of giving new content to language deliberately readopted after this Court has construed it. For us to make such an assumption is to discourage, if not to deny, legislative responsibility. By thus adopting and confirming this Court's construction of what Congress had enacted in the Naturalization Act of 1906 Congress gave that construction the same legal significance as though it had written the very words into the Act of 1940.

NOTES AND QUESTION

1. Is there more than one type of Congressional "silence" at work here? If so, what are they? Does the majority deem congressional silence irrelevant?

2. Why is *Apex Hosiery Co. v. Leader*, 310 U.S. 469, 488–89 (1940), which Chief Justice Stone quotes from in his dissent, not controlling in the *Girouard* context?

3. Remember the point made by Justice Brandeis in *Erie Railroad v. Tompkins*, 304 U.S. 64, 77 (1938): "If only a question of statutory construction were involved, we should not be prepared to abandon a doctrine so widely applied throughout nearly a century." What convinced the *Erie* Court to abandon the doctrine?

4. Professor Horack criticized *Girouard* in *Congressional Silence: A Tool of Judicial*

Supremacy, 25 Tex. L. Rev. 247 (1947). Why would he contend that *Girouard* preserved *judicial* supremacy? *See also* Laurence H. Tribe, *Toward a Syntax of the Unsaid: Construing The Sounds of Congressional and Constitutional Silence,* 57 Ind. L.J. 515 (1982).

FRANK E. HORACK, JR.,
CONGRESSIONAL SILENCE: A TOOL OF JUDICIAL SUPREMACY,
25 Texas Law Review 247, 251–52, 254–55 (1947)*

. . . .

After the decision, whether the Court correctly or incorrectly interpreted the statute, the law consists of the statute *plus* the decision of the Court. Thus, at the time a second case comes before the Court, the law on the particular point is both clear and determinate. The only undetermined question is whether the facts of the second case bring it within the rule of the prior decision.

Even assuming that the prior interpretation was incorrect, if the Court now reverses the position it took in the first case it is affirmatively changing an established rule of law under which society has been operating. This is explicitly and unquestionably the exercise of a legislative function. The correctness or incorrectness of the prior rule is less important than the fact that the members of society have acted upon it.

The judicial change of a legislative rule occurs without any of the safeguards normally surrounding legislative action. The change is not made by elected representatives. It is not formulated into a written proposal upon which interested persons can express their opinion formally before the committees of Congress or informally by petition and through the press and on the air. There is no compliance with the bicameral principle of equal state representation in the upper house and popular representation in the lower. There is no opportunity for executive veto.

. . . .

For example, those who support the decision in the *Girouard* case argue in this fashion: after congressional enactment the Court in a given case must determine whether the statute is applicable and, if so, its meaning. In determining its meaning the Court must follow the intent of Congress. If, after the Court has determined the legislative intent, Congress takes no further action, there is no formal congressional expression of approval or disapproval of the first interpretation. Therefore, in a subsequent case there is no additional legislative intent which the court need consider binding. Consequently, so far as the principles of statutory construction are concerned, the Court is as free in the second case as it was in the first to determine congressional intent. Thus, it is entirely appropriate for the Court to change its interpretation and reverse the prior decision if it decides that that decision was erroneous.

This proposition is carried one step further in the *Girouard* case to include the situation where there has been re-enactment of the original statute without any change in the act directly affecting the question previously decided. It is argued that in this situation there is likewise no indication of legislative intent beyond that expressed in the first enactment and that therefore the re-enactment has no greater significance than the silence or inaction of Congress considered in the first example.

The proposition obscures a more significant postulate which may be stated thus: that in case of doubt the Court is accepting its own determination of policy in preference to any interpretation which may be drawn from subsequent congressional action.[24] The result is that an affirmative duty is placed on Congress to express itself in such positive

---

* Copyright 1947 by the Texas Law Review Association. Reprinted by permission.

[24] "Action" should include "inaction" for it has the same result. "Inaction" continues the rule of law as originally interpreted. The rule is enforced during the period of "legislative inaction" so that if enforcement is contrary to the legislative intent it should be anticipated that demands would arise for a change in the rule.

and compelling language subsequent to a judicial interpretation of the statute that the Court would be unable to escape the effect of its statement. In short, the *Girouard* case, extends judicial supremacy into the field of legislative policy except in those instances where Congress affirmatively and explicitly acts.

Those who find difficulty with the judicial method of the *Girouard* decision emphasize the fact that the Court's function is not to determine policy but to apply it and that as a consequence until Congress indicates *affirmatively* that it is not satisfied with the result achieved by prior judicial interpretation it must be presumed that the prior interpretation is consistent with the original intent of Congress or at least with the intent of subsequent congresses.

MONELL v. DEPARTMENT OF SOCIAL SERVICES OF NEW YORK
436 U.S. 658 (1978)

[This case is included in Chapter 7 for its consideration of legislative history. In addition, it overruled an established precedent. That discussion is included here.]

III

Although we have stated that *stare decisis* has more force in statutory analysis than in constitutional adjudication because, in the former situation, Congress can correct our mistakes through legislation, *see, e.g., Edelman v. Jordan*, 415 U.S. 651, 671, and n. 14, 39 L. Ed. 2d 662, 94 S. Ct. 1347 (1974), we have never applied stare decisis mechanically to prohibit overruling our earlier decisions determining the meaning of statutes. *See, e.g., Continental T.V., Inc. v. GTE Sylvania, Inc.*, 433 U.S. 36, 47–49, 53 L. Ed. 2d 568, 97 S. Ct. 2549 (1977); *Burnet v. Coronado Oil & Gas Co.*, 285 U.S. 393, 406 n. 1, 76 L. Ed. 815, 52 S. Ct. 443 (1932) (Brandeis, J., dissenting) (collecting cases). Nor is this a case where we should "place on the shoulders of Congress the burden of the Court's own error." *Girouard v. United States*, 328 U.S. 61, 70, 90 L. Ed. 1084, 66 S. Ct. 826 (1946).

First, *Monroe v. Pape, supra*, insofar as it completely immunizes municipalities from suit under § 1983, was a departure from prior practice. *See, e.g., Northwestern Fertilizing Co. v. Hyde Park, supra; City of Manchester v. Leiby*, 117 F.2d 661 (Cal. 1941); *Hannan v. City of Haverhill*, 120 F.2d 87 (Cal. 1941); *Douglas v. City of Jeannette*, 319 U.S. 157, 87 L. Ed. 1324, 63 S. Ct. 877 (1943); *Holmes v. City of Atlanta*, 350 U.S. 879, 100 L. Ed. 776, 76 S. Ct. 141 (1955), in each of which municipalities were defendants in § 1983 suits. Moreover, the constitutional defect that led to the rejection of the Sherman amendment would not have distinguished between municipalities and school boards, each of which is an instrumentality of state administration. *See supra*, at 673–82, 56 L. Ed. 2d 625–30. For this reason, our cases — decided both before and after *Monroe* . . . — holding school boards liable in § 1983 actions are inconsistent with *Monroe*, especially as *Monroe*'s immunizing principle was extended to suits for injunctive relief in *City of Kenosha v. Bruno*, 412 U.S. 507, 37 L. Ed. 2d 109, 93 S. Ct. 2222 (1973) . . . . Thus, while we have reaffirmed *Monroe* without further examination on three occasions, it can scarcely be said that *Monroe* is so consistent with the warp and woof of civil rights law as to be beyond question.

. . . Far from showing that Congress has relied on *Monroe*, . . . events since 1961 show that Congress has refused to extend the benefits of *Monroe* to school boards and has attempted to allow awards of attorneys' fees against local governments even though *Monroe, City of Kenosha v. Bruno, supra*, and *Aldinger v. Howard*, 427 U.S. 1, 49 L. Ed. 2d 276, 96 S. Ct. 2413 (1976), have made the joinder of such governments impossible.

Finally, even under the most stringent test for the propriety of overruling a statutory decision proposed by Mr. Justice Harlan in *Monroe* — "that it must appear beyond doubt from the legislative history of the 1871 statute that [*Monroe*] misapprehended the meaning of the [section]," 365 U.S., at 192, 5 L. Ed. 2d 492, 81 S. Ct. 473 (concurring opinion) — the overruling of *Monroe* insofar as it holds that local governments are not "persons" who may be defendants in § 1983 suits is clearly proper. It is simply beyond doubt that, under the 1871 Congress' view of the law, were § 1983 liability unconstitutional as to local governments, it would have been equally unconstitutional as to state officers. Yet everyone — proponents and opponents alike — knew § 1983 would be applied to state officers and nonetheless stated that § 1983 was constitutional . . . . And, moreover, there can be no doubt that § 1 of the Civil Rights Act was intended to provide a remedy, to be broadly construed, against all forms of official violation of federally protected rights. Therefore, absent a clear statement in the legislative history supporting the conclusion that § 1 was not to apply to the official acts of a municipal corporation — which simply is not present — there is no justification for excluding municipalities from the "persons" covered by § 1.

For the reasons stated above, therefore, we hold that stare decisis does not bar our overruling of *Monroe* insofar as it is inconsistent with Parts I and II of this opinion.

. . . .

Mr. Justice Rehnquist, with whom The Chief Justice joins, dissenting.

Seventeen years ago, in *Monroe v. Pape*, 365 U.S. 167, 5 L. Ed. 2d 492, 81 S. Ct. 473 (1961), this Court held that the 42d Congress did not intend to subject a municipal corporation to liability as a "person" within the meaning of 42 U.S.C. § 1983. Since then the Congress has remained silent, but this Court has reaffirmed that holding on at least three separate occasions. *Aldinger v. Howard*, 427 U.S. 1, 49 L. Ed. 2d 276, 96 S. Ct. 2413 (1976); *City of Kenosha v. Bruno*, 412 U.S. 507, 37 L. Ed. 2d 109, 93 S. Ct. 2222 (1973); *Moor v. County of Alameda*, 411 U.S. 693, 36 L. Ed. 2d 596, 93 S. Ct. 1785 (1973). *See also Mt. Healthy City School Dist. v. Doyle*, 429 U.S. 274, 277–79, 50 L. Ed. 2d 471, 97 S. Ct. 568 (1977). Today, the Court abandons this long and consistent line of precedents, offering in justification only an elaborate canvass of the same legislative history which was before the Court in 1961. Because I cannot agree that this Court is "free to disregard these precedents," which have been "considered maturely and recently" by this Court, *Runyon v. McCrary*, 427 U.S. 160, 186, 49 L. Ed. 2d 415, 96 S. Ct. 2586 (1976) (Powell, J., concurring), I am compelled to dissent.

I

As this Court has repeatedly recognized, *Runyon, supra,* at 175 n. 12; *Edelman v. Jordan*, 415 U.S. 651, 671 n. 14 (1974), considerations of stare decisis are at their strongest when this Court confronts its previous constructions of legislation. In all cases, private parties shape their conduct according to this Court's settled construction of the law, but the Congress is at liberty to correct our mistakes of statutory construction, unlike our constitutional interpretations, whenever it sees fit. The controlling principles were best stated by Mr. Justice Brandeis:

Stare decisis is usually the wise policy, because in most matters it is more important that the applicable rule of law be settled than that it be settled right . . . . This is commonly true even where the error is a matter of serious concern, provided correction can be had by legislation. But in cases involving the federal Constitution, where correction through legislative action is practically impossible, this Court has often overruled its earlier decisions.

Burnet v. Coronado Oil & Gas Co., 285 U.S. 393, 406–07, 76 L. Ed. 815, 52 S. Ct. 443 (1932) (dissenting opinion) (footnotes omitted). Only the most compelling circumstances can justify this Court's abandonment of such firmly established statutory precedents. The best exposition of the proper burden of persuasion was delivered by Mr. Justice Harlan in *Monroe* itself:

From my point of view, the policy of *stare decisis*, as it should be applied in matters of statutory construction, and, to a lesser extent, the indications of congressional acceptance of this Court's earlier interpretation, require that it appear *beyond doubt* from the legislative history of the 1871 statute that [*Classic v. United States*, 313 U.S. 299 (1941)] and [*Screws v. United States*, 325 U.S. 91 (1945)] misapprehended the meaning of the controlling provision, before a departure from what was decided in those cases would be justified.

Monroe, supra, at 192 . . . (concurring opinion) (footnote omitted; emphasis added).

. . . .

Thus, our only task is to discern the intent of the 42d Congress. That intent was first expounded in *Monroe*, and it has been followed consistently ever since. This is not some esoteric branch of the law in which congressional silence might reasonably be equated with congressional indifference. Indeed, this very year, the Senate has been holding hearings on a bill, S. 35, 95th Cong., 1st Sess. (1977), which would remove the municipal immunity recognized by *Monroe*. 124 Cong. Rec. D117 (daily ed. Feb. 8, 1978). In these circumstances, it cannot be disputed that established principles of *stare decisis* require this Court to pay the highest degree of deference to its prior holdings. *Monroe* may not be overruled unless it has been demonstrated "beyond doubt from the legislative history of the 1871 statute that [*Monroe*] misapprehended the meaning of the controlling provision." *Monroe, supra*, at 192 . . . (Harlan, J., concurring). The Court must show not only that Congress, in rejecting the Sherman Amendment, concluded that municipal liability was not unconstitutional, but also that, in enacting § 1, it intended to impose that liability. I am satisfied that no such showing has been made.

. . . .

The Court is probably correct that the rejection of the Sherman Amendment does not lead ineluctably to the conclusion that Congress intended municipalities to be immune from liability under all circumstances . . . .

Whatever the merits of the constitutional arguments raised against it, the fact remains that Congress rejected the concept of municipal tort liability on the only occasion in which the question was explicitly presented. Admittedly this fact is not conclusive as to whether Congress intended § 1 to embrace a municipal corporation within the meaning of "person," and thus the reasoning of *Monroe* on this point is subject to challenge. The meaning of § 1 of the Act of 1871 has been subjected in this case to a more searching and careful analysis than it was in *Monroe*, and it may well be that on the basis of this closer analysis of the legislative debates a conclusion contrary to the *Monroe* holding could have been reached when that case was decided 17 years ago. But the rejection of the Sherman Amendment remains instructive in that here alone did the legislative debates squarely focus on the liability of municipal corporations, and that liability was rejected. Any inference which might be drawn from the Dictionary Act or from general expressions of benevolence in the debate on § 1 that the word "person" was intended to include municipal corporations falls far short of showing "beyond doubt" that this Court in *Monroe* "misapprehended the meaning of the controlling provision." Errors such as the Court may have fallen into in *Monroe* do not end the inquiry as to *stare decisis;* they merely begin it. I would adhere to the holding of *Monroe* as to the liability of a municipal corporation § 1983.

. . . .

PATTERSON v. McLEAN CREDIT UNION
485 U.S. 617 (1988)

Per Curiam.

This case is restored to the calendar for reargument. The parties are requested to brief and argue the following question:

"Whether or not the interpretation of 42 U.S.C. § 1981 adopted by this Court in

Runyon v. McCrary, 427 U.S. 160 (1976), should be reconsidered?"

One might think from the dissents of our colleagues from the above order that our decision to hear argument as to whether the decision in *Runyon v. McCrary* . . . should be reconsidered is a "first" in the history of the Court. One would also think from the language of the dissents that we have decided today to overrule *Runyon v. McCrary.*

. . . .

In addition, we have explicitly overruled statutory precedents in a host of cases . . . . These actions do not mean that the Court has been insensitive to considerations of *stare decisis*, but only that we recognize it as " 'a principle of policy and not a mechanical formula,' " *Boys Markets, supra*, at 241, (quoting *Helvering v. Hallock*, 309 U.S. 106, 119 (1940) (Frankfurter, J.)) . . . .

Justice Blackmun, with whom Justice Brennan, Justice Marshall, and Justice Stevens join, dissenting.

. . . .

Twelve years ago, consistently with our prior decisions . . . we observed that it is "well established" that 42 U.S.C. § 1981 "prohibits racial discrimination in the making and enforcement of private contracts." *Runyon v. McCrary*, 427 U.S. 168. We reaffirmed our reading of the legislative history and language of the statute as reaching private acts of racial discrimination, and emphasized that in the years since *Jones*, Congress specifically had considered and rejected legislation to override our interpretation of the Civil Rights Act of 1886 . . . . Writing for the Court, Justice Stewart noted:

> There could hardly be a clearer indication of congressional agreement with the view that § 1981 *does* reach private acts of racial discrimination . . . . In those circumstances there is no basis for deviating from the well-settled principles of *stare decisis* applicable to this Court's construction of federal statutes.

Id., at 174–175 . . . . (emphasis in original).

. . . .

. . . The parties in this case have not informed us of anything that suggests Congress has reconsidered its position on this statutory matter in light of *Runyon* and subsequent cases. I see no reason whatsoever for the Court deliberately to reach out in the manner it does today.

NOTES AND QUESTIONS

1. Why should the doctrine of *stare decisis* be viewed differently in statutory, as opposed to constitutional or common-law, cases? *See generally* Earl M. Maltz, *The Nature of Precedent*, 66 N.C. L. Rev. 367 (1988); F. Reed Dickerson, The Interpretation and Application of Statutes 252–55 (1975).

2. What if a court interprets a statute in a certain way and, after a period of years, reverses that interpretation, and the legislature "acquiesces" in both, contradictory, judicial interpretations?

PATTERSON v. McLEAN CREDIT UNION
491 U.S. 164 (1989)

Justice Kennedy delivered the opinion of the Court.

. . . .

. . . We conclude after reargument that *Runyon* should not be overruled, and we now reaffirm that § 1981 prohibits racial discrimination in the making and enforcement of private contracts . . . . We have said also that the burden borne by the party advocating the abandonment of an established precedent is greater where the Court is asked to overrule a point of statutory construction. Considerations of *stare decisis* have special force in the area of statutory interpretation, for here, unlike in the context of constitutional interpretation, the legislative power is implicated, and Congress remains free to alter what we have done.

. . . .

We conclude, upon direct consideration of the issue, that no special justification has been shown for overruling *Runyon*. In cases where statutory precedents have been overruled, the primary reason for the Court's shift in position has been the intervening development of the law, through either the growth of judicial doctrine or further action taken by Congress. Where such changes have removed or weakened the conceptual underpinnings from the prior decision, *see, e.g., Rodriguez de Quijas v. Shearson/American Express, Inc.*, 490 U.S. 477 (1989); *Andrews v. Louisville & Nashville R. Co.*, 406 U.S. 320, 322–323 (1972), or where the later law has rendered the decision irreconcilable with competing legal doctrines or policies, *see, e.g., Braden v. 30th Judicial Circuit Ct. of Ky.*, 410 U.S. 484, 497–499 (1973); *Construction Laborers v. Curry*, 371 U.S. 542, 552 (1963), the Court has not hesitated to overrule an earlier decision. Our decision in *Runyon* has not been undermined by subsequent changes or development in the law.

Another traditional justification for overruling a prior case is that a precedent may be a positive detriment to coherence and consistency in the law, either because of inherent confusion created by an unworkable decision, *see, e.g., Continental T.V., Inc. v. GTE Sylvania, Inc.*, 433 U.S. 36, 47–48 (1977); *Swift & Co. v. Wickham*, 382 U.S. 111, 124–125 (1965), or because the decision poses a direct obstacle to the realization of important objectives embodied in other laws, *see, e.g., Rodrigues de Quijas, supra*, at ___; *Boys Markets, Inc. v. Retail Clerks, supra*, at 240–41. In this regard, we do not find *Runyon* to be unworkable or confusing.

. . . .

Finally, it has sometimes been said that a precedent becomes more vulnerable as it became outdated and after being " 'tested by experience, has been found to be inconsistent with the sense of justice or with the social welfare.' " *Runyon*, 427 U.S., at 191 (Stevens, J., concurring), *quoting* B. Cardozo, The Nature of the Judicial Process 149 (1921). Whatever the effect of this consideration may be in statutory cases, it offers no support for overruling *Runyon*. In recent decades, state and federal legislation has been enacted to prohibit private racial discrimination in many aspects of our society. Whether *Runyon*'s interpretation of § 1981 as prohibiting racial discrimination in the making and enforcement of private contracts is right or wrong as an original matter, it is certain that it is not inconsistent with the prevailing sense of justice in this country. To the contrary, *Runyon* is entirely consistent with our society's deep commitment to the eradication of discrimination based on a person's race or the color of his or her

. . . .

We decline to overrule *Runyon* and acknowledge that its holding remains the governing law in this area.

III

Our conclusion that we should adhere to our decision in *Runyon* that § 1981 applies to private conduct is not enough to decide this case. We must decide also whether the conduct of which petitioner complains falls within one of the enumerated rights protected by § 1981. [The Court went on to conclude that the conduct complained of did not come within the language of § 1981. — Eds.]

. . . .

[The Court went on to rule on the merits that, although it would not overrule *Runyon*, Section 1981 only applied to discrimination in the "making and enforcement" of contracts and not to the discriminatory *termination* of contracts]

NOTES AND QUESTIONS

1. Could the Court's decision in *Patterson* on the *stare decisis* issue be seen as an example of "*judicial* supremacy"?

2. For extensive discussions of statutory precedents and *stare decisis*, see William N. Eskridge, *Overruling Statutory Precedent*, 76 GEO. L.J. 1361 (1988), and William N. Eskridge, *Interpreting Legislative Inaction*, 87 MICH. L. REV. 67 (1988). Each article contains an extensive appendix listing cases in which the Supreme Court has overruled a statutory precedent.

3. Professor Larry Marshall defended the rule of absolute *stare decisis* in statutory interpretation cases in Larry Marshall, *"Let Congress Do It": The Case for an Absolute Rule of Statutory Stare Decisis*, 88 MICH. L. REV. 177 (1989) and Larry Marshall, *Contempt of Congress: A Reply to the Critics of an Absolute Rule of Statutory Stare Decisis*, 88 MICH. L. REV. 2467 (1990). Professor William Eskridge had been one of the critics, writing a fictional opinion considering whether to overrule the *Caminetti* case in William N. Eskridge, *The Case of the Amorous Defendant: Criticizing Absolute Stare Decisis for Statutory Cases*, 88 MICH. L. REV. 2450 (1990).

4. Should the majority's decision not to overrule *Runyon* in the *Patterson* case be seen as adherence to "neutral principles"? *See* Earl M. Maltz, *Critical Theory, Neutral Principles, and The Future of Legal Scholarship*, 43 U. FLA. L. REV. 445, 454–60 (1991).

5. The holding in *Patterson* was overruled by Congress in the 1991 Civil Rights Act. The question of whether that statutory amendment was retroactive was decided in the negative in *Rivers v. Roadway Express, Inc.*, appearing in Section [D] of this Chapter.

WILLIAM N. ESKRIDGE, JR., OVERRULING STATUTORY PRECEDENTS,
76 GEORGETOWN LAW JOURNAL 1361 (1988)[*]

In a few cases, though, the acquiescence argument has a more plausible appeal, because a case can be made that the legislature's acquiescence bespeaks deliberation about and approval of the interpretation. For example, *Flood v. Kuhn* acknowledged the "illogic" of continuing to exempt professional baseball from the antitrust laws but justified adherence to stare decisis in large part on grounds of implicit legislative approval. The Court noted that after *Toolson* (the 1953 decision upholding the baseball exemption) more than fifty bills were introduced in Congress in connection with the Court's decisions.[210] While some of the bills sought to strip baseball of its exemption, most sought to expand the exemption to other professional sports . . . .

Although *Flood v. Kuhn* is an unusually strong case for the acquiescence argument, its analysis is problematic from at least three different perspectives, each of which suggests that little meaning can usually be derived from Congress' inaction. The first perspective is proceduralist. Legal process theory poses the question: "If a legislature has discretion whether to legislate or not to legislate, how can significance rationally be attached to its decision not to do so?"[213]

Congress' failure to modify the illogical exclusion of baseball, and only baseball, from the antitrust laws might be the result of any combination of reasons:

(1)   positive legislator approval of the Court's decisions;

---

[*] Reprinted with permission of the publisher, © 1988. The Georgetown Law Journal Association and Georgetown University.

[210] *Flood*, 407 U.S. at 281–82.

[213] H. Hart & A. Sacks, The Legal Process: Basic Problems in the Making and Application of Law 1395 (tent. ed. 1958).

(2) legislator apathy concerning the application of antitrust rules to professional sports;

(3) legislator disapproval of the Court's decisions, but disagreement among legislators as to what should be done (e.g., overrule the baseball exemption or expand it to other sports);

(4) legislator disapproval of the Court's decisions, but procedural roadblocks to proposed legislation (e.g., committee or subcommittee opposition, House Rules Committee opposition, Senate filibuster, threatened presidential veto);

(5) legislator disapproval of the Court's decisions, but other issues more important for the legislative agenda and no time to deal with the baseball exemption;

(6) legislator disapproval of the Court's decisions and no opposition to legislation, but legislation still forestalled due to compromises and logrolling.

As a matter of the legal process, "[i]t would require very persuasive circumstances enveloping Congressional silence to debar this Court from reexamining its own doctrines," argued Justice Frankfurter. Because of the many possible reasons for legislative inaction, "we walk on quicksand when we try to find in the absence of corrective legislation a controlling legal principle."[215]

   . . . .

This legal process argument, of course, suggests a response. Since most of the legislative activity sought to expand the exemption to other sports, it would be anomalous for the Court to move in the opposite direction by overruling *Federal Baseball* and *Toolson*. This is a good argument, and probably persuaded a majority of the Court, but it is subject to a powerful counter-argument. That is, "public choice theory," the application of economic insights to political behavior, suggests that the pattern of legislative proposals following *Toolson* is a predictable response of the political process but illustrates the chief systemic problem of the political process — its tendency to pander to small, well-organized groups. In a nutshell, public choice theory predicts that groups will tend to organize politically more often when they are small and well-defined, and when they are seeking concentrated benefits (such as subsidies) or opposing concentrated costs (such as special taxes or user fees). Groups will not organize as often to seek or oppose legislation that distributes benefits to the general population or is paid for generally. Much of the legislative agenda is dictated by the formation and activity of interest groups.

Baseball club owners are a small, well-organized group intensely interested in preserving their exemption from antitrust law and can be expected to lobby hard against any proposal to overturn *Flood v. Kuhn*. Those primarily hurt by the sport's exemption are the millions of spectators who buy tickets (and, arguably, pay higher prices because of the owners' cooperative behavior). We are largely ignorant of any injury we have suffered and are, in any event, unlikely to organize politically because whatever harm we have suffered individually is quite small. Baseball players were harmed by the reserve clause throughout the 1960s, but like consumers they were not politically well organized until 1966. On the other hand, the owners in other professional sports, such as football, are also likely to be politically well-organized and might be expected to press for legislation expanding the antitrust exemption to other professional sports, as indeed they did. That Congress, even under continuous special interest pressure, refused to expand baseball's exemption to other sports is persuasive evidence that the deliberative procedures of Congress were "working," and rebuffed the demands of the special interest groups. In my view, this history on the whole supports cancellation of the exemption by the Court that blunderingly created it . . . . Our political organs are much more reluctant to take away entitlement than to grant

---

[215] *Helvering v. Hallock*, 309 U.S. 106, 119–21 (1940) . . . .

new ones, a tendency greatly exacerbated by the "dilemma of the ungrateful electorate." According to this theory, the things an elected representative does for interest groups will be remembered and felt much less strongly than the things she does to penalize those groups. Yet most legislators are regularly reelected. Legislators accomplish this trick by refusing to make political choices harming important interest groups. Legislators will do almost anything to avoid making hard political choices, and Congress' decade of grappling with the immunity issue illustrates the operation of this avoidance. When hard political choices must be made, legislators prefer to draft general statutes and leave the specific decisions to someone else, mainly judges and administrators. Most legislators would have been perfectly happy for the Court to have overruled *Federal Baseball* (preferably prospectively). Baseball owners would have objected, but legislators could have deferred to the Court (a perfect avoidance strategy) and perhaps even legislated some relief concerning the reserve clause. Hence, the Court in *Toolson* and *Flood v. Kuhn* was doing Congress no favor when it dumped the baseball exemption back into the legislative lap.

A third perspective, political decision making theory, supports my skepticism about the meaning of legislative inaction and suggests that the Court's adherence to ridiculously incoherent statutory precedents may in fact disrupt the legislative process. Political scientist John Kingdon posits that Congress is an "organized anarchy" whose deliberations are best characterized by the theory of "garbage can decision making." Congress is an organized anarchy because it enjoys fluid participation in decision making, works, haphazardly by trial and error, and does not operate according to fixed and rigid substantive preferences. In such an anarchy, there will not be linear and rational decision making, but the legislative agenda will be quite limited because the deliberative energy of its participants is limited. Salient concerns of national policy, proposals to deal with those concerns, and political opportunities to do something will coexist as separate streams in the "garbage can." Public policy will typically be made when the streams fortuitously come together: A concern is recognized as salient, a well-considered solution is available that fits in with current thinking about other arenas of policy, and the political climate is ripe for change (the change fits in with the agendas of important participants in the process, and constraints do not inhibit action).

Garbage can decision making gives us little confidence that the Supreme Court's shuttling a problem of statutory interpretation back to congress will result in any serious consideration of the issue. In many cases, the Court's decision will not make the issue salient enough to find a place on the legislative agenda, and even when the issue is salient (as the baseball immunity issue has been) nothing will be done unless there is a well-considered proposal that fits in with the drift of public thinking and the personal agendas of important participants. Moreover, the garbage can model suggests that the legislative agenda is not infinitely elastic. The insertion of one issue into the agenda crowds out other issues. Is it desirable for the Court to add to the clutter? The issue of baseball's exemption from the antitrust laws is a worst case for such an addition: The issue is at bottom trivial, yet it is so controversial that it is bound to command legislative attention, especially in light of the patent "illogic" of the exemption.

In conclusion, none of the traditional arguments for the super-strong presumption against overruling statutory precedents is persuasive in *Flood*, which is a strong case for the legislative acquiescence argument. Normal stare decisis concerns, chiefly baseball's reliance on the antitrust immunity, still made *Flood* a difficult case. The Court could have — and can still — overrule *Federal Baseball* prospectively, with a transition period if necessary.

III.

Applying the Evolutive Approach to Overruling Statutory Precedents

The super-strong presumption against overruling statutory precedents is rhetoric that the Supreme Court ought to discard. It has become riddled with exceptions and is only selectively followed, and it rests upon either a confused formalism or a naive view of the political process. In my view, statutory precedents are entitled only to normal stare decisis effect. Thus, the Supreme Court can overrule them if they are clearly wrong, produce bad policy consequences, and have not generated an undue amount of public and private reliance.

NOTES AND QUESTIONS

1. For a highly controversial disagreement over the role of *stare decisis* in statutory interpretation cases, see *Johnson v. Transportation Agency, Santa Clara Cty.*, 480 U.S. 616 (1987).

2. The *Johnson* decision is also discussed in William N. Eskridge, *Overruling Statutory Precedents*, 76 Geo. L.J. 1361 (1988). *See also* William N. Eskridge, *Interpreting Legislative Inaction*, 87 Mich. L. Rev. 67, 92–95, 104–08 (1988); William N. Eskridge, *The Case of the Amorous Defendant: Criticizing Absolute Stare Decisis for Statutory Cases*, 88 Mich. L. Rev. 2450 (1990).

WILLIAM N. ESKRIDGE, JR., OVERRIDING SUPREME COURT STATUTORY INTERPRETATION DECISIONS,
101 Yale Law Journal 331 (1991)*

As if to debunk the conventional wisdom, the 101st Congress busied itself with efforts to override numerous Supreme Court decisions construing federal statutes. Successful legislation overrode eight recent opinions interpreting federal statutes. Overturning an older decision, another law for the first time rejected a Supreme Court interpretation discriminating against bisexuals, gay men, and lesbians. Even abortive override efforts in the 101st Congress illustrated Congress' attention to the Court's statutory interpretation cases. Most prominent among the unsuccessful override efforts was the vetoed Civil Rights Act of 1990, which would have overturned nine recent decisions narrowly construing Title VII of the Civil Rights Act of 1964 and related statutes. A similar Civil Rights Act of 1991, however, was enacted into law by the 102d Congress.

Congress' attention to the Court's statutory decisions raises issues that are critically important to statutory interpretation scholarship. Specifically, Congress' recent override activity presents scholars with an opportunity to revisit longstanding academic debates about (1) congressional awareness of, and responsiveness to Supreme Court decisions in general; (2) political theories that realistically describe both the legislative process and the interaction between the Court and Congress; and (3) the ramifications of the first two debates for the theory and practice of statutory interpretation.

Three obstacles thus far have hindered academic debate on these topics. First, and most important, existing scholarship has not yielded much reliable data about when and how often Congress overrides the Court. Even the leading empirical studies by political scientists are, on the whole, disappointingly incomplete. Second, theoretical literature on the legislative process is divided into opposing viewpoints that fail to recognize alternative approaches. One side views the political process as dominated by rent-seeking interest groups, while the other sees politics as deliberation about the common

---

*   Reprinted by permission of The Yale Law Journal Company and Fred B. Rothman & Company.

good. Without a consensus, or even dialogue between the competing camps, political science scholarship is not as helpful to legal scholarship as it might be. Third, legal theories touching on the political process do not represent the most up-to-date political science data and theory. Hence, even if reliable empirical data and useful theoretical consensus existed, they would not necessarily inform legal discourse.

Based on more comprehensive empirical evidence documenting congressional responses to the Court's statutory interpretation decisions, this Article presents a revised view of the legislative process and the interaction between the Court, Congress, and the President. It further discusses the implications that this revised discourse has for the theory and practice of statutory interpretation. Part I and the appendices to this Article report the results of an empirical survey of congressional overrides of Supreme Court — as well as lower court — interpretations of federal statutes. It concludes that Congress and its committees are aware of the Court's statutory decisions, devote significant efforts toward analyzing their policy implications, and override those decisions with a frequency heretofore unreported. Congressional overrides are most likely when a Supreme Court interpretation reveals an ideologically fragmented Court, relies on the text's plain meaning and ignores legislative signals, and/or rejects positions taken by federal, state, or local governments.

The Article then uses the empirical data and case studies to develop a theoretical model that deepens our understanding of the interaction between the Court, Congress, and the President. Part II develops the model by drawing insights from competing distributive and deliberative theories of legislation. The model posits that a dynamic game exists between the Court, the relevant congressional committees, Congress, and the President. In this game, ultimate statutory policy is set through a sequential process by which each player — including the Court — tries to impose its policy preferences. The game is a dynamic one because each player is responsive to the preferences of other players *and* because the preferences of the players change as information is generated and distributed in the game.

Part III applies the data and the sequential game model to rethink legal issues of statutory interpretation. Descriptively, a central theme is that the Court's statutory interpretation decisions are more responsive to the expectations of the current Congress than to those of the enacting Congress. But the Court is also responsive to its own institutional and personal preferences — especially its preference for coherence and predictability in the law. This descriptive analysis provides new insights into several otherwise puzzling doctrines of statutory interpretation, including the Court's invocation of special *stare decisis* for statutory precedents, its willingness to find meaning in legislative inaction, and its reliance on subsequent legislative history.

Normatively, this Article analyzes the Court's traditional role as an important player contributing to the operation of the pluralist political process. The Court facilitates the operation of pluralism over time by updating statutes to reach new situations, to reflect new values, and to accommodate the current preferences of governing political forces. Current critics, however, believe that the Court should not pay attention to current legislative preferences in statutory interpretation and instead should attend only to statutory text or original intent. This Article argues that the Court's traditional practice survives this objection but is more vulnerable to another objection: that the Court's practice fails to give sufficient attention to interests and perspectives that are unrepresented in our pluralist political system.

NOTES AND QUESTIONS

1. Professor Eskridge's full article is recommended for its reconsideration of the notion that legislators do not pay attention to judicial interpretations of statutes. What are the implications of his findings?

2. For further consideration of this question, see Michael E. Solimine & James L.

Walker, *The Next Word: Congressional Response to Supreme Court Statutory Decisions*, 65 TEMPLE L. REV. 425 (1992).

B. DEFERENCE TO PRIOR ADMINISTRATIVE DETERMINATIONS

The question of institutional competence emerges with the growth and proliferation of the administrative state.

The following provisions of the Administrative Procedures Act (A.P.A.), 5 U.S.C. § 701, § 706, speak to the applicability and scope of judicial review of questions of law:

§ 701. Application; Definitions

(a) This chapter applies, according to the provisions thereof, except to the extent that —

(1) statutes preclude judicial review; or

(2) agency action is committed to agency discretion by law.

§ 706. Scope of Review

To the extent necessary to decision and when presented, the reviewing court shall decide all relevant questions of law, interpret constitutional and statutory provisions, and determine the meaning or applicability of the terms of an agency action. The reviewing court shall —

(1) compel agency action unlawfully withheld or unreasonably delayed; and

(2) hold unlawful and set aside agency action, findings, and conclusions found to be —

(A) arbitrary, capricious, an abuse of discretion, or otherwise not in accordance with law;

(B) contrary to constitutional right, power, privilege, or immunity;

(C) in excess of statutory jurisdiction, authority, or limitations or short of statutory rights.

Questions of law subject to judicial review arise in the context of specific provisions of the diverse assortment of statutes conferring decision-making authority on a heterogeneous set of agencies including the Federal Reserve, the armed services, and the Environmental Protection Agency.

Initial judicial responses to the issue of judicial review of an agency's legal interpretations were defensive, asserting the continued primacy of the judiciary in resolving interpretive questions. Thus, the Supreme Court stated that "the interpretation of the meaning of statutes . . . is exclusively a judicial function." *United States v. American Trucking Associations, Inc.*, 310 U.S. 534, 544 (1940). A more pragmatic approach took hold in subsequent cases.

The state of the law is well summarized in the following comment:

THOMAS W. MERRILL,
JUDICIAL DEFERENCE TO EXECUTIVE PRECEDENT,
101 YALE L.J. 969, 972–975 (1992)*

A. *Pre-*Chevron*: The Multiple Factors Regime*

Prior to 1984, the Supreme Court had no unifying theory for determining when to defer to agency interpretations of statutes. The approach was instead pragmatic and contextual. One feature of the Court's practice was that deference could range over a spectrum from "great" to "some" to "little" (although no attempt was ever made to calibrate different degrees of deference with any precision). A particularly common approach was to cite the views of those charged with administration of the statue as one of several reasons for adopting a particular construction. Thus, the Court might embrace a particular interpretation (1) because it was supported by the language of the text, (2) because it was consistent with the legislative history, and (3) because it was the longstanding construction of the administrative agency.[9] To be sure, there were also decisions at the polar extremes during this era — either ignoring the agency view or treating it as virtually dispositive.[10] But in practice, deference existed along a sliding scale, bridging these outer limits.

In addition, in deciding what degree of deference to give an executive interpretation, the Court relied on an eclectic cluster of considerations[11] Although there was no explicit rationale linking the various factors together, the overall approach had an implicit logic. The default rule was one of independent judicial judgment. Deference to the agency interpretation was appropriate only if a court could identify some factor or factors that would supply an affirmative justification for giving special weight to the agency views. Admittedly, the factors tended to be invoked unevenly. But in this respect, they probably functioned in a manner not too different from the way the canons of interpretation operate in statutory interpretation cases.[12] The pre-*Chevron* deference factors may be classified in various ways. For present purposes, I will group them into three categories: (1) factors addressed to Congress' interpretative intent (that is, whether Congress intended courts to defer to an agency's interpretation of a statutory provision); (2) factors addressed to the attributes of the particular agency decision at issue; and (3) factors thought to demonstrate congruence between the outcome reached by the agency and congressional intent regarding that specific issue.

---

*   Reprinted by permission of The Yale Law Journal Company and Fred B. Rothman & Company.

[9] For example of this approach, see *Bell v. New Jersey*, 461 U.S. 773 (1982); *Blum v. Bacon*, 457 U.S. 132 (1982); *United States v. Clark*, 454 U.S. 555 (1982); *Federal Election Comm'n v. Democratic Senatorial Campaign Comm'n*, 454 U.S. 27 (1981).

[10] *Compare Newport News Shipbuilding & Dry Dock Co. v. EEOC*, 462 U.S. 669 (1983) (Court discusses EEOC guidelines with no suggestion that they are entitled to deference), *with Heckler v. Campbell*, 461 U.S. 458, 466 (1983) (Court states that its review is limited to determining whether Secretary's regulations are arbitrary or capricious).

[11] For useful accounts of the multiple factors employed during this period, see Colin S. Diver, *Statutory Interpretation in the Administrative State*, 133 U. PA. L. REV. 549, 562 n.95 (1985); Ernest H. Schopler, Annotation, *Supreme Court's View as to Weight and Effect to be Given, on Subsequent Judicial Construction, to Prior Administrative Construction of Statute*, 39 L.R.A.2d 942 (1975); David R. Woodward & Ronald M. Levin, *In Defense of Deference: Jusicial Review of Agency Action*, 31 ADMIN. L. REV. 329, 332–4 (1979).

[12] The dominant view for many years, following Llewellyn, was that the canons are mutually contradictory, and hence are of little or not value in guiding judicial decisionmaking. *See* Karl N. Llewellyn, *Remarks on the Theory of Appellate Decision and the Rules or Canons About How Statutes Are to Be Construed*, 3 VAND. L. REV., 395, 401–06 (1950). More recently, a revisionist trend has set in, and commentators have begun to take a more sympathetic attitude toward the canons. *See* CASS R. SUNSTEIN, AFTER THE RIGHTS REVOLUTION: RECONCEIVING THE REGULATORY STATE 111-92 (1990); William N. Eskridge, Jr., *Public Values in Statutory Interpretation*, 137 U. PA. L. REV. 1007 (1989); Geoffrey P. Miller, *Pragmatics and the Maxims of Interpretation*, 1900 WIS. L. REV. 1179.

The first factor focused on Congress' probable interpretative intent. The important distinction was between "legislative rules" and "interpretative rules." Legislative rules were the product of a specific delegation of authority from Congress to an administrative agency to interpret a specific statutory term or fill in a statutory gap. Interpretative rules were executive interpretations not backed by this type of specific delegated authority. The Supreme Court on several occasions suggested that interpretation in the former category were entitled to great deference, but those falling within the latter category were entitled only to whatever persuasive effect they might have.[14]

A second group of factors focused not on the agency's authority, but rather on various attributes of its decision. One factor was whether the issue fell within an area of agency "expertise."[15] The idea was that courts are generalists, whereas agencies are specialists. Specialists usually have a better grasp of technical terms[16] or the practical consequences of a decision,[17] and thus their views should be given deference by generalists. Another important factor was the notion that "longstanding," "consistent," or "uniform" administrative interpretations (the terms were used more or less interchangeably) are entitled to special deference.[18] A third factor in this category was that interpretations supported by a reasonable analysis were entitled to deference. The most prominent statement to this effect is found in *Skidmore v. Swift & Co.*,[19] where the Court stated that the weight to be given to an agency interpretation will depend upon "the thoroughness evident in its consideration, the validity of its reasoning, its consistency with earlier and late pronouncements, and all those factors which give it power to persuade, if lacking power to control."[20] A final decision-related factor, encountered less often, was whether multiple agencies agreed or disagreed about the correct interpretation of the statute.[21]

A third set of factors was designed to measure the degree to which the specific outcome reached by an agency was likely to reflect the intent of Congress. One old idea was that an executive interpretation is entitled to extra weight "when it involves a contemporaneous construction of a statute by the men charged with the responsibility of setting its machinery in motion."[22] Contemporaneous interpretations were thought to be especially probative of congressional intent, either because the administrators had themselves participated in the drafting process[23] or because such an interpretation was

---

[14] *See, e.g., Heckler v. Campbell*, 461 U.S. at 466–68 & n.10 (deferring to rule promulgated under grant of general rulemaking power); *Herweg v. Ray*, 455 U.S. 265, 274-74 (1982) (deferring to interpretation with "legislative effect"); *Batterton v. Francis*, 432 U.S. 416, 424–26 & nn.8–9 (1977) (distinguishing delegated "legislative power" from nondelegated "interpretative power" and according great deference to agency interpretation using former).

[15] *See, e.g., Aluminum Co. of Am. v. Central Lincoln Peoples' Util. Dist.*, 467 U.S. 380, 390 (1984).

[16] *See, e.g., E.I. du pont de Nemours & Co. v. Train*, 430 U.S. 112, 134–35 & n.25 (1977).

[17] *See, e.g., NLRB v. Seven-Up Bottling Co.*, 344 U.S. 344, 348.

[18] *See United States v. Clark*, 454 U.S. 555, 565 (1982); *Haig v. Agee*, 453 U.S. 280, 291 (1981); *NLRB v. Bell Aerospace Co.*, 416 U.S. 267, 275 (1974); *Udall v. Tallman*, 380 U.S. 1, 16 (1965). *Compare Nashville Gas Co. v. Satty*, 434 U.S. 136, 142 n.4 (1977) (consistently maintained EEOC Guideline given significant weight by Court), *with General Elect. Co. v. Gilbert*, 429 U.S. 125, 142–43 (1976) (EEOC Guideline that conflicts with earlier agency weight.)

[19] 323 U.S. 134 (1944).

[20] *Id.* at 140; *see also Adamo Wrecking Co. v. United States*, 434 U.S. 275, 287 n.5 (1978) (quoting *Skidmore*, 323 U.S. at 140); *SEC v. Sloan*, 436 U.S. 103, 117–18 (1978); *Investment Co. Inst. v. Camp*, 401 U.S. 617, 626–27 (1971).

[21] *See North Haven Bd. of Educ. v. Bell*, 456 U.S. 512 (1982); *General Elec. Co. v. Gilbert*, 429 U.S. at 144–45.

[22] *Norwegian Nitrogen Co. v. United States*, 288 U.S. 294, 315 (1933).

[23] *See United States v. Moore*, 95 U.S. 760 (1878).

"itself evidence of assumptions — perhaps unspoken by either the administrators or Congress — brought to a regulatory problem by all involved in its solution."[24] In addition, there was the recurrent notion that executive interpretations are entitled to special deference if they have been ratified in some fashion by Congress. The notion of what would count as a ratification was never very precise. The paradigm situation was when Congress, after being informed of an agency's construction, reenacted a statute without any relevant modification.[25]

Standing alone, these factors did not comprise, either individually or collectively, what could be described as a coherent doctrine. No attempt was made to connect the various factors together or to explain their relevance in terms of a model of executive-judicial relationship. Indeed, my own attempt to organize them in functional categories may impose a greater sense of order than the cases themselves warrant. Moreover, there is little evidence that the factors had much predictive or constraining power. To take but one example, in *SEC v. Sloan*[26] the Securities and Exchange Commission argued that its interpretation not only was entitled to deference because the interpretation was longstanding and consistent but also because it had been ratified by Congress when its construction was cited with approval in a committee report at the time the statute was reenacted.[27] The Court rejected these arguments, noting that the interpretation was not supported by a careful analysis of the statutory language and that evidence of congressional ratification was not enough if "based only upon a few isolated statements in the thousands of pages of legislative documents."[28]

As *Sloan* suggests, application of the various factors in individual cases is manipulable. Still, it would be presumptuous to dismiss them as empty rhetoric. Some factors — such as the importance of longstanding and consistent or contemporaneous administrative constructions — have been invoked as reason for deferring to executive interpretations for over 150 years.[29] Given the durability of these factors, it is plausible to view them as reflecting deep-seated judicial intuitions about the kinds of considerations that ought to bear on the decision to defer. If they do not determine the outcome of cases with logical certainty, neither does any other "traditional tool" of statutory interpretation. At least the factors turned the attentions of courts and litigants — including administrators — toward relevant considerations that presumably shape the judicial response.

CHEVRON, U.S.A. INC. v. NATIONAL RESOURCES DEFENSE COUNCIL, INC.,
467 U.S. 837 (1984).

Justice Stevens delivered the opinion of the Court.

In the Clean Air Act Amendments of 1977, Pub. L. 95-95, 91 Stat. 685, Congress enacted certain requirements applicable to States that had not achieved the national air quality standards established by the Environmental Protection Agency (EPA) pursuant to earlier legislation. The amended Clean Air Act required these nonattainment States

---

[24] *SEC v. Sloan*, 436 U.S. at 126 (Brennan, J., concurring).

[25] *See, e.g., NLRB v. Hendricks County Rural Elec. Corp.*, 454 U.S. 170, 177 (1981); *NLRB v. Bell Aerospace Co.*, 416 U.S. 267, 275 (1974); *Red Lion Broadcasting Co. v. FCC*, 395 U.S. 367, 381 (1969).

[26] 436 U.S. 103 (1978).

[27] *Id.* at 117–20.

[28] *Id.* at 121.

[29] *See, e.g., Brown v. United States*, 113 U.S. 568, 570–71 (1884) (longstanding and contemporaneous construction); *United States v. Moore*, 95 U.S. 760, 763 (1878) (contemporaneous construction); *Edward's Lessee v. Darby*, 25 U.S. (12 Wheat.) 206, 210 (1827) (contemporaneous construction); *United States v. Powell*, 9 U.S. (5 Cranch) 368 (1809) (longstanding construction); *see also* Annotation, *Effect of Practice or Administrative Construction of a Statute on Subsequent Judicial Construction*, 73 L. Ed. 322 (1929) (citing hundreds of state and federal cases discussing deference to executive views).

to establish a permit program regulating new or modified major stationary source of air pollution. Generally, a permit may not be issued for a new or modified major stationary source unless several stringent conditions are met.[1] The EPA regulation promulgated to implement this permit requirement allows a State to adopt a plantwide definition of the term stationary source.[2] Under this definition, an existing plant that contains several pollution-emitting devices may install or modify one piece of equipment without meeting the permit conditions if the alternation will not increase the total emissions from the plant. The question presented by these cases is whether EPA's decision to allow States to treat all of the pollution-emitting devices within the same industrial grouping as though they were encased within a single bubble is based on a reasonable construction of the statutory term stationary source.

I

The EPA regulations containing the plantwide definition of the term stationary source were promulgated on October 14, 1981. 46 Fed. Reg. 50766 Respondents filed a timely petition for review in the United States Court of Appeals for the District of Columbia Circuit pursuant to 42 U.S.C. § 7607(b)(1). The Court of Appeals set aside the regulations . . . .

The Court observed that the relevant part of the amended Clean Air Act does not explicitly define what Congress envisioned as a stationary source, to which the permit program . . . should apply, and further stated that the precise issue was not squarely addressed in the legislative history. In light of its conclusion that the legislative history bearing on the question was at best contradictory, it reasoned that the purposes of the nonattainment program should guide our decision here.[5]

Since the purpose of the permit program — its raison d'etre, in the court's view — was to improve air quality, the court held that the bubble concept was inapplicable in these cases under its prior precedents. It therefore set aside the regulations embodying the bubble concept as contrary to law. We granted certiorari to review that judgment, . . . and we now reverse . . . .

The basic legal error of the Court of Appeals was to adopt a static judicial definition of the term stationary source when it had decided that Congress itself had not commanded that definition.

---

[1]　Section 172(b)(6), 42 U.S.C. § 7502(b)(6), provides:

　　"The plan provisions required by subsection (a) shall —

　　. . . .

　　"(6) require permits for the construction and operation of new or modified major stationary sources in accordance with section 173 (relating to permit requirements)." 81 Stat. 747.

[2]

　　"(i) Stationary source means any building, structure, facility, or installation which emits or may emit any air pollutant subject to regulation under the Act.

　　"(ii) Building, structure, facility, or installation means all of the pollutant emitting activities which belong to the same industrial grouping, are located on one or more contiguous or adjacent properties and are under the control of the same person (or persons under common control) except the activities of any vessel." 40 CFR §§ 51.18(j)(1)(I) and (ii) (1983).

[5]　The court remarked in this regard:

　　"We regret, of course, that Congress did not advert specifically to the bubble concept's application to various Clean Air Act programs, and note that a further clarifying statutory directive would facilitate the work of the agency and of the court in their endeavors to serve the legislators' will."

II

When a court reviews an agency's construction of the statute which it administers, it is confronted with two questions. First, always, is the question whether Congress has directly spoken to the precise question at issue. If the intent of Congress is clear, that is the end of the matter, for the court, as well as the agency, must give effect to the unambiguously expressed intent of Congress.[9] If, however, the court determines Congress has not directly addressed the precise question at issue, the court does not simply impose its own construction on the statute, as would be necessary in the absence of an administrative interpretation. Rather, if the statute is silent or ambiguous with respect to the specific issue, the question for the court is whether the agency's answer is based on a permissible construction of the statute.[11]

The power of an administrative agency to administer a congressionally created . . . program necessarily requires the formulation of policy and the making of rules to fill any gap left, implicitly or explicitly, by Congress. *Morton v. Ruiz*, 415 U.S. 199, 231 (1974). If Congress has explicitly left a gap for the agency to fill, there is an express delegation of authority to the agency to elucidate a specific provision of the statute by regulation. Such legislative regulations are given controlling weight unless they are arbitrary, capricious, or manifestly contrary to the statute. Sometimes the legislative delegation to an agency on a particular question is implicit rather than explicit. In such a case, a court may not substitute its own construction of a statutory provision for a reasonable interpretation made by the administrator of an agency.

We have long recognized that considerable weight should be accorded to an executive department's construction of a statutory scheme it is entrusted to administer, and the principle of deference to administrative interpretations has been consistently followed by this Court whenever decision as to the meaning or reach of a statute has involved reconciling conflicting policies, and a full understanding of the force of the statutory policy in the given situation has depended upon more than ordinary knowledge respecting the matters subjected to agency regulations.

If this choice represents a reasonable accommodation of conflicting policies that were committed to the agency's care by the statute, we should not disturb it unless it appears from the statute or its legislative history that the accommodation is not one that Congress would have sanctioned.

In light of these well-settled principles it is clear that the Court of Appeals misconceived the nature of its role in reviewing the regulations at issue. Once it determined, after its own examination of the legislation, that Congress did not actually have an intent regarding the applicability of the bubble concept to the permit program, the question before it was not whether in its view the concept is inappropriate in the general context of a program designed to improve air quality, but whether the Administrator's view that it is appropriate in the context of this particular program is a reasonable one . . . .

IV

The Clean Air Act Amendments of 1977 are a lengthy, detailed, technical, complex, and comprehensive response to a major social issue. A small portion of the statute — 91 Stat. 745–751 (Part D of Title I of the amended Act, 42 U.S.C. §§ 7501–7508) —

---

[9] The judiciary is the final authority on issues of statutory construction and must reject administrative constructions which are contrary to clear congressional intent . . . . If a court, employing traditional tools of statutory construction, ascertains that Congress had an intention on the precise question at issue, that intention is the law and must be given effect.

[11] The court need not conclude that the agency construction was the only one it permissibly could have adopted to uphold the construction, or even the reading the court would have reached if the question initially had arisen in a judicial proceeding.

expressly deals with nonattainment areas. The focal point of this controversy is one phrase in that portion of the Amendments.[22] . . .

The 1977 Amendments contain no specific reference to the bubble concept. Nor do they contain a specific definition of the term stationary source contained in § 111(a)(3), applicable by the terms of the Act to the NSPS program. Section 302(j), however, defines the term major stationary source as follows:

> "(j) Except as otherwise expressly provided, the terms major stationary source and major emitting facility mean any stationary facility or source of air pollution which directly emits, or has the potential to emit, one hundred tons per year or more of any air pollutant (including any major emitting facility or source of fugitive emissions of any such pollutant, as determined by rule by the Administrator)." 91 Stat. 770.

V

The legislative history of the portion of the 1977 Amendments dealing with nonattainment areas does not contain any specific comment on the bubble concept or the question whether a plantwide definition of a stationary source is permissible under the permit program. It does, however, plainly disclose that in the permit program Congress sought to accommodate the conflict between the economic interest in permitting capital improvements to continue and the environmental interest in improving air quality. Indeed, the House Committee Report identified the economic interest as one of the two main purposes of this section of the bill . . . .

VI

As previously noted, prior to the 1977 Amendments, the EPA had adhered to a plantwide definition of the term source under a NSPS program. After adoption of the 1977 Amendments, proposals for a plantwide definition were considered in at least three formal proceedings . . . .

In August 1980, however, the EPA adopted a regulation that, in essence, applied the basic reasoning of the Court of Appeals in these cases. The EPA took particular note of the two then-recent Court of Appeals decisions, which had created the bright-line rule that the bubble concept should be employed in a program designed to maintain air quality but not in one designed to enhance air quality. Relying heavily on those cases, EPA adopted a dual definition of source for nonattainment areas that required a permit whenever a change in either the entire plant, or one of its components, would result in a significant increase in emissions even if the increase was completely offset by reductions elsewhere in the plant. The EPA expressed the opinion that this interpretation was more consistent with congressional intent than the plantwide definition because it would bring in more sources or modifications for review, 45 Fed. Reg. 52697 (1980), but its primary legal analysis was predicated on the two Court of Appeals decisions.

In 1981 a new administration took office and initiated a Government-wide reexamination of regulatory burdens and complexities. 46 Fed. Reg. 16281. In the context of that review, the EPA reevaluated the various arguments that had been advanced in connection with the proper definition of the term source and concluded that the term should be given the same definition in both nonattainment areas and PSD areas.

In explaining its conclusion, the EPA first noted that the definitional issue was not squarely addressed in either the statute or its legislative history and therefore that the issue involved an agency judgment as how to best carry out the Act. *Ibid.* It then set

---

[22] Specifically, the controversy in these cases involves the meaning of the term major stationary sources in § 172(b)(6) of the Act, 42 U.S.C. § 7502(b)(6).

forth several reasons for concluding that the plantwide definition was more appropriate. It pointed out that the dual definition can act as a disincentive to new investment and modernization by discouraging modifications to existing facilities and can actually retard progress in air pollution control by discouraging replacement of older, dirtier processes or pieces of equipment with new, cleaner ones. Ibid. Moreover, the new definition would simplify EPA's rules by using the same definition of source for PSD, nonattainment new source review and the construction moratorium. This reduces confusion and inconsistency. *Ibid.* Finally, the agency explained that additional requirements that remained in place would accomplish the fundamental purposes of achieving attainment with NAAQS's as expeditiously as possible. These conclusions were expressed in a proposed rulemaking in August 1981 that was formally promulgated in October. *See id.*, at 50766.

VII

In this Court respondents expressly reject the basic rationale of the Court of Appeals' decision. That court viewed the statutory definition of the term source as sufficiently flexible to cover either a plantwide definition, a narrower definition covering each unit within a plant, or a dual definition that could apply to both the entire bubble and its components. It interpreted the policies of the statute, however, to mandate the plantwide definition in programs designed to maintain clean air and to forbid it in programs designed to improve air quality. Respondents place a fundamentally different construction on the statute. They contend that the text of the Act requires the EPA to use a dual definition — if either a component of a plant, or the plant as a whole, emits over 100 tons of pollutant, it is a major stationary source. They thus contend that the EPA rules adopted in 1980, insofar as they apply to the maintenance of the quality of clean air, as well as the 1981 rules which apply to nonattainment areas violate the statute.

Statutory Language

The definition in § 302(j) tells U.S. what the word major means — a source must emit at least 100 tons of pollution to qualify — but it sheds virtually no light on the meaning of the term stationary source. It does equate a source with a facility — a major emitting facility and a major stationary source are synonymous under § 302(j). The ordinary meaning of the term facility is some collection of integrated elements which has been designed and constructed to achieve some purpose. Moreover, it is certainly no affront to common English usage to take a reference to a major facility or a major source to connote an entire plant as opposed to its constituent parts. Basically, however, the language of § 302(j) simply does not compel any given interpretation of the term source.

Respondents recognize that, and hence point to § 111(a)(3). Although the definition in that section is not literally applicable to the permit program, it sheds as much light on the meaning of the word source as anything in the statute. As respondents point out, use of the words building, structure, facility, or installation, as the definition of source could be read to impose the permit conditions on an individual building that is a part of a plant. A word may have a character of its own not to be submerged by its association. On the other hand, the meaning of a word must be ascertained in the context of achieving particular objectives, and the words associated with it may indicate that the true meaning of the series is to convey a common idea. The language may reasonably be interpreted to impose the requirement on any discrete, but integrated, operation which pollutes. This gives meaning to all of the terms — a single building, not part of a larger operation, would be covered if it emits more than 100 tons of pollution, as would any facility, structure, or installation. Indeed, the language itself implies a bubble concept of sorts: each enumerated item would seem to be treated as if it were encased in a bubble. While respondents insist that each of these terms must be given a discrete meaning, they also argue that § 111(a)(3) defines source as that term is used in § 302(j). The latter section, however, equates a source with a facility, whereas the former defines source as a facility, among other items.

We are not persuaded that parsing of general terms in the text of the statute will reveal an actual intent of Congress. We know full well that this language is not dispositive; the terms are overlapping and the language is not precisely directed to the question of the applicability of a given term in the context of a larger operation. To the extent any congressional intent can be discerned from this language, it would appear that the listing of overlapping, illustrative terms was intended to enlarge, rather than to confine, the scope of the agency's power to regulate particular sources in order to effectuate the policies of the Act.

Legislative History

In addition, respondents argue that the legislative history and policies of the Act foreclose the plantwide definition and that the EPA's interpretation is not entitled to deference because it represents a sharp break with prior interpretations of the Act.

We find that the legislative history as a whole is silent on the precise issue before U.S. It is, however, consistent with the view that the EPA should have broad discretion in implementing the policies of the 1977 Amendments.

. . . .

Our review of the EPA's varying interpretations of the word source — both before and after the 1977 Amendments — convinces us that the agency primarily responsible for administering this important legislation has consistently interpreted it flexibly — not in a sterile textual vacuum, but in the context of implementing policy decisions in a technical and complex arena. The fact that the agency has from time to time changed its interpretation of the term source does not, as respondents argue, lead us to conclude that no deference should be accorded the agency's interpretation of the statute. An initial agency interpretation is not instantly carved in stone. On the contrary, the agency, to engage in informed rulemaking, must consider varying interpretations and the wisdom of its policy on a continuing basis. Moreover, the fact that the agency has adopted different definitions in different contexts adds force to the argument that the definition itself is flexible, particularly since Congress has never indicated any disapproval of a flexible reading of the statute.

Significantly, it was not the agency in 1980, but rather the Court of Appeals that read the statute inflexibly to command a plantwide definition for programs designed to maintain clean air and to forbid such a definition for programs designed to improve air quality. The distinction the court drew may well be a sensible one, but our labored review of the problem has surely disclosed that it is not a distinction that Congress ever articulated itself, or one that the EPA found in the statute before the courts began to review the legislative work product. We conclude that it was the Court of Appeals, rather than Congress or any of the decision makers who are authorized by Congress to administer this legislation, that was primarily responsible for the 1980 position taken by the agency.

Policy

The arguments over policy that are advanced in the parties' briefs create the impression that respondents are now waging in a judicial forum a specific policy battle which they ultimately lost in the agency and in the 32 jurisdictions opting for the bubble concept, but one which was never waged in the Congress. Such policy arguments are more properly addressed to legislators or administrators, not to judges.

In these cases, the Administrator's interpretation represents a reasonable accommodation of manifestly competing interests and is entitled to deference: the regulatory scheme is technical and complex, the agency considered the matter in a detailed and reasoned fashion, and the decision involves reconciling conflicting policies. Congress intended to accommodate both interests, but did not do so itself on the level of specificity presented by these cases. Perhaps that body consciously desired the Administrator to strike the balance at this level, thinking that those with great expertise and charged with responsibility for administering the provision would be in a better position to do so; perhaps it simply did not consider the question at this level; and perhaps Congress was unable to forge a coalition on either side of the question, and those on each side decided to take their chances with the scheme devised by the agency. For judicial purposes, it matters not which of these things occurred.

Judges are not experts in the field, and are not part of either political branch of the Government. Courts must, in some cases, reconcile competing political interests, but not on the basis of the judges' personal policy preferences. In contrast, an agency to which Congress has delegated policy-making responsibilities may, within the limits of that delegation, properly rely upon the incumbent administration's views of wise policy to inform its judgments. While agencies are not directly accountable to the people, the Chief Executive is, and it is entirely appropriate for this political branch of the Government to make such policy choices — resolving the competing interests which Congress itself either inadvertently did not resolve or intentionally left to be resolved by the agency charged with the administration of the statute in light of everyday realities.

When a challenge to an agency construction of a statutory provision, fairly conceptualized, really centers on the wisdom of the agency's policy, rather than whether it is a reasonable choice within a gap left open by Congress, the challenge must fail. In such a case, federal judges — who have no constituency — have a duty to respect legitimate policy choices made by those who do. The responsibilities for assessing the wisdom of such policy choices and resolving the struggle between competing views of the public interest are not judicial ones: Our Constitution vests such responsibilities in the political branches. *TVA v. Hill*, 437 U.S. 153, 195 (1978).

We hold that the EPA's definition of the term source is a permissible construction of the statute which seeks to accommodate progress in reducing air pollution with economic growth. The Regulations which the Administrator has adopted provide what the agency could allowably view as . . . [an] effective reconciliation of these twofold ends . . . . *United States v. Shimer*, 367 U.S. at 383.

The judgment of the Court of Appeals is reversed.

It is so ordered.

Reread *Immigration and Naturalization Service v. Cardoza-Fonseca, supra,* Chapter 7, Section [B][1], with the addition of the following excerpt from the decision:

IV

. . . .

The INS's second principal argument in support of the proposition that the "well-founded fear" and "clear probability" standard are equivalent is that the BIA so construes the two standards. The INS argues that the BIA's construction of the Refugee Act of 1980 is entitled to substantial deference, even if we conclude that the Court of Appeals' reading of the statutes is more in keeping with Congress' intent. This argument is unpersuasive.

The question whether Congress intended the two standards to be identical is a pure question of statutory construction for the courts to decide. Employing traditional tools of statutory construction, we have concluded that Congress did not intend the two standards to be identical. In *Chevron U.S.A. Inc. v. Natural Resources Defense Council, Inc.*, 467 U.S. 837 (1984), we explained:

"The judiciary is the final authority on issues of statutory construction and must reject administrative constructions which are contrary to clear congressional intent. [Citing cases] If a court, employing traditional tools of statutory construction, ascertains that Congress had an intention on the precise question at issue, that intention is the law and must be given effect." *Id.*, at 843, n.9 (citations omitted).

NOTES AND QUESTIONS

1. A recent survey indicates that *Chevron* has been cited in more than 7,000 cases and in more than 3,600 articles available on LEXIS. Thomas W. Merrill, *The Story of Chevron: The Making of an Accidental Landmark, in* PETER L. STRAUSS, ED., ADMINISTRATIVE LAW STORIES 399, 399–400 (2006). Justice Stevens, author of the opinion, insists that he regarded the decision "As simply a restatement of the existing law, nothing more or less." *Id.* at 420. Professor Merrill, however, thinks that the decision "contains three significant innovations relative to previous judicial discussion." *Id.* at 400.

> First, the Court laid down a new two-step framework for reviewing agency statutory interpretations . . . .
>
> Second, *Chevron* departed from previous law by suggesting that Congress has delegated authority to agencies to function as the primary interpreters of the statutes they administer . . . .
>
> Third, *Chevron* broke new ground by invoking democratic theory as a reason for deferring to agency interpretations of statutes they administer . . . .

Id. at 400–401.

2. In *Chevron*, the Court adopts a two step approach when reviewing an agency's construction of the statute which it administers. Step one is determining "whether Congress has directly spoken to the precise question at issue."

Recall Counselor Nunez's grid in Chapter 7[A]. How likely is it that the text of the statute itself will address the precise question at issue?

Mr. Nunez singles out the definition section, the preamble, or explicit recitals of policy as the hardest evidence of legislative intent. Should a definition section be dispositive? Reread *Train v. Colorado Public Interest Research Group*, 426 U.S. 1 (1976) in Chapter 7[B][1].

Justice Scalia had this to say about the search for legislative intent in the context of *Chevron*:

> In the vast majority of cases I expect that Congress *neither* (1) intended a single result, *nor* (2) meant to confer discretion upon the agency, but rather (3) didn't think about the matter at all. If I am correct in that, then any rule adopted in this field represents merely a fictional, presumed intent, and operates principally as a background rule of law against which Congress can legislate.

Antonin Scalia, *Judicial Deference to Administrative Interpretations of Law*, 1989 DUKE L.J. 511, 517.

3. In *Cardoza-Fonseca*, the Court made it clear that it would employ the "traditional tools of statutory construction" by elevating footnote nine in *Chevron* to the text. However, Professor Grad in Chapter 1A argues that "some of the older rules of statutory construction seem hardly relevant in their application [to programmatic legislation]."

a. Consider the following cases in which the Supreme Court applied the canons of statutory construction to programmatic legislation.

In *Washington State Department of Health and Social Services v. Guardianship Estate of Keffler*, 537 U.S. 371, 384–85, 389–90 (2003), a unanimous Court invoked *ejusdem generis* and *noscitur a sociis* to confine the meaning of "other legal process" while finding that the phrase "best interests of the beneficiary foster child" to be an open-ended and potentially vague term meriting *Chevron* deference.

In rejecting an agency's claim to *Chevron* deference, the Supreme Court invoked the *noscitur a sociis* canon and a statutory provision declaring Congress' purpose in enacting the statute. *Dole v. United Steel Workers of America*, 494 U.S. 26, 36–38 (1990).

In *Barnhart v. Thomas*, 540 U.S. 20, 26 (2003), the Court applied "the rule of the last antecedent" in overturning the Third Circuit's interpretation of the Social Security Act.

b. Consider the fate of arguments that evidence of alternative dictionary definitions of the word or phrase in controversy triggers *Chevron* deference.

In *National Railroad Passenger Corp. v. Boston and Maine Corp.*, 503 U.S. 407, 418 (1992), the Court observed, in affording Chevron deference to the ICC's interpretation of "required," that "few phrases in a complex scheme of regulation are so clear as to be beyond the need for interpretation when applied in a real context."

In *MCI Telecommunications Corp. v. American Telephone and Telegraph Co.*, 512 U.S. 218, 225–30, 241–43 (1994), the Court split 5 to 3 over whether the term "modify" unambiguously foreclosed the FCC's detarrifing policy, with both sides engaging in a battle of conflicting dictionary definitions.

In *Babbitt v. Sweet Home Chapter of Communities for a Great Oregon*, 515 U.S. 687, 697, 717–20 (1995), the battle of the dictionaries resulted in affirmance of the Secretary of the Interior's expansive understanding of the phrase "to take" as encompassing significant habitat modification that kills or injures wildlife.

In *Verizon Communications Inc. v. Federal Communications Commission*, 535 U.S. 467, 498–501 (2002), the Court deferred to the FCC's interpretation of the term "cost," rejecting arguments that the term has a fixed technical meaning in the fields of utility rate-making, economics, or accounting. According to the Court, "cost" is a chameleon, citing an accounting dictionary for the proposition that "cost" is "virtually meaningless."

4. Much controversy exists over the scope of the term "traditional tools of statutory construction." In rejecting *Chevron* deference to the EEOC's interpretation of the term "age" in the Age Discrimination in Employment Act, the Court relied on a broad spectrum of interpretive tools, as the following excerpt indicates:

> . . . Even for an agency able to claim all the authority possible under *Chevron*, deference to its statutory interpretation is called for only when the devices of judicial construction have been tried and found to yield no clear sense of congressional intent. *INS v. Cardoza-Fonseca*, 480 U.S. 421, 446–48 (1987) (citing *Chevron supra*, at 843, n.9), Here, regular interpretive method leaves no serious question, not even about purely textual ambiguity in the ADEA. The word "age" takes on a definite meaning from being in the phrase "discriminate . . . because of such individual's age," occurring as that phrase does in a statute structured and manifestly intended to protect the older from arbitrary favor for the younger.

IV

> We see the text, structure, purpose, and history of the ADEA, along with its relationship to other federal statutes, as showing that the statute does not mean to stop an employer from favoring an older employee over a younger one.

General Dynamics Land Systems, Inc. v. Cline, 540 U.S. 581, 600 (2004).

In 1989, Justice Scalia commented that:

> Surely one of the most frequent justifications courts give for choosing a particular construction is that the alternative interpretation would produce absurd results, or results less compatible with the reason or purpose of the statute. This, it seems to me, unquestionably involves judicial consideration and evaluation of competing policies, and for precisely the same purpose for which (in the context we are discussing here) *agencies* consider and evaluate them — to determine which one will best effectuate the statutory purpose. Policy

evaluation is, in other words, part of the traditional judicial tool-kit that is used in applying the first step of *Chevron* — the step that determines, *before* deferring to agency judgment, whether the law is indeed ambiguous

Antonin Scalia, *supra* 1989 DUKE L.J. at 515. If Justice Scalia is correct, how much interpretative ground has the *Chevron* court truly ceded to the "political branches of Government"?

5. Reread Karl Llewellyn's article in Chapter 8[A] and Jane Schacter's article in Chapter 7[B]. To what extent does the Court's use of the traditional canons of statutory construction shift policy-making authority from program administrators to agency lawyers and judges?

6. In *Food and Drug Administration v. Brown & Williamson Tobacco Corp.*, 529 U.S. 120 (2000), by a 5-4 vote, the Court invalidated federal regulations of cigarettes under the FDA Act that restricted sale and distribution of cigarettes and smokeless tobacco to children. The FDA had used its jurisdiction over "drugs" and "devices" to protect children from nicotine which it found to be a drug, and cigarettes, which it found to be "drug delivery devices." Manufacturers had argued that they didn't intend for cigarettes to be a means to "alter functions of the body," a definition of a drug under the Act. The FDA had maintained that cigarettes were intentionally designed by manufacturers to provide active doses of nicotine to consumers. The Court held that the FDA's claims to jurisdiction were contravened by the clear intent of Congress reflected by the "overall context" of the legislation.

Acknowledging that its analysis was constrained by *Chevron* deference, the Court avoided the doctrine by holding that under step one of the analysis, Congress had specifically addressed the question at issue. Refusing to be bound to the statutory language "in isolation," the Court found that "in context," the FDA had consistently disavowed jurisdiction over cigarettes throughout its history. The FDA response to that argument was that it had extended its jurisdiction based on the recently discovered evidence that manufacturers had *intentionally* controlled the level of nicotine in cigarettes for the purpose of addicting consumers into a smoking dependence. The Court also found the FDA's restriction of this "drug" only as to children was inconsistent and contradictory of the agency's obligation to assure that all drugs and devices was safe as marketed, since the agency had not generally prohibited sale of tobacco and cigarettes as unsafe.

Thus, the majority found the context of the legislation and the agency's prior actions counseled against an implicit delegation to FDA of regulatory jurisdiction over cigarettes. As Professor William Funk pointed out, "the difficulty with a 'contextual' analysis as Justices Scalia and Thomas usually point out, is that it empowers judges to make subjective decisions based on their own preferences masked as an interpretation of the context . . . ." 25 ADMINISTRATIVE AND REGULATORY LAW NEWS 4 (Summer 2000) at p. 9. Using the total context of a statutory scheme to determine if Congress directly addressed an issue, Professor Funk noted, is hardly inconsistent with *Chevron*, which originally stated that courts should employ "traditional tools of statutory construction" to answer that question.

7. In *Brown and Williamson Tobacco Corp.*, the Court also set forth criteria for judicial review of an agency's interpretation. The Court determined that a reviewing court: a) should not confine itself to examining a particular statute in isolation but as part of a "symmetrical and coherent" regulatory scheme; b) should consider whether the meaning of one statute is affected by other statutes "particularly when Congress has spoken subsequently and specifically to the topic at hand"; and c) should "be guided to a degree by common sense as to the manner in which Congress is likely to delegate a policy decision of such economic and political magnitude to an administrative agency." 529 U.S. at 133. Do any or all of these considerations fit within the box containing the "traditional tools of statutory construction"? Do any of them involve resort to legislative

history of a kind disfavored by Justice Scalia? If so why did he join in the opinion of the Court?

8. In *National Cable and Telecommunications v. Brand X Internet Services*, 545 U.S. 967, 982–83 (2005), the Court held that a prior judicial construction of a statute trumps *Chevron* deference only if the prior interpretation "unambiguously forecloses the agency's interpretation, and therefore contains no gap for the agency to fill . . . ." Does this holding square with your understanding of the role that *stare decisis* plays in statutory interpretation based on the materials in section A of this Chapter?

9. Step two looks to whether the agency's construction of the statute is "permissible" or "reasonable." To what extent does step two overlap with the scope of review spelled out in § 706(2)(A) of the Administrative Procedure Act, which empowers the reviewing court to "hold unlawful and set aside agency action, findings, and conclusions found to be — arbitrary, capricious, an abuse of discretion or otherwise not in accordance with the law," 5 U.S.C. § 706(2)(A)?

UNITED STATES v. MEAD CORP.
533 U.S. 218 (2001)

Justice Souter delivered the opinion of the Court.

The question is whether a tariff classification ruling by the United States Customs Service deserves judicial deference. The Federal Circuit rejected Customs's invocation of *Chevron U.S.A. Inc. v. Natural Resources Defense Council, Inc.*, 467 U.S. 837 (1984), in support of such a ruling, to which it gave no deference. We agree that a tariff classification has no claim to judicial deference under *Chevron*, there being no indication that Congress intended such a ruling to carry the force of law, but we hold that under *Skidmore v. Swift & Co.*, 323 U.S. 134 (1944), the ruling is eligible to claim respect according to its persuasiveness.

I

A

Imports are taxed under the Harmonized Tariff Schedule of the United States (HTSUS), 19 U.S.C. § 1500(b) provides that Customs shall, under rules and regulations prescribed by the Secretary [of the Treasury,] . . . fix the final classification and rate of duty applicable to . . . merchandise under the HTSUS. Section 1502(a) provides that

> "[t]he Secretary of the Treasury shall establish and promulgate such rules and regulations not inconsistent with the law (including regulations establishing procedures for the issuance of binding rulings prior to the entry of the merchandise concerned), and may disseminate such information as may be necessary to secure a just, impartial, and uniform appraisement of imported merchandise and the classification and assessment of duties thereon at the various ports of entry."[1]

The Secretary provides for tariff rulings before the entry of goods by regulations authorizing ruling letters setting tariff classifications for particular imports. 19 CFR § 177.8 (2000). A ruling letter

> "represents the official position of the Customs Service with respect to the particular transaction or issue described therein and is binding on all Customs Service personnel in accordance with the provisions of this section until modified or revoked. In the absence of a change of practice or other modification or

---

[1] The statutory term ruling is defined by regulation as a written statement . . . that interprets and applies the provisions of the Customs and related laws to a specific set of facts. 19 CFR § 177.1(d)(1) (2000).

revocation which affects the principle of the ruling set forth in the ruling letter, that principle may be cited as authority in the disposition of transactions involving the same circumstances." § 177.9(a).

After the transaction that gives it birth, a ruling letter is to be applied only with respect to transactions involving articles identical to the sample submitted with the ruling request or to articles whose description is identical to the description set forth in the ruling letter. § 177.9(b)(2). As a general matter, such a letter is subject to modification or revocation without notice to any person, except the person to whom the letter was addressed, § 177.9(c), and the regulations consequently provide that no other person should rely on the ruling letter or assume that the principles of that ruling will be applied in connection with any transaction other than the one described in the letter, *ibid.* Since ruling letters respond to transactions of the moment, they are not subject to notice and comment before being issued, may be published but need only be made available for public inspection, 19 U.S.C. § 1625(a), and, at the time this action arose, could be modified without notice and comment under most circumstances, 19 CFR § 177.10(c) (2000). A broader notice-and-comment requirement for modification of prior rulings was added by statute in 1993, Pub.L. 103–182, § 107 Stat. 2186, codified at 19 U.S.C. § 1625(c), and took effect after this case arose.[3]

Any of the 46 port-of-entry Customs offices may issue ruling letters, and so may the Customs Headquarters Office, in providing [a]dvice or guidance as to the interpretation or proper application of the Customs and related laws with respect to a specific Customs transaction [which] may be requested by Customs Service field offices . . . at any time, whether the transaction is prospective, current, or completed, 19 CFR § 177.11(a) (2000). Most ruling letters contain little or no reasoning, but simply describe goods and state the appropriate category and tariff. A few letters, like the Headquarters ruling at issue here, set out a rationale in some detail.

B

Respondent, the Mead Corporation, imports day planners, three-ring binders with pages having room for notes of daily schedules and phone numbers and addresses, together with a calendar and suchlike. The tariff schedule on point falls under the HTSUS heading for [r]egisters, account books notebooks, order books, receipt books, letter pads, memorandum pads, diaries and similar articles, HTSUS subheading 4820.10, which comprises two subcategories. Items in the first, [d]iaries, notebooks and address books, bound; memorandum pads, letter pads and similar articles, were subject to a tariff of 4.0% at the time in controversy.

Between 1989 and 1993, Customs repeatedly treated day planners under the other HTSUS subheading. In January 1993, however, Customs changed its position and issued a Headquarters ruling letter classifying Mead's day planners as Diaries . . . , bound subject to tariff under subheading 4820.10.20. That letter was short on explanation, but after Mead's protest, Customs Headquarters issued a new letter, carefully reasoned but never published, reaching the same conclusion. This letter considered two definitions of diary from the Oxford English Dictionary, the first covering a daily journal of the past

---

[3] As amended by legislation effective after Customs modified the classification ruling in this case, 19 U.S.C. § 1625(c) provides that a ruling or decision that would modify . . . or revoke a prior interpretive ruling or decision which has been in effect for at least 60 days or would have the effect of modifying the treatment previously accorded by the Customs Service to substantially identical transactions shall be published in the Customs Bulletin. The Secretary shall give interested parties an opportunity to submit, during not less than the 30 day period after the date of such publication, comments on the correctness of the proposed ruling or decision. After consideration of any comments received, the Secretary shall publish a final ruling or decision in the Customs Bulletin within 30 days after the closing of the comment period. The final ruling or decision shall become effective 60 days after the date of its publication.

day's events, the second a book including printed dates for daily memoranda and jottings; also . . . calendars . . . .

Customs concluded that diary was not confined to the first, in part because the broader definition reflects commercial usage and hence the commercial identity of these items in the marketplace. Customs concluded that HTSUS was not referring to bookbinding, but to a less exact sort of fastening described in the Harmonized Commodity Description and Coding System Explanatory Notes to Heading 4820, which spoke of binding by reinforcements or fittings of metal, plastics, etc.

Customs rejected Mead's further protest of the second Headquarters ruling letter, and Mead filed suit in the Court of International Trade (CIT). The CIT granted the Government's motion for summary judgment, adopting Customs's reasoning without saying anything about deference.

The Federal Circuit, however, reversed the CIT and held that Customs classification rulings should not get *Chevron* deference. Rulings are not preceded by notice and comment as under the Administrative Procedure Act (APA), 5 U.S.C. § 553, they do not carry the force of law and are not, like regulations, intended to clarify the rights and obligations of importers beyond the specific case under review. The appeals court thought classification rulings had a weaker *Chevron* claim even than Internal Revenue Service interpretive rulings, to which that court gives no deference; unlike rulings by the IRS, Customs rulings issue from many locations and need not be published.

The Court of Appeals accordingly gave no deference at all to the ruling classifying the Mead day planners and rejected the agency's reasoning as to both diary and bound. It thought that planners were not diaries because they had no space for relatively extensive notations about events, observations, feelings, or thoughts in the past. *Id.*, at 1310. And it concluded that diaries bound in subheading 4810.10.20 presupposed unbound diaries such that treating ring-fastened diaries as bound would leave the unbound diary an empty category.

We granted certiorari, 530 U.S. 1202, 231 (2000), in order to consider the limits of *Chevron* deference owed to administrative practice in applying a statute. We hold that administrative implementation of a particular statutory provision qualifies for *Chevron* deference when it appears that Congress delegated authority to the agency generally to make rules carrying the force of law, and that the agency interpretation claiming deference was promulgated in the exercise of that authority. Delegation of such authority may be shown in a variety of ways, as by an agency's power to engage in adjudication or notice-and-comment rulemaking, or by some other indication of a comparable congressional intent. The Customs ruling at issue here fails to qualify, although the possibility that it deserves some deference under *Skidmore* leads us to vacate and remand.

II

A

When Congress has explicitly left a gap for an agency to fill, there is an express delegation of authority to the agency to elucidate a specific provision of the statute by regulation, *Chevron* 467 U.S., at 843–844 and any ensuing regulation is binding in the courts unless procedurally defective, arbitrary or capricious in substance, or manifestly contrary to the statute. APA, 5 U.S.C. §§ 706(2)(A), (D). But whether or not they enjoy any express delegation of authority on a particular question, agencies charged with applying a statute necessarily make all sorts of interpretive choices, and while not all of those choices bind judges to follow them, they certainly may influence courts facing questions the agencies have already answered. [T]he well-reasoned views of the agencies implementing a statute constitute a body of experience and informed judgment to which courts and litigants may properly resort for guidance, *Skidmore*, 323 U.S., at 139–140,

[w]e have long recognized that considerable weight should be accorded to an executive department's construction of a statutory scheme it is entrusted to administer . . . . *Chevron, supra,* at 844.

The fair measure of deference to an agency administering its own statute has been understood to vary with circumstances, and courts have looked to the degree of the agency's care, its consistency, formality, and relative expertness, and to the persuasiveness of the agency's position, *see Skidmore, supra,* at 139–140. The approach has produced a spectrum of judicial responses, from great respect at one end . . . . to near indifference at the other . . . . Justice Jackson summed things up in *Skidmore v. Swift & Co*:

> "The weight [accorded to an administrative] judgment in a particular case will depend upon the thoroughness evident in its consideration, the validity of its reasoning, its consistency with earlier and later pronouncements, and all those factors which give it power to persuade, if lacking power to control." 323 U.S., at 140.

Since 1984, we have identified a category of interpretive choices distinguished by an additional reason for judicial deference. This Court in *Chevron* recognized that Congress not only engages in express delegation of specific interpretive authority, but that [s]ometimes the legislative delegation to an agency on a particular question is implicit. 467 U.S., at 844. Congress, that is, may not have expressly delegated authority or responsibility to implement a particular provision or fill a particular gap. Yet it can still be apparent from the agency's generally conferred authority and other statutory circumstances that Congress would expect the agency to be able to speak with the force of law when it addresses ambiguity in the statute or fills a space in the enacted law, even one about which Congress did not actually have an intent as to a particular result. *Id.,* at 845. When circumstances implying such an expectation exist, a reviewing court has no business rejecting an agency's exercise of its generally conferred authority to resolve a particular statutory ambiguity simply because the agency's chosen resolution seems unwise, *see id.,* at 845–846, but is obliged to accept the agency's position if Congress has not previously spoken to the point at issue and the agency's interpretation is reasonable, *see id.,* at 842–845, *cf.* 5 U.S.C. § 706(2) (a reviewing court shall set aside agency action, findings, and conclusions found to be arbitrary, capricious, an abuse of discretion, or otherwise not in accordance with law).

We have recognized a very good indicator of delegation meriting *Chevron* treatment in express congressional authorizations to engage in the process of rulemaking or adjudication that produces regulations or rulings for which deference is claimed. *See, e.g., EEOC v. Arabian American Oil Co.,* 499 U.S. 244, 257 (1991) (no *Chevron* deference to agency guideline where congressional delegation did not include the power to promulgate rules or regulations' (quoting *General Elec. Co. v. Gilbert,* 429 U.S. 125, 141 (1976))); *see also Christensen v. Harris County,* 529 576, 596–597 (2000) (Breyer, J., dissenting) (where it is in doubt that Congress actually intended to delegate particular interpretive authority to an agency, *Chevron* is inapplicable). It is fair to assume generally that Congress contemplates administrative action with the effect of law when it provides for a relatively formal administrative procedure tending to foster the fairness and deliberation that should underlie a pronouncement of such force.[11] Thus, the overwhelming number of our cases applying *Chevron* deference have reviewed the fruits of notice-and-comment rulemaking or formal adjudication. That said, and as significant as notice-and-comment is in pointing to *Chevron* authority, the want of that procedure

---

[11] *See* Merrill & Hickman, Chevron's *Domain,* 89 Geo. L.J. 833, 872 (2001) ([I]f *Chevron* rests on a presumption about congressional intent, then *Chevron* should apply only where Congress would want *Chevron* to apply. In delineating the types of delegations of agency authority that trigger *Chevron* deference, it is therefore important to determine whether a plausible case can be made that Congress would want such a delegation to mean that agencies enjoy primary interpretational authority).

here does not decide the case, for we have sometimes found reasons for *Chevron* deference even when no such administrative formality was required and none was afforded, *see, e.g., NationsBank of N.C., N.A. v. Variable Annuity Life Ins. Co.*, 513 U.S. 251, 256–257 (1995). The fact that the tariff classification here was not a product of such formal process does not alone, therefore, bar the application of *Chevron*.

There are, nonetheless, ample reasons to deny *Chevron* deference here. The authorization for classification rulings, and Customs's practice in making them, present a case far removed not only from notice-and-comment process, but from any other circumstances reasonably suggesting that Congress ever thought of classification rulings as deserving the deference claimed for them here.

B

No matter which angle we choose for viewing the Customs ruling letter in this case, it fails to qualify under *Chevron*. On the face of the statute, to begin with, the terms of the congressional delegation give no indication that Congress meant to delegate authority to Customs to issue classification rulings with the force of law. We are not, of course, here making any global statement about Custom's authority, for it is true that the general rulemaking power conferred on Customs, *see* 19 U.S.C. § 1624, authorizes some regulation with the force of law, or legal norms . . . . It is true as well that Congress had classification rulings in mind when it explicitly authorized, in a parenthetical, the issuance of regulations establishing procedures for the issuance of binding rulings prior to the entry of the merchandise concerned, 19 U.S.C. § 1502(a). The reference to binding classification does not however, bespeak the legislative type of activity that would naturally bind more than the parties to the ruling, once the goods classified are admitted into this country. And though the statute's direction to disseminate information necessary to secure uniformity, *ibid.*, seems to assume that a ruling may be precedent in later transactions, precedential value alone does not add up to *Chevron* entitlement; interpretive rules may sometimes function as precedents, *see* Strauss, *The Rulemaking Continuum*, 41 DUKE L.J. 1463, 1472–1473 (1992), and they enjoy no *Chevron* status as a class. In any event, any precedential claim of a classification ruling is counterbalanced by the provision for independent review of Customs classifications by the CIT, *see* 28 U.S.C. §§ 2638–2640 . . . . It is hard to imagine a congressional understanding more at odds with the *Chevron* regime.

It is difficult, in fact, to see in the agency practice itself any indication that Customs ever set out with a lawmaking pretense in mind when it undertook to make classification like these. Customs does not generally engage in notice-and-comment practice when issuing them, and their treatment by the agency makes it clear that a letter's binding character as a ruling stops short of third parties; Customs has regarded a classification as conclusive only as between itself and the importer to whom it was issued, 19 CFR § 177.9(c) (2000), and even then only until Customs has given advance notice of intended change, §§ 177.9(a), (c). Other importers are in fact warned against assuming any right of detrimental reliance. § 177.9(c).

Indeed, to claim that classifications have legal force is to ignore the reality that 46 different Customs offices issue 10,000 to 15,000 of them each year. Any suggestion that rulings intended to have the force of law are being churned out at a rate of 10,000 a year at an agency's 46 scattered offices is simply self-refuting. Although the circumstances are less startling here, with a Headquarters letter in issue, none of the relevant statutes recognizes this category of rulings as separate or different from others, there is thus no indication that a more potent delegation might have been understood as going to Headquarters even when Headquarters provides developed reasoning, as it did in this instance.

Nor do the amendments to the statute made effective after this case arose disturb our conclusion. The new law requires Customs to provide notice-and-comment procedures only when modifying or revoking a prior classification ruling or modifying the treatment accorded to substantially identical transactions, 19 U.S.C. § 1625(c); and under its regulations, Customs sees itself obliged to provide notice-and-comment procedures only when changing a practice so as to produce a tariff increase, or in the imposition of a restriction or prohibition, or when Customs Headquarters determines that the matter of sufficient importance to involve the interests of domestic industry, 19 CFR §§ 177.10(c)(1), (2) (2000). The statutory changes reveal no new congressional objective of treating classification decisions generally as rulemaking with force of law, nor do they suggest any intent to create a *Chevron* patchwork of classification rulings, some with force of law, some without.

In sum, classification rulings are best treated like interpretations contained in policy statements, agency manuals, and enforcement guidelines. *Christensen*, 529 U.S., at 587. They are beyond the *Chevron* pale.

To agree with the Court of Appeals that Customs ruling letters do not fall within *Chevron* is not, however, to place them outside the pale of any deference whatever. *Chevron* did nothing to eliminate *Skidmore*'s holding that an agency's interpretation may merit some deference whatever its form, given the specialized experience and broader investigations and information available to the agency, 323 U.S., at 139, and given the value of uniformity in its administrative and judicial understandings of what a national law requires, *id.*, at 140.

There is room at least to raise a *Skidmore* claim here, where the regulatory scheme is highly detailed, and Customs can bring the benefit of specialized experience to bear on the subtle questions in this case: whether the daily planner with room for brief daily entries falls under diaries, when diaries are grouped with notebooks and address books, bound; memorandum pads, letter pads and similar articles, HTSUS subheading 4820.10.20; and whether a planner with a ring binding should qualify as bound, when a binding may be typified by a book, but also may have reinforcements or fittings or metal, plastics, etc., Harmonized Commodity Description and Coding System Explanatory Notes to Heading 4820, p. 687. A classification ruling in this situation may therefore at least seek a respect proportional to its power to persuade, *Skidmore*, *supra*, at 140 . . . . Such a ruling may surely claim the merit of its writer's thoroughness, logic, and expertness, its fit with prior interpretations, and any other sources of weight.

D

Underlying the position we take here, like the position expressed by Justice Scalia in dissent, is a choice about the best way to deal with an inescapable feature of the body of congressional legislation authorizing administrative action. That feature is the great variety of ways in which the laws invest the Government's administrative arms with discretion, and with procedures for exercising it, in giving meaning to Acts of Congress. Implementation of a statute may occur in formal adjudication or the choice to defend against judicial challenge; it may occur in a central board or office or in dozens of enforcement agencies dotted across the country, its institutional lawmaking may be confined to the resolution of minute detail or extend to legislative rulemaking on matters intentionally left by Congress to be worked out at the agency level.

Although we all accept the position that the Judiciary should defer to at least some of this multifarious administrative action, we have to decide how to take account of the great range of its variety. If the primary objective is to simplify the judicial process of giving or withholding deference, then the diversity of statutes authorizing discretionary administrative action must be declared irrelevant or minimized. If, on the other hand, it is simply implausible that Congress intended such a broad range of statutory authority to produce only two varieties of administrative action, demanding either *Chevron* deference or none at all, then the breadth of the spectrum of possible agency action must be taken into account. Justice Scalia's first priority over the years has been to limit and simplify. The Court's choice has been to tailor deference to variety. This acceptance of the range of statutory variation has led the Court to recognize more than one variety of judicial deference just as the Court has recognized a variety of indicators that Congress would expect *Chevron* deference . . . .[18]

We think, in sum, that Justice Scalia's efforts to simplify ultimately run afoul of Congress's indications that different statutes present different reasons for considering respect for the exercise of administrative authority or deference to it. Without being at odds with congressional intent much of the time, we believe that judicial responses to administrative action must continue to differentiate between *Chevron* and *Skidmore*, and that continued recognition of *Skidmore* is necessary for just the reasons Justice Jackson gave when that case was decided.

Since the *Skidmore* assessment called for here ought to be made in the first instance by the Court of Appeals for the Federal Circuit or the CIT, we go no further than to vacate the judgment and remand the case for further proceedings consistent with this opinion.

Justice Scalia, dissenting.

I

Only five years ago, the Court described the *Chevron* doctrine as follows: We accord deference to agencies under *Chevron* . . . because of a presumption that Congress, when it left ambiguity in a statute meant for implementation by an agency, understood that the ambiguity would be resolved, first and foremost, by the agency, and desired the agency (rather than the courts) to possess whatever degree of discretion the ambiguity allows, *Smiley v. Citibank (South Dakota), N.A.*, 517 U.S. 735, 740–741. Today the Court collapses this doctrine, announcing instead a presumption that agency discretion does not exist unless the statute, expressly or impliedly, says so. While the Court disclaims any hard-and-fast rule for determining the existence of discretion-conferring intent, it assets that a very good indicator [is] express congressional authorizations to engage in the process of rulemaking or adjudication that produces regulations or rulings for which deference is claimed. Only when agencies act through adjudication[,] notice-and-comment rulemaking, or . . . some other [procedure] indicat[ing] comparable congressional intent [whatever that means] is *Chevron* deference applicable — because these relatively formal administrative procedure[s] [designed] to foster . . . fairness and deliberation bespeak (according to the Court) congressional willingness to have the agency, rather than the courts, resolve statutory ambiguities. Once it is determined that *Chevron* deference is not in order, the uncertainty is not at an end — and indeed is just beginning. Litigants cannot then assume that the statutory question is one for the courts to determine, according to traditional interpretive principles and by their own judicial lights. No, the Court now resurrects, in full force, the pre-*Chevron* doctrine of *Skidmore* deference, *see Skidmore, supra,* whereby [t]he fair measure of deference to an agency administering its own statute . . . var[ies] with circumstances, including the degree of the agency's care, its consistency, formality, and relative expertness, and . . . the persuasiveness of the agency's position. The Court has largely replaced *Chevron*, in other words, with that test most beloved by a court unwilling to be held to rules (and most feared by litigants who want to know what to expect): th' ol' totality of the circumstances test.

The Court's new doctrine is neither sound in principle nor sustainable in practice.

---

[18] It is, of course, true that the limit of *Chevron* deference is not marked by a hard-edged rule. But *Chevron* itself is a good example showing when *Chevron* deference is warranted, while this is a good case showing when it is not. Judges in other, perhaps harder, cases will make reasoned choices between the two examples, the way courts have always done.

A

As to principle: The doctrine of *Chevron* — that all *authoritative* agency interpretations of statutes they are charged with administering deserve deference — was rooted
in a legal presumption of congressional intent, important to the division of powers
between the Second and Third Branches. When, *Chevron* said, Congress leaves an
ambiguity in a statute that is to be administered by an executive agency, it is presumed
that Congress meant to give the agency discretion, within the limits of reasonable
interpretation, as to how the ambiguity is to be resolved. By committing enforcement of
the statute to an agency rather than the courts, Congress committed its initial and
primary interpretation to that branch as well.

There is some question whether *Chevron* was faithful to the text of the Administrative Procedure Act (APA), which it did not even bother to cite.[2] But it was in accord with
the origins of federal court judicial review. Judicial control of federal executive officers
was principally exercised through the prerogative writ of mandamus. *See* L. Jaffe,
Judicial Control of Administrative Action 166, 176–177 (1965). That writ generally would
not issue unless the executive officer was acting plainly beyond the scope of his
authority.

Statutory ambiguities, in other words, were left to reasonable resolution by the
Executive.

The basis in principle for today's new doctrine can be described as follows: The
background rule is that ambiguity in legislative instructions to agencies is to be resolved
not by the agencies but by the judges. Specific congressional intent to depart from this
rule must be found — and while there is no single touchstone for such intent it can
generally be found when Congress has authorized the agency to act through (what the
Court says is) relatively formal procedures such as informal rulemaking and formal (and
informal?) adjudication, and when the agency in fact employs such procedures . . . .

B

As for the practical effects of the new rule:

The principal effect will be protracted confusion. As noted above, the one test for
Chevron deference that the Court enunciates is wonderfully imprecise: whether
Congress delegated authority to the agency generally to make rules carrying the force
of law, . . . as by . . . adjudication[,] notice-and-comment rulemaking, or . . . some
other [procedure] indicati[ng] comparable congressional intent . . . .

Worst of all, the majority's approach will lead to the ossification of large portions of
our statutory law. Where *Chevron* applies, statutory ambiguities remain ambiguities
subject to the agency's ongoing clarification. They create a space, so to speak, for the
exercise of continuing agency discretion. As *Chevron* itself held, the Environmental
Protection Agency can interpret stationary source to mean a single smokestack, can
later replace that interpretation with the bubble concept embracing an entire plant, and
if that proves undesirable can return again to the original interpretation. 467 U.S., at
853–859, 865–866. For the indeterminately large number of statutes taken out of
Chevron by today's decision, however, ambiguity (and hence flexibility) will cease with
the first judicial resolution. *Skidmore* deference gives the agency's current position
some vague and uncertain amount of respect, but it does not, like *Chevron*, leave the
matter within the control of the Executive Branch for the future . . . .

And finally, the majority's approach compounds the confusion it creates by breathing
new life into the anachronism of *Skidmore*, which sets forth a sliding scale of deference
owed an agency's interpretation of a statute that is dependent upon the thoroughness

---

[2] Title 5 U.S.C. § 706 provides that, in reviewing agency action, the court shall decide all relevant questions
of law — which would seem to mean that all statutory ambiguities are to be resolved judicially.

evident in [the agency's] consideration, the validity of its reasoning, its consistency with earlier and later pronouncements, and all those factors which give it power to persuade, if lacking power to control; in this way, the appropriate measure of deference will be accorded the body of experience and informed judgment that such interpretations often embody, 323 U.S., at 140. Justice Jackson's eloquence notwithstanding, the rule of *Skidmore* deference is an empty truism and a trifling statement of the obvious: A judge should take into account the well-considered views of expert observers.

It was possible to live with the indeterminacy of *Skidmore* deference in earlier times. But in an era when federal statutory law administered by federal agencies is pervasive, and when the ambiguities (intended or unintended) that those statutes contain are innumerable, totality-of-the-circumstances *Skidmore* deference is a recipe for uncertainty unpredictability, and endless litigation. To condemn a vast body of agency action to that regime (all except rulemaking, formal (and informal?) adjudication, and whatever else might now and then be included within today's intentionally vague formation of affirmative congressional intent to delegate) is irresponsible.

III

To decide the present case, I would adhere to the original formulation of *Chevron*. The power of an administrative agency to administer a congressionally created . . . program necessarily requires the formulation of policy and the making of rules to fill any gap left, implicitly or explicitly, by Congress, 467 U.S., at 843. We accordingly presume — and our precedents have made clear to Congress that we presume — that, absent some clear textual indication to the contrary, Congress, when it left ambiguity in a statute meant for implementation by an agency, understood that the ambiguity would be resolved, first and foremost by the agency, and desired the agency (rather than the courts) to possess whatever degree of discretion the ambiguity allows, *Smiley*, 517 U.S., at 740–741. *Chevron* sets forth an across-the-board presumption, which operates as a background rule of law against which Congress legislates: Ambiguity means Congress intended agency discretion. Any resolution of the ambiguity by the administering agency that is authoritative-that represents the official position of the agency-must be accepted by the courts if it is reasonable.

Nothing in the statute at issue here displays an intent to modify the background presumption on which *Chevron* deference is based . . . .

NOTES AND QUESTIONS

1. Although *Mead* was decided 17 years after *Chevron*, the *Mead* Court majority sets forth a framework for addressing a question that is logically prior to the application of *Chevron* analysis — to what extent has Congress indicated, either explicitly or implicitly, that Congress has "delegated authority or responsibility to implement a particular provision or fill a particular gap" to the agency that administers the statute? And so, before reaching *Chevron's* two steps, the Court holds that administrative interpretations qualify for *Chevron* deference only when a prior two step analysis is undertaken:

1) " . . . when it appears that Congress delegated authority to the agency generally to make rules carrying the force of law . . ."

2) " . . . and that the agency interpretation claiming deference was promulgated in the exercise of that authority . . ."

Mead at 226–27.

2. Note the sources of evidence that the *Mead* Court recognizes in determining whether a particular agency's interpretation of a particular statutory provision meets the two-step *Mead* criteria:

Delegation of such authority may be shown in a variety of ways, as by an agency's power to engage in adjudication or notice-and-comment rulemaking, or by some other indication of a comparable congressional intent.

Mead at 227.

Two of indicia of congressional intent are clearly textual. Does the phrase "some other indication" open the door to arguments based on legislative purpose or legislative history?

3. Professor Adrian Vermeule has proposed the following interpretation of *Mead* in relation to *Chevron*:

> The *Chevron* opinion itself is best read as an attempt to simplify and clarify the preexisting, and notoriously muddled, law of deference to agency interpretations. Doctrinally, *Chevron* announced a straightforward set of ideas: Congress sometimes intends to delegate lawmaking authority to agencies; such delegations may be express or implied; statutory ambiguities and gaps will be taken as implied delegations of agency authority to make law by interpreting the ambiguity in one direction or the other, or by filling in the gap. From this follows the famous *Chevron* two-step, under which courts first ask whether Congress has spoken clearly to the question at hand, and, if not, whether the agency interpretation is reasonable. The first question asks whether there is an ambiguity or a gap to be filled, the second asks whether the agency's chosen interpretation falls, permissibly, within the domain of the ambiguity, or impermissibly outside it. On this view, the key innovation of *Chevron* is to create a global interpretive presumption: ambiguities are, without more, taken to signify implicit delegations of interpretive authority to the administering agency.
>
> *Mead* reverses this global presumption. Rather than taking ambiguity to signify delegation, *Mead* establishes that the default rule runs against delegation. Unless the reviewing court affirmatively finds that Congress intended to delegate interpretive authority to the particular agency at hand, in the particular statutory scheme at hand, *Chevron* deference is not due and the Chevron two-step is not to be invoked.

Introduction: Mead *in the Trenches*, 71 GEO. WASH. L. REV. 347, 348 (2003).

Do you agree that the *Mead* majority opinion supports his interpretation?

4. The Court reversed the Federal Circuit for failure to apply *Skidmore* deference to the Customs Services tariff classification ruling. Compare the variable criteria set forth in *Skidmore* with the pre-*Chevron* deference criteria laid out by Professor Merrill in the article excerpted earlier in this Chapter. Does the comparison illustrate the proverb "what is past is prologue"?

5. A former General Counsel of the E.P.A. observed:

> Courts used to conceive of a statute as a package of instructions that, once decoded, will answer every conceivable question that might arise. In *Chevron*, however, the Court adopted the far more realistic view that most members of Congress probably never even think about many questions that might arise subsequently under a statute they enact, much less form a consensus on them. This first move in *Chevron* rejected the prior legal fiction that Congress had an imminent, if unconscious, "intention" on every conceivable question that might arise and that it was the role of courts to "find" Congress' intentions on every question when interpreting a statute.
>
> The fundamental difference between the role of EPA OGC (and probably in any other agency as well) pre-*Chevron* and post-*Chevron* is this: pre-*Chevron*, OGC usually gave its legal advice as a point estimate, e.g., "the statute means this. There is only one meaning to the statute. We in OGC are the keepers of what the statute means. The statute speaks to every question, and you must follow what we in OGC tell you is the correct/best interpretation of the statute

or you will lose in court." In other words, the pre-*Chevron* conception of a statute was as a prescriptive text having a single meaning, discoverable by specialized legal training and tools. This "single-meaning" conception of statutes created a very powerful role for lawyers and OGC within agencies. The privileged role for lawyers in defining what the statute required on every issue in turn led to a great deal of implicit policy-making by lawyers in OGC. They may have in all good faith believed that they were divining the one true and correct meaning of the statute, but intentionally or unintentionally, they may have smuggled a great deal of their policy preferences into their legal advice. As EPA's General Counsel, I tried to get our lawyers to separate their legal opinions from their policy advice and to differentiate between the two.

Post-*Chevron*, the form of OGC opinions is no longer a simple point estimate of what a statute means. Rather, OGC opinions now attempt to describe a permissible range of agency policy-making discretion that arises out of a statutory ambiguity. Post-*Chevron*, a statute no longer possess a single prescriptive meaning on many questions; rather, they describe what I call a "policy space," a range of permissible interpretive discretion, within which a variety of decisions that the agency might make would be legally defensible to varying degrees. So the task of OGC today is to define the boundaries of legal defensibility, and thereby to recognize that often there is more than one possible interpretation of the meaning of key statutory terms and concepts. The agency's policy-makers, not its lawyers, should decide which of several different but legally defensible interpretations to adopt . . . .

Within this realm of discretion, it is neither a legislative nor judicial function, but rather an executive function for an agency, acting under presidential supervision, to answer statutory questions left open by Congress. The "answer" that an agency chooses will reflect the agency's policy choices, as supervised by the White House. This is a major shift of power to the Executive Branch and away from congressional staff and lower federal courts.

One result of this *Chevron* induced shift of power to agencies within the Executive Branch, as mentioned earlier, is that agency experts are making more policy decisions rather than agency lawyers and federal courts. Thus, *Chevron* represents a culmination of the vision articulated by the first generation of administrative lawyers in the 1930s that "expertise" would play a greater role than "legalism" in our law. For example, James Landis, the intellectual father of administrative agencies in the 1930s, wrote "[t]he administrative process is, in essence, our generation's answer to the inadequacy of the judicial and legislative processes." Landis and his colleagues argued that the common law tends to become a closed system that is not sufficiently receptive to information from other disciplines. They argued for a system in which technical knowledge and expertise from disciplines in addition to law would play a larger role in shaping public policy. In the words of Landis' Harvard contemporary, Felix Frankfurter, the role of expertise would be to expand "the area of accredited knowledge as the basis of action" in the "intricate and technical facts" of a complex modern society.

E. Donald Elliott, *Chevron Matters: How the Chevron Doctrine Redefined the Roles of Congress, Courts and Agencies in Environmental Law*, 16 VILL. ENVTL. L.J. 1, 7, 11–12, 14 (2005).

Will the *Mead* case shift power from experts and policy-makers to agency lawyers and lower federal courts?

6. If the *Nix v. Hedden* case in Chapter 6[B] were to arise today, would the Supreme Court defer to the customs collector's determination that tomatoes are "vegetables" rather than "fruits"? Note that the Customs Service in its tariff ruling in *Mead* relied on the Oxford English Dictionary's definition of "diary" in classifying Mead's day planners as subject to tariffs.

7. For a comprehensive discussion of the variety of deference doctrines recognized in administrative law, see *Gonzalez v. Oregon*, 546 U.S. 243 (2006).

C. SEVERABILITY

When a provision in a statute is held unconstitutional and therefore invalid, a number of issues arise as to the continued validity of the remaining parts of the statute. Is the surviving part unaffected? Or must the entire statute or even an entire Act be rejected because the legislature intended to pass all of the law or none of it? How does the court determine whether the invalid provisions are such that the legislature would not have intended the remainder to survive after the invalid part is invalidated?

You may have encountered phraseology in contracts and in legislation that recite an intention that if any provisions are held invalid it is intended that the remaining portions continue to be enforceable. To what extent can a court reasonably rely upon such a severability clause in determining the intent of the legislature regarding whether an invalid provision may be severed from the remaining portions which will continue to have validity? There can be additional complexities. A statute can be valid if applied to some classes of cases, but void if applied to others. Statutes may be valid if applied in the future, but invalid if applied retroactively, for instance.

Courts are not authorized to declare the remainder of a statute invalid simply because a part of it is unconstitutional unless all provisions are related by subject matter, are interrelated and operate for the same purpose or are connected to each other in some meaningful way. Constitutionally valid and unconstitutional provisions can be found in the same provision, yet because they are sufficiently distinct, they can be considered severable. One test sometimes used is whether, when the invalid portion is stricken, the remainder is complete in itself and capable of standing alone or being enforced consistent with apparent legislative intent. The difficulty faced by interpreters of such statutes is how to determine whether the invalid and valid parts of the statute are capable of being separated. Guidance can be found from a contemplation of the statute and of the purpose to be accomplished by it. Asked another way, the theoretical question is whether the legislature would have passed the statute if it could not be upheld in its entirety? Different sets of issues arise when the statute contains an *inseverability clause*.

UNITED STATES v. JACKSON
390 U.S. 570 (1967)

Mr. Justice Stewart delivered the opinion of the Court.

The Federal Kidnaping Act, 18 U.S.C. § 1201 (a), provides:

> "Whoever knowingly transports in interstate . . . commerce, any person who has been unlawfully . . . kidnaped . . . and held for ransom . . . or otherwise . . . shall be punished (1) by death if the kidnaped person has not been liberated unharmed, and if the verdict of the jury shall so recommend, or (2) by imprisonment for any term of years or for life, if the death penalty is not imposed."

This statute thus creates an offense punishable by death "if the verdict of the jury shall so recommend." The statute sets forth no procedure for imposing the death penalty upon a defendant who waives the right to jury trial or upon one who pleads guilty.

On October 10, 1966, a federal grand jury in Connecticut returned an indictment charging in count one that three named defendants, the appellees in this case, had transported from Connecticut to New Jersey a person who had been kidnaped and held for ransom, and who had been harmed when liberated. The District Court dismissed this count of the indictment, holding the Federal Kidnaping Act unconstitutional because it makes "the risk of death" the price for asserting the right to jury trial, and thereby "impairs . . . free exercise" of that constitutional right. The government appealed directly to this Court, and we noted probable jurisdiction. We reverse.

We agree with the District Court that the death penalty provision of the Federal Kidnaping Act imposes an impermissible burden upon the exercise of a constitutional right, but we think that provision is severable from the remainder of the statute. There is no reason to invalidate the law in its entirety simply because its capital punishment clause violates the Constitution. The District Court therefore erred in dismissing the kidnaping count of the indictment.

. . . .

The remaining question is whether the statute as a whole must fall simply because its death penalty clause is constitutionally deficient. The District Court evidently assumed that it must, for that Court dismissed the kidnaping indictment. We disagree. As we said in *Champlin Rfg. Co. v. Commission*, 286 U.S. 210, 234:

> "The unconstitutionality of a part of an Act does not necessarily defeat- . . . the validity of its remaining provisions. Unless it is evident that the legislature would not have enacted those provisions which are within its power, independently of that which is not, the invalid part may be dropped if what is left is fully operative as a law."

Under this test, it is clear that the clause authorizing capital punishment is severable from the remainder of the kidnapping statute and that the unconstitutionality of that clause does not require the defeat of the law as a whole. *See McDowell v. United States*, 274 F. Supp. 426, 429. *Cf. Spillers v. State*, 84 Nev. 23, 27, 436 P.2d 18, 23–24.

The clause in question is a functionally independent part of the Federal Kidnaping Act. Its elimination in no way alters the substantive reach of the statute and leaves completely unchanged its basic operation. Under such circumstances, it is quite inconceivable that the Congress which decided to authorize capital punishment in aggravated kidnaping cases would have chosen to discard the entire statute if informed that it could not include the death penalty clause now before us.

In this case it happens that history confirms what common sense alone would suggest: The law as originally enacted in 1932 contained no capital punishment provision. A majority of the House had favored the death penalty but had yielded to opposition in the Senate as a matter of expediency. Only one congressman had expressed the view that the law would not be worth enacting without capital punishment. The majority obviously felt otherwise. When the death penalty was added in 1934, the statute was left substantially unchanged in every other respect. The basic problem that had prompted enactment of the law in 1932 — the difficulty of relying upon state and local authorities to investigate and prosecute interstate kidnaping — had not vanished during the intervening two years. It is therefore clear that Congress would have made interstate kidnaping a federal crime even if the death penalty provision had been ruled out from the beginning. It would be difficult to imagine a more compelling case for severability.

In an effort to suggest the contrary, the appellees insist that the 1934 amendment "did not merely increase the penalties for kidnaping; it changed the whole thrust of the Act." They note that Congress deliberately limited capital punishment to those kidnapers whose victims are not liberated unharmed. Such a differential penalty provision, the appellees argue, is needed to discourage kidnapers from injuring those whom they abduct. The appellees contend that, without its capital punishment clause, the Federal Kidnaping Act would not distinguish "the penalties applicable to those who do and those who do not harm or kill their victims." Stressing the obvious congressional concern for the victim's safety, they conclude that "it is doubtful that Congress would intend for the statute to stand absent such a feature." This argument is wrong as a matter of history, for Congress *enacted* the statute "absent such a feature." It is wrong as a matter of fact, for the length of imprisonment imposed under the Act can obviously be made to reflect the kidnaper's treatment of his victim. And it is wrong as a matter of logic, for nothing could more completely obliterate the distinction between "the penalties applicable to those who do and those who do not harm or kill their victims" than the total invalidation of *all* the penalties provided by the Federal Kidnaping Act — the precise result sought by the appellees.

Thus the infirmity of the death penalty clause does not require the total frustration of Congress' basic purpose — that of making interstate kidnaping a federal crime. By holding the death penalty clause of the Federal Kidnaping Act unenforceable, we leave the statute an operative whole, free of any constitutional objection. The appellees may be prosecuted for violating the Act, but they cannot be put to death under its authority.

The judgment is reversed and the case is remanded for further proceedings consistent with this opinion.

It is so ordered.

NOTES AND QUESTIONS

1. How does one determine whether "what is left is fully operative as a law"? Is this determination dependent on the legislative history? The Court states the Act is fully operative as a matter of fact, history, and logic. What should happen in a situation where logic or history leads to the opposite conclusion of a provision's viability after severance?

2. What is the test for the independence of statutory provisions? Is functional independence the only test, or is it one of several?

3. How did the Court determine the operability of the remaining provisions from the legislative history? What was Congress' intent?

4. How much of the statute is severed? In other words, what portion of the statute is the "death penalty clause"? How did the Court define it? Does it help here that the clause was added as an amendment? Which alternative makes more sense in severing the statute: (a) to remove all of the provision (1) and the second clause of (2), or (b) remove just the second clause of (1)? If the first alternative is used, what is left of the statute? Which alternative would more clearly reflect the intent of Congress?

5. What penalty will the defendants be subject to under the remaining part of the Act? Can a stiffer penalty be imposed for persons convicted of kidnaping in which the victim is harmed? Does imprisonment for a term of years or life turn on the decision of the trier of fact not to impose the death penalty? The defendants' claim was limited to the right to a jury trial. Under the holding in this case, what language should Congress use to enact a death penalty clause in the Federal Kidnapping Act which is not dependent on a jury determination? Is it still possible to discourage harm to kidnaping victims?

CARTER v. CARTER COAL CO.
298 U.S. 238 (1936)

Mr. Justice Sutherland delivered the opinion of the Court.

The purposes of the "Bituminous Coal Conservation Act of 1935," involved in these suits, as declared by the title, are to stabilize the bituminous coal-mining industry and promote its interstate commerce; to provide for cooperative marketing of bituminous coal; to levy a tax on such coal and provide for a drawback under certain conditions; to declare the production, distribution, and use of such coal to be affected with a national public interest; to conserve the national resources of such coal; to provide for the general welfare, and for other purposes. C. 824, 49 Stat. 991. The constitutional validity of the act is challenged in each of the suits . . . .

[The Court held the labor provisions of the Act unconstitutional.]

Seventh. Finally, we are brought to the price-fixing provisions of the code. The necessity of considering the question of their constitutionality will depend upon whether they are separable from the labor provisions so that they can stand independently. Section 15 of the act provides:

> If any provision of this Act, or the application thereof to any person or circumstances, is held invalid, the remainder of the Act and the application of such provisions to other persons or circumstances shall not be affected thereby.

In the absence of such a provision, the presumption is that the legislature intends an act to be effective as an entirety — that is to say, the rule is against the mutilation of a statute; and if any provision be unconstitutional, the presumption is that the remaining provisions fall with it. The effect of the statute is to reverse this presumption in favor of inseparability and create the opposite one of separability. Under the non-statutory rule, the burden is upon the supporter of the legislation to show the separability of the provisions involved. Under the statutory rule, the burden is shifted to the assailant to show their inseparability. But under either rule, the determination, in the end, is reached by applying the same test — namely, What was the intent of the lawmakers?

Under the statutory rule, the presumption must be overcome by considerations which establish "the clear probability that the invalid part being eliminated by the legislature would not have been satisfied with what remains," *Williams v. Standard Oil Co.*, 287 U.S. 235, 241 *et seq.*; or, as stated in *Utah Power & L. Co. v. Pfost*, 286 U.S. 165, 184–85, "the clear probability that the legislature would not have been satisfied with the statute unless it had included the invalid part." Whether the provisions of a statute are so interwoven that one being held invalid the others must fall, presents a question of statutory construction and of legislative intent, to the determination of which the statutory provision becomes an aid. "But it is an aid merely; not an inexorable command." *Dorchy v. Kansas*, 264 U.S. 286, 290. The presumption in favor of separability does not authorize the Court to give the statute "an effect altogether different from that sought by the measure viewed as a whole." *Railroad Retirement Board v. Alton R. Co.*, 295 U.S. 330, 362.

The statutory aid to construction in no way alters the rule that in order to hold one part of a statute unconstitutional and uphold another part as separable, they must not be mutually dependent upon one another. Perhaps a fair approach to a solution of the problem is to suppose that while the bill was pending in Congress a motion to strike out the labor provisions had prevailed, and to inquire whether, in that event, the statute should be so construed as to justify the conclusion that Congress, notwithstanding, probably would not have passed the price-fixing provisions of the code.

. . . .

With the foregoing principles in mind, let us examine the act itself. The title of the act and the preamble demonstrate, as we have already seen, that Congress desired to accomplish certain general purposes therein recited. To that end it created a commission, with mandatory directions to formulate into a working agreement the provisions set forth in § 4 of the act. That being done, the result is a code.

. . . .

. . . Following the requirement just quoted, and, significantly, *in the same section* (*International Textbook Co. v. Pigg*, 217 U.S. 91, 112–13) under appropriate headings, the price-fixing and labor-regulating provisions are set out in great detail. These provisions, plainly meant to operate together and not separately, constitute the means designated to bring about the stabilization of bituminous-coal production, and thereby to regulate or affect interstate commerce in such coal. The first clause of the title is: "To stabilize the bituminous coal-mining industry and promote its interstate commerce."

Thus, the primary contemplation of the act is stabilization of the industry through the regulation of labor *and* the regulation of prices; for, since both were adopted, we must conclude that both were thought essential. The regulations of labor on the one hand and prices on the other furnish mutual aid and support; and their associated force — not one or the other but both combined — was deemed by Congress to be necessary to achieve the end sought. The statutory mandate for a code upheld by two legs at once suggests the improbability that Congress would have assented to a code supported by only one.

This seems plain enough; for Congress must have been conscious of the fact that elimination of the labor provisions from the act would seriously impair, if not destroy, the force and usefulness of the price provisions. The interdependence of wages and prices is manifest. Approximately two-thirds of the cost of producing a ton of coal is represented by wages. Fair prices necessarily depend upon the cost of production; and since wages constitute so large a proportion of the cost, prices cannot be fixed with any proper relation to cost without taking into consideration this major element. If one of them becomes uncertain, uncertainty with respect to the other necessarily ensues.

So much is recognized by the code itself. The introductory clause of Part III declares that the conditions respecting labor relations are "To effectuate the purposes of this Act." And subdivision (a) of Part II, quoted in the forepart of this opinion, reads in part: "In order to sustain the stabilization of wages, working conditions, and maximum hours of labor, said prices shall be established so as to yield a return per net ton for each district in a minimum price area, . . . equal as nearly as may be to the weighted average of the total costs, per net ton . . . ." Thus wages, hours of labors, and working conditions are to be so adjusted as to effectuate the purposes of the act; and prices are to be so regulated as to *stabilize* wages, working conditions, and hours of labor which have been or are to be fixed under the labor provisions. The two are so woven together as to render the probability plain enough that uniform prices, in the opinion of Congress, could not be fairly fixed or effectively regulated, without also regulating these elements of labor which enter so largely into the cost of production.

These two sets of requirements are not like a collection of bricks, some of which may be taken away without disturbing the others, but rather are like the interwoven threads constituting the warp and woof of a fabric, one set of which cannot be removed without fatal consequences to the whole. Paraphrasing the words of this Court in *Butts v. Merchants Transportation Co.*, 230 U.S. 126, 133, we inquire — What authority has this Court, by construction, to convert the manifest purpose of Congress to regulate production by the mutual operation and interaction of fixed wages and fixed prices into a purpose to regulate the subject by the operation of the latter alone? Are we at liberty to say from the fact that Congress has adopted an entire integrated system that it probably would have enacted a doubtfully-effective fraction of the system? The words of the concurring opinion in the *Schechter* case, 295 U.S. at pages 554–55, are pertinent in reply. "To take from this code the provisions as to wages and the hours of labor is to destroy it altogether . . . . Wages and the hours of labor are essential features of the plan, its very bone and sinew. There is no opportunity in such circumstances for the severance of the infected parts in the hope of saving the remainder." The conclusion is unavoidable that the price-fixing provisions of the code are so related to and dependent upon the labor provisions as conditions, considerations or compensations, as to make it clearly probable that the latter being held bad, the former would not have been passed. The fall of the latter, therefore, carries down with it the former.

. . . .

It is so ordered.

Separate opinion of Mr. Chief Justice Hughes.

. . . .

Upon what ground, then, can it be said that this plan for the regulation of transactions in interstate commerce in coal is beyond the constitutional power of Congress? The Court reaches that conclusion in the view that the invalidity of the labor provisions requires us to condemn the Act in its entirety. I am unable to concur in that opinion. I think that the express provisions of the Act preclude such a finding of inseparability.

This is admittedly a question of statutory construction; and hence we must search for the intent of Congress. And in seeking that intent we should not fail to give full weight to what Congress itself has said upon the very point. The Act provides (§ 15):

> If any provision of this Act, or the application thereof to any person or circumstances, is held invalid, the remainder of the Act and the application of such provisions to other persons or circumstances shall not be affected thereby.

That is a flat declaration against treating the provisions of the Act as inseparable. It is a declaration which Congress was competent to make. It is a declaration which reverses the presumption of indivisibility and creates an opposite presumption. *Utah Power & Light Co v. Pfost*, 286 U.S. 165, 184.

The above quoted provision does not stand alone. Congress was at pains to make a declaration of similar import with respect to the provisions of the Code (§ 3):

> "No producer shall by reason of his acceptance of the code provided for in section 4 or of the drawback of taxes provided in section 3 of this Act be held to be precluded or estopped from contesting the constitutionality of any provision of said code, or its validity as applicable to such producer."

This provision evidently contemplates, when read with the one first quoted, that a stipulation of the Code may be found to be unconstitutional and yet that its invalidity shall not be regarded as affecting the obligations attaching to the remainder.

I do not think that the question of separability should be determined by trying to imagine what Congress would have done if certain provisions found to be invalid were excised. That, if taken broadly, would lead us into a realm of pure speculation. Who can tell amid the host of divisive influences playing upon the legislative body what its reaction would have been to a particular excision required by a finding of invalidity? The question does not call for speculation of that sort but rather for an inquiry whether the provisions are inseparable by virtue of inherent character. That is, when Congress states that the provisions of the Act are not inseparable and that the invalidity of any provision shall not affect others, we should not hold that the provisions are inseparable unless their nature, by reason of an inextricable tie, demands that conclusion.

. . . .

MR. JUSTICE CARDOZO (dissenting).

. . . .

Undoubtedly the rules as to labor relations are important provisions of the statute. Undoubtedly the lawmakers were anxious that provisions so important should have the force of law. But they announced with all the directness possible for words that they would keep what they could have if they could not have the whole. Stabilizing prices would go a long way toward stabilizing labor relations by giving the producers capacity to pay a living wage. To hold otherwise is to ignore the whole history of mining. All in vain have official committees inquired and reported in thousands of printed pages if this lesson has been lost. In the face of that history the Court is now holding that Congress would have been unwilling to give the force of law to the provisions of Part II, which were to take effect at once, if it could not have Part III, which in the absence of agreement between the employers and the miners would never take effect at all.

. . . .

NOTES AND QUESTIONS

1. Why does the Court discuss a presumption against severability in *Carter* but not in *Jackson*? Is this because the Court wanted to come out the other way on the issue of severability? Should there be such a presumption?

2. The Congress decided to deal with the problem of potential partial unconstitutionality of the Act at issue by inserting a severability clause. What real effect does such a clause have? What good does the clause do in reversing the presumption and burden of proof regarding severability when the test is still congressional intent? Indeed, why is the severability clause rebuttable? Should not such a clause conclusively determine the legislative intent? In his separate opinion, Chief Justice Hughes states that "the question of severability should [not] be determined by trying to imagine what Congress would have done if certain provisions found to be invalid were excised." Why not?

3. Is there a point at which what is left of an act after severance is not enough to stand on its own? How is this point to be determined? Is it significant that the Act does not speak of "labor provisions," but of "stabilization"? How important is the fact that the labor-regulating and price-fixing provisions are set out in the same section? What would Congress do if the provisions here were held severable?

4. An article by Robert L. Stern, *Separability and Separability Clauses in the Supreme Court*, 51 HARV. L. REV. 76 (1937), examines the Court's behavior and indicates that a presumption of severability or inseverability has not been controlling. He found cases were decided on the basis of how the Court viewed the constitutional claim and the legislative intent. With the wholesale use of severability clauses by legislatures in the vast majority of enactments, he feels such a presumption has become even less desirable. He suggests that the legislature's use of severability clauses would be more effective if the clauses were made specific by precisely indicating which provisions can be severed without affecting the overall legislative intent. What problems do you foresee such severability provisions would create? Would the legislative specifications actually bind the Court?

5. The decision in *Immigration & Nat'n Serv. v. Chadha*, 462 U.S. 919 (1983), that declared legislative veto provisions unconstitutional has generated renewed examination of the severability issue, since over 200 existing federal statutes were subject to such veto provisions. The one House veto provision of the Immigration and Nationality Act gave either House the power to override a decision of the Attorney General to suspend deportation proceedings on any given alien. The Act also contained a severability clause.

In determining the severability of the veto provision from the remainder of the statute, the Court utilized the *Champlin Refining* severability test it had outlined in *Jackson*. It did so, however, by indulging in a two-part test that was not applied in *Champlin. Champlin Refining* held a presumption of severability existed if it was not evident otherwise that Congress would not have intended severability. In *Chadha*, for similar reasons, the Court presumed severability. It stated that it need not "embark on that elusive inquiry" since Congress, by incorporating a severability clause in the Act, had answered that question, and a presumption of severability existed.

The Court examined the historical background of congressional handling of these matters and determined that the presumption could not be overcome. Thus, even though Congress had shown reluctance to delegate "final" authority over the cancellation of deportations and had often handled these matters by "private" legislative acts, these actions were not sufficient to rebut the presumption raised by the severability clause.

In the second part of its analysis, the *Chadha* Court reinforced its initial presumption that the veto provision was severable by asking whether that which remained was "fully operative as a law." The Court answered by perfunctorily stating that the Act was fully operative as workable administrative machinery absent the veto provision.

Did the Court create an additional presumption in the second question it asked, one that was absent in *Champlin Refining?* If so, will this lead more often to a finding of severability? Is this inquiry any different than that which the Court addressed in the *Carter Coal* case?

6. Because of the potentially great impact of *Chadha*, Congress examined

alternatives to its veto power to control its delegation of authority to the Executive Branch. *See* The Supreme Court in *INS v. Chadha* and Its Implications for Congressional Oversight and Agency Rulemaking, Hearings Before the Subcomm. on Administrative Law & Governmental Relations of the House Comm. on the Judiciary, 98th Cong., 1st Sess. 24-102 (1983). No specific alternatives ultimately evolved, however.

STILP v. COMMONWEALTH
905 A.2d 918 (Pa. 2006)

[Editors' Note: In 2005, the Pennsylvania Legislature exacted a comprehensive pay raise for all three branches of state government (Act 44 of 2005). Because the state constitution prohibited a *legislative* pay raise from taking effect during the current term of the Legislature, the statute provided for "unvouchered expenses" in the exact amount of the legislative pay raise that would take effect after the next election. A political firestorm ensued, and later in 2005, the Legislature passed an act repealing Act 44 in its entirety. *But*, the state constitution also prohibited a *decrease* in judicial pay. Therefore, the original *legislative* "pay raise" was arguably unconstitutional, but the later repeal of the *judicial* pay raise was also arguably unconstitutional. A taxpayer, Gene Stilp, filed an action challenging the original Act 44, which contained an inseverability clause.]

. . . .

F. Nonseverability Provision

- 1 -

The final interpretive issue, arising by virtue of our finding above that the unvouchered expense allowance in Act 44 is unconstitutional, is the legal effect of the nonseverability provision included in the Act. That the Act contains a nonseverability provision is remarkable in and of itself, because the general rule set forth in Section 1925 ("Constitutional construction of statutes") of the Statutory Construction Act, 1 Pa.C.S. § 1501 *et seq.*, establishes a presumption of severability:

> The provisions of every statute shall be severable. If any provision of any statute or the application thereof to any person or circumstance is held invalid, the remainder of the statute, and the application of such provision to other persons or circumstances, shall not be affected thereby, unless the court finds that the valid provisions of the statute are so essentially and inseparably connected with, and so depend upon, the void provision or application, that it cannot be presumed the General Assembly would have enacted the remaining valid provisions without the void one; or unless the court finds that the remaining valid provisions, standing alone, are incomplete and are incapable of being executed in accordance with the legislative intent.

1 Pa.C.S. § 1925. This Court has deemed the presumption in Section 1925 so fundamental to our task, when confronted with a finding that a provision of a statute is invalid, that we have invoked Section 1925 even where the parties failed to argue severability. *See, e.g., Mockaitis*, 834 A.2d at 502. In addition to applying to "every" statute and employing mandatory terms, Section 1925 is notable because it is not merely boilerplate. Thus, Section 1925 does not mandate severance in all instances, but only in those circumstances where a statute can stand alone absent the invalid provision. Section 1925 sets forth a specific, cogent standard, one which both emphasizes the logical and essential interrelationship of the void and valid provisions, and also recognizes the essential role of the Judiciary in undertaking the required analysis.

Though now embodied in a legislative command, the principle of severability, and the standard by which severability is measured, has its roots in the common law. For example, in *Rothermel v. Meyerle*, 136 Pa. 250, 20 A. 583 (1890), this Court stated the following standard:

> A statute may be void only so far as its provisions are repugnant to the constitution. One provision may be void, and this will not affect other provisions of the statute. If the part which is unconstitutional in its operation, is independent of, and readily separable from, that which is constitutional, so that the latter may stand by itself, as the reasonable and proper expression of the legislative rule, it may be sustained as such; but, if the part which is void is vital to the whole, or the other provisions are so dependent upon it, and so connected with it, that it may be presumed the legislature would not have passed one without the other, the whole statute is void.

Id. at 587–88. The standard now contained in Section 1925 merely codified this settled decisional law.

The practice of severing and striking only the unconstitutional provision of a larger legislative enactment, in instances where the legislation is otherwise self-sustaining and valid, has its origins in principles of jurisprudential restraint. *See generally* John Copeland Nagle, *Severability*, 72 N.C. L. Rev. 203, 212–18 (1993); *accord* Fred Kameny, *Are Inseverability Clauses Constitutional?*, 68 Alb. L. Rev. 997, 1002 (2005). The development of the doctrine has been described as follows:

> The *Champlin*[38] test has its origins in Chief Justice Lemuel Shaw's 1854 opinion for the Supreme Judicial Court of Massachusetts in *Warren v. Mayor & Aldermen of Charlestown*, [68 Mass. 84, 2 Gray 84 (1854),] the first case holding that an unconstitutional statutory provision rendered an entire statute invalid. Prior to *Warren*, the severability of statutory provisions was usually assumed. In the earliest cases questioning the constitutionality of a federal statute, the United States Supreme Court gave no indication that the unconstitutionality of one provision — or its application — would render an entire statute invalid. In *Marbury v. Madison*, [5 U.S. 137, 1 Cranch 137, 2 L. Ed. 60 (1803),] for example, the unconstitutionality of section 13 of the Judiciary Act of 1789 did not render the entire Act invalid. As Chief Justice Marshall later wrote, "If any part of the act be unconstitutional, the provisions of that part may be disregarded while full effect will be given to such as are not repugnant to the constitution of the United States . . . ." As a result of this lack of guidance, some courts invalidated statutes "so far as" they were unconstitutional, while a few courts suggested that severability depended on the ability of the remaining provisions to function absent the unconstitutional provision.

Then came *Warren*. . . . Chief Justice Shaw agreed with those courts that had found that a statute could be constitutional in part and unconstitutional in part. But he quickly added:

> [T]his must be taken with this limitation, that the parts, so held respectively constitutional and unconstitutional, must be wholly independent of each other. But if they are so mutually connected with and dependent on each other, as

---

[38] *Champlin Refining Co. v. Corporation Commission*, 286 U.S. 210, 234, 52 S. Ct. 559, 564–65, 76 L. Ed. 1062 (1932), *overruled by Phillips Petroleum Co. v. Oklahoma*, 340 U.S. 190, 71 S. Ct. 221, 95 L. Ed. 204 (1950). Under *Champlin*, the severability of a statute depends upon two factors: legislative intent, and whether the statute can function without the offending provision. This Court has employed the same standard. *See, e.g.*, *Saulsbury v. Bethlehem Steel Co.*, 413 Pa. 316, 196 A.2d 664, 667 (1964). *Cf. Rutenberg v. City of Philadelphia*, 329 Pa. 26, 196 A. 73, 79 (1938) ("The test of severability may be stated in simple terms as follows: After the invalid portion of the act has been stricken out, whether that which remains is self-sustaining and is capable of separate enforcement without regard to that portion of the statute which has been cast aside. If this be true the statute should be sustained to the extent of that which remains.").

conditions, considerations or compensations for each other, as to warrant a belief that the legislature intended them as a whole, and that, if all could not be carried into effect, the legislature would not pass the residue independently, and some parts are unconstitutional, all the provisions which are thus dependent, conditional or connected, must fall with them.

Nagle, *Severability*, 72 N.C. L. REV. at 212–13 (citing *Warren*, 68 Mass. 84, 2 Gray at 99) (footnotes omitted).

No doubt because the severance principle has its roots in a jurisprudential doctrine (and the standard itself reflects the experience of the common law), the courts have not treated legislative declarations that a statute is severable, or nonseverable, as "inexorable commands," but rather have viewed such statements as providing a rule of construction.

Nor is the fact that the ordinances contain a severability clause controlling. As stated by Mr. Justice Brandeis in *Dorchy v. State of Kansas*, 264 U.S. 286, 44 S. Ct. 323, 68 L. Ed. 686 (1924), the clause "provides a rule of construction . . . in determining [legislative] intent. But it is an aid merely; not an inexorable command." As ruled by this Court in *Pennsylvania R.R. Co. v. Schwartz*, 391 Pa. 619, 139 A.2d 525 (1958), while a severability clause must be given due weight, it is not to be accepted judicially as conclusive if the unity of the general legislative scheme is completely destroyed by a severance of its provisions.

Saulsbury v. Bethlehem Steel Co., 413 Pa. 316, 196 A.2d 664, 667 (1964) (additional U.S. Supreme Court citations omitted). *See also Pennsylvania Fed'n of Teachers v. School Dist. of Philadelphia*, 506 Pa. 196, 484 A.2d 751, 754 (1984) (holding nonseverability provision inapplicable where Act is unconstitutional only as applied to persons who were members of retirement system at time of the enactment, but constitutional as applied to those who became members of the retirement system subsequent to the effective date of the Act); *accord Louk v. Cormier*, 218 W. Va. 81, 622 S.E.2d 788, 803 (2005) ("[W]e now hold that a non-severability provision contained in a legislative enactment is construed as merely a presumption that the Legislature intended the entire enactment to be invalid if one of the statutes in the legislation is found unconstitutional. When a non-severability provision is appended to a legislative enactment and this Court invalidates a statute contained in the enactment, we will apply severability principles of statutory construction to determine whether the non-severability provision will be given full force and effect."); *Stiens v. Fire and Police Pension Assoc.*, 684 P.2d 180, 184–85 (Colo. 1984) (nonseverability clause, like severability clause "is not conclusive as to legislative intent" but "gives rise only to a presumption that, if the unconstitutional parts of an act were eliminated, the legislature would not have been satisfied with what remained"; ultimately holding that "the presumption of unseverability has been overcome"); *Legislative Research Commission v. Brown*, 664 S.W.2d 907, 919–20 (Ky. 1984) (declining to enforce nonseverability clause because to do so would violate separation of powers, in that it would "unconstitutionally limit[ ] and interfere[ ] with the governor's mandated duties"); *Biszko v. RIHT Fin. Corp.*, 758 F.2d 769, 773 (1st Cir. 1985) ("Although . . . a non-severability clause cannot ultimately bind a court, it establishes a presumption of non-severability.").

The willingness of courts to look behind legislative provisions concerning severability in appropriate cases apparently derives, at least in part, from a historical uneasiness with the notion that legislatures could dictate the conclusion of what had long been a judicial inquiry:

The first severability clauses appeared late in the nineteenth century, and they became much more common around 1910. These clauses were a reaction to those courts that were aggressively holding statutes nonseverable. The earliest legislative statements that statutory provisions should be construed as being severable were taken at face value by the courts. But courts soon soured on express legislative statements concerning severability. State courts and commentators refused to accept the proposition that legislatures had authority to dictate to the courts the appropriate decision regarding severability.

Nagle, *Severability*, 72 N.C. L. REV. at 222 (footnotes omitted). The severability standard adopted in Section 1925's presumption does not pose the historical issue Nagle describes because it is not a boilerplate directive. Instead, Section 1925 adopts the historical judicial standard which governed severability inquiries, and then statutorily mandates the Judiciary to make the ultimate determination of severability.

We have no doubt that the unconstitutional legislative unvouchered expense provision is severable from the remaining, valid (although now repealed) provisions of Act 44, under the substantive standard set forth in Section 1925. In Act 44, the General Assembly adopted a comprehensive new compensation system governing the three branches of government, a system which employed formulas tying the compensation paid Pennsylvania officials to that provided for corresponding federal officials, albeit in a stepped-down fashion. Insofar as the Act adopted the new compensation system for the legislative branch, that system could go into effect, without violating Article II, Section 8 of the Pennsylvania Constitution, with the commencement of the next term of office for each legislative seat. A major and new perceived benefit of this system of compensation consisted in the fact that, by tying salary to the federal structure, the issue of raising official compensation would be de-politicized. This new system of compensation, however, was not "essentially and inseparably connected with" the legislative unvouchered expense provision, much less did it "depend upon" that provision. *See* 1 Pa.C.S. § 1925. The remaining valid (but repealed) provisions are easily capable of being executed in accordance with the General Assembly's manifest intention of providing a new and permanent compensation structure for officials in all three branches of government. In contrast, the legislative unvouchered expense provision had nothing to do with the new, comprehensive compensation system. Instead, that provision sought to avoid a constitutional limitation particular only to the legislative branch, which cannot increase its own salary or mileage during the same legislative term in which such a law is passed. Whatever may have been the motivation behind the unvouchered expense provision, it is clear that the provision was not integral to the workings of the comprehensive system of governmental compensation otherwise adopted in Act 44.

But, of course, the issue is not so simple because the General Assembly included in Act 44 a boilerplate nonseverability provision, which reads as follows:

> The provisions of this act are nonseverable. If any provision of this act or its application to any person or circumstance is held invalid, the remaining provisions or applications of this act are void.

Act 44, § 6. This nonseverability provision is unlike the general provision ensconced in Section 1925 in that it sets forth no standard for measuring nonseverability, but instead, simply purports to dictate to the courts how they must decide severability. If this nonseverability clause is not controlling, the unvouchered expense provision, as noted, can be severed from the remaining valid provisions of Act 44. If the nonseverability clause is controlling, however, and validly operates to dictate to the Judiciary the effect of a finding of unconstitutionality as to any individual provision in Act 44, then Act 44 would of necessity be invalidated in its entirety. In the latter instance, this Court would have to proceed to the Judges' claim that invalidation of the entirety of Act 44, and the attendant reduction of judicial compensation that action would entail, would violate Article V, Section 16(a) of the Pennsylvania Constitution.

- 2 -

While maintaining his primary argument that Act 44 violates the procedural provisions of Article III of the Pennsylvania Constitution, and therefore, the severability issue is moot, Stilp argues, in the alternative, that the nonseverability provision must be deemed to have no valid legal effect. Stilp submits that the General Assembly obviously included the nonseverability clause for the sole purpose of coercing the courts not to strike Act 44's unconstitutional legislative unvouched expense provision: "The General Assembly shrewdly calculated that the courts would not want to jeopardize their own raise, but would instead look the other way . . . ." Stilp's Brief at 26. Stilp argues that the General Assembly's attempt to influence and control judicial consideration of the constitutionality of Act 44 and its individual provisions violates the separation of powers doctrine. Therefore, according to Stilp, if this Court were to find the unvouched expense provision unconstitutional but the rest of the Act valid, the provision should be severed.

. . . .

- 3 -

The issue of the enforceability of the nonseverability provision is not a question of legislative intent; the provision itself makes clear the legislative desire that no court invalidate a single provision of the Act without invalidating the whole. The question is whether and when the General Assembly may dictate the effect of a judicial finding that a provision in an act is "invalid." There is no controlling authority on this point. The *Gmerek* OISA, cited by both legislative appellees, was not a majority opinion and, in any event, merely would have applied the nonseverability provision without inquiring into its legitimacy. *See Gmerek*, 807 A.2d at 819 ("Given the explicit dictates of Section 1311(b) of the Act [regarding nonseverability], the entire Act must be declared invalid."). Likewise, although this Court in *Pennsylvania Fed'n of Teachers, supra*, declined to enforce a nonseverability provision, we did not discuss whether or when such provisions should be deemed binding. Moreover, the only Pennsylvania state appellate decision this Court has found which discusses a constitutional challenge to a nonseverability clause is *Kennedy, supra*, and that case is unhelpful to the present inquiry.

Kennedy involved comprehensive public official compensation legislation which was similar to Act 44 in that it increased the salaries of legislators, the Judiciary, and high-ranking executive officials, and contained a nonseverability provision worded identically to the nonseverability provision later found in Act 44. *See* The Act of July 3, 1987, P.L. 193, No. 28. The *pro se* appellants in *Kennedy*, a member of the Pennsylvania House and two private citizens, raised several claims, including a multi-pronged challenge to the nonseverability clause. The appellants challenged the provision on grounds that it: gave the Judiciary an interest in the statute because it linked an increase in judicial compensation to unvouched expense allowances; effectively denied the appellants their right to legal representation because no attorney would likely represent a party challenging an act that included a raise in judicial compensation for fear of alienating the Judiciary; violated the spirit of Article III, Section 27 of the Pennsylvania Constitution; and was contrary to public policy, which presumes severability. The appellants did not explicitly claim, however, that the provision violated the separation of powers.

The Commonwealth Court *en banc* panel in *Kennedy* first held that the appellants were not denied access to the courts because they had in fact received judicial consideration of their claims. The *en banc* panel then dismissed the appellants' public policy argument as unripe, noting that nonseverability was an issue only if another provision of the act was found to be unconstitutional, and that condition precedent was not satisfied because the *en banc* panel upheld the unvouched expense provision which had been challenged. Finally, the *en banc* panel found the Article III, Section 27

challenge moot. The *Kennedy* court did not address the appellants' first argument —
i.e., that the nonseverability clause improperly tied the increase in judicial compensation
to the legislative unvouchered expense provision — the claim that is most like the
separation of powers issue before the Court in the case *sub judice. Kennedy*, 546 A.2d
at 738–39.

By definition, a legislative provision concerning severability or nonseverability exists
only in anticipation of judicial review. In the ordinary case, a standard-less nonseverability clause is superfluous since the Legislature, once confronted with a judicial ruling
that a provision of a statute is unconstitutional, may always revisit the subject anew,
irrespective of whether the court deemed the unconstitutional provision severable. Such
a practice leaves it to the legislative body to assess whether the statute, as affected by
the judicial interpretation, is acceptable. Indeed, this practical fact may account for the
relative rarity of nonseverability provisions. Having said this, for purposes of this
appeal, we may assume that, as a general matter, nonseverability provisions are
constitutionally proper. There may be reasons why the provisions of a particular statute
essentially inter-relate, but in ways which are not apparent from a consideration of the
bare language of the statute as governed by the settled severance standard set forth in
Section 1925 of the Statutory Construction Act. In such an instance, the General
Assembly may determine that it is necessary to make clear that a taint in any part of the
statute ruins the whole. *See generally* Kameny, *Are Inseverability Clauses Constitutional?*, 68 ALB. L. REV. at 1000 (arguing that severability determinations are "guess-
work by definition, and it is understandable for legislators to fear that the courts might
guess wrong."). Or, there may be purely political reasons for such an interpretive
directive, arising from the concerns and compromises which animate the legislative
process. *See* Michael D. Shumsky, *Severability, Inseverability, and the Rule of Law*, 41
HARV. J. ON LEGIS. 227, 267–68 (2004) ("When [a legislature] includes an inseverability
clause in constitutionally questionable legislation, it does so in order to insulate a key
legislative deal from judicial interference."); Israel E. Friedman, *Comment, Inseverability Clauses in Statutes*, 64 U. CHI. L. REV. 903, 914 (1997) ("[I]nseverability clauses
serve a key function of preserving legislative compromise;" they "bind[ ] the benefits and
concessions that constitute the deal into an interdependent whole."). In an instance
involving such compromise, the General Assembly may determine, the court's application of the logical standard of essential interconnection set forth in Section 1925 might
undo the compromise; a nonseverability provision, in such an instance, may be essential
to securing the support necessary to enact the legislation in the first place. Once again,
this is a concern that would not necessarily be apparent to a court analyzing the bare
language of the statute.

On the other hand, this Court is not naive, and we recognize that a nonseverability
provision is a legislative practice that, in certain instances, may be employed as a sword
against the Judiciary or the Executive, rather than as a shield to ensure preservation of
a legislative scheme or compromise.[46] Where the provision appears to be aimed at
securing a coercive effect upon the Judiciary, it necessarily implicates the separation of
powers. Although there is little authority or commentary concerning nonseverability
provisions (indeed, what commentary there is notes the lack of authority), those

---

[46] A nonseverability provision could also be employed, in conjunction with a relatively minor but
constitutionally suspect provision in a bill, in the hope that the courts will strike down legislation that the
legislative body did not truly support, but passed for reasons of political expediency. *See generally* Kameny,
Are Inseverability Clauses Constitutional?, 68 ALB. L. REV. at 1001 ("The other questionable use of
inseverability, a sort of poison-pill device . . . , involves an attempt to sabotage a statute. The legislators
might assume that the statute contains some unconstitutional provision already . . . , or they might insert
both an inseverability clause and a new provision whose unconstitutionality was fairly plain . . . . Such a
clause can serve a dual purpose: it can ensure invalidation of the law, and at the same time legislators who
oppose the bill in principle, but whose constituents favor it, can feel comfortable voting for the bill and gaining
political advantage without concern that the bill might survive judicial scrutiny.").

authorities to consider the matter have distinguished (and rightfully so, in this Court's view) between appropriate uses of nonseverability clauses and uses which are more problematic in light of separation of powers concerns. Kameny, whose point of departure was the Commonwealth Court's opinion in *Kennedy*, described the compensation statute and nonseverability provision at issue there as follows:

> Pay increases for government employees are never politically popular, but this bill seemed unremarkable — although one could question the propriety of having the increase in expense allowances take effect immediately, so that the legislators were in effect voting an increase for themselves. Yet the truly extraordinary feature of the bill was not the hint of self-dealing, but rather the way in which the legislators sought to clothe the self-dealing in protective garb. For the bill contained the following language: "The provisions of this act are nonseverable. If any provision of this act or its application to any person or circumstance is held invalid, the remaining provisions or applications of this act are void." The implications of this clause are inescapable: there was some question as to the constitutionality of having legislators increase their own expense allowances; the legislature foresaw that a constitutional challenge was possible; and the inseverability clause ensured that if a court struck down the increase in legislators' expense allowances, the increase in judicial salaries would be sacrificed as well.

Kameny, *Are Inseverability Clauses Constitutional?*, 68 ALB. L. REV. at 997–98. Kameny describes this use of a nonseverability provision as "serv[ing] an in terrorem function, as the legislature attempts to guard against judicial review altogether by making the price of invalidation too great." *Id.* at 1001. This sort of practice, he continues, is "especially troubling" because it "represent[s] an attempt by the legislature to prevent the judiciary from exercising a power that rightly belongs to it . . . . These clauses, in other words, amount to coercive threats." *Id. See also* Friedman, *Inseverability Clauses in Statutes*, 64 U. CHI. L. REV. at 919–20 (although nonseverability clauses should generally be honored and should be shown more deference than severability clauses, "courts' deference to the plain meaning of inseverability clauses should not be unlimited. If giving effect to an inseverability clause would result in overstepping the bounds of legislative or judicial authority, then the clause should not be followed."). *Accord Brown*, 664 S.W.2d at 920 (declining to enforce nonseverability clause because "[t]he restriction placed on the executive by [the nonseverability clause] effectively and unconstitutionally limits and interferes with the governor's mandated duties.").

As we have noted above, this Court has never deemed nonseverability clauses to be controlling in all circumstances. And, in the case *sub judice*, given the separation of powers concerns that arise from inclusion of the clause in a statute such as Act 44, which includes compensation provisions for the Judiciary, we hold that the clause is ineffective and cannot be permitted to dictate our analysis. Although we have confidence that no member of the Pennsylvania Judiciary in a position to pass upon the statute in fact would allow the effect of the clause to influence the analysis of any constitutional challenge, the fact remains that the clause, if deemed effective, acts as an incentive to engage in a less exacting constitutional inquiry. As the *Jorgensen* Court noted, in discussing the importance of the separation of powers, "[r]etribution against the courts for unpopular decisions is an ongoing threat." 811 N.E.2d at 660. In this case, the potential "retribution" is built into the statute itself in the would-be automatic effect of the nonseverability provision. It is improper, to say the least, for the Legislature to put a coequal branch of government in such a position. Whether this effect is the sole or primary purpose of the nonseverability provision, and whether it is entirely deliberate, is of less importance than the fact of its existence in such legislation, and the obvious influence such a provision might be designed to exert over the independent exercise of the judicial function. In a case such as this, we conclude, enforcement of the clause would intrude upon the independence of the Judiciary and impair the judicial function.[48] Accordingly, we will not enforce the clause but instead we will effectuate our independent judgment concerning severability. Therefore, and consistently with our severability analysis above, we hold that the unvouchered expense provision, which plainly and palpably violates Article II, Section 8 of the Pennsylvania Constitution, is severable from the otherwise-constitutionally valid remainder of Act 44.

NOTES AND QUESTIONS

1. The court's decision not to enforce the nonseverability clause had the effect of upholding the original *judicial* pay raise, on the ground that the state constitution barred a reduction in judicial pay once it has taken effect, but permitting the later repeal to cancel the legislative and executive pay raises. This created a new political firestorm with its focus on the elected Pennsylvania judiciary.

2. In the absence of the kind of legislative coercion noted by the court (certainly an unusual circumstance), should inseverability clauses be routinely enforced?

D. RETROACTIVE APPLICATION OF STATUTES: THE INTERPRETATION QUESTION

LANDGRAF v. USI FILM PRODUCTS
511 U.S. 244 (1994)

JUSTICE STEVENS delivered the opinion of the Court.

The Civil Rights Act of 1991 (1991 Act or Act) creates a right to recover compensatory and punitive damages for certain violations of Title VII of the Civil Rights Act of 1964 . . . . The Act further provides that any party may demand a trial by jury if such damages are sought. We granted certiorari to decide whether these provisions apply to a Title VII case that was pending on appeal when the statute was enacted. We hold that they do not.

I

From September 4, 1984, through January 17, 1986, petitioner Barbara Landgraf was employed in the USI Film Products (USI) plant in Tyler, Texas. She worked the 11 p.m. to 7 a.m. shift operating a machine that produced plastic bags. A fellow employee named John Williams repeatedly harassed her with inappropriate remarks and physical contact. Petitioner's complaints to her immediate supervisor brought her no relief, but when she reported the incidents to the personnel manager, he conducted an investigation, reprimanded Williams, and transferred him to another department. Four days later petitioner quit her job.

. . . .

On July 21, 1989, petitioner commenced this action against USI, its corporate owner, and that company's successor in interest. After a bench trial, the District Court found that Williams had sexually harassed petitioner causing her to suffer mental anguish. However, the court concluded that she had not been constructively discharged. The court said:

---

[48] We find further support for our conclusion in the fact that none of the arguments in favor of enforcing this nonseverability provision offer any persuasive explanation of how it served some benign legislative purpose other than to attempt to influence and burden judicial review. For example, Speaker Perzel suggests that the provision merely shows that the General Assembly sought to ensure a "complete review and overhaul of public officials' compensation" and not to tackle the task in "piecemeal fashion." But the unvouchered expense provision obviously was not necessary to the comprehensive overhaul itself; that was already complete. Moreover, it is notable that here, unlike in *PAGE*, for example, the General Assembly included a global and boilerplate nonseverability provision, and not a partial, targeted, or specific one.

"Although the harassment was serious enough to establish that a hostile work environment existed for Landgraf, it was not so severe that a reasonable person would have felt compelled to resign. This is particularly true in light of the fact that at the time Landgraf resigned from her job, USI had taken steps . . . to eliminate the hostile working environment arising from the sexual harassment. Landgraf voluntarily resigned from her employment with USI for reasons unrelated to the sexual harassment in question." App. To Pet. for Cert. B-3-4.

Because the court found that petitioner's employment was not terminated in violation of Title VII, she was not entitled to equitable relief, and because Title VII did not then authorize any other form of relief, the court dismissed her complaint.

On November 21, 1991, while petitioner's appeal was pending, the President signed into law the Civil Rights Act of 1991. The Court of Appeals rejected petitioner's argument that her case should be remanded for a jury trial on damages pursuant to the 1991 Act. Its decision not to remand rested on the premise that "a court must 'apply the law in effect at the time it renders its decision, unless doing so would result in manifest injustice or there is statutory direction or legislative history to the contrary.' *Bradley [v. School Bd. of Richmond*, 416 U.S. 696, 711, 94 S. Ct. 2006, 2016, 40 L. Ed. 2d 476 (1974).]" 968 F.2d 427, 432 (CA5 1992). Commenting first on the provision for a jury trial in § 102(c), the court stated that requiring the defendant "to retry this case because of a statutory change enacted after the trial was completed would be an injustice and a waste of judicial resources. We apply procedural rules to pending cases, but we do not invalidate procedures followed before the new rule was adopted." *Id.*, at 432–433. The court then characterized the provision for compensatory and punitive damages in § 102 as "a seachange in employer liability for Title VII violations" and concluded that it would be unjust to apply this kind of additional and unforeseeable obligation to conduct occurring before the effective date of the Act. *Id.*, at 433. Finding no clear error in the District Court's factual findings, the Court of Appeals affirmed the judgement for respondents.

. . . .

We . . . assume, *arguendo*, that if the same conduct were to occur today, petitioner would be entitled to a jury trial and that the jury might find that she was constructively discharged, or that her mental aguish or other injuries would support an award of damages against her former employer. Thus, the controlling question is whether the Court of Appeals should have applied the law in effect at the time the discriminatory conduct occurred, or at the time of its decision in July 1992.

II

Petitioner's primary submission is that the text of the 1991 Act requires that it be applied to cases pending on its enactment. Her argument, if accepted, would make the entire Act (with two narrow exceptions) applicable to conduct that occurred, and to cases that were filed, before the Act's effective date. Although only § 102 is at issue in this case, we preface our analysis with a brief description of the scope of the 1991 Act.

The 1991 Act is in large part a response to a series of decisions of this Court interpreting the Civil Rights Acts of 1866 and 1964. Section 3(4), 105 Stat. 1071, note following 42 U.S.C. § 1981, expressly identifies as one of the Act's purposes "to respond to recent decisions of the Supreme Court by expanding the scope of relevant civil rights statutes in order to provide adequate protection to victims of discrimination." . . .

Other sections of the Act were obviously drafted with "recent decisions of the Supreme Court" in mind . . . .

A number of important provisions in the Act, however, were not responses to Supreme Court decisions . . . . Among the provisions that did not directly respond to any Supreme Court decision is the one at issue in this case, § 102.

. . . .

Before the enactment of the 1991 Act, Title VII afforded only "equitable" remedies. The primary form of monetary relief available was backpay. Title VII's backpay remedy, modeled on that of the National Labor Relations Act, 29 U.S.C. § 160(c), is a "make-whole" remedy that resembles compensatory damages in some respects . . . . However, the new compensatory damages provision of the 1991 Act is "in addition to," and does not replace or duplicate, the backpay remedy allowed under prior law. Indeed, to prevent double recovery, the 1991 Act provides that compensatory damages "shall not include backpay, interest on backpay, or any other type of relief authorized under section 706(g) of the Civil Rights Act of 1964." § 102(b)(2).

Section 102 significantly expands the monetary relief potentially available to plaintiffs who would have been entitled to backpay under prior law . . . .

Section 102 also allows monetary relief for some forms of workplace discrimination that would not previously have justified *any* relief under Title VII. As this case illustrates, even if unlawful discrimination was proved, under prior law a Title VII plaintiff could not recover monetary relief unless the discrimination was also found to have some concrete effect on the plaintiff's employment status, such as a denied promotion, a differential in compensation, or termination . . . .

In 1990, a comprehensive civil rights bill passed both Houses of Congress. Although similar to the 1991 Act in many other respects, the 1990 bill differed in that it contained language expressly calling for application of many of its provisions, including the section providing for damages in cases of intentional employment discrimination, to cases rising before its (expected) enactment. The President vetoed the 1990 legislation, however, citing the bill's "unfair retroactivity rules" as one reason for his disapproval. Congress narrowly failed to override the veto. *See* 136 Cong. Rec. S16589 (Oct. 24, 1990) (66 to 34 Senate vote in favor of override).

The absence of comparable language in the 1991 Act cannot realistically be attributed to oversight or to unawareness of the retroactivity issue. Rather, it seems likely that one of the compromises that made it possible to enact the 1991 version was an agreement *not* to include the kind of explicit retroactivity command found in the 1990 bill.

The omission of the elaborate retroactivity provision of the 1990 bill — which was by no means the only source of political controversy over that legislation — is not dispositive because it does not tell us precisely where the compromise was struck in the 1991 Act. The Legislature might, for example, have settled in 1991 on a less expansive form of retroactivity that, unlike the 1990 bill, did not reach cases already finally decided. A decision to reach only cases still pending might explain Congress' failure to provide in the 1991 Act, as it had in 1990, that certain sections would apply to proceedings pending on specific preenactment dates. Our first question, then, is whether the statutory text on which petitioner relies manifests an intent that the 1991 Act should be applied to cases that arose and went to trial before its enactment.

III

Petitioner's textual argument relies on three provisions of the 1991 Act: §§ 402(a), 402(b), and 109(c). Section 402(a), the only provision of the Act that speaks directly to the question before us, states:

> "Except as otherwise specifically provided, this Act and the amendments made by this Act shall take effect upon enactment."

That language does not, by itself, resolve the question before us. A statement that a statute will become effective on a certain date does not even arguably suggest that it has any application to conduct that occurred at an earlier date.[10] Petitioner does not argue otherwise. Rather, she contends that the introductory clause of § 402(a) would be superfluous unless it refers to §§ 402(b) and 109(c), which provide for prospective application in limited contexts.

. . . .

According to petitioner, theses two subsections are the "other provisions" contemplated in the first clause of § 402(a), and together create a strong negative inference that all sections of the Act not specifically declared prospective apply to pending cases that arose before November 21, 1991.

Before addressing the particulars of petitioner's argument, we observe that she places extraordinary weight on two comparatively minor and narrow provisions in a long and complex statute. Applying the entire Act to cases arising from preenactment conduct would have important consequences, including the possibility that trials completed before its enactment would need to be retired and the possibility that employers would be liable for punitive damages for conduct antedating the Act's enactment. Purely prospective application, on the other hand, would prolong the life of a remedial scheme, and of judicial constructions of civil rights statutes, that Congress obviously found wanting. Given the high stakes of the retroactivity question, the broad coverage of the statute, and the prominent and specific retroactivity provisions in the 1990 bill, it would be surprising for Congress to have chosen to resolve that question through inferences drawn from two provisions of quite limited effect.

Petitioner, however, invokes the canon that a court should give effect to every provision of a statute and thus avoid redundancy among different provisions . . . . Unless the word "otherwise" in § 402(a) refers to either § 402(b) or § 109(c), she contends, the first five words in § 402(a) are entirely superfluous. Moreover, relying on the canon "[e]xpressio unius est exclusio alterius," see *Leatherman v. Tarrant County Narcotics Intelligence and Coordination Unit*, 507 U.S. 163, 168, 113 S. Ct. 1160, 1163, 122 L. Ed. 2d 517 (1993), petitioner argues that because Congress provided specifically for prospectivity in two places (§§ 109(c) and 402(b)), we should infer that it intended the opposite for the remainder of the statute.

. . . .

It is entirely possible that Congress inserted the "otherwise specifically provided" language not because it understood the "takes effect" clause to establish a rule of retroactivity to which only two "other specific provisions" would be exceptions, but instead to assure that any specific timing provisions in the Act would prevail over the general "take effect on enactment" command. The drafters of a complicated piece of legislation containing more than 50 separate sections may have inserted the "except as otherwise provided" language merely to avoid the risk of an inadvertent conflict in the statute. If the introductory clause of § 402(a) as intended to refer specifically to

---

[10] The history of prior amendments to Title VII suggests that the "effective-upon-enactment" formula would have been an especially inapt way to reach pending cases. When it amended Title VII in the Equal Employment Opportunity Act of 1972, Congress explicitly provided:

"The amendments made by this Act to section 706 of the Civil Rights Act of 1964 shall be applicable with respect to charges pending with the Commission on the date of enactment of this Act and all charges filed thereafter." Pub.L. 92-261, § 14, 86 Stat. 113.

In contrast, in amending Title VII to bar discrimination on the basis of pregnancy in 1978, Congress provided:

"Except as provided in subsection (b), the amendment made by this Act shall be effective on the date of enactment." § 2(a), 92 Stat. 2076. The only Courts of Appeals to consider whether the 1978 amendments applied to pending cases concluded that they did not . . . ."

If we assume that Congress was familiar with those decisions, *cf. Cannon v. University of Chicago*, 441 U.S. 677, 698–699, 99 S. Ct. 1946, 1958–1959, 60 L. Ed. 2d 560 (1979), its choice of language in § 402(a) would imply nonretroactivity.

§§ 402(b), 109(c), or both, it is difficult to understand why the drafters chose the word "otherwise" rather than either or both of the appropriate section numbers.

. . . .

IV

It is not uncommon to find "apparent tension" between different canons of statutory construction. As Professor Llewellyn famously illustrated, many of the traditional canons have equal opposites. In order to resolve the question left open by the 1991 Act, federal courts have labored to reconcile two seemingly contradictory statements found in our decisions concerning the effect of intervening changes in the law. Each statement is framed as a generally applicable rule for interpreting statutes that do not specify their temporal reach. The first is the rule that "a court is to apply the law in effect at the time it renders its decision," *Bradley*, 416 U.S., at 711, 94 S. Ct., at 2016. The second is the axiom that "[r]etroactivity is not favored in the law," and its interpretive corollary that "congressional enactments and administrative rules will not be construed to have retroactive effect unless their language requires this result." *Bowen*, 488 U.S., at 208, 109 S. Ct., at 471.

We have previously noted the "apparent tension" between those expressions. *See Kaiser Aluminum & Chemical Corp. v. Bonjorno*, 494 U.S. 827, 110 S. Ct. 1570, 1577, 108 L. Ed. 2d 842 (1990); *see also Bennett*, 470 U.S., at 639–640, 105 S. Ct., at 1560. We found it unnecessary in *Kaiser* to resolve that seeming conflict "because under either view, where the congressional intent is clear, it governs," and the prejudgement interest statute at issue in that case evinced "clear congressional intent" that it was "not applicable to judgements entered before its effective date." 494 U.S., at 837–838, 110 S. Ct., at 1577. In the case before us today, however, we have concluded that the 1991 Act does not evince any clear expression of intent on § 102's application to cases arising before the Act's enactment. We must, therefore, focus on the apparent tension between the rules we have espoused for handling similar problems in the absence of an instruction from Congress.

We begin by noting that there is no tension between the *holdings* in *Bradley* and *Bowen*, both of which were unanimous decisions. Relying on another unanimous decision — *Thorpe v. Housing Authority of Durham*, 393 U.S. 268, 89 S. Ct. 518, 21 L. Ed. 2d 474 (1969) — we held in *Bradley* that a statute authorizing the award of attorney's fees to successful civil rights plaintiffs applied in a case that was pending on appeal at the time the statute was enacted. *Bowen* held that the Department of Health and Human Services lacked statutory authority to promulgate a rule requiring private hospitals to refund Medicare payments for services rendered before promulgation of the rule. Our opinion in *Bowen* did not purport to overrule *Bradley* or to limit its reach. In this light, we turn to the "apparent tension" between the two canons mindful of another canon of unquestionable vitality, the "maxim not to be disregarded that general expressions, in every opinion, are to be taken in connection with the case in which those expressions are used." *Cohens v. Virginia*, 6 Wheat. 264, 399, 5 L. Ed. 257 (1821).

A

As Justice Scalia has demonstrated, the presumption against retroactive legislation is deeply rooted in our jurisprudence, and embodies a legal doctrine centuries older than our Republic. Elementary considerations of fairness dictate that individuals should have an opportunity to know what the law is and to conform their conduct accordingly; settled expectations should not be lightly disrupted. For that reason, the "principle that the legal effect of conduct should ordinarily be assessed under the law that existed when the conduct took place has timeless and universal appeal." *Kaiser*, 494 U.S., at 855, 110 S. Ct., at 1586 (Scalia, J., concurring). In a free, dynamic society, creativity in both commercial and artistic endeavors is fostered by a rule of law that gives people confidence about the legal consequences of their actions.

It is therefore not surprising that the antiretroactivity principle finds expression in several provisions of our Constitution . . . .

The Constitution's restrictions, of course, are of limited scope. Absent a violation of one of those specific provisions, the potential unfairness of retroactive civil legislation is not a sufficient reason for a court to fail to give a statute its intended scope.[21] Retroactivity provisions often serve entirely benign and legitimate purposes, whether to respond to emergencies, to correct mistakes, to prevent circumvention of a new statute in the interval immediately preceding its passage, or simply to give comprehensive effect to a new law Congress considers salutary. However, a requirement that Congress first make its intention clear helps ensure that Congress itself has determined that the benefits of retroactivity outweigh the potential for disruption or unfairness.

. . . .

The largest category of cases in which we have applied the presumption against statutory retroactivity has involved new provisions affecting contractual or property rights, matters in which predictability and stability are of prime importance. The presumption has not, however, been limited to such cases . . . .

Our statement in *Bowen* that "congressional enactments and administrative rules will not be construed to have retroactive effect unless their language requires this result," 488 U.S., at 208, 109 S. Ct., at 471, was in step with this long line of cases. *Bowen* itself was a paradigmatic case of retroactivity in which a federal agency sought to recoup, under cost limit regulations issued in 1984, funds that had been paid to hospitals for services rendered earlier, *see id.*, at 207, 109 S. Ct., at 471; our search for clear congressional intent authorizing retroactivity was consistent with the approach taken in decisions spanning two centuries.

The presumption against statutory retroactivity had special force in the era in which courts tended to view legislative interference with property and contract rights circumspectly. In this century, legislation has come to supply the dominant means of legal ordering, and circumspection has given way to greater deference to legislative judgements. *See Usery v. Turner Elkhorn Mining Co.*, 428 U.S., at 15–16, 96 S. Ct., at 2892–2893; *Home Building & Loan Assn. v. Blaisdell*, 290 U.S. 398, 436–444, 54 S. Ct. 231, 239–242, 78 L. Ed. 413 (1934). But while the *constitutional* impediments to retroactive civil legislation are now modest, prospectivity remains the appropriate default rule. Because it accords with widely held intuitions about how statutes ordinarily operate, a presumption against retroactivity will generally coincide with legislative and public expectations. Requiring clear intent assures that Congress itself has affirmatively considered the potential unfairness of retroactive application and determined that it is an acceptable price to pay for the countervailing benefits. Such a requirement allocates to Congress responsibility for fundamental policy judgements concerning the proper temporal reach of statutes, and has the additional virtue of giving legislators a predictable background rule against which to legislate.

B

Although we have long embraced a presumption against statutory retroactivity, for just as long we have recognized that, in many situations, a court should "apply the law in effect at the time it renders its decision," *Bradley*, 416 U.S., at 711, 94 S. Ct., at 2016, even though that law was enacted after the events that gave rise to the suit. There is, of course, no conflict between that principle and a *presumption* against retroactivity when the statute in question is unambiguous . . . .

Even absent specific legislative authorization, application of new statutes passed after

---

[21] In some cases, however, the interest in avoiding the adjudication of constitutional questions will counsel against a retroactive application . . . .

the events in suit is unquestionably proper in many situations. When the intervening statute authorizes or affects that propriety of prospective relief, application of the new provision is not retroactive . . . .

We have regularly applied intervening statutes conferring or ousting jurisdiction, whether or not jurisdiction lay when the underlying conduct occurred or when the suit was filed . . . .

Changes in procedural rules may often be applied in suits arising before their enactment without raising concerns about retroactivity . . . .

Petitioner relies principally upon *Bradley v. School Bd. of Richmond*, 416 U.S. 696, 94 S. Ct. 2006, 40 L. Ed. 2d 476 (1974), and *Thorpe v. Housing Authority of Durham*, 393 U.S. 268, 89 S. Ct. 518, 21 L. Ed. 2d 474 (1969), in support of her argument that our ordinary interpretive rules support application of § 102 to her case. In *Thorpe*, we held that an agency circular requiring a local housing authority to give notice of reasons and opportunity to respond before evicting a tenant was applicable to an eviction proceeding commenced before the regulation issued. *Thorpe* shares much with both the "procedural" and "prospective-relief" cases. *See supra*, at 1501–1502. Thus, we noted in *Thorpe* that new hearing procedures did not affect either party's obligations under the lease agreement between the housing authority and the petitioner, 393 U.S., at 279, 89 S. Ct., at 524–525, and, because the tenant had "not yet vacated," we saw no significance in the fact that the housing authority had "decided to evict her before the circular was issued," *id.*, at 283, 89 S. Ct., at 527. The Court in *Thorpe* viewed the new eviction procedures as "essential to remove a serious impediment to the successful protection of constitutional rights." *Ibid. Cf. Youakim v. Miller*, 425 U.S. 231, 237, 96 S. Ct. 1399, 1402–1403, 47 L. Ed. 2d 701 (1976) (*per curiam*) (citing *Thorpe* for propriety of applying new law to avoiding necessity of deciding constitutionality of old one).

Our holding in *Bradley* is similarly compatible with the line of decisions disfavoring "retroactive" application of statutes. In *Bradley*, the District Court had awarded attorney's fees and costs, upon general equitable principles, to parents who had prevailed in an action seeking to desegregate the public schools of Richmond, Virginia. While the case was pending before the Court of Appeals, Congress enacted § 718 of the Education Amendments of 1972, which authorized federal courts to award the prevailing parties in school desegregation cases a reasonable attorney's fee. The Court of Appeals held that the new fee for services rendered before the effective date of the amendments. This Court reversed. We concluded that the private parties could rely on § 718 to support their claim for attorney's fees, resting our decision "on the principle that a court is to apply the law in effect at the time it renders its decision, unless doing so would result in manifest injustice or there is statutory direction or legislative history to the contrary." 416 U.S., at 711, 94 S. Ct., at 2016.

Although that language suggests a categorical presumption in favor of application of *all* new rules of law, we now make it clear that *Bradley* did not alter the well-settled presumption against application of the class of new statutes that would have genuinely "retroactive" effect. Like the new hearing requirement in *Thorpe*, the attorney's fee provision at issue in *Bradley* did not resemble the cases in which we have invoked the presumption against statutory retroactivity. Attorney's fee determinations, we have observed, are "collateral to the main cause of action" and "uniquely separable from the cause of action to be proved at trial . . . ." Moreover, even before the enactment of § 718, federal courts had authority (which the District Court in *Bradley* had exercised) to award fees based upon equitable principles . . . .

In approving application of the new fee provision, *Bradley* did not take issue with the long line of decisions applying for the presumption against retroactivity. Our opinion distinguished, but did not criticize, prior cases that had applied the antiretroactivity canon . . . . The authorities we relied upon in *Bradley* lend further support to the conclusion that we did not intend to displace the traditional presumption against applying statutes affecting substantive rights, liabilities, or duties to conduct arising before their enactment . . . .

When a case implicates a federal statute enacted after the events in suit, the court's first task is to determine whether Congress has expressly prescribed the statute's proper reach. If Congress has done so, of course, there is no need to resort to judicial default rules. When, however, the statute contains no such express command, the court must determine whether the new statute would have retroactive effect, *i.e.*, whether it would impair rights a party possessed when he acted, increase a party's liability for past conduct, or impose new duties with respect to transactions already completed. If the statute would operate retroactively, our traditional presumption teaches that it does not govern absent clear congressional intent favoring such a result.

V

We now ask whether, given the absence of guiding instructions from Congress, § 102 of the Civil Rights Act of 1991 is the type of provision that should govern cases arising before its enactment. As we observed *supra*, there is no special reason to think that all the diverse provisions of the Act must be treated uniformly for such purposes. To the contrary, we understand the instruction that the provisions are to "take effect upon enactment" to mean that courts should evaluate each provision of the Act in light of ordinary judicial principles concerning the application of new rules to pending cases and preenactment conduct.

Two provisions of § 102 may be readily classified according to these principles. The jury trial right set out in § 102(c)(1) is plainly a procedural change of the sort that would ordinarily govern in trials conducted after its effective date. If § 102 did no more than introduce a right to jury trial in Title VII cases, the provision would presumably apply to cases tried after November 21, 1991, regardless of when the underlying conduct occurred.[34] However, because § 102(c) makes a jury trial available only "[i]f a complaining party seeks compensatory or punitive damages," the jury trial option must stand or fall with the attached damages provisions.

Section 102(b)(1) is clearly on the other side of the line. That subsection authorizes punitive damages if the plaintiff shows that the defendant "engaged in a discriminatory practice or discriminatory practices with malice or with reckless indifference to the federally protected rights of an aggrieved individual." The very labels given "punitive" or "exemplary" damages, as well as the rationales that support them, demonstrate that they share key characteristics of criminal sanctions. Retroactive imposition of punitive damages would raise a serious constitutional question. *See Turner Elkhorn*, 428 U.S., at 17, 96 S. Ct., at 2893 (Court would "hesitate to approve the retrospective imposition of liability on any theory of deterrence . . . or blameworthiness") . . . .

Before we entertained that question, we would have to be confronted with a statute that explicitly authorized punitive damages for preenactment conduct. The Civil Rights Act of 1991 contains no such explicit command.

The provision of § 102(a)(1) authorizing the recovery of compensatory damages is not easily classified. It does not make unlawful conduct that was lawful when it occurred; as we have noted, *supra*, at 1490–1491, § 102 only reaches discriminatory conduct already prohibited by Title VII. Concerns about a lack of fair notice are further muted by the fact that such discrimination was in many cases (although not this one) already subject to monetary liability in the form of backpay. Nor could anyone seriously contend that the compensatory damages provisions smack of a "retributive" or other suspect legislative purpose. Section 102 reflects Congress' desire to afford victims of discrimination more

---

[34] As the Court of Appeals recognized, however, the promulgation of a new jury trial rule would ordinarily not warrant retrial of cases that had previously been tried to a judge. Thus, customary practice would not support remand for a jury trial in this case.

complete redress for violations of rules established more than a generation ago in the Civil Rights Act of 1964. At least with respect to its compensatory damages provisions, then, § 102 is not in a category in which objections to retroactive application on grounds of fairness have their greatest force.

Nonetheless, the new compensatory damages provision would operate "retrospectively" if it were applied to conduct occurring before November 21, 1991. Unlike certain other forms of relief, compensatory damages are quintessentially backward looking. Compensatory damages may be *intended* less to sanction wrongdoers than to make victims whole, but they do so by a mechanism that affects the liabilities of defendants. They do not "compensate" by distributing funds from the public coffers, but by requiring particular employers to pay for harms they caused. The introduction of a right to compensatory damages is also the type of legal change that would have an impact on private parties' planning. In this case, the event to which the new damages provision relates is the discriminatory conduct of respondents' agent John Williams; if applied here, that provision would attach an important new legal burden to that conduct. The new damages remedy in § 102, we conclude, is the kind of provision that does not apply to events antedating its enactment in the absence of clear congressional intent.

In cases like this one, in which prior law afforded no relief, § 102 can be seen as creating a new cause of action, and its impact on parties' rights is especially pronounced . . . .

It will frequently be true, as petitioner and *amici* forcefully argue here, that retroactive application of a new statute would vindicate its purpose more fully. That consideration, however, is not sufficient to rebut the presumption against retroactivity. Statutes are seldom crafted to pursue a single goal, and compromises necessary to their enactment may require adopting means other than those that would most effectively pursue the main goal. A legislator who supported a prospective statute might reasonably oppose retroactive application of the same statute. Indeed, there is reason to believe that the omission of the 1990 version's express retroactivity provisions was a factor in the passage of the 1991 bill. Section 102 is plainly not the sort of provision that *must* be understood to operate retroactively because a contrary reading would render it ineffective.

The presumption against statutory retroactivity is founded upon sound considerations of general policy and practice, and accords with long held and widely shared expectations about the usual operation of legislation. We are satisfied that it applies to § 102. Because we have found no clear evidence of congressional intent that § 102 of the Civil Rights Act of 1991 should apply to cases arising before its enactment, we conclude that the judgement of the Court of Appeals must be affirmed.

RIVERS v. ROADWAY EXPRESS, INC.
511 U.S. 298 (1994)

Justice Stevens delivered the opinion of the Court.

Section 101 of the Civil Rights Act of 1991, Pub.L. 102-166, 105 Stat. 1071, defines the term "make and enforce contracts" as used in § 1 of the Civil Rights Act of 1866, Rev. Stat. § 1977, 42 U.S.C. § 1981, to include "the making, performance, modification, and termination of contracts, and the enjoyment of all benefits, privileges, terms, and conditions of the contractual relationship." We granted certiorari to decide whether § 101 applies to a case that arose before it was enacted. We hold that it does not.

I

Petitioners Rivers and Davison were employed by respondent Roadway Express, Inc., as garage mechanics. On the morning of August 22, 1986, a supervisor directed them to attend disciplinary hearings later that day. Because they had not received the proper notice guaranteed by their collective-bargaining agreement, petitions refused to attend. They were suspended for two days, but filed grievances and were awarded two days' backpay. Respondent then held another disciplinary hearing, which petitioners also refused to attend, again on the ground that they had not received proper notice. Respondent thereupon discharged them.

On December 22, 1986, petitioners filed a complaint alleging that respondent had discharged them because of their race in violation of 42 U.S.C. § 1981. They claimed, *inter alia*, that they had been fired on baseless charges because of their race and because they had insisted on the same procedural protections afforded white employees.

On June 15, 1989, before the trial commenced, this Court announced its decision in *Patterson v. McLean Credit Union*, 41 U.S. 164, 109 S. Ct. 2363, 105 L. Ed. 2d 132. *Patterson* held that § 1981 "does not apply to conduct which occurs after the formation of a contract and which does not interfere with the right to enforce established contract obligations." *Id.*, at 171, 109 S. Ct., at 2369. Relying on *Patterson*, the District Court held that none of the petitioners' discriminatory discharge claims were covered by § 1981, and dismissed their claims under that section . . . .

While petitioners' appeal was pending, the Civil Rights Act of 1991 (1991 Act or Act) became law. Section 101 of that Act provides that § 1981's prohibition against racial discrimination in the making and enforcement of contracts applies to all phases and incidents of the contractual relationship, including discriminatory contract terminations. Petitioners accordingly filed a supplemental brief advancing the argument that the new statute applied in their case.

We granted certiorari . . . on the sole question whether § 101 of the 1991 Act applies to cases pending when it was enacted and set the case for argument with *Landgraf v. USI Film Products* . . . .

II

In *Landgraf*, we concluded that § 102 of the 1991 Act does not apply to cases that arose before its enactment. The reasons supporting that conclusion also apply to § 101, and require rejection of two of petitioners' submissions in this case . . . .

III

Petitioners rely heavily on an argument that was not applicable to § 102 of the 1991 Act, the section at issue in *Landgraf*. They contend that § 101 should apply to their case because it was "restorative" of the understanding of § 1981 that prevailed before our decision in *Patterson*. Petitioners advance two variations on this theme: Congress' evident purpose to "restore" pre-*Patterson* law indicates that it affirmatively *intended* § 101 to apply to cases arising before its enactment; moreover, there is a "presumption in favor of application of restorative statutes" to cases arising before their enactment. Brief for Petitioners 37.

A

Congress' decision to alter the rule of law established in one of our cases — as petitioners put it, to "legislatively overrul[e]," *see id.*, at 38 — does not, by itself, reveal whether Congress intends the "overruling" statute to apply retroactively to events that would otherwise be governed by the judicial decision.[5] A legislative response does not necessarily indicate that Congress viewed the judicial decision as "wrongly decided" as

---

[5] Congress frequently "responds" to judicial decisions construing statutes, and does so for a variety of reasons. According to one commentator, between 1967 and 1990, the Legislature "overrode" our decisions at an average of "ten per Congress." Eskridge, *Overriding Supreme Court Statutory Interpretation Decisions*, 101 Yale L.J. 331, 338 (1991). Seldom if ever has Congress responded to so many decisions in a single piece

an interpretive matter. Congress may view the judicial decision as an entirely correct reading of prior law — or it may be altogether indifferent to the decision's technical merits — but may nevertheless decide that the old law should be amended, but only for the future. Of course, Congress may also decide to announce a new rule that operates retroactively to govern the rights of parties whose rights would otherwise be subject to the rule announced in the judicial decision. Because retroactively raises special policy concerns, the choice to enact a statute that responds to a judicial decision is quite distinct from the choice to make the responding statute retroactive.

Petitioners argue that the structure and legislative history of § 101 indicate that Congress specifically intended to "restore" prior law even as to parties whose rights would otherwise have been determined according to *Patterson*'s interpretation of § 1981. Thus, § 101 operates as a gloss on the terms "make and enforce contracts," the original language of the Civil Rights Act of 1866 that was before this Court in *Patterson*. Petitioners also point to evidence in the 1991 Act's legislative history indicating legislators' distress with *Patterson*'s construction of § 1981 and their view that our decision had narrowed a previously established understanding of that provision. Taken together, petitioners argue, this evidence shows that it was Congress' sense that *Patterson* had cut back the proper scope of § 1981, and that the new legislation would restore its proper scope. Regardless of whether that sense was right or wrong as a technical legal matter, petitioners maintain, we should give it effect by applying § 101's broader definition of what it means to "make and enforce" a contract, rather than *Patterson*'s congressionally disapproved reading, to cases pending upon § 101's enactment.

We may assume, as petitioners argue, that § 101 reflects congressional disapproval of *Patterson*'s interpretation of § 1981. We may even assume that many or even most legislators believed that *Patterson* was not only incorrectly decided but also represented a departure from the previously prevailing understanding of the reach of § 1981. Those assumptions would readily explain why Congress might have wanted to legislate retroactively, thereby providing relief for the persons it believed had been wrongfully denied a § 1981 remedy. Even on those assumptions, however, we cannot find in the 1991 Act any clear expression of congressional intent to reach cases that arose before its enactment.

The 1990 civil rights bill that was vetoed by the President contained an amendment to § 1981, identical to § 101 of the 1991 Act, that assuredly would have applied to pending cases . . . .

The statute that was actually enacted in 1991 contains no comparable language. Instead of a reference to "restoring" pre-existing rights, its statement of purposes describes the Act's function as "*expanding* the scope of relevant civil rights statutes in order to provide adequate protection to victims of discrimination." Act of 1991 § 3(4), 105 Stat. 1071 (emphasis added). Consistently with that revised statement of purposes, the Act lacks any direct reference to cases arising before its enactment, or to the date of the *Patterson* decision. Taken by itself, the fact that § 101 is framed as a gloss on § 1981's original "make and enforce contracts" does not demonstrate an intent to apply the new definition to past acts . . . .

The legislative history of the 1991 Act does not bridge the gap in the text. The statements that most strongly support such coverage are found in the debates on the *1990* bill. Such statements are of questionable relevance to the 1991 Act, however, because the 1990 provision contained express retroactively provisions that were omitted from the 1991 legislation . . . .

. . . .

Patterson did not overrule any prior decision of this Court; rather, it held and

---

of legislation as it did in the Civil Rights Act of 1991. *See Landgraf v. USI Film Products*, 511 U.S., at 250–251, 114 S. Ct., at 1489–1490.

therefore established that the prior decisions of the Courts of Appeals which read § 1981 to cover discriminatory contract termination were *incorrect*. They were not wrong according to some abstract standard of interpretive validity, but by the rules that necessarily govern our hierarchical federal court system . . . . It is this Court's responsibility to say what a statute means, and once the Court has spoken, it is the duty of other courts to respect that understanding of the governing rule of law. A judicial construction of a statute is an authoritative statement of what the statute meant before as well as after the decision of the case giving rise to that construction.[12] Thus, *Patterson* provides the authoritative interpretation of the phrase "make and enforce contracts" in the Civil Rights Act of 1866 before the 1991 amendment went into effect on November 21, 1991. That interpretation provides the baseline for our conclusion that the 1991 amendment would be "retroactive" if applied to cases arising before that date.

Congress, of course, has the power to amend a statute that it believes we have misconstrued. It may even, within broad constitutional bounds, make such a change retroactive and thereby undo what it perceives to be the undesirable past consequences of a misinterpretation of its work product. No such change, however, has the force of law unless it is implemented through legislation. Even when Congress intends to supersede a rule of law embodied in one of our decisions with what it views as a better rule established in earlier decisions, its intent to reach conduct preceding the "corrective" amendment must clearly appear. We cannot say that such an intent clearly appears with respect to § 101. For this reason, and because it creates liabilities that had no legal existence before the Act was passed, § 101 does not apply to preenactment conduct.

Accordingly, the judgement of the Court of Appeals is affirmed, and the case is remanded for further proceedings consistent with this opinion.

Justice Scalia, with whom Justice Kennedy and Justice Thomas join, concurring in the judgements.

I

I of course agree with the Court that there exists a judicial presumption, of great antiquity, that a legislative enactment affecting substantive rights does not apply retroactively absent *clear statement* to the contrary. *See generally Kaiser Aluminum & Chemical Corp., v. Bonjorno*, 494 U.S. 827, 840, 110 S. Ct. 1570, 1578–1589, 108 L. Ed. 2d 842 (1990) (Scalia, J., concurring). The Court, however, is willing to let that clear statement be supplied, not by the text of the law in question, but by individual legislators who participated in the enactment of the law, and even legislators in an earlier Congress which tried and failed to enact a similar law. For the Court not only combs the floor debate and Committee Reports of the statute at issue, the Civil Rights Act of 1991 (1991 Act), Pub. L. 102-166, 105 Stat. 1071, *see* 511 U.S. at 262–263, 114 S. Ct. at 1495–1496, but also reviews the procedural history of an earlier, unsuccessful attempt by a *different* Congress to enact similar legislation, the Civil Rights Act of 1990, S. 2104, 101st Sess. (1990), *see id.*, at 255–257, 263, 114 S. Ct. at 1491–1493, 1496.

This effectively converts the "clear statement" rule into a "discernible legislative intent" rule — and even that understates the difference. The Court's rejection of the

---

[12] When Congress enacts a new statute, it has the power to decide when the statute will become effective. The new statute may govern from the date of enactment, from a specified future date, or even from an expressly announced earlier date. But when this Court construes a statute, it is explaining its understanding of what the statute has meant continuously since the date when it became law. In statutory cases the Court has no authority to depart from the congressional command setting the effective date of a law that it has enacted. Thus, it is not accurate to say that the Court's decision in *Patterson* "changed" the law the previously prevailed in the Sixth Circuit when this case was filed. Rather, given the structure of our judicial system, the Patterson opinion finally decided what § 1981 had always meant and explained why the Courts of Appeals had misinterpreted the will of the enacting Congress.

floor statements of certain Senators because they are "frankly partisan" and "cannot plausibly be read as reflecting any general agreement" *ante*, at 1495, reads like any other exercise in the soft science of legislative historicizing,[1] undisciplined by any distinctive "clear statement" requirement. If it is a "clear statement" we are seeking, surely it is not enough to insist that the statement can "plausibly be read as reflecting general agreement"; the statement must *clearly* reflect general agreement. No legislative history can do that, of course, but only the text of the statute itself. That has been the meaning of the "clear statement" retroactivity rule from the earliest times . . . .

NOTES AND QUESTIONS

1. In *Landgraf*, Justice Stevens acknowledged the apparent tension between two seemingly applicable but opposite canons, citing Llewellyn. Did he resolve the tension? Could the two lines of cases be reconciled?

2. William Eskridge and Philip P. Frickey assert that the canons of statutory interpretation comprise part of an "interpretative regime."

> An interpretive regime is a system of background norms and conventions against which the Court will read statutes. An interpretive regime tells lower court judges, agencies, and citizens how strings of words in statutes will be read, what presumptions will be entertained as to a statute's scope and meaning, and what auxiliary materials might be consulted to resolve ambiguities . . . . The integrity of an interpretive regime provides some degree of insulation against judicial arbitrariness; by rendering statutory interpretation more predictable, regular, and coherent, interpretive regimes can contribute to the rule of law. This goal is subject to Llewellyn's criticism, but the Supreme Court is itself aware of that criticism and can therefore be expected to counteract its force. For example, Justice Stevens's opinion in *Landgraf* adverted to Llewellyn and acknowledged two "seemingly contradictory statements found in [the Court's] decisions concerning the effect of intervening changes in the law." But the remainder of his opinion sought to reconcile those statements and resolved whatever contradictions there had been in favor of a strong presumption against the application of statutes to nonlitigation events completed before the statute's enactment. For issues of statutory retroactivity, *Landgraf* greatly diminishes the force of Llewellyn's criticism.

William N. Eskridge & Philip P. Frickey, *The Supreme Court 1993 Term: Foreword: Law As Equilibrium*, 108 Harv. L. Rev. 26, 66 (1994).

3. What is different about the retroactivity question in *Rivers* from that decided in *Landgraph*?

4. Justices Scalia, Kennedy and Thomas, concurring in *Rivers*, make reference to a "clear statement" requirement for retroactivity. This requirement, in other contexts, is explored in the next section.

5. For a detailed analysis and application of *Landgraf*, see *Mathews v. Kidder, Peabody & Co.*, 161 F.3d 156 (3d Cir. 1998).

6. In 2001, the Illinois Supreme Court adopted the *Landgraf* approach. *Commonwealth Edison Co. v. Will*, 749 N.E.2d 964, 968–72 (Ill. 2001).

7. A very important category of retroactive lawmaking is the category of "curative acts." These are laws passed to cure defects in prior statutes or to ratify past official conduct that is out of compliance with statutory requirements. *See* 2 Norman J. Singer,

---

[1] In one respect, I must acknowledge, the Court's effort may be unique. There is novelty as well as irony in its supporting judgement that the floor statements on the 1991 Act are unreliable by citing Senator Danforth's floor statement on the 1991 Act to the effect that floor statements on the 1991 Act are unreliable. *See* 511 U.S., at 262–263, n. 15, 114 S. Ct. at 1495, n. 15.

STATUTES AND STATUTORY CONSTRUCTION § 41.11 (6th ed., 2001). Such acts are, by their terms, intended to apply retroactively.

UNIFORM STATUTE AND RULE CONSTRUCTION ACT (1995)[*]

§ 8. Prospective Operation.

A statute or rule operates prospectively only unless the statute or rule expressly provides otherwise or its context requires that it operate retrospectively.

E.   CLEAR STATEMENT REQUIREMENTS

PENNHURST STATE SCHOOL & HOSPITAL v. HALDERMAN
451 U.S. 1 (1981)

JUSTICE REHNQUIST delivered the opinion of the Court.

At issue in these cases is the scope and meaning of the Developmentally Disabled Assistance and Bill of Rights Act of 1975, 89 Stat. 486, as amended, 42 U.S.C. § 6000 et seq. (1976 ed. and Supp. III). The Court of Appeals for the Third Circuit held that the Act created substantive rights in favor of the mentally retarded, that those rights were judicially enforceable, and that conditions at the Pennhurst State School and Hospital (Pennhurst), a facility for the care and treatment of the mentally retarded, violated those rights. For the reasons stated below, we reverse the decision of the Court of Appeals and remand the cases for further proceedings.

. . . .

Turning to Congress' power to legislate pursuant to the spending power, our cases have long recognized that Congress may fix the terms on which it shall disburse federal money to the States. *See, e.g., Oklahoma v. CSC*, 330 U.S. 127 (1947); *King v. Smith*, 392 U.S. 309 (1968); *Rosado v. Wyman*, 397 U.S. 397 (1970). Unlike legislation enacted under § 5, however, legislation enacted pursuant to the spending power is much in the nature of a contract: in return for federal funds, the States agree to comply with federally imposed conditions. The legitimacy of Congress' power to legislate under the spending power thus rests on whether the State voluntarily and knowingly accepts the terms of the "contract." *See Steward Machine Co. v. Davis*, 301 U.S. 548, 584–598 (1937); *Harris v. McRae*, 448 U.S. 297 (1980). There can, of course, be no knowing acceptance if a State is unaware of the conditions or is unable to ascertain what is expected of it. Accordingly, if Congress intends to impose a condition on the grant of federal moneys, it must do so unambiguously. *Cf. Employees v. Department of Health and Welfare*, 411 U.S. 297 (1973); *Edelman v. Jordan*, 415 U.S. 651 (1974). By insisting that Congress speak with a clear voice, we enable the States to exercise their choice knowingly, cognizant of the consequences of their participation.

Indeed, in those instances where Congress has intended the States to fund certain entitlements as a condition of receiving federal funds, it has proved capable of saying so explicitly. *See, e.g., King v. Smith, supra* at 333 (Social Security Act creates a "federally imposed obligation [on the States] to furnish 'aid to families with dependent children . . . with reasonable promptness to all eligible individuals,'" quoting the Act). We must carefully inquire, then, whether Congress in § 6010 imposed an obligation on the States to spend state money to fund certain rights as a condition of receiving federal moneys under the Act or whether it spoke merely in precatory terms.

. . . .

We are persuaded that § 6010, when read in the context of other more specific provisions of the Act, does no more than express a congressional preference for certain kinds of treatment. It is simply a general statement of "findings" and, as such, is too

---

[*] Reprinted with permission.

thin a reed to support the rights and obligations read into it by the court below . . . .

The fact that Congress granted to Pennsylvania only $1.6 million in 1976, a sum woefully inadequate to meet the enormous financial burden of providing "appropriate" treatment in the "least restrictive" setting, confirms that Congress must have had a limited purpose in enacting § 6010. When Congress does impose affirmative obligations on the States, it usually makes a far more substantial contribution to defray costs. *Harris v. McRae, supra.* It defies common sense, in short, to suppose that Congress implicitly imposed this massive obligation on participating States.

Our conclusion is also buttressed by the rule of statutory construction established above, that Congress must express clearly its intent to impose conditions on the grant of federal funds so that the States can knowingly decide whether or not to accept those funds. That canon applies with greatest force where, as here, a State's potential obligations under the Act are largely indeterminate.

NOTES AND QUESTIONS

1. For discussions of this "clear statement" requirement in statutory interpretation, see Stewart A. Baker, *Making the Most of Pennhurst's "Clear Statement" Rule*, 31 Cath. U. L. Rev. 439 (1982); Luneburg, *Justice Rehnquist, Statutory Interpretation, The Policies of Clear Statement, and Federal Jurisdiction*, 58 Ind. L.J. 211 (1982); Note, *Intent, Clear Statements, and the Common Law: Statutory Interpretation in the Supreme Court*, 95 Harv. L. Rev. 892 (1982).

2. Can you reformulate the clear statement approach in the language of presumptions? In the language of strict construction?

3. What other areas of law might be susceptible to a clear statement requirement? Are there areas of state law to which this approach might be applied? *See Gould v. O'Bannon*, 770 S.W.2d 220, 221 (Ky. 1989) ("A statute has no retrospective application unless it is specified in the statute expressly.").

4. For other expressions of the clear statement requirement, see *Board of Educ. v. Rowley*, 458 U.S. 176, 204 n.26 (1982); *Wright v. Roanoke Redev. & Hous. Auth.*, 479 U.S. 418, 423 (1987); *Wilder v. Virginia Hosp. Ass'n*, 58 U.S.L.W. 4795 (June 14, 1990).

5. The *Pennhurst* approach was reaffirmed by the Court in *Arlington Central School Dist. v. Murphy*, 548 U.S. 291, 126 S. Ct. 2455, 2458–60 (2006).

ATASCADERO STATE HOSPITAL v. SCANLON
473 U.S. 234 (1985)

Justice Powell delivered the opinion of the court.

This case presents the question whether States and state agencies are subject to suit in federal court by litigants seeking retroactive monetary relief under § 504 of the Rehabilitation Act of 1973, 29 U.S.C. § 794, or whether such suits are proscribed by the Eleventh Amendment.

. . . .

II

. . . [I]n *Hans v. Louisiana*, 134 U.S. 1 (1890), the Court held that the Amendment barred a citizen from bringing a suit against his own State in federal court, even though the express terms of the Amendment do not so provide.

There are, however, certain well-established exceptions to the reach of the Eleventh Amendment. For example, if a State waives its immunity and consents to suit in federal court, the Eleventh Amendment does not bar the action. *See, e.g., Clark v. Barnard*, 108 U.S. 436, 447 (1883). Moreover, the Eleventh Amendment is "necessarily limited by the enforcement provisions of § 5 of the Fourteenth Amendment," that is, by Congress' power "to enforce, by appropriate legislation, the substantive provisions of the

Fourteenth Amendment." *Fitzpatrick v. Bitzer*, 427 U.S. 445, 456 (1976). As a result, when acting pursuant to § 5 of the Fourteenth Amendment, Congress can abrogate the Eleventh Amendment without the States' consent. *Ibid.*

But because the Eleventh Amendment implicates the fundamental constitutional balance between the Federal Government and the States, this Court consistently has held that these exceptions apply only when certain specific conditions are met. Thus, we have held that a State will be deemed to have waived its immunity "only where stated 'by the most express language or by such overwhelming implication from the text as [will] leave no room for any other reasonable construction.'" *Edelman v. Jordan*, 415 U.S. at 673, quoting *Murray v. Wilson Distilling Co.*, 213 U.S. 151, 171 (1909). Likewise, in determining whether Congress in exercising its Fourteenth Amendment powers has abrogated the States' Eleventh Amendment immunity, we have required "an unequivocal expression of congressional intent to 'overturn the constitutionally guaranteed immunity of the several States.'" *Pennhurst II*, 465 U.S., at 99, quoting *Quern v. Jordan*, 440 U.S. 332, 342 (1979). *Accord, Employees v. Missouri Dept. of Public Health and Welfare*, 411 U.S. 279 (1973).

. . . .

. . . For these reasons, we hold — consistent with *Quern, Edelman*, and *Pennhurst II* — that Congress must express its intention to abrogate the Eleventh Amendment in unmistakable language in the statute itself.

NOTES AND QUESTIONS

1. The outcome in *Atascadero State Hospital* was overturned by Congress in the Rehabilitation Act Amendments of 1986. Pub. L. No. 99-506, § 1003, 100 Stat. 1807, 1845 (1986) (codified at 42 U.S.C. § 2000d-7) (maintaining that "[a] State shall not be immune under the Eleventh Amendment . . . from suit in federal court . . . ."). Should this have any effect on the Court's clear statement requirement for Eleventh Amendment waiver arguments?

2. *See also Welch v. Texas Dep't of Hwys. & Pub. Transp.*, 483 U.S. 486, 474 (1987); *Hoffman v. Connecticut Dep't of Income Maintenance*, 492 U.S. 96, 101 (1989); William N. Eskridge, *Public Values in Statutory Interpretation*, 137 U. PA. L. REV. 1007, 1031–32, 1055–57 (1989). What would be the "public value" at work in the clear statement requirement in interpreting the Eleventh Amendment waivers?

3. The United States Supreme Court requires Congress to be "clear and plain" when it intends to intrude on Native American treaty rights, but it will accept legislative history. *See, e.g., United States v. Dion*, 476 U.S. 734, 738–40 (1986).

In *Dellmuth v. Muth*, 491 U.S. 223, 230 (1989), the Supreme Court held that the Education of the Handicapped Act did not waive Eleventh Amendment immunity. Justice Kennedy stated:

> Our opinion in *Atascadero* should have left no doubt that we will conclude Congress intended to abrogate sovereign immunity only if its intention is "unmistakably clear in the language of the statute." *Atascadero, supra* at 242, 105 S. Ct. at 3147. Lest *Atascadero* be thought to contain any ambiguity, we reaffirm today that in this area of the law, evidence of congressional intent must be both unequivocal and textual. Respondent's evidence is neither. In particular, we reject the approach of the Court of Appeals, according to which, "[w]hile the text of the federal legislation must bear evidence of such an intention the legislative history may still be used as a resource in determining whether Congress' intention to lift the bar has been made sufficiently manifest." 839 F.2d, at 128. Legislative history generally will be irrelevant to a judicial inquiry into whether Congress intended to abrogate the Eleventh Amendment. If Congress' intention is not unmistakably clear, recourse to legislative history will be futile, because by definition the rule of *Atascadero* will not be met.

WILLIAM N. ESKRIDGE,
THE NEW TEXTUALISM,
37 UCLA L. REV. 621, 683–84, 688 (1990)*

. . . .

Indeed, there is something of a "bait-and-switch" feature to the new textualism in actual practice. That is, Congress enacts a statute against certain well-established background assumptions, many of which the Court created for it. The Court then switches those assumptions and interprets Congress' work product in ways that no one at the time would have, or perhaps even could have, intended. Bait-and-switch is an unfair con game in general, and when the victim of the con game is Congress it may be unconstitutional as well.

Recall *Dellmuth v. Muth* where the Court found no waiver of eleventh amendment immunity in the Education of the Handicapped Act of 1975 (EHA), even though (*inter alia*) the sponsor of the Act specifically stated that the Act contemplated lawsuits against the states.[243]

Under the Supreme Court's prevailing eleventh amendment precedents in 1975, the general jurisdictional language and specific legislative history were enough to demonstrate that the states could be sued and that Congress had exercised its power to abrogate the states' immunity.[244]

In 1985, the Court changed the rule to require explicit statutory language to abrogate state immunity and held that the Rehabilitation Act of 1973 did not abrogate state immunity.[245]

Sensing that the rules had changed, Congress in 1986 enacted the following statute: "A State shall not be immune under the Eleventh Amendment . . . from suit in Federal Court for a violation of [enumerated provisions of the Rehabilitation Act], or the provisions of any other Federal statute prohibiting discrimination by recipients of Federal financial assistance."[246] Congress grumbled that its intent had been slighted by the Court and that it had to take the trouble to restate what it thought it had stated in 1973 (the Rehabilitation Act) and thereafter. Three years later, in *Dellmuth*, the new textualists ruled that the EHA did not abrogate state immunity, and that even the 1986 statute did not render the original legislative intent clear![247] Outraged dissenters argued, with justification, that "the Court ignores Congress' actual intent to abrogate State immunity . . . instead resorting to an interpretative standard that Congress could have anticipated only with the aid of a particularly effective crystal ball."[248]

. . . .

2. Prospective Clear Statement Rules

I believe, with the new textualists, that clear statement rules can be a useful way of avoiding unnecessary recourse to legislative history. The best cases for such a rule are those in which there are constitutional concerns. *Dellmuth* holds that any Congressional abrogation of state's eleventh amendment immunity must be clear on the

---

* Originally published in 37 UCLA L. REV. 621. Copyright 1990, The Regents of the University of California. All Rights Reserved.

[243] 121 Cong. Rec. 37, 415–416 (1975) (statement of Sen. Williams).

[244] *See Employees of the Dept. of Pub. Health & Welfare v. Department of Pub. Health & Welfare*, 411 U.S. 279, 283–85 (1973) (general language plus confirming legislative history indicative of legislative intent to abrogate state immunity).

[245] *Atascadero State Hosp. v. Scanlon*, 473 U.S. 234 (1985).

[246] 42 U.S.C. § 2000d-7(a)(1) (Supp. IV 1986).

[247] *Dellmuth*, 109 S. Ct. at 2400–02.

[248] *Id.* at 2407 (Brennan, J., dissenting).

face of the statute. Other similar rules could be constructed: Statutes, and agency rules pursuant to statute, cannot be applied retroactively unless explicitly authorized by clear text. Jury trials are required under any federal statutory scheme authorizing damage remedies, unless specifically negated by statutory language. And so forth.

The Court ought to be formulating such rules, but it ought not make them applicable retroactively, as in *Dellmuth*, because of the bait-and-switch problem. Prospective rulemaking might obviate that problem.

NOTES AND QUESTIONS

1. Why does Eskridge support prospective, but not retroactive, clear statement requirements? Are not all statutory interpretation approaches, in a sense, retroactive?

2. *See generally* William N. Eskridge & Philip P. Frickey, *Quasi-Constitutional Law: Clear Statement Rules as Constitutional Lawmaking*, 45 VAND. L. REV. 593 (1992).

3. *See generally* John Copeland Nagle, *Waiving Sovereign Immunity in an Age of Clear Statement Rules*, 1995 WIS. L. REV. 771 (1995).

4. Are there areas of state law where "clear statement" rules might be asserted by counsel or required by the courts? *See Summer v. Teaneck Twp.*, 251 A.2d 761, 764 (N.J. 1969):

> A municipality may not contradict a policy the Legislature establishes . . . . Hence an ordinance will fall if it permits what a statute expressly forbids or forbids what a statute expressly authorizes. Even absent such evident conflict, a municipality may be unable to exercise a power it would otherwise have if the Legislature has preempted the field. This follows from the basic principle that local government may not act contrary to State law. But an intent to occupy the field must appear clearly.

F.   STATE AND FEDERAL COURT STATUTORY INTERPRETATION

1.   State Statutes in Federal Court

It is, of course, often the case that *state* courts must interpret *federal* statutes, and *vice versa*. When this is the case, must these courts follow the statutory interpretation approaches of the other judicial systems? In *Tunick v. Safir*, 209 F.3d 67 (2d Cir. 2000), Judge Calabresi confronted this problem. An artist had challenged a New York statute banning public nudity in federal court based on federal question jurisdiction. The Second Circuit had to decide whether to send a certified question to the New York Court of Appeals because the state statute had not received any authoritative interpretation, particularly in the context presented in the litigation. Part of Judge Calabresi's reasoning in favor of certification had to do with the institutional competency of federal courts interpreting state statutes:

> B.

> Given the shared goals of *Pullman* abstention and of the device of certifica-tion, the factors counseling the former are also suggestive of when the latter is desirable. As a result, *Arizonans*, *Quill*, and *Glucksberg* in no way lessen the significance of these *Pullman* factors. They do, however, put a gloss on them, while also pointing to other factors that are relevant to the question of certification.

> Thus, the Supreme Court in *Arizonans* emphasized the relationship of certification to the canon of statutory construction under which statutes are to be read to avoid constitutional difficulties. *See Arizonans*, 520 U.S. at 78, 117 S.

Ct. 1055. When a *state* statute is at issue, the Court pointed out, those difficulties are not comfortably avoided by a *federal* court interpretation. The task, instead, properly belongs to a state court, which must decide which canons of construction it can and should apply. *Cf. id.* at 78–79, 117 S. Ct. 1055.[10] The federal court should certify, and not interpret, because it "risks friction-generating error when it endeavors to construe a novel state Act not yet reviewed by the State's highest court." *Id.* at 79, 117 S. Ct. 1055. The object, the avoidance of unnecessary, and hence premature, constitutional decisions, remains the same whether a state or federal statute is involved. *See generally* Alexander M. Bickel, *The Least Dangerous Branch: The Supreme Court at the Bar of Politics* (1962). But, because a state law is at play, only the state court can ultimately determine whether a saving interpretation is appropriate under the canons of interpretation of the particular state whose statutes it is called upon to construe.

This teaching of the Supreme Court is fundamental and may result in some state courts having *more* and others *less* power than do federal courts to interpret state statutes to avoid constitutional difficulties. Because they are supreme in their power, under state law, to decide the meaning of state statutes, state courts are neither bound to follow, nor limited by, federal canons of interpretation, including those that speak to avoiding constitutional issues. It follows that a state court, under state canons, may be unwilling to do to a state statute what federal courts are expected to do to a federal one, *see, e.g., Califano v. Yamasaki*, 442 U.S. 682, 692–93, 99 S. Ct. 2545, 61 L. Ed. 2d 176 (1979) (in a suit involving payments under the federal Social Security Act, the Supreme Court noted that federal courts "presented with both statutory and constitutional grounds to support the relief requested usually should pass on the statutory claim before considering the constitutional question" in order to avoid "unnecessary constitutional adjudication"). But it is also possible that state law would allow state courts to rewrite state statutes to a degree that would be impermissible for federal courts dealing with federal laws. *Compare, e.g., Reno v. American Civil Liberties Union*, 521 U.S. 844, 884, 117 S. Ct. 2329, 138 L. Ed. 2d 874 (1997) (emphasizing, in a First Amendment challenge to the federal Communications Decency Act, that federal courts "may impose a limiting construction on a [federal] statute *only if* it is 'readily susceptible' to such a construction" (emphasis added)), *with National Ass'n of Indep. Insurers v. State*, 89 N.Y.2d 950, 952, 655 N.Y.S.2d 853, 678 N.E.2d 465, 466 (1997) ("A presumption of constitutionality attaches to [a New York law], and [New York courts are] *required* 'to avoid interpreting [it] in a way that would render it unconstitutional if such a construction can be avoided.'" (quoting *Alliance of Am. Insurers v. Chu*, 77 N.Y.2d 573, 585, 569 N.Y.S.2d 364, 571 N.E.2d 672 (1991)) (emphasis added)); *A Woman's Choice-East Side Women's Clinic v. Newman*, 671 N.E.2d 104, 111 (Ind. 1996) (Dickson, J., concurring) (noting that Indiana courts have an *"overriding obligation* to construe [their] statutes in such a way as to render them constitutional if reasonably possible" (emphasis added)).

This question of the extent to which the state court can go when interpreting its own laws is paradigmatically one of state law, and it is one that federal courts are singularly unsuited to answer. *Compare Blue Cross & Blue Shield of Alabama, Inc. v. Nielsen*, 116 F.3d 1406, 1413 (11th Cir. 1997) ("The final arbiter of state law is the state supreme court, which is another way of saying that Alabama law is what the Alabama Supreme Court says it is . . . . At the threshold, the answer to [the question before this court] depends upon reconciliation of the competing trajectories of a number of canons of statutory

---

[10] In fact, as the Supreme Court noted, Arizona has adopted the federal canon under which statutes are to be interpreted to avoid constitutional difficulties. *See id.*

construction. Given the nature of the overlapping and somewhat contradictory canons of statutory construction arguably applicable to this case, and the competing interests and policies at stake, the task is less like applying a scientific formula and more like painting a picture. We . . . are not at all confident our painting would resemble the one that the Alabama Supreme Court would have produced."), *with Hope Clinic v. Ryan*, 195 F.3d 857, 865–69 (7th Cir. 1999) (en banc) (Easterbrook, J.) (applying federal models of statutory construction in order to limit the enforcement of two state statutes banning partial-birth abortions to their "central core of meaning," such that the statutes could be enforced to prohibit only the abortion procedure known as dilation and extraction, even though the statutes themselves did not refer to this procedure), *petitions for cert. filed*, 68 USLW 3461 (Jan. 10, 2000), 68 USLW 3480 (Jan. 14, 2000). For that reason, too, certification — if otherwise appropriate — is particularly germane.

At the same time, *Arizonans* does not mean that a federal court must certify whenever (1) it has grave doubts about a state statute that has not yet been authoritatively interpreted by the state's highest tribunal and (2) those doubts could conceivably be avoided by an interpretation from a state court. The limits placed on *Pullman* by *Baggett* and *Procunier* remain crucially relevant. And the Court's decision, after *Arizonans*, on the merits of the constitutional issues in the right-to-die cases, *see Glucksberg*, 521 U.S. at 706, 117 S. Ct. 2258; *Quill*, 521 U.S. at 797, 117 S. Ct. 2293, must mean that in some circumstances — even when a state statute raises serious constitutional questions that could be avoided by a state court interpretation and even when the *Pullman* factors do not counsel against certification — certification may not be warranted.

Tunick v. Safir, 209 F.3d 67, 75–77 (2d Cir. 2000).

NOTES AND QUESTIONS

1. The concerns raised by Judge Calabresi, about a state court providing a limiting statutory interpretation to avoid federal constitutional questions, will arise regularly, but not that often. On the other hand, in the garden variety federal court litigation under diversity jurisdiction and supplemental jurisdiction, matters in which the federal courts apply state law, would it not be true that it would be very common for federal courts to have to decide whether to apply state statutory interpretation canons and other techniques? Conversely, given the concurrent jurisdiction that state courts have over most federal law questions, would not the same issue arise as to whether *state* courts would have to apply *federal* statutory interpretation canons and other techniques?

2. Judge Calabresi made the following observations in footnote 9:

The issue is a different one from the question of when certification is appropriate in diversity cases. *See Liriano v. Hobart Corp.*, 132 F.3d 124, 132 (2d Cir. 1998) ("Certification is particularly appropriate when the state's highest court has cast doubt on the scope or continued validity of one of its earlier holdings, or when there is some law in the intermediate state courts, but no definitive holding by the state's highest tribunal."); *McCarthy v. Olin Corp.*, 119 F.3d 148, 153–54 (2d Cir. 1997) (finding sufficiency of guidance in state caselaw to be determinative of whether a federal court should certify in diversity case). Uncertainty in state law is central to both situations. *See id.* and *infra* Part IV.E. But what is in play in diversity situations, *see id.* at 157 (Calabresi, J., dissenting) (noting that certification in diversity cases serves to avoid the evil "of forum shopping that *Erie R.R. Co. v. Tompkins*, 304 U.S. 64, 73–77, 58 S. Ct. 817, 82 L. Ed. 1188 (1938), was intended to prevent"), is quite different from what is involved when the validity of a state statute under the federal constitution is at stake. Accordingly, considerations relevant to certification in one context do not necessarily control in the other.

3. In *Town of Castle Rock v. Gonzalez*, 545 U.S. 748, 777–79 (2005) (Stevens, J., dissenting), another federal question case, Justice Stevens contended the question of *state* statutory interpretation, which was central to the *federal* constitutional claim, should have been certified to the state court.

2. Federal Statutes in State Court

ANTHONY J. BELLIA,
STATE COURTS AND THE INTERPRETATION OF FEDERAL STATUTES[*]
59 Vand. L. Rev. 1501 (2006)

Introduction

In the debate over how federal courts should interpret federal statutes, "faithful agent" theories stand pitted against "dynamic" theories of statutory interpretation. The following questions lie at the heart of the debate: Is the proper role of federal courts to strive to implement the commands of the legislature — in other words, to act as Congress's faithful agents? Or, is the proper role of federal courts to act as partners with Congress in the forward-looking making of federal law — in other words, to interpret statutes dynamically? Proponents of faithful agent theories include both "textualists" and "purposivists." Textualists have argued that federal courts best fulfill their responsibility to serve as faithful agents of Congress by interpreting statutes according to the meaning that their texts most reasonably impart. Certain purposivists have argued that federal courts best fulfill their responsibility to act as faithful agents of Congress by interpreting statutes according to statutory purposes, even where those purposes might contradict the most reasonable import of statutory text. Proponents of dynamic theories of statutory interpretation reject the premise that federal courts should strive to act as faithful agents of Congress. Dynamicists cast federal courts as "cooperative partners" with Congress in the federal lawmaking enterprise, rather than as Congress's agents.

Scholars have debated the constitutional legitimacy of these interpretive theories in separation of powers terms: Which interpretive methodology best comports with the federal "judicial power" of Article III relative to the federal "legislative powers" of Article I? Most notably, Professors William Eskridge and John Manning have debated whether, as a matter of original understandings of the constitutional structure, the Article III "judicial power" of federal courts is a power to interpret statutes as "faithful agents" of Congress, or as agents of "the People," empowered to establish federal policy in partnership with Congress.[6]

This Article argues that how courts ought to interpret federal statutes is not only a "horizontal" question of the separation of powers between federal courts and Congress, but also a "vertical" question of the proper relationship between Congress and state courts — in other words, a federalism question. State courts play an important, often

---

[6] *See* William N. Eskridge, Jr., *All About Words: Early Understandings of the "Judicial Power" in Statutory Interpretation, 1776–1806*, 101 Colum. L. Rev. 990 (2001); John F. Manning, *Deriving Rules of Statutory Interpretation from the Constitution*, 101 Colum. L. Rev. 1648 (2001) [hereinafter Manning, *Rules of Statutory Interpretation*]; John F. Manning, *Textualism and the Equity of the Statute*, 101 Colum. L. Rev. 1 (2001) [hereinafter Manning, *Equity of the Statute*]. In the last decade or so, other scholars, too, have examined the methods of statutory interpretation that prevailed in English and American courts around the time of the American Founding. *See* William D. Popkin, Statutes in Court: The History and Theory of Statutory Interpretation (1999); John Choon Yoo, *Marshall's Plan: The Early Supreme Court and Statutory Interpretation*, 101 Yale L.J. 1607 (1992).

independent, role in the interpretation of federal statutes. Accordingly, the question of how they ought to interpret federal statutes should figure prominently in federal statutory interpretation debates. The answer to this question does not depend on what, as a matter of separation of powers, constitutes the judicial power of the federal courts. It depends, rather, on what, as a matter of federalism, is the judicial power of state courts when they enforce federal statutes.

. . . .

When state courts interpret federal statutes, they act as more than mere adjuncts to the Supreme Court of the United States. The Constitution itself limits the Supreme Court's jurisdiction to review state court determinations of federal law. Moreover, Congress has authority under the Constitution to limit the jurisdiction of the Supreme Court to review federal determinations made by state courts. In reality, state court judgments resting upon the interpretation of federal statutes may — indeed, in the overwhelming majority of cases today, do — govern the rights and duties of parties subject to them without Supreme Court review. Unless and until the Supreme Court interprets a federal statute differently, state court judgments can constitute the final word on the meaning of federal law within a state court system, as the courts of many states do not consider themselves bound to follow the decisions of lower federal courts on questions of federal law.[14]

Thus, the following is a question of real constitutional significance: How should state courts interpret federal statutes? To put the question in terms of statutory interpretation debates, should state courts strive to act as faithful agents of Congress, or as partners with Congress in the forward-looking making of federal law?

Part I of this Article describes relevant practices of state courts in interpreting state statutes during the years immediately following ratification. Certain scholars have observed that during the Founding period state courts invoked doctrines such as "equity of the statute" in interpreting state statutes to enforce statutory meanings that expanded or limited the plain import of a statute's "letter." Scholars have disputed, however, whether the fact that state courts "equitably" interpreted state statutes in certain cases evidences a constitutional understanding that the judicial power of the United States is a power to interpret statutes dynamically, rather than as faithfully as possible to congressional directives. An important question, however, that has not yet factored into this debate is whether state courts interpreted federal statutes in the same ways that they interpreted state statutes. This Part undertakes an independent examination of the practices of state courts in interpreting state statutes during the Founding period and years immediately following ratification. Drawing upon the foundations of English practice, this Part discusses the role of legislative intent in state court interpretive practice and reveals significant distinctions among the ways in which state courts justified equitable interpretations. This Part lays the groundwork necessary for understanding how the practice of state courts in interpreting federal statutes differed from their practices in interpreting state statutes.

Part II explains how the practices of state courts in interpreting federal statutes differed from their practices in interpreting state statutes. In interpreting federal statutes, state courts did not invoke equity of the statute or other interpretive principles to justify departures from the search for actual legislative intent. Rather, state courts employed a host of interpretive techniques that uniformly — by nature or by explanation of the court — were geared toward implementing congressional intent. State courts appear to have uniformly understood their role in interpreting federal statutes to be to abide by the directives of Congress, as best they could discern them — and this during decades when state actors and institutions often questioned the

---

[14] *See* Donald H. Zeigler, *Gazing into the Crystal Ball: Reflections on the Standards State Judges Should Use to Ascertain Federal Law*, 40 WM. & MARY L. REV. 1143, 1153–57 (1999) (describing the varying weights that state courts give to different kinds of federal law determinations by federal courts).

legitimacy of federal action. Part II further provides a possible explanation of why state courts uniformly strove to implement congressional directives without invoking doctrines of equitable interpretation that operated without regard for manifest legislative direction. Not only was there a trend in English and American state courts at the time favoring interpretations that implemented actual legislative intent, but state courts may have understood the Supremacy Clause to specifically require them to recognize congressional supremacy.

Part III tentatively examines the implications of this analysis for the debate over how federal courts should interpret federal statutes. Unless federal courts properly may approach the enterprise of interpreting federal statutes differently than state courts, an understanding that state courts must strive to implement actual congressional directives suggests that the federal judicial power entails the responsibility to strive to implement actual congressional directives as well. This Part explores, at least preliminarily, whether federal and state courts should be understood to have different powers when interpreting federal statutes. In other words, it explores whether the substance of federal law should vary in certain instances depending on whether a federal court or a state court is interpreting a federal statute.

. . . .

II. State Courts, Federal Statutes, and Federalism

This Part explains how the practices of state courts in interpreting federal statutes differed from their practices in interpreting state statutes. Specifically, it summarizes an analysis of 74 state court cases decided between 1789 and 1820 that involved a question of federal statutory interpretation. This set of cases emerged from a search for all reported cases involving a question of federal statutory interpretation that state courts decided during this period.

. . . .

4. Tentative Observations

The point of this analysis is that state judges interpreted federal statutes during the first three decades following ratification in ways geared toward implementing legislative directives. In not one case did a state court invoke the equity of the statute doctrine in interpreting a federal statute or otherwise expressly profess to be equitably interpreting one. Rather, state courts most often interpreted federal statutes according to the import of statutory language, a means understood to be geared toward the implementation of actual legislative directives. Where state courts employed less text-focused means of statutory interpretation (for example, by examining purposes or consequences), they did so either to support independent textual analyses or for the stated purpose of giving effect to congressional intent . . . .

It suffices for present purposes to observe that state courts generally understood their proper role in interpreting federal statutes to be that of discerning and enforcing the directives of Congress. How courts can best fulfill this role, and how helpful the concept of legislative intent is to answering this question, is beyond the scope of this Article. The point for now is that state courts did not manifest an understanding that their role in interpreting federal statutes was to act as agents of "We the People of the United States," empowered to make federal law accord with reason or policy in forward-looking ways without regard for discernable expectations of Congress.

B. Why State Courts Did Not Make Reason-Based
Equitable Interpretations of Federal Statutes

This Section suggests a possible explanation of why state courts did not make the kind of reason-based equitable interpretations of federal statutes that they sometimes made of state statutes. As explained in Part I, there was movement on the part of some (perhaps a predominance of) English and American state judges at the time of the American Founding toward interpretive principles understood to implement the law as made by the legislator. One theory behind this movement, as explained, was respect for legislative supremacy. If the supremacy of state legislatures was a disputed matter among some state judges, the supremacy of Congress when it properly exercised its enumerated powers under the Constitution may have been deemed indisputable in light of the Supremacy Clause.

. . . .

Conclusion

The question of how courts ought to interpret federal statutes implicates not only the horizontal relationship between the legislative power of Congress and the judicial power of federal courts; it also implicates the vertical relationship between the federal legislative power and state judicial powers. In the first three decades following ratification, state courts interpreted federal statutes in ways understood to be geared toward implementing actual congressional directives. If state courts interpreted their own statutes in certain cases without apparent regard for actual legislative expectations, the practice of state courts in interpreting federal statutes may well evidence an understanding that state courts were bound to interpret federal statutes according to manifest congressional expectations. This understanding certainly accords with the import of the Supremacy Clause: to ensure that state courts faithfully enforce as the "supreme law of the Land" federal statutes that Congress has properly enacted. This understanding may have implications for the interpretation of federal statutes by federal courts. Specifically, it may suggest that to respect the federal lawmaking procedures that the Constitution provides and to safeguard the supremacy of federal law enacted pursuant to those procedures, federal courts should strive to interpret federal statutes as faithful agents of Congress as well.

This Article does not address whether, today, some form of textualism or purposivism would better serve as a means of implementing congressional directives in any given case. As explained, there are examples of state courts in the decades following ratification seeking to implement actual congressional intent through both textual and purposive analyses. The point for now is that state courts, employing various interpretive principles, appear to have understood their role in interpreting federal statutes during the first three decades of the Union to be to implement actual directives of Congress.

NOTES AND QUESTIONS

1. Consider the type of argument, and support, you would need to make to convince a state judge to interpret federal statutes using a more textual technique than she might use for state statutes. Is that what Professor Bellia is proposing?

2. Is this a new argument for textualism, specifically under the circumstance where a federal statute applies to a state court action? Do you agree? Would you want to know more about what modern state courts, particularly those in *your* state, have been doing when they interpret federal statutes? Could the courts in different states take different approaches?

TABLE OF CASES

[References are to pages]

1

[References are to pages]

[References are to pages]

[References are to pages]

[References are to pages]

[References are to pages]

(Rel. 0-0/1960 Pub.3086)

INDEX

[References are to pages.]

[References are to pages.]

[References are to pages.]

[References are to pages.]

SPEECH OR DEBATE CLAUSE—Cont.

Newsletters and press release, immunity for Congress Member for defamatory statements in . . . 298-307

Official report, libel read from . . . 307-308

Press release and newsletters, immunity for Congress Member for defamatory statements in . . . 298-307

Representation by legislature and . . . 105-107

Session adjournments, immunity applicability to senators during . . . 309-311

Sphere of legislative activity analysis for application of . . . 290-291; 292-293

Subpoena issuance by Congress and applicability of . . . 290-291; 295-298

STAFF FOR LEGISLATORS

Committee staff (See COMMITTEES)

STANDING COMMITTEES (See COMMITTEES)

STARE DECISIS (See PRECEDENTS)

STATUTE, ENACTMENT OF

Pending litigation, as resolving . . . 30-34

STATUTORY INTERPRETATION OF LEGISLATION (See INTERPRETATION OF LEGISLATION)

SUBJECT MATTER

Governor's call, limitation of subject matter to . . . 358-362

Title of legislation and one-subject rule . . . 214-227

SUBPOENAS

Investigative powers of legislature . . . 288-292; 295-298

Presidential communications, confidentiality of . . . 297-298

Session adjournments, immunity applicability to senators during . . . 309-311

SUNDAYS

Closing laws . . . 268-272

Prohibition of activities on . . . 353

SUPREME COURT JUSTICES

Nomination of Judge Souter, hearings and reports on . . . 539-541

T

TEXAS

Legislative history, compiling . . . 577-580

TITLE OF LEGISLATION

Interpretation of legislation . . . 624-625

One-subject rule . . . 205-206; 214-227

State constitution requirements . . . 205

TORT LAW

Preemption, implied . . . 66-74

Statutory compliance as defense . . . 64-65

TRANSITIVE STATUTE

Defined . . . 9

Intransitive statute compared . . . 9

U

UCC (See UNIFORM COMMERCIAL CODE (UCC))

UNIFORM COMMERCIAL CODE (UCC)

Anticipatory breach doctrine under Section 2-609; sale of goods . . . 58-60

Common law and . . . 47-51

Construction, rules of . . . 47

Influence of . . . 50

Modification of contracts . . . 10-11

Purpose of . . . 47-49

Variation by agreement . . . 47-48

Warranties (See WARRANTIES)

UNIFORM ELECTRONIC SIGNATURE ACT

Validity of electronic signature under . . . 11

UNIFORM STATUTE AND RULE CONSTRUCTION ACT

Applicability . . . 396-398

Canons of statutory interpretation . . . 600

Common and technical usage . . . 398

Common law, statutes in derogation of . . . 642-643

Conflict, statutory . . . 411

Incorporation by reference . . . 398

Judicial assumptions of legislative consideration . . . 652

Legislative history . . . 474-475

Legislative intent . . . 461

Penal statutes, construction of . . . 634-635

Provisions . . . 368-371; 386

Retroactive application of statute . . . 719

Technical usage . . . 398

V

VETO POWER OF EXECUTIVE

Generally . . . 313-315

Gubernatorial veto

    Generally . . . 341

    Amendatory veto . . . 352-353

    California Constitution . . . 341

    Example of state provisions . . . 341-343

    Indiana Constitution . . . 342-343

    Item veto . . . 343-350

    New York Constitution . . . 341

    Oregon Constitution . . . 342

    Washington Constitution . . . 342

Item veto

    Gubernatorial veto . . . 343-350

    Presidential veto . . . 325-341

Line item veto (See subhead: Item veto)

Pocket veto power of president . . . 321-325

Presidential veto

    Generally . . . 316-321

    Constitutional provisions . . . 315; 318-321

    Defined . . . 316

    Item veto . . . 325-341

    Legislative function of president . . . 316-317

    Memoranda on approval, presidential . . . 319-321

    Overriding veto, difficulty in . . . 317-318

    Pocket veto power . . . 321-325

    Two-thirds vote requirement for overriding . . . 317

[References are to pages.]

W